THE
Sealed Portion
THE FINAL TESTAMENT OF JESUS CHRIST

Translated by

Christopher

The Sealed Portion of the Book of Mormon—The Final Testament of Jesus Christ

Text and cover design copyright © 2008 http://wwunited.org
Worldwide United Foundation Organization, Inc. (WUF)

All rights reserved. No part of this book may be used or reproduced in any manner whatsoever without written permission of the author or publisher, except by a reviewer who may quote brief passages.

Trademarks: The Worldwide United Foundation name featured herein, and its logo are the exclusive property of the Worldwide United Foundation.

FRIST PUBLISHED APRIL 2005
SOFTCOVER SECOND EDITION PUBLISHED MAY 2008
ISBN: 978-0-9785264-6-7

Library of Congress Catalog Number: 20088928908

Worldwide United Publishing
A division of the Worldwide United Foundation—http://wwunited.org
http://wupublishing.com—1.888.499.9666

Printed in The United States of America

Come unto me, O ye Gentiles, and I will show unto you the greater things, the knowledge which is hid up because of unbelief.

Come unto me, ...and it shall be made manifest unto you how great things the Father hath laid up for you, from the foundation of the world; and it hath not come unto you, because of unbelief.

Behold, when ye shall rend that veil of unbelief which doth cause you to remain in your awful state of wickedness, and hardness of heart, and blindness of mind, then shall the great and marvelous things which have been hid up from the foundation of the world from you—yea, when ye shall call upon the Father in my name, with a broken heart and a contrite spirit, then shall ye know that the Father hath remembered the covenant which he made unto...you.

And then shall my revelations which I have caused to be written by my servant John be unfolded in the eyes of all the people.

Remember, when ye see these things, ye shall know that the time is at hand that they shall be made manifest in very deed.

Therefore, when ye shall receive this record ye may know that the work of the Father has commenced upon all the face of the land.

Therefore, repent all ye ends of the earth, and come unto me, and believe in my gospel, and be baptized in my name; for he that believeth and is baptized shall be saved; but he that believeth not shall be damned; and signs shall follow them that believe in my name.

And blessed is he that is found faithful unto my name at the last day, for he shall be lifted up to dwell in the kingdom prepared for him from the foundation of the world. And behold it is I that hath spoken it. Amen.

Ether 4:13–19

TABLE OF CONTENTS
THE SEALED PORTION OF THE BOOK OF MORMON

Chapter 1 2	Chapter 35 218	Chapter 69 420
Chapter 2 3	Chapter 36 229	Chapter 70 427
Chapter 3 4	Chapter 37 236	Chapter 71 431
Chapter 4 7	Chapter 38 243	Chapter 72 436
Chapter 5 11	Chapter 39 249	Chapter 73 440
Chapter 6 16	Chapter 40 256	Chapter 74 446
Chapter 7 19	Chapter 41 261	Chapter 75 450
Chapter 8 23	Chapter 42 267	Chapter 76 454
Chapter 9 28	Chapter 43 273	Chapter 77 458
Chapter 10 23	Chapter 44 281	Chapter 78 461
Chapter 11 39	Chapter 45 285	Chapter 79 462
Chapter 12 47	Chapter 46 290	Chapter 80 466
Chapter 13 56	Chapter 47 296	Chapter 81 469
Chapter 14 60	Chapter 48 300	Chapter 82 474
Chapter 15 65	Chapter 49 306	Chapter 83 479
Chapter 16 70	Chapter 50 311	Chapter 84 486
Chapter 17 81	Chapter 51 317	Chapter 85 493
Chapter 18 90	Chapter 52 324	Chapter 86 497
Chapter 19 97	Chapter 53 329	Chapter 87 503
Chapter 20 105	Chapter 54 335	Chapter 88 509
Chapter 21 115	Chapter 55 342	Chapter 89 517
Chapter 22 123	Chapter 56 347	Chapter 90 519
Chapter 23 130	Chapter 57 352	Chapter 91 524
Chapter 24 135	Chapter 58 358	Chapter 92 532
Chapter 25 145	Chapter 59 363	Chapter 93 538
Chapter 26 153	Chapter 60 368	Chapter 94 544
Chapter 27 163	Chapter 61 373	Chapter 95 548
Chapter 28 171	Chapter 62 381	Chapter 96 552
Chapter 29 176	Chapter 63 385	Chapter 97 554
Chapter 30 182	Chapter 64 391	Chapter 98 564
Chapter 31 189	Chapter 65 399	Chapter 99 567
Chapter 32 197	Chapter 66 402	Chapter 100 573
Chapter 33 207	Chapter 67 407	
Chapter 34 213	Chapter 68 414	

Appendix 1

The Coming Forth of The Sealed Portion 577
How I Received the Gold Plates of Mormon 582

Appendix 2

The Book of Lehi

The Lost 116-page Manuscript 591
Chapter 1 599
Chapter 2 604
Chapter 3 607
Chapter 4 611
Chapter 5 615
Chapter 6 621
Chapter 7 623
Chapter 8 626
Chapter 9 629

Appendix 3

The First Vision

Introduction 635
The First Vision 637

Appendix 4

The Fullness of the Gospel of Jesus Christ

Introduction 643
Matthew 5 647
Matthew 6 650
Matthew 7 652

The Sealed Portion of The Book of Mormon

AN ABRIDGMENT OF THE VISION AND WORDS OF THE BROTHER OF JARED
WRITTEN AND SEALED UP BY MORONI, THE SON OF MORMON

Therefore, these things shall remain sealed and hidden from the eyes of all men except it be unto those to whom the Lord shall reveal them. And I, Moroni, have written upon these plates the things that the Brother of Jared saw. And I have made these plates after the pattern that hath been shown unto me by my father. And the Lord hath commanded me that I should seal up these things; that in the day that one shall be found worthy, even one who shall demonstrate faith in the Lord, even as the Brother of Jared did upon the mount; that in that day these things shall be delivered unto him with the interpreters thereof. And a commandment I give unto him who shall receive these things, that he shall leave this portion of the plates sealed until the day cometh that he shall receive a commandment of the Lord to translate them. And thou shalt translate these things by the gift and power of God. Therefore, I have sealed up the interpreters with this record according to the commandment of the Lord so that thou shalt be able to translate therewith.

And he that will contend against these things, let him be accursed; and also he that shall deny these things, let him also be accursed; for unto them I will show no greater things, saith the Lord. For in that day that men shall begin to exercise faith in me, even as the Brother of Jared did, then will I manifest unto them these things, even unto the unfolding unto them all of my revelations, saith the Lord, even Jesus Christ.

Come unto the God of Israel, Oh, ye Gentiles, and he will show unto you the knowledge which is hid up because of your unbelief. Come unto the Lord of Hosts and it shall be made manifest unto you the great things which the Father hath laid up for you from the foundation of the world, and it hath not come unto you because of your unbelief and the hardness of your hearts.

Behold, when ye shall rend that veil of unbelief which causeth you to remain in your awful state of wickedness, and hardness of heart, and blindness of mind, then shall the great and marvelous things which have been hidden from the foundation of the world from you, shall be made known unto you. Therefore, when ye shall receive this record of the writings of the Brother of Jared, then shall ye know that the work of the Father hath commenced upon the face of all the earth. And if ye shall call upon the Father in the name of Jesus with a broken heart and a contrite spirit, then ye shall know that the Father hath remembered the covenants which he hath made unto the house of Israel and unto all the world.

TRANSLATED BY CHRISTOPHER MARC NEMELKA

CHAPTER 1

Moroni writes the things revealed to the Brother of Jared. He testifies that Jesus Christ came to the Nephites. He exhorts all to have faith and obey the commandments of God.

AND now I, Moroni, proceed to write the great and marvelous things that the Lord hath made manifest unto the brother of Jared.

2 And I write these things according to the commandment of the Lord in the which he hath commanded me, saying: A commandment I have given unto thee, that thou shalt write the things which I have shown unto the Brother of Jared at the time he presented himself before me and manifested great faith in my name, evensomuch that I could not withhold my spirit from before him.

3 And again, a commandment I give unto thee, that thou shalt include these things with the record of my people who are the children of Lehi, who came out of Jerusalem, whose seed is a remnant of the house of Israel.

4 Behold, I have prepared these two stones as interpreters inasmuch as I have caused the language of the Jaredites to be confounded. This I have done to hide these things from the eyes of the world. For behold, there are none, save a few only, who have faith enough to behold the things that the Brother of Jared saw.

5 And I have shown unto him all the inhabitants of the world which have been, and all those which shall live upon the earth on which thou standest. Behold, I could not withhold them from his sight, even unto the ends of the earth.

6 For behold, I have covenanted with the children of men from the beginning that if it so be that they exercise faith in me and keep my commandments in all things, believing that I can show unto them the mysteries of godliness, behold, I will come unto them by the power of the Holy Ghost; and he shall teach them whatsoever their hearts desire, if it so be that they ask in righteousness.

7 Nevertheless, thou shalt seal up the words of the brother of Jared until I have manifested myself in the flesh unto my people.

8 And now, I, Moroni, have written the things which the Lord hath commanded me upon the plates which I have formed with my own hands according to the pattern shown unto me by my father. And upon these plates of my father hath an account of the resurrection of Jesus Christ been given.

9 Behold, it hath truly been manifested herein that Jesus did come unto his people. Not only did he visit the Jews who were his people at Jerusalem, but he did also manifest himself unto my fathers according to the promises which he hath made unto them. For my fathers were separated from the Jews at Jerusalem through the mercy and for the purposes of the Lord.

10 Therefore, I, Moroni, write the words of the brother of Jared according to the commandment which the Lord hath given me. Nevertheless, these things shall be sealed up and shall not be given to the children of men with the first part of the record which my father, Mormon, hath made upon these plates of ore.

11 And the Lord hath made it known unto me that these things shall be withheld from the children of men until the day that they begin to exercise faith in God and also in His Son, Jesus Christ, even as the Brother of Jared did; that they also may be sanctified by the Holy Spirit, having overcome the sins and temptations of the world.

12 And inasmuch as they shall do these things, the Lord shall make manifest unto them all the things which the brother of Jared beheld; and all of the revelations of Jesus Christ, the Son of God; yea, even all things which have been given unto the children of men from the foundation of the world shall be revealed unto them.

13 And when the children of men begin to exercise this faith of which I have spoken, then shall the Lord reveal these things unto them.

14 And it shall come to pass that when these things shall be revealed unto them, there shall be none, save a few only, who shall understand them and receive them into their hearts. And the Spirit shall witness the truthfulness of these things unto them.

15 And many shall mock at these things and contend against the word of the Lord. Behold,

thus saith the Lord unto those who shall mock and deny these things: Let them be accursed from hence forth and forever. For they have sealed unto themselves eternal damnation, insomuch that I will show no greater things unto them.

16 But those unto whom I shall reveal these things shall be laid under a strict command that they shall only reveal unto the children of men the words which I shall give unto them. For this reason have I caused these things to be written and preserved until the appointed time when all things shall be revealed for the salvation of mine elect.

17 And it shall come to pass, that those who shall receive the words of the brother of Jared and accept them with gladness, and harden not their hearts, to them shall be given the greater portion of my word—which is my gospel of truth—until they know the mysteries of God in full.

18 And they shall receive a new name which shall only be known and understood by those who receive it. And they shall become my friends, and I will be their God.

19 Now I, Moroni, do plead with my brethren and also my sisters, yea, even with all those who shall receive these things who are of the house of Israel, and also those among the Gentiles who shall receive these things; Yea, I say unto you: Come unto the Lord, even Jesus Christ, and he will show unto you the great and marvelous things of God which He hath caused to be hidden from the eyes of the world because of wickedness and unbelief.

20 Behold, I say unto you, that when ye shall begin to rend that veil of unbelief which causeth the Spirit of the Lord to withdraw from you; yea, when ye shall cast off the chains of the devil with which he hath you bound, then my beloved brothers and sisters, shall these great and marvelous things which have been hid from the foundations of the world be made known unto you.

21 Oh, my beloved brethren, how long will the Lord, our God, allow the earth to lie under such bondage of sin? How long can He remain merciful unto you in your wickedness?

22 My soul is harrowed up in sorrow because of the things which the brother of Jared hath written concerning you. Behold, it is because of your wickedness that the Lord hath withheld these things from you; and behold, these same things shall condemn you at the last day.

23 And it shall come to pass in that day, that the books shall be opened, and ye shall read of your corruptions and deceptions, and ye shall weep and wail and gnash your teeth as ye behold the wickedness of your ways and the deceptions of your hearts.

24 Even as the Lord requested of the Father, even so I would that this bitter cup be allowed to pass from before my lips that I might not drink thereof and sorrow because of your sins. Nevertheless, the Lord hath commanded me and I must obey.

25 For behold, the words of the brother of Jared are great and marvelous, and if ye mock them, ye mock God. For they are the words of Christ given unto all those who do his will and call upon his holy name with a broken heart and a contrite spirit.

CHAPTER 2

Moroni begins the record of the Brother of Jared. The Brother of Jared is shown the spirit body of Jesus and the kingdoms of the Father, and also the kingdom where the spirits of the children of men were created and raised by their Eternal Mothers.

AND now I, Moroni, will proceed with the account of the Brother of Jared, which translation was given unto me by the gift and power of God through the Urim and Thummim, which, being interpreted, is light and perfection.

2 And it came to pass that the brother of Jared was carried away by the Spirit of the Lord upon the mount called Shelem.

3 And after he had beheld the spirit body of Jesus, the brother of Jared marveled exceedingly that his mortal eyes could perceive such things.

4 And it came to pass that the Lord perceived the thoughts of the brother of Jared and said unto him: Marvel not that this thing hath come to pass. For behold, thou canst not see spiritual things with mortal eyes. Nevertheless, I have caused a change to come over thy mortal body that thou might behold my work and my glory, which is the work and glory of my Father, whom I serve.

5 And it came to pass that the eyes of his understanding were opened and the brother of Jared beheld as it were many worlds and kingdoms without end.

6 And he marveled exceedingly and exclaimed, yea his entire soul being filled with the Spirit of God: Oh, great God, Lord of all, yea, even the Father of all things in the heavens and all those things which are upon earth, what are these worlds which appear to men as the stars in the night sky?

7 And it came to pass that the Lord answered him saying: All these are the kingdoms of my Father and also the kingdoms of His fathers before Him.

8 For behold, the world upon which thou standest is a creation of my Father, who is the father of my spirit and also the father of thy spirit. Behold, our Father hath created many such worlds and the numbers of His creations are numberless; nevertheless, He knoweth them and they are His.

9 And it came to pass that the Brother of Jared was taken, as it were, to one of the worlds which he beheld.

10 And this world was like unto the world in which we live. Yea, there were many strange and marvelous buildings, the construction of which he had never before beheld. And even I, Moroni, am forbidden to describe the exactness of their form and the glory of their architecture.

11 And it came to pass that the brother of Jared was overcome by the strangeness of these things, insomuch that he inquired of the Lord as to the meaning of the things which he beheld.

12 And the Lord answered him saying: Behold, this is the kingdom and the glory of our Father. It was on this world that our Father begat His posterity, even the spirits of all the children of men which live upon the world on which thou standest. And this was once a world like unto the world on which thou livest, and is where our Father learned the mysteries and responsibilities of godhood.

13 And behold, it is upon this same world where the mothers of the spirits of all the children of God reside with the Father.

CHAPTER 3

The Brother of Jared meets the Father and is overcome by His spirit. He meets his heavenly Mother and is commanded to obey the commandments of the Lord.

AND it came to pass that as the brother of Jared looked upon the world where the Father dwelleth in all His glory, he beheld many people talking and reasoning one with another. And he beheld their dress that it was of a whiteness that was most exquisite and exceeded any that he had beheld before.

2 And as he pondered on the beauty of the people, he looked thereon and beheld plants and vegetation which grew in the likeness of those upon this earth; nevertheless, they grew spontaneously as if they were compelled to grow without the aid and toil of man. And this vegetation was not like any that he had known upon the earth.

3 And the people came forth and partook of the fruit of the vines and of the trees, yea, even of all the vegetation that produced flowers and fruits which were pleasing to the desires of the people.

4 And he beheld the people partaking of this fruit freely, taking only that which they desired to make themselves happy. For behold, the people appeared as though they never hungered, neither did they thirst, nor did they take more than that which they needed; yea, they partook of the fruit only to make themselves joyous and fulfill their desires of happiness.

5 And the brother of Jared continued his description of this world, saying: And I beheld that the moment that one of these fruits was plucked from the vines or from the trees, that another one would immediately begin to grow in the stead thereof, insomuch that the trees and

vines were always full of fruit, and also of beautiful flowers.

6 And my soul desired that I might also partake of this fruit that I might not hunger or thirst again.

7 And as I approached the people who were partaking of the fruit, I beheld a man among them who was of such familiarity to me that it caused me to be drawn immediately to his presence, as a small boy would be drawn to his father in a strange crowd. Nevertheless, I was not a stranger among them.

8 And as the brother of Jared drew near unto this man of whom he spoke, his heart and soul were filled with an unspeakable love and warmth.

9 And the brother of Jared continued his words saying: His radiance filled my entire soul, evensomuch that it did cause me to shrink from his presence. For my tongue seemed bound in that I could not speak. And I did fall to the ground because my limbs could no longer support me; and I became, as it were, a small child who knew not how to move his limbs or use his tongue.

10 And this man reached forth and took me by the hand commanding me to rise. And no sooner had I touched His hand, than I immediately received my strength once again and stood before this wondrous being.

11 And He spoke unto me saying: My son, from whence cometh thou and for what purpose dost thou desire to speak unto thy Father?

12 But I still could not speak, my soul being filled with an essence of the spirit which came directly from the soul of my Father. But I did attempt to cry to Jesus that he might assist me in speaking to the Father. For behold, the Spirit bore witness unto me that this man was indeed my Father and also the Father of Jesus.

13 And Jesus did appear at my side and spake unto the Father on my behalf saying: My Father, this, Thy son, hath come unto Thee to receive the further light and knowledge which Thou hast promised unto all those who believe in me and keep my commandments; yea, even all those who come unto me with a broken heart and a contrite spirit.

14 Behold, my Father, I could not restrain him from beholding these things and coming forth unto Thee. For he hath manifested the faith which the eternal laws require before any of Thy children can behold Thee and come into Thy presence. He is of the world that Thou hast placed in my power and under my authority, and he is my disciple.

15 And the Father spake unto Jesus saying: Well done, my beloved Son. There are, save a few only, who have prepared themselves for this moment in mortality. And I say unto thee, that never before hath such faith been manifested by any of the inhabitants of the earth that I have placed in thy power. Therefore, this, my son, shall know me and thee, for we are one, yea the very Eternal God; and he shall know the things which have been reserved since the beginning for those who belong to our Order, and he shall be one with us and be received into our Order.

16 And thou knowest, my Son, that all those who manifest this faith and keep thy commandments shall belong to this same Order, and it is this Order which shall rule and reign forever, worlds without end.

17 Nevertheless, thou shalt command him to keep these things from the rest of my children who reside in thy kingdom, until they, too, repent and work righteousness, having faith in the things which thou shalt teach unto them by thine own mouth and also by the mouth of the Holy Ghost, which I have placed under thy authority.

18 Instruct this, my son, to remember the things which he hath seen, and also the things which he shall be shown hereafter. Command him to write these things and seal them up to come forth at the time appointed for them, yea, even according to the commandments that I have given unto thee.

19 And Jesus answered the Father saying: Thy will be done my Father, as it always hath and shall always be done, and the glory be Thine forever.

20 And it came to pass that the Father led the Brother of Jared and the Son forth among the people. And the people were exceedingly beautiful and happy. Yea, never were there known to be such a happy people. And they truly loved one another.

21 And the Brother of Jared wrote, saying: I beheld their beauty and the peace of their souls, and I was desirous to be a part of them.

22 And there were many women among the people, and some men, but there appeared to be more women than there were men.

23 Nevertheless, there was no lasciviousness, coveting, or evil thoughts among them. For all seemed to know all as they are known and see others as they are seen.

24 And as I wandered forth among them, I beheld that some of these women greeted the Father with a kind bow, a handclasp, and a tender kiss. I marveled greatly at the tenderness the Father had for each one.

25 And I asked the Father, saying: Who are these women who encompass Thee with such admiration and love?

26 And the Father stretched forth his hand and beckoned unto one of the women and brought her forth and placed her before me. And I beheld her beauty and her fairness, which surpassed that of any woman I had ever known.

27 And her radiance caused my limbs that they did once again lose their strength that they could not support my body.

28 But behold, my Lord, even Jesus Christ, was at my side and did support me that I did not fall.

29 And the woman spake unto me saying: Behold, my son, I am the mother of thy spirit and my name is Marihala. I am she that provided the materials necessary so that thy Father, who is my brother and my friend, could create thy spirit.

30 And the woman turned to the Father and said: Elohim, my soul is filled with joy because of this, our son, who hath proven himself worthy to know us and become one with us. Alas, my soul sorroweth for the majority of our children who inhabit the world which Thou hast placed in the authority of his elder brother Jesus, the Christ.

31 I pray that Thou wilt bless this, our son, that he may continue in righteousness and may one day join our Holy Order which hath existed from the beginning to bring about the eternal life and happiness of our children.

32 And the Father looked upon the woman; and He truly loved this woman with all of His soul; and the Father answered her, saying: My dearly beloved, I also share Thy sorrow and anguish because of the wickedness of our children which belong to the kingdom under the authority of our son, even Jesus Christ.

33 Behold, this, our son, shall be the means by which many of our children are brought to repentance and understanding that they might also work righteousness and prepare themselves for their inheritance in our eternal worlds.

34 And it came to pass that the spirit Mother of the brother of Jared did embrace Her son, and his heart was filled with exceeding great joy. And the Woman blessed him saying: Go, my son, and do the things that the Lord hath commanded thee to do. And blessed art thou for that which thou art about to see and write unto the children of men.

35 For behold, it shall shine unto them out of the darkness and shall be brought to the knowledge of the people according to the wisdom and power of God. And because of thy words, many of my own children shall one day return unto me and know that I am, and that I am their Mother as thou now knowest.

36 And now my son, I would that thou shouldst remember to build thy foundation upon the rock of thy Redeemer, even Jesus Christ, thy elder brother, a son of God who hath been appointed to rule and reign over the kingdom of the Father to which thou belongest.

37 And if thou shalt do these things and obey his words in all things whatsoever he shall command thee, behold, thou shalt receive eternal life and one day thou shalt return unto me and thy Father, and then thou shalt sorrow no more. And thou shalt know me as I am and we shall share eternal happiness forever.

38 And this, my son, is salvation and eternal life.

39 And now, my son, I bid thee farewell that thou mightest go and do the things which have been commanded of thee.

40 And it came to pass that the Mother of his spirit left the brother of Jared. Nevertheless, Her radiance did not leave him for sometime thereafter; for he felt as though he was a part of Her and She a part of him.

41 And the Brother of Jared praised and worshipped his Eternal Mother as he did his Eternal Father. And there were other fathers and mothers in this world, but of those the brother of Jared wrote little, as they were not his eternal parents.

CHAPTER 4

The brother of Jared sees many worlds and kingdoms of the Father. He receives many mysteries and knowledge because of his faithfulness. The Father outlines his mission. He distinguishes between the spirit body and the mortal body, and introduces the three degrees of glory in the kingdom of God.

AND it came to pass that the brother of Jared continued on his journey accompanied by the Father and the Son.

2 And they did show unto him many great and marvelous things. And they presented before his eyes many kingdoms and worlds. And the eyes of his understanding were opened, and he understood that the worlds which he was beholding appeared as the stars in the night sky from the earth from whence he came.

3 And it came to pass that Jesus spake unto him saying: My son—and the brother of Jared was truly the son of Jesus inasmuch as Jesus was appointed to be the God of this world by the Father—and Jesus said unto him: Thou hast beheld that which no mortal hath beheld before.

4 Behold, there have been many righteous men who have lived upon the earth who have desired to see that which thou hast beheld. But because of the wickedness of the men who lived among them, I could not show unto them such great and marvelous things.

5 For behold, their hope and faith was sufficient enough for them; and with this faith, they waited patiently upon the Father to reveal unto them these mysteries in His own due time.

6 For this purpose I have led thee and thy brother and thy friends from among the wicked; yea, even that I might raise up a righteous branch unto the Father.

7 And it was because of thy faith, and also the faith of thy brother, Jared, that I have done these things. And because I have led thee away from among the wicked, I am permitted by the Father to show unto thee the things which thou beholdest.

8 And thou shall behold many more of the mysteries of God, which shall be shown unto thee, that thou might teach thy brethren these things.

9 And if it so be that thy brethren turn from me and keep not my commandments, after they have received these things from thy hand, and have been taught my commandments by thee, then I will withdraw my spirit from before them and they shall be left unto themselves.

10 And those who do not repent, and remain in their wickedness, shall be in the power of Satan, and he shall rule over them, for he desireth to have them.

11 Now, I, Moroni, continue to relate the words of the brother of Jared which he wrote pertaining to the glorious vision that he had seen pertaining to the world in which the spirits of all men reside.

12 For behold, all of the spirits of every man and woman who have lived upon this earth were born unto eternal Mothers and Fathers in the world that the brother of Jared beheld. And it was on this world that our spirits received the learning and the nurturing of our Heavenly Parents, like unto that which we give our mortal children. Nevertheless, we were taught the eternal laws that pertained unto that world, or in other words, the world on which we were created.

13 And this world that the brother of Jared beheld shall be known in mortality as the Celestial Glory, which is the highest degree of glory of all the glories in the kingdom of God.

14 And it is a planet like unto the one on which we reside; and it is in another part of the kingdom of God, which kingdom is vast and eternal, in other words, it hath no beginning and no end, thus it is eternal.

15 And it was on this earth where the Fathers and Mothers of our spirits were born into mortality and passed through the days of their probation, proving Themselves worthy of the blessings and power of the Celestial glory.

16 And after They had proven Themselves worthy of this power and glory, the planet on which They passed the days of their probation was transformed and renewed and received its paradisical glory, which glory was that of a Celestial glory.

17 And there are other Gods that live on the same world on which reside our Eternal Father and Mothers. And these other Gods have other worlds that They have created on which They have placed Their spirit children, so that Their children might also pass through the days of their probation like unto us.

18 Nevertheless, the Lord hath commanded me that I touch not on these other worlds that the brother of Jared saw, but that I relate the words of the brother of Jared that pertain unto us and the world on which we reside.

19 But I have been commanded to reveal this mystery unto those of you who shall receive these things, even this knowledge that there are many earths like unto the one where we reside, and there are many Gods and many Christs that pertain unto these worlds. And these Gods and these Christs are the creators and the leaders of these worlds.

20 And many of these mysteries will be revealed unto you through the words of the brother of Jared, but of the worlds that do not pertain unto us, I make no further mention upon these plates. But know this, that these Gods and these Christs of which I have spoken are bound by the same eternal laws by which our God and our Christ are bound.

21 Therefore, the works of our Father and the works of our Christ are the same works that are done in other worlds; and the number of these worlds are without beginning and without end, thus they are eternal. And also these Gods and these Christs of which I have spoken are also eternal, therefore they have no beginning and they have no end.

22 And this is the mystery that was revealed unto the brother of Jared by the Lord. And because of this eternal truth, many have stumbled and have erred in their desire to know and understand the truth regarding these things, yea, even regarding the very foundation of the kingdom of God.

23 For behold, there are many who believe that there was a beginning, or in other words a creation of matter. But in this they do err and understand not the truth regarding these things. For howbeit that there is a beginning if there is not an end? And also, howbeit that there is an end if there is no beginning?

24 And since there have always been Gods, then there hath always been matter. Nevertheless, this matter existeth in an unorganized state. And it is the power of the Gods to organize this matter and cause it to appear as the worlds in which life existeth.

25 And these Gods also possess the power to create spirits, or in other words, organize matter into a spirit form like unto the bodies that They possess. And there are irrevocable eternal laws that determine how this matter is organized. And this matter is organized inside the eternal bodies of Eternal Mothers, who are the Mothers of our spirits. And They receive the commands thereof from the bodies of Eternal Fathers, who are the Fathers of our spirits. And in this way is all life created—male and female Gods and Goddesses organizing matter according to the eternal laws of heaven.

26 And it came to pass that the brother of Jared beheld the spirits that were born unto the Father, and also unto those Women who had chosen the Father and existed in the world that the brother of Jared beheld. Nevertheless, our Eternal Father was not the only eternal Father who resided in that world, and there were also many other Women who resided therein who did not pertain to the world on which we live.

27 And the brother of Jared was shown all of the spirits that were children of our Father, which spirits were created from the bodies of our Eternal Mothers. And these same spirits were raised by their Mothers like unto children that are raised by mortal mothers; nevertheless, there was no pain and toil in childbirth, neither was there any tribulation in the rearing of these spirit children.

28 And it came to pass that these spirit children grew in stature and in knowledge, and they lived among their eternal parents who taught them all things whatsoever they were required to know in their spiritual state. And as these spirit children grew in knowledge, they began to realize that they were different from their parents, insomuch that they did not have a body of flesh and bone like unto their Eternal Parents, who were exalted beings.

29 And they realized that they did not understand the happiness that their Eternal Parents enjoyed, nor did they understand the requirements of this happiness. For behold, they saw these Gods eat and find joy therein. And they saw them physically enjoin one with another and also find pleasure therein. But these spirits could not understand this pleasure, nor this joy, having a different body than that which their Eternal Parents possessed.

30 And they were taught by their Mothers that this pleasure and joy could only be experienced when the spirit matter from which they were created interacteth with other matter from which these feelings of joy shall come. And it was this other matter that the spirit children did not possess.

31 And it came to pass that the Father called His children unto Him and counseled with them. And He taught them many more things pertaining to that which would be required of them so that they would have a body with which they might also experience the things that He enjoyeth.

32 And He taught them that very few of His children would have bodies like unto His body and the bodies of their Mothers, for these type of bodies are reserved for those who would prove themselves worthy to have the power that these bodies possess, even the power of creation. And these bodies are Celestial bodies.

33 And there are other bodies that would be created and provided for the majority of His children, so that they, too, could partake of eternal happiness and joy according to the desire of happiness that each spirit possesseth. And these bodies are Terrestrial and Telestial bodies, having been thus explained to them by the Father.

34 And the Father taught His children that in His kingdom there would be three degrees of happiness, or in other words, degrees of glory in which His children would dwell according to each of their individual desires of happiness.

And these degrees of happiness would have each, three separate degrees, and each of these degrees would be instituted for the pleasure and happiness of those who reside therein.

35 Thus there are bodies Celestial, and bodies Terrestrial, and bodies Telestial—each pertaining to the state of happiness that its inhabitants desire.

36 And these are the glories in the kingdom of God. And to each glory there are laws and blessings assigned to govern those who dwell therein.

37 For behold, the Celestial glory is where they who are like unto the Father dwell. Yea, these are they who derive their happiness in the continual service of others, and they do nothing for themselves; but their actions and their desires are eternally directed to the service of their creations, as well as to the service of each other. And their pleasure cometh solely from this selfless service.

38 And because of their selflessness, they become Gods and Goddesses to rule and reign forever in worlds without end. For behold, only These have the power and the authority to create other beings and other worlds and oversee the eternal work that is required by the laws of heaven. And They have the proper bodies to perform this work—male and female—and They are the only ones that can partake of the joy that is a cause of the union between a male and a female.

39 These have overcome all things and have proven Themselves worthy to possess the exceedingly miraculous powers that all Gods possess. And if it so be that They could possibly be selfish in Their desires, then They would disrupt the order of the heavens and would create things for Their own pleasure and for Their own joy, and the eternal work of God would cease.

40 But it is impossible that the work of God should cease, for then all would be for naught; then the world would not be, and we could not exist.

41 And now I, Moroni, have been wrought upon greatly by the spirit of God, insomuch that I have been commanded to explain further some other things pertaining to the position of those

who are Gods, yea even those that exist in a exalted Celestial state of happiness.

42 And many of these things were touched upon by the prophets and are also touched upon in the holy scriptures that are among the children of men in our world. But there are few that understand the meaning of these things. And others have been led to believe that because God cannot be corrupt without destroying the work of God, then those who are His chosen leaders among the children of men cannot be corrupt, because they, too, would destroy the work of God.

43 Behold, those that believe this are in great error, and are susceptible to the enticings of the devil, which are given unto them by those men and women who make such a claim. For those who claim that a leader of the church of God will never be allowed to mislead them, are being misled by those who proclaim this. For they have taken an eternal principle and made it carnal to fit their foolish and selfish desires.

44 For behold, the Lord alloweth the children of men to be led according to the desires of their hearts. And if their desires are evil, then they will be led unto evil. And if the desires of their hearts be good, then are they led in righteousness.

45 Therefore, the leaders of the people will be as evil or as good as the people who they lead. And also the people will be as good or as evil as those who lead them.

46 For the eternal laws of heaven cannot be altered, and by these laws are all the children of God guaranteed their agency—which is a power to act according to the dictates of their own conscience, according to each, by their own desires of happiness.

47 And no man or woman can be forced to follow a leader without his or her consent. For if this were the case, then the eternal law of agency would be for naught, and then God would be for naught, and His work would cease.

48 And if a man followeth blindly and sayeth unto himself: I have accepted this leader as my leader and will trust in him; and if it so be that this leader leadeth me wrongly, then I will not be responsible for my actions, but my sin will fall upon the head of my leader.

49 Now, this man who thinketh this is in grave danger of being led into misery and sorrow. For behold, all the creations of God are responsible to the God who gave them life and who hath also granted unto them their agency to choose their own actions, which actions will lead to their own misery, or to their own happiness.

50 However, woe be unto those who set themselves up as leaders among men, for not only will they suffer for their own sins, but they must suffer also for the sins of their followers. And therefore, their state is much worse than that of their followers. But their followers shall also suffer with them.

51 Now this is the thing that the Spirit hath instructed me to explain in this record, even that those who are our leaders, or our Gods, that lead us in righteousness, shall partake of our happiness also. Yea, we shall receive eternal happiness if it so be that we follow Their guidance, but They, too, shall receive more happiness than us, having added to Theirs because of our own.

52 Now this is the state of those that live in the Celestial glory in the kingdom of God. Therefore, because Their happiness is directly correlated to the happiness that we receive, They strive to give us this happiness, thus affecting Their own.

53 For this reason they are our servants and are eternally bound by their own natures to assure us continual happiness.

54 And it hath been taught by the precepts of men that those who are Celestial beings become Gods and Goddesses to rule and reign in the eternities, while those who are not Celestial become the servants of these Gods and Goddesses and serve them forever in worlds without end.

55 And this doctrine is contrary to the laws of heaven and also contrary to the laws that govern the Celestial glory. For behold, God is our servant and will remain so forever.

56 And we have chosen These Beings who are our servants. In other words, we have chosen our God and have accepted Him as our leader and our creator, knowing that according to the unalterable laws of heaven, He will serve us by bringing us the joy and happiness that we seek.

57 For behold, did not our God, yea, even our Lord Jesus Christ come down to this earth and take upon him flesh and blood so that he could serve us? Even though he was made in the image of his Father, and therefore is in his Father as his Father is in him, thus becoming a mortal God, did he not put himself below all of us?

58 Yea, now this is what is meant by the condescension of God. For behold, he was born into the world amongst animals of a lower order—a place that most would consider unclean for the birth of a child. And as he grew and came to know that his Father was God, he became even more humble still.

59 And did he not teach his disciples that the least among them was the greatest of all? And when he came down to the children of Lehi, did he not bring the children unto him and bless them and cause the angels to minister unto them? And many of the things that he said unto the children, and also many of the things that he said unto his Father in heaven could not be written by my father in that part of his record. And it is those things that I am explaining now, even those things that my father was forbidden to write. But I write them according to the commandment of the Spirit which is in me.

60 Doth the record of my father not say that no tongue can speak, nor can it be written by any man the great and marvelous things that the children of Lehi heard Jesus speak when he prayed for them unto the Father?

61 And doth it not say that no one can conceive of the joy which filled their souls, yea, even the exceeding joy that overcame the multitude that heard the prayer of Jesus unto the Father on their behalf?

62 And my father, Mormon, continued in his record, saying, And they arose from the earth, and he spake unto them, and bade them arise. And they arose from the earth, and he said unto them: Blessed are ye because of your faith. And now behold, my joy is full. And when he had said these words, he wept.

63 Now I, Moroni, do testify unto you that the tears that Jesus wept were tears of exceeding great joy and happiness. And this happiness is the happiness that I have explained to you that is felt by those who are Celestial beings, yea even those who are Gods.

64 Behold, these people heard the Lord glorifying them and praying to the Father that they would understand his mission and his glory. He expressed his deep love for the people and told them that he was their eternal servant who had been chosen by them to lead them and teach the laws of salvation unto them so that they could enjoy the fruits of eternal happiness.

65 And he made an intercessory covenant with the Father in behalf of the people that he would assure their eternal salvation by teaching them the things that they must do to gain this salvation. And in an incredible demonstration of his love for them, Jesus promised all the people who were in the land of Bountiful, yea, even all those who had died, who were their relatives and their friends, that he would go and prepare a place in the kingdom of God for each of them, thus assuring them their eternal happiness forever.

66 Now this is why the people were filled with exceedingly great joy, and this is also why Jesus said that his joy was full.

CHAPTER 5

The spirit children of God are taught the plan of salvation. The rebellion of Lucifer and the great debate in heaven is mentioned. The state of those who followed Satan is revealed.

Now, I, Moroni, continue with the vision that the brother of Jared saw pertaining to the spirit children of God.

2 And it came to pass that the Father showed all of His children examples of the kingdoms that He had already created; yea, even those kingdoms of glory that appear as the stars in the night sky to our mortal eyes.

3 And He explained unto them that these were the works of His own hands, and that after their pattern He would prepare the worlds wherein these spirits would reside and enter into their second estate, or in other words, mortality.

4 Behold, the first estate of all beings is that in

which they were created as spirits. And it is this estate in which the brother of Jared found himself in his vision. And the second estate of which he hath written is the state in which we are now upon this earth.

5 And this second estate is a time of probation for all the spirits of the children of God to see if they are willing to do all things whatsoever they are commanded to do by the Lord.

6 And it is also a state in which all spirits shall prove to themselves that the degree of glory in the kingdom of God to which they belong is justifiable, and it shall be proven unto them to be the only place where they can find a fullness of joy according to the happiness that each of them desireth.

7 For behold, all spirits are taught the laws that govern the different degrees of glory in the kingdom of God. And each spirit knoweth at the time the Father presenteth the examples of His kingdom before them, which degree of glory best suiteth their desires for happiness, having thus determined these desires while growing up and progressing as a spirit being.

8 And the laws and happiness of the Celestial glory are shown unto them, and also the laws and happiness of the Terrestrial and Telestial kingdoms are also shown unto them. And each spirit recognizeth that which he desireth to make him happy.

9 Nevertheless, to the Terrestrial and Telestial glories there are eternal penalties affixed, thus distinguishing them from the glory of the Celestial, which hath no penalty affixed to it.

10 And the penalty of the Terrestrial glory is that the inhabitants thereof will not have the power of creation. In other words, they will have no ability to experience posterity, having not the body that can create these beings. Yea, there will be no male or female among them, having no need for the different sexes, and no need for those relations that are enjoyed by a man and a women in the course of creating a new life.

11 And those of this glory will not have the knowledge or the power to create other worlds, or the animals, or the plant life that is necessary to produce life on these other worlds.

12 Nevertheless, they will have exceedingly great joy and live peacefully one with another, having no concern for their well being, having all things provided for them from the administration of those in the Celestial glory. And these will also administer to their own needs and find much joy and pleasure therein.

13 And these are those who are the majority of the spirits of the children of men.

14 And those who inherit the Telestial glory will receive a penalty like unto that received by those in the Terrestrial glory, even that they will have no power of creation or the blessings that go with this power. Nevertheless, they will forever live with the realization that they belong to the order of a Telestial glory, which is the lowest order of the kingdom of God, and this because of their very selfish natures and desires. And this is the penalty affixed to the Telestial glory, even this knowledge that will burn in their breasts forever.

15 Nevertheless, these also shall experience exceedingly great joys, which joys we are accustomed to feeling in our second estate, or in the world in which we live, but they shall live without the sorrows that we presently experience during the days of our probation.

16 And I, Moroni, was about to write more regarding the wonderful blessings and joys that Telestial beings will enjoy in that glory of the kingdom of God, but the Spirit hath forbidden me at this time, and thus I end my description of the Telestial glory.

17 And it came to pass that as the Father presented this plan of salvation to His spirit children, one of them stood up and questioned the Father, and wondered why it should be that all spirits should not have the full blessings of the Celestial glory like unto the Father.

18 And this spirit was a great one among those that the Father had created, and his name was Lucifer, he being a spirit who was the firstborn of his Eternal Mother and a leader among the spirits.

19 And Lucifer questioned the Father saying: Oh, my Father, forgive the boldness of my words and allow me the agency that Thou hast granted unto all Thy creations. For behold, there are many among us that know that they will not become Gods, and have thus accepted their

place in thy kingdom in the glories that will bring them their chosen happiness, but to which certain penalties have been affixed.

20 And now my Father, why is it that these must suffer so and not become as Thou art and also as our Mothers are—powerful and blessed with the ability to have posterity and the joys that thou enjoyest in Thy kingdom?

21 We know that Thou art God, and that Thou hast the power to give these things unto us if it so be Thy desire.

22 And Thou hast spoken unto us of our probation and hast shown unto us examples of the pain and suffering that we must go through during the days of this probation. And I ask of Thee, why is it necessary that we must suffer so, seeing that we already realize which glory in Thy eternal kingdoms is most satisfactory unto us?

23 Is it not possible that Thou canst create our eternal bodies for us and prepare the worlds in which we can live and give these things unto us without suffering and without passing through so much affliction and sorrow?

24 And when Lucifer had spoken these words unto the Father, many of the other spirits began to voice their concerns unto the Father also, evensomuch that there arose a mighty contention among the spirits who had gathered to hear the words of the Father.

25 And there were many spirits who sided with Lucifer and joined him in what they thought were righteous and just desires.

26 And there were many spirits that fought against Lucifer and argued with him, explaining to those that followed after him that they must do the things that the Father hath instructed them to do, and how these things have always been done according to the laws of heaven.

27 And it came to pass that the Father rose up and quieted his children, saying: My beloved children, do not be angry at the words of Lucifer, for he is justified in his right to say that which he believeth to be just. And for thy own instruction and learning, I would that ye should discuss these things amongst yourselves and determine for yourselves that which ye believe to be the best for each of you.

28 And it came to pass that another of the spirits stood up among them. And this spirit was also the firstborn of the Father, but not from the same Mother as Lucifer. And the mother of this spirit was Marihala, the same woman that had embraced the brother of Jared and called him her son. And his name was Jehovah.

29 And Jehovah was also a leader among the spirits, being the first born of many, and had been blessed exceedingly in all the wisdom of his Father. And he spake unto all the spirits, saying:

30 Know ye not that the laws that have been set forth from the foundation of time and all eternity are unalterable and necessary for our salvation? Why do ye think that the Father hath taught these things unto us? Do ye not have faith in His words?

31 And the Father smiled upon the words of Jehovah, nevertheless He did not interfere with the discussions that were taking place among His children.

32 Thus we see the great wisdom and love that the Father hath for His children. In patience and mercy He alloweth us to work out our own salvation, knowing beforehand that we will come to the only conclusion that can be made—that we must honor and obey the eternal laws of heaven.

33 Nevertheless, in His omniscient wisdom, He knoweth that we must be given the chance to learn these things by faith without His force, or without His intervention, thus securing us the free agency that He hath granted unto us.

34 And after Jehovah had spoken these words, Lucifer rose again and contended with the words of Jehovah, saying:

35 We know that there are laws that have been declared unto us as being eternal, but are not these laws those that others have made to serve their own purposes? And is it not true that in order for these laws to be binding upon us, that we must first agree to them and confirm that they are the laws by which we wish to live?

36 And if by using our agency we choose to live by other laws of our own choosing, are we not then bound by these laws that we have chosen for ourselves and not by the laws that have been chosen for us by others?

37 Behold, I am a Celestial spirit and it is my desire to be a servant unto others, and by the

course of my power—that I know I will have because of the joy that I receive in serving others—I will create more joy among them. And with this power I will cause that new laws are formed which guarantee that all of the spirits that I create will become like unto me and have the power and glory that I have.

38 Is this not a righteous desire? I do not do this for myself, but to serve the just cause of eternal happiness, yea, even by giving this happiness to all without the pain and sorrow of which our Father hath spoken.

39 And Jehovah responded to the words of Lucifer, saying: And how dost thou suppose that we learn about this pain and sorrow of which the Father hath spoken if we do not first experience it? And how dost thou suppose that we comprehend the happiness and joy of eternity if we do not know what causeth them?

40 Behold, thou knowest that one of the eternal laws stateth that there is an opposite to all things. If this were not the case, then we could not know anything. For if there was no dark, how could we comprehend the light? And if there was no bad, how could we comprehend good? And if there is no pain and sorrow, how can we understand what joy and happiness are?

41 And these things are according to our feelings. But even so if there were not cold, how could we know warmth. Yea, even if there were no rocks, then there would be no earth, which is softer than a rock, yet made up of the same elements.

42 How canst thou, being a Celestial being, expect to serve thy creations by taking away the only source of the joy that thou supposeth to give to them? Thou knowest that this is not possible. Let us listen to the words of the Father and trust in His glory, that He will provide the means whereby we may experience happiness according to our desires of happiness.

43 And Lucifer rebuked Jehovah and railed against him, evensomuch, that the Father stood up again amongst all of His spirit children and beckoned them to listen to Him.

44 And Lucifer stood forth amongst those who stood with him and rebelled against the Father. And the Mothers of these spirits stood with the Father and pled with their spirit children to listen to their Father. But the words of Lucifer were convincing unto them, they being mostly Telestial beings who understood that their eternal lot was that of a Telestial glory and they understood the penalties that were affixed to that kingdom.

45 And these Eternal Mothers wept for their spirit children, but They knew that the laws of agency could not be breached, and thus They saw the rebellion of Their beloved children.

46 And truly the Father hath shown His great mercy towards His children in their iniquities, insomuch that after the rebellion of Lucifer and a host of spirits, the Father cast them out of His kingdom and they were cut off from the kingdom of God forever.

47 Now I, Moroni, would that ye should know that the things that the brother of Jared saw are taught symbolically unto the children of men in the temples that the Lord suffereth to be built among them for their sanctification and their instruction.

48 And this great endowment of knowledge was given unto Adam and passed down from generation to generation to teach the children of men the mysteries of God in a form that they will not understand without the Spirit to guide them. And in this way the Lord keepeth his mysteries hidden from those who have not received his Spirit by keeping his commandments.

49 And now these great mysteries are taught in the temples of the Lord as he instructeth his children in mortality; for truly Lucifer and his followers did not keep their first estate, which estate is represented by the new name that one receiveth when endowed in the temple of the Lord.

50 Behold, this new name is the name of a righteous soul who hath passed through the trials and tribulations of mortality and hath proven him or her self worthy to proceed in the kingdom of God—in other words, this new name representeth our spiritual existence.

51 Therefore, he who abideth not by the laws of the Holy Priesthood that govern this spirit world shall be cut off from the kingdom of our Father—symbolically represented as if he were to lose his head—the head symbolizing the

kingdom and glories of our Father.

52 And they who keep not this first estate will have no part in the kingdom of the Father from the time of their rebellion henceforth and forever.

53 Nevertheless, the great wisdom and love of our Father hath prepared a place for them in the eternities—a place where they, too, will forever feel the love and mercy of their creator.

54 This place shall be known in mortality as outer darkness where there shall be weeping and wailing and gnashing of teeth. This place of torment shall not be known at this time or forever by those who keep their first estate, but will only be known by those who inherit it.

55 And the Father shall make Himself known unto His children in outer darkness and they too shall feel of His mercy and love. This shall be their torment; yea, that they feel the love of the Father and partake of His mercy, but know forever of their iniquities and their rebellion against Him. Nevertheless, they too shall receive of the love of the Father.

56 Now I, Moroni, was about to write more of the words of the brother of Jared that he wrote concerning the mercy and love of the Father for those who are cast out of his kingdom. But the Lord hath forbidden me saying: Stay thy hand and write no more concerning these things. For behold, many of my children might take these words and the knowledge that is given unto them and justify the wicked desires of their own hearts; desiring to join Lucifer and his followers seeing that their lot is just and merciful.

57 And it is my work and glory to prepare the souls of all men to be found spotless before God and His angels, that they might partake of the glorious blessings of His kingdom.

58 Behold, Lucifer and his followers have no part in the atonement that I have caused for the children of men, thus their sins and iniquities shall be present in their minds forever; and this is what is meant by endless torment.

59 And I would that all men shall know that I have felt the pain of these souls. And this pain caused me to shrink before the Father, even so much that I asked that I might be delivered of this pain and sorrow—praying to the Father that this cup pass from me.

60 And this pain did cause me to bleed as if from every pore of my body, and the pain thereof cannot be explained in words that thou wouldst understand.

61 And this is the work that I took upon myself when Lucifer rebelled against the plan of salvation. In his rebellion, he sealed his fate and that of those who follow after him; insomuch that they have no part in the redemption of my work and glory; and the atonement hath no affect on them because they have rejected the words of the Father.

62 Behold, they shall feel the pain and sorrow of their iniquities and know the anguish that no other mortal, except me, knoweth. For this reason my soul doth sorrow.

63 And I, Moroni, marveled greatly at the love that Jesus had for these rebellious spirits. For he truly loved them as much as he did those who did not rebel against the Father and kept their first estate.

64 And it came to pass that I pondered these things and my heart and soul were filled with exceedingly great joy. For I knew of the love and mercy that the Father had for His children, and this love and mercy gave me great hope for the souls of my brethren who had perished in battle—which battle raged in their hearts because of their wickedness and hath caused their destruction.

65 And it came to pass that the brother of Jared saw the workings of Lucifer and his followers as they went throughout the earth deceiving the children of men and turning many away from the precepts of God.

66 And behold, there were many spirits which did possess the bodies of many of the sons of Adam insomuch that they did that which is contrary to the will of God by desiring their brethren in a way that a woman desireth a man.

67 And the Lord was merciful unto these sons of men and understood the reason for their unnatural state. And I marveled at the love the Lord had for these brethren who were possessed with the spirits of those who would have been women had they been allowed to pass through their second estate.

68 And they were meek and compassionate, having many of the qualities of a righteous woman, yet they were mortal men having a body that was like unto their mortal fathers.

69 And the brother of Jared beheld that these men were despised by their brethren and mocked and ridiculed for their manner of speech and the workings of their nature.

70 Nevertheless, these were loved by God. For behold, the Father loveth all of His children, and those of His children that rebelled against Him in the spirit realm are loved by Him as well as are all of those who did not rebel against Him.

71 And thus hath He commanded us to love our enemies and those that are not like us, yea, even those that we do not understand, and do good unto them, all of us being the children of God.

CHAPTER 6

The Father introduces Jehovah, Michael, and Seriphia to his spirit children. He establishes their calling and authority over the children of men. The Father concludes his instructions to his spirit children and places Adam and Eve in the garden of Eden.

AND the brother of Jared beheld the legions of souls which were cast out of the presence of God going to and fro throughout the earth deceiving the sons and daughters of Adam and corrupting their souls and turning them away from the plan of salvation.

2 Nevertheless, the armies of God were also organized in the spirit realm and were sent forth to battle against the armies of Lucifer. And the Lord Jesus, the Christ, stood at the front of the battle and led the armies of God in righteousness until the time was appointed that he should give this authority to the Holy Ghost.

3 And it is under this direction in the spirit world that the spirits of the children of men are saved from the enticings of the evil one, if it so be that they give heed to the promptings of the spirits who are called to protect them.

4 And I return again to the vision of the brother of Jared in the spirit world and to the counsel in which the Father instructed His children.

5 And it came to pass that after Lucifer and his followers were cast out from among the rest of the spirits that resided in the kingdom of God, the Father stood before His children and explained unto them that He had chosen a leader from among them to watch over His work in this part of His kingdom.

6 And the Father called forth Jehovah from among the other spirits and presented him before them as the one that He had chosen.

7 And it came to pass that another valiant spirit was called forth and presented unto the spirits by the Father. And the brother of Jared continued his writings, saying:

8 And the Father brought forth one of the spirits and presented him to the other spirits that resided there. And I beheld that this spirit was Michael, who would become the mortal father of all the children of men.

9 And the Father called him Adam, meaning the Son of Man. For it was this spirit that was chosen from among all of the spiritual children of the Father to be the first to take upon him mortality and receive a body of flesh and bone.

10 And Michael knelt before the Father and before the Son, who had now taken his place on the right hand of the throne of the Father. And the Father raised Himself up and stood before Michael and commanded him to rise.

11 And Michael rose up and embraced the Father. And as the Father embraced him, a change came over Michael, even so much that many of the spirits did marvel at that which they beheld. For at the touch and command of the Father, Michael was given a body of flesh and bones like unto the body of the Father.

12 And I marveled at this mystery and was amazed at the beauty and perfection of the body that was created for Adam. And I did not at this time comprehend how the spirit body of Michael was transferred into the tabernacle like unto the Father, but even so, it was.

13 And the Father bent His head towards Michael and whispered words that were not heard or understood by any present. And Adam took his place at the left side of the throne of the Father, directly across from the Lord, even Jesus the Christ.

14 And now I, Moroni, cannot begin to

explain the feelings of joy and complete awe that I felt as I read the description of what the brother of Jared saw. For he truly beheld the Godhead in its fullness.

15 There before the throne of the Eternal Father, even Elohim, stood Jehovah, even Jesus the Christ, and Michael, the father of all the children of men, even the man Adam. And every knee bowed and every soul sang praises to this Holy Trinity.

16 And the brother of Jared continued his description saying: There appeared a sea of many souls, even more numerous than the sands upon the sea shore, each singing praises of glory towards the throne of God, and all kneeling in honor of their Father and their God.

17 Then appeared directly behind the throne of God numerous women who were Goddesses, the Mothers of the spirit children that resided in this world; and among them I found my mother, Marihala, who was also the mother of Jehovah. And my soul rejoiced and my heart once again desired to hold Her as I had once before.

18 And the Father gestured towards these women and gave them glory and honor. Never have I seen such beautiful women, and never have I felt the joy of a family as I witnessed my Eternal Mother standing directly behind my Father, with my brothers, Jehovah and Michael, at His side.

19 And I looked and beheld all the spirit children of the Father; and my heart rejoiced in the thought that all of these were part of my eternal family.

20 And the Father presented the Mothers of heaven to the sea of souls who were still praising these glorious Beings. And the spirits arose and came forth and surrounded the throne of the Father, each taking a place nearest to the Goddess that had given them life.

21 And thus were the families of heaven divided at this time. Oh, how great was the love and joy that was felt among the spirits at this time. And I beheld Marihala, my Mother, and saw my brother, Jared, and many of the spirits that would one day be my other mortal brothers and sisters surrounding Her and bowing to Her graciously and giving Her glory.

22 And She tenderly touched each one and smiled upon them. And my joy was too much to bear; and I fell to the ground weeping and giving thanks to the Lord for the wonderful vision that I was having. For I truly had an eternal family, and in this I did rejoice.

23 And it came to pass that the brother of Jared wrote of the tenderness and pride of the Father as He smiled upon His children as they surrounded their Mothers. And Their children were praising Them and giving Them glory. For the Father stood in the midst of Them all, but gave all the glory to the Mothers of His children.

24 And it came to pass that the Father called forth another spirit from among the others and presented her before Adam. And this spirit was extraordinarily beautiful and pure. And her name was Seriphia.

25 And Adam was well pleased and praised the Father and the Son.

26 And Seriphia knelt before the Father. And upon commanding this spirit child to rise, the Father bent his head towards this spirit child and whispered words that could only be heard by Seriphia.

27 And the Father embraced her in the same manner that He had embraced Michael; and Seriphia was given a body of flesh and bones like unto that which Adam had received from the Father. And Seriphia was again presented to Adam and placed on his right side. And Adam called her Eve, for she was to be the mother of all living.

28 And the Father presented Michael and Seriphia to the rest of His spirit children and blessed them, saying: Unto you I give these, my children. They shall be the first among you to take upon them a mortal body preparatory for entrance into a probationary state upon one of the planets that I have created and placed in this part of my kingdom.

29 And they shall be known as Adam and Eve, and shall be they through whom the rest of my beloved children shall be blessed with mortal bodies. Nevertheless, for a time, they shall reside in a state of glory like unto the glory in which I now reside. For behold, their present bodies are made of the same materials as the body which I now possesseth.

30 Yea, they shall live in this state forever,

unless they are willing to use their agency to fulfill my commandments and bring to pass my work and my glory, which is to help bring to pass your immortality and eternal life.

31 Nevertheless, they cannot be forced to perform this work, but must make this choice of their own free will. And to them I will give the great commandments which are unalterable and have existed forever.

32 These laws are irrevocable and cannot be altered, even by me. Behold, I have prepared my son, even Jehovah, to be a redeemer that shall satisfy the consequences of these laws, so that all of you may be like unto me if it so be that this be the desire of your happiness.

33 Even so, because of Adam and Eve—if it so be that they choose to use their agency to do so—all of you can pass through mortality and take upon you the trials and tribulations of your second estate.

34 Behold, there is a law irrevocably decreed in heaven that maintaineth that power and glory can only be given to those who prove themselves worthy to use this power for the purposes for which it existeth. This law requireth that a soul shall fall and experience the vicissitudes of pain and sorrow, which shall be given to you in your second estate.

35 Upon experiencing this period of probation, a soul must lose all power over the elements and nature and be subject to the power of natural effects, which wield the soul weak and debilitated, even unto death.

36 And there must be one who submiteth completely to all the vicissitudes of this probationary state, and doth so in perfection, never deviating from the laws of heaven. This one will comply with all the laws of heaven and remain faithful and stalwart all the days of his probationary period.

37 This one shall overcome all things and satisfy the demands of the law so that death shall have no power over him. And voluntarily, this one must offer his soul up as a sacrifice to satisfy the demands of the law for the rest of the spirits of my children.

38 And Jehovah, who shall be known among you as Jesus the Christ, is he who shall comply with the law and cause death to lose its power over my children. Even so as in Adam all of my children will suffer in death, even so in Christ shall all be made alive. And all things must be done through the voluntary will of those that I have chosen according to the eternal law of agency.

39 And now my children, I present to you your brothers, Jehovah and Michael, who will give you life in mortality and life forever.

40 It is Michael who shall take Seriphia into the world that I have created for you. There shall they be given the laws that they must obey in order to carry on the work which I have started there.

41 And Lucifer have I cast into this world to tempt Michael and Seriphia, as the law requireth. Yet, I would that ye should know that Lucifer knoweth the eternal laws of heaven and he must also abide by them. Yea, he shall play his part in the fulfilling of these laws so that he, too, might one day be lifted up as a God in his own glory and be redeemed for what he hath done.

42 Nevertheless, he hath lost his glory, and this glory and birthright hath been given to my son, Jehovah. Before him ye shall bow your knee and give glory unto me, and in his name shall my work and my glory be done.

43 Behold, Michael shall go unto the earth and perform his work and then return again to the spirit world where he will take his place at the right hand of Jehovah.

44 And when Jehovah hath accomplished his work and satisfied the demands of the law according to the commandments that I shall give unto him in mortality, then he shall return to the spirit world for a short time. And during this time, then he shall relinquish all power therein to Michael who shall be known as the Holy Ghost.

45 And then shall Jehovah take upon himself a body like unto mine and come unto me and dwell with me in my kingdom. Nevertheless, he will be an emissary between you and me forever. Therefore, ye shall pray to me in his name, and by the power of the Holy Order of the Son of God established in the spirit world, and under the direction of Michael, shall your prayers be answered.

46 And now my beloved children, I give my power and glory to your elder brother, Jesus, the Christ. He is my beloved Son and from this time forth this power shall be held in the Order of his name, or in other words, the Holy Order of the Son of God.

47 And all of you shall belong to and partake of this Holy Order. And ye shall do this by keeping the commandments that he shall give unto you. And he shall give these commandments unto you only by and through my own command, for he is your brother and I am your God.

48 And he will call others to help him in my work. They, too, shall belong to this Holy Order; and all things shall be done in righteousness with an eye single to my glory, which glory is in your eternal joy and happiness.

49 And there shall be great power in this Holy Order of the Son of God; and this power shall be given by the laying on of hands. And as I have touched Michael and Seriphia, and by the power of this Order caused their bodies to be transformed, even so shall this power be transferred in this manner among the children of men so that order might be preserved among them.

50 Now, my children, I must go to other parts of my kingdoms and perform the work that I have taken upon myself to do. I leave you in the power of your brother, even your Lord, Jesus the Christ, and those whom he shall choose to lead you.

51 Honor them and obey their counsel. By the power of this Order established in this spirit world shall I be with you. Yea, by the power of the Holy Ghost shall you be blessed and have my spirit to be with you always.

52 I love you, my children, and will never forsake you. Amen.

53 And it came to pass that after the Father had given these final instructions to His spirit children, He took Michael and Seriphia and led them from among the multitudes of spirits and took them to one of the worlds that He had created in the part of His kingdom that pertaineth unto us.

54 And it came to pass that all of His spirit children followed the Father into the world that was created for Adam and Eve. Nevertheless, the spirits existed in a different realm of this world—in an ethereal state did they exist.

CHAPTER 7

The brother of Jared is shown the world as it appeared at the time of the garden of Eden. He witnesses the creation of the sun and the planets and the glories of the kingdom of God are set forth. The order of nature is also set forth. The spirit and mortal worlds are described and their orders set forth.

AND it came to pass that Adam and Eve were placed in this world in a part thereof that was separated from the rest of this world that had already been created, and they were separated by many waters.

2 And this part was known as the garden of Eden. And this garden was like unto the world that the brother of Jared had described when he visited the kingdom of the Father and met his Eternal Mother for the first time.

3 And the brother of Jared beheld that the rest of the world was inhabited by all manner of beasts and fowl, and that fishes were abundant in the seas and in the oceans. Nevertheless, Adam knew nothing of these other beasts and fowls and fishes.

4 Behold, there were also animals that appeared like unto Adam and Eve, they having lived among the order of animals in the other parts of the world. But Adam and Eve knew nothing of them, nor did these other mortal beings know about Adam and Eve.

5 And there were animals in the garden that was prepared for Adam and Eve, yet they were different from those that had been created in the other parts of this world. Nevertheless, the part of the world in which the garden of Eden was placed also had many other animals, which were also in other parts of the world but were no longer living there when the garden was prepared for Adam and Eve.

6 And the brother of Jared wrote concerning the many different animals that he had never before seen until this great vision, and marveled at their greatness and numbers.

7 And it came to pass that the Lord spake unto the brother of Jared, saying: Behold, these other creatures are those that the laws of nature require in order for all things to be brought to pass in order.

8 Behold, one day all creatures will be known by the inhabitants of the earth, so that they may understand how the laws of nature and heaven cannot be altered or changed.

9 For many changes will take place in the parts of the world separated from the garden in which Adam and Eve have been placed. And these changes will prepare the earth to pass through its probationary state, so that it, too, can receive its paradisiacal glory.

10 Now, I Moroni, will not dwell much on the things which the brother of Jared learned at this time from the Lord. For these things will be made known at a later time in this record where the discovery and understanding of these changes in nature, and also of these animals, will be discovered and understood by the children of men.

11 It sufficeth me to say that the Lord worketh with the laws of nature as they have been decreed from the beginning. Behold, these laws cannot be altered and must be obeyed in order for any eternal work to progress. Even God cannot alter the laws of nature, which are the eternal laws of heaven; nevertheless, He useth them for His purposes and for His glory.

12 And now, I, Moroni, find it expedient to expound upon the words of the brother of Jared which he wrote concerning the creation of this world, and also the worlds that are nearest unto the sun which was created by the Father.

13 For it came to pass that Jesus made these things known unto him and commanded him that he should write the things which he beheld.

14 And the brother of Jared was taken by the Father to an expanse of space that had no light, therefore it was filled with darkness and void of any light as it appeareth unto us on this earth.

15 And as he looked behind him, he could see the great expanse of the heavens, and he recognized this expanse by the stars that appeared immediately behind him. But in front of him there were no stars, neither was there any light that he could behold. And the great expanse of darkness was endless as his eyes beheld it.

16 And the Father stopped at the edge of the heavenly expanse that was recognizable by the brother of Jared.

17 And the Father commanded both the brother of Jared and Jesus to remain at the edge of this great void in the expanse of the heavens. And the Father continued on for a time into the great expanse until the brother of Jared could not see Him any longer.

18 And Jesus spake to the brother of Jared, saying: The Father hath found a place in the greatness of the expanse of heavens where He will create a sun like unto the one that giveth light to the earth to which we belong.

19 And this power and knowledge is reserved for those who have proved themselves worthy of such power, therefore, we are not able to see this great work performed, or hear the wonderful commands that the Father giveth to the elements that are necessary to create the power and glory of the sun.

20 And it came to pass that there immediately appeared an exceedingly bright flash of light, the size and breadth of which hath never been described by man until the brother of Jared attempted to describe that which the Father caused to come to pass as the brother of Jared wrote concerning this miraculous creation in the words of his vision.

21 And he wrote saying: And this exceedingly immense light began to spin perpetually. And as it spun, other elements were present and were attracted to the motion of the spinning body of this exceedingly great light.

22 And there were motions of many elements that I was unable to comprehend and the end of which I did not understand. But as I watched the Father perform His work, I noticed that other balls of matter spun off the great ball of fire that He had created. And when they had been thrown out into the expanse of the darkness, they began to cool and became round like unto a ball. And these reflected the light from the new sun that the Father had created. And they became lights in the expanse of the great darkness.

23 And these balls of element did also spin in the same direction and in the like manner that they had been thrown off by the great sun. And from their own spinning, other balls were thrown off and cooled close unto the balls from which they were formed.

24 And in this manner did I witness the Father creating a sun and the worlds that belong to that sun, in the like manner of those that are next to the earth on which I reside.

25 And the Father appeared before me and my brother, even Jesus Christ, and said unto me: My beloved son, these are like unto the world on which thou liveth. Behold, these are my creations and belong to my kingdom like those that belong to the kingdom that I have placed in the authority of thy elder brother, Jehovah.

26 Behold, one day these planets and these moons, which appear as the stars in the sky to thee and thy brethren on the world in which thou liveth, shall be the glories of my kingdoms for the children which I have created for this kingdom.

27 And there are three degrees of glory in my kingdom, and each degree hath three degrees, and to each of these pertaineth one of these planets which I have caused to be created.

28 And that planet closest to the sun shall be the highest degree in the Celestial degree of glory. And the next unto it shall be the next degree, or in other words, the lower degree, and likewise shall all the degrees of glory in my kingdom be laid out before me until they once again reach the borders of this great darkness which thou beholdest in the distance beyond the worlds that I have just created.

29 Behold, there is no glory that is lower than the next, for they lay before me in a perfect line, each in its own orbit circling the great light that I have caused to be created to give life unto them.

30 But the degrees of these glories shall differ as the brightness of the sun differeth from the brightness of the moon and also from the brightness of the stars. Nevertheless, even the moon and the stars receive their light from the sun. And likewise shall all my glories receive the same light, even my light, in my kingdom. However, each will have a different degree of that light and be empowered with different powers and limitations depending upon the amount of light each receiveth from the sun, or in other words, from me.

31 Now this is the great mystery that thy brethren do not understand. And they will not have this understanding, nor will they have this power, yea, even the power of creation, unless they receive it from me. And only those who inhabit those degrees of glory in my kingdom that are closest unto me, shall receive this power. And to the rest will I give a portion of this power according to the rights and privileges associated to the degree of glory to which they belong.

32 And now, my beloved son, it must needs be that the laws of nature are satisfied according to their foundation. And they have been founded on the eternal laws of heaven which are unalterable and cannot be changed, but must be abided by in order to bring about the immortality and eternal life of my children.

33 And there must needs be order in all things. And with this order cometh the preservation and continuation of lives.

34 And it came to pass that the Father showed the brother of Jared how He separated the waters above the earth from the waters below the earth; in other words, He caused the air to appear and the rain to fall down perpetually upon the earth.

35 And there were seeds of all kinds brought unto the Father; and He blessed them and pronounced that they were good. And there went out many Beings, who had bodies like unto the Father, to the earth that was created and these Beings spread the seeds throughout the entire earth.

36 And these seeds began to grow and take power from the sun and transform this power into the atmosphere in which life could be brought forth. And these plants began to grow exceedingly, insomuch that they began to cover the entire earth.

37 And it came to pass that many strange and marvelous animals were brought before the Father from other worlds that were known unto Him. And He took these animals and blessed them and placed them upon the earth to eat the

plants that had overgrown the earth, thus assuring a natural balance in all things.

38 And these animals were exceedingly large and plentiful, evensomuch that they were able to eat the plants and assure that this natural balance was established and maintained. And other animals were brought to the Father and blessed and placed in the world to assure the delicate balance of those animals that received their nourishment from the plants. And these other animals could not eat plants, but received their nourishment from the flesh of those that ate the plants.

39 And there were exceedingly great numbers of these animals, and soon the earth was covered with them, each assuring that a natural balance was maintained.

40 And it came to pass that the animals that received their nourishment from the flesh of other animals began to rise up and destroy those that received their nourishment from the plants. And after they had eaten all those that they could find and catch, they began to eat each other until there were no more large animals upon the face of the whole earth.

41 And this is the plan and order of nature. For had the plants been allowed to grow unchecked, they would have overcome the world, and the balance of nature would be thwarted. And had those that consumed the plants been allowed to grow and produce unchecked, they would have eaten all the plants of the earth, and then there would be no air to breathe, thus the process of life could not continue.

42 And it was wisdom in the Father, according to the laws of nature, that those animals that fed upon the flesh of others should consume all those that they could catch, thus preparing the earth for the eventual habitation of His children and the days of their probation.

43 And there were other animals that existed whose bodies became like unto the bodies that the Father had created for Adam and Eve. And these began to use their bodies to rule and reign over the other creatures that lived with them on the world in which they were created.

44 Nevertheless, they were not the bodies that were prepared by the Father for His children to inhabit. And the Father gave a commandment unto Adam and Eve that they should not intermarry or create offspring with these other animals, or they would disobey the natural laws and create chaos in the world in which they were placed.

45 And it came to pass that after the Father had cleared the earth of the creatures that consumed the flesh of other animals, He prepared a garden in which He placed Adam and Eve.

46 And there were no animals that were in this garden that ate the flesh of those animals that received their sustenance from the plants. And Adam and Eve did not eat the flesh of any animal, and were commanded to abstain from such things; that it was an abomination to consume the flesh of any other animal that partook of the fruit of the plants and of the trees that the Father had caused to grow perpetually upon the earth.

47 Nevertheless, in other parts of the world the Father allowed there to remain many animals that ate the flesh of other creatures to maintain the balance of nature that was intended from the beginning. But in the garden of Eden, there were none.

48 And those animals in the other parts of the earth that were like unto Adam and Eve did also consume the flesh of other animals, but in this they did disobey the laws of nature and died unnatural deaths because of the things that they did eat.

49 And Adam and Eve lived in the garden of Eden peacefully. And they did not grow old, nor did they clothe themselves and cover their nakedness. For behold, they did not know that they were naked, for they had never seen an animal that was not naked. And in this state of innocence did they exist forever.

50 And in this state the Father allowed Adam and Eve to live to show unto all of His children the state in which all would remain if it so be that they did not enter into mortality and be subjected to the vicissitudes and sorrows of mortal life. And Adam and Eve were ignorant of their nakedness, or in other words, they did not know right or wrong and were like unto little children.

51 And because they did not understand pain and misery, neither did they understand joy and happiness, and thus they could not understand the felicity of eternal happiness that their Father had explained unto them as spirit children.

52 And while Adam and Eve were living in the garden of Eden, the rest of the spirit children of the Father were observing all things whatsoever were occurring unto them in the world that the Father had caused to be created for them. And they also beheld the animals and the other creatures that inhabited the other parts of the world which were separated from the garden that was placed in the land that the Father called Eden.

53 And all the spirits observed these as they lived without the laws of God, having been created with instincts that require them to live their lives according to the laws of nature. Nevertheless, these did not have free agency and were bound by the laws of these instructions that held them in the sphere of their individual creation, which had been given unto them by the Father who had created them.

54 And it was in this way that the Father caused to be taught those of His spirit children who had resided with their Eternal Mothers in His kingdom.

55 For behold, it was the purpose of the Father to teach His spirit children the laws that pertain to the eternal happiness that they desire.

56 And the Father caused a veil to be placed in the world that He had created. And this veil allowed those that were made of spiritual element to observe all things whatsoever that transpired in the mortal world, but did not allow those of the world, or those who were mortal, to observe the things of the spirit world.

57 And this He did by way of the eternal laws of nature. And this law is predicated upon the functions of light which are reflected, according to the element to which they react, thereby causing some things of element to be seen by the mortal eye, and other things to be seen only by and through the power of the spirit.

58 For behold, even the wind that bloweth upon the face of the earth is the transference of eternal elements from one place to another that cannot be seen by the mortal eye.

59 And a spirit can also move in the realm in which it hath been placed. And when it moveth, being created of eternal element, it also displaceth the other elements that exist, and in this way a spirit createth the sensation of wind that is felt by a mortal. Nevertheless, a mortal cannot see the spirit unless he or she is allowed this privilege by the gift and power of God.

60 And so it is that all of the children of the Father, whether they are spirit children, or those spirits which have taken upon themselves a body of flesh and bone, which is mortality, exist in the same world that was created for them. Therefore there is a mortal world and also a world of spirit.

61 And in this spirit world the children of the Father observe and learn all things whatsoever they might learn from observing the actions of those in the mortal realm, which these spirits have either once been a part of, or of which they will one day be a part.

62 Thus we can see the wisdom of God in allowing His children to view the experiences of mortality whether they are a spirit or a living soul. And in this way the spirit children were able to observe the lives of Adam and Eve in the garden of Eden.

CHAPTER 8

The government of the spirit world is explained. The Holy Ghost is revealed and the workings of the spirit world within the mortal world are described—How prayers are received and answered and inspiration given through the ministrations of the Spirit.

AND now, I, Moroni, have been commanded by the Holy Spirit to explain more, even in its fullness, the spirit world which I have mentioned in the vision of the brother of Jared. And the brother of Jared did truly witness all these things, yea even all the workings of the spirit world. Nevertheless, these things were made known unto me long before I used the interpreters to read the words of the brother of Jared.

2 And these things were made known unto me by the power of the Holy Spirit who is the God of this spirit world, or in other words, its leader. And my father also knew of the workings of this spirit world of which I have made mention. Nevertheless, he was commanded not to write the things that he knew concerning it, and the things that he knew were the same things that I know, and also the same things that have been written of by the brother of Jared.

3 And these things have been withheld from the world because of the wickedness and unbelief of the children of men. Behold, these things have been reserved for the faithful who have for a long time sought to understand the workings of the spirit realm and the mysteries of God that pertain unto it.

4 And many have believed that there existeth a spirit realm that cannot be seen with mortal eyes, nevertheless, they do not understand this realm, nor do they understand its operations and its government.

5 Behold, after the Father hath created the world on which He will allow His children to be tried and tested and prove to themselves what degree of happiness best suiteth their individual needs and desires of happiness; yea, after He hath created this world, He confineth all of his children to this world and giveth a commandment unto them that they shall remain therein until He hath finished His work and His glory and hath prepared the mansions where each shall dwell according to each of their desires of happiness.

6 Therefore, all spirits are confined to the atmosphere of the world in which they live; and they cannot exist outside of the boundaries that the Father hath set according to the laws of nature that govern the boundaries of all the planets that are capable of producing and sustaining life.

7 And within these boundaries, the spirits interact with the spirits of those that are confined to a body of flesh and bone during the days of their probation.

8 And it came to pass that after the Father had presented Jehovah to be our leader, or in other words, our God, in this part of His kingdom, He returned once again to His own planet where we, as His children, were created. And the Father gave a commandment unto Jehovah that only he would be allowed to leave the confines of the boundaries that were set to govern the world that the Father had created, but only at the appointed time according to the commandment which the Father had given unto him.

9 And in this way Jehovah became our emissary between the world in which we live and the kingdom of the Father.

10 And Jehovah was the leader of the spirit world after the Father had left this part of His kingdom, he having all the power that was given unto him by the Father.

11 And it came to pass that Michael went down and passed through the days of his probation and died; yea, even so, he returned once again to the world of spirits from whence he came.

12 And Michael ruled at the right hand of Jehovah and reigned in his stead when the time came for Jehovah to pass through the days of his probation.

13 And when Jesus was among his disciples at Jerusalem, yea even when he was among the children of Lehi on this continent, he taught them that after he was gone from among them, he would send the Holy Ghost unto them to direct and guide them.

14 For behold, after the resurrection of Jesus, he could no longer reside in this world without being beheld by mortal eyes, having received his eternal body of flesh and bone like unto the Father.

15 For behold, when Jesus presented himself once again to his disciples at Jerusalem after his resurrection, and then again to the Nephites and the Lamanites who were gathered in the land of Bountiful, they did see him descend and ascend up into the sky. And in this resurrected state he could not enter again into the spirit world as he had before, but was given power to leave the boundaries of the earth according to the commandment that he received from the Father in the beginning.

16 And for the small space of time in between the death of his mortal body and his resurrection, Jesus entered once again into the spirit world and bestowed upon Michael all the

powers and authority that he had received from the Father, so that Michael could rule and reign in the spirit world.

17 And now, this is the mystery that hath not been revealed except unto those who have been faithful and received the knowledge of God by way of the spirit of God. For behold, Michael is the other member of the Godhead, yea even the Holy Ghost.

18 And when the Lord entered the spirit world after his mortal death, he gathered all of those who would rise with him, even immediately after his resurrection, he being the first fruit of the resurrection. And these were the souls of the righteous who had lived in mortality and chosen for themselves to obey the law of the gospel as it had been taught to them by the Father.

19 And these were ready for their degree of glory in the kingdom of the Father, and who after their resurrection, went unto the Father in His kingdom to await the time when the worlds would be prepared that pertain to each of their degrees of glory. And they reside with the Father to this day.

20 But Michael would not take upon himself a resurrected body, but was called and chosen to rule and reign in the spirit world as the Holy Ghost until the work of the Father, concerning His children that belong to this part of His kingdom, is finished.

21 And as many of the children of God, yea even the spirits who are ready and willing to obey the law of the gospel, or in other words, the law that governeth the kingdom of God; even when any one of these is ready to be resurrected, he shall receive his eternal body and return again to the kingdom of the Father to await the end of His work in this part of His kingdom.

22 And those spirits who are not ready to obey the law of the gospel, and also those spirits who have been chosen to serve the Lord and his purposes, either continually in the spirit world, or in the flesh upon the earth, are not resurrected. And these remain as spirits until those who have rejected the gospel of Jesus Christ have accepted this gospel and can live by it forever.

23 And many of these spirits must return again to the earth, even as many times as it is required of them to learn the things that they must learn in order to be able to reside in the kingdom of the Father forever as an immortal being.

24 And it is under the direction of the Holy Ghost that the determination is made whether or not an individual spirit is ready to be resurrected. And this is what is meant by having your calling and election made sure. For this election is sealed unto those who have prepared themselves for the resurrection by the power and authority of the Holy Ghost. And they are chosen and anointed unto the resurrection based on the works that they do during the course of the days of their probation.

25 And if during the course of the days of their probation they listen to the promptings of the Holy Spirit and follow the commandments which shall be given unto them by the chosen prophets and revelators of the word of God in mortality, and also by the power of the Holy Ghost in the spirit world, then they shall be received back into the spirit world into a state of happiness, according to their desires of happiness, waiting patiently in joy for the eventual day that they are called forth by the Holy Ghost to receive their resurrected body and return to the kingdom of their Father.

26 And those who waste the days of their probation, yea, even those who spend their days seeking after the things of the world and seeking for the honor and praise of men; yea, and those who live in riotous living unbridled in their lusts and passions, disobeying the commandments of God as they are presented to them by His prophets and revelators; yea, even these shall return again to the spirit world and be received into a state of misery and pain knowing that they have disobeyed the commandments of God.

27 These shall find themselves unprepared for the kingdom of God and shall have to return once again to mortality to learn the lessons that they did not learn during the days of their probation.

28 And this is the patience and the love and the mercy that the Father hath for His children, even so much that He giveth them many opportunities to learn the things that they must learn in order to live in His kingdoms forever.

29 And there are many who have lived in

mortality many times. And the most righteous spirits lived at the times when it was the hardest for the children of men to live upon this earth, yea, even in the times of the greatest hardships and miseries. And these are those who are of a Celestial glory. And most of them will have already been resurrected and shall come with the Lord when he once again returneth to the earth in his glory to prune his vineyard for the last time.

30 Nevertheless, there are many noble and great spirits who chose not to be resurrected and have elected to stay in the spirit world, or who come back to the earth to help their fellowmen learn the gospel of Jesus Christ and help prepare the spirits of all men for the kingdom of God.

31 And those who are weaker spirits, and who have chosen their desire of happiness as that of a Terrestrial and Telestial state and would not have been able to handle the hardships of mortality, yea, even many of these are living in the last days before the coming of the Lord in his glory, even when the power of Satan hath taken away many of the vicissitudes and hardships of life and given unto them things that were forbidden to come forth in the days of the hardships of their ancestors.

32 And many of these will find their happiness in the last days and will search out the things of the world and aspire to the honors and praises of men, thus straying away from the gospel of Jesus Christ which would cause them to search first for the kingdom of God.

33 But because of the happiness that Satan hath been allowed to provide for them, they believe in their hearts that they do not need the kingdom of God. And there will be many of them that are convinced by the precepts of men that the kingdom of God hath already come, and that they belong to this kingdom, and in this kingdom they believe that they have found their happiness.

34 And there will be many spirits that will not be ready for the resurrection when the Lord cometh in his glory, but will be given another chance to learn the gospel of Jesus Christ when he ruleth and reigneth once again in his glory upon the earth.

35 And now, it is expedient that I, Moroni, explain how those in the spirit world interact with those in mortality. For behold, this is what is meant by being wrought upon by the Spirit, or touched by the spirit of God, or embraced by the spirit of Jesus.

36 For behold, many of you do err in your perceptions and in your beliefs pertaining to these things. Behold, the spirit of God, the Father, is eternally bound to the laws of a resurrected and eternal body of flesh and bone. His spirit is confined to this eternal body never to leave it again. And the spirit of Jesus is also bound like unto the spirit of the Father.

37 Therefore, their spirits cannot be with any mortal, and they have nothing directly to do with the revelations and inspiration given to the children of men, being confined to the kingdom in which they now reside. Nevertheless, the Holy Ghost is one with them and inspireth as both the Father and the Son would so inspire.

38 Behold, if Jesus, or God the Father, was near unto you, your mortal eyes would behold them and they would minister unto you according to the workings of the eternal elements that make up their bodies. And in this manner they would communicate with you. And this communication is like unto that which we experience as mortals.

39 But the Spirit doth not have a body of flesh and bone, and therefore, cannot produce the sounds that our mortal ears can distinguish; or in other words, we cannot hear the words of the Spirit as we do the words of another mortal.

40 And our mortal bodies limit the ability of our spirits to interact with other spirits. Yea, our mortality prohibits us from remembering the spirit world from whence we came; and this so that we may live by faith and prove to ourselves the degree of happiness that we desire without the law of free agency being interfered with by the pure knowledge that we received as spirits.

41 Nevertheless, there are changes that can be made to the elements that make up our mortal bodies which allow us to see into the spirit realm and understand the things that we were once taught by the Father. And in this way the brother of Jared was able to behold the things that the Lord showed unto him as a spirit. Yea, this change came over his mortal body and caused him to have the ability to enter once again into

the spirit world, and witness things therein as a mortal man.

42 And there are those among us that have special gifts and skills that are accentuated by the power of their spirit. And there are those among us that have mortal bodies that can perceive things of the spirit that many of us cannot perceive with the mortal bodies that we possess.

43 And this is the way that we receive direction and guidance from the spirit world under the direction of the Holy Ghost.

44 And when we pray, though in His glory our Father receiveth His joy, and in the name of Jesus we approach the Father, our prayers are not heard by the Father, nor are they heard by the Son, but they are heard and attended to according to the workings of the Holy Ghost.

45 Behold, when we die and leave mortality we are received once again into the spirit world and are greeted and received by those who were the most familiar to us as mortals. And in this way we are assured an easy transition from a mortal state to a spiritual state.

46 And once we are received therein, we can go wherever our desires lead us and see the things of mortality in spiritual ways that we could never see, or perceive, as a mortal.

47 And most of us will go to those that we left in mortality, yea even unto our children, or unto our wives, or unto our friends, for it is our choice to go where we choose according to our desires of knowledge.

48 And when as a spirit we see those that we once loved in mortality, we will mourn for them as they mourn, we will rejoice with them as they rejoice. And when they pray to the Father, we will see that there is not the Father to hear and answer their prayers, but that there are others who have been assigned to them by the power and authority of the Holy Ghost. And these shall attempt to give those in mortality, who pray unto God, guidance, and answer their prayers according to the guidelines and instructions of the Holy Ghost whom they serve.

49 And those of us who are dead, being a spirit in the like manner as those ministering spirits who attend to the prayers of the children of men, yea, even we will make an attempt to communicate with our loved ones and make an intercession on their behalf to those in authority in the spirit world.

50 And behold, we will see others there also who are those spirits who followed Lucifer and were cast out from the presence of the Father. These were cast out of the kingdom of God and confined to the earth to which they would have belonged had they not rebelled against the plan of God.

51 These also have a government in the spirit world, and they are led by Lucifer. And they make every attempt they can, if possible, to deceive the children of men and answer their prayers according to the laws of their own government which is not under the authority and guidance of the Holy Ghost, but under their own authority.

52 And in this way, Michael, who is the Holy Ghost, is known as the archangel who is in constant battle for the souls of men with Lucifer, who is also known as the devil.

53 For behold, Lucifer and his minions can communicate with us in the very same manner like unto the Holy Ghost. Yea, he can cause us to receive all manner of revelation and inspiration that maketh us feel as if we were receiving it from God. And in this way he deceiveth the children of men.

54 Nevertheless, for this cause the Lord hath called his disciples and his prophets and the leaders of his church to guide and direct the children of men in the way that they should go.

55 For behold, it is much easier for the children of men to follow the words of another mortal than it is for them to follow the dictates of the Holy Spirit. Nevertheless, there are many instances when the people are deceived by their leaders, who pretend to be teaching the words of the Holy Ghost when they are actually teaching the words that Satan hath put into their hearts.

56 And for this reason the Lord hath prepared the written word as a reference and also as a standard of his laws and commandments. And he hath caused that the words that are written should be passed down from one generation to another, so that all might receive his words, and so that all might judge their actions according to the words of the prophets and revelators that he hath called to teach them these words.

57 And now, I, Moroni, was about to write other mysteries pertaining to the spirit world in which the spirits of all men reside, but the Spirit hath restrained me from revealing any more of the mysteries of God pertaining to the spirit world in this record.

58 Behold, I know the rest of these mysteries, and they are glorious and wonderful unto those who receive them. And because I have received them from the Spirit, I know that ye can also receive them from this same source, if it so be that ye comply with the laws that are predicated upon receiving such things.

59 And if ye are to know the remainder of the things concerning the spirit world, then ye must ask in faith, giving reverence to the Father, in the name of Jesus; in other words, by keeping the commandments of the Father, even the words of his eternal gospel.

60 And again I say unto you, that except ye keep the commandments that ye shall receive from the mouth of Christ, yea, even those words that are written in this record, and also in the record of my father, and also in the record of the Jews, and by the mouth of the holy prophets who have been chosen by the Lord to teach his words; yea, except ye shall keep these commandments, the laws that govern the spirit world will not allow the Holy Ghost to teach you the mysteries of God.

61 And if ye do not have the Holy Ghost to guide you in your lives, you will be under the power of Satan, or ye will be misled by the precepts and doctrine of men, which have the appearance of godliness, but deny the power thereof.

62 And this is the power of the priesthood which hath been conferred upon those in authority in the spirit world, and which power cannot be controlled except upon the principles of righteousness, which principles are based upon the words of Christ.

CHAPTER 9

The Holy Priesthood is explained. The rights and the power of the priesthood are described. The way to distinguish between a righteous and an evil priesthood are set forth.

AND now, I, Moroni, have been instructed by the Spirit to write an explanation of the priesthood of God which I have mentioned previously in this record. And this explanation is also taken from the words of the brother of Jared. But again I say unto you, that I knew the true meaning of this priesthood, having received this knowledge from the Spirit of God that hath accompanied me all the days of my life.

2 And it shall come to pass that the knowledge of this priesthood shall be had among the Jews and the Gentiles in the last days. Nevertheless, they shall not understand this priesthood, nor shall they have the Spirit to teach them the truth regarding these things, because they choose not to follow the words of Christ in righteousness, and therefore, have forfeited the right to know these things.

3 For it shall come to pass that this priesthood shall be misunderstood and misused in such a way that men will begin to exercise control and dominion over the souls of the children of men; because in their pride, they will claim that they have been given the authority to do so by those who have the authority to give this power unto them.

4 In the beginning there existed no priesthood of God, for all were equal like unto the Son of God, therefore there was no need for this priesthood.

5 Behold, there existed an Order of spirits that committed themselves to the plan that the Father had presented unto them. And this Order of spirits promised the Father that they would follow the commands of His Son according to all things whatsoever he would command them.

6 And this Order became known as the Holy Order of the Son of God, having been organized and ordained by those spirits in the kingdom of the Father who were the firm supporters of the plan of salvation as presented unto us by the Father.

7 And it were these same spirits who kept their first estate and entered into mortality where they would pass the days of their probation.

8 Behold, it was during the times of the wickedness of the children of men that the Lord allowed to be instituted upon the earth symbolic representations of this Holy Order. For behold, it is his desire, and hath always been the desire of the Lord, to teach all of his children the same things that each heard when each of them was present in the spirit world listening to the teachings of our common Eternal Father.

9 But because of the frailties and wickedness of the children of men, the Lord allowed to be established a Holy Priesthood which would officiate in the offices necessary to teach the people the things that they would need to do to keep them in remembrance of him and his commandments.

10 And it is this priesthood after the Order of the Son of God that the Lord alloweth to be established in the churches that he suffereth the children of men to organize among themselves so that they can worship him and learn of his commandments. Now, I say that the Lord suffereth these things to take place among the children of men because this is not the plan or the purpose of the Lord.

11 For as I have said, the children of men find it easier to hear the word of God from mortals, who share their same means of communication, than they do by listening to the promptings of the Holy Spirit of Promise.

12 Behold, the Lord sorroweth in the formation of any organized form of religion where men are called upon to perform in the offices and appendages of the Holy Priesthood. For many times these ordained leaders become wicked and mislead the people away from his commandments and cause the heavens to withdraw themselves. And when the heavens withdraw themselves from among the people, the spirit of the Lord is grieved. And when the spirit of the Lord is grieved, there can be no more power in this priesthood, and it becometh a thing of naught.

13 Nevertheless, because the children of men refuse to obtain their knowledge and their direction directly from the Holy Ghost, who hath the proper authority to bestow it upon them, the Lord suffereth his children to hear the words of salvation from leaders who have been ordained to a position of authority in the Holy Priesthood and have received this authority according to the formation of the religions that he suffereth to be created among the children of men for their sake.

14 And this he suffereth that there may exist some order upon the earth regarding the preaching of his gospel and the establishment of the religions of men to teach this gospel unto the people.

15 And again, I, Moroni, caution you to beware of the religions and priesthoods of men, especially those that shall be established for the sake of the children of men in the last days.

16 Behold, for this purpose the Lord hath caused to be written the holy scriptures, even those things which ye are now reading from the works of my hands. Yea, the fullness of the gospel of Jesus Christ can be found in these writings, and with these writings the children of men can judge their leaders whether they have power in their supposed priesthood or not.

17 And because of the weakness of the Nephites and the Lamanites when the resurrected Lord visited them, according to the record of Nephi, the Lord suffered a church to be established among them.

18 And he called forth twelve men to whom he gave the authority to teach the people. And now, my beloved brothers and sisters, what was it that the Lord commanded his disciples to teach unto the people?

19 Do ye believe that these people were spared from the great destruction wrought throughout the promised land because they were righteous? Behold, if ye believe this, then ye do not understand the record that my father hath prepared for you.

20 Behold, I say unto you that these people were not righteous. For did not the Lord proclaim unto them, even out of the great darkness that did cover the land of Bountiful: Oh, all ye that are spared because ye were more righteous than they, will ye not now return unto me, and repent of your sins, and be converted, that I may heal you?

21 Behold, the Lord knew that these people would not listen to the promptings of the Holy Ghost, and therefore it was necessary that he set up a church among them and establish an order in this church according to the ministrations of a holy priesthood.

22 And he commanded those whom he had called to teach the people to go forth and baptize the people and teach them the commandments of the Father that he would give unto them.

23 And the Lord commanded the people that they should offer up no more sacrifices by the shedding of blood as they had been taught in their traditions according to the law of Moses.

24 And he said unto them: And ye shall offer for a sacrifice unto me a broken heart and a contrite spirit. And whoso cometh unto me with a broken heart and a contrite spirit, him will I baptize with fire and with the Holy Ghost, even as the Lamanites, because of their faith in me at the time of their conversion, were baptized with fire and with the Holy Ghost, and they knew it not.

25 And now my beloved brothers and sisters, how can it be that the Lamanites were baptized with fire and with the Holy Ghost seeing as they had no church established among them, yea neither did they have any type of priesthood to administer this ordinance unto them?

26 Yea, many of the Lamanites were brought unto God by the preaching and patience of the prophets of God who lived among them. And these same prophets of God surely belonged to the Holy Priesthood after the Holy Order of the Son of God, yet they did not have authority to perform the ordinances and act in the authority of a church, nevertheless they were prophets of God.

27 And according to the record of my father Mormon, the people of King Limhi, who were Nephites, accepted the gospel of Jesus Christ as it had been taught to them by Ammon. And King Limhi and his people were desirous to be baptized and form a church among them, not understanding the workings of the Holy Ghost which had been the cause of their conversion.

28 But Ammon refused to use his authority to organize a church among them and baptize them. For Ammon knew that it was not his mission to form a church among them, and that the authority to do this was passed down by a holy anointing given by those in authority in the church of God.

29 And the church of God had become corrupt because the wicked King Noah and the High Priests of the church had caused the people to commit many sins against God because of their examples. And was not Alma one of these wicked priests who had been anointed by the church to perform the ordinances therein?

30 And even though Alma was wicked, he still maintained his standing in the Holy Priesthood that was set up within the church to maintain order therein. And after Alma heard the words of the prophet Abinadi, he fled from before the other High Priests and lost his standing in the church. Nevertheless, he did not lose his priesthood authority.

31 For this reason the people of Limhi sought out Alma and his priesthood authority so that they could be baptized as a witness and a testimony that they were willing to serve God with all their hearts and keep his commandments.

32 And these commandments of God are the words that the resurrected Lord gave unto the Nephites and the Lamanites that were spared in the land of Bountiful because they were more righteous than those that were killed.

33 And these were the same commandments that Jesus gave unto the Jews when he lived among them at Jerusalem. And he also suffered that a church was organized among the people at Jerusalem. And he laid his hands upon his apostles and commissioned them, or in other words, gave them the authority to act in his name according to the commandments that he had given unto them to teach to the people, thus showing them an example of how he suffereth the Holy Priesthood to be instituted properly in the religions of men.

34 And now my beloved brothers and sisters, what efficacy do ye suppose this calling and authority of the priesthood hath in the kingdom of God?

35 Behold, before ye are allowed to enter into the kingdom of God ye are required to have the capacity and the understanding of living

according to the commandments of the gospel of Jesus Christ, and have proven yourselves worthy to live by this standard forever. Therefore, what need do ye think ye will have of a church? And what need will there be for a holy priesthood if there is no church established among you?

36 And those of you who belong to the Holy Order of the Son of God, of what need will there be to have prophets and apostles, yea, even the scriptures that teach you the commandments by which ye should live, when ye already belong to an Order of men and women that knoweth and liveth by these things?

37 Therefore, I say unto you, that the priesthoods of men are suffered by the Lord so that he might teach his children his words in a way that they might understand them. And these priesthoods are necessary for the order of his church, which church only pertaineth to the children of men in the flesh.

38 And in the spirit world there is also an order established, even a church, which is under the priesthood authority of the Holy Ghost, who administereth unto the children of men in the flesh, and also unto those in the spirit world according to the ministrations of this priesthood.

39 Behold, there is save one true church of God, which is the church of the Lamb of God, who is Jesus Christ. And any church that doth not teach the words of Christ, or the words that he taught the people when he came down among them, is not the church of the Lamb of God. And these churches that teach not the words of the Lamb of God do not have the priesthood authority to act in the name of God according to the commandments that He hath given unto the children of men through his Son, Jesus Christ.

40 And this is what Jesus meant when he commanded the people to call the church in his name saying: Therefore, whatsoever ye shall do, ye shall do it in my name: therefore ye shall call the church in my name.

41 And many believe that this meant that the Lord would only sanction a church if it was called after his name. Now this is not what the Lord meant. For behold, there are many churches built up that are called after the name of Jesus Christ, nevertheless, they are not built upon his gospel, which are the commandments that he gave unto his disciples as I have explained it unto you.

42 For behold, the Lord commanded the church to be called in his name, which signifieth that it doeth the things that he hath shown it to do. For the name of the Lord hath reference to his works, and it is customary among the Jews, as it is among us, that our works constitute the name by which we are known.

43 Therefore, if a church is built in the name of Jesus Christ, then it will do the works that he hath commanded. And it mattereth not whether this church is named after any other thing, for its works shall be shown within it and it shall only be accepted by the Father according to its works.

44 Now, it is expedient that I make this clear unto the faithful who shall receive this record, even this sealed portion of the plates that I have made with mine own hands.

45 For behold, in the last days there shall be many churches set up among the children of men that are called after the name of Jesus Christ, nevertheless, they are not built upon his gospel, but are built upon the works of men or the works of the devil. And their works follow after them.

46 And ye shall have this record and also the record of the Jews as two testimonies of the teachings of Jesus Christ. And if any church teacheth more or less than Jesus taught the people, ye shall surely know that these churches are called after his holy name and not in his name as I have explained it unto you.

47 And whosoever preacheth the words of Christ hath the blessing and authority of the Holy Priesthood of God. And whosoever teacheth more or less than the words of Christ, though they might have the priesthood conferred upon them, they have not the sanctification of the Holy Spirit, and therefore, have no power in their priesthood. For behold, many are called, but few are chosen.

48 And there will be many of you who question the authority of those who teach the words of Christ because they do not have the authority of the church to do so. Beware of this

fallacy in your thinking, my beloved brothers and sisters, for so thought the Jews at Jerusalem when they rejected the prophets who were sent to preach repentance unto the church that was set up among them. For the Lord hath said: For he that is not against us is for us.

49 And if a man can cast out devils in the name of Jesus and doeth many wonderful works also in his name, then that man belongeth to the church of the Lamb of God, whether he belongeth to an organized church upon the earth, or whether he doeth it on his own, it is the same.

50 For any man or woman that obeyeth the gospel of Jesus Christ as he hath given it unto us, hath the priesthood of God and can act in the name of God according to the words of Christ.

51 And if it so be that this man or this women desireth to establish a church in the name of Christ, and call it after his or her own name, then it will be counted as righteousness before the Father and He will send the Holy Ghost to sanction it.

52 Now this is the mystery of the priesthood which the Spirit hath commanded me to explain unto you. And there are other things about the priesthood that I have not explained. But the most important part, which is for your understanding, I have explained upon these plates.

CHAPTER 10

The Holy Endowment is introduced and explained. Moroni uses the account of the presentation of the endowment given to Adam and Eve by Jehovah. The First Token of the Aaronic Priesthood is introduced and explained.

AND now, I am constrained by the Spirit to explain further some of the things that the Lord suffereth to be given to the children of men that they might be kept in remembrance of him, that they might always remember him and keep his commandments which he hath given unto them, so that the Holy Ghost may always be with them during the course of the days of their probation.

2 And many of these things are taught unto the people symbolically through the administrations of the Holy Priesthood that hath been established in the churches that he hath suffered to be built up among the children of men.

3 And many of these things are taught in the temples of the Lord, as they are called by the church, and are the basis of an endowment of great understanding and teaching unto the children of men.

4 Behold, the Lord showed this endowment unto Adam and his posterity and commanded them to teach their children this sacred ordinance as a way to keep them in remembrance of him.

5 And this endowment was given unto many of the prophets of God to give unto the people a symbolic representation of the plan of salvation, and also to teach them many of the truths that the Father revealed unto His children in His kingdom before He placed them in the world that He had created for them.

6 And this endowment was given unto Nephi who passed it down from generation to generation, and it was taught in the temples that he caused to be built among his people.

7 And it was a cause of exceeding joy to the people of Nephi that they had the opportunity to go to a temple dedicated to the teachings and instructions of the Lord.

8 And at this time, or during the time of the reign of Nephi, there was none that was prohibited from partaking of the ordinance of the endowment, it being taught to the people symbolically with signs, tokens, penalties, and symbols that no one could understand unless he was given this knowledge and understanding by the gift of the Holy Ghost, which gift was only given to those who were righteous.

9 And it was the purpose of Nephi and his brothers, who were anointed High Priests, to teach the people the words of Christ, that all people should be allowed to have the endowment presented before them, thus with the hope that they might be encouraged to seek an understanding of the mysteries of God.

10 And in its purity this holy endowment is a

perfect representation of the plan of salvation and giveth the children of men all the understanding that they need in order to work out their own salvation before the Lord.

11 Now, I, Moroni, have seen the church of God established in the last days and have seen the reestablishment of this holy endowment and the construction of many temples dedicated to the purpose of giving the children of men the opportunity to receive the endowment that they might also be encouraged to seek out its meaning and abide by the principles taught therein.

12 And I have seen that this endowment was revealed in its pure form, which form had been previously adulterated by the precepts and learning of men, which learning was not based upon the gospel of Jesus Christ, but upon the precepts of men.

13 And the same prophet, seer, and revelator who shall bring this record to the world, shall also be given this endowment in its pure form as it was in the beginning. And he shall set up a school of learning in which this endowment shall be presented to the people like it was in the time of Nephi, and Jacob and Joseph, his brothers.

14 And it shall come to pass that the people of the church that he shall establish shall reject the pure message of the gospel of Jesus Christ and be given lower laws of sacrifice and ordinances like unto the children of Israel when they desired that Moses be their leader.

15 And because of the wickedness of this church, this prophet shall be taken from among them. And because he is taken from among them, they are left to themselves to establish a church according to the dictates of their own conscience, which dictates are not based upon the words of Christ as I have explained them in this record.

16 And because the church is named after the name of Jesus Christ and not in his name, or in other words, based upon his gospel, this holy endowment shall be changed and modified according to the desires and precepts of the leaders of this church, who do so because of the praise of the world.

17 And my soul is burdened exceedingly as I read the words of the brother of Jared who hath seen the coming forth of this church among the Gentiles, yea even the very same church which shall preach the words of the record of my father, and also many of my own words, and carry them forth to many parts of the world.

18 For behold, it shall come to pass that this church shall begin to deny the children of God from partaking of this holy ordinance, and few will be given the opportunity to be encouraged by its wonderful teachings and the hidden messages of its extraordinary symbolism.

19 And of those that do receive this endowment, few will understand its meaning because of the many changes that have been done to it because of the misunderstanding and wickedness of the leaders of the church that is called after the name of Jesus Christ.

20 Behold, in their pride they shall believe that if a person doth not abide by the commandments of the church, then he will not be allowed to behold this holy endowment, which is a blessing from God unto all of His children.

21 Yea, there shall be found among them those who follow the words of Christ and obey them with a broken heart and a contrite spirit. Nevertheless, because these do not obey the commandments of the church and its leaders, which commandments are not the words of Christ, but the precepts of men, they are not allowed to enter into the temples which have been dedicated to the Lord for the edification and perfection of his children.

22 And it is for this reason that the Spirit hath commanded me to explain these things in this part of my record. And according to the commandment that I have been given, I will explain this holy endowment in its pure form, giving all the signs, tokens, and penalties, and all of its symbolism, and also an explanation of all of these things.

23 And these things shall reveal many of the things that the brother of Jared saw in his vision and of which he wrote. And the majority of the explanation that I shall give of the Holy Endowment, I shall take from his words, for they are great, and his words compensate for the weakness of my own writing.

24 And the brother of Jared watched by the

power of the Spirit as Adam and Eve were given the endowment and taught the way in which they should present it to their children; and this according to his words that are written:

25 And I saw the Holy Endowment that was prepared from the foundation of the world to give the children of Adam the opportunity to learn the things that they cannot see beyond the veil that hath been placed over their minds through the effects of mortality.

26 And they received these things by the mouth of Jehovah, who had been given the authority to teach these things unto them by the Father. And Jehovah said unto them:

27 And ye shall build houses of learning and instruction for thy children that they may have a place dedicated to the learning of the plan that the Father hath given unto them.

28 Inasmuch as ye were created by the Father and formed from element and given intelligence in this form, even so ye shall teach this to your children by the symbolic ordinance of washing. For of the eternal elements, of which water is a part, ye were created.

29 And ye shall wash them in a manner that is archetypal of the creation of their spirit form, starting from their head and washing to their feet. Behold, ye shall do this as a preparatory stage that prepareth them to receive an opportunity to become as the Father is, even an eternal God who ruleth and reigneth in His own kingdom forever.

30 And then ye shall anoint them with oil to become Kings and Queens unto the Most High God. And only an oil which hath been consecrated for this purpose shall ye use. For behold, this oil is not of the eternal elements, but is processed by the works of the hands of men, which symbolically representeth that no man or woman shall become a God or a Goddess like unto the Father, except it be through the works of their own hands. Nevertheless, all have been created as spirits, which is from eternal element that no man hath touched.

31 And this oil shall be processed from the olive tree, which is a symbol of peace and purity. And it shall be pure olive oil and shall be forbidden from mixtures of any other type, thus maintaining its purity that symbolizeth righteousness.

32 And this washing shall be sealed upon the head of him who shall receive it, thus symbolizing that all have been created as spirits and given the agency to act in the sphere of their own consciousness and are responsible for their own choices.

33 But the anointing with oil shall only be confirmed upon their head and shall not be sealed. For behold, though the ability to become as the Father is given to them, or in other words, confirmed upon them, they are not sealed unto this end, and shall not see the sealing of this confirmation except it be by their righteous works and desires.

34 And after they have been washed and anointed, ye shall place a garment upon them which symbolizeth the receiving of a body of flesh and bone, in other words, it representeth their entrance into mortality.

35 Ye shall explain unto them and give them a commandment to wear this garment throughout the remainder of their lives, representing the fact that they will have their mortal body all the days of their probation.

36 Ye shall explain to them that if they do not defile this garment, or in other words, if they do not defile their body, by disobeying the covenant that they make in obeying the law of the gospel, then they shall be protected against the power of Satan until they finish the days of their probation.

37 And ye shall give unto them a new name and command them that they should always remember it, but that they should never reveal it to any other person for the rest of their mortal lives. And this new name shall be the name of a righteous person who is still in the spirit world, or who hath lived through mortality and hath returned to the spirit world.

38 And this new name is symbolic of their spirit existence which they cannot remember in mortality, a veil of forgetfulness being placed upon them by cause of the functions of their mortal bodies—thus the reason why it is never revealed during their lifetime. It is a name that they were symbolically called by in the preexistence before they entered mortality.

Nevertheless, it is not important that they be given the actual name that they received from their Eternal Mother, for it is from Her that they received it, but a name of a righteous spirit will suffice for the representation of their spirit existence.

39 And this name, as well as all the other names that shall be given in this endowment, representeth the actions, desires, and responsibilities of the individual who is receiving this endowment according to the name that they shall be instructed to use at the appropriate time.

40 In other words, their new name is a symbolic representation of their works in the spirit world before they entered mortality. And ye shall instruct them to use their own given name, as it shall be explained unto you, which representeth their actions, desires, and responsibilities, or in other words, their works in mortality. For this name was given unto them during the days of their probation. And thus ye shall instruct them.

41 Ye shall give a brief introduction to them about the endowment and its purpose. And this introduction shall be symbolic of the great council that the Father called in His kingdom, wherein He presented the plan of salvation unto all of His spirit children. And ye shall give all those who would receive the endowment the solemn choice to proceed with the presentation of the endowment or withdraw, thus symbolizing the law of free agency afforded to all the children of God.

42 Ye shall call those who shall help you present this endowment to your children. And these shall play the parts representative of the Father and all those who have a part in the presentation and fulfillment of the plan of salvation that the Father presented unto them as spirits in His kingdom.

43 And as all the spirit children of God were shown the plan of the Father and witnessed the mystery of His work and His glory, so shall ye present the endowment unto your children in a like manner.

44 Ye shall show unto them the creation of the world and show the stages in which the Father caused to be created the world on which they live.

45 Ye shall present unto them the creation of their world to show that each of them participated in the decisions that were made pertaining unto the world where they would pass through the days of their probation. Yea, ye shall call upon one to play the part of Michael, who representeth all of the children of God in their spirit form; for thus ye shall call Michael who was known in the spirit world as such, but who became the man Adam when he entered mortality.

46 And now, I, Moroni, would that ye should understand that this is an important part of the mysteries of God. Yea, even that we all participated in the formation of the world on which we live.

47 Behold, I have already given unto you an explanation of the laws of heaven pertaining unto our freedom to choose for ourselves and act according to the dictates of our own conscience. And it is requisite of this law that we all be in one accord with the laws that we covenant to obey.

48 And for this reason Lucifer presented his opinion, saying: And if by using our agency we choose to live by other laws of our own choosing, are we not then bound by these laws that we have chosen for ourselves and not by the laws that have been chosen for us by others?

49 Behold, truly he did understand the laws of heaven and used them accordingly to seek his own glory.

50 And because of this law, it was a requirement that each of us agree to the way and means whereby we would be tried and tested during the days of our probation. Therefore, it was requisite that we be involved in the organization of the world on which we live.

51 Though we do not have the power to command the elements as doth the Father, we have the right to voice our opinion on how His command and power should be used for the purposes of our own happiness. And in this way, our God is our servant forever, as I have previously explained it unto you.

52 And just as the Father gave us the privilege to discuss among ourselves whether or not the plan of Lucifer was what we wanted for ourselves, so doth the Father allow us to create our own world within the parameters of the eternal laws to which He is subjected by the power that hath been given unto Him by and through the Celestial glory.

53 And this is the reason why the endowment is presented in the way that it is in the beginning; even that God commandeth Jehovah—who is the overseer of His will and assureth that the eternal laws are abided by, and Michael, who representeth all of us as spirits—to go out and organize a world on which we can live according to the worlds that the Father had created before.

54 And during the course of this symbolic creation, it is imperative, according to the law of free agency, that Michael agreeeth with all the commands and instruction that Jehovah giveth unto him.

55 And it is also imperative that Jehovah repeateth the commands of the Father precisely as they are given unto him, thus showing the authority given unto Jehovah to do the will of the Father in all things. But in all these things, Michael, who symbolizeth each of us, must agree.

56 And now I will return to the explanation of the endowment as given in the vision of the brother of Jared. But before I return once again unto the words of the brother of Jared, the Spirit constraineth me to speak once again unto the church of Jesus Christ, or that church that is called after his name in the last days:

57 Behold, because of your ignorance, which hath been brought upon you by your works, which are not the works based on the words of Christ, but are works based on the precepts and understanding of men, therefore ye have not the Holy Ghost to guide you; yea, because of this ignorance, ye present the Holy Endowment in a way that doth not follow the original purpose of its presentation.

58 Behold, ye do not understand the First Token of the Aaronic Priesthood which hath been given unto you, and ye have interpolated it at a time in the presentation of the endowment where it is not intended to be; yea, because ye have done these things, ye have corrupted its holy meaning.

59 This token is symbolic of the acceptance of the plan of salvation and our acceptance of Jehovah as he who will present himself as a sacrifice so that we might all be saved by his name, or in other words, by his works. Thus this token being called the Law of Sacrifice.

60 And this token is that which was given to us as spirits in the kingdom of our Father.

61 For this purpose the token is symbolically given to those who receive it through the presentation of the endowment, by clasping the right hands and placing the joint of the thumb in between the first and second knuckles of the hand, demonstrating that it is received in a body without flesh and bone, the bone of the hand being the key, and the thumb symbolizing the giving unto the participant a spirit body without bone present.

62 Behold, I have read the words of the brother of Jared in which he describeth the endowment and warneth those who would officiate in it and present it to the children of men, that they do not change the manner in which the endowment is given, thus confusing the children of men and corrupting the word of God.

63 And now, I, Moroni, return once again to the words of the brother of Jared concerning the continuation of the presentation of the endowment:

64 And after ye have given unto them this token, which ye shall call the First Token of the Lower Priesthood, because it is administered unto all the children of men; and the offices of this lower priesthood, which I have suffered you to establish in my church, administereth to the needs and wants of all the children of men; yea, after they have received this token as I have described it unto you, ye shall give unto them the accompanying name, sign, and penalty.

65 The name of this token is the new name that ye were given as it was previously explained to you. In other words, that this token was given unto you when ye resided as spirits in the kingdom of the Father.

66 The sign is made by bringing the right

arm to the square, the palm of the hand to the front, the fingers close together and the thumb extended.

67 Behold, this sign symbolizeth the straight and narrow path which hath been laid out for you from the foundation of the world—of which the square is indicative—and that this path is one of righteousness—of which the right arm is used to indicate this upon forming the square; and that the palm is faced front, signifying that you have accepted the plan of the Father which is before you, or in front of you, and that you accept it by the uplifting of your hand.

68 The execution of the penalty of this token is represented by placing the thumb under the left ear, the palm of the hand down, and by drawing the thumb quickly across the throat to the right ear, and dropping the hand to the side.

69 The execution of the penalty is symbolic of the penalty of all those who do not accept the plan of the Father and the election of me as a Savior, who will give myself as a sacrifice for the children of men. The head representeth the kingdom of God, or the Godhead that resideth in that kingdom and who presented the plan of salvation unto us.

70 The thumb being drawn quickly across the throat symbolizeth he who rejecteth the plan of the Father, being cut off, or severed from the head, or from the kingdom of God. And this is the penalty that Lucifer and those that followed after him received from the Father, even that they were cut off from the Godhead forever, and this because they rejected, or revealed—as it is presented symbolically—the Law of Sacrifice, which is the First Token of the Lower Priesthood.

71 For behold, it is the authority of this lower priesthood, and those that fall under its authority to administer in the ordinance of sacrifice by cutting the throats of pure animals selected from among all others. And this sacrifice is also done in similitude of the First Token that I have caused to be given unto you in the Holy Endowment as I have just explained it unto you.

72 And after ye have given unto the participants the First Token of the Lower Priesthood, ye shall present to them a representation of the garden of Eden, in which the creation of your mortal bodies will be presented unto them by those who are examples of me and our Father. And after the world hath been created in symbolic form, the Father shall go down with Jehovah into the earth that hath been formed and create a body for Michael, who, upon his entering the newly formed body, shall be known as Adam. And ye shall give unto them a brief description in the form of an archetype regarding your experience in the garden of Eden.

73 Ye shall show the innocent state in which ye resided in the garden of Eden, and show unto them that ye still had a knowledge of the Father and the world from whence ye came. Nevertheless, ye shall not divulge any portion of the truth regarding the actual way in which Eve was tempted and lost her power over death and was cast out of the garden of Eden. For behold, these things shall not be known by any man except it be unto those whom I choose to reveal these things.

74 Behold, in your innocence you transgressed the laws of God, and you are not to be held accountable for that which ye did not understand, having been deceived by the power of Satan. And if the children of men knew the truth regarding your expulsion from the garden of Eden, then they would begin to blame all women for the problems of the world, and believe that because of them, all is lost. Thus blaming you, their first parents, for their own wickedness and sins.

75 Behold, it was necessary that Lucifer be allowed to tempt Eve in the manner that he did that ye might know that which ye did not consider before. And because of these things, the plan of salvation, yea, even the plan of eternal happiness could proceed.

76 Behold, I would that ye should teach your children a representation that is symbolic of the plan that Lucifer presented in the kingdom of our Father, which we rejected. Yea, teach them that the garden of Eden is symbolic of this life with the Father, and that Lucifer is trying to entice the children of God to follow his plan according to his own desires of how this plan should be.

77 Teach the receiver of the endowment the ways in which Lucifer promised to possess the mortal bodies that ye shall provide for the spirits of the children of God, even with the enticements of the treasures and glories of the earth. And finally have him cast out from the garden of Eden, symbolically representing that he was cast out of the kingdom of God as a spirit being.

78 Then shall ye present cherubim and a flaming sword to guard the Tree of Life, which representeth the veil placed over the minds of the children of men, so that they might live by faith, and so that they shall not remember—excepting they are wrought upon by the Holy Spirit—the place from whence they came, or the things which were taught unto them.

79 And ye shall teach your children that when they enter into mortality, the hardships and vicissitudes of life shall be for their own good. And Eve shall explain unto them the pain and sorrow in her conception, which is opposed to the joy that is felt by our Eternal Mothers when They conceive and bring forth a spirit child in the kingdom of our Father.

80 And Adam shall explain unto them that the earth shall produce food and raiment unlike the manner in which they are produced in the kingdom of our Father. And that this food and raiment will not be given freely and without toil, but shall be provided by the earth only by the hardships that shall teach you and give you experience.

81 And this so that one day ye shall know the exceeding joy that those who reside in the kingdom of God experience. For behold, they do not toil, neither do they experience any hardships, because the food and raiment that brings them this joy will be freely provided for them forever.

82 And in this state of mortality Adam shall have a body that is much stronger than the body of Eve, and with this body he shall rule over her in righteousness. Nevertheless, this rule will only last through the days of your probation and shall not continue in the kingdom of God. For behold, all are equal in the kingdom of God, and there is none that ruleth over another, everyone having received the same fullness of the kingdom of glory that they have chosen for themselves according to their desires of happiness.

83 And in mortality it will be expected of Adam to provide for the needs of Eve, this because she shall be engaged in a constant awareness of her children and their needs. And it must needs be that Adam be allowed to call upon the Father for guidance and instruction, thus becoming the Head over Eve according to the commandments that I shall give unto him.

84 And Adam shall lead her in righteousness, covenanting before the Father that he will do the will of the Father in all things. And if he doeth the will of the Father, then he will love his wife with all of his heart and serve her for the remainder of his days, for this is the will of the Father.

85 And Eve shall be subjected to the will of her husband as long as he is righteous before the Lord. But if he doeth not those things which the Lord shall command him, and beginneth to exercise unrighteous dominion over her, then she shall not be bound any longer to the covenant that she shall make with him.

86 Behold, the Father loveth our Eternal Mothers, yea, He loveth all those who have the power to create bodies for His children. And because of this power that the daughters of Eve shall possess, they shall be more compassionate, and docile, even that they shall exhibit more of the attributes of their Eternal Mother than the sons of Adam exhibit of their Eternal Father.

87 And the glory of a woman shall one day be known by all the children of the Father. Yea, they shall know that the woman hath infinitely more power than the power given unto many men. For what need do we think that our Father hath for those of us who shall take a body of a male in mortality? Could not the Father command his holy angels to bring forth children of the mortal bodies provided for the daughters of Eve?

88 And if this be the case, why doth He need a man to do His will? Behold, without a mortal woman it is impossible for any of the spirit children of the Father to gain their second estate, even the state of mortality.

89 And this shall be shown unto you when the Father commandeth a chosen mortal woman to become my earthly mother. And is this woman in need of a man to bring to pass my mortal body? And in the same way could the Father provide all the mortal bodies necessary for all of His spirit children. Nevertheless, he hath commanded the sons of Adam to care for their wives and hold them in high esteem, lest in their dishonor of them they lose their righteous reward, which is their strength over them in mortality.

90 And by following the commandments that I shall give unto you by way of my gospel, ye shall be taught the ways of righteousness, even the manner in which a husband shall treat his wife.

CHAPTER 11

The explanation of the presentation of the endowment is continued. The Second Token of the Aaronic Priesthood and the Law of the Gospel is explained as well as the tokens and laws of the higher, or Melchizedek Priesthood. The explanation of the endowment is completed.

Y<small>E</small> shall continue the presentation of the endowment by symbolically introducing Adam and Eve into the Telestial glory, or the world as it will be known unto your children in mortality.

2 Behold, this world will be very much like unto the worlds that exist in the Telestial glory of the kingdom of our Father. And those who reside therein shall partake of the same experiences that bring them joy in this world, except it be that there shall be no pain or sorrow, nor will there be any sickness or death anymore.

3 But in the Telestial glory there shall be a penalty affixed which shall be an eternal penalty that those who reside in that glory will always remember. And those who receive this penalty are those who did not obey the law of the gospel in mortality, thus symbolically revealing the token and receiving the penalty that is affixed to it.

4 And since the presentation of the endowment is presented in a world that representeth this glory, I would that ye should introduce this penalty, along with its name and sign, as I have shown unto you, like unto the first token that is called the First Token of the Lower Priesthood.

5 And this token shall be called the Second Token of the Lower Priesthood. And this token shall be given unto the participants that are receiving this endowment along with the law of my gospel, which I shall give unto them in the written word of the holy scriptures, which I shall instruct your children to keep a record of for their instruction and their learning.

6 For behold, there shall come a time when your children will rebel against the things that ye shall teach unto them, yea even those things which ye shall teach unto them in their purity, having received them from mine own mouth.

7 And they shall forget these things and live according to the lusts of their flesh, which Satan will entice them to do. And as he promised in the beginning to take the treasures and things of the earth and build up kingdoms of men that do not follow the laws of the gospel, so shall he therefore have great power over the hearts of the children of men.

8 And instead of looking unto the God who gave them life, many of them will look unto the earth for their happiness. And with the things that are upon the earth shall they find their joy. And this according to the designs and plans of Satan, who would have them turn away from me and the gospel that I have given unto you for their sake.

9 And ye shall teach these things to your posterity during the presentation of the Holy Endowment. Ye shall show how Satan useth his cunningness and the things of this world to turn the hearts of the children of men away from our Father.

10 And there are those who the Father hath given unto me to help me in His work. And these shall be those among you who are the prophets, and the seers, and the revelators of my words. They shall be my disciples and go forth among the people and teach them the things that I shall give unto them.

11 And these prophets shall be men, because of the burden of childbearing that shall come upon the daughters of Eve, and these men, not having this burden, can dedicate their mortal days in the service of preaching and calling the children of men to repentance. However, there shall be many more women than men who already know the gospel and live according to the things that they shall receive by the ministrations of the spirit world. And these ministrations I shall cause to be given unto these women because of their righteousness, they being more righteous than the sons of Adam.

12 And during the presentation of this endowment ye shall call others to play the roles of my servants, the prophets. And these shall give unto those who are receiving this endowment the law of my gospel and command them that they shall covenant before God that they will obey the law of the gospel as it is given unto them through the holy scriptures that I shall cause to be written, as well as from the mouths of my servants, the holy prophets.

13 And as the endowment hath thus far progressed to a representation of mortality, ye shall symbolically give unto them the Second Token of the Lower Priesthood by clasping the right hands and placing the joint of the thumb directly over the first knuckle of the hand, thus symbolizing receiving a body of flesh and bone, the thumb resting on the bone of the hand for emphasis that they are receiving a body of flesh and bone.

14 The name associated with this token is the first given name of the participants, or in other words, the name by which they are known in mortality, thus signifying that they shall be judged according to their works and their desires and their responsibilities that they have accomplished during the mortal days of their probation.

15 And inasmuch as they are in what symbolically representeth the Telestial glory, ye shall give unto them the penalty of this kingdom of glory. For if they choose this glory they shall suffer this penalty.

16 The sign is given by bringing the right hand in front of you in a cupping shape and the right arm forming a square, and the left arm being raised to the square, thus symbolizing the presentation of their works—being cupped in the hand as if presenting them to the Lord—and the left arm to the square demonstrating that they did not follow the path of righteousness; for righteousness is represented by the right arm forming the square. And the execution of the penalty is represented by placing the right hand on the left breast—thus signifying the place where feelings are perceived to be experienced and felt by a mortal body—and then drawing the hand quickly across the body, and dropping the hands to the side.

17 The penalty that the inhabitants of the Telestial glory receive is the knowledge and the everlasting feeling that they reside in the lowest kingdom of glory in the kingdom of God. Though they will have exceeding joy in this kingdom, they will have humble hearts and contrite spirits forever because of the glory that they have chosen; thus is the symbolic representation of the penalty of the Second Token of the Lower Priesthood.

18 And I have called it the Second Token of the Lower Priesthood because it is by the authority of this priesthood that my word is taught to the children of men. For I have suffered them to have churches and administrations of my word among them, and through these administrations I will command them to establish this lower priesthood and its authority to teach the people of these churches my gospel.

19 And all those who enter the kingdom of God must abide by the law of the gospel as it was presented unto them in the beginning by the Father. For if they cannot abide, they cannot be eternal. For behold, the laws of this gospel will ensure that all of those that will live forever, shall live together in peace and happiness; and for this end is the law of my gospel given.

20 For behold, this gospel teacheth all the children of God the proper way to interact one with another. Yea, it giveth unto them the standard that is necessary to live by in order to assure this eternal peace and happiness. For if the law of the gospel did not exist, then there would be wars and contentions and all manner of chaos in the kingdoms of the Father.

21 But there are not wars and contentions, nor is there chaos in the kingdoms of God.

Therefore, he that cannot abide by the law of the gospel will not be resurrected into an eternal body until he hath proven himself ready and able to abide by these eternal laws forever.

22 And this is what is meant by being saved in the kingdom of God. And also this is what is meant by the saving power of my sacrifice for you.

23 For behold, I shall teach you this gospel when I come down on the earth as a mortal. And I shall sacrifice my own safety and my own life in presenting this gospel unto you. Now this is what is meant by the atonement that I shall accomplish for you. Yea, I shall sacrifice my life in order to teach you those things that shall make you one again with the Father. For the Father and I are one.

24 And because I shall teach these things, which are the pure and simple truths of salvation, many shall be angered with me and claim that I am a deceiver who is trying to change the holy ordinances and traditions that I have suffered to be given unto them by their fathers.

25 And because the children of men are so easily led by other mortals who have received their power over the hearts of the children of men by their mysterious words and their supposed understanding of the mysteries of God—this power consecrated unto them by the voice of the people; and because they are led this way, they shall reject the simplicity and pureness of the gospel that I shall give unto them.

26 And for this reason I am burdened by that which I must do in order to keep the children of men in continual remembrance of the plan of salvation given unto them by the Father.

27 And because I will suffer that the children of men establish churches among them, they are led in such a manner that in many instances they do err because they are taught the precepts of men who do not understand the mysteries of God; nor are they righteous enough to receive the help of those who would minister it unto them from the spirit world.

28 And it burdeneth me that I must give unto you this holy endowment so that ye might teach it unto your posterity and give them another opportunity to hear the words of the Father that they so easily forget. And I know that this endowment will also be corrupted by the men who have no understanding of its meaning and its intent.

29 But I will raise up prophets who shall be given the endowment in its purity, and they shall teach the people the truths that are hidden therein, if it so be the desire of the people to know the mysteries of godliness, which mysteries are not mysterious unto those who know and understand them. But unto those who do not understand them, they are a mystery and will remain so unless the people repent and obey the law of the gospel.

30 And it mattereth not unto me in what manner you shall present the plan of salvation unto your posterity during the presentation of this endowment. But it is vital to their understanding and crucial to the plan itself that each of them be given all the symbolic tokens along with their names and their signs, and their penalties, which are representations of the stages of their existence that they must go through in order to reside in the kingdom of God.

31 I would that ye impress upon the minds of those who shall receive these things, the importance of not revealing or forsaking these tokens that they receive; or in other words, that they be willing to accept what these tokens represent, for they truly represent what hath already occurred in the course of the plan of the Father, and also what shall occur in the futures of all of His children.

32 And those who shall be called by my hand to be the prophets and the revelators among my people shall know the proper way to present these things. And in each of their dispensations they shall conform this holy endowment to the needs and the cultures of the people to whom I have sent them. But the tokens with their accompanying names, signs, and penalties shall be everlasting, for these represent those things that are unchangeable and everlasting.

33 And with the law of my gospel that those who are receiving the endowment shall covenant to obey, ye shall reiterate unto them the importance of avoiding those things that distract from the Holy Spirit and cause the children of men to lose the companionship of those who have been assigned to them as their spiritual guides.

34 Ye shall command them to not speak evil of their brothers and their sisters, who are their neighbors, and who have been anointed as Kings and Queens, Priests and Priestesses unto the most high God. For if they judge their neighbor wrongly, and their neighbor becometh exalted in the kingdom of the Father, and they do not receive this exaltation, Oh, how great will be their disappointment and their torment forever in the presence of those who they have wrongfully judged.

35 And ye shall charge them to not take the name of God in vain. Yea, he will not be held guiltless who taketh the name of God in vain. In other words, if a man accepteth the message of the gospel and taketh upon him the name of God, in that he maketh a covenant with Him to obey His commandments; and if this man doth not obey the commandments of God after he hath made a covenant to do so, then this man hath taken the name of God in vain and will not be held guiltless for not keeping these commandments.

36 And in all these things ye shall teach your posterity that they shall be taught the commandments of God by the mouth of His holy prophets. And these prophets shall teach the leaders of the churches that I shall suffer to be built up among the children of men.

37 And I have mentioned the lower priesthood and its authority, which authority giveth unto the children of men to administer the outward ordinances of the church, which priesthood I have suffered to be established in the church for the edification and instruction of my people.

38 And ye shall also give unto the participants who are receiving this holy endowment the First Token of the Higher Priesthood, which priesthood hath the power and the authority to have the privilege of receiving the mysteries of the kingdom of heaven, to have the heavens opened unto them, and to commune with me, who is your arbitrator with the Father.

39 And this token shall be given in the course of the presentation of the endowment in the Terrestrial kingdom of glory. And those who have chosen the Terrestrial glory as their state of happiness shall also receive a penalty for that which they have chosen for themselves.

40 And these shall go throughout the days of their probation as honorable men who are blinded by the craftiness of men and who are deceived by the riches and the glory and the praise of the world. These are they who generally obeyed the law of the gospel, but did not accept me as their Savior and take my yoke upon them, and become one with me. And these are they which are the majority of the children of God.

41 And because the main focus of this token is the ability of a man or a woman to look unto me and follow my example, as it will be shown unto them when I visit the earth in the flesh; yea, because I am the center of a selfless life, which is a life like unto that which existeth in the kingdom of glory of our Father, therefore the name of this token shall be the Name of the Son.

42 For behold, I shall live my life according to all the commandments that I have received of the Father. And the works that I shall do and the desires that I shall have and the responsibilities that I shall be given shall be representative of my name, which shall be the Son of God.

43 And those who are deserving of a Terrestrial glory cannot take upon them my name and bear the cross that I shall bear, neither shall they desire to live for the sake of others. And in this way do these reveal the First Token of the Higher Priesthood.

44 And the token shall be given as a symbolic representation of the manner in which I shall be sacrificed because of the things that I shall teach to the children of men, and which things many of them shall reject.

45 And it shall be a sacrifice because I shall willingly give up my life, knowing that I could save myself from the persecution and eventual death which I shall experience, which death shall be the most cruel and painful death that any of the children of men shall ever experience.

46 And the token shall be given by placing the tip of the forefinger in the palm, and the thumb opposite on the back of the hand of the one who is receiving the token, thus signifying the final stage of the fulfillment of my name, or of my works, as I have explained it unto you, which is also the name of the token.

47 The sign of the token is made by bringing the left hand in front of you with the hand in cupping shape, the left arm forming a square; the right hand is also brought forward, the palm down and the fingers close together and the thumb extended—thus symbolizing the presentation of their works to the Lord—and using the right arm to show that they are committed to accepting a lower kingdom of glory that is below the head, which representeth the Celestial kingdom of God, signifying this by the gesture of the palm pointing downward.

48 The execution of the penalty is represented by placing the right thumb on the left side of the womb area and drawing it quickly across the body, thus signifying that those who inherit the Terrestrial kingdom of glory will never be able to produce offspring, or in other words, they will live without the power of creation that is reserved for those of a higher glory. And those of the Telestial glory will also receive this penalty as well as the penalty that they receive in the Telestial kingdom of glory.

49 And these shall remain with a body of flesh and bone that is eternal, but there shall be no gender among them—male and female there shall not be.

50 For behold, when a spirit child is conceived and raised up by its Eternal Mother, it is neither male nor female, having no need for a distinction in its gender. And when the spirit children of the Father enter mortality, they shall be given the body that they desire, or the body that will benefit them during the course of the days of their probation depending on those things that they need to learn, or depending on those things that they need to overcome; and also depending on those things that might be required of them by the Lord.

51 For this purpose ye shall give at this time in the presentation of the endowment the Law of Chastity, which is that your sons and daughters shall not have sexual relations with anyone who is not their spouse.

52 Behold, this law is given because of the great sin of lasciviousness and immorality that existeth in mortality. And this desire to create children is a natural desire that is enhanced by the carnality of the children of men. And those who cannot control themselves in this thing shall not be trusted to have this power in the worlds to come.

53 For behold, this power is reserved for those who will use it for the purpose for which it was intended. And because of this purpose, there are great blessings attached to the ability to use this power. And these blessings are the ultimate feelings of joy and happiness, and will only be experienced by those of the highest glory in the kingdom of God. Yea, these blessings coalesce the most powerful joys that a body and spirit can produce together.

54 And it is because of the joy that is felt from these blessings that the children of men misuse and abuse this power that they have been given in mortality to provide the bodies for the rest of the spirits that reside in the spirit world.

55 Nevertheless, this power and this joy shall be taken from the majority of the children of God and given only to those who shall selflessly serve others forever, this joy being one of their greatest rewards.

56 And those who inherit the Telestial and the Terrestrial kingdoms of glory shall not receive the body necessary to experience this joy, nor will they crave this joy. But they shall remember that it existed in the mortal world where they learned to distinguish between those things that gave them joy and those things that gave them pain.

57 And they will often suffer from the knowledge that they were not righteous enough to enjoy this blessing like unto their Father, nor will they experience the great joys that come from being an eternal parent. And thus is the penalty received by those of a Terrestrial glory, and also by those of a Telestial glory.

58 And all these shall be saved in the kingdom of God because of their worthiness in keeping the law of the gospel that I have given unto them as it is incorporated in the law of sacrifice, meaning that they have received this law because of the sacrifice that I have

performed for them. And for this reason shall the First Token of the Higher Priesthood be according to my name.

59 And as the other tokens of the lower priesthood are symbolic of the works that the children of God showed both in their first estate, which is the state of spirit, and also in their second state, which is the state of mortality, even so it is that the tokens of the higher priesthood are symbolic of works that others have done for them on their behalf.

60 And these works are done on their behalf by me and my Father. And I have administered these works unto them according to the order of the priesthood that the Father established in the beginning, even that which is called the Holy Priesthood after the Order of the Son of God.

61 Therefore, whosoever belongeth to this Order shall have the privilege to communicate with the Father and also with me, the mediator of the covenant with the Father, and receive the mysteries of godliness that pertain to the kingdom of glory of which they are worthy.

62 And those who shall inherit the Terrestrial glory in the kingdom of God shall not do so, except it be by me. And I shall administer unto them the blessings thereof, which blessings are great and glorious, even so much that those who inherit that kingdom shall experience exceeding joy and happiness therein according to their desires of happiness. And I shall be their servant assuring that they receive the desires of their happiness forever.

63 For this reason this first token and its name and symbol refer to me and the work that I shall do for them.

64 And after ye have given unto those who receive this holy endowment, the First Token of the Higher Priesthood, ye shall teach unto them the Law of Consecration which is associated with the Second Token of the Higher Priesthood.

65 And ye shall teach them that the law of consecration is the holiest and most sacred law of all the laws of God. And it is this law that governeth the Celestial glories of the kingdom of God. Behold, it is this law that bringeth the greatest amount of joy and happiness to an eternal soul.

66 And if it so be that ye could teach this law unto your children and cause them to live by this law in mortality, then would they have peace and happiness among them all the days of their probation. Nevertheless, the requirements of this law are opposed to the plan of Lucifer, whose purpose and intent hath always been centered in selfishness; and he hath great power and influence over the hearts of the children of men, and this because of the veil that hath been placed over their minds that they do not remember the things of the Father.

67 For the law of consecration is this: That all those who live this law shall give of all that they have been blessed with, yea, even from each according to his abilities to each according to their needs, that all might be blessed equally according to their needs and their wants. And their wants shall only be those things that they shall need, and they shall not want that which they do not need.

68 And under this law there shall be no rich because there are no poor; all having access to that which all possess. And they shall possess only that which they need for their happiness. And their desires of happiness shall be in providing from their abilities for the needs of others.

69 Therefore, if they receive their happiness by giving of themselves unto others, then they shall receive from others that which they give; and in this way their joy shall be continually full and they shall want for nothing.

70 And those who abide by this law shall see as they are seen and know as they are known, thus being equal with all those who share the same glory.

71 And there is no selfishness among them because they find no pleasure or joy in doing that which doth not benefit another. But their selfishness is in the joy that they receive from giving joy to others. And when they have given this joy to another, they do rejoice for that which they have done, thus receiving this joy twofold, having administered it in joy and sharing in the joy that they have administered.

72 And such are those who shall reside in the Celestial kingdom of glory. And these shall receive all of the blessings that the Father hath received; and they shall receive these blessings from the Father.

73 And ye shall present the Second Token of the Higher Priesthood, without its name, to those who are receiving the endowment, from those who are administering it unto them. For its name shall be given to them symbolically by him who shall play the part of the Father during the presentation of the endowment.

74 And the sign of the Second Token of the Higher Priesthood is associated with the name of this token. In other words, the sign is made by raising both hands into the air and while lowering the hands repeating the words, Oh, God, hear the words of my mouth. This sign signifieth the desire of the person to have communion with the Father, in that he offereth to the Father, by uplifting his hands, all that he possesseth and is. The hands are slowly lowered while repeating the phrase three distinct times in reference to the holiness of the Holy Trinity and the respect that each member of the Godhead deserveth.

75 And the name shall be symbolic of the blessings that a Celestial being shall receive from the Father. And ye shall give this name by saying unto them: Health in the navel, and marrow in the bones, and strength in the loins and in the sinews; thus signifying the great powers that the bodies that those who receive a Celestial glory shall possess.

76 And ye shall continue, saying: Power in the priesthood be upon me and upon my posterity through all generations of time, and throughout all eternity; thus signifying the ability of a Celestial soul to continue the work of the Father forever, or in other words, that which is done by the power and authority of the Holy Priesthood which is given after the Holy Order of the Son of God.

77 And all those who reside in the Celestial glory shall be one with the Father and shall know Him as they are known by Him. And for this reason ye shall give the name of this token to them who are receiving this endowment upon the five points of fellowship, which are given to show the representation of being one with the Father in all things.

78 And it shall be given along with the Second Token of the Higher Priesthood that pertaineth to the kingdom of the Celestial glory by clasping the right hands and interlocking the little fingers, and placing the tip of the forefinger upon the center of the wrist of them that are receiving the endowment, thus representing a surety that they will be held in the hand of fellowship by the Father, thus having become one with Him.

79 And ye shall place the inside of the right foot by the side of the right foot of the person that is receiving the endowment, thus signifying that this person hath followed in the footsteps of the Father, or in other words, hath lived his life as the Father hath commanded him. The knee shall be to the knee and the breast to the breast, showing that the person hath bowed his knee in worship and prayer unto the Father all the days of his probation, and that the Father hath given him a burning in his bosom, or in other words, a feeling of peace in answer to his prayers.

80 And ye shall place your left hand on the back of the person that is receiving his endowment, thus signifying the closeness and acceptance of the Father, having been embraced by Him in this manner.

81 And your mouth shall be near unto the ear of the person receiving the endowment, that they might hear the name of the Second Token of the Higher Priesthood, signifying the sacredness and the secrecy of the power with which those who receive the Celestial glory will be blessed. For behold, they shall have the power to command the elements; and this power shall be shown unto them by the Father according to the laws that restrict this power and reserve it only unto those who are worthy of it.

82 And ye shall administer these things unto those who receive this endowment at a place that is symbolically represented as the veil that hath been placed over their minds, thus signifying that in mortality, they cannot see or remember their previous life with the Father.

83 And ye shall present those who are receiving this endowment at the veil. And he who representeth the Father shall put forth his hand and test the knowledge of them to see if they have remembered the tokens which they have been given during the presentation of the endowment.

84 And this ye shall do to show that the Father will not allow anyone to enter His presence unless they have passed through the stages that were presented in the plan of salvation.

85 For behold, it is a requisite of all of us to accept the plan that the Father presented to us as spirit children when we were taught by Him in His kingdom. And if we chose not to follow this plan, we were cut off from the kingdom of God. And those of us who kept this first estate in that we did not reveal the token that we received in association with the law of sacrifice that was presented to us by the Father, or in other words, we did not rebel against the law of sacrifice that was presented to us as spirits, are able to continue to our second state, which is mortality.

86 And in mortality ye shall be given the law of the gospel that shall be taught unto you through the ministrations of the holy prophets and the scriptures that I shall cause to be written for the benefit of the children of men; and also by the words of my own mouth.

87 And those who keep this second estate and do not reveal the token that is associated with the law of the gospel, shall be candidates of the Terrestrial glory in the kingdom of our Father. And those who reveal this token, or sell this token for money, or in other words, set their hearts and desires upon the things of the world and aspire to the honors of men, shall be candidates of a Terrestrial or a Telestial state, according to their works and desires of happiness.

88 And those of us who did not give in to the lusts of the flesh, even the lusts that so easily consume the spirits of the children of men, yea, even those that obey the law of chastity as it was previously explained unto you, these shall have the privilege of receiving the Celestial glory in the kingdom of our Father.

89 And those who revealed the token associated with the law of chastity, or those who were honorable men and women upon the earth, yet gave in to the lusts of the flesh, shall be given the Terrestrial glory in the kingdom of our Father as I have explained it unto you previously.

90 And those of us who receive the token that is associated with the law of consecration, which is the law that governeth the Celestial glory in the kingdom of our Father, shall receive no penalty. For behold, what penalty think ye that they who are in the Celestial glory receive? For unto them is given everything that the Father hath, therefore, they suffer no penalty.

91 And ye shall teach unto them the true order of prayer. For behold, the children of men will offer up many prayers unto the Father in my name; and these prayers shall be in vain except they shall be given in the true order according to the way that I shall show unto you.

92 And if they shall not be given in the true order of prayer, then when the children of men spread forth their hands unto me, yea, when they make many prayers, I will not hear them.

93 For behold it is not conducive unto the Spirit who heareth and answereth these prayers that they be given with much repetition and with much frequency. Nevertheless, I have commanded you to pray always lest ye enter into temptation because of the power of Satan, who is also there in the spirit world, and can also listen to your prayers.

94 Now I did not mean that you should always be in the action of prayer, but I have commanded you to be in the attitude of prayer, or in other words, that ye are always aware of the presence of those who are spirits, whom I have commissioned to hear and answer your prayers.

95 And I do not require it of you to pray for all things whatsoever ye shall do, but that ye shall do all things in my name, or as I would do them.

96 For behold, there are many who pray over their food to bless it that it may nourish and strengthen their bodies. And in this they use vain repetition because the food is the blessing that they ask for, and a further blessing shall not be given.

97 And many of the children of men pray for things that they should not, believing that they shall receive that which they pray for if they but ask of the Father. Behold, the Father already knoweth what ye are in need of before ye ask it of Him, therefore ye use vain repetition in your prayers. And the only thing for which ye should

ask the Father, is that His will be done concerning you.

98 For behold, if there is one sick among you and it is appointed unto him to die, what doth it profit you to fight against the will of God? Yea, why should ye pray unto the Father that He might change His will concerning the time that He hath appointed this one unto to death? Do ye not believe that this spirit child of the Father is loved by Him and that He knoweth what is best for His children?

99 And ye shall teach the true order of prayer by instructing those who are receiving their endowment to form a circle, both male and female, side by side. And this circle representeth eternity, in which the true order of prayer is practiced forever.

100 And ye shall command anyone that hath aught against anyone else in the circle to withdraw from the circle. For behold, the Spirit of God doth not reside with those who are angry, or those who have judged their neighbor, or those who consider another to be their enemy.

101 And ye shall instruct those who are in the circle to make all the signs of the tokens that they have received during the presentation of the endowment and execute the penalties pertaining to each one, thus signifying unto each other that they have all passed through the stages of the plan of salvation and are blessed with eternal life because of their righteousness.

102 For behold, there are no prayers that are heard by those whom the Father hath commissioned to hear and answer prayers on His behalf, that are given in unrighteousness. And for this reason ye have been commanded to pray in my name.

103 For behold, my name is symbolic of my works, which I have previously explained to you during the presentation of this holy endowment. And it is not requisite that ye use my name when ye pray. But before ye pray, see that ye do the things that ye see me do, or the things that I shall command you to do according to the ministrations of those whom I have instructed to hear your prayers.

104 And he who prayeth and useth my name in vain, or in other words, doeth not the things that I have commanded of him, shall not be held guiltless and his prayer shall not be heard. And I have commanded all the children of men to not be angry with one another and to love their enemies and refrain from judging each other, so that my spirit may be with them. And if they do these things, then truly they shall have my spirit to be with them.

105 And ye shall instruct those of the circle to take one another in the Second Token of the Higher Priesthood, as it hath been explained unto you, thus symbolizing the firm unity in the Order to which they belong. And they shall belong to the Holy Order of the Son of God, which is my Order, and shall be the Order of all those who keep the commandments that I shall give unto them.

106 And ye shall instruct those of the circle to make the sign of the square with their left arm, thus signifying their unrighteous acts done in the flesh, and they shall place their left elbow upon the shoulder of the person to their left, thus signifying that all shall bear the burdens of each other, and support one another in their sins and in their afflictions.

107 And in this way shall ye teach the true order of prayer to those who are receiving this holy endowment.

CHAPTER 12

Moroni further expounds on the purpose of the endowment. He sees the latter-day church and the corruption of the endowment. He condemns those who are fixated on genealogy work and reveals the corrupt state of the latter-day church and its leaders.

AND now, I, Moroni, have written many of the words of the brother of Jared concerning the Holy Endowment that the Lord gave unto Adam and Eve and commanded them to present to their children so that they might have some measure of knowledge regarding the plan of salvation that the Father gave unto them in His kingdom, but which the children of men cannot remember in mortality.

2 And this same endowment was given unto Lehi when he entered the land of promise. And Lehi taught these things unto his son Nephi, who caused temples to be built in the land of Lehi-Nephi for the instruction and edification of the Nephites.

3 And I have the large plates of Nephi in which are written these things. Nevertheless, the Lord commanded my father Mormon not to include them on the plates upon which he hath abridged the record of Nephi.

4 And in the day of my father, and also in my own day, this holy endowment hath been corrupted by the church and its leaders. But this church and these leaders have all been destroyed by the Lamanites. And they have also destroyed the temples and the places that were dedicated to teach these things unto the people.

5 However, it would not have mattered to the Lord if his people received the endowment that was being taught by the church in my day, because it was changed and corrupted, evensomuch that it did not have the signs or the penalties of which the brother of Jared hath written.

6 And it confused the people who received it more than it lifted them up and taught them the mysteries of God.

7 And the people were required by the leaders of the church to keep the endowment secret and not to discuss it among themselves. Behold, how is that they should learn about it and find its true meaning, if it so be that it cannot be discussed among them? And because it cannot be discussed among the people, they do not understand it. And because of their unrighteousness, they did not have the Holy Spirit to help them understand its meaning.

8 And in this way the leaders of the people did corrupt the pure and simple truths of God. For they presented the endowment as something that it was not, believing that it was necessary for their salvation. And thus they begin to put themselves up above those that were not in the church.

9 And they did that which shall be done in the last days by the church that shall have the fullness of the Holy Endowment revealed unto them, even that they shall forbid those who do not obey the commandments of the church from receiving the endowment.

10 And those of my own day began to believe that the ordinances that were done for those that were dead were ordinances of salvation for the dead, assuming in and of themselves that the dead could not be saved unless these ordinances were done by the living of the church, thus making themselves saviors of men.

11 And this is not what was intended by the Lord when he commanded Lehi to teach this holy endowment unto his children.

12 And I have searched among the records of the Nephites and I have found the record wherein are written the instructions of Lehi that were given unto him by the Lord pertaining to this endowment and its presentation.

13 And Lehi wrote saying: And inasmuch that it is necessary that we understand that the plan of salvation, which includeth all the covenants that we make concerning the laws that we receive during the Holy Endowment, is in effect eternally, whether we are dead or alive, we should administer these things symbolically for those who have died and did not have the chance to receive this endowment during the days of their probation.

14 And also, this will give us an opportunity to perform this ordinance more often, which will help us to remember the things that we have covenanted to do. And also that we might understand its meaning more fully and learn the things that the Lord would have us learn from its presentation.

15 And we shall do these things for our own sake, for thus was this endowment given, and not for the salvation of the dead. For behold, they know the plan of the Father concerning them, having the veil of forgetfulness lifted upon their entrance once again into the spirit world.

16 But I would that it should be taught unto all, that whether alive or dead, we must all accept the words of God as shall be given unto us by the Holy Ghost, and also by the mouth of the Lord when he shall reveal himself unto us in the flesh. And those who are in the spirit world must also accept these things.

17 And now, I, Moroni, am burdened in that

which I have seen concerning these things that shall be revealed in the last days unto the church that shall call itself after the name of the Lord, even Jesus Christ.

18 For behold, they shall do that which was done by those leaders who corrupted the Holy Endowment in the days of my father, and also in the days of his father.

19 For the leaders shall teach the people that the endowment is a necessary ordinance that must be performed in order for one to enter the kingdom of God.

20 And in that day they shall build many temples unto the Lord and dedicate them to the Lord in hopes that they will be accepted as places where this holy endowment can be presented unto the children of men. And they shall adorn these temples with all manner of fine things; and they shall gain much praise of the world because of the adorning of their temples.

21 And they shall set requirements on the children of men, allowing only those to enter the temple to receive this endowment who have fulfilled the requirements that they have set.

22 And these requirements shall be given by the leaders of the church according to the precepts of men who do not have the Holy Spirit to guide them and give them direction. And these requirements shall include the payment of a tithe to the church in order for one to enter into the temple.

23 And if there is one who is poor among them that cannot afford to pay a full tithe unto the church, then this person shall be denied the opportunity of entering into the temple of the Lord and having the endowment presented unto him. And thus shall the leaders of this church corrupt the holy things of God; and they shall change His holy ordinances, and teach for doctrine the commandments of men.

24 And these leaders shall require that no one can enter the temple who doth not accept them as the only true prophets, or the only true givers of the words of God. And in this way they shall deceive the people and cause many to err and follow them in their foolish doctrine, which doctrine is fashioned after the praise of the world.

25 And this church shall set itself up above all other churches. And because of the gospel that it shall have among them, which is the only true gospel of the Lord, they shall think of themselves like unto the Zoramites who lived in the days of Alma, of which my father wrote in his record.

26 And like the Zoramites, these people who shall call themselves the Saints of God, and they shall gather themselves together on one day of the week, which day they shall call the day of the Lord.

27 And according to the vision that my father had concerning them, and also according to the words of the vision of the brother of Jared, I have seen their works and their manner of worship. Yea, even on this one day of the week they shall rise to a pulpit which is in the center of their synagogue, which is according to the words that my father wrote concerning the Zoramites:

28 For they had a place built up in the center of their synagogue, a place for standing, which was high above the head, and would only admit one person.

29 And in the last days, the leaders of this church shall also place themselves above the people of the church and shall speak unto them from this pulpit, and shall teach the people that they are the elect of God, and that God hath separated them from the rest of the world and given unto them the only true gospel, and that they are a chosen and a holy people.

30 And because they shall believe in Christ and shall call their church after his name, they believe that they are not like unto the Zoramites, who did not believe in Christ, and of whom they have a record before them, which is the record that my father and I have prepared for them.

31 And they shall be taught by their leaders that the day that hath been chosen as the day of the Lord is the only day that they should gather together and do the things that the Lord requireth of them. And thus they deceive themselves. For if they have chosen only one day of the week to worship the Lord, whom do they worship the rest of the days of the week?

32 And I have seen their works and the desires of their hearts, and I know that the rest of the days of the week their hearts are set upon gold, and upon silver, and upon the money that they might obtain because of this gold and this silver, and all manner of fine goods, thus following the example of the Zoramites in all things, even that their hearts are lifted up unto great boasting in their pride.

33 And according to the words of Alma, my soul doth also cry unto the Lord because of the things that I have seen in the latter days.

34 Behold, Oh, God, they cry unto thee, and yet their hearts are swallowed up in their pride. Behold, Oh, God, they cry unto thee with their mouths, while they are puffed up, even to greatness, with the vain things of the world.

35 Behold, Oh, my God, their costly apparel, and their ringlets, and their ornaments of gold, and all their precious things which they are ornamented with; and behold, their hearts are set upon them, and yet they cry unto thee and say— We thank thee, Oh, God, for we are a chosen people unto thee, while others shall perish.

36 And I, Moroni, have seen the manner in which the leaders of this church in the latter days present the Holy Endowment unto the people. And after the people have paid their money to the church, and after the church hath taken this money and constructed all manner of fine temples and adorned them with the fine things of the world; yea, even after they have done all these things, they shall prohibit those who are poor and needy, even those who are unable to comply with the requirements of the church, from receiving this endowment.

37 And they have changed the ordinance of the Lord and have broken his everlasting covenant. They seek not the Lord to establish his righteousness, but every man walketh in his own way, and after the image of his own god, whose image is in the likeness of the world, and whose substance is that of an idol that they do worship, instead of worshiping the Lord and doing the things that he hath commanded them.

38 And I know that the Lord condemneth those who have used the ordinances that he suffereth the children of men to have in the flesh, according to the administrations of the priesthood which he hath given them, for their own gain, or for the gain of their church.

39 For behold, these ordinances were given by the Lord freely unto all of his children. And they are given for the edification of all; and it is not important to the Lord whether or not his children can pay a tithe unto him. Behold, this is not the sacrifice that he requireth of them; for he requireth a broken heart and a contrite spirit.

40 And all those who come unto him with a broken heart and a contrite spirit shall receive the gift of the Holy Ghost as it hath been explained previously in the words of the brother of Jared. And the Holy Ghost shall teach them all things whatsoever they need to do in order to enter into the kingdom of God.

41 And I have the gift of the Holy Ghost, and it hath been my constant companion all the days of my life, and it doth not tell me that I need to participate in the presentation of the endowment to be saved in the kingdom of God. Behold, nowhere in the words of Christ doth he command his people to receive an endowment that they might be saved. And in this way shall the word of God be changed by the church in the latter days. And this because the spirit is not among them, and they listen to the vain words of their leaders and follow their examples, which are not the examples of Christ, but are the examples of men.

42 And hath not the church that is called after the name of Jesus Christ in the latter days fulfilled the prophecy of the prophet Zenos which he gave unto the Jews in the allegory of the tame and wild olive trees?

43 For did not Zenos say unto them: And in the latter days before God once again sendeth His Son among the people, yea, even in all his glory like unto the glory that he showed unto the Nephites and the Lamanites in the land of Bountiful, God shall once again bring the knowledge of His gospel unto the Gentiles and then unto the Jews, that the last may be first, and the first may be last.

44 And it shall come to pass that the gospel shall be established in all the parts of the world, in other words, the Lord shall graft in the wild branches into the natural olive trees and the natural branches into the wild trees, that he might once again obtain fruit that is pleasing unto him.

45 And after this gospel shall be preached in all the parts of the world, yea, even after the voice of Jesus Christ shall be heard among all

men, then still shall the Lord of the vineyard weep and say unto his servants: What could I have done more for my vineyard?

46 For behold, all the trees of the vineyard shall be corrupt. And the Lord will ask of his servants what was the cause of the corruptness of his vineyard.

47 Then shall the servant of the Lord say unto his master: Is it not the loftiness of thy vineyard—have not the branches thereof overcome the roots which are good? And because the branches have overcome the roots thereof, behold they grew faster than the strength of the roots, taking strength unto themselves.

48 And it came to pass that Zenos expounded the meaning of the parable unto the High Priests, saying: Behold, in the latter days the church of God shall be like unto this church at Jerusalem. For the Lord will give unto them the pureness of his everlasting gospel and provide for them a way whereby they might be saved in the kingdom of God at the last day.

49 Nevertheless, because of the branches, or in other words, because of the church of God and its supposed greatness, the roots of the tree, which is the pure gospel of God, shall be overcome. Yea, the leaders and members of the church of God shall become lofty and prideful, and their desires shall be towards the church and not set upon the gospel, which is the root of the tree, thus the branches overcome the roots that are good.

50 And now I, Moroni, do mourn exceedingly for the Gentiles to whom the pure form of the gospel shall be given. And I would that the Lord would command me to refrain from writing further concerning your wickedness and the corrupt state of the church of God in the latter days. For as I write, my soul is harrowed up in sorrow because of your pride. And because of your pride, ye do not see that in which ye have corrupted the words of Christ.

51 And now if it is not enough that I should be harrowed up in great sorrow because of you, the Lord hath commanded me to include in this record what I have seen concerning the work that ye do for those who are dead, yea, even the work that ye do in your temples for the dead, which work hath only the efficacy of salvation as I have explained it unto you according to the words of Lehi.

52 Instead of feasting upon the words of Christ and patterning your lives after his example, ye search the genealogies of your ancestors, believing that without you, they cannot be saved in the kingdom of God. And ye waste away your time in vain searching out these things when ye should be searching the words of Christ and living by the precepts that he hath given unto you.

53 Did ye not read in the record of my father the words of Nephi concerning the genealogy of his fathers? Do ye not realize that Nephi gave little importance to the traditions of his father and their lineage, or in other words their genealogies? Did not Nephi write, saying:

54 And now I, Nephi, do not give the genealogy of my fathers in this part of my record; neither at any time shall I give it after upon these plates which I am writing; for it is given in the record which hath been kept by my father; therefore, I do not write it in this work.

55 For it sufficeth me to say that we are descendants of Joseph.

56 And it mattereth not to me that I am particular to give a full account of all the things of my father, for they cannot be written upon these plates, for I desire the room that I may write of the things of God.

57 For the fullness of mine intent is that I may persuade men to come unto the God of Abraham, and the God of Isaac, and the God of Jacob, and be saved.

58 Therefore, the things which are pleasing unto the world I do not write, but the things which are pleasing unto God and unto those who are not of the world.

59 Therefore, I shall give commandment unto my seed, that they shall not occupy these plates with things which are not of worth unto the children of men.

60 Now, how can ye misunderstand the simplicity of the words of Nephi? For truly he hath shown unto you that your genealogy work is vain and useless before God. Behold, the people of the world are concerned about their ancestry. And the work of genealogy doth nothing to bring the children of men unto the God of which Nephi hath spoken, which is Jesus Christ, that they might be saved.

61 How can ye waste your time and your money and your efforts in such things, yet ye suffer the poor and the needy, the sick and the afflicted, and those who are imprisoned to pass by you that ye notice them not?

62 How can ye deny the blessing of the endowment, insomuch that it is only a representation of the plan of salvation that hath been given to all the children of God, to all those who ye believe are sinners, or to those who cannot pay you the tithe that ye require of them?

63 Yea, how can ye believe that by your works, even the work of your genealogies, your ancestors will be saved? Know ye not that this is blasphemous before the Lord? For it is only by his works, after all we can do, that we are saved. And your works are in vain, and shall not be counted as righteousness before the Lord because ye consume them upon the pride of your hearts.

64 For in your pride ye look towards your ancestors in hopes that ye might be related to one who was mighty and great among men. And if ye are the descendants of one that was mighty and great among men, what reason have ye to be prideful? These are the things that are pleasing unto the world and which are not pleasing unto God.

65 Behold, your leaders have misled you and have destroyed the righteous ways of the Lord. And they are like unto the leaders of the church of God at Jerusalem at the time that Zenos preached repentance unto them. And if ye continue to allow your leaders to mislead you in this thing, then shall the all the words of Christ be fulfilled, which he said:

66 And I say unto you, that if the Gentiles do not repent after the blessing which they shall receive, after they have scattered my people;

67 Then shall ye, who are a remnant of the house of Jacob, go forth among them; and ye shall be in the midst of them who shall be many; and ye shall be among them as a lion among the beasts of the forest, and as a young lion among the flocks of sheep, who, if he goeth through both treadeth down and teareth in pieces, and none can deliver.

68 Thy hand shall be lifted up upon thine adversaries, and all thine enemies shall be cut off.

69 And I will gather my people together as a man gathereth his sheaves into the floor.

70 For I will make my people with whom the Father hath covenanted, yea, I will make thy horn iron, and I will make thy hoofs brass. And thou shalt beat in pieces many people; and I will consecrate their gain unto the Lord, and their substance unto the Lord of the whole earth. And behold, I am he who doeth it.

71 And it shall come to pass, saith the Father, that the sword of my justice shall hang over them at that day; and except they repent it shall fall upon them, saith the Father, yea, even upon all the nations of the Gentiles.

72 Now, I, Moroni, say unto you, what do ye think is the blessing that you have received of the Lord? Behold, it is his gospel in its pure form, yea, even this record that my father and I have prepared for you. And it is also the revelation of the Holy Endowment that hath been explained unto you.

73 And even after all these things shall be given unto you, ye shall deny the power of the Holy Ghost and seek after the things of the world and desire its power and its glory, which is in the likeness of ancient Babylon, even that great city that did fall because of the judgments of the Lord.

74 Behold, I say unto you, shake off the chains by which ye are bound. Do not use the ordinances of God to justify your desires to please the world and be a part thereof. Do not follow the examples of your leaders in these things.

75 Behold, I know that your leaders teach you the words of Christ, but they do not follow these words for themselves, but use them as a guise to keep you under their authority and to keep you under their power, which power is given unto them by the devil, who is the God of this earth.

76 Seek out the words of Christ and know that the ordinances of your church were established to teach you the words of Christ. And if ye do not have the ordinances, ye still have the words

of Christ. And these words are the only way that ye can be saved. And your ordinances are good for nothing, except it be for the words of Christ which they represent.

77 And now, I say unto you, Repent and work righteousness. Deny no one the opportunity to have the Holy Endowment presented unto him. Present it unto him in the form that it hath been revealed unto you in this record according to the words of the brother of Jared. Give it freely to all the children of men, so that they might be encouraged to come unto the Holy One of Israel and partake of the salvation that he hath to give unto them.

78 And this salvation cometh only by his words, and also by his name, which is the only name under the heavens and in the earth by which all the children of men can be saved.

79 Behold, know ye not that the Lord giveth his salvation freely unto all those who call upon his name, repenting of their sins and covenanting with him to keep his commandments?

80 And ye are like unto the Zoramites, who cast out the poor because of the coarseness of their dress. And ye say to yourselves: We do not cast out the poor. Yet, ye treat those who would enter into one of your synagogues, or into one of your temples, with contempt, if it so be that they are not dressed like unto you. And thus also did the Zoramites justify themselves by casting the poor from among them because of their apparel.

81 And I saw your day and have spoken unto you, and ye have my words in the part of this record that hath been circulated and read among you.

82 And I wrote concerning you, saying: Behold, I speak unto you as if ye were present, and yet ye are not. But behold, Jesus Christ hath shown you unto me, and I know your doing.

83 And I know that ye do walk in the pride of your hearts; and there are none save a few only who do not lift themselves up in the pride of their hearts, unto the wearing of very fine apparel, unto envying, and strifes, and malice, and persecutions, and all manner of iniquities; and your churches, yea, even every one, have become polluted because of the pride of your hearts.

84 For behold, ye do love money, and your substance, and your fine apparel, and the adorning of your churches, more than ye love the poor and the needy, the sick and the afflicted.

85 Oh, ye wicked and perverse and stiffnecked people, why have ye built up churches unto yourselves to get gain? Why have ye transfigured the holy word of God, that ye might bring damnation upon your souls?

86 Oh, ye pollutions, ye hypocrites, ye teachers, who sell yourselves for that which will canker, why have ye polluted the holy church of God? Why are ye ashamed to take upon you the holy name of Christ? Why do ye not think that greater is the value of an endless happiness than that misery which never dies because of the praise of the world?

87 Why do ye adorn yourselves with that which hath no life, and yet suffer the hungry, and the needy, and the naked, and the sick and the afflicted to pass by you, and notice them not?

88 Yea, why do ye build up your secret abominations to get gain, and cause that the widows should mourn before the Lord, and also the orphans to mourn before the Lord?

89 Now, I, Moroni, would that I might write unto you the pleasing words of Christ in which my soul rejoiceth. But I am constrained by the Spirit to speak to you of your sins and the great hypocrisy that hath arisen in the latter days because of a great church that hath risen up out of obscurity and is called after his name.

90 And I know that ye do not see yourselves as sinners, and that your leaders do preach unto you the pleasing words of Christ, yet they do not require them at your hand. Yea, they have required of you the things that the world requireth of you, and not that which the Lord requireth of all those who call themselves after his Holy Name.

91 Do ye believe that those who do not receive the Holy Endowment, yea even those who cannot enter into one of your temples to receive this endowment because of the requirements that ye first ask of them; do ye believe that these shall be damned? I say unto you that they shall not be damned, but that it is good that they are not allowed to enter into your temples and into your synagogues. For by not entering therein, they might have a chance to humble themselves and hear the words of Christ by the mouth of his holy angels.

92 And this is what Alma taught the people who were poor and could not enter into the places of worship of the Zoramites. Did he not say unto them: Behold I say unto you, do ye suppose that ye cannot worship God save it be in your synagogues only? And also, I would ask, do ye suppose that ye must not worship God save it be only one day in a week?

93 And Alma taught the people that it was necessary that they repent of their sins and come unto God and believe on His word. And if they believe on His word, and repent of their sins, then they shall find mercy. And he that finds mercy and endureth to the end, the same shall be saved in the kingdom of God.

94 And Amulek also spake unto them commanding them to exercise faith and repent of their sins and call upon the Lord for mercy. And after he had preached these things unto the people, he said unto them: And now behold my beloved brethren, I say unto you, do not suppose that this is all; for after ye have done all these things, if ye turn away the needy, and the naked, and visit not the sick and afflicted, and impart of your substance, if ye have, to those who stand in need; I say unto you, if ye do not any of these things, behold, your prayer is vain, and availeth you nothing, and ye are as hypocrites who do deny the faith.

95 And now, I, Moroni, know that ye have read these things, but have ye obeyed the commandment of the Lord in which he hath commanded you, saying: Behold, I have caused to be written many of the words of my holy prophets and also others have I commanded to keep an account of my works among the children of men. And these are my holy scriptures, which I have suffered to be written that they might profit the children of men and be a blessing unto them. And I would that ye should liken all scripture unto yourselves. For behold, that which is past hath been that which is present, and that which is present shall be that which shall come to pass.

96 Verily I say unto you, before the throne of God there is no history of His works—for His works are eternal and are encompassed into one eternal round, from which He observeth all the works of His hands and receiveth of the joy therein.

97 Therefore, the actions of those who have lived before shall imitate the actions of those who shall live in the present, and also those that shall live in the future. For unto all of the children of men are the same commandments given; and these commandments are the words that I have given unto you.

98 And as it shall pass in one generation—even the sins of that generation—so shall it come to pass in the next generation, because the same spirit that existeth among the children of men, yea, even that spirit that causeth them to sin, shall exist among them of the next generation even until the time of the end of the earth.

99 And for this reason I have called my holy prophets and have commanded them to write the things that they are taught by the Holy Ghost. For from the Holy Ghost, who is one with my spirit, shall the things of my spirit, or my words, be given unto the children of men.

100 And now, I, Moroni, have testified unto you that the Holy Ghost hath been my constant companion all the days of my life. And I have written the things upon these plates that he hath commanded me to write. And I shall write the rest of the words that I shall be commanded by this same spirit, which is also the spirit of Christ, as he hath explained it unto you.

101 And I write these things unto you of the latter days, even unto all those who shall receive my words which shall be sealed up and not given unto the world at the time of my other words, even those of my words which were included in the record that my father Mormon commanded me to hide up in the earth that they may come forth unto you and be a blessing unto you; and so that they might profit you according to the word of the Lord.

102 And many of these things I was desirous to include with the words of my father, but I was forbidden by the Lord and commanded that I should not write these things unto you. But now I have received a commandment to write these

words unto you and seal them up that they may come forth in the own due time of the Lord.

103 And I know that they shall come unto you in the latter days when that which I have spoken of shall come to pass, even the sins that ye do, which are like unto those of the Zoramites.

104 And I say unto you, repent and take hold of the rod of iron that shall lead you to eternal life, yea, even the words of Christ which are also written herein. Do not think that your ordinances shall save you in the day that the Lord shall come and demand from you an accounting of your works, even according to the things that he hath suffered to be revealed unto you.

105 For the fullness of his gospel is contained in the record that ye have received, even this record which ye now read. And there is nowhere to be found in the record of my father, or in this record that I write pertaining to the vision of the brother of Jared, or anywhere in the holy scriptures, that commandeth a man or a woman to receive the Holy Endowment as a means by which they may be saved.

106 And if these records contain a fullness of the gospel, and ye cannot find any reference to the saving power of this ordinance in this record, then what doth it profit you to believe that this ordinance can save you?

107 But ye have been commanded to be baptized in the name of the Father and of the Son, and of the Holy Ghost. And this ordinance is part of the fullness of the gospel of Jesus Christ. Nevertheless, this ordinance was given unto you as a representation of the things that ye should do if ye have made a covenant to serve God and keep His commandments.

108 And as the symbolic representation of a name hath been taught unto you in the words that the brother of Jared wrote concerning the Holy Endowment that the Lord gave unto Adam and Eve, even so shall ye recognize that when ye make a covenant unto God, ye shall do so by doing the same works, and having the same desires, and having the same responsibilities as the Father, and as the Son, and as the Holy Ghost. Now, this is why ye are baptized in their names.

109 And I have also given unto you the proper manner in which the elders and the priests should administer the flesh and blood of Christ unto the church, even as the disciples were taught by Jesus. And many of you, even if not all of you, partake of the flesh and blood of Christ unworthily.

110 And these ordinances are also part of his commandments concerning the administration of his gospel unto his people. But these things are not his gospel, but administer it unto the church, which are his people.

111 For behold, when the Lord taught the Jews at Jerusalem his gospel, he said unto them: Except ye eat of my flesh and drink of my blood, ye shall in no wise inherit the kingdom of God. And those that heard this were angry with him and understood not what he meant, because the Lord taught them in parables. And in this manner doth he teach his people who have taken upon them his name.

112 And if ye look to the words of the administration of the bread, or the flesh of Christ as it is represented, ye will notice that the blessing includeth the words: that they are willing to take upon them the name of thy Son, and always remember him, and keep his commandments which he hath given them.

113 And if ye take upon you the name of the Son, then ye will do the same works that he did, and have the same desires that he had, and have the same responsibilities towards your neighbor that he had. This is what representeth the name of the Son, or in other words, his works. And ye will also remember the works that he did, and keep his commandments which he hath given unto you. This is what is meant by eating the flesh of Christ.

114 And if ye look to the words of the administration of the wine, or the blood of Christ as it is represented, ye will notice that these words are not included therein, even the words that ye shall take upon you his name and keep his commandments. And these words have been excluded because the blood is symbolic of the spirit which giveth life unto the body of the flesh. And by drinking the blood of Christ, ye are covenanting that ye are doing the works that he did for the same purpose, or with the same intent in which he did his works, thus the blood of Christ representing his spirit, or the attitude in which he performed his works.

115 For if ye do the works of Christ without the spirit of Christ, how can they be his works? And if ye have the spirit of Christ, ye shall do his works. And if ye do not drink the blood of Christ, then the works that ye do are not his works. And these works are done in vain. In other words, ye have taken the sacrament of the Lord unworthily and have presented yourselves before him as hypocrites.

116 And again I say unto you, if a man or a woman doeth the works of Christ in the spirit of Christ and doth not receive the ordinance of baptism, or doth not partake of the ordinance of the sacrament, then this man or woman is already doing the will of the Lord and is justified therein. For the Lord judgeth all the children of men according to their works, according to the desires of their hearts.

117 And if their works are righteous, then the ordinances that have been established in the church profit them nothing. And if their works are evil, then the ordinances of the church also profit them nothing.

118 And I have seen your works, and they are not the works of Christ, but are the works of men, which are evil. And because your works are evil, your ordinances profit you nothing, and ye shall drink of the wine of the wrath of God, which is poured out without mixture into the cup of his indignation. And ye shall be tormented with fire and brimstone in the presence of the holy angels, and in the presence of the Lamb. And the smoke of your torment shall ascend up forever and ever, and ye shall have no rest day or night.

119 And now, I, Moroni, am desirous to continue my abridgment of the glorious vision that was given unto the brother of Jared. And many of these things concerning this church of which I have spoken will be given hereafter as the latter days are unfolded unto us through the words of the brother of Jared. But this I say unto the church that calls itself the church of Jesus Christ of the latter days: Yea, repent and turn again unto the words of Christ which have been revealed unto you. For my testimony and the testimony of my father shall stand against you before the judgment bar of Christ. And the books that the Lord hath caused to be written by my hand, and also by the hand of my father, shall be opened up, and ye shall be judged by the things that we have written, which things were commanded of us by the Lord.

120 And if ye do not repent, then I bid you farewell forever, for ye shall receive the just reward for your works. And by these works shall ye be known forever. Amen

CHAPTER 13

Moroni details the explanation of a righteous government. The power of Celestial Beings is touched upon. The establishment of the government of each degree of glory is explained.

AND before I return once again to the account of the brother of Jared and his vision regarding Adam and Eve and their expulsion from the garden of Eden, the Spirit hath commanded me to explain further the kingdom of the Father and the eternal laws that constitute the government of the eternal worlds, even all the worlds that are, which are worlds without end.

2 And there existeth only one pure form of government that hath always existed, and shall continue to exist in worlds without end.

3 And this government hath one purpose and priority in which are incorporated all the eternal laws that manage this government and cause it to function for the purpose for which it existeth. And that purpose for which it existeth is for the eternal happiness of those whom it serveth.

4 And the first principle and law of this government, is that this government shall never be self-serving, or in other words, it shall never act in and of itself and of its own accord for the sake of its own existence.

5 And this government is restricted in its power according to the restrictions that are necessary to ensure that it abideth by this first principle and law.

6 For behold, this government serveth those that benefit from its existence, and those who benefit from its existence are those who give it the power that it hath received. And the power that it hath received hath been given to this government to serve those who have given it its power.

7 And the power of this government resideth in the eternal physical bodies of those who exist to serve in this government. And this power is restricted to the Celestial kingdom of glory in the kingdom of God.

8 And I have previously explained unto you what the desires of happiness are of those who reside in the Celestial kingdom of God. And I have also explained unto you that these beings exist to serve us, and also to assure us the eternal happiness that each of us desireth according to each of our individual desires of happiness.

9 And I also have shown unto you that a Celestial Being shall do nothing except it benefit those whom it hath been given the power to serve. And by serving others and bringing them happiness, this Celestial Being receiveth its happiness, which is its own eternal reward.

10 And with a Celestial body, a God can command the elements and they obey Him. And this is the thing that the Spirit restraineth me to explain further unto you.

11 For behold, even by our own spirit do we control the elements that make up our mortal flesh. And by commanding these elements, we are able to act. And because of these commands, our bones move and permit us to do with our bodies that which we desire. Even so, our bodies are made up of eternal elements, even the same elements that exist in all parts of the kingdom of God.

12 However, we are limited in our ability to command the elements of our environment; even our mortal flesh doth inhibit our ability to command these elements, because our spirit is confined to the elements that make up our mortal bodies, and these are the only elements that we can command.

13 Nevertheless, we are not able to command all the elements that make up our mortal bodies. For even as it hath been demonstrated unto us by the functions of our mortal bodies; yea, even that we know that we cannot stop our hearts from acting in their own environment, according to the power that hath commanded them to function and act for our benefit.

14 And many of the elements that were used by the bodies of our mortal mothers to create our own bodies cannot be controlled by us directly. And for this reason, the heartbeat of a growing body is recognized in the womb of its mother. And the mother hath received the commands necessary to begin the creation of our bodies from our mortal fathers. Yet, neither our mothers or our fathers can control the elements of our mortal bodies.

15 And when our spirit entereth the mortal body, it can then begin to command many of the elements of which it is made. But it cannot command all of the elements, for the power to do this is not given to our spirits while they are confined to this mortal body.

16 Nevertheless, this power hath been reserved unto us, or in other words, this power can be developed and taught to us, and with this power, we can begin to control all of the elements of our bodies. And if it so be that we could control all the elements of our mortal bodies, then we would live forever, and our bodies would not die, for we could command the elements to act in the environment and function in which they have been created, thus assuring ourselves that our bodies would remain mortal forever.

17 Now, this is what is meant by the Lord commanding that cherubim and the flaming sword be placed to guard the Tree of Life, lest Adam and Eve put forth their hand and partake thereof, and live forever in their sins.

18 For if Adam and Eve could remember the commands that they understood as spirit children of the Father, then they would be able to control all the elements of their mortal bodies. And with this power, they and their children would be able to command the elements that make up their bodies. And they could command these bodies to live forever, thus making the plan of salvation null and void.

19 In other words, none of the children of men could have received any of the glories of the kingdom of God with a resurrected body that pertaineth to that kingdom, because they would remain forever in a mortal state.

20 And when the Father created the mortal bodies that were given unto Adam and Eve, He limited the ability of these bodies to exercise complete control over all of the elements from which these bodies were created. And there hath been none of the children of Adam and Eve that hath been given this power, because the bodies of their children are patterned after the mortal bodies that the Father created for Adam and Eve, which do not have this power.

21 Now, I say unto you, that none of the children of Adam and Eve hath ever been given this power, but in this do not assume that this power hath not been given by God to a mortal man. For behold, His Son, even Jesus, the Christ, did possess this power; yea, even the power to control the elements, of which he was created, and command them at his will. But I said unto you, that none of the children of Adam and Eve hath ever been given this power. But Jesus is not a son of Adam, but the son of the Father.

22 For behold, the Father used the power at His command to cause the elements that were given unto the mortal mother of Jesus to create a body that was patterned after His own. And because His own body—which is also a body of flesh and bone, nevertheless it is an exalted body, even a Celestial body—was not inhibited or restricted in its ability to command all matter of element, then neither was the body that He caused to be created for Jesus.

23 And Jesus was and is the only mortal who hath ever lived upon this earth who hath had the power of the Father, even this great power to command the elements. And in this way, he was able to perform the many miraculous things that he did perform during the days of his own probation. And because of this power, he gave up his life. And at any time he could have commanded all the elements of his body and they would have done that which he commanded them.

24 Now, this great power that belongeth to those of a Celestial order hath been given unto them according to the laws of heaven, so that these might act in positions of authority in the eternal government of heaven.

25 And the second principle and law of this eternal government is that it will guarantee the freedom, or the free agency, of all those whom it serveth. And this free agency that it guaranteeth, restricteth those whom it serveth from infringing on the free agency of another, or from having another infringe upon the free agency that each of those it serveth possesseth.

26 And this government will do nothing that infringeth upon the free agency of those whom it serveth, except in defending the free agency of another from being infringed upon.

27 And now this is the reason that Lucifer was allowed to rebel against God and follow the dictates of his own conscience, by which he establisheth laws for himself and also for those who follow him. And by the rights granted them by the government that serveth them, even by the power which the Father hath given unto them, they are able to act according to their own desires, as long as these desires do not act upon another, in that the free agency of another is infringed upon.

28 For this reason, Satan and his followers are forbidden to tempt a man beyond his ability to resist the temptation that hath been given him. For if the laws of the government of heaven did not restrict Satan, then he would control the children of men, and they would lose their free agency, and then personal responsibility for sin would not exist.

29 And the third principle and law of this eternal government is that it shall provide the means whereby those whom it serveth may have an equal opportunity to experience the happiness that they desire. And because it was not the choice of those that it serveth to exist, this government must provide those things that are necessary to fulfill the measure and purpose of their creation, which purpose is their individual happiness.

30 Now, I would that ye should understand, that even though the eternal government doth provide the means whereby we might find eternal life and happiness, it cannot compel us to use those things which it hath provided for us, so that we might find the happiness that we desire. For if this government were to compel us in any of these things, then it would break the second law that governeth it, by taking away our free agency.

31 For behold, it would have been the desire

of the Eternal Mothers of the spirits that followed Lucifer to compel Their children to follow the plan that the Father presented unto them, which these Mothers knew would bring Their children happiness. But these loving Mothers were restricted in Their desire by the laws of the government that existeth in the Celestial kingdom of glory, in which glory They reside.

32 Behold, it was the desires of these Eternal Mothers that caused the creation of these spirit children by the Father. For They desired happiness. And They receive Their happiness according to the happiness that Their children receive, and this according to the nature of a Celestial being as it hath been explained unto you.

33 And because it was the desire of their Eternal Mothers, these spirits did not have a choice to exist. And because they did not have a choice to exist, the means for their happiness is provided for them according to the principles and laws of the government that assureth the order of the kingdom of God.

34 And these are the three main principles and laws of the eternal government of heaven, which government controlleth all things both in heaven and on earth, both in the kingdom of the Father, and also in the kingdoms of His father, which are worlds without end.

35 And these principles and laws of government exist to serve those whom have established this government. And they exist to assure the freedom of those whom this government serveth. And they exist to provide equality for all those whom this government serveth.

36 And under these three main principles and laws are sub-laws and sub-principles, which are set forth to assure the adherence to these three main laws. But these sub-forms of principles and laws of this government shall not be mentioned. But I say unto you, that all these laws are perfected in the structure for which they have been formed. And this structure assureth the order of all things.

37 And all these principles and laws and sub-principles and sub-laws are part of the government of the Celestial glory in the kingdom of God.

38 But in the Terrestrial kingdom of glory, only the second and third principles and laws of government exist. For the first is not needed therein.

39 And in the Telestial kingdom of glory only the third principle and law of this government existeth. For the first and the second are not needed and do not pertain to the worlds that make up that glory. For those who are of the Telestial glory are not permitted to act according to the free agency that hath been granted to those of the Celestial and Terrestrial glories.

40 For in this kingdom of glory, the bodies of the spirits that inherit this kingdom are restricted like unto the bodies that we receive as mortals, except that their bodies shall be immortal and live forever in the state that they have been given according to their desires of happiness.

41 Now this doth not mean that they do not have their free agency to act as they wish according to the power given unto them by the eternal body that they receive, but this only meaneth that this free agency is restricted by the principles and laws that govern that kingdom of glory.

42 And those of the Telestial glory shall be provided with all the necessary elements and things that they need to fulfill their desires of happiness, but these desires will be restricted to the bodies that they possess. And thus also will the desires of the Terrestrial beings be restricted according to the bodies that Terrestrial beings possess.

43 But unto those of a Celestial state, there are no restrictions given. And these can act according to the desires of their hearts, which desires are unrestricted in the bodies that they possess. Thus, these are those who are the leaders of the government as I have explained it unto you. And these live by the principles and the laws that pertain to this government, which are the principles and laws of the Celestial kingdom of glory.

44 And this same government which is in heaven hath been explained and given unto the children of men through the prophets of God

who have lived among them, and also from the ministrations of the Holy Ghost.

45 And the prophets have instructed the children of men to pattern their governments after the government which is in heaven, even the eternal government that assureth peace and order in all the worlds that exist, which worlds are without end.

46 And according to the words of the brother of Jared, yea, even according to the words of my ancestors, and also according to my own experience, when the children of men attempt to pattern their governments after the pattern that hath been revealed unto them, then peace existeth upon the earth.

47 But if they stray from the pattern that hath been shown unto them, then there are wars and chaos and famine and all manner of destruction among them.

48 And the reason why they stray from the pattern shown unto them, is because they reject the words of the holy prophets, or they offend the Spirit, in that it withdraweth itself from them. And when the Spirit withdraweth from them, they have no ministrations to teach them the proper way that a government should work.

49 And when this pure form of government hath been established among them by those in authority, even those who have listened to the voice of the prophets, or who have the Holy Ghost as their constant guide, then peace and prosperity reign among them, evensomuch that there existeth no poor or needy among them.

50 And in this state, the Nephites and also the Lamanites found themselves many times. Yea, when they were righteous and listened to the prophets that the Lord suffered to come unto them, then they were happy and there were no contentions and disputations among them, and they did deal justly one with another. And they had all things in common among them; therefore there were not rich and poor, bond and free, but they were all made free, and partakers of the heavenly gift. And this according to the record of my father.

51 But when their leaders depended on their own wisdom, and the flesh of their own arm, and cast out the holy prophets, and began to seek after gold and silver and all the vain things of the earth; yea, even when they began to establish their own forms of government among them, which are not established according to the laws of heaven, but according to the laws of men; yea, when they began to do these things, they were eventually destroyed.

52 And thus hath the history of the children of men followed this pattern since the time that Adam and Eve left the garden of Eden and entered into the mortal world.

CHAPTER 14

Moroni explains how the Bible and other scriptures have been changed and corrupted. He acknowledges other religions and names by which Jesus Christ might be known and worshipped. He writes plainly to the understanding of all.

AND now, I, Moroni, return once again to the vision of the brother of Jared in which he saw all things that have transpired among the children of men, even all things that shall transpire according to the vision that was given unto him by the Lord.

2 And many of the words of the brother of Jared will confound the foolish doctrines that have been passed down from generation to generation according to the traditions and understanding of the children of men.

3 Even the holy scriptures have been corrupted by evil men, whose responsibility it was to watch over these holy records and ensure that they remained untouched by the interpretations and opinions of men.

4 And there shall be many sources of scriptures upon the earth in the latter days. And these scriptures shall be had among all the different peoples of the earth, according to each of their cultures, and each of their capabilities of learning and understanding.

5 And when these scriptures were given by the mouth of the holy prophets, who the Lord suffered to teach the people of the earth according to their cultures and according to their learning and understanding, they were pure and unadulterated by the hand of man.

6 And over the course of time, the commandments and the instructions of the Lord became unclear and confusing to the children of men who read from these sources of scripture. And many of the children of men are led by others whom they have accepted as their leaders and their spiritual guides. And these leaders have caused their own interpretations and opinions to be mingled with the mistranslations and misquotations of the holy scriptures that the Lord hath caused to be written for their benefit and for their instruction.

7 And even the Lord himself knew of the frailties and the works of men, who in their attempt to understand the things of God, without the spirit of God, mislead and corrupt the hearts of the children of men. And for this reason the Lord left no written record of those things which he taught.

8 And for this reason he commanded his disciples, who were at Jerusalem, to write nothing that he had said unto them while he was with them in the flesh, except it be given unto them after he had sent the Holy Ghost unto them.

9 And this he did that he might maintain a sense of integrity of the words that he had spoken unto the children of men. And he knew that by the power of the Holy Ghost his disciples would be given that which he would have them write. And it would be known that it was his disciples who wrote these things, and that these things were not written by his own hand; for if these things were one day corrupted by the workings and opinions of men, then there would be no cause that any would have to say that the Lord wrote that which he did not.

10 And the Lord hath sent his holy prophets among all the people of the earth, and hath suffered the children of men to be taught and instructed according to the way in which they have been accustomed to living according to the traditions and customs of their fathers.

11 For behold, because of the law of free agency, the children of men are allowed to live upon the earth according to the desires of their hearts. And because the desires of our hearts are as distinct and as individual as each of our spirits, therefore our cultures and our traditions differ one from another.

12 And according to these cultures and traditions, we have been taught the gospel of Jesus Christ. Nevertheless, this gospel is not called the gospel of Jesus Christ according to the traditions and customs of the many different peoples of the world.

13 And it doth not matter to the Lord in what name he is called, for it is his desire to give unto all the laws of his gospel, let these laws be called by whatever name they might be called. And also, let him be called by whatever name he may be called according to the different cultures and traditions of the children of men.

14 And the Lord spoke unto my fathers when he visited them after his resurrection and ascension, and he said unto them: And verily, verily, I say unto you that I have other sheep, which are not of this land, neither of the land of Jerusalem, neither in any parts of that land round about whither I have been to minister.

15 For they of whom I speak are they who have not as yet heard my voice; neither have I at any time manifested myself unto them.

16 But I have received a commandment of the Father that I shall go unto them, and that they shall hear my voice, and shall be numbered among my sheep, that there may be one fold and one shepherd; therefore, I go to show myself unto them.

17 Now I, Moroni, ask of you, Do ye know the name by which the Lord is called by these other sheep who had not yet heard his voice at the time he presented himself to my fathers? Do ye not know that his name is not important to him, if it so be that the people believe in him and keep his commandments?

18 And what say ye of those who are reading this record that the Lord hath commanded me to make, and hath instructed me to write the things that the Spirit whispereth unto me; again, what say ye, if ye heard me pronounce the name of the Lord Jesus Christ according to my own language, which was taught to me by the traditions and culture of my fathers? Would ye understand of whom I speak?

19 Behold, I say unto you, that ye would not understand the words that I would speak, and likewise, I would not understand the words that ye would speak. And if I pronounce the name of the Lord in a different manner, or if I call him by a different name than you, what think ye then about the name of Jesus Christ?

20 And if my Lord and my God is called Cummenkinin, and it is this being whom I worship and obey, what say ye of my righteousness then? And if it so be that Cummenkinin hath established a church among my people, which is established according to our traditions and our culture, which of a surety is different than your own, is it then a sin to worship our God in this manner, who is not called Jesus Christ by us, but who is the same God whom ye worship according to your traditions?

21 And if our prophets, whom we call Serihlibiem, teach us the law of Cummenkinin, and teach us that we should love our enemies and do good to them that hate us and persecute us, and if we live our lives in harmony with the spirit of Cummenkinin, as we are taught by our Serihlibiem, are we to be condemned for not taking upon us the name of Jesus Christ only because we do not understand this name, and it cannot be understood by us according to our language and our culture?

22 Behold, I say unto you, that when the Lord shall visit these people, who are some of the other sheep that have not heard his voice, he shall allow them to call him Cummenkinin, or by whatever name they have been taught to worship by their Serihlibiem.

23 And this doth not take away the efficacy of the holy name of Christ, by which all men shall be saved. For I have written upon this record the meaning of the symbolism of which a name is given. And again, I say unto you, that all names are symbolic of the works that are associated with that name.

24 And is it not by the works of Christ, or Cummenkinin, or by whatever name he might be called, that we are saved? I say unto you, that it is by the works, which the name of Christ doth symbolize, by which we are saved. Behold, we are not saved by his name, but by that which he hath accomplished for us.

25 Therefore, it mattereth not unto the Father by what name we call Him or those whom He hath commissioned to serve us and bring us back to His kingdom.

26 And if there are churches and religions that are named according to the customs and traditions of the different peoples of the world; and if these have their own written word, which is their holy scripture, then what difference would they have in the eyes of the Lord, if it so be that they teach his gospel?

27 I say unto you, that there is no difference. And if these teach the words of the gospel of Christ, then they are accepted by him.

28 Now this is what was meant by the prophecy of Nephi wherein he saw a vision of the latter days. And Nephi wrote, saying: And it came to pass that when the angel had spoken these words, he said unto me: Rememberest thou the covenants of the Father unto the house of Israel? I said unto him, Yea.

29 And it came to pass that he said unto me: Look, and behold that great and abominable church, which is the mother of abominations, whose founder is the devil.

30 And he said unto me: Behold there are save two churches only; the one is the church of the Lamb of God, and the other is the church of the devil; therefore, whoso belongeth not to the church of the Lamb of God belongeth to that great church, which is the mother of abominations; and she is the whore of all the earth.

31 And it came to pass that I looked and beheld the whore of all the earth, and she sat upon many waters; and she had dominion over all the earth, among all nations, kindreds, tongues, and people.

32 And it came to pass that I beheld the church of the Lamb of God, and its numbers were few, because of the wickedness and abominations of the whore who sat upon many waters; nevertheless, I beheld that the church of the Lamb, who were the saints of God, were also upon all the face of the earth; and their dominions upon the face of the earth were small, because of the wickedness of the great whore whom I saw.

33 And now, I, Moroni, ask if ye believe that

there are more than two churches only? I say unto you, that according to the words of Nephi, and I know that his words are true, there are save but two churches only.

34 Behold, if ye do not belong to the church of the Lamb of God, or in other words, if ye do not believe in the gospel of His Son, which is the Lamb of God, and keep his commandments which he hath given unto you by the words of his own mouth in this gospel, then ye belong to the great and abominable church that Nephi saw in his vision.

35 And the words of Nephi are not intended to mean that there is any one church that is the church of the Lamb of God, or that any one church is the church of the devil. But his intent was that ye either believe in the words of the Lamb of God and keep his commandments, or ye follow the works of the world, which are the works of the devil.

36 For did not Nephi describe this church in his writings? And he wrote, saying: And the angel said unto me: What beholdest thou? And I said: I behold many nations and kingdoms.

37 And he said unto me: These are the nations and kingdoms of the Gentiles.

38 And it came to pass that I saw among the nations of the Gentiles the formation of a great church.

39 And the angel said unto me: Behold the formation of a church which is most abominable above all other churches, which slayeth the saints of God, yea, and tortureth them and bindeth them down, and yoketh them with a yoke of iron, and bringeth them down into captivity.

40 And it came to pass that I beheld this great and abominable church; and I saw the devil that he was the founder of it.

41 And I also saw gold, and silver, and silks, and scarlets, and fine-twined linen, and all manner of precious clothing; and I saw many harlots.

42 And the angel spake unto me, saying: Behold the gold, and the silver, and the silks, and the scarlets, and the fine-twined linen, and the precious clothing, and the harlots, are the desires of this great and abominable church.

43 And also for the praise of the world do they destroy the saints of God, and bring them down into captivity

44 Now, I, Moroni, ask if ye do not now see the meaning of the words of Nephi, which he hath written concerning the description of this great church. For behold, a church is the people who belong to it and do its works. Yea, a church can be judged by the works of its members, and if their works are the works of the world, or if they do the things that Nephi observed that were done by the church of the devil, then they belong to the church of the devil, whether they attend a church named after the name of Jesus Christ, or after some other name.

45 And the church that is called after the name of Jesus Christ in the latter days, of which I have previously spoken, belongeth to the church of the devil. For behold, the members of this church seek after the vain things of the world and aspire to the honors of men.

46 Nevertheless, there are those who are members of this church who are the humble followers of Christ, nevertheless, they are led, that in many instances they do err because they are taught by the precepts of men, and this is also according to the words of Nephi.

47 And it shall come to pass that these humble followers of Christ shall have the words which I am writing unto them at this time. And they shall humble themselves before the Lord whom they seek, and repent of the things in which they have been misled by the precepts of men. And it shall come to pass that they will leave the church of the devil and join the church of the Lamb of God.

48 And there will be many others in the latter days who shall receive my words, and many of these shall belong to other churches who call themselves, some by one name and some by another. And when they shall read these things, they shall be wrought upon by the Holy Ghost, and he will testify unto them of their wickedness, and cause them to repent and forsake the church of the devil that they might join the church of the Lamb of God.

49 And then shall the rest of the words of Nephi come to pass, which he wrote, saying: And it came to pass that I beheld that the great mother of abominations did gather together multitudes upon the face of all the earth, among all the nations of the Gentiles, to fight against the Lamb of God.

50 And it came to pass that I, Nephi, beheld the power of the Lamb of God, that it descended upon the saints of the church of the Lamb, and upon the covenant people of the Lord, who were scattered upon all the face of the earth; and they were armed with righteousness and with the power of God in great glory.

51 And it came to pass that I beheld that the wrath of God was poured out upon that great and abominable church, insomuch that there were wars and rumors of wars among all the nations and kindreds of the earth.

52 And as there began to be wars and rumors of wars among all the nations which belonged to the mother of abominations, the angel spake unto me, saying: Behold, the wrath of God is upon the mother of harlots; and behold, thou seest all these things.

53 And when the day cometh that the wrath of God is poured out upon the mother of harlots, which is the great and abominable church of all the earth, whose founder is the devil, then, at that day, the work of the Father shall commence, in preparing the way for the fulfilling of his covenants, which he hath made to his people.

54 And it came to pass that the angel spake unto me, saying: Look!

55 And I looked and beheld a man, and he was dressed in a white robe.

56 And the angel said unto me: Behold one of the twelve apostles of the Lamb.

57 Behold, he shall see and write the remainder of these things; yea, and also many things which have been. And he shall also write concerning the end of the world.

58 Therefore, the things which he shall write are just and true; and behold they are written in the book which thou beheld proceeding out of the mouth of the Jew; and at the time they proceeded out of the mouth of the Jew, or, at the time the book proceeded out of the mouth of the Jew, the things which were written were plain and pure, and most precious and easy to the understanding of all men.

59 And behold, the things which this apostle of the Lamb shall write are many things which thou hast seen; and behold, the remainder shalt thou see.

60 But the things which thou shalt see hereafter thou shalt not write; for the Lord God hath ordained the apostle of the Lamb of God that he should write them.

61 And also others who have been, to them hath he shown all things, and they have written them; and they are sealed up to come forth in their purity, according to the truth which is in the Lamb, in the own due time of the Lord.

62 And now, I Moroni, would that ye should know that the brother of Jared is he of whom the angel spoke unto Nephi as being one of the others who hath been shown all things. And these things which he saw, I am making an abridgment of according to the commandments that my father received from the Lord, and also according to the commandments that I have received from the Lord.

63 And I have been commanded to seal these things up to come forth in the own due time of the Lord, which, if ye are reading these things, then ye know that that time hath come.

64 And the things that I write shall make known unto all those who have the record of the Jews among them, and also many of the records that the Lord hath caused to be written among the many other peoples, the things that were plain and pure and most precious and easy to the understanding of all men, according to the words of Nephi.

65 And for this reason the Lord hath commanded me to write plainly and without parable or allegory, even without the words that are hard to the understanding of men, that these things might be easy for the children of men to read and understand.

66 And because these things shall be easy to understand, many shall be offended by them, and many shall reject them because of their simplicity. For there are many who would want that the things of God remain mysterious unto them, so that they might not understand the things of God and be held accountable to His commandments.

67 For behold, the Lord doth not hold those accountable who do not understand his words. But when they come to an understanding of his

words, then they are held accountable for what they understand.

68 And because these things that I write are easy to the understanding of all the children of men, then all shall be responsible for their understanding. And if there are those who do not read these words when they are available unto them to read, then they will be held accountable before the Lord for that which they should have understood had they read these things.

69 For out of the words that have been revealed unto the children of men in the books that the Lord hath caused to be written, shall the world be judged according to its works.

70 And it shall come to pass that the world shall have these things which the Lord hath caused to be written by my hand, yea, even according to the vision of the brother of Jared, in which he saw all things. And they shall be available unto all. And they shall be plain and easy to understand. Therefore, the world shall be judged by these things.

71 And when these things have become available to the world in the day that the Lord shall bring them forth, then shall the world know that the Lord hath begun to prepare his saints, by gathering them out of the great and abominable church of the devil. And he shall gather out his saints and give them the mark in their foreheads that the apostle John hath described in the record of the Jews. And when he hath marked his saints in their foreheads, then shall he release his judgments upon the great church, which is the mother of all abominations before him.

CHAPTER 15

The true reason behind the fall of Adam and Eve is revealed. The situation of the world at the time of their expulsion is explained. Adam and his posterity begin to spread throughout the world.

AND now I, Moroni, continue with my abridgment of the vision of the brother of Jared.

2 And it came to pass that the brother of Jared observed Adam and Eve in the garden of Eden; and he watched to see in what manner came the cause of their fall from this state.

3 And this fall hath been represented in many different ways in the holy scriptures according to the traditions and interpretations of men.

4 For the Lord hath not revealed the full effect of their fall and the way in which it came about unto the children of men. And he commanded Adam and Eve to teach their children a different version of what actually transpired in the garden of Eden, even how Eve fell before Adam.

5 And the Lord instructed them, saying: Nevertheless, ye shall not divulge any portion of the truth regarding the way in which Eve was tempted and lost her power over death and was cast out of the garden of Eden. For behold, these things shall not be known by any man except it be unto those whom I choose to reveal them.

6 And I, Moroni, would that ye should know that unto some the truth of these things was revealed. And this truth hath been corrupted and changed over the course of the history of the children of men. For some have written concerning a fallen angel who came down upon the earth and enticed the daughters of men to engage in sexual intercourse.

7 And others have misinterpreted the words that are found in the book that proceeded out of the mouth of the Jew, in which they say: The sons of God saw the daughters of men that they were fair; and they took them wives of all which they chose.

8 And many thought these sons of God meant the angels of God. And in this they do err considerably. For behold, there are no angels or servants of God who have the body necessary to produce offspring with a daughter of a mortal man. And those who have interpreted these things in this way do not understand the workings of the Father.

9 Nevertheless, many things that are written in the books of the children of men have portions of the truth hidden amongst the stories and the myths that have been passed down from generation to generation. But in the beginning, Adam taught his children the truth that the Lord had revealed unto him, and commanded his posterity to teach their children the truth in all things, except for those things forbidden of them by the Lord.

10 And Adam caused to be written many of his teachings that they might be passed down from one generation to the next, thus preserving the plain and simple truths from the mouth of God that Adam received while in the garden of Eden.

11 But as I have previously explained it unto you, many of these things have been lost in translation and corrupted by the works of men. And the language in which Adam wrote these things unto his children hath been lost from among all the languages of the world. And it was in this tongue that Adam learned from the Father. And it is in this tongue, even the Adamic tongue, that the Father speaketh unto those who hear His voice.

12 And now, I, Moroni, refer to the words of the brother of Jared which he wrote concerning Adam and Eve:

13 And I saw the lands that surrounded the great land wherein was placed the garden of Eden. And these lands were great. And there were a great many waters that separated these lands from each other. But in the beginning of the creation, this was not so. For the land was one of itself, this being the purpose of the Father in allowing the plants to grow and populate themselves one with another that there might be air to breath and an atmosphere created upon the planet that He had formed into a world for His children. And the flowers and the plants that He caused to grow upon the earth and cover it with their abundance, could not do so, except that the land was one of itself.

14 And I saw many animals that appeared very similar to the bodies that the Father had created for Adam and Eve. And these animals were like unto Adam and Eve, nevertheless, they lived by their instincts without the spirit that God had created for the order of species of the bodies that he had created for Adam and Eve.

15 And these animals that were similar to them were separated by the many waters; and there were none of these upon the land in which the Lord had planted and cared for the garden in the land of Eden.

16 And I looked and beheld the organization of the communities of these animals. And they did not have a spoken language among them; and they did not know right from wrong, but lived according to their natural desires that perpetuated their lives.

17 And I also saw Lucifer with the many spirits that were following him. And they were wandering to and fro upon the earth wondering how they could institute the plans that they had created for their own form of government and for their own happiness.

18 And these spirits had the power given unto them, like unto all spirits, to inhabit temporally, the mortal body of any animal that they desired. Nevertheless, according to the restrictions placed upon them by the eternal laws of heaven, they could not use these animals in anyway to hurt the children of men, thus interfering with the free agency of the children of God.

19 But because there were no children of men created from the bodies of Adam and Eve, Lucifer could find no animals, whereupon entering their mortal body, he could experience joy. For upon entering the body of an animal that was not prepared to house the spirit of a child of God inside of it, the animal was confused and thrashed its body considerably in an attempt to rid itself of this unnatural imbalance.

20 And thus Lucifer and those that followed after him found little success among the animals that were created by God to serve the measure of their creation and then become extinct for the rest of the probationary days of His children.

21 And after many years of going to and fro upon the earth, Lucifer and his followers began to have some considerable success with some species of animals that possessed bodies like unto the bodies that God had created for Adam and Eve. And with the limited power that Lucifer was permitted by the laws of heaven to have over them, he began to interbreed certain species with other species until he had formed an animal that was very much like unto the bodies that were created for Adam and Eve.

22 And after much time had passed in refining this breeding process, the followers of Lucifer began to possess the bodies of these animals and cause them to act according to their own desires, which desires gave them a limited amount of happiness.

23 Nevertheless, these animals were not given the exact same bodies that were created for Adam and Eve, and therefore, Lucifer and his followers could not experience a fullness of the joy that had been described to them by the Father in the beginning. For these animals did not have a kingdom of glory prepared for them in the kingdom of the Father. And they were of a much lower order of element, because their creation and their purpose was to bring about the earth, and prepare it for the probationary days of the children of God.

24 And Lucifer became incarnate, and took upon himself one of the bodies that he found best suitable for that which he was wont to do.

25 And the desire of Satan was to go into the garden of Eden and entice Eve and cause her to obey the eternal laws of the Father that he might take the glory upon himself.

26 And Satan designed a type of ship in which he traveled over the many waters. And when he reached the land in which was centered the garden of Eden, he continued his travels up a large river of water until he came upon the borders of the garden of Eden.

27 And the Lord did not stop Satan from doing that which he was wont to do, and this because of the law of free agency.

28 And Satan spent many days in the body of this creature; and the creature appeared very much like unto a man. And for many days he secretly watched the goings and comings of Adam and Eve in the garden of Eden. And when there came a time that Eve was alone washing herself on the borders of the garden, Satan came forth out of his hiding place and introduced himself unto Eve.

29 And Satan caused the creature to speak unto Eve in the voice of a man in the language of the Father, a language that had been spoken in the kingdom of the Father in which all spirits were created.

30 And Satan spake unto her, and Eve was not afraid. For Eve knew not what to be afraid of, she being innocent in the garden of Eden.

31 And Satan touched Eve in a manner that Eve had never been touched before. And when he touched Eve, she was surprised and astonished at the feeling that it caused to come over her.

32 And Satan said unto her: Knowest thou not that these feelings that thou art experiencing at this time are those blessings that the Father hath given unto thee that thou mightest partake of the joy of which He partaketh?

33 And Eve answered him, saying: I do not know about the feeling of joy of which our Father hath spoken, for I have not yet experienced this joy in all things. But in the things that I have experienced, I do not know what joy I should feel.

34 And Satan said unto her: When I touch thee in this way, doth it not give unto thee the feelings of joy? And these feelings are the only way that thou canst comply with all the commands of the Father. For did not the Father command thee and Adam to multiply and have joy in your posterity? And how can ye have joy in something that ye do not have?

35 And Satan enticed Eve, and showed unto her the pleasures of which he had spoken. And Satan took Eve and showed unto her the way that the other animals, that were like unto him, whose body Satan had possessed, produced their offspring.

36 And Eve gave in to the enticings of Satan and conceived within her.

37 And immediately upon knowing that Eve had conceived within her womb, Satan departed from the creature whose body he had possessed. And immediately upon departing, the creature fell dead into the water and was washed away by the great waters of the river that ran near unto the garden of Eden.

38 And Eve knew not that she had conceived a child within her. And immediately there appeared at her side, Marihala, who was the mother of her spirit. And Marihala counseled with Eve and explained unto her what Satan had done.

39 And Eve was saddened greatly for that which she had done and found little solace in the comforting words of her Eternal Mother. For Marihala had counseled with Eve and told her to go unto Adam without revealing unto him that which had transpired with Satan, and that she should say nothing unto him regarding the child that was conceived in her womb.

40 But that she should speak to Adam and tell him of the commandment of the Father, and that she should show unto Adam the things that she had learned pertaining to the way in which the child was conceived.

41 And Eve went unto Adam and touched him. And Adam felt the joy from the touch of Eve. And Adam said unto Eve: How didst thou know the way that we can experience this joy together? And Eve did not reveal unto Adam these things, but she kept them unto herself according to the counsel of her Mother.

42 And Eve explained to Adam that this was the only way that they could obey the commandments of the Father and multiply and have joy in their posterity. But Adam refused to listen to Eve because he did not understand that which he was to do. For the feelings that he felt from the touch of Eve were foreign to him, and he dared not touch her in a like manner, unless he received a commandment of the Father.

43 And Eve wept before Adam. And Adam said unto her: Why dost thou weep? And what is the cause of thy emotion, which emotion we do not experience here in the garden of Eden?

44 And Eve continued to weep before Adam, begging him that he would come unto her and complete the plan that the Father had for them. But Adam remained steadfast and firm in his desire to do only those things that he had been taught by the Father.

45 And Eve said unto him: Dost thou believe that the Father shouldst command us in all things? Dost thou know the way in which our spirits were created by our Father and our Mother? Dost thou not take into account that these things were hidden from our view while we lived with the Father in his kingdom? Could it not be the will of the Father that we learn these things of ourselves?

46 Behold, because I desire these things, I shall be forced to leave the security of the garden of Eden and search the world that the Father hath created for us and commanded us to explore and care for. And because of thy stubbornness, thou shalt be alone in the garden of Eden and unable to fulfill the commandments of the Father that He hath given unto us.

47 And after much conversation with Adam, Eve was successful in explaining to him the plan of the Father, and the only way that it could be carried out.

48 And Adam gave to Eve that which she desired. And it was very pleasurable unto him, evensomuch that he thanked Eve for that which she had done.

49 And from that time forth, Adam and Eve perceived each other differently than they had before. Their bodies began to crave the feelings that they had experienced as a man and a woman. And they realized that they were naked.

50 And the Father came down with Marihala to the garden of Eden and visited with Adam and Eve. Behold, Marihala had gone back to the kingdom of the Father and brought him word of all the things that Satan had done in the world that He had created for His spirit children. And the Father smiled upon Marihala, indicating that His plan would now go forth according to the laws of heaven, which laws had restricted him from interfering with the free agency of those whom He hath created, even all of His spirit children.

51 For the Father could only give the commandments, but of none can He require to keep His commandments, unless they willingly do so of their own accord.

52 And Satan knew the plan of the Father, and thought that if he could do this thing unto Eve, and get her to obey the command of the Father, and begin the mortal lives for His spirit children, that the Father might see in him the glory that he desired. For behold, the plan of the Father could not progress without the choice of Adam and Eve to do what they did without the intervention of the Father.

53 But Satan, for his own glory, desired these things, and thus broke the first principle and law of the government of heaven.

54 And Lucifer presented himself before the Father and told Him the things that he had done. And the Father rejected the pleas of Lucifer because of the laws that he had broken to accomplish the thing that he thought would bring him his glory. And Lucifer left the presence of the Father and went back unto the earth.

55 And when the Father had visited Adam and Eve, he found that they were timid and shy of their nakedness. And the Father inquired of them as to whether or not they had experienced the joy that cometh from becoming a parent. And Adam told the Father that Eve had enticed him to do this thing.

56 And the Father rebuked Adam for his lack of understanding, and blessed the actions of Eve in that she had figured out the way that His plan could progress. And Adam was commanded to stay with Eve from that time forth, and that he should care for her and also for the child that was conceived in her womb.

57 And Adam knew not that the child was not his own, and the Father did not reveal this unto him at this time, because He wanted Adam to love the child as if it were his own.

58 And the Father touched Adam and Eve and therewith commanded the elements of their bodies to change in such a way that they begin to die from that day forward. Nevertheless, the Father gave unto them laws and commandments that they should live by so that they could live healthy and vibrant lives, thus having the ability to provide more bodies for His spirit children who were waiting for the days of their probation to begin.

59 And the Father made some commands that I did not understand, but from that time forth, the borders of the garden of Eden were no longer, and Adam and Eve were left to go into the world wherever the desires of their hearts would lead them.

60 And the Father had given them instructions to eat of the fruit of all the land, and that they might do so for their health and strength. And they were instructed to cultivate the earth and raise the fruit of the tree, and of the vine to eat, and also the roots of the plants that required the movement of that part of them that appeared above the ground to ensure the perpetuation of its species.

61 And Adam went forth and planted vineyards and fruit trees, taking with him some of the seeds that the Father had provided for him from the garden of Eden.

62 For in the garden of Eden, the plants continually grew according to the command of the Father. And in the seeds of these plants God provided perpetual life for each species of plant. And these seeds would be the means of eternal life for each type of plant in its own environment. And some of these plants were specifically chosen by the Father to bring considerable joy to Adam and Eve as they ate them. And it was these plants that the Father instructed them to eat.

63 And there were many other plants that God had placed on the earth to provide food for other animals, but mostly to produce the atmosphere wherein life could exist.

64 And Adam and Eve were forbidden to eat the flesh of another animal, for their bodies were not built for this type of nourishment. And Adam and Eve knew nothing about cooking their food, because they did not need to cook food in the garden of Eden, nor was it part of the plan of God.

65 For inside the food that they were commanded to eat, even the fruit that provided the seed of itself, and also those roots which needed to be pulled up in order to spread their seeds by the hand of an animal; even inside all of these were the necessary nourishment that Adam and Eve needed to keep themselves healthy and strong all the days of their probation.

66 And in the communities of the other animals, even those whose bodies were being possessed by Satan and his followers, they did eat the flesh of other animals, and they did cook their food. And when they did cook the food which they did eat, the heat from the fire destroyed those nutrients that God had established in the food to provide for the health and strength of the animal that would eat it.

67 And amongst these creatures, death did enter therein swiftly and take their lives from the causes of the disease and pestilence that were created from the food that they had eaten. For fire destroyeth all things that it toucheth, and it is a process of destruction that was not taught unto Adam and Eve from the beginning.

68 And at the time of the expulsion of Adam and Eve from the garden of Eden, or at the time the Father changed the make-up of the garden, and also the make-up of the bodies of Adam and Eve, the rest of the world was abiding in its course according to the time that God had set for it.

69 And Satan commanded his followers to entice the creatures that were like unto Adam and Eve to travel the course across the waters to the land in which Adam and Eve could be found. And this he did that he might cause the bodies of Adam and Eve to become corrupted by the seed of the creatures whose bodies were of a lower order than the bodies created for Adam and Eve.

70 And these creatures were wise, as it were, according to the order in which they had been created. But they became wiser still because of the success that Satan had in possessing their bodies and in influencing their minds.

71 For after many years of inhabiting the bodies of this type of animal, Satan had caused them to become much like Adam and Eve, evensomuch, that only the darkness of their skin distinguished them from the bodies created for Adam and Eve.

72 And Satan taught them many things, and patterned many of the things that he taught them after the things that he had learned from the Father, even the manner in which the Father had planted the area known as the garden of Eden.

73 And these also lived near nigh unto the great rivers that ran throughout the world. For it was in the most fertile parts of the earth that these had gathered to find the food that they needed.

74 And I saw that the world was divided in its land mass, even that there were seven separate areas of the world where the creations of God had wandered according to their individual abilities and their desires for food. And this great division was a new understanding unto me. Yea, I had thought the earth was one land mass surrounded by many waters.

75 And of these great land masses, only two were inhabited by the majority of those of whose bodies Satan and his followers possessed. And they congregated around four great river areas of the earth. And in the valleys of these rivers they did prosper and begin to cultivate the land and make it their own.

76 And even as the righteous spirits who resided in the spiritual part of the world did administer unto Adam and Eve and their posterity, even so did those spirits therein that chose not to follow the plan of the Father, did administer their ministrations unto these creatures.

77 But this order of animal did not have the capacity to allow a spirit child of God to inhabit its body for a great length of time. For if they were possessed for a great length of time, they would be fatigued and would soon die because of their inabilities, which were caused by the order of their natures that had been given unto them by the Father.

78 And Satan showed them the way whereby they could cross the many waters and travel to the great continent where Adam and Eve lived. And thus some of them began their journeys thereto.

CHAPTER 16

Beneli is the first mortal child born to Adam and Eve. He discovers that he is not Adam's son. Beneli discovers his true father and begins to deceive the other children of Adam and Eve. Cain is born and is influenced by Beneli to slay Able.

AND it came to pass that the brother of Jared saw many things pertaining to the way in which Adam and Eve began to have dominion over the earth, and also over the beasts of the field, and this because of the intelligence of Adam and Eve, and the things that they had learned of the Father. For the beasts were created on a lower order than the children of men. And these beasts were driven by their instincts, not knowing right or wrong, and therefore, not being able to partake of the joys of which the children of men partake.

2 And when the time arrived for the birth of the child conceived in the garden of Eden, both Adam and Eve rejoiced in his birth. And they called his name Beneli, which being interpreted means, a son of God.

3 And it came to pass that Adam and Eve had many sons and daughters. And these grew and were taught to worship the Lord according to the manner in which Adam and Eve were instructed by the Lord in the garden of Eden, and also by way of the Holy Endowment that hath been explained unto you previously in this record.

4 And the Lord also suffered that Adam should organize a church for the benefit of his children, and also that the Holy Priesthood of God, with its lower and higher appendages, should be established among them for their instruction and their learning.

5 For behold, the children of Adam and Eve were not in the garden of Eden, and they did not know the Lord, nor had they ever seen him with their mortal eyes. And it was required of them to live by faith, even faith in the words that Adam taught unto them.

6 And the ministrations of the Holy Ghost began to fall upon the children of Adam, which ministrations bear record of the Father and of the Son and of the plan that they have established for the children of Adam.

7 And it came to pass that after many years Adam also began to doubt that which he had experienced before in the garden of Eden, even believing that it had been a dream. And thus was the power that Satan had over the hearts of all men, even unto the convincing of the very elect, if it were possible, that they should not believe that which they cannot see with their eyes or listen to that which they do not hear with their ears.

8 And the Father sent an angel from His kingdom unto Adam to help him remember the things that he had forgotten by faith. For behold, in the beginning, Adam did not have faith, for he knew that the Father existed, and that he was begotten of the Father, this having been taught to him by Jehovah immediately after being expelled from the garden of Eden, and also by his own personal experiences with the Father.

9 And it is the condition of mortality that causeth a pure and simple knowledge to become a matter of faith after a long time; and this because of the manner of thought which is permitted by a mortal body. For it was necessary that the Father limit the ability of the children of men to remember their lives before their births, thus ensuring that they do not reach forth and partake of the Tree of Life and live forever in their sins as I have previously explained it unto you.

10 And Adam kept all the commandments that he had received from Jehovah when he was expelled from the garden of Eden. And he taught these commandments to his children according to the manner that was shown unto him.

11 And it came to pass that Beneli grew and became a popular man among the other children of Adam. And he began to notice a difference in his appearance from those who were the other sons and daughters of Adam. For his skin was darker, and his features were different than the rest of his brothers and sisters. And his father Adam did not think anything of the differences that were obvious in the appearance of Beneli, even because he did not understand all of the

mysteries of God pertaining to the creation of a mortal body at this time, and therefore accepted that Beneli was conceived of him.

12 And Beneli went unto his mother Eve and questioned her concerning these things. And Eve could not hide the truth from Beneli any longer, and explained unto him that which had occurred in the garden of Eden.

13 And Eve petitioned fervently unto her son and asked that he would promise her that he would not reveal these things unto Adam, who did not know that this thing had happened, and who loved Beneli with all of his heart. And Beneli loved his mother and hearkened unto her, and promised her at this time that he would not tell Adam that which she had revealed unto him.

14 But from that time forth, Beneli began to search out his natural father, even that he began to pray unto Satan and ask for his guidance and his blessing. And Satan came unto Beneli, calling him his son and giving unto him all that he desired.

15 And Beneli began to teach his other brothers and sisters the things which he had learned from Satan, which things were contrary to the commandments that Adam had taught unto them. And because the words of Beneli were enticing unto many of his brothers and sisters, they began to rebel against the words of their father Adam and follow the commandments of Satan that were taught unto them by their eldest brother, Beneli.

16 And in this way did Satan begin to have success in possessing the bodies that the Father had created for Adam and Eve. And from that time forward, men began to be carnal and sensual and devilish in their ways.

17 And the Lord raised up prophets among the children of Adam and gave unto them the Holy Ghost, and commanded them to preach repentance unto their brothers and sisters. And Adam did spend much of his time counseling and directing the church through the priesthood that had been established among them, that he might also bring many of his children unto repentance.

18 And it came to pass that the creatures that had been possessed by Satan and his followers found their way into the land in which lived the children of Adam and Eve. And the sons and daughters of Adam and Eve, who did not hearken to the words of their father, or to the words of their brothers who had been called by the Lord as prophets to preach repentance unto them; yea, even these began to breed with those creatures who were not created by the Father to house the spirits of His children.

19 And from these unions there came to be many different peoples upon the earth. And the bodies that were created by these unions begin to be the vessels in which the Father was required by the eternal laws of heaven to put the spirits of His children. And thus had Satan corrupted the natural bodies that God had created for Adam and Eve.

20 Nevertheless, all this was done according to that which the Father had already known and that which He had expected. For in this same manner did the other worlds in which life was created bring about the mortal bodies for the spirits of the children of God.

21 And all these things were necessary so that the children of God might partake of that which is imperfect, so that they might know that which is perfect. And the bodies that the Father created for Adam and Eve were perfect according to the laws of the nature in which they were formed. And their bodies were also like unto the bodies that He and their Eternal Mothers possess.

22 And how is it that we might know that these bodies are perfect, unless it so be that we experience the effects of a body that is imperfect, and therefore, have some type of comparison that we might know these things?

23 And Satan continued to do that which had been done before in the worlds that were created for the salvation and happiness of the children of God.

24 Therefore, in the beginning, the children of men were given a body like unto that of the Father, and they were also given commandments pertaining to this body that it might not be defiled. But in the space of not many generations, all of the children of men began to possess bodies that were imperfect and unlike the perfect bodies that had been created for Adam and Eve.

25 And it came to pass that the brother of

Jared wrote concerning Adam and his efforts to teach his children the commandments of God. For behold, the major part of them had rebelled against these commandments.

26 And because of the agency given unto his children, Adam could not force them to do his will. And he saw the effects of his sons and daughters who were creating children with those that were not chosen vessels of the Father. And Adam saw the effects of his eldest son Beneli as he set himself up as a leader among them, and also as he began to persuade his brothers and sisters to disregard the commandments of God and seek after the things of the earth.

27 And it came to pass that Eve bore another son unto Adam and called his name Cain, believing that he was one that she could raise up righteously before the Lord, and that he would obey the commands of his father.

28 And it was also the desire of Adam that he might preserve in the next generation the similitude of the physical body that he had received from the Father, and therefore Adam was desirous that Cain follow in his footsteps and maintain this purity.

29 And Eve conceived again and bore unto Adam another son and called his name Abel.

30 And it came to pass that as Cain and Abel grew together in the house of their father, that Cain began to become jealous because of the love that he perceived his father Adam had for Abel. And truly Adam loved all of his children the same, but this was not the perception of Cain.

31 And Cain became familiar with the teachings of his eldest brother, Beneli, and went unto him and inquired of the things that he had taught his other brothers and sisters. And Beneli was glad that his younger brother had come unto him, and he blessed him and treated him like his own son.

32 And Cain began to follow the words of Beneli and reject the things that his father had taught unto him.

33 But Abel grew and became righteous and did those things which were expected of him by his father, and also the things that were commanded him of the Lord. And Abel became a High Priest in the church that Adam had established among them. And Able began to preach repentance to his brothers and his sisters.

34 And it came to pass that Abel went unto the house of his eldest brother, Beneli, to inquire of him as to why he had corrupted the teachings of their father, and why he did not worship God as he had been commanded.

35 And Abel said unto him: How is it that thou, being our eldest brother, persuadeth us to disobey father? Knowest thou not that our father hath taught the truth unto us concerning the beginning of our existence in this world, and that he and our mother Eve were commanded by the Lord to teach us the laws that are necessary for our happiness?

36 And Beneli answered him, saying: I have said nothing about our father. For he is a man of many dreams and visions and his imagination doth cause him to believe things that do not exist. And this happiness of which thou hast spoken?—Are we not a happy people? Do we not enjoy our wives and our children and live in peace and happiness? And behold the work of our hands and the accomplishments that we have done with the things of the earth, do they not bring us the joy of which thou speaketh?

37 Did not our father give unto us a commandment that we should multiply and replenish the earth and have dominion over the beasts of the field and the fowls of the air and the fish that are in the water? And do we not have dominion over these things and find joy therein?

38 I say unto thee, that we do find joy in these things, and that we shall continue to find joy in these things all the days of our lives.

39 And Abel rebuked his brother, saying: The joy of which thou speakest is not the everlasting joy of which our father hath taught us existeth in the kingdom of God, and which shall be given unto all those who believe in Him and keep His commandments.

40 The joy of which thou speakest shall only last among thee and those who follow thee for a short time. And the causes of this joy shall require that ye continually pursue that which hath given you this joy for a short season only. But ye do not consider that which shall come to pass by the pursuit of this joy. Yea, neither do

ye consider those things that shall also be the cause of much sorrow among you because of this joy that ye seek.

41 For behold, ye do eat the flesh of beasts and of fowl, and of the fishes in the water, which example hath not been given unto you by our father, but hath been given unto you by those beings whom ye have taken as your wives, and unto whom ye give your daughters that they might bring forth children unto you. And these are not those of the children of our father who have the pure blood within them, but ye have corrupted this blood because of your unions with them.

42 And because ye do eat the flesh of the beasts and also the flesh of the fowls and the flesh of the fish in the waters, ye have also corrupted and defiled your own bodies, which bodies were not intended to partake of such things. And even if ye were hungry, and forced by famine to eat the flesh of a creature, ye would not receive the nourishment that your bodies require to live in this joy of which thou speakest. For ye have caused the destructive force of fire to destroy the nutrients that the Father hath placed in the flesh of these animals and also in the plants that these animals eat to gain their nourishment.

43 And because ye have become used to the taste of seared fat and boiled plants and fruits, yea, because ye receive this joy from eating that which hath none of the natural nutrients that the Father hath provided therein to give our bodies health and strength, ye have caused that disease and pestilence should come upon you. And can ye call this an everlasting joy?

44 And thou hast taught thy followers that it is not a sin to take from the earth more than what is necessary to sustain their lives, because thou hast taught them that there is no life after this life in which we find ourselves, and that they should eat and drink and be merry and take unto themselves of all the fine things of the earth that they might have an abundance for themselves.

45 And with these teachings thou hast caused them to become selfish and carnal and share none of the joy of which thou hast spoken with their neighbors, or with their friends, but that they should hoard all that they can for the benefit of their own wives and their own children.

46 And in separating yourselves into these family units in which ye have found this joy of which thou hast spoken, ye have destroyed the sense of fellowship and unity that our father taught us should exist among us. For do we not all share the same father and the same mother? Therefore, to whose family do we pertain, seeing that we are all brothers and sisters?

47 And the ramifications of this joy that you describe are that there shall be contentions among you, in that ye will be more concerned about the welfare of your own family and the things that ye have hoarded from the earth for its welfare, than you will be about sharing that which ye have with those who do not have that which ye have hoarded, because ye have taken it all unto yourselves.

48 And your joy will cause the misery of others. And these—because they, too, want the same joy of which thou hast spoken—will take by force, if necessary, those things that ye have hoarded for the benefit of your own family. And thus will contentions and disputations arise among you. And these things would not arise among you. if ye would do the things that our father hath commanded us.

49 And our father hath given unto us the commandments that he received from the mouth of God when he was banished from the garden of Eden. And ye know that this garden did exist because ye have seen its borders and have experienced the exceedingly verdant nature that existeth therein, which nature is not like any that we can find in other parts of the land in which we live.

50 And even though it is also subjected to the laws of nature, which laws will cause all things therein to decay and to die a natural death, even so, its beauty and exceedingly great natural order doth even now continue to exist. And if this garden of which our father hath spoken doth exist, then why thinkest thou that the God who created this garden doth not exist? And if God doth not exist, then where did our first parents come from? For behold, they are unlike all the other animals that exist upon this land.

51 And even this land, from where thinkest thou that it came? And seest thou not the great order of nature that is all around us? How can this order exist except there be laws given that establish this order and cause it to remain in the state in which it hath been established?

52 And if these laws were given unto nature to keep it in its proper order by Him who created it, then why thinkest thou that this same Being would not give unto us laws that would help us maintain order among ourselves?

53 For we are not of the same order as the order of the nature that is around us. And by these natural laws we do not need to abide. For in this nature it is requisite that only that which is needed to sustain life is taken from it, and under this law are all the creatures that dwell on this world with us subjected.

54 But we are not subjected by this law. And ye have proven this by your actions, even that which ye take from nature; of which ye have no need except to consume it upon the lusts that ye have for this temporary joy that ye pursue.

55 And it is also a law of this nature that those who are subjected to it shall live in a symbiotic state with it, in that they give to its order as it giveth unto them. But what is it that thou supposeth that ye give unto nature from which ye receive many things? Behold, ye give nothing unto nature, but it provideth for you all the things that ye desire.

56 And because thou and thy followers are not subjected by all the laws of nature, by what laws are ye subjected? I say unto thee, that thou and those who follow thee are subjected under your own laws, which are laws of selfishness and carnality, and which shall bring about more sorrow and misery for you than the short time that ye shall experience the joy which ye seek.

57 But there is one law of nature to which ye are all subjected, which law was brought to pass because of the choice of our first parents to provide bodies for us and allow us to enter into mortality with them. And this law is the natural law of death, to which all things in nature are subjected.

58 And thou knowest this law, and hath convinced these people that there is no escaping this law under which we are subjected, thus giving them reason to live their lives as if the only joy that they can experience is that joy that they receive here in mortality.

59 But I have already shown unto thee that we are not subjected to the laws of nature as are the rest of the creations that are found therein. But we are subjected to the laws of the God by whom we were all created.

60 And if it so be that we are subjected to His laws, then there must be a law that He is subjected to that supercedeth the law of nature that we have been subjected to because of the desires of our parents.

61 And because we are not a part of this nature, we are not subjected to its laws, but because we live in this order of nature at this time, and take from it that which bringeth us joy, we are forced into submission to its laws. And for this reason we shall die, thus submitting to the laws of nature.

62 But when we are no longer a part of this nature, then we are no longer subjected to its laws. And after our spirits depart from this mortal body, which was created from this nature, we are no longer a part of it, and are therefore subjected to other laws which govern the environment in which we will find ourselves.

63 And in this spiritual state, or this spirit environment, we shall be subjected to the laws of Him who created our spirits, or to Him from whom we shall receive our joy. And if it so be that we do not abide by His laws, then we cannot receive any joy from Him. And if we do not receive any joy from Him, then we shall be miserable forever in the state in which we shall find ourselves.

64 And there is a law of God that compensateth for the law of nature, or the law of death. And even as it was death that came upon us and cut short the joy that we find in this natural environment, even so shall this law of God be given that we shall once again find life. And this life shall be eternal, for such are all the laws of God.

65 And the law of sacrifice which our father hath given unto us is in similitude of this law that shall give us eternal life and eternal joy.

66 And this law shall be given unto us by the Son of God, who shall come down among us and teach us all the laws of God that shall bring us eternal life, in which we shall experience eternal joy and happiness.

67 And he shall sacrifice his own life for us by presenting himself as a sacrifice for all of us, in that he will teach us the laws of God that we must be subjected to in order to be saved in the kingdom of God, where the laws of happiness and joy are eternal, as well as the laws of life, which are also eternal.

68 And now, I would that thou shouldst know that these are the things which our father hath taught us. And these are the things that we must live by in order to find the happiness and joy that we seek, both in this state of nature, and also in the spiritual state of our God who hath created us.

69 And it came to pass that Abel did confound Beneli in all of his words. And because of the words of Abel, many people left from following Beneli and followed once again after the things that they had been taught by their father.

70 But there were also many others who did not listen to the words of Abel. And many of these were those who had been born into the imperfect bodies as I have explained it unto you. Nevertheless, there were some of those who were born of the imperfect body who did follow the counsel of Abel and sought out Adam to hear his words. And there were also those who had the similitude of the perfect body, in that they were direct descendants of the sons of Adam and the daughters of Eve, and some of these did remain under the power of Beneli.

71 And from that time forth Beneli was wroth with Abel and devised a way in which he could destroy him.

72 And Beneli called Cain unto him and spoke with him, saying: Thou knowest that I love thee as my own son and that I would give my life for thee if it so be that I could save thee. And thou also knowest that I have provided a means whereby these people, even our brothers and our sisters, might find great joy. And this joy is that for which I would give my life.

73 Behold, our brother Abel hath come among us and hath taken away the joy of many of our brothers and sisters and hath caused them to feel guilty for feeling the joy that they have experienced. And he hath caused considerable damage to our families, claiming that our family units are not important, and that they are not part of the laws of this God whom none of us hath seen.

74 And in this way he hath deceived us by taking away our means of this joy that we have experienced. And he doeth this that he might take that which we possess unto himself. For did he not say unto us, that we should impart of our substance unto those who do not have that which we possess? And he doth not have that which we have. And by his cunningness, he desireth to take from us so that he can have part of all that we have.

75 And thou seest that this, our brother, hath lied unto us, for he hath said unto us that we should not take from nature except that we should give back in the same portion of which we have taken. Yet, he offereth up for sacrifice the firstlings of his flocks unto this unknown God, and pretendeth that it hath been commanded of him by God. And he shedeth their blood, but doth not partake of their flesh. And in this way he taketh away from nature without giving back any portion of that which he hath taken.

76 And even thou strugglest all of thy days to grow food from the earth. And thy sweat is the testimony of the hard work that is the lot that hath been given unto thee by our father Adam. And doth not our brother Abel eat of the fruit of thy hands? Doth he not take from thee even that which he doth not return?

77 And is it fair of our father that he requireth of thee to toil in this manner to provide food for thy brother, whose only toil is watching after his flocks and tending to their needs, which needs do not come by his hand, but by the hand of nature that hath given these flocks unto him?

78 And who is he that he thinketh that he shall rule over me, who is his eldest brother, and also over thee who is his elder brother?

79 And it came to pass that by the words of Beneli, the heart of Cain was hardened against his brother Abel.

80 And Beneli entered into a secret pact and

covenant with Cain, that if he would kill Abel, he would be protected and watched over by Beneli and those who follow him. And Beneli convinced Cain that the things that he was to do would bring a greater peace and happiness among the people, and that he would be held in respect among them for that which he would do.

81 And they made this pact according to all that Beneli had learned from his father, who was Satan in the beginning. And this pact was held secret among them. And thus began the children of men to form alliances and make covenants one with another in secret that they might get gain and destroy those who prevented them from getting that which they desired.

82 And Cain did that which Beneli desired of him. And he went unto Abel while he was tending to his flocks, and slew him. And this was the first time that a child of Adam was slain by the hand of another. And thus began murder to enter into the hearts of the children of men.

83 And Beneli and those who followed after him came to Cain and gave unto him the title of Master Mahan, which title was given to him of the highest order of this secret society, which society was set up to get gain and maintain power among the people. And Beneli also gave one of his daughters unto Cain as his wife for that which he had done.

84 And those who belonged to this society did not think of themselves as evil men, but they thought of themselves as the most righteous among the people. And they took upon themselves oaths and covenants that would protect them, and also protect their desire for gain and power among the people.

85 And their desire for power, as they had convinced themselves, was to assure the prosperity and freedom of all those who belonged to this secret order. And they took the endowment that they had learned from Adam and changed the signs and the symbols and the penalties to fit the desires of their secret society.

86 And they began to convince themselves that their ways and their teachings were the right ways, and that if there was a God, then that God would want the same things that they desire, which things are joy in their families, and joy in their worldly possessions, and joy in their freedom.

87 And this society began to enforce the desires of their hearts upon the people throughout the land. And if any man or woman refused to live by the laws that they had established according to these desires, then they would call upon those who had taken the secret oaths and covenants to protect their society to kill this man or this woman.

88 And they began to set up a system of law that served this society and its desires, even the desire to get gain and hold on to this gain for the benefit of their families. And in this way did the laws of men begin to supercede the laws of God. And in this way did Lucifer do that which he had promised upon being cast out of the presence of the Father, even that he would take the treasures of the earth, and with gold and silver, he would buy up the means of force, and that he would buy up the means of justice and laws that the children of men would be subjected to through the governments and religions of men, and reign with blood and horror upon the earth.

89 And this society began to use gold and silver and the precious elements of the earth to measure and control the gain that they desired. For behold, among the children of Adam there did not exist a means whereby the value of the things of the earth was measured. For all things were free unto all. And everyone did that which they could, according to their individual abilities, and all received according to their individual needs. And this was done by the sweat of their brow, which was commanded of them by the Father in the beginning.

90 Nevertheless, it had come to pass earlier among the children of Adam, that there lived some who did not want to work by the sweat of their own brow, but who had put themselves up above their brothers and their sisters. And these thought that because of their words, or because of their intelligence, they should not have to work by their own sweat.

91 And it was the eldest son of Adam, even Beneli, who had learned from Satan a way in which he could get gain by not working with his hands. And he had been convinced by Satan that because he was the eldest, and one of the most intelligent among them, that he should not be required to toil like unto the others.

92 And it came to pass that Beneli spent many days wandering throughout the land observing the toil and labor of the rest of his brothers and sisters, and even of his father Adam and his mother Eve, whom he loved.

93 And he was shown by Satan the gold that glittered in its natural state, and that it was beautiful to the eyes and smooth to the touch, even that it was everlasting and that which could not tarnish and age with time. And he also knew that this gold, and also silver which had the same attributes of gold, was sparse and was not found in abundance throughout the land.

94 And Beneli gathered up a large quantity of this gold and this silver and began to shape jewelry in a fashion that was most beautiful to be seen, and most comfortable against the skin of those who would wear it. And he went unto his wife and adorned her with the jewelry which he had made and convinced her to show it unto her friends and her neighbors and let them touch it and see its beauty.

95 And the other women began to covet the things of the wife of Beneli; and they desired of their husbands that they might have jewelry like unto hers. But these men did not know where to get this gold and this silver of which to make these things. And when they searched throughout the land, they could not find any, because of that which Beneli had taken unto himself.

96 And when their wives knew that their husbands could not find that which they desired, they pleaded with them to go unto Beneli and request of him some of his gold and his silver that they might have these things.

97 And the men went unto Beneli and asked of him that he might give unto them some of his gold and his silver, even that which he had gathered up in abundance unto himself

98 And Beneli answered them, saying: My dear brethren, it is my utmost desire that I should share that which I have with each of you, so that ye might give unto your wives that which I have given unto my wife, even that which hath given her great joy and pleasure. Yet, I would ask of you if it is fair that I give unto you that which I have toiled to obtain, even for many days have I toiled and labored with my own hands that I might acquire these things. And with my own hands have I fashioned these things into that which bringeth joy to my wife, and which your wives also desire.

99 And ye spend your days in toil by the sweat of your brows for the benefit of all, even the food that we eat and the homes that we live in and the clothes that we wear. And how is it then, that your toil is more important than mine? For behold, ye toil to assure that we live. Yet, what type of life do we live, if we do not have the joy and the pleasure that this life can bring? And ye have beheld that I have provided my wife with that which bringeth her this pleasure and this joy, even beyond that which ye have provided unto your own wives.

100 But I want that ye have the ability to give unto your wives this pleasure and this joy. Therefore, I would that ye should trade with me your labor and that which your labor produceth for that which my labor hath produced, even that which will bring joy unto your wives.

101 And it came to pass that with his words, Beneli convinced the men to give unto him of their labors and of their food and of their clothes. And he caused them that they should build houses for him and fences in which he could mark the land that was his, even that for which he had traded in his dealings with these men.

102 And it came to pass that the gold and the silver of the land became more valuable to the people than their food, and their homes, and their raiment. And Beneli controlled the trading of the gold and the silver, evensomuch that he became very rich among the people and possessed much more than his other brothers and sisters.

103 And many others coveted the things that Beneli had; and they wanted to become rich like unto him. And in this way the children of men began to divide themselves into classes, even into the poor and the rich, or those who had much and those who had little. And those who had little coveted that which the rich possessed. But because gold and silver were so rare and precious among them, these poor could not

become like unto the rich. And there were those among the poor who began to steal from the rich. And these justified their actions because they felt that they should have that which the rich kept from them, even their gold and their silver, which they could not find in the land.

104 And thus the children of men began to come under the control of Satan. And he did rage in their hearts and became their God.

105 And Adam labored all of his days to convince them of their errors and to turn them once again to the commandments that he had taught them, which were given unto him by the Lord.

106 And it came to pass that after the death of Abel, Adam called all those who listened to his words and kept the commandments of the Lord. And there were many strong and agile men among them, nevertheless, they had never fought with their brethren, being taught that even anger towards another was not justifiable in the eyes of God.

107 But Adam explained unto them concerning the wickedness and corruption of those among them who did not keep the commandments of God; and that these had caused many sorrows to enter in among them, and that if they allowed this wickedness to continue, that it would surely lead to their destruction.

108 And the children of Adam who followed him were not as many as those that followed after the order of Beneli and Cain. Nevertheless, these had the spirit of God among them. And they had not defiled their bodies with the flesh of animals or with food that had been cooked. And these were strong men and had much more stamina and vigor than those who followed Satan.

109 And Adam spoke unto these strong ones who worshipped the Lord and kept his commandments, and said unto them: I would that ye should know that my heart is burdened by the actions of your brothers and sisters who have disregarded the commandments of God and have established their own laws among them.

110 And I have spent many years preaching unto them and counseling with them with a hope that they would see the error of their ways and return again unto God. But my works among them have been in vain. And they have slain my son Abel, who was your beloved brother, and also a prophet of God. And because they have chosen to rid themselves of all those who do not bow down to their form of government and take the oaths and covenants of that secret society among them, I am afraid that they might come among those of us who keep the commandments of God and live according to His word, and destroy us.

111 Therefore, it is my desire that I should speak unto them one last time and ask them in all humility, even with the love that I have for them as their father, that they change their ways and bring peace once again throughout the land.

112 And if it so be that they refuse to listen to my words and give heed unto my counsel, then I am constrained by the spirit of God, yea, even by the spirit of peace and harmony; which is the spirit of God, that I banish them from this land and command them to leave and go back the way in which those came who do not have the pure blood of the bodies that the Father created for the spirits of His children; even those who are now our brothers and our sisters, but who do not have the pure blood.

113 And I would that ye should know, that it mattereth not whether their bodies are of the pure blood or not. For it is the spirit that commandeth the body. And if their spirit is good, then it shall command the body in righteous works. And there are many among us who keep the commandments of God who do not have the pure blood, and many of these are more righteous than those who have the pure blood. Therefore, it mattereth not unto me, nor unto God, which body they possess, for by their works shall they be known.

114 And if the works of your brothers and sisters were righteous, then there would be no need for that which I must command of them, if it so be that they repent and turn to God.

115 And now, I, Moroni, find it necessary that I write that the sons and daughters of Adam had much respect and honor for Adam and for Eve. Yea, even those who did not follow the commandments of God, still did honor their father and their mother.

116 And Adam and Eve were loved and respected above all others upon the land. And I have shown unto you before that Beneli had a great love for his mother Eve. And he did also love his father Adam, but did not that which he was commanded by his father, and this because he was persuaded by Satan, who had possessed the body of him who was his natural father. And the children of Beneli did also honor Adam and Eve, even for many years after the death of Beneli, who was their father and their leader, who had died many years before this time, because of the imperfections and defilement of his body.

117 And it was the desire of Adam to gather all of his children upon the face of the whole land, even all those who were his sons and daughters, and also their sons and daughters. And there were numerous people upon the face of the earth in and around the place where the Lord had planted the garden of Eden, it being the center and also the borders of their land.

118 Now in this day, Adam was five hundred and two years old when he made a proclamation throughout the land that all the people therein should gather themselves together to hear his words. And it had been over five hundred years that the sons and daughters of Adam had gone two by two upon the face of the land and raised up children. Therefore, the lands round and about the borders of the garden of Eden were full of many people.

119 And in the church of God that had been established by Adam there were many wise and righteous leaders, they being direct descendants of Adam and having the Holy Priesthood passed down through the patriarchal order of the sons of Adam.

120 For after the death of Abel, which death had occurred many years before the time of the gathering of the people to listen to the words of Adam, Eve conceived and bore Seth unto Adam.

121 And now I, Moroni, have once again been constrained by the Spirit to give unto you, yea, even those who shall receive this record, a proper accounting of the years and time of Adam. Behold, when Adam was cast out of the garden of Eden he was a grown man who had reached the age of mortality of thirty and three years; and his wife, Eve, was younger in mortal years, she being the age of mortality of eighteen years when she was deceived by Satan and cast out of the garden with her husband. Now this was according to the years of man, for unto God the time of man doth not exist.

122 Now the bodies that were given to Adam and Eve in the beginning were formed like unto those of a man of thirty and three years old, and of a woman of eighteen years old. And these are the ages in mortality when the children of men are fully mature and have reached the pinnacle of strength and vitality. For according to the laws of nature, yea, even according to the laws that we are subjected to during the days of our probation, our bodies reach this pinnacle after thirty and three years for a man and after eighteen years for a woman.

123 And because Adam and Eve were given perfect mortal bodies that were not defiled by the forbidden things from which God had commanded them to abstain, they lived for many years. And at the age of the pinnacle of health and strength to which they grew, their bodies remained in this state for many years. For this reason, those who carried within them undefiled blood lived for hundreds of years, whereas those who had defiled their blood with the things that had been forbidden, began to die after the pinnacle of their mortality was reached. And in a matter of a few years, they who had defiled their bodies began to grow old and lose the strength and vitality that they had experienced at this pinnacle.

124 And those who had eaten the flesh of other animals and cooked their food, thus destroying the vital nutrients that nature hath provided for their health and strength; and also those who had mixed their blood with the blood of other animals that were not given the same bodies that were given to Adam and Eve; yea, even those whose bodies had been possessed by Lucifer and his followers for many years; yea, even these did not reach the age of longevity with which the pure sons and daughters of Adam and Eve were blessed.

125 And this was also the wise purpose of the Lord. For the Lord knew that the sons and daughters of Adam and Eve would begin to follow the enticings of Satan and turn against the commandments that he had given unto them. And since there are always upon the earth those who disobey the laws of God and follow the enticings of Satan; yea their numbers being exceedingly greater than those who keep His commandments; therefore, in the beginning God assured a balance of righteousness so that the righteous would not be overwhelmed by the wicked.

126 And the days of Adam were eighty and two when he begot Cain. And two years after the birth of Cain did Eve conceive and give birth to Abel. And Abel was thirty and three years old when he began his ministry in the church of God. And he taught in the church for five years and preached many things unto his brothers and sisters. And his father placed him over the flocks of the field, even those flocks that were raised for the sacrifices that they performed according to the commandments of God. And when he was thirty and eight years old, his brother Cain slew him.

127 And now I, Moroni, would that ye should know somewhat more concerning the jealousy that Cain had towards his younger brother Abel. For behold, Adam had given each of his sons the work that each of them should do according to each of their abilities and their strengths. And Cain was much stronger than Abel, he having received of his father a body that was exceedingly stronger than the bodies of most other men.

128 And Adam saw the strength of Cain and blessed him and put him over the work that was done in the fields, even the tilling and the planting and the harvesting of the fruits and the plants that the people harvested for food.

129 And even at a young age, Cain became an expert at his trade and demonstrated great skill in his ability to produce food for the people, evensomuch that he produced an abundance of food, and was known throughout the land for his husbandry.

130 But his brother Abel was short of stature and weak in the strength of his hands, evensomuch that he did not contribute to the physical tasks that were required of the men to produce and harvest the food that the house of Adam needed for sustenance. Therefore, Adam assigned Abel to tend the flocks.

131 And he became exceedingly proficient in organizing and caring for the flocks and preparing them for that which they were being raised. And they were being raised exclusively for a sacrifice unto God, as they had been commanded by Him, this being in similitude of the law of sacrifice that was given to Adam and Eve in the Holy Endowment.

132 And it came to pass that Cain did not understand why the works of his hands were not acceptable unto God as a sacrifice like unto those of his brother Abel. And Cain brought forth and placed the works of his hands on the altar that Adam had commanded to be constructed to perform the law of sacrifice. And when he had done this thing, Adam rebuked his son and commanded him to bring no such offering unto the Lord, except it be that the Lord shall command it.

133 And Adam loved his son and made an attempt to explain to him that the law of sacrifice was symbolic of a law that would be fulfilled without the works of man. And as his offering was the work of the hands of men, and the offering of a beast, that God had created, had nothing consistent with the works of man, then his offering was not consistent with the intent of the symbolism of the law of sacrifice.

134 And Cain became angry with his father and jealous of his brother, and went unto the eldest son of Adam, even Beneli, that he might seek his advice, which advice he took unto himself and did those things that Beneli required of him.

135 And it came to pass that eight years had passed after the murder of Abel. And during these eight years Adam did mourn because of the loss of his son, and he did also morn because of such a terrible thing that had come to pass among his children. For there had never been a murder committed during the days of Adam until that time.

136 And after eight years of mourning the loss of her son Abel, Eve conceived again and gave unto Adam another son. And he called his name, Seth. And the Lord had great compassion upon Adam, and made Seth in an exact likeness of his father, evensomuch that Eve rejoiced therein and knew that the Lord had done this to ease the pain of Adam.

CHAPTER 17

The great meeting at Adamondiahman is held and Adam gives his counsel to his children. He explains the meaning of the probationary period in mortality. He teaches his children more about their Heavenly Mother. Moroni gives his admonition regarding the plurality of wives and the honor and respect that should be given to all women.

AND Seth grew in righteousness and followed in the footsteps of his father and did all things whatsoever the Lord commanded him. And Seth had the pure blood of Adam within him, and he had many sons and daughters born unto him. And he begot a son and called him Enos. And Enos also grew in the righteousness of the Lord.

2 And Enos begot a son and named him Cainan. And Cainan also followed in the footsteps of his fathers. And Cainan was a very strong man among men, and was pleasant to look upon, and the desire of many women. Nevertheless, he was faithful to the commandments of God and the counsel of his fathers in all things. And he became one of the most popular leaders among those who were righteous.

3 And Cainan begot a son and named him Mahalaleel, and he also followed in the footsteps of his father.

4 And Mahalaleel begot Jared, who was like unto his fathers in all things. And Jared was ordained in the Holy Priesthood and served with his fathers in the church of God that existed among them. And it was in the early ministry of Jared that Adam called his children from all parts of the land to give them his counsel.

5 And the people gathered themselves together, even those who belonged to the church of God, and also those who did not belong to the church. And the descendants of Beneli had gathered themselves on one side, and the sons of Seth were gathered on the other. And Seth sat with his father, Adam, among the people. And Enos, and Cainan, and Mahalaleel, and Jared also sat among the people, as Adam had instructed of those who lead the church of God.

6 For behold, Adam would not suffer that the leaders of the people place themselves above or in front of those whom they serve. And it was customary among the leaders of the church that they sit with the congregation of those who had gathered to hear their words. And when it was time for them to speak, this leader would rise up from among the people and take his place in front of them and deliver that which he was inspired to teach unto them. And immediately after preaching unto the people, this leader would return once again to his place among the people.

7 And in this way, the people were taught that their leaders were their servants and that the people should not envy their leaders, neither should they bow down and worship them, this thing being an abomination before God.

8 Now, I, Moroni, would that ye should know, that Cain was not present at this meeting in Adamondiahman. For he was banished by his father Adam from among the people after it was made known unto Adam that which he had done to his brother Abel.

9 And Cain was given the land east of the garden of Eden and commanded to stay in that part of the land and not partake of the law of consecration with the rest of the posterity of Adam. And Adam and his people did not support Cain and his posterity according to the laws which were established among them. Nevertheless, they suffered that they should live in the borders of their lands as long as they did not come in among them.

10 But the descendants of Beneli supported Cain and his people, as was promised him by way of the secret covenants that they had made with him. And a way of commerce and trade was opened up between them that greatly benefited them both. And the posterity of Cain grew and became numerous upon the land, but they could not come unto the children of Adam and partake of their sustenance, which sustenance was provided for them by the laws that Adam had established according to the laws of God.

11 And Cain and his posterity became a loathsome people unto the rest of the children of men. For they would go about the land naked.

And after a few generations, the effects of the sun on their naked bodies defiled their bodies even more than they had hitherto been defiled, and they became darker still. And they were afflicted with disease and sores upon their bodies that made them easy for the people of Adam to recognize, and thus forbid them from entering into their lands.

12 And after many generations, the sores left a mark upon them, even that their appearance was not like that of the sons and daughters of Adam any longer. And they wandered the land wither they desired to go, but they dared not come into the land of Adamondiahman. And for this reason, none of the posterity of Cain was present when Adam called the people together.

13 And Adam was five hundred and two years old when he called his posterity together. And even after these many years, he was exceedingly vibrant and strong and was able to do all things that were expected of him. And Eve was like unto Adam, even that in childbirth she continued to thrive above all other women.

14 And it came to pass that Adam came forth from among the people and took his place in the middle thereof. And a day and an hour were chosen in which there were no wind or natural causes that would keep the posterity of Adam, which was great, from hearing his voice. For the leaders of the people had chosen a spot in a valley where Adam could speak unto the people. And the people sat themselves upon the hills that surrounded this valley. And when Adam spoke unto them his voice would resonate throughout the valley and follow up the course of the hills that surrounded him.

15 And Adam spoke unto them, saying: My beloved children, yea, even all of you who have come forth from my loins and the loins of your dear mother Eve. Truly the Lord, our God, hath blessed us and hath given unto us this earth on which we live, and hath prepared it so that we might enjoy the life that he hath also given unto us.

16 And without regret I can say unto you that I have loved you all the days of my life. And I have watched you grow and prosper and experience this life and find joy therein. And I have also witnessed the sorrows and the tribulations that ye have experienced by way of the choices that ye have made because of the freedom that we enjoy, having been given this freedom to act according to the desires of our hearts from the God who hath created us.

17 And without force or intervention He hath granted unto us the freedom to live out the days of our probation as we feel so compelled according to our individual desires of happiness. And because He hath created us and hath given us this free agency to act according to the dictates of our own conscience; yea, because we did not have a choice in our own creation, or in the creation of our own spirit, He hath granted unto us all things that are necessary so that we might fulfill the desires of our happiness.

18 And He hath granted unto us all the gift of mortality, which gift He hath given unto us so that we may understand this happiness that we desire; and that we may be able to recognize the good by experiencing the bad. And it is in this way that all knowledge is received. For without the opposition in all things, nothing can be understood and experienced. And for this reason He hath given unto us mortality.

19 And for the space of many years He allowed your mother Eve and me to dwell in the garden that He placed in this land that He hath called Eden. And in this garden He gave unto us bodies of flesh and bone that were created in His own image. Yea, even in the image of the Gods did he create our bodies—both male and female.

20 And now my beloved children, do ye suppose that if we were created in the image of the Gods—both male and female—that this image is only that of a man? Ye know well that there are females among us, and are not their bodies also created in the image of God? And I say unto you that they are also created in the image of God, and that God is not our Father alone, but that we also have an Eternal Mother, who is also a God.

21 And these things I have caused to be taught unto you by faith, knowing that ye have never seen the Father and the Mother of whom I speak. For they are the father and the mother of your spirits, which spirits ye also cannot see with your mortal eyes. Nevertheless, our Eternal Father and Mother are not made of spirit matter of which our spirits are made, but they have bodies of flesh and bone like unto ours. And our mortal bodies were created in the image of their eternal bodies, which are perfect. And our mortal bodies, which are imperfect, were made in the image of their bodies, but not in an exact likeness like unto our spirits.

22 For behold, our spirits are an exact likeness of our eternal parents in a similar way as your mortal bodies are a likeness of your mortal parents. And ye have beheld the body that I possess, and also the body that your mother Eve possesseth. And we were not born of mortal parents, therefore our bodies were not created in the likeness of imperfection, but were created after the pattern of the bodies of our Father and Mother in heaven. And for this reason ye have beheld that we have maintained our strength and our vitality even unto a very old age. And your mother Eve is like unto her daughters in every way, even that she hath lived many years past the deaths of many of her daughters, even those who have defiled their bodies and made them impure by those things which were forbidden unto them.

23 And as I have said unto you that I have taught you to believe in our Eternal Parents by faith, because ye have not seen Them with your own eyes; I would that ye should know that I do not believe in Them by this faith of which I have spoken. For behold, my eyes have beheld Them, and I know that They are. And Eve also knoweth that They are, even her knowledge of Them hath never been tarnished by the effects of time as mine was for a brief moment.

24 Yea, after many years had passed since I last saw my Father and my Mother in the garden of Eden, I began to be drawn in by the effects of mortality, and I began to doubt that which I had once known. But your mother Eve did not doubt these things, and she hath been a source of much strength and comfort to me all the days of my life.

25 And the Father sent an angel unto me and shocked me into my senses, that I once again knew of those things that ye accept by faith. Yet, I should have known these things by the examples of this knowledge that hath been with me all the days of my life, even the mortal body which I have, yea, even the knowledge that this mortal body that I possess hath no mortal parents. But as are the frailties of mortality, more especially among those of us who are men, I lost the effects of this pure knowledge to the weakness of my mortality, in that I was not humble in my assumptions.

26 And Eve brought this knowledge back to my attention many times, but I would not listen to her because of my pride; yea, even the pride that a man doth feel because of the strength that he hath been given over a woman. Yet this strength that I have been given over Eve was not the strength of the spirit, which strength she hath in a greater abundance than I. And for this reason, my beloved sons, I would that ye should look unto your wives and your mothers; yea, in many instances, even unto your daughters for this spiritual strength that will keep you humble during the days of your probation here in mortality.

27 And now, as I have mentioned to you concerning the days of your probation, I would that ye should understand more concerning this probationary period, which hath been granted unto each of us that we might live in mortality and experience the opposite nature of those things which are good; that we might understand them and know them and appreciate that which is good.

28 And I plead unto all of you that ye would listen to my words and accept them on faith, and ponder upon them and apply them in your lives. And if ye accept them on faith, then ye shall ponder upon them. And after ye have pondered upon them, ye shall know that they are true, and ye will begin to apply them in your lives. And if ye shall apply them in your lives, then ye will realize that they were true by the test of the application that ye have given unto them. And the end result of this test shall be the happiness which ye desire.

29 For I know that many of the things that I shall teach unto you shall be those things that ye cannot see with your mortal eyes. Yea, this faith is the substance of the things for which ye hope. And ye do hope for happiness, for this is the end of your desires. For in all things we desire to be happy. And if ye act upon this hope and are given happiness, then ye have received an

evidence of those things that ye cannot see; and then ye shall begin to exercise greater faith, until your faith becometh a knowledge.

30 And by exercising your faith, ye shall eventually be led to the knowledge which ye desire, or in other words, the happiness for which ye hope. Therefore, my beloved children, listen to my words and exercise your faith upon them.

31 And now, before I can explain further unto you regarding the days of probation of which I have spoken, which is your life here upon this earth, even the days from the day and hour of your birth to the day and hour of your death, which death ends the days of your probation, behold it is necessary that I explain unto you how this became a probationary period for you.

32 Now, in general terms a probationary period means a period in which a critical examination or evaluation, yea even the subjection to this critical examination or evaluation, is performed. This period, or trial of subjection, is necessary to ascertain fitness, or in other words, worthiness.

33 And in order to find out with certainty if we are worthy, we must know of what worthiness we are being required to ascertain. In other words, by what standard of worthiness are we trying to know of a certainty.

34 Now, our hope by which we act and think, is that we might find joy and happiness. This happiness is a state of well-being and contentment, which is experienced concurrently with joy, which is the emotion or feeling that we experience by the prospect of possessing that which we desire. And that which we desire is happiness. And for this purpose were we created, that we might have this joy and happiness forever.

35 And now my beloved children, I would that ye should know that before we came to this earth, even to this part of this great universe, which expanse of space we can see with our mortal eyes; yea, even before we came to this planet upon which we now live and pass through the days of this probation, we lived on another planet with our Eternal Parents, who is the God that I have taught you to believe in all the days of my life.

36 And we were created from the materials from our Eternal Mother, having received the instructions for the creation of our spirits from our Eternal Father. And this process took place in a similar fashion like unto the conception of a child here in mortality. Nevertheless, this conception was perfect and refined according to the laws of the planet on which our Eternal Parents live.

37 For we are subjected under different laws while in mortality; these laws being the laws of this natural world; whereas the laws of Their world are the laws of an eternal world. Thus there are natural laws and there are eternal laws, the one being parallel with the other. Nevertheless, the natural laws are patterned after those that are eternal.

38 For even as all things pass away by the laws of nature, even so shall all things remain eternal by the eternal laws, which laws are the laws to which all the universe is subjected. And even these natural laws shall pass away, but these eternal laws must abide forever in the state in which they are given—even an eternal state.

39 And the laws of nature are established that they may fulfill the purposes and requirements of the eternal laws. Therefore, all natural law is subjected unto eternal laws, and are therefore sub-laws which are given for eternal purposes. And the end for which all eternal law is given is the joy and happiness of which I have spoken.

40 And since God is subjected to these eternal laws, then the purpose of God must be His own happiness. And this happiness, which is the purpose of these eternal laws, cometh to Him because of the happiness that He can give to others. And if there are no others to which He can give this happiness, then He cannot have this happiness for Himself. For this purpose we were created, even that He might give unto us this happiness so that His happiness might be fulfilled, and also that He might comply with the eternal laws.

41 And I would ask of you, for what other purpose is a law given except that it bring forth the happiness that I have explained unto you? And what other purpose would God have, except to obey the law and provide those who He hath created with this happiness?

42 And our Mothers who brought us forth from Their own bodies began to teach us these eternal laws of happiness. Yea, even from the day of our spiritual birth we were continually taught and raised by our Mothers to know this happiness. And by teaching us about this happiness, our Eternal Mothers received their own happiness.

43 And this is the work and the glory of an eternal woman who hath the power and the ability, which Her exalted body provideth, even to bring forth spiritual offspring, which are Her eternal children, which She shall know forever.

44 But the Father hath other works that He doeth, even according to the eternal laws of happiness that govern Him. For while our Eternal Mother is caring for our spirit and bringing other spirits into being, that our spirit might not be alone; yea, even as She is engaged in the desires of Her own happiness, so is our Father engaged in the performance of His labors, which labors shall provide for us the means by which we shall be able to know the happiness that our Mothers desire for us.

45 Behold, our Eternal Mothers perform the labors that are necessary for our first estate, which estate is the state in which we find ourselves as spirits in the kingdom of our Eternal Parents. But our Eternal Father performeth the labors that are necessary for our second estate, which estate is the state of the days of our probation, or the days of our mortality.

46 And because our Mothers are busy with their labors in our first estate, They do not concern Themselves with the cares and labors of our second estate. And our Father doth not concern himself with the affairs of our first estate, in which estate the labors of our Mothers are performed. For what purpose would we need a mother if it was that our father could provide for all of our needs? And again, what purpose would we need a father, if our mother could provide us with all that we need?

47 For this reason the Gods are male and female; nevertheless, they are equal in all things, having the same glory and the same power.

48 And now, I, Moroni, would that ye should know that this thing of which Adam hath spoken is a mystery which hath caused some manner of confusion and disputation among the children of men. For there are those who feel that a woman is inferior to a man, and that if our Father is a male, then that must be an indication that a man is the preferred gender, and one of a higher order than that of a female.

49 And ye also know that our Eternal Mothers are not mentioned in the scriptures that ye have before you. Yea, at very few times hath there been made proper mention of our Eternal Mothers throughout the history of the children of men. Yet, ye will see as the vision of the brother of Jared is unfolded unto you, that the children of men will begin to worship female Goddesses, and this hath been done in times of old by those who do not understand the mysteries of God, but have changed them by the foolish traditions that have crept in among them because they do not follow the commandments of the Father.

50 For behold, because our Eternal Mothers have little to do with this world and the state of our probation, as Adam hath described it unto you, They are not mentioned in the holy scriptures. And this because this is the work of the Father, and He deserveth the glory from that which is required of Him by the eternal laws that He obeyeth.

51 Now this doth not mean that the honor and glory of an Eternal Mother is taken away. For she received the major portion of the honor and glory while we existed in our first estate. And as spirits in our first estate, we had very little to do with our Father, because of the work that was required of Him in other worlds that He had created for the spirits of those that were created before our spirits were created.

52 For this is not the only world on which existeth the spirit children of the Father and of our Eternal Mothers. For after a spirit reacheth an age of maturity and is raised to this state by an Eternal Mother, then that spirit is presented to the Father that it might be prepared for its second estate, which is the work of the Father. And after it hath passed through its second estate, then it shall receive its eternal glory in the kingdom of the Father. And then shall the work of the Father, and also of our Eternal Mothers be completed.

53 And when this work is completed, then shall the Father and our Eternal Mothers partake of the honor and glory together, having earned this honor and glory according to the works of each, in the estate that They were involved with according to the eternal laws of the kingdom of God.

54 And after this work is completed, do ye think that the work of the Father and our Mothers is complete? I say unto you that it is not complete, because Their work is eternal and cannot end. Therefore, They will continually seek the happiness that They desire by doing what bringeth Them this happiness. And this happiness cometh by way of the happiness that They can provide for others, which others are Their spiritual children.

55 And I would that ye should understand that a man and a woman are equal in all things. Yea, I would that those of you who think that a man is greater than a woman would know that a woman is even more precious unto the Lord than a man. And this because of her power of creation as it hath been explained previously unto you.

56 Behold, a righteous man can bring forth many children, but these children cannot be righteous except that they are taught by their mothers who are righteous. And if it were in the best interest of the purpose of creation, then God would rid Himself of most men, but keep unto Himself the women. For within one man is the power to create many children, but within a woman is the power by which she might only create one child at one time. And this righteous man might be the means by which many women may bring forth children.

57 And this thing was known from the beginning, even according to the words of Adam. And at certain times the Lord commanded chosen men to allow their wives to give unto them other wives for the purpose of creation. Nevertheless, these were righteous men who were chosen specifically by the Lord to do this thing. But unto the rest of the children of men, he hath commanded that they have but one wife only, and this because of their unrighteousness.

58 And in the record of my father is given instruction, even by the mouth of Jacob, the brother of Nephi, concerning these things. And my father wrote the words of Jacob in which he said: For behold, thus saith the Lord: This people begin to wax in iniquity; they understand not the scriptures, for they seek to excuse themselves in committing whoredoms, because of the things which were written concerning David, and Solomon his son.

59 Behold, David and Solomon truly had many wives and concubines, which thing was abominable before me, saith the Lord.

60 Therefore, thus saith the Lord, I have led this people forth out of the land of Jerusalem, by the power of mine arm, that I might raise up unto me a righteous branch from the fruit of the loins of Joseph.

61 And I the Lord God will not suffer that this people shall do like unto them of old.

62 Therefore, my brethren, hear me, and hearken to the word of the Lord: For there shall not any man among you have save it be one wife; and concubines he shall have none. For I, the Lord God, delight in the chastity of women. And whoredoms are an abomination before me; thus saith the Lord of Hosts. And this people shall keep my commandments, saith the Lord of Hosts, or cursed be the land for their sakes.

63 For if I will, saith the Lord of Hosts, raise up seed unto me, I will command my people; otherwise they shall hearken unto these things. For behold, I, the Lord, have seen the sorrow, and heard the mourning of the daughters of my people in the land of Jerusalem, yea, and in all the lands of my people, because of the wickedness and abominations of their husbands.

64 And now, I, Moroni, know that the plurality of wives is an abomination in the sight of God, except it be according to the exceptions of which I have mentioned. But I know that there are many of you who shall receive this record that shall believe that ye are justified in this thing, because of the exceptions which I have mentioned. But I say unto you, that in the latter days, there shall be no exceptions except they be given unto you by him who shall bring forth this record. And only by the power which he hath been given shall he command any man to allow his wife to give unto him another.

65 And this power and this authority shall not be passed down from one generation to the next according to the transference of authority as it is suffered in the priesthood and in the church of God that shall be among you.

66 And unless he who shall bring forth this record shall give this power and authority unto another by the direct laying on hands, and this power be sealed by the Holy Ghost, this authority shall not be used. And unto those to whom he shall give this power, they shall have no power in the priesthood to transfer it to any other.

67 But I say unto you, that he shall not give this power unto any other, but this power shall reside solely in him who hath received all the keys of the kingdom of God. And this power is not transferable with the keys that are required of the priesthood to preach the gospel unto the world. For this is not part of this gospel. And the gospel of Christ requireth a man to love his wife and cleave unto her and none else. And if a man even looketh upon another woman, that is not his wife, to lust after her, he hath committed a grave sin, and except he repent, he shall be condemned before God. For God loveth his daughters and will protect them from the lusts and desires of men.

68 And this power shall be used to create bodies for the spirit children of God. But in the latter days, there will be no need that more bodies be created for the spirits of the children of God, like unto days of old. And there will not be many men who are worthy enough to be allowed to take more than one woman as a wife.

69 Yea, the power of Satan will rage in the hearts of men in those days, and they will begin to lust exceedingly after the daughters of men, even unlike at any other time during the history of the children of men. And their sins shall be like unto those of Sodom, even according to the prophecy of Isaiah, which he prophesied, saying: The show of their countenance doth witness against them, and doth declare their sin to be even as Sodom, and they cannot hide it. Woe unto their souls, for they have rewarded evil unto themselves!

70 And these men that shall read these things shall suppose that Isaiah is referring to the sins of Sodom and Gomorrah as have been misinterpreted in the Bible. And it was true that in the city of Gomorrah there were many men who were lustful one towards another, this lust being that which is sinful in the sight of God, and not the love that a man might have for another man. But Isaiah specifically mentioneth Sodom, which city was full of all manner of lasciviousness, and it was full of men that lusted continually after the women of the city. And there were many therein that took many wives and concubines that they might consume them on their lusts.

71 And even as Jacob was grieved because of that which he was commanded to speak unto the Nephites, when he would have rejoiced in preaching unto them the pleasing word of God, so am I grieved because I must leave the great words of Adam to admonish those men in the latter days, who have taken to themselves more than one wife, because they pretend to be complying with the commandments of God.

72 And they have grieved the spirit of God and it is not with them. And because of the things which they shall do, they shall be a scourge unto the Gentiles, and the Gentiles shall persecute them and hate them for that which they do. And their children shall begin to rebel against these men and bring dishonor unto them.

73 But the women who have chosen to subject themselves unto these men shall be blessed. Yea, these women shall subject themselves under the dominion of the unrighteousness of their husbands because they understand the role of their Eternal Mothers, and are desirous to be like unto Them. And in great faith, shall these righteous women bring forth children and subject themselves under the law of their husband, because of their faith.

74 And it shall come to pass that when the words of this record shall come forth among them, they shall read of the wickedness of their husbands and know of the deception under which these men have held them. And they shall know that the authority of this great sealing power was not given unto their husbands, and that they are living a law of the Celestial glory in which their husbands cannot abide. But all that which these women have done shall be counted unto them for righteousness.

75 And I say unto you, who are my sisters that live under the dominion of a man, even a man that you know within your heart that ye do not love. Nevertheless, ye love God more than ye love this man, and ye subject yourselves to this man because ye have been misled in the laws of God by a man. And do ye not now realize that if a man establisheth laws for himself, then that man will establish laws that he can consume upon his lusts? And these are the laws that have been established by any man that is desirous to have more than one wife.

76 And in the words of Christ, there existeth no such commandment, but he condemeth any man from lusting after a woman who is not his wife. And unless your husband hath been directly commanded by him who hath the authority to authorize the taking of more than one wife—and not a man who thinketh he hath this authority that is not transferable through the lines of authority in the priesthood as it hath been explained unto you—then your husband is living in sin, and shall in no wise inherit the kingdom of God unless he repenteth of the thing which he hath done.

77 But ye are not living in sin, but are being glorified in that which ye have done. For your desires are given unto you by the example of our Eternal Mothers, who in the kingdom of the Father, share in the power of the Father for the purpose of their own happiness, as Adam hath explained it unto you.

78 Behold, ye do not sin in desiring a righteous man as a husband. And ye know that the curse of mortal men, even in their prideful state, can cause that a husband of this nature doth bring more misery on you than the joy that ye would think a husband should provide for you. And because there are few men that are righteous, ye are justified in desiring to share those who are true men of God. Nevertheless, a righteous man would not take more than one wife, unless the Lord commanded it of him. And the Lord would not command a man to do this thing, but he hath given this power and authority unto one man only. And only from this man, whom the Lord hath anointed unto this power, can the permission to do such a thing be granted.

79 And now my beloved sisters, I write these things unto you that ye might know the way in which ye should judge the men that ye would take as your husbands. Ye know that ye have received these things which have been written by my hand and which the Lord hath commanded me to be written unto you. And the spirit of God hath wrought upon you and testified of the truthfulness of these things.

80 And how have ye received these things except it be from the hand of a mortal man who hath been raised up by the Lord to bring these things forth unto you? And it is this man to whom ye should listen and abide by his precepts in all things whatsoever he shall command you concerning these things. And it is only by the hand of this man who can authorize another man that he take more than one wife.

81 And behold, I say unto you that this man will not command these things of any man who is not worthy of such things. And there are few men who are worthy of these things, and even fewer who exist upon the earth in the latter days, or in the days that these things shall be revealed unto you.

82 And this man is a prophet of God, a bearer of Christ, who shall direct you to the words of Christ. And if ye shall abide by the words of Christ, then ye shall have the husband that ye desire, whether in this world, or in the next, ye shall be blessed with that which will bring you the joy and happiness that ye seek.

83 And now my beloved sisters, remember who is your Father in heaven. Remember that ye have a Mother there also. Yea, remember that ye were created in the image of your Eternal Mother, and that She loveth you and desireth that ye have the happiness that ye desire. Ye are daughters of an Eternal Father and Mother. Ye deserve the respect and honor of a daughter of these Eternal Beings. Be ye not deceived by your brothers who lust after you and would take you away from the words of Christ.

84 Behold, Christ is your brother, but he doth not lust after you, nor doth he desire that ye become his wife. He desireth to bring you happiness, and he will accomplish this desire by preaching repentance unto your brothers, and teaching them his ways that they may prepare themselves to be your husbands and the fathers of your spirit children, which will bring you joy and happiness forever.

85 Behold, thus saith the Lord unto all of the daughters of God: My beloved sisters, I would that ye should know the love by which ye are loved, and the honor by which this love cometh. Behold, of all the creations of the Father, none are as beautiful and more consistent to the glory of His kingdom than are ye.

86 Remember to keep my commandments that ye may always have my spirit to be with you. And if ye have my spirit with you always, ye shall not be deceived by your brothers. And through the ministrations of the Holy Ghost ye shall be able to discern which of your brothers are worthy of your companionship.

87 Learn of me and my spirit. Defile not the temple that I have given unto you and blessed with the power of creation. If any man would be your husband, let him prove himself worthy of you by keeping my commandments and following in my footsteps.

88 Behold, I have given unto men the pattern that they should follow to become righteous husbands for you. And I have given my life as an example unto them. And if men learn of me and follow my example in all things, then shall they be worthy of you. And if they follow not my example, then they will not be like unto me. And I love you and serve you and do those things that bring you happiness. And if men do not follow in this example, then they are not worthy of you.

89 And if they are not worthy of you in this life, by following the example that I have given unto them, then they will not be worthy of you in the kingdom of my Father. And if they are not worthy of being a husband in the kingdom of my Father, then what purpose do ye have for them, except as salt which hath lost its savour and is henceforth good for nothing, but to be cast out and to be trodden under the foot of men.

90 Behold, a commandment I give unto you, even that ye wait patiently upon me, and I will prepare a husband for you. And he will be like unto me, and will do unto you that which I would do unto you if I were your husband. And that which I would do unto you shall bring you exceedingly great joy and be the means of your eternal happiness.

91 I love you my beloved sisters, and leave upon you my blessing. Amen.

CHAPTER 18

Adam continues his sermon and counsel to his posterity at Adamondiahman concerning our probationary state. He introduces the law of the gospel. Moroni expounds upon this law and writes of the great apostasy from this law in the latter days, and also of the hypocrisy of the Church of Jesus Christ of Latter-day Saints.

AND now, I, Moroni, continue with the words of Adam that he spoke unto those who were gathered in the valley of Adamondiahman:

2 And when the Mothers of our spirits have raised their children to maturity in the world of our Eternal Parents, then each is ready to determine for itself what kind of happiness that each desireth. For they have experienced the happiness that existeth among those who live in the world in which they were created, in other words, they have experienced the type of life, and the types of things that are done in this world that bring happiness to those therein.

3 And we were taught that these exalted Beings experience a fullness of joy, and because of their joy, they dwell in a state of happiness forever.

4 In order to teach us so that we could understand, our Mothers showed us the fruits of the joy that they experienced. For an example unto us, They would pluck a piece of fruit from off of a tree and show that fruit unto us. And They would describe its shape and its size and the texture of its skin unto us, and allow us to hold the fruit in our hands and feel that of which They describe. But to us, as spirits who did not know the difference between good and bad, or between soft and hard, nor did we know the difference between hunger and the feeling of being satisfied, we did not understand completely the feeling of joy that our Mothers tried to explain unto us.

5 And They would eat the fruit and make the sounds of enjoyment as They tasted the sweetness thereof. And a smile would form upon Their face, and a happy sensation would exude from within Their perfected body. And we could sense the joy that was felt by our Mothers, but we did not understand it.

6 And when They smiled, we could sense the joy of Their smile, but we did not understand what it was that made Them smile in this manner. And when They sang to us, we could hear the words of Their voice and the tenderness of the melody that resonated throughout our spirits, but we could not understand why it should cause us to be joyful. Nevertheless, our Mothers received much joy from singing to us and teaching us to sing. And though there were those among us who could sing the songs and melodies that our Mothers taught unto us, none of us could understand the reason that these brought so much joy to Their hearts.

7 And They would hold us gently next to Them and cry upon us, which crying was caused from the exceeding joy that They felt because of us. Yet, we could not understand the cause of Their tears. And when Their tears would fall upon us, we did not have the capability of determining the wetness thereof.

8 And though we could sense a change in the sensations of our own spiritual body when these tears would touch us, we could not determine for ourselves the meaning of such sensations.

9 And we did not understand the peace and harmony that existed among those who dwelt on this world with our Father and our Mothers. For there were other Fathers and other Mothers that did not pertain unto us and were not part of our eternal family. And there were other spirits there also which were not created from the directions that our Father provided, but were given bodies of their own Eternal Mothers and Fathers. And this world was great and glorious; and it was filled with eternal families of eternal parents creating spirit children.

10 And when the work of the Eternal Fathers was complete in one part of the vast expanse of the heavens; yea, even when They had placed Their spirit children on the planets in that part that They had prepared for them, these Fathers would then go to another part and create other worlds for the spirit children that were being born unto the Eternal Mothers that resided in this world.

11 But this peace and harmony and cooperation we did not understand, for we had not experienced anything but that which had always existed there. And we took for granted the greatness and glory of this world in which we were created; and we assumed that all worlds were like unto this one, having not experienced anything different.

12 And now, my beloved children, if it were that we could eat a piece of fruit that is good to the taste and which maketh us happy, why is it that we would not want to continue to partake of this fruit and the joy that it provideth forever? And this is the thing that our Mothers explained unto us.

13 And we could see that the make-up of Their bodies was different than our own. And we could see that unless we had a body like unto Theirs, we could never partake of the fullness of joy of which They partake forever.

14 And it became apparent unto us that not all of us were the same, even that our spirits were very individual with different desires and traits that made us unique in and of ourselves. And we knew that there was also much joy in these differences, yet we did not understand these differences.

15 But as we grew in spirit matter, our Eternal Mothers began to discern our spirits and teach unto us the types of joy that would suit each of us, and bring us the state of happiness that would best fit the make-up of our spirit, and that which would best compliment our personalities and the traits that made us unique in and of ourselves.

16 And they introduced to us the varying states of happiness that exist in the kingdom of God. And from the choices that were presented unto us, we determined for ourselves which state of happiness was that which we desired. And when we arrived at the state of maturity when this self-realization had taken place, then we waited upon the Father to create for us the kingdoms in which we would dwell and experience the state of happiness that we had chosen for ourselves.

17 And now, I, Moroni, shall not repeat all the words of Adam concerning the plan of salvation that was presented unto the children of God when they resided with him as spirits. For this thing hath already been given in this record according to the vision that the brother of Jared received regarding it. And the words of Adam are also from the record of the brother of Jared, in which he saw in vision Adam and his posterity and wrote the things which he saw.

18 But I will continue with the words of Adam as he taught his posterity the law of the gospel as it had been given unto him by the Lord after he was banished from the garden of Eden. And this law was given unto him as a prototype of the laws that govern all the glories of the kingdom of God. And it is this law that teacheth a man and a woman the manner in which they must live to maintain peace and harmony one with another.

19 And it is this law that a spirit must be willing and able to abide by in order for it to be allowed to live forever in one of the glories in the kingdom of God. And if a spirit cannot abide by the law of the gospel, it shall not be allowed to enter the kingdom of God.

20 For if a spirit is one that would create problems with others in the world in which it is placed forever, then there would be problems among those who reside in this world forever. But there are no problems in the kingdom of God, and those who reside therein do not have the capacity to cause these problems, having overcome this propensity during the days of their probation.

21 Therefore, the law of the gospel is the most important law that the children of men can learn during the days of their probation. And it was this law that Jesus taught unto his disciples and unto the people. And it was this law that his disciples were commanded to teach unto the people after he was gone. And it is by the law of the gospel that Jesus taught that all the children of God are saved.

22 And again I say unto you, for this reason Jesus, the Christ, is our Savior, in that he is the giver of this law. And there is nothing that Jesus can do for us that will save us in the kingdom of God, except teach unto us this law, which are the commandments of God. And again I say unto you, that there was nothing that Jesus did for us when he was upon this earth that shall save us, except give us the law of the gospel.

23 And there will be many in the latter days that shall believe that by the blood of Christ we are saved; and that the blood of Christ hath atoned for our sins, and that we must only believe in Christ and we will be saved in the kingdom of God. And in these beliefs many people do err and are being led away from the law of the gospel and are taught the precepts of men.

24 And I say unto those of you who believe these things; yea, even as I have said unto you before, even in this record have I said these things unto you: Ye do not understand the scriptures and have not inquired of the Holy Ghost for an understanding of the atonement and what the Lord intended by this. For the intent of the Lord was to make us one with God, even he commanded us that we should be perfect as our Father in Heaven is perfect.

25 And do ye think that ye can become like unto our Father if ye do not understand the things that the Father doeth? And the Father obeyeth the law of the gospel in all things, and He hath commanded His Son, even Jesus the Christ, to teach us this law that we might learn to live by it. And if we live by the same law by which our Father liveth, then we become one with Him, and then the atonement is fulfilled.

26 And I wish that I could write pleasant words unto you like unto the words of Adam which he gave unto his children in the land of Adamondiahman; for these words feel good to your souls and cause you to feel a spirit of joy and optimism, even that they cause you to weep with exceeding joy because of the things that he hath said unto his children.

27 But I am constrained by the Spirit and commanded by the Lord, that I speak unto you the truth in plainness so that ye might understand and have no more excuse for your unrighteousness and your evil ways, which ways are contrary to the law of the gospel, which I shall allow the words of Adam to teach you in this record. And in the part of this record that was unsealed and came unto you with the record of my father, Mormon, I was commanded by the Lord not to reveal these things unto you in their plainness, but that I should give unto you the similitude and symbolism of these things.

28 And it is my duty towards you as my

brothers and my sisters that I teach you these things, even that I might bring you unto repentance and prepare you for that great and dreadful day of the Lord, when he shall return once again to this earth with all those who have been resurrected after him, even the righteous who are ready and willing to obey the law of this gospel of which I have spoken.

29 And why do ye suppose that it is called the great and dreadful day of the Lord? Should it not be a day of comfort and of joy? Should it not be a day of rejoicing in which ye shall feel those special feelings of the mercy of his atoning blood that ye have deceived yourselves into feeling all the days of your probation?

30 Yet, nowhere is it written in the holy scriptures that the day of the Lord shall be filled with the feelings of joy that ye express when ye think about him upon the cross; yea, when ye think of his hands pierced and bleeding to pay the debt of your sins. For behold, he did not pay any debt for your sins. For ye shall pay your own debts. And these debts shall be required of you because ye have failed to keep his commandments and abide by the law of his gospel that he hath given unto you.

31 Thus is the day of the Lord great and dreadful, even full of the wine of the wrath of God, which is poured out without mixture into the cup of his indignation. And ye shall be tormented with fire and brimstone in the presence of the holy angels, and in the presence of the Lamb. And your smoke of your torment shall ascend up forever and ever, and ye shall have no rest day or night. And all these things shall come to pass according to the prophecies of all the holy prophets who have ever been.

32 And what then shall ye think who believe that the Lord hath died for your sins and taken upon himself your debts? What then shall ye think who have felt the false sensations of security and peace that the devil hath caused to come over you when ye look upon the cross of Christ as the way by which ye shall be forgiven for the evil that ye do?

33 Will ye feel this sense of peace and security in his presence, yea even in the presence of the Lamb as it hath been prophesied? I say unto you that ye shall not feel these things, but shall shrink from before him and wish that ye could command the rocks to fall upon you and hide you from the countenance of the Lord.

34 For he shall come down in all of his glory and give unto you once again his gospel, which is the same gospel that he gave unto the Jews, and which ye have written in the Bible which proceedeth forth from the mouth of the Jew. And ye shall also have these same words in the record of my father in that part of this record that was not sealed. And then ye shall once again hear these things from his own mouth. And then ye shall have three testimonies of the word of God. And then shall the law be fulfilled which hath been spoken by the Father that in the words of three I will establish all of my words.

35 But this is not all, for ye shall have my words which shall be given unto you in this part of the record of my father which hath been sealed. And this shall be the final testimony of the gospel of Jesus Christ. And my words shall be plain and simple to understand. And if after reading my words, ye still do not understand the meaning of these things, then ye must remain until ye hear them from the mouth of God himself.

36 And if it so be that ye do not understand and accept this gospel, and live by its precepts as it hath been given unto you in all these testimonies that ye shall receive, then when ye hear it from the mouth of God, ye shall hear it to your condemnation, because ye have chosen, even three times, to disregard His words.

37 And now I write to you in plainness concerning these things. And these things I say unto all the world; for by the things that I say unto you in plainness ye shall be judged in the last day when the Lord cometh in his glory with his holy angels:

38 Behold, all religions, all doctrines, all principles, all beliefs, all scriptures, all writings, all holy men, all holy prophets, all institutions, all churches, all governments, all priesthoods, all laws, all sealings, all ordinances, all sacrifices, all traditions, all customs, yea, even everything that is done upon this earth among the children of men, are of no effect and have no power out of this world. In other words, they mean nothing in the kingdom of God.

39 The only thing that hath any meaning in the kingdom of God is the law of the gospel and the commandments that are given therein.

40 Therefore, if there are any among you who hear these things and keep the law of the gospel, then this person is ready for the resurrection and the eternal kingdom of God. They are those who will not cause any contentions in these kingdoms and shall live forever with those of their likeness in the worlds that the Father hath prepared for us.

41 And if there are any among you who think that ye shall be saved in any other way, even in that ye believe that you need the ordinances and doctrines of a church, then ye do not understand the plainness of my words, and shall be one of those to whom the Lord will say: Many will say to me in that day, Lord, Lord, have we not prophesied in thy name? And in thy name have cast out devils? And in thy name done many wonderful works? And then will I profess unto them, I never knew you, depart from me, ye that work iniquity.

42 And why shall the Lord say this unto them? Because they did not keep the law of the gospel as he was commanded by the Father to give unto them. For the things which he shall command of them, this is the will of the Father.

43 Behold, I have seen the last days, both in my own vision, and also through the words of the brother of Jared of which I am making an abridgment and writing to you at this time. And in those days, there are none, no not one, save it be a few only who are the humble followers of Christ who live by the law of this gospel.

44 And your churches and the leaders of your churches to whom ye look to be taught the will of God mislead you and cause you to err and teach not the law of the gospel as it hath been given unto them through the holy scriptures. And more especially, I speak unto those of you of the church of Jesus Christ, even those of you who call your church after his holy name but not in it.

45 Behold, ye are so centered on your church and the ordinances and functions therein, that ye have very little time and effort to spend obeying the law of the gospel. And ye have been taught by your leaders that these ordinances and these functions are saving ordinances which are necessary for your salvation. And in this ye are deceived and are being led captive by the devil.

46 And the words of Nephi are being fulfilled in you, in which he wrote, saying: And others will he pacify, and lull them away into carnal security, that they will say: All is well in Zion; yea, Zion prospereth, all is well—and thus the devil cheateth their souls, and leadeth them away carefully down to hell.

47 And because your church prospereth exceedingly, yea, even above any other church that is built up among the children of men, ye have become a rich and powerful people in the world. And the money that hath come from this prosperity, that should be going to the poor and the needy, the sick and the afflicted, and those that are imprisoned; yea, ye use this money to build up houses of worship which ye go to on one day a week and which are left empty for the rest of the week when they could be used to help the poor and the needy in their afflictions.

48 And if I could stop from condemning you before God, that ye might repent without searing your souls further with the heat of my words, I would. But I have seen the great temples that ye have caused to be constructed. And these ye have constructed to present the Holy Endowment that hath been explained unto you herein. And they are full of the fine things of the world, evensomuch that ye have received much praise from the world because of them.

49 And ye enter into these temples and think that ye are saviors of men, even that the endowment that ye receive is necessary for your salvation. And even this is not the end of your pride and your abominations before the Lord; for ye also believe that the work of your hands, even the work that ye perform within these temples will save those who are dead, which thing is most abominable before God.

50 Oh, my brethren, ye are those that shall suffer the most in the great and dreadful day of the Lord. Ye shall listen to his words in that day and quickly realize that he did not command that these things be done among the children of men. Ye will realize that the only concern that he hath for the world, is that they live by the law of his gospel, which law ye do not teach in your churches and in your temples.

51 And those who belongeth to your church shall watch in horror as the Lord calleth his own servants from among those who do not belong to your church, yea, even those who do not have the priesthood that ye think ye have. Then what shall ye say at that time of the works that ye have accomplished during the days of your probation? What shall ye think when ye are considered a thing of dross by the Lord, and that he giveth no attention to the glory and greatness of your church?

52 And why is it that ye shall suffer more than those who are not of your church? Yea, why do ye believe that the Lord will hold you accountable for more than he will hold the rest of those who have been deceived by the means of the miracles that Satan hath caused to be wrought among you? I say unto you that ye shall be held more accountable because ye have already two witnesses of the gospel of which I have spoken, even the words of Christ that he gave unto us, which is this gospel.

53 And no other people on earth will have these two testimonies which the Lord hath given unto the children of men. And the Lord will use your pride and your arrogance against you. For in your pride and arrogance, ye think ye are better than the rest of your brothers and sisters in the world, and that ye enjoy a happiness that they do not enjoy. And with this pride, ye send out missionaries to take your message of pride throughout the world.

54 And ye shall carry the record of my father with you, and pretend that ye believe in this record. And ye shall testify unto the world that the fullness of the gospel of Jesus Christ is contained in this record. And in this ye testify correctly, but by so testifying, ye are securing your own damnation. For ye testify of those things that ye do not do. And though the Lord will have exceedingly great mercy for the sinner, he shall condemn and punish the hypocrite.

55 And these words which I write unto you at this time, even in the sealed part of the plates upon which my father and I have written, and which I have been commanded to complete and hide in the earth to come forth in the own due time of the Lord; even these things shall ye reject because they were not given unto you by the leaders of your church, which leaders are all men of the world, which have received the fine things of the world and the praises and honors of men.

56 But these things shall condemn you and shall confound your false doctrines and the traditions that ye have allowed to creep into the foundations of the church that is called after the name of Jesus. For in the beginning, the foundation of your church was given in its purity, and the Lord suffered it to be organized according to the power of the Holy Priesthood and under the direction of the Holy Ghost.

57 But ye shall reject the pure foundation that was given unto you by him who shall receive this record from the place wherein I shall hide it. And because of your wickedness, the world will reject you and shall murder him who hath given these things unto you.

58 But another like unto him shall the Lord raise up to bring the sealed part of this record forth among you. And he shall have power given unto him, even the power of the Holy Spirit, to confound you and preach repentance unto you, and show you the wickedness of your ways.

59 And ye shall become like unto the Jews at Jerusalem who were the murderers of the prophets of old. And ye shall call upon your secret combinations, which combinations ye think are of God, and which ye think are righteous even like unto them of old. Yea, ye shall call upon these to murder this prophet.

60 Yea, ye shall become like the Nephites at the time Samuel the Lamanite was called by the Lord to preach repentance unto them. For when Samuel went forth to speak the truth concerning the wickedness of the church of God that was among them, they wanted to kill him and cast him away from them, so that they might not hear his preaching. But the Lord protected him, even that their bows and their arrows could not hit him.

61 And he who shall bring forth the sealed part of this record shall flee unto the rest of the world for protection, even unto those who are not of your church. And they shall protect him and give him sanctuary until he hath done all that which hath been commanded him by the Lord.

62 For it was the world that was responsible for the death of him that brought forth the portion of this record that was unsealed. And it was the cause of the wickedness of the church of God that caused his death. And now this same church shall seek the death of the prophet of God who shall bring these things forth unto you. And it shall be the world that openeth up its mouth and consumeth the flood of water that is issued forth from the mouth of the serpent that hath control of this church of which I have spoken.

63 Then shall the words of John be fulfilled which he wrote, saying: And when the dragon saw that he was cast unto the earth, he persecuted the woman which brought forth the man child.

64 And to the woman were given two wings of a great eagle, that she might fly unto the wilderness, into her place, where she is nourished for a time, and times, and half a time, from the face of the serpent.

65 And the serpent cast out of his mouth water as a flood after the woman, that he might cause her to be carried away of the flood.

66 And the earth helped the woman, and the earth opened her mouth, and swallowed up the flood which the dragon cast out of his mouth.

67 And the dragon was wroth with the woman, and went to make war with the remnant of her seed, which keep the commandments of God, and have the testimony of Jesus Christ.

68 For behold, the prophets of God have been persecuted by the wicked ever since they were first called to bring the law of the gospel unto the children of men. And a true prophet of God is always persecuted and hated by the world. And this is the thing that I ask of ye that belongeth to this great church in the latter days: Are your leaders hated by the world? Do those who have set themselves up as your prophets receive the afflictions of the prophets of old?

69 I say unto you that they do not. And why do they not receive this persecution as a true prophet of God should? Because they are of the world, and they seek the praise of the world more than they seek to teach unto you the law of the gospel.

70 And in the day that ye shall read my words, even in the day when the Lord shall give unto the world the words of the brother of Jared, ye shall see your leaders rise up and condemn this work. And they shall condemn this work because it testifieth against them and bringeth to your attention the truth regarding their wickedness and abominations.

71 And they shall say unto you: Behold, these things are not of the Lord. For the Lord would not give unto you anything except he do so through the authority of the church, which is held in the authority of those who have been called of God to serve in his Holy Priesthood.

72 And they shall speak unto you in kindness and smoothness, and in the gentle natures that ye have become accustomed to hearing their words. But in this same way, did Beneli entice and convince Cain that he should reject the words of Abel and rise up and murder him.

73 And they shall teach unto you their precepts that justify the wickedness of your ways. And they shall justify unto you the need for your churches and your temples and the fine things of the world. And they shall do that which hath been done by all the leaders of religions that are not set up according to the principles and laws of the gospel of Christ.

74 And now, I, Moroni, have shown unto you the wickedness of some of those who profess to be the followers of Christ, but deny the power of Christ, which power can only come by keeping the commandments of his gospel. But the whole world lieth under sin and shall come under severe condemnation, except that the children of men shall repent and turn their hearts towards the gospel that was given unto their fathers. And if they do not do this, then the whole earth will be destroyed at his coming.

75 And this is what was meant by the prophet Malachi, of whom the Lord spake when he visited my fathers in the land of Bountiful. And he said unto them: Remember ye the law of Moses, my servant, which I commanded unto him in Horeb for all Israel, with the statutes and judgments.

76 Behold, I will send you Elijah the prophet before the coming of the dreadful day of the Lord;

77 And he shall turn the heart of the fathers to the children, and the heart of the children to their fathers, lest I come and smite the earth with a curse.

78 And now, I, Moroni, ask of you: What was the law of Moses with it statutes and judgments which the Lord had given unto Moses in the land of Horeb? Yea, even that law that was given unto him upon the mount? I say unto you, it was the law of the gospel, or the words of Christ, who was the giver of this law.

79 And when Moses descended down from upon the mount and witnessed the great wickedness of the children of Israel, he threw down the law and gave unto them a lower law, which was a law of sacrifice and ordinances and rituals that pointed them towards the higher law, or in other words, the law of the gospel.

80 And when Jesus came into the world, he testified unto the people that he had come to fulfill the law which Moses had given unto the children of Israel. And he gave unto them the exact same law, or the exact same gospel, that he had given unto Moses before the rebellion of the children of Israel.

81 And this same law that he gave unto the children of Israel, he did give unto the Jews at Jerusalem. And this same law was given unto my fathers, and this law was also given unto others who are not of the house of Israel, but who dwell upon the earth in other parts that were unknown at the time of my fathers. Yet he had received a commandment of the Father to give these peoples the law of the gospel also. And this he did according to their language and their culture and according to their understanding.

82 And in the last days, the world shall have this gospel preached unto all peoples throughout the world. And it shall be carried unto all the ends of the world until all have heard it according to their own language and their own understanding.

83 And those of you who belong to this great church which is called after the name of Jesus Christ, who believe that it is by your words that the world shall receive these things, I say unto you, that it is because of your pride that ye believe these things. For when this gospel shall come unto you by way of the record of my father, behold, in that day, this same gospel shall already be among many of the peoples of this earth. And because it was given unto them according to their own traditions and customs and understanding, ye shall not recognize it. But if it teacheth the law of the gospel, it is recognized by God.

84 And now I would that all the world should have the words of this gospel and live by the commandments which are given therein, which commandments not only shall save you in the kingdom of God, but shall bring peace and happiness upon the entire earth.

85 And this gospel was taught to the children of Adam in the beginning in such a way that they could not misunderstand that which he spoke. Therefore, I return once again unto the words of Adam, according as they are given by the brother of Jared upon the record that he caused to be written. For they are plain and simple and easy to the understanding of the children of men, and in this way, hath the Lord commanded me to present these things.

CHAPTER 19

Adam explains in plainness the law of the gospel and the commandments of Jesus Christ. Love your neighbor as yourself. He explains the sacredness and importance of fidelity in marriage.

AND Adam continued his teachings, saying: Our Eternal Mothers taught us that we must obey the laws of the kingdom of God in order to ensure that we would be guaranteed the happiness that each of us desired for ourselves.

2 And now, I would that ye should know that these laws were also given unto your mother Eve and me upon our expulsion from the garden of Eden. Behold, these laws are eternal and are the same in the world in which our Eternal Parents reside, as well as in all the kingdoms that exist. And these laws ensure order in the universe; and that the end of these laws, which

is happiness, may be realized by all those subjected to these laws.

3 And if ye abide by these laws throughout the days of your probation upon this earth, then ye shall also have peace and order among you here. And for this purpose were they given unto us after we left the garden of Eden.

4 And these laws are based upon one great law which encompasseth all of the commandments that God hath given us. Yea, it encompasseth all of the commandments that shall ever be given unto you and your children forever.

5 And this is the law on which all other commandments are based, that was given unto us by the Lord, even that ye should do unto others what ye would have them do unto you.

6 Now, from this law the Lord hath given us specific instructions, or commandments, that we must follow to accomplish the purpose of this law.

7 For he hath commanded us that we should not be angry one with another; and that we should have a respect for the opinions of each other; and rejoice in the freedom that we each have to express our own opinion without the fear of repression or anger from another.

8 For this anger can cause us to strike out at our neighbors and harm them for that in which we feel that they have wronged us. And why is it that we feel that they have wronged us? Is it not that they do that which doth not agree with us? And why should we believe that our opinion of that which they think or do, is that which is right? Yea, it might be right for us, but might not be right for our neighbor.

9 And this anger can escalate and cause ye to strike out against your neighbor. Now I say unto you, that this is most abominable before God, even that ye should touch your neighbor without first receiving the permission to do so. For upon doing so, ye have taken away the free agency of your neighbor. For they have the right not to be touched by you, if it so be their desire.

10 And the eternal law that is violated by anger, is the law of free agency, which guaranteeth to each of us the right to act according to the desires of our hearts. And according to this law, ye have the right to become angry with your neighbor if that be your desire, even though your desire would be contrary to the commandments of God. But ye do not have the right to strike out in anger and harm another. For your neighbor did not use his free agency to desire that ye should strike him.

11 Therefore, ye have been commanded to respect one another and give unto each other this worthy respect that each of us deserveth. And ye should not be angry because ye do not understand that which your neighbor doeth with his free agency. For he will be held accountable for that which he doeth, and ye will not be held accountable, therefore, why should ye be angry?

12 And the Lord hath commanded us to have kind thoughts towards each other, and to not be involved in rumors or gossip in any manner concerning another. For if we, with our own eyes, do not see that which our neighbor hath done, then why think ye that ye can trust the words of another to tell you the truth regarding that which they claim they have seen? For that person who is making an account unto you of the actions of another would not do so unless he was angry with another. For what other purpose would there be a reason for rumor and gossip, except to make an account of those actions with which we do not agree?

13 And the Lord hath commanded us to refrain from listening to those who would make a bad account of the actions of another. And he would that we should know, that even if the account of these actions is true, we should respect that this person hath his free agency to act. And he hath commanded us not to become angry when another person useth his free agency to act according to his will.

14 For our Father allowed Lucifer and those that followed after him to act according to the laws of free agency. And He did not become angry with them, but He loved them and blessed them. Nevertheless, He was bound by the eternal laws of heaven in the limit of that which He could do to save them, they having acted according to the law, using their own free agency.

15 And nothing good can come from an angry heart; for he who is angry placeth his spirit in a state of rebellion with his body, and for this reason, the body reacteth to the anger of the spirit, thus causing sickness and poor health.

16 And the Lord hath given this commandment unto us that there might not arise contentions and disputations among us. For where there are contentions and disputations, war soon followeth, and many souls are sent home to the God who gave them life unprepared for the state in which they shall be received.

17 And it hath been with great sadness that I have watched death by the hand of another enter in among you because of the anger of which I have spoken. For even my beloved son Cain did submit to the anger of his heart and murdered his brother Abel. And that day I lost two sons. For it became necessary that I banish my beloved son Cain and his wives and his sons and daughters from among us, that we might guard ourselves against these terrible things.

18 And I would that ye should know that I counseled with Cain and commanded him that he should repent of the thing which he had done. But his heart was hardened against my words, and he would not give heed to the tenderness of my love for him. And he kept the anger that he felt for his brother inside of him and would not release it from his soul.

19 And the Lord hath commanded us that if we have something amiss between each other, that we should reconcile our differences between ourselves in love, not allowing anger to control us and cause us to hate.

20 And it is also with great sorrow that I was forced to construct prisons among us wherein we could hold those who would not give heed unto the commandments of the Lord, and who could not control their anger. And in these prisons, I have caused that they should be taught and counseled and have shown unto them a greater love than that which they experience without the walls of the prisons, that they might know in what way they should act when they are released from these prisons.

21 For if these are imprisoned because of their anger, and are therefore shown greater examples of anger and hate within prison, then when they are released, they shall be much worse off than when they first entered into prison. Thus have I commanded our prisons to be places of instruction and love and tender feelings, that they who are therein might have an example set for them.

22 And the Lord hath commanded us that we should not return evil for evil, but that we should return good unto all. For this is what we would have others do unto us. For when your neighbor doeth something evil unto you, he doth not believe at the moment that he is doing this thing unto you that his actions are wrong. For if he believed that his actions were wrong at the time that he doeth evil unto you, or if he believed that his actions were evil, then he would not have done this thing unto you.

23 And Satan hath been given power to tempt us and cause us to take that which is good as something that is evil; and likewise he causeth us to take that which is evil as something that is good. And in the moment that our neighbor is enticed to do evil unto us, Satan can tempt him, and cause him to justify this evil thing as a thing that is good at that moment. Nevertheless, Satan doth not have the power to tempt us beyond our ability to resist him, thus making us fully responsible for our own actions.

24 But because of the power of Satan, and the weakness of our neighbor in resisting his enticements, many times our neighbor will do evil unto us believing that it is good. And if it so be that we do evil back to him, even though at the moment we might justify it as that which is good—because of the thing that he hath done unto us—we have disobeyed the commandments of the Lord.

25 And the Lord gave us this commandment, saying: Behold, I say unto you, that ye shall not resist evil, but whosoever shall smite thee on thy right cheek, turn to him the other also.

26 And if any man will sue thee at the law and take away thy coat, let him have thy cloak also. And whosoever shall compel thee to go a mile, go with him twain.

27 For there have been many of you who have come before the judges that I have caused to be set up among you to administer the laws that we have established among us to maintain peace and order. And ye bring unto them grievances against your neighbor. Now, when ye do this ye have already broken the commandments of God in that ye have become angry with your neighbor and have the desire to take the matter of your anger against him before a judge. And in this ye do sin. But this is not the end of your sin, for ye cause him whom you have sued to also sin, because in his anger, he will defend himself before the judge.

28 And no good can come of the grievance between you. But the Lord hath commanded any of you who are taken before a judge by your neighbor who hath a grievance against you, to give unto your neighbor all things that he hath asked of you in his grievance against you. In other words, he hath commanded you to not defend yourself, but to submit to the demands of the grievance.

29 And if ye submit to the demands of the grievance against you, then ye are not angry because of it. And if ye give what is asked of you by your neighbor, then ye have stopped the cause of the anger that your neighbor hath against you.

30 And if ye are struck by your neighbor, and ye return the blow unto him, then ye are angry when ye deliver this blow unto him. And in his anger he will return again and strike you. And then the anger of both of you will rise and cause that ye both shall sin before God, even until ye have committed the most grievous sin before Him, even the sin of murder.

31 Therefore, the Lord hath commanded you to turn the other cheek that your neighbor may strike you again in his anger. But ye shall not be angry and strike back. And when ye have offered both of your cheeks unto him that he may strike them, then the end of his anger might be satisfied and both your lives may be saved.

32 And the Lord hath commanded us, saying: Behold I say unto you, love your enemies, bless them that curse you, do good to them that hate you and pray for them who despitefully use you and persecute you, that ye may be the children of your Father who is in heaven.

33 Now, this commandment which he hath given unto us cannot be given with any more plainness than that which the Lord hath spoken.

34 Behold, we are commanded to love each other, in spite of what might be done unto us. For are we not all brothers and sisters who belong to the same Father who hath created us? And doth not the Father love each of us the same? Yea, I know that the Father loveth each of us the same, for He is no respecter of persons and loveth the sinner like unto the prophet. And he loveth Satan as he loveth each of us, for behold, Satan was our brother in the beginning.

35 And we have been commanded to do good in all situations, and love our enemies as well as our friends. And it is easy to love our friends, for even the most evil among us love their friends and hate their enemies.

36 But a sure judge of the righteousness of a man or woman is not in how they love their friends, but in how they love and treat their enemies. And if there are any among you who hate another, then what reward have ye when ye love your friends? For ye shall be loved also by your friends, and this is your reward. But when ye love your enemies, then they will not return unto you this love, but your reward will be given unto you by God.

37 And now my beloved children, I would that ye should understand that this flesh meaneth nothing before God, but that which is in the flesh is of God. And if ye lose this flesh by obeying the commandments of God, then by losing this flesh ye shall be received by God. But if ye keep this flesh because ye have disobeyed the commandments of God, then ye will not be received by God, but will receive the rewards of the flesh, which rewards are contrary to the happiness of God.

38 And I know that when my son, Cain, confronted his brother, Abel, in the field, his brother did not become angry with him, nor did he fight back to save his life. But in his final words, he blessed his brother Cain and forgave him for that which he was about to do unto him. And my son, Abel, was received by God and given a just reward.

39 And Cain hath received a just recompense for that which he hath done. And his reward was that of the flesh, which flesh became his curse and caused him to lose the happiness that he could have enjoyed among us if he would have obeyed the commandments of God.

40 And if your neighbor riseth up against you to take your life, trust in the commandments of God, and bless your neighbor and do not fight against him. And if ye will do this, ye shall be received by God. And if ye defend yourself and take up arms against your neighbor, then ye shall gain the reward of the flesh. And this reward shall be the continual hatred and anger that shall exist among you for many generations. And there shall be no peace among you.

41 And I ask of you, Is it not better that ye die without anger at the hand of your enemy and be received by God, than it is to be slain in anger in a war against him? For in one instance ye shall die in righteousness; and in the other ye shall die in your sins. And if ye believe that by your strength ye can slay your enemy before he slayeth you, then ye are preparing the way whereby the war that ye have caused shall be the means of slaying many of your sons and daughters by the hand of the sons and daughters of the enemy that ye have slain.

42 And if ye have hate towards another, ye shall not experience the state of happiness with the Father that He hath promised you after ye are dead. For ye will be in the spirit world with those whom ye have hated. And in that world, ye shall not have the flesh that ye have at this time. And without this flesh, what cause can ye give unto your anger for another? And your anger shall cause you to remain in a state of misery, and without the flesh, ye will be unable to act upon this anger.

43 And ye shall see all of your brothers and sisters and realize that we all share the same Eternal Parents. And ye shall realize that ye have disobeyed the commandments that They have given unto you concerning the way that ye should act towards each other. And do ye think that ye can exist in a state of happiness knowing these things?

44 Therefore hath the Lord given unto us these commandments that we might live together in peace and harmony, one with another, enjoying the wonderful blessings that the Father hath provided for us as His children in His eternal worlds.

45 And if we do not learn these commandments and we are not able to abide by them forever, then we will not be able to dwell in His kingdom. For He alloweth none who do not obey His commandments to enter therein.

46 And He hath commanded us, saying: Verily, verily, I say unto you that ye judge not, that ye be not judged. For with what judgment ye judge, ye shall be judged; and with what measure ye mete, it shall be measured to you again.

47 And why beholdest thou the mote that is in the eye of thy brother, but considerest not the beam that is in thine own eye. Or how wilt thou say to thy brother: Let me pull the mote out of thine eye, and behold, a beam is in thine own eye?

48 Thou hypocrite, first cast the beam out of thine own eye; and then shalt thou see clearly to cast the mote out of the eye of thy brother.

49 Now, this doth not mean that the Lord doth not want us to discern between good and evil and choose the good over the evil and cling to it. But who among us hath the right to determine what is good and what is evil? For unto some what is evil might be good unto others. And to others, what is evil might be good unto some. Therefore, if we must judge the actions of others, we must make a righteous judgment.

50 But I say unto you, my dear children, that it is better that ye do not judge at all, but leave all judgment to our Father, who hath created us all, and hath given us our free agency to choose for ourselves that which is good and that which is evil. And He loveth all of His children, whether their actions be good or whether they be evil, He loveth them the same.

51 For what think ye, that ye are better fathers than our Father in heaven? And if one of your children doeth evil in your judgment, do ye love him less than those of your children that do that which ye judge to be good? And if ye, being evil fathers, desire good for your children, then how much more would our Father, who is righteous, desire good for all of His children?

52 And it is a hard thing that ye should determine what is good and what is evil on your own accord. For ye know not the circumstance in which the action of another hath taken place; and therefore, ye have no way to judge righteously whether or not this action is good or evil. For in one circumstance the action could be good, but in another circumstance it could be evil.

53 And if ye judge an action of another to be evil, and it is actually good, then the condemnation resteth upon your shoulders for the judgment ye have rendered. And if ye judge an action of another to be good, and it is actually evil, then this condemnation also resteth upon your shoulders.

54 For if ye judge the action of another, and ye have determined in yourselves that this action is evil, then ye shall show prejudice and bias against this action, which prejudice and bias cause you to have anger against this person.

55 And with this anger, ye have sealed yourselves up to the prison, or the state of misery in the spirit world of which I have spoken. And if ye find out after death that the action that ye have judged was not an evil action, but a righteous action, then ye will not have the power to reconcile with him whom ye have misjudged in the flesh—because ye are in the spirit—and a recompense for prejudice and bias and anger cannot be given in the spirit world. And ye shall not come out of this prison, or in other words, ye shall remain in this state of misery, until the consequences of your judgment hath ended in the flesh.

56 And now, my children, I shall give unto you an example of that which I have spoken, so that ye shall not be confused in this thing. For I have seen this among you, even this judgment which ye have made of something that is good as being evil, and because of this thing that I have seen, and the judgments ye have made, there is much contention among you, and there will be many of you who shall suffer because of these things in the spirit prison as I have explained it unto you.

57 Behold, there are those among you who have condemned others in that which they eat and drink. Yea, there are those of you who have cursed your neighbors because they eat the flesh of beasts and cook their food, which the eating of flesh and cooking are contrary to the strict laws of health that the Lord hath given unto us. And ye believe that because they eat this flesh and cook their food, that they shall be condemned before God and chastised by Him.

58 And in this thing ye have caused much anger and contention among yourselves. But in this thing ye have judged your neighbors incorrectly, and ye have become angry against them and prejudiced your minds and hearts against them that do these things. And your children see your examples and grow up with this prejudice already in their hearts. And this prejudice turneth them cold towards those who do the things that your children have been taught are evil.

59 And because of this anger and this prejudice towards them, ye have caused those who do these things that ye perceive to be evil, to have anger and prejudice towards you. And they also teach their children this prejudice, which divideth us further into families and factions that have anger one towards another. And in this anger ye are disobeying the commandments of God, and not in that which ye eat.

60 For the laws of health associated with that which we should eat, and that which we should abstain from eating, pertain only to this world and our mortal flesh. And those who use their free agency to disobey the laws of health, receive the recompense for their disobedience in this world. And this recompense is the poor health and diminished strength and the disease and pestilence that causeth them to suffer during the days of their probation. But once they are dead, and have cast off the flesh, that is the end of their punishment, and they will receive no further punishment for that which they have chosen to eat and drink.

61 But those of you that have become angry with them and have hardened your hearts against them because of your prejudice and your bias against the things that ye have judged to be evil, will suffer the recompense of your anger, not only in this life, but in the prison of the next as I have explained it unto you.

62 And when, as a spirit, ye observe that your children and their children, even unto many generations, do carry on the hate and the prejudice that ye have caused because of your misjudgment, then ye shall suffer in this state of misery until the end of the cause of this hate and prejudice that ye have taught unto your children.

63 Therefore, my beloved children, love one another and do good to each other. And I would that ye should know that it doth not matter to the

Lord what goeth in the mouth of another according to his free will and choice. But it mattereth to him how ye treat one another, and this is the only thing that mattereth unto him.

64 And I would that ye should remember the things that I have spoken unto you regarding the kingdom of God and the different glories that pertain thereto, which are the glories of happiness that all the children of God shall inherit according to the individual desires of happiness of each.

65 Remember that I have explained unto you that each of us determined before we were born into mortality which of these glories of happiness best suited our own desires of happiness. And this time of probation was the time that we would prove to ourselves that the choice that we have made for ourselves is indeed that which we desire.

66 And since each of our desires of happiness are different, then those things that we believe are good for us, might be things that are evil unto another. And likewise, those things that might be evil for us, might bring happiness to another. And for this reason it would be hard to make a righteous judgment.

67 But the commandments of the Lord that I am giving unto you at this time must be obeyed by all. For they are truly commandments that will bring us the happiness that we all desire. And if another chooseth an action for himself that is not contrary to the commandments of God, even the commandments of His gospel, which are the commandments that I am giving unto you at this time; then that person is justified in this action if it bringeth him joy.

68 And we do not do anything except that we might have joy therein. And the things that we do that do not bring us joy, then we may know for a surety that they are evil to us. And those things that bring us joy, are surely good and righteous to us. But remember again, my beloved children, that what bringeth joy to one person doth not mean that the same joy will be experienced by another.

69 Therefore, I would that ye judge not at all, but let our Lord be the judge of us all. And this is what I have caused to be taught among you, even in the churches that the Lord hath suffered us to establish among us for our sake. Even that all of us shall be brought before the judgment bar of God and be judged according to the commandments that he hath given unto us.

70 And for this reason, I give unto all of you these commandments. And if a commandment is not given by me at this time, then that commandment was not given unto me and your mother Eve by the Lord. And therefore, this commandment cannot be a commandment of God, but is a commandment of men. And if it is a commandment of men, then you will not be held accountable for it at the judgment bar of God.

71 And now I would that ye should beware of the commandments of men, for these commandments of men shall usually lead you away from the commandments of God. Therefore, I speak plainly unto you of those commandments that we have received from the mouth of God.

72 And the Lord commanded us, saying: Thou shalt not commit adultery. And whosoever looketh on a woman, to lust after her, hath committed adultery already in his heart. Behold, I give unto you a commandment, that ye suffer none of these things to enter into your heart.

73 Verily, verily, I say unto you, that whosoever shall put away his wife, saving for the cause of fornication, causeth her to commit adultery; and whoso shall marry her who is divorced, committeth adultery.

74 And now I would that ye should know, that in the garden of Eden the Lord commanded me to cleave unto Eve and become one with her. And I was commanded to care for her and stay at her side all the days of my life. And because she was to be engaged in the bringing forth of children, I was commanded that I should make sure she was provided with those things that she desired to make her happy, and to sustain her life and the lives of our children.

75 And ye are all our children. And ye also know that I have spent all the days of my life in labor to sustain your lives and give unto you those things that make you happy. But in all these things, I have depended upon Eve as my companion, and it is she whom I have been commanded to love and honor. And she hath loved me and honored me all the days of my life, which hath brought me much joy and hath fulfilled my desires of happiness concerning her.

76 But even though I was commanded to love and honor her by the Father, I did not need to be commanded in this thing, for I truly do love her, and it is I that am indebted to the Father because of her.

77 And I have caused to be taught among you that it is not the right of a man to ask that a woman be his wife. For it is the responsibility of a man to live his life honorably, and cause that a woman should desire him. And if the woman hath desired him as her husband, then it is because she believeth that he will fulfill the desires of her happiness.

78 And this is the law of the heavens which I have caused to be taught unto you in mortality, because of the physical strength that a mortal man hath over a woman. For if a man was left to the carnal desires of his heart, then he would force himself upon a woman and cause her to accept him by his brute strength over her. But this thing is most abominable before God, and any man that doeth this thing shall be condemned by God.

79 And again, any man that would do this thing shall not be given the eternal body of a man in the kingdoms of glory that permit this type of body. And only those spirits that are worthy of this body, and desire it to serve others, shall receive this power in the kingdom of God. And those spirits who desire to be women, in this same glory, shall choose for themselves the man that they would have as a husband. And they shall do this according to their knowledge of this man and his righteousness.

80 And I am saddened that there are many of you, my sons, among us, who have corrupted the law of marriage, as I have caused it to be taught unto you. For ye deceive the women, and pretend to be righteous, and pretend that ye are willing to fulfill her desire of happiness, so that the woman will choose you and desire to make you her husband. And ye lust after her and the dowry that is given and not that ye should serve her and provide for her happiness.

81 And because it is by the free will and choice of a woman to make a man her husband, she is bound by the covenant that she shall make unto him. And through this covenant, she hath obligated herself to this man all the days of her life. And for this reason, a man hath no right to put away his wife, if it so be that he accepteth her desire to make him her husband.

82 And a man shall not be compelled in this world or in the next—in the glory that permitteth eternal unions—to accept the desire of a woman. Nevertheless, in the glory of the kingdom of God where these unions are permitted, there will be only righteous men, and a righteous man shall never deny a desirous woman from being his eternal companion. And they shall only desire this union to serve others, for in this, their blessing and their joy are complete.

83 And ye shall not engage in any sexual relations of any kind, even those actions that lead up to the desire of these relations, unless ye have been chosen by a woman to be her husband. And the woman shall remain pure and untouched by other men until the day that she maketh a decision regarding her choice of a husband.

84 For every woman shall one day be the wife of a husband, if she so chooses. And if it so be that a woman commiteth fornication, or anything like unto it, she shall commit adultery against her future husband. And any man that commiteth fornication, or anything like unto it with another woman, hath committed adultery with the future wife of another man, who the woman hath not yet chosen for herself.

85 And if a woman hath committed fornication, or anything like unto it, and maketh a lie to the man that she is desirous to take unto herself as a husband, and presenteth herself as clean and pure before him, then she can be put away, or divorced from him to whom she made the lie. But if that man be a righteous man, then he shall forgive his wife for the things which she hath done before she made the covenant with him. And her sins will be remembered no more before the Lord. And it will be counted unto the man as righteousness.

86 But if he doth not desire to have her as a wife, he shall be justified before the Lord in a divorcement. And likewise also, shall it be for the woman who hath been lied to by a man.

87 And there shall be no other reason that a divorcement shall be given. For this reason, the daughters of God must be cautious, and prove those whom they would have as their husbands. Yea, they must assure themselves that the man whom they choose as their husband is worthy before God. And ye shall test them and see if they live by the commandments of God, and not by the commandments of men. And if they live by the commandments of God, then ye shall receive from them the happiness that ye desire. But if they live by the commandments of men, then ye shall experience misery and strife in a union with them.

88 And there is a sure test, my beloved daughters, that will help you that ye shall know whether a man followeth the commandments of God, or the commandments of men. For behold, it is the natural desire of all men to engage in fornication, and anything like unto it, whenever they are allowed to do so by a woman. Therefore, if a man attempteth fornication with you, or anything like unto it, then ye shall know that he disregardeth the commandments of God and hath followed the instincts of his own carnal desires. And if it so be that ye still desire this man, then you shall experience the strife of which I have spoken, and in the eternal worlds, your union shall not exist.

89 And it shall be that there are very few men who are righteous and are willing to obey the commandments of God in all things. And ye shall realize that if it so be that you depend on the righteousness of men to give you children, then ye would be barren and childless all the days of your life.

90 And if ye are a righteous woman and are desirous to have children, then ye shall be justified in creating these children with an unrighteous man, if it so be that he is chosen by you because ye cannot find a righteous man among you.

91 And if your desires are righteous, then shall the Lord ease the burden of this strife between you and your unrighteous husband, and shall bring you great joy in your posterity. And if ye remain faithful all the days of your life, even that ye keep all the commandments of the Lord, then shall ye be blessed with the choice of a righteous husband in the kingdom of God, if that so be your desire.

92 But if your husband is unrighteous, and obeyeth not the commandments of the Lord in all things, then are ye justified in a divorcement from him. But in all these things ye shall judge only according to the commandments of God, and not according to the commandments of men. Beware that ye are not deceived by men who put themselves up above you and give you commandments that are not of God.

93 Let no man deceive you, and say unto you that the Lord hath commanded him to take another wife unto himself. For the Lord would never command such a thing. For as it hath been explained unto you, it is the choice of a woman to choose a husband. And if a woman cometh unto you and desireth to take your husband also as her own husband, then ye shall have the decision to take her unto yourself as a sister wife to your husband. But if ye do this thing to your sister, then ye must know that she shall be equal to you in the eyes of your husband.

94 And there shall be no man that shall be given the power and authority to give a woman to another man, neither shall the power be given to any to choose a husband for any woman. But unto some, who are righteous men of God, the Lord suffereth to be given the authority to counsel with the women who find themselves without husbands because of the wickedness of men. And it will be given unto this righteous man to seal this covenant before God.

95 And if any woman taketh a sister wife unto herself for her husband, then it will be counted unto her as righteousness before God. But if she doth not allow another woman to take her righteous husband as her own, then it shall not be counted unto her as unrighteous before God. For the Lord delighteth in the chastity and honor of women.

96 Behold, I have been loyal and faithful to Eve all the days of my life. In honor I sustain her and cherish each moment I am blessed with her presence. I have had no lascivious thoughts, and no lustful desires have entered into my heart all the days of my life. And I am one with her. And because of these things, we enjoy a fullness of happiness in the union within which we have been blessed.

97 And now I say unto you, if ye shall love your spouses as we have loved one another, then ye also shall have this joy, which joy causeth the happiness that we share. And because of this happiness, the Lord hath established this union of a man and a woman, and hath given unto us the commandments pertaining to this union that shall be maintained in righteousness. And because of righteousness, this union shall exist in the kingdom of the Father forever.

CHAPTER 20

Adam continues to explain the gospel and the commandments of Jesus Christ. He explains the evil of money and worldly possessions and gives the commandments pertaining to them. He expounds on and explains the evils of the family unit.

And the Lord continued his commandments unto us, saying: Lay not up for yourselves treasures on earth, where moth and rust doth corrupt, and thieves break through and steal; but lay up for yourselves treasures in heaven, where neither moth nor rust doth corrupt, and where thieves do not break through nor steal.

2 For where your treasure is, there will your heart be also. And the light of the body is the eye; if, therefore, thine eye be single, thy whole body shall be full of light. But if thine eye be evil, thy whole body shall be full of darkness. If, therefore, the light that is in thee be darkness, how great is that darkness.

3 No man can serve two masters; for either he will hate the one and love the other, or else he will hold to the one and despise the other. Ye cannot serve God and Mammon.

4 And when we received these commandments from the Lord, we did not understand the meaning of them. For we had no desire for any of the treasures of the earth. Yea, we did not know what we should even consider as treasures of the earth. Therefore, we could not lay up for ourselves those things that we did not understand. Nevertheless, we covenanted to obey this commandment without fully understanding it at the time it was given unto us. And this we did, because of our faith in the word of the Lord.

5 And we remembered the words of Satan when he was cast out of the kingdom of the Father, in which he said that he would take the treasures of the earth, and with gold and silver he would buy up great armies of men, and that he would buy up the means of justice and laws that the children of men would be subjected to through his governments and his religions, and that he would reign with blood and horror upon the earth.

6 And when the Lord gave unto us the Holy Endowment as an instrument to give our children the opportunity to know the plan of salvation that he hath provided for us, we were commanded to demonstrate the great enticement that the treasures of the earth would have upon the souls of the children of God. But even then, we did not fully understand that which was commanded of us.

7 And it was my hope that through my daily administrations among you, and also by the preaching of those who have been given the authority to teach you in the church that the Lord hath suffered to be established among us, that these things might not come to pass among you, in other words, that we might not see the necessity of these commandments.

8 But it was our eldest son Beneli, who first introduced gold and silver among us and deceived his other brothers and sisters, and taught them that these things were precious things of the earth. And as ye have these many years developed a system of money, which is based on these things which ye believe are precious, these commandments have become necessary and vital to our salvation and happiness.

9 For ye have used these things to form inequalities among you. And ye began to covet those things of your neighbor that ye do not possess, which things are not the things of God, and have nothing to do with your eternal salvation. Yea, these things also have nothing to do with the sustaining of your lives upon this earth.

10 For who among you can eat gold and silver and obtain nourishment from them? And can ye form them into raiment that can shield your flesh from the ill effects of the laws of nature? And who among you can find use for them in the construction of your houses in which ye live? Yea, what use do these things have unto you, except to deceive you, and give unto you a means whereby ye might disobey the commandments of God?

11 Behold, in the beginning I taught unto you the law of consecration, which is the law of the Lord pertaining to all of the children of God, and the means whereby all of us receive that which we are in need of, according to our individual needs. And by this law, we existed in peace and harmony with each other, having food and raiment and houses to satisfy the needs of all.

12 And there were no poor or rich among us. For how can there be poor, if there are no rich? And how can one man be considered rich, if he hath only that which he needeth, like unto all those whose needs are also filled? And what purpose would a man gain, if he owned more than that which he needed to sustain his life? The only purpose would be so that he could consume the excess of that which he possesseth on the pride of his heart. And it is this pride in his heart that alloweth him to consider himself rich.

13 And when the pride of his heart hath consumed him, in that he spendeth his days counting his abundance and thinking up ways in which he can increase this abundance, then doth the light which entereth his eye causeth his whole body to be full of darkness. Yea, the obscurity of the darkness within him overcometh any light that he once possessed.

14 And we were commanded from the beginning to work by the sweat of our brow in order to eat the food that would bring us nourishment. And the commandment did not say, that we shall live by the sweat of the brow of our brother, but it said, by the sweat of our own brow.

15 And there are those of you who are rich and have justified your laziness because ye think that ye can take advantage of another because of his words. Or in other words, because he is not as intelligent as you. But this I say unto you, I am equally as intelligent as any of you, and I have worked by the sweat of my own brow all the days of my life. And your mother Eve hath worked along with me at my side. And we are not rich, nor do we have more than that which we need.

16 And because ye have placed value upon gold and silver and other things that ye have made precious among you, ye have caused much misery to come to pass among you. For in the beginning there was no need of a commandment that thou shalt not steal. For everything was provided for and offered free to all without a price. And there were no prices or worth affixed to anything upon this earth.

17 But now ye have placed value upon each other, even that the worth of a man and his trade hath a price. And in this, not only do ye sin in the treatment of each other, but ye sin against God, who hath commanded us to love one another and do unto each other what we would have others do unto us.

18 Now, what man among you would want others to consider you of less value than that value which they consider of themselves? And who among you would want to be known for your little value? And what of those that carry the buckets of our waste and bury them outside of our cities, that we should not behold our waste and cause our cities to stink? Of what value do these have unto us?

19 I say unto you, that I would rather live in a clean city that is unburdened by our waste, than I would in a city, where those therein wear fine linens and clothing where moths make their own waste thereon. And we value the dressmaker and the cobbler more than we value he who carrieth our waste from among us. Yet, if we had not the dressmaker and the cobbler among us, we could make our own clothes, though not finely made as they might be, but sufficient for our needs.

20 And if there were none to carry forth our waste from among us, then our cities would begin to stink and we would suffer because of their absence. So I say unto you, which of these should be of more value unto us?

21 And those of you who think that your

intelligence should be rewarded at a higher value than the work of those that till our fields and harvest the foods that we eat; yea, what think ye, if they became intelligent like unto yourselves, and thought themselves above the sweat that produceth this food? What then would ye eat?

22 Behold, your intelligence cometh from your deceptions and the advantage that ye have taken of others because of their words. For ye have convinced those who carry forth the waste, and also those who bring forth the fruits of the field, that your gold and your silver are most precious and are desirous to possess. And because of your many words and your deceptions, those who work by the sweat of their brow to support you depend on you for this gold and this silver that they might live.

23 And ye have taken that which they produce and have convinced them who have produced it that its worth is less than the worth that ye know it to be. And then in your deception, ye take that which ye have purchased for little, and sell it for much, so that ye might get gain in this profit and add to the abundance that ye already have.

24 And ye enter into covenants with each other that ye might control those who work by the sweat of their brow to support you. And ye have used your gold and your silver to buy protection for your evil plans; and to hire those who make laws and ordinances. And these laws and ordinances assure that ye might continue to get gain without the consequences of the law to interfere with you.

25 And once ye have established these laws among you, ye use these laws to justify your actions. And before long, your whole body shall be full of darkness, according to the words of the Lord, and Oh, how great is that darkness.

26 I would that ye would take away the gold and the silver from among you, so that Satan can have no more power over you. For if the things of this earth have no value to you, except that it be to sustain your lives and give you joy therein, then shall ye begin to lay up for yourselves treasures in heaven, where neither moth nor rust doth corrupt, and where thieves do not break through and steal.

27 And if ye had all things in common, like it was in the beginning; yea, even like unto the church that we have established for your instruction, then there would be no thieves, because there would not be anything to steal. And if the things of the earth had no value, then why would ye keep unto yourself more than what ye needed to sustain your lives?

28 And ye are beginning to establish borders and fences among you. And how do ye think that ye can do these things and comply with the commandments of God? Behold, the earth is not ours to own, for we will soon die and leave it to another and take none of it with us. Then what is the cause in which ye think ye are justified in the ownership of land, which doth not belong to you?

29 And if it doth not belong to you, then ye are thieves who claim it as your own. And if ye are thieves who have claimed it as your own, then ye give the right unto others to enter in among you and take that which is not yours to have. And this will be the cause of much war and contention among you. And with these wars and this contention cometh the anger that the Lord hath commanded us not to have in our hearts.

30 And this desire to own that which is not yours hath caused you to divide yourself throughout the land into families and communities. And when ye have thus divided yourselves, ye cause your thoughts to center on your families instead of on all people, who are your brothers and your sisters. And this family unit shall be the cause of much heartache and contention among you.

31 For ye have begun to believe that your families are more important than the rest of your brothers and sisters, who are your neighbors. And because ye believe this, ye shall concentrate all of your efforts on acquiring the things of the world to care for your family in the flesh. And your children shall become selfish and centered in themselves because of the example of the things that ye have shown unto them.

32 And they shall begin to think that they have no other brothers and sisters, except those with whom they share the same parents. And they shall begin to believe that their family unit is better than that of their neighbor, and that they should put their own family and its needs above the needs of their neighbor.

33 And this belief shall cause pride to overcome them; and they shall begin to think of themselves above all others who do not belong to their own family. And because of this pride, family shall fight against family for the land that ye have divided amongst yourselves for the purpose of providing for the needs of your own family.

34 And ye shall believe that your needs are greater than the needs of your neighbors. And ye shall withhold your substance from your neighbors, and justify the withholding of your substance, because ye believe that if ye give unto them, ye shall not have enough for your family.

35 And because of this family unit in which ye have divided yourselves, ye shall begin to put even more value upon your own lives in comparison to the lives of your neighbors. And ye shall strive to be rich and have more than others. And in your desire to be rich, ye shall make many of your brothers and your sisters—yea, even your brothers and your sisters before God—poor.

36 And ye shall begin to teach your children to focus their lives on learning the ways of the world, that they might get gain therein, and receive the honors and praises of men for the gain that they have received. And your children shall begin to search for gold and silver, and for fine linens, and all the fine things of the world. And they shall make these things their idols, for they shall fall down before them and worship them, in that their hearts and desires are continually focused upon them.

37 And ye have already begun to teach your children that these family units are sanctioned by God, and that it is the most important unit among you. And ye believe that the things that ye have acquired of the world are the blessings of God, and that He hath given you these things because of your righteousness in your families.

38 But I say unto you, these family units are an abomination before God. Behold, they divide the children of God against each other and cause the spirit of God to withdraw itself from you. And when the spirit of God hath withdrawn itself from among you, then ye are left unto yourselves. And when ye are left unto yourselves, Satan beginneth to have power over you.

39 And when Satan hath power over your hearts, he beginneth to convince you that that which is evil and of him, is good, and that which is good and of God, is evil. And in this way he misleadeth you and lulleth you away into carnal security, carefully leading your souls away from God and down to hell.

40 And this hell is not a place where ye shall go after this life, for all of us will return to the spirit world from whence we came. But this hell is a state of being which is either on this earth, or in the spirit world.

41 And it is easy to tell whether or not a thing is from God, or if it is from Satan. For the things of God shall lead you to do the will of God. And when ye do the will of God, then ye are happy. And if ye are not happy, then ye are not doing the will of God. And Satan will allow you to rejoice in your wickedness for a time, but he will not stand by you for long. And when he turneth his back on you, ye shall no longer remain happy in the evil thing that ye are doing.

42 And I know that ye do rejoice in the concept of your family unit, and that ye rejoice in your children, and your spouses, and in the things of this world that ye have accumulated to support them in their needs. And because ye find joy therein, ye believe that these things must be from God. But I say unto you, that these things are not from God. And if ye continue in these things, or in other words, the division of yourselves into separate family units, ye shall reap the recompense of this sin.

43 For once ye have divided yourselves into families, then ye shall divide yourselves into communities of families; and once ye have divided yourselves into communities of families, then ye shall divide yourselves into countries and nations. And ye shall place borders around the lands of your nations, and cause that any that enter into the borders of your nations to be bound by the laws which ye have set for this nation, which laws are based on the things that ye have taught your children in the family units that ye have created.

44 And in your desire to protect your families and those things in which ye believe, which things ye have convinced yourself are from God, ye shall raise up armies and means of force that shall protect the borders of your lands; and ye shall cause to be killed any whom ye believe shall threaten the family units that ye have set up among yourselves.

45 And in anger shall nation rise against nation. And ye shall have diverse wars and contentions among you. And these wars and these contentions shall be caused because ye think in and of yourselves that ye are more righteous than those of other nations. And these other nations are also created by family units, which believe differently than you do, and which also think that the beliefs of their families are more righteous than yours.

46 And ye shall follow the leaders of these nations, and they shall lead you into battle against your brothers and sisters. And ye shall kill them in anger. And they, in recompense for what ye have done unto them, shall kill you. And if it so be that they are a nation of people who do not have the strength to kill you, then their children and the children of their children, even for many generations, shall wait until the time that they are strong enough to rise up against you, and then they shall make war against you because of the things that ye have done unto their families.

47 And ye shall begin to follow the doctrine and commandments of men, and shall cause to be established among you divers religions and priesthoods that conform to the beliefs that ye have taught your children, which beliefs are contrary to the gospel and the commandments of God that I am giving unto you at this time.

48 And these religions, and these churches, and the leaders that ye follow, shall cause you to hold fast to the family divisions that ye have created for yourselves. And they shall preach gentle words unto you that will keep you lulled away in carnal security, while many of your brothers and sisters who live in other families in other nations beyond the borders of your own, shall suffer because of you.

49 But ye shall not concern yourselves about those in another nation, or in another family, because they are not of your family, and they do not believe the same things that ye believe. And because they do not believe the same things that ye believe, ye shall consider them unworthy of the blessings of God, which blessings ye believe are the things of this world. And ye believe that these blessings of God are your gold and your silver and all of the precious things that ye have accumulated for your family.

50 And then shall the words of Lucifer, which he spoke unto the Father in the beginning, come to pass, in which he said: And with the enmity that thou hast placed between me and the children of men, I will take the treasures of the earth, and with gold and silver I will buy up armies and the means of force and priesthood and religions, and I will reign with blood and horror on this earth.

51 Now, I would that ye should understand what Lucifer meant by this enmity that the Lord hath placed between him and the children of men, which are all of us. For Lucifer had a desire to gain glory for himself. And this is contrary to the first law and principle of the government of the heavens that stateth that this government shall never be self-serving, and it shall never act in and of itself and of its own accord for the sake of its own existence.

52 And the plan that Lucifer had presented to us as spirits was rejected by the majority of us, and was a plan that could not be accepted because of its violation of the eternal laws of heaven that cannot be violated. But there were many of the spirits that desired the things which Lucifer presented unto them. And these followed him and were cut off from the kingdom of God at that time.

53 And they have been with us here upon this earth in the realm of the spirits since the beginning. And Lucifer hath also been here among us. And he tempted Eve, and she gave in to his enticements and disobeyed the commandments of God. But Satan, as he is known among us in mortality, justified that which he had done unto Eve, claiming that it was necessary in order to bring about the mortality of the children of God, as it had been done in other worlds.

54 But Satan did these things of his own

accord, and wanted the glory for himself. And he did these things that he might corrupt and possess the bodies that the Father hath created for us.

55 And Satan hath his own kingdom and receiveth his own glory upon this earth among those that follow him and keep his commandments, which are the same commandments and precepts of men. And his kingdom consisteth of all of you who disobey the commandments of God and follow his enticements.

56 And God said unto Lucifer: I will place enmity between thee and the seed of the woman. Thou mayest have power to bruise his heel, but he shall have power to crush thy head.

57 And now, my beloved children, I have caused these things to be taught unto you in the Holy Endowment that ye all have the opportunity to receive. But many of you think this endowment is foolish, and ye do not understand the things that are taught therein. And there are many of you who have received this endowment, but do not ask for understanding and have confused yourselves because of it.

58 And if ye would have inquired of me, I would have revealed unto you all of its meanings, for it is not a secret thing among us and hath been taught openly in the churches that I have caused to be established among you. But many of you do not attend these churches and listen to the words of the leaders, who have been given the authority to teach these things unto you.

59 And ye would not need these leaders or these churches if it were that ye obeyed the commandments of God. And if ye obey the commandments of God, ye shall have the Spirit of God to be with you. And by this same Spirit, ye shall know the truth of all things.

60 But I would that ye should understand these things, and also that ye should understand the commandments of God that ye must live by in order to have the Spirit as your constant companion all the days of your lives. And for this purpose have I gathered you together, even that I might teach these things unto you.

61 And as it is that your feet take you through this life, and make a record, as it were, of all those things that ye do during your life; yea, even that your feet carry you forth unto works of righteousness or works of evil, according to the law of free agency which hath been given unto you; therefore, Satan hath power to bruise your heel, in that he causeth you often to do evil, and bruiseth the works that ye do during the days of your probation.

62 And these bruises can cause you to stumble and walk unsurely in the straight and narrow path that the Father hath prescribed for us and hath directed us to follow. And Satan hath been given power to bruise our heels all the days of our lives.

63 But in the end; yea, when we finally come to an understanding of the righteousness of the Father and the commandments that he hath given unto us; then shall we have power to crush the head of Satan, or in other words, destroy his kingdom with righteousness.

64 And the Lord hath placed enmity between Satan and us. And this enmity that he hath placed between us is the feelings that we receive when we work righteousness, in that we are happy and feel joy. And this enmity is also the feelings that we receive when we do evil, in that we are miserable, where there is an absence of joy, in other words, this enmity is our conscience.

65 And Satan hath taken these feelings, or this enmity, and hath deceived us into thinking that evil is good and good is evil. And he hath accomplished this with gold and silver and the fine things of the earth. And he hath done this with the families in which he hath caused you to divide, so that ye shall hate one another, and put yourselves above others.

66 For when ye are engaged in the pursuit of the things of the world, or Mammon as it hath been called, then ye make that pursuit your God, and it is from this that ye receive your happiness. And ye are happy when ye think on the things that ye own, even your houses, and your clothes and your possessions, and all the things to which ye have given a value that do not sustain your life—even a life that requireth only food, and simple raiment, and a simple shelter to survive.

67 And ye are happy when ye see your families prospering and enjoying the things that ye have provided for them. And ye take no thought of others, for in the happiness of your families ye find your joy.

68 And ye find joy in your religions and your beliefs and in the leaders that teach you the things that ye want to hear, even preaching those things that support you in that which ye believe. And ye shall find happiness and joy in the pride of your nations, and your countries, and the armies, and the means of force that protect you within the borders thereof.

69 And in this way hath Satan used the enmity, that the Lord hath placed between him and us, to deceive us and lull us away into carnal security. And he lulleth us carefully, without our knowing, and leadeth us down into the misery of hell.

70 And I would that ye should know, my beloved children, that any institution that is set up among you that shall be a cause of your disobedience of the commandments of God, shall also cause your destruction.

71 And it is the commandment of the Lord that we should love each other according to the eternal laws of heaven. For it was according to these laws that we were created. And we are all the children of the same Eternal Father. And He hath used these same laws, by which He also liveth, to afford us the opportunity to become like Him and live forever in happiness, according to our desires of happiness.

72 And all of the unions that we create among ourselves, as well as the covenants, contracts, bonds, obligations, oaths, vows, performances, connections, associations, or expectations that we enter into during the days of our probation, have an end when we are dead.

73 And after we are dead, we shall be judged according to the works that we have done, even according to our obedience and conformity to the laws of heaven. And these same laws exist forever in the eternal worlds that have existed long before this mortal state in which we find ourselves. And these same laws shall exist in the eternal worlds after this mortal state, even forever.

74 And all things that are not established by the Lord, according to his word, which word is given according to these eternal laws of heaven, shall be thrown down and shaken and destroyed, and shall not remain after we are dead.

75 And these family units in which ye have divided yourselves are not according to the word of the Lord; and he hath commanded us against such things. Therefore, they are not eternal and shall not last after ye are dead.

76 And what think ye shall come to pass when ye are dead? Do ye think that in the kingdom of the Father we shall be divided into families? Do ye believe that ye shall take the pride which ye feel for your spouses and your children into the kingdom of God, and claim your stake there? I say unto you that ye shall not do any such thing.

77 For those of your own household are also your brothers and your sisters before God. And have ye not heard my words and my teachings concerning the creation and growth of a spirit? Did I not speak clearly unto you, and teach you that there existeth no marriage or families in the kingdom of the Father? For there are no such beings as male spirits or female spirits.

78 Yea, there are those spirits which were given a male body according to the flesh, and there were also those spirits that were given a female body according to the flesh. But in the kingdom of the Father there were no male spirits, neither were there females spirits, but we were all children of the Father, and had not yet determined for ourselves which gender we would take upon ourselves to bring us the happiness that each of us desired.

79 And when we return again to the kingdom of the Father, or in other words, to the spirit world from whence we came, we will return again as spirits without a gender.

80 And after the resurrection, there will be very few among us who will be blessed with the exalted bodies that the Gods possess, which bodies are male and female, and are given according to the eternal laws that govern the Celestial glory in the kingdom of our Father. And these bodies are given for the purposes of creation, and also for the fullness of joy of those who deserve the power that these bodies possess.

81 And I say unto you, that except ye abide by the commandments and laws of God, ye cannot attain to this glory. For strait is the gate, and narrow the way that leadeth unto the exaltation and the power of the continuation of lives, and few there be that find it. And ye do not find it because ye know not God. But if ye receive the commandments of God in the flesh, and abide by them, then shall ye know Him. And if ye know Him, ye shall receive your exaltation, and ye shall be in the same kingdom of glory in which God dwelleth.

82 For behold, this is eternal lives; even that ye might know the only wise and true God, who is our Father.

83 And broad is the way, which leadeth to destruction, and many there be who go in thereat; and this according to the commandments and the words that the Lord hath given unto us.

84 And because Satan hath entered in among us, there shall be many that come in among you in the clothing of sheep, but inwardly are ravening wolves. These shall call themselves prophets of God and set themselves up as your leaders and begin to teach unto you the flattering words that ye would desire of them.

85 And the Lord hath shown unto us the way in which we can judge these who would make such a claim. And I say unto you, that I will show you a sure way that ye might know how to judge a false prophet. For ye shall judge him by his works. And the flatteries of his mouth shall not uncover his unrighteousness. For Satan shall inspire him to speak unto you according to the peace that you have been taught shall be given unto you by the Holy Spirit. And Satan shall mimic this feeling and cause you to believe the words of the false prophet, as if they were the words of God.

86 And ye shall judge all men according to the commandments of God that I am giving to you this day, and which shall be taught unto you in the same likeness and in the same words by all the true prophets of God. And a true prophet of God will not add to or take away from these commandments that I have given unto you, and which I shall continue to give unto you.

87 And I know that God himself, shall come down among those of our posterity in the flesh. And when he is among them, he shall be known as the Son of God. And he shall be the Son of God. But because the Son shall be in the exact likeness of the Father, and shall have the power and authority of the Father, he shall be our God.

88 And he shall also give unto you the commandments that I am giving to you this day, which are the exact commandments that your mother Eve and I received from him after we left the garden of Eden. And these shall be the same words that he shall always speak unto the children of men, regardless in what time period they are given. Whether they be given unto them today, or yesterday, or tomorrow, they are the same.

89 For these commandments are eternal. And if they are eternal, then they are from God, and shall last beyond the days of our probation, even forever.

90 And any of those among you who claim that they are prophets of God, shall teach these things unto you. And again, I say unto you, that they shall not add to or take away from, nor shall they change these commandments in any way. And if they add to, or take away, or cause any of these things to be changed, then ye shall know of a surety that these are not men of God, but are false prophets.

91 And there shall be many false prophets who shall come among you preaching what they claim to be the words and commandments of God. And many of you shall be deceived by their words. And ye shall be deceived because ye do not keep the commandments of God. And many of you shall think that the commandments of God are too hard to keep, and that they do not bring you the joy that ye have been promised.

92 Ye shall say that it is vain to serve God; and what profit is it that we have kept his commandments and have walked mournfully before the Lord all the days of our lives? And we call the proud happy; yea, they that work wickedness are set up, and they who tempt God are even delivered in their time of need.

93 And in this way Satan shall have power over you and lull you away, in that ye will begin to believe that there is no heaven, nor is there a hell, and that there is no Satan, therefore there is no God. And many of you shall say amongst yourselves: Let us eat and drink and be merry,

for tomorrow we die, but it shall be well with us.

94 For we will fear God. And by fearing Him, He will justify us in committing a little sin; yea, we can lie a little and take advantage of our neighbor because of his words; and we can dig a pit for our neighbor, so that our own family might not fall therein. And if we do all these things, and tomorrow we die, it shall be well with us. And God will beat us with a few stripes, but in the end, we will be saved in His kingdom.

95 And these things shall be taught unto you by those who are false prophets among you. Therefore, I would that ye should know these things, that ye might not be deceived by them.

96 And do not think that when ye stand before the judgment bar of God that these things will not be known. For ye shall know those things which ye did that were contrary to the commandments of God. But even so, there will be many of you who shall say unto the Father in that day: Oh, Father, have we not prophesied in Thy name, and in Thy name cast out the evil that is among us, and in Thy Holy Name done many wonderful works? Did we not take unto ourselves wives as Thou hast commanded us and brought up unto Thee many children whom we have taught to honor and respect Thee? And in the abundance of that which we took from the earth, did we not dedicate a portion thereof unto Thee?

97 And then will the Father say unto them: Ye did nothing in my Holy Name. For of all the things that I have required of you, ye have done none. For I was hungered and ye gave me no food; and I was thirsty and ye gave me no drink; and I was a stranger and ye took me not in, and was naked and ye clothed me not; I was sick and ye did not attend unto me. And I was imprisoned and ye visited me not.

98 And then ye shall answer the Father, saying: Oh, Father, when did we see Thee hungered, or athirst, or a stranger, or naked, or sick, or in prison, and did not administer unto Thee? And in all these things have we taken care of the needs of our families as Thou hast commanded us.

99 And when they were hungered, we fed them; and when they were thirsty, we gave them to drink; and when they were naked, we clothed them with all manner of fine clothing; and when they were sick, we administered unto their needs; and if any of them were in prison, we visited them.

100 And strangers we were counseled by our leaders to avoid, lest they come in among us and destroy our families and our beliefs.

101 But Oh, Father, when saw we Thee an hungered, or athirst, or a stranger, or naked, or sick, or in prison, and did not minister unto Thee? For had we known Thee, then we would have given all unto Thee, as Thou hast commanded us.

102 And then shall the Father say unto them: Yea, it is because ye did not know me that ye did not recognize me. Verily I say unto you, inasmuch as ye did it not to one of the least of those among you, ye did it not to me.

103 For behold, ye think that those of your own family are they which are the greatest among you. And ye have given these things unto them. But I did not command you to divide yourselves into these families in which ye have placed your priorities. And those who are the least among you are those who are not of your family, but whom I have commanded you to do unto as ye would have them do unto you.

104 And would ye not want that when ye are hungered, or athirst, or a stranger, or naked, or sick, or in prison, that others would attend to your needs, whether they are members of your family or not?

105 Yea, I never knew you, and you never knew me. For if ye had known me, then ye would have known that I am the Father of all, and that ye are all my children. And I have given you a commandment to do unto all of my children, which include the very least among you.

106 And ye have judged the beggar that is one of the least among you, and have denied him your sustenance because ye have said that he hath brought upon himself his own misery, therefore I will stay my hand and will not give unto him of my food, nor impart unto him of my substance that he may not suffer, for his punishments are just, because he hath offended God in his laziness.

107 And how can ye say that this beggar, who is my child, hath offended me, when ye do not know me? Know ye not that the world that I have caused to be created is for all of my children? And do ye not know, that my kingdom is for those who are the least among you?

108 Yea, blessed are the poor in spirit, for theirs is the kingdom of heaven. And blessed are they that mourn, for they shall be comforted. And blessed are the meek, for they shall inherit the earth when I finish my work thereon. And blessed are they which do hunger and thirst after righteousness, for they shall be filled. And blessed are the merciful, for they shall obtain mercy. And blessed are the peacemakers, for they shall be called the children of God. And blessed are the pure in heart, for they shall see God.

109 And these are those who are the least among you. And they are my children and belong to my family, which is the only family that I have ever caused to be organized among you. And because ye did not keep my commandments, ye are not pure in heart. And because ye are not pure in heart, ye shall not see me, neither shall ye know me. Depart from me ye that work iniquity.

110 And Adam continued his words, saying: And now, my beloved children, see that ye learn these commandments which I have given unto you, and also those which I am about to give unto you. And if ye keep these commandments, ye shall have a pure heart, and ye shall know God, and not be cast out of His presence.

CHAPTER 21

Moroni explains the reason why his writings and the writings of his father, and the words of all prophets of God are similar, if not exact in their wording. He describes and explains the workings of the Urim and Thummim and expounds on the latter day missions of Joseph Smith Jr. and Christopher Marc Nemelka.

AND now I, Moroni, am again constrained by the Spirit to write unto you concerning the manner in which these things are written upon the plates which I have made with my own hands.

2 And I have seen the day that these things shall come unto you. And there shall be many in that day who shall mock these things, and also him by whom these things shall be given unto you. And many of you shall think that these things were copied from the writings of others who have come before us.

3 And I have also seen many of the scriptures which shall come forth unto you. And many of the things that are written upon these plates shall be similar to, if not in the exact likeness of many of those things that have been written by the hand of other prophets of God.

4 And this is the will and the command of the Lord concerning all things that shall be written. For if a man hath the spirit of prophecy, then he shall write the same words, in the same likeness, of all those who have been given this spirit of prophecy by the Lord. And this spirit of prophecy is a gift given unto a chosen vessel who hath been preordained and chosen by the Lord to do the thing that shall be required of him.

5 And there are many gifts of the spirit. To some is given one, and to some is given another, that all the children of God might profit thereby.

6 And again I say unto you that a man must be called by God and anointed to the calling that he shall receive, according to the order of the kingdom of God. And before this world was created, even in the kingdom of God, the plan was set forth, and the prophets of God were foreordained and given their specific mission and calling. And each of us hath been given a time and a season for the fulfilling of our calling.

7 And we belong to the Holy Order of the Son of God. And what one of us believeth, so do the rest, who belong to this Holy Order. Therefore, if the word of God is given by one, then this same word, which is eternal and never changing, shall be given unto all the rest of those who belongeth to this Holy Order.

8 And as pertaining to this work that my father hath been commanded to perform for the benefit of all those who shall receive these things; yea, pertaining to this work, I have seen and conversed with all those who have been called by God to bring this work forth. And I have conversed with them in the flesh, or in the spirit; for whether in the flesh, or in the spirit, it is the same to a man of God.

9 And there have been two of us, one who hath lived, and I who am still living, who have been commanded by the Lord and have been foreordained and given the power necessary to bring this work to light among the children of men. And there shall be two more among you in the latter days that are like unto us, and these shall be given the gifts and power of God to bring these things forth.

10 And these two prophets in the latter days shall increase in wisdom beyond the wisdom that we possessed in our days. And the first among you shall bring forth the part of this record that is not sealed. And he shall allow the interpreters to be kept secure by the church which he shall cause to be established among you. But the plates that I have made with my own hands shall remain in my custody and in my power, until I shall deliver them up for the last time to the Lord, who shall show them unto all the world as a testimony of the things that he hath caused to be written for the benefit of the children of men.

11 And this first shall be taken from among you because of the wickedness of the Gentiles, to which he shall reveal the part of this record that is unsealed. And he shall join me and the brother of Jared in the kingdom of the Father where we shall wait upon the Lord and the time that the fullness of these things shall be revealed unto you.

12 For behold, we shall be three, yea, even three witnesses of the truthfulness of this work, that shall be resurrected and live in the kingdom of the Father until the time cometh that the sealed part of this record shall come forth.

13 And while we are in the kingdom of the Father, there shall be others appointed in the spirit world, under the direction of the Holy Ghost, who shall prepare the final of the four of us who have been ordained unto this thing.

14 And when this last prophet shall be raised up and prepared for that work which he shall be commanded to do, then shall all of us sit in counsel and determine that which is best for this work, according to the commandments of the Lord that we shall receive concerning it.

15 And now, I would that ye should know the name of him who shall be called to bring forth the sealed part of this record unto you. For he shall be hidden from the knowledge of all the children of men until he hath passed through the tribulations and trials that shall test him, and prove him therewith, to see if he is willing to do all things whatsoever the Lord shall command him.

16 And the first part of his name shall be called after the mission that he is to perform. And since his mission is to bring to the world the final testament of the words of Christ, he shall be known by his first name, which shall be a bearer of Christ.

17 And the second part of his name shall be given unto him as a symbolic representation of those who shall aid him and watch over him in the spirit world. And this name shall be called after the brother of his father, which brother the Lord shall take, even at a very young age, in order that he might aid in the spiritual upbringing and care of him who hath been chosen.

18 And likewise shall the Lord do unto the brother of the first prophet that shall live among you in the latter days, even him who shall bring forth the unsealed portion of this record. And his brother is he who was called in the spirit world to help in the spiritual guidance of this first chosen one for the latter days.

19 And because the brother of Jared and I, shall be resurrected beings at this time, even during the latter days, we shall not be able to reside in the spirit world, for we shall have already received our eternal bodies of flesh and

bone. But power shall be given unto us to visit these two latter-day prophets and give them counsel and support in the calling that they have received from the Lord.

20 And for this reason the Lord hath given instructions to the Holy Ghost to assure that these two men are watched over by those in the spirit world. And because the children of men shall be divided into families, the members of these families shall be most familiar with the circumstance of their own family. And for this reason, the Lord shall choose one member of each of the families of these final two prophets, who shall be taken home to the spirit world at an early age, to aid in the guidance that each of these last two shall receive therein.

21 And the last name by which this final prophet shall be known among the children of men, shall be by the name of the family in which he shall be born. And this name shall mean an enemy of all evil spirits, or a nemesis of that which is not of God. And by these names shall ye know this last prophet of God, who shall be given the power to bring forth this work unto you.

22 And he shall be looked upon as a thing of naught; and he shall be refined with the refining fire of the Lord, until he is ready to fulfill the purpose for his creation. And he shall not be like unto the rest of those of his family. And he shall be ridiculed and persecuted by those who share his name. And in their pride, they shall think of him as those among the Jews thought of the Lord.

23 And it is written, saying: Is not this the son of a carpenter? Is not his mother called Mary? And are not his brethren called James, and Joses, and Simon, and Judas? And his sisters, are they not all with us? Whence then hath this man all these things? And they were offended in him. But Jesus said unto them: A prophet is not without honor, save in his own country, and in his own house.

24 And I have written this thing that ye might see that it is possible that the Lord commandeth his prophets to write his words according to the understanding and cultures of those who receive his words.

25 For behold, I, Moroni, have written upon these plates the things that I have just written according to the power of the Spirit that is within me. And this same Spirit guideth my hand in this thing. And the form of the language in which I write these things was known unto my fathers, but hath been altered by us, and was given unto my father and me by the power of this same Spirit.

26 And its form shall not be known upon the earth at the time that these things shall be given to the children of men in the latter days. For this reason, the Lord hath given the interpreters that have been passed down from the brother of Jared, even until they are in my possession.

27 And the form of language that the brother of Jared used to write the account of his vision, yea, even the account that is written upon the twenty-four plates that were found by the people of Limhi, is also unknown unto us. And only by the power of the interpreters can these things be made known.

28 And the reason why the Lord hath commanded that these things be written in a language that is unknown among the children of men, is because of the things that are written therein.

29 For the things that are written therein, are many things that the Lord doth not want the children of men to have until the fullness of times, in which all things shall be revealed. For if all things were revealed unto the children of men, then they would know many of the mysteries of God, and knowing these things would cause them to not live by faith, in order that they might be tried and tested during the days of their probation.

30 But most importantly to the Lord, is that the power of Satan is not revealed until the time shall come that he shall be released and have complete power over his own dominion. And if this power of Satan was allowed to come forth unto the children of men in times of old, then they would have destroyed themselves because of it, and the work and purposes of the Lord would have been frustrated.

31 For the earth must remain in the state in which it hath been created according to the time of the Lord, which exact time is only known by him. And if many of the things regarding the power of Satan were revealed unto the children of men too early in the days of their probation, then life would end because of their wickedness.

32 And if mortal life would end, then those who are left in the spirit world, who have not had the opportunity to pass through the days of their probation, would be continually waiting upon the Lord until another earth could be created and pass through its times and its seasons, until it reacheth the point of its nature wherein the children of God could be clothed with mortality and placed upon it.

33 For ye of the latter days shall come to know the great seriousness of your situation because of the power that hath been given unto Satan over his own dominions. And with that power, Satan shall bring forth many of the things that he hath learned from the eternal laws of God, and introduce them unto the children of men, that he might turn them from God and take the glory unto himself.

34 And if the days of your lives were not shortened, yea, if the Lord did not provide a time for his work to end, or a time of his final work to begin, then with the miracles and power that Satan shall give unto you, ye shall destroy each other from off the face of the earth.

35 And many of these things are written upon the twenty-four plates that the prophet Ether caused to be safeguarded and given unto the people of Limhi. And these plates were passed down from generation to generation, even from the time of Jared. And had they been written in a language that could be understood by the children of men, then the plates could have fallen into the wrong hands. And in the wrong hands, because of the things that were written thereon, the people would have destroyed themselves.

36 For this reason, Alma gave a commandment concerning these things to his son Helaman, saying: And now, I will speak unto you concerning those twenty-four plates, that ye keep them; that the mysteries and the works of darkness, and their secret works, or the secret works of those people who have been destroyed, may be made manifest unto this people; yea, all their murders, and robbings, and their plunderings, and all their wickedness and abominations, may be made manifest unto this people; yea, and that ye preserve these interpreters.

37 For behold, the Lord saw that his people began to work in darkness, yea, work secret murders and abominations; therefore the Lord said, if they did not repent they should be destroyed from off the face of the earth.

38 And the Lord said: I will prepare unto my servant Gazelem, a stone, which shall shine forth in darkness unto light, that I may discover unto my people who serve me, that I may discover unto them the works of their brethren, yea, their secret works, their works of darkness, and their wickedness and abominations.

39 And now, my son, these interpreters were prepared that the word of God might be fulfilled, which he spake, saying: I will bring forth out of darkness unto light all their secret works and their abominations; and except they repent I will destroy them from off the face of the earth; and I will bring to light all their secrets and abominations, unto every nation that shall hereafter possess the land.

40 And now, my son, we see that they did not repent; therefore they have been destroyed, and thus far the word of God hath been fulfilled; yea, their secret abominations have been brought out of darkness and made known unto us.

41 And now, my son, I command you that ye retain all their oaths, and their covenants, and their agreements in their secret abominations; yea, and all their signs and their wonders ye shall keep from this people, that they know them not, lest peradventure they should fall into darkness also and be destroyed.

42 For behold, there is a curse upon all this land, that destruction shall come upon all those workers of darkness, according to the power of God, when they are fully ripe; therefore I desire that this people might not be destroyed.

43 Therefore ye shall keep these secret plans of their oaths and their covenants from this people, and only their wickedness and their murders and their abominations shall ye make known unto them; and ye shall teach them to abhor such wickedness and abominations and murders; and ye shall also teach them that these people were destroyed

on account of their wickedness and abominations and their murders.

44 For behold, they murdered all the prophets of the Lord who came among them to declare unto them concerning their iniquities; and the blood of those whom they murdered did cry unto the Lord their God for vengeance upon those who were their murderers; and thus the judgments of God did come upon these workers of darkness and secret combinations.

45 Yea, and cursed be the land forever and ever unto those workers of darkness and secret combinations, even unto destruction, except they repent before they are fully ripe.

46 And now, my son, remember the words which I have spoken unto you; trust not those secret plans unto this people, but teach them an everlasting hatred against sin and iniquity.

47 And now, I, Moroni, would that ye should know concerning the interpreters that I have mentioned. And these interpreters are the same Urim and Thummim that I have mentioned to you in the first part of this record, even that which I used to translate the words of the brother of Jared that he had caused to be written in the language that the Lord commanded him to use, which language was also taught to him by the Holy Spirit.

48 And these same interpreters have been passed down from generation to generation and have been handled by many hands, and have been seen many times by the children of men. Nevertheless, these interpreters do not allow all who touch them to translate therewith. For the interpreters are directly associated with the spiritual energy that emanates from the person who is touching them. And this doth not mean that any righteous man can make them work. For my father, Mormon, was a righteous man, but he could not make them work. And he did not know beforehand what he should do with them.

49 But it came to pass that as I grew, I being very curious in my youth, even that I took an interest in the work in which my father was engaged concerning the records of the Nephites; and I would often sit among the records and read the words that I could, and try to understand their meaning, having very little knowledge of the things of God because of my youth.

50 And it came to pass that while I was thus engaged in the curious nature of my intentions, I noticed the Urim and Thummim as it sat among the records that had been given to my father. And it appeared unto me as two stones that were clear and smooth to the touch. And when I picked them up, to my great astonishment, they began to produce light, and startled me. And in my excitement, I ran to my father and told him what had happened to me.

51 And my father went with me to the place where he had hidden all the records that had been given unto him. And he placed the Urim and Thummim once again into my hands, and it again produced light, and this left my father exceedingly delighted in the thing that he beheld.

52 For behold, my father had known for a long time that the interpreters would not work for him. And even though he prayed with all of his heart that he might know how to use it, he could never cause the Urim and Thummim to produce light.

53 And the Spirit of the Lord came unto my father and revealed unto him the calling for which I had been conceived. And the nature of my flesh corresponded with the nature of the Urim and Thummim. And because of this, my touch was all that was needed for the interpreters to work.

54 And it came to pass that I grew in the Lord and passed through many days of tribulation and learning. And my father taught me the things that would be required of me concerning this record and the abridgment that I would make of the record of the brother of Jared. And his commandments unto me were like unto those that Alma gave unto his son Helamnan.

55 And when I was thirty and two years old, the time came that the Lord commanded me to translate the words of the brother of Jared. And I was commanded by my father, and also by the spirit of the Lord, to end the record of my father with these things. And my father was dead, having been killed in battle with the Lamanites. And I was left alone, for the Lord had not permitted me to take a wife and bear children.

56 And as I used the Urim and Thummim to translate the words of the brother of Jared, I was overcome with the Spirit because of the things which I read. And his words were powerful, even that they did overwhelm me, that I lost all the strength within me. And this was not the only reason that I lost this strength. For the Urim and Thummim cannot produce light in and of itself, but it dependeth on the energy of him who actuateth its properties for the light which it produceth.

57 And I begin to see the great physical toll that using these interpreters had on the body of a mortal man. And for this reason, the Lord gave me the commandment to use these things in my youth, even at the time of my greatest strength.

58 And it shall come to pass that the two future prophets who shall also use these interpreters shall be men of uncommon physical strength and ability. And they shall use it also in their youth, that they might have the strength within them to do that which hath been commanded of them by the Lord.

59 And to none other shall the Lord grant the power and the ability to use these interpreters. For a man must be called by God and raised up from the beginning to have this power. And if this man doth not do the will of the Lord in all things, the power that hath been given unto him shall be taken away.

60 But the work of God shall continue, and His eternal purposes shall roll on until all of His promises that He hath made unto His children are fulfilled.

61 And because of the great power of Satan in the last days, all of the children of men shall be corrupt. And the elect shall be deceived by the enticements of Satan, and also by the words of the false prophets that shall preach the supposed word of God unto them. And because of this great wickedness, this last prophet of whom I have spoken, yea, even he who shall bring forth the sealed portion of this record, shall be alone in that which he hath been called and ordained to do.

62 And he shall make an attempt to find others to help him in this work. But because of the power of Satan, and this great and abominable church that Satan hath caused to be established among you, he shall find very few who can be trusted to aid him in his calling.

63 And as I was alone, so shall he be. Nevertheless, after these things shall be revealed unto the children of men, then shall he find those of the elect who shall help him to bring this work unto all the children of men. And the elect shall begin to gather from the four corners of the earth. But this gathering shall not be done in haste, nor shall it be a physical gathering. But it shall be a spiritual gathering that is done in wisdom and according to the guidance of the Holy Ghost.

64 And this last prophet shall be visited and supported by the disciples of Jesus who desired to tarry in this land after the Lord had given unto them the desires of their hearts. And they shall be a source of inspiration and strength unto him, as they were unto me, and also as they shall be unto the first who hath been taken from among you. And these have administered unto me in my times of need. And they shall minister unto the needs of these final two prophets who the Lord shall raise up in the latter days.

65 And these things which are sealed shall come forth to the world to confound all false doctrine. And they shall be a source of great inspiration and guidance to the elect of God. For these things shall show unto the elect the ways in which they have been deceived by the enticements of Satan. And the dark works of the children of men shall be revealed unto them, so that they might know these things and avoid them; and also that they might begin to repent of their sins and their misunderstandings and come unto God and know Him by the power of His Holy Spirit.

66 And through the words of Christ shall the elect know these things. For the words of Christ shall teach them all things necessary that they might keep the commandments of God in all things. And if they keep the commandments of God in all things, then shall they know Him, and He shall make them His elect.

67 And for this purpose the Lord hath caused the translations that come through the Urim and Thummim to reproduce the exact likeness of his words that have been given to the children of

men in times of old. And he doeth this so that he might plant in the hearts of the children the promises made to the fathers, and the hearts of the children shall turn to their fathers. For if it were not so, the whole earth would be utterly wasted at his coming, and this according to the words of the prophets.

68 And these promises which the Lord hath made with the children of men are the same promises that the Father gave unto us in His kingdom before the creation of this world. And these promises are eternal, therefore they are unchangeable and cannot be altered. Therefore, what the Lord promiseth in one generation shall be the same that he promiseth in future generations, even to all of his children.

69 Therefore, why would ye think that the Lord would not command his holy prophets to write the same words unto the children of men in times present, that were given unto them in times past? For if he did not give unto them the same promises and the same commandments, then those of one generation might suppose that they were cheated, and that their promises were not as great as the promises he made at other times. And they might suppose that the commandments that the Lord hath given unto their generation are harder and more difficult to abide by than those that he hath given unto another generation.

70 And this is not the intent of the Lord to cause this confusion and feelings because of his words. For his words do not confuse, but uplift and create peace and harmony among the children of men. But the words and the commandments of men, yea, even the promises of men, these create confusion and strife and persecutions and all manner of wickedness among the children of men.

71 And it shall come to pass that when these last two prophets, of whom I have spoken, receive this record so that it might be translated into the language that shall exist in this future generation, even in the latter days, then they shall be commanded by the Spirit to search the scriptures and compare the words that they receive from the Urim and Thummim with the words that have already gone forth among the children of men.

72 And they shall be commanded to transpose the words that they receive from the Urim and Thummim, even the translation of this record, so that they correspond as closely as possible with the words that are already had among them. And in this way, the words of the former shall testify of the words of the present. And the children of men shall understand the words of the former more clearly because they shall be given in the context of the present. And thus shall these things be done for the profit of those who shall receive this record.

73 And I would that ye should know, that the interpreters do not always give unto him—who hath been given the power to use them—the words which he shall write. But many times images are projected upon them. And it will be given unto him by the Spirit what things he shall write to explain the images that he shall behold thereon. And after he hath written the interpretation of these images according to the Spirit of God, then shall he conform those words as closely as possible to the words that have already gone forth among the children of men.

74 And I give unto you an example of these things, even some of these things that ye have already received from the mouth of a Jew. And I would direct you to the words of the revelation of John, which is included in the record that shall come forth from the mouth of the Jew.

75 And if ye observe carefully the things which John hath written, ye will see that he hath also conformed that which he hath written to those things which had already been given to the children of men in his generation. For many of the symbols and allegories and explanations that he useth therein, are directly related, if not word for word in some instances, to the scriptures that he had in his day.

76 For behold, as Nephi beheld the time of John, and the things which he would write, even concerning the words that the angel spake unto him, saying: And behold, the things which this apostle of the Lamb shall write are many things which thou hast seen: and behold, the remainder shalt thou see. But the things which thou shalt see hereafter thou shalt not write; for the Lord God hath ordained the apostle of the Lamb of God that he should write them.

77 And also others who have been, to them hath he shown all things, and they have written them; and they are sealed up to come forth in their purity, according to the truth which is in the Lamb, in the own due time of the Lord.

78 And I, Nephi, hear and bear record, that the name of the apostle of the Lamb was John, according to the word of the angel.

79 And now, I, Moroni, would that ye should search the words of John and compare them with the words of Daniel and Ezekiel and Jeremiah, which words ye have among you. And if ye search these things, ye shall know the way in which the Lord hath commanded his prophets to write his words unto you.

80 And behold, I say unto those of you who would mock these things and try to discredit these prophets of God, and say that they have used the words of others to bring forth their own words. Yea, ye are deceived by Satan, who would have ye believe these things. Yea, again I give unto you the words of my father Nephi, for he speaketh unto those of you who would mock these things:

81 Oh, that cunning plan of the evil one! Oh, the vainness, and the frailties, and the foolishness of men! When they are learned they think they are wise, and they hearken not unto the counsel of God, for they set it aside, supposing they know of themselves, therefore, their wisdom is foolishness and it profiteth them not. And they shall perish.

82 But to be learned is good if they hearken unto the counsels of God. But woe unto the rich, who are rich as to the things of the world. For because they are rich they despise the poor, and they persecute the meek, and their hearts are upon their treasures; therefore, their treasure is their God. And behold, their treasure shall perish with them also.

83 And woe unto the deaf that will not hear; for they shall perish. Woe unto the blind that will not see; for they shall perish also. Woe unto the uncircumcised of heart, for a knowledge of their iniquities shall smite them at the last day. Woe unto the liar, for he shall be thrust down to hell. Woe unto the murderer who deliberately killeth, for he shall die. Woe unto them who commit whoredoms, for they shall be thrust down to hell.

84 Yea, woe unto those that worship idols, for the devil of all devils delighteth in them. And, in fine, woe unto all those who die in their sins; for they shall return to God, and behold His face, and remain in their sins.

85 Oh, my beloved brethren, remember the awfulness in transgressing against that Holy God, and also the awfulness of yielding to the enticings of that cunning one. Remember, to be carnally-minded is death, and to be spiritually-minded is life eternal.

86 Oh, my beloved brethren, give ear to my words. Remember the greatness of the Holy One of Israel. Do not say that I have spoken hard things against you; for if ye do, ye will revile against the truth; for I have spoken the words of your Maker. I know that the words of truth are hard against all uncleanness; but the righteous fear them not, for they love the truth and are not shaken.

87 Oh, then, my beloved brethren, come unto the Lord, the Holy One. Remember that his paths are righteous. Behold, the way for man is narrow, but it lieth in a straight course before him, and the keeper of the gate is the Holy One of Israel; and he employeth no servant there; and there is none other way save it be by the gate; for he cannot be deceived, for the Lord God is his name.

88 And whoso knocketh, to him will he open; and the wise, and the learned, and they that are rich, who are puffed up because of their learning, and their wisdom, and their riches; yea, they are they whom he despiseth; and save they shall cast these things away, and consider themselves fools before God, and come down in the depths of humility, he will not open unto them.

89 But the things of the wise and the prudent shall be hid from them forever, yea, that happiness which is prepared for the saints.

90 Now, I, Moroni, have caused to be written the words that Nephi spoke, which words have already been received by those of you who are reading this portion of the record of my father which was sealed.

91 And when this final prophet of the latter days, of whom I have spoken, shall use the Urim and Thummim to translate the words that I have caused to be written upon these plates, the Spirit shall instruct him to search the words of Nephi that have already gone forth among you, Yea, he shall be commanded by the Spirit to make any adjustments to the words which he hath translated, so that the words which he hath translated shall conform exactly with the words that ye already have among you.

92 And the words that are written in this sealed portion shall testify of the words that have already gone forth among you. And the words that have already gone forth among you shall testify of these things. Nevertheless, the words that I have been commanded to write unto you, even in this sealed portion of the record of my father, shall be more clear and precise in their explanation of the commandments and the mysteries of God. And for this purpose were these things prepared.

93 For there shall be many of the elect who shall be deceived by the words of the learned and those who think that they are wise. And there shall be many churches built up and led by those who think that they are wise, and who are learned and have received the glories and honors of men, because of the things that they think they know. And the elect of God shall not know where they must go to hear the pure word of God. And because they do not understand fully the things of God, and His commandments for them, they do not have the Spirit to give them the guidance that they need.

94 And the words of this sealed portion shall be given unto them that they might know more fully the things of God. And with the words that are written herein, the elect of God can remove themselves from the world, and cause that the Lord shall seal in their foreheads his Holy Name, so that at his coming, they do not burn with fire, and be tormented with brimstone in the presence of the holy angels, and in the presence of the Lamb, even according to the words of the apostle of the Lamb.

95 And then shall the elect know the true intent and purpose of the word of God that hath already gone out among them. And then shall they know the truth of all things. And their religions and their churches, and their governments, and their leaders; even all these shall lose the respect that they do not deserve. For the Lord deserveth the respect of all the children of men. And the elect shall give unto him his due respect.

96 And the elect shall realize that pure religion that is undefiled before God and the Father is this: To visit the fatherless and widow in their affliction, and to keep himself unspotted from the world. And I say unto you, there is no other religion of the Father.

CHAPTER 22

Adam continues his counsel to his children and finishes explaining the commandments and the law of the gospel. Taking the Lord's name in vain is expounded on and the proper way to pray and fast explained. The purpose and intent of baptism is given.

AND now, I, Moroni, return once again to the words that the brother of Jared wrote concerning the counsel of Adam to his posterity. Behold, Adam taught his children the ways and commandments of the Lord according to the commandments that he received from God. And by the power of the Spirit Adam expounded these commandments unto his posterity that they might have no confusion on the points of doctrine concerning them.

2 And Adam continued speaking unto them, saying: And now my beloved children, I would that ye might know the commandments of the Lord pertaining to his requirements of us in relationship to the Father, or in other words, the things that we must do to be like unto the Father, so that we might show this example to our children.

3 And the Lord spoke unto us, saying: Verily, verily, I say unto you, I give unto you to be the salt of the earth; but if the salt shall lose its savor, wherewith shall the earth be salted? The salt shall be thenceforth good for nothing, but to be cast out and to be trodden under foot of men.

4 Verily, verily, I say unto you, I give unto you to be the light of your posterity, that your light might shine forth out of the darkness. And when your light shineth forth, it giveth its light unto all that are in the land. And ye shall be as a city that is set high upon a hill from wherewith ye send forth this light. And this light shall shine forth as a beacon unto them, that they might come into the city and bask in the light. And a city that is set on a hill cannot be hid.

5 Behold, do men light a candle and put it under a bushel? Nay, but on a candlestick, and it giveth light to all that are in the house; therefore let your light so shine before your posterity that they may see your good works and glorify your Father who is in heaven.

6 Now the Lord did not only give this commandment unto us as your parents, but he hath given it unto all of us who have taken upon ourselves the name of the Lord, or in other words, who have covenanted with him to obey his commandments. And when we have covenanted with him to obey his commandments, then we become an example for others to follow, or the light that he hath mentioned.

7 And he hath commanded us that we shall not take the name of the Lord in vain, and that he shall not be held guiltless who taketh the name of the Lord upon himself in vain. And this meaneth that we shall not be held guiltless if we say that we are godly, and that we have taken upon ourselves his name, yet do none of the things that he hath commanded of us. Behold, this is what he meaneth by taking his Holy Name in vain.

8 And I have heard it said among you that the taking of the name of the Lord in vain refereth to saying his name in an inappropriate or indifferent manner. And ye have commanded your children that they should not say the name of the Lord in this manner, thinking that this is what the Lord meant by this commandment. And this ye teach unto your children because ye do not want to acknowledge that ye are taking his name in vain by not keeping his commandments.

9 And I say unto you that it mattereth not to the Lord in what manner his name is used, for it is just a name, or a word that we have given unto him. But to take the name of the Lord upon ourselves, by covenanting with him to keep his commandments, and doing this thing in vain, because we do not obey his commandments, now this is the sin against God, and shall be punished according to the punishment that is affixed to this commandment.

10 But the Lord careth nothing for the words that come forth out of your mouths, as long as those that do come forth, come forth with love and not anger. For words are just words, but the feeling and enmity behind the words that we say, are those things which condemn us. Therefore, I would that ye would not teach your children these things to justify your own complacency in obeying the true meaning of this commandment.

11 And the Lord gave unto us commandments regarding the oaths and covenants and the contracts that we make between ourselves. For there are many among you who forswear yourselves to your fellowmen by an oath to God. And this ye do that ye might prove to each other the seriousness and trust of these oaths. For ye believe that if ye swear by saying, so help me God, that ye shall not lie unto him to whom ye are swearing.

12 But the Lord hath commanded us, saying: Verily, verily, I say unto you, swear not at all; neither by heaven, for it is the throne of God; nor by the earth, for it is His footstool; neither shalt thou swear by thy head, because thou canst not make one hair black or white;

13 But let your communication be yea, yea, or nay, nay; for whatsoever cometh of more than these is evil.

14 And now my beloved children, ye have caused much misery among yourselves because of your failure to keep this commandment among you. And because ye have failed to keep this commandment, ye have caused much anger and contention among you. And ye disobey one commandment, even that ye should not forswear yourselves, and it causeth you to disobey another commandment, which is even greater, even that ye should not become angry one with another.

15 And all of the commandments of God are based upon the great law that I have explained unto you, even that ye should do unto others as ye would have them do unto you.

16 And if your neighbor sweareth a thing unto you, then would ye not expect that he doeth the thing that he hath sworn? Likewise, ye would expect, that if ye swear a thing unto him, that the thing which ye have sworn shall also be done. And in these things, ye have opened up the possibility that ye might disobey the commandments of God in many ways.

17 As an example, I would that ye should consider that which ye would borrow from your neighbor. Foremost, if ye did not place value on your possessions, and would make them free unto all according to their needs, then ye would not need to borrow anything from your neighbor.

18 But if ye do borrow a thing from your neighbor, and ye forswear yourselves that ye shall return to him the thing that ye have borrowed, according to the contract and the oath that ye have made between you; and if ye swear to this thing, and for some reason or another ye cannot do the thing that ye have sworn to do, then ye have lied to your neighbor, and have broken the oath that ye have made unto him. And your lie will be a cause that your neighbor shall become angry. Therefore, not only have ye sinned, but ye have also caused your neighbor to sin.

19 And I have seen great contention among you because of the worth that ye have placed upon your gold and your silver. For there are those of you who do not have gold and silver, and because ye do not have these things, ye covet the gold and silver of your neighbors.

20 And if this coveting was not enough to turn you against the commandments of God, ye have done that which is most abominable before Him. For ye have made yourselves dependent upon this gold and this silver, because of the value that ye have placed upon all the things that ye possess, even those things that God hath provided freely to us all to sustain our lives.

21 And this value that ye have placed upon these things is according to your gold and your silver and other precious things. And this system of exchange that ye have based upon these useless elements, hath been, and shall be, the cause of much conflict and contention among you. Yea, even that there shall be many wars among you because of this value that ye have placed upon the things of the world.

22 And when one of you coveteth a thing that he doth not possess, then ye make contracts with each other in order that ye might possess those things that ye do not have.

23 And those of you who have an abundance of gold and of silver, approach him that coveteth, and offer unto him a contract, in that ye shall lend to him the gold and the silver that he requireth to purchase that which he coveteth. And in your contract with him, ye have made stipulations that he must return unto you more than that which ye have given unto him in the first place.

24 And he forsweareth himself that he will do this thing, so that he might have that which he coveteth. Therefore, this man hath disobeyed the commandment that he shall not covet, and furthereth his disobedience to the commandments of God by forswearing himself, as he hath been commanded not to.

25 And if this man, in the course of the time of his sworn contract, is called home to the God who hath given unto him these commandments, or in other words, if this man dieth, then what shall become of that which he hath sworn to do?

26 And I know that it is a common practice among you to make his children comply with the oath that this man hath made; but the children did not make this oath. And if they do not comply with the contract of their father, then ye demand justice from them, in that ye take all of their possessions, or ye take them before a judge to be tried and sentenced according to a crime that they did not commit.

27 And if the man doth not die, but cannot pay back the gold and silver that he hath forsworn himself to do, then ye demand the same justice of him. But this is not all in which ye do sin, for your demands are made in anger.

28 And those of you who charge usury in these things have been the cause of much wickedness among us. For ye entice your brothers and sisters to covet that which they do not have, thus being emissaries of Satan in this thing. For is it not Satan that enticeth the children of men with the things of the world, so that they do not give heed to the commandments of God?

29 And first ye entice others to covet that which they do not have. And then ye entice them to forswear themselves unto you, that they might have the thing that they covet. And then ye sin yourselves, in that ye get gain without work, which is contrary to the laws of God. And ye get this gain by the usury that ye charge those who have forsworn themselves unto you.

30 And as emissaries of Satan, ye are the means of much contention and misery among us. And I say unto you, except ye shall see the error of your ways and stop that thing in which ye are sinning against God, and causing others to sin against God; yea, except ye stop these things, ye shall become the salt that hath lost its savor and is thenceforth good for nothing but to be cast out and to be trodden under foot of men.

31 And ye shall be trodden on by those whom ye have charged usury. For they shall come forth out of the prisons in which ye shall cast them, and in their anger, they shall hew you down and take from you the abundance that ye have received from them.

32 Behold, the Lord hath commanded us, saying: Give to him that asketh of thee, and from him that would borrow of thee, turn thou not away. And if ye charge usury to him that would borrow of thee, then ye shall have your reward in the usury that ye have charged. And this reward shall be according to the rewards of Satan, whom ye serve. And ye shall be miserable like unto him.

33 Verily, verily, I say unto you that I would that ye should do alms unto the poor; but take heed that ye do not your alms before men to be seen of them; otherwise ye have no reward of your Father who is in heaven.

34 Therefore, when ye shall do your alms, do not make an announcement before you, as shall the hypocrites do in the churches and in the streets, that they may have glory of men. Verily, I say unto you, they have their reward. But when thou doeth alms, let not thy left hand know what thy right hand doeth; that thine alms may be in secret; and thy Father who seeth in secret, Himself shall reward thee openly.

35 And now, my beloved children, I would that ye should know that those of you who get gain without work, and who have an abundance of the things of this world, in that ye are considered rich among us, do not give alms unto the poor as the Lord hath commanded.

36 Yea, I know that of your abundance, ye do give unto others according to the desires of your hearts. And ye desire that the things that ye give have your names attached thereto, so that ye might justify yourselves before others, and show that ye give to the poor. And ye do this that ye might receive the glory and honor of men.

37 And in this glory and honor, ye receive your reward, and shall receive no reward from your Father in heaven. And it is easy to tell the difference between a reward of the Father, which is given unto you through the ministrations of the Spirit, and a reward from Satan, which is given to you according to that which ye desire in this world, which is according to the flesh.

38 And the rewards of the Spirit are different than the rewards of the flesh. For the flesh lusteth against the Spirit, and the Spirit against the flesh, and these are contrary the one to the other, so that ye might know that which ye should not do, and this is the enmity of which I have spoken.

39 And for this same reason, the Father placed enmity between us and Satan. For each of us knoweth that which leadeth to the fruit of the Spirit, and that which leadeth to the fruit of the flesh.

40 For the fruit of the flesh is made manifest by the abundance that ye have received from it. And because of your abundance, ye cause yourselves to have lasciviousness among you, which leadeth you to adultery and fornication. And ye have variance from that which ye know to be good, and emulations of that which is evil. And wrath and strife, seditions and heresies, loneliness and depression, self-indulgence and the defilement of the body, envyings and murders, drunkenness and revellings; and all things like unto these are the fruits of the flesh.

41 But the fruit of the Spirit is love and joy, peace and longsuffering, gentleness and goodness, faith and meekness, and temperance, and all things like unto these. And ye that give without thinking beforehand of what ye do, are those of whom the Lord hath said that give

without the left hand knowing what the right hand doeth. For ye give to the poor from your hearts, which desires are known by the Father.

42 And ye shall receive the fruits of the Spirit as your reward. And see that ye are not deceived because of the rewards of the flesh that are received by those who disregard the commandments of God.

43 For many of you have thought that the Father rewardeth His children with the things of this earth. But He doth not reward His children with the things of this earth, for the whole earth is the reward of those who love Him and keep His commandments.

44 And the Father liveth by the Spirit, and hath commanded us to live by this same Spirit. And if it so be that we live by this same Spirit, then shall our rewards be those of the Spirit, and not of the flesh. And when ye ask anything of the Father, I would that ye should follow the commandments of the Lord concerning these things. And he commanded us, saying: And when thou prayest, thou shalt not be as the hypocrites are, for they love to pray standing in the synagogues and in the corners of the streets, that they may be seen of men. Verily, I say unto you, they have their reward.

45 But thou, when thou prayest, enter into thy closet, and when thou hast shut thy door, pray to thy Father who is in secret; and thy Father, who seeth in secret, shall reward thee openly. But when ye pray, use not vain repetitions, as the heathen do, for they think that they shall be heard for their much speaking. Be ye not therefore, like unto them, for your Father knoweth what things ye have need of before ye ask him. Even after this manner, therefore, pray ye: Our Father which art in heaven, Hallowed be thy name. Thy kingdom come; Thy will be done, in earth, as it is in heaven. Give us this day our daily bread, and forgive us our debts, as we forgive our debtors. And lead us not into temptation, but deliver us from evil. For thine is the kingdom, and the power, and the glory, for ever. Amen.

46 For if ye forgive men their trespasses, your heavenly Father shall also forgive you. But if ye forgive not men their trespasses, neither shall your Father forgive your trespasses.

47 Moreover when ye fast, be not as the hypocrites, of a sad countenance, for they disfigure their faces, that they may appear unto men to fast. Verily I say unto you, they have their reward. But thou, when thou fastest, anoint thine head, and wash thy face; that thou appear not unto men to fast, but unto thy Father which is in secret. And thy Father, which seeth in secret, shall reward thee openly.

48 And now, my beloved children, I would that ye should know somewhat more concerning these commandments that the Lord hath given unto us. For the Lord would that we pray always, yea, even a commandment he hath given unto us, that we should pray always lest we enter into temptation.

49 And how can it be that we shall pray always, as we have been commanded? For if we were always praying as ye have accustomed yourselves to pray, then ye would be doing nothing else in your lives. But indeed we were commanded to pray always, and this ye can do if it so be that ye understand prayer, and pray according to a true understanding of its power and purpose.

50 For many of you suppose that when ye pray unto the Father, that He personally heareth your prayers, and answereth these prayers forthwith. But I say unto you, how can the Father possibly hear your prayers, when He is continually engaged in other work; and when He resideth in His kingdom, where only those who are in front of Him can communicate with Him according to the laws that govern the Celestial body that he possesseth?

51 And what of the prayers that ye offer unto Him? For many of you pray for that which ye should not. And many of you pray unto God that He would bless you with the things of the earth and the successes and honors and glories of men. And why do ye suppose that the Father would bless you with such things, or help you acquire these things, when He hath commanded you to avoid such things?

52 And why do ye pray over your food that He might bless it to nourish and strengthen your bodies and do you the good that ye need? Do ye not know that the food in and of itself is a blessing of God? And why should ye ask a

blessing on the food that He hath already provided for us as a blessing?

53 And ye cause this food to pass through fire in the procedures that ye have established among you for the cooking of your food. And ye have taken something wholesome, in which God hath provided all the nourishment that ye need for your bodies, and have destroyed it with the heat of your fires. And why then do ye ask Him to bless it that it might nourish and strengthen you, after ye have changed that with which He hath already blessed you? How can ye suppose that such hypocrisy and vain repetition of prayer are acceptable and justifiable before God?

54 And the Father already knoweth that in which ye are in need before ye ask it of Him. And He hath given unto us all the things that we need according to the flesh. And we should only want that which we need to eat to sustain us on a daily basis.

55 And He hath established the laws and government of the Spirit world to administer to us according to our spiritual needs. And it is our Lord, who is His Son, and our elder brother according to the Spirit, that ruleth in the kingdom of the Spirits at this time.

56 And if we obey the commandments of God, then we shall have the ministrations of this spirit world with us always. And if the Spirit is with us, we shall not be led into temptation, and we will always be delivered from evil.

57 Now, I would that ye should know, that to pray always, meaneth that we are constantly aware of the commandments of God, and that we are continually striving to keep them, so that we may have this Spirit to be with us.

58 And obedience is the attitude of prayer. For it is by obedience that we obtain the Spirit, and it is by this Spirit that we receive all things which we need to be happy. And the thing that shall make us happy is the fruit of the Spirit as I have explained it unto you.

59 And if ye use vain repetition in your prayers, do ye not think that these exact same words have been heard time and time again by those in the spirit world who are assigned to administer unto you and answer your prayers? Now, I would ask if ye would want to hear the same prayers day after day, time after time, knowing that these prayers can only be answered with the rewards of the Spirit?

60 For most of the prayers that ye offer up unto God are for the things of the flesh, with which He doth not bless us. Therefore, when ye offer up such prayers, ye are certainly answered therein, but ye are answered by him who hath authority to give unto you the rewards of the flesh, for they are in his power. And from Satan, who is the god of this world, ye shall receive these things, for he also is in the spirit world listening to your prayers. And ye shall receive that which ye have asked for and reap the rewards of the same.

61 And the Lord hath commanded us to fast and pray always. And if we fast as ye are accustomed to fast, how is it that we shall live? For ye think that this fasting also hath to do with the things of the flesh. But it hath nothing to do with the things of the flesh, but the things of the Spirit.

62 And when we fast, we are commanded to give up the things of the flesh that we might concentrate more on the things of the Spirit. And it is possible that ye can fast all the days of your lives, as ye have been commanded. And if ye give up the things of the flesh, ye do not necessarily give up the food with which the Father hath blessed us.

63 Behold, the food that we eat doth not cause us to follow after the lusts of the flesh. Yet, there are those foods that we eat that we consume upon the lusts of our flesh, which lusts cause us to receive the rewards of the flesh, which are laziness and obesity and all manner of gluttonous excess.

64 But when we fast, which we are commanded to do always, lest we enter into temptation, we should only eat our daily bread, or that which shall sustain our lives. For anything more than this, quickly leadeth us into the temptations of the flesh.

65 For if ye notice the beasts of the field and the fowls of the air, ye shall notice that they do not fast, neither do they pray, yet the Father hath provided for them in all things. But we are not of their order, and for this reason, we should fast and pray for that which shall sustain the order from which we were created. And the order from which we were created is a spiritual order. And our spirits need the things of the Spirit, of which things the beasts and fowl are not in need.

66 And the Father hath established the power and authority of the Spirit world to administer to us in all of our spiritual needs. And the Lord said unto us: Ask, and it shall be given you; seek, and ye shall find; knock, and it shall be opened unto you. For every one that asketh, receiveth; and he that seeketh, findeth; and to him that knocketh, it shall be opened.

67 Or what man is there of you, whom if his son ask bread, will he give him a stone? Or if he ask a fish, will he give him a serpent? If ye then, being evil, know how to give good gifts unto your children, how much more shall your Father which is in heaven give good things to them that ask him?

68 And now, my beloved children, I would that ye should remember to ask not amiss, and trust that the will of the Father shall be done on this earth as it is in heaven.

69 Behold, these are the commandments of God that were given unto us after we left the garden of Eden. They have been given unto us to help us during the days of our probation. And these commandments are the laws by which we will be required to live in the kingdom of God.

70 And for this purpose were they given unto us, that we might learn them and prepare ourselves to enter the kingdom of God and live forever in the glory that we have chosen for ourselves according to our desires of happiness.

71 And there are no other laws or commandments that we shall be required to live by in order to be saved in the kingdom of God. And all these commandments are encompassed in the one great commandment that I have given unto you, even that all things whatsoever ye would that men should do to you, do ye even so to them. For on this commandment is based the entire law, even all of the words of the prophets.

72 And the Lord hath given us a commandment to be baptized for the remission of sins, and that the Holy Ghost shall be given to us as our constant companion. And this baptism is our covenant with the Father, which covenant we make before all men, that they might be witnesses thereof of the covenant that we make with God.

73 And with this covenant we are born anew, and become sanctified in the works that we have covenanted with the Father to do.

74 For this reason, the ordinance of baptism shall be administered in a symbolic representation of being buried, by the full immersion into the water, and by coming forth out of the water as a new person; yea, even one who hath been washed of all his former sins and hath been born again.

75 And in the Holy Endowment, that ye have available to you for your edification and instruction, this baptism is symbolized by the removal of your shoes from off of your feet in the room which is a representation of the Telestial kingdom, or the world on which we now live. And the removal of your shoes symbolizeth that ye have removed all that which ye have done in the past, your shoes having carried you forth in the works that ye have done.

76 And with this covenant that ye shall make with the Father, ye shall take upon you the name of the Father, and the name of the Son, and the name of the Holy Ghost. And this meaneth that ye covenant to be perfect as your Father which is in heaven is perfect, and that ye shall do so by following the example which the Son shall show unto you, that ye might have the Holy Ghost to guide you in these things.

77 And this is why it hath been taught unto you, that except ye be born again, even of the water and of the Spirit, ye shall in no wise enter into the kingdom of God. In other words, those who are not baptized shall not inherit the kingdom of God.

78 Now, I know that this doctrine hath caused some contention and disputes among you. For there are those of you who believe that the actual ordinance of baptism must be performed by all of us, whether we are alive, or dead, according to the ordinance of baptism for the dead, which thing we also perform according to the will of the Lord.

79 And now, I would that ye should know, that baptism is only a symbolic ordinance that the Lord hath suffered to be given unto us to keep us in remembrance of the plan of salvation

and those things that we must do to be saved in the kingdom of God, as I have previously explained them unto you.

80 And we perform baptisms for the dead as a symbolic representation, that whether we are alive or dead, we must keep the commandments of God in order to be saved in His kingdom. And these baptisms for the dead are for our instruction and our learning. For the dead know much more than we do, and have no need for a baptism according to the things of the flesh. But those in the spirit world, who were wicked during the days of their probation, shall also be required to be baptized, but their baptism shall be one of fire, for they shall be in a state of misery for that which they have done in mortality.

81 And many of them must return again to this earth and go through more days of probation, wherein they must prove themselves worthy of the kingdom of God.

82 And all that have died without receiving a baptism and making this covenant with God, who would have received it if they had been permitted to tarry, shall be heirs of the kingdom of God. And also all that shall die henceforth without this baptism, who would have received it, shall be heirs of the kingdom of God.

83 For the Lord judgeth all men according to their works, according to the desires of their hearts. And baptism availeth a man nothing, if it so be that he doth not keep the commandments of God. And if he keepeth the commandments of God, then this baptism availeth him nothing, except that he keepeth the commandments of God in receiving it.

84 And now, my beloved children, I would that ye should remember all these commandments that I have given unto you this day. Yea, I would that ye should remember that I love each of you, and want only those things that shall bring happiness unto you. And I would that ye should love one another as I have loved you.

85 And if ye remember none of my words this day, I would that ye would remember to love one another as ye would have them love you. For my words shall not save you in the kingdom of God, but they shall witness against you when ye stand before God to be judged in the spirit according to the things that ye have done in the flesh. And for this reason, the Lord hath commanded me to write these things down that ye may always have my words among you.

86 And if ye shall keep these things among you, and teach them unto your children, then they shall know the commandments of God. But if ye do not keep these things among you, then ye shall not have a true record of the commandments of the Father. And without a true record of these things, ye shall be led by the precepts and commandments of men, who shall receive their guidance from those in the spirit world who fight against the plan that the Father hath given unto us for our salvation.

87 And thus it is, my beloved children. Amen.

CHAPTER 23

Many of the children of Adam rebel against his counsel. Adam is commanded to leave the land of Eden in North America and travel to the continent of Africa. His children divide themselves and spread throughout the land. Those who remain in the Land of Eden destroy themselves. Moroni explains why the history of the world is important.

AND it came to pass that after Adam had spoken unto his children at Adamondiahman, he caused to be written all those things which he had said. And when these things had been written according to his commandment, he sent them unto all parts of the land unto all of his posterity.

2 And he gave special instructions to those who carried these words forth, even that they should go in among the children of Cain and the descendants of Beneli and give unto them the commandments of the Lord.

3 And it came to pass that as soon as those who carried forth his words entered in among the children of Cain, they were bound and tortured and slain, and the words that they carried forth were destroyed.

4 And when word came unto Adam that his words had been destroyed, and that those that had carried them forth had been killed, he became desirous that he should go personally to his children who had rejected his words, and who truly were his beloved children, that they might show unto him respect; and that they might listen to him.

5 But the sons of Adam, and those whom he had gathered together that they might discuss this matter, dissuaded him that he might not go in among them. For the Cainites had become a wild and ferocious people and had been taught to hate their brothers and sisters who were the other sons and daughters of Adam; even those who had not been banished out of the land by Adam in the day of their father, Cain.

6 And the descendants of Beneli were the more intelligent of those who did not give heed unto the words of Adam. And these Benelites stirred up the Cainites to anger against the sons and daughters of Adam who did not belong to their families and to their communities.

7 For the Benelites had for many years established a means of trade and industry with the Cainites, even that the Cainites performed all the labors for the Benelites, so that these did not have to work with their own hands.

8 And because the words of Adam condemned their works, and would be the means of ending their trade with the Cainites, thus forcing them to work by the sweat of their own brow, these Benelites stirred up the Cainites to anger against the children of Adam, even those who listened to his words. For the Cainites were a very strong people as to the strength of a man, because of the labors that they performed for the Benelites.

9 And the righteous sons of Adam were also strong as to the strength of a man. Yet their strength was in the health of their marrow and the strength of their bones, which strength was increased by the Spirit of God, which was in them. But the Cainites were much stronger than the other sons of Adam, because of the intense physical labor that they did perform daily to sustain the lives of the Benelites, who they had accepted as their leaders.

10 And at this time, ore and iron and steel, nor any other metal, had not yet been discovered among the children of men. For these things were not necessary to sustain life, but were introduced later to the children of men by Satan, who used these things to augment the means of force and the armies that he useth to cause wars and horror upon the earth as he had promised.

11 And during the time of Adam, the men did often engage in feats of strength, but these games were done in love and compassion for those with whom they competed. And it did not matter among them who was stronger than another, for they that were strong used their strength for the benefit of the weak.

12 And among the righteous children of Adam, the men did not know how to use their strength to take the life of another, nor were they trained in using their strength to defend themselves.

13 But the Cainites were experts at the art of fighting and conquering. Yea, the games among them were fought to the death. And he that was victorious over another received great honor and distinction among them. Therefore, they were strong as to the skills that were necessary to conquer another.

14 And it came to pass that the Benelites organized the Cainites into armies and elected captains and chiefs among them. And their desire was that they should become sufficiently strong enough to invade the land of Eden and take the sons and daughters of Adam captive so that they could be the leaders of the whole land.

15 And it came to pass that Adam was given word of the preparations of the Benelites and the Cainites to come in among them and take over the land. And because of this, Adam became exceedingly sorrowful and mourned many days before the Lord, praying unto him that this thing might not come to pass.

16 And the voice of the Lord came unto Adam, saying: Behold, it is expedient in me that I allow this thing to come to pass. For I have granted unto the children of men their agency to choose for themselves the laws by which they shall live and the happiness that they would desire.

17 And it is necessary that they experience all the vicissitudes of mortality so that they shall understand the great necessity in keeping my commandments which I have given unto them.

18 And now my beloved son, lift up your head

and be of good cheer; for behold, thou hast kept my commandments and hast done all those things which I have commanded thee to do. And it is not because of your sins that your children desire to disobey my commandments, for thou hast taught them what they should do. And their sins shall be answered upon their own heads.

19 And now, a commandment I give unto thee, that thou, and those who follow thee, should leave the land of Eden, and make vessels in which ye can cross the great waters and enter into a land that hath been prepared for you. And this land is not as verdant and comely as the land of Eden, but it is the land that I desire that the generations of men inhabit for their own sake.

20 For the land of Eden shall be withheld from the knowledge of the children of men until the time that I shall make it again known unto them.

21 And because the children of men choose to disobey my commandments, and this because of the state of the flesh in which they are in, there shall be much wickedness throughout the world during all the future generations of thy posterity.

22 And I will make this land of Eden a promised land unto those whom I will. And I will cause that it shall be a place of refuge and freedom for those of thy posterity that honor me and keep my commandments.

23 And if I did not save a promised land for this purpose, then the wicked of the earth would soon overcome the righteous, and the ends of the creation of the earth would be frustrated and complicated. For the wicked shall destroy the wicked, and unless I take the righteous from among them, they will destroy the righteous also.

24 And I would that ye should teach your children to keep my commandments in all things. And I have commanded you to love one another and to give to him that asketh of thee, and that if ye are struck on the left, turn again the right that it might also be struck. And I have commanded you to love your enemies and do good to them that hate you and persecute you and despitefully use you.

25 And I have covenanted with you, that if ye shall do these things, then ye shall prosper in the land. But if ye do not do these things, then ye shall perish in the land with the wicked.

26 And if thou art to be an example to thy children of the way that they shall live, then I say unto thee, that thou shalt not fight thy enemy, but shall give unto him that which he desireth. But thou shalt not allow thy enemy to hurt you or take advantage of the purity and chastity of your women. But ye shall flee before them and allow them to have the land of Eden.

27 And if ye shall do these things and keep my commandments, ye shall be blessed, and I will prepare a way whereby thou and thy posterity might be saved.

28 Now go my son, and teach these things unto thy children. Remember that I have said, that he that shall find his life, shall lose it. And he that loseth his life for my sake, shall find it. And if ye lose your life in keeping the commandments of God, then shall ye be received in the kingdom of God in a state of never ending happiness. But if ye live or die in your sins, ye shall be received in a state of misery. These are my words and commandments unto thee.

29 And it came to pass that when Adam had received the word of the Lord, he called unto him all those that would give heed to his words. And when they had gathered before him, Adam recounted unto them all the words of the Lord.

30 And there were those among them that were angered because of these words. And it was their desire that they should stand up to the Benelites and the Cainites and defend the land against them. And there were two mighty and strong men among the sons of Adam, and their names were Amoran and Amalek.

31 And these had many sons who were like unto their fathers. And these stood forth and pledged their support to their fathers, and wanted that Adam would allow them to stand and fight the Cainites.

32 But Adam rebuked them, saying: Do ye know what ye are asking? Do ye realize that ye are desirous to disobey the commandments that the Lord hath given unto us? I say unto you, that if we stay and fight against the Cainites, we shall perish with them. Behold, your anger is caused by your pride; and this pride hath been put into your hearts by Satan, who would have us destroyed.

33 And now my beloved children, let us make haste and gather up the provisions that we are in need of and leave this land according to the commandments of the Lord.

34 And Amoran and Amalek did not agree with their father, Adam. Nevertheless, they knew that their numbers were not sufficient enough that they should stand alone and fight against the Cainites.

35 And the Benelites had placed spies among the children of Adam. And these spies acted as if they were righteous, and that they were desirous to hear the words of Adam. And after hearing the words of Adam, these spies returned again to their leaders and told them all the things that Adam had said, and revealed unto their leaders the plans that Adam was making to depart out of the land.

36 And it came to pass that the Benelites were so darkened and corrupted by the power of Satan, that they did not want Adam and those who would follow him to leave the land undisturbed. And they knew that they were going to inherit the land of Eden, for this had been one of the purposes for which they had stirred up the Cainites to anger against the other sons and daughters of Adam. But their utmost desire was to enslave the children of Adam so that they would not have to work with their own hands.

37 And the leaders of the Benelites called together their captains and their chiefs and gave unto them a commandment that they should immediately go in among the people of Adam and keep them from leaving the land of Eden.

38 And it came to pass that as the Cainites were gathering their armies together to do that thing that they were commanded, an exceedingly great storm gathered in their lands. And there came great whirlwinds that carried many of them away, and destroyed their homes and their precious things.

39 And the Cainites became sore afraid, and did not unite at this time to go up against the people of Adam.

40 And thus we can see that the promises of the Lord shall be fulfilled unto all those who keep his commandments.

41 And it came to pass that Adam, and those who followed him, were guided by the Spirit whither they should go. And they constructed ships that they had never before seen among them, even according to the Spirit that directed them in the construction of these ships.

42 And they carried forth many of the seeds that they had harvested in the land of Eden. And they also took with them many of the animals that they had trained to help them till the earth and harvest the fruits thereof.

43 And it came to pass that they set forth upon the many waters and traveled until they came to a great continent that they had never seen before. And they entered into a waterway that carried them into the middle of this continent. And when they had entered into this passage between the lands, they traveled for a time on the great expanse of sea that was enclosed by these great continents.

44 And they traveled upon this sea until they came to a great river that flowed into it. And they found that the borders of this river were verdant and bountiful, like unto the land of Eden. Nevertheless, these borders were limited in their expanse, and were surrounded by deserts and desolate land that was uninhabitable for the children of men.

45 And they also found in these lands, other beings of a lower order that were like unto them, even the descendants of those who had found their way to the land of Eden. And these beings were descendants of those who had bred with the children of Adam and had corrupted the bodies that God had created for them.

46 And there were many among the children of Adam, who had chosen to leave the land of Eden and follow him across the great waters, that were descendants of Beneli and of those who did not have the pure blood of Adam.

47 And it came to pass that as they began to settle in this new land, many of them began to explore the land in search of other areas where they could live. And as they traveled eastward, they found other great rivers which spilled their waters into the oceans that surrounded the land. And these great continents were exceedingly large.

48 And it came to pass that the sons and daughters of Adam began to inhabit these lands, many of them finding the great rivers that existed there and settling in the borders thereof.

49 And after many years of inhabiting these lands, the children of Adam were interspersed with those other beings of a lower order that were like unto them. And it came to pass that these beings ceased to exist, for they had been driven out of their lands by the children of Adam, or mixed in with them, contrary to the commandments of God concerning this thing.

50 And Amalek and Amoran rebelled against Adam, and were desirous to return again to the land of Eden and take back the land that they had left for the Benelites and Cainites to possess. And because they rebelled against Adam, they did not carry with them the words that he had caused to be written, which words contained the commandments of God.

51 And because they had no other form of writing among them, which to use as an example to teach their children, their language became corrupt.

52 And it came to pass that all those who did not carry forth the words that Adam had caused to be written soon found that their languages and manner of communication had become corrupted.

53 And in this way the peoples of the earth began to divide themselves and create their own languages and cultures among them. But among those who listened to the words of Adam, and obeyed the commandments of God, and carried this written word among them; yea, even among these, they did retain the pure language that Adam had received from the Father.

54 And it came to pass that in the land of Eden there begin to be many wars and contentions among the Cainites. And after not many years, the contentions increased to such a degree that the Benelites could not maintain control over them any longer.

55 And the Cainites had organized themselves into tribes that consisted of the leaders that the Benelites and caused to be formed among them, even their captains and their chiefs. And these captains and these chiefs were ferocious warriors. And they began to divide the land among themselves and take that which they wanted by force.

56 And because the Spirit of the Lord had ceased to administer among them, they were left to themselves. And when a carnal man is left to himself, he becometh even more carnal, and beginneth to think and act like the animals of a lower order, which are driven by their instincts alone.

57 And it came to pass that the Cainites and their leaders would no longer listen to the flattering words of the Benelites, whose wisdom and intelligence they did not understand. And the Cainites sought out the Benelites and killed every one of them, and also their women and their children, so that not one Benelite remained upon the land.

58 And the wars and contentions between the leaders of the Cainites became exceedingly fierce. And there were some among them who were more pacified in their natures. And these fled towards the lands northward, which lands were not inhabitable because of the cold that had overcome them. But in order to save their lives, these fled from among the Cainites. And they traveled into the lands of snow and ice where they would not be destroyed by the wars and the contentions that existed among the rest of the Cainites.

59 And not many years had passed before the Cainites were all destroyed upon the face of the whole land of Eden. And there were some of those who escaped the wars and the contentions, who had fled to the great waters. And they made crude ships after the manner of him who had first deceived Eve in the garden of Eden.

60 And because these ships were not like unto the ships that the sons of Adam constructed according to the manner shown unto them by the Spirit of God, they could not travel as far. And many of them found the islands of the great oceans. And they began to inhabit these islands, which supported their needs.

61 But because they did not have the word of God among them, their manner of language was also corrupted. And when the children of men corrupt the language that they have been given, and have no example in writing of this language, then they do not retain the ability to keep a record of their history. And this because they do not know how to write the written words of their languages, not having an example to follow.

62 Thus we can see the importance of the commandments of God pertaining to the words of the prophets that He hath commanded the children of men to keep among them. And thus we can see the importance of keeping a record of the people.

63 And the brother of Jared saw all these things, according to the manner in which it was presented unto him by the Spirit. And, I, Moroni, can only write a small part of all that the brother of Jared saw pertaining to the children of Adam and their history.

64 But the things that I do write, are the things that the Spirit hath commanded me. And the Spirit shall command me according to the will of the Father. For the Father would that many of these things shall be made known unto His children in the latter days, so that they might know the plan that He hath outlined for their salvation.

65 And the things concerning the history of the children of men that I write in this record shall confound the written histories that the children of men have caused to be written among them. For those histories that they have caused to be written among them, are not always according to the truth. For those who have written these histories were not present when the events occurred, even all those events that have taken place among the children of men since the beginning.

66 And many of their records are from testimonies of others who were also not present when these events occurred. Therefore, all the histories among the children of men have been corrupted by the precepts and opinions of the men who have taken upon themselves to write these histories.

67 But if a man is not there at the time that an event occureth, then how shall he make the claim that his interpretation of that event is the truth regarding it? But the prophets of God know the history of men. And these prophets do not know the history of men by the power of their own sight, or by their own understanding. But these things are given unto them by the power of the Spirit.

68 And those that are in the spirit world see all things that occur among the children of men in mortality. And a record of these events is recorded by those who have been given this calling by the Father, under the direction of the Holy Ghost.

69 And there are also those who travel between the planet on which we live and the planet on which the Father liveth. And these also take a record of that which is occurring on this earth and present it unto the Father, that He might know all things pertaining to this earth that He hath created for His children.

70 And for this reason, the words of the brother of Jared are a more true and accurate account of the history of the children of men. And there hath been no other account that hath been given by the children of men that shall present the truth regarding the events of the past, than the words of the brother of Jared.

71 For this reason, the Lord hath caused that his words were sealed up and kept from the children of men until the fullness of time when all things shall be known among them. And when these things come forth, they shall confound the hearsay, and the speculations, and the theories, and the misperceptions of men who are not given the truth of these things according to the Spirit of God.

72 And according to the Spirit of God, a man may know the truth of all things and have the mysteries of God given unto him.

73 And now my beloved brothers and sisters, even all those unto whom this record shall come, the words that are written herein are true. And they shall teach you the truth regarding many of the events that occurred during the history of the earth.

74 Nevertheless, I cannot include all things herein, for there is not space upon the plates which my father and I have made for this purpose, and ore I have none. Therefore, the things that I write, are according to the abridgment that I have taken from the words of the brother of Jared.

75 And I write the things that the Spirit whispereth unto me to write. And what the Spirit shall command me, that I shall write.

76 And I know that there are those among you who would that I write the names of peoples,

and places, and times, and events, according to the language that ye understand, but these things are not important to the end for which the Lord hath commanded these things to be written. For what is called a name by one people, might be called differently by another, and therefore, these things can cause contention among you.

77 And the things that are written upon these plates shall be written to bring to pass your salvation, which salvation can only come in and through the words that Christ hath given unto you.

78 Nevertheless, by reading the accounts of the history of the children of men, ye shall begin to see the importance of the words of Christ, which he hath given unto us. And ye shall begin to realize why it is necessary that we abide by them. And this is the purpose of these things, and there shall be no other purpose given for them.

CHAPTER 24

The sons of Adam establish righteousness among them. The death of Adam is described. Many people begin to introduce idolatry and the worship of strange gods invented by the precepts of men. Moroni describes the wicked state of the world and its nations and kingdoms.

AND it came to pass that after more than two hundred years had passed away since Adam gave his counsel in the valley of Adamondiahman, he dwelt with his sons and his daughters in the new land where the Lord had led him.

2 And shortly after they came into this land, Jared, the son of Mahalaleel begat a son and called his name Enoch.

3 And these were the generations of the patriarchal order that Adam had set up in the church that he had established among them. And Adam caused that temples should be built throughout the land, so that the people could meet together often and hear the words of those who had been called to serve in the church. And also, that the people could receive the Holy Endowment, so that they might know the plan of salvation more fully.

4 And at the time of the birth of Enoch, the sons and daughters of Adam began to once again rebel against the commandments of God. And they began to search for gold and silver and the precious things of the earth, and place value upon them like unto the Benelites in the land of Eden.

5 And Cainan, the son of Enos, searched the new land for many years and came upon a land that was eastward and that bordered the great sea. And this land was a land also like unto the land of Eden. And he had taken Amoran and Amalek with him and had shown unto them this land that they might be satisfied therein and not desire to return to the land of Eden as had been their intention, contrary to the commandments of the Lord.

6 And Amoran and Amalek were pleased with the land. And it came to pass that each took a section thereof for the inheritance of their children. And thus the children of men began to once again divide up the land amongst themselves according to their families, which was contrary to the commandments of the Lord and the words of Adam.

7 And this whole part of the land that Cainan had discovered was called the land of Cainan. And the children of men began to name their lands after their fathers and after themselves. But Cainan did not want this land named after him, for he was a righteous man who loved the Lord and obeyed the words and counsel of Adam. Nevertheless, thus it was called.

8 And it came to pass that Cainan returned to the land where Adam dwelt, and beckoned unto him that he might bring himself and Eve, and all those who would follow him, and come over into the land of Cainan where they could once again worship the Lord according to the ways of the Lord.

9 And Adam hearkened unto his words and followed him into the land of Cainan. And Adam blessed the land, and he began once again to establish righteousness among his people.

10 And Adam was a righteous man all the days of his life. And he did not search for gold or silver or any of the precious things of the

earth. And would not allow that any part of the land should be called after his name. And he kept all the commandments of God that had been given unto him.

11 And his sons were also righteous men among the people; and these righteous sons were the leaders of the church that was established among them. For they did worship the Lord. And they did always unto others what they would have had done unto them. And at this time, the people of the land of Cainan did prosper exceedingly, and there was peace throughout the land.

12 And Enoch grew in the Lord and became exceedingly righteous before God, even so much, that many of the things that were revealed unto the brother of Jared, were also revealed unto Enoch, and this because of his exceeding faith, wherein the Lord could not deny him this thing.

13 And Enoch begot Methuselah. And Methuselah begot Lamech. And it was this same Lamech who was the father of Noah.

14 And it came to pass that in the days of Lamech, Adam began to be old and was ready to return to the spirit world and serve with Jehovah there for the sake of all the children of God.

15 And before he died, Adam called unto him all of his children once again. And Adam knew that his death was near. And it was his desire to die at the appointed time that the Lord had given him. For Eve had died ten years after the birth of Lamech, the son of Methuselah, who was a direct descendent of her son, Seth, she having fulfilled the commandments of the Lord in providing many bodies for the spirit children of the Father.

16 And Eve became honored exceedingly after her death. And many of her daughters made statues and idols unto her and worshiped her. And in this thing Adam was exceedingly sorrowful, and counseled with his daughters that they should not do this thing; for Eve would not have wanted this thing done unto her, because she understood that the Father deserved all the glory.

17 But many of the daughters of Eve rebelled against Adam and formed their own society of women, and took upon themselves honor that esteemed them above others. And this honor and esteem that they desired, these women did not feel that they received from the men, because of the patriarchal order that had been established among them.

18 And it came to pass that on the day that Adam knew he was to die, he called his sons before him. And according to the words of the brother of Jared, the meeting was exceedingly renown. For surrounding the bed on which Adam lay, even taking his last breath as a mortal, were his son, Seth, and the son of Seth, who was Enos, and Cainan and Mahalaleel, and Jared, and Enoch, and Methuselah, and Lamech, who were some of the most righteous men who have ever lived upon the face of the earth.

19 And Adam reminisced on many of the days of his life, and smiled upon them, knowing that he was faithful in keeping the commandments of the Lord during all the days of his probation.

20 And Adam called many of his daughters and granddaughters unto him. And his sons made way whereby these women could approach their father, Adam, and hear his words unto them. And their eyes were full of tears and anguish, for they knew that they were about to witness the death of the greatest man whom they had ever known.

21 And Adam took one of the daughters of Eve by the hand, even a daughter who appeared in the flesh in the same likeness as her mother, Eve. And he spake unto all of them who were surrounding him, saying: Oh, my beloved daughters, I would that ye should be the last on this earth to see my face; and that ye also are the last thing that I see with my mortal eyes before I give up the flesh and return home to the spirit realm of the Father.

22 And I know that ye have been engaged in childbearing all the days of your lives, in which ye have received much joy and happiness, in spite of the tribulations that exist because of the flesh. And thy brethren have been commanded to watch over you and lead you. Yea, they have been given the responsibility to teach you the things that the Lord taught unto me and your mother, Eve in the garden of Eden.

23 And they do not take upon themselves the honor and glories of men, but these things are given unto them by those who do not understand the mysteries of God and His will concerning those who are called to serve His children. But I understand these mysteries. And I say unto you, that none of them hath the power and deserveth the glory that ye do.

24 Behold, none of these men were with me in the garden of Eden. Yea, no other man was there, but your mother, Eve. And she was my companion, my helpmeet, my sister and my friend. Oh, how I loved her so. Oh, how I have missed her these many years since her death. And without her, I have felt a great loss and am unable to be comforted at night when I should be holding her next to me.

25 And when the Lord commanded that we should be one flesh, surely this came to be through the many years that we were together. And when I would cry over my children, even because of their wickedness, she would be there for me, holding me and wiping away my many tears.

26 And when I had forgotten my Lord, and thought that our life in the garden of Eden in the presence of the Father was just a dream, she was there with exceeding faith to bring these things once again to my memory, and to show unto me the righteous ways of the Lord.

27 And in exceeding strength and faith in the Lord, she did bring forth many children unto me. And she caused these children to laugh and smile and know her tender ways all the days of their youth. And even those children, who as adults, have rebelled against me; yea, these could not rebel against their mother. For she was gentle and kind to everyone all the days of her life.

28 And when she died, I held her flesh next to me for many hours, weeping exceedingly, because she had left me alone in the flesh. And my beloved wife could sense my anguish in the spirit world and came unto me unseen, and gave unto me once again her exceeding love and support. And without her I am nothing.

29 And now, my beloved daughters, I would that ye should hold me one more time, that I might feel the softness of your touch, and the gentleness of your ways. Yea, I would that ye gather around me and take my hands in yours, that I might once again think of my beloved Eve as I leave this flesh to once again be reunited with her in the spirit. For behold, I came into this world with her at my side. And now I shall go out with the freshness of her daughters at my side, who are in her likeness and her glory.

30 And the daughter who was like unto Eve fell upon Adam and wept upon him. And the other women who were there came close unto him and took his hands in theirs and wept exceedingly.

31 And the brother of Jared wrote, saying: And because I was in the Spirit, I could behold all the spiritual beings who had also surrounded Adam to welcome him back into the spirit world from whence he came. And Seriphia was in the forefront and smiled upon the words that Adam spoke concerning her. And Jehovah was also there, rejoicing in the mortal death of his brother and friend, Michael.

32 And with his last breath, Adam kissed the daughter of Eve upon her face. And Adam gave up the ghost.

33 And I beheld the spirit matter of Michael leave the body of Adam and enter into the spirit realm where he was greeted with the applause and love from all of those who attended his reentrance into this world. And with Seriphia at his side, Michael disappeared from before my eyes that I could see him no longer.

34 And now, I, Moroni, did also weep at the words that the brother of Jared wrote concerning the death of Adam. For I had not been allowed by the Lord to marry during the days of my probation. Nevertheless, I knew that one day I would be blessed with a woman like unto Seriphia, who was the woman Eve in the flesh. And I was desirous to feel the exceeding love and devotion that Adam had for his wife. For I knew that without the woman, a man cannot receive a fullness of joy in exaltation. And in the knowledge that one day I would experience this joy, I did rejoice.

35 And I would rejoice in this forever, if I did not have the commandment to write this record. For behold, I am forced to write concerning the great wickedness that befell the posterity of Adam upon the earth.

36 And it came to pass that many peoples did inhabit different parts of the earth. And there have been some records kept regarding the history of these peoples, but in most cases, there was no written history kept among the early peoples that inhabited the earth. But the sons of Adam did keep a record, and they passed it down from generation to generation until it hath come to the knowledge of all the earth.

37 And this is the record of the Jews, which is recorded in the Bible that ye already have among you. And because ye have this record among you, the Lord hath commanded me to write much concerning the history of the other children of Adam who did not keep a written history among them. And this he hath commanded, so that ye might have a more accurate record of their history, than that which ye shall be given in the latter days.

38 And it came to pass that when Adam and his sons came into the land of Cainan, many of his children were left in the land in which they had first arrived when they crossed the great waters from the land of Eden. And those who stayed in this part of the land were many notable sons and daughters of Adam, who were very wise as to the things of the world.

39 Nevertheless, they were not wise as to the things of God. For they took upon themselves their own wisdom, and began to believe that the things that Adam had taught unto them were foolish and vain things that profited them nothing. And they began to believe that the things of God profited them nothing, because they could not behold them with their eyes, or sense them with the course of the flesh.

40 And they began to find meaning and understanding only in the things that they could see with their eyes and sense with the feelings of the flesh. And in many instances, these things became their gods, and the things that they would worship, and to which they would pray and offer up sacrifice.

41 And they began to concentrate the efforts of their being on the things of the earth and the daily labors that were necessary to sustain their lives.

42 And because they had rejected the words of Adam, they also rejected the Holy Endowment and changed its form and meaning to represent their own beliefs, which arose from their different systems of culture that they began to establish among them.

43 And during the course of many years, there arose many great kingdoms and nations and governments among them. But of all these kingdoms and nations and governments, none was based upon the gospel of Christ. Neither were they based upon the Spirit of God that would lead a man or a woman to the gospel of Christ.

44 And Satan had tremendous power over them, evensomuch that he caused them to take that which is of God, and pronounce it as an evil thing before the gods that they had invented for themselves. And that which is evil, they pronounced as good and righteous before the gods that they had created—their gods being based on that which they believed.

45 And the children of men created many gods and many devils, each according to their traditions and their beliefs and the cultures that rose up among them.

46 And the family unit became the foundation of these cultures and these beliefs. And from these family units into which they had divided themselves, contrary to the commandments of God, selfishness and pride overcame the children of men.

47 And the words of Adam, which he spoke unto his posterity in the valley of Adamondiahman, began to come true throughout the whole world. And because Satan had convinced them that good was evil, and evil was good, he became their God, and also their gods.

48 Behold, it did not matter to Satan in what the children of men believed, as long as they did not understand the truth as was presented by the Father in the beginning.

49 And it was not the intent of Satan, ostensibly, to subvert the plan of God, but to prove that the plan that Lucifer had presented in the beginning was a plan that would be successful in bringing more happiness unto the children of God, than the plan that was presented unto them by the Father.

50 And power was given unto Satan, in that

he was allowed to rule and reign over the earth according to the heed that the children of men gave unto his enticings. Nevertheless, he was bound by certain laws that kept him from allowing the earth to be destroyed. For had Satan been released in the beginning, and given power over all his dominions, he would have caused the earth to be destroyed prematurely according to the plan of the Father.

51 And this because he would have revealed unto the children of men many of the powers and mysteries of the heavens that must be controlled upon the principles of righteousness. And if they are not controlled upon the principles of righteousness, then they can be misused to bring great misery, instead of the happiness for which they were intended.

52 And now, I would that ye should understand, that Satan did not want to destroy the earth, but to prove to the Father, and to all those who had rejected his plan, that his plan could succeed.

53 And he influenced the greatness and worldliness of the kingdoms and nations of men. And he inspired them to set up governments and laws according to the idea that he had in mind in the beginning, in which he desired to bring to pass the happiness that he believed was more righteous and just to all than was the plan of the Father.

54 And all of the kingdoms of Satan, yea, even all of the greatest nations that have ever existed among the children of men, did not last, and were destroyed off the face of the earth. And it was not the Lord who destroyed them, for the Lord shall do nothing that interfereth with the agency that was given to the children of God in the beginning, and this according to the eternal laws of heaven by which the Lord is bound.

55 And it was by the agency that was given unto the children of men that the kingdoms of the earth were destroyed. And in each kingdom, Satan attempted to establish new laws and new governments that he caused to be changed from time to time, with the purpose of finding the right government that would follow the plan that he had devised for our salvation.

56 And with much patience and love, the Father allowed Satan to try his hand, and incorporate his plan into the lives of the children of men. For the Father knew that all of the attempts of Lucifer to prove his plan worthy of consideration would fail.

57 For behold, the laws of heaven cannot be altered, for they are eternal, which meaneth they cannot change. Yet, they have always been the same, and shall always be the same. But it is the desire and work of the Father that He prove all of His words unto us, so that when we receive our eternal bodies, and are subjected forever to these eternal laws, that we might understand that they are righteous laws, and that there is no other way, except by these laws, that we can receive eternal joy and reside in happiness in the eternal worlds that He hath prepared for us.

58 And so it is that He alloweth the kingdoms and empires of the children of men to be established among us; that we might learn from our own experience that His plan is the best plan for us; yea, that His plan is the only plan that we can follow to find the peace and happiness that we all desire.

59 And from the time that Adam and Eve were banished from the garden of Eden, even from the time that the children of men began to spread themselves into all parts of the earth, the Lord hath established his Holy Order, both in the spirit world and upon the earth, to save the souls of his children.

60 And by way of this Order, he bringeth the truth of the plan of the Father unto us. For it is also necessary that we experience righteous living, or in other words, governments and peoples that understand and live by the gospel and the commandments of the Lord.

61 And for this purpose, the Lord hath called his holy prophets in mortality to go in among the people of the culture in which they are born, and give unto the people of the earth his gospel according to their understanding and their cultures, so that they might have a choice by which to live.

62 And there were times upon the earth that the children of men lived in righteousness and obeyed the commandments of God. And when they did this, they prospered in the land, and there existed great peace and harmony among them. But when they disobeyed His commandments, and lived by the commandments and precepts of men, then there were all manner of persecutions, strifes, idolatries, lasciviousness, and chaos among them.

63 And these are the things which Nephi saw in his vision. Behold, Nephi saw the whole earth and the formation of a great and abominable church that was established by Satan. And the angel spake unto him, saying: Look! And I looked and beheld many nations and kingdoms.

64 And the angel said unto me: What beholdest thou? And I said: I behold many nations and kingdoms. And he said unto me: These are the nations and kingdoms of the Gentiles.

65 And it came to pass that I saw among the nations of the Gentiles the formation of a great church. And the angel said unto me: Behold the formation of a church which is most abominable above all other churches, which slayeth the saints of God, yea, and tortureth them and bindeth them down, and yoketh them with a yoke of iron, and bringeth them down into captivity.

66 And it came to pass that I beheld this great and abominable church; and I saw the devil that he was the founder of it. And I also saw gold, and silver, and silks, and scarlets, and fine-twined linen, and all manner of precious clothing; and I saw many harlots.

67 And the angel spake unto me, saying: Behold the gold, and the silver, and the silks, and the scarlets, and the fine-twined linen, and the precious clothing, and the harlots, are the desires of this great and abominable church. And also for the praise of the world do they destroy the saints of God, and bring them down into captivity.

68 And now, I, Moroni, would that ye should know that this great and abominable church is the nations and the kingdoms of the world, even all those that have been and all those that shall be upon the face of the earth until the Lord cometh again in his glory to reclaim the earth and take it back from Satan.

69 And the formation of this church began in the days of Adam, when his eldest son, Beneli, gave in to the enticings of his natural father. And since that time, the natural man hath been an enemy of God, and will be part of this great and abominable church forever and ever, unless he yieldeth to the enticings of the Holy Spirit, and putteth off the natural man and becometh a saint through the atonement of Christ the Lord, and becometh as a child, submissive, meek, humble, patient, full of love, willing to submit to all things which the Lord seeth fit to inflict upon him, even as a child doth submit to his father—and this according to the words of King Benjamin which are given in the record of my father.

70 And when the Lord hath reclaimed the earth, he shall once again teach his gospel unto the children of men in the same manner that he taught it unto the Jews, and also unto the Nephites and the Lamanites who were in the land of Bountiful.

71 And his gospel shall spread throughout the earth and be established in all the corners thereof. And then shall come to pass the words of Isaiah, which he wrote, saying: And it shall come to pass in the last days, that the mountain of the house of the Lord shall be established in the top of the mountains, and shall be exalted above the hills; and all nations shall flow unto it.

72 And many people shall go and say, Come ye, and let us go up to the mountain of the Lord, to the house of the God of Jacob; and he will teach us of his ways, and we will walk in his paths: for out of Zion shall go forth the law, and the word of the Lord from Jerusalem.

73 And he shall judge among the nations, and shall rebuke many people: and they shall beat their swords into plowshares, and their spears into pruninghooks: nation shall not lift up sword against nation, neither shall they learn war any more.

74 Oh, house of Jacob, come ye, and let us walk in the light of the Lord.

75 Therefore thou hast forsaken thy people the house of Jacob, because they be replenished from the east, and are soothsayers like the Philistines, and they please themselves in the children of strangers.

76 Their land also is full of silver and gold, neither is there any end of their treasures; their land is also full of horses, neither is there any end of their chariots: Their land also is full of idols; they worship the work of their own hands, that which their own fingers have made And the mean man boweth not down, and the great man humbleth not himself; therefore forgive them not.

77 Enter into the rock, and hide thee in the dust, for fear of the Lord, and for the glory of his majesty. The lofty looks of man shall be humbled, and the haughtiness of men shall be bowed down, and the Lord alone shall be exalted in that day.

78 For the day of the Lord of hosts shall be upon every one that is proud and lofty, and upon every one that is lifted up; and he shall be brought low. And upon all the cedars of Lebanon, that are high and lifted up, and upon all the oaks of Bashan; and upon all the high mountains, and upon all the hills that are lifted up, and upon every high tower, and upon every fenced wall, and upon all the ships of Tarshish, and upon all pleasant pictures.

79 And the loftiness of man shall be bowed down, and the haughtiness of men shall be made low: and the Lord alone shall be exalted in that day. And the idols he shall utterly abolish.

80 And they shall go into the holes of the rocks, and into the caves of the earth, for fear of the Lord, and for the glory of his majesty, when he ariseth to shake terribly the earth.

81 In that day a man shall cast his idols of silver, and his idols of gold, which they made each one for himself to worship, to the moles and to the bats; to go into the clefts of the rocks, and into the tops of the ragged rocks, for fear of the Lord, and for the glory of his majesty, when he ariseth to shake terribly the earth.

82 Cease ye from man, whose breath is in his nostrils: for wherein is he to be accounted of?

83 And now, I, Moroni, would that ye should know, even all of you who shall receive these things, which were sealed to come forth at the time of the commencement of the work of the Father, that the words of Isaiah shall not be fulfilled until the Lord cometh in his glory and seteth up his kingdom for the last time.

84 Behold, I know that there are those of you in the latter days who believe that your churches are the kingdom of God, and that He hath established you according to the words of Isaiah. And that God hath exalted you, even so that ye believe that those who join your church are those who are flowing unto it from all nations of the earth.

85 Oh, the pride and arrogance and wicked ways of the children of men. Why are ye so prideful in your hearts and so unwise in your speculations, that ye do not understand the word of the Lord when it is given unto you in such plainness?

86 Behold, do ye not have the words of Nephi among you? And if ye have his words, why do ye not read them, and understand them according to the Spirit of the Lord, which shall reveal unto you the truth thereof?

87 Behold, the reason why ye do not understand them is because ye do not have the Spirit of the Lord with you, but ye have the Spirit of the devil. And ye belong to the church of the devil, and not to the church of the Lamb of God, as ye suppose.

88 And did not Nephi explain unto you that there are save, two churches only upon the face of the whole earth? The one is the church of the Lamb of God, and the other is the church of the devil.

89 And did he not say unto you that if ye belongeth not to the church of the Lamb of God, then ye belongeth to the church of the devil? And how is it that ye do not understand these things?

90 And I know that there are many religions and beliefs among you, and that ye have organized yourselves into churches according to these beliefs, and also according to your traditions. Yet, ye still do not understand the meaning of two only?

91 There are not many churches of God, save it be but one. And a church doth not mean the religions to which ye belong; a church is made up of a group of people who believe a certain way. And because of the way that they believe, their works manifest that they belong to this church.

92 And ye cannot say that the church might be evil, but its beliefs are righteous. For a church consisteth of those who believe and act upon those beliefs. Therefore, if the works of those who belongeth to a church are evil, then that church is also evil. And if the works of those who belongeth to a church are righteous, then that church is also righteous.

93 And likewise there are not many churches of the devil, there is but one. And one and one are two. Therefore, there are save two churches only.

94 And many of you believe in your hearts that ye belong to the church of the Lamb of God, and that your neighbor belongeth to the church of the devil. But I say unto you, that ye all belongeth to the church of the devil, and this because of your works. For ye do the works of the devil and have the desires of his church.

95 And again, can I speak unto you more plainly? Have I not repeated the words of Nephi, which ye have among you, and which ye proclaim to believe, yet ye understandeth them not? Do ye not desire gold, and silver, and silks, and scarlets, and fine-twined linen, and all manner of precious clothing?

96 And are not gold, and the silver, and the silks, and the scarlets, and the fine-twined linen, and the precious clothing, the desires of your church? And are ye not constantly engaged in acquiring these things?

97 And your temples and your churches, are they not made from the fine things of the world; yea, even so exceedingly fine that ye rob the poor because of them? And do ye not construct them in a way that ye might receive the praise of the world?

98 And also for the praise of the world ye do destroy the saints of God, and bring them down into captivity.

99 And ye say amongst yourselves: We do not destroy the saints of God, for we are the saints of God. Nor do we bring any into captivity because of the righteousness of the laws of our nation, and also the teachings of our church, which forbid such things.

100 Behold, I, Moroni, say unto you, that ye have mistaken that which is good to be evil, and that which is evil, ye have accepted it as good. For ye would believe that this destruction and captivity, yea, even the persecution and murder of these saints, are things that ye do not do. And ye believe this, because ye think that this is a physical thing that ye do unto them. But these things have nothing to do with the things of the flesh, but with the things of the spirit.

101 And ye do not realize how ye destroy the true saints of God and lead them into captivity. And ye do not understand these things, because ye do not understand the words that ye have before you, even the words of the holy scriptures, which have been given unto you in the record of my father.

102 Yea, it hath been explained unto you how the devil useth his subtlety to deceive the people, and this subtlety causeth them to not understand the things of God. And this subtlety he useth as a snare, which he hath laid to catch the saints of God, that he might bring them under subjection unto him, that he might encircle them about with his chains, and that he might chain them down to everlasting destruction, according to the power of his captivity. And ye also use these same chains to lead into captivity the true saints of God.

103 And I say unto you, how many of you know and understand the mysteries of God, yea even in full? And I have heard your words according to the things that the Lord hath shown unto me concerning you. And ye say amongst yourselves: It is not necessary that we understand all the mysteries of God; for they are not that we should understand them. For if we were to understand them, then God would reveal them to the leaders of our church, and only through them shall we be led in all things. But of the mysteries of God, we should not speak amongst ourselves.

104 Oh, ye wicked and perverse people, how long shall the Lord suffer you to destroy the righteousness of the true saints and lead them into captivity because of your ignorance? Behold, ye have the words of Alma, but ye do not have the Spirit to help you understand them. And ye do not have the Spirit, because your hearts are set upon your gold and your silver and your precious things.

105 Behold, Alma explained what is meant by the captivity in which ye have led the saints of God. And my father wrote the words which Alma spake concerning these things. And he wrote, saying: And therefore, he that will harden

his heart, the same receiveth the lesser portion of the word; and he that will not harden his heart, to him is given the greater portion of the word, until it is given unto him to know the mysteries of God, until he know them in full.

106 And they that will harden their hearts, to them is given the lesser portion of the word until they know nothing concerning his mysteries; and then they are taken captive by the devil, and led by his will down to destruction. Now this is what is meant by the chains of hell.

107 And now, I would ask you if these things are not plain enough for your understanding? Behold, there are a few humble followers of Christ among you who are the true saints of God. And these are being deceived and held captive by the subtlety of the devil, and also by your precepts and doctrines, which ye have taught them.

108 For ye have changed the Holy Endowment and introduced doctrine and precepts, which are the doctrine and precepts of men. And ye follow the examples of your leaders, which examples follow after the works of the great and abominable church. Nevertheless, ye say that your leaders are righteous because they persuade you to read the words of Christ.

109 But I have already shown unto you that ye do not understand the words of Christ. And your leaders also do not understand them. And therefore, your leaders and their examples cause you to justify your own wickedness.

110 And ye have changed the commandments and ordinances of God, so that ye might not be ridiculed by the world. And because ye have done these things, the members of your churches are in captivity, even being led captive by the devil and his angels.

111 And this is what is meant by their being murdered and destroyed by you. For they are destroyed as to things of righteousness. And ye murder them as Alma hath expressed his remorse, even in the way in which he misled and deceived the saints of God in his day. Even Alma said: Yea, and I had murdered many of his children, or rather led them away unto destruction; yea, and in fine, so great had been my iniquities, that the very thought of coming into the presence of my God did rack my soul with inexpressible horror.

112 Oh, my beloved brothers and sisters, if only the Lord would do unto you what he did unto Alma to cause him to recognize the sins and the murders and the destruction that he caused among the people. Oh, that ye might realize what ye have done before it is too late, and before ye feel this inexpressible horror in the presence of God.

113 And now, I would that ye should know, that thus it is with all the kingdoms of the world that are not set up according to the words of Christ.

114 And it is expedient in the Lord, that the record of the brother of Jared come forth among you that ye might revisit the kingdoms and governments of men that have gone before you. And this that ye might see the reason for their destruction, and also the patience and mercy that the Lord hath had for them.

115 And ye shall read of the prophets that were called of God and sent among them to bring the people back to the church of the Lamb, and teach them His laws, that they might be saved, not only in the kingdom of God, but upon the earth.

116 And the covenant of the Lord that he hath made to all of his children, is this: Inasmuch as ye shall keep my commandments, ye shall prosper in the land. And inasmuch as ye keep not my commandments, ye shall be destroyed and led into captivity.

117 And the Lord hath promised that in the latter days he shall plant in the hearts of the children the promises made to the fathers, and the hearts of the children shall turn to their fathers.

118 And ye shall know of these promises by reading the holy scriptures, which ye already have among you. But the final testament of Jesus Christ, yea, even the words of the brother of Jared, which have been sealed up and preserved for the latter days, shall give unto you all of these promises.

119 And these words shall demonstrate the great mercy that the Lord hath for all of us. And then ye will understand the words that Lehi spoke after he had seen these things in a vision. And Nephi wrote these words of his father, saying: Great and marvelous are Thy works, Oh, Lord God Almighty! Thy throne is high in the heavens, and Thy power, and goodness, and mercy are over all the inhabitants of the earth; and because Thou art merciful, Thou wilt not suffer those who come unto Thee that they shall perish.

120 And I, Moroni, would that ye should know, that the words of Nephi are true regarding the kingdoms and nations which have been upon the earth, and which shall be upon the earth.

121 And as ye read of these great nations and kingdoms, ye shall begin to see why there are very few humble followers of Christ. And when there are humble followers of Christ, they are persecuted and murdered, as I have explained this unto you, and thrown out of the churches and kingdoms of men.

122 But in the end, the righteous shall prevail. And when ye receive this final testament of Jesus Christ, then shall ye know that the work of the Father hath commenced upon the face of the earth in preparing the way for the fulfilling of the promises that He made to our fathers. And Nephi wrote, saying: And it came to pass that I looked and beheld the whore of all the earth, and she sat upon many waters; and she had dominion over all the earth, among all nations, kindreds, tongues, and people.

123 And it came to pass that I beheld the church of the Lamb of God, and its numbers were few, because of the wickedness and abominations of the whore who sat upon many waters; nevertheless, I beheld that the church of the Lamb, who were the saints of God, were also upon all the face of the earth; and their dominions upon the face of the earth were small, because of the wickedness of the great whore whom I saw.

124 And it came to pass that I beheld that the great mother of abominations did gather together multitudes upon the face of all the earth, among all the nations of the Gentiles, to fight against the Lamb of God.

125 And it came to pass that I, Nephi, beheld the power of the Lamb of God, that it descended upon the saints of the church of the Lamb, and upon the covenant people of the Lord, who were scattered upon all the face of the earth; and they were armed with righteousness and with the power of God in great glory.

126 And it came to pass that I beheld that the wrath of God was poured out upon that great and abominable church, insomuch that there were wars and rumors of wars among all the nations and kindreds of the earth.

127 And as there began to be wars and rumors of wars among all the nations which belonged to the mother of abominations, the angel spake unto me, saying: Behold, the wrath of God is upon the mother of harlots; and behold, thou seest all these things.

128 And when the day cometh that the wrath of God is poured out upon the mother of harlots, which is the great and abominable church of all the earth, whose founder is the devil, then, at that day, the work of the Father shall commence, in preparing the way for the fulfilling of his covenants, which he hath made to his people who are of the house of Israel.

129 And I, Moroni, would that ye should give great heed to the words of Nephi. And as ye read this abridgment that I have been commanded by the Lord to make for you, ye shall see that the words of Nephi were fulfilled in every instance, according to the kingdoms and nations and governments of men. And ye shall read the truth regarding them herein.

130 And ye shall also read the truth regarding your own nation and its government. And ye shall read of your wickedness and your abominations before the Lord, which abominations make the whole land desolate of righteousness. And this is what is meant by the abomination of desolation spoken of by Daniel, the prophet.

131 And if ye do not read these things and humble yourselves before God, and begin to work righteousness before him; yea, even if ye do not stand in a holy place, and join the church of the Lamb of God, ye shall be destroyed and led into captivity.

132 And your captivity shall be that of the devil, who is desirous to have you. And when the Lord cometh to his church, which church is the church of the Lamb of God, ye shall stand without and weep and wail and gnash your teeth.

CHAPTER 25

Moroni continues his abridgment of the vision of the brother of Jared concerning the early kingdoms of the world. The Egyptian nation is introduced. The city of Enoch is described, and the great flood is discussed. The purpose for the written history of the nations of the earth is expounded on.

AND now I will return once again to the words of the brother of Jared concerning those of the children of Adam who began to establish kingdoms and nations among them.

2 And it came to pass that those of the children of Adam who stayed behind in the land that bordered on the great river, even that great river that Adam and those that followed him encountered in this new world; and these begin to divide themselves up into areas, according to their individual families.

3 And these families sought out the most fertile parts of the land where they could plant their seeds and raise their food. And they began to cultivate the land that was fertile in such a way that they began to raise much more food than was necessary for their daily sustenance.

4 And they began to take the water from this great river and dig canals and ditches wherein it would flow into places that there had not been water before. And in this way they did increase the harvest of their crops.

5 And this work was done by many families in cooperation with each other, having elected one to oversee the construction of their canals, and their waterways, and their dams. For the people felt that it was better that one man should have the authority over many in order to eliminate contention and disputations among them.

6 And in this way these people began to form their governments and elect their leaders from among their own families.

7 And it came to pass that these leaders became wealthy; and they did not work by the sweat of their brow, but required a payment for their services. And because of their positions, which had been given unto them by the people, these leaders began to develop schemes and plans whereby they could control more of the daily activities of the people, than the activities that they had been elected to perform.

8 And it was a benefit to the families that they had established among them to choose these men to whom they gave this power and authority from within their own families.

9 And in this way the children of men began again to allow Satan to exercise power over them. For according to the word of the Lord, a leader of the people should be the servant of all. And because they did not have the Holy Spirit to guide them, these peoples did not understand the principles and laws of heaven for the establishment of a righteous government.

10 And the only concern of the people was that they could feed their families, and have shelter from the elements, and have clothes to wear. And the majority of them spent their days providing for their own needs, and also for the needs of those whom they had elected to have power over them.

11 Now, this was the thing that Satan desired. For he knew that if he could assure that the power and control over the people fell into the hands of a few men, then he could control the rest of the people by the power and the authority that these leaders had been given by the people. For this was an eternal law by which even Satan had to abide. Even the law that giveth all the children of God the right to choose the leaders whom they would follow, and also the laws by which they would live.

12 And if Satan could convince the people to accept their leaders as chosen men of God, then he would have an even greater control over their hearts and their minds. And this was the desire of Satan from the beginning, even that he should maintain control over the hearts and minds of all the children of God, so that he could force them to obey the laws of heaven, without giving them the choice to do so by their own choosing.

13 And it came to pass that these leaders of the people, who were those who did not work with their own hands for their own support, began to introduce ideas to the rest of the people about the world and its creation, and its times and its seasons.

14 For behold, time is also something that

Satan desired to give unto the children of men. For if they had a sense of time, then they would believe that there was a beginning of their lives. And if there was a beginning of their lives, then they would realize that there was also an end. And thus making the concept of eating, drinking, and making merry all the days of your life, consistent with the cognitions that Satan intended for them.

15 And these lazy men began to look to the stars, and to the moon, and to the other planets in the heavens for the signs and symbols that they thought were necessary to keep the people under their submission.

16 And this great river of which I have written became known as the Nile River. And it came to pass that the people near the mouth of this great river, even that part that emptied into the great sea, became known as the people of the lower Egypt. And those in the southern part of the great river were known as the people of upper Egypt.

17 And there arose a mighty man among the people of upper Egypt, who became a king and a ruler among the people. And this man was not elected by the voice of all the people, but was given his power by the voice of the other leaders, who had for many years lived upon the spoils of those who tilled and watered the ground and brought forth the fruit thereof.

18 And it came to pass that this great king united the peoples of the upper and lower Nile and brought them under his rule. And he introduced unto them the idea that his family was of royal blood, and that only through the blood of his family could the ruling class be brought forth.

19 And this he had taken from the corrupt teachings that had been passed down among them regarding Adam and the pure blood of the bodies that the Father had given to Adam and Eve.

20 And now we can see how easy it is for a man to take a principle of righteousness and make it a principle that satisfieth his own selfish demands.

21 And because the people did not have the written word that Adam had caused to be written and carried forth among them, they did not have a correct interpretation of the truth.

22 And it came to pass that the numbers of these people grew exceedingly. And they were a delightsome and a fine looking people, they having the remnants of the dark skin that had been passed down from those who had defiled themselves with the beings of a lower order that had crossed over into the land of Eden during the early days of Adam. But as their generations passed, and as these people mixed with the pure blood of Adam and Eve, they became an exceedingly beautiful people.

23 And it came to pass that the people were convinced that the doctrine of their king was correct, in that the ruling class consisted of special men and women who had been chosen by the gods to rule over them.

24 And among the people of Egypt, many forms of gods were created and taught unto them. And they worshipped these gods according to the abilities of each, in other words, according to what each of these gods contributed to their daily lives.

25 And the majority of the people were taught that these rulers were partly gods themselves; and that the gods had come down among them and established these few for the sake of the majority.

26 And because of their deception and manipulation of the people, these rulers became very rich and fared sumptuously off of the labors of the people who followed them and bowed down before them. And they caused that great houses be built in their names. And they became the great pharaohs of the Egyptian nation.

27 And these pharaohs established a priesthood among them; and they called priests to administer in this priesthood, which priesthood served the ruling class and its needs and desires.

28 And the people were taught that the success of this life was based upon the material things of the world. And they were divided into classes of three; the first being the ruling class, which consisted of the pharaohs, who were the few; and the next class among them consisted of the priests and those who administrated the laws to the majority.

29 But the majority of the people were of the

lower class. And this class of people did all the manual labor that was necessary to gain this worldliness for their pharaohs, who they worshipped as their gods.

30 And thus had Satan entered into their hearts; and with the treasures of the earth, he began his reign of horror as he had promised.

31 And it came to pass that the Egyptians began to have some strife among the ruling class. And there began to be minor wars among them.

32 And there were other peoples upon the earth that were not of their land, and who did not believe as the Egyptians, but who were also under the great power and influence of Satan.

33 And great trade routes were established among the nations that existed upon the earth. And when one nation would hear of the contentions within another, this first nation would come quickly to that nation ripe with contention and make war with its people, that they might take its gold and its precious things and enslave its people, so that they would not have to work with their own hands.

34 And this was the purpose of all the leaders of the great nations that existed on the earth at this time. And this will also be the purpose of all the leaders of the nations of future generations of the children of men that shall be established after this time.

35 Nevertheless, in the early days of the history of the children of men, the sons of Adam tried hard all the days of their lives to live according to the principles of the gospel that had been given unto them.

36 But even among their own people, the lure of worldliness and the fine things of the world was too great, and their children began to succumb to the enticings of Satan.

37 And at this time, Enoch had established a city in the land of Cainan, in which lived the many generations of his children.

38 And they became an exceedingly righteous people. And they did not divide themselves into family units, nor did they have gold or silver or any fine things of the world among them. And they ate the fruit of the vine and of the ground, even those things that perpetuated themselves forever for their nourishment. And they ate no flesh, neither did they cook their food.

39 And they obeyed the commandments of God in all things. And the men of the city of Enoch were exceedingly righteous, each of them having only one wife, and concubines they had none; for there was no lasciviousness among them.

40 And their women were the most beautiful women upon the face of the earth. For Enoch and his posterity had maintained the pure blood that had been passed down to them from their father, Seth, who was created in the exact likeness of his parents, Adam and Eve.

41 And they had all things in common among them. And they had a church established among them after the Holy Order of the Son of God. And the leaders of this church worked by the sweat of their own brow and took nothing from the people.

42 And there was no government set up among them. For all of their children were taught the commandments of God from the day of their birth. And because there was no desire among them to acquire or seek out material things, there was no need for laws to be established to govern the things of the world.

43 And the only laws among them were the laws and the commandments contained in the law of the gospel that had been given unto them by the mouth of Adam.

44 And there were no taxes, for there was no need for them, as all people shared in the responsibilities of the needs of the city. And all gave according to their abilities, and received according to their needs.

45 And there did not exist, nor hath there ever existed, a people like unto them on the face of the earth.

46 And it came to pass that the other sons of Adam, who had corrupted themselves with the things of the world, began to desire the daughters of the city of Enoch because of their beauty and their grace. And they also desired to bring the men of the city of Enoch under subjection and make them pay taxes to the governors of their own cities and nations.

47 But these people had kept all of the commandments of God. And therefore, the Father was bound by the covenant that He had made with them. And because they had kept all

His commandments, yea, even every one of them, the Lord was bound by his word.

48 And it came to pass that the Lord sent Enoch out among the people that were not part of his city to preach repentance unto them in an attempt to turn their hearts back to God, so that they would not come into the city of Enoch and destroy it.

49 And the Lord did this that he might warn the other people of the earth of his indignation, if it so be that they would harm the people of the city of Enoch.

50 But even so, it came to pass that the wicked men came up into the borders of the city of Enoch.

51 And the faith of Enoch was exceedingly great, and when the enemies of his people came upon them, Enoch spoke the word of the Lord and the earth trembled, and the mountains fled, even according to his command. And the rivers of water were turned out of their course by the cause of the great earthquakes that were commanded by the word of Enoch.

52 And these great floods consumed the enemies of the city of Enoch. And the other peoples of the nations that were established in the other parts of the land, felt the rumbling of the earth, and heard the great noise of violence that was taking place in that part of the world. And they were all afraid, and dared not to come up against Enoch and the people of his city. And the fear of the Lord was upon all nations of the earth.

53 And it came to pass that the Lord spake unto Enoch and showed unto him many of the things that had been shown unto the brother of Jared, and this because of his exceeding faith and righteousness before the Lord.

54 And it came to pass that according to the words of the brother of Jared, he saw, that in the spirit world, Jehovah was well aware of the city of Enoch and its righteousness. And Jehovah went unto the Father and described to Him the things that were happening upon the earth. And he presented unto the Father the righteousness of Enoch and his people.

55 And it was because of this report from Jehovah that the Father sent some of His angels, who had power over the elements of this world, to watch over Enoch and do whatsoever Enoch would command. And these angels, who were servants of God, and were also exalted beings like unto the Father, came down upon the earth in disguise. Yea, they made themselves appear as mortal men, even those who were the most despised among men, that they might not be recognized and discovered.

56 And these watched over the people of Enoch. And when Enoch made a command in the name of the Lord, these angels of God did that thing to the earth which he had commanded.

57 For behold, no mortal man hath the body or the ability to exercise control over the elements of the earth. For this power resideth only in the knowledge and body of an exalted being. For this reason, the Father sendeth angels unawares unto us that they might do the will of the Father according to the faith that the children of men have in Him.

58 And these same angels were commanded by the Father to prepare the city of Enoch to be taken from among the people of the earth. For behold, the people of Enoch had passed through the days of their probation without sin. And they were ready to inherit the kingdoms of their happiness, which is their glory in the kingdom of the Father.

59 And because they had done all these things, the Father was not restricted in what He could do for them. And these angels caused a deep sleep to come upon all the inhabitants of the city of Enoch. And according to the words of the brother of Jared, they were taken up into the heavens.

60 And the brother of Jared wrote, saying: And I beheld columns of light coming down from the heavens upon the people who were fast asleep in the city of Enoch. And by the power of God, which is unknown by men, these were lifted out of their beds and out of their houses, and anywhere that they had fallen into a deep sleep by the commands of the angels of God.

61 And these angels caused this great sleep to come upon them by introducing a mixture of elements into the air that was in and around the city of Enoch. And all the people fell fast asleep by breathing this mixture of elements that was put into the air by the angels of God.

62 And these great columns of light were many, and were exceedingly great and wondrous. And upon these beams of light, were all the people of the city of Enoch taken up into the heavens.

63 And they were taken to the planet on which our Father dwelleth. And they were still asleep as they rested in the kingdom of the Father.

64 And the Eternal Mothers of these spirits, and also the Father, went forth and touched each one. And as these Eternal Parents touched their spirit children, each awoke and glorified their Mothers and the Father whom they immediately recognized, having had the veil removed from their minds by the touch of their Mothers, and some by the touch of the Father.

65 And the people of Enoch were accepted by the people who lived on the planet with the Father. And they could now understand all things that they had been taught as spirits by the Father, and also by their experiences during the days of their probation.

66 And many of their mortal relatives, who had died, were still in the spirit world upon the earth waiting for the day of their resurrection, but the people of Enoch resided with the Father.

67 And the Father explained unto them that they would not be given a body of exalted flesh and bone at this time, because it was necessary that they one day return unto the earth and be presented to all the world as an example that it is possible to live in mortality and keep all of the commandments of God.

68 And now, I, Moroni, would that ye should understand that there are many spirits who would want to believe that the plan of salvation that the Father presented unto us is unfair, in that it is impossible to keep all of the commandments that He hath given us. And for this reason, the Father took the people of Enoch unto Himself. And one day, these shall return once again to the earth and show themselves unto the children of men.

69 And they shall show that they still have mortal bodies, and with these mortal bodies, they shall keep all the commandments of God. And then shall the wicked see them and know that it is possible to do all things whatsoever the Father hath given us to do; and then they shall have no excuse for their wickedness.

70 And it came to pass that the Lord caused the city of Enoch that was left behind, yea, even its buildings and all the things therein, to be buried in the depths of the sea. And when the other nations of the earth found that the great city of righteousness had vanished by the fierce power of the Lord, they began to invent all kinds of stories as to why this occurred, using many of these stories to keep the majority of the people subjected under the power and authority of their gods.

71 And it came to pass that the children of men became very wicked, and there were none who were found to be righteous like unto the people of Enoch. Nevertheless, the sons of Adam, even the fathers of Enoch, which were Seth and Enos, and Cainan, and Mahalaleel, and Jared, the father of Enoch, and Methuselah, the son of Enoch; yea, all these did remain upon the earth that they might preach repentance unto the remainder of the children of men, so that they might persuade them to establish righteousness upon earth.

72 And it came to pass that Seth died and was buried next to his father Adam in the land of Cainan. And shortly after the death of Seth, Lamech bore a son and called his name Noah. And it is this same Noah of which the record of the Jews maketh a recording.

73 And for the sake of the room that will be needed for the other part of the history of the children of men, I do not make a full account of Noah and what transpired during the days of his probation. For ye have the record of the Jews, and that record is sufficient for the purposes of the Lord.

74 Nevertheless, the Lord hath commanded me that I should make mention of the account of the great flood that is recorded in this record. For behold, the great flood did not cover the entire earth, but only covered that land in which Noah and his sons dwelt.

75 For in that time, the people of the land did not know the great vastness of the earth. And when this great flood came upon the land, they assumed that the entire earth was flooded.

76 And this thing was taught correctly by Noah and his sons, but because of the traditions and corrupt nature of the men who would make

their own history, according to their own foolishness, the truth regarding this flood was not recorded properly.

77 But as to the record of the Jews, there was no need for them to know anything else that transpired outside the realm of the land in which they lived, even the land of Cainan.

78 And it came to pass that after the great flood, the children of Noah once again began to populate the earth and mix their seed with the seed of other peoples who were not affected by the flood in the land of Noah.

79 For behold, the brother of Jared was not a direct descendent of Noah, but he and his brother, Jared, lived in the land east of the land of Cainan many years after the great flood had subsided off of that part of the earth.

80 And the time of the brother of Jared was about the time that this great king of Egypt began to unite the people of the lower and upper valleys of the Nile River.

81 And if ye read the book of the Jew, ye shall find many of the errors of those who recorded this history. For after the days of Noah, the record saith that the nations of the earth were divided by the families of the sons of Noah, saying: These are the sons of Shem, after their families, after their tongues, in their lands, after their nation. But after this passage was written, the record then saith: And the whole earth was of one language, and of one speech.

82 Now, how can the families of Shem be divided after their tongues, if it so be that the whole earth was of one language and one speech?

83 And there are many discrepancies in the record of the Jews. For the Jews are a proud people, and would want that the whole world believe that all life came through them. And in a way, they are correct in what they believe. For the Jews are the chosen people of God.

84 Nevertheless, they are not chosen because of their righteousness, nor are they the chosen people from whom came forth the rest of the peoples of the earth. But they are the ancestors of Jesus, the Christ, who shall come into the world from their loins, or in other words from the generations of the Jews.

85 And in this way, they are the chosen people, only in that their lineage is the lineage that was chosen by the Father from which to have his Son come forth according to the flesh. Nevertheless, the Father could have chosen any of the other peoples of the earth to be the chosen lineage of the Son of God.

86 But it was through the lineage of Abraham that the Lord promised, that through his loins shall all the nations of the earth be blessed. And the nations of the earth have been blessed by the Son of God being born into the Jewish lineage.

87 For behold, there are no people on the earth that are the chosen people of God. For the Father esteemeth all flesh as one, and is not a respecter of any people or of any person. For we are all His children, even all the nations of the earth.

88 And in this the Jews do err because of the pride and the wickedness that is among them. For whosoever keepeth the commandments of God, is His chosen people.

89 And the Jews do not keep the commandments of God, for they esteem themselves above the rest of the children of God, and therefore cannot be His chosen people. But from their lineage the earth was blessed by the birth of Christ. And the Jews have rejected Christ. Therefore, how can they think that they are His chosen people, if it so be that they have rejected Him and keep not His commandments?

90 And in their pride, the Jews shall be condemned and allowed to be persecuted by the rest of the nations of the earth because of this exceeding pride, believing that they are a chosen people above all others.

91 And it came to pass that the sons of Noah traveled to the east to the land of Shinar and dwelt there. For the sons of Noah had dwelt in the land west of the land of Shinar.

92 And because the king of Egypt had made his proclamation of uniting the kingdoms of Egypt, it was voiced throughout the other nations of the earth that he might gain power over the whole earth.

93 And there were great warriors that had developed in the eastern part of the land, which came forth to go up into that part of the land in which it had been voiced that the Egyptians were uniting themselves. And these warriors joined with the people who had fled the land of Cainan after the great flood.

94 For most of the people in the land of Cainan were destroyed by the flood according to the record of the Jews. And the posterity of Noah was afraid that the floods would come again upon that part of the earth, so they fled eastward towards the valleys that surrounded the other great rivers in the land that would be called Mesopotamia, or in other words, the land between the rivers.

95 And in the land of Shinar, which it was called at this time, according to the record of the Jews, the people united with the great warriors from the East.

96 Now, the intent of the posterity of Noah was to build a city that could not be affected by any flood that might be sent up again upon the earth. And they began the foundation of a great city, even the city of Babel that is mentioned in the record of the Jews.

97 And the people were taught in one language, which was the language that Noah had spoken, even the Adamic tongue that had been passed down from generation to generation from the time of Adam.

98 And because much of the pure language had been corrupted by men because of the lack of the written word, which most did not have among them, the posterity of Noah caused that all of their children should be taught once again this true form of language, so that they could communicate one with another and build this great city that would never again be consumed by the floods of the earth.

99 And when the Lord saw that which they would do; even that they would not submit to his will and obey his commandments, but believeed that in and of themselves they could supercede the will of God by the works of their own hands; yea, the Lord did not allow them to gather themselves together and preserve the pure language among them.

100 And the great warriors from the East could not learn the language that the posterity of Noah had attempted to teach unto them. And because they could not learn the language of Adam, they became frustrated with the people of Babel and began to destroy them and bring them under bondage, even before they had a chance to build up the great city that they had intended to build up among them.

101 And they took many of the people of Babel as slaves and servants for themselves, and caused these slaves and these servants to be taught in their own language, which was a corrupted form of the pure language, which the ancestors of these warriors had spoken.

102 For when the sons of Adam had come into this land during the days of Adam, then did the whole earth speak the same language. But many of his posterity went into different parts of the land and did not carry with them the language that Adam had caused to be written for the purpose of preserving the words of God, which were given in the pure Adamic tongue from the beginning.

103 For Adam had caused these words to be written upon clay tablets and subscribed with tools that created the symbols for the words that he taught unto his children. And they also used the skins of animals to write these symbols thereupon. Nevertheless, the skins of animals did not last like unto the tablets made of clay, and therefore, over time, they were destroyed.

104 And the tablets of clay were given unto those who would carry the record forth with them and teach the things written thereon unto their children. And the ancestors of the brother of Jared had these clay tablets among them.

105 And their ancestors had spread forth upon the land and were not affected by the floods that destroyed the people in the land of Cainan. But the incident of the great flood was taught unto them by their fathers. For their fathers were familiar with Noah, he being a great one among them who had preserved the pure blood of Adam through his seed.

106 And the ancestors of the brother of Jared had also preserved the pure blood of Adam among them. And at the time of the brother of Jared, he and his brother Jared, and their friends and their families, were the only ones upon the face of the whole earth who still had the pure blood of Adam, which was undefiled. For the posterity of Noah had mixed their blood with the other peoples of the earth after the great flood.

107 And the brother of Jared came up into the land of Shinar to help build the city. And his intention in helping build the city was not to escape the judgments of God, but to build a city

like unto the city of Enoch. But when he could see that the others who had come over from the land of Cainan, even the posterity of Noah, did not have the same intention as he had, the brother of Jared sought out the Lord and what he should do, so that he and his brother and their friends might not have their language corrupted under the subjection of the warriors from the East.

108 And the Lord commanded the brother of Jared to flee the land. And because of his righteousness, and also to preserve the pure blood of Adam upon the earth, the Lord led the brother of Jared to the land of Eden, which was the land of promise that the Lord had covenanted to give to them that serve him and keep his commandments.

109 And before the brother of Jared arrived in the promised land, the Cainites and the Benelites had all been destroyed, or the remnants of them had departed from the land to the isles of the seas, or to the frozen land northward.

110 And the rest of the history of the brother of Jared and his posterity is given in the record of my father, even the part of their history that the Lord commanded me to write concerning them.

111 And now, I return once again to the history of the people of the earth of which we do not have a recorded history, even a true history that hath not been defiled by the precepts and ignorance of men.

112 And the record which ye have of the Jews, even the Bible, as ye call it, is not a perfect record, nevertheless, it giveth a more accurate account of the nations that arose from the descendants of Noah than doth any other record that was caused to be written at that time by the children of men.

113 And the vision of the brother of Jared giveth a true and accurate account of all the peoples of the world. But there were numerous peoples and many nations upon the earth, some of these were great nations, which were the nations of the great empires that arose and conquered most of the children of men under the power of their dominions.

114 But there were other nations that were not great, yea, even smaller nations that were hidden from the knowledge of the greater nations by the hand of the Lord. For if there were a righteous people like unto Jared and his brother, then the Lord gave unto them commandments that they should leave the lands that had been conquered by the great nations and controlled by the power of Satan, that he might lead them to a promised land where they could keep his commandments and have peace and harmony among them.

115 And the world soon became covered by many peoples. And even the smaller nations, which were hidden from the dominions of the larger ones, became corrupted in time, evensomuch, that by the latter days, all the nations and kingdoms of the world shall be wicked and under the power of Satan.

116 And the purpose of this record is to present unto you, even unto all those who are the elect who shall receive these things in righteousness, the history of many of these great nations, and also many of these smaller nations that were led from among the great ones.

117 And these histories that shall be given herein shall demonstrate to you the great patience and mercy that the Lord hath had with the children of men. And they shall also show unto you the great wickedness of the children of men, and the ways that Satan useth to deceive those that give heed unto his enticings.

118 And when the children of men give heed unto his enticings, then he hath them encircled with his chains, which chains cause them to kill each other and hate each other and do all manner of evil to each other, until their nations are completely destroyed.

119 And after ye have read these things herein, ye shall know that which ye must do in order to prepare yourselves, and also the earth, for the coming of the Lord in all his glory.

120 And if ye prepare yourselves, ye shall be saved at the great and terrible day of the Lord. And if ye do not prepare yourselves; yea, if ye do not read these things that have been prepared for you, and learn what the Lord would have you learn, according to the power of the Holy Ghost, ye shall not be prepared in the day of the Lord, and ye shall join the wicked who shall weep and wail and gnash their teeth when the Lord revealeth their wickedness unto them.

121 Therefore, I beseech you, even with all of my soul, that ye read these things carefully and ponder them in your hearts. Behold, live by the commandments of God, even by the words of Christ, in all things, and ye shall have the Holy Ghost to teach the truthfulness of these things unto you.

CHAPTER 26

Moroni recounts the history of Egypt, the first great empire. He explains why the histories of the human race are one-sided and seldom tell the whole truth. The pharaoh Akhenaton is introduced, and is befriended by the prophet Ubaid. The Egyptian nation is a great nation, which is later destroyed because of wickedness.

AND now, I return again to the history and works of the children of men according to the nations into which they have divided themselves.

2 And it came to pass that this unification of Egypt made that part of the land strong in their trade and in their commerce with each other. And these people were like unto the Benelites in every way. For they loved their families, and thought of their family units above those of their neighbors. And in their commerce and their trading they became exceedingly prosperous as to the things of the world; and they began to spread throughout the land.

3 And their rulers were put up before them as sons of the gods, even the literal descendants of their gods. And the people did worship them and give reverence unto them. And the priests, who had been chosen by their rulers to teach the people the ways of their gods, were also revered and put up above the people.

4 And because they were divided into classes, according to their positions in society and also according to their wealth, those of the lower classes became unhealthy, and their mortality greatly increased because of their poverty.

5 But this did not concern the upper class of people, who were supported by the lower classes, for they had been convinced, that the gods had given unto each man his own destiny. And if the destiny of a man caused that he was born into a lower, or laboring class, then it was the will of their gods that this man remain a servant to the rulers forever.

6 Nevertheless, there were some instances when a member of the lower class might became a member of the upper class, if it so be that he demonstrated a special skill or a knowledge that would benefit the rulers of the upper class. But in most cases, the majority of the laboring class of people remained so throughout the generations of their children.

7 And the people of the upper class began to enjoy peace and harmony. But this peace and harmony was not felt among those of the lower class. For these were in constant fear for their lives. For they knew that they were destined to be servants unto the gods that they served, and therefore, they did everything that was possible to please these gods, which included their rulers, the pharaohs.

8 And they believed that the desires of these gods were the desires of the leaders and the priests, who had invented these gods and presented them unto the people. And those who had invented these gods were like unto Beneli, in that they knew that they were inventing gods that would keep the people under subjection, and assure that they would not have to work with their own hands for their sustenance.

9 And the poor, who were the servants, and also who were the majority of the people, were not allowed to question the power and authority of their rulers and their priests. For they were taught from their childhood that the gods had given to the people these rulers for their benefit and protection. And they were taught that these gods would give no instruction unto them, unless the instruction was given unto them through their rulers and their priests.

10 And in this way, Satan began to breakdown the authority and means of ministrations of the Holy Spirit. For the people knew not that they could pray and ponder and receive revelation and knowledge from their true Father, who had set up the authority and administrations of the spirit world to give unto all of His children any revelations and instructions that they needed.

11 And when the Lord calleth a prophet to preach repentance unto the children of men, this prophet doth not set himself up as a leader among the people, nor doth this prophet instruct the people that only through him, can they receive revelation and inspiration from God.

12 For this is not the intent of the Father in calling a prophet for the people. For the Father loveth all of His children, and would that all of them know Him and receive the mysteries of

His kingdom in the way that He hath set forth by the ministries of the Spirit world.

13 And a true prophet of God would teach the people the commandments of God that they must obey in order to be worthy of the ministrations of the Spirit of God. And if the people repent of their wickedness and begin to obey the law of the gospel, then they shall be worthy of knowing all of the mysteries of God.

14 And if they know all of the mysteries of God, for what purpose would they then need a prophet? Yea, for what purpose would they need a ruler, or a priest, to teach these things unto them? And I say unto you, that they would not need a ruler, or a priest, or a prophet, or even a church in which to learn these things.

15 For they would already have the spirit of Christ, which spirit is received by keeping the words of Christ. And if they have the spirit of Christ, then they become prophets, seers, and revelators in and of themselves.

16 But this is the thing that Satan did not want in the beginning. For if the children of God did not need a leader to give unto them the blessings and wisdom of the Father, then there would be no glory in being a leader among them. And it was this glory after which Satan sought.

17 And Satan put his desires into the hearts of the rulers of the nations of the children of men. And he introduced to them the laws and the order that these leaders needed to establish in their kingdoms to keep the children of men under their subjection, and give unto them the glory that they desired.

18 And with these laws, the rich and powerful are given the better part of the things of the world. And because they are given the better part of the things of the world, they are envied by those who are poor. And because of this envy, they are worshipped and honored by those who envy them.

19 Nevertheless, the joy and peace that the rich receive in the flesh is the temporary joy of which Abel spoke when he confounded Beneli in the land of Eden.

20 And it came to pass that the upper class of the Egyptians fared exceedingly well for many years. And because they had peace and prosperity among them, they believed that the gods were pleased with them.

21 But there were not peace and prosperity among the majority of the people. But of the majority of the people, the historians who were called by their rulers to keep an accurate history of the nation, did not mention. For there was no king who wanted to be known for his injustice and ill treatment of those whom he ruled. Therefore, those who kept the history of the nations, yea, even those who were commissioned by the rulers, were biased in their reports.

22 For they did not report of the wickedness, and the poverty, and the suffering of the masses, but they wrote only of those things that would bring honor and glory to the ruler, or to the leader who had given them the authority and the commission to write this history.

23 And thus it hath been throughout the history of the children of men. For there have been, but a few, who have written the truth regarding the leadership of the rulers of the nations in which these historians lived. And if there was one who wrote the truth regarding the lifestyle and the suffering of the poor and the working class among them, which were the majority of the children of men, then that historian was killed or decommissioned for the things that he had written, which things were contrary to the order and principles of the ruler of the nation in which he lived, and the things which he had written would be destroyed.

24 And there were many rulers among the nations of the earth who were oblivious to the plight of the poor and the needy, and also of those who provided the labor by which the great nations of the earth were built.

25 For these rulers had nothing to do with those of a lower class. And anything that was reported unto them, was reported by a priest, or a religious leader, who had been called by these rulers to bring word unto them concerning the plight of their people. And it was the duty and commission of these religious leaders to teach the people, and assure that they followed the laws that were established by the rulers.

26 And if there were contention and misery among the people, then the ruler would place blame upon the heads of those whom he had commissioned to watch over the people, believing that those who were commissioned were the cause of the misery and contention of the people.

27 And these religious priests and leaders, who had been commissioned by the king, or the ruler, would not tell the truth about the plight of the people, fearing for their own position of authority; even that the ruler would find another who could bring him good word about the people.

28 Therefore, the majority of the children of men, throughout the written histories that have been given of them, have not been given a truthful representation of their misery and their strife and the great wickedness that was caused among them, because of the wickedness of their leaders.

29 And it came to pass that as the Egyptian nation was prospering, yea, as the upper classes of this nation were prospering, there were other nations upon the earth that were also prospering and doing the will and the desire of Satan in all things.

30 And of these other nations, I shall abridge the words of the brother of Jared in a way that might maintain a sense of order and understanding regarding them.

31 For behold, there are many prophecies written about these nations in the holy scriptures that ye have before you in the latter days. But because the leaders of the people were intolerant of any man who would speak against their glory, as I have just explained it unto you, these prophets wrote their prophecies in symbolism and in allegories and in parables.

32 And when the leaders, or their priests, read the words of the prophets, they could not understand the symbolism and the allegories and the parables that were given unto them by the prophets of God. But he who hath the spirit of prophecy, which is the ministrations of the spirit world as it hath been explained unto you, even this person shall understand the symbolism and the allegories and the parables, which have been given by those who share the same Spirit.

33 And in the course of my abridgment of the vision of the brother of Jared, I, Moroni, will attempt to give unto you the proper explanation of this symbolism that is given in the scriptures that ye already have among you. And by this ye shall know that all the words of the holy prophets have come true, or shall come true according to the time in which they were given.

34 And the truth of all these things shall be known unto you in this record. For behold, this record shall come forth at a time when the people shall be given a greater knowledge of the wickedness and the corruption of their leaders.

35 And there will not exist a law among those of you in the latter days to whom these things shall come, that prohibiteth a person from speaking the truth regarding the things that the leaders of the people do to cause misery among those whom they lead.

36 And the plight of the poor, who shall always be the majority, shall be known by way of this record, and also by way of the words of others who have reported these things to the people.

37 And the words of the prophets shall come to pass in that day, in which they have said: Hearken, Oh, ye people of my church, even the church of the Lamb of God, saith the voice of him who dwells on high, and whose eyes are upon all men; yea, verily I say: Hearken ye people from afar; and ye that are upon the islands of the sea, listen together.

38 For verily the voice of the Lord is unto all men, and there is none to escape; and there is no eye that shall not see, neither ear that shall not hear, neither heart that shall not be penetrated. And the rebellious shall be pierced with much sorrow; for their iniquities shall be spoken upon the housetops, and their secret acts shall be revealed.

39 And the voice of warning shall be unto all people, by the mouths of my disciples, who I have chosen in these last days. And they shall go forth and none shall stay them, for I the Lord have commanded them.

40 And now, I, Moroni, would that ye should ponder these things in your heart, even those of you who have received this sealed part of the gold plates that my father hath prepared for you. For ye shall begin to understand in what way the iniquities of your leaders shall be spoken of upon the housetops.

41 For ye shall have the ability to be in your homes and in your places of business, and see

and hear the reports of the actions of your leaders and your rulers.

42 And your leaders shall attempt to hide their wickedness from before you, but their attempts shall be in vain. Behold, the Lord shall use the miracles that Satan hath introduced among you to do his will. And it is by way of these miracles, that ye shall hear of their iniquities upon your housetops.

43 Nevertheless, I would that ye remember the commandments of the Lord, in that he hath commanded us to not judge with an unrighteous judgment. Therefore, it is necessary that ye have the Spirit with you in order to be able to discern for yourselves the truth regarding the things that ye shall hear.

44 For ye shall hear many things, and most of that which ye shall hear shall be that which Satan would have you hear. For Satan would have you hear that which are the things of God; and he shall convince you that they are evil; and the things that are evil, he shall convince you that they are good. For this reason this record hath been prepared for you.

45 But ye shall not understand this record, nor shall ye understand the truth, unless you have the spirit of truth within you. And if ye have the spirit of truth within you, then ye shall not be deceived by your leaders, and ye shall know the truth of all things.

46 And I have shown unto you the way whereby ye must live in order to have this spirit of truth with you always so that ye are not deceived.

47 And again I say unto you, read the words of Christ, and follow in his footsteps, then and only then, can ye have this spirit to be with you.

48 And it came to pass that the Egyptians did not have the Spirit with them, because they did not keep the commandments of God as they were taught by their father Adam.

49 For there was great lasciviousness among them. And they justified their adultery because they were taught the precepts and commandments of men concerning these things. And they were taught the importance of fidelity in marriage, but their marriages were given more for the sake of worldly possessions, than they were that the man and the woman should be one.

50 And this fidelity in marriage was hard for many of them to abide by because of the lasciviousness that they were allowed until they were married. And before they were married, the men had been with many different women before they made a commitment to the woman who would be their wife. And the women had also been with many men who were not their husbands.

51 And when a man married a woman, he would think often of those with whom he had been before his marriage, thus committing adultery against his wife in his thoughts. And these thoughts would eventually lead to the act of adultery outside the bonds of their marriage.

52 And because of the examples of their rulers and their priests, the people became exceedingly wicked. Nevertheless, they did not believe that they were wicked because of the prosperity of their rulers and their cities. For if their rulers and their cities prospered, then the people felt that the gods were pleased with them, and that they were living in righteousness.

53 And because the Lord loveth his children, he desireth that they should be stirred up in remembrance of their sins. And this because he understandeth that in their sins, they cannot find the eternal peace that he hath prepared for them. Yea, even because of his love for them, he alloweth their destruction.

54 Now this is the thing that ye should understand. For behold, the Lord doth not command a nation to rise up against another and destroy it. For the Lord would never command his children to disobey one of his own commandments. And he hath commanded us to love our enemies and do good to them that persecute us and hate us and despitefully use us.

55 And the Lord doth not want evil to come upon any of his children. Nevertheless, he hath the power to defend us against another, and save our lives and the lives of our children for many generations, if it so be that we love him and keep his commandments as he hath covenanted with us.

56 And thus it is, that at times, the hand of the Lord is stayed in our defense, if it so be that we have forgotten him and keep not his commandments. And for our own sake, he alloweth us to be led into captivity, that we may experience misery and strife and hardships. And his desire is that these things might be the cause of our humility, which might cause us to have a contrite spirit, which shall allow us to approach him through the ministrations of the Holy Spirit and be blessed by him.

57 And it came to pass that after many years of peace and prosperity, the Lord suffered the warriors from the East, of whom I have given an account unto you at the time of the city of Babel, to come in among the Egyptians and destroy their ways and throw down their gods.

58 And the cause of their destruction came from within their own nation, which was weak from internal disorder. For such shall be the destruction of all nations that have forgotten the Lord and keep not his commandments. For his commandments were given unto the children of men to guard against this internal disorder and contention.

59 And if a nation turneth again to the Lord, and repenteth of their sins, in that they remember him and the things that he taught unto them, then this internal disorder and civil unrest can be reversed, and peace shall once again be experienced in a nation that is repentant.

60 And it came to pass that the people of Egypt were not warriors and were not trained in the art of warfare, having never experienced these things before.

61 And they began to learn this art from those who had conquered them. And with this knowledge of war, they did unite themselves once again, and rose up and overcame their conquerors, and once again established peace throughout all of Egypt.

62 But this peace that they had once again established, was not established according to the spirit of the Lord. And because it was not established according to his spirit; yea, because it was established according to the principles of warfare that they had learned from those who had conquered them, the people continually feared for their safety.

63 For had they established this peace according to the Spirit of the Lord, they would not fear, but their peace would be everlasting.

64 And this fear led them to establish armies and navies and means of force that would pacify the fear that they felt in their hearts.

65 And again, it had come to pass that the words of Satan were fulfilled in which he said that with gold and silver he would buy up the means of force to reign with blood and horror upon this earth.

66 And it came to pass that the nation of Egypt became exceedingly great among all the nations of the earth. And they trained armies to protect them, and they caused that great cities were built up according to their traditions and the worship of their gods.

67 And it came to pass that there was a son of a pharaoh, whose name was Akhenaton. And during the days of his youth, Akhenaton played among the slaves, which were in the service of his father.

68 And among those with whom he played, was a boy whose name was Ubaid. And Ubaid had been foreordained by the Lord to become a great prophet to the Egyptian people. For the parents of Ubaid were a humble people who did not accept the many gods that were worshipped in Egypt.

69 Nevertheless, they were forbidden by law to speak their minds concerning theses things. And they were mindful of the plight in which the poor class of the people found themselves under the reign of the pharaohs.

70 And they began to teach their son that there was but one God, and that God would not want that any of His children suffer as the poor were being forced to suffer because of the wickedness of the rich. And they were gentle people who gave what they could to relieve the suffering of those who suffered.

71 And the father of Ubaid was one of the chief laborers who was assigned to the upkeep and maintenance of the statues of the gods that adorned the great houses in which the Pharaoh and his wives dwelt. For the Pharaoh had many wives, he being considered a god who had this right.

72 And the Pharaoh trusted the father of Ubaid and gave unto him great authority over all those who were his servants in his own household. And the father of Ubaid was a just man who dealt justly with all the servants of the

Pharaoh, and therefore, was highly esteemed among them for the way that he exercised the authority that he had been given over them by the Pharaoh.

73 And for this reason, Akhenaton was allowed to play with Ubaid all the days of their youth. For it was not permitted by their laws, that the upper class had established for them, that their children, who were esteemed above the children of the lower class, should play with or associate with other children who were not of their own class.

74 But it came to pass that Akhenaton became like a brother unto Ubaid. And while in the house of Ubaid, he would listen to the words of the father of Ubaid and ponder upon them in his heart.

75 And it came to pass, that at a certain time, it was required of Ubaid that he pass through the circumcisions that were customary among the people of Egypt in introducing their young males into adulthood. But among the upper class, it was not a requirement for them. For they had more sanitary environments in which they lived. But of the lower classes, it was a law that all males receive this circumcision.

76 And Akhenaton was forbidden from that time forward to associate with the children of the servants of his father, the Pharaoh. And Akhenaton was exceedingly sorrowful because of the loss of his friend. And he kept this sorrow in his heart because of the power of his father; and also his fear of the judgment of his father, the Pharaoh.

77 But Akhenaton wanted to be circumcised like unto his friend Ubaid so that he could always remember the friendship that they enjoyed as children.

78 And it came to pass that Ubaid grew and was wrought upon by the Holy Ghost. And he was taught the commandments and laws of God, and also the truth pertaining unto God. And he was called to preach repentance to the Egyptian people and show unto them the things wherein they had corrupted the truth concerning the commandments of the Father.

79 And it came to pass that as Ubaid taught the people these things, he was bound and imprisoned by those priests who were threatened by what he preached. And these priests, who were the holy priests of the gods in which the people had been taught to believe, had him bound according to the laws of the land, which did not permit anyone to speak contrary to the teachings of the priests of Pharaoh.

80 And Ubaid was held in captivity for many days and was given little to eat and drink. And his father went unto the Pharaoh and threw himself at the feet of his master and begged for mercy for his son.

81 And the Pharaoh knew not that which had been done by his priests, for they had hidden this thing from him. And the Pharaoh commanded that his priests give unto him an account of all that they had done unto Ubaid, and also an account of why they had done these things.

82 And the priests came before the Pharaoh and told unto him all manner of lies concerning the effect that the preaching of Ubaid was having on the people of Egypt.

83 And now, it would have been no great thing, if Ubaid had spoken of his beliefs and kept them to himself. But when his beliefs began to cause contentions and disputations among the people of Egypt, as the wicked priests reported to the Pharaoh, the Pharaoh was obligated by the laws of their nation to take the life of him who causeth contention, so that the peace of the kingdom would not be affected.

84 But in this thing, his priests had lied unto him. For the words of Ubaid were not contentious, but were the simple words of love that the Spirit had taught unto him. Yea, they were the words of Christ, and the law of the gospel as it hath been presented in this record. And because of the teachings of Ubaid, many of the people began to question the priests in whom they believed, but there was no contention among them.

85 But the priests knew that they could not reveal the true nature of the teachings of Ubaid unto the Pharaoh, for it would usurp the authority that they had received by the office of their calling, which was given unto them by the Pharaoh. For the Pharaoh depended on his priests for advice and counsel in the ways that he should govern the people of his kingdom.

86 And if their advice caused contention and

disputations among the people of Egypt, then the Pharaoh would require this at the hands of those to whom he had given the commission to watch over the people. For this reason, the priests of the Pharaoh lied to him about the effect of the words of Ubaid.

87 And the Pharaoh was bound by his word, and also by the traditions of his forefathers, to take the life of whomever disrupted the peace of the kingdom, which peace was only experienced among the upper class as it hath been explained unto you.

88 And it came to pass that the father of Ubaid pled even more exceedingly for the life of his son. But the Pharaoh had spoken; and nothing the father of Ubaid could say would save the life of his son.

89 And Akhenaton did not know concerning these things at the time that they occurred. And the father of Ubaid went unto the house of Akhenaton. And because he was not a servant of that house, and was not assigned by law to the house of Akhenaton, he was not permitted to enter therein.

90 But the father of Ubaid tore at his clothes and wept exceedingly and made his voice loud so that all could hear his pleas.

91 And it came to pass that Akhenaton heard the commotion that was being made in front of his house, and went for himself to see that which was occurring. And when he recognized the father of Ubaid, he immediately commanded his guards to release him and allow him to come into his house.

92 And the father of Ubaid recounted all the things that the priests of his father had done unto Ubaid. And Akhenaton wept also for Ubaid, for he knew that there was nothing he could do to save his friend because of the word that had been spoken by his father.

93 Nevertheless, Akhenaton went unto his father and pled for the life of his friend. And the Pharaoh did not have compassion on the words of his son, and forbade him from ever speaking of the matter before him again. But in one final effort to do what he could for Ubaid, Akhenaton pleaded with his father that he, who was one of the royal sons, could administer this sentence of death unto Ubaid.

94 And because of the laws that were among them, the Pharaoh could not forbid his son from doing that which he desired. For it was a long standing tradition among them that the sons of the pharaohs be given the opportunity to carry out the commands of their fathers, and in this way, show their loyalty and integrity to the throne, which one of them would receive upon the death of the reigning pharaoh. And because of this thing that Akhenaton desired of his father, the Pharaoh; even that he would take the life of his beloved friend for the sake of the law and order that had been established among them; Akhenaton showed his loyalty to his father and to all of Egypt.

95 And because of this thing, the Pharaoh pronounced upon him that he would inherit the throne upon his death. And when the Pharaoh had announced this, it became law.

96 And this was not the desire of the priests, for they were enjoined in their desire to have another of the sons of the Pharaoh inherit the throne, even one that they had taught themselves, since the day of his birth.

97 But in this, their plan was spoiled, for the word of the Pharaoh when spoken, was like unto the word of God to the people. And Akhenaton was anointed to be their Pharaoh and their God, and in this, the wicked priests were uneasy, but they had no choice but to submit themselves to the word of the Pharaoh.

98 And it came to pass that there was not a set time that the sentence of death had to be administered unto Ubaid. And Akhenaton went into Ubaid in captivity, and wept upon him, and told his friend that which he had to do.

99 And Ubaid smiled upon his beloved friend, and held him close to his bosom and said unto him: Oh, my beloved Akhenaton, cry not for me, for to this end was I called before this world was. Behold, dost thou not realize, that because of this thing, thou shall sit upon the throne of thy father and rule and reign over this people? And dost thou not realize that we have been forbidden to see each other for these many years, even since the days of our youth? And if this thing had not come to pass, then we might not have ever seen each other again.

100 And it came to pass that Ubaid spent

many hours reminiscing with Akhenaton about the happy times of their youth. And Akhenaton was comforted by these things, and stopped his weeping for a time

101 And Ubaid continued, saying: Behold, I have been called by God to preach repentance unto this people, and to teach them the truth regarding those things that they have been taught by the traditions of their fathers, which are the precepts of men. For the things that they have been taught are contrary to the laws of happiness by which God would have us live, so that we might be happy upon this earth, and also, that we might be happy when we return once again to live with Him in His kingdoms.

102 And Akhenaton was confused, and said unto him: Of which of our gods dost thou speak? And what is it that thou hast said concerning this happiness in the kingdoms of this God? And I know that when we die, we go unto the land of Osiris, and there we will be placed according to our status here upon this earth. And for this reason we have the priests of Osiris to teach us the things that we must do to prepare ourselves for this afterlife.

103 But I do not know of what happiness to which thou referest thyself, when thou sayest that we shall be happy when we live with Him in His kingdoms. For it hath been taught unto us that there is only one kingdom after this life, and that it is the kingdom of Osiris.

104 And when I die, it hath been taught unto me by the priests of Osiris, and also the priests of our other gods, that I shall rule and reign in the afterlife, as I shall rule and reign here. And that all men shall fulfill the destiny that the gods have given unto them, both here upon this earth, and in the afterlife.

105 And Ubaid answered him, saying: What thinkest thou, my friend, of my life and the position in this life that I hold? Dost thou not know the suffering of those that are not of thy class? Is it so, that we must suffer in the afterlife, because we are not of the class to which thou belongest?

106 And would thou wantest that I suffer in the afterlife as I have suffered here, as a servant to thy father and to his priests? Remember when we played together in our youth, and I was elected pharaoh over us, and you subjected yourself unto me, that we might play out the desires of our hearts as children?

107 Were we not happy believing that we were equal, and that we were brothers? And did thou not findest joy and acceptance and love in my house with my parents and with my brothers and my sisters? Rememberest thou the time, when thou wanted to change places with me, and have me dress in thy royal garments, and have my garments, even the vestment of a slave, put upon thee? And we exchanged our clothes, and laughed and played in them.

108 And thou would bow down before me and do what I commanded of thee. Rememberst thou, what it was that I commanded thee to do at that time? Behold, I commanded thee to always be my best friend and my brother, and always remember me when thou sittest upon the throne of thy father? And thou promised me that I would always be thy friend, and that thou wouldst never have a cause to forget me. And in this promise, thou hast been faithful.

109 And because of the promise of thy love for me, thou hast taken it upon thyself to administer the sentence that thy father hath pronounced upon my head. And with this pronouncement, thou shalt be able to keep the rest of the promise that thou madest unto me in our youth, even that thou wouldst always remember me.

110 And after hearing these words from Ubaid, Akhenaton fell again upon his friend and wept, saying: Oh, my beloved Ubaid, I shall never forget thee. I beg of thee, tell me that which thou wouldst have me do in honor of thy memory, that thou mightest know that I shall keep the promise I have made unto thee all the days of my life.

111 Now, this was the thing that Ubaid had hoped his friend would say. For he knew that the word of the son of a pharaoh was just as binding as the word of the Pharaoh himself. And Ubaid spoke again, saying: I would that thou spendest the last few days of my life with me, that I might teach unto thee all the things which I have learned from the God of which I have spoken.

112 And after thou hast listened to my words, I would that thou shouldst remember these words, even as thou sittest upon the throne of thy father. And even if thou should only remember my words, then that would be the greatest honor that I could receive from thee as my friend.

113 And it came to pass that Akhenaton did that which Ubaid had requested of him. And for many days he would go into the prison where Ubaid was being held captive and listen to the words of this prophet of God.

114 And the Holy Ghost came upon Akhenaton, and he believed the things which he had been taught by Ubaid. And in this manner, the Lord prepared a way whereby the Egyptian nation could receive his words, even by way of one of their kings.

115 And it came to pass that the day arrived in which Akhenaton was forced to administer the sentence of death unto Ubaid. And this administration of death was done according to the desire of he who was administering it.

116 And Akhenaton had searched among all the land for that which would administer death in such a way that Ubaid would not feel any pain. And he found a poison that would do this thing. And this poison would cause Ubaid to fall asleep before taking his life.

117 And with great anxiety and heaviness of heart Akhenaton went in unto his friend for the last time. And he wept exceedingly upon the breast of Ubaid. And Ubaid did also weep with him.

118 And when the time came for the administration of the poison, Akhenaton could not administer it unto Ubaid. And Akhenaton took the poison in his hand and was desirous to take it himself, not wanting to see his beloved friend die before his eyes.

119 But Ubaid reached forth his hand and stopped his friend from administering the poison unto himself. And Ubaid could not take the poison himself, for it was required by the law that it be administered unto him by the hand of Akhenaton. For if he would have taken the poison himself, Akhenaton would not have kept the oath that he had made to his father and to the people of Egypt, and then would the death of Ubaid be for nothing, and Akhenaton would lose the throne of his father.

120 And it came to pass that with the last strength that he had in him, Ubaid took hold of the wrists of Akhenaton, and he folded his hands around the trembling hands of his friend. And with much struggle at first, Ubaid forced the hand of Akhenaton to administer the poison unto him.

121 And upon eating the poison from the hand of Akhenaton, Ubaid looked at his friend for the last time, and smiled upon him, and said unto him: Remember the thing that thou hast promised me. I am your friend and your brother forever. It is done. And with these words, Ubaid gave up the ghost. And Akhenaton held the body of Ubaid for many hours thereafter. And as a spirit, Ubaid was then able to speak the consoling words of comfort to his friend, Akhenaton. And through the ministrations of the spirit world, Akhenaton was comforted.

122 And it came to pass that Akhenaton sat upon the throne of Egypt after his father died. And he caused the things that he had learned from Ubaid to be taught to the people. And he also withdrew the government support previously given to the priests of the other gods, and caused all to worship one god, even the God that he had been taught to worship by Ubaid.

123 And it came to pass that while Akhenaton lived and sat upon the throne of his fathers, many of the people began to turn from the traditions of their fathers and worship God. But the priests were numerous and influential among the people, evensomuch that they succeeded in terrifying the fearful people into believing that if they obeyed Akhenaton, they would suffer the wrath of the other gods that they had been taught to believe in by their ancestors.

124 And it came to pass that after the death of Akhenaton, the priests of Egypt once again turned the people to all manner of wickedness and idolatry.

125 And for many years the Egyptian nation was revered throughout the earth as a great nation to be feared. And it was under the rule of one of its pharaohs that the sons of Israel were subjected to slavery, according to the record of the Jews which ye already have among you. And because ye already have these things among you, I will save these plates for other things.

126 But I would that ye should know the reason why the slavery of the children of Israel, and also the deeds and works of Moses are not mentioned in the history that was recorded by those who had received the commission of historian by the pharaohs of Egypt.

127 Behold, I have already explained unto you that these historians were forbidden to write anything that would shed a bad light upon the actions and reign of the pharaohs. And for this reason, nothing was recorded regarding the dealings of the Egyptians with the children of Israel.

128 Behold, there were many more things that were not recorded regarding the Egyptians and their great sins and wickedness among them, as well as among the other nations that they conquered with their armies.

129 And it came to pass that after many years, the nation of Egypt was overrun and subdued by other nations, who were like unto them, in that they were under the power and influence of Satan.

CHAPTER 27

The reason why political leaders of nations have power and riches is expounded upon. The spiritual state of two slain soldiers that died in war is revealed. War is expounded upon, and the commandments of the Lord are given concerning the defense of a nation by going to war against another nation.

NOW, this power of Satan was over the entire earth during the reign of the kings and the civilizations that existed in and around the fertile river valleys of the earth. And because of his power, no one kingdom or empire could survive for long periods of time. Nevertheless, there were some that survived longer than others depending on the inner conflicts that arose within each empire.

2 For when the leaders could no longer subdue the majority of the people of another nation, which were the poor and the laboring class, then they would turn their armies against their own people. And this would cause brother to rise up against brother and family against family, thus eroding the uniting principle upon which these nations were founded.

3 But in all the nations of the earth, during the time of the Egyptians until the latter days, the rich and powerful, which were the few among many, ruled over and subdued the majority.

4 And the desires of the rich and powerful were given unto them by their God, who is Satan. And the cause of their power did not come from the strength of their own arm, neither did it come from the strength of their friends, or of their families. For the friends and the families of the rich and powerful, even the leaders of all the nations, are weak like unto themselves.

5 Behold, their strength and their power cometh from their armies and their navies, even the means of force that Satan hath built up to protect and provide his servants with the blessings that he hath promised them.

6 And if money had not been introduced among the children of men, or if a value had not been placed upon the things of the earth that have no intrinsic value as to the sustaining of our daily lives, then these rich and powerful would have nothing with which to pay their soldiers and their generals and their captains. And if they cannot pay their soldiers and their generals and their captains then they would not have armies and navies.

7 And the riches which they receive to pay for the means of force that they set up for their protection, do not come from their own work, neither from the sweat of their own brow.

8 But these riches come unto them like they came unto Beneli, who first introduced the system of value, or money, in the beginning. For Beneli used flattering words and taught the people to have pride in themselves and also in their families. And this same pride was a tactic that hath been used by many leaders to bring the minds and hearts of the majority under their control.

9 For these leaders speak of the greatness of their nation as if it was the only nation that mattered upon the earth. And they stir up the people to patriotism and hate for all other nations of the earth.

10 And with this feeling of patriotism, the poor send their sons to serve in the armies of these leaders, believing that by so doing, their sons would bring honor to their family; in that their sons have stood to defend their country and their lands from the wickedness of other nations.

11 And they would be convinced by the leaders of their own nation, that the works of other nations are evil, and that these evil works threaten the security of their own nation.

12 And when the people are thus convinced, then they are willing to give all that they can as a tax to these leaders, believing that they are supporting their freedom and their nation. And in this way do the peoples of the earth divide themselves.

13 And each nation putteth itself above another. And when they go to war with each other, the soldiers of the armies do not think that they are killing their brothers and their sisters, but that they are killing an enemy, who is a possible threat to their own families and their own nation.

14 And now, I, Moroni, have seen these great nations and their armies, and the great power that the leaders of these nations have over the hearts of the children of men. And the brother of Jared wrote concerning that which he beheld occurring in the world to which all the spirits of the children of men would return when they are murdered or slain in battle for the sake of their nations and their leaders.

15 And it came to pass that the brother of Jared wrote of two men, whose names were Selethared and Ameago. And they were both soldiers who were engaged in battle in a war that took place between the armies of the nation of the Hittites and the nation of the Babylonians.

16 And as these two soldiers were thus engaged in fighting one another, they rose up against each other and thrust their daggers deep into the heart of the other. And as they felt the searing heat of the pain entering their hearts from the cut of the daggers, they looked into the eyes of each other, and wondered for that moment, why they had done this.

17 And in the tongue that each spoke, and with their last breath, they did curse each other and died.

18 And the brother of Jared wrote concerning them, saying: And each of their spirits left the mortal flesh and entered into the dimensions of the spirit world. And they were each greeted by those who were dead, even those who had been the most familiar to them while they were mortal.

19 And each of them forgot for that moment what had been the cause of their deaths, for they were overwhelmed by the great love of those spirits who had surrounded them and welcomed them into the spirit world.

20 And without the flesh, their memories were enhanced, and they began to remember their existence as spirits prior to the days of their probation in mortality. And after a time, it was brought to their remembrance the cause of their death, and also their works and actions during the days of their probation upon the earth in the flesh.

21 And in the course of the spirit, Selethared went back to the battle field and saw his flesh thereupon, and also the flesh of Ameago, the man in whom he had thrust his dagger. And Selethared returned again to the reception area of the spirit world in which the spirits of all the children of God are received upon their death, to be greeted by their loved ones who had preceded them in death from mortality.

22 And he searched out this man whom he had killed on the battlefield. And Selethared found Ameago among the other spirits who had met him upon his entrance into the spirit world. And Selethared approached Ameago and was wont to speak with him.

23 And because the spirit was not burdened by the flesh and its limited means of communication, both of these spirits recognized each other from their thoughts, and began to hate one another for what they had done to each other during battle.

24. And there was a great silence among those spirits who were there surrounding Selethared and Ameago. And these two spirits stood in front of each other for a time, perceiving the thoughts and the memories of one another; yea, they truly were becoming aware of the experiences and the past life of each other through the communication and power of the spirit.

25 And Ameago spoke unto Selethared, saying: I know you now. You were my friend in this same spirit world before we entered into mortality. And you entered into mortality first, that you might begin the days of your probation as a man amongst the Hittite people of the earth in a family that you had chosen for the days of your probation.

26 And I watched you grow as a child, and I wondered upon you before I left this place and entered into mortality into a Babylonian family.

27 And why was it that our final thoughts of each other in this spirit world were thoughts of love and respect, even thoughts of genuine concern for our plights during the days of our probation. Yea, and our final thoughts of each other in the flesh were thoughts of hate and prejudice, even that we did curse each other with our final breaths?

28 Do we not even now remember our lives as spirit children of our Father? And can we not remember the experiences of our mortal probation, even all the days of our lives among the peoples and the nations to which we were born?

29 And how can we have this hate for each other, which was garnered and perpetuated by the nations and the families to which we belonged in mortality? Yea, how can we continue to have this hate now that we are spirits again and understand all these things? Are we not both children of the same God, even of the same eternal family to which all of these spirits belong?

30 And Selethared and Ameago pondered briefly upon the situation in which they found themselves. And they realized what had happened to them during the days of their probation. And they embraced each other by the power of the spirit, and were in a state of torment for a time for the way that they had felt about each other in the flesh.

31 And they wondered on the cause of such wickedness to which they had let themselves be submitted in the flesh. And as they wondered upon these things, the spirit who had been the father of Selethared in mortality did appear before them.

32 And Selethared did not have memories from mortality of this spirit being as his father, but he did recognize him as his friend, whom he had known in the spirit world before he had entered into mortality. For the father of Selethared was a righteous man who had been killed by the Babylonians in the flesh while Selethared was still a young child at the knee of his mother.

33 And this spirit bade that Selethared and Ameago follow him into the world. And the three of them went unto the house of Selethared among the people of the Hittites.

34 And there they saw the mother of Selethared weeping exceedingly because of the report she had received that her son had died in a battle against the Babylonians. And the mother of Selethared carried within her heart an extreme hatred for the Babylonians. And Selethared knew of this hate, having had it taught unto him all the days of his youth.

35 For he was taught by his mother to hate the Babylonians for what they had done to his father. And as a youth in the flesh, Selethared began to curse the Babylonians and dream of vengeance upon their heads for that which they had done to the father that he never knew.

36 And his heart was full of anguish and hate because of the things that were taught to him by his mother. And these three spirits could sense this hate, and this anguish, and the exceedingly great pain of the mother of Selethared.

37 And there was another son, who was the younger brother of Selethared, and he was attempting to console his mother, saying: My dearest mother, cry not for thy son, even for my brother Selethared; for I will avenge his death upon the Babylonians who have taken from thee thy husband and thy son.

38 And the spirits could perceive the intense anger and hate that swelled up in the heart of the brother of Selethared as he thought on killing the Babylonians who had killed his brother and also the father that he never knew.

39 And as a spirit, Selethared tried to comfort his mother and his brother through the ministrations of the spirit world in which he was confined.

40 But they would not listen to his gently

promptings because of the hate and the anguish that filled their souls. And Selethared began to feel this anguish and this misery, which is described as the state of misery that the souls of the wicked experience when they return to the spirit world and begin to ponder on the works that they did in the flesh, and also upon the things that they did in the flesh to cause so much pain and anguish to others.

41 And Selethared could not relinquish the misery which he felt, for it engulfed his whole spirit. For he had hated the Babylonians, even with all of his soul, during the days of his probation. And he had taught his younger brother, according to the flesh, this hate and this prejudice against those who had killed their father.

42 And now he could see the fruits of his labors. For he knew that his brother would go up to battle against the Babylonians, and that his brother would be destroyed, like he was destroyed, because of the strength and the great numbers of the Babylonians, but also from the blind hatred that swelled in the heart of his brother.

43 And there was nothing that he could do for his mother or for his brother to relieve them of their misery. And as he observed and felt their misery, it increased his own, and he was in a state of hell.

44 And the spirit who was his mortal father spoke unto him, saying: For so many years I tried desperately to speak the consoling words of comfort to thee and thy mother, that ye might not hate the Babylonians, who are the children of God, and with whom we share the same Father who hath placed us upon this earth, both as spirits, and also according to the flesh.

45 But the hate of thy mother was too strong, and she influenced thy hate, and I could not convince either of you to listen to the promptings of the spirit that I would give unto you.

46 And now, my friend, for truly thou art my friend, and also my brother in the Father, here is thy spiritual friend Ameago, who was with thee before thy entrance into the days of your probation. And he is a Babylonian whom thou hatest and whom thy mother and thy mortal brother hate, even with all of their souls.

47 And ye have killed each other according to the flesh, but see each other according to the spirit. And what is the cause of this hate that ye had between you in the flesh? Can ye see the great turmoil that Lucifer hath caused among us, because it was his desire that we be divided into families and into nations?

48 And because ye were divided into families and into nations, and because ye had forgotten your spiritual existence before entering into mortality, ye began to hate each other. And the only time that ye met in mortality was upon the field of battle in which ye were both killed in hatred and anger by the hand of the other.

49 And there are many spirits who have returned to the spirit world who have hated others during the days of their probation. And there are many spirits that have killed others because of this hate and this prejudice.

50 Now let us go unto the house of Ameago and see his family and that which they are doing at this time. And the three of them went unto the house of Ameago.

51 And at this time, the family of Ameago had not yet received the news of the death of their son in battle. For the battle was decisively won by the Babylonian forces, and the entire army of the Hittites was destroyed in this battle.

52 And because the Babylonians were victorious, they were celebrating in the streets of their cities; and they were praising the names of their gods for the death that they had caused to come upon the nation of the Hittites.

53 And all of the soldiers had not yet returned to their families from the field of battle. And the family of Ameago assumed that their son would arrive with the returning armies and rejoice with them in the destruction of their enemies.

54 And as a spirit, Ameago could perceive the thoughts and the desires of his family. And they were drunken with the wine of celebration and filled with exceeding pride for what they perceived to be the death of their enemies. And their dancing and their drunkenness and their wantonness were all done in celebration of this victory.

55 And Ameago became exceedingly sorrowful in the spirit, because of the things which he beheld. And he also made an attempt to speak to the souls of his father and his family, even according to the ministration of the Holy Spirit, as it was allowed to be administered in the spirit world according to the laws that govern that dimension of this mortal world.

56 But his family would not take notice of that still small voice that penetrateth deep within the hearts of the children of men, yet cannot be perceived in wickedness. And Ameago knew that he was also drunken with pride and hate for his enemy, the Hittites, while in the flesh, and that he would be considered a great hero among those of his family for having died in such a victorious battle.

57 And Selethared and Ameago were both exceedingly sorrowful for that which they witnessed as spirits among the people of the nation to whom they belonged during the days of their probation.

58 And they wondered between themselves what was the true cause of the wars that existed between the two nations to which they belonged.

59 And the spirit who was the mortal father of Selethared, beckoned to them that they would follow him. And they went unto the house and the palaces of the kings and the leaders of the nation to which they had belonged. And among the Babylonians there was much celebration, even exceeding pride and arrogance of those who led the people.

60 And these leaders lived in luxury and pomp, having received all these things from the people whom they led. And Ameago and Selethared could discern the hearts of their leaders. And their hearts were set upon their riches and their comforts and the security of their own families.

61 And these spirits could perceive the apathy that these leaders had for the families of the poor and the majority, who had sacrificed their sons and their fathers for the battles against their enemies, who were in actuality only the enemies of the rich and of their leaders.

62 And these spirits could see that the cause of the battles between them was for land and gold and silver and the fine things of the earth, after which their leaders lusted for themselves and also for their families.

63 And these leaders had convinced the people of their nations that their own nation was greater than any other upon the face of the earth. And they were convinced and deceived by their leaders and the rich who controlled these leaders, and who paid for the armies that secured their borders so that they could enjoy peace with their families.

64 But for the people and the families of the other nations, they did not care, for these were of no concern to them, having thought of these other nations and peoples as their enemies.

65 And the people thought of these other nations and these other peoples as their enemies because of the flattering words of patriotism and courage that were given unto them by their leaders. For the leaders had convinced the people that they should fight for their country with pride and patriotism, and if they should die in defense of their country, then they would die as heroes of the nation.

66 And Selethared and Ameago realized that they did not die for their country, but they had died for their leaders, that these leaders might continue to have the riches and the prosperity that they desired. And also that these leaders and the rich might continue to have the power over the land and over the hearts and minds of the people.

67 And Selethared and Ameago were in a miserable state in the spirit world for that which they saw among those who were their families and their friends, even those of their own nation to which they belonged in the flesh. And in this state of misery, they dwelt in the spirit world without the ability to change what they had done during their mortality and the days of their probation.

68 And now, I, Moroni, would that ye should consider the things that the brother of Jared wrote concerning Selethared and Ameago and liken these things unto yourselves. For behold, throughout the history of the children of men there have been countless wars and much misery because of the families and the nations that ye have allowed to exist among you.

69 And I have seen in the latter days that this same pride and arrogance that is spawned by the feeling of family and country, even this same

feeling of hatred of other nations, is the cause that sendeth many souls into the spirit world unprepared for what they shall experience there.

70 For there shall be many, who are soldiers, who shall die in battle thinking that they are heroes, and that they have died defending their country. But they shall enter into the spirit world and remain in a state of misery and hell as they observe the real intent of their leaders in sending them to war against their brothers and their sisters of another country.

71 And they shall see the spirits of those whom they have killed. And they shall recognize these spirits as the children of the same Father, even their own Eternal Father. And they shall see the anguish that their mortal families have because of their death; and also the pride that they shall have, because in their anguish, these families want to believe that their sons and their daughters fought for a righteous cause, and that they died as heroes.

72 But I say unto you, that they are not heroes, but are in a state of hell and misery because of the things that were taught unto them as children; yea, even this pride and this arrogance that their parents and their leaders have caused them to feel for their country, and their flags, and the symbols of their countries that cause this pride to rise in their hearts.

73 Oh, ye wicked and perverse people, what shall ye think in the presence of the Father of us all? What then shall ye think of the pride and patriotism that ye feel for your nations and your families?

74 Will ye begin at that time to justify the killing of other children of God, whom ye have killed in your pride and your arrogance? Do ye think that the Father shall look at you and justify the murder of any of His children for the cause of patriotism and pride? Do ye think that in any of these things ye shall be justified?

75 I say unto you that ye shall not be justified, but ye shall be damned, and ye shall not partake of the holiness of the Father, or of His kingdom, unless ye repent of this pride and begin to realize that ye are all His children and there existeth no nation or family under God.

76 And now, I would that ye should know that there hath existed war and carnage among the peoples of the earth ever since they begin to place a value upon the things of the earth and divide themselves into these family units.

77 And there hath not been a time when there have not existed these wars and rumors of wars according to the desires of Satan. And those of you that shall receive these things shall read of some of the great wars that have existed among the children of men, and among the nations of the earth. And there is no such thing as a righteous war.

78 Yea, there is no such thing as a war that was started and blessed by the Father. For behold, God would never command His children to kill one another. But these wars are caused by the God of this world, who is Satan. And it is Satan that hath blessed these wars and given the power to one nation to destroy another.

79 Nevertheless, the Lord can aid in the defense of a nation. And only in this defense doth he suffer that any of the children of men should take up arms against their brothers and their sisters. Yea, even in the defense of your lives ye have been given specific commandments, which if ye adhere to them, ye shall be blessed and receive the blessings and assistance of the Lord.

80 And these are the commandments of the Lord pertaining unto the defense of your nations: And the Lord hath spoken to his prophets regarding the defense of the governments that have been set up among the children of men.

81 And all governments and constitutions and laws of the same, must support the principle of freedom in maintaining rights and privileges for all. And any law or constitution given by a government that guaranteeth these rights and privileges of freedom shall be supported and befriended by all. And this is as it pertaineth to the law of man, for whatsoever is more or less than this, cometh of evil.

82 And the Lord hath spoken, saying: I, the Lord God make you free, therefore ye are free indeed; and the law should also make you free. Therefore, I would that ye should seek diligently out from among you those who are honest and wise to be your leaders.

83 And these should not be given to riotous

living, neither should they be those who have set their hearts upon gold and silver and the precious things of the earth. Yea, there are many among the poor who are wise and honest, and even these, who have not set their hearts upon the things of the world, shall govern you in the service of love, and not for the money that ye would pay them to be your leaders.

84 And your leaders should not receive for payment that which is greater than what they who are of a majority do receive for their sustenance. And ye should not seek out your leaders from among the rich and the successful pertaining to the things of this world, for they have proven themselves already by their works.

85 Nevertheless, those who would be your leaders, even those whom ye would choose from among the poor; yea, these should not want to take from those, who are rich, the desires of their hearts. For if ye take from the rich the desires of their hearts, which are the fine things of this world, then ye have taken away their freedom to pursue those things which cause their happiness.

86 And a wise and righteous leader among you shall respect the desires of happiness of all of those whom he serveth, whether they be rich or poor. But his desires should not be for the things of this earth, but his desire should be to serve you and give you freedom to pursue your desires of happiness.

87 And good men and wise men ye should observe to uphold; otherwise whatsoever is less than these cometh of evil. And I give unto you a commandment, that ye shall forsake all evil and cleave unto all good, that ye shall live by every word which proceedeth forth out of the mouth of God.

88 For He shall give unto the faithful line upon line, precept upon precept; and I shall try you and prove you herewith. And whoso layeth down his life in my cause, for the sake of my name, shall find it again, even life eternal.

89 Therefore, be not afraid of your enemies, for I have decreed in my heart that I will prove you in all things, whether ye shall abide in my covenant, even unto death, that ye may be found worthy before our Father. For if ye shall not abide in my covenant, then ye are not worthy of me. Therefore, renounce war and proclaim peace, and seek diligently to turn the hearts of the children to their fathers, and the hearts of the fathers to their children, even according to the covenants that I have made since the beginning, lest I come and smite the whole earth with a curse, and all flesh be consumed before me.

90 For if I shall find no righteousness among you, then what cause would I have that would keep me from consuming all flesh? Let not your hearts be troubled; for in the house of my Father there are many mansions, and I have prepared a place for you; and where my Father and I am, there ye shall be also, if ye keep the covenant that I have given unto you. And if I will, I shall chasten the nations of the earth and will do whatsoever I list, if they do not repent and observe all things whatsoever I have said unto them.

91 And again I say unto you, if ye observe to do whatsoever I command you, I, the Lord, shall turn away all the wrath and indignation from you, and the gates of hell shall not prevail against you.

92 Now, I speak unto you concerning the families that ye have set up among you, and also the nations which exist because of these families, which ye have set up contrary to the commandments that I have given unto you. But because ye have desired these things, I have suffered that they should remain among you according to the desires of your hearts.

93 And if any nation shall rise up and smite you once, and ye bear it patiently and revile not against them, neither seek revenge, ye shall be rewarded. But if ye bear it not patiently, it shall be accounted unto you as being meted out as a just measure unto you.

94 And again, if your enemy shall smite you the second time, and you revile not against your enemy, and bear it patiently, your reward shall be an hundredfold. But if ye bear it not patiently, even this second time, then ye shall be justified in your actions, but ye shall receive no reward from me.

95 And again, if your enemy shall smite you the third time, and ye bear it patiently, your reward shall be doubled unto four-fold. And these three testimonies shall stand against your enemy if he repent not, and shall not be blotted out, and I shall remember them always and bring my vengeance upon them for your sake.

96 And now, verily I say unto you, if that enemy shall escape my vengeance, that he be not brought into judgment before me in the flesh, then ye shall see to it that ye warn him in my name, that he come no more upon you, neither upon your families or your nation unto the third and forth generation.

97 And then, if he shall come upon you, I have delivered your enemy into your hands, and you can do unto them that which ye shall desire to protect yourselves from him, or destroy him before you.

98 But if ye shall spare him, ye shall be rewarded for your righteousness. Nevertheless, your enemy is in your hands; and if you reward him according to his works, then ye are justified before me.

99 Yea, if he hath sought your lives, and your lives and your freedom are endangered by him, then he is in your hands, and ye are justified. Behold, this is the law that I have caused to be given to all my prophets. And I have commanded them to teach these things unto the children of men in all the nations of the earth.

100 And again, this is the law that I gave unto them, that they should counsel with the leaders of the nations that they should not go out unto battle against any nation, kindred, tongue, or people, save I, the Lord commanded them. But I do not want my children to hurt one another, but that they should love their enemies and do good unto them.

101 Nevertheless, because of the power of Satan, it is necessary at times that the righteous defend themselves against that which is evil. And if any nation, tongue, or people should proclaim war against them, they should first lift a standard of peace unto that people, nation, or tongue.

102 And if that people do not accept the offering of peace, neither the second nor the third time, then shall the testimonies of which I have spoken be brought before me. Then I, the Lord, would give unto them a commandment, and justify them in going out to battle against that nation, tongue, or people in defense of their freedom.

103 And only in the defense of their freedom shall they fight. For if there is a people, or a nation, or a tongue that doth not desire the freedoms, or the laws, or the constitution of freedom, then they shall not be forced to accept these freedoms, or these laws, or this constitution.

104 And there shall never be a war of the offense given by my command. And if ye have abided by my commandments concerning these things, then I, the Lord, shall fight your battles, and the battles of your children, and the battles of the children of your children, until they have avenged themselves on all their enemies, to the third and forth generation.

105 Behold, this is an ensample unto all people, saith the Lord your God, for justification before me. For I shall never command you contrary to the law of the gospel that I have given unto you.

106 Nevertheless, I shall not allow you to be destroyed, if ye are abiding in the law of the gospel, which is the covenant that I have given unto your fathers. And again, verily I say unto you, if after your enemy hath come upon you the first time, and he repenteth and cometh unto you praying for your forgiveness, ye shall forgive him, and shall hold it no more as a testimony against your enemy.

107 And this ye shall do unto the second time and the third time, and as oft as your enemy repenteth of the trespass wherewith he hath trespassed against you, ye shall forgive him, until seventy times seven.

108 And if your enemy trespasseth against you and repenteth not the first time, nevertheless ye shall forgive him. And if you enemy trespasseth against you and repenteth not the second time, nevertheless ye shall forgive him. And if your enemy trespasseth against you and repenteth not the third time, ye shall also forgive him.

109 But if he trespasseth against you the fourth time, and he repenteth not for that which he hath done, then ye shall not forgive him, but shall bring these testimonies before the Lord; and they shall not be blotted out before me until he repenteth and rewardeth to you four-fold in all things wherewith he hath trespassed against you.

110 And if he doeth this, ye shall forgive him with all of your heart, but if he doth not do this, then I, the Lord will avenge you of your enemy an hundred-fold. And upon his children and the children of his children of all them that hate me, unto the third and fourth generation.

111 But if the children of your enemy repent, or the children of his children, and turn to the Lord their God with all their heart and with all their might, mind, and strength, and restore four-fold for all their trespasses wherewith they have trespassed, then your indignation shall be turned away from them, and ye shall remember no more the trespasses of their fathers against you.

112 And vengeance shall no more come upon them, saith the Lord, your God, and their trespasses shall never be brought any more as a testimony before the Lord against them.

113 And now, I, Moroni, have included these commandments of the Lord, which he hath suffered to be given unto us because of the wickedness of the trespasses that are prevalent among the children of men.

114 And it is the nations with the most evil leaders that take an offense against another nation. And the purpose of their offense is for gain. For they desire this gain that they might not work by the sweat of their own brow.

115 And they love the honor and the praise of those whom they subject to their laws, which laws are set up to protect their riches and their honor and their glory among men.

CHAPTER 28

The power of Satan reveals to the human race the technological advances that can cause their destruction. The cause of the rise of the Hebrew nation is explained. Moroni explains some of the symbolism of Revelation concerning time and times, and half a time. Satan's ability to deceive the human race with technology and scientific advances is touched upon. The prophet Zarathustra is introduced.

AND it came to pass that the Hittite nation was weakened somewhat by the power of the Babylonians, who had established written laws among themselves and began to prosper because of these laws.

2 For not all the laws that were introduced among the children of men were evil. There were some leaders who were more compassionate than others.

3 And the commandments of God that were given to Adam were passed down among the people and corrupted with time; but in some instances, the remnants of the gospel were recognizable among the laws of the peoples who chose to worship their own gods according to their customs and their traditions.

4 And the Lord sent his prophets throughout the land. And these prophets went unto any people that would receive them and listen to the gospel as they preached it unto them. But in most instances, these prophets were persecuted or slain by the leaders of the nations, and this because the law of the gospel would take away their riches and their power and make them equal to all people.

5 And if there were a people, or a nation, that listened to the prophets and began to introduce the principles of the gospel among them, then Satan would do whatever he could to cause discontent and turmoil, so that he could maintain control over the children of men and their leaders.

6 And Satan was bound, as I have explained it unto you, as to what he could inspire those who followed him to do. Nevertheless, he was allowed some leeway in his desires. And his desires were to make a nation of those who would worship him strong and efficient in warfare so that they could conquer other nations.

7 And through the ministrations of the spirit world, Satan began to introduce certain ores and the manufacture of metals, which would greatly improve the ability of the armies of the nations to kill one another.

8 And when the knowledge of copper and bronze was given unto the children of men by Satan, his desire was to give them more reasons to fixate their hearts upon the things of the world. For copper and bronze were beautiful, like unto gold, and were easy to form into their precious things.

9 But they were soft metals and had not the ability to kill as efficiently as Satan would want them to, according to the death of the flesh.

10 And it came to pass that Satan introduced iron ore into the nation of the Hittites, and they began to manufacturer weapons of war. And these new weapons quickly made them one of the most powerful nations upon the earth.

11 And it came to pass that they overcame the land of Mesopotamia and brought the people under their subjection. For there was not any army in the land that could stand against their iron weapons, more especially against their iron tipped arrows, which would rip through the flesh and bone of any man.

12 And when the pharaohs of the great nation of Egypt learned of the great armies of the Hittites, they sent their own armies, which had become exceedingly strong and powerful, to contend against them. And these two nations were at war one with another for many years.

13 And after so many years of war, the great nations of the Hittites in Mesopotamia and the Egyptian nation in the land of the Nile began to weaken.

14 And it was in this weakened state that the Hebrew nation was allowed once again to inherit the land of Cainan, and this nation began again to worship the Lord as they had been commanded by him.

15 And the record of their history ye already have with you in the book of the Jews. And according to the word of the Lord, and also the words of the brother of Jared, there are some minor errors that were recorded therein, which are not of such an extent that would cause me to take up room on these plates to correct them.

16 It sufficeth me to say, that because of the weakness of the great nations that Satan had caused to be established upon the earth; yea, because of their wars and continual contention, Abraham was able to set up a people and begin a nation in which the covenant of the Lord could once more be established in the earth.

17 But this was not the only people to whom the Lord had given his laws and his gospel and had blessed with the Priesthood that would allow the children of men to establish churches and places of worship among them.

18 And I have explained unto you that the Lord is no respecter of persons; and that one nation is just as important to him as another. And he sendeth forth his prophets among all his children, even unto as many as will hear his words.

19 And there are times when there hath existed righteous peoples upon the earth, yet there have been many times when there existed no living soul who obeyed the law of the gospel and who was blessed with the Spirit of the Lord.

20 Now, here is a mystery that I am commanded to explain unto you; yea, even a great mystery that is written in the holy scriptures that ye already have among you. And it is again from the words of John, which words were given unto my father, Nephi, from which I take my interpolation.

21 And it is written according to the words of John: And to the woman were given two wings of a great eagle, that she might fly into the wilderness, into her place, where she is nourished for a time, and times, and half a time.

22 Now, this symbolism was also know before the time of John. For it was Daniel who first used this symbolism to describe that which I am about to explain unto you. And the words of Daniel are written, saying: And he shall speak great words against the most High, and shall wear out the saints of the most High, and think to change times and laws, and they shall be given into his hand until a time and times, and the dividing of time.

23 And later in the words of Daniel, it is written: And I heard the man clothed in linen, which was upon the water of the river, when he held up his right hand and his left hand unto heaven, and sware by him that liveth forever that it shall be for a time, times, and an half.

24 And now, my beloved brothers and sisters, even all of you who are the elect that shall receive these words and wonder on the great mysteries of the scriptures. Behold, the promise of the Lord is that he shall make known unto you all of his mysteries until you know the mysteries of God in full.

25 Therefore, I give unto you an explanation of these things: For in the beginning, the Spirit of God and His gospel, and also the Holy Order of the Son of God existed. And these are those things that nourished the woman in the wilderness, or in other words, the children of men, according to the words of John.

26 And these things were given unto the children of men for a period of time in the beginning before the Lord withdrew his Spirit from the earth and allowed the children of men to live according to the power of Satan. Or in other words, Satan was given an opportunity to incorporate his plan into mortality, and prove it therewith to see if it was good.

27 And without the Spirit of the Lord, or the ministrations of the Holy Ghost, or the administrations of the Holy Order of the Son of God, which includeth his holy prophets, the world is left in the power of Satan, and this because of the desires of the children of men.

28 For if they use their free agency to choose the plan of Lucifer over the plan of the Father, then that is their choice. But if that is their choice, then they can receive no part of the blessings of the Father. Therefore, the gospel in its purity lasted for a period of time, in the beginning, before it was taken from the earth.

29 And after this time, of which John hath written, then this gospel was once again reestablished in the earth among the children of men for a period that was twice as long as the period in which it was upon the earth in the beginning, even before it was taken off the earth after the first period of time.

30 And this is what is meant by times, or in other words, time by twice.

31 And then, after it is taken off the earth for the second time, it shall one day be restored for the final time, for a period that is one half as long as the first period of time that it existed upon the earth, in the beginning, or in other words, half a time.

32 And I was about to write further concerning the symbolism of these time periods, but the Spirit forbade me. For if these time periods were revealed unto you, then the children of men would know the time when they should look for the coming of the Lord, even for the last time in his glory, to cast Satan out and once again establish his gospel for the last time throughout the whole earth.

33 And if these times were known among you, then it would give unto you an excuse to delay the time of your repentance and your righteous works. But I say unto you, do not delay your repentance and your righteous works; for in a time that ye think not, the Lord will come; or perhaps, you will be called home to the spirit world, and thus shall end the days of your probation and the time of your repentance according to the flesh. Therefore, the exact periods of this time, and times and half a time, shall not be given unto you at this time.

34 And during the times that the gospel of the Lord did not exist upon the earth, then the children of men were greatly influenced by the power of Satan. And he doeth great wonders, so that he maketh fire come down from heaven on the earth in the sight of men. And he deceiveth them that dwell on the earth by the means of those miracles which he had power to give unto them, and this according to the words of John.

35 And now, I would that ye should know that Satan hath shown many miracles unto the children of men, but most of the miracles that he hath shown unto them have only been those that he hath been allowed to show unto them according to the will of the Father.

36 For if Satan had his choice, he would show unto the children of men all the miracles that he knoweth. And these miracles include all of his evil works and the works of his secret combinations that are set up to get gain and maintain power, and also the natural powers and wonders of science that he shall give unto the children of men in the latter days when he shall

no longer be forbidden by the Father in that which he shall give unto the children of men.

37 And I have explained unto you before that many of the prophets of God who understand these great miracles were forbidden to write about them in the words that they were commanded to include in the records of the people. For had the people been given all the miracles that Satan would give unto them, except he be commanded not to by the Father, the children of men would have destroyed themselves off the face of the earth many years ago.

38 And it shall be revealed unto you in this record the time in which Satan shall be released and have power over all of his dominion. And at that time, the advancement and knowledge of the miracles that Satan shall introduce among the children of men shall threaten the very existence of the earth.

39 And iron ore is one of these miracles. For with its introduction, Satan was able to raise up great armies among the nations that followed him and chose him as their god, or as their gods—for it doth not matter to Satan how many gods are used to keep the children of men deceived and under his power.

40 And it came to pass that a great nation began to form, even the great Assyrian nation. And this nation began to use its weapons of warfare to overcome all the nations of the earth. And they began to destroy the people of the earth and take them captive.

41 And it came to pass that because their nation was so vicious, even to the point of extreme barbarism, it did not last for many years. And it was the Chaldean empire that rose up and conquered the Assyrians and destroyed them from off the face of the earth, and this because many of the people of the earth began to repent of their sins and look to God for their protection. For there were many prophets sent once again throughout the earth to teach the people the things of God.

42 And it came to pass that there lived a man and his wife in the eastern part of the wilderness that surrounded the great land of Mesopotamia. And his name was Pouruchathpa, and the name of his wife was Dughdova.

43 And Dughdova was a chosen daughter of God who had the spirit of the Lord with her since the days of her youth. And in the days of her youth she dreamed a dream, in which she saw a great camel descend upon the home of her father. And the camel was golden in color and spoke in her tongue, calling her by name and saying unto her:

44 Behold, truly thou art blessed above all those of the earth. For thou shalt bring forth a son and he shall bring about much righteousness in the land of thy fathers. And in thy heart thou shalt know the things that thou should teach unto him; but the things of thy fathers, even those things which thou hast been taught, teach them not unto him, for he hath been chosen by the great Ahura Mazda, who is thy Lord.

45 And it came to pass that as she grew in stature she kept these things in her heart. And she married Pouruchathpa and did not divulge these things unto him.

46 And Pouruchathpa was an honorable man, who had much business among the merchants of his town. And when Dughdova was ready to deliver her child, she called Pouruchathpa unto her and recounted unto him the dream that she had as a youth.

47 And there were midwives there who heard the things that she told unto her husband. And they immediately spread what they had heard throughout the city. And the priests, who were those that had been appointed over the people to keep them in subjection to the gods that they worshipped, even these did come into the house and mocked Dughdova for the things which she had said concerning her child.

48 And because of the things that they said unto her, she became exceedingly sorrowful and cried that her husband would come in unto her. And when Pouruchathpa had heard all that the priests had said to his wife, he was filled with anger, and he cursed them and their gods and threw them out of the house.

49 And the priests commanded the people of the city to avoid the house of Pouruchathpa and his wife, and their child; for they were condemned from that time forth by the gods of the people. And because of the condemnation of the priests, the midwives did leave the side of Dughdova and would not return again unto her.

50 And Pouruchathpa shut the door of the house and went in unto his wife. And Dughdova cried in pain and delivered the child. And as the child was born, the sun shone down upon the house. And its reflection caused the people of the city to become terrified at the sight, and they ran in among the priests and told them of the great light that shined down upon the house.

51 And the priests surrounded the house and condemned it before their gods. And they commanded the people to cast Pouruchathpa and his wife out from among them. And before an hour had passed after the birth of their son, Pouruchathpa and Dughdova were forced out into the wilderness by the people.

52 And it came to pass that the Lord was with them, and they found shelter and sustenance in the wilderness. And they came upon the house of a man who had lost his sight many years ago from the effects of the sun. And this man was poor and had little effects, but those that he did have, he offered to Pouruchathpa and Dughdova and their son.

53 And they called their son Zarathustra, which being interpreted means, golden camel, after the vision that his mother had in her youth. And it came to pass that Zarathustra spent the days of his childhood in the house of the blind man. But as the days went on according to the days of Zarathustra, even unto the days of his youth, the blind man began to receive his sight. And he looked upon Zarathustra and thanked the gods for that which had been done unto him.

54 But Dughdova rebuked the man and explained unto him, instructing him that he would not teach her son concerning the gods of her fathers, which gods were of the priests that had cast them out of the city.

55 And it came to pass that Zarathustra grew, and he was wrought upon by the ministrations of the spirit world and taught those things that he would one day teach unto the people. And when the days of the pinnacle of his manhood was reached, the Lord sent an angel unto Zarathustra and gave unto him the laws of the gospel and taught unto him all those things that had been corrupted among the children of men.

56 And the Lord called Zarathustra to be a prophet and preach the things that he had learned from the angel, and also those things that he had learned from the ministrations of the Spirit in his youth. And he was taught the plan of God, who was called Ahura Mazda according to the language and the customs of the people.

57 And he also knew of the plan of Lucifer, who was called Ahriman, according to the words of the people.

58 And now, I, Moroni, would that ye should realize, even those who have received these things, that the Father hath allowed his prophets to teach His gospel unto all of His children in their own tongue and according to their customs and traditions, as I have previously explained it unto you in this record.

59 And Ahura Mazda shall be known in the world as the God of Zarathustra, a prophet of God. But this Ahura Mazda is the Father of whom I have spoken of in this record. Thus can ye see that the names which the children of men give unto Him are of little importance to our Father.

60 For the words of Zarathustra were given in their purity to the children of men in the beginning. And he become a prophet to his people. And there were many that followed after his teachings.

61 And it came to pass that he taught the gospel to one of the great kings who was among the people. And this king accepted the teachings of Zarathustra and caused them to be taught throughout the land. Nevertheless, the King would not allow those teachings of Zarathustra to be taught, which would usurp his authority among the people, or in other words, the things that would take away from his own divinity.

62 And Zarathustra taught in the court of the King for many years. But after a time, he went back among the people and began to preach the gospel unto them. And because of his teachings to the King, the people, who were of the nation of the great Persian Empire, which had risen to power after the Babylonian Empire, were ruled with justice.

63 Nevertheless, they were not given a voice in their own government as Zarathustra had taught was the will and commandment of Ahura Mazda. But the people were allowed to think for themselves and act according to the dictates of their own conscience as long as they did not violate the law and mandates of the King.

64 And because many of them did began to think for themselves, the Holy Ghost was able to communicate with them. And thus began the ministrations of the spirit world to the children of men once again.

65 And thus began the period of the times of which I have spoken. And this I shall reveal unto you, even that the time hath passed, and the times shall be ended during the days of not many generations of my descendants. And ye who shall receive this sealed portion of the record of my father, even ye are in the half of time. He who hath wisdom, let him understand.

CHAPTER 29

Why the children of God can receive their own revelation and guidance without trusting in the arm of flesh. The elect of God need no prophets or religious leaders. Moroni reveals more of the wickedness of the modern-day LDS Church.

AND it came to pass that when the ministrations of the spirit world began once again to have some effect on the children of men, the people begin to search their hearts and ponder on their plight in life.

2 For it is sad to report, that most of the children of God, while they are in mortality, and having been caused by the flesh to forget the Father and the things that they experienced in His kingdom; yea, because of these things, most of them rely on the arm of flesh, or in other words, they rely on their leaders to teach them what they should know pertaining to the kingdom of God.

3 And this is not, nor hath it ever been, nor will it ever be the will of the Father concerning His children. And again I say unto you that God is no respecter of persons, and He would that all of His children come unto Him and know Him. And it is possible that all the children of men can come to know Him and His ways.

4 And I have explained unto you previously that no man or woman called of God to preach His gospel to His children would teach anything more or less than this.

5 For behold, the prophets of God are commanded to preach repentance only unto the children of men, and teach them the commandments of God that they should live by so that they may have His spirit to be with them.

6 And I have also explained unto you that having His Spirit to be with you doth not mean that the Father is present constantly with you in the flesh. For He resideth on the planet where he passed through the days of His own probationary period prior to becoming an exalted being, even of the Celestial glory.

7 But having His Spirit to be with you meaneth that you have the ability to communicate with those in the spirit world, which is another dimension of this world in which we live, as it hath been previously explained unto you. And the spirits that are assigned to support us and inspire us and give us counsel throughout our lives, can only do so when we listen to their promptings and follow their gentle persuasions, which persuasions are felt by our conscience.

8 For behold, all of us have been given the ability to know right from wrong. And again, this was the enmity that the Father placed between Lucifer and our spirits, even that we would know right from wrong. But if we have been deceived by the flatteries and manipulations of another, then we will not listen to the promptings of the Spirit, and we will be led wherever those who are manipulating us desire to lead us, according to the desires of their hearts, which are full of evil because they are not from God.

9 Therefore, it is expedient that ye understand this principle. And it is of such importance that I shall reiterate it unto you time and time again throughout my abridgment of the vision of the brother of Jared. And if ye understand this principle, which is also an eternal law, it shall be hard for you to be misled by another who is not of God.

10 For it came to pass that the brother of Jared wrote of the times on the earth when the ministrations of the spirit world had stopped among the children of men, and the Holy Priesthood, and all the holy prophets, and the pure gospel of the Lord, did cease to exist upon the earth among the children of men.

11 And of these times he wrote, saying: And the children of men knew not where they should turn for that which they sought to know and understand for themselves. For every man was led in his own way, which way was determined by the leaders in whom he chose to trust and believe.

12 And the women during these times did not have a choice in that which they should think, for the men began to exercise their superior physical strength over them. And after the nations of the great Queens were subdued and overrun by the strength and the weapons of the men, the daughters of God were forced to become submissive and subservient to the men. And those who did not do this, were often beaten into this submission because of their lack of strength over the men.

13 And the leaders of the nations, who were led by Satan, did cause that all men should think the way that these leaders would have them think. And if there were any among them who dissented from the ways of the leaders, they were killed, or subdued by the armies of the leaders and forced to submit to the will and mind of their leaders.

14 And the religions and beliefs among the children of men were created by false prophets and sorcerers, even all those who possessed the ability to gain power over the minds and hearts of a leader of a nation. And they would cause this leader to worship the gods that these prophets and sorcerers had invented.

15 And it came to pass that there were times when the only ministrations of the spirit world were coming from Lucifer and those who followed him And these evil spirits inspired the false prophets and the sorcerers, and gave unto them their inspiration and their revelations, and also their magic and their pretended powers.

16 And the false prophets and the sorcerers taught the leaders of the people. And these leaders were forced into subjection to the words of the false prophets and the sorcerers, because the word of God was nowhere to be found upon the earth to dispute the words that were given unto them.

17 Therefore, whatsoever these leaders felt was right—according to the conscience which they had been given by God—that they would do, but only if it agreed with the counsel and advice that they received from those whom they had accepted as the mouthpieces of God—even the false prophets and the sorcerers.

18 And because of this conscience, or this enmity—and this enmity is our ability to know right from wrong, which our Father hath given to all of His children—the children of men began to wonder about themselves. And they began to realize that they were much different than the other animals with which they shared the earth. For the other animals do not wonder about themselves, nor do they have the freedom to think outside of the laws that these of a lower order have been given to fulfill the measure of their creation.

19 For when we look up into the night sky, we wonder on the great stars which hang motionless in the great expanse of space. And we also wonder on the sun, and on the moon, and on their times and their seasons, and this wondering began to influence the thinking and beliefs of the children of men. And we concern ourselves regarding why we exist. And these things are unique to our natures, the other animals having no such nature.

20 And because we wonder on these things, it is easy for us to be led away from the truth of God and accept things that might be in the similitude of godliness, but are not of Him. And an understanding of these things we often receive from those whom we have accepted as our leaders.

21 And as the children of men wondered concerning themselves, Lucifer and his followers became exceedingly adroit in their ability to inspire and give revelation unto them. And the inspirations and revelations of Satan were subtle, and similar to the ministrations of the righteous spirits who were supportive of the plan of the Father.

22 And it became much easier for the children of men to receive their answers to their wonderings, and also their inspirations and their revelations from other mortals, even from their leaders and their false prophets, than it was for them to live their lives by the word of God, so that they might receive a personal and direct answer from the Holy Spirit themselves, without trusting in the arm of flesh for their answers.

23 And thus it was throughout the earth between the times that the word of God was upon the earth, even between the times which John and Daniel have described in symbolism. And when the gospel was upon the earth during the time, and times, and the dividing of time, it was given unto the children of men, both through the ministrations of the spirit, and through the words of the holy prophets of God by the power of the Holy Order of the Son of God, by which they were called.

24 And now the Lord hath commanded me to give unto you a reference in the history of the house of Israel, even the Jews, regarding the manner in which the Lord desireth to give unto us his revelations and his words according to the principle and the eternal law that I have explained unto you.

25 And this reference shall come forth from the Bible, which ye have already among you. And he who is using the Urim and Thummim to translate this record, shall be commanded to interpolate the exact text as it is written in the history of the Jews, according to the Bible. For my words shall be an abridgment of the words that are written upon the plates of brass, which have been passed down to me from my fathers.

26 For in this reference, it shall be shown unto you the exactness of the principle that the Lord would have you understand. For it is the desire of the Lord to speak directly with the children of men, from his own mouth, or according to the ministrations of his Holy Spirit, which are administered in the spirit world.

27 And if the children of men would sanctify themselves and live according to the covenant of the Lord, then they should have no need of a prophet, or apostles, or leaders to lead them. And this was the intent of the Lord for the house of Israel after they had been delivered out of the hands of the Egyptians.

28 And it was the desire of the Lord to allow the people of Israel to hear his voice and know for themselves that the commandments that he would give unto them were directly from his own mouth. For the Lord would that all of the house of Israel be priests and prophets before him, even a holy nation above all that were upon the earth at that time.

29 And here are the words given from the account of the Jews: In the third month, when the children of Israel were gone forth out of the land of Egypt, the same day came they into the wilderness of Sinai.

30 For they were departed from Rephidim, and were come to the desert of Sinai, and had pitched in the wilderness; and there Israel camped before the mount.

31 And Moses went up unto God, and the Lord called unto him out of the mountain, saying, Thus shalt thou say to the house of Jacob, and tell the children of Israel: Ye have seen what I did unto the Egyptians, and how I bare you on the wings of eagles, and brought you unto myself.

32 Now therefore, if ye will obey my voice indeed, and keep my covenant, then ye shall be a peculiar treasure unto me above all people; for all the earth is mine: And ye shall be unto me a kingdom of priests, and an holy nation. And these are the words which thou shalt speak unto the children of Israel.

33 And Moses came and called for the elders of the people, and laid before their faces all these words which the Lord commanded him. And all the people answered together, and said, All that the Lord hath spoken we will do. And Moses returned the words of the people unto the Lord.

34 And the Lord said unto Moses, Lo, I come unto thee in a thick cloud, that the people may hear when I speak with thee, and believe thee forever. And Moses told the words of the people unto the Lord.

35 And the Lord said unto Moses, Go unto the people, and sanctify them today and tomorrow, and let them wash their clothes, and be ready against the third day: for the third day the Lord will come down in the sight of all the people upon mount Sinai.

36 And thou shalt set bounds unto the people round about, saying, Take heed to yourselves, that ye go not up into the mount, or touch the border of it: whosoever toucheth the mount shall be surely put to death: There shall not an hand touch it, but he shall surely be stoned, or shot through; whether it be beast or man, it shall not live: when the trumpet soundeth long, they shall come up to the mount.

37 And Moses went down from the mount unto the people, and sanctified the people; and they washed their clothes. And he said unto the people: Be ready against the third day: come not at your wives.

38 And it came to pass on the third day in the morning, that there were thunders and lightnings, and a thick cloud upon the mount, and the voice of the trumpet exceeding loud; so that all the people that were in the camp trembled.

39 And Moses brought forth the people out of the camp to meet with God; and they stood at the nether part of the mount.

40 And mount Sinai was altogether on a smoke, because the Lord descended upon it in fire: and the smoke thereof ascended as the smoke of a furnace, and the whole mount quaked greatly.

41 And when the voice of the trumpet sounded long, and waxed louder and louder, Moses spake, and God answered him by a voice. And the Lord came down upon mount Sinai, on the top of the mount: and the Lord called Moses up to the top of the mount; and Moses went up.

42 And the Lord said unto Moses, Go down, charge the people, lest they break through unto the Lord to gaze, and many of them perish. And let the priests also, who come near to the Lord, sanctify themselves, lest the Lord break forth upon them.

43 And Moses said unto the Lord: The people cannot come up to mount Sinai: for thou chargedst us, saying, Set bounds about the mount, and sanctify it.

44 And the Lord said unto him, Away, get thee down, and thou shalt come up, thou, and Aaron with thee: but let not the priests and the people break through to come up unto the Lord, lest he break forth upon them. So Moses went down unto the people, and spake unto them.

45 And now I, Moroni, have been commanded by the Lord to expound somewhat on that which hath been interpolated herein from the record of the Jews.

46 For at this time, the Lord, even Jehovah, was a spirit that resided in the dimensions of the spirit world. And it is requisite that the natural body be changed to some degree in order for it to be able to communicate with spirit matter.

47 But in this instance, the Lord commanded that the elements of the earth be arranged in such a way so that the people could hear his voice, but not see him in the spirit. For it was not expedient that all the bodies of the children of Israel be changed so that they could behold spirit matter with their natural eyes.

48 But even so, it was the will of the Lord that they should hear his voice with their natural ears. And that which they have described in their records as the great sound of a trumpet, was that which was done unto the elements of the earth, so that they could hear the voice of the Lord as he spoke as a spirit, according to the spirit matter from which the body of Jehovah was created.

49 And the bounds that he set around the mount were to protect the natural bodies of the children of Israel from the effects of the spiritual change that the elements surrounding the mount were subjected to, so that all could hear the actual voice of the Lord.

50 And sadly, as I have explained it unto you previously, it is much easier for the children of men to receive their guidance and revelation and inspiration from the voice of another mortal, with whom they are accustomed to communicate.

51 Therefore, the children of Israel became afraid of the Lord and did not want to speak with him directly. And they sent Moses to speak with him, saying: Moses, thou art the chosen one of God, and we have received your counsel through your servant Aaron. And it is easy to understand his words. Therefore, we shall accept thee and sustain thee as our prophet, and through the ministrations of Aaron, receive thy words. Now let it be thee who speaketh unto God on our behalf.

52 And the desire of the children of Israel was

contrary to the principle and eternal law of heaven as it hath been explained unto you.

53 For as a mortal, we cannot know for a surety that we are receiving the words of God, unless we hear them from His own mouth. And how can we hear them from His own mouth, unless we hear them with our own ears?

54 And we did hear the words of the Father from His own mouth before we were placed in the confines of this earth. And we cannot hear the words of the Father presently, except it be from His own mouth in His kingdom wherein He resideth. But He hath given unto us the words of Jehovah, which are His own words.

55 And at the time of Moses, Jehovah was in the spirit world where he could give unto us the words of the Father according to the ministrations of this spirit world. And it is the desire of the Father that we do not receive His words except it be from His own mouth, or the mouth of His Son, because they are the exact same words.

56 For the Son would do nothing, nor say anything, except it be given unto him of the Father. And if we receive the words of the Father directly from His own mouth, then what need do we have for prophets, and apostles, and priests among us?

57 And those who are led by the Lord, or who receive his words directly from his own mouth, do not need these leaders. But sadly, the majority of the children of men trust in the arm of flesh. And they find more comfort in words that are given unto them according to the ministrations of the flesh, than they do when they are wrought upon by the Holy Spirit of God.

58 And in this way they are led that in many instances they do err because they are taught the precepts of men, who have not been given these precepts from the Lord. For the children of men have become accustomed to receiving their knowledge and understanding from their leaders.

59 And the leaders of the people receive their knowledge and understanding from their prophets, and their priests, and their sorcerers. And these prophets, and priests, and sorcerers receive their understanding and guidance from the ministrations of Lucifer in the spirit world. And in this way, Lucifer hath complete control over the hearts of the children of men.

60 And now, I, Moroni, once again am constrained by the Spirit to speak unto you as plainly as possible that ye might not misunderstand these things. And now, I say unto you that there is no man, or woman, or leader, or prophet, or priest, or apostle; no, there is no one who hath any more privilege or power to communicate with the Spirit of God and receive His will and revelation concerning us, than the power that hath been given unto all of us by the Father.

61 For behold, we are all equal in the eyes of God. And if we keep His commandments, which He hath given us through His Son, even Jesus Christ, or by whatever name he might be known in the different cultures of the children of men. Yea, if we keep His commandments, then any of us hath the right to the ministrations of the Holy Spirit.

62 And His commandments are not the commandments of men, who are the false prophets who Satan hath inspired to lead us away from the true commandments of God. And I have shown unto you many of the works of this great church in the latter days that calls itself after the name of Jesus Christ, yea, even the very church that shall receive the unsealed record of my father. And I have shown unto you that they have their prophet and their apostles, and their leaders to whom the members of this church look for guidance and inspiration.

63 And because the people look to their leaders for this inspiration, they are led away from the true commandments of the gospel. For they are like unto the church of Jerusalem in the days of Lehi, in that they look to the commandments of the church and their leaders before they look to the commandments of God.

64 And I have shown unto you that this church requireth that its members perform the ordinances of this church, which ordinances they are led to believe shall save them. And in order to perform these ordinances, a man or a woman must keep the commandments of this church and its leaders, even that they must covenant with a sacred covenant that they shall accept their prophet and their apostles and their leaders as the mouthpieces of God, even the only true mouthpieces of God upon the earth.

65 And they do not realize that this is a part of the plan of Lucifer, which plan he hath caused to be incorporated into this church by his subtleness, to lead them further away from the pure gospel of Jesus Christ.

66 For behold, these are part of the covenants of the secret combinations of old, even that its members would swear that they uphold the leaders and the High Priests of these combinations, and that only these leaders and these High Priests can receive the direct revelation and inspiration from God concerning their secret society.

67 And this church shall make it a requirement to pay money in the form of a tithing to God, as I have explained it unto you previously, or its members shall not be permitted to receive the ordinances that they are taught to believe are the saving ordinances of God. And this is also a part of the secret combinations of the devil. For the devil requireth a payment of money before a man is given the knowledge available in his secret societies, which are set up for gain and to maintain control over the hearts and minds of the children of men.

68 And in this way Satan hath again deceived them and hath bound them with his everlasting chains. And if there be a man or a woman among them that covenanteth to obey the words of the leaders of the church, even that they sustain these leaders as the mouthpieces of God; and if this man or woman payeth a full tithe to this church, then they are afforded the opportunity to receive the ordinances that they have been convinced shall save them in the kingdom of God.

69 And if this same man or woman is angry with their neighbor, or lusteth after another, or sueth in a court of law, or taketh advantage of their neighbor because of his words, or seeketh after the riches of the world; yea, even if these hate their enemies and impart not of their substance unto the beggar who putteth up his petition before them; yea, to my great astonishment, these shall receive all the blessings and ordinances of this church.

70 Oh, ye wicked and corrupt church. Know ye not that ye are leading the souls of many down to hell? Know ye not that it is an abomination before God to put one man above another and claim that it is possible that one man hath more authority and right to receive the revelations of God than another?

71 Why have ye put restrictions on those who would keep the pure gospel of the Lord, and allow them not to enter into your temples to receive the ordinances that ye erroneously teach as being saving ordinances, when ye allow those who pay you money and worship you as the only mouthpieces of God on earth, to enter therein whether they obey the words of Christ or not?

72 Yea, it is my hope that my words speak unto many of the members of your church out of the dust, that they might come to a realization of the great wickedness by which they have allowed themselves to be deceived. It is my hope that my words shall convince them that they should not give unto you of their money, nor should they worship you and put you up above themselves as prophets and apostles of the Lord, when ye are prophets and apostles of Satan.

73 For ye do the works of Satan. And by your examples, ye cause those who look to you for guidance and inspiration to do the works of Satan also. And ye are like unto the wicked priests of old who condemned my father Lehi, even that they did not believe that they were wicked, but that they were righteous men who had been called by the Order of the Holy Priesthood that was instituted among them.

74 And I say unto you, if they were righteous, then why did the Lord cause his holy prophets to go in among them and preach repentance unto them? And if ye are righteous, why is it that I must spend the precious space of these plates to condemn you and reveal unto the elect of your deceptions and your wickedness?

75 For behold, Satan hath lulled you into carnal security. And ye say within yourselves, All is well in Zion; yea, Zion prospereth, all is well, therefore, we must be righteous leaders of God.

76 But I say unto you that ye are not righteous leaders of God, but are being deceived by your

own pride and the inspirations that Satan hath given unto you.

77 And do ye think that the Lord hath caused your Zion to prosper? I say unto you that he hath not. But that it is your god, even Satan whose works ye do, that doth cause ye to prosper. And this is what Nephi meant when he said that ye shall be pacified and lulled away into carnal security. And this carnal security is your prosperity, and it hath been given unto you by Satan to deceive you and cheat your souls.

78 And now, I, Moroni, must once again return to the vision of the brother of Jared. Behold, my soul is torn because of the wickedness of the latter days, which things I have seen.

79 For behold, my father prepared these plates and gave me commandments concerning them that they might come forth in the latter days for the benefit of the whole world. But the church that hath been established because of these things, hath corrupted the truth and turned the hearts of the children of men towards this church, taking strength unto itself, and not towards Christ.

80 And my soul is burdened because I feel that the work that my father hath done, and also my own work, hath been done in vain, and this because ye have our work among you and ye do not understand it, nor do ye live by its precepts. And for this reason I am wont to spend the precious space of these plates to write unto you of your wickedness and your abomination, so that perhaps, there might be some elect among you who will turn to Christ; and then shall our work, which the Lord hath commanded of us, not be in vain.

81 And if it was by way of my own desire, I would fill these plates with the plainness of my words and reveal unto the elect, even unto all those who shall receive these things, the many ways in which Satan hath deceived the children of men and led them away from the simplicity and purity of the gospel of Christ. And this will be shown unto you in many ways in this record.

82 Nevertheless, my will is overcome by the will of the Spirit, which will is more subdued than my own spirit. And my spirit causeth me to depart from my abridgment of the glorious vision of the brother of Jared to expound on the wickedness of the men of the latter days, when these things shall be revealed unto them, and more especially on the wickedness of this church to which these things shall be revealed.

83 And I know that I can write in plainness, and that the words which I shall write shall stand as a testimony and a warning against those of the latter days that have set themselves up as prophets of God, when they are not.

84 And it is necessary that ye understand how the Lord hath worked with the children of men since the beginning, that ye might learn from their histories and liken them unto yourselves, or unto the present day in which ye live. And if ye liken these things unto yourselves, ye shall learn that which the Lord would have you learn from them.

CHAPTER 30

The rise of the democracy. The nation of Greece is introduced. The prophets Antioch, Socrates, and Sythipian are introduced. The administration of dreams are explained and expounded upon.

FOR it came to pass that as the Spirit began once again to work with the children of men upon the earth, there arose a great nation of thinkers and philosophers who began to be inspired by the Holy Spirit and to teach others the things which they had learned.

2 And the principle of democracy began to come forth among the children of men in the islands of Aegean, or the nation of Greece, as it is known among you. And this occurred about the same time that the Lord sent his prophets to the city of Jerusalem unto the house of Israel to preach repentance to the Jews. For Israel had fallen under the subjection of the Babylonian nation, which had risen up after it had once been destroyed.

3 And it was about this time, according to the record of Lehi, that the prophets Zenos and Zenock were sent unto the High Priests at Jerusalem. And ye already have this account,

but it sufficeth me to say, that about this time there began to be many prophets sent throughout the world to the different cultures and tongues and peoples to teach them the gospel according to their understanding, and according to their traditions, even according to those things that each people could understand and accept.

4 And at about this time in the islands of the Aegean world, tyrants, as they were called, rose up and began to seize power from the small communities of people that were controlled by the nobles, or those who had been given authority over them.

5 And this was not the thing that Satan wanted for his people. For a tyrant was a maverick leader who took it upon himself to cast out the nobles and turn the power and control of the government over to the people. For Satan knew that if the people were not controlled in their thoughts, then it would be easier for the Spirit of God to work with them, and also it would be easier for the Lord to send prophets unto the people to teach them the pure gospel. And the rise of these tyrants led in the direction of a democracy, which is a government by the people.

6 And it came to pass that a prophet of God, who was named Antioch, traveled in the area of the Aegean islands. And he was befriended by the farmers and the peasants, even those who were the majority of the people, and who struggled to pay their debts to the rich who held power over them.

7 And the people loved Antioch and began to believe on the words which he taught unto them concerning the justice and equality that God wanted for all men. Nevertheless, these poor farmers were subjected to the rich and the noblemen who had power over them.

8 And it came to pass that Antioch traveled up into the land of the noblemen and came upon the house of Solon, who was a great leader among them. And there was a great celebration being held at the house of Solon. And all those who were the relatives of Solon came unto his house to celebrate with him.

9 And there were many of them without the house of Solon who were poor, and who did not dress in the fine linens and fabrics of the rich. And these were forbidden to enter into the house of Solon and eat at the same table as those whose garments were made of fine linens and fabrics.

10 And Antioch was dressed like unto those who were without the house of Solon. And because Antioch knew the will of God pertaining to the equality of all men, he entered straightaway into the house of Solon and inquired as to the meaning of the celebration.

11 And when Antioch entered the dining hall, which was decorated with exceeding opulence and with many of the precious and fine things of the world, the audience therein refrained from speaking and gave unto Antioch their attention. For never before had any one entered therein who was dressed in the garments of the poor.

12 And Antioch looked around and found the place where the table was set, upon which were placed the finest foods and wines that were available in all the land. And he went to the table and began to taste of the food thereupon to the utter astonishment of all those in the room.

13 And as he tasted of the food, he again inquired as to the meaning of the celebration. And Solon arose from his seat and smiled pretentiously upon Antioch because of the thing which he had done.

14 And Solon said unto him: I am Solon, the Archon of this province, and these people are of my family which have come into my house to celebrate the day of my birth. But as to you, I do not know you as one of my family.

15 And with his mouth yet partially full of the food that he had taken from off the table, Antioch responded to Solon, saying: And why wast thou born, good Sir, that it should be a cause of such a celebration?

16 And for a moment Solon did not know how he should respond to such a question. Nevertheless, the audience of his relatives was silent in its desire to hear his response to the question of Antioch.

17 And when Solon did not speak forthwith, Antioch continued, saying, Was thou not born so that thou couldst partake of this food that it might bring thee joy? And this joy that thou desirest, is this not why thou wast born?

18 And Solon knew that he was being watched by those within his house as to the answers that he would give unto Antioch. And he answered Antioch, saying: I think that might be one of the reasons for which I was born. But I also think that I was born, so that I could share this joy with others, even those that are here today in my house. And this he said because he was trained in the art of rhetoric, which manner of speech was customary among the leaders of his day.

19 And Antioch said unto him: Surely, this food doth bring great joy to our souls, and for this do we have thee to thank? Yea, from whence did this food come? Did it not come from the vineyards and the gardens of those farmers who depend on thee for thy leadership and thy protection? And if it came unto thee from them, why is it not possible that they, too, share in the celebration of thy birth?

20 And Solon did not know how to answer him in this, for the farmers were burdened with that which they were required to provide for the leaders who received of the labors of the farmers as payment for their leadership. And after the farmers had paid this tax according to the desires of their leaders, there was very little left for themselves and for their own families.

21 And Antioch knew these things. And it was for this purpose that he had come unto the house of Solon.

22 And Antioch continued, saying: And are not those which are in the courtyard of thy house, even those of thy own family? And do they not also deserve to partake of the joy of which thou hast spoken?

23 And I say unto thee, that the Father of us all hath made us in His own image, and in His likeness were we all born. And because we are all similar one to another, even in the likeness of God, it is requisite of Him, who hath created us, that we treat each other as equals.

24 And God would have us all give according to our abilities to all according to their needs; and if we would do this thing, then all of us may partake of the joy which thou hast said was a reason for which thou wast born.

25 And it came to pass that Antioch continued teaching Solon and all those who were present the pure gospel that had been given unto him by the power of the Holy Spirit.

26 And after he had concluded his speaking unto them, Solon opened up the doors to the outside of his house and beckoned unto all those without that they might enter within and partake of the bounteous food of which those who were finely dressed were partaking.

27 And Antioch stayed with the people all that day. And when they retired to their own houses at the night, Solon beckoned that Antioch stay within his walls to teach him more concerning the things that he had said concerning this great Father who had given these commandments.

28 And Antioch did not stay in the house of Solon, desiring to return once again unto the people with whom he was more comfortable residing.

29 And after this celebration, Solon began to reason with the other leaders of the people to see what could be done to relieve the burden of the farmers. And it came to pass that the farmers were somewhat relieved by the things which Solon did for them.

30 And thus we can see how the gospel can become instrumental in the good of the people, if it so be that their leaders abide by its precepts.

31 And there were those who were present at this celebration who were affected by the words of Antioch. And one of these was a very young boy who remembered all of the words of Antioch. And when he became a man, he became a great leader among them and began to redistribute the land and the property of the nobles among the poor and those who had no land. And his name was Pisistratus.

32 And thus were the beginnings of democracy laid by these men who had been affected by the words of a prophet of God. And when the people began to repent and work righteousness, according to the gospel, then the Lord was bound by his covenants to protect them and defend them against other nations that would destroy them.

33 And it came to pass that the great nation of Persia rose up to battle against the Greeks to take control of their cities and their government. For the people of Greece began to prosper exceedingly because of the laws of trade and equality that they had established among them.

34 And the kings of Persia were desirous to have the fine things that Greece could provide for them. But as they came to war against the Greeks, yea, even so much that the Greeks were greatly outnumbered by the Persians, the Lord aided the people of the Aegean islands and kept the Persians from overrunning their countries.

35 And in one instance, the great navies of Persia set sail upon the waters that divided the two countries, so that they might come upon them and attack them with their great force. And the Lord caused an exceedingly powerful storm to come upon the sea, unlike any storm that had ever been encountered by the Persians. And this great storm destroyed the navies of the Persians and caused them to retreat.

36 And the Persian nation had changed the laws from those which Zarathustra had given unto them; and they became corrupt in a manner of only a few years, because of their exceeding prosperity and their powerful armies.

37 But when they came again upon the people of Greece, the Lord would do that which he could to repel their armies. And there was one great battle in which the men of the great city of Athens had called upon the warrior state of Sparta to come to their aid and fight at their side against the great army of Persia.

38 And before the Athenians departed to the battlefield, each of them was blessed by his mother. Yea, their mothers did pray for their safe return, which did cause many of the Athenians to desire to fight for the sake of their mothers.

39 And the state of Sparta was a warrior state, which was the home of the finest warriors that the world had yet known. For they were trained from their youth to fight against those who would take away their freedom. And they were feared by all the other people of the Aegean lands.

40 And when the day of the great battle came, the Spartans could not come down to the battlefield to aid the Athenians, because they were counseled against the day on which the battle was to take place by the priests of their gods, whom they had set up among themselves. And this Satan caused in order to allow the Persians the ability to destroy the army of Athens.

41 And when the Athenians came upon the battlefield, they saw the Persians arrayed in their armor with their archers and their horses, and all manner of weapons which they had brought with them to destroy the armies of the Greeks.

42 And the Athenians beheld the numbers of their enemies, and the numbers of the Persian army far exceeded the number of their own army. And the Athenians were not as valiant warriors like unto the soldiers of Sparta. Nevertheless, the few men that they did have, thought upon their mothers who had blessed them.

43 And they also knew that if they did not conquer the Persians, then they would lose their freedoms, and their mothers might be slain before them. And with the thought of their mothers fresh in their minds, the Athenians began to run at a great speed towards the armies of the Persians.

44 And there was a great distance between the two armies, but the Athenians did not slow their pace, and continued to run ferociously towards the Persians. And when the armies of the Persians beheld the men of Athens running towards them without horses, without heavy armor, even without archers, they did laugh amongst themselves at the sight that they beheld.

45 And they said amongst themselves: Who are these fools from Athens who think that their small number of men shall stand a chance against our great army? And even if they could fight against us, how do they think they can stand and fight against us after exhausting themselves by the greatness of the distance that they have run?

46 And the Persians knew nothing of the blessing of their mothers, nor did they realize that the Lord had commanded the angels of God to stand ready to aid the Athenians in their battle.

47 And these angels were unseen and dispersed themselves among the armies of the Persians. And when the Athenians reached near unto the armies of the Persians, their leaders commanded their archers to shoot arrows and cut them down before they reached their front lines.

48 But the angels of God that were among the Persians, unseen, misdirected their arrows so that they fell aimlessly away from the Athenians. And before the Persian archers could take up another arrow and set it in their bows, the armies of the Athenians were upon them, and they slew them as they reached for their arrows.

49 And the rest of the Persian army fell into the battle with the Athenians. And the angels of God made the arms of the Persians heavy so that they missed their mark with each blow. But with each blow of the Athenians, a Persian soldier was sent home unprepared to the spirit world.

50 And when these Persian soldiers were in the spirit world, they could then discern the angels of God that were among their armies helping the Athenians defeat them. And they did not understand the cause of this, but soon learned by the power of the Spirit, that they were wicked in their offense against the Greeks.

51 And many of them were received that day in a state of misery in the realm of the spirit world.

52 And now, I, Moroni, would that ye should know that the Lord hath always blessed a nation and its people when they begin to turn to him and keep his commandments. Yea, when they begin to set up governments among them that are based upon the commandments of God; even the greatest commandment of all, which is that ye should love another as ye would have them love you; then will the Lord open up a way whereby that nation might enjoy the peace and happiness that he hath promised to the children of men according to his covenants with them.

53 But when they begin to turn from these commandments and begin once again to set up classes of people among them, and treat one group of his children above those of another group, then he doth not defend that nation, and in time, that nation is allowed to be destroyed by the nations that are led by Satan.

54 And it came to pass that the Greek nation flourished for a time. And they introduced a democracy among them that allowed most of the people to have a say in that which the government did for them. However, they did not include everyone in this voice, and because of this, their nation did not come to know the fullness of the truthfulness of the things of God.

55 But the Spirit did come upon many of the people, and many great men and also women began to question the governments that they had set up among them.

56 And there was one among them who was called Socrates. And he was a prophet of God, who had been given the gift and power of the Holy Ghost all the days of his life. And he began to teach the people that within every person, the full knowledge of the truth was contained within the soul.

57 And he taught them that a person need only to reflect upon the inner feelings that are felt as the promptings of the Holy Spirit are given, in order to find the truth of all things. And Socrates was like unto many of the prophets of God who made an attempt to teach the people according to their understanding and with the words that they were accustomed to hearing, even those that they had learned in their culture.

58 And because of the blessings of the Lord, in that Greece was protected from the offenses of other countries, the people began to prosper exceedingly. And as they began to prosper, they also began to sin and forget the things that had been taught unto them by Antioch and the other prophets who had been sent by the Lord among them.

59 And Socrates began to condemn the injustice in the Athenian society. And because he criticized the rich and the powerful, and the laws that these had established for themselves, thus creating the classes of people that the Lord had forbidden among his children; yea, because of his preaching unto them, they were wont to prosecute him and exile him from their nation.

60 But many people loved Socrates, many of them being the youth who had not yet been set firmly in their ways, and who would listen to the words of Socrates and rise up in rebellion against their elders, even against those of the government who held power over them.

61 Now, it would have been no great thing had the words of Socrates not caused rebellion among the youth of the nation, but because the youth who listened to him would not submit to the established laws of the land, which were established to protect the rich and powerful and their glory, the leaders of the people felt threatened.

62 Now, this is the way that Satan worketh among the children of men. For he shall make many wicked men and women the leaders of the people, and he shall reward them with prosperity, and power, and riches. But also, he rewardeth them with that thing which he sought in the beginning, even the glory of those whom he would lead.

63 And it was this glory for which he sought that caused him to rebel against the Father and be cast out of the kingdom of God. For the plan of the Father gave no glory to those who would serve and lead another.

64 For the first principle and law of heaven pertaining to a government is that this government shall never be self-serving, or in other words, it shall never act in and of itself and of its own accord for the sake of its own existence.

65 And this government is restricted in its power according to the restrictions that are necessary to ensure that it abideth by this first principle and law.

66 For behold, this government serveth those who benefit from its existence; and those who benefit from its existence are those who give it the power that it hath received. And the power that it hath received hath been given to this government to serve those who have given it its power. And this according to the words that I have previously given unto you, according to the words of the brother of Jared.

67 And in the beginning, the democracy of the people in setting up the laws of the government in the Greek nation was done according to these righteous principles, the leaders having been influenced by the teachings of Antioch.

68 But during the time of Socrates, the leaders of this government began to follow the desires of Satan and consume the power that they had received from the people upon their lusts.

69 And it came to pass that Socrates would not depart out of the land of his birth, for it was the land in which the Lord had commanded him to preach the gospel. And with his refusal to depart out of the land, a death sentence was pronounced upon his head, and he was killed in a similar manner as was Ubaid among the Egyptian people.

70 And as I read the words of the brother of Jared concerning these two great prophets, and also many of his words concerning many of the prophets of God who have been sent forth upon the earth under command of the Holy Spirit to preach repentance unto the people and turn their hearts towards the gospel, I, Moroni, began to see that the words of the Lord were verified, when he said: Verily I say unto you, before the throne of God there is no history of His works—for His works are eternal and encompassed into one eternal round, from which He observeth all the works of His hands and receiveth of the joy therein.

71 Therefore, the actions of those who have lived before, shall imitate the actions of those who shall live in the present, and also those who shall live in the future. For unto all of the children of men are the same commandments given, and these commandments are the words that I have given unto you.

72 And as it shall come to pass in one generation—even the sins of that generation—so shall it come to pass in the next generation, because the same spirit that existeth among the children of men, yea, even that spirit that causeth them to sin, shall exist among them of the next generation, even until the time of the end of the earth.

73 And for this reason I have called my holy prophets and have commanded them to write the things that they are taught by the Holy Ghost. For from the Holy Ghost, who is one with my spirit, shall the things of my spirit, or my words, be given unto the children of men.

74 And Socrates was truly a prophet of God and did those things which were commanded of him by the Holy Spirit according to the culture and traditions of the people of the Greek nation.

75 And he left no written record of the things which he had taught the people, not wanting to take any glory upon himself. And also, because he knew that in many instances, the children of men corrupt the written word and change it according to their own whims and according to their own understanding.

76 And when they have changed the written word, then they present it as being the literal words of him whom they claim to others hath written that which they have caused to be changed. And for these very same reasons, there are no written words of Jesus when he preached during the days of his ministry unto the people at Jerusalem.

77 And it came to pass that because Socrates had taught the people to search inside themselves for the kingdom of God, there began to be many people who would not listen to the precepts of men, even those men who were being led by Satan And these began to think for themselves, with help from the ministrations of the spirit world.

78 And it came to pass that the great nation of Greece began to become weakened from the contentions and strife among its own people. For there were many who disagreed with the government and argued for more just laws and statutes that would return more control of the government to the people.

79 But the people were not righteous in their desires, because they did not care about their neighbor, but only about their own selves and their own families, and thus they began to prosper in their wickedness and were led away by Satan into carnal security.

80 And when Satan had finally won their hearts, he turned his back on them when they would not give him the glory that he sought.

81 And it came to pass that a great prophet was sent among the people, and his name was Sythipian. And Sythipian dreamed a dream in which he saw a vision of an allegory pertaining to the destruction of the Greek nation and their captivity. And he went unto the people and told them all that he had dreamed in the dream, and all that he had seen in the vision, which he had received from the ministrations of the spirit world.

82 And now, it is expedient according to the commandment of the Lord given unto me by the Holy Ghost, that I explain unto you the purpose and realization of dreams, so that ye might not be misled by those who dream, and also that ye might not be misled by your own dreams.

83 And I have previously explained to you the workings of the spirit world and how those who reside therein communicate with us in the flesh. And because of the restrictions of the flesh, we are unable to communicate with these spirits, except it be through the medium of our own spirits when we are concentrating, or directing our spirit matter towards these ministrations.

84 And because most of the children of men are so enticed by the things of this world, and the problems and stresses therein, yea, most of them do not direct the medium of their spirit towards these ministrations, because according to the flesh, we can only be concentrating on one thing at a time.

85 Nevertheless, when we are asleep, our flesh sleepeth, but our spirit is free to be directed according to its desires, or it is directed according to the desires of those in the spirit world who have the power and authority to direct our spiritual thoughts.

86 And there are many dreams in which our own spirit useth its own medium to reflect the desires of our own heart, and these are the dreams that come to us according to our free agency.

87 But there are also those dreams that are given unto us by those in authority in the spirit world to teach us and guide us, or to give us directions that we might share the things that we dream with others for their instruction and profit.

88 And now, here is a mystery that ye should know and understand: Behold, Lucifer and those who did not follow the plan of the Father, even all those in the spirit world who do not accept the plan of the Father, are given no authority to cause us to dream.

89 For if Satan had this ability, then it would be that much easier for him to deceive us. For when we are asleep, our flesh giveth in to the needs of itself, but our spirit doth not require sleep and is alive in each of us, but only according to the limits of the flesh in which it was confined upon our birth into mortality.

90 Therefore, all dreams are either a cause of our own free agency, or are given unto us by the power and authority of the Holy Spirit for our own benefit or the benefit of others.

91 And it is important that ye understand that if ye receive a dream, and in this dream ye are commanded in any way to disobey the law of the gospel in any manner, then ye may know that this dream was initialized and perpetuated by your own thoughts, which are evil.

92 And this dream should be a cause of your repentance of that which ye desire to do in the spirit, but have not yet done in the flesh.

93 For while ye are awake and conscious of the world in which ye reside, Satan useth all of his powers and his deceptions to persuade you to do evil. And if he hath affected you to a great extent, because ye have allowed him to, then ye will be affected in your dreams according to his will and your own free agency.

94 And now that is the mystery of dreams that the Spirit commanded me to write unto you in this record.

95 For it came to pass that the Holy Spirit caused Sythipian to dream a dream in which he saw a great tree begin to grow from a seed planted in the northern part of the land of Greece. And this tree grew exceedingly and caused its branches to extend over the whole nation of Greece, evensomuch that the rays of the sun where blotted out.

96 And there was an abundance of fruit upon this tree of which the people partook according to their desires. And the men of Greece were desirous to once again see the sun and partake of its warmth, therefore, they took up their axes to cut down the tree, or at least clear a way whereby they might see the light of the sun once again. But as they began to cut the tree, the branches thereof shook before them and the fruit fell to the ground.

97 And from the seeds of the fruit, more trees were spawned, which quickly grew and overcame the men that were wont to cut down the first tree. And because the fruit of the tree contained many seeds, the new trees began to grow and spread throughout all parts of the earth.

98 And Sythipian explained to the leaders of the people the meaning of the dream. And he told them that the tree represented a great king of the land northward who was nourished by the nation of Greece in his knowledge and in his wisdom, but that he would rise up against them one day to overcome them and take them into captivity.

99 And this great king would make friends with them and give them of his own kingdom until they began to see his power and make an attempt to sever the friendship and bonds which they had created between them.

100 And this great king would be killed by them, but his son would rise up and grow in knowledge and wisdom, being nourished from all the knowledge and understanding of the wisest and most noble Greeks among them.

101 And this son would conquer them and lead them into captivity, and would spread his kingdom throughout that part of the earth.

102 And it came to pass that the Greeks mocked Sythipian and cast him out from among them and called him a fool for revealing unto them such a dream. And their leaders mocked him, saying: Dost thou think that this great nation can be overrun by another? Behold, there is no nation upon this earth that hath the power and the unity that we have. And our leaders are of the greatest minds the world hath ever known. And our gods protect us. And they have protected us because we worship them, and honor them, and give them glory.

103 And if thou thinkest that this great nation shall be destroyed because of thy dream, then it is because thou desirest this thing of thyself. And because thou desirest this thing, thou art an enemy of the state, and are thus sentenced to death.

104 And the leaders of the Greeks put Sythipian to death for the dream that he had.

105 And it came to pass that not many years later, King Philip of the Macedonians rose up and was desirous to take them captive. And when he was murdered, his son, Alexander, did rise up and take the whole land of Greece, and many other parts of the world under his control.

106 And now we can see that in all the history of the world, among all the children of men, the Lord sendeth forth his prophets to warn them of impending danger and captivity.

107 And if the children of men heed the words of the prophets and turn to God, even that they begin to keep His commandments, then He will bless them according to His covenants which He hath made to their fathers.

108 But if they will not turn their hearts to their fathers and the covenants that the Lord hath made with them, which are the same covenants that the Lord maketh to all the children of men in all generations of time, then the Lord is not bound by these covenants, and they will be left to be dealt with according to the will of the god whom they worship, even Satan.

109 And Satan shall reward them according to his own will and covenants.

CHAPTER 31

The rise of the Great Roman Empire and the explanation of the great beast by John in Revelation. The Roman Empire is one beast, and the great European Empire and the United States are some of the other beasts described by John. The book of Revelation is expounded on extensively.

AND now it is convenient at this point in my abridgment that I introduce the next great nation that arose after the nation of the Greeks. And this great nation is that Roman Empire, even that same nation that ruled most of the earth in the present day of my fathers on the other continent of the earth, even that continent out of which traveled my fathers.

2 And about this present time, the Roman Empire shall be wounded exceedingly because of its great sins before the Lord, evensomuch that it shall be destroyed by a deadly wound, according to the words of John that are written in the Bible, which ye have already among you.

3 But from its wounds, the rise of another great nation shall come to pass. And this nation shall be known as the great European Empire. And from that great empire, Satan shall make his final stand against the saints of God, even before the Lord cometh again in his glory to claim that which hath been placed in his power by the Father.

4 For Satan shall cause to be established a powerful nation among the Gentiles that shall strike fear in all the other nations of the world. And with this great nation, Satan shall begin to rule and reign over his own dominion without the restrictions that were placed on him by the Father in the beginning.

5 And this shall be the final opportunity of Satan to show unto the children of God that his plan can bring happiness and joy to those who follow him and give him the glory that he seeketh. And this great nation shall be known as the United States, for they shall be united in their desire to worship Satan and his image, and this because of their works.

6 And unknowingly they shall be led subtlety to believe that Satan is their God, even the very eternal Father. And they shall support and worship his image, and cause all other nations who do not support and worship the image of Satan, to be condemned or destroyed.

7 And now, all these things shall come to pass according to the words of the brother of Jared. And I shall hereafter give unto you an abridgment of how these things shall come to pass. Nevertheless, it hath been commanded me by the Spirit to give unto you the words of John, which are written in the book of the Jews. For the words of John are the final words of this book, and shall give unto the children of men all the knowledge that they shall need in order that they might understand that which Satan hath done to deceive them and lead them away from the words of Christ and into captivity, being bound by the chains of Satan.

8 And the words of the brother of Jared shall show unto the elect the way in which Satan rewardeth those who follow his plan and keep his covenants. And he rewardeth them with peace and carnal security as it hath been explained unto you previously in this record.

9 And all of the prophets of God have seen this time when Satan shall be released by the Father and given power over his own dominions without the restrictions that were placed upon him from the beginning.

10 For Lucifer hath complained unto the Father that the presentation of his plan and its incorporation into mortality cannot take a full effect, nor can it be given the proper chance, so that the children of God can make a fair choice of which plan is the best and most righteous for all, if he is not allowed to give unto them some indication and example of the eternal laws that have been established for their happiness.

11 Therefore, the Father hath chosen a time when peace shall be taken from the earth for the last time and Lucifer shall have power over his own dominions. And at this time, the plan of Lucifer shall be shown in its full effect unto the children of God. Whether they are alive in mortality, or alive according to the manner of the spirit in the dimensions of the spirit world; yea, all the children of God shall witness these last days, and see the plan of Lucifer in its glory.

12 And after it hath failed miserably, then

shall every knee bow, and every tongue confess that the plan of salvation which was given unto us by the Father, is the only plan that is possible whereby we might have eternal peace and happiness, even that eternal joy that the Father hath promised unto all of us in the beginning.

13 And since all the prophets of God have seen these latter days, and these prophets know the will of God concerning them; yea, because they have known these things, many of them have touched upon them in their writings, which are contained in the holy scriptures that are upon the earth in the latter days.

14 Nevertheless, the Lord hath not permitted any of them to reveal unto the children of men the entire truth regarding these things. But some of them have revealed many things by way of symbolism and allegory, which was commanded of them by the Lord, so that the children of men would be inspired to seek the meaning of these things from him, or in other words, from his Holy Spirit.

15 And he who shall be the bearer of Christ, even he who shall bring forth the sealed portion of this record unto the world, shall have the power to discern all the symbolism and the allegories that have been given unto the children of men by the prophets of old. And those things that are not revealed in the portion of this record that is sealed, shall be revealed through him. And by the power of the Spirit he shall discern all things which have been written.

16 Nevertheless, I, Moroni, have been commanded to explain unto you the words of John that pertain to the great Roman Empire, and also that great nation that shall rise up because of the Romans, even the great European Empire, and also the last great nation that shall rise up above all other nations upon the earth in the latter days.

17 And this last nation shall be the seat of Satan, where he shall sit and rule and reign throughout the world, even in the final stages of his power and dominion.

18 And they who shall bring these things forth unto the world shall be among those of this last nation. And the first of these last two prophets of God in the latter days shall be at the beginning of this nation, and the last shall be near the end thereof, or at the time when the words of the Lord shall be fulfilled pertaining unto the time when the work of the Father shall commence in gathering the saints from among the wicked before the great and dreadful day of the Lord.

19 For unto the saints of God, the day of the Lord shall not be dreadful, but shall be that day for which they have waited in patience. But unto the wicked, which are all those who worship the beast, who is Lucifer, the day of the Lord shall indeed be great and terrible.

20 And then shall the words of John be understood and fulfilled, which he wrote, saying: And after these things I saw another angel come down from heaven, having great power; and the earth was lightened with his glory.

21 And he cried mightily with a strong voice, saying, Babylon the great is fallen, is fallen, and is become the habitation of devils, and the hold of every foul spirit, and a cage of every unclean and hateful bird. For all nations have drunk of the wine of the wrath of her fornication, and the kings of the earth have committed fornication with her, and the merchants of the earth are waxed rich through the abundance of her delicacies.

22 And I heard another voice from heaven, saying, Come out of her, my people, that ye be not partakers of her sins, and that ye receive not of her plagues. For her sins have reached unto heaven, and God hath remembered her iniquities. And then shall the saints of God lift up their voice unto the Lord, and the voice of all the holy prophets shall cry unto the Lord, saying: Reward her even as she rewarded us, and double unto her double according to her works; in the cup which she hath filled, fill even to her double as she hath done unto us.

23 How much she hath glorified herself, and lived deliciously of our labors and our sorrow, so much torment and sorrow give double unto her: for she saith in her heart, I sit a queen, and am no widow, and shall see no sorrow.

24 Therefore shall her plagues come in one day, death, and mourning, and famine; and she shall be utterly burned with fire: for strong is the Lord God who judgeth her. And the kings of the earth, who have committed fornication and

TSP 31:25– 31:36

lived deliciously with her, shall bewail her, and lament for her, when they shall see the smoke of her burning. And they, standing afar off for the fear of her torment, shall lament her, saying, Alas, alas that great city Babylon, that mighty city! for in one hour is thy judgment come.

25 And the merchants of the earth shall weep and mourn over her; for no man buyeth their merchandise any more, even the merchandise of gold, and silver, and precious stones, and of pearls, and fine linen, and purple, and silk, and scarlet, and all manner of vessels of ivory, and all manner of vessels of the most precious wood, and of brass, and iron, and marble, and cinnamon, and odours, and ointments, and frankincense, and wine, and oil, and fine flour, and wheat, and beasts, and sheep, and horses, and chariots, and slaves, and all the souls of men that have been held captive by her.

26 And the fruits that thy soul hath lusted after are departed from before thee, and all the things which were dainty and goodly are departed from thee, and thou shalt find them no more at all. And the merchants of these things, which were made rich by her, shall stand afar off for the fear of her torment. And they shall weep and wail, saying: Alas, alas that great city, that was clothed in fine linen, and purple, and scarlet, and decked with gold, and precious stones, and pearls.

27 Yea, even that great city from which we received our riches and our power and our glory; for in one hour so great riches is come to naught. And every shipmaster, and all the company in ships, and sailors, and as many as trade by sea, stood afar off, and cried when they saw the smoke of her burning, saying: What city is like unto this great city! And what is the cause of its destruction?

28 And they shall cast dust upon their heads, and cry, weeping and wailing, saying: Alas, alas that great city, wherein we were made rich, even all that had ships in the sea by reason of her costliness. For in one hour is she made desolate.

29 Rejoice over her, thou heaven, and ye holy apostles and prophets; for God hath avenged you on her. And a mighty angel took up a stone like a great millstone, and cast it into the sea, saying: Thus with violence shall that great city Babylon be thrown down, and shall be found no more at all. And the voice of harpers, and musicians, and of pipers, and trumpeters, shall be heard no more at all in thee.

30 And no craftsman, of whatsoever craft he be, shall be found any more in thee; and the sound of a millstone shall be heard no more at all in thee. And the light of a candle shall shine no more at all in thee; and the voice of the bridegroom and of the bride shall be heard no more at all in thee. For thy merchants were the great men and leaders of the nations of the earth. For by thy sorceries were all nations deceived.

31 And in her was found the blood of the holy prophets, and of the saints, and of all that were slain upon the earth, even all those who trusted in God and kept the commandments that were given unto them.

32 And now I, Moroni, would that ye should understand that the nations of the earth have caused that many of the prophets of God have been slain because they have tried to teach unto them the plan of the Father, which plan is diametrically opposed to the plan of Lucifer.

33 And when a nation would rather live by the plan of Lucifer, or in other words, do his will, then these same nations seek to destroy the prophets of God because of the words of God that these prophets preach unto them, which words condemn them.

34 And it shall come to pass that the words of the prophets contained in the book of the Jews, or the Bible, and the words of the prophets of this record, which is the record of my father, Mormon; yea, in the last days these two records shall be represented symbolically as these last two prophets of whom John spoke when he wrote, saying: And there was given me a reed like unto a rod: and the angel stood, saying, Rise, and measure the temple of God, and the altar, and them that worship therein.

35 But the court which is without the temple leave out, and measure it not; for it is given unto the Gentiles. For they shall tread under foot the holy city for forty and two months. But I will give power unto my two witnesses, and they shall prophesy a thousand two hundred and threescore days, clothed in sackcloth.

36 Behold, these are the two olive trees, and

the two candlesticks standing before the God of the earth. And if any man will hurt them, fire proceedeth out of their mouth, and devoureth their enemies; yea, if any man will hurt them, he must in this manner be killed.

37 And these shall have power to shut heaven, that it rain not in the days of their prophecy. And they shall also have power over the waters to turn them to blood, and to smite the earth with all of their plagues, as often as they will, according to the heed that is given unto them.

38 And when they shall have finished their testimony, the beast that ascendeth out of the bottomless pit shall make war against them, and shall overcome them, and kill them. And their dead bodies shall lie in the street of the great city, which spiritually is called Sodom and Egypt, where also our Lord was crucified, because the holy city gave no heed unto the words of his prophets.

39 And they of the temple of God, which are the people and kindreds and tongues and nations of the earth, shall see their dead bodies three days and an half, and shall not suffer their dead bodies to be put in graves.

40 And they that dwell upon the earth shall rejoice over them, and make merry, and shall send gifts one to another; because these two prophets tormented them that dwelt on the earth.

41 And now, I, Moroni, give unto those of you who are the elect, the explanation of these things; for they are glorious things, which can only be made known unto you by the Spirit of God. But I know that many of you have been led by the precepts of men for so long, that it is difficult for ye to discern that which is of the Spirit, and that which is of men.

42 For Satan whispereth a portion of the truth unto many, that he might convince them of his power. And he introduceth his own precepts, mingled with the truth, to deceive you. And for this reason, this record hath been prepared and sealed up to come forth unto you to help you discern the truth of all things.

43 For behold, John hath revealed unto you the time of the Lord in that which he wrote, saying: For they shall tread under foot the holy city for forty and two months; and I will give power unto my two witnesses, and they shall prophesy a thousand two hundred and threescore days, clothed in sackcloth; And they of the temple of God, which are the people and kindreds and tongues and nations of the earth, shall see their dead bodies three days and a half, and shall not suffer their dead bodies to be put in graves.

44 And now, I would that ye should know that forty and two months are a thousand two hundred and threescore days. And a thousand two hundred and threescore days are three years and a half, or in other words, three days and a half, according to the symbolism that John hath used to describe these things.

45 And these days represent years. Therefore, a thousand two hundred and threescore years shall pass until all these things shall be fulfilled. Now here is the understanding of the wise. A time and two times, and a half of time is three and a half. He who hath the Spirit and receiveth these things according to the spirit of prophecy, shall understand and not be afraid of that which is to come.

46 And the Bible and the record of my father shall be upon the earth for a thousand two hundred and threescore years before the words of the Lord shall be fulfilled in all things that he hath given unto the children of men through the mouths of his holy prophets. And these two great prophets of which John hath written shall be a witness unto the world of its wickedness, in the same manner and likeness as the words of a holy prophet shall witness in the flesh of the wickedness of a nation.

47 And the people and kindreds of the earth shall have them available to them, but shall not give heed unto them. And those who do give heed unto them, shall not live by their precepts. And this is what is meant by the people and kindreds and tongues and nations of the earth, which shall see their dead bodies three days and a half, and shall not suffer their dead bodies to be put in graves.

48 For behold, Satan hath deceived the whole earth and hath caused the children of men to disregard these two testimonies of the words of Christ. And now, when John wrote, saying: These are the two olive trees, and the two candlesticks standing before the God of the earth. And if any man will hurt them, fire proceedeth out of their mouth, and devoureth their enemies: and if any man will hurt them, he must in this manner be killed.

49 Yea, John was giving reference to the warning that he also hath given at the end of the Bible, in which he wrote, saying: For I testify unto every man that heareth the words of the prophecy of this book, that if any man shall add unto these things, God shall add unto him the plagues that are written in this book. And if any man shall take away from the words of the book of this prophecy, God shall take away his part out of the book of life, and out of the holy city, and from the things which are written in this book. And he of which this book testifieth, saith: Surely I come quickly. Amen. And I saith: Even so, come, Lord Jesus.

50 And now, I, Moroni, testify to those of you who shall receive these things, that the sealed portion of this record shall be that which the Lord hath prepared to stand as a witness of the truth regarding the holy scriptures that ye have among you.

51 And whatsoever ye find in the scriptures that ye have among you that doth not agree with that which ye shall receive in this record, then ye shall know that it hath been changed and added to or taken away from. And if it hath been changed in this manner, then the words of this record can help you to know the truth regarding these changes, even the truth that was meant to be known by those who have written these things.

52 And when John wrote, saying: And these shall have power to shut heaven, that it rain not in the days of their prophecy. And they shall also have power over the waters to turn them to blood, and to smite the earth with all of their plagues, as often as they will, according to the heed that is given unto them.

53 Yea, he meant that if the children of men abide by the words of Christ in these books, or of these two prophets, then they shall be blessed according to the covenants that the Lord hath made with their fathers. And if they do not abide by their words, then shall the earth be cursed for their sakes, even that they might repent. For the rain from heaven is the revelation that is given unto the children of men through the ministrations of the Holy Ghost, according to the heed that they give unto the words of Christ.

54 And when John wrote, saying: And when they shall have finished their testimony, the beast that ascendeth out of the bottomless pit shall make war against them, and shall overcome them, and kill them. Yea, he meant that Satan shall deceive the children of men to such an extent that the words of the holy scriptures shall have no effect upon them.

55 And the hearts of the children of men shall be set so much upon the things of this world, and the desire for the honors of men, that the holy scriptures shall be dead unto them, because they do not have a desire to read them. And when they do read them, they do not understand them.

56 And then shall ye understand more fully the words of John which he wrote, saying: And they that dwell upon the earth shall rejoice over them, and make merry, and shall send gifts one to another; because these two prophets tormented them that dwelt on the earth. For the children of men shall began to believe that these holy scriptures are not the words of God, but are myths and fantasies created by other men to deceive them. And this is what Satan would have them believe.

57 And now, I would that ye should understand the words of John pertaining unto these great nations of which I have spoken, which shall be set up upon the earth in order to give Satan the time of his power and his glory.

58 And John wrote of the Roman Empire, saying: And I stood upon the sand of the sea, and saw a beast rise up out of the sea, having seven heads and ten horns, and upon his horns ten crowns, and upon his heads the name of blasphemy. And the beast which I saw was like unto a leopard, and his feet were as the feet of a bear, and his mouth as the mouth of a lion: and the dragon gave him his power, and his seat, and great authority.

59 Now this beast which John describeth is the power of Satan that is over the entire earth, even upon the seven continents, which are the seven heads. And this power is in ten of the great empires or nations, which are the ten horns upon which are ten crowns.

60 And John continueth his words, saying: And they worshipped the dragon which gave power unto the beast and to them that were the leaders among men. And they worshipped the beast, saying: Who is like unto the beast? Who is able to make war with him? And there was given unto him a mouth speaking great things and blasphemies; and power was given unto him this time to continue forty and two months.

61 And he opened his mouth in blasphemy against God, to blaspheme his name, and his tabernacle, and them that dwell in heaven. And it was given unto him to make war with the saints, and to overcome them by the words of the leaders of the nations to whom he hath given his power. And this power was given him over all kindreds and tongues and nations. And all that dwell upon the earth shall worship him, whose names are not written in the book of life, which is the church of the Lamb of God who was slain from the foundation of the world.

62 If any man have an ear, let him hear; For he that leadeth into captivity shall go into captivity, and he that killeth with the sword must be killed with the sword. Here is the patience and the faith of the saints.

63 Now, I, Moroni, would that ye should understand that thus hath been, and is, and will be the state in which the children of men shall find themselves among all the nations of the earth since the beginning. And I have previously explained unto you that Satan shall use the power that he hath over the leaders and rulers of the nations of the earth to subdue the truth of God and slay the prophets who shall preach the truth unto them.

64 And it is only by the sword that Satan shall be able to enforce his will upon the earth. And any nation that submiteth to the will of Satan and taketh up a sword against another nation, shall be destroyed by the sword. Thus it hath been, thus it is, and thus it shall always be until the Lord cometh in his glory.

65 And for this reason the Lord hath commanded me to make a record of the histories of these nations, so that ye might see the fulfillment of all the words of the Lord concerning these things. For behold, every nation that hath lived by the sword, hath died by the sword. And every nation that taketh another nation captive, shall be led into captivity according to the word of the Lord, which word hath been given to all the nations of the earth through his holy prophets.

66 And John continueth his words, saying: And I saw one of his heads as it were wounded to death; and his deadly wound was healed: and all the world wondered after the beast. Now, this is the head that representeth the Roman Empire. For ye shall see how this great nation shall rise above all other nations and wield its power throughout the entire earth.

67 And its system of government shall eventually fall, which is what is meant by being wounded to death. But this same system of government and laws shall once again rise up on the earth, which is what is meant by his deadly wound being healed.

68 And all the world shall wonder after this system of government and its laws, and they shall be led to believe that this system of government and its laws are the most righteous that have ever been upon the earth.

69 And it is this system of government and these laws that shall be the medium for the plan of Lucifer. And John continueth his words concerning this government and its laws, or in other words, this power, saying: And I beheld another beast coming up out of the earth; and he had two horns like a lamb, and he spake as a dragon. And he exerciseth all the power of the first beast before him, and causeth the earth and them which dwell therein to worship the first beast, whose deadly wound was healed.

70 Now this hath reference to the great European Empire, which shall eventually be divided into ten major nations, or horns. And a beast shall be among them, even a beast with two horns. And this beast shall have two horns, one shall be known as the British Empire, and the other of these horns shall be the colonial states, which shall be separated from the main land of this empire by many waters.

71 And these two nations, which are from the beast, were one in the beginning and shall be one in the end, and shall base their system of government upon many of the laws and ideas of the Roman Empire, which government and laws were wounded to death, but then healed, or revived by the later great European Empire from which these two nations shall rise. And these two nations shall promote peace, as the two horns like a lamb represent. Nevertheless, this peace shall be the peace and carnal security into which Satan shall lull them.

72 And John gave another representation of this, in which he wrote, saying: And there came one of the seven angels which had the seven vials, and talked with me, saying unto me, Come hither; I will shew unto thee the judgment of the great whore that sitteth upon many waters, with whom the kings of the earth have committed fornication, and the inhabitants of the earth have been made drunk with the wine of her fornication.

73 And now, I, Moroni, would that ye should understand that this is the great and abominable church of which Nephi hath written in his vision, which is the same vision that was given unto John. And I have explained this great and abominable church unto you previously. Therefore, it is important that ye reference these things that ye might understand them more fully.

74 And John continued with his words, saying: So he carried me away in the spirit into the wilderness: and I saw a woman sitting upon a scarlet coloured beast, full of names of blasphemy, having seven heads and ten horns. And the woman was arrayed in purple and scarlet colour, and decked with gold and precious stones and pearls, having a golden cup in her hand full of abominations and filthiness of her fornication.

75 And upon her forehead was a name written, Mystery, Babylon The Great, The Mother Of Harlots And Abomination Of The Earth. And I saw the woman drunken with the blood of the saints, and with the blood of the martyrs of Jesus.

76 And when I saw her, I wondered with great admiration. And the angel said unto me: Wherefore didst thou marvel? I will tell thee the mystery of the woman, and of the beast that carrieth her, which hath the seven heads and ten horns.

77 The beast that thou sawest was, and is not; and shall ascend out of the bottomless pit, and go into perdition: and they that dwell on the earth shall wonder, whose names were not written in the book of life from the foundation of the world, when they behold the beast that was, and is not, and yet is.

78 And here is the mind which hath wisdom. The seven heads are seven mountains, on which the woman sitteth. And there are seven kings: five are fallen, and one is, and the other is not yet come; and when he cometh, he must continue a short space.

79 And now, I, Moroni, think that it should be easy to understand these words of John. For behold, the five great nations that have fallen before the great Roman Empire, which is the nation that is upon the earth at the time of John, are the nations of the Egyptians, the Hittites, the Assyrians, the Persians, and the Greeks.

80 And the one that is yet to come, according to the time of John, is the great European Empire.

81 And now, I, Moroni, have seen the words of John which have been given in the Bible. And I would that ye should remember the words of Nephi which he wrote, saying: Thou seest that after the book hath gone forth through the hands of the great and abominable church, that there are many plain and precious things taken away from the book, which is the book of the Lamb of God.

82 And after these plain and precious things were taken away it goeth forth unto all the nations of the Gentiles; and after it goeth forth unto all the nations of the Gentiles, yea, even across the many waters which thou hast seen with the Gentiles that have gone forth out of captivity, thou seest—because of the many plain and precious things which have been taken out of the book, which were plain unto the understanding of the children of men, according to the plainness which is in the Lamb of God— because of these things which are taken away out of the gospel of the Lamb, an exceedingly great many do stumble, yea, insomuch that Satan hath great power over them.

83 Now, I, Moroni, would that ye should understand that the two prophets that shall be among you in the latter days, even those who shall bring this record forth unto you, shall have

the power and authority given unto them to discern which of the plain and precious things have been taken out of the Bible. And they shall be commanded to put these plain and precious things back into the holy scriptures according to the revelations that they shall receive of the Holy Spirit, which shall be with them.

84 And they do not add to, nor do they take away from that which is written, but they put back the things which have been taken out by the great and abominable church of which Nephi hath spoken. And I have also been given this power and authority of the Spirit.

85 Therefore, I have given unto you the words of John in their original state, even that state in which John hath written them, even most plain and precious so that ye may understand the truth regarding them.

86 And John continueth more specifically in what he hath written, saying: And the beast that was, and is not, and yet is, hath given his full power unto an eighth, and this eighth is of the seventh, and this eighth shall worship the beast. And this beast is he that goeth into perdition. And the ten horns which thou sawest are ten kings, which have received no kingdom as yet; but receive power as kings one hour with the beast. These have one mind, and shall give their power and strength unto the beast.

87 Now this eighth nation of which John hath written is the United States of the last days, and it is of the seventh, or of the great European Empire. And ten major nations shall arise of the great European Empire and shall reign for a short time And unto the nation of the United States, Satan shall begin to show forth his power and establish his plan among the people of the earth.

88 And this first prophet of the latter days, even he that shall bring forth the unsealed portion of this record, shall be given a revelation from God in which he shall warn the people of the earth that the time is not yet, but is nigh at hand when Satan shall be released and have power over his own dominion.

89 And this revelation shall be given unto the children of men just before the day and the hour that the Father shall take off the chains by which Satan hath been bound, even that He shall no longer forbid Satan from showing forth his power unto the children of men.

CHAPTER 32

The voice of warning given by Joseph Smith is given and the book of Revelation is further expounded on. The beast and the power and influence of money are explained as well as the marks of the beast. Those who have the mark of the Lamb in their foreheads are the elect of God. Moroni describes the difference between a righteous and an evil nation.

AND I have been commanded to include this voice of warning upon these plates as it shall be given unto the world by the first prophet of the latter days: Hearken, Oh, ye people of the church of the Lamb of God saith the voice of him who dwelleth on high, and whose eyes are upon all men.

2 Yea, verily I say, hearken ye people from afar, and ye that are upon the islands of the sea, listen together; for verily the voice of the Lord is unto all men, and there is none to escape, and there is no eye that shall not see, neither ear that shall not hear, neither heart that shall not be penetrated.

3 And the rebellious shall be pierced with much sorrow, for their iniquities shall be spoken upon the housetops, and their secret acts shall be revealed. And this voice of warning shall be unto all people, by the mouths of my disciples, whom I have chosen in these last days, and they shall go forth and none shall stay them, for I the Lord have commanded them.

4 Behold, this is mine authority, and the authority of my servants, which I have given them to preach unto you, Oh, inhabitants of the earth; therefore fear and tremble, Oh, ye people, for what I the Lord have decreed, in them, shall be fulfilled.

5 And verily, I say unto you, that they who go forth bearing these tidings unto the inhabitants of the earth, to them is power given to seal, both on earth and in heaven, the unbelieving and rebellious; yea, verily, to seal them up unto the day when the wrath of God shall be poured out upon the wicked without measure; even unto the day when the Lord shall come to recompense unto every man according to his work, and measure to every man according to the measure which he hath measured to his fellow man.

6 Therefore the voice of the Lord is unto the ends of the earth, that all that will hear may hear. And this voice is like one that cryeth in the wilderness, saying: Prepare ye, prepare ye for that which is to come, for the Lord is nigh; and the anger of the Lord is kindled, and his sword is bathed in heaven, and it shall fall upon the inhabitants of the earth.

7 And the arm of the Lord shall be revealed unto the ends of the earth. And the day cometh that they who will not hear the voice of the Lord, neither the voice of his servants, neither give heed to the words of the prophets and apostles, shall be cut off from among the people.

8 For they have strayed from mine ordinances, and have broken mine everlasting covenant. They seek not the Lord to establish his righteousness, but every man walketh in his own way, and after the image of his own god, whose image is in the likeness of the world, and whose substance is that of an idol, which waxeth old and shall perish in Babylon, even Babylon the great, which shall fall.

9 Therefore, I the Lord, knowing the calamity which should come upon the inhabitants of the earth, have called upon my servants and spake unto them from heaven, and gave unto them commandments that they should proclaim these things unto the world; and all this that it might be fulfilled, which was written by the prophets, that the weak things of the world shall come forth and break down the mighty and strong ones, that man should not counsel his fellow man, neither trust in the arm of flesh.

10 But that every man might speak in the name of God the Lord, even the Savior of the world. And that faith also might increase in the earth; that mine everlasting covenant might be established and that the fullness of my gospel might be proclaimed by the weak and the simple, unto the ends of the world, and before kings and rulers.

11 Behold, I am God, and have spoken it; these commandments are of me, and were given unto my servants in their weakness, after the manner of their language, that they might come to understanding; and inasmuch as they erred it might be made known; and inasmuch as they sought wisdom they might be instructed; and inasmuch as they sinned they might be chastened, that they might repent; and inasmuch as they were humble, they might be made strong, and blessed from on high, and receive knowledge from time to time.

12 And after having received the record of the Nephites, yea, even my servants the prophets, might have power to translate, through the mercy of God, by the power of God, the Book of Mormon. And also those to whom these commandments were given might have power to lay the foundation of this church, even the church of the Lamb of God and to bring it forth out of obscurity, and out of darkness, the only true and living church upon the face of the whole earth, with which I the Lord am well pleased, speaking unto the church collectively and not individually.

13 For I the Lord cannot look upon sin with the least degree of allowance; nevertheless, he that repenteth and keepeth the commandments of the Lord shall be forgiven; and he that repenteth not, from him shall be taken even the light which he hath received. For my Spirit shall not always strive with man, saith the Lord of Hosts.

14 And again, verily I say unto you, Oh, inhabitants of the earth, I, the Lord, am willing to make these things known unto all flesh, for I am no respecter of persons, and will that all men shall know that the day speedily cometh—the hour is not yet, but is nigh at hand—when peace shall be taken from the earth, and the devil shall have power over his own dominion.

15 And also the Lord shall have power over his saints, and shall reign in their midst, and shall come down in judgment upon the world. Verily, I say unto you, search these commandments, even the words that shall be given unto you by my servants, for they are true and faithful, and the prophecies and promises which are in them shall all be fulfilled.

16 And what I, the Lord, have spoken, I have spoken, and I excuse not myself; and though the heavens and the earth pass away, my words shall not pass away, but shall all be fulfilled, whether by mine own voice, or by the voice of my servants, it is the same.

17 For behold, and lo, the Lord is God, and

the Spirit beareth record, and the record is true, and the truth abideth for ever and ever. Amen.

18 And now, I, Moroni, have given unto you these words of warning. And these words shall be given at the time just before the day and the hour that Satan is released by the Father as I have explained it unto you.

19 And the words of John describe this day, saying: And he doeth great wonders, so that he maketh fire come down from heaven on the earth in the sight of men, and deceiveth them that dwell on the earth by the means of those miracles which he had power to do in the sight of the beast.

20 And he shall say to them that dwell on the earth, that they should make an image to the beast, which had the wound by a sword, and did live.

21 And he had power to give life unto the image of the beast, that the image of the beast should both speak, and cause that as many as would not worship the image of the beast should be killed.

22 Behold, when Satan is released, he shall begin to inspire the children of men with great advancements in technology and science, even advancements that shall turn the hearts of the children of men away from God.

23 And these advancements are based upon powers that are eternal, which the Father forbade Lucifer to give to the children of men, so that they would not destroy themselves in their wickedness. And up to the time that he was released, Satan was allowed to introduce some of these technologies and advancements, but only according to the wisdom of the Father.

24 For the Father knoweth all things. And He hath seen many earths come and go, even those which He hath prepared for other of His children. And He knoweth what the children of men can endure in their times and in their seasons. And He also knoweth the effects that these technologies and advancements shall have on the hearts of His children. And not only on His children, but on the earth that He hath created for them.

25 For it is the desire of Lucifer to give unto all the great blessings and powers of the Celestial glory, or the glory of the Father. Now, this desire would not be such a bad thing, except that these powers are reserved for those who will use them in the service and for the benefit of those whom they serve, according to the laws that govern the Celestial kingdom.

26 But Lucifer argued in the beginning that all of the children of God are capable of enjoying the power and blessings of the Celestial glory, if they are given unto them.

27 And Jehovah argued against the plan of Lucifer, saying: And if these great powers are given unto those who are not restricted in their use, according to the restrictions set by the laws of the kingdom of happiness in which they exist, then they shall use these powers for their own enjoyment and benefit without regard for that which the use of these powers might do to another.

28 For in the Terrestrial and Telestial glories there are no restrictions or laws that prohibit the use of any of the eternal laws that they are given in those kingdoms. For the powers that shall be given unto them, are given for their own enjoyment, which is according to their own desires of happiness.

29 And these eternal laws constitute these powers. And if these powers are used in selfishness, then there shall be no way that these beings can be restricted from harming one another, if it so be that these powers bring joy to the individual who useth them for his own happiness, in spite of how it might affect another.

30 And if this be the case, then there shall be much contention and discord among those in the glories whose desires of happiness are self-serving and centered only in their own happiness.

31 Behold, those of a Celestial glory only use those powers in the service of others and never for Their own benefit or glory, and this is according to the laws of this kingdom of glory. And if these powers are only used for the benefit of others, then what shall be the cause of any contention among those who reside in this type of kingdom?

32 And Lucifer argued that because we are inexperienced in the use of these powers, how is it that we should not be given the chance to have these powers, even all of the children of God, so that we might see for ourselves if we can live in peace and harmony with them.

33 And so it is that the plan of Lucifer is not that there should be contention and discord among us, but that we should all have the power and blessings of the Father, or those who are Celestial. And for this reason, the Father allowed him to incorporate many of the powers of heaven into the lives of the children of men in the latter days, even that his argument—which was made through the free agency that the Father hath given unto all of His children—might be proven.

34 And many of the ancient prophets of God saw the latter days and beheld the great wickedness that would exist among the children of men because of the miracles, or the powers that Satan shall give unto them.

35 For even with the great advancements of technology and science, of which advancements ye shall know, even those of you who have received this record, the children of men do not live in peace and harmony one with another, but have separated themselves into families, and communities, and nations, which are even more isolated and more selfish than at any other time upon the earth.

36 And many of these things shall be revealed in this record as I approach the time period of the latter days after I have explained unto you the way that Satan eventually prepareth the children of men for the day of his glory.

37 And ye shall see how the God of the latter days, who is Lucifer, hath lifted himself up and hath deceived those upon the earth to such an extent that they shall think that he is their Father in heaven, and that the true Lord is the devil.

38 And one of the ways that ye might know these things is by the money that ye shall have among you in the latter days. And if ye look at this money, ye shall notice that which Satan hath caused you to inscribe thereon, even the words: In God We Trust.

39 And ye do trust in this god, even the money on which ye have inscribed these words. But in the Lord, ye do not trust, for ye have been led to believe that his ways are of the devil.

40 And this money shall become the thing that shall take you away from the gospel of Christ, even that ye shall forget about his words and put your trust in this money.

41 And John wrote concerning this, saying: And he causeth all, both small and great, rich and poor, free and bond, to receive a mark in their right hand, or in their foreheads. And that no man might buy or sell, save he that had the mark, or the name of the beast, or the number of his name.

42 Here is wisdom. Let him that hath understanding count the number of the beast: for it is the number of a man; and his number is Six hundred threescore and six.

43 And now, in order for ye to understand this riddle that John hath given unto you, it is necessary that ye understand somewhat concerning the customs of the Jews, from which culture John was, that ye might understand that which he hath written unto you.

44 For it was customary among the Jews to equate that which a man doeth in his life, or his works, with a mark upon his right hand, in that his hand doeth that which he performeth in his life, even his works, which is his name. And the thoughts of that man are indicative of a mark in his forehead, or in other words, the desires of his heart, or the reason for which he doeth the works that he performeth.

45 And it shall come to pass in the latter days that he who doth not have money, or who doth not participate in the economy of the nations of the world, which economies shall revolve around the seat of the beast, or the money of the nation of the United States, then he shall be killed, for he cannot survive in a system of economy that is based upon this money.

46 And all people, yea, even everyone who liveth upon the earth, shall receive the mark in their right hands; or in other words, they shall be forced to participate in this economy which shall be set up and based upon money. And this money is the system of exchange by which the whole world shall live. And this money is the number of the beast.

47 And John has given a riddle unto those who have wisdom to understand his words. And he wrote, saying: Here is wisdom. Let him that hath understanding count the number of the

beast: for it is the number of a man; and his number is six hundred threescore and six.

48 And because there shall be very few of you who have the spirit of understanding, which is only given to those who have the Spirit of God, most of you shall be unable to solve this riddle, and shall come up with all manner of speculation and answers to the meaning of this man and his number, which is six hundred threescore and six.

49 Yet, ye already have the answer to this riddle among you. Now here is wisdom, only those who are true prophets of God would know this answer, for it is simple and easy to understand. And it is written in the Bible, even the source of most of the symbolism of the words of John.

50 Yea, it is written: Now the weight of gold that came to Solomon in one year was six hundred threescore and six talents.

51 And now my beloved brothers and sisters, is this thing so hard to understand? Is it so hard that ye must look past the mark and look for meaning in something beyond your understanding? Know ye not that the Spirit of the Lord is there, willing and able to guide you in your understanding of all of his words, which words are given unto you by his holy prophets?

52 Oh, ye of little faith, who have set up stumbling blocks before you because ye do not ask of the Lord concerning these things. But do not think that ye can just ask the Lord and he shall give these things unto you. For if ye do not obey his words, then ye are not worthy of his understanding.

53 And now, I, Moroni, give unto you a way in which ye can tell whether or not ye are inspired by the words of Christ, and are given the truth of all things according to the Holy Ghost, or if ye are receiving your inspiration from your own god, even Satan.

54 Behold, before reading these words herein, did ye understand the meaning of the riddle which John hath given unto you? If ye did not, and I know that ye did not, for there are few in the latter days that have the Spirit with them, then ye are under the influence of Satan, and are being led to believe that which he would have you believe, so that he can keep you under his power.

55 And under his power, ye shall never understand the mysteries of God. For it would not behoove the plan of Lucifer if ye understood that money was the cause of all of your wickedness. Yea, it would be contrary to the plan of happiness that he hath established for you if ye did not have money and the fine things of the world. And without money, how would ye obtain the fine things of the world? Yea, without money, how would ye live in the kingdom of Satan that he hath established among you?

56 Behold, there shall be no way that a man can live in the latter days except he have the mark of the beast in his right hand. Nevertheless, that doth not mean that he must have the mark of the beast in his forehead.

57 And the beast shall cause all to receive this mark in their right hand, but he shall not have the power over you to make you receive it in your foreheads. In other words, your minds and your hearts can be centered in Christ, even though ye are forced to participate in the economy that hath been established among you.

58 And if your hearts are centered in Christ, then ye shall use the economy of the beast to do the works of Christ. And ye will use your money to do good, to clothe the naked, and to feed the hungry, and to liberate the captive, and administer relief to the sick and the afflicted; in other words, ye shall work with the mark of the beast in your right hand, with your heart and mind centered on Christ.

59 And do not think that ye can have your heart and your mind centered on Christ if ye do not do the works of Christ. For even Jesus had the mark of the beast in his right hand. And for this purpose was Judas called, so that he might carry the bag among the apostles of Christ, so that they could participate in the economy of the beast, so that they would not be killed by the beast, whose only desire is the number of its name.

60 Nevertheless, Christ had a mark in his forehead that was a name that only he knew. In other words, only he understood the things that he did, and only he had the intent to do the works that he did.

61 Now, this is the thing that John meant when he wrote, saying: His eyes were as a flame of fire, and on his head were many crowns; and he had a name written upon his forehead that no man knew, but he, himself.

62 And John wrote also concerning those who followed the example of Christ and had his name, or the name of the Father—it is the same—written in their foreheads. And he wrote, saying: Hurt not the earth, neither the sea, nor the trees, till we have sealed the servants of our God in their foreheads.

63 And I looked, and lo, a Lamb stood on the mount Sion, and with him an hundred forty and four thousand, having the name of his Father written in their foreheads.

64 And there shall be no more curse; but the throne of God and of the Lamb shall be in it; and his servants shall serve him; and they shall see his face; and his name shall be in their foreheads.

65 And now, to those who do not have the mark of the Lamb in their forehead, even the majority of you in the latter days, more especially those of you of this eighth kingdom that hath risen out of the seventh, John also giveth you warning, saying: And it was commanded them that they should not hurt the grass of the earth, neither any green thing, neither any tree; but only those men which have not the seal of God in their foreheads.

66 And the third angel followed them saying with a loud voice, If any man worship the beast and his image, and receive his mark in his forehead, or in his hand, the same shall drink of the wine of the wrath of God, which is poured out without mixture into the cup of his indignation; and he shall be tormented with fire and brimstone in the presence of the holy angels, and in the presence of the Lamb.

67 And I saw thrones, and they sat upon them, and judgment was given unto them: and I saw the souls of them that were beheaded for the witness of Jesus, and for the word of God, and which had not worshipped the beast, neither his image, neither had received his mark upon their foreheads, or in their hands; and they lived and reigned with Christ a thousand years.

68 And now, I, Moroni, have been instructed by the Spirit to speak somewhat concerning that which is evil and of Satan, compared with that which is righteous and of God. For it shall come to pass that there shall be many of you in the latter days that shall not understand how your nation can be under the power of Satan and be an evil nation, when ye believe that ye are happy therein and prosper, and seem to be blessed by the hand of God. And there shall be many of you that shall judge other nations as being evil, when ye judge your own to be righteous.

69 Now, I would that ye should understand that anything that goeth contrary to the eternal plan of salvation that the Father hath set up for us, and which He presented to us in the beginning in His kingdom, is evil and is considered of Satan. And I would that ye should also know, that the plan of Lucifer is not considered an evil thing to Him, nor to those who followed Lucifer in the beginning.

70 Behold, I have explained already unto you that the argument of Lucifer, or his plan, was a wonderful and righteous plan to many of those who heard it; evensomuch, that these rebelled against their own Eternal Father and their Eternal Mothers, who these spirits knew understood all things, and to whom all the eternal powers of heaven had been given.

71 Yet, even upon beholding these eternal beings in all their glory, Lucifer and many of the children of God rebelled against Him and came up with a plan that they felt was more righteous than the plan of the Father.

72 Therefore, to Lucifer and those who followed after him, the plan of the Father is evil, being contrary to their plan, which they believe is righteous. Now, this is how Satan is able to convince the children of men that he is not Satan, but is God; and that God is not our true Father, but is the devil. The one on the one hand, and the other on the other.

73 And it is a prerequisite of our free agency that we choose for ourselves which plan is righteous, and which plan is evil.

74 But the words of the prophets of God, even the words of the holy scriptures, which are written by these prophets, support the plan of the Father. Therefore, they consider the plan of Lucifer to be evil, and the plan of the Father to be righteous.

75 And the prophets of God are called by the Holy Order of the Son of God to teach the plan of the Father only. And that which is not of God, they teach as being evil and of Satan, and therefore, they condemn these things before the children of men.

76 And for this reason, it becometh very difficult for the children of men to discern which plan they are following. For when they are following the plan of Lucifer, he pretendeth to be their God, and blesseth them according to his will and the covenants that he maketh with them.

77 And all of the blessings which Satan bestoweth upon the children of men are material blessings, or things of the earth. And he can bless with riches and power and prosperity; yea, he can even bless with wisdom and understanding.

78 But the Father only blesseth His children, or those who follow His plan, in one way; and that way is complete and eternal happiness.

79 Now, Satan can also bless us with a state of happiness and euphoria, but this state will only be temporary, and will change from time to time according to the way in which Satan chooseth to bless us.

80 Therefore, it should be easy for a person to tell whether or not the state of happiness that they are experiencing is a blessing from God, or a blessing from Satan. For if it is a blessing from God, then this state of happiness shall never cease.

81 But if it is a blessing from Satan, it shall cease one day. And when the day cometh that his blessing of happiness ceaseth, then the misery that followeth shall be greater than that misery that a person felt before they were blessed with a state of happiness by Satan.

82 Now, this is one way that ye shall be able to tell whether or not ye are following Satan, or following God. For if ye are in a state of never ending happiness, in that your joy is full, then ye are following God.

83 And if your happiness is completely dependent on a temporary state, even the state of the flesh in which we temporarily find ourselves in mortality, then ye can be certain that ye are following the plan of Lucifer. And there is another way that ye can discern between a nation that followeth the plan of God, and one that is under the power of Satan.

84 For the plan of God is based upon eternal laws that govern the eternal worlds. And these laws are administrated by an eternal government. And this government is based upon three eternal principles that I have already explained unto you previously in this record. Therefore, if a nation and its government are based upon these eternal principles, then it is a nation under God. And any nation that is based upon these principles shall not allow any of its subjects to go without the necessary means that are needed so that these subjects might live peacefully and be able to pursue happiness according to each individual desire for happiness.

85 And here again are the three principles of a righteous government: The first principle and law of this government is that this government shall never be self-serving, or in other words, it shall never act in and of itself and of its own accord for the sake of its own existence.

86 And this government is restricted in its power according to the restrictions that are necessary to ensure that it abideth by this first principle and law.

87 For behold, this government serveth those who benefit from its existence, and those who benefit from its existence are those who give it the power that it hath received. And the power that it hath received hath been given to this government to serve those who have given it its power.

88 And the second principle and law of this eternal government is that it will guarantee the freedom, or the free agency, of all those whom it serveth. And this free agency that it guaranteeth, restricteth those whom it serveth from infringing on the free agency of another, or from having another infringe on the free agency that each of those it serveth possesseth.

89 And this government will do nothing that infringeth upon the free agency of those whom it serveth, except in defending the free agency of another from being infringed upon.

90 And the third principle and law of this eternal government, is that it shall provide the

means whereby those whom it serveth may have an equal opportunity to experience the happiness that they desire. And because it was not the choice of those whom it serveth to exist, this government must provide those things that are necessary to fulfill the measure and purpose of their creation, which purpose is their individual happiness.

91 And now, I have made it easy for you to discern whether or not the government of the nation to which ye belong in the latter days, or the governments of the nations that shall be made known unto you; even those of whose histories I have touched upon, or which I shall touch upon in this abridgment; yea, it should be easy for ye to determine if they are a nation under God, or one under the power and influence of Satan.

92 And if your nation hath no poor among you that have not been provided with the means whereby they might have an equal opportunity to experience the happiness that they desire, then that nation is under God.

93 But be careful that ye do not deceive yourselves; for there shall be many of you that shall claim that your nation giveth equal opportunity to all of its subjects to pursue the happiness that each desireth. Yet if there is one among you—and it is important that ye remember that this one did not make a choice, according to the flesh, to be born, but that choice was made by the parents of this one—yea, if this one maketh a choice to sit idle all the days of his life, then doth not this one have the right and free agency to do this according to the laws of a righteous government?

94 And should not his food, and shelter, and raiment be provided for him according to the laws of a righteous nation under God? I say unto you that he doth have a right to those things. And I am not the only one who saith this thing. For the Lord, even Jesus Christ hath said the same thing unto you in the form of a parable, which hath been given unto you in the Bible.

95 And the parable was given, saying: There was a certain rich man, who was clothed in purple and fine linens, and fared sumptuously every day. And there was a certain beggar named Lazarus, who was laid at his gate, full of sores, and desiring to be fed with the crumbs which fell from the table of the rich man; moreover the dogs came and licked his sores.

96 And it came to pass that the beggar died, and was carried by the angels into the bosom of Abraham; the rich man also died, and was buried. And in hell he lifted up his eyes, being in torment, and seeth Abraham afar off, and Lazarus in his bosom.

97 And he cried and said, Father Abraham, have mercy on me, and send Lazarus, that he may dip the tip of his finger in water, and cool my tongue; for I am tormented in the flame.

98 But Abraham said, Son, remember that thou in thy lifetime receivedst thy good things, and likewise Lazarus evil things? But now he is comforted, and thou are tormented. And beside all this, between us and you there is a great gulf fixed; so that they which would pass from hence to you cannot; neither can they pass to us, that would come from thence.

99 Then he said, I pray thee therefore, Father, that thou wouldst send him to the house of my father; for I have five brethren; that he may testify unto them, lest they also come into this place of torment.

100 Abraham saith unto him, They have Moses and the prophets; let them hear them. And he said, Nay, Father Abraham; but if one went unto them from the dead, they will repent. And he said unto him, If they hear not Moses and the prophets, neither shall they be persuaded, though one rose from the dead.

101 And now, I, Moroni, would ask of you of the latter days, even ye of the eighth nation of which John hath spoken, which is the seat of Satan. Yea, how many beggars are there in your nation like unto Lazarus?

102 Do they not sit before you idly on their hands, and do not have the capacity to work? And do they not want that ye should feed them from the crumbs that fall off of your tables, even those crumbs that would sustain their lives and give them the sustenance that they need to survive?

103 And how many are there among you who are rich and who fare sumptuously like unto the rich man of whom Jesus spoke? Yea, how many of you turn away from the poor and

the needy of your great nation, because ye do not want to notice them in their miserable state? And how many of you blame this state of theirs upon those who beg for their existence and do not work with their own hands to obtain these things, because ye believe that they are lazy and are of no use to you because of the sores of their poverty, or the sores of their lack of education, or the sores that have been forced upon them by their parents, who brought them into this world by no choice of their own, according to the flesh?

104 And the dogs that lick their sores, are they not the dogs to which ye feed the scraps and crumbs that fall from your table? Let him that hath understanding know the full meaning of this parable.

105 For the seat of Satan, even that great nation, shall not suffer that the beggars among you should have that which they need. But ye shall send the dogs that feed from your own tables unto them to lick their sores. But when they die, and when ye die, which of you shall be received in the spirit world in a state of happiness, and who shall be received in a state of misery?

106 I say unto you, that those of you who believe that your nation is one under God, shall be received in a state of misery, when, as a spirit, ye discover that the nation to which ye belonged during the days of your probation was in actuality the seat of Satan.

107 And the seat of Satan siteth firmly upon those who prosper exceedingly because of the blessings that Satan giveth unto them. And these blessings are power and glory, and the fine things of the world, even those things which ye of this nation seek

108 And Satan shall give unto you peace and carnal security, until the day of the Lord cometh upon you like a thief in the night. And ye shall be unprepared to meet him.

109 And then shall all the words of John be fulfilled concerning you.

110 And the poor and the meek, and the peace makers and those who mourn, and the merciful and the pure in heart, even all these shall inherit the earth. And ye of this great nation shall be tormented by the presence of the Lord, when ye finally realize whose seat ye sit upon.

111 For a nation under God hath no borders that separate it from the rest of the nations of the world that are inhabited by other sons and daughters of God. And the leaders of a nation under God serve its people and not themselves. And this nation tendeth to the needs of all of the people and provideth for them all the sustenance that they need to sustain their lives and pursue the happiness that each of them desireth, according to each of their individual desires for happiness.

112 And this nation would not cause that the sword of war should fall upon any other people. And only in the defense of this nation, shall it raise the banner of war against another, and only to protect its people in their rights and in their freedoms.

113 And a nation under God would protect the earth and its resources and use them according to that which is good for the earth, and also that which is good for its people.

114 And the leaders of a nation under God would not have cause to hide their works, or their words, or any of their secret agendas or alliances, which are the secret combinations that are spoken of by the holy prophets. For if this government is set up to serve those who have given unto it its power, or in other words, the people of this nation, then the very least among them should understand its workings and its words.

115 And a government of a nation under God would judge its success and its compliance with the laws of a righteous government, which laws have been established for all governments that are of God, which shall last forever; yea, this government shall judge its success by looking at the least among its people. For this nation shall be judged by God according to the manner in which it serveth the very least amongst it.

116 For behold, the plan of the Father was established according to these eternal laws. And all of the children of God are served by this eternal plan. And it mattereth not unto God which kingdom of glory that His children decide for themselves best suiteth their individual desires of happiness.

117 For this reason, He hath established three degrees of glory, and within these three, He hath established another three. And these nine worlds shall each have their times and their seasons. And each of them shall have all the means necessary, so that the inhabitants of these worlds may pursue their desires of happiness in their fullness.

118 And it doth not matter to the Father if one of His children decideth that his desire of happiness is best suited for a life of no work, or a life of laziness according to the flesh. For it is not laziness according to the Father, but a choice that this child of God hath made pertaining unto his own desire of happiness, which is guaranteed to this child, if he accepteth the plan of salvation that the Father hath established.

119 For what is laziness unto God, when his own Son taught, saying: Therefore I say unto you, Take no thought for your life, what ye shall eat, or what ye shall drink; nor yet for your body, what ye shall put on. Is not the life more than meat, and the body more than raiment? Behold the fowls of the air; for they sow not, neither do they reap, nor gather into barns: yet your heavenly Father feedeth them. Are ye not much better than they?

120 Which of you by taking thought can add one cubit unto his stature? And why take ye thought for raiment? Consider the lilies of the field, how they grow; they toil not, neither do they spin; and yet I say unto you, That even Solomon in all his glory was not arrayed like one of these. Therefore, if God so clothe the grass of the field, which today is and tomorrow is cast into the oven, shall He not much more clothe you, Oh, ye of little faith?

121 Therefore take no thought, saying, What shall we eat, or what shall we drink, or wherewithal shall we be clothed. For after all these things do the Gentiles seek. For your Heavenly Father knoweth that ye have a need of all these things. But seek ye first the kingdom of God, and his righteousness; and all these things shall be added unto you. Take therefore no thought for the morrow; for the morrow shall take thought for the things of itself. Sufficient unto the day is the evil thereof.

122 And now, I, Moroni, ask all of you that shall receive these things: Do ye not realize that the Son of God knew the Father, and that he only taught the people the things that the Father had given unto him to teach? And do ye think that the fowls of the air are lazy, in that they do not work for their food, but all that they need to sustain their lives is given unto them by the Father?

123 Now, this is what a righteous government under God would do for all of its subjects. For this is what the Father doeth for all of His children in the eternal worlds that He hath prepared for them. And for this reason He hath been given the great power and knowledge of a God. For He is a righteous God, who hath proven Himself worthy to serve us forever.

124 And what better way can He serve us forever than to give unto us those things that we desire to make us happy? But remember, my beloved brothers and sisters, that the happiness that God giveth unto us is an everlasting happiness, and not a happiness that we can consume upon the lusts of our flesh.

125 But the governments of men, or those who are under the power and influence of Satan, give unto the people of their nations all the things that they can consume upon the lusts of the flesh. But this happiness that they enjoy is a temporary happiness that shall end when they are dead.

126 For instead of providing for the needs of the least among them, the leaders of the nations of Satan provide for their own needs, and the needs of their own families, and care not about those whom they believe are evil, because—according to the perception of these leaders and the wicked part of these nations, which are the rich—they do not work.

127 But ye shall see as the works and the secret combinations are revealed unto you in this record, even those works and the secret combinations of this great nation of the United States of the latter days, and also of the great churches of the latter days of which I have spoken, and more especially that church through which the record of my father hath come forth unto you; yea, ye shall see that they do not do the work of the Father, and care not for those who are the least among them.

128 For they are prideful. and suppose that because of the success of their great

government, and the success of this great church, they have been blessed by God for their righteousness. And they truly have been blessed by God for their righteousness. And the god that hath blessed them, is he who hath rewarded them for their righteousness in obeying his commandments. And Satan hath rewarded them according to the things of the flesh, which are temporary.

129 And when the true God sendeth His Son, even in all of his glory unto the earth to establish for the last time a true nation under God, yea, even a nation without borders, then shall this other nation, and this great church that hath been established within it, realize who the God is that they have worshipped and by which they have been blessed.

130 And it would have been better for them both had they had a millstone hung about their neck, and that they were drowned in the depths of the sea, because of the offenses that they have caused against the least among them, which are the children of the kingdom of God.

131 And woe unto the world because of its offenses towards these little ones. For it must needs be that offenses come; but woe to that nation by which the offense cometh! And this according to the words spoken by the mouth of the Son of God.

132 And now it is once more expedient that I, Moroni, return again to the history of the world according to that which the brother of Jared hath written concerning his vision. And as the formation and the foundation of these last great nations are revealed unto you, ye shall see how subtle Satan is in his designs to incorporate his plan among the children of men.

133 But ye shall also see the great mercy and patience of the Lord and the saints who are continually burdened with the unrighteous power and dominion that their brothers and sisters, even the children of God, exercise over them because of the influence of Satan and their selfish desires for the things of the world.

134 And from time to time I shall revisit the words of John and shall explain them further unto you as they become relevant to the abridgment that I am making of the great vision of the brother of Jared, in which he saw all things according to the power of the Spirit.

CHAPTER 33

The reason why the first name of the brother of Jared is not given in this record. The Roman Empire is established and occupies much of the earth. Because of the Romans, the Jews were able to return to Jerusalem and establish themselves preparatory for the birth of the Christ.

AND it came to pass that there arose a people from one of the sons of Joktan, who was a direct descendent of Seth, the son of Adam, through the lineage of Noah; and the name of this son was Ophir; yea, this son was one of the thirteen sons of Joktan who were known throughout the world at that time as the most righteous sons of God that had ever lived upon the earth after the days of the great flood in the land of Cainan.

2 And this same Joktan was the brother of Peleg who was the father of Mahonjad, who was one of the loyal friends who had come to know Jared and his brother, from whose record I am compiling these words and making my abridgment.

3 And it came to pass that because of the exhortation and words of the brother of Jared unto the sons of Joktan, they all followed him, except for Ophir, into the wilderness before their language was corrupted by those who had invaded and conquered the great city of Babel.

4 And now, it hath been whispered to me by the Spirit that an error that is written upon the plates of brass shall be the cause of some contention and misunderstanding among the children of men, especially among those who believe that they are learned, having learned all that they know from their study of the histories of the children of men that they have among them.

5 And I have explained unto you that these histories are many times incorrect and bias towards the truth depending upon him who writeth this history. And many of them are incomplete and do not give a full account of the history of the people.

6 And upon the plates of brass it is written that in the days of Peleg, the earth was divided. Now, this hath led many to believe that the great land masses of the continents of this earth, which were once one, were divided at this time. But this is not what was meant by the words that were written upon the plates of brass regarding the history of the Jews, for the land masses of the earth were one many years before Adam and Eve were placed in the garden of Eden.

7 For in the days of Peleg, and he lived two hundred and thirty and nine years, the brother of Jared began to preach unto the people who would listen to him concerning the great vision that he had received of the Lord.

8 And it came to pass that in this day, the sons of Joktan were known throughout the whole earth as exceedingly righteous men, and it was their popularity among the people that led Jared and his brother to them. And they became friends and were united in their desire to serve God and keep His commandments.

9 And because of the wickedness and pride of the rest of the children of men, the sons of Joktan were desirous to follow Jared and his brother into the wilderness in search of the promised land that Jared had seen in his great vision, and to which he was commanded by the Lord to travel with his family and his friends.

10 And when the sons of Joktan had departed from among the people, then it was voiced throughout the land that the earth had been divided, or that the Lord had caused a division between the wicked and the righteous, even the sons of Joktan, who followed the brother of Jared, and the rest of the people.

11 And he who wrote the history of the Jews did not mention Jared and his brother, because they were sorely disliked by the people for taking away such righteous men from among them.

12 And as it is with most righteous men, the sons of Joktan did not like the accolades of the people, neither did they think of themselves as more righteous than any other. Therefore, in the history of the people of Jared and his brother, they wanted no glory for themselves, and made it a requirement that their names were not mentioned in the history of the people of the brother of Jared. Therefore the record refereth to them as the friends of Jared, and the friends of the brother of Jared and their families.

13 And now, I would that ye should also know the reason for which the brother of Jared is not known by his first given name, even that name which he received from his father when he entered into mortality.

14 Behold, the brother of Jared saw all the days of the children of men, and he beheld how they began to worship individual men and make sacrifice and homage unto their names. And these things are an abomination to him, in that he desireth that all the glory be given to Him who deserveth this glory, even to God, our Father.

15 And for this reason, he hath commanded all those who have written a history concerning him, that they refrain from using his given name. And this commandment he hath given as a token of his reverence and humility before the Lord, and also that his name might not be worshipped like the names of other prophets of God who did not make similar restrictions in the use of their names.

16 And I, Moroni, will not give the name of the brother of Jared in this record. But I know his name, and will do his will concerning it. And for these same reasons, the sons of Joktan restricted the use of their names also.

17 Nevertheless, I know by giving the names of the sons of Joktan in this record, it might clear up some of the confusion as to why the record of the Jews readeth the way that it readeth, and perhaps, a better understanding of the truth may come forth. For it came to pass that after the sons of Joktan had departed, his brother, whose name was Shemlem, changed his name to Peleg, in remembrance of the time when he saw the departure of his beloved son Mahonjad and his righteous nephews, indicating the division of the righteous from among the wicked.

18 And Peleg did not follow the brother of Jared, but stayed in the land that perhaps he might be the means whereby others of his children might be turned to God and keep His commandments. And this was also the desire of Joktan and his son, Ophir.

19 And it came to pass that the descendants of Ophir were the Latins who settled in the area of the great Tiber River.

20 And after many years, the descendants of Ophir became wicked, and because of their

wickedness, the Lord suffered a powerful group of people from the north to enter in among them and conquer them. And these conquerors were the descendants of one of the other brothers of Jared, who did not believe in the words of his brother and remained in the land in which they were born.

21 And from this other brother of Jared came forth a great civilization that had hidden itself from the invasions of other great nations and flourished hidden for many years.

22 And it came to pass that they became a powerful people and carried with them for a time, all the words and commandments that Adam had caused to be written and given unto his children. And for this reason they had a written language among them, which over time, had been corrupted by the influence of their customs and their cultures, yet it was the language which was most like the pure language of the Adamic tongue.

23 And from their language the Greeks and many other nations were able to develop their own form of language and writing. And these people would become known as the Etruscan people among the children of men. And after they had conquered the small Latin tribes that existed in that area of the land, they began to introduce their laws and their customs among them.

24 And like all nations under the influence of Satan, the Etruscan people were subjected to the ruling of the few, who were the rich and powerful among them. And it came to pass that a revolt occurred in which the man who had been elected king by the rich was overthrown, and the new nation of the Romans began to be established.

25 And like all new governments that are supported by the majority of the people—and the poor among the Romans were known as the plebeians—the rich received the vote and the consent of the plebeians because of their promises of equality for all, and a fair representation for all, and a voice for all in their own government.

26 Now, this was the guise and subtlety of Satan. For he knew that if he could get the majority of the people to trust in their leaders, then he would only have to influence one man in order to influence many people. And to the one man who allowed himself to be influenced, even as a leader of the people, Satan would reward him with glory and riches, which are the things that he sought from the Father in the beginning.

27 And the plebeians were promised many things, and because they did not understand the workings of Satan, for at that time there were no prophets of God among them to teach them the truth to counter the deception of Satan, they were led wherever the rich and powerful would lead them.

28 And it came to pass that the Roman Empire began to grow exceedingly. And their entire form of government was established and run by those who were influenced by Satan. And their politicians, as they were known among the people, were of the rich class; therefore, the poor did not receive the representation that they had been promised.

29 And the rich among them were known as patricians, or the fathers of the state. And it were these who inspired the people to fight against the Etruscans and win their freedom. Now, these patricians did not care for the plebeians and their plight; yea, the only reason why these patricians cared about the plebeians, was because the plebeians performed all the labor and paid the tax of their labors unto them.

30 And if it so be that there were no plebeians, then the patricians would have to work for their own sustenance by the sweat of their own brow, which they were not accustomed to doing.

31 And these rich became the leaders of the people and influenced the people according to their own selfish desires. For the government among them was set up and presented to all the people as a fair representation of all the people.

32 And they set up their consuls and their Senates, which groups maintained the order and established the laws for all the people. Nevertheless, only a patrician could become a consul or serve in the Senate. And these allowed the plebeians to set up their own assemblies among them. But this, these politicians allowed, that they might pretend to give unto the poor the representation that they had promised unto them.

33   Yet, in order for the poor to have representation with power and authority, they were forced to choose one from among the rich class to represent them. And it came to pass, that with this form of government, the rich became exceedingly rich and the poor became even poorer having a tax placed upon them that supported their government.

34   And the poor were told that without a strong government, which comprised not only of the governing counsels of politicians to establish the order of law among them, but also comprised of a strong military presence in the land; yea, without this strong government, invaders would come into the land and take away their lands and their families. And in this way the leaders of the people used fear to ensure that the people would support them in their laziness and also in their lust for riches and power.

35   And in this promise the Roman government had many examples to show unto the people the strength of their military and the protection of their lands. For there were many invaders that came into the land.

36   And it came to pass that a strong nation came into their lands and burned Rome to the ground. And this bred great fear into the hearts of the people, and they became disconcerted with their leaders for that which they had been promised, even that for which they had paid such a high tax to avoid.

37   But before the people could rise up against their leaders and demand a reform for that which they had given of their hard labor, the leaders of the people made a contract with those who had invaded them. And this contract involved the payment of a tribute to them if they would withdraw out of their lands. And the rich paid this tribute out of the tax that they had placed upon the poor.

38   But the poor did not know of the payment of this tribute, for the contract was made between their rich leaders and the rulers of the invading armies. And when the invaders had departed out of the land, the politicians convinced the people that because of their leadership, or in other words, because of their great skill in their politics, they had brought peace and safety again to the land.

39   And because of their flatteries and their lies, the people once again began to believe in their leaders and support them.

40   And it came to pass that there arose contention among the leaders of the early Roman people, and the land was divided by the powers that were in control at that time. But after a few years of this discord, the powerful Roman military took control of the whole land and unified the people under one rule.

41   And the leaders became exceedingly wise in their positions of authority and in their dealings with the other rulers of the nations of the earth that did not belong to the Roman Empire. But their wisdom was not given unto them by the Holy Spirit, but was given unto them by Satan, who had promised in the beginning to use the treasures of the earth to possess the hearts and souls of the children of men. And through the Roman Empire he began to see exceeding success in his desires.

42   And it came to pass that a large part of the success of the Roman government came because of the training and dedication of the Roman military.

43   Now, these soldiers were of the plebeian class and were easily manipulated and controlled by their leaders. And when the sons of the plebeians heard the words of the politicians, they began to become exceedingly prideful in their hearts because of these words. And they were convinced that the Roman nation was the greatest nation upon the earth and that it must be protected at all costs.

44   And when their politicians had a desire to conquer another people, and usually this desire was based upon what the other nation could provide for them to increase their power and their riches, then these politicians would devise some secret plan through their secret combinations to make the citizens of the nation believe that they must stand up to this other nation or they would lose their freedoms and their rights, and also their pretended representation in the government.

45   And the people were easily deceived by their leaders because the spirit of God was not with them. And the soldiers and their families were convinced that their sons were fighting for

the greatness of their nation, and that if they would die in battle, then they died for their nation, and thus in their death they would become a hero.

46 And now again, this was the plan of Lucifer from the beginning. For if a man could be convinced that he was dying a hero for the cause of freedom, when in actuality he was dying to increase the land holdings and the riches of his leaders, then Satan could use this man to do anything that would further the realization of his plan.

47 And the leaders were experts at rallying the citizens of their nation to war. And they would speak unto them of patriotism, which was loyalty to the patricians, who were the rich. And the people were deceived considerably, evensomuch that the Roman military soon became the most powerful military the world had yet to know at that time.

48 But there began to be some among the poor who could see beyond the deceptions and intentions of the rich leaders. And as these spoke out, they were quickly destroyed by the workings of these secret combinations that were among them.

49 And the soldiers would make solemn pacts according to the outline taught unto them in their training. And these pacts were created from the workings of these secret combinations. And these soldiers would carry out the orders given unto them by their leaders, even if the orders put their own life or the life of their family and friends in danger.

50 And the solider received his wages accordingly. And because of these wages, more devotion and dedication was given to the leaders who gave them the wage that they received. And because of the devotion and dedication of soldiers, the politicians became exceedingly powerful and used this power to crush anyone who spoke against them.

51 And the leaders of the people became wise in their dealings with the people that they conquered. For they would allow the people to live according to their own traditions and customs as long as they paid a tribute, or a tax to the government that would protect them within their own borders.

52 And these people who were conquered did pay the tax as was required of them because they were afraid of the armies of the Romans who had conquered them. And in this manner most of the world became subjected to the Romans and their government.

53 And it was because of this form of government that the children of Abraham, or the Jews, were able to once again enter into the land of Cainan and establish the church of God as it had been given unto them by their fathers.

54 For it came to pass that the Romans destroyed all other great nations, even the Babylonians, and the Assyrians, and all those who had held their own power upon the earth.

55 And now we can see that Satan doth not back up those who serve him in the time of their need. For if he can find another nation which is more powerful, even one that he can deceive and bind with his chains, even one that will serve his purposes more efficiently, then he will choose the strong one over the weak to accomplish his purposes.

56 Now, having the Jews return again to Jerusalem was also part of the plan of Lucifer. For he knew that if he could keep the Jews isolated under the power of the Roman government, which he had established, then he could control the church and its leaders.

57 And if the prophets of God were to once more come in among the people, then they would also be subjected to the authority of the Roman government, which he controlled. And thus is the plan of Lucifer to control the temporal and the spiritual governments of the children of men.

58 And because Satan enticeth the children of men with the lusts of the flesh, then the only way that he can control them is by the flesh. And for this reason he hath set up the great armies and navies and means of force throughout the earth. For it is only by fear that the leaders of the people maintain their control over the children of men.

59 And without the fear of the sword, they would have no power. And because of the sword, the leaders are able to control the people and subject them to laws that protect their riches and their glory, which riches and glory they receive from the people.

60 But the people are also under the influence of Satan, even the very poor among them. For the poor envy their leaders and lust after the things that their leaders possess, even the things that these poor covet for themselves.

61 And this envy of their leaders causeth them to give unto their leaders a respect and honor that they do not deserve. For all men who are not of God, yea even all those who do not have the name of the Lamb in their foreheads, lust after honor and glory and the riches of the earth.

62 And because they lust after these things, they give honor and respect unto their leaders who have the things which they desire. And this honor and respect that the people give unto their leaders alloweth their leaders to control them and subject them under their laws, which are set up to benefit the rich.

63 And it came to pass that there were very few among the Romans who lived the gospel of Christ and obeyed the commandments of the Father. And the Lord had withdrawn his spirit from among them in order to allow the plan of Lucifer to be given the chance that Lucifer desired.

64 Nevertheless, the Lord knew that he could not allow Satan to give the children of men many of the powers and the understanding that would be given unto them in the latter days. And even without these things that Satan was forbidden to give unto them, the Roman Empire became exceedingly powerful and prosperous, but this prosperity was limited only to the upper classes of the people. And the gap between those who were rich and those who were poor grew exceedingly.

65 And at the height of the power and glory of the Roman Empire, the Holy Ghost had ceased to communicate with the children of men. Nevertheless, it was still in the period of the times, as was spoken of by John and Daniel, in that the Spirit and authority of God was not entirely taken from off of the earth.

66 For Lehi had departed out of Jerusalem before the rise of the Roman Empire. And he took with him the authority of God. And the Spirit was also with my fathers, even as it is with me at this time. And the beginning of the period of the times began just before the time of Lehi, and it shall end shortly after my time.

67 But before the Spirit of God is taken off the earth for the second time, another great prophet shall rise up after my time and before the time of the two prophets of the latter days.

68 And this great prophet that shall rise up after my time, shall be the last and final prophet that the Lord shall send forth upon the earth, until the latter days. And he is the last prophet of the period of the times, even the second period that the children of men shall be given the authority of God and the Spirit to inspire them. And after this period of the times shall end, there shall be great spiritual darkness upon the earth.

69 And this prophet shall be called Mohammed, and from him shall a great nation rise upon the earth. And an account of this nation shall be given hereafter in this record.

70 But now it is required by the Spirit of the Lord, and also by the commandment that the brother of Jared hath given in his record; and it is also my greatest joy and desire to abridge the vision of the brother of Jared which he saw pertaining to the coming forth of the Son of God into mortality.

71 And it is this great event that all the children of God have looked forward to since the beginning. And it is this event that shall mark the meridian of all time upon this earth, as well as the meridian of the times, of which I have spoken.

72 And with exceeding anticipation, all of the holy prophets that have been, and all the holy prophets that shall be upon the earth, shall look forth to the day of the arrival of the Savior of the world, even the Son of God to come forth into mortality.

73 And those in the spirit world shall witness all things pertaining to his life and his mission. And these things were shown unto the brother of Jared, of which he rejoiced exceedingly for the opportunity to see these things before they occurred, yet mourned even more exceedingly because of the way that the Son of God, even the perfect example of the Father in the flesh, shall be treated by the children of men.

CHAPTER 34

The stage is set for the birth of Christ. The Spirit World prepares for the entrance of Jehovah into mortality. The family and preparation of Mary, as the mother of Jesus, is introduced. Misconceptions about when the spirit enters the body are cleared up, as well as the literal creation of the mortal body of Jesus. The Lord is born into the world.

AND it came to pass that the part of the world from which my fathers had departed in the days of Lehi was under the complete control and domination of the Roman Empire. And with this domination, the government provided freedom for its citizens to practice their religious beliefs according to the dictates of their own conscience.

2 For the Romans had many gods among them whom they worshipped and honored. And their leaders pretended that they also worshipped these gods. Nevertheless, they allowed the religions and beliefs of the people to give them their hope and their patience, which hope and patience caused peace throughout the land. But the majority of the leaders did not, in and of themselves, believe in the faith of the people, but made a pretend in their beliefs so that the people would accept them and honor them as the leaders that their gods had anointed to lead them.

3 And every citizen of Rome was given the freedom to worship how and where and what they desired. And with this freedom, many of the people began to organize themselves into different factions and religions that were ramifications of each other.

4 For if a man did not believe in his religious leaders, then he was not forced to follow them, but could choose for himself the religion and the leader that satisfied his desires of faith.

5 And the leaders of the Romans knew that this freedom would keep the people happy and distracted from the heavy tax burden that the government had placed upon them. For the leaders of the Romans cared about the fine things of the world which they received by way of this tax, and cared not whether there was a true God or not. And this tax was the only thing that they required of the people.

6 And because of the rule of the Romans, the Jews were once again able to return to Jerusalem and establish themselves as a people within the borders of the Roman Empire. And they were protected by the armies of the Romans and given freedom to live according to their customs and their traditions.

7 And there lived a man and his wife among the Jews who had listened to the leaders of the church of God which had been reestablished among them. And they had for a long time been wrought upon by the Holy Ghost regarding the true nature and purpose of religion among the children of men. And they knew that the church of God at Jerusalem had been corrupted by the examples of the leaders.

8 For they were not leaders as God had instructed, even leaders who were servants of the people. For they had set themselves above the people and lived their lives according to the success that they had in the material things of the world, which things were given unto them by the people according to the commandments that had been given by Moses pertaining to those who serve the people of the church of God.

9 And the name of the man was Jacob, and the name of his wife was Sara. And they had grown up in the church of God according to the customs and conditions of the church at that time. But while they attended to the commandments of the church, there were those in the spirit world that were preparing them for even a greater mission, even that they would have a daughter who they would raise up to become the mother of the Son of God.

10 Now, it came to pass that the brother of Jared described many of the things that were happening in the spirit world up until the time that Jesus was born into the world. And there was one of the spirits who was the chosen one who would become known in the flesh, as the mother of Jesus.

11 And this spirit was close to her mother, even the great Eternal Mother Marihala, who was the eternal mother of Jehovah and the brother of Jared. And all of the spirits that

were in this world knew of this one spirit; for this spirit was the one that would take the body of a woman in mortality and become the mother of the body of flesh and bone that would house the spirit of Jehovah, the God of the spirit world, even the Lord of all this part of the kingdom of God, which had been given unto him by the Father.

12 And this spirit was called after the name of her Eternal Mother. And she was known in the spirit world by the same name by which she shall be known in mortality, thus being called Mary, which means, she that came from Marihala.

13 And Mary, as a spirit, and also knowing the role that she was going to play in the plan of the Father, was one of the spirits who was instrumental in instructing Jacob and Sara in that which they should know and feel towards the truth as it was given unto them by the ministrations of the spirit world, which was under the direction of Jehovah at this time.

14 And under the influence of the Spirit, Jacob and Sara departed out from the main city of Jerusalem, and dwelt in the wilderness that surrounded that city.

15 And now, Jacob had gained much respect among the people at Jerusalem because of his honesty and his integrity among them. For he was assigned by the high priests to raise up the animals that were used by the people for their sacrifices. And he was to sell them for a profit, which profit would be given unto the priests for their sustenance.

16 But Jacob was just in his business and could not make the profit that the church expected of him. And there was one of the high priests whose name was Zacharias who was the brother in law of Jacob, and also his friend. And Zacharias did everything in his power to persuade his friend to sell the animals in a way that would bring more profit to the church.

17 But if there was a poor man or woman among them who did not have the money to buy an animal that was required of them as a sacrifice before the church, then Jacob would give unto this person the animal that they would need without charge.

18 And the poor of the people knew that they could go unto Jacob and that he would give unto them without charge. And this is the thing that disturbed the high priests of the church. For they knew that the poor who could not afford the price of a sacrificial animal, could also not afford to pay a tribute, or a tithing to the church.

19 Therefore, the poor were less desirable to the high priests than those who could give a tithing to the church for its sustenance.

20 And Zacharias sat with the counsel that was desirous to release Jacob from his business. And he defended his friend, saying: How is it that we can deny those among us who are poor from making the sacrifices that they need for their own salvation? Do they not have the right to these sacrifices as well as the rich? How is it that we can forbid them from doing these things which we have commanded of them according to the words and laws of Moses, because in their poverty, they have not that with which to pay their tithes, or purchase the means of their sacrifice?

21 And one of the other high priests rebuked him, saying: Those who are poor have no reason to be in the situation that they find themselves. Behold, there are plenty of opportunities for them to work among the people and show forth their faith unto God by paying a portion of their income to the church. And if their faith is not great enough to cause them to do these things, then how can they be worthy to make such a sacrifice?

22 And when the other priests concurred with these things, Zacharias became silent and would speak no further concerning these things.

23 But the Spirit wrought upon him all the days of his ministry in the church. But because of his family and his position, even the honor that he received from the people of the church because of his position as a high priest among them, he would not speak those things which the Spirit witnessed unto him.

24 And it came to pass that Jacob was released from his business. And after he was released by the high priests, Jacob took Sara and they wandered out into the wilderness and found a good piece of land where they could worship God according to the dictates of their own conscience.

25 And Sara was from a very wealthy family among the Jews. And her family was distraught with her decision to leave the church and go into the wilderness. But Sara loved Jacob, even with all of her soul, and stayed with her husband all the days of her life.

26 And she had a sister, and her name was Lydia. And it was this same Lydia who was the wife of the High Priest, Zacharias, who was the friend of Jacob. And Lydia would visit her sister Sara in the wilderness and bring her news of her family and of the people who lived in the city of Jerusalem. And from time to time, Zacharias would accompany his wife to see his friend and brother Jacob.

27 And it came to pass that Zacharias had a son, and he was called after the name of his father. And he was the eldest son of Zacharias. And this son, even Zacharias, followed in the same order of the priesthood in which his father had ministered all the days of his life. And he married the daughter of one of the other high priests, and her name was Elizabeth.

28 And it came to pass that Sara began to bear children unto Jacob. And when the time came for the birth of Mary, Sara had come to believe that the days of her ability to give birth were passed; for she had given birth unto seven children, and they were all sons.

29 But from the spirit world, Mary spoke unto her earthly mother and assured her by the ministrations of the spirit that she would have one more child.

30 And it came to pass that as the children of Zacharias and Lydia grew, they began to accompany their parents into the wilderness to the house of Jacob. And Zacharias, the younger, also came many times unto the house of Jacob with his wife Elizabeth.

31 And Sara would talk with her sister, Lydia, and also with her niece, Elizabeth, about the workings of the Spirit within her concerning the birth of her last child, which she now believed would be a daughter from her.

32 And the spirit of Sara was strong, evensomuch that Elizabeth was overcome by this valiant women who had left her life in Jerusalem and had raised seven sons in the wilderness. And Elizabeth loved Sara.

33 And it came to pass that Elizabeth dreamed a dream in which she saw Sara clothed in a garment of gold with seven stars in her left hand and a stem of a rose bush in the other. And the fragrance of the flower overcame all those who came close unto Sara, evensomuch that they all became desirous to smell the flower and bask in its fragrance forever.

34 And the flower began to grow in the hand of Sara until it became too heavy for her to hold with one hand. And she threw the seven stars in her right hand high into the heavens where they remained. And with both of her hands she upheld the flower. But it continued to grow until it became an exceedingly large bush and had surrounded her and lifted her up into its branches.

35 And the fragrance of the bush was exceedingly wondrous, and she was desirous to eat thereof. But Sara believed that the flower bush was poison, as this had been taught to her all the days of her life.

36 But she began to hunger and wanted to taste of the flowers that supported her and gave off such a wondrous odor. And Sara reached forth her hand and partook of the flowers, and they were exceedingly sweet in her mouth, but in her belly they became bitter and she was wont to die because of them. And the thorns of the bush began to prick her and cause her pain, evensomuch that she could not bear to remain in the flower bush any longer.

37 And the seven stars that were in the heavens descended upon her and lifted her up out of the bush and took her into the heavens with them.

38 And it came to pass that after Elizabeth had dreamed this dream, she hurried to the house of Jacob and told all these things unto Sara. But Sara did not understand the meaning of the dream.

39 And it came to pass that Elizabeth kept this dream in her heart, until the next night, when she was given the interpretation of the dream by an angel of God.

40 And the angel spake unto her, saying: Behold, the aunt of thy husband shall conceive and bring forth a daughter. And she shall be the mother of the Christ. And her sons shall be

sacrificed to save the life of her daughter, even that this last daughter might grow and be prepared to give birth to the Son of the very Eternal Father.

41 And she shall live to see the birth of her grandson, even he who shall be the Savior of the world. And she shall know by the Spirit that her daughter is a blessed woman, even the most blessed among all the daughters of men for that which shall come forth from her womb.

42 And this is the odor that thou smelled in thy dream. And Sara shall witness before the people that her daughter hath been blessed by the hand of God, and this is why the flower tasted good in her mouth. But she shall see the end of the life of her grandson, and in this she shall feel the pains of her bosom, or that which in her belly is bitter.

43 And she shall die in bitterness, having felt the pains of losing her seven sons, and seeing the exceeding pain of her grandson, who shall be the Christ.

44 And she shall be lifted up in death and join her sons and her husband, and together they shall witness the completion of the purpose for which the life of her grandson was given.

45 And in the spirit world, she shall know him for who he is, even the Savior of the world, and shall praise him, and she shall be glorified forever for her part in his mortal mission.

46 And thou shalt not reveal these things unto her, for her sake; but shalt keep these things hidden in thy heart until the day that the Christ is lifted up once again into the spirit world, and then to the kingdom of the Father.

47 And it came to pass that Elizabeth did keep these things in her heart. And because of the position of her husband, even as a high priest in the church, Elizabeth did not visit Sara for many years.

48 And Sara conceived in the wilderness and brought forth a daughter whom she named Mary.

49 And it came to pass that the Romans went throughout the land collecting taxes from all of the people in the land round and about Jerusalem. And the tax collectors came unto the house of Jacob and demanded of him an accounting of his taxes.

50 And Jacob stood boldly before the tax collector and said unto him: For what desirous thou that I pay taxes? I did not receive this land from the Romans, but I received it from God.

51 And one of the soldiers that stood nearby struck Jacob and forced him to his knees before the Roman authority.

52 And Jacob stood boldly once again and rebuked the Romans, saying: If I cannot live a free man then I shall die a free man. And after he had said these words, he was slain by the sword of the soldier who had struck him.

53 And the sons of Jacob rushed forth and fell upon the tax collector; and in their anger slew him and the soldier who had slain their father. And the other soldiers who were experts in the art of warfare, fell upon the sons of Jacob and slew them all.

54 And Sara was hiding in the house with her daughter Mary. And she sheltered Mary, that she would not behold the things that were done unto her brothers and her father, she being in her youth.

55 And it came to pass that Sara buried her husband and her sons and lived alone with her daughter, Mary. And Mary became the joy of her life.

56 And when Zacharias had heard of that which had happened unto the sister of his wife and his friend, he appealed before the consul of the Romans for that which they had done unto Jacob. But the consul did nothing for them, because Jacob had refused to pay tribute to the government according to the laws that had been established among them.

57 And Zacharias pled with Sara that she should move back to Jerusalem and have a place in his house where he could protect her and Mary. But Sara would not leave the place in the wilderness where she had buried her husband and her sons.

58 And it came to pass that Zacharias sent his sons to watch over Sara and Mary from time to time and assure their safety. And they carried provisions unto them; yea, in everything that they needed, Zacharias provided for them.

59 And it came to pass that the brother of Jacob, even Heli of Nazareth, learned of the death of his brother and sent his sons unto the house of Jacob to give unto them that which they needed. And Joseph was one of the sons of Heli who was sent into the wilderness unto Sara and Mary.

60 And Joseph fell in love with Mary and was wont to marry her. For Mary was exceedingly beautiful and had reached the age of the pinnacle of her flesh, even eighteen years old, when Joseph became desirous to marry her.

61 And now, ye have already before you the account of the marriage of Joseph and Mary, and also the visitations that were given unto both of them regarding the birth of Jesus. And generally, the record, which hath proceeded forth out of the mouth of the Jew, is correct in its rendition of those things.

62 Nevertheless, I would that ye should know a few more things concerning that which ye have already before you. For there are some things that have given a cause of contention among you; yea, even trivial things concerning the account that hath been written by the Jews in the Bible.

63 And I have been given a commandment to clear up these arguments so that ye might know the truth regarding these things, and that there might be no further contention among you.

64 And the first of these contentions is the manner in which the Father gave his seed, or the instructions for the body of Jesus to be created within the womb of Mary.

65 For there are many of you who have argued that the Father had sexual intercourse with his daughter, and in incest brought forth His son.

66 Now, this hath come among you from unwise stewards of the accounts which ye have been given. For the Father would do no such thing unto one of his daughters. And there is no God in the heavens that would do such a thing.

67 And the record that you find already among you should read: And Mary was wrought upon by the Holy Ghost. And through the power that had been given by the Father to those in authority in the spirit world, the body of Jesus was created within the womb of Mary.

68 And now, I, Moroni, shall give unto you a brief explanation of these things. For behold, power hath been given unto matter that is spiritual to command, from time to time, matter that is of the flesh. And with this very same type of power can we command the functions of our flesh by the power of our spirit.

69 And when our spirit maketh its commands on our flesh, the flesh obeyeth these commands, having received them by that which is spiritual.

70 And if we, who have very limited knowledge at this time, can command the flesh and it obeyeth our commands, then why do ye think that those in authority in the spirit world cannot command the flesh according to the power and the knowledge that they have been given by the Father?

71 And it was Jehovah, who was the main authority in the spirit world, who commanded the elements of the body of Mary to be patterned after the elements of his own spirit, which spirit was in the exact likeness of the Father. And with his command, Mary did conceive.

72 And also ye have confused yourselves about the time that a spirit entereth the body of flesh and is confined therein until the end of the days of probation of that soul. For it is written among you: And it came to pass, that, when Elizabeth heard the salutations of Mary, the babe leaped in her womb; and Elizabeth was filled with the Holy Ghost.

73 And now, ye think that this meaneth that the spirit of John was already in the body that had been created for him by his earthly parents. But I say unto you, that the spirit doth not enter the body, except it be when the body exiteth the womb and taketh its first breath.

74 And the body inside the womb is affected by the emotions and stimulations of its mother. And when Elizabeth was aware that it was Mary who was before her, and that she was with child, then she remembered the things of which she had dreamed, and also those things which had been commanded of her by the angel of God. And by her own emotions, which were caused by the testimony of these things from the Holy Ghost, did the body in her womb react.

75 And this mystery can be further verified in the record of my father. For the Lord was still in the spirit world the day before he was to come into the world as the son of Mary and Joseph in Jerusalem.

76 Nevertheless, on this continent he spoke unto Nephi, saying: Lift up your head and be of good cheer; for behold, the time is at hand, and on this night shall the sign be given, and on the morrow come I into the world, to show unto the world that I will fulfill all that which I have caused to be spoken by the mouth of my holy prophets.

77 Now, how do ye think the spirit of Jesus could have spoken unto Nephi in the flesh, if it was confined to the body within the womb of Mary on the other side of the earth?

78 O, ye fools! Why is it that ye shall cause yourselves such contention when the truth is right before you? Why is it that ye cannot find this truth by the ministrations of the same Spirit that can teach you the truth of all things? Is it that ye want that for which ye can contend?

79 Behold, Jehovah reigned in the spirit world from the beginning, until the time of his birth, according to the time of the flesh. And he instructed Michael, who was Adam, who had died, to rule and reign in that world while he was going through the days of his mortality.

80 And by the power of his spirit was he conceived; and by the power of the Father was he created.

81 And on a chosen night near the town of Bethlehem, the Lord, even Jesus the Christ; who is Jehovah, the chosen one of the Father, and unto whom the Father hath given all of His powers and knowledge; yea, on this night entered he into his mortal flesh.

82 And upon his first breath, his spirit was confined to the flesh that was created within the womb of his mother, Mary.

83 Behold, I, Moroni give this final testimony of him; even that he came into the world to save us all, thus becoming our Savior. And the heavens rejoiced, even the whole of the spirit world did rejoice, as we all witnessed the birth of our Lord and our King, even Jesus Christ, who is my brother and my friend.

CHAPTER 35

Moroni's meeting with the Savior. He is commanded to give a more precise version of the life of Christ. The importance of the life of Christ is explained. The reason the Lord was called Jesus in the flesh is explained. Moroni expounds upon the importance of the Sealed Portion of the Book of Mormon and exhorts all to read it and ponder its meaning. The Sealed Portion shall take away all of the stumbling blocks of the elect. (Compare 2 Nephi 26 & 27)

AND now, I have been commanded by the Lord; yea, I have been given the greatest commandment of all pertaining to the commission that I have received regarding these plates and the record that I have been instructed to write upon them.

2 For behold, nothing that hath ever been written can compare in importance and necessity to the purpose for which the literal Son of God was born into this world.

3 And now, I would that ye should understand, that the commandment I have received pertaining to these things, not only hath been given unto me by the Holy Spirit; though it is through the ministrations of the Holy Ghost from which I receive the inspiration to know what to write; nevertheless, this commandment hath been given unto me by the Lord himself.

4 For as it is that I have been alone for many years, hiding and fleeing the wars of the Lamanites; and my own people having been completely destroyed because of their wickedness; and I being alone; yea, even in my despair I did cry mightily unto the Lord that he would support me and assuage the inner loneliness that I felt.

5 And I found myself in this state as I continued the promise I had made to my father to protect this record, as well as all the records which Nephi had commanded his posterity to keep among them. And I have hidden most of the records which I have received concerning the children of Lehi; and carry with me only those records that I feel are necessary to finish the translation of the words of the brother of Jared, and seal these things up according to the

command of the Lord, which commandment I had received through my father Mormon.

6 And I have been visited from time to time by the apostles of the Lord who have remained among us upon this earth, having been given this opportunity by their own desires at the time when the Lord gave unto them the desires of their hearts.

7 And when they visited me I was uplifted and received much strength and joy from their companionship. And they taught me many things and helped me to understand some points of doctrine and belief that I had not understood clearly by myself. For it had been necessary that I fight in the wars against the Lamanites in defense of my people, even though I realized that our efforts were in vain. But I did fight; and this fighting kept the Holy Spirit away from my mind and caused me to lose precious times of learning in which I could have been engaged had I not been fighting.

8 And during this time, these three disciples of Jesus did visit me and encourage me in the commandments that I had received from my father, and also they did give unto me further commandments concerning this record that shall be sealed and that shall not come forth unto the world until the last days, even in the days in which the Father shall begin his last work upon this earth.

9 And this work shall be a marvelous work and a wonder. And it shall mark the start of the gathering of the elect, even that God might gather them unto Himself, that they may not be tormented and destroyed at the final coming of His Son, even Jesus Christ.

10 And now this glorious day of the second coming of Christ would not have been possible except that he had once lived upon this earth. And now, this is the commandment that I have received from his own mouth, even that I should write concerning the days of his mortality upon these plates.

11 For behold, he did visit me in my affliction, and brought me close to him, and put his arms around me and held me to his bosom, even like a loving brother would hold another brother who was afflicted.

12 And he sat with me for a time, conversing with me concerning the events that had transpired upon the earth, and also about the future events that would also transpire upon the earth according to all the words that he had caused to be given unto the children of men by the mouths of his holy prophets. And I rejoiced exceedingly in all that he revealed unto me at this time.

13 And the Lord smiled upon me and conversed with me as his friend; and he would not allow me to fall down before him and worship him, as was my desire when he first appeared unto me. For he treated me like unto a brother, and commanded me to treat him like a brother, yea, both of us being sons of the very Eternal Father.

14 And he reviewed his life with me in preparation for that which I was about to write upon these plates concerning the days of his mortality. And we laughed at many things—his love and spirit abiding in all the senses of joy that are experienced in the flesh.

15 And it came to pass that the time came for him to once again return to the kingdom of the Father until a future time when he would visit the earth once again to call another prophet, even the final prophet of the period of the times, of which I have spoken concerning the symbolism that was used by Daniel and also by John.

16 And after he hath called this prophet, yea, even after this prophet hath made one last attempt to give the words of God to the children of men, then the Lord shall not return again to the earth until he shall come unto the two prophets of the latter days, of which I have written.

17 And I was exceedingly saddened that he had to leave my presence; and I beckoned unto him that he would stay with me a little while longer, even that he would teach me more of the glorious truths that he understood and had taught to many of the prophets that have lived upon the earth. Nevertheless, most of these prophets did not have the glorious experience of having the glorified Lord come unto them and administer unto them in the flesh.

18 And he administered his words unto them by the power and the ministrations of the spirit

world where he resided until he came into mortality and was born of Mary.

19 And I cried unto the Lord, saying: My Lord;

20 And now, in this he did once again reprimand me, saying: My dear brother, I have suffered that the children of men give unto me this title and this glory only because of their hardheartedness and their stiffneckedness and their lack of understanding pertaining to the mysteries of godliness. But from thee, I cannot accept this title.

21 For behold, I am thy brother and thy friend; and I am also thy servant. And I tried to teach these things unto my disciples. For there arose disputations among them as to which of them should be the greatest, they having given unto me the title of Christ, which they did not understand at the time.

22 And they did not understand these things concerning me at the time because the Holy Ghost had not yet descended upon them to testify unto them concerning the truth of these things concerning me. And because they had given unto me this title, and worshipped me, they each wanted that I make him greater than his fellow disciple, that he might stand next to me in authority.

23 And when I had perceived that which they desired to understand, even which one of them that I should put above the others; yea, when I began to see their own stiffneckedness and their own hardheartedness, I took a child and brought him forth and placed him in front of them and said unto them: Whosoever shall receive this child in my name receiveth me. And whosoever receiveth me receiveth Him that sent me, even the Father.

24 And he who is least among you all, the same shall be the greatest among you. For even this child in all of his glory is greater than any of you.

25 For ye have been called by the Father to be a servant unto all. Therefore, how can the servant be greater than his master?

26 Ye know that the princes of the world, which are the servants of Satan, exercise dominion over the children of men, and they have received the glory of men, in which they are perceived as being great. And with this glory, which hath been given unto them by the children of men, they exercise authority upon them.

27 But it shall not be so among you. But whosoever will be great among you, let him be your servant. Behold, I did not come into this world, nor have I been commanded of the Father, to be ministered unto, but I have come into the world to minister and serve the children of God, and give my life as a ransom for all those who will listen to the words of the Father, which are given through me, even all those who shall have eternal life in the kingdoms prepared for them by the Father.

28 Behold, the scribes and Pharisees sit in the seat of Moses and teach unto you the words of Moses and the laws that have pointed you in the straight course, which course is the words and the gospel that I have given unto you.

29 And these hypocrites have preached these things unto you all the days of your lives. Therefore, all that they bid you to observe, that observe and do; but do not ye after their works; for they preach the pleasing words of the gospel unto you, but they do not do that which they preach.

30 For they bind heavy burdens upon you that are grievous to be borne, even the commandments of men that they require ye to do. And these commandments of men they do, because these commandments are their own commandments, which make it so that they shall not be burdened by the true law, which is grievous for them to bear, and which they lay upon the shoulders of the children of men, but they themselves will not move with one of their fingers to obey these true commandments.

31 But all the works that they do, they do to be seen of men; and they make broad their phylacteries, and enlarge the borders of their garments, and love the uppermost rooms at feast, and the chief seats in the synagogues. And they love the greetings in the market, and to be called of men, Rabbi, Rabbi.

32 But ye shall not be called Rabbi, for one is your Master, who is not your Rabbi or your master, but your servant; and all ye are his brethren. And call no one your creator upon the earth, or your heavenly father; for one is

your creator and Heavenly Father, even He who is in heaven. Neither are any of you to be called Masters; for one is your Master, even he whom your Heavenly Father sent, which is Christ; for He hath sent him among you that ye may have life.

33 But even he, who is the greatest among you, shall be your servant. And whosoever shall exalt himself shall be abased; and he that shall humble himself shall be exalted. And therefore, my beloved friend Moroni, thou shalt refer to me as thy friend and thy brother from this time forth.

34 And I will suffer that the children of men worship me according to their understanding. For it is better that they worship me and look to me as their example and their Lord, than it would be that they look to Satan, who would have them believe that he is their Lord. For behold, Satan is the Lord over the whole earth and hath spread his influence among all the nations of the earth.

35 And I have sent forth prophets unto all these nations that I might bring the children of men unto repentance, that they might recognize their true Lord and keep the commandments that I have given unto them. But those prophets shall know me for who I am, and they shall be my friends and my brothers and my sisters.

36 And it came to pass that the Lord stayed with me for a short time after I had pled with him that he might remain. And he taught me many more things pertaining to this work that shall give an account of his life and his ministry, even a greater account than that which is given in the Bible from the mouth of a Jew.

37 For at the time it proceeded forth from the mouth of the Jew, it was more pure, even as it hath been explained unto you previously. And many precious things were taken out and discarded by the great and abominable church, even as Nephi hath given an account in his record.

38 But I was commanded by the Lord to give a better account, even a more pure and precious account of his life and his ministry, so that the elect who shall receive these things in the latter days might know him as I know him and become his brothers and sisters and his friends.

39 For truly, Jehovah was given the power and authority of the Father to act and do all the things that the Father would do, he being a perfect example of the Father in all things. And because he is a perfect example of the Father in all things, he was called and foreordained in the beginning, even by the Father, and also by the voice of all of the children of God, except those who followed the plan of Lucifer.

40 And he was ordained and sustained to be the God and leader of the kingdom of the Father in this part of the universe, even over the planets that rotate in their positions around the sun. And in this, some symbolism hath been given of his power and his authority.

41 For even as the planets are subjected to the will and power of the sun, having been created by its force and from its elements, even so shall all the children of God who belong to this earth on which we live, be subjected to the will and power of the Son of God, who is Jesus Christ.

42 And it came to pass that I watched as my friend and brother, even Jehovah, who is Jesus the Christ, was lifted up and carried into the heavens upon the beam of light on which he came unto me.

43 And tears of joy filled my eyes and my heart rejoiced exceedingly because of the great love that I felt for him, and also for the great love that I felt that he had for me. And because of his ministrations unto me, I received much strength to continue with this abridgment and fulfill the commandments that I have been given concerning this thing.

44 And now it is expedient that ye have an understanding of the importance of the mission and life of Jesus Christ. And I would that all the earth should know that Jesus Christ is the true God of this part of the kingdom of the Father.

45 And he shall be called many names by the children of men, these names having been given him because of the different traditions and customs among them. And I have previously explained unto you the insignificance of the name that is given to the Lord, or to God, the Father.

46 For it mattereth not what They are called, only that Their commandments are obeyed. For some shall call Them one thing, and some shall call Them another, but that which is important is that which the name of the Lord representeth. For the Lord was known in the flesh as Jesus, which was a very common name among the children of men in his day.

47 And now, I would that ye of the latter days, even those who shall have the record of the Jews translated in the same language in which this record is translated, even in that which shall be known among you as the English language; I would that ye should know that your translation of the name Jesus is not consistent with the true translation of the language in which the reports of the life of Jesus were originally written.

48 For this name should have been translated, Joshua, which is the more correct translation of the original language. And now, this should be a thing of humility and learning unto you, even that ye now know that the name of Jesus hath no effect whatsoever on your righteousness, for it should read Joshua the Christ.

49 And now what think ye of the name of Jesus? Do ye think that by the name of Jesus ye shall be saved? Yea, I say unto you that by the name of Joshua ye shall be saved, for it is this name that should be recorded in your language according to the correct translation. And again I say unto you, that by neither name shall ye be saved, but by the works that ye do because of the name given unto the Christ; yea, by these things shall ye be saved.

50 And now, I would exhort you to consult with those who are learned among you; for they shall verify and testify that the things that I have said unto you regarding the translation of the name of Jesus in the Bible, is correct. And then what shall ye say?

51 Nevertheless, so that there shall be no confusion and contentions among you, yea even for the purpose of this record and all the scriptures that pertain to the mortality of Jehovah, the Son of God, I shall use the name of Jesus, instead of Joshua, for this is the name that ye have become accustomed to hearing when ye think of the Savior of the world.

52 And the purpose for this name was to signify the commonality that he representeth to the children of men. And those who were called Jesus, or Joshua, of his day were those among the poor class of the people.

53 And it was Joseph who gave this name unto him, having been commanded by the voice of an angel. But the family of Joseph was not pleased with the name that was given unto the son of Mary, for they thought that the child was the son of Joseph.

54 And his family was rich and prosperous among the people, and felt that the child should be given a more prestigious name that would fit more properly with the names of their family. And they were further distraught when Joseph disregarded his family and left his riches and the glory that belonged
to the house of Heli, and lived among the poor in Nazareth.

55 And when they had heard the account of the birth of Jesus, even that he was born in a manger that was unclean, this did impede their pride even further, and they thought that Joseph had gone mad. And it came to pass that they ostracized him from among them. But Joseph knew of that which he had been commanded by the angel, and he did those things which were commanded of him.

56 And now, there are many things that I have been commanded to correct about the account given of the life and ministry of the Lord as it hath been given unto you in the Bible. Nevertheless, the Spirit hath commanded me that I should give those things which I have translated from the vision of the brother of Jared.

57 And a commandment shall be given unto him who shall bring these things forth in the latter days, even this bearer of Christ, who shall be the second of the latter-day prophets who shall live among you.

58 Behold, he shall be commanded to follow the translation as given through the Urim and Thummim; nevertheless, he shall be commanded to use the Bible as a reference of those things which he shall receive through the Urim and Thummim. And if it so be that the translation is similar to the words of the Bible, then he shall use the words that are found in the Bible and interpolate them into this record and make all things of one, witness of the other; or in other words, make one record concise and in agreement with the other.

59 And this would not be necessary if it were not for the wickedness and lack of faith of the children of men. For if this record contradicteth those scriptures that ye already have among you, and which ye have already accepted as the word of God, then ye might have reason to believe that this record is not the word of God.

60 But I say unto you, that this record is plain and pure and hath not been translated by the hands of men various times, evensomuch that it hath become corrupted by the hand of man. But this record shall be translated once, and its translation shall be true, and shall be given unto him who shall translate these plates upon which I write these things, through the gift and power of God, which he shall have with him.

61 And these words shall be more precise and easy to the understanding of men, evensomuch that none shall have an excuse to disobey the words of Christ because of the mistranslations and interpretation of men.

62 For this record shall be the final testimony of Jesus Christ, and shall include all things which God shall reveal unto the children of men in the latter days to prepare their hearts and minds for the coming of His Son in his glory.

63 Therefore, this record shall be the greatest source of scripture that hath ever been given to the world. And if it so be that the children of men only had this one scripture, then that would be all that they would need in order to prepare themselves to be saved in the kingdoms of the Father.

64 And there shall be no other scripture given, except it be by the mouth of this last prophet by which these things shall come forth. But this last prophet shall say nothing contrary to that which is given in this record.

65 And he shall restrain himself from giving any more of the mysteries of God, except for those mysteries that are given with this record; for this record shall include all things that the Father would want His children to know, even all things which have been among the children of men, and which ever shall be even unto the end of the earth, even until His Son cometh again in the flesh and teacheth them from his own mouth.

66 But the things that he shall teach them with his own mouth shall be those things which are written herein. Therefore, I admonish you to read these things and feast upon them. Yea, ye should read these things in the morning, and in the midday, and in the evening, even that ye should ponder them in your bed at night and live your life according to the words of Christ that are written herein, that ye may be worthy of the Spirit which shall teach you all of the mysteries of God until ye know them in full.

67 And now, because of the misinterpretations of the record of the Jews, and also because of the things that my father and I were commanded not to write unto you in the portion of this record that is unsealed; yea, even many of those things that we wrote in the unsealed portion of this record, which were given unto you according to your traditions and your customs; yea, because of these things, it is necessary that I give unto you in plainness the explanation concerning the true nature of the mission of Christ and the atonement of the Savior; even that I explain unto you why my friend and brother, Jesus Christ, is considered a savior unto you, when he hath already told us that he is only our servant.

68 And these things were not revealed unto you in the unsealed portion of this record, nor have they been revealed in any other record that the Lord hath suffered to be written and given unto the children of men, because of their wickedness and their lack of faith.

69 For the things which have been written are available to all to read and ponder. Yea, they are read by many who are wicked and who teach for doctrine and principles the things which are written therein, yet they deny the confirmation and the understanding of these things, which can only be given unto them by the Holy Ghost.

70 And a man cannot have the Holy Ghost unless he obeyeth the words of Christ and keepeth his commandments. And the words of Christ are given in their entirety, yea, even all the commandments by which he expecteth the children of men to live, are given in the Bible, which hath come forth because of the Jews.

71 And also this record, which was made by the hand of my father, hath given an account of the words of Christ as they were given unto the Nephites and the Lamanites who were left in the land of Bountiful after his death and resurrection among the Jews.

72 And I have already explained the importance of these words unto you. And many of the prophets who have written in these records have expressed the importance of these words unto you. For they are the words of Christ, and the only words that ye need to read in order to find out how ye must live in order to have the Holy Ghost as your constant companion.

73 And if ye have the Holy Ghost as your companion, then ye shall be taught the mysteries of God which are contained within the portion of this record which is sealed, but hath now been revealed unto you.

74 And there shall be many of you who are wicked who shall read these things, and if ye do not have the Holy Ghost as your companion, then ye shall reject these things and not understand them, thinking that ye know of yourselves what is the truth.

75 But I say unto you, if ye do not have the fruits of the Spirit, then ye do not have the Spirit to guide you. And if ye do not have the Spirit to guide you, then ye shall not accept these things, but shall be angered because of them. And anger is not a fruit of the Spirit.

76 And ye shall be angered because the things that are written herein shall testify of your wickedness and your carelessness in understanding the truth of God.

77 And the things that have been given unto you in the scriptures that ye have before you are those things which the Lord suffered to be given unto you in your wickedness. And even those things which he hath suffered to
come forth unto you, ye shall read, but ye shall not understand.

78 And this is what is meant by the stumbling blocks that the prophets referred to in their writings. Yea, these stumbling blocks are the things that the Lord hath suffered to be given unto you in your wickedness, even those things which he gave unto you in parables and allegories, and in the likeness of things that ye could not understand, except by the Spirit.

79 And if ye had hearkened unto the words of the Lamb of God, which were given unto you in the unsealed portion of this record, but shall also be given unto you more fully in this sealed portion that hath now been revealed unto you, then ye could have had these stumbling blocks removed from before you.

80 And then ye would have understood the words of Nephi more clearly which he wrote, saying: And it came to pass that the angel of the Lord spake unto me, saying: Behold, saith the Lamb of God, after I have visited the remnant of the house of Israel, and this remnant of whom I speak is the seed of thy father; therefore, after I have visited them in judgment, and smitten them by the hand of the Gentiles; and after the Gentiles do stumble exceedingly, because of the most plain and precious parts of the gospel of the Lamb which have been kept back by that abominable church, which is the mother of harlots, saith the Lamb, I will be merciful unto the Gentiles in that day, insomuch that I will bring forth unto them, in mine own power, much of my gospel, which shall be plain and precious, saith the Lamb.

81 For, behold, saith the Lamb: I will manifest myself unto thy seed, that they shall write many things which I shall minister unto them, which shall be plain and precious; and after thy seed shall be destroyed, and dwindle in unbelief, and also the seed of thy brethren, behold, these things shall be hid up, to come forth unto the Gentiles, by the gift and power of the Lamb.

82 And in them shall be written my gospel, saith the Lamb, and my rock and my salvation. And blessed are they who shall seek to bring forth my Zion at that day, for they shall have the gift and the power of the Holy Ghost; and if they endure unto the end they shall be lifted up at the last day, and shall be saved in the everlasting kingdom of the Lamb; and whoso shall publish peace, yea, tidings of great joy, how beautiful upon the mountains shall they be.

83 And it came to pass that I beheld the remnant of the seed of my brethren, and also the book of the Lamb of God which had proceeded forth from the mouth of the Jew, that it came forth from the Gentiles unto the remnant of the seed of my brethren. And after it had come forth unto them, I beheld other books which came forth by the power of the Lamb, from the Gentiles unto them, unto the convincing of the Gentiles and the remnant of the seed of my

brethren, and also the Jews who were scattered upon all the face of the earth, that the records of the prophets and of the twelve apostles of the Lamb are true.

84 And the angel spake unto me, saying: These last records, which thou hast seen among the Gentiles, shall establish the truth of the first, which are of the twelve apostles of the Lamb, and shall make known the plain and precious things which have been taken away from them; and shall make known to all kindreds, tongues, and people, that the Lamb of God is the Son of the Eternal Father, and the Savior of the world; and that all men must come unto him, or they cannot be saved.

85 And they must come unto him according to the words which shall be established by the mouth of the Lamb; and the words of the Lamb shall be made known in the records of thy seed, as well as in the records of the twelve apostles of the Lamb; therefore they both shall be established in one; for there is one God and one Shepherd over all the earth.

86 And the time cometh that he shall manifest himself unto all nations, both unto the Jews and also unto the Gentiles; and after he hath manifested himself unto the Jews and also unto the Gentiles, then he shall manifest himself unto the Gentiles and also unto the Jews, and the last shall be first, and the first shall be last.

87 And it shall come to pass that if the Gentiles shall hearken unto the Lamb of God in that day, then he shall manifest himself unto them in word, and also in power, in very deed, unto the taking away of their stumbling blocks.

88 And I, Moroni, have given unto you the words of Nephi which he wrote concerning these things that ye have received. And it is expedient that ye understand that the portion of this record that was unsealed and given unto you by the first of these last two latter-day prophets among you, did also contribute to the stumbling blocks that the Lord hath placed before you because of your inability to abide by his words.

89 And if ye had hearkened unto the words of Christ that he hath given you in the unsealed portion of this record, then the Lord would have taken away your stumbling blocks and given unto you the Spirit, that ye might have these things, even this portion that hath been sealed and reserved to come forth at the set given time of the Lord.

90 And now I give unto you a mystery and an understanding of this time of the Lord: Behold, these things shall come forth unto the world exactly two thousand years from the birth of Christ, even according to the calendar that ye have established among you in the latter days.

91 And there shall be some discrepancies in the manner of your accounting of the years of your history, yet ye shall know by this record of the exactness of these things.

92 And this record, even this sealed portion, shall take away your stumbling blocks and give unto you the plain and precious things that the Lord would have you know concerning his gospel.

93 For it shall come to pass that the elect of God in the latter days shall pray unto the Lord, even as Nephi did pray, saying: Oh, Lord, wilt thou encircle me around in the robe of thy righteousness! Oh, Lord, wilt thou make a way for mine escape before mine enemies! Wilt thou make my path straight before me! Wilt thou not place a stumbling block in my way, but that thou wouldst clear my way before me, and hedge not up my way, but the ways of mine enemy.

94 And it shall come to pass that the Lord shall give unto his elect the words of this record and it shall clear the way before them and shall cause to be removed the stumbling blocks that have been placed before them.

95 And the Lord and his gospel shall be as a sanctuary for the elect of God, but to their enemies, even all those who shall reject these things, he shall be as a stumbling block, even according to the words of Isaiah, which he wrote, saying: Sanctify the Lord of Host himself, and let him be your fear, and let him be your dread. And he shall be a sanctuary; but for a stone of stumbling, and for a rock of offense to both the houses of Israel, for a gin and a snare to the inhabitants of Jerusalem.

96 And these words of Isaiah have all been fulfilled. For behold, Jesus was truly a cause of the exceeding stumbling of the Jews in his days, and he was indeed a rock of offense to them. For they would not give heed unto his words,

and looked upon him as a thing of naught, and thought that his words, which is his gospel, were too easy and simple to the understanding of men, and that the things of God should be more mysterious and sacred.

97 And because they desired those things that they could not understand, they did stumble exceedingly and were eventually destroyed because of the stumbling blocks which Christ had placed before them.

98 And now, the Lord gave many things unto Nephi, and showed him all that he desired, even in removing all the stumbling blocks before him that he might understand these things. And Nephi prophesied concerning these things, even unto those of the latter days unto which these things shall be revealed.

99 And he wrote, saying: But behold, I prophesy unto you concerning the last days; concerning the days when the Lord God shall bring these things forth unto the children of men. After my seed and the seed of my brethren shall have dwindled in unbelief, and shall have been smitten by the Gentiles; yea, after the Lord God shall have camped against them round about, and shall have laid siege against them with a mount, and raised forts against them; and after they shall have been brought down low in the dust, even that they are not, yet the words of the righteous shall be written, and the prayers of the faithful shall be heard, and all those who have dwindled in unbelief shall not be forgotten.

100 For those who shall be destroyed shall speak unto them out of the ground, and their speech shall be low out of the dust, and their voice shall be as one that hath a familiar spirit; for the Lord God will give unto him power, that he may whisper concerning them, even as it were out of the ground; and their speech shall whisper out of the dust.

101 For thus saith the Lord God: They shall write the things which shall be done among them, and they shall be written and sealed up in a book, and those who have dwindled in unbelief shall not have them, for they seek to destroy the things of God. Therefore, as those who have been destroyed have been destroyed speedily; and the multitude of their terrible ones shall be as chaff that passeth away; yea, thus saith the Lord God: It shall be at an instant, suddenly.

102 And it shall come to pass, that those who have dwindled in unbelief shall be smitten by the hand of the Gentiles. And the Gentiles are lifted up in the pride of their eyes, and have stumbled, because of the greatness of their stumbling block, that they have built up many churches; nevertheless, they put down the power and miracles of God, and preach up unto themselves their own wisdom and their own learning, that they may get gain and grind upon the face of the poor.

103 And there are many churches built up which cause envyings, and strifes, and malice. And there are also secret combinations, even as in times of old, according to the combinations of the devil, for he is the founder of all these things; yea, the founder of murder, and works of darkness; yea, and he leadeth them by the neck with a flaxen cord, until he bindeth them with his strong cords forever.

104 For behold, my beloved brethren, I say unto you that the Lord God worketh not in darkness. He doeth not anything save it be for the benefit of the world; for he loveth the world, even that he layeth down his own life that he may draw all men unto him. Therefore, he commandeth none that they shall not partake of his salvation.

105 Behold, doth he cry unto any, saying: Depart from me? Behold, I say unto you, Nay; but he saith: Come unto me all ye ends of the earth, buy milk and honey, without money and without price. Behold, hath he commanded any that they should depart out of the synagogues, or out of the houses of worship? Behold, I say unto you, Nay. Hath he commanded any that they should not partake of his salvation? Behold I say unto you, Nay; but he hath given it free for all men; and he hath commanded his people that they should persuade all men to repentance.

106 Behold, hath the Lord commanded any that they should not partake of his goodness? Behold I say unto you, Nay; but all men are privileged the one like unto the other, and none are forbidden. He commandeth that there shall be no priestcrafts; for, behold priestcrafts are that men preach and set themselves up for a light unto the world, that they may get gain and praise of the world; but they seek not the welfare of Zion.

107 Behold, the Lord hath forbidden this thing; therefore, the Lord God hath given a commandment that all men should have charity, which charity is love, and except they should have charity they were nothing. Therefore, if they should have charity they would not suffer the laborer in Zion to perish. But the laborer in Zion shall labor for Zion; for if they labor for money they shall perish.

108 And again, the Lord God hath commanded that men should not murder; that they should not lie; that they should not steal; that they should not take the name of the Lord their God in vain; that they should not envy; that they should not have malice; that they should not contend one with another; that they should not commit whoredoms; and that they should do none of these things; for whoso doeth them shall perish.

109 For none of these iniquities come of the Lord; for he doeth that which is good among the children of men; and he doeth nothing save it be plain unto the children of men; and he inviteth them all to come unto him and partake of his goodness; and he denieth none that come unto him, black and white, bond and free, male and female; and he remembereth the heathen; and all are alike unto God, both Jew and Gentile.

110 But, behold, in the last days, or in the days of the Gentiles; yea, behold, all the nations of the Gentiles and also the Jews, both those who shall come upon this land and those who shall be upon other lands, yea, even upon all the lands of the earth, behold, they will be drunken with iniquity and all manner of abominations.

111 And when that day shall come they shall be visited of the Lord of Hosts, with thunder and with earthquake, and with a great noise, and with storm, and with tempest, and with the flame of devouring fire. And all the nations that fight against Zion, and that distress her, shall be as a dream of a night vision; yea, it shall be unto them, even as unto a hungry man which dreameth, and behold he eateth but he awaketh and his soul is empty; or like unto a thirsty man which dreameth, and behold he drinketh but he awaketh and behold he is faint, and his soul hath appetite; yea, even so shall the multitude of all the nations be that fight against Mount Zion.

112 For behold, all ye that doeth iniquity, stay yourselves and wonder, for ye shall cry out, and cry; yea, ye shall be drunken but not with wine, ye shall stagger but not with strong drink. For behold, the Lord hath poured out upon you the spirit of deep sleep. For behold, ye have closed your eyes, and ye have rejected the prophets; and your rulers, and the seers hath he covered because of your iniquity.

113 And it shall come to pass that the Lord God shall bring forth unto you the words of a book, and they shall be the words of them which have slumbered. And behold the book shall be sealed; and in the book shall be a revelation from God, from the beginning of the world to the ending thereof. Therefore, because of the things which are sealed up, the things which are sealed shall not be delivered in the day of the wickedness and abominations of the people. Therefore, the book shall be kept from them.

114 But the book shall be delivered unto a man, and he shall deliver the words of the book, which are the words of those who have slumbered in the dust, and he shall deliver these words unto another; But the words which are sealed he shall not deliver, neither shall he deliver the book. For the book shall be sealed by the power of God, and the revelation which was sealed shall be kept in the book until the own due time of the Lord, that they may come forth; for behold, they reveal all things from the foundation of the world unto the end thereof.

115 And the day cometh that the words of the book which were sealed shall be read upon the house tops; and they shall be read by the power of Christ; and all things shall be revealed unto the children of men which ever have been among the children of men, and which ever will be even unto the end of the earth.

116 Therefore, at that day when the book shall be delivered unto the man of whom I have spoken, the book shall be hid from the eyes of the world, that the eyes of none shall behold it save it be that three witnesses shall behold it, by the power of God, besides him to whom the book shall be delivered; and they shall testify to the truth of the book and the things therein. And there is none other which shall view it, save it be a few according to the will of God, to bear testimony of his word unto the children of men; for the Lord God hath said that the words of the faithful should speak as if it were from the dead.

117 Therefore, the Lord God will proceed to bring forth the words of the book; and in the mouth of as many witnesses as seemeth him good will he establish his word; and wo be unto him that rejecteth the word of God!

118 But behold, it shall come to pass that the Lord God shall say unto him to whom he shall deliver the book: Take these words which are not sealed and deliver them to another, that he may show them unto the learned, saying: Read this, I pray thee. And the learned shall say: Bring hither the book, and I will read them. And now, because of the glory of the world and to get gain will they say this, and not for the glory of God. And the man shall say: I cannot bring the book, for it is sealed. Then shall the learned say: I cannot read it.

119 Therefore it shall come to pass, that the Lord God will deliver again the book and the words thereof to him that is not learned; and the man that is not learned shall say: I am not learned. Then shall the Lord God say unto him: The learned shall not read them, for they have rejected them, and I am able to do mine own work; therefore thou shalt read the words which I shall give unto thee.

120 Touch not the things which are sealed, for I will bring them forth in mine own due time; for I will show unto the children of men that I am able to do mine own work. Therefore, when thou hast read the words which I have commanded thee, and obtained the witnesses which I have promised unto thee, then shalt thou seal up the book again, and hide it up unto me, that I may preserve the words
which thou hast not read, until I shall see fit in mine own wisdom to reveal all things unto the children of men.

121 For behold, I am God; and I am a God of miracles; and I will show unto the world that I am the same yesterday, today, and forever; and I work not among the children of men save it be according to their faith.

122 And again it shall come to pass that the Lord shall say unto him that shall read the words that shall be delivered him: Forasmuch as this people draw near unto me with their mouth, and with their lips do honor me, but have removed their hearts far from me, and their fear towards me is taught by the precepts of men

123 Therefore, I will proceed to do a marvelous work among this people, yea, a marvelous work and a wonder, for the wisdom of their wise and learned shall perish, and the understanding of their prudent shall be hid. And woe unto them who seek deep to hide their counsel from the Lord! And their works are in the dark; and they say: Who seeth us, and who knoweth us?

124 And they also say: Surely, your turning of things upside down shall be esteemed as the clay of the potter. But behold, I will show unto them, saith the Lord of Hosts, that I know all their works. For shall the work say of him that made it, he made me not? Or shall the thing framed say of him that framed it, he had no understanding?

125 But behold, saith the Lord of Hosts: I will show unto the children of men that it is yet a very little while and Lebanon shall be turned into a fruitful field; and the fruitful field shall be esteemed as a forest.

126 And in that day shall the deaf hear the words of the book, and the eyes of the blind shall see out of obscurity and out of darkness. And the meek also shall increase, and their joy shall be in the Lord, and the poor among men shall rejoice in the Holy One of Israel.

127 For assuredly as the Lord liveth they shall see that the terrible one is brought to naught, and the scorner is consumed, and all that watch for iniquity are cut off; and they that make a man an offender for a word, and lay a snare for him that reproveth in the gate, and turn aside the just for a thing of naught.

128 Therefore, thus saith the Lord, who redeemed Abraham, concerning the house of Jacob: Jacob shall not now be ashamed, neither shall his face now wax pale. But when he seeth his children, the work of my hands, in the midst of him, they shall sanctify my name, and sanctify the Holy One of Jacob, and shall fear the God of Israel. They also that erred in spirit shall come to understanding, and they that murmured shall learn doctrine.

129 And now, I, Moroni, would that ye should know, that this marvelous work which shall be done among this people, yea, even this marvelous work and a wonder, is the coming forth into the world the things which are sealed, even this record that hath been revealed unto you.

130 And the wisdom of the wise and the learned shall perish, and the understanding of the prudent shall be hid, because of the things that are written herein. And the elect of God that erred in spirit shall come to understanding, and they that murmured shall learn doctrine.

131 And this doctrine of which Nephi hath spoken is the true doctrine of Christ. And it is this doctrine that I am about to give unto you. Yea, even my whole soul is overcome by this part of the abridgment of the vision of the brother of Jared, and also that which is from my own understanding, having received this understanding from the mouth of the Lord; even that which I have been commanded to give unto you concerning the life of Jesus Christ.

CHAPTER 36

The scriptures are not as complete in the truth as is the truth when given by the Spirit. The written word of scripture is of men who are inspired, but this written word is susceptible to man's corruption. The light of Christ hath been given to us to discern all truth, and is given to us by the gift of the Holy Ghost. The atonement is again expounded on.

AND it shall come to pass that as the record which hath come forth from the mouth of the Jews giveth an account of the birth and life and the ministry of Jesus Christ in the flesh, so hath this same record been given unto the world by the works of men.

2 For Jesus did not write those things which he would have the children of men know concerning his life and those things which he did according to the commandments that he had received from the Father.

3 For behold, all things whatsoever that the Lord would have the children of men learn and know of the Father, he would have them receive these things through the Holy Spirit, which is the way that the Father instituted in the beginning for His children to receive His guidance and His instruction.

4 Nevertheless, the Lord hath commanded his prophets that they should write unto the children of men and give unto them in writing the things which they receive from him through the Spirit, as the Father had commanded. But this is not the will of the Father concerning His children; nevertheless, in many instances it is the only way whereby He might give unto His children His commandments, which commandments will bring them eternal peace and happiness.

5 For the children of men do not live according to the Spirit, and therefore they cannot discern between good and evil by this Spirit. And if they could discern between good and evil from the Spirit, which is by the ministrations of the Holy Ghost, then they would not need the written word to inspire them to turn to God and keep His commandments.

6 For behold, the Spirit would whisper these things unto them. And all of the words that are given unto the children of men, even those that they have accepted as the word of God, or as the holy scriptures which contain the word of God; yea, even all these words that are written, are written by the hand of a man.

7 And if they are written by the hand of a man, how can another be sure that they are the words of God and not the words of the man who hath written them? For there have been many things written by many of the prophets of God in many parts of the earth unto many different peoples and cultures, even according to their knowledge and understanding, or their ability to accept the word of God that hath been given them through the prophet that hath been chosen by the Lord to give unto the people his words.

8 And all of these things are the words of men, and are not the words of God. For God doth not speak to man through the written word. For if a man readeth the words that are written, then he hath read the words, and hath not heard them by the voice of God.

9 Behold, God speaketh unto His children with His own voice and not through the voice of a man. And because God, who is our Eternal Father, doth not reside here on our planet, then He cannot speak unto us that we may hear His words. For this reason He hath set up the ministries of the Spirit that are administered unto the children of men by the power of the Holy Ghost.

10 For the Holy Ghost is also a member of the Godhead. And this Holy Trinity exemplifieth the essence of the Father; in other words, that which is done by the Father, is the same thing that is done by the Son. And that which is done by the Son, is the same thing that is done by the Holy Ghost. And if it was done by the Son, then it was the same thing that would have been done by the Father.

11 Thus, the Father, the Son, and the Holy Ghost are one God, even the very Eternal Father. And for this reason the Lord is referred to at times as the Son, and some times as the Father. And this is why the Son is referred to, at times, as the Father. And this is why the Holy Ghost is also referred to as the Spirit of God.

12 Behold, it mattereth not which of them shall give a command unto the children of men, for if a command is given by one, then it is sanctioned by the other two; and in this way all three of them are the Father, even the very same Eternal Father that hath given us all things since the beginning.

13 And in the beginning the Father gave Jehovah the power and authority over this solar system, or this part of His kingdom. For the Father hath other kingdoms, for His works are endless and eternal. And since He cannot be in two places at once, He giveth His power and authority unto others who do His will in all things.

14 And to those whom He giveth this power and authority, to them is given His word, which is this power and this authority. And this power and authority was given unto Jehovah who was among the great spirits that existed in the kingdom of the Father in the beginning.

15 And by this word, or by Jehovah, everything that would be given unto us, who are the literal spiritual offspring of the Father, and who pertain to this part of the kingdom of God in which hath been established our sun and our planets; yea, everything that would be given unto us by the Father is given by and through our Lord, who is Jehovah.

16 And Jehovah is the same spirit whom we all confirmed and agreed to lead us and be our Head, even in this part of the kingdom of the Father that He hath prepared for us. And Jehovah was this Word and was given the authority of God. And this Word was in the beginning, and this Word was with God, and this word became God, by the authority of the Father, and also by our sustaining vote.

17 For behold, from the beginning, we were given the agency to do that which we would want for ourselves. And Lucifer and many of the children of the Father, would not sustain Jehovah, nor would they sustain the eternal plan of the Father which was presented unto them.

18 And because they would not sustain Jehovah and accept him as their God, even the God and leader over this solar system, they were forbidden to come upon this earth into mortality and receive a body of flesh and bone and partake of that which the Father commanded Jehovah to create for us.

19 For the Father created the solar system, which consisteth of the sun and the planets from this sun, but then He commanded that the earth be given life by the work and commands of those whom He hath put in authority in this solar system.

20 But even this work was done by the Father, under the direction and through the authority of the Son, and through the Holy Ghost, who is Michael, who are one God.

21 Therefore have the prophets written of this God. And sometimes this God, of whom they have written, might refer to the Son; and at other times this God might refer to Michael, or the Holy Ghost; and at times this God of whom the prophets have written might refer to the very Eternal Father, who is the essence of all eternal good, or in other words, He is God.

22 But it mattereth not to the Father if a work be done by His own hand or by the hands of those whom He hath called and given the authority and power to do His work. For these

could not do His work, save that He commanded them. Therefore, if He hath commanded them, then it is still His work.

23 Therefore, the scriptures are written, at times, that they might be a stumbling block unto the children of men because of their lack of faith; and this as I have explained it unto you previously.

24 For it is written in the Bible, even given as the word of God and accepted by you of the latter days; yea, it hath been written, saying: In the beginning was the Word, and the Word was with God, and the Word was God. The same was in the beginning with God. And all things were made by him, and without him was not any thing made that was made. In him was life, and the life was the light of men.

25 And the light shineth in darkness; and the darkness comprehended it not. And that was the true Light, which lighteth every man that cometh into the world. He was in the world, and the world was made by him, and the world knew him not. He came unto his own, and his own received him not. But as many as received him, to them gave he power to become the sons of God, even to them that believe on his name.

26 And these which believe on his name do his works and are received by him. And they are born unto him, which were born, not of blood, nor of the will of the flesh, nor of the will of man, but of the will of God.

27 And this Word that was in the beginning with God was made flesh, and dwelt among us; and we beheld his glory, the glory as of the only begotten of the Father, who is full of grace and truth.

28 And now I, Moroni, would ask of you that have received these things; yea, even those of you who have received the words that have proceedeth forth out of the mouth of a Jew, even the Bible; How is it that this Word, of which hath been written, can light every man that cometh into the world, even with this true Light? And how is it that these that receive this Light, or this Word, are not born of the flesh, or the will of man, but of the will of God?

29 For are we not all of the flesh? Behold, have we not all been born of the will of the flesh, even the will of our mortal parents? Now, I say unto you, that Jehovah resided in the spirit world, which is not of this flesh, until he came into mortality. And he continued in the spirit world to do the will of the Father in all things.

30 And the will of the Father is that all of His children be given His commandments by which they should live, that they might find happiness. Now, this is the light that hath been given to every man and woman who hath been born into the flesh. Yea, this is the life and the light of men, even a light that shineth in darkness; and the darkness comprehended it not.

31 Behold, this is the light of Christ that is given unto us through the ministrations of those in the spirit world under the direction of the Holy Ghost. But before the Word was made flesh, he was the authority of the spirit world and directed the functions and administrations thereof. And before he left the spirit world and entered into mortality, he gave the power and authority of the spirit world to Michael, who was once Adam in mortality, who became known as the Holy Ghost.

32 And it was the desire of Michael that he be known to the children of men as the Holy Ghost. For it is the will of all righteous souls to not want glory for themselves, but that the glory be given unto the Father. And Michael, or Adam, did not want men to worship him while he was in their service, even while he was administering the will of the Father in the spirit world. Therefore, he is only known by the name of the Holy Ghost.

33 And this light of Christ of which I have spoken is the same light of which I have spoken in the portion of this record that is unsealed and which ye already have among you. And I have already written unto you, saying: For behold, the Spirit of Christ is given to every man, that he may know good from evil; therefore, I show unto you the way to judge; for every thing which inviteth to do good, and to persuade to believe in Christ, is sent forth by the power and gift of Christ; therefore ye may know with a perfect knowledge it is of God.

34 But whatsoever thing persuadeth men to do evil, and believe not in Christ, and deny him, and serve not God, then ye may know with a perfect knowledge that it is of the devil; for after

this manner doth the devil work, for he persuadeth no man to do good, no, not one; neither do his angels; neither do they who subject themselves unto him.

35 And now, my brethren, seeing that ye know the light by which ye may judge, which light is the light of Christ, see that ye do not judge wrongfully; for with that same judgment which ye judge, ye shall also be judged.

36 Therefore, I beseech of you, brethren, that ye should search diligently in the light of Christ that ye may know good from evil; and if ye will lay hold upon every good thing, and condemn it not, ye certainly will be a child of Christ.

37 And now, my brethren, how is it possible that ye can lay hold upon every good thing? And now, I come to that faith of which I said I would speak; and I will tell you the way whereby ye may lay hold on every good thing. For behold, God, knowing all things, being from everlasting to everlasting; behold, He sent angels to minister unto the children of men, to make manifest concerning the coming of Christ; and in Christ there should come every good thing.

38 And God also declared unto prophets, by his own mouth, that Christ should come. And behold, there were divers ways that he did manifest things unto the children of men, which were good; and all things which are good cometh of Christ; otherwise men were fallen, and there could no good thing come unto them.

39 Therefore, by the ministering of angels, and by every word which proceeded forth out of the mouth of God, men began to exercise faith in Christ; and thus by faith, they did lay hold upon every good thing; and thus it was until the coming of Christ.

40 And after that he came, men also were saved by faith in his name; and by faith, they become the sons of God. And as sure as Christ liveth, he spake these words unto our fathers, saying: Whatsoever thing ye shall ask the Father in my name, which is good, in faith believing that ye shall receive, behold, it shall be done unto you.

41 And now, I would that ye should understand the simplicity of my words. For the light of Christ is given unto every man and women who entereth into mortality. And it is by this light that we can judge good from evil, or in other words, this is the enmity that the Father caused to be placed between those who followed Satan and those who are the children of Adam and Eve, or the children of men according to the flesh.

42 For as soon as any spirit leaveth the spirit world and entereth into mortality, they are caused by the flesh to forget their former existence that they might more fully be tried and tested during the days of their probation.

43 And immediately upon arriving to an age of understanding, Satan beginneth to make an attempt to influence them and enticeth them to accept his plan, they becoming susceptible to his enticings because of the flesh.

44 But the ministrations of the spirit world, which is the ministering of angels, minister unto us every word that proceeded forth out of the mouth of God, as I have explained it unto you and as I have previously written.

45 And these ministering angels, or these ministering spirits, are provided by the Father to inspire us to do good, and they also keep Satan and those who follow him in check, that they might not tempt us or entice us beyond our capabilities to resist their temptations.

46 And for this reason Satan is powerless to tempt and entice children, or those who have not reached the age of understanding. And I have also caused to be written the words of my father, Mormon, which he wrote unto me concerning the baptism of little children. For this is a mockery of the purpose for which baptism was given. For what infant among you can choose to make a covenant with God? And they are innocent until they reach the age of accountability and understanding.

47 And these ministering spirits, or angels of God, are subject unto the Lord, or Jehovah, who overseeth the work in the world in which these spirits reside. And they minister according to the word of his command, showing the truth and giving understanding unto them of strong faith and of a firm mind in every form of godliness.

48 And the office of their ministry is to call men unto repentance, and to fulfill and to do the work of the covenants which the Father hath made with his children from the beginning.

49 And these spirits declare the words of Christ unto the prophets of God and give unto them the knowledge and the understanding that they need that they might be sent forth unto the children of men to teach the words of Christ.

50 And by the mouths of these prophets, the Lord hath given unto the rest of the children of men, even those who are not strong in faith and firm in every form of godliness, a way whereby they might hear the word of God and begin to exercise faith in Christ, that they may have the privilege of receiving the mysteries of the kingdom of heaven for themselves, and to have the heavens opened unto them that they might know the will and mind of the Father in all things.

51 And now, this is one of the covenants that the Father made unto us in the beginning; even that if we obey His commandments, then we shall have His spirit to be with us that we might be one with Him.

52 And becoming one with the Father is the purpose of the atonement of Christ, or in other words, to make us one with God. And he cannot make us one with God, except it be according to the manner that the Father has covenanted with us in the beginning, even that we should first keep His commandments in all things.

53 And these commandments are the things which the Lord giveth to us through the Spirit, and which he taught to us when he came down into the world in the flesh.

54 And so, my beloved brothers and sisters, once again I shall speak to you in plainness that ye might not err any longer concerning this thing, even concerning the atonement of Jesus Christ. For the mission of our Lord was to teach unto us the commandments of the Father that we might be one with the Father, as he is one with the Father.

55 And because of the flesh, we are weak and understandeth not the things of God. And because of the flesh, the words which Jesus spake unto the children of men in the flesh were not understood; for they looked beyond the mark and the standard that he had given unto them, which were the commandments that he had received of the Father, even the same commandments that we all received in the beginning as spirits in the kingdom of our Father.

56 And he is our Savior because of the things that he taught unto us, even the commandments of the Father. For behold, if we do not keep the commandments that he hath given unto us, then we shall not be saved in the kingdom of God.

57 And now, I cannot be more plain in my words that ye might understand the mission and calling of Jesus Christ. And many of the prophets who have been wrought upon by the Holy Spirit and who have been ministered unto by these angels of God; even that the eyes of their understanding have been opened up that they have seen God, and not according to the flesh but according to the spirit; even these prophets have written that which they have been inspired to write by these spiritual ministrations.

58 And these things are the holy scriptures that ye have among you. And because they are the words of men, which are written unto you in the language of men, they are susceptible to the weaknesses of men and the corruption of men.

59 And these writings of the prophets of God, even these men who write unto the children of men according to the inspiration that they receive from the Holy Ghost, cannot be understood in their intent and purpose, except that the person who hath received them and readeth them hath been given an understanding of them by the power of the Spirit of God.

60 For this reason, Jesus did not keep any written record of his words, or his works, or his prophecies that he gave unto the children of men in the flesh. And while he was alive in the flesh, he did not allow his disciples to keep an account of the things that were done among them.

61 For his disciples did not have the Holy Ghost to help them understand the mission and purpose of the Savior. And if any of them would have attempted to write an account of the works and teachings of Jesus without the Spirit to guide him in that which he should write, then his account might be susceptible to his own interpretation and perception of the teachings of Jesus, and not necessarily of the truth.

62 And it was after Jesus was resurrected and had sent unto them the Holy Ghost; or in other words, after he had commanded those in the spirit world to minister to his disciples in the flesh, according to the workings and administrations of the Holy Ghost; that the disciples began to understand the true purpose and intent of his earthly mission, yea, even all things that they desired to know.

63 For Jesus taught his disciples, saying: Whatsoever thing ye shall ask the Father in my name, which is good, in faith, believing that ye shall receive it, behold, it shall be done unto you.

64 And the disciples later learned by the Spirit that the name of Jesus symbolized the works that he did among them. Therefore, they understood that praying to the Father was in vain unless they did so in the name of Jesus, or in other words, unless they did the things that Jesus did, which works are symbolic of his name.

65 And now, I would that ye should know of the time that the Holy Ghost was given unto the disciples of Jesus, and also that which transpired to cause them to understand the things which they did not understand without the Spirit.

66 And according to the words of the brother of Jared, which he wrote, saying: And the twelve who had been chosen by God to serve under Jesus were gathered together on the day of Pentecost according to the traditions of the Jews. And they were gathered together in one place and were enclosed within the house in which they had gathered.

67 And I beheld the ministering spirits in the spirit world who had been organized and called by Michael to teach these disciples the things that they did not understand pertaining to the works of Christ that they had witnessed. And Michael did these things according to the commandments that he had received from Jehovah, who had returned to the spirit world for a brief time between the death of his flesh and his resurrection.

68 And as these spirits entered into the same room where these disciples were sitting, their spiritual bodies, which were made of element, even element that was not seen by the mortal eye; yea, when these spirits entered into the room, the elements of their spiritual bodies displaced the elements of the air that were already present there.

69 And when the elements of the air were displaced by the spiritual matter that made up the bodies of these ministering angels, the disciples felt the displacement of this air around them rush towards them, even to such an extent that they felt a rush of a mighty wind which forced itself upon them as if it came from heaven.

70 And when these spirits began to speak unto the disciples in the flesh, according to the power of the spirit, the disciples were overcome with emotion, evensomuch that it appeared to them that their bosoms were on fire within them, because of the manner of communication that was used by the spirits to communicate with their flesh.

71 And then the minds and the hearts of the disciples in the flesh began to communicate with the spirits that were speaking unto them. And this manner of communication was two types of communication, or divided, even in the tongue of the language that was understood by the disciples, and in the tongue that was spoken by those in the dimension of the spirit that was among them.

72 And now, I, Moroni, give the rest of this account according as it hath been given in the Bible, which ye already have among you. And this I do by way of the Spirit which whispereth these things to me. But he who shall translate these things shall give unto you those things which ye already have among you, according to the words that are written, even that ye might understand the things that ye have already accepted as the word of God.

73 And the record is written, saying: And when the day of Pentecost was fully come, they were all with one accord in one place. And suddenly there came a sound from heaven as of a rushing mighty wind, and it filled all the house where they were sitting.

74 And there appeared unto them cloven tongues like as of fire, and it sat upon each of them. And they were all filled with the Holy Ghost, and began to speak with other tongues, as the Spirit gave them utterance.

75 And it came to pass that these apostles began to preach unto the people in the tongue that each could understand, having this given unto them by the power of the Holy Ghost, or by

the power of the communication process that was used with them by the spirits who had entered into the house to teach them.

76 And the people began to gather and mock them and accuse them of being drunk with wine because of that which they heard but could not understand.

77 And the apostle, who was called Peter, stood up and said unto them: Ye men of Judea, and all ye that dwell at Jerusalem, be this known unto you, and hearken to my words: For these are not drunken, as ye suppose, seeing it is but the third hour of the day. But this is that which was spoken by the prophet Joel, which he said: And it shall come to pass in the last days, saith God, I will pour out my Spirit upon all flesh: and your sons and your daughters shall prophesy, and your young men shall see visions, and your old men shall dream dreams; and on my servants and on my handmaidens I will pour out of my Spirit in those days; and they shall prophesy.

78 And now, my beloved brothers and sisters, I, Moroni, have given unto you an explanation of the true mission and purpose for which the Son of God was born unto us in the flesh. And this is the main purpose for his mission, even to teach unto us the commandments of the Father that we might have the Spirit of the Father bear witness unto us of the Father.

79 And if we bear witness of the Father, then shall we know the Father; and if we know the Father, then we shall be accepted by the Father and be allowed to live in one of the kingdoms of glory that He hath established in His kingdom.

80 And I have explained unto you that the Lord hath given unto the children of men prophets and apostles, and others who have the Spirit of God with them, that they might persuade the children of men to repent of their sins and turn to God and keep His commandments, that they might have His Spirit to be with them.

81 And these prophets and apostles have written the word of God and have given it unto you in the scriptures that ye have before you. But because these words of these prophets and these apostles have been given unto you second hand, there is no way that ye can possibly understand the things that have been written except that ye have the same Spirit by which these things were written.

82 And because those of you in the latter days, even those of you who shall read my words; which words I testify unto you have been given unto me by this same Spirit that hath inspired all the prophets of God since the beginning; yea, because ye are wicked and are taught the precepts and commandments of men, which are not given by this Spirit, which is the light of Christ as I have explained it unto you, then it is expedient that the Lord hath caused that these things are written unto you by His Spirit, so that ye might have a better understanding of the things that the Spirit would have taught unto you, if ye were righteous.

83 Behold, the scriptures that ye have before you have been translated by men who often did not have the spirit of prophecy and discernment among them. And when they would think it was in the best interests of their own understanding, they would change that which was written by the prophet who gave them the word of God in written form.

84 And for this reason, many of the prophets of God have written the mysteries of God in symbolism and in ways that could not be understood, except it be given unto him who hath the Spirit of God always with him.

85 And now, it is easy for you to determine whether ye have the Spirit with you or not. For if ye read the words of the prophets that have been given unto you, and ye understandeth them not, then ye do not have the Spirit with you. And ye do not have the Spirit with you, because ye are not worthy of this Spirit, and ye have not asked the Father for understanding.

86 Nevertheless, I would that ye should be aware of those who would make you believe that they understand the words of the prophets, and who give unto you their interpretations and perceptions of these words. For many times their words are the interpretations and perceptions of men who will cause you to be misled and cause you to err in your understanding of the words of the Father which He would give unto you.

87 And the Lord hath given you a sure way

that ye shall know a prophet of God from a prophet of Satan. And the way to determine this is as simple as the understanding of this way.

88 For behold, a true prophet of God would only teach unto you the words of Christ. And he cannot teach unto you the words of Christ, except he be given the light of Christ. And he cannot have the light of Christ, except that he do the works of Christ. Therefore, ask yourselves this: Do the actions of this prophet follow after the name of Christ? Or in other words, if Christ were this prophet, would he do the works that this prophet doeth before you?

89 For behold, in the latter days there shall be many who claim to preach unto you the words of Christ, and there shall be many who shall preach unto you the words of Christ. But they are all corrupt and have not the light of Christ in them, because of their works.

90 For by the material things that they possess ye can determine for yourselves that they are not true prophets of God. For would the Christ have more than his neighbor? Yea, would the Christ put himself above another even to the wearing of very fine apparel and having all of the fine things of the world, which are not a necessity for the calling of a true prophet of God, who would only possess that which would sustain his life?

91 Yea, I say unto you, go unto these prophets in their own houses and see that which they possess away from their pulpits of their preaching and their vain words. Witness for yourselves that which they give unto their children, even that which they command to be built up as sanctuaries unto God, even the churches, and the synagogues, and the temples among you. Are these the works of Christ?

92 I say unto you that they are not the works of Christ, but that they are the works of men, who seek for the praise and glory of the world. For thus taught Jesus Christ when he lived his life in the flesh. For the works that he did, he expecteth of all those who know him and understand the commandments of the Father.

93 And all true prophets of God pattern their lives after Christ in all things. And did Christ own a home in which he accumulated the fine things of the world? I say unto you that he did not. And did Christ purchase, with the money that was given unto him for the ministry, that which did not sustain the simplicity of his life? I say unto you that he did not.

94 And this is the sure way, my beloved brothers and sisters, that ye can tell if those who lead you and pretend to be the mouthpieces of God, are true prophets of God. But I say unto you, that there are very few prophets of God in the latter days. And those that are shall be made known unto you by their works.

95 And they shall not be of the world, for the world shall hate them and persecute them because of the things that they testify concerning the wickedness of the world; and also because of their lifestyle, which is the lifestyle that Jesus Christ lived in the flesh during the days of his life and ministry.

CHAPTER 37

The lineage of Jesus is given in its proper perspective as it is written in the Bible in Matthew and Luke. The life and ministry of John the Baptist is explained and expounded upon. John begins his ministry among the people.

AND now, I will begin the account of the life and ministry of Jesus. And it is written in the Bible, which ye have among you, the genealogies of the lineage of Christ, both according to the flesh, and according to the lineage of the Priesthood that was given unto the men at Jerusalem according to the traditions and beliefs of the Jews.

2 And ye shall have two versions of the lineage of Jesus given unto you, which shall be a cause of much contention among you because of these two different accounts of his lineage.

3 And now, I would that ye should know that the first lineage that ye shall read in the book which proceedeth forth from the mouth of the Jew, is the literal lineage of Jesus according to the flesh. But I ask ye, how can this be the literal lineage of Jesus according to the flesh, when the Father of Jesus was not according to the flesh? And he who hath understanding will understand that the generations between Abraham and Jesus are forty and two, which correspond to that which hath been spoken of by John, even of the one thousand, two hundred and sixty days. He who heareth, let him listen.

4 And now, it was common practice among the Jews that the lineage of a man be given through the father, or through patriarchal lines, thus reserving the sense of authority that men believe that they have over the women.

5 Nevertheless, he who wrote the first account of the life of Jesus that ye have among you, even he whom ye shall know as Matthew; yea, he disregarded the traditions of the Jews according to their ways and their customs. And the lineage that he hath given of Jesus is the lineage of his mother, Mary, whose lineage was the only lineage of the flesh that could be properly accounted as being true of Jesus, who had no father according to the flesh.

6 And when he gave his account in the beginning, it was correct and read according as ye have it before you beginning with Abraham and continuing until it cometh to Eliud, the son of Achim. And then Matthew proceeded to give the lineage according to the matriarchal order, because Jesus was born of Mary in the flesh and not of any man.

7 And when the words of this apostle, even Matthew, were reviewed by those who would assign themselves to compile the writings that were to be permitted in the Bible as pertaining to the life of Jesus, they, not having the Spirit to guide them in all things, thought that Matthew had erred in his judgment when he began to follow the lineage of Mary concerning Jesus.

8 But he did not err, and he wrote it properly, saying: And Eliud begot Eleazar, and Eleazar begot a daughter and called her name Rebecca. And Rebecca married Matthan; and from this marriage was begotten Jacob, who was the father of Mary, of whom was born Jesus, who is called Christ.

9 And now, it is not a hard thing to see the error of those who have changed these things because of their pride in that which they believe should be the right of a man to have all things bear witness of his patriarchal order; for the lineage of Joseph, the husband of Mary is given in the account of another of the apostles of Jesus, even he whom ye shall know as Luke.

10 For behold, Luke giveth a true account of the lineage of Joseph, who was the husband of Mary. And from this lineage is given the lines of priesthood authority that were given unto Joseph according to the customs and traditions of the Jews. And it was through this line of the Priesthood that Jesus justified his calling to the ministry when he reached the age in which he could minister to the Jews according to their traditions.

11 And now, Joseph was the son of Heli, who was the son of Matthan. And Heli was the brother of Jacob, the father of Mary.

12 And these genealogies are the things of men given to satisfy their pride in their ancestors. But God careth nothing for these things as I have previously explained it unto you. Nevertheless, the Spirit commanded that these two lineages be included in the accounts of the life of Jesus, that they may come forth in the latter days as a further testimony of Jesus; and also that the pride and stiffneckedness of the Jews, and those who have put themselves above another because of the name of Jesus, might be taken away in the thing in which they are prideful.

13 And all these things have been done in a likeness of things that are past, and also of things that are present, and things that are in the future, so that the Lord can show forth the foolishness of those who are prideful and think that they are great, even that they think of themselves above another.

14 For behold, according to the flesh, the fathers of Jesus were the most corrupt of the sons of their fathers, and were the fruits of grave sins which were committed by his ancestors, in which no one can have a sense of pride and envy.

15 For if ye were to take the lineage of Jesus back through his fathers, and this according to the lineage of his mother, who gave unto him the flesh, then ye would see that Jesus came from the lineage of Solomon, who was conceived from the womb of Bathsheba, she that was taken in sin by David.

16 And the account of Matthew maketh specific mention of this grave sin that it should be known. For there is no other mention of the wife of any other of the fathers in the lineage of Jesus, except for that in which David did sin grievously before God.

17 And Solomon did also sin before God and lived a corrupt life that introduced much strife and misery among the people of his kingdom.

18 And now the mention of these fathers is important to understand. For if the pure lineage of a man was important to the functions of his mission, or his calling from God, then ye would think that the Father would have brought forth his son, even according to the flesh, among righteous men. But Solomon, who was wicked, was chosen over his brother, Nathan, who was a righteous man of God, who was named by his father David after the prophet Nathan, who ministered unto David.

19 And Solomon was chosen as the direct ancestor of Jesus, whereas Nathan was chosen as the direct ancestor of Joseph, the husband of Mary, who provided Jesus with the justification for which he was allowed to preach according to the laws and the customs of the Jews in his day.

20 And this whole thing was given and directed by the Lord that he might abase those who would exalt themselves, and exalt those who would be abased. For the Lord careth nothing for the things of the flesh; and it is not important to him that his ancestors were wicked, for he came into the world to save all men from their wickedness and turn them towards God.

21 And he loveth the sinner and those who fall in the weakness of the flesh that they may be humble. And how can he save a man who hath no need of saving? And how can he turn a man to God who is already in that straight and narrow path?

22 Therefore, the Lord hath once again shown his love for the sinner and his contempt for those who would set themselves above another because of the things of the flesh.

23 For behold, in the last days there shall be some among you who would like to think that because of their lineage, or because of the color of their skin, that they are better than their brothers and their sisters.

24 But I say unto you who shall think these things, yea, study the lineage of Christ according to the flesh. And if ye study the lineage of Christ according to the flesh, ye shall find that he hath the blood of the Canaanite, which is the dark blood of those whom ye condemn because of their bloodlines.

25 And from all the sons of Jacob, one of the most wicked, even Judah, was chosen to be the direct ancestor of the Christ.

26 And also this thing hath been done that it might show unto the Jews in the latter days of their own foolishness, which foolishness hath come to them from the vanity and pride of their fathers.

27 For in that day, the Jews shall become prideful of their heritage and think of themselves above their neighbors. And this pride shall lead them to be placed under the power of Satan, even that there shall be no peace among them because of this pride that they have.

28 And under the power of Satan, they shall be led to fear for their lives all the days of their probation. And there shall be many wars among them and great destruction shall come upon them because they do not keep the commandments of God, but in their pride are being led by Satan.

29 For they think that because they are descendants of Abraham, they are special, even that they deserve a special place upon the earth. And they do not understand the words of the prophets that have been given unto them. For the words of their prophets have testified concerning Christ and his mission. But the Jews have rejected Christ and his mission and the commandments that he hath given unto them.

30 For behold, according to the traditions of the Jews, Jesus was only a prophet who was sent among the people of Jerusalem to preach repentance unto them and not to fulfill the laws that Moses had given unto them. And they do not accept that he was the great Jehovah who gave them these laws, according to their records.

31 And it came to pass that this was taught unto them by their own prophets, even a great prophet who came among them before the ministry of Christ began. And he said unto them: Why is it that ye receive not the preaching of him whom God hath sent? If ye

receive not this in your hearts, ye receive not me; and if ye receive not me, ye receive not him of whom I am sent to bear record; and for your sins ye have no cloak.

32 Repent, therefore, and bring forth fruits meet for repentance. And think not to say within yourselves, Abraham is our father; we have kept the commandments of God, and none can inherit the promises but the children of Abraham; for I say unto you that God is able of these stones to raise up children unto Abraham.

33 And thus did the Lord also give unto the Jews and all those who have taken stock in their lineage, an example through his own lineage of the unimportance of the genealogies and traditions of men. For behold, we are all equal in the eyes of the Father, and He hath chosen no people over another.

34 And this prophet among the Jews whom I have just mentioned shall be known in the record of the Jews as John the Baptist.

35 And now, it is expedient herein that I give unto you a brief account of the life and ministry of John, even that which ye do not have among you in the accounts that have been given unto you in the Bible. For John was accepted by the Jews in his day as a holy prophet among them, and the people having accepted him, rejected the words of Christ, whom John preached unto them.

36 And now, it is important that it be shown unto you the manner in which the children of men believe and accept those whom they would have as their prophet. For when a prophet speaketh unto the people, they accept his words as one with authority, but also as one who is an outcast and derelict among them. Therefore, they have little reason to pattern their lives after the example that a prophet would set for them.

37 And the prophets do not speak of themselves, but of God. And because they speak not of themselves, but of God, it is easier for the children of men to accept them and give heed unto their counsel, if the people believe that they are doing the will of God, and not the will of men.

38 But Jesus Christ came in among the people not as a prophet, but he who called the prophets, even he of whom the prophets have spoken and written. And because he spoke of himself, he was rejected by the people. For the people cannot accept things that are plain and simple to their understanding, nor can they accept that even God can have flesh and be subjected to the vicissitudes of the flesh.

39 And for this reason John was called and ordained to prepare the way for Jesus, even that he would testify before the people of the divinity of Christ, who was among them. And thus the Father commanded, so that the hearts of the people might be more open to receive the message of His Son.

40 For it came to pass that John was born of his mother Elizabeth; and when he was a young child, John would accompany his mother into the desert unto the house of Sara, whom she continued to visit for many years.

41 For Mary had moved out of the wilderness and lived with her husband Joseph near unto the city of his fathers in Nazareth.

42 And Sara loved John, even as her own son, and asked many times of his mother that she would leave him with her that she might have joy in his presence.

43. And it came to pass that John grew to love Sara, even as he did his own mother. And he became well adapted to the wilderness in which she lived, and was wont to abide there as he grew older.

44 For it had come to pass that as John began to grow, he also began to grow in the Lord, for the Spirit was with him all the days of his life. And John was taught by his mother of the wondrous dream that she had concerning the daughter of Sara. And in this way John began to learn of the mission of Jesus, who was the grandson of Sara, whom he loved.

45 And Sara also told John of Mary and the miraculous thing that had been done to her by the power of the Holy Ghost. For Sara knew her daughter Mary, and knew that she was a virgin who had never been with a man, even until the birth of Jesus.

46 And John began to study the prophets of old, and was also ministered unto by those in the spirit world who were called to prepare him for his mission.

47 And for the early part of his life, John dwelt in the house of his father Zacharias. And Zacharias was a High Priest in the church at Jerusalem.

48 And it came to pass that John did not like that which was done by his father, who was a high priest in the church at Jerusalem. For he began to see the great hypocrisy of the leaders of the church, and also the great wickedness of the Jews because of their leaders and their church.

49 And it came to pass that John rebelled against his father and was cast out of his house for that which he began to speak against the church at Jerusalem. And he cast off the clothes that he had been accustomed to wearing in the house of his father.

50 For he had argued with his father that the tithing of the people should not be used to purchase the fine things of the world for those who would serve in the church, but that they should be examples for the people and only have the things that were necessary to sustain their lives, and that they should not take from the people to get gain for themselves and their families.

51 And John forsook the things of the world and began to fast and pray and study the word of God that was given unto the people, even the words of all the holy prophets before him. And he committed his entire life to the cause of truth and to God.

52 And he went into the wilderness and lived with Sara for many years, even until the time that he was called forth by the Lord to go unto the people of Jerusalem and preach repentance unto them and prepare the way for his cousin, Jesus, who was the Christ.

53 For he had been taught by Sara and his mother concerning the Christ who should come among them, and that this Christ was the son of Mary, whom he had never met, for she was with her husband, Joseph, in the land of his fathers.

54 And John grew exceedingly in the Spirit; and he gave up all of the lusts of the flesh that he might be filled constantly with the Holy Ghost.

55 And because of his father, and according to the traditions of the church, he was given the authority to baptize the people by his father when he lived with Zacharias. And with this authority, he began to go forth and teach the people that the church of God at Jerusalem was corrupt, and if they wanted to serve God and keep His commandments more fully, that they should come unto Him and learn the true commandments of God and be baptized so that they could recommit themselves unto God.

56 And the people began to listen to John because of his father, who was a leader among them. But his father would not listen to his son, but rebuked him for that which he taught the people against the church.

57 And Zacharias rebuked John, saying: How is it that thou, being my son, canst turn these people away from the church of God, because ye have taken it upon yourself to be a prophet unto them, but have not been given the authority of the church in this thing?

58 Behold, I know that thou wast conceived by the gift and power of God, for I know that an angel of the Lord did visit me at thy conception and gave me commandments concerning thee. But the angel said unto me that thou wouldst bring joy and gladness unto me and that many should rejoice because of thee. And that thou wouldst turn the hearts of the fathers to the children and the disobedient to the wisdom of the just.

59 And how is it that thou canst do these things by turning the people away from the church, which hath been established by the power of God for the salvation and happiness of the people? And because of thy example, many people have a hard time in listening to the words that I give unto them according to the position of authority that I hold in the church, which hath been given unto me by my father and by his father, even unto Moses, who gave us the laws of salvation.

60 And I know that thou hast been called of God to preach unto this people and prepare the way of salvation, for this knowledge was given unto me by the Spirit of God after I received my voice, which was taken from me as I doubted upon the Lord. And the Holy Ghost taught me many things concerning your mission and that which ye should do among us.

61 But how is it, my son, that these things, of which the angel hath spoken, can come to pass concerning thee when thou hast forsaken the church of God and hast taught these people to forsake the church also?

62 And John looked upon his father

Zacharias, and said unto him: My beloved father, O, how can so many simple things be shown unto thee, yet thou failest to understand them because of the traditions of thy fathers? And I know that thou didst think that I would grow up in the church and take the mantle from thee, even the mantle of the Holy Priesthood, which was given unto thee by the laying on of hands by those who are in authority in the church. And I, too, have received of this authority from thee, according to the administrations of the Aaronic Priesthood.

63 But thou hast erred in thy understanding of how these things, which were given unto thee by the Spirit, should come to pass. For behold, these things shall not come to pass by way of the church, which hath been given unto us because of our sins and our inabilities to receive the things of the Father from the Spirit, by which He hath established the way from the beginning to teach us these things.

64 And the Christ shall not come forth from the church, nor shall he be given the power and authority of the Priesthood of the church. For the church shall reject him and mock him, and thy peers shall want to kill him and stop him from turning the people away from the church and its authority.

65 For the Christ shall teach the people that they do not need the church, nor its leaders, nor its authority to receive the gifts of the Spirit that the Father hath promised unto all of His children. Yea, he shall teach them that they must obey the commandments of God, and then all these things shall be given unto them without having to depend on the arm of flesh to provide for them these things.

66 For dost thou not see the great abomination in the dealings of the church regarding the manner in which the people of the church are forced to accept its authority and the words of the High Priests, as the only words of God that are true?

67 Behold, thou hast been influenced by the traditions of the church and have been swayed to believe and follow the commandments of the church because of thy peers. And the law of Moses that thou preachest unto the people, knowest thou not for what purpose this law was given unto the children of Israel? Was it not given unto them in their wickedness because they were afraid of God and wanted not to hear the voice of God for themselves, but wanted only that they receive the word of God through the voice of Moses?

68 And these laws that were given unto them are not the laws of salvation, which the leaders of the church would have its members believe, but they point a soul towards Christ, who shall teach the people the laws that they need to live by in order to be saved. And in this way shall the Christ fulfill the law of Moses, even that it shall become a thing of naught among them.

69 And these are the things that shall be taught by the prophet of the Highest, even the Christ that hath been prophesied of by all the holy prophets. And if I am to go and prepare a way for him, even give knowledge of salvation unto this people that they might repent of their sins and be baptized and prepare themselves for the words of Christ that shall be given unto them, then how is it that I can direct these people towards the church?

70 And I have been commanded to direct this people towards the Christ, who is not of the church, and who shall discover unto the people the wickedness of the church and its leaders, of which thou art a part.

71 And now, my beloved father, I would that thou shouldst repent of the things that thou knowest are not good in the church, and come unto me and let me baptize thee of a new, that thou mightest be prepared to hear the words of the Christ. Come out of the church, my father, and have nothing more to do with its sins and its hypocrisy, and prepare thyself for the coming of the Christ, who is Jesus, the son of Mary, whom thou knowest.

72 And after Zacharias had heard these words of his son, he did not contend with him any further. But Zacharias could not leave the seat of authority that he had been given by the church, for he did not want to be mocked by the church and his family and their friends.

73 But from that time forth, Elizabeth did not support her husband in his calling in the church, but turned to her son and was baptized by him.

74 And it came to pass that John began to preach to the people throughout the land of Jerusalem concerning the Christ. And it was voiced throughout the land that a prophet had come unto them and preached the word of God.

75 And when the people would gather together to hear the words of John, he would preach unto them repentance of their sins. But the people who belonged to the church at Jerusalem, and who listened to the leaders of the church, did not think that they were in need of repentance, because they believed that they were keeping the commandments of God according to the law of Moses that had been taught unto them by the church.

76 And the people believed that they had already been baptized by those in authority in the church of God, and that they did not need any other baptism. And they did not believe that their leaders were corrupt and misleading them, owing to the prosperity of the church of God among them.

77 But John said unto them: Oh, ye generation of vipers, who hath warned you to flee from the wrath to come? Do your leaders warn you of these things? Or do they give unto you the pleasant words that ye are wont to hear that they may continue to receive your respect and support? For if the leaders of your church were to preach unto you of the wrath of God, which shall come to pass upon the wicked and upon all those who shall reject the Christ, then ye shall leave from following them and would not give unto them of your support.

78 And ye believe that the works that ye do are keeping the commandments of God. But I say unto you that they are not the commandments of God, but the commandments of men, and that ye should repent of these things and bring forth fruits worthy of repentance and say not within yourselves, Abraham is our father; we have kept the commandments of God, and none can inherit the promises but the children of Abraham; for I say unto you, That God is able of these stones to raise up children unto Abraham.

79 And the root of the tree which hath sprung forth among you, even the true gospel of God, hath become corrupted by the branches, which is ye of the church. And the fruit of this tree is your works, which are not the works of God, but the works of men, which are evil. And now also the axe is laid unto the root of the trees; and every tree therefore which bringeth not forth good fruit is hewn down, and cast into the fire.

80 And the people answered John, saying: We have kept the law of Moses in all things according to the commandments that our leaders have taught to us in the church of God. And we attend the synagogues regularly as is required of us, and make sacrifices in the temple of God, according to the law of Moses. And we honor our mothers and our fathers and do all else that the Lord hath commanded us by way of his leaders in the church. Therefore, what more shall we do then?

81 And John answered them, saying: Even in all these things that ye have done, ye have not kept the commandments of God in any. For the Lord hath not commanded these things of you, but they have been given unto you as commandments of men. And also, ye have been given the lower law of Moses, which is not the law of the Father, but a law that should point you towards the Father, that ye might have His Spirit to be with you.

82 And the commandments of the Father are that ye do unto others as ye would have others do unto you, even that ye shall give of your abilities to each according to his needs. Therefore, he that hath two coats, let him impart to him that hath none; and he that hath meat, let him do likewise.

83 Now these are commandments of the Father, and the only commandments that shall save any of you in His kingdom.

84 And it came to pass that the people began to believe upon the words of John; for they began to see the hypocrisy of the church and the wickedness of its leaders, who had set themselves up above them and who had the fine things of the world, while many of them had none.

85 And the people began to believe that John was the Christ of whom the prophets had testified would come into the world. But he rebuked them, saying: I indeed baptize you with water; but one mightier than I cometh, the latchet of whose shoes I am not worthy to unloose; and he shall baptize you with the Holy Ghost and with fire.

86 For ye shall learn the commandments of God from him. And after ye have been given the commandments of God, then if ye shall live by them, then ye shall receive the Holy Ghost, which shall burn in your bosom as a fire and testify unto you of all the things of God which are necessary for your salvation.

CHAPTER 38

The preaching of John the Baptist. Moroni compares his preaching with that of Abinadi in the unsealed part of the Book of Mormon and uses Abinadi's words to expound upon the preaching of John.

AND now, in everything that John did, he prepared the people for the ministry of Christ. For there began to be many among them who believed on the words of John, because they accepted him as a prophet of God.

2 But the leaders of the church, and also many of the members of the church who had placed their trust in their leaders, did not believe that John was a prophet of God, but that he said these things of himself, having alienated himself from the church because of his disagreements with his father who was a high priest of the church.

3 And Zacharias had known of the calling of John since his conception. Nevertheless, he had convinced himself that John would one day be a great high priest in the church, in which he would prepare the people for the coming of the Messiah, upon whom the church waited for their salvation.

4 For upon his birth, Zacharias regained his ability to speak, and he prophesied that which the Spirit gave unto him, saying, Blessed be the Lord God of Israel; for he hath visited and redeemed his people, and hath raised up an horn of salvation for us in the house of David, as he spake by the mouth of his holy prophets, which have been since the world began; that we should be saved from our enemies, and from the hand of all that hate us; to perform the mercy promised to our fathers, and to remember his holy covenant, even the oath which he sware to our father Abraham, that he would grant unto us that we, being delivered out of the hand of our enemies, might serve him without fear, in holiness and righteousness before him, all the days of our life.

5 And thou, child, shalt be called the prophet of the Highest: for thou shalt go before the face of the Lord to prepare his ways; to give knowledge of salvation unto his people by the remission of their sins, through the tender mercy of our God; whereby the dayspring from on high hath visited us, to give light to them that sit in darkness and in the shadow of death, to guide our feet into the way of peace.

6 And now, Zacharias had given this prophecy according to his own understanding, which had been given him by the traditions and customs of the church at Jerusalem. For the church taught that the Messiah would be from the house of David, and that this Messiah would save them from their enemies.

7 And the Jewish nation had been destroyed many times, and they were led away into captivity by their enemies. Therefore, it was this enemy that the people believed the Messiah would overthrow and from which he would bring them forth out of captivity and give unto them the land of their inheritance, even that land which they believed they had been promised by the holy prophets, and also according to their understanding of the covenant that the Lord had made with Abraham.

8 And these beliefs of the church led many of the Jews to reject the words of John; for John preached unto them, saying: Why is it that ye think that ye are such a chosen people of God? Behold, your pride blindeth your minds and causeth your stiffneckedness and your inability to understand the truth.

9 Do ye not realize that there were others upon the earth at the time of Abraham who were also the children of God? And do ye not think that they also deserved His love and mercy like unto Abraham? And do ye think that the covenants of God only pertain unto you, because ye are the children of Abraham?

10 And this church, which is established among you according to the law of Moses; what think ye, that this church is the only true and living church upon the face of the whole earth, and that unless a man listeneth to the leaders of this church and receiveth the ordinances therein, that he cannot be saved?

11 And ye believe that ye live by the law of Moses; yet the law of Moses is specific in many things, even in the commandments that the Lord gave unto Moses when your fathers rejected the opportunity to hear them from his own mouth.

And do ye think that in obeying these commandments that ye shall be saved?

12 And ye have already convinced yourselves that ye are obeying the law of Moses, as ye believe, yet ye are in captivity and have been destroyed many times by your enemies, even while ye have been keeping these commandments of Moses as ye suppose them to be kept.

13 And this covenant that the Lord, God made with Abraham, what think ye of it? Behold, the record which ye have among you hath not given you the full account of this covenant that the Lord made with Abraham. For the record speaketh only that the Lord will give unto Abraham and his seed—which ye believe that ye are—the lands of their inheritance.

14 But why is it that ye do not have the lands of your inheritance? Is it that the Lord hath made a lie unto Abraham and hath not done the things which he hath covenanted to do? Behold, I say unto you that the Lord doth not lie, nor can he make a lie.

15 But ye have not remembered the full covenant that he gave unto Abraham. And the full covenant is the same covenant that he giveth unto all of the children of God, even that inasmuch as ye shall keep the commandments of God, ye shall prosper, and shall be given a land of promise; yea, even a land which hath been prepared for you; yea, a land which is choice above all other lands.

16 Now, is not this land of which the Lord hath spoken the land of your fathers? And how is it that ye still do not have this land as your own? Yea, how is it that ye do not prosper in the land of your fathers, but are being held captive by the Romans, who are your leaders? I say unto you, it is because ye do not keep the commandments of God. For if ye would keep the commandments of God, then He would fulfill the covenant that He hath made unto you.

17 And now, all of the holy prophets since the beginning have prophesied and given this covenant unto all the peoples of the earth that they might know God and keep His commandments. And these prophets have given these things unto you as shadows and types of those things which are in heaven.

18 For behold, the covenant of the Father, which is given unto all of His children, is: that if they obey His commandments, then they shall be given a land of promise, even a part of His kingdom and a glory therein.

19 Now, this is the land of promise, even a land of milk and honey, which He hath promised unto all of His children if they keep His commandments. And if they do not keep His commandments, then they shall be in the captivity of Satan, who is the enemy of the covenant of the Father.

20 And now, I say unto you: It mattereth not, according to the flesh, if ye are held in captivity by another nation, for ye have been held in captivity most of the days of your fathers since the days of Abraham, and this because of your wickedness; yea, it mattereth not to God concerning the captivity of the flesh, or that ye do not have a land that ye can call your own. But it mattereth unto God that your souls are not held in captivity by the enemy of all righteousness, who is Satan.

21 And now, the words of prophecy that my father spoke concerning me were true. Nevertheless, they are a type and a shadow of things which are spiritual and not the things which are temporal as ye have supposed.

22 For the church that is among you is a temporal church, which teacheth you of temporal things. But the Spirit is not of the flesh, therefore, it doth not give unto you things that are temporal, but things that are spiritual.

23 And now, my father spoke concerning me, according to the Spirit which gave unto him the words that he did speak, but these things were spiritual because they were given by the Spirit.

24 But ye who are of the flesh and do not have the Spirit cannot understand the things of the Spirit, which are spiritual, but ye suppose all things to be temporal, because that is the only thing that ye understand. And ye have been given this understanding from the church, which is also temporal, and administereth to your temporal needs.

25 And ye are indeed in captivity according to that which is temporal, having been subdued and brought under captivity by the Romans, who have overthrown the other nations that once held the house of Israel captive.

26 But ye are also held captive by Satan, according to things that are spiritual, and it is this captivity and this enemy of which the Spirit spoke by the mouth of my father.

27 And now, so that ye may know without misunderstanding the words of the Spirit that my father spake unto you concerning me, let me give again the words that were given unto my father. But I shall give them in plainness, even according to the Spirit that is in me at this time, so that there shall be no way that ye can misunderstand them:

28 Yea, blessed be the Lord God of Israel; for he shall soon visit his people that he may redeem them of their sins which have held them in captivity. And who hath raised up an horn to sound loud and long, even an horn of salvation that shall sound for us in the house of his servant David.

29 Yea, even as he hath spoken by the mouth of his holy prophets, who have been since the world began, that we should be saved from the captivity of Satan, who is an enemy of God, and from the hand of all those who hate God and keep not His commandments.

30 And that He shall perform mercy to us, that we, the children, might turn our hearts to our fathers, and to remember the holy covenant that He gave unto them, even that if we obey His commandments, then we shall be given a land of promise, even a part of the kingdom of God and a glory therein.

31 And that He would grant unto us, that we, being delivered out of the hand of Satan by which we are bound because of our wickedness, might serve Him without fear of Him, even that we might not fear facing Him at his judgment bar where we shall be judged for the works that we have done. For we shall not fear Him if we live in holiness and righteousness before Him all the days of our life.

32 And thou, child, shalt be called as one of the prophets of the Highest, for like those who have gone before thee, thou shalt go before the face of the Lord, who is shortly to come, to prepare his ways and teach his people his true commandments, which they do not receive in the church to which they belong; to take away their stumbling blocks that they may be prepared to learn the true doctrine of Christ, and give unto them knowledge of eternal salvation, so that they might keep the true commandments of God and receive a remission of their sins through the tender mercy of our Father.

33 And this mercy which hath been given unto us is already among us and shall come as the dayspring from on high to give light to all of us who sit in darkness. And in the shadow of death that shall come upon us because of our sins, we shall receive the light that will light the path which is straight and narrow that will guide our feet into the way of eternal peace in the kingdom of our Father.

34 And now, this light that I have described unto you, even that which will light the path of righteousness that ye must follow, is the very Christ who shall save you from the enemy of all righteousness.

35 And he shall not save you from your temporal enemies, which are the other nations of the earth that hold you captive, for these temporal things are not as important to him as the things that are spiritual.

36 And the Messiah, who hath been spoken of by all the holy prophets since the beginning, is a Savior who shall save you in the kingdom of the Father; yea, even a kingdom that was made without the hands of man.

37 And this kingdom is an eternal kingdom where there shall be peace and happiness, which is the milk and honey according to the blessings and the covenant that the Father hath promised us from the beginning.

38 And he shall save you by teaching you the true commandments of God, which are much more than the law of Moses, which law was given to point us towards this Messiah, who shall give us the law of God.

39 For if it is the law of Moses, then it is the law of a man, and is given unto us for our temporal salvation. But the laws of God are eternal and have been given for our eternal salvation.

40 And if ye would have kept the law of Moses, then it would have been possible that ye would have not been held in captivity by your enemies which are temporal.

41 And the law of Moses taught you, saying: I am the Lord thy God, who hath brought thee out of the land of Egypt, out of the house of bondage. Thou shalt have no other God before me. Thou shalt not make unto thee any graven image, or any likeness of any thing in heaven above, or things which are in the earth beneath.

42 And now, have ye done all this? I say unto you, that ye have not done these things. And your church and your leaders have spoken these words unto you, but they do not keep these words, and have pretended to give unto you examples of righteousness by their works; but their examples have been the cause of your own unrighteousness.

43 For ye believe that the leaders of your church are the mouthpieces of God, and that there are no other mouthpieces of God on earth. Yet, they have given you the law of Moses by their mouths, but they do not obey it, and cause you to not obey it by their own examples.

44 For the commandment is that ye shall not make unto you any graven image, or any likeness of any thing in heaven above, or things which are in the earth beneath.

45 And what think ye of your riches, and the riches of your church and its leaders? Yea, even the glorious synagogues and temples that ye have caused to be constructed among you; are not these things which are in the earth beneath?

46 Do ye think that a house of God would be made in such worldly glory and splendor? And the ostentatiousness of these things, do ye believe that God is pleased with these things when there are those among you who do not have enough food to eat, or raiment to wear, or a shelter in which to live? Do ye think that God dwelleth in tabernacles made by the hands of men, even those that are made and dedicated unto Him, while His children sleep without its walls without shelter?

47 Behold, I say unto you, that your riches and your precious things and your desires for these things are your gods, and in this way ye disobey the law of Moses. And because of these things, ye have caused other nations to lust after and covet your riches and come in among you and destroy you and carry off your riches and your precious things.

48 And because ye suffered that the majority among you do not have sufficient for their needs, they could not raise their hand in your defense, nor did they desire to do so, believing that they might receive for their sustenance from the nations that came upon you.

49 And now, I, Moroni, have translated many of the words that the brother of Jared wrote concerning that which he saw of John and his preaching.

50 And John continued his preaching to the people and to the church at Jerusalem. And as I read the words of the brother of Jared, which he wrote concerning John, I saw the similarity of the words that John spoke to the words that my father wrote concerning the prophet Abinadi, which he spoke unto the church among the Nephites that had become corrupt under the reign of the wicked King Noah and his priests.

51 And I have been instructed by the Spirit to finish the words of John by the words which Abinadi spoke, thus showing unto those who receive this record how the Lord speaketh the same words to one prophet that he speaketh to all of his prophets.

52 And both John and Abinadi spoke very much the same words, saying: And now I read unto you the remainder of the commandments of God, for I perceive that they are not written in your hearts; I perceive that ye have studied and taught iniquity the most part of your lives.

53 And now, ye remember that I said unto you: Thou shalt not make unto thee any graven image, or any likeness of things which are in heaven above, or which are in the earth beneath, or which are in the water under the earth. And again: Thou shalt not bow down thyself unto them, nor serve them; for I the Lord thy God am a jealous God, visiting the iniquities of the fathers upon the children, unto the third and fourth generations of them that hate me; and showing mercy unto thousands of them that love me and keep my commandments.

54 Thou shalt not take the name of the Lord thy God in vain; for the Lord will not hold him guiltless who taketh his name in vain.

55 Remember the sabbath day, to keep it holy. Six days shalt thou labor, and do all thy work, but the seventh day, the sabbath of the Lord thy

God, thou shalt not do any work, thou, nor thy son, nor thy daughter, nor thy man-servant, nor thy maid-servant, nor thy cattle, nor the stranger that is within thy gates; for in six days the Lord made heaven and earth, and the sea, and all that in them is; wherefore the Lord blessed the sabbath day, and hallowed it.

56 Honor thy father and thy mother, that thy days may be long upon the land which the Lord thy God giveth thee.

57 Thou shalt not kill. Thou shalt not commit adultery. Thou shalt not steal. Thou shalt not bear false witness against thy neighbor. Thou shalt not covet the house of thy neighbor, thou shalt not covet the wife of thy neighbor, nor his man-servant, nor his maid-servant, nor his ox, nor his ass, nor anything that is of thy neighbor.

58 Have ye taught this people that they should observe to do all these things for to keep these commandments? I say unto you, Nay; for if ye had, the Lord would not have caused me to come forth and to prophesy evil concerning this people.

59 And now, ye have said that salvation cometh by the law of Moses. I say unto you that it is expedient that ye should keep the law of Moses as yet; but I say unto you, that the time shall come when it shall no more be expedient to keep the law of Moses.

60 And moreover, I say unto you, that salvation doth not come by the law alone; and were it not for the atonement, which God himself shall make for the sins and iniquities of his people, that they must unavoidably perish, notwithstanding the law of Moses.

61 And now, I say unto you that it was expedient that there should be a law given to the children of Israel, yea, even a very strict law; for they were a stiffnecked people, quick to do iniquity, and slow to remember the Lord their God; Therefore there was a law given them, yea, a law of performances and of ordinances, a law which they were to observe strictly from day to day, to keep them in remembrance of God and their duty towards him.

62 But behold, I say unto you, that all these things were types of things to come. And now, did they understand the law? I say unto you, Nay, they did not all understand the law; and this because of the hardness of their hearts; for they understood not that there could not any man be saved except it were through the redemption of God.

63 For behold, did not Moses prophesy unto them concerning the coming of the Messiah, and that God should redeem his people? Yea, and even all the prophets who have prophesied since the world began, have they not spoken more or less concerning these things? Have they not said that God himself should come down among the children of men, and take upon him the form of man, and go forth in mighty power upon the face of the earth?

64 Yea, and have they not said also that he should bring to pass the resurrection of the dead, and that he, himself, should be oppressed and afflicted?

65 I would that ye should understand that God himself shall come down among the children of men, and shall redeem his people. And because he dwelleth in flesh, he shall be called the Son of God, and having subjected the flesh to the will of the Father, being the Father and the Son; the Father, because he was conceived by the power of God; and the Son, because of the flesh; thus becoming the Father and Son; and they are one God, yea, the very Eternal Father of heaven and of earth.

66 And thus the flesh becoming subject to the Spirit, or the Son to the Father, being one God, suffereth temptation, and yieldeth not to the temptation, but suffereth himself to be mocked, and scourged, and cast out, and disowned by his people.

67 And after all this, after working many mighty miracles among the children of men, he shall be led, yea, even as Isaiah said, as a sheep before the shearer is dumb, so he opened not his mouth. Yea, even so he shall be led, crucified, and slain, the flesh becoming subject even unto death, the will of the Son being swallowed up in the will of the Father.

68 And thus God breaketh the bands of death, having gained the victory over death; giving the Son power to make intercession for the children of men. Having ascended into heaven; having the bowels of mercy; being filled with compassion towards the children of men;

standing betwixt them and justice; having broken the bands of death and taken upon himself their iniquity and their transgressions; having redeemed them and satisfied the demands of justice.

69 And now, I say unto you, who shall declare his generation? Behold, I say unto you, that when his soul hath been made an offering for sin, he shall see his seed. And now what say ye? And who shall be his seed?

70 Behold I say unto you, that whosoever hath heard the words of the prophets, yea, all the holy prophets who have prophesied concerning the coming of the Lord, I say unto you, that all those who have hearkened unto their words, and believed that the Lord would redeem his people, and have looked forward to that day for a remission of their sins, I say unto you, that these are his seed, or they are heirs of the kingdom of God.

71 For these are they whose sins he hath borne; these are they for whom he hath died, to redeem them from their transgressions. And now, are they not his seed? Yea, and are not the prophets, every one who hath opened his mouth to prophesy, who hath not fallen into transgression, I mean all the holy prophets ever since the world began?

72 For were it not for the redemption which he hath made for his people, which was prepared from the foundation of the world, I say unto you, were it not for this, all mankind must have perished.

73 But behold, the bands of death shall be broken, and the Son reigneth, and hath power over the dead; therefore, he bringeth to pass the resurrection of the dead. And there cometh a resurrection, even a first resurrection; yea, even a resurrection of those who have been, and who are, and who shall be, even until the resurrection of Christ.

74 And now, the resurrection of all the prophets, and all those who have believed in their words, or all those who have kept the commandments of God, shall come forth in the first resurrection; therefore, they are the first resurrection. They are raised to dwell with God who hath redeemed them; thus they have eternal life through Christ, who hath broken the bands of death.

75 And these are those who have part in the first resurrection; and these are they who have died before Christ came, in their ignorance, not having salvation declared unto them. And thus the Lord bringeth about the restoration of these; and they have a part in the first resurrection, or have eternal life, being redeemed by the Lord. And little children also have eternal life.

76 But behold, and fear, and tremble before God, for ye ought to tremble; for the Lord redeemeth none such that rebel against him and die in their sins; yea, even all those who have perished in their sins ever since the world began, who have wilfully rebelled against God, who have known the commandments of God and would not keep them; these are they who have no part in the first resurrection.

77 Therefore ought ye not to tremble? For salvation cometh to none such; for the Lord hath redeemed none such; yea, neither can the Lord redeem such; for he cannot deny himself; for he cannot deny justice when it hath its claim.

78 And now, I say unto you that the time shall come that the salvation of the Lord shall be declared to every nation, kindred, tongue, and people. Yea, Lord, thy watchmen shall lift up their voice; with the voice together shall they sing; for they shall see eye to eye, when the Lord shall bring again Zion. Break forth into joy, sing together, ye waste places of Jerusalem; for the Lord hath comforted his people, he hath redeemed Jerusalem.

79 The Lord hath made bare his holy arm in the eyes of all the nations; and all the ends of the earth shall see the salvation of our God. Yea, the time shall come when all shall see the salvation of the Lord; when every nation, kindred, tongue, and people shall see eye to eye and shall confess before God that his judgments are just.

80 And then shall the wicked be cast out, and they shall have cause to howl, and weep, and wail, and gnash their teeth; and this because they would not hearken unto the voice of the Lord; therefore the Lord redeemeth them not. For they are carnal and devilish, and the devil hath power over them; yea, even that old serpent that did beguile our first parents, which was the cause of their fall; which was the cause of all mankind becoming carnal, sensual, devilish, knowing evil from good, subjecting themselves to the devil.

81 Thus all mankind were lost; and behold, they would have been endlessly lost were it not that God redeemed his people from their lost and fallen state. But remember that he that persisteth in his own carnal nature, and goeth on in the ways of sin and rebellion against God, remaineth in his fallen state and the devil hath all power over him. Therefore, he is as though there was no redemption made, being an enemy to God; and also is the devil an enemy to God.

82 And now if Christ had not come into the world there could have been no redemption. And if Christ is not risen from the dead, or if he doth not break the bands of death that the grave should have no victory, and that death should have no sting, there could be no resurrection.

83 But there is a resurrection, therefore the grave hath no victory, and the sting of death is swallowed up in Christ. He is the light and the life of the world; yea, a light that is endless, that can never be darkened; yea, and also a life which is endless, that there can be no more death.

84 Even this mortal shall put on immortality, and this corruption shall put on incorruption, and shall be brought to stand before the bar of God, to be judged of him according to their works whether they be good or whether they be evil.

85 If they be good, to the resurrection of endless life and happiness; and if they be evil, to the resurrection of endless damnation, being delivered up to the devil, who hath subjected them, which is damnation, having gone according to their own carnal wills and desires; having never called upon the Lord while the arms of mercy were extended towards them; for the arms of mercy were extended towards them, and they would not; they being warned of their iniquities and yet they would not depart from them; and they were commanded to repent and yet they would not repent.

86 And now, ought ye not to tremble and repent of your sins, and remember that only in and through Christ can ye be saved? Therefore, if ye teach the law of Moses, also teach that it is a shadow of those things which are now among you. Teach them that redemption cometh through Christ the Lord, who is the very Eternal Father.

CHAPTER 39

The apostolic calling and preparation of the twelve apostles is explained. The latter day LDS Church leaders are commanded to repent. All prophets and apostles are given the experiences that will help them perform their missions. The opinions of the apostles differ from that which they receive from the Spirit.

AND it came to pass that after John had spoken these words unto the people, his father Zacharias withdrew himself from John and would have nothing further to do with his son, and this because of his pride and his position in the church.

2 But it came to pass that there were many, more especially among the poor, who came unto John and were baptized again—they having first been baptized in the church, according to the law of Moses—that they might make a new covenant with God to keep the commandments that John had given them, and which they would receive from the Christ.

3 Yet, the people believed on John, and knew not of the Christ of whom he spoke. And there were many among them who were young and of the age of maturity where they were no longer under the supervision and authority of their parents.

4 And there were those who became the disciples of John, because they had witnessed the hypocrisy of the church and found out for themselves that the leaders of the church at Jerusalem were misleading the people and teaching things which caused discord and confusion among them.

5 And there was a certain group among them that met often and discussed the things of God, and also those things of the church which they knew were not the things of God.

6 And they were Andrew and his brother, who was called Simon, who was also known as Peter, and Philip and Nathanael, who was also known as Bartholomew.

7 And these were from a city near unto Jerusalem. And they would meet together often and become distressed in the spirit because of the things that they witnessed of the people of

the church at Jerusalem. And they spoke of the scriptures and searched them when they could that they might gain a better understanding of the words of the prophets than that which the leaders of the church had taught them.

8 And these were being wrought upon by the Spirit and by the ministrations of the spirit world to prepare them for their foreordained callings as apostles of Jesus, even the twelve who would be commissioned to preach the gospel of Christ after his ascension to the Father.

9 And the brother of Jared saw the lives, in brevity, of each of the disciples of Christ who would become his apostles while he was with them on the earth. And they were righteous men who were curious in nature and unable to accept the orthodox views and teachings of their fathers.

10 And the brother of Jared gave particular mention unto Nathanael, who was one of the most learned among them. For he had studied much concerning the ways of the world, and also the things of God.

11 And he could not understand the reasons for the contentions and misery of the people when there was so much knowledge among them that could create peace and happiness.

12 And he strove for many days with the Spirit that he might understand the things which were true, even those things that he could do to bring peace among his people.

13 And he had a place where he would go of which no one of his friends or family knew. And in this place, he would ponder the things of God and pray for understanding and wisdom. And he sat for many days under a fig tree that he had chosen for a rest, and up against which he struggled with his intellect and the gentle persuasions that were given unto him by the Spirit.

14 Yet, he was prideful in that which he had learned among men, and did not give in to the enticings of the Spirit until it came to pass that Jesus told him of the fig tree under which he strove with the Spirit, and of which he had told no living soul.

15 And because Jesus knew these things of him, Nathanael was converted and became a great asset unto the twelve after the ascension of the Lord.

16 And now, the record of the Jews accounteth for very little of the lives of the men who were the apostles of Christ during mortality.

17 But the brother of Jared saw the workings of those who would bring forth the Bible and include therein some of the accounts of those who were with Jesus when he ministered unto the people.

18 And those who brought forth this work, or in other words, those who prepared that which was to be included in the Bible as the testament of the life of Christ, were rich men who were proud of their positions of authority in the church that had been formed among them at the time that the canon of this scripture was organized and presented to the world as the only authority of the works and life of Christ.

19 And these leaders formed a council to represent them. And they had records which were written by the original apostles of Jesus Christ among them. But these rich leaders were prideful and knew that their own lives did not exemplify the lives of the men who had been chosen by Jesus to be his apostles.

20 And for this reason, they did not include many of the words of the apostles, nor did they give a full accounting of their works or their lives before they became apostles of the Lord.

21 And it shall be revealed in this record of the coming forth of the Bible and the manner in which it shall come forth. And I know that this record hath recently come forth among those on the other continent where the Jews reside, for the Lord hath discussed these things with me when he visited me and gave me a greater insight into his life and those things that he would have me include in this record concerning his life and his ministry.

22 And the purpose of the Lord is to show unto the elect that he loveth them, and that he is their brother, and that he is very much like them in every way, even that he laugheth and he crieth, and he feeleth pain and sorrow. And he would that we should know that he was like unto all of us during the days of his probation, but that he lived below all men that he might be a means whereby others might be lifted up because of him; he being an example of one who is abased who shall be exalted.

23 And those whom he called to be his apostles were men who were not chained with the yoke of customs and traditions that keep the children of men from finding the truth. They were men of integrity and curiosity who were often considered outcasts and nonconformists in the society of people in which they lived.

24 And they did not accept the teachings of those in authority over them as the infallible truth; for their hearts told them otherwise; and it was in this that they were influenced and administered to by the Holy Ghost from their youth.

25 And they were gentle men, who were peacemakers, yet who stood for that which they felt was right, even if it meant giving up their families and their traditions and their beliefs to pursue that which they believed was right.

26. And they were men who were humble as to the things of the world, for they desired not riches and worldly success, nor did they aspire to the honors and glories of men.

27 And this Nathanael of whom I have made mention, was educated and instructed in many things, even many of the ways of the Romans and their government. And he was also instructed in the traditions of his father, which were the strict traditions of the Sadducees among the Jews, who dealt more directly with the letter of the law, which was believed among them.

28 But Nathanael believed not in the opinions that others of his same level of education had concluded, and knew within himself that there existed a way that all men and woman could be treated with justice and equality, both by the Roman government, and also by the church of the Jews. And because of his beliefs, he was an outcast who had very few friends with whom he could speak concerning those things which he felt within him.

29 And he became friends with the sons of Jonah, which Jonah was a high ranking official in the church of the Jews that controlled many of the affairs of the people under the guidance of the high priests.

30 And it had happened that Peter and Andrew were present when John had argued with his father Zacharias, a high priest, when Zacharias was engaged in officiating in his office and calling within the church. And they believed on the words of John; and from that time forward did not return again unto the church, nor did they pay their tithes and offerings, because of those things which they heard from the mouth of John concerning the abuses of the church.

31 And they met often with Phillip who was also in attendance at the church when John rebuked his father before the people. And they were all in their youth at this time, but held all these things in their hearts and contemplated that which the Spirit bore witness unto them as they grew in maturity.

32 And when John returned once again into the land of Jerusalem and began to preach unto the people, Andrew was among those whom he taught at the time he baptized the Lord and witnessed of his divinity to the people.

33 And now, it is expedient that ye understand the reason why the Lord doth not choose his leaders from among the rich and the successful and those who have received the honors and glories of men.

34 For I say unto you, that no prophet or apostle of God hath ever been, nor ever shall be chosen from among those who are rich and successful and have the honors and glories of men, except it be that they first acknowledge the errors of their ways and humble themselves and cast these things from them; that they might prove unto the people, whom they would lead, that they are the humble followers of Christ, who are committed to following in his footsteps.

35 And now, concerning the latter days and this great church in which shall come forth the unsealed portion of this record, I have seen your works, and I know that ye choose from among you those who are rich and successful and who have been given the honors and glories of men to be your prophets and your apostles.

36 And by this shall the people know that ye are not inspired men of God, but that ye are servants of Satan who blind the eyes and harden the hearts of the children of men to the fruits of the Spirit, because ye enjoy the fruits of the flesh in abundance.

37 And because ye enjoy the fruits of the flesh in abundance, ye have convinced the people that these fruits are evidence of your callings as apostles and prophets, because ye suppose that the Lord hath blessed you with these things.

38 But I have already explained unto you that the Father doth not bless His children that they might put themselves one above another, but He hath commanded them against such a thing.

39 And ye of the latter days are like unto those at the time of Jesus, who persecuted him and mocked him, and also who mocked his apostles because they were not rich and successful and did not aspire to the honors and glories of men.

40 And ye are those of whom Jesus spoke when he said: The scribes and the Pharisees sit in the seat of Moses; all therefore whatsoever they bid you observe, that observe and do; but do not ye after their works; for they say, and do not.

41 For behold, in the Spirit, I have seen the manner in which ye deceive the people. And I have also read much concerning you in the words of the brother of Jared, which he wrote, saying: And they speak in kindness, using gentle voices, which appear unto the people as the servants of God, who are humble and contrite.

42 And their manner of speech is the same, even that they practice that which they give unto the people before they give it, so that it may conform with the gentleness and manner that the people have been accustomed to hearing from them.

43 And they speak the words of Christ, and tell the people in their kind words and their pretended mannerisms, that they are the prophets, seers, and revelators of the Lord, and that the people should listen to their words, and that they will not be misled by them.

44 And with their words and their mannerisms and the means of the great church which they have caused to be established among them, even with the riches and fine things of the world, they lead the people away carefully and subtlety from the true gospel of Christ and teach unto them of their traditions and their customs, which are the precepts and commandments of men.

45 For they deny the Holy Ghost and dare not speak unto the people by the power of the Holy Ghost, which hath given utterance unto all the prophets of God since the beginning. For their speeches and their mannerisms are given unto them by their church, which shall establish for them the way that they should speak and what things they should say unto the people.

46 And now, I, Moroni, ask of ye of the latter days, How can these leaders be true prophets of God? Have ye heard a true prophet of God speak? I say unto you that ye have not. For ye are like unto the Jews, who were accustomed to listening to their leaders, which leaders taught them all that they desired to understand.

47 And when a true prophet of God came among them, they did not recognize him, having been conditioned to only hear the words as they are given by their leaders, which are not inspired by the Holy Ghost, but by the workings of men.

48 For behold, when a prophet speaketh with the power of the Spirit, he speaketh with authority, even an authority which causeth all the wicked to be angry at that which he speaketh. And are all the Jews righteous? Yet, when their leaders speak, they are not angry, but they feel the Spirit, as they suppose, which causeth them to justify their complacency in keeping the true commandments of God.

49 For their leaders do not say anything that will stir up anger among the people; for if the people are angry, then they will withdraw their support from their leaders and seek out other leaders which will preach unto them the things that will not cause them to be angry.

50 And for this reason the Lord calleth forth those who are not of the world, and who are not bound down by the foolish traditions of men to be his prophets and his apostles.

51 And I say unto those of you of the latter days, even ye who have put yourselves up as the prophets and apostles of Christ; Yea, seek out he who hath given unto you this sealed portion, and cause him to speak unto you by the power of the Holy Ghost.

52 And I say unto you, that he shall condemn you in your words and shall make ye a thing of naught among the people who might be listening to you, even as John did his father

Zacharias, which caused many to think on the things of the church and reject those things which are not of God. Yea, seek out this bearer of Christ that shall have this record.

53 But I have seen your works already. And I know that ye shall not seek out this last prophet of God who shall give unto you this sealed portion of the record of my father, for ye are afraid that he will rebuke you and take away the authority of your words from among you, even in front of the people.

54 For if the people would hear his words, even if they could see the manner in which he speaketh and by what spirit he speaketh, then they shall see the difference between him and you, even that he hath the Spirit of God, and ye do not.

55 And his knowledge of the mysteries of God shall astound you and make you afraid lest the people follow him and not you. But he shall not allow the people to follow him as ye have allowed them to follow you. For he shall give the glory and honor to the Father, who deserveth this glory and honor, which is not a glory and honor of men, which ye have, but is the glory and honor of the Spirit, which ye do not have.

56 And in your pride ye shall seek deep to hide your counsels from the Lord and shall make an attempt to make this prophet a thing of naught among the people. And this ye shall do by your lies and your deceitfulness and by your secret combinations which ye have established among you.

57 And ye shall wonder after this prophet and shall imagine in your hearts that ye had the ability that he shall have in bringing forth the truth unto the people.

58 And when the day of the Lord shall come, what say ye then when the Lord shall call forth this prophet, whom ye have attempted to make a thing of naught among you, and shall make him a ruler over you; and show unto all the people of your sins and your wickedness, even as ye have proclaimed unto them that ye were prophets and apostles of the Lord.

59 And now, I would that ye should know, even ye leaders of the church of Jesus Christ of the latter days, that this doth not have to come to pass in this manner. For the arm of the Lord shall be outstretched unto you all the days of your lives. And if ye shall accept these things that shall come forth unto you, and also accept him who shall bring these things among you, even this bearer of Christ of whom I have spoken, then shall the Lord soften the hearts of the people that they shall understand your follies and your misunderstandings.

60 And if ye repent and follow the counsel and advice of this prophet of God, who shall be patient with you and give you all things in kindness and with understanding, then ye shall maintain your positions and authority among the people and be a means of much righteousness among the people in preparing the elect for the great and wondrous day of the coming of the Lord in all of his glory.

61 But if ye persist in your pride, and reject these things as it hath been shown unto me, then the day of the Lord shall be great and dreadful unto you, and ye shall be cast aside as a thing of naught and the whole world shall see you and mock you for that which ye thought of yourselves.

62 And now, my beloved brethren, yea, even those of you who have put yourselves up as prophets and apostles of the Lord Jesus Christ, repent ye and come unto the Lord. Preach unto the people the words of Christ, which are already among you, and which shall be given unto you in this record.

63 Embrace these words and cause the world to rejoice in that which the Father hath done to redeem all of His children. Yea, be a friend of Christ, and not his enemy.

64 And now, I have said these things unto you that ye might know further concerning the manner of men that the Lord calleth to serve him as apostles and prophets. For in their youth, they are tried and tested by and through all the follies and experiences of youth.

65 And in many instances they do err and keep not the commandments of God in all things, and run contrary to the Spirit that hath been given unto them to prepare them for the work which they have been foreordained to do.

66 For by their experiences, they shall have a greater understanding of that which they shall preach unto the people. For how can a man among you preach concerning that which ye should do, when he hath not done that thing which he expecteth of you? In other words, how can he know for a surety that that which he requireth of you is that which he knoweth shall bring you happiness, if it so be that he hath not experienced the opposite of this happiness himself?

67 And for this reason, all the prophets and apostles of the Lord shall be refined and taught in their youth, that they may be more fully prepared for that which they have been called to do. And this refinement shall cause many of you to look at them as sinners, for as such viewed them the Jews, who witnessed the types of men that Jesus had called.

68 Nevertheless, except in a few instances, shall any of these men, who have been called of God, do unto others that which they would not have done unto them. For this is the essence of their spirits, and it is also the essence of all the true commandments of God.

69 But those who pass through the fires of refinement shall know of their sins, and these sins shall cause them immediate unhappiness. And those who do not pass through this fire, receive no such unhappiness from the sins that they do. And because most do not experience immediate unhappiness in their sins, they begin to justify their actions as righteousness, and this because of their pride.

70 Nevertheless, in the end, shall all experience the punishment of their sins. But he who hath passed through the fire of refinement shall acknowledge all of his sins and justify none.

71 And all of the men who were called to be apostles to the Lord during the time of his ministry were refined men, who have been through the refining fire of the Spirit and have been prepared from the beginning.

72 And now, it is not important to point out the various facts of the individual lives of these apostles. And if ye knew of their lives as I know of them, then I would think that those among you, who are wicked, would misjudge them and concern yourselves more with your judgments of them than ye would with the message that they were commanded to give unto the world.

73 Nevertheless, there is one thing that the Spirit would have me write unto you concerning these apostles of the Lord. For I have seen that this thing hath been a source of much contention and misery among you of the latter days. And this contention hath been caused because ye do not understand the words of Christ, nor do ye have the Spirit of Christ, which would keep you from becoming contentious one with another.

74 And now, it is written among you in the words of a later apostle of Christ, even he who was once called Saul, and who, upon changing his life and repenting of his sins, became known as Paul.

75 And many of the words that ye have been given in the scriptures that ye accept as the words of God, are the words of Paul. And there are some of the words of Paul that were inspired of the Holy Ghost, yea, even most of the words of Paul were so inspired.

76 But if ye read the record, ye shall come to know of some contention between Paul and other of the disciples that were with Jesus in the flesh. And the record reads, saying: And some day after Paul said unto Barnabas, Let us go again and visit our brethren in every city where we have preached the word of the Lord, and see how they do.

77 And Barnabas determined to take with them John, whose surname was Mark. But Paul thought it not good to take him with them, who departed from them from Pamphylia, and went not with them to the work. And the contention was so sharp between them, that they departed asunder one from the other; and so Barnabas took Mark, and sailed unto Cyprus; And Paul chose Silas, and departed, being recommended by the brethren unto the grace of God.

78 And now, I, Moroni, have been commanded by the Lord himself to correct this account of the record, that ye shall know the truth behind the contentions of Paul and Barnabas.

79 And that which I shall reveal unto you shall be a means of much rejoicing unto many of our brothers and sisters in the latter days, yea, even many of the children of God who have lived in fear of repression and persecution for that happiness which they have chosen for themselves.

80 For behold, Barnabas and John were

united as one in the flesh, evensomuch that they loved each other and slept with each other as a man sleepeth with a woman.

81 And Paul knew of this before and had brought the matter before the other apostles of the Lord who had been with the Lord in the flesh. For Paul was not with the Lord in the flesh and did not see those things which were done among them in the flesh.

82 And Barnabas and John were united in the flesh even in the presence of the Lord, who upon seeing them together said of them: Surely these two love each other exceedingly. O, that there was a man that could love his wife even as John loveth Barnabas. Truly they shall be together in the kingdom of our Father as one.

83 And now, this caused some contention among the other apostles at the time, but they did not rebuke the Lord in that which he said, knowing of themselves that he was truly the Son of God.

84 And now, I, Moroni, have been commanded to expound upon these things that I have revealed unto you. For I have already written unto you that we all have our choice of happiness, according to our individual desires of happiness.

85 And those of our brothers and sisters who desire to be with another brother or sister, who is of the same gender, are justified in this thing according to the flesh.

86 Nevertheless, they are under the same commandments that the Lord hath given to a man concerning a woman, even that a man shall not lust after another man, or a woman, if he hath so committed himself to another.

87 And if a man loveth another man, in which way doth he disobey the words of Christ? Did Christ not teach us that we should love one another? And why should we think that these men who desire to be with each other shall be condemned for that which they do, when we sin in becoming angry at them and persecuting them contrary to the words of Christ?

88 Behold, I say unto you, that they shall also be saved in the kingdom of God. Now they shall not inherit the Celestial kingdom of God, which is reserved for those who use the power of procreation to serve others by providing bodies for the spirit children of God. But they shall be together as friends in the other kingdoms of glory that the Father hath prepared for us based upon our individual desires of happiness.

89 And again, I say unto you, search the words of Christ. Wherein doth he command a man that he shall not lie with another man? I say unto you that he doth not. Behold, the words of Paul say these things, and the words of others who have not spoken by the power of the Spirit, but by the power of their own minds, which have been prejudiced and biased by the traditions and customs among them.

90 And if ye could have all the words of Christ, which he taught to his disciples, then ye would know of these things. But the leaders who have brought forth the words of the Bible, have kept these things from you, believing that they are not the words of Christ, nor should they be made known, and that this thing should not be justified among those of their church.

91 And again, all of the commandments of God are based upon this one true commandment that ye shall love another as ye would have them love you. Therefore, search the words of Christ, not the words of men.

92 And it came to pass that Paul could not travel with Barnabas and John together; though with one, he could do that which the Lord had commanded him, having been chastened by the other apostles in his views that a man should not be with another man.

93 Nevertheless, Paul preached his own doctrine at times unto the people, and misled them in that which he wrote unto them, having given unto them his own opinions and not according to the Spirit of God.

94 Nevertheless, had those who brought forth the words of the Bible left it untouched and unedited by their own hands, which editions were guided by their prejudices and biases, then the full truth regarding these things might have been made known unto the world.

95 And if these things had been made known at the time these things came forth among the children of men, then there would have been less suffering and persecution of those who love one another.

96 And it is important that ye should remember not to judge those who have been called of God to give unto you His gospel, but of their works which are present, shall ye judge them.

97 For that which is in their past shall manifest itself in the works that they perform in the future, or which are manifested in the present. For if they are truly called of God, then at their appointed time, even the time that they shall be called forth to come unto you by the power of the Holy Spirit, then ye shall know of a surety that they shall be ready; and they shall give unto you the words of Christ.

98 And ye shall prove them therein; and if they do the works of Christ, which they show unto you, then ye shall have a sure witness that they have been called of God.

99 And each of the apostles of God were chosen and foreordained to do that which they were appointed to do in the beginning. And each was prepared from the beginning to do that which they were appointed to do. And surely, they have all done that which they were appointed to do, even giving their own lives for the words of Christ.

CHAPTER 40

The baptism of Christ is explained and John prophesies of the Christ. Moroni uses the words of Nephi to reiterate the words of John that he saw in a vision. John's mission in the latter days is revealed. Moroni concurs with the testimony of Nephi and John.

AND now, it is expedient once again to return to the account of the prophet John who prepared the way for the introduction of the Christ unto the people.

2 For it came to pass that the time finally arrived when the Lord was allowed to begin his ministry among the Jews according to their laws and customs.

3 For in all things the Lord obeyed the laws of the Jews, that he might draw them unto him and not push them away from him, giving them a cause to harden their hearts against his word.

4 For behold, the church was established among them; and if the Lord could have gone unto the leaders of the church and given them his words, that they might then give them unto the people, who already had accepted the leaders of the church as the mouthpieces of God; yea, if he could have done this thing, then he would have found a means; even the very means for this purpose that he suffered to be established among them in the days of Moses, even that he might more successfully give his words unto the people of the church.

5 But the leaders of the church had already rejected him, he having been among them previously and taught them his words as they sat in their temples and in their synagogues.

6 And Jesus waited patiently until the time came that he reached the age that a man was accepted as worthy and ready to preach the word of God. And because a church had been established among them, it was a necessity that he do those things which were expected of the church, even that he should be baptized according to their traditions.

7 And this the Lord hath commanded of all of his prophets, even that they try first to give his words to the churches which have been established among the children of men, from which the children of men are accustomed to hearing the words of God.

8 And if the leaders of these churches repent and accept the words of God, then the prophet that hath given these words unto them, shall be commanded to act as a counselor and an adviser to them, so that the authority and order of the priesthood is not disrupted.

9 For if the authority of the priesthood is disrupted, then the children of men might not know where they should go for direction, and this because they do not have the Spirit to guide them.

10 And thus it is that order may be established in all things. For all things which are temporal are given in a likeness of those things which are spiritual. And there is an order in heaven, and the authority to maintain this order resideth in the power and authority of the Holy Order of the Son of God, this being the Holy Priesthood that the Father established to do His will.

11 And the temporal ordinances that are given unto the children of men in their churches, are given unto them as examples and in the likeness of those things which are done in heaven.

12 And Jesus knew that he had to maintain this order and set an example of himself that others should follow, even that they should know that they should be humble and comply with the ordinances of the priesthood in the flesh, if these ordinances are given in the likeness of the things which are in heaven, and are administered by those who are righteous.

13 And for this reason, the Lord did not go unto the church of God at Jerusalem to be baptized, but sought out John and commanded him that he should baptize him to fulfill all righteousness and maintain the order of which I have spoken.

14 For John had already been rejected by the church, and was baptizing the people anew and giving unto them the new and everlasting covenant, which was the commandments that the Lord would give unto them by the Holy Ghost and also by his own words.

15 And now, I, Moroni, once again call upon the words that have already been revealed unto you, even in the part of this record that was not sealed, to teach you further of these things.

16 For once again John spoke these exact same words unto the Jews, even the words which Nephi beheld that John would give unto them in the vision that Nephi received from an angel of God.

17 And after Nephi had seen these things, he remembered the words which John spoke after he had baptized the Lord and witnessed the sign of the dove, which had been prophesied unto him in his youth by an angel of God, that he might know that he had completed the mission that was required of him.

18 For it came to pass that many of the Jews who were gathered unto John and witnessed the baptism of the Lord, these did question John and ask of him concerning the Lord and why the Christ was in need of a baptism, seeing that it was by him that they were covenanting with the Father, as John had taught them.

19 And John answered them. And the words that he answered to them were the same words that Nephi heard of him in his vision. And John answered them, saying: And now, if the Christ, he being holy, should have need to be baptized by water, to fulfill all righteousness, oh then, how much more need have we, being unholy, to be baptized, yea, even by water?

20 And now, I would ask of you, my beloved brethren, wherein the Christ did fulfill all righteousness in being baptized by water? Know ye not that he was holy? But notwithstanding he being holy, he showeth unto you that, according to the flesh, he humbleth himself before the Father, and witnesseth unto the Father that he would be obedient unto Him in keeping His commandments.

21 Therefore, after he was baptized with water, the Holy Ghost descended upon him in the form of a dove, which ye have witnessed at this time. And again, it showeth unto you the straightness of the path, and the narrowness of the gate by which ye should enter, he having set the example before you.

22 And now, I say unto you that ye should follow him, yea, even he hath commanded you to follow him. Therefore, my beloved brethren, can we follow Jesus save we shall be willing to keep the commandments of the Father?

23 And the Father said: Repent ye, repent ye, and be baptized in the name of my Beloved Son. And also, the voice of the Son hath witnessed unto you this day, saying: He that is baptized in my name, to him will the Father give the Holy Ghost, like unto me; therefore, follow me, and do the things which ye have seen me do.

24 Therefore, my beloved brethren, I know that if ye shall follow the Son, with full purpose of heart, acting no hypocrisy and no deception before God, but with real intent, repenting of your sins, witnessing unto the Father that ye are willing to take upon you the name of Christ, by baptism; yea, by following your Lord and your Savior down into the water, according to his word, behold, then shall ye receive the Holy Ghost; yea, then cometh the baptism of fire and of the Holy Ghost; and then can ye speak with the tongue of angels, and shout praises unto the Holy One of Israel.

25 But, behold, my beloved brethren, after ye have repented of your sins, and witnessed unto the Father that ye are willing to keep his commandments, by the baptism of water, and have received the baptism of fire and of the Holy Ghost, and can speak with a new tongue, yea, even with the tongue of angels, and after this should deny him, it would have been better for you that ye had not known him.

26 Yea, he that endureth to the end, the same shall be saved. And now, my beloved brethren, I know by this that unless a man shall endure to the end, in following the example of the Son of the living God, he cannot be saved.

27 Therefore, do the things which your Lord and your Redeemer hath done before you this day; for, for this cause hath he come unto me to be baptized, even that ye might know the gate by which ye should enter. For the gate by which ye should enter is repentance and baptism by water; and then cometh a remission of your sins by fire and by the Holy Ghost.

28 And then are ye in this strait and narrow path which leadeth to eternal life; yea, ye have entered in by the gate; ye have done according to the commandments of the Father and the Son; and ye have received the Holy Ghost, which witnesseth of the Father and the Son, unto the fulfilling of the promise which he hath made, that if ye entered in by the way ye should receive.

29 And now, my beloved brethren, after ye have gotten into this strait and narrow path, I would ask if all is done? Behold, I say unto you, Nay; for ye have not come thus far save it shall be by the word of Christ with unshaken faith in him, relying wholly upon the merits of him who is mighty to save.

30 Therefore, ye must press forward with a steadfastness in Christ, having a perfect brightness of hope, and a love of God and of all men. Therefore, if ye shall press forward, feasting upon the word of Christ, and endure to the end, behold, thus saith the Father: Ye shall have eternal life.

31 And now, behold, my beloved brethren, this is the way; and there is none other way nor name given under heaven whereby man can be saved in the kingdom of God.

32 And now, behold, this is the doctrine of Christ that I have preached unto you this day; and it is the same doctrine that hath been preached unto our fathers by all the holy prophets since the beginning; and the only and true doctrine of the Father, and of the Son, and of the Holy Ghost, which is one God, without end.

33 And now, behold, my beloved brethren, I suppose that ye ponder somewhat in your hearts concerning that which ye should do after ye have entered in by the way. But, behold, why do ye ponder these things in your hearts? Do ye not remember that I said unto you that after ye had received the Holy Ghost ye could speak with the tongue of angels?

34 And now, how could ye speak with the tongue of angels save it were by the Holy Ghost? Angels speak by the power of the Holy Ghost; therefore, they speak the words of Christ. Therefore, I said unto you, feast upon the words of Christ; for behold, the words of Christ will tell you all things what ye should do.

35 Therefore, now after I have spoken these words, if ye cannot understand them it will be because ye ask not, neither do ye knock; wherefore, ye are not brought into the light, but must perish in the dark.

36 For behold, again I say unto you that if ye will enter in by the way, and receive the Holy Ghost, it will show unto you all things what ye should do. Behold, this is the doctrine of Christ, and there shall be no more doctrine given of him from my mouth, until ye shall hear his words from his own mouth. And when ye have heard these words from him, the things which he shall say unto you shall ye observe to do.

37 And now, my beloved brethren, I am left to mourn because of the unbelief, and the wickedness, and the ignorance, and the stiffneckedness of men; for they will not search knowledge, nor understand great knowledge, when it is given unto them in plainness, even as plain as word can be.

38 And now, my beloved brethren, I perceive that ye ponder still in your hearts; and it grieveth me that I must speak concerning this thing. For if ye would hearken unto the Spirit which teacheth a man to pray, ye would know that ye must pray; for the evil spirit teacheth not a man to pray, but teacheth him that he must not pray.

39 But behold, I say unto you that ye must pray always, and not faint; that ye must not perform any thing unto the Lord save in the first place ye shall pray unto the Father in the name of Christ, that he will consecrate thy performance unto thee, that thy performance may be for the welfare of thy soul.

40 And it came to pass that after John had finished his preaching unto the people, he left them and would not allow them any more to follow him, directing his disciples to find the Christ and follow him and give heed unto his words.

41 And now, this same John, of whom I have written, was ordained from the beginning to prepare the way whereby the children of men could receive the words of Christ and understand them by the Spirit.

42 And his mission was a preparatory mission to open up the hearts of the children of men that they might receive the gospel of Jesus Christ, even in turning the hearts of the children to the promises of the fathers.

43 And the way that a person prepareth to accept the gospel of Christ, is for him to cast off the sins of his past and be born again and make a new covenant before God, even a covenant that can be seen of others, being an example to them that he is willing to obey the law of the gospel.

44 And after he hath made this covenant, then he shall be given the law of the gospel from the mouth of Christ, or from the mouth of his apostles, which shall teach the commandments of the Christ unto them, and give unto them the gift of the Holy Ghost, which is given according to their compliance with the covenant that they have made with the Father.

45 And it shall come to pass that in the latter days, the power and authority of John shall be given to the first of these two prophets of which I have written of the latter days.

46 And this power shall be given unto him by the hand of John, even that he might have the authority to baptize all those who are willing to take upon them the name of Christ and obey his commandments.

47 And after John hath given unto this prophet this authority, then shall the Lord send his apostles, even three of them as an established witness unto him, and they shall give unto him the power and authority to give the words of Christ to the people, or the gospel of Jesus Christ.

48 And in this way the order of the priesthood shall be preserved and given unto the children of men in a likeness of those things which are in heaven.

49 And it shall come to pass that after the Gentiles shall reject the gospel that hath been given unto them by the first of these prophets, then the Lord shall take this power and this authority from among the children of men once again, for there shall not be one left who is righteous enough to have this power and authority bestowed upon them.

50 And since these things are in a similitude of things which are spiritual, the last of these two latter day prophets shall be given the authority to baptize and teach the words of the gospel of Jesus Christ in a like manner as the first. Nevertheless, he shall be commanded to teach the children of men the similitude of these things, that they might prepare their spirits for that which is to come among them, even the coming of the Lord in all of his glory to teach unto the whole earth his gospel from his own mouth.

51 And when the Lord cometh in the glory of the Father, he shall fulfill all the temporal laws and ordinances which he hath suffered to be given unto the children of men to point them towards the laws of the Father, which laws must be taught unto them to prepare them for their eternal inheritance in the kingdoms of the Father.

52 And at that day shall this final prophet be called forth from among the people and he shall stand with John and the other prophets who have gone before him, and he shall witness unto the Lord that he hath done all those things which he hath been commanded.

53 And then shall the books be opened up, and from the mouth of the Lord all the ends of the earth shall hear of their great wickedness and corruption.

54 But the elect shall rejoice in that which they already know among them, even that which they have been given through the books which have been given unto them by the holy prophets; and also that which they have been given by the Holy Ghost.

55 And I, Moroni, shall stand with the Lord and with the other prophets and apostles of God, and we all shall testify unto the ends of the earth of those things which we have done to bring the children of men unto repentance.

56 And all of these things did Nephi see in his vision but was forbidden to write at that time. But I have written them in this sealed portion of the record.

57 And Nephi sealed up his testimony of these things unto you, saying: And now, I, Nephi, cannot write all the things which were taught among my people; neither am I mighty in writing, like unto speaking; for when a man speaketh by the power of the Holy Ghost the power of the Holy Ghost carrieth it unto the hearts of the children of men.

58 But behold, there are many who harden their hearts against the Holy Spirit, that it hath no place in them; therefore, they cast many things away which are written and esteem them as things of naught.

59 But I, Nephi, have written what I have written, and I esteem it as of great worth, and especially unto my people. For I pray continually for them by day, and mine eyes water my pillow by night, because of them; and I cry unto my God in faith, and I know that he will hear my cry.

60 And I know that the Lord God will consecrate my prayers for the gain of my people. And the words which I have written in weakness shall be made strong unto them; for it persuadeth them to do good; it maketh known unto them of their fathers; and it speaketh of Jesus, and persuadeth them to believe in him, and to endure to the end, which is life eternal.

61 And it speaketh harshly against sin, according to the plainness of the truth; therefore, no man will be angry at the words which I have written save he shall be of the spirit of the devil.

62 I glory in plainness; I glory in truth; I glory in my Jesus, for he hath redeemed my soul from hell. I have charity for my people, and great faith in Christ that I shall meet many souls spotless at his judgment seat. I have charity for the Jew; I say Jew, because I mean them from whence I came. I also have charity for the Gentiles.

63 But behold, for none of these can I hope except they shall be reconciled unto Christ, and enter into the narrow gate, and walk in the strait path which leadeth to life, and continue in the path until the end of the day of probation.

64 And now, my beloved brethren, and also Jew, and all ye ends of the earth, hearken unto these words and believe in Christ; and if ye believe not in these words believe in Christ. And if ye shall believe in Christ ye will believe in these words, for they are the words of Christ, and he hath given them unto me; and they teach all men that they should do good.

65 And if they are not the words of Christ, judge ye, for Christ will show unto you with power and great glory at the last day that they are his words; and you and I shall stand face to face before his bar; and ye shall know that I have been commanded of him to write these things, notwithstanding my weakness.

66 And I pray the Father in the name of Christ that many of us, if not all, may be saved in his kingdom at that great and last day.

67 And now, my beloved brethren, even all those who are of the house of Israel, and all ye ends of the earth, I speak unto you as the voice of one crying from the dust: Farewell, until that great day shall come. And ye that will not partake of the goodness of God, and respect the words of the Jews, and also my words, and the words which shall proceed forth out of the mouth of the Lamb of God, behold, I bid you an everlasting farewell, for these words shall condemn you at the last day.

68 For what I seal on earth, shall be brought against you at the judgment bar; for thus hath the Lord commanded me, and I must obey. Amen.

69 And now, to the words of Nephi, I, Moroni, give my own testimony, even so, Amen.

CHAPTER 41

An explanation of the true character of the Christ and of the Father. The voice of the Father is given differently than the voice of mortal prophets. People need prophets because they won't listen to the Spirit, which is the voice of the Father.

AND now, my beloved brothers and sisters, even all of you of the latter days, and those of you who have passed through the days of your probation and reside in the spirit world and wait patiently on the Lord that he might bring about the resurrection of your souls; and also those of you who remain in the spirit world in a state of torment because ye now know that which ye did not consider while ye existed in mortality, even as ye went through the days of your probation and did not partake of the goodness of God which He hath given us through His Son, Jesus Christ.

2 I say unto all the children of God no matter where they might reside: How do ye think that ye shall come to know the Father, except ye shall first know His Son, who is in the exact likeness of the Father, and who hath been given to us as an example to follow in all things?

3 And now, how can ye expect to know yourselves, except ye first know Him who hath created you? Now, this thing ye know of a surety, even that ye do exist. And if ye think not that ye exist, then I say unto you, find the highest point of earth on which ye can tread, and go unto this point and cast yourselves off of this terrestrial apex.

4 And as ye fall to the earth to your death, know ye not that ye are alive? For if ye are not alive, then why should ye fear death? And what would be the cause of your fear, if it so be that ye do not exist?

5 And while ye are falling, and know that ye shall die, to whom shall ye call on to save you? I say unto you, that ye shall call upon someone, even it so be that ye call upon yourselves. And if ye call upon yourselves, then ye have a witness that ye do exist.

6 And ye cannot exist and have a knowledge of this existence except ye have a knowledge of the Father who hath created you. And because ye cannot see the Father, ye do not know that he existeth. For if ye could see Him, then ye would know for a surety that He doth exist and that He hath created you.

7 And if He hath created you, and ye do indeed exist, then there must be some reason for which the Father hath created you. And if there is a reason that He hath created you, then the reason must be His reason and not your own, because ye did not exist to have a reason to create yourselves.

8 And if the Father had a reason, or a purpose for which He created you, then would not it be appropriate that the Father teach unto you the reason for your creation, or rather, the reason for which He caused you to be created?

9 And now, I say unto you, that the Father hath given unto us the reason why we have been created. And do ye think that He caused us to be created that we might be miserable and unhappy forever?

10 For what purpose do ye think that God would have in using His omnipotence to create something that would be miserable and unhappy forever? Yea, what kind of God can ye imagine in your hearts would do such a thing?

11 I say unto you, that God created us that we might have joy, yea, even eternal happiness. And now, do ye think that if He hath created us so that we might have this joy, that He would not provide for us the means and the way whereby we might have this eternal joy and happiness?

12 Do ye think that He would create us, and then leave us to ourselves to create our own happiness and provide for our own means whereby we might obtain this happiness?

13 And how is it that ye can think that we would have an idea of where we could find this happiness or those things that we must do to provide for ourselves the means of this happiness? For behold, we have no experience in this thing. And we have no experience in this thing because we did not exist until we were created.

14 And from the moment that we are created, we begin to have experiences, and thus begin our ability to become an individual and think and act for ourselves, independent of the control

of others, even independent of the control of Him who had created us.

15 For if the Father had not given unto us our independence from His own experience, distinguishing the one from the other, then we would not know this happiness or joy for ourselves, being created for His experience and not for our own.

16 And He already knoweth this joy and happiness; and He knoweth this from His own experience. And because He had the experience to know these things, He knoweth that He is eternally happy in His own existence.

17 And because He knoweth and understandeth this eternal happiness, it is His desire to give this happiness unto us, who are His children, or His creations who have been created by Him that we might have the experiences that He hath had that have brought Him this happiness.

18 And this happiness can only come through independence and free agency, or in other words, having the ability to be independent of the Father and gain from our own experiences our own happiness.

19 And now, once we have had these experiences and have felt this joy, even this state of eternal happiness, to whom do ye think that we shall give praises and thanksgiving for this happiness that we enjoy? Do ye think that we shall thank ourselves for giving us this happiness?

20 Do ye think that we shall thank others for this happiness, even those who did not create us and had nothing to do with making us independent so that we could experience and gain this happiness?

21 I say unto you, that ye shall one day give praise and glory only to the Father and our Eternal Mothers for the experiences and the joy and happiness that ye shall have forever in the kingdoms of the Father, which kingdoms He hath created for us to provide the means for us to experience this happiness.

22 And now, I would that ye should consider this thing: If ye are of a family, and ye have brothers and sisters; and if ye all have a father and a mother who have given unto all of you, who are their children; yea, even those who were born of them without a choice of their own, but by the choice of them who are the parents;

23 Yea, and your parents have given equally unto you great and glorious blessings, even all of their riches and all of their possessions, and all of their lands and their fine things, even everything that bringeth them happiness; if the children of this family have been given all these things of their parents, then who shall receive the thanks and the glory for these things?

24 Shall the brother or the sister say unto another, I thank thee dear brother for all that which thou hast given unto me? And will that brother say unto the others, Ye are welcome for that which I have given unto you, and I deserve and am worthy of your praise and your glory?

25 And if it so be that the father and the mother of this family shall be gone into another country, and shall leave all of their possessions and their lands, and their fine things, even all things which they possess that make them happy, and give unto the oldest son the power and authority to give unto their children equally all that they possess and have worked for all of their lives for the sake of their children;

26 And if this oldest son hath this authority and this power, shall he then be worthy of the praise and the glory of the other children, when they receive all these things through him, even those things that their parents commanded should be divided equally unto all of their children?

27 I say unto you, that a wicked son would take the glory for himself and think not to turn the hearts of the children to the parents who have provided these things freely unto them all. Yea, a wicked son would not divide the possessions of the parents equally, but would give of the finest parts to himself and to those whom he loveth, or to those who look up to him and give him the glory that he thinketh that he deserveth because of the power and authority that hath been given him by the parents.

28 But I say unto you, that a righteous son would show unto the rest of his brothers and his sisters that he hath been chosen only to give unto them what their parents have commanded of him; and he shall give equally unto all the portion that they deserve, all being equally loved by their parents.

29 And what glory and praise shall this righteous son desire, knowing that he did not provide his brothers and sisters with their inheritance, but that it came from their parents, and he was only chosen because of his righteousness in administering the will of his parents according to their desires?

30 And now, if the father and the mother wanted to make sure that all of their children would receive an equal part of the inheritance that they have left for their children, then which son would they choose to administer their will?

31 And when they return home to their children, who then shall the children worship and honor? Would they honor their brother, or would they not honor the father and the mother who have provided for them equally in all things?

32 And if their children still praise this righteous son, would this son want this of himself, or would he not direct the glory of his siblings to their parents, who deserve this glory?

33 And what then shall be the reason for the glory and praise of the unrighteous son, who being the oldest among them, sought for praise and honor for himself?

34 Then shall the other siblings see him for who he really is, a devil, a charlatan whose only desire was to take glory upon himself for that which he had nothing to do with in the first place. And then shall the Father cast out this unrighteous son and all those who were desirous to take more of the inheritance than their other brothers and sisters.

35 But if the righteous son hath done all things that the father hath commanded of him, then the father shall thank that son and give unto him his equal portion with the rest of his brothers and sisters.

36 And all of the children shall worship the father and the mother and give glory and praise unto them forever, thanking them for their inheritance, and also thanking them for leaving the power and authority of dividing this inheritance in the hands of the righteous son.

37 And now, my brothers and sisters, I am about to take away from you a great stumbling block that hath been placed before you because of your wickedness. And this wickedness of which I speak is that ye have given credit and praise and glory where this credit and praise and glory is not due, neither is it expected of him to whom ye give it. And because ye have done these things, ye have had these stumbling blocks placed before you.

38 And this wickedness of which I speak is like unto the parable that I have given unto you, even like unto those children who gave honor and praise to the unrighteous son who wanted this praise and glory for himself, knowing fully that he had nothing to do with the inheritance that the parents had left for all of their children equally.

39 For behold, ye seek for that which shall make you unequal with your other brothers and sisters; and ye seek for someone that ye might worship and honor and who hath given unto you what ye believe is the greater part of the inheritance of the Father.

40 And I speak specifically unto you of the latter days who shall have these things revealed unto you. For there are many of you, yea, even all of you, except it be for the very few elect, who have chosen for yourselves this oldest son whom I have given as an example in the parable.

41 For there are many of you who have placed Jesus and others above you and have given unto them the glory that ye should be giving unto the Father in all things.

42 And because ye have done this, Christ hath become a stumbling block unto you, even that ye do stumble and err in your understanding of truth. And the true Christ that ye have accepted and that ye think ye know, ye know not.

43 For he is not the true Christ of which I have spoken, and of which all the holy prophets have written and spoken since the beginning. For ye worship the unrighteous son and call him your Christ and your Lord and give unto him glory and praise, which is the thing that the righteous son would not accept of you.

44 And now, it is this thing that I have been commanded to reveal unto you by the true Lord, even Jesus Christ himself, the righteous Son of God, which he commanded me when

he visited with me and conversed with me and taught me many things concerning him and his life, which things he hath commanded me to include in this record.

45 Yea, Jesus Christ hath commanded me to make this thing plain unto you that ye might have no more excuses in your wickedness, and that ye might come to know the true Christ. For if ye come to know the true Christ, then ye shall come to know the true Father, which is the Father of Christ as well as our own Father, and who is the Creator of all things.

46 Behold, He hath created us and hath given unto us all of His blessings equally. And He gave the power and authority to His Son, even Jehovah, or Jesus Christ, as he shall be known among the Jews and the Gentiles, to represent Him and do His will in this part of His kingdom.

47 And His will is that all of His children return unto Him and partake of the eternal happiness of His kingdom. And this happiness He hath given unto all of His children equally according to their desires of happiness.

48 And He doth not say to one, Thy happiness shall be less than that of thy brother. Nor doth He say to another, Thy happiness is greater than that of thy brother. But He sayeth unto all, Thy happiness is a fullness of all I can give unto thee according to thy own desires and choices of happiness.

49 And this is the eternal plan of the Father, and it is also the desire of our Eternal Mothers, who work for our happiness with our Father.

50 And now, it is the Son of whom I must speak and give unto you an understanding. For ye give praise and glory unto the Son which he doth not deserve, neither doth he want the praise and the glory that ye give unto him.

51 And it saddeneth his heart when ye give unto him this praise and this glory, even that praise and glory that he desireth that the Father receive from you. And he knoweth that in your wickedness, or in your darkness, ye cannot give unto the Father the praise He deserveth, because ye do not see the Father. But ye have seen him and know that he hath lived among you. And for this reason, ye worship him and give unto him glory contrary to that which he hath commanded you.

52 And in all things he hath attempted to turn your hearts towards the Father that ye might be taught by the Father as he was taught by the Father, having received a fullness of the Father, which fullness is offered unto all of the children of God equally.

53 And in sorrow he suffereth you to worship him and use his name in vain, giving unto him the glory that he would force you to give unto the Father, if he could. But he cannot force you to do that which ye do not desire, according to the free agency that ye have received from the Father.

54 And the Father hath also commanded him to not force you, but that he should love you and allow you to worship the Father in his name, that ye might know the Father through the Son, because of your wickedness.

55 For what righteous father among you would truly want any of his children to come unto him by way of a brother? I say unto you, that if ye are a righteous father, then ye would want to speak to all of your children and love them each as ye do the others.

56 But if your children fear you, because they do not know you, and they choose to come unto you only through their brother, then they shall not be in your presence and know you, but they shall only know the brother that they have chosen to come unto you on their behalf.

57 But ye shall still love your children and want them to be happy; therefore, ye shall allow them to speak with you through their brother. But ye would be saddened that your children would not come unto you personally and sit upon your knee and embrace you and speak to you like you speak with their brother, whom they have chosen and to whom they speak instead of you.

58 And would it not frustrate this brother, if he were a righteous son, and he knew that all of his brothers and sisters could approach their father and sit upon his knee and converse with their father, yet they will not do this because they fear him? Would not this brother make every attempt that he could, to get his siblings to know their father and come unto him?

59 And now, I will give unto you examples of this thing both in the record of the Jews, and also

in the record of my father which hath already come forth among you. And these examples have been hidden from you because of your wickedness and the stumbling blocks that the Lord hath placed before you.

60 But I will explain these things unto you in plainness, and ye shall see your errors and take notice of your ignorance of those things that ye should have understood. But without the Spirit to guide you in your understanding, there is no way that ye could have understood these things.

61 Behold, the written word hath caused much contention among you because of the way that these words have been written and given unto you. But if ye would not have the spirit of contention among you, then ye would have understood these things.

62 And because ye had this contention, which is contrary to the spirit of Christ, then ye did not have the spirit of Christ, and therefore, could not understand these things when they were presented unto you already in plainness.

63 And now, I would that ye should make reference to the words of my father, Mormon, which he hath given unto you concerning the coming of Jesus Christ unto the people who were gathered in the land of Bountiful after he was resurrected.

64 And now, I would that ye should know that the Father hath suffered that the children of men be given the opportunity to hear His words by those whom they will accept as His mouthpiece.

65 And I have already shown unto you that if the children of men are willing, then they can receive the words of God directly from His mouth, even from the Holy Ghost, who is one with the Father in all things, and is the voice of the Father, and is the way that the Father hath established to teach unto the children of men His will in all things.

66 And this way He hath established so that His children will not give undeserved praise and glory to their other brothers and sisters, who did not create them, nor do they have anything to do with their eternal salvation, except it be giving His words unto them that they might turn to Him and keep His commandments, which were given so that they might have joy and happiness.

67 And because the children of men do not recognize the way which the Father hath established to teach them, even that they cannot hear and understand his voice, He hath suffered that they be taught the only way that they might understand and accept His words.

68 And He hath suffered that the children of men should worship others of their brothers, even the holy prophets who have been sent unto them, that they might at least have some contact with Him and receive His word in some way.

69 Now, this communication with the Father, even the desire of the Son to turn the people to their Father, was given as an example in the record of my father, and he wrote, saying: And now it came to pass that there was a great multitude gathered together, of the people of Nephi, round about the temple which was in the land Bountiful; and they were marveling and wondering one with another, and were showing one to another the great and marvelous change which had taken place.

70 And they were also conversing about this Jesus Christ, of whom the sign had been given concerning his death.

71 And it came to pass that while they were thus conversing one with another, they heard a voice as if it came out of heaven; and they cast their eyes round about, for they understood not the voice which they heard; and it was not a harsh voice, neither was it a loud voice; nevertheless, and notwithstanding it being a small voice it did pierce them that did hear to the center, insomuch that there was no part of their frame that it did not cause to quake; yea, it did pierce them to the very soul, and did cause their hearts to burn.

72 And it came to pass that again they heard the voice, and they understood it not.

73 And again the third time they did hear the voice, and did open their ears to hear it; and their eyes were towards the sound thereof; and they did look steadfastly towards heaven, from whence the sound came.

74 And behold, the third time they did understand the voice which they heard; and it said unto them: Behold my Beloved Son, in whom I am well pleased, in whom I have glorified my name; hear ye him.

75 And now, I, Moroni, give unto you an

explanation of these things. For behold, whose voice did the people hear that testified unto them of His Son? Was it not the voice of the Father?

76 And why is it that they did not understand this voice when it was given unto them the first time? And even a second time it was given unto them and they did not understand it. And this voice was given unto them by their loving Father in heaven, who loveth them all and desireth to give unto all of His children His words by His own mouth.

77 And the voice of the Father is not a harsh voice, like the voice of a prophet at times, neither is it a loud voice, with which a prophet at times doth proclaim his message and teacheth repentance. But it was a small voice that did pierce them that did hear to the center, insomuch that there was no part of their frame that it did not cause to quake; yea, it did pierce them to the very soul, and did cause their hearts to burn.

78 And this burning was caused because the voice was recognizable by the spirit of these people, but the flesh could not understand these things, because it was not heard in their ears as they were accustomed to receiving communication.

79 Now behold, these people understood the voice of Jesus, of whom they had been given the signs and the testimonies of the prophets, to whom they had listened with the means of communication of which they were accustomed in the flesh.

80 And they did previously, to this time, yea, even just before the Father made an attempt to speak unto them with His own voice, they did hear the voice of Christ in the darkness.

81 Now, why is it that these people could hear the voice of Christ in the darkness, when he spoke unto them from the heavens, but they could not perceive and understand the voice of the Father, when He spoke unto them from the same heavens in the light?

82 And what is it that the Father was trying to tell the people, even through the manner of communication that they could not understand, yea, even through this still small voice?

83 Behold, these things were shown unto the people that were preserved in the land of Bountiful as a similitude of those things which are upon the earth.

84 For the Father made twice the attempt to speak unto His children, but they could not understand the words which He gave unto them. And they did not know Him, therefore, they did not recognize His voice.

85 Nevertheless, He knew that they were conversing about His Son, even Jesus Christ, who Samuel the Lamanite had prophesied would come into the world. And they were conversing about Jesus Christ just before they heard the voice of the Father speak unto them from the heavens.

86 And the Father knew that these people were not ready to hear from His own mouth that which He would gladly teach unto them. For He knew that they could not listen to that still small voice that spoke directly to their spirit—He being the Creator of their spirits—and not to their ears, which were of the flesh.

87 And when He had made the attempt twice, He turned them over to the Son, that He might teach them through His Son. And He spoke unto them this time in the manner of communication that they could understand in their wickedness.

88 And for this reason, it is written: And behold, the third time they did understand the voice which they heard; and it said unto them: Behold my Beloved Son, in whom I am well pleased, in whom I have glorified my name; hear ye him.

89 And with this the Father gave the children of men the opportunity to hear His words the only way that they could understand them, even the way that they had been taught by their customs and their traditions. Nevertheless, it was better that they hear His words in this way, than that they should not hear any of His words.

CHAPTER 42

Moroni gives a more in depth description of the intercessory prayer of Jesus that he gave among the Nephites and the Lamanites. The Father reveals Himself to all humankind through the innocence and love of little children.

AND it came to pass that Jesus came down among them, and they fell before him and worshipped him. But in this thing the Lord was not pleased, but suffered it to be because of the commandment that he had received of the Father. And the will of the Father is that He would have His children receive His word as they could understand it through the means that they would accept.

2 And my father, Mormon, was forbidden to write many of the things which he read of the account which the people had recorded concerning the visit of Jesus Christ in the days of his fathers. And he was forbidden to write this thing, because it behooveth the Father that the children of men be given only those things that they can understand and accept.

3 And because the Father knew that in the latter days, even at the time these things shall be given unto the children of men, that they would already honor Jesus Christ and give unto him the glory of the Father. Yea, because He knew these things, He commanded His Son to suffer it to be that He might save as many of His children as He can by turning them from their sins by the words of and the glory of Jesus.

4 And the record readeth that Nephi bowed and kissed the feet of Jesus. And the Lord commanded that he should arise and do not these things unto him, but that he should worship the Father and give all glory unto Him.

5 But Nephi and the people were overwhelmed by the greatness of the appearance of the resurrected Christ among them, even they were still overcome by the words that they heard him speak unto them in the darkness.

6 And now, this thing is also an example and a similitude unto you; For behold, did not Jesus speak unto the people in darkness? And in the darkness the people understood his voice.

7 Yet when it was light, whose voice did they first hear? Yea, in the light, did not the Father make an attempt to speak unto His children?

8 And this thing was the will of the Son that he might show unto the children of men that while they are in darkness, they shall hear his voice, but when they are in the light, or rather, when they have the Spirit, who is with them, because in them dwelleth light, then the Father speaketh unto them Himself.

9 And in this way ye shall know if ye are in the darkness or in the light according to your works. For behold, if ye can only hear the words of Jesus and those whom he hath commissioned to teach you and preach repentance unto you, then ye shall know of a surety that your works are works of darkness, for in darkness ye shall be given their words.

10 But if your works are righteous, or are in the light, then ye shall be given the mysteries of godliness by the voice of the Father as I have explained it unto you.

11 And now, I would that ye should continue in the record of my father and follow the course that the Lord took as he taught unto the people the words of the Father.

12 For behold, because these people were in darkness, according to the Spirit, he called others among them to preach unto them. And these others were his disciples whom he commanded to baptize the people according to their traditions that they could understand and accept.

13 For when Jesus spake unto the people in the darkness, before they were given the chance to receive the words directly from the Father, he said unto them: And as many as have received me, to them have I given to become the sons of God; and even so will I give to as many as shall believe on my name, for behold, by me redemption cometh, and in me is the law of Moses fulfilled. I am the light and the life of the world. I am Alpha and Omega, the beginning and the end.

14 And ye shall offer up unto me no more the shedding of blood; yea, your sacrifices and your burnt offerings shall be done away, for I will accept none of your sacrifices and your burnt offerings.

15 And ye shall offer for a sacrifice unto me a broken heart and a contrite spirit. And whoso cometh unto me with a broken heart and a contrite spirit, him will I baptize with fire and with the Holy Ghost, even as the Lamanites, because of their faith in me at the time of their conversion, were baptized with fire and with the Holy Ghost, and they knew it not.

16 Behold, I have come unto the world to bring redemption unto the world, to save the world from sin. Therefore, whoso repenteth and cometh unto me as a little child, him will I receive, for of such is the kingdom of God. Behold, for such I have laid down my life, and have taken it up again; therefore repent, and come unto me ye ends of the earth, and be saved.

17 And now, I, Moroni, ask of ye, wherein did the Lord command anyone to be baptized by immersion into water in the words which he spoke unto the people in darkness?

18 Behold, he said unto them that he had fulfilled the law of Moses, and the law of Moses commanded baptism as a similitude of those things which were to come.

19 And Jesus said these things unto the people in the darkness to prepare their minds and their hearts that they might hear and understand the words that the Father would speak unto them in the light.

20 But when the Father spoke unto them in the light, they did not understand the words that the Father said unto them. And had they heard the words that the Father spoke unto them, or had they been more righteous and receptive to the Holy Ghost, which is the voice of the Father, then they would have heard all things from the Father.

21 But because they could not listen and understand in this way, the Father sent His Son down among them and instituted the ordinances that He would require of them to point them towards the Father, even the ordinance of baptism by immersion according to their customs and their traditions, which they could understand.

22 And if they had listened to and heard the voice of the Father, then the only thing that would have been required of them would have been a broken heart and contrite spirit.

23 And with this broken heart and contrite spirit, the Holy Ghost would have given them all the understanding and knowledge that they needed to be saved in the kingdom of God, despite the law of Moses, which was fulfilled in Christ.

24 And it came to pass that after Jesus had taught the people the will of the Father and given unto them all of the commandments of the Father, yea, even those commandments that were necessary that they might have the joy and happiness that the Father had promised them; yea, after Jesus had given unto them these things, he said unto them, Behold, my time is at hand. I perceive that ye are weak, that ye cannot understand all my words which I am commanded of the Father to speak unto you at this time.

25 Therefore, go ye unto your homes, and ponder upon the things which I have said, and ask of the Father, in my name, that ye may understand, and prepare your minds for the morrow, and I come unto you again. But now I go unto the Father and also to show myself unto the lost tribes of Israel, for they are not lost unto the Father, for he knoweth whither He hath taken them.

26 And it was the will of the Lord and his desire to leave the people at this time and go unto others who had been prepared to receive him as a resurrected being, even unto those who were the other sheep of whom he gave mention.

27 And he had commanded the people to go home and pray unto the Father for understanding, hoping that by doing this, they might be wrought upon by the Spirit and be given understanding.

28 But as he was about to leave, he beheld the people, that they were still weak in their understanding and still in an attitude of worship of him; even in their tears, he had compassion on them.

29 And the Lord told me of this time and he said unto me: Behold, I had commanded the people that they might go unto their homes and call upon the Father and give glory unto Him, that He might send the Holy Ghost unto them so that they might have understood better the things that I had taught unto them.

30 But I could perceive their ignorance and their inability to show faith, even the faith in that which they could not see. And because they saw me, they did worship me.

31 And it came to pass that Jesus said unto them: Behold, my bowels are filled with compassion towards you. Have ye any that are sick among you? Bring them hither. Have ye any that are lame, or blind, or halt, or maimed, or leprous, or that are withered, or that are deaf, or that are afflicted in any manner? Bring them hither and I will heal them, for I have compassion upon you; my bowels are filled with mercy.

32 For I perceive that ye desire that I should show unto you what I have done unto your brethren at Jerusalem, for I see that your faith is sufficient that I should heal you. And it came to pass that when he had thus spoken, all the multitude, with one accord, did go forth with their sick and their afflicted, and their lame, and with their blind, and with their dumb, and with all they that were afflicted in any manner; and he did heal them every one as they were brought forth unto him.

33 And they did all, both they who had been healed and they who were whole, bow down at his feet, and did worship him; and as many as could come of the multitude did kiss his feet, insomuch that they did bathe his feet with their tears.

34 And now, it was in this thing that the Lord was troubled, but he did not have the will to say unto the people that they should not bow down before him and worship him in this manner. For he loved them and did not want them to have that taken away which brought them such joy.

35 But he wanted them to come to know the Father. And he thought of a way by which he might bring the Father to them, that they might know Him and understand Him, that they would not fear Him, and that they might give all the glory to the Father and not to him.

36 And it came to pass that he commanded that their little children should be brought. So they brought their little children and set them down upon the ground round about him, and Jesus stood in the midst; and the multitude gave way till they had all been brought unto him.

37 And it came to pass that when they had all been brought, and Jesus stood in the midst, he commanded the multitude that they should kneel down upon the ground.

38 And it came to pass that when they had knelt upon the ground, Jesus groaned within himself, and said: Father, I am troubled because of the wickedness of the people of the house of Israel.

39 And now, I, Moroni, would ask of ye, why do ye think that the Lord groaned within himself and said unto the Father that he was troubled because of the wickedness of the people? I say unto you, that he was troubled because they were like unto the Jews who were at Jerusalem. For they had faith which was sufficient that he should heal them, but they did not have enough faith that they could receive the things which they should know from the Holy Ghost, which was from the Father.

40 And he groaned that he could not tell them in plainness concerning these things and turn them to the Father who deserved all the glory and praise that the people were giving unto him.

41 Nevertheless, the Lord was commanded by the Father to suffer it so for the sake of His children. For even the Father himself doth not take upon Himself glory as ye have supposed.

42 And this is the mystery and the understanding that the Lord hath commanded me to give unto you in plainness. Even that the Father of us all, the Great Creator, who hath given us life and all things for our happiness, even this wondrous Being doth not take glory unto Himself.

43 For His work and His glory is to bring to pass the immortality and eternal life of all of His children. This is His glory, and the praise and honor of His children He doth not require of them. The only thing that He requireth of them is that they have eternal joy in a state of happiness forever.

44 Now, this is the thing that I am to teach unto you, even this great mystery that hath not been revealed unto you because of the stumbling blocks that have been placed before you because of your wickedness and your lack of understanding.

45 And now, I would that ye should imagine in your minds and hearts the image of a wonderful Father who loveth all of His children and desireth that all of them be happy. Do ye think that this Father would have His children fall down at His feet and kiss His feet and bow down before Him and worship Him?

46 Do ye not think that this loving Father would want all of His children to come unto Him and embrace Him and laugh with Him, and sit upon His knee and smile with Him and be joyous in His presence?

47 Now, which of these Fathers would ye choose for yourselves; yea, even a Father who would command you and expect you to bow down low before Him, or a Father whom ye could embrace and with whom ye could laugh and smile?

48 And now, I know what ye have been taught by your traditions and your customs and the precepts of men that have been taught among you, but these are not the precepts and the truths of the Father.

49 For behold, the Father did not create you that ye should worship Him. But He hath created you that ye might partake of the happiness that He hath to offer you.

50 And when ye worship God as ye are accustomed to worship Him in your churches and your synagogues, even in the privacy of your own homes, are ye happy in this attitude of worship? Is not your countenance of a sad nature, even that ye feel a spirit of sadness that causeth you to frown?

51 But if ye could smile and rejoice and sing praises unto God, yea, even that your Father would sing praises and songs with you, would ye not then be happy?

52 And now, after the Lord had groaned within himself and was troubled because of the wickedness of the people, he knelt upon the earth and prayed unto the Father.

53 And the things which he prayed could not be written in the record of my father because of the stumbling blocks that were in place because of the wickedness of those who would receive this record.

54 And not only did the people hear the words of the prayer, but they beheld with their eyes things that could not be written. For it was not an usual prayer, like unto those that ye are accustomed to hearing and observing among you.

55 For when ye pray, what is there that the eye might see, except ye, kneeling in sorrow and covering your head and closing your eyes and falling to the ground in what ye perceive is humility before God?

56 But these people did indeed see something with their eyes. And that which they saw, my father was forbidden to write. But my father was overwhelmed by those things which he read concerning that which the people both saw and heard.

57 And because he was so overwhelmed, he wrote, saying: And after this manner do they bear record: The eye hath never seen, neither hath the ear heard before, so great and marvelous things as we saw and heard Jesus speak unto the Father; and no tongue can speak, neither can there be written by any man, neither can the hearts of men conceive so great and marvelous things as we both saw and heard speak; and no one can conceive of the joy which filled our souls at the time we heard him pray for us unto the Father.

58 But now, I am about to reveal unto you the things that Jesus prayed unto the Father, even those things that my father was commanded should not be given unto the children of men in the unsealed portion of this record.

59 Behold, these things were not given, so that the faith and resolve of the elect might be tried and tested, even that they might have an opportunity to understand these things by the Holy Ghost, or the voice of the Father in the light.

60 But because of the great wickedness that is among those of you of the latter days, even that many of the elect have been misled by the precepts of men, I have been commanded to give unto you the words of this great and marvelous prayer that the Lord offered to the Father, and also those things which the people saw, and of which they bore record, but of which my father was forbidden to write.

61 But my father did write many things in his record concerning that which the people heard and beheld. Nevertheless, he did so in a way that the full truth of these things might not be known, except it be known through the ministrations of the Holy Ghost unto those who would receive his words.

62 And the Lord prayed, saying: Oh, My Father, behold these little ones whom I have placed before Thee that they might behold Thee as I have beheld Thee. Oh, My Father, these are those among this people who have not yet turned their hearts from Thee, even that they have not been led away from Thee because of the traditions of their fathers.

63 And in the innocence of these little ones, they love one another as Thou hast commanded their parents to love each other.

64 And in their eyes shineth Thy glory and the sparkle of Thy countenance aboundeth in them.

65 And their countenances have been preserved in righteousness from their birth, even that they look in their innocence unto their parents for guidance and instruction and love without condition or fear.

66 And now, dear Father, I would that Thou wouldst come down amongst us and show unto this people Thy true nature, even the nature of Thy Being, which they know not, neither do they understand, because Thou hast kept this from them for their own sakes.

67 But these innocent children can behold Thy face, for they do not fear Thee, but know Thee. For behold, from Thee, their spirits were created, and of Thy Spirit their hearts are shorn.

68 And when Jesus had spoken these words, the heavens opened up and a great pillar of light appeared directly over the children and the Lord. And within the pillar of light appeared a man and others, who were women, with him.

69 And they came down upon the earth and dispersed Themselves among the children; and They took the children in Their arms and smiled upon them and kissed their faces and sat them upon Their knees.

70 And the children had no fear of these glorious beings. And they ran joyously from one being to another jumping into Their arms and climbing upon Them, playing carefree with all of the beings who had descended from within the pillar of light.

71 And these beings were dressed in robes of white, which whiteness exceeding any other whiteness upon the earth.

72 And the children began to laugh and play with the Father. And the Father laughed and played with them. And the Lord did also play with the little ones for a time. And it came to pass that Jesus embraced the Father, and walked off a ways with the Father, before the people.

73 And the people were astonished at the things which they saw. And the parents of the children were even more astonished still at the ease of their children around these Goddesses, and also the gentleness and love that were shown unto their children by Them.

74 And they saw Jesus speak unto the Father, saying: Father, behold this people which have been spared because they have faith in me. How is it that I can take from Thee the honor that these give unto me because of Thee? And what is it that I must do that I might turn them to Thee that they might know Thee and be one with Thee as I am one with Thee?

75 And the Father answered Jesus, saying: My beloved Son, it is a hard thing which thou asketh of these, thy brothers and sisters. Behold, because of the veil that I have caused to be placed over their memories due to the flesh in which their spirits reside, they do not remember me. Behold, they have been convinced by the flesh that they cannot know me.

76 But behold, my beloved Son, they do know me. For it is written in their hearts, even as they hold their own children in their arms do they witness of me and my glory.

77 And when they hold their child, even as a newborn infant, in their arms, they feel of my love and learn of me. And when that infant smileth upon them and they see the light within it through the gentleness of its eyes, behold they see me and know me.

78 And when that child crieth and is in need of comfort and succor that can only be given by its parent; yea, when that child crieth for its parent and is comforted in their arms, then they feel of my spirit and know of me.

79 And in their children they find the hope of their future, for I have given them this hope through the smile and the innocence of a child. And in the eyes of a child they behold me. And in the touch of a child they feel me. And in its love they long for me.

80 For I have given unto all of my children the innocence of a child, that they might have an example of me before them always.

81 And when a child cometh unto them and asketh of them a certain thing, who among them can deny the child that which it desireth? And in this they know of my mercy and compassion for them.

82 Behold, in all things my love is shown unto them through the love of a child. And I love them as they love their children. And I love them as their children love them.

83 And if my children would look unto the examples that I have given unto them of me, even if they would look within their own children according to the flesh, then they shall find me.

84 For what greater happiness can come unto them than that which cometh of a child?

85 And after the Father had said these things unto Jesus, He turned and smiled upon the people. And for the first time since their births into mortality, the people beheld the face of their Eternal Father.

86 And His countenance shown upon them and they fell to the earth and became as little children, having the love of the Father penetrate to the very center of their souls. Yea, even every one of them did fall to the ground and began to worship the Father and call upon His name.

87 And in this the joy of the Lord was full and he wept before them. For the people had seen the Father and known Him as Jesus knew Him, and they worshipped Him as they had worshipped Jesus; and this is the thing that Jesus wanted of the Father.

88 And the Father departed from before Jesus and the people and beckoned unto the others who were there with Him that they should go with Him back into the pillar of light that did hover directly above them.

89 And now, I know that these others were our Eternal Mothers. And they were the most beautiful women the people had ever seen. And as these Eternal Mothers picked up each child and held them and kissed their faces, they would turn towards the people and smile upon them.

90 And their countenance did shine like unto the countenance of the Father, and the people were overwhelmed by them, even as they were by the Father.

91 And it came to pass that these wondrous beings disappeared within the light from which they came. But before They disappeared into the light, They waved, each of Them, to the people and to the children.

92 But the people were still on the ground and were still overwhelmed from that which they both saw and heard.

93 And when the light had gone up into the heavens from whence it came, Jesus continued his prayer to the Father, saying: Oh, My Father, we thank Thee for that which we have witnessed this day, which Thou hast shown unto us, even who Thou art.

94 And we thank Thee that we now know where we must look to find Thee, that we might always remember Thee and strive to become like Thee.

95 And I ask of Thee, that Thou mightest bless these people that they become as their little children and love Thee as their children love them. I pray, Father, that Thou wouldst help them to know Thee through their children, and become like unto a child that they might be able to accept Thee and keep Thy commandments that they might be saved in Thy kingdoms forever.

96 And forgive them that they do worship me, but suffer that they might do this thing that they might look unto me as an example. For I love Thee as a little child loveth his father. And I have done all things that I have been commanded to do, even like a little child. And I am their brother and one of Thy children.

97 Therefore, I pray for them that they might understand these things and come unto Thee and hear all things from Thine own voice, that they might give glory to Thee and not to me.

98 But when they worship me, they are worshipping Thee, Oh, Father, because I have been given unto them as an example of Thee. I pray Thee, Oh, My Father, that if they worship me, that Thou wouldst suffer that they might have Thy Spirit to be with them, that they might also become one with Thee as I am one with Thee.

99 And if they fail me, Oh Father, they have not failed Thee. For I am in the flesh and have given them of Thee in the flesh. And their flesh turneth them from me, but their spirits shall always abide in Thee.

100 Therefore, forgive them of all things whatsoever they might do in the flesh because of me, and take them in the spirit back to Thee and give them that which Thou hast promised unto them from the beginning, and which Thou hast promised them through me.

101 Oh, My Father, let not one of them be lost, but redeem them all according to the spirit, and I will redeem them according to the flesh. But if I cannot redeem them according to the flesh, then Oh, Father, I know that Thou shalt redeem them according to the Spirit.

102 For we are all Thy children and Thou art our Father. We love Thee, Father, and we cannot help but give Thee glory and praise forever. Amen.

103 And now these are the things that happened and were accounted for in the record of my father.

104 And there are differences in that which I have written unto you and also that which is written in the record of my father, Mormon. But these differences are only those that were made by each of us according to our weaknesses.

105 But I have given unto you herein the truth regarding these things; and my father was under a commandment that he not give all these things in that part of the record which is unsealed.

106 Therefore, if there are differences, then they are minor and are made by the writing style and interpretation of what we both beheld. And my father took his interpretation from the records of the Nephites, but I have given mine from the commandment that I received from the mouth of the Lord.

107 And I know that the record of my father is correct according to that which the Lord wanted to come forth unto the children of men who received the unsealed portion of this record.

108 And this part of the record, which shall be sealed, shall be the standard of truth for the unsealed record of my father and all the scriptures that the Lord hath suffered to be given to the children of men.

109 Therefore, do not mock the things of God. And if ye must mock something, then mock me and my father for our weaknesses, and not for the words that we have been commanded to give unto you.

110. And now, I, Moroni, am going to return to the vision of the brother of Jared, which he gave concerning the Lord and the life of the Lord as a child.

111 And the Lord hath commanded me to include these things that ye might know of him, that he is your brother and doth not want to be set up above any of you, even according to the doctrine and mystery of godliness that I have just revealed unto you.

CHAPTER 43

Written scripture given through revelation can sometimes be misunderstood because of faulty translation. The reasons why Jesus is not mentioned in most historical documents. The early years of Christ with his family, which consisted of Joseph, his mother Mary, and his brothers, Joseph Jr., James, Simon, and Judas, and his sisters Sariah, Rachael, Elizabeth and Anah.

AND it shall come to pass that those who have set themselves up as leaders among the people, even those who are leaders of the religions of men, and also the governments of men, shall decide amongst themselves that history which they shall allow those under their subjection to receive. Or in other words, the written accounts of the histories of the children of men which are kept and sent forth as truth shall be determined by these leaders.

2 And the truth regarding what actually happened among the children of men shall not be made known. But the history that shall be presented shall be that truth which these leaders would want the people to believe.

3 And I have already explained unto you that the leaders of the nations shall not cause anything to be written that might cause them to be seen in a bad light unto future generations. For these leaders and rulers seek the glory of men, and want that all should remember them for that which they did that was righteous among the people of their kingdom.

4 And they would not allow to be written that which was contrary to their command. And if something was written which was contrary to their command, or which spoke the truth of their atrocities, or their murders, or their unjust actions among those of their kingdom, then they would cause these things to be destroyed along with the man or woman who had written these things.

5 And for these reasons, the truth regarding the childhood of Jesus was not had in the record of the Jews. For behold, those who transcribed the testimonies of the eyewitnesses to the life of Jesus would not allow to be written that which would throw a light upon Jesus that did not conform with the perception that these scribes had of him.

6 For this reason, many plain and precious things were left out of the record of the Jews. For the later leaders of those who followed the doctrine of Jesus, who would be known as Christians, had made Jesus into a God and gave him praise and glory and worshipped him, thus taking away from the glory of the Father, which Jesus had given unto the Father during the days of his earthly ministry.

7 And because these Christian leaders wanted the people of their churches to know and worship Jesus according to their own precepts, they caused the canon of holy scriptures, which they allowed the people to receive, to be confined to those things that supported their precepts and their beliefs.

8 And in the latter days when all things concerning the works of the children of men shall be revealed, many things shall come to light that the early Christian leaders did not know, neither did they understand because they did not have the Spirit of the Lord to guide them in that which they allowed to be given unto the people.

9 Nevertheless, the Lord fulfilleth his words and causeth his works to be done, not only through the righteous, but also through the works of the wicked. For in many ways, the things that were written of and that came forth unto the world in the Bible, which is the canon of scripture that the later Christian leaders caused to be given unto the people; yea, in many instances these things were acceptable to the Lord because of the wickedness of the people.

10 For Christ became their stumbling block because they would not humble themselves before the Father and do His will that they might receive the truth of all things from the Father as the Lord had commanded of all men.

11 And because of their wickedness, many of these plain and precious things pertaining to the truth and the life of Jesus were withheld from them, even according as it hath been explained unto you.

12 But the Lord hath commanded me that I should write somewhat concerning those things which were kept out of the canon of the holy scriptures that have been presented in written form and known in the latter days as the New Testament of the Bible.

13 And he hath commanded me that I include these things in this sealed portion of the record of my father, so that the world shall not have them until the Father commenceth His final work upon this earth, even when He shall begin to separate the tares from the wheat, or the evil from the righteous, as it hath been explained unto you in the holy scriptures.

14 And the righteous shall receive these things with gladness and rejoicing, for that which they did not understand shall be made known unto them by the gift and power of the Holy Ghost. And they shall begin to rejoice as they read the words of truth, which the Lord hath commanded me through the Holy Ghost to write unto them.

15 For the truth shall set them free from the chains by which Satan hath had them bound because of the traditions and beliefs of their fathers, which tradition and beliefs were not correct, according to the truth of God.

16 For it shall come to pass that the true history of the people shall be so polluted and corrupted by the desires of the rich and the powerful, as they make an attempt to hide their works of darkness from the eyes of the children of men, that the truth will hardly be known among them.

17 And for this reason these things which I

have written unto you, and also those things which I shall write unto you hereafter, shall come forth and reveal unto you the truth concerning the histories of men. And they shall reveal unto you the hidden works of darkness that your leaders have hidden from you because of their wickedness and personal agendas.

18 And their agendas and desires are that they should receive praise and honor of men, caring not for that which is of God. For inasmuch as they proclaim that the things which they do are the works of God, their hearts shall be uncovered in that which they do, and the people shall know of their wickedness. And it shall come to pass that those who follow them shall see their nakedness and mock them for that which they have tried to hide from them.

19 And at the time of the birth of Jesus there was a great king who was known as Herod according to the record of the Jews. And he had commanded that all the children under the age of two years be killed according to the beliefs of the Jews that a Messiah should be born among them at the time when the sign was given, and should come forth and save them.

20 And these beliefs were those things that were taught among the people by the leaders of the Jews who had read the words of the holy prophets and taken it upon themselves to give unto the people the meaning and understanding of these prophecies.

21 And this Herod, knew not the exact time of the birth of this Christ of which the prophets had spoken, but he knew that Bethlehem was to be the place of his birth. And according to his command, the children under the age of two were all killed in the city of Bethlehem.

22 Now, this thing was a gross tragedy and vicious atrocity to the people of Bethlehem, who were many of the poor among the people, but to the government of the Romans, it meant nothing. For Herod did many things away from which the Romans turned their cheeks, he being greatly honored among them.

23 And the people of the city of Bethlehem were few, and of their children there were sixty and three slain by the command of Herod. And what would be the reason for those who kept a history of the people to report such a minor loss to the Roman government? For who were the Jews to them? And why would they concern themselves of the beliefs and prophecies of the Jews?

24 But King Herod was a superstitious king who had his own priests and counselors who informed him of all things among the people. And when the prophecy of the birth of a Messiah was shown unto him, he commanded that the prophesied city be placed under his executive order, even that by his command were all the infants of this city killed, and this also according to the prophecies of the holy prophets.

25 Nevertheless, immediately after the birth of Jesus, Joseph was warned of the intent of Herod and took him and fled into Egypt. And immediately after these things, even immediately after he had given his executive order, a sore disease came upon Herod and he died a terrible death, having been cursed by the Lord because of his great wickedness.

26 And now this thing hath been a cause of contention among those of you in the latter days, even among those of you who claim that because the histories of the Romans and the Jews do not include these atrocities committed against the Jews by Herod, that they did not occur.

27 But I say unto you, ye have only one record, and that record hath been written according as I have explained it unto you. And do ye think that the leaders among the people of the Jews and the Romans would include any account of a man who caused a rift and a division among them? Yea, even one whom others testified of as being the Son of God?

28 For the Jews did not accept Jesus as the Messiah who should save them. And if they did not accept him as the Messiah of whom had been prophesied by all the holy prophets who had written concerning the coming of a Messiah, then why would ye think that their scribes and their historians would count him worthy of their attention?

29 And the Romans thought nothing of Jesus and the religion of the Jews. Therefore, why do ye think that they would have caused an account of him to be written?

30 And for these reasons which I have given

unto you, the written history of Jesus Christ is not had among the histories of the world, except it be among those who believed on his name and called themselves Christians and who were converted by the preaching and teachings of the twelve apostles that Jesus had chosen during his ministry.

31 But the accounts of these apostles have been changed and abridged and edited in such a way that they do not give the full truth of that which was written by the apostles concerning their time with Jesus in the flesh. And this time of Jesus in the flesh is not according to the calendars of time that ye keep among you in the latter days. Here is wisdom to him that hath understanding: even that the true day of the Lord in the flesh is within ten years of your accepted times; and by this knowledge ye can attempt to reckon the true time of the Lord.

32 And now, the Lord hath commanded me that I speak somewhat concerning his family, which consisted of Joseph, his father according to the flesh, his mother Mary, his younger brothers who were Joseph, who was the first born of Joseph, and James, Simon and Judas, and his sisters Sariah, Rachael, Elizabeth and Anah.

33 And these dwelt in the land of Nazareth, Joseph and Mary having traveled out of Egypt to inherit the land of their fathers when the Lord had commanded them by the Spirit.

34 And while they sojourned in Egypt, Joseph was born of Mary, yea even one year after the birth of Jesus, Joseph was born and called after the name of his father.

35 And when they returned to the land of Nazareth, Joseph went in unto the house of his father, Heli, and asked of him some of the land that was promised unto Joseph according to the laws and customs of the Jews pertaining to the inheritance of the sons from the father.

36 But Heli would not give unto Joseph that part of his inheritance, and this he withheld from him because Joseph had disgraced the name of Heli with his marriage to Mary and the birth of Jesus, who was not called after the name of those in their family.

37 But when Heli came to know that there was another son, even Joseph, who had taken the name of his father, then Heli gave unto Joseph a portion of that inheritance which he desired. And upon that inheritance Joseph began to raise his family according to the customs and traditions of the Jews.

38 And Jesus grew as a child. And from time to time he would go with Mary into the wilderness to visit her mother. And it was in the wilderness that Jesus came to know John, the son of Zacharias, who lived with the mother of Mary in the wilderness.

39 And when Jesus would visit his grandmother as a child, she would hold him tenderly and weep upon him, for she truly knew who he was and for what purpose he had been born into the world.

40 And it came to pass that as the mother of Mary showered these feelings upon Jesus, the other sons of Mary did notice that which they did perceive were adorations that they did not receive from their grandmother.

41 And because of this thing, Joseph, the eldest son of Mary and Joseph, did complain unto his father. And Joseph took Mary apart from their children and said unto her: How is it that thy mother can give this special attention and love unto Jesus, yet suffer that the children of my flesh receive no special bond with her? Should they not be treated like unto him in all things?

42 And Mary answered her husband, saying: My mother doth not look upon Jesus as she doth our other children, because he is not like our other children, for they are not of the Spirit as is our Lord Jesus, who was conceived of the Spirit and not of the flesh to save us all from our sins. And shall he not save me and my mother and our children? Yea, shall he not also save thee of thy sins according to the words of the angel that thou hast heard concerning him?

43 And from that time forth Joseph became jealous of Jesus, and began to mistreat him with indifference and inequality, not like unto his other children.

44 And it came to pass that Joseph sought out the help and advise of his father and also his uncle who were High Priests of the church at Jerusalem. And he was convinced by them that Jesus was not the Messiah, but that he might be a great prophet among them, owing to the great words which Jesus could speak unto them even as a youth, but that he could not be the great Messiah of which the prophets have prophesied.

45 And Joseph believed on the words of the leaders of the church and did not keep in remembrance those things which were given unto him by an angel of God. And all the days of the youth of Jesus were filled with this treatment of inequality from Joseph.

46 And now, these things were not included in the Bible according to the words of the Jews, because the leaders did not want it discovered that Joseph was an unrighteous man, who was against Jesus all the days of his life.

47 But Jesus remained a faithful son, according to the flesh, to Joseph. For whatever was required of him, that did Jesus do. And Jesus was given those tasks which were the most arduous and time consuming of all the commands that Joseph gave unto his sons in the course of their daily labors.

48 And Jesus did not complain of these things, and did those things which were expected of him according to the will of Joseph. And not in anything did Jesus give Joseph a reason that he should have been treated unequally, but thus he was.

49 And the other sons of Joseph began to mock Jesus and take cause up against him with their father for that which they wanted to cause the hardship and turmoil of Jesus.

50 For it came to pass that in a particular city that was near unto Nazareth, Joseph had made a contract with a certain rich man to build a house with his sons. And the contract was according to the time that was allowed by the rich man to Joseph and his sons to build the house.

51 And it came to pass that Joseph put his son Joseph in authority over Jesus and commanded him to build the house according to the desires of the rich man. And Joseph exercised this authority over Jesus, evensomuch that he did nothing with his own hands to build the house.

52 And he commanded his other brothers to help Jesus, but that they should rest when they were desirous and drink when they were thirsty. But Joseph had set certain times that Jesus, who was even his elder brother, could drink and rest from his labors.

53 And when they would meet their father coming from another place in which he was engaged in other matters of his business, Joseph would report on the progress of the house and explain unto Joseph of the laziness and ineptness of Jesus in doing those things which he had commanded him to do according to the power and authority that he had been given over him by their father. And to these charges, Jesus would not respond.

54 And Joseph rebuked Jesus, saying: Who thinkest that thou art? I know that thou hast been taught by thy mother that thou art special and have a mission that is to be performed when thou hast reached the age of maturity, but what thinkest thou of us, who are thy family and who provide for thee and give unto thee all that thou needest to eat and a place to sleep? Canst thou not even for a few years of thy life give unto me thy respect and obedience for that which I provide for thee?

55 And Jesus looked upon his brother Joseph, and said unto his father: Ask of him at what stage of building we are according to the design and the contract that thou hast made with the owner of the house.

56 And Joseph inquired of his son Joseph as to the stage of the building. And Joseph said unto his father: We are yet in the first stage because of the works of Jesus, who refuseth to do those things which I have required of him.

57 And Jesus said unto his father, Joseph: It is true, my father, that the work of Joseph is yet in the first stage, for that is the work that he hath done. But the work that I have done thou shall see on the morrow in the light, for that which hath been required of the contract shall be done by my Father.

58 And these words were spoken in respect by Jesus unto Joseph. Nevertheless, Joseph ridiculed Jesus and fell upon him and knocked him to the ground for that which he had said, thinking that Jesus had said these things to mock him, believing that Jesus had referred to him as his father.

59 And on the morrow Joseph went with his sons unto the place where they were building. And he went with them that there would be no further contention among them, and so that he could work with them and fulfill the terms of the contract which he had made.

60 And when they reached the house, the rich man was waiting there outside with full payment in his hand for that which had been done. For when they came unto the house and looked, it was complete according to all the specifications that had been given them. And they were all, except Jesus, astonished at the precision and the beauty of the house, which had been finished in one night.

61 And the rich man said unto them: When I arrived in the early hour of the morning, I saw those who were finishing up the house according to the design that I had given unto you. And after they were finished, I offered this payment unto them thinking that they were of thy hire, and that they had been commanded of thee to finish this work before the terms of our contract required.

62 And because of their work, which I supposed was commanded of thee, I offered them double of that amount that we had agreed upon because of the speed and the fineness of the work. But they refused to take my money, but instructed me to give it unto him who had commanded them. And when I asked of them who it was that had commanded them to work through the night by the light of their fires to complete this thing, they said Joseph, thy son, had commanded it of them.

63 And with these words the rich man gave Joseph, the son, the money that he had brought with him to pay for the terms of the contract which had been completed by the angels of God, according to the will and desire of Jesus.

64 And Joseph accepted the money not knowing what it was that he should say to his father concerning those who had completed this work.

65 And Jesus perceived the perplexity of Joseph and spoke unto his father, saying: It was this thing that our brother Joseph did not want to explain unto thee, not knowing if thou wouldst become angered because of the hires that he made without thy permission, seeing that I could not do those things which he had commanded of me.

66 And Joseph, the son, looked upon Jesus in wonder and amazement and did not have that which he should say.

67 And Joseph said unto his son: That which thou hast done is a good work. Now, go and take some of this money and pay those whom thou hast hired to do this thing. And Joseph gave unto his father all the money except that which his father had determined was sufficient to pay those whom he supposed his son had hired.

68 And Jesus smiled upon his brother Joseph. And it came to pass that Jesus left with his father and his other brothers while Joseph stood with the money that his father had given unto him to pay the hirelings.

69 And when Joseph had counted out the money that his father had given unto him, he counted exactly thirty pieces of silver. And at the exact moment that he had counted out this amount, he looked back towards the way wherein his father and brothers were going, and Jesus looked back upon him and smiled once again upon Joseph.

70 And now, Joseph had been taught by his father, and also by the leaders of the church, that Jesus was not the Messiah, but a man who might have a mission of prophecy unto the people, but that unless the church sanctioned his preaching and his ministry, then it could not be from God.

71 And because of the words which Jesus had taught unto them as a child, even the words of wisdom that even they could not understand, the leaders wanted to know all things concerning him throughout the days of his life.

72 And for this reason, the leaders of the church made the son of Joseph a spy for them of all that which Jesus said and did during the course of his life with his family.

73 And it came to pass that Joseph took the money that his father had given unto him and went unto the High Priest and told him all things which were done that day.

74 And the High Priest commanded Joseph to speak to no one concerning this thing, but that he should take no more authority over Jesus in the course of the business of his father.

75 And the High Priest took the money, even the thirty pieces of silver, and put it in a secret place that it might be used against Jesus if it were possible. For behold, if money was needed against Jesus, the High Priest felt that he could not use the money of the church, nor should he use his own money to do that which was needed against a wicked man as he supposed.

76 And this was done that the words of the prophet might be fulfilled which he spoke, saying: And I said unto them, If ye think good, give me my price; and if not forbear. So they weighed for my price thirty pieces of silver.

77 And from that time forth, Joseph did not command Jesus in anything, neither did he mock him or make cause against him before his father Joseph, and this according to the instructions that he had received from the High Priest.

78 And Jesus continued to work for his father Joseph and do those things which were required of him.

79 And as he worked in the course of the days of his youth and early adulthood, Mary would send her daughter Sariah to carry water and provisions unto her brothers while they worked.

80 And Sariah loved Jesus, even with all of her heart, and looked to him with pride and adoration as her older brother and as her friend. And Jesus also loved Sariah and played with her often in her infancy and in her youth. And he came to love Sariah, even with all of his soul.

81 And Sariah would sit upon his knee in her youth and converse with Jesus for many hours, learning of him the things that he would teach unto her. And Jesus taught Sariah many things which he had learned from the Spirit according to the will of the Father.

82 And Jesus made Sariah promise him that she would keep all these things in her heart and tell no one, except she should speak to their mother Mary concerning them.

83 And it came to pass that while Jesus was engaged in building again according to the command of Joseph, and he worked with Joseph on this particular day; and on this day Rachael and Elizabeth ran unto their father and told him that Sariah had fallen from her labors and was taken suddenly ill.

84 And Joseph and Jesus immediately left that which they were doing and ran unto their house. And when they were come into the house, Mary was in the doorway with Anah weeping exceedingly. And Jospeh hurried into the room where his oldest daughter was lying ill.

85 And Jesus held his mother and took Anah from her as she fell to the ground before her son pleading with him that he might save his sister from the illness that had quickly befallen her.

86 But Joseph returned again to Mary and took her in his arms and wept exceedingly with her, for Sariah had died.

87 And Jesus gave Anah unto his brother Joseph, whose countenance had fallen at the news of the death of his sister, and who was with his other brothers who were there beholding their parents as they wept for Sariah. And they also wept great tears of sorrow for their sister, for she was dearly beloved by all of them.

88 And Jesus went straightaway into the room where the body of Sariah was laid. And he took her into his arms and held her close to him and wept exceedingly upon her, evensomuch that his tears wet her face and the pillow upon which she lay.

89 And Jesus thought within himself that he should use the power that the Father had given unto him to bring back his beloved sister. And when he had thought on these things, yea, even when he was about to issue forth the command in his sorrow, a voice spoke unto him near unto the bed where the flesh of Sariah lay.

90 And he looked up and saw the departed spirit of his sister near unto him. And as a spirit, Sariah whispered unto him, saying: My Lord, I know that thou hast the power that thou hast been given of our Father to command my spirit to enter again into my body that I might once again take upon me the flesh that I received when I entered into mortality. But I beg of thee that thou shouldst not do such a thing, for that which hath been done is according to my own will, and hath been granted unto me by our Father.

91 Behold, thou art my beloved brother and my friend. All the days of my life hast thou loved me and kept me safe and secure in the arms of thy love, evensomuch that many times I was overwhelmed by the love that thou showed unto me as a child.

92 And thou spoke unto me of those things that thou hast commanded me not to share with any other in the flesh. And I did that which thou didst command of me all the days of my life. But in the night before the dawn of today, I received a dream in the which I saw thee and that which would befall thee in the flesh, even that thou wouldst be scourged and beaten and lifted upon the cross to die an unnatural death, even a death that no other man in the flesh could suffer.

93 And in sorrow I did rise to face another day of knowing you in the flesh and being at your side and loving you as my brother. And the thought of the pain that I would suffer, knowing that these things would one day happen unto thee, brought me even unto the door of the death of my soul.

94 For behold, how could I live to see this happen to my beloved brother? Yea, how could I, in the flesh, see thou sufferest because of the sins and wickedness of the world, even when thou art innocent of all sin?

95 And I prayed with all my soul that the Father would take me home to Him that I might not be a witness of your death in the flesh. And I prayed with all of the energies of my heart and made a promise that if the Father did not take me, then I would take my own life this day, so that I would not have to behold these things concerning you in the flesh.

96 But as a spirit, I can behold these things and understand them. Yea, even as a spirit I can be at thy side and uphold thee and give thee strength even at the time of thy greatest need.

97 Behold, in the flesh I could not do these things. Now, wantest thou that I suffer so in the flesh? Thou knowest of the glory of the spirit world. Thou knowest of the peace and happiness of the souls that enter therein without sin. Thou knowest that they rest from all of their worries and are not burdened with the things of the flesh any longer. And now, my beloved brother, even my Lord Jesus Christ, what wouldst thou want for me?

98 And after the spirit of Sariah had said these things unto Jesus, he was comforted in his pain; and he did not command that her spirit enter again into her body. And he said unto her: Of thy spirit, I have renewed my own. Go in peace, my beloved sister, and I will come unto thee soon.

99 And now, when the brother of Jared had witnessed these things in his vision, it caused him exceeding love for his sisters who were of his family. For he also had a sister who had died in her youth, and her name was Herithany.

100 And he requested of the Lord in his vision that he might be visited by her, that he, too, might receive the comfort which he beheld concerning Jesus and Sariah.

101 And the Lord had compassion upon the brother of Jared and commanded the spirit of Herithany to come forth according to the power of the Spirit by which he beheld these things. And she came forth; and with her was another spirit. And the brother of Jared immediately recognized the other spirit as that of Sariah who would one day come into mortality as the sister of Jesus.

102 And both of them smiled upon the brother of Jared and gave unto him the comfort that he desired. And in this thing the brother of Jared was overwhelmed by the Spirit, evensomuch that he could not go on in the vision according to the flesh.

103 But Jehovah once again supported him and gave him the strength that he needed to continue with his glorious vision.

CHAPTER 44

More of the youth of Jesus is described. He is forbidden by the Father to use his powers and knowledge unwisely. The body of flesh that was given Jesus is explained and is the means whereby he can do the miracles that he does. The theory of evolution is touched upon when Moroni gives an account of Jesus commanding a change in the state of nature to benefit one species of an animal over another.

AND it came to pass that the brother of Jared wrote much concerning the life of Christ. Nevertheless, I, Moroni, have been commanded to include in this record only a small part of the things which the brother of Jared saw, and also many of the things which the Lord hath commanded me to include in this record when he visited me.

2 And it came to pass that as the Lord grew in the flesh, the Holy Ghost was with him and taught him many things which were commanded of the Holy Ghost by the Father.

3 And Jesus was commanded to not use the powers of his body for that which was not commanded of the Father. For Jesus began to see that his body of flesh was different from that of his other brothers and his sisters. For if he cut his flesh, he could command it to be restored unto its original state like unto that which is of new, and it was immediately done unto him as he had commanded.

4 Now this he could do, as well as many other miracles, wherein he commanded the elements, because of the body that he had received of the Holy Ghost, which was given unto him by the command of the Father.

5 Now, in the latter days it shall be made known unto you—even Satan shall cause these things to be known unto you, believing that he shall receive the glory of this knowledge—the manner in which the body of flesh is created by the pattern which it receiveth from the mother and the father.

6 And this pattern is followed precisely as the laws of nature direct the creation of this body. For behold, all things that are flesh follow the course of flesh in which they are created. And in order for anything in the flesh to be created, it must follow a pattern that hath been given unto it according to the eternal laws of nature, which the Father hath commanded shall be used upon this earth according to the order of the flesh which He hath given unto us, and with which we pass through the days of our probation.

7 And these laws of nature, even the laws by which we exist, require that a pattern be given by the mother and also that a pattern and a direction be given by the father.

8 Now, I have said that a pattern is required of the mother, but not necessarily a direction. Behold, the mother hath only to give a pattern of the flesh unto the body that she would create, but the father shall give a pattern and a direction according to the will of the Father, which is the will of the Spirit.

9 For all spirits are without gender, and it is determined by the Father, according to the spirit, which gender the body of the flesh shall be. And this determination is made by the spirit child of God, and it is made according to that desire of happiness that this spirit hath chosen for itself.

10 And when a spirit maketh a determination of its gender, then through the spirit, which again is the will of the Father, the command is given through the body of the mortal father, who unknowingly giveth direction unto the body of the mother of which gender should be produced.

11 And after the determination of gender is made, then the pattern that is given with this direction from the father unto the mother is used, as well as the pattern of her own body, which pattern hath always been with the mother since the creation of her flesh.

12 And these two patterns shall cause to be created a new body that shall be of the mother until a new spirit entereth into the newly created body upon birth.

13 And a woman hath been given the power to create after the power of her own body since her birth. For inside the woman hath the pattern been already given.

14 But the man cannot have this power except it be allowed of him by the power of his spirit, which shall be the direction in which his own pattern shall be used, along with the pattern of a woman, to create the new body of flesh.

15 Now in the creation of the body of Jesus, the pattern of the mother was used as I have explained it unto you. And the direction came directly from the power of the Father, through the administrations of the spirit world, which gave the direction and the pattern that should be used for his body.

16 And the direction was for the creation of a male body like unto that of the Father. And the pattern was given in the exact likeness of the Father, which upon combining with the pattern provided by the body of Mary, created a body of flesh that was both eternal and immortal, yet subject to the flesh, or the nature to which our mortal bodies are created.

17 And when the pattern was followed, which gave unto Jesus the example of that portion of the body which shall be called the cerebrum in the latter days, he was given the pattern also of the cerebrum of the Father, which provided for him certain means whereby the transmissions of his cerebrum can command more elements—which elements have been restricted by the laws of our mortal nature, even the nature of the flesh. But the cerebrum of the Son is not restricted, like unto the Father, and it can command more element than the cerebrums of those who have two mortal parents, who have each contributed a pattern for its creation.

18 Now, here is somewhat of a mystery that I will explain unto you of the latter days: For I have explained unto you what Cherubim and the flaming sword symbolizeth, even that it symbolizeth the veil of forgetfulness that is placed upon us so that we cannot remember, in the flesh, those things which occurred before the days of our probation, that we may be more thoroughly tested by faith.

19 And this Cherubim and the flaming sword symbolizeth the formation of our mortal cerebrum which cannot be used to produce those memories which our spirit can readily recall. For if a spirit is placed in a body where the cerebrum hath not been patterned after the limitations that the Father hath set by the representation of the Cherubim and the flaming sword, then that spirit would be able to react with this cerebrum of flesh and remember all things.

20 For behold, the spirit was created of eternal elements which cannot be seen by mortal eyes, but which existeth as I have explained it unto you previously. And when the spirit entereth into the body, it is able to send certain commands to the elements of the flesh, or of nature, according to the type of cerebrum that hath been given unto the body of flesh.

21 And Jesus was given a cerebrum that was patterned partially after the cerebrum of the Father, who is eternal and who can command all elements. Therefore, the cerebrum of Jesus was so constructed, that the spirit of Jesus, who was Jehovah, could command the elements like unto the Father, but was restricted in some senses because of the order of nature in which he was created by his mother Mary.

22 And Jesus could also remember things that had occurred before he was born into mortality, not having the fullness of the Cherubim and the flaming sword placed before him; or in other words, not having a cerebrum that was affected by all the restrictions placed upon the cerebrums of the other children of Adam and Eve.

23 And he could also communicate with the Spirit—which is the means given by the Father to communicate with His children—in a much more concise and consistent manner than that which the rest of us in mortality can do.

24 And so it was that Jesus was born into the world with powers that no other mortal man had ever, nor would ever be given. And he was commanded by the Father, through the ministrations of the Spirit, that he should not use these powers except it be according to the commandments that he shall receive from the Father.

25 And now, in this thing was the righteousness of Christ proven in all things. For behold, he had the power to do many things, yea, even the power to give life after the order of the flesh, and take life from this same order of flesh.

26 And if it were his desire, he could command the elements at his will, having the ability to do so because of the body that he received from the direction and pattern of the Father.

27 And the Father could not prohibit Jesus

from using these powers as he wished because of the eternal laws of nature that are given unto them who have this type of body. For they are not restricted in anything that they would do.

28 Nevertheless, the Father could give unto him commandments. But it was by the free will and choice of Jesus that would determine whether or not he would keep the commandments of the Father. And for this reason, very few are allowed to have this type of power, which cometh from a body like unto the Father.

29 And Jesus kept the commandments of the Father in all things from the beginning. And the Father knew that Jesus would keep His commandments, and this was the only reason that the Father allowed His Son to have a body patterned after His own.

30 And so it is with all of those who shall receive a body like unto the Father, or a Celestial body, that shall have the power and glory of the Father, according to the order in which it is created.

31 And once a spirit hath been given this body, it shall have the powers of this body. And the powers of this body shall be under the direct control and will of the spirits who possess it. And for this reason, the spirits of all men and women are tested and tried to see if they are worthy of this type of body.

32 And if they are worthy of this type of body, which is Celestial, then they shall have all the power of the Father, becoming one with Him in all things. And those of the flesh that shall one day receive the power of the Father, even a body that is patterned after His Celestial body; and given direction according to their desires of happiness, whether their desires be male or female; yea, these shall be proven to see if they shall do the will of the Father in all things.

33 And the will of the Father in all things are the words of Christ according to the flesh. And in this way is Christ the supreme example for us all. For he shall prove unto all of us that he is willing and able to do the will of the Father in all things, thus proving himself eligible for the power of the Father.

34 And he hath come into the flesh to show unto us all that those who shall receive this power of the Father are fully able to abide the will of the Father in all things whatsoever He shall command them.

35 And in this way the plan of Lucifer is destroyed, even the desire of Lucifer to give unto all the children of God the power of the Father in providing for them a Celestial body that alloweth them this power.

36 For the majority of all spirits cannot abide in righteousness in the flesh, but use the limited capacity of their body to disobey the commandments of the Father.

37 And because Jesus hath lived his life as an example unto them, they cannot say that it is impossible to live a life in the flesh according to the will of the Father in all things. For Christ hath already shown unto them that it can be done. Therefore, if Christ can do it, even having the power of the Father, or no limitations on his power, then any spirit that is righteous can do it.

38 And it is much easier for those who have limited power to live according to the will of the Father, for they cannot be tempted to use the power that they do not have. For can ye imagine a world wherein all the bodies of the children of men possess the power of the Father?

39 What would then become of the lusts of men? Could they not create from the dust that which they would consume upon their lusts?

40 And what of the anger and prejudice of men? Would not they destroy any thing that upset them or which did not fit into their own desire of happiness? And how would they destroy their enemy by the power of their word, when by the power of the word of their enemy, their enemy could be saved?

41 And those who desire more power and riches than another; yea, what would be the end of their creation of gold and silver and the precious things of the earth? For when one by his own command can create a mountain of gold, then another by his own command shall make a mountain even higher than the mountain of the first. And once the first seeth the mountain of the second, then would he not covet a mountain that is even bigger still?

42 And after he had created another mountain, which is bigger still, then would the second create still a bigger mountain until it reached

forever into the heavens without end. And thus we can see why the children of men are limited in the powers that they possess.

43 But Jesus was not limited in the powers that he possessed, but he restricted himself in these powers according to the will and the commandments of the Father.

44 Even as a child, Jesus refrained from using his powers. And there were some instances in which he did use his powers, but he did so as he was commanded by the spirit, or when he knew that the use of his power would bring about that which was good.

45 And it came to pass that on one occasion the young Jesus of about ten years of age was upon the edge of a river where he would retire to be by himself and communicate with his Father through the Spirit.

46 And on this occasion he took it upon himself to observe the animals that lived in the orders in which they were created. And he noticed a particular group of birds that was at the waters edge and which was voraciously devouring the eggs of a certain type of frog that existed along the edge of the river in the shallows thereof.

47 And he had observed that there were many birds which had discovered that the eggs of the frog were pleasant to their taste and that they were nutritious for them.

48 But the birds threatened the existence of this particular frog, which species of frog could only be found along the edge of this one river.

49 And Jesus had compassion upon the frog and commanded the elements of its eggs that they would not be nutritious unto the birds, but that the birds would, by their nature, devour the eggs of the frogs, but in their stomachs the eggs would maintain their life giving essence and be passed out of the bird in its time of excrement.

50 And the birds would deposit these eggs at other places along the river according to their time of excrement, thus assuring the survival and perpetuation of that species of frog.

51 And now, this is another mystery that shall be known unto you in the latter days. For among you shall be those who think that the order of nature itself might cause this gradual formation of an egg that shall be adapted to the survival of the species which it representeth, so that it is not completely destroyed.

52 And ye shall think that this gradual adaptation of a species shall take place over many years in a process that ye shall call evolution. But I say unto those of you who shall believe these things: Yea, what if the Lord had not commanded the elements of the eggs of these frogs? Would they have survived the hunger of the birds? I say unto you that they would not have survived the hunger of the birds and would have become extinct in a manner of a short time according to the knowledge of the birds and their hunger.

53 And do ye not believe that by the spirit, even according to the power that is held in the spirit world, that these things can be commanded to take place instantaneously, so that one species of animal or plant might not overrun another?

54 And I say unto you that believe this thing, are not your own bodies created of the same elements of which are created the plants and the animals within the order of nature to which ye belong?

55 And do ye not control the elements of your own body in a limited manner? I say unto you, that ye do command these elements, even the elements that cause ye to breath and which cause your muscles to move.

56 But with your limitations, ye cannot command the elements of another, or of that which is outside of your flesh. Nevertheless, the Lord alloweth examples of this ability to be among you.

57 For are there not those among you who exhibit extraordinary feats which would require the effects of the cerebrum on outside elements? I say unto you that there are those among you who can do these things, but they are restricted in a limited manner as I have explained it unto you.

58 And if ye, with your limitations, can command matter, then how much more can be done by one who doth not have the limitations that ye possess?

59 And there are those among you who do not have the limitations that ye possess, but they are under strict command to not use this power

unless they are commanded by the Father, according to the ministrations of the Spirit.

60 But unto the body of Jesus there were no limitations given, and thus he was able to do the miracles that he did during the days of his ministry.

61 And there were other miracles that he wrought as a youth, but none of significance for the purpose of this record. And one of the first miracles that he did perform before the eyes of all men, he did perform at his own wedding.

CHAPTER 45

Jesus is married to Martha and Mary, and later to Mary Magdalene, who becomes the closest to him in the flesh. He is not allowed to have children for the sake and the glory that he desires for the Father. The relations between a Celestial husband and wife are set forth and explained. A man will have only one eternal mate. Mary Magdalene is the eternal mate of Jesus and will be at his side at the Second Coming.

AND now it was the purpose of those who organized the canon of scripture that gave an account of the life of Jesus in the record of the Jews to not include the account of the marriage of the Lord to Martha, who was the daughter of Amasiah, and the sister of Mary and also of Lazarus, who was a childhood friend of Jesus.

2 For behold, Lazarus had known Jesus most of his life; and they had played together in many instances as children when their fathers were engaged in the course of their businesses.

3 But this Lazarus and his family moved away from Nazareth and settled closer unto Jerusalem in the town of Bethany. And when Jesus was of the age of maturity according to their customs, even that he was no longer subjected to the will and dominion of his parents, he left Nazareth and went unto Bethany and found Lazarus and dwelt there for sometime while he prepared for the day of his ministry.

4 And while in the house of Amasiah, Jesus preached the gospel unto them of the whole house, and they were converted unto the gospel of which he spoke, which gospel he had received of the Father.

5 And Amasiah loved Jesus as his own son, and also as his Lord, having been given a witness of him by the Spirit as he listened to the gospel of the Father that was taught unto him by Jesus.

6 And Amasiah desired that Jesus take his eldest daughter, Martha, as his wife, that he might have companionship during the days of his ministry.

7 Now, this was the custom of the Jews, even that the father might have some direct involvement in choosing a husband for his daughters.

8 But Jesus had taught unto them the will of the Father concerning the marriage of a man and a woman and said unto Amasiah: Behold, it is not given unto me to choose that woman who would be my wife, but she must choose me for herself. And the law of Moses hath been fulfilled in me, even in this thing which thou desirest of me.

9 But thy daughter is of an age and of a sound mind that she might choose for herself the man with whom she shall covenant as her husband. And if she chooseth me of her own free will and choice, then I will be her husband according to the commandments of the Father.

10 For the Father doth not respect a man over a woman, and hath given unto each woman the right to choose for herself her own husband. But this I have been commanded to tell unto thee from the Father, even that if thy daughter chooseth me to be her husband, then she shall have no children from the union.

11 For the Father hath commanded me that I shall not leave a posterity in the flesh. For if I were to leave a son or a daughter in the flesh, then the glory of that son or daughter would one day overshadow the glory of the Father, which glory is meant to be given with an eye single to His glory and not to any person in the flesh.

12 And if it is the will of thy daughter that she be my wife, then she shall be barren all the days of her life and shall have no child with me, but shall be my companion during the time of my life, which shall not be many years.

13 But if she is righteous and doeth that which is required of her by the Father, then she shall be with me forever in the kingdom of the Father where we shall one day experience the joy of eternal children, even as the Father doth experience the joy of His own.

14 And it came to pass that Martha chose Jesus to be her husband according to that which she had been taught by him.

15 Now, this thing was hard for Martha to do because of the traditions and the customs of the Jews, which were taught unto her all the days of her life. But she had also been converted by the Lord and given the Holy Ghost that convinced her that Jesus was the Savior of the world, and the Son of the Eternal Father who had been sent to save the world from its sins by teaching the people the will of the Father.

16 And because she had received this witness of him, she knew that she could not have a child by him, according to his words. And Martha reasoned in herself for some time. And she knew that the opportunity to be at the side of Jesus for as long as he was among the people in the flesh would be a blessing enough for her. And she wanted that Jesus be her husband, and went unto him and requested of him this thing.

17 And because of the Jews and their customs and traditions, Jesus suffered that Martha marry him according to this manner. And it was this wedding of which is briefly spoken of in the record of the Bible which ye already have before you.

18 For it was customary that the family of the groom provide the wine and the food for those who were in attendance at the wedding. And Mary, the mother of Jesus, did not think that Jesus would submit himself to the traditions and customs of the Jews, therefore, she did not prepare the wedding on her part according to these customs.

19 And when the hour of the wedding arrived, Jesus was made aware that there had been no wine brought by his mother according to the tradition. And he smiled upon his mother and said unto her: Behold, for my wife I do these things and have submitted to these things for her enjoyment and the enjoyment of those of her family.

20 And where are those of my own family? Did they not think that I would do this thing because of that which I have been given to do by my Father? Behold, my hour is not yet for that which I must do for my Father. Therefore, what wilt thou have me to do for thee? That will I do; for mine hour is not yet come.

21 And it came to pass that Mary sent the servants of the wedding to Jesus and commanded them to do that which he would tell them, that she might fulfill all those things which were required of her family by the traditions of the Jews.

22 And Joseph, the firstborn of Joseph, and his other brothers and his other sisters were forbidden to come to the wedding by the commandment of Joseph, their father. For at this time, Joseph had rebelled against Jesus and remembered not the things which he knew to be true about him, even those things which were given unto him by an angel of God. And he taught his other children, who were from Mary, that Jesus was like unto them.

23 Nevertheless, Mary knew of the divinity of her son and kept all these things in her heart, for she loved Joseph and submitted herself unto him according to the traditions of the Jews.

24 But when it came to Jesus, Mary would not submit to the will of Joseph, but did those things which were given unto her by the power of the Spirit, or by the voice of her son, whom she knew was also the Savior of the world.

25 And the reason why the publishers of the Bible and the account of the life of Jesus presented therein, did not want it known that Jesus was married was because of their own beliefs that those who would have the priesthood of God should not be married and partake of the relations that a man enjoyeth with a woman who is his wife.

26 And this they believed only because of their own misunderstandings of the scriptures and that which they felt was proper for the people to know concerning Jesus whom they had set up with much glory among the later Christians, contrary to that which the Lord had taught to his disciples.

27 And because they did not have the Spirit to guide them, they did not understand that the

relationship between a man and a woman was the only way whereby eternal happiness could be perpetuated and given unto others.

28 And Jesus was the example in the flesh unto the people in all things. And if it was required of him to be a perfect example of the Father, then it would be requisite that Jesus be the perfect example of the Father in all things.

29 And before the Father became a father, He was first an husband, even the husband of an Eternal Mother, who is his wife. For a man cannot become a father, even an Eternal Father, save he shall first be a husband who hath been chosen by a woman to fulfill the measure of her happiness by creating children within her by her husband.

30 And thus was it necessary that Jesus give unto the world the example of a righteous husband in all things. And the account of his marriages, which were three in the flesh, were all given in the accounts of the apostles who were called by him to preach his gospel to the people.

31 And now, I have revealed unto you that Jesus was married thrice during the days of his probation. And it is this thing that I must explain unto you: But because of the wickedness of the later Christian leaders, many of these plain and precious things were taken out of the accounts of the apostles.

32 Behold, the first marriage was according to the traditions and the customs of the Jews, which was the marriage of Jesus to Martha, the eldest daughter of Amasiah, the father of his friend Lazarus.

33 And the younger sister of Martha, who was Mary, also desired to be the wife of Jesus according to the new law which Jesus had taught unto them pertaining to marriage.

34 And it came to pass that Mary went unto her sister Martha and desired that she, too, could be the wife of Jesus according to that which they had been taught by Jesus.

35 And Jesus had taught unto them the eternal law of marriage, which is the same law that Adam taught unto his children, and which I have given unto you in an earlier part of this record.

36 And this law was given unto all the daughters of Adam and Eve, even that if a woman cometh unto another woman and desireth to take her husband also as her own husband, then that wife shall have the choice to take her unto herself as a sister wife to her husband. But if she doeth this thing to her sister, then she must know that this sister shall be equal to her in the eyes of her husband.

37 And if any woman taketh a sister wife unto herself for her husband, then it will be counted unto her as righteousness before God. But if she doth not allow another woman to take her righteous husband as her own, then it shall not be counted unto her as unrighteous before God. For the Lord delighteth in the chastity and honor of women.

38 And it came to pass that Martha gave Mary unto Jesus to be his wife according to the desire of Mary, her sister.

39 And now, the third wife of Jesus of which I have spoken was she who was also called Mary, even she who is referred to as Mary Magdalene in the accounts of the apostles.

40 And this Mary also came unto Martha and Mary after she was cleansed from all of her sins; and she desired to be the wife of Jesus with them.

41 And Mary loved Mary Magdalene, even with all of her heart, and wanted her to be a sister wife with them. But Martha thought upon the things, even that which the Lord had said that it would not be counted unto her as unrighteous before God if she did not accept another woman to share her husband.

42 And she thought many days on that which Mary Magdalene had desired of her. And she knew that none of them could have children by Jesus, and that each of them would be equal in his eyes and loved according to the just love that the Lord had for all people.

43 And after she prayed unto the Father concerning this thing, even as Jesus had taught her, she accepted Mary Magdalene also as a wife of Jesus.

44 And it came to pass that this second Mary became the closest to Jesus in the flesh, even that she became his close friend in whom he would confide many things of his heart.

45 And on one occasion, Jesus said unto this Mary, even Mary Magdalene: Behold, my beloved, the Father knoweth of thy desires and He knoweth of my love for thee. And the love that I have for thee is an eternal love that cannot be broken in the flesh, nor in the Spirit in which it is given.

46 And thou art sealed up to be my wife and my friend according to the eternal laws of heaven which allow a man and a woman to be sealed together forever as a couple that shall not be separated.

47 And the Father, even at this time, is preparing other men for Martha and Mary that they might also have a husband who loveth them as I love thee, and as thou lovest me, if it so be that they shall have the desire to have an eternal mate.

48 But for their sakes, I have given myself unto them in the flesh according to the commandments that the Father hath given unto me pertaining to marriage. For it was their desire that I be their husband according to the flesh, which desire I was commanded to fulfill according to the commandment given to me by my Father.

49 Behold, in the kingdom of the Father there are those women who do not have husbands, because in a husband they do not find a friend of happiness. Nevertheless, they are righteous women who have chosen to be Eternal Mothers forever in the kingdom of the Father.

50 And they shall conceive like unto my mother, Mary, who conceived by the power of the Father through the Holy Ghost. And they shall be the Eternal Mothers of all the spirit children of the Father, but they are His sisters who desire the more righteous part of being a mother.

51 For behold, the Father hath only one wife, and her name is Marihala, and she is the mother of my spirit. And only with Marihala doth the Father engage in those relations that bring Him the joys of the flesh, which are given through this union.

52 And now my Dear Beloved, keep these things in thy heart and tell them not unto thy sister wives according to the flesh, for they are not ready that they might be able to accept these things.

53 But thou knowest that I love them, even with all the love that a husband can have for his wife, but this love is according to the flesh and not according to the Spirit.

54 But I love thee according to the Spirit, and it is by this same spirit that our marriage hath been sealed by the Holy Spirit of promise that giveth us the promise that we shall be together in the kingdom of the Father forever.

55 And now, I, Moroni, have been commanded by the Lord to reveal this mystery unto you, even those things which the Lord said unto Mary Magdalene, who was sealed to him by the Holy Spirit of promise.

56 And this he hath commanded me because of the wickedness of the men in the latter days who shall receive these things. For behold, they shall not understand the principle of eternal marriage as it hath been established according to the eternal laws of heaven.

57 For there are many of you who shall believe that ye shall have more than one wife in the Celestial kingdom of the Father. Behold, it is true that ye might have many wives, even hundreds and thousands of wives who shall choose you, if ye are righteous, to take from you the power that ye have, according to the Spirit, to give direction and a pattern unto them that they might conceive and bring forth spirit children unto you.

58 But ye shall not have sexual relations with any, save it be but one, who shall be sealed unto you by the Holy Spirit of promise that the Lord hath spoken of to Mary.

59 Now, I am commanded to give unto you a brief explanation of the way in which the body of Jesus, according to the flesh, was conceived inside the womb of Mary.

60 And I have already given this explanation to you. And in this same way, shall ye, who are righteous, be the Eternal Fathers of many spirit children according to the desires of the woman who shall reside in the Celestial glory with you.

61 But do ye think that ye shall consume upon your lusts the relations that are pure and precious and which are reserved as a blessing unto those who have used the power of creation to serve others? Yea, do ye think that ye shall have these sexual unions with the hundreds and

thousands of women who shall be desirous to be an Eternal Mother in the Celestial kingdom?

62 I say unto you, that if ye think these things then ye are not righteous men and shall have no part in the Celestial kingdom of God, nor shall ye be given the power to create spirit children, nor shall ye have the body of a man and those parts of the body that are necessary to have sexual relations with a woman.

63 For if ye think that the Father engaged in this type of sexual relation with His own daughter to create the body of His Son according to the flesh, then ye are more unrighteous still.

64 And if ye would think that the Father would do this thing to his daughter, then ye have already justified this action in your own hearts as that which is righteous, and ye are even more wicked still. For would ye do that to your own daughter? Behold, all ye that think these things shall look up from hell and remain in a state of awful indignation until ye have repented of such a thing.

65 For behold, each woman who is righteous shall be given the choice of whether or not she desireth to have a husband, who is righteous, to give her children. And if she is righteous, then she doth not desire this man so that she can consume her lusts upon him, but she desireth this man because he is righteous.

66 And if her heart is pure, then she shall receive the blessings that come from having a husband, even those sexual relations that bring joy to the flesh and to the spirit. And she shall not be required to share that relation with any other woman, except it be in the flesh to bring forth children and posterity in righteousness according to the commandments of the Father.

67 And there shall be many women in the Celestial glory who shall choose a righteous man that he might only give children unto them. But this shall be done unto them by the power of the spirit of that righteous man, even as it was done unto Mary by the Father.

68 But now, do ye suppose that these shall not have those sensations of joy that are the blessings reserved for those who are righteous in bringing forth children in eternity?

69 Yea, these shall have the power and the ability to feel these sensations according to their own will and pleasure. And those sensations which they shall experience shall be much greater and more enhanced than any such feeling that they have ever experienced in the flesh.

70 But if they desire to have a husband with whom they shall be able to enjoy these feelings, then it shall be granted unto them according to their desire.

71 Behold, the prophet Isaiah prophesied somewhat concerning the many righteous women that shall be left after the wicked have been destroyed from off the face of the earth, even most of the wicked who are men. And he wrote, saying: And in that day seven women shall take hold of one man, saying, We will eat our own bread, and wear our own apparel; only let us be called by thy name, to take away our reproach.

72 In that day shall the branch of the Lord be beautiful and glorious, and the fruit of the earth shall be excellent and comely for them that are escaped of Israel.

73 And Isaiah wrote these things according to the things which he understood pertaining to the kingdom of the Father, which shall be set up upon this earth after it hath been purified of all unrighteousness.

74 Yea, even this very earth shall be a kingdom in the Celestial glory, which shall have for its inhabitants those who have the power to create children, even those who are men and women forever.

75 And in the Celestial glory there are three degrees, which correspond to the other two planets that reside in their creation closer yet to the sun. For our earth is the third planet from the sun and shall receive the paradisiacal glory that pertaineth unto it, which is a degree of glory in the Celestial kingdom.

76 And those women who choose not to be with a man to have children, but choose to be a mother of spirit children, shall inherit a glory in the Celestial kingdom that is different than that glory in which reside those who have chosen for themselves a man to be their friend and their eternal mate forever.

77 But these same women who reside in these

other glories of the Celestial kingdom must choose for themselves the man from which they shall receive the pattern and direction to create their children according to the Spirit as I have already explained it unto you.

78 And these men who shall be the Eternal Fathers of their children, shall be responsible for creating the kingdoms in which their spirit children shall reside according to all things which have been done unto all the children of God in their first estate, which is their spiritual preexistence in the kingdom of the Father, and also in their second estate, which is the days of mortality, and in their third and final estate, which is the kingdom of glory that they have chosen for themselves according to their desires of happiness.

79 And it came to pass that Mary kept these things in her heart all the days of her life. And the Jews knew that Jesus had taken Martha as his legal wife, therefore, they looked upon him as a sinner in that they perceived that her sister Mary, and also Mary Magdalene were his concubines.

80 And in this he was mocked and ridiculed by the Jews of the church at Jerusalem, which gave unto them further cause to hate him and persecute him.

81 For how could it be that Jesus is the Messiah and the Son of the living God, if it so be that he had concubines? But in this the Jews were in error, not understanding the things which Jesus had taught unto them.

CHAPTER 46

Jesus begins his ministry. His words were very plain to the Jews, but they refused his doctrine because it went against all the traditions that they had been taught by the laws of Moses. He gives the laws of salvation, which is the gospel of Jesus Christ. He is the bread of life that all must eat in order to be saved.

AND it came to pass that the time of the age of his ministry arrived; and Jesus went forth among the people and began to teach them after he had been baptized by John the Baptist.

2 And the men whom he had chosen to be his apostles were men who were not accepted by the church at Jerusalem as being righteous men, for each of them had in some way alienated himself from the church of the Jews.

3 Now, it was this church that sought to silence Jesus and keep him from preaching against the words and commandments of the church that were given unto the people by the high priests.

4 For the people were taught that the church was the only true church of God upon the earth, and that the Jews were an holy and peculiar people who were the only ones who had been blessed with the truth.

5 And the laws of salvation were taught unto the people according to the precepts of the leaders of the church. And these leaders told the people that God would not give any new revelation unto the world, except it be given through the leadership of the church at Jerusalem.

6 And the people were taught that the Lord would not allow them to be misled by the leaders of the church, and that if there was something that the Lord wanted to tell the people, then he would only tell them through the established lines of ecclesiastical authority that were established in the church.

7 Now, this was the main thing that Jesus spoke against; yea, in many things he did speak against the church and its leaders because they had corrupted the word of God and taught for doctrine the commandments of men, denying the power of the Father to teach His own children, but believing that the Father had given all His power and authority unto men.

8 But Jesus taught the people that they were all children of God, and that they did not need a church or leaders to go unto the Father and receive from Him any instructions that He might have for them.

9 And Jesus began to usurp, as the leaders of the church supposed, the authority of the leaders of the church by teaching these things to the people.

10 And he taught the people that the ordinances and doctrines of the church would not save them, but that the only way that they could be saved was by keeping the commandments of the Father, which he was commanded to give unto them.

11 And he taught the people that he had been sent by the Father to give unto them these commandments, and that only by way of these commandments could they be saved.

12 And these commandments were not the commandments of the church, for the church required things of the people which were not commandments of God, but were the commandments of men.

13 And Jesus taught the people that the synagogues and temples that were built among them were useless in the purpose for which they believed that they were created, even that they were houses of God. For he taught them that the Father would never reside in a house built by the hands of men, but that He dwelt in the hearts and minds of each of His children according to the power of His spirit, which was the Holy Ghost.

14 And many of the things that Jesus taught to the people were hard for them to accept; yea, none of the things which he taught unto them were hard to understand, but they were hard to accept. For the people were so entrenched in their traditions and in their customs that they could not accept that a man, who was not set apart and ordained by the leadership of the church, could teach them the things of God.

15 And Jesus began to teach the people that they should not support the church and its wickedness by the payment of tithes and offerings, but that they should give that which they could afford to the poor and those who have less than they do.

16 And Jesus condemned the rich and also the leaders of the church for the luxurious lifestyles that they lived, having received these things because of that which the people gave unto the church.

17 Now, the people of the church were led to believe that their leaders were men who had been blessed with riches because of their righteousness before God. And they supposed that if riches meant righteousness, then they should covet and seek after these riches, that they might prove to their neighbor that they were righteous like unto the example of their leaders, whom the people believed were the examples of God pertaining to righteousness.

18 And the people of the church were prejudiced and biased towards those who did not belong to their church, even those whom they called Gentiles among them. And they would command their children not to play with those who were not members of their church, thus committing great sin and wickedness among them and teaching these abominations unto their children.

19 And Jesus reiterated the words of John, even those words which he spoke concerning the genealogies and the pride of the church in thinking that they were the only people of God upon the earth.

20 And Jesus spoke in many instances regarding his other sheep which were in other parts of the world, but were unknown to the Jews. For behold, the Jews knew nothing of us in the promised land; but we knew of them, our fathers having come forth from among them.

21 And Jesus taught the people that all the people of the earth were the children of God and loved by the Father the same, and that the Father had no respect for any church that was set up according to the commandments and precepts of man, which were not His commandments and precepts, and which placed one of his children above another.

22 And Jesus taught the Jews the commandments of the Father, even the same commandments that he gave unto Adam and Eve after they were banished from the garden of Eden.

23 And now, my beloved brothers and sisters, yea, even all of you who are upon the earth at the time ye shall receive this record, which shall come forth unto you as the final testimony of Jesus Christ; yea, listen all ye ends of the earth, even those of you who are upon the isles of the sea, and who are upon all the continents of land which are inhabited by the children of men.

24 Behold, Jesus taught the law of the gospel, which are the commandments of the Father, which He hath given unto us all to prepare us to inherit the kingdoms which He shall prepare for us.

25 Yea, Jehovah taught this gospel first to Adam and Eve, and then to all the holy prophets who have ever lived upon the earth. And these prophets taught this gospel unto all of you in all parts of the world according to your own language and your own understanding.

26 And then he came in the flesh and taught the Jews the exact same things that he had taught unto Adam and Eve. And then after he had died and was resurrected, he taught the exact same words unto my fathers who were in the land of promise, even the land where Adam was placed in the beginning.

27 And after he had taught these exact same things to my fathers, he went unto other sheep to whom the Father commanded him to go, even unto all the people of the earth that they might have this good news given unto them; even the good news that the Father loveth all of His children and hath prepared a way that all of them might be saved in His kingdoms.

28 And now, what do ye think are the words that he shall speak unto you when he cometh in the glory of the Father, yea, even with all the holy angels at his side and in the power of the Father; yea what shall he say unto the people of the world at this time?

29 Behold, he shall say the same things and give the exact same commandments that he hath given to the Jews and the Gentiles, even to all the ends of the earth.

30 And how can I, Moroni, be more plain in that which I have written? How can I further impress upon your weak minds and your hardened hearts that ye must obey the words of Christ or ye cannot be saved?

31 Behold, ye have the Bible, which is one testimony of these words, even the first testimony of Jesus Christ. And ye have the record of my father, which is among you and hath come to be known as the Book of Mormon, another testament of Jesus Christ, and now ye have these things which have been sealed up, which is the final testament of Jesus Christ.

32 Behold, how many more witnesses do ye need to show unto you the path that ye must follow in order to be saved in the kingdom of God?

33 And those of you in other countries who have not received the Bible, or the Book of Mormon, or the Sealed Portion of the Book of Mormon, do ye not have among you the words of the prophets that have been sent by the Father unto you?

34 And do not the words of your books have the exact same words of Christ that are given in the books that came forth because of the Jews?

35 I say unto you that ye do have the words of Christ. And how shall ye know that they are the words of Christ if they do not specifically speak of Christ?

36 Now this thing I will tell unto you. All of the words of Christ, yea, even the entire gospel of Jesus Christ is encompassed in one great commandment, which is the one commandment upon which all other commandments are based, even that ye should love your neighbor as ye would have them love you.

37 And now, I say unto those of you of other cultures, even of other countries who do not yet have access to the records of the Jews, or the record of my fathers, and also this record which I make with my own hand; yea, I say unto you, search those scriptures and holy books which ye have among you. Do they not also have commandments that are based upon this one great commandment that I have explained unto you?

38 I say unto you that they do. And they have these commandments, which are the words of Christ, because Christ visited your ancestors and spoke unto your prophets and your holy priests, and the holy men that ye accept as your prophets. And unto these, Christ gave the words of the Father, which are the same words and commandments that have been given unto all the children of God.

39 And now, I say unto you, then in which church shall the truth be found? Yea, which church is the church of the Lamb of God? Yea, the church that teacheth the words of Christ and obeyeth them, this is the church of the Lamb of God.

40 And every other church that hath been established and set up among the children of men that doth not teach the words of Christ, and doth not obey his words; yea, even those churches who have added other things to the words of Christ, or who have taken away from these words of Christ; yea, I say unto you that these are the churches of the devil.

41 And ye do not need a church or a leader of a church to teach you the words of Christ. For they are not his words, but the words of the Father. And the Father will speak unto you and give unto you all of His words, IF ye obey His commandments.

42 Yea, if ye treat your neighbor as ye would have your neighbor treat you, then ye are obeying the commandments of the Father and He will give unto you an understanding of all things that ye need for your happiness.

43 And these are the things that Jesus taught unto the Jews at Jerusalem; and the words of Jesus were plain and easy to understand. But because the people were so convinced that salvation came by another way, even by the way that the leaders of the church had showed unto them, they could not accept the simple and plain words of Christ.

44 And Jesus taught them, saying: All things are delivered unto me of my Father: and no man knoweth these things of the Son, but first he knoweth these things of the Father; neither knoweth any mortal man the things of the Father, save he first know the things which he hath heard of the Son, and he to whomsoever the Son will reveal these things unto him.

45 And these things of the Father are those things which He hath given unto me to give to you that ye might rest from the stress of life and have hope and faith in Him through me. Come unto me, all ye that labor and are heavy laden, and I will give you rest. Take my yoke upon you, and learn of me; for I am meek and lowly in heart: and ye shall find rest unto your souls. For my yoke is easy, and my burden is light.

46 And now, my beloved brothers and sisters, what suppose ye are the things which the Lord received from the Father, except it be the words that he hath given unto you in his gospel, even the gospel of Jesus Christ?

47 And did he not say unto you that ye have first heard these things of the Father before ye heard them from the Son? Yea, ye heard these things of the Father as His spirit children in His kingdom in your first estate.

48 And the Father gave His power to Jehovah, who is Jesus, to give unto us these things in the flesh, or in mortality, which is our second estate.

49 And these commandments of the Father are much easier and will bring you much more happiness than the commandments that ye are given in your churches by your leaders.

50 For what can be hard about loving your neighbor as ye would have him love you? Yet, your churches require much more of you than these things.

51 Yea, there are many of your churches that teach the words of Christ, even that ye should love your neighbor as yourself, but they do not require this thing of you to be a member in good standing in the church, because it is possible that ye can be a member of the church of the devil without obeying the commandments of the Lamb.

52 And hath Jesus required of you that ye should pay unto his church tithes and offerings? I say unto you that he doth not, but hath commanded you to give unto the poor and those who are in need of your sustenance. And if ye believe that ye are giving of your money to the Lord, I say unto you, in what need is the Lord that he should want your money?

53 And doth he command you to attend church and worship him in a synagogue and a temple that ye supposeth hath been dedicated to him? I say unto you that he doth not. But ye can worship him in your fields as ye reap and as ye sow. Ye can worship him on the street and in the places of your businesses and in all places where ye might be.

54 And in what way doth he require you to worship him except it be in keeping his commandments, which commandments are those that are based on the commandment to love your neighbor and do unto him that which ye would have him do unto you?

55 And doth he condemn you for that which ye eat or drink, or that which ye wear? I say unto you that he doth not condemn you in these things, but has said unto you: Bring unto me of your poor and your hungry and your naked and your sick and afflicted and I shall feed them with that which shall fill them, even that they shall not hunger again, nor shall they thirst anew, neither shall they be naked.

56 For I shall give unto them the kingdom of my Father wherein they shall live forever and have all things provided for them in all that they need for their happiness.

57 And now, in this way did the Lord teach the Jews at Jerusalem. And many followed after him. But they did not follow after him that they might learn of him and keep the commandments that they had received from him, but they followed him because of the miracles which he did among them.

58 And he was allowed by the Father to perform these miracles because of the weakness of the children of men in accepting his words.

59 And the Father commanded Jesus to give every opportunity available to the people to receive his words. And on one occasion the people came unto him and desired more of him. And Jesus answered them and said, Verily, verily, I say unto you, Ye seek me, not because ye are willing to do the will of the Father which hath been given unto you through me, but because ye saw the miracles, and did eat of the loaves and were filled.

60 And I say unto you, Labor not for the meat which perisheth, but for that meat which endureth unto everlasting life, which the Son of man shall give unto you, even unto him that God, the Father, hath sealed by the Holy Spirit of promise, which shall assure him a place in the kingdom of the Father.

61 Then said they unto him, What shall we do, that we might work the works of God? And this they said because they did not understand that the only things which were required of them were the things that Jesus had already taught unto them; and it was that which they should do.

62 And Jesus answered and said unto them: This is the work of God, that ye believe on him whom the Father hath sent and do those things which He hath commanded you through me, who hath been sent unto you by the Father.

63 And they said therefore unto him: What sign shewest thou then, that we may see, and believe in thee? What work dost thou do that we might know that thou hast been sent from heaven from the Father?

64 For the bread that thou hast offered unto us is not like the bread that came down from heaven unto our fathers; for they did eat manna in the desert; as it is written, He gave them bread from heaven to eat.

65 Then Jesus said unto them, Verily, verily, I say unto you, Moses gave you not that bread from heaven, except it came forth unto you by the command of the Father. But this day my Father giveth you the true bread from heaven.

66 For the bread of God is he who cometh down from heaven, and giveth life unto the world by giving unto the world the only bread which they shall eat in order to be saved, as your fathers were thus saved in similitude of these things in the wilderness by the bread sent down from the Father.

67 Then said they unto him, Lord, evermore give us this bread. And Jesus said unto them, I am the bread of life: he that cometh to me and believeth in my words, which are the words of the Father, shall never hunger; and he that believeth on these words which cometh of me shall never thirst.

68 But I have said unto you, that ye also have seen me in the flesh and believe not though ye can see me. But blessed are those who believe on my words without seeing me in the flesh, for they shall be given this bread of life by the Father, they having been given to me by Him.

69 And all those whom the Father giveth me shall come to me; and he that cometh to me and believeth on my words I will in no wise cast out. For I came down from heaven, not to do mine own will, but the will of Him who sent me.

70 And this is the will of the Father who hath sent me, that of all those whom He hath given me I should lose none of them, but should raise them up again at the last day.

71 And this is the will of Him who sent me, even that everyone who seeth the Son, and believeth on his words, may have everlasting life: and I will raise him up at the last day.

72 And the Jews then murmured at him, because he said, I am the bread which came down from heaven. And they said, Is not this Jesus, the son of Joseph, whose father and mother we know? How is it then that he saith, I came down from heaven?

73 Jesus therefore answered and said unto them, Murmur not among yourselves, for no man can come to me, except he doeth the will of my Father who hath sent me. And this is the will of Him who hath sent me, that ye receive the Son; for the Father beareth record of him; and he who receiveth the testimony, and doeth the will of Him who sent me, I will raise him up in the resurrection of the just at the last day.

74 It is written in the prophets that they shall be all taught of God. Every man therefore, that hath heard my words and hath learned of the Father, which understanding cometh unto him by the Spirit, cometh unto me. Not that any man hath seen the Father in the flesh, save he hath seen him who was sent of God; and if ye see me, who is he who hath been sent, then ye have seen the Father.

75 Verily, verily, I say unto you, he that believeth on me and the words which I have given unto you, hath everlasting life. I am that bread of life. Your fathers did eat manna in the wilderness, and are dead. But my word is the bread which cometh down from heaven, that a man may eat thereof, and not die.

76 Behold, I am the living bread which came down from heaven, and if any man eat of this bread, he shall live forever. And the bread that I will give is my gospel, which I give unto you in the flesh, which flesh I will give for the life of the world.

77 And still the Jews did not understand his words and therefore strove among themselves, saying, How can this man give us his flesh to eat? Then Jesus said unto them, Verily, verily, I say unto you, Except ye eat the flesh of the Son of man, and drink his blood, ye have no life in you. Whoso eateth my flesh, and drinketh my blood, hath eternal life; and I will raise him up at the last day. For my flesh is meat indeed, and my blood is drink indeed.

78 He that eateth my flesh, and drinketh my blood, dwelleth in me, and I in him. And as the living Father hath sent me, and I live by the Father, so he that eateth me, even he shall live by every word that proceedeth forth from the mouth of God, which are the words that I shall give unto him.

79 This is that bread which came down from heaven: not as your fathers did eat manna, and are dead, but he that eateth of this bread shall live forever.

80 And these things said he in the synagogue, as he taught in Capernaum. And many of his disciples, when they had heard this, said: This is a hard saying; who can hear it? When Jesus knew in and of himself that his disciples murmured also at this doctrine, he said unto them, Doth this offend you?

81 What and if ye shall see the Son of man ascend up where he was before? Yea, then shall ye believe that I came down from heaven, even from the presence of the Father? Behold, it is the spirit that quickeneth; the flesh profiteth nothing: the words that I speak unto you, they are of the spirit, and they are those words that can give unto you eternal life.

82 But there are some of you that do not understand and believe not. For Jesus knew from the beginning who they were that believed not, and who should betray him because they believed not in him.

83 And he said, Therefore said I unto you, that no man can come unto me, except it were given unto him of my Father.

84 And now, I, Moroni, have used the record of the Jews to give unto you the words that Jesus spoke unto the Jews concerning his gospel. And these words have reference to the ordinance of the sacrament which I have previously explained unto you, saying: And these ordinances are also part of his commandments concerning the administration of his gospel unto his people. But they are not the gospel, but administer it unto the church, which are his people.

85 For behold, when the Lord taught the Jews at Jerusalem his gospel, he said unto them: Except ye eat of my flesh and drink of my blood, ye shall in no wise inherit the kingdom of God. And those that heard this were angry with him and understood not what he meant, because the Lord taught them in parables. And in this manner doth he teach his people who have taken upon him his name.

86 And if ye look to the words of the administration of the bread, or the flesh of Christ as it is represented, ye will notice that the blessing includeth the words: that they are willing to take upon them the name of thy Son, and always remember him, and keep his commandments which he hath given them.

87 And if ye take upon you the name of the Son, then ye will do the same works that he doeth, and have the same desires he hath, and have the same responsibilities towards your neighbor that he hath. This is what representeth the name of the Son, or in other words, his works. And ye will also remember the works that he did and keep his commandments which he hath given unto you. This is what is meant by eating the flesh of Christ.

88 And if ye look to the words of the administration of the wine, or the blood of Christ as it is represented, ye will notice that these words are not included therein, even the words that ye shall take upon you his name and keep his commandments. And these words have been excluded because the blood is symbolic of the spirit which giveth life unto the body of the flesh.

89 And by drinking the blood of Christ, ye are covenanting that ye are doing the works that he would do for the same purpose, or with the same intent in which he doeth his works, thus the blood of Christ representing his spirit, or the attitude in which he performed his works.

90 For if ye do the works of Christ without the spirit of Christ, how can they be his works? And if ye have the spirit of Christ, ye shall do his works. And if ye do not drink the blood of Christ, then the works that ye do are not his works. And these works are done in vain. In other words, ye have taken the sacrament of the Lord unworthily and have presented yourselves before him as hypocrites.

91 And again I say unto you, if a man or a woman doeth the works of Christ in the spirit of Christ and doth not receive the ordinance of baptism, or doth not partake of the ordinance of the sacrament, then this man or woman is already doing the will of the Lord and is justified therein. For the Lord judgeth all the children of men according to their works, according to the desires of their hearts.

92 And if their works are righteous, then the ordinances that have been established in the church profit them nothing. And if their works are evil, then the ordinances of the church also profit them nothing.

93 And now, I, Moroni, have repeated these things unto you a second time because of their importance, for thus the Lord hath commanded me.

94 And all these things were taught unto the Jews by the mouth of Jesus. And the priests of the church at Jerusalem were exceedingly angered at that which Jesus taught unto the people.

CHAPTER 47

What the calling and title of Elijah or Elias means. What is significant about turning the hearts of the children to their fathers. Latter day temple work for the dead is an abomination before God. Prophets are taught by the still small voice, which is the voice of the Father. They are taught to teach people to love one another.

AND now, I have been commanded by the Lord to give unto you an explanation of the calling of the prophet Elijah. For this is the thing that caused much confusion among the Jews, and also shall be the cause of much confusion and contention among those of you in the latter days, even unto you to whom this sealed record shall be revealed.

2 And the Jews believed that the prophet Elijah, who was among their fathers, even among the house of Israel, would one day return to the earth and turn the hearts of the fathers to the children, and the hearts of the children to their fathers, and this according to the prophet Malachi, who was revered among them as a holy prophet of God.

3 And in the latter days the first prophet among you shall be visited by the prophet Elijah in vision and similitude, and he shall be given the authority to establish a priesthood among you so that the gospel of Jesus Christ might be preached unto the world, and, therefore, the promises made to the fathers can be planted in the hearts of the children, so that the hearts of the children can turn to the fathers.

4 And now, I have touched somewhat upon

these things already in this record, nevertheless, it is expedient according to the commandment of the Lord that I explain these things unto you more clearly that there might be no further disputations among you regarding this thing.

5 For in your understanding of these things ye do err as did they of old in the time of John the Baptist when he came into the land preaching unto the people.

6 And the Jews asked John if he was the prophet Elijah who had been sent by God according to the words of the prophets. And thus they were confused as to their understanding of these things.

7 For they did not understand how the hearts of the children could be turned to the fathers, and how the hearts of the fathers could be turned to the children, so that the earth would not be smitten with a curse according to the words of the prophet.

8 And in the latter days, ye shall also be confused about this meaning, evensomuch that ye shall begin to commit great abominations before God in the work that ye assume ye are doing—being the children—for the dead—being your fathers—as ye have perceived it through your genealogies, even that ye have set yourselves up as saviors of the dead according to your misperceptions and pride.

9 And how do ye think that ye shall save the dead? Do ye think that by your vicarious ordinances ye shall save the dead? Yea, ye shall think this to your own damnation, which cometh because of your stiffneckedness and your inability to understand the truth regarding these things according to the Spirit.

10 And like the Jews of old, ye shall crucify the Christ once again in the flesh by rejecting the pureness and simplicity of his gospel. And will ye think of yourselves greater than he is, in that ye can save those who are dead, when even Christ could not save them by his own works in the flesh?

11 And now, I have been commanded to give unto you in plainness the things that ye have misunderstood and which have been hidden from you because of your wickedness and your pride

12 For behold, the first prophet among you in the latter days shall give unto you a revelation that he received in a vision in the presence of a witness who shall stand with him in this vision and know of the things which he shall reveal unto you.

13 And this revelation shall be given in truth according to the understanding that shall be had among you of the latter days.

14 And this revelation begins, saying: The veil was taken from our minds, and the eyes of our understanding were opened. And we saw the Lord standing upon the breastwork of the pulpit before us; and under his feet was a paved work of pure gold, in the color like amber.

15 And now, do ye of the latter days know what it meaneth to have the eyes of your understanding open? Yea, it is by these eyes that this vision shall be given. For behold, by his mortal eyes this first prophet of the latter days shall see nothing, neither shall his companion who shall be with him on this occasion.

16 Behold, when ye are gathered together and begin to be enlightened by the Spirit of God, even when the Father sendeth His Spirit among you so that ye might begin to rejoice with an understanding of the things which ye are discussing amongst you; yea, this is having the eyes of your understanding opened up unto you.

17 And when ye begin to understand the things of God, do not your souls rejoice in that which ye begin to understand? Yet, what behold ye with your mortal eyes? Yea, ye behold nothing.

18 And on the occasion of this vision, this prophet and his companion shall see nothing with their mortal eyes, but the heavens shall be opened unto them according to the knowledge of their understanding.

19 And because the companion of this prophet shall see nothing with his mortal eyes, except those things which they shall discuss among them in the Spirit, having the eyes of their understanding opened unto them by faith; behold, because of these things, this companion shall reject this first prophet and fall away from the truth and begin to persecute this prophet and cause all manner of wickedness because of his lack of faith in that which he saw by the eyes of his understanding, and not with his mortal eyes that he might not doubt.

20 For these two did have the heavens opened up to the eyes of their understanding and there appeared unto them Moses, and Elias, and Elijah, and committed unto them the keys of administration in the priesthood, so that these could go forth into the world and begin to preach the gospel of Jesus Christ.

21 But on this occasion, there was no physical or mortal contact with Moses, or Elias, or Elijah, but these things were done by the eyes of their understanding being opened up unto them. And these things were done in similitude of those things which were done among their fathers, even among the Jews and those of my fathers who were upon the land in which these two in the latter days shall dwell in the latter days.

22 And this first prophet shall say unto his companion: Thou knowest that the people of this world are prideful in that which they believe. Behold, they can hardly accept the revelations of God that have been given unto them already. And except they believe that an angel of God hath given these things unto us, they shall not believe that we have been given the authority to preach the gospel of Jesus Christ, which we have been called to preach.

23 Therefore, let us give unto the world the words of our understanding that we have received this day in the house of the Lord, so that they might be accepted by the people as that for which they are waiting and anticipating.

24 And with this first prophet, his companion shall agree and make a solemn promise that he shall never reveal unto the world that Moses, Elias, and Elijah did not actually appear unto them in the flesh, but according to the Spirit, which is having the eyes of their understanding opened unto them.

25 And now, this prophet did nothing contrary to the will of the Lord in this thing. For behold, the children of men are slow to learn the things of God and are even slower to righteous works. And for this reason, the Father alloweth His servants to teach the people according to their understanding and prepare a way whereby they might be more receptive to His words.

26 Now, in order to prepare the people to be more receptive to His words, which are the words of Christ, or the gospel of Jesus as it hath been explained unto you, the Lord sendeth forth an Elias before any great work that is to be done among the children of men.

27 And this word Elias is the same as Elijah and meaneth the same in the tongue in which it was formed, or being translated means, Jehovah is God. Now, the Lord hath given the title of Elias, or Elijah unto all those who are called to do a preparatory work for the greater work of a prophet that shall come after them. And the reason for this is in the similitude of the original Elijah of whom it is spoken in the record of the Jews.

28 For Elijah prepared the way for his successor, Elisha, to come forth and take the glory of his mantle; or in other words, to prepare the people that they might be better receptive of the words and works that Elisha did among them.

29 Now, Elijah was like unto John the Baptist, who prepared the way for the coming of Jesus who did even a greater work among the people. And as John lived in the wilderness and dressed in animal skins and ate that which was unbecoming, so did Elijah, in whose similitude he came.

30 And Elias dwelt in a city, like unto Jesus, until he was called forth to the ministry and to do a greater work than that which his predecessor, or his preparer, did for the children of men.

31 And so it was that John was the Elijah of whom the scriptures had spoken.

32 And the disciples of Jesus did not understand the title of Elijah, or Elias—for they are the same calling—and questioned the Lord, saying: Why then say the scribes that Elias must first come? And this they asked after they had received a witness from the Father that Jesus was surely the Christ. For according to the leaders of the church at Jerusalem and their scribes, Christ would not come, except that Elias should come first to restore all things and prepare for his coming.

33 And Jesus answered his disciples, saying unto them: Elias truly shall come and restore all things, even that he shall turn the hearts of the children to the promises that the Father hath made with their fathers, who are of the house of Israel.

34 But I say unto you, That Elias is come

already, and they knew him not, and understood not that which he said unto them concerning me. And they have done unto him whatsoever they desired. And these things which they have done unto him, they shall also do unto me, and if ye shall receive it, I am Elias.

35 And now, if I, Moroni, have not explained the calling and office of an Elijah, or an Elias, unto you, even that ye cannot misunderstand these things, then I will give unto you in more plainness that ye might in no way be mistaken:

36 For behold, Abinadi was the Elijah that prepared the way for the coming of Alma to do a mighty work among the people of my fathers. And Samuel the Lamanite was the Elijah that prepared the way for our father Nephi to prepare the people for the birth of the Lord Jesus Christ.

37 And there are other prophets who have been called according to the calling of Elijah and who have been sent forth unto other peoples of the earth to prepare them for the words of another who shall work a greater work of faith among the people.

38 And in the latter days, the first prophet among you shall be called by the calling of Elijah to prepare the children of men for the second prophet among you, even this bearer of Christ from whom ye shall receive these things.

39 And this second latter day prophet shall be the final Elijah who shall be in the office of this calling, even that he might bring these things forth and prepare the people of the earth for the coming of the Lord Jesus Christ.

40 Yea, each prophet of God doth that which he hath been foreordained to do in the dispensation of time in which he hath been called by the Lord.

41 And all those who shall do a preparatory work for a greater prophet than themselves, or better, for a greater work to be done among the children of men, shall be killed by the children of men, or sought out to be killed by them.

42 And this is a sure sign that this man hath been called according to the office of Elijah, even that he shall seal his testimony with his blood, or be willing to do so, if it so be required of him.

43 And each of these prophets who shall hold this calling of Elijah, shall attempt to turn the hearts of the children of men to the gospel of Jesus Christ and help the people better understand those things that the people shall eventually receive from the prophet that cometh after the preparatory prophet, or he who is called as was Elijah.

44 Now, the Jews did not understand these things, and they questioned John as to whether he was the Elias of which their scribes and leaders had spoken. And John answered them that he was not. And in this he did not lie, for he was not the Elias which they sought according to their understanding.

45 But Jesus testifieth that John the Baptist truly was this Elias, even he who was acting in the position and with the authority of Elijah to prepare the way before him.

46 And the Jews could not understand these things in the day of Jesus. And they shall not understand these things in the latter days, neither shall they who are not the Jews, but are the Gentiles, who have received the gospel of Jesus Christ among them, but have rejected it.

47 And this first prophet of the latter days shall give direction unto the people in the vision of which I have just spoken. Yea, he shall give these words by revelation, saying: For behold, I have accepted this house, and my name shall be here; and I will manifest myself to my people in mercy in this house. Yea, I will appear unto my servants, and speak unto them with my own voice, if my people will keep my commandments, and do not pollute this holy house.

48 And now, I, Moroni, know that the people unto whom this revelation and vision were given have polluted the house of God. And because they have polluted the house of God, even that they do that which is most abominable before God in a house that is dedicated to the name of the Lord; even these baptisms and these ordinances of salvation for the dead; yea, because of these abominations, he hath not appeared unto them and they have not heard his voice, but he hath taken from them his priesthood and the keys which were committed unto the first of these two latter day prophets.

49 And if the people shall repent in that day that their wickedness and abomination shall be

made known unto them by way of the second of these two latter day prophets, even by way of the coming forth of these things, then shall the Lord once again fulfill his promise which was given unto the first.

50 And he shall appear unto his servants and speak unto them with his own voice. And now, this voice that they shall hear shall be the same voice that was heard by Elijah.

51 And the record of the Jews hath been written, saying: And he said, Go forth, and stand upon the mount before the Lord to receive his word concerning the people. And behold, as the Lord passed by, a great and strong wind rent the mountains, and brake in pieces the rocks before the Lord; but the Lord was not in the wind: and after the wind was an earthquake; but the Lord was not in the earthquake; And after the earthquake a fire; but the Lord was not in the fire; but the word of the Lord was like unto a burning fire in his bosom, even a still small voice.

52 And now, this is the voice of the Father which is given unto all of His children according to the heed that they give unto Him in keeping His commandments.

53 And those who are called according to the calling of Elijah hear the voice of the Lord in this manner, even in a still small voice that they understand.

54 And this voice whispereth unto them: Preach my gospel to my children and bring them home unto me. Teach them to love one another and do good to each other.

55 Behold, this is the only voice of the Father unto those who hold the office and calling of Elijah, and is His only commandment unto them.

CHAPTER 48

Why Jesus began to speak in parables to the people. The way to understand the parables and symbolism of the scripture is given. The final latter day prophet will be given the ability to understand and explain all parables that have been given, but will only do so according to the commandment of the Spirit. The rich are condemned.

AND now, I have been given a commandment of the Lord; yea, this is the commandment that I have rejoiced in all the days of my life, even the one that I have waited for all of my life to expound upon and speak about with all the energies of my soul.

2 Behold, I have been given the commandment to explain in plainness the mission and purpose of the life of Jesus Christ and the reason why it was necessary that he come into the world and live his life as he did, and teach the things that he taught unto all of us, according to our cultures and our abilities to understand him.

3 And throughout the scriptures that ye have among you in the latter days, and also throughout this sealed portion of the record of my father, many of the holy prophets have taught you many of the things that I am about to expound unto you.

4 And many times they were commanded that they should speak unto you in parables and allegories, even in great similitude and symbolism of that which I have now been given permission by the Lord to give unto you in plainness.

5 Even the Lord himself began to speak unto the people in parables after he had given unto them his gospel in plainness concerning the things that I am about to explain unto you. And the Lord would have continued to speak unto the people in plainness had they not rejected the simplicity of his words and his message.

6 And his disciples came, and said unto him: Why speakest thou unto them in parables? And he answered and said unto his disciples: Because it is given unto you to know the mysteries of the kingdom of heaven, but to them it is not given.

7 For whosoever receiveth, to him shall be given, and he shall have more abundance, but whosoever continueth not to receive, from him shall be taken away even that he hath.

8 Therefore, speak I to them in parables, because they seeing, see not; and hearing, they hear not, neither do they understand. And in them is fulfilled the prophecy of Isaiah, which saith: Go and tell this people, Hear ye indeed, but understand not; and see ye indeed, but perceive not. Make the heart of this people fat, and make their ears heavy, and shut their eyes; lest they see with their eyes, and hear with their ears, and understand with their heart, and convert, and be healed.

9 Yea, by hearing they shall hear, and shall not understand; and seeing they shall see, and shall not perceive. For the hearts of the people are waxed gross, and their ears are dull of hearing, and their eyes they have closed; lest at any time they should see with their eyes and hear with their ears, and should understand with their heart, and should be converted, and I should heal them.

10 But blessed are your eyes, for they see, and your ears, for they hear. For verily I say unto you, that many prophets and righteous men have desired to see those things which ye see, and have not seen them; and to hear those things which ye hear, and have not heard them.

11 And now, this Jesus said unto them regarding the prophets who had been given the gospel of Christ by the ministrations of the Spirit, but not by the literal voice of Christ in the flesh.

12 And now, I, Moroni, say unto all of you of the latter days who shall receive these things, even all the children of men of every tongue and every religion and every culture and every nation upon the face of the earth: Yea, all of you have shut your eyes and have closed your ears and have hardened your hearts that ye do not understand the simplicity of the message of Christ that hath been given unto you.

13 And ye have been taught by parables and symbolism, and a similitude of the plainness that ye could have received from the Spirit of Christ if ye were doing the works of Christ. And every parable, every teaching, every doctrine, every statement, every principle, every word that Christ spoke in the flesh taught the simple truths of his gospel.

14 But because of its simplicity, ye refuse to accept it and open your eyes that ye might see, and your ears that ye might hear, and your hearts that ye might understand.

15 And now, I have been commanded to give unto you in plainness the message and understanding of all the parables, the teachings, the doctrine, the statements, the principles, and all the words of Christ. And all these things that Christ did, he did to teach us the will of the Father; yea, even the will of the very Eternal Father who created all of our spirits and set in motion the nature of the world on which we reside.

16 And the message of the Father is this: Behold, my beloved children, I have given unto you all these things that ye might find joy therein. And I am no respecter of persons, and would that ye should know that I esteem all flesh as one.

17 Yea, there is not one of my children that I do not esteem and love as much as the others. And to show this example of my love unto you, I have given unto you mine Only Begotten Son according to the flesh, and have bestowed upon him all of my powers and my authority, and have commanded him to do unto you as I would do unto you.

18 And I do not esteem him above any of you, but have given him unto you as your servant to teach you all the things that ye need to understand, so that it might be possible that ye might have this joy of which I have spoken.

19 Behold, I have created you that ye might have joy; and for no other purpose have I created you. For behold, I did not create you that ye might serve me, but that I might serve you, by giving unto you this joy.

20 And the commandments that I have given unto My Beloved Son are those commandments that I have given unto him to give to you. And only by these commandments can ye be assured of the joy of which I have spoken.

21 And I do not force any of you to obey these commandments, but have given unto each of you the ability to choose for yourselves how ye should live and how ye should act.

22 Nevertheless, I know that ye cannot find joy and live in eternal happiness unless ye obey the commandments that he hath given unto you.

23 Behold, my commandments are that ye love one another and do unto each other as ye would have another do unto you. And if ye follow this simple commandment, ye shall be happy.

24 And I have commanded you to give according to each of your abilities, and take according to each of your needs, esteeming one another as equal in all things.

25 And I have not commanded you to give glory unto any man. Yea, I have commanded against such things, even that ye put one man above another among you. For ye are all my children, and regardless of what each of you do in the flesh, I will love and esteem you all the same.

26 And I do not love mine Only Begotten Son any more or less than I love any of you, but have given him unto you that he might teach unto you these things. And he loveth you as I love you and hath commanded you to love one another as I have loved you.

27 And he seeketh not for your glory or that ye should worship him, for he is your brother, and seeketh not the glory, but only the joy that he might receive from giving unto you the things which he hath received from me.

28 Behold, I am your Father, and have created you that ye might have joy, not that ye should honor me. For what manner of Father would I be if I created you only that ye should honor me and give me glory?

29 Again, I say unto you, I did not create you to worship me, but to find joy in me. And for this reason, I have given unto you my commandments, even that ye should love one another and do unto others as ye would have them do unto you.

30 And now, my beloved children, I plead with you to act upon my promise, even that ye shall find joy if ye keep the commandments that I have given unto you through mine Only Begotten and Beloved Son, Jesus Christ.

31 Yea, keep his commandments and ye shall find joy; and if ye find joy, then ye are worshipping me. And in my kingdom ye shall find this joy and eternal happiness forever. Amen

32 And now, I, Moroni, do testify unto you that this is the message that the Father hath given since the beginning of time, and it shall be the message that He shall give until the end of time; and there is no other message that he shall give unto His children.

33 And it is this message that He spoke in the light immediately after the darkness had lifted from up off the earth at the time my fathers were gathered in the land of Bountiful.

34 And because they did not have the ability to receive His words through the Spirit at this time, they could not understand the Father. And for this reason, the Father introduced His Son, Jesus Christ, unto them that they might hear His Son in the flesh.

35 And now, in the time of Jesus, when he began to teach these things unto the Jews, they could not accept the simplicity of this message; for they believed that they were saved by their works in the flesh, which works were taught unto them by their leaders.

36 Yea, the Jews believed that in the sacrifices and the ordinances that were administered unto them in the temples of God by those who had been given the authority of God, were they saved. And these are the only works that they believed that they needed to do to be saved.

37 And when Jesus explained unto them that they did not need to do any of these things to be saved, but that they only needed to love their neighbor as themselves, they could not accept these things, because of their traditions and their faith and their trust in the leaders of their church.

38 And it shall come to pass in the latter days, even among those who shall belong to the church called the Church of Jesus Christ of the latter days, that they shall be like unto the Jews in every way.

39 For they shall be taught by their leaders that a person must be baptized by one who hath authority in their church and receive all the ordinances of the temple of God, or this person will not be saved in the kingdom of God.

39 And like the Jews in the time of Christ, they shall forget the simplicity of the message of Christ and do the things that are required of them by their church. But they shall be angry one with another, and they shall put themselves

above their neighbor, even that they shall command their daughters that they shall not marry any man that is not a member of their church because of their pride.

40 And they shall command their children that they shall not play with those who are not of their faith. And they shall not allow in their churches and their temples those who do not abide by the commandments of the church according to the words of its leaders, even though these that they do not allow into their church might abide by all the words of Christ.

41 And they shall sue in the courts of law one another and seek for glory and riches of the world, and set themselves up as a light unto the world and send forth missionaries into every part of the world that they might convert all the children of men to their religion.

42 And when they find one that will give heed unto their words, they shall testify to him that they believe in Christ and that they are the only true church of Christ upon the earth. Nevertheless, they shall not require that that person obey the words of Christ, but the words of their church.

43 And Satan shall use this church to deceive the earth and turn the people further from the message of Christ. And this church shall grow in strength, even by the power that Satan shall give unto it. But its numbers shall be few, and the strength that they shall receive shall be the strength that Satan shall give unto them because of their riches and the money that they have taken from the people in their tithes and offerings.

44 And they shall be involved in many of the governments of the earth and exercise their influence over many people because of their riches and the secret combinations that they have established to do the will of the Lord, as they suppose. Now, this is the exact situation in which the church at Jerusalem found itself among the Jews at the time of Christ.

45 And this last prophet who shall be among them in the latter days, even he who shall bring forth this record unto them, shall preach repentance unto them and attempt to give unto them the simplicity of the gospel of Christ, even in its fullness.

46 And they shall reject him as the Jews rejected Christ, he being a bearer of Christ, calling him a devil and an apostate of the truth and filled with all manner of wickedness in that which he shall teach the people.

47 And as the Jews regarded Jesus a sinner among them, so shall this latter day church regard this last of the two prophets of which I have spoken to you concerning this record.

48 And this prophet, who is the bearer of Christ, shall act in the calling of Elijah and make one final attempt to turn the hearts of the children to their fathers, even in teaching them the words of the Father, that they should love one another and do unto others what they would want others to do unto them.

49 But because he shall usurp the authority of this church of the latter days, they shall reject him and make an attempt to turn the people against him.

50 But this record shall go forth before him and shall testify of him, and it shall also testify of Christ and give unto the world the gospel of Christ and explain in simplicity and plainness all of the works of Christ, which are the works of the Father.

51 But behold, the people of the Church of Jesus Christ of the latter days, as well as all the earth, shall have an opportunity to humble themselves and repent of their iniquities and their sins and open up their eyes that they might see and their hearts that they might understand.

52 And because the Lord shall no longer command this final prophet to speak to the people in parables, he shall give unto the people all things in plainness that they cannot err in their understanding.

53 And if the people of the latter days begin to repent of their sins and turn once again to the words of Christ, then the Father will send forth His Spirit unto them and heal them and gather them up against the wicked, which shall be many upon the earth.

54 Then shall the words of the first prophet of the latter days be fulfilled, which he wrote, saying: And also the Lord shall have power over his saints, and shall reign in their midst, and shall come down in judgment upon Idumea, or the world.

55 Therefore, the Lord hath given unto you a commandment by the voice of this prophet that ye should search these commandments, for they are true and faithful, and the prophecies and promises that are in them shall all be fulfilled. What I the Lord have spoken, I have spoken, and I excuse not myself; and though the heavens and the earth pass away, my word shall not pass away, but shall all be fulfilled, whether by mine own voice or by the voice of my servants, it is the same.

56 For behold, and lo, the Lord is God, and the Spirit beareth record, and the record is true, and the truth abideth forever and ever.

57 And now, the Lord hath commanded me to explain in simplicity and plainness some of the parables that ye have received in the accounts that ye have before you, even that ye might better understand the things that Jesus taught unto his disciples. For unto his disciples, Jesus spoke in simplicity and plainness as it hath been explained unto you.

58 And now, everything that Jesus taught can be correlated to the commandment of the Father that we should love each other as ourselves.

59 And for this reason the Lord condemneth the rich and those who have more than others. And he taught his disciples of the great evils that come about because of money. And his teachings are plain and easy to understand regarding these things. But those of you in the latter days who call yourselves Christians, and who are rich, do not have eyes that see, neither do ye have ears that hear, and ye do not understand that if ye are rich, then ye are wicked.

60 For there is no man who is rich who shall see the kingdom of God in any way unless he repenteth of that which he hath done to become rich. Now, it mattereth not to the Lord how much income a man might make, but it mattereth to the Lord how that income was made and why that man useth that income to consume it upon the lusts of his own flesh.

61 And ye of the latter days shall convince yourselves that your riches are a blessing of your industry and that ye have received of your riches because of the sweat of your own brow. And Satan would have ye believe these things that ye might justify that which ye have. And if ye truly understood the words of Jesus, then ye cannot be rich, for it would be impossible.

62 And for this reason there shall be many of the rich of the latter days that belong to this church that calls itself after the name of Jesus Christ. For the commandments of this church are easy for them to obey, and these commandments of men help them to justify their riches and that which they have been deceived into believing hath been given unto them by God.

63 And they think they are righteous because they obey all the commandments of the church. And they are like unto the young man who came unto Jesus, and in his pride thought of himself as righteous, and said unto Jesus: Good Master, what good thing shall I do, that I may have eternal life?

64 And he said unto him, Why callest thou me good? There is none good but one, that is, God, who is our Father, and we brothers, are His sons. But if thou wilt know the Father and enter into life, then ye must keep the commandments of the Father

65 And the young man saith unto Jesus: Which commandments of the Father shall I keep? And Jesus perceived his thoughts and knew of the commandments that the young man had kept according to the law of Moses.

66 And Jesus said: thou shalt do no murder, thou shalt not commit adultery, thou shalt not steal, thou shalt not bear false witness, Honour thy father and thy mother; for all these are the law that hath been given unto you by the scribes and Pharisees.

67 But the commandment of the Father hath fulfilled all these things and is encompassed into a commandment that thou keepest not, but which thou must keep in order to inherit the kingdom of the Father, even that thou shalt love thy neighbour as thyself.

68 And the young man saith unto him, All these things have I kept from my youth up; what lack I yet to show unto the Father that I love my neighbor as myself?

69 And Jesus said unto him, If thou wilt be perfect, even as our Father which is in heaven is perfect, then go and sell all that thou hast, and

give to the poor, and come and follow me, and thou shalt have treasure in heaven. But when the young man heard that saying, he went away sorrowful: for he had great possessions.

70 Then said Jesus unto his disciples: Verily I say unto you, that a rich man shall hardly enter into the kingdom of heaven because of his riches which he
imparteth not unto those who are in need.

71 And again I say unto you, It is easier for a camel to enter into the city through the gate, which is the eye of the needle, than for a rich man to enter into the kingdom of God. For in order for a camel to enter into the city through the eye of the needle, it must first be relieved of that which burdeneth it, so that it can get on its knees and pass through the gate into the city.

72 Likewise, if a man is rich, he must relieve himself of his abundance and humble himself before God before he can enter into the kingdom of God.

73 And when his disciples heard it, they were exceedingly amazed, saying: Who then can be saved? But Jesus perceived their thoughts, and said unto them: With men this is impossible; but if they will forsake all things for my sake, with God whatsoever I speak is possible.

74 Then answered Peter and said unto him, Behold, we have forsaken all, and followed thee; what shall we have therefore, in the kingdom of God?

75 And Jesus said unto them, Verily I say unto you, That ye who have followed me and believed in me and have obeyed the commandments of the Father in all things, in the resurrection when the Son of man shall sit in judgment of those who have rejected these things before the throne of the glory of the Father, then ye also shall sit in judgment, judging the twelve tribes of Israel, because unto them shall I send you to preach unto them these things.

76 And because we have preached these things unto them, our testimony shall be given before the Father, that they might be judged according to those things which we preached unto them, and our testimonies against them shall stand before the Father, even that they were given the chance to obey His commandments.

77 And our testimonies and our words shall judge them before the Father, because they did not believe in that which we were sent to teach unto them.

78 And every one of you that hath forsaken houses, or brethren, or sisters, or father, or mother, or wife, or children, or lands, for the sake of my name, shall receive an hundredfold of the happiness that these things would have brought unto you in the flesh. And these shall inherit everlasting life.

79 But many unto whom we preach these things, which are first, shall be last in the resurrection, because they refuse the commandments of the Father as we have given them.

80 And many of them that shall receive this gospel after it hath been rejected by the Jews, yea, even the Gentiles, which are the last, shall be first to be resurrected unto everlasting life, because they rejoiced in the Father and kept his commandments.

81 But in the end, all those who are first shall be last and those that are last shall be first, for the Father shall save all of His children as soon as they are willing to keep His commandments, which He hath commanded me to give unto them.

82 And all shall be equally blessed of the Father, whether they were resurrected first or last, all shall be heirs of His kingdom and given that which the Father promised them in the beginning.

83 For the kingdom of heaven is like unto a man that is an householder, which went out early in the morning to hire laborers into his vineyard. And when he had agreed with the laborers for a penny a day, he sent them into his vineyard.

84 And he went out about the third hour, and saw others standing idle in the marketplace, and said unto them; Go ye also into the vineyard, and whatsoever is right I will give you. And they went their way.

85 Again he went out about the sixth and ninth hour, and did likewise.

86 And about the eleventh hour he went out, and found others standing idle, and saith unto them, Why stand ye here all the day idle? They say unto him, Because no man hath hired us. He saith unto them, Go ye also into the vineyard; and whatsoever is right, that shall ye receive.

87 So when even was come, the lord of the vineyard saith unto his steward, Call the laborers, and give them their hire, beginning from the last unto the first.

88 And when they came that were hired about the eleventh hour, they received every man a penny. But when the first came, they supposed that they should have received more; and they likewise received every man a penny.

89 And when they had received it, they murmured against the good man of the house, saying: These last have wrought but one hour, and thou hast made them equal unto us, which have borne the burden and heat of the day.

90 But he answered one of them, and said: Friend, I do thee no wrong. Didst not thou agree with me for a penny? Take that thine is, and go thy way. For I will give unto this last, even as unto thee.

91 Is it not lawful for me to do what I will with mine own? Is thine eye evil, because I am good?

92 And thus spoke Jesus in parable that his disciples might understand that the last shall be first, and the first shall be last in the kingdom of the Father. For many are called, but few chosen, and they are not chosen because they complain against the Father who rendereth equally in all things which pertain unto His children.

CHAPTER 49

Jesus continues his teaching against inequality. Families and money are the main cause of the inequality among the people of the earth. Moroni further condemns the modern LDS Church for doing what the Jews did in requiring money in the form of tithing. He also condemns them for making statues of him that are placed on the LDS temples. The words of King Benjamin are used as an example.

AND now, Jesus taught many things unto his disciples concerning the equality of the children of God. And the cause of this inequality among the people was due to their division into families, and also because of the riches that some had over another.

2 And Jesus commanded against riches because he knew that when one had more than another, then he who had more cared little for the way in which he received his riches, nor did he care for those who had less than himself.

3 And Jesus taught the people that the leaders of the church were wealthy men who enjoyed the things of the world and the associations that they had with those in power outside of the church, even the politicians and the leaders of the governments under which the church was subjected according to the laws of the land.

4 And the only income that came into the church came by way of the tithes and offerings that the people gave unto the church, as they were commanded by their leaders.

5 And the Jews who were rich were prideful in that which they gave unto the church because they gave much more than the poor, thus justifying themselves in their wickedness believing that because of the abundance of which they gave unto the church, they were more blessed than the poor who gave little or nothing at all.

6 And now, I have given unto you a brief account of Jacob, the father of Mary, who was assigned by the church to sell those animals to the people that came up to the temple to worship and make sacrifice unto God according to the law of Moses.

7 And in the time of Jesus, the law of Moses had been corrupted and changed considerably, even that the original purpose and meaning of the sacrifice of animals, as well as the manner in which they were sacrificed, had been changed, so that the people did not understand that which they did in offering up sacrifices. But the people did these things according to their traditions that they might fulfill the requirements of salvation as they had been taught to believe by their leaders.

8 And Jacob, being employed by the church to sell for money the animals that the people needed to make the appropriate sacrifices, as they supposed, knew that the church had corrupted the laws of God and replaced them with the commandments and precepts of men.

9 And because he knew these things, he could not sell the animals that he had raised by command of the church, and who had set the price for them, to those who were poor and could not afford to pay for that which they needed to participate in what they believed to be the ordinances of their salvation.

10 And Jesus also knew of these things. And when he had come into Jerusalem according to the tradition of the Passover, he found in the temple those who sold oxen and sheep and doves, and also the money changers who had been commissioned by the church to accept the money of the people no matter in what form it was received.

11 And everything that was done by the church was done for a profit; for the leaders believed that it was within their stewardship to make sure that the money that was received in the name of the Lord should be used wisely to make more money for the church, which they believed was the will of the Lord. For this reason, they had commanded Jacob to make a profit of everything that he sold.

12 And when Jesus beheld these things, his spirit groaned exceedingly within him and he left that place and withdrew himself a ways off from among the people.

13 And he cried unto the Father, saying: Oh, My Father, how is it that Thou canst suffer such wickedness of Thy children. Behold, they are taught to believe that by their money they shall buy their salvation and assure a place in Thy kingdom because of the things of the world that they believe they give unto Thee as tithes and offerings.

14 Oh, My Father, forgive me, Thy Son, for my sorrow and that which I am about to do. Behold, I cannot bear to see the people do this thing and disgrace that which should be sacred and available to all of Thy children for their instruction, but which their leaders have turned into a den of thieves.

15 And Jesus became aware of his own indignation which he had for the people who were desecrating the temple. But he did not act upon the emotions of his anger, and held all these things within him in control according to the commandment of the Father.

16 For the Spirit of God alloweth reproving at times with sharpness, when moved upon by the Holy Ghost; but then a showing forth afterwards of an increase of love towards them who have been reproved, lest they esteem him that reproveth to be their enemy.

17 But Jesus was already hated by the Jews, even though he had showed forth exceeding love for them. And he thought in himself that perhaps a reproof of their sins with sharpness, might be the cause of some of them listening better to his words.

18 And after he had prayed to the Father, Jesus made a scourge of small cords and took the time to ponder on that which he was about to do.

19 And with the whip that he had made, he drove them all out of the temple with the sheep and the oxen, and poured out the money of the changers and overthrew their tables. And he could not drive out the doves that were in cages, but had compassion on them in their state of captivity and did not overturn them, but commanded those who sold them, saying: Take these things hence; make not the house of my Father a house of merchandise.

20 And now, all these things were in similitude of that which shall come to pass in the latter days among those of you who belong to the church of Jesus Christ of the latter days, yea, even your temples and your church shall be like unto the temple of the Jews.

21 For ye shall believe that it is necessary that ye receive the ordinances of salvation, as ye suppose, and cause that any who would receive these things should pay money for that which they receive. And in the tithing that ye require of them, ye make it requisite that it be paid in full before ye allow any to enter into the temple and perform what ye believe are the saving ordinances of God.

22 Now, are not your works the same works as the works of the Jews? Yea, do not your leaders command these things of you? And do they not take the money which ye give unto them in the name of the Lord and use it to buy up the things of the earth that they might gain honor and glory of men and the praise of the world?

23 Yea, ye perceive in your hearts that because your church is rich and your synagogues and your temples are of such beauty and exquisite workmanship, that the people of the world will be drawn unto you.

24 But when they are drawn unto you, and they begin to believe that they shall find the words of Christ within you, even because ye have more testimonies of these words than they have; yea, when they come unto you, do ye not make it a requirement that they purchase their salvation by the payment of tithes and offerings to the church?

25 Now, in what difference can ye justify your actions compared to the actions of the Jews who sold for a price the means of salvation among them? And how can ye not understand the words which I wrote unto you in the part of this record that shall not be sealed and is already among you?

26 Did I not prophesy concerning you, even that I said unto you and caused to be repeated already in this sealed record, that my words might penetrate the shell of your stiffneckedness and hardheartedness? I wrote unto you: Behold, I speak unto you as if ye were present, and yet ye are not. But behold, Jesus Christ hath shown you unto me, and I know your doing.

27 And I know that ye do walk in the pride of your hearts; and there are none save a few only who do not lift themselves up in the pride of their hearts, unto the wearing of very fine apparel, unto envying, and strifes, and malice, and persecutions, and all manner of iniquities; and your churches, yea, even every one, have become polluted because of the pride of your hearts.

28 For behold, ye do love money, and your substance, and your fine apparel, and the adorning of your churches, more than ye love the poor and the needy, the sick and the afflicted.

29 Oh, ye pollutions, ye hypocrites, ye teachers, who sell yourselves for that which will canker, why have ye polluted the holy church of God?

30 Why are ye ashamed to take upon you the name of Christ? Why do ye not think that greater is the value of an endless happiness than that misery which never dies because of the praise of the world?

31 Why do ye adorn yourselves with that which hath no life, and yet suffer the hungry, and the needy, and the naked, and the sick and the afflicted to pass by you, and notice them not?

32 Yea, why do ye build up your secret combinations to get gain, and cause that widows should mourn before the Lord, and also orphans to mourn before the Lord, and also the blood of their fathers and their husbands to cry unto the Lord from the ground, for vengeance upon your heads?

33 Behold, the sword of vengeance hangeth over you; and the time soon cometh that he avengeth the blood of the saints upon you, for he will not suffer their cries any longer.

34 Behold, do not my words have any meaning unto you? Do ye not yet understand them when they are written in such plainness?

35 Why do ye think that ye can take the money that ye receive in the name of the Lord from the people and do with it that which is an abomination in his sight?

36 And now, if these things of which I have prophesied concerning you could have been the only abominations that ye shall do before God, I might have more hope for your souls. But ye have caused that my own name shall be raised up in glory and presented unto the world in a manner which is most abominable before our Father, and of which I am exceedingly ashamed.

37 Behold, ye have made statues of gold, and have called them by my name, and have placed them upon your temples, even these houses of

Satan that ye believe are the houses of holiness unto the Lord.

38 And in sorrow I have seen these things and shrink from the knowledge that ye have used my name and my persona in this manner.

39 And I have asked the Lord that if it be possible, that he make an intercession and stop this abomination in my name. But he hath suffered it according to his will that the judgments that he shall pour out upon you shall be justified when he avengeth the blood of the true saints of God and gathereth his elect from among you.

40 And those of you who are rich and believe that ye give much unto God by the abundance that ye give unto your church. I ask of you, do ye think that the Lord is in need of your money and your abundance?

41 Know ye not that he can create gold from dust and cause that which is gold to return to the dust from which it was made? Then why think ye that your money is a gift or a righteous offering unto him?

42 Behold, hath he not commanded you to do unto others as ye would have them do unto you? And what if your neighbor who doth not belong to your church is in need of something? Would you give unto him that which he desireth of you?

43 And now, if ye were poor and had not the things that the rich possess, would it not be that ye would want the rich to feed you, even if it meant from the scraps of their tables? And I say unto you who are rich, that the scraps from your tables are all that is required of you to give unto to those that are poor. And if ye do this, then can ye rejoice in the riches that ye desire.

44 But if your scraps fall into the mouths of ravenous dogs, then what shall be left for those that would gain from your scraps?

45 And your leaders and your church are these dogs that steal from the poor because of their fine clothing and their fine buildings and the adorning of their temples. Therefore, why should ye give of your scraps unto them?

46 I say unto you, give your scraps to the poor who are in need of them to improve their lot. And if ye allow them your scraps, then your Father will justify that which ye covet for yourselves.

47 But if ye say within yourselves: The dogs are of my own house, therefore, they alone shall eat of my scraps; yea, even if ye continue to give of your abundance to the church to which ye belong, ye shall have no reward in heaven, but shall be condemned for that which ye have above those who are your brothers and sisters before God.

48 And Jesus spoke likewise unto the Jews when on one occasion he had been questioned by the leaders of the Jews. And in order to teach unto them this principle that I have just given unto you, he said unto them in his doctrine: Beware of the scribes, which love to go in long clothing, and love salutations in the marketplaces, and the chief seats in the synagogues, and the uppermost rooms at feasts, who devour the houses of widows, and for a pretense make long prayers: these shall receive greater damnation.

49 And to show to his disciples what he meant concerning the wickedness of the leaders and the rich who supported these leaders, he took his disciples and sat over against the treasury, and beheld how the people cast money into the treasury. And many that were rich cast in much. And there came a certain poor widow, and she threw in two mites, which make a farthing.

50 And he called unto him his disciples, and saith unto them: Verily I say unto you, That this poor widow hath cast more in, than all they which have cast into the treasury: For all they did cast in of their abundance; but she of her want did cast in all that she had, even all her living.

51 And of a truth I say unto you, that this poor widow hath cast in more than they all: For all these have of their abundance cast in unto the offerings of God: but she of her penury hath cast in all the living that she had.

52 And his disciples began to understand the words of Jesus; and they beheld the temple and how it was adorned and the amount of money that was required for its upkeep and maintenance.

53 And as they spoke of the temple and how it was adorned with goodly stones and gifts, Jesus said unto them: As for these things which ye behold, the days will come, in the which there shall not be left one stone upon another, that shall not be thrown down.

54 And now, I, Moroni, do prophesy unto ye of the latter days: Yea, if ye do not repent of the great abominations that ye have committed in the name of the Lord, even in all those things that I have just explained unto you, then at the day of the Lord, shall every one of your temples be thrown down and destroyed according to his words.

55 And then shall I have my vengeance upon you for that which ye have done with my name. For behold, the statues that ye have erected of me shall sit upon the mounds of rubble that were once your great temples of gold and silver and all manner of precious things.

56 And now, Jesus hath shown unto us in many ways in the records that ye already have among you how the rich are cursed while the poor are blessed. Yet, the rich justify that which they have over another because in their pride, they think that they deserve their riches because of the work that they did to obtain these riches, and that the beggar in his laziness is justified in that he hath nothing.

57 And in this ye are mistaken, and except ye repent and begin to understand the will of the Father concerning all of His children, ye shall be in a state of hell when ye die.

58 And the Lord gave another parable concerning these things unto the Jews, saying: There was a certain rich man, who was clothed in purple and fine linen, and fared sumptuously every day because of that which he acquired of his business.

59 And there was a certain beggar named Lazarus, who was laid at his gate, full of sores. And desiring to be fed with the crumbs which fell from the table of the rich man, was laid close upon the gate by those of the church who would not help him.

60 But the church did give unto Lazarus just that which would keep him alive; moreover the dogs came and licked his sores in similitude of the things that he received from the church.

61 And it came to pass, that the beggar died, and his spirit was carried by the angels into the spirit world where he was received into the bosom of his fathers, or those who were there to greet him in the spirit world.

62 And the rich man also died, and was buried, and his spirit was also carried into the spirit world. But he was received not in a state of joy and rest as was Lazarus, but in a state of hell where he lifted up his eyes, being in the state of torment that is given unto them that have done wickedly in mortality.

63 And he seeth the righteous fathers afar off, and Lazarus in their bosom. And he cried and said, Oh, righteous Father Abraham, and this he said because of his traditions not knowing the true Father, have mercy on me, and send Lazarus, that he may dip the tip of his finger in water, and cool my tongue and forgive me for that which I did not do unto him in mortality. For I am tormented in this flame of my soul.

64 But the righteous spirits said unto him, Son, remember that thou in thy lifetime receivedst thy good things, and likewise Lazarus evil things: but now he is comforted, and thou art tormented.

65 And beside all this, between the spirit world and mortality there is a great gulf fixed, so that they which would pass from the state of your misery back into mortality to change their actions in life cannot; neither can they which are mortal pass unto us, even those who shall come from thence.

66 For thou canst not enter back into mortality and change that which thou hast done seeing that thou art now dead.

67 Then he said, I pray thee therefore, righteous Father, that thou wouldst send Lazarus as a spirit to the house of my father; for I have five brethren; that he may testify unto them, lest they also come into this place of torment.

68 And the righteous spirit saith unto him: They have Moses and the prophets and all the commandments and laws that these have given unto thy brethren; therefore, let them hear them.

69 And he said, Nay, righteous Father, but if one went unto them from the dead, they will repent.

70 And the spirit said unto him: If they hear not Moses and the prophets and obey not their words, neither will they be persuaded, though one rose from the dead.

71 And now, this is the state of all of you who are rich and have set yourselves above your brother in the things which ye possess, even that ye withhold from him that which might make him happier than the state in which he suffereth.

72 And now, I would once again refer you to the great discourse given unto the people of Zarahemla by King Benjamin, who had witnessed this wickedness of which I have spoken among his own people.

73 And he caused all the people of the land to be gathered together and he said unto them: My brethren, all ye that have assembled yourselves together, ye who can hear my words which I shall speak unto you this day; for I have not commanded you to come up hither to trifle with the words which I shall speak, but that ye should hearken unto me, and open your ears that ye may hear, and your hearts that ye may understand, and your minds that the mysteries of God may be unfolded to your view.

74 I have not commanded you to come up hither that ye should fear me, or that ye should think that I of myself am more than a mortal man. But I am like as yourselves, subject to all manner of infirmities in body and mind; yet I have been chosen by this people and consecrated by my father, and was suffered by the hand of the Lord that I should be a ruler and a king over this people; and have been kept and preserved by his matchless power, to serve you with all the might, mind and strength which the Lord hath granted unto me.

75 I say unto you that as I have been suffered to spend my days in your service, even up to this time, and have not sought gold nor silver nor any manner of riches of you; neither have I suffered that ye should be confined in dungeons, nor that ye should make slaves one of another, nor that ye should murder, or plunder, or steal, or commit adultery; nor even have I suffered that ye should commit any manner of wickedness, and have taught you that ye should keep the commandments of the Lord, in all things which he hath commanded you

76 And even I, myself, have labored with mine own hands that I might serve you, and that ye should not be laden with taxes, and that there should nothing come upon you which was grievous to be borne, and of all these things which I have spoken, ye yourselves are witnesses this day.

77 Yet, my brethren, I have not done these things that I might boast, neither do I tell these things that thereby I might accuse you; but I tell you these things that ye may know that I can answer a clear conscience before God this day.

78 Behold, I say unto you that because I said unto you that I had spent my days in your service, I do not desire to boast, for I have only been in the service of God. And behold, I tell you these things that ye may learn wisdom; that ye may learn that when ye are in the service of your fellow beings ye are only in the service of your God.

79 Behold, ye have called me your king; and if I, whom ye call your king, do labor to serve you, then ought not ye labor to serve one another? And behold also, if I, whom ye call your king, who hath spent his days in your service, and yet hath been in the service of God, do merit any thanks from you, Oh, how ye ought to thank your heavenly King.

CHAPTER 50

Moroni extols the words of King Benjamin. The latter day Worldwide United Foundation is introduced and explained. Christopher is to guide its establishment and function in righteousness. The evil of the family unit is expounded on, and the abomination of the teachings of the modern LDS doctrine regarding an eternal family unit is foretold.

AND now, I, Moroni, have included these words, which my father hath already given in the part of this record that is unsealed, in this part that is sealed, because they are exceedingly wonderful words which were given by the Spirit of God through King Benjamin.

2 And because his words testified of the Christ, I have included them in this part of the record. And the words which he spake concerning the works that are required of all of us who take upon ourselves the name of Christ, are the things that I would have you know were taught by Jesus during the days of his ministry.

3 And as I was about to write the words that I

thought were appropriate enough to teach you these things according to the commandment that the Lord hath given unto me concerning this record, I remembered the words of King Benjamin, which were written by my father on these plates. And the words of King Benjamin were given by the same Spirit which giveth unto me the words that I write by my own hand.

4 But the words which King Benjamin spake unto the people are much greater than my words, he being stronger in speaking than I am in writing, and for these reasons I have included these things at this time in this portion of these plates that I shall seal up according to the commandment of the Lord.

5 And now, from that which I have caused to be written in this record, I hope that in its plainness ye can begin to understand the will of the Father concerning those of you that are rich as pertaining to the things of the world.

6 Now, if in your riches ye find happiness, then ye shall have these riches in the kingdom that the Father shall provide for you. However, in that kingdom, there shall be no rich among you, because all will partake of these riches which are the desires of happiness of those that pertain to that kingdom.

7 And it is not in the riches that the Father hath condemned you, but in the inequality that these things create among His children. And if this inequality did not exist among you, then ye would be justified in your riches.

8 But when ye begin to think that because ye are rich ye are more blessed than your brother who is poor, then in this ye do err considerably. And if ye give of your abundance unto a cause that doth not do the will of the Father, or which doth not use your money to create equality among you, then ye give your money in vain and it profit you nothing before the Father.

9 Therefore, the Lord hath commanded you that are rich to give unto the poor and not to the churches that consume that which ye give unto them upon their lusts for the praise of the world.

10 And in the latter days, even after this record shall come forth among you, this last prophet who shall give these things to you, shall direct you in the way that ye shall give of your abundance to help the poor among you.

11 And he shall do this with an eye single to the glory of God, in that he shall establish a way whereby the children of God might become equal one with another. And this he shall do according to the Spirit of God which is in him and not for the glory and praise of the world.

12 And he shall do nothing in secret, as those who are not of God work according to their secret combinations, but he shall establish a foundation and a means for those that have an abundance, so that these might be able to give to those that have not, in such a way, that all things shall be known concerning the manner and the means that he shall accomplish these things among you.

13 And it shall not be required of you to give all that ye possess unto the poor, for by doing so, ye shall become poor also. But if ye do give all that ye possess, and ye do this with an eye single to the glory of God, then ye are justified and shall remain among the poor all the days of your life, and shall be assured of a state of happiness when ye die; but this thing shall not be required of you.

14 But ye should give of your abundance; and that which ye shall give shall be used by him to whom ye shall give it according to the commandments of God, which commandments are the words and will of Christ, which he hath given unto you.

15 But those of you that are like unto the Lord in all things, even those of you who are the elect of God, ye shall have no rich among you, but shall have all things in common. And if ye are elect, ye shall not be rich, for ye cannot become rich unless ye have set your hearts and desires upon these things.

16 And the elect shall not set their hearts and desires upon these things, but shall give all, even as the widow gave of her mite, to the kingdom of God to which they belong; for these are the Celestial spirits that shall be one with the Father in all things.

17 And now, during the ministry of Jesus he taught these same things unto his disciples. And he also taught them of the evils of the family unit which was established among the children of men since the days of Adam, in which his son Beneli taught the people that they should think of themselves and their wives and their children above their neighbors, and that they should separate themselves from the families of others.

18 But this thing is an abomination before the Father who hath created all of His children to be equal in all things. For behold, if ye separate yourselves into families, ye are not equal in all things, but think more for the needs of your families than ye do for those of your other brothers and sisters who are not of your own family.

19 And now, the commandments and words of Christ which he gave unto his disciples concerning the evils of this family unit is one of the things which was taken out of the accounts that ye have before you by those who organized the canon of scripture that ye have in the Bible. And they did not include these things therein because they were already unequal in their dealings with their fellowmen, and dedicated to their own family units, thus making an attempt to hide their abominations from the eyes of the world.

20 And this thing, or the family, hath been suffered by the Lord since the beginning because of the will of the children of men to divide themselves in this way. And because the children of men divide themselves in this way, he hath given specific commandments at times for the benefit of these family units, which are set up according to the free agency of the children of God.

21 But because they create such inequality among us, they are not part of the gospel of Jesus Christ, and cannot be found in any of his commandments that pertain unto our salvation, and will not be part of the kingdom of God in any manner once we are dead.

22 For I have already explained unto you that in the glories of the kingdom of our Father, there existeth no male and female, except it be in the Celestial glory of the Father. And if there is no male and female, then there can be no man and wife. And if there be no man and wife, then there can be no children who pertain unto this man and wife. Therefore, the eternal family doth not exist, except it be in the kingdom of the Father as I have explained it unto you.

23 But this eternal family to which the elect of God shall belong is not divided into husbands and wives, but is a kingdom of brothers and sisters who are the children of the Father and our Eternal Mothers, even a holy Order of individuals who are one with the Father and the Son.

24 Therefore, all of those who dwell upon this earth have no children in and of themselves. For behold, are not your children still your brothers and sisters in the eyes of the Father?

25 I say unto you, that they are your brothers and sisters; and after they have passed through the days of their infancy and childhood, which time hath been given unto them that ye might have an example of the love of the Father; yea, even after this time, they shall be mature adults like unto their parents; and the relationship that they once had as a child and parent, will be no more among them. But the relationship that they have as brothers and sisters before God shall be with them forever.

26 And the things which Jesus taught were plain and forthright concerning the family unit and the wickedness which it causeth among the people. But many of the things which he said concerning it were taken out or excluded in the record of scripture that ye have already among you.

27 Nevertheless, there are some indications in the records that ye have among you of his teachings, and it is this that the Lord hath commanded me to explain unto you, so that there might exist no more contentions among you concerning these things which ye already accept as the words of God.

28 And Jesus did not teach that ye should not love your mortal sons and your daughters, who are your spiritual brothers and sisters before God, neither did he command you not to love those of your families, but he taught that besides them, ye should love your neighbors as you do them.

29 And he knew that the gospel that the Father had sent him to teach would be the cause of much division in the family because of the equality that the Father expecteth from all of His children. And of this equality Jesus spoke as he was about to send his apostles into the world to preach the gospel of the Father unto people.

30 And he spake unto them, saying: Behold, I send you forth as sheep in the midst of wolves. For those to whom I send you will want to turn you from my flock that they may devour you and destroy my flock. But ye must not fear them and what they can do to your flesh, but fear what they can do to your soul.

31 Be ye therefore wise as serpents, and harmless as doves, in that ye avoid the traps that they will set for you. But in return for that which they do to you, ye shall not cause harm or malice to them.

32 But beware of men who come to you in the clothing of sheep and would make you think that they are friendly towards you. For once they have steered ye away from the flock, they will deliver you up to the councils, and they will scourge you in their synagogues. And they shall bring you before governors and kings for my sake, because of the testimony that ye give against them and the Gentiles.

33 But when they deliver you up, take no thought how or what ye shall speak, for it shall be given you in that same hour what ye shall speak. For it is not ye that speak, but the Spirit of your Father which speaketh in you.

34 And because of the things which ye shall testify of them, even of the wickedness of their works, the wicked brother shall deliver up the righteous brother to death, and the wicked father shall deliver up the righteous child to death. And the wicked children shall rise up against their righteous parents, and cause them to be put to death.

35 And because ye cause the families of the children of men to divide themselves for the sake of my gospel, ye shall be hated of all men for the sake of my name because they believe that their families are good, and that anyone who speaketh against the family cannot be of God, but must be of Satan.

36 But he that forsaketh his family and followeth after me and endureth to the end shall be saved in the kingdom of God where there are no families, but children under one God, who is our Father in heaven.

37 But when they persecute you in this city for that which ye preach unto them, flee ye into another and preach my gospel there. And when they persecute you in that city, flee yet into another, even unto all the nations of the earth. For verily I say unto you, Ye shall not have gone over all the cities of the earth, till the Son of man cometh in the glory of the Father.

38 And remember that ye do the things that I have commanded you to do, that ye may be one with the Father as I am one with Him. And remember that the disciple is not above his master, nor the servant above his lord. It is enough for the disciple that he be equal to his master, and the servant equal to his lord, for thus it is in the kingdom of God.

39 And if they have called the master of the house Beelzebub, how much more shall they call them of his household who are equal to him? Fear them not because of the works that they do in darkness and those sins which they have covered before the people. For the Father knoweth all things, therefore, there is nothing covered, that shall not be revealed; and there is nothing that they have hid, that shall not be known.

40 What I tell you about those that are in darkness, that speak ye in light, making known unto them of their sins that they might repent and come unto the Father through me.

41 And what ye hear in the ear by the still small voice of the Father, which is the Spirit that will be given unto you, that preach ye upon the housetops.

42 And fear not them which kill the body, but are not able to kill the soul. But rather fear him which is able to destroy both soul and body in hell. And your Father knoweth those that would destroy you and take you away from him. And He is aware of you at all times in all places.

43 And are not two sparrows sold for a farthing? Yet, one of them shall not fall on the ground without your Father knowing. Nevertheless, the very hairs of your head are all numbered, for ye are His children. Fear ye not, therefore, ye are of more value unto the Father than many sparrows.

44 Whosoever therefore shall confess me and teach my gospel before men, him will I confess also before my Father which is in heaven. But whosoever shall deny me and my gospel before men, him will I also deny before my Father which is in heaven.

45 Behold, the gospel which I have sent you forth to teach is a gospel of peace unto all that believe in me and keep the commandments of the Father. But this earth is not the kingdom of the Father, but the kingdom of the devil, who hath deceived the children of men and hath taken away the peace which their Father would give unto them if they would keep His commandments.

46 And I cannot bring peace to a kingdom that is not of the Father. Therefore, think not that I am come to send peace on earth, which is the kingdom of Satan; I came not to send peace, but a sword, even the sword of rigteousness.

47 For I am come to teach unto the children who belongeth to the family of Satan, the gospel of the Father. And this gospel will set a man at variance against his father, and the daughter against her mother, and the daughter in law against her mother in law.

48 And because of the wickedness of the children of men, the foes of a man shall be they of his own household. But he that loveth his father or mother more than me is not worthy of me; and he that loveth son or daughter more than me is not worthy of me. And he that taketh not his cross, which is the cross that I bear because of the wickedness of the children of men, and followeth after me, is not worthy of me.

49 For the world persecuteth me for that which I testify is wicked among men. And they want to kill me for that manner of life that I lived away from them, and which I could not find among them in the world and have peace. But he who seeketh to save his life in this world, even that he shall find peace in the kingdom of Satan, shall lose it. And he that loseth his life in this world for my sake shall find it in the kingdom of my Father.

50 For he that receiveth you, receiveth me, and he that receiveth me receiveth him that sent me. And he that sent me is the Father who receiveth all those who receiveth Him. Verily, I say unto you, it mattereth not unto the Father by what name the children of men shall call Him, if it so be that they receiveth him who the Father sendeth unto them.

51 And there shall be prophets and righteous men sent among the children of men in all parts of the world to teach them the will of the Father. And he that receiveth a prophet in the name of a prophet shall receive the reward of that prophet; and he that receiveth a righteous man in the name of a righteous man shall receive the reward of a righteous man.

52 And these shall be my disciples who shall give all the children of men a cup of cold water that shall be in them a well of water springing up into everlasting life. And whosoever drinketh of this water shall never thirst again.

53 And I am unable of myself to give this drink unto all the nations of the earth. And for this reason I send ye forth unto the world in my name. And if they do not believe on my name, then let them believe on your name that they might be saved through repentance and in keeping the commandments that they shall receive because of you.

54 And whosoever shall give to drink unto one of these little ones a cup of cold water only in the name of a disciple, verily I say unto you, he shall in no wise lose his reward.

55 And now, I, Moroni, would that ye should know that the gospel of Jesus Christ will never be accepted by the whole world while it is under the control of Satan. And in darkness the light of the gospel shall shine forth unto any that will see it and let it guide them through this darkness.

56 And the disciples of Christ are those who hold up a torch of light in the darkness and beckon unto all to come unto Christ that all might see the straight and narrow path through the darkness of the world.

57 And any of you who preach the words of Christ, and live by the words of Christ, are a torch bearer of the light of Christ. And if ye have desires to serve God, then are ye called to the work and become His torchbearers. But ye shall not hold up his light except by your examples before men.

58 And Adam gave these same instructions unto his children, which were the same instructions that Jesus gave unto the Jews. And I have given the words of Adam unto you in this record, even those things which he said: Verily, verily, I say unto you, I give unto you to be the light of your posterity, that your light might shine forth out of the darkness. And when your light shineth forth, it giveth its light unto all that are in the land.

59 And ye shall be as a city that is set high upon a hill from wherewith ye send forth this light. And this light shall shine forth as a beacon unto them, that they might come into the city and bask in the light. And a city that is set on a hill cannot be hid.

60 Behold, do men light a candle and put it under a bushel? Nay, but on a candlestick, and it giveth light to all who are in the house; Therefore let your light so shine before your posterity, that they may see your good works and glorify your Father who is in heaven.

61 Now the Lord did not only give this commandment unto us as your parents, but he hath given it unto all of us who have taken upon ourselves the name of the Lord, or in other words, have covenanted with him to obey his commandments. And when we have covenanted with him to obey his commandments, then we become an example for others to follow, or the light that he hath mentioned.

62 And these words of Adam were given unto his children by the Holy Ghost, who at the time of Adam, was Jehovah. Therefore, Adam gave the words of Christ unto his children.

63 And now, my beloved brothers and sisters, I would ask of ye in the latter days, do ye have the light of Christ? Do ye let your light shine so that others might see your good works and glorify your Father in heaven? Or are your works the works of darkness, which drown out the light?

64 I say unto you that I have seen your works, and I know that your works are the works of darkness. For there are many among you who believe that your families are the most precious things to you. And this church that hath been established among the Gentiles, even the church that is called after the name of Jesus Christ in the latter days, hath caused the people to worship their families more than they worship the Father.

65 For they believe that their family units are eternal, and that unless this family unit is sealed for eternity, or in other words, unless the mother and father are sealed together and the children are sealed to them, then they cannot inherit the kingdom of God. And this they believe because of the precepts of men that are taught among them.

66 And they are like unto the Benelites of old, and also the Zoramites in the time of my fathers. Yet they are worse than these, because in their pride, they have shown forth an example unto the world that turneth the children of men away from the words of Christ, which they have in abundance among them.

67 And they send forth their ministers into the world to convince the world that the only way whereby they might be saved; yea, the only way whereby they might be an eternal family unit forever, is to join with them and keep the commandments of their church, which they present to the people as the gospel of Jesus Christ.

68 And they say unto the world: Come unto us for we have the fullness of the gospel of Jesus Christ. And we believe the Bible to be the word of God, and we also believe the Book of Mormon to be the word of God. And in these books can be found the fullness of the everlasting gospel of the Father and all of His commandments which must be obeyed in order for a man to be saved in His kingdom.

69 And now, this which they proclaim is the truth. For behold, I, Moroni, give unto you who shall receive these things, my testimony that the fullness of the gospel of Jesus Christ is contained within the Bible and the Book of Mormon as I have previously explained it unto you.

70 But unto this church of Jesus Christ of the latter days, I say unto you: Search the Bible, and also the record of my father, yea, even search all the words of Christ that are given unto all the nations of the earth according to their learning and their traditions. Now, in your search, can ye find one word, yea, even a jot or a tittle in reference to an eternal family and the necessity that a man hath of being sealed to his wife and to his children as an eternal family unit?

71 I say unto you that ye shall find no such thing, for this thing is not a commandment of the Lord, nor hath it ever been, nor shall it ever be. But the Father hath commanded against such things.

72 And ye shall say within your hearts: The Lord hath given us this new revelation through our prophets and our apostles who are the high priests of our church and only to whom the Lord shall reveal all things concerning his will for the children of men.

73 But I say unto you, that if this be the case, then why do ye lie to the people of the world and testify unto them that the fullness of the gospel is contained in the scriptures that I have mentioned?

74 Yea, how can a glass be full, yet still there be room for more water? Why do ye not say unto the world that the fullness of the gospel is not fully contained within the scriptures; for the Lord is a respecter of persons and shall not give his will concerning all of the children of God to any, except it be through the leaders of your church, who are his apostles and his prophets?

75 Are ye afraid to tell the truth unto the world concerning your pride? Are ye afraid that your works of darkness shall be spoken of upon the housetops and that ye shall be discovered for who ye really are and whom ye really serve?

76 Are ye afraid to tell the world that they cannot be sealed to their families forever unless they pay one tenth of all that they earn to your church in the form of tithing to be used for the purposes that your leaders see fit?

77 And for what purpose do your leaders see fit to use the money that is paid unto them, so that a man might be sealed to his family forever? Is it not to build the temples that are required to administer these sealings unto the people?

78 Behold, in these things ye have grossly corrupted the gospel of Jesus Christ, and except ye repent for that which ye have done, ye shall suffer the wrath of God to come down upon you and destroy you before His Son cometh once again upon the earth to teach his true gospel in its fullness.

79 And hath he not already taught his gospel to the children of men in its fullness? I say unto you that he hath taught unto them this gospel, because He doth not choose one child over another and teacheth His will to all of His children in whatever form they might worship Him.

80 And in the words that he taught his disciples, the Lord condemned the family unit that ye have set up among you. Even his own mother and his brothers came up to see him on one occasion while he yet talked to the people. And his mother and his brethren stood without, desiring to speak with him. Then one said unto him, Behold, thy mother and thy brethren stand without, desiring to speak with thee.

81 But he answered and said unto him that told him: Who is my mother and who are my brethren? And he stretched forth his hand towards his disciples, and said: Behold my mother and my brethren; for whosoever shall do the will of my Father which is in heaven, the same is my brother, and sister, and mother.

82 And now, I, Moroni ask of you of the latter days: Who of ye are his brother, his sister, or his mother?

CHAPTER 51

Moroni is commanded to include a retranslation of the gospel account of John, which includes all the plain and precious things that were taken out to please those who canonized the New Testament of the Bible. Jesus explains his anger in clearing the temple. He teaches the gospel to the Samarians, who are despised by the Jews.

AND now, I, Moroni, have been commanded by the Lord to give unto you the rest of the account of his life according to that which ye have already received among you in the record of the Jews.

2 Behold, there were many accounts given of the life and ministry of Christ. And that council of men of which I have spoken, who decided among themselves which of the accounts of the life and ministry of Jesus they would allow to be published unto the world of Christendom many years after the death of Christ; yea, when these men read these accounts, they changed the wording thereof and transcribed the accounts according to that which they believed was the truth regarding the life and ministry of Christ according to their own beliefs and traditions.

3 And they included the accounts of the apostles who were eyewitnesses, who lived and preached with Jesus during the days of his ministry. And to emphasize that which they wanted the people to believe and accept, this council of men chose those records that testified of each other, even those accounts that related that which they wanted the people to accept and understand.

4 And though the Spirit of God was not with them individually, the Spirit was there to guide somewhat in that which was included; and in many instances the Spirit covered the understanding of these men of the council, so that they would include many things that they would not have included of their own free will and choice according to their understanding and perceptions of Christ.

5 Now, in this, their free agency was not infringed upon because the scripture and the accounts were already written before hand, and these men used the words that were written to interpolate their own doctrine and precepts. And this they did by not including some words, and taking others out of context, so that the meaning of the original account conformed to their desires.

6 And in the latter days, the Urim and Thummim shall be used by these last two prophets to bring back the things that were taken out of these accounts, so that a more true account can be given of the life and the ministry and the words of Christ.

7 And the first of these two prophets shall do a small part of giving a more full account of the New Testament, as it shall be known among you. And he shall only reveal a small part of the true account, because of the time of the Lord, even that the people to whom these things shall come shall reject the fullness of the gospel of Jesus Christ, and these shall not have the full truth at that time.

8 But the second of these latter day prophets, even he from whom ye shall receive this sealed portion of the record of my father; yea, he shall give unto the world a more full account as he shall receive it through the Urim and Thummim.

9 And I have seen this record of the account of the life and ministry and the words of Christ through the same Urim and Thummim which I will hide up with these records that it might be available to these last two latter-day prophets of whom I have spoken.

10 And each of them shall be commanded by the Lord to use the Urim and Thummim to translate the portion of the record that he hath been commanded to translate. But unto the first prophet, even he who shall translate the unsealed portion of this record, the Lord shall give a commandment to use the Urim and Thummim to give a small part of the corrections that need to be made to the record of the Jews, according to that which the Lord desireth that shall be revealed unto the people at that time.

11 But the second of these prophets shall translate directly from these plates as he shall be commanded. And upon these plates, I will give the account of the life and ministry and the words of Christ according as I have been commanded.

12 For behold, I have seen these records by the power and means provided through the Urim and Thummim, and I will take my account of these things from these translators. And he who shall use the Urim and Thummim to translate these things shall not add to or take away from anything that I write herein.

13 Nevertheless, he shall be commanded to compare that which I shall write unto you with that which hath already gone forth among you, and if that which I have written needeth to be changed in some minor way that it might more fully testify of the things that ye already have among you, then the Spirit shall command him to make those adjustments according to the Spirit of God and the power and means of the Urim and Thummim.

14 And in this way, the Lord hath commanded us so that a more complete and true account of his ministry might be given unto the world. And in those accounts which ye already have among you, there are those who have included many of the parables which Jesus spoke unto the Jews.

15 Now, these parables were not understood by the men of the council who allowed them to be included in the record that ye have before you. And if they would have understood the true meaning of some of these parables, then they would have known that they testify in symbolic form of their own wickedness and their pride, which keepeth them from having the Holy Ghost to guide them in that which they should do.

16 And of those accounts, even those accounts that contain many parables given by the Lord, I make little mention except where the explanation of a parable might be

necessary to expound upon the message of the Lord more fully.

17 But the Lord doth not speak in parables to the elect of God, for he hath nothing to hide from them; for they are the sheep who hear his voice and follow him. And this record which is sealed is for the elect of God; and for this reason, the Lord hath commanded me to take most of my account of his life from that which was written by his closest friend, even his beloved apostle, John, whom he loved.

18 For John doth not give so many parables in his record, having his intent fully directed towards the true message of Jesus Christ, his friend and Savior.

19 And now, through the power of the Spirit and the means and power of the Urim and Thummim, I will give unto you a more true accounting of the life of Christ, which I have not yet given unto you.

20 And I say unto you who shall receive these things, even the elect who hear the voice of the Lord and understandeth him; yea, I say unto you: Rejoice in Christ. Ponder in Christ. Make Christ your friend that ye might know him as your friend and brother.

21 Worship him only as he hath commanded you, which commandments give all the glory to the Father in all things. Become one with him and ye shall have the Holy Ghost to bear witness of him. And when ye have the testimony of the Spirit, ye shall be one with him.

22 And so that ye might more fully know him, I continue with an account of his life according to the words of his beloved apostle, who was an eyewitness to the life and the words of the Christ in the flesh.

23 And it came to pass that immediately after the Lord had cleared the temple, he threw the whip that he had made to the ground and smiled upon his disciples, having once again regained his countenance of peace and tranquility that exuded from his soul continually.

24 And in a smiling humility he said unto them: Behold, and now shall my enemies become greater because of that which I have done herein. Well did David prophesy a song unto me when he wrote, saying: They that hate me without a cause are more than the hairs of mine head; they that would destroy me, being mine enemies wrongfully, are mighty. For I have restored that which I took not away.

25 Oh, God, thou knowest my foolishness; and my sins are not hid from thee. Let not them that wait on thee, Oh, Lord God of hosts, be ashamed for my sake. Let not those who seek thee be confounded for my sake, Oh, God of Israel, because for Thy sake I have borne reproach; shame hath covered my face.

26 I am become a stranger unto my brethren, and an alien unto the children of my mother, for the zeal of thine house hath eaten me up; and the reproaches of they who reproached thee are fallen upon me.

27 And this Jesus said to his disciples because he knew of those things which would come because of his actions in the temple that day. And his disciples kept in their remembrance what Jesus said unto them and that it was written: The zeal of thine house hath eaten me up.

28 And there were Jews within the temple that confronted him and asked of him concerning the zeal of which he had spoken. And Jesus perceiving their thoughts, said unto them: The zeal came from within my own house, which is my body. And my indignation did eat me from within because of the wickedness of those who are within the walls of this house, which ye suppose ye have dedicated unto my Father.

29 And these Jews which questioned him had heard of the many miracles that Jesus had wrought, and these wanted to see a miracle at his hand so that they could consume it upon their lusts, because they did not believe in him.

30 Then answered the Jews and said unto him, what sign shewest thou unto us, seeing that thou doest these things and hath claimed that this is the house of thy Father? For if thou art the son of God as thou pretendest, then show forth unto us a sign of thy power.

31 Jesus answered and said unto them, Destroy this temple, and in three days I will raise it up.

32 Then said the Jews: Forty and six years was this temple in building, and wilt thou rear it up in three days? But he spake of the temple of his body and did not reveal unto them the intent and meaning of his words, they being wicked and unbelievers. And straightaway he left them.

33 When therefore he was risen from the dead, his disciples remembered that he had said this unto them; and they believed the scripture, and the word which Jesus had said.

34 Now, when he was in Jerusalem at the Passover, on the feast day, many believed in his name when they saw the miracles which he did among them. But Jesus did not reveal himself unto them, nor did he teach them further the mysteries of godliness that he had been commanded by the Father to teach unto them, because he knew all things and knew that these men did not believe on his name and only sought him out because of the miracles which he did.

35 But he needed not that any man should testify of the Son of man—as he called himself because he was a servant to all men, even as a son serveth his father—for he knew that the Spirit which was within each man would testify of him according to that spirit that was in that man.

36 And there came a man of the Pharisees, named Nicodemus, a ruler of the Jews; this same man came to Jesus by night, and said unto him: Rabbi, we know that thou art a teacher come from God, for no man can do these miracles that thou doest, except God be with him. Therefore, I beg of thee that thou wouldst teach me that which I must do that I may also have this power and be a servant in the kingdom of God.

37 And this Nicodemus said unto him because he did not believe in Jesus, but marveled within himself at the miracles which he performed and were testified of by the people.

38 And Jesus answered, and said unto him: Verily, verily, I say unto thee, ye cannot have this power except ye see the kingdom of God. And except a man be born again, he cannot see the kingdom of God.

39 And Nicodemus saith unto him: How can a man be born when he is old? Can he enter the second time into the womb of his mother and be born?

40 Jesus answered, Verily, verily, I say unto thee, Except a man be born of water as he cometh forth from the womb of his mother in the flesh, and also of the Spirit, he cannot enter into the kingdom of God. For that which is born of the flesh followeth after the things of the flesh; and that which is born of the Spirit followeth after the things of the spirit.

41 Therefore, marvel not that I said unto thee, Ye must be born again, for that which is flesh must return to the dust from which it cometh, and then there is only spirit left. And except a man repent of his sins and prepareth his spirit when the flesh is cast off, he shall in no wise enter the kingdom of God.

42 And Nicodemus said unto him: I can see my flesh, but I cannot see my spirit; and I know I am of the flesh because I was born into that which I can see. How, then, can I know of this spirit of which thou speakest?

43 And Jesus answered him, saying: The wind bloweth where it listeth, and thou hearest the sound thereof, but canst not tell whence it cometh, and whither it goeth. And of the same matter from which the wind is made, so is every one that is born of the Spirit.

44 Nicodemus answered and said unto him, How can these things be?

45 Jesus answered and said unto him, Art thou a master of Israel, and knowest not these things? Verily, verily, I say unto thee, we speak that of which we do know, and testify of that which we have seen; and ye receive not our witness because the Spirit of God is not with you to teach you these things.

46 If I have told you concerning earthly things that ye understand and can see, and ye believe not, how shall ye believe, if I tell you of heavenly things which ye cannot see?

47 And no man hath ascended up to heaven, except it be by him who came down from heaven, even the Son of man who is not in heaven, but among you, even him whom ye do not believe.

48 And as Moses lifted up the serpent in the wilderness, even so must the Son of man be lifted up by those who sit in the seat of Moses, even by thee who art among them. And he is lifted up because of the things which he hath taught you, which ye believe not.

49 But he hath taught you these things that

whosoever believeth in him should not perish, but have eternal life. For God so loved the world, that he gave his only begotten Son, that whosoever believeth in him should not perish, but have everlasting life.

50 For God sent not his Son into the world to condemn the world; but that the world through him might be saved. He that believeth on him is not condemned; but he that believeth not is condemned already, because he hath not believed in the name of the only begotten Son of God, which before was preached by the mouth of the holy prophets; for they testify of me.

51 And this is the condemnation of those who believeth not in me, even that light is come into the world, and men loved darkness rather than light, and would not come to the light and be saved, because their deeds were evil.

52 For every one that doeth evil hateth the light, neither cometh to the light, lest his deeds should be reproved. But he that doeth truth cometh to the light that his deeds may be made manifest by the fruits of the Spirit, which will testify that they are wrought in God

53 And from that time forth Nicodemus believed in the words of Jesus. But he was a rich man who was in authority in the church of the Jews. And because of his riches and his pride, even that he did not want to incur the ridicule of the other leaders of the church, he did not openly confess Jesus, but kept all these things within him.

54 After these things came Jesus and his disciples into the land of Judea, and there he tarried with the people; and his disciples baptized all those that came unto them and wanted to make a new covenant with God to keep the commandments that Jesus had given unto them.

55 And Jesus suffered that the ordinance of baptism be taught to the people to keep them in remembrance of the covenant that they would make with the Father. For the people found more purpose in those things that they could see with their mortal eyes, than that which the Spirit would give unto them, which they could not see.

56 And for this reason, the Father suffered that Jesus allow the people to be required to be baptized according to the laws of their traditions. But Jesus would not baptize the people, but gave the authority to do so to his apostles.

57 And John also was baptizing in Aenon near to Salim, because there was much water there; and many people came, and were baptized of John, for John was not yet cast into prison.

58 Then there arose a question between some of the disciples of John and the Jews about whether or not they were purified by his baptism, because he had taught them that the baptism which Jesus would give unto them was greater than his own.

59 And this the people believed because they thought that baptism washed away their sins and purified their souls, having been taught this by their traditions.

60 And they came unto John, and said unto him, Rabbi, he that was with thee beyond Jordan, to whom thou bearest witness, behold, the same baptizeth, and all men come to him.

61 John answered and said, Oh, ye wicked and perverse generation. How long shall the Lord suffer you to wallow in your ignorance? Truly a man can receive no understanding of the Spirit, except it be given him from heaven.

62 Ye yourselves bear me witness, that I said, I am not the Christ, but that I am sent before him. He that hath the bride is the bridegroom; but the friend of the bridegroom, which standeth and heareth him, rejoiceth greatly because of the voice of the bridegroom.

63 And because ye now bear witness unto me that the people are going to the Christ, in this my joy therefore is fulfilled. He must increase, but I must decrease.

64 He that cometh from above is above all. But ye are of the earth and are earthly, and speaketh of the earth and understandeth not that which is from above. Behold, he that cometh from heaven is above all. And what he hath seen and heard of our Father in heaven, that he testifieth of; and no man receiveth his testimony, except he hath the Spirit of the Father within him.

65 He that hath received his testimony, hath set to his forehead the seal of the Father, and testifieth that the testimony of God, which he hath received from him who was sent from the

Father, is true. For he whom God hath sent speaketh the words of God, for God giveth him not the Spirit by measure, for he dwelleth in him, even the fullness of the Father.

66 The Father loveth the Son, and hath given all things into his hand for the sake of all of His children. And he who believeth on the Son hath everlasting life; and shall receive of his fullness. But he who believeth not the Son shall not receive of his fullness; for the wrath of God abideth on him because of the works which he doeth, which are against that which the Father hath commanded.

67 And when, therefore, the Lord knew how the Pharisees had heard that Jesus made and baptized more disciples than John—though Jesus himself baptized not, but his disciples only—he left Judea, and departed again into Galilee. And this he did that he would not disrupt further the work that John was doing in that part of the land, because the Jews accepted John as a prophet, but rejected him.

68 And on his way to Galilee he must needs go through Samaria. Now, the Jews hated the Samarians and were taught by the leaders of their church that these were unclean and that they should not marry them or allow their children, or the children of their children, to associate with them.

69 And thus all the Jews believed because of their traditions and that which they had been taught, even that they were a peculiar and a chosen people, being the children of Abraham.

70 And Jesus came into a city of Samaria, which is called Sychar, near to the parcel of ground that Jacob gave to his son Joseph. Now the well of Jacob was there, but the Samarians were not allowed near unto the well in the presence of a Jew.

71 Jesus, therefore, being wearied with his journey, sat thus on the well knowing that he could show an example to his disciples of the foolishness of the traditions of the Jews.

72 And it was about the sixth hour when Jesus tarried there, for he knew that soon there would be some who would come to the well for water. And there cometh a woman of Samaria to draw water; and so that he could show the example to his disciples—for his disciples were gone away unto the city to buy meat—Jesus tarried there with the woman and engaged her time that she would not leave. And he saith unto her: Give me to drink.

73 Then saith the woman of Samaria unto him: How is it that thou, being a Jew, askest drink of me, who is a woman of Samaria, for the Jews have no dealings with the Samarians?

74 Jesus answered and said unto her: If thou knewest the gift of God that He hath given to all of His children, and who it is that saith to thee, Give me to drink; thou wouldst have asked of him, who is this gift, and he would have given thee living water.

75 The woman saith unto him: Sir, thou hast nothing to draw with, and the well is deep; from whence then hast thou that living water? Art thou greater than our father Jacob, who gave us the well, and drank thereof himself, and his children, and his cattle?

76 Jesus answered and said unto her: Whosoever drinketh of this water shall thirst again. But whosoever drinketh of the water that I shall give him shall never thirst; but the water that I shall give him shall be in him a well of water springing up unto everlasting life.

77 The woman saith unto him, Sir, give me this water, that I thirst not, neither come hither to draw. And this she said because she did not understand the words of Jesus and was wont to mock him for that which he said unto her.

78 And Jesus perceived her mockery and saith unto her: Go, call thy husband, and come hither. The woman answered and said, I have no husband.

79 And Jesus said unto her: Thou hast well said, I have no husband, for thou hast had five husbands; and he whom thou now hast is not thy husband: in that saidst thou truly.

80 And then the woman began to believe on him and saith unto him: Sir, I perceive that thou art a prophet. But if thou art a prophet, then tell me why our fathers worshipped in this mountain; and ye say, that in Jerusalem is the place where men ought to worship, and hateth us for not worshiping as thou, who art a Jew, worshipeth.

81 And Jesus saith unto her: Woman, believe me, the hour cometh, when ye shall neither in this mountain, nor yet at Jerusalem, worship the

Father. Ye worship ye know not what because ye are taught the traditions of your fathers which are the commandments and precepts of men that confuse you.

82 We know what we worship, for salvation is of the Jews according to the prophets that have preached unto your fathers. And I am he of whom they preached and am here among you to give unto you the commandments of the Father that ye may know that the Father loveth you like unto the Jews from whence I came.

83 But the hour cometh, and now is, when the true worshippers shall worship the Father in spirit and in truth; for the Father seeketh such to worship him, for he needeth not that a religion be set up among men to teach of Him.

84 For God is the father of the spirit; and they that worship Him must worship Him in spirit and in truth. And if it so be that they worship Him in spirit and in truth, then He shall send His Spirit unto them to teach them of Him, for He is no respecter of persons and loveth all people, both the Jew and the Gentile, they are all His children.

85 And the woman saith unto him: I know that the Messiah cometh, which is called Christ according to the words of the prophets unto our fathers; and when he is come, he will tell us all things.

86 Jesus saith unto her: I that speak unto thee am he who the prophets prophesied shall come into the world to save the world from sin. And I shall save the world by teaching them the will of the Father concerning them, that they might prepare themselves to enter into the kingdoms that the Father hath prepared for them.

87 For this purpose have I been sent unto the Jews first, and unto the Gentiles last. For the first shall be last and the last shall be first, making all things equal in the eyes of the Father, who is our God.

88 And upon this came his disciples, and marvelled that he talked with the woman, yet none among them said unto the woman, What seekest thou? Nor did any ask of the Lord, Why talkest thou with her? For they knew that the Lord understood all things concerning the manner in which they should treat one another in spite of their traditions.

89 And the disciples of Jesus then understood that all were equal under God, and that Jesus had been sent unto the whole world that it might be saved, not only to the Jews.

90 And it came to pass that the woman being astonished at the things which Jesus had told her left her water pot, and went her way into the city, and saith to the men of the city: Come, see a man, who told me all things that ever I did; is not this the Christ of whom our fathers spoke? Then they went out of the city, and came unto him.

91 In the meanwhile his disciples prayed him, saying: Master, eat that which we have purchased for thee from the Samarians.

92 But he said unto them: I have meat to eat that ye know not of. And the meat that ye have purchased from the Samarians shall be returned to them a hundred fold in the blessings which they shall now receive from my Father.

93 Therefore saith the disciples one to another: Hath any man brought him ought to eat?

94 Jesus saith unto them: My meat is to do the will of Him that sent me, and to finish His work, which is to teach His commandments to the world, that all those that keep these commandments might have His Spirit to be with them.

95 Do ye not say that there are yet four months, and then cometh harvest? Behold, I say unto you, lift up your eyes, and look on the fields; for they are white already to harvest.

96 And he that reapeth receiveth wages of Him that sendeth you forth to reap. And if ye reap with all your heart, might, mind, and strength, then ye shall gather fruit unto life eternal; for that which ye shall teach unto this people shall give them eternal life. Therefore, if these receive eternal life, then both he that soweth and he that reapeth may rejoice together.

97 And herein is that saying true, One soweth, and another reapeth. Behold, my Father hath sowed the seeds of His Spirit within all the children of men, who are all His children. And He hath done this by commanding me to send forth His holy prophets that His children might have His commandments; and that by keeping His commandments have His Spirit to be with them always.

98 And these prophets are those who have sown before you, for the people believe on the prophecies that these holy prophets have given unto them concerning me. Therefore, I have sent you to reap that whereon ye bestowed no labor, for other men, who are the prophets of God who have come before you, have labored, and ye are entered into their labors.

99 And many of the Samarians of that city believed on Jesus for the saying of the woman, which she testified, saying, He told me all that ever I did. So when the Samarians were come unto him, they besought him that he would tarry with them and teach them the commandments and will of the Father as he had explained it unto the woman.

100 And he abode there two days and taught them the things which he had taught unto the Jews at Jerusalem.

101 And many more believed because of his own word; and those who believed on him said unto the woman: Now we believe, not because of thy saying; for we have heard him ourselves, and know that this is indeed the Christ, the Savior of the world.

CHAPTER 52

The account of John continues. Jesus' family turns the people against him. He heals on the sabbath and is mocked because of it. The dead in the spirit world hear the words Christ teaches in the flesh. Jesus testifies of his work in the spirit world. He condemns the leadership of the church and prays to the Father to stop showing miracles to the people.

Now, after two days Jesus departed thence, and went into Galilee. For Jesus himself testified, that a prophet hath no honor in his own country. For his father Joseph and his brothers who did not believe in him turned the hearts of the people of Galilee against him, proclaiming that he was a man like all other men, and that he was not the Christ.

2 Then when he was come into Galilee, the Galilaeans received him because of the miracles that he performed among the people, having seen all the things that he did at Jerusalem at the feast; for they also went unto the feast of the Passover according to their traditions.

3 So Jesus came again into Cana of Galilee, where he was married to Martha and made the water wine. And there was a certain nobleman, whose son was sick at Capernaum, who, when he heard that Jesus was come out of Judea into Galilee, went unto him, and besought him that he would come down, and heal his son; for his son was at the point of death.

4 Then said Jesus unto him: What is it that thou wantest from me, seeing that thou dost not believe in that which I have preached unto thee, but only those miracles that the Father hath commanded me to give unto thee. Behold, except thou seest signs and wonders, thou wilt not believe.

5 But the nobleman persisted in his tears and begged of the Lord that he would heal his son, saying unto him: Sir, come down ere my child die. And Jesus had compassion on him according to the commandment that he had received of the Father, even that he should show forth the power which was in him, that others might, per chance, come unto him and listen to his words and be saved.

6 And Jesus saith unto him: Go thy way; thy son liveth. And the man believed the word that Jesus had spoken unto him, and he went his way. And as he was now going down, his servants met him, and told him, saying: Thy son liveth. Then enquired he of them the hour when he began to mend; for he began to doubt the word of the Lord after leaving his presence, because he did not believe in him according to the Spirit, but because of the testimonies of others that Jesus truly could perform miracles.

7 And they said unto him: Yesterday at the seventh hour the fever left him. So the father knew that it was at the same hour, in the which Jesus said unto him, Thy son liveth. And the man fell to his knees and began to repent of his sins and his unbelief. And he himself believed, and he also taught those of his whole household, who also believed because of the miracle that had been done.

8 This is again the second miracle that Jesus did, when he was come out of Judea into Galilee of which the people testified before the high priests at Jerusalem. And after this miracle, there was a feast of the Jews; and Jesus went up to Jerusalem according to the traditions of the Jews. For Jesus truly respected the religions and traditions of all men, though he believed in none of them.

9 Now, there is at Jerusalem by the sheep market a pool, which is called in the Hebrew tongue Bethesda, having five porches, on which lay a great multitude of impotent folk, of blind, halt, and withered, all waiting for the moving of the water according to their traditions.

10 For the people were taught by their traditions that an angel went down at a certain season into the pool and troubled the water; whosoever then first, after the troubling of the water, stepped in, was made whole of whatsoever disease he had.

11 And a certain man was there, which had an infirmity thirty and eight years. And when Jesus saw him lie, and knew that he had been now a long time in that case believing in the foolish tradition that the people were taught, he saith unto him: Wilt thou be made whole?

12 And the impotent man answered him, saying: Sir, I have no man, when the water is troubled, to put me into the pool; but while I am coming, another steppeth down before me.

13 And Jesus had compassion on him because of his patience in his belief of this tradition, and saith unto him: Rise, take up thy bed, and walk. And immediately the man was made whole, and took up his bed, and walked.

14 And this was done on the same day as the sabbath. And the Jews who had not seen Jesus heal the man and did not recognize this man as he who lay for so many years at the pool, therefore said unto him that was cured: It is the sabbath day and it is not lawful for thee to carry thy bed.

15 And the man answered them, saying: He that made me whole, the same said unto me, Take up thy bed, and walk. Then asked they him, saying: What man is that which said unto thee, Take up thy bed, and walk? And he that was healed wist not who it was, for there was a multitude being in that place, and Jesus had conveyed himself away secretly so that others would not take notice of that which he had done for the man.

16 Afterward, Jesus findeth the man whom he had healed in the temple offering sacrifice unto the church and worshipping the leaders of the church for that which he thought was a miracle wrought by the power and authority of the Priesthood of the church as he had been taught.

17 And when Jesus saw that which he offered in thanksgiving unto the church, he saith unto him: Behold, thou art made whole, therefore, sin no more in supporting the wickedness of this church and its leaders, lest a worse thing come unto thee. For behold, they do not worship the true God, who hath healed you.

18 And because they have rejected my gospel, they belong to the church of the devil. And that which thou giveth unto them supporteth them in their sins. And the man did not believe on the words of Jesus, though he was healed by him, because of that which he spoke against the church.

19 And the man, being old, knew only the church and its leaders whom he accepted as the mouthpieces of God and the only ones with authority to do the will of God.

20 Therefore, the man departed and told the Jews that it was Jesus, who had made him whole, and told them all the things that Jesus had said unto him concerning the wickedness of the church and their leaders.

21 And therefore did the Jews mock and persecute Jesus, and sought to slay him, because he had done these things on the sabbath day and had said that he was the true God who had healed the man.

22 But Jesus answered them, saying: My Father worketh hitherto on the sabbath, and I do the work that I see my Father do.

23 Therefore the Jews sought the more to kill him, because he not only had broken the sabbath, but had said also that God was his Father, making himself equal with God.

24 Then answered Jesus and saith unto them: Verily, verily, I say unto you, the Son can do nothing of himself, but what he seeth the Father do; for whatsoever things He doeth, these also doeth the Son likewise. For the Father loveth the Son, and sheweth him all things that He Himself doeth. And the Son will shew unto you greater works than these, that ye may marvel, because the Father hath given His power unto the Son that he might do these things before you.

25 For as the Father raiseth up the dead, and quickeneth them; even so the Son quickeneth he who listeneth to the words of the Father, given unto him by the Son. For the Father judgeth no man, but hath committed all judgment unto the Son, so that the Son can judge men by those things which the Son hath given unto them, which are the commandments of the Father.

26 And the Father hath given His power unto the Son in the flesh that all men should honor the Son, even as they honor the Father. He that honoreth not the Son honoreth not the Father which hath sent him.

27 Verily, verily, I say unto you, He that heareth my word, and believeth on Him that sent me, hath everlasting life, and shall not come into condemnation; but is passed from death unto life, and this is what I meant when I said that the Son quickeneth whom he will, even that those who believe on that which I teach them of the Father shall be saved in the kingdom of the Father.

28 Verily, verily, I say unto you, The hour is coming, and now is, when the dead shall hear the voice of the Son of God in the flesh, but they being in the spirit shall also see that which is done in mortality, they being aware in the spirit of all things. And they who hear that which the Son shall teach, and keepeth the commandments of the Father, shall live forever in the kingdom of the Father.

29 For as the Father hath the power to give life in himself; so hath he given this power to the Son to have life in himself. And hath given him authority to execute judgment also, because he is the Son of man, who hath been called by the Father to teach the laws of salvation unto all the children of men, who are all the spirit children of the Father.

30 Marvel not at this; for the hour is coming, in the which all that are in the graves shall hear his voice; for the Son shall enter again into the spirit world from whence he came and give all the authority that he hath received of the Father to the Holy Ghost, who shall teach the spirits of those who are dead the gospel of the Son.

31 And they shall come forth; they who have done good, unto the resurrection of life; and they who have done evil, unto the resurrection of damnation.

32 I can, of mine own self, do nothing in the flesh, for as I hear with my mortal ears, I judge, and my judgment is just; because I seek not mine own will, but the will of the Father who hath sent me.

33 Therefore, if I bear witness of myself, my witness is not true, for it cometh of my flesh, which ye hear according to the flesh. However, there is another that beareth witness of me in the flesh; and I know that the witness which he witnesseth of me ye have accepted as being true, because ye accept him and not me.

34 Ye sent unto John, and he bare witness unto the truth. But I am not received by those who receive their testimony from a man. But I am received by those who have been given a testimony of me by the Father who knoweth the truth of all things, and administereth His truth to all of His children through the Holy Ghost.

35 But these things I say of John, even that ye should believe on his word, that ye might be saved. He was a burning and a shining light sent forth of the Father in the spirit of Elias. And ye were willing for a season to rejoice in his light.

36 But I have greater witness than that of John; for the works which the Father hath given me to finish, the same works that I do bear witness of me, that the Father hath sent me. And the Father Himself, which hath sent me, hath borne witness of me.

37 Ye have neither heard the voice of the Father at any time with your mortal ears, nor have ye seen his shape with your mortal eyes, because he administereth the truth by the power of His Spirit, which is the Holy Ghost.

38 And because ye do not have the Holy Ghost with you, ye have not His truth abiding in you; for whom He hath sent, him ye believeth not.

39 Search the scriptures; for in them ye think ye have eternal life because ye have been taught this by your leaders who do not have the Spirit of the Father. And ye do not need your leaders

to teach unto you that which your Father will give to you freely if ye but ask it of Him.

40 And if ye ask of Him, He will bear witness to you of the scriptures, that they are they which testify of me. But because ye listen to your leaders and believe that only through them can ye receive the truth, ye will not come unto me, who hath been sent by the Father, and of whom ye receive a witness by the Holy Ghost, that ye might have eternal life.

41 I receive not honor from men as do the leaders of your church. But the honor that I receive is given unto me by the Father. And this honor which he hath given unto me is the love of God that I feel within my spirit.

42 But I know you, that ye have not the love of God in you, because ye do not listen to the Spirit within you, but to your leaders, who do not have the love of God, or His Spirit.

43 I am come in the name of my Father, and ye receive me not, because ye are taught by your leaders that God shall only give unto you his truths through them. And if one of your leaders, whom ye accept as the mouthpiece of God, shall come in his own name, him ye will receive.

44 How can ye believe, which receive honor one of another, and seek not the honor that cometh from God only, which is the love of God felt through His Spirit? And the honor that cometh from God is an honor that is bestowed upon all men equally.

45 Therefore, ye have no need for those who sit in the seat of Moses and who are the leaders of your church. For they accuse you for that which ye do not do according to the commandments of the church.

46 Do not think that I will accuse you to the Father, even though He hath given unto you His commandments through me. Yea, there is one that accuseth you, even those who sit in the seat of Moses, in whom ye trust.

47 For had ye believed Moses, ye would have believed me; for he wrote of me. But ye do not believe the words of Moses, but ye believe the words of those whom ye believe have his authority and who have told you not to accept me.

48 Yet, ye have his writings before you, and they are not the words of your leaders, but the words of Moses himself. But if ye believe not his writings, how shall ye believe my words?

49 And after he had said these things, Jesus went over the sea of Galilee, which is the sea of Tiberias. And a great multitude followed him, because they saw his miracles which he did on them that were diseased. For the people still could not accept him as the Messiah because of the things that they were taught by their leaders.

50 And Jesus went up into a mountain, and there he sat with his disciples and taught them and answered all their questions which they asked concerning those things which he had taught to the people.

51 And the disciples were perplexed with many of the words of Jesus which he taught unto the Jews. And the Passover, a feast of the Jews, was nigh. When Jesus then lifted up his eyes, he saw a great company come unto him because the news of his miracles had spread quickly throughout the land.

52 And he saith unto Philip: Whence shall we buy bread, that these may eat? And this he said to prove him, for he himself knew what he would do. And Philip answered him, saying: Two hundred pennyworth of bread is not sufficient for them, even if every one of them taketh a little.

53 One of his disciples, Andrew, the brother of Simon Peter, saith unto him: There is a lad here, who hath five barley loaves, and two small fishes; but what are they among so many?

54 And Jesus said: Make the men sit down. Now there was much grass in the place. So the men sat down, in number about five thousand.

55 And Jesus took the loaves; and when he had given thanks, he distributed to the disciples, and the disciples to them that were set down; and likewise of the fishes as much as they would.

56 And when they were filled, he said unto his disciples: Gather up the fragments that remain, that nothing be lost. Therefore they gathered them together, and filled twelve baskets with the fragments of the five barley loaves, which remained over and above unto them that had eaten.

57 Then those men, when they had seen the miracle that Jesus did, said amongst themselves: This is of a truth that prophet that should come into the world.

58 When Jesus, therefore, perceived that they would come and take him by force to make him a king because of the miracles which he performed, he departed again into a mountain himself alone.

59 And Jesus was by himself upon the mountain and groaned within him because of the wickedness of the people. For he had given them the commandments of the Father, which were commandments of love and mercy, and which would create peace and harmony among them.

60 But his words meant nothing to the people; but the people were drawn unto him by the miracles which he performed, and not by the words which he gave unto them of the Father.

61 And while upon the mount, Jesus was once again alone in spirit, and he wept exceedingly because of the people. For the people would make him a king and give him the glory of men, which he had already taught them was an abomination before God.

62 And he had many who had offered him for a price that he might do a miracle for money. And Jesus did nothing for money, nor did he do anything for the glory of men, but he did only those things which the Father commanded him, believing that these things would glorify the Father who had sent him.

63 And the Lord prayed mightily at this time unto the Father. And these things which he prayed are recorded in the vision of the brother of Jared, for his disciples were not present at the time of his prayer, he being upon a mount away from them.

64 And the Lord did not command me to include this prayer in this record. But the Spirit commandeth me; not that the Lord had forgotten these things, only that in his humility, he wanted only that which would glorify the Father included in this record.

65 But it was Michael, the Holy Ghost, who hath commanded that I give unto you in this record the account of the meeting with the Father and the Son upon this mountain near unto the Sea of Galilee.

66 And Michael hath received his commandment directly from the Father, who knoweth that Jehovah hath never wanted any glory, but that it be given to the Father in all things.

67 And Jesus prayed unto the Father, saying: Oh, My Father, I have done those things which Thou hast commanded of me, even I have given unto this people Thy words, and have taught unto them the things which Thou hast given unto me to teach them.

68 Yet, they do not hear, for Thy Spirit is not yet with them. And Thou hast commanded me to show unto them Thy power, which is in me, by healing them and doing the miracles which are of Thy power.

69 And Thou hast had much mercy upon them by allowing me to show unto them these things. But Father, forgive me for questioning Thy great wisdom in these things, for I know that Thou knowest all things, and Thou hast given this knowledge unto me, but my soul groaneth within me because of this people.

70 For they follow me to see more miracles and witness Thy power within me by the means of the flesh, which Thou hast provided for them in the days of their probation. Yet, it is the senses of their flesh that testifieth unto them that I am Thy Son and that Thou hast sent me unto them.

71 For when they see a miracle wrought by my hand, then they marvel amongst themselves and give glory unto me for the power which Thou hast given unto me. And I have tried, Oh, Father, to dissuade those whom I have healed by Thy power from revealing unto the rest from whence the healing was received, except that they give glory to Thee and praise Thy Holy Name for that which they have received of Thee.

72 But they do not see Thee, My Father, but they see me with the eyes of their flesh, and it is me whom they honor. And I fear, My Father, that in these things, Thy honor is diminished and mine is increased; but only because of their flesh in which they behold me, but they see not Thee in the spirit.

73 And if Thou wouldst send unto them the power of the Holy Ghost, which Thou hast established to communicate with them; yea, even if Thou wouldst but speak unto them with Thy still small voice, then shall the glory be taken from me and given unto Thee.

74 Oh, Father, I know that I speak against Thy will as Thou hast already explained it unto me, but I cannot bear to see Thy children worship me, their brother, when they should worship Thee, who is their Father and Creator, even my Father and my Creator.

75 And in great anguish and tears did the Lord plead unto the Father because of the honor that the people gave unto him because of the miracles that he performed by the power of the Father.

76 And the rest of his prayer I have been commanded not to write at this time. But it came to pass, that the Father descended down upon that mount in a pillar of light on which he traveleth throughout the great expanse of space.

77 And he came down to his Son, and came close upon him while he was praying. And the Father embraced the Son as a loving father would embrace his mourning son; and He held him close upon His breast and whispered unto him according to the communication of the flesh which Jesus had received from his mother Mary.

78 And the words which the Father whispered unto him were great and marvelous, even the loving words of a father. And the brother of Jared heard the words that the Father whispered unto the Son.

79 And I, Moroni, have read the words which the brother of Jared hath written, and in these words I am stricken with great wonder and amazement at the patience and love and exceeding mercy of the Father towards His children, even towards all the children of men.

80 For truly the Father esteemeth all flesh as one, and maketh no distinction between any man or woman when it cometh to the love that He hath for each one of them.

81 And I was about to write the words of the Father, which He whispered unto the Son, but I was forbidden by the Spirit, and commanded that these things shall never be heard by any man or woman, except it be given unto them through the Spirit, which is given of the Father.

82 And I know that after this sealed portion of this record shall come forth unto the world in the latter days, that many of the wicked shall have it and read its words and mock the things that are written herein. But if they were to hear the words of the Father, even those words that he whispered unto the Son upon this mount near unto the Sea of Galilee, then they would know more than that which the Father would have them know in their wickedness.

83 But unto those of you who are the elect, I say unto you, Pray unto the Father and he shall give unto you these words by the power of His Holy Spirit. And by the power of the Holy Ghost ye shall have all of the words of the Father, even all those which are necessary for your salvation.

CHAPTER 53

The Father commands Jesus to continue to do miracles. Jesus walks on the water. The leaders of the church confuse the people in their understanding of Christ's simple message. His words offend the people and also the twelve apostles. (Compare John Ch. 6)

AND now, Jesus was greatly concerned that the people believed more in the leaders of their church and their traditions and the ordinances and doctrine of their church than they did in the words that he had given unto them.

2 And the miracles which he performed among them did not take them away from their church or their leaders, nor did it lead the people towards the true doctrine of the Father.

3 Nevertheless, the Father commanded Jesus to continue in the things that He had commanded of him from the beginning and to not concern himself if he received the glory of men; for the Father cared not for the glory of men, but He wanted only the love and devotion of His children, who are those who hear His voice and do the things that He hath commanded of them.

4 And Jesus knew of this great love which the Father had for all of His children; and in all things he tried to turn the hearts of the people towards their Father, without, if possible, taking the glory of the Father upon himself.

5 And the Lord spent much of that day and into the evening talking with the Father away from his disciples.

6 And when evening was now come, his disciples went down unto the sea and entered into a ship, and went over the sea towards Capernaum. And it was now dark, and Jesus was not come to them. And the sea arose by reason of a great wind that blew.

7 And the cause of this great wind was the myriads of spirits in the spirit world who were present with the Lord at this time because of their observance of the meeting of the Son with the Father. For as their spirits displaced the elements immediately around them, they created a great wind, as it hath been explained unto you previously.

8 So when the disciples had rowed about five and twenty or thirty furlongs, they saw Jesus walking on the sea, and drawing nigh unto the ship walking on the water amidst the great wind which was about to capsize their ship; and they were afraid of that which they saw, for they did not know it was the Lord coming unto them.

9 But Jesus said unto them in a loud voice over the wind that blew: It is I; be not afraid. And Peter recognized the Lord and marveled that he could walk on water.

10 And Jesus perceived the thoughts of Peter and beckoned unto him with a smile that he should leave the ship and walk unto him. And Peter was afraid and looked at the Lord without faith in his words.

11 And the Lord held out his hand and beckoned unto Peter that he should come. And Peter saw the smile of the Lord and was comforted therein, and left the ship and walked also upon the water for a short distance with his eyes fixated upon the Lord.

12 And while his eyes were set upon the Lord, he did walk upon the water, for the Lord had commanded the elements of his body to do that which was necessary to allow him buoyancy. But the moment that Peter turned his eyes from the Lord, even because he became afraid of the waves that lapped at his feet, he lost this buoyancy and began to sink.

13 And he cried unto the Lord that he would save him. And the Lord reached forth his hand and again looked into the eyes of Peter and smiled. And when the Lord took his hand and looked into his eyes, Peter once again regained his buoyancy and they came into the ship.

14 And the other disciples marveled at that which they beheld, and they willingly received them into the ship. And when the Lord had entered the ship, it was immediately at the land whither they went, having been taken there by the spirits who controlled the wind at this time.

15 And it came to pass that the day following, when the people which stood on the other side of the sea saw that there was none other boat there, save that one whereinto his disciples were entered, and that Jesus went not with his disciples into the boat on the previous day, but that his disciples were gone away alone—howbeit there came other boats from Tiberias nigh unto the place where they did eat bread, after that the Lord had given thanks—but when the people therefore saw that Jesus was not there, neither his disciples, they also took shipping, and came to Capernaum, seeking for Jesus.

16 And when they had found him on the other side of the sea, they said unto him: Rabbi, when camest thou hither?

17 And Jesus answered them and said: Verily, verily, I say unto you, ye seek me, not because ye desire to keep my sayings, neither because ye saw the power of my Father and His testimony of me by way of the miracles, but because ye did eat of the loaves, and were filled.

18 And the Lord then gave unto them the words that I have already included in this record previously, even that he was the bread that they should eat and the water that they should drink so that they would not hunger nor thirst any more.

19 But as it was with most of the words of Jesus, the people understood him not, being prejudiced against him by their leaders who were always among them watching Jesus.

20 And when Jesus spoke in profundity, even that the people began to understand him and believe in him, the leaders of the church would send forth their scribes and the Pharisees and confuse the people once again into believing more in the traditions of the Jews and the law of Moses than in the simple words of Christ.

21 And because of their confusion, the people were convinced that Jesus was a deceiver and a devil, and that by the power of the devil he performed the miracles that he performed.

22 But the people did not care by whom they witnessed these miracles, for the children of men are always drawn to that which satisfieth the desires of their flesh, than to that which would heal the sorrows which burn in their souls.

23 And many of the things which Jesus taught unto the people were not things that could be understood by the senses and desires of the flesh, but could only be understood by the Spirit.

24 Many, therefore, of those who followed him, who were his disciples, when they had heard his sayings, said: This is an hard saying; who can hear it and accept it as that which is from God?

25 And when Jesus knew in himself that his disciples murmured at it, he said unto them, Do these things offend you? What and if ye shall see by the senses of the flesh the Son of man ascend up where he was before? Then would ye believe because ye see these things according to the flesh? And ye shall see these things.

26 But it is the spirit that quickeneth the flesh and giveth understanding to my words. The flesh profiteth nothing, for nothing of the Father can be understood by the flesh. And the words that I speak unto you are from the Father, therefore, they are of the spirit, and they have the power to give unto you eternal life.

27 But there are some of you who believe not in the things of the Father, for ye do not have His Spirit to bear witness to you; but ye have me. Nevertheless, there are some who do not believe in me, who was sent unto you by the Father to teach you according to the flesh the things of the Father, which ye cannot receive because ye do not have His Spirit.

28 For Jesus knew from the beginning who among his disciples believed not him, but followed him because of the things that they gained from him in the flesh. And he also knew who should betray him.

29 And he continued, saying: Therefore said I unto you, that no man can come unto me, except it were given unto him of my Father. And ye should know by the flesh if the Father hath born witness unto you of me, because when He speaketh unto you by the Spirit, it causeth the peace of the flesh.

30 And if ye do not know who I am and that the Father hath sent me to bring salvation unto you by my words, then ye are the children of Satan, for ye follow his words, which are the words of your church and its leaders.

31 And after he had said these things unto them, from that time many of those who followed him went back to their church and their traditions, and walked no more with him.

32 Then said Jesus unto the twelve, for they were also discouraged by that which he said unto them; and he asked them: Will ye also go away?

33 Then Simon Peter answered him saying: Lord, to whom shall we go? We know that thou hast the words of eternal life, and we believe and are sure that thou art that Christ, the Son of the living God.

34 Jesus answered them: Have not I chosen you twelve from among the people because ye feel the peace that the Father hath given to you by the Spirit, which testifieth of me, yet one of you is a devil? And he spake of Judas Iscariot, the son of Simon: for he it was that should betray him, being one of the twelve.

35 And after these things Jesus walked in Galilee; for he would not walk in Jewry, because the Jews sought to kill him, because the people had returned unto the church at Jerusalem and reported to their leaders all those things that Jesus had said unto them.

36 And the leaders of the church knew that for righteousness sake, as they supposed, they would have to get rid of Jesus. Therefore, they went unto the politicians and those whom they knew held power over the people of the land. And there was a judge who had been appointed by the Romans to issue warrants and judgment in that part of the empire.

37 And this judge was a Jew who was a member of the church at Jerusalem and would do anything that was bidden of him by the High Priest of the church. And the High Priest called forth this judge in secret and commanded that a warrant be issued for the arrest of Jesus.

38 And the judge issued forth the warrant unto the soldiers of the Romans, and sent forth a command that when Jesus was arrested, that he should be brought forthwith to the judgment seat to be judged by the laws of the Romans. But this judge was in the pockets of the high priests, and would use his power to deliver Jesus first unto them, and then to the Romans that he might have the law of the Romans exercise justice upon him.

39 And this the leaders of the church did that the people might not know that it was they who wanted to kill Jesus, believing that the people would think that the Romans did this unto to Jesus because he had broken their laws.

40 Now, the feast of tabernacles of the Jews was at hand. And Jesus had returned to his home to see his mother, Mary. And his father, Joseph, and his brethren were embarrassed by his presence and wanted not that he stay in their house because of the people who hated Jesus for what he spoke against the church, who were their friends.

41 And they knew of the warrant that had been issued against Jesus, but Mary stood between them and would not let her other sons and daughter, neither would she let Joseph turn in her son to the authorities.

42 His brethren, therefore, said unto him: Depart hence, and go into Judea, that thy disciples there might also see the works that thou doest. For they have heard of thy works, which we know are the works of the devil.

43 For there is no man who doeth any thing in secret and hideth himself from the law of the land, and he himself seeketh to be known openly by the words which he speaketh. If thou doest these things, shew thyself to the world. For neither did his brethren believe in him, and they wanted him to be arrested and put away from among them.

44 Then Jesus said unto them: My time is not yet come to be taken away from the people to whom I have been sent to save, but your time with them is already, for ye are like them and do that which they do who are of the world. The world cannot hate you; but me it hateth, because I testify of it, that the works thereof are evil.

45 Go ye therefore up unto this feast without me for I will not reveal myself to those who would kill me. I go not up yet unto this feast with you, for ye shall reveal me unto the Jews, but I cannot be taken, for my time is not yet fully come.

46 And when he had said these words unto them, he abode still in Galilee where his mother, Mary, was staying with his wives. But when his brethren were gone up, then went he also up unto the feast, not openly, but as it were in secret.

47 Then the Jews sought him at the feast, and said, Where is he of which the people speak? And there was much murmuring among the people concerning him; for some said, He is a good man, and others said, Nay; but he deceiveth the people. Howbeit no man spake openly of him for fear of the leaders of the Jews.

48 For the people feared that if they spoke of him openly, then they would be judged as one who believed in him, and this would bring upon them persecution from their friends who thought that he was of the devil.

49 And they were also afraid that the leaders of the church would find out that they had spoken of him; and because they had spoken of him, they would be cast out of the church for that which they spoke which was good about him.

50 And it came to pass that about the midst of the feast, Jesus went up into the temple and taught in disguise, not wanting the people to discover him at this time, but wanting to teach the people who had gathered there.

51 And the Jews did not recognize him because of his disguise and marveled, saying: How knoweth this man letters, having never learned? And this they said because there were few people among the Jews who could read and write their language.

52 And the church had appointed those who were learned to be the scribes who would read the word of God to the people. And the high priests would also read the word of God to the people mingled with their own interpretations and their own doctrines, which they wanted the people to believe. But because the majority of the people could not read or write, they were led to believe whatever their leaders wanted them to believe.

53 And when they did not recognize Jesus as a learned man among them, or one who had been authorized by the church to administer the word to the people, they questioned who he was.

54 And Jesus answered them, and said: My doctrine is not mine, but His that sent me. And the Father hath sent me unto you to teach you His will. And the doctrine that I give unto you is His will. If any man shall do His will, he shall know of the doctrine, whether it be of God, or whether I speak of myself.

55 He that speaketh of himself seeketh his own glory: but he that seeketh the glory of Him that sent him, the same is true, and no unrighteousness is in him.

56 For those who give unto you the law of Moses seek the glory of men for themselves. And they do not teach the will of God, but the will of men. And they pretend to give unto you the word of God according to the law of Moses in which ye have been taught to believe.

57 Did not Moses give you the law, and yet none of you keepeth the law? Why go ye about to kill me?

58 The people answered and said, Thou hast a devil; who goeth about to kill thee? And this they said because they did not recognize him for who he was. Neither did the people know that their leaders were conspiring to kill him.

59 And Jesus took the cloak off and the hood that had hidden him from the people. And when he had done this, a great murmur went up among the people for they knew him.

60 Jesus answered and said unto them: I have done one work, which is the work of my Father on the sabbath, even that I caused a man to take up his bed and walk, and ye all marvel.

61 And Jesus said these things because the high priests had brought this allegation publicly against him and had presented him to the people as one who had no respect for the church, or the law of Moses, in which all the people believed.

62 And he said unto them: Moses gave unto you circumcision—not because it is a requirement of God, but because your fathers wanted this thing—and ye on the sabbath day circumcise a man. If a man on the sabbath day receive circumcision, that the law of Moses should not be broken; are ye angry at me, because I have made a man every whit whole on the sabbath day?

63 Judge not according to your traditions, which are the appearance of the work, but judge a righteous judgment of the purpose of the work. For man was not made for the sabbath, but the sabbath was made by man to satisfy his need to justify his wickedness of the rest of the week.

64 For are there not seven days of the week? Yet, is it only on one day that ye dedicate yourselves to God? And to whom do ye dedicate yourselves the other six days? I say unto you, that ye dedicate the majority of the week to the god that ye serve, who is Satan.

65 And there were the high priests, who when they heard that Jesus taught in the temple, went up that they might take him and serve the warrant upon him. But when they came into the temple, they feared the people that they would see them for the servants of Satan that they were, instead as the humble men of God whom they pretended to be in front of the people.

66 Then said some of them who had heard the High Priest who had secured the warrant against Jesus at Jerusalem: Is not this he, whom they seek to kill? But, lo, he speaketh boldly, and they say nothing unto him. Do the rulers know indeed that this is the very Christ? Howbeit, we know this man whence he is, for he was born among us and was raised in the house of Joseph, and his brothers and his sisters, are they not also among us? But we have been taught by our leaders that when Christ cometh, no man knoweth whence he is.

67 Then cried Jesus in the temple as he taught, saying: Ye both think that ye know me, and think ye know from whence I am. But have ye asked of Joseph if I am the son of his flesh? Yea, if ye would ask this of him, then he would tell you the truth, for I am not the son of his flesh. And if I were the son of his flesh, then he would believe in me.

68 But ye have my mother before you; ask of her who it is that is my father, and she will tell you the truth concerning my conception.

69 For behold, I am not come of myself and present myself as true, but He who sent me is true, whom ye know not. But I know Him because He is my true Father, and I am from Him, and He hath sent me unto you to bring you salvation.

70 And is this not the promise of the Christ that hath been prophesied of by all the holy prophets? Are not the words that I have given unto you the words of God, which teacheth a man to love his neighbor and do good to his enemies?

71 And because I have said these things unto you in plainness, and have taught you that ye do not need a church nor its leaders to know these words of salvation, ye do not believe that I am the Christ.

72 And because of your unbelief in me, and because ye believe in the traditions of your fathers and the words of your leaders, which are not the words of salvation, which turn a man to love his neighbor as himself; but their words turn you against your neighbor that they might get gain and glory from you; yea, because I speak of these things in plainness before you, ye believe me not.

73 But the Father hath suffered that I perform many miracles by the power which He hath given unto me. And what of this power that ye have witnessed? Do the leaders of your churches have this power? I say unto you that they do not have the power of God, because it is only given to those who have true faith in God and work in righteous works.

74 Then the leaders of the church sought to take him away from among the people, so that the people could not hear any more of his words. But no man laid hands on him, because his hour was not yet come.

75 And many of the people believed on him, and said: When Christ cometh, will he do more miracles than these which this man hath done? The Pharisees heard that the people murmured such things concerning him; and the Pharisees and the chief priests sent officers to take him.

76 Then said Jesus unto them: Yet a little while am I with you, and then I go unto Him who sent me. Ye shall seek me, and shall not find me; and where I am, thither ye cannot come.

77 Then said the Jews among themselves: Whither will he go, that we shall not find him? Will he go unto the dispersed among the Gentiles, and teach the Gentiles? What manner of saying is this that he said, Ye shall seek me, and shall not find me, and where I am, thither ye cannot come?

78 For they did not understand that Jesus spoke of the kingdom of the Father where no one will be permitted to enter unless he can abide by the words which Jesus taught unto them.

79 And Jesus made his way from among the people that day so that the priests could not lay their hands on him.

80 But on the last day, that great day of the feast, Jesus stood and cried again unto the people, saying: If any man thirst, let him come unto me, and drink. He that believeth on me, as the scripture hath said, out of his belly shall flow rivers of living water. But this spake he of the Spirit, which they who believe on him should receive by keeping the commandments which he had given unto them.

81 For the Holy Ghost was promised unto all them who believe, after that Jesus was glorified, because Jesus was not yet glorified by the Father. And whether the people receive the words of the Father by the Son in the flesh, or by the Holy Ghost in the spirit, it is the same.

82 Nevertheless, the power of the Holy Ghost can overcome the flesh and therefore speaketh directly to the spirit of a man. But the words of Christ were given according to the flesh, and could not be received except that the flesh be first overcome.

83 Many of the people therefore, when they heard his words, said: Of a truth this is the holy prophet, Elias, who we know is to come to prepare the way for the Christ. And others said: This is the Christ. But some said: Shall Christ come out of Galilee? Hath not the scripture said that Christ cometh of the seed of David, and out of the town of Bethlehem, where David was? And this the people said amongst them because they did not know of the circumstance that surrounded the birth of Jesus.

84 So there was a division among the people because of him. And some of them would have taken him, but no man laid hands on him because of the others who believed that he was a good man who had done nothing wrong.

85 Then came the officers who were sent by the chief priests and Pharisees to arrest Jesus, and the priests said unto them: Why have ye not brought him? And the officers answered: Never hath a man spake like this man speaketh to the people.

86 Then answered them the Pharisees, saying: Are ye also deceived? Have any of the rulers or the Pharisees, who know the law and and the will of God for the people, believed on him? But this people who knoweth not the law are cursed because they believe on him. For that which he speaketh, speaketh against the law, and God hath said that cursed are those who speaketh against his law.

87 And Nicodemus, he who came to Jesus by night, being one of them who was among the chief priests, and who secretly believed in Jesus, saith unto them: Doth our law judge any man, before it heareth him, and knoweth what he doeth?

88 They answered and said unto him, Art thou also of Galilee? Search the scriptures of yourself, and look at the words of the prophets which the Lord hath given unto us; for out of Galilee ariseth no prophet.

89 And Nicodemus was afraid from that time forth to speak in defense of Jesus, for fear of being persecuted and cast out from among his peers.

90 And while the chief priests were discussing what was to be done with Jesus amongst themselves, Jesus found his way through the crowd and left the temple unnoticed.

91 And every man went unto his own house, but Jesus went unto the mount of Olives to pray again to his Father and to be alone to contemplate those things which he should do. For many of the Jews who were in the temple and heard his words wanted him to return again on the morrow and preach more of his words unto them.

CHAPTER 54

Mary Magdalene is brought to be condemned by Jesus. Jesus recognizes her as his eternal wife. Jesus continues his teachings of the Father, spiritual bondage, and the truth shall set you free. He heals the blind man, who confounds the leaders of the church.

AND Jesus was by himself alone as he contemplated the things which had been said, and also those things which he should say unto the people on the morrow to bring them unto the Father.

2 For the intent of the Lord in all things was to bring the children of God to their Eternal Father, and that they might live peacefully with love one towards the other in the flesh. And upon these things the Lord thought much and prepared himself against the morrow that he might know what he should do.

3 For behold, the Lord did not speak according to the promptings of the Holy Spirit, for he had no need of its help, he being the giver of the Spirit before he came into mortality.

4 And he knew all things of the Father; and in him was no sin; therefore, being perfect, he had a perfect light which gave unto him all knowledge and understanding of truth.

5 And early in the morning he came again into the temple to teach the people as they so desired, and all the people came unto him, and he sat down, and taught them.

6 And to tempt the Lord that they might catch him in a lie and turn the people against him, the scribes and Pharisees brought unto him a woman taken in adultery. And when they had set her in the midst, they said unto him: Master, this woman was taken in adultery, in the very act.

7 Now, Moses in the law commanded us that such should be stoned for that which she hath done unto a man who is married amongst us. And we know that the man hath committed no sin against her, for she lied unto him and told him that she was a virgin and desired to be his wife. But what sayest thou?

8 This they said, tempting him, that they might have cause to accuse him, because the people had been taught the law of Moses, which had been corrupted among them since the time that it was first given unto Moses by the Lord.

9 For the Lord never gave a commandment to his children that they should kill one another, not for any crime or sin that they might commit among them, but that forgiveness should be given to those who would repent, except it be those who murder another, but even these should not be killed, but taught the gospel while they are in prison to prepare them for the spirit world when they should die.

10 But the children of Israel had corrupted the law of Moses and taught that murder of another was justifiable under the law unto those who committed specific sins among them.

11 And that which hath been recorded in the Bible, which are the words of the Jews, hath been passed down from generation to generation since the laws were first given by Moses, and these laws were changed to fit the fancies and desires of men.

12 For the law stateth that if a man find a damsel who is a virgin, which is not betrothed, and lay hold on her, and lie with her, and they be found; then the man who lay with her shall give unto the father of the damsel fifty shekels of silver, and she shall be his wife; because he hath humbled her, and he may not put her away all of his days.

13 And in this law the man had justified his actions unto the Pharisees who had brought the woman before Jesus. But Jesus knew the woman immediately and recognized her by her spirit, and knew that she was Mary Magdalene who would be his wife forever.

14 And Jesus also knew that Mary had been married, and that her husband had beat her with a rod and had thrown her out of his house because she was not clean when she married him. And Mary was not clean because her father and her brother had forced themselves upon her in her youth, and would not admit this to any man.

15 But when Mary was espoused to her husband, in her despair, she told her husband what had been done unto her in her youth. And her husband became angry and jealous in his countenance. But he did not become angry with those who had defiled his wife in her youth, for they denied all these things; but he became angry with Mary and beat her and cast her out of his house, because he thought that she had lied unto him.

16 And because she was cast out of the house of her husband, Mary had nowhere to go, and no other man would take her because of the things said about her by her husband.

17 And the people scourged Mary with their words and cast her out from among them. And Mary lived where she could find shelter; and to get the money that she needed to eat, and to clothe herself, she would entice the men of the city to be with her for money. And she was a very beautiful woman who was much desired by those who would pay her money.

18 And the Pharisees knew of Mary, because many of them had paid her money and had committed adultery with her. And those who were not married, lusted after Mary and paid her to satisfy their lusts and their wants. And for this reason, they brought her before Jesus, knowing her from their own experience.

19 And Jesus knew all of these things, but did not look at Mary, but stooped down, and with his finger wrote upon the ground, as though he heard them not.

20 And now, Jesus did not write words that any man knew, nor did he intend to write that which one could read, but he used the time of this writing to thank his Father for bringing Mary unto him, calling on the Father to sanctify her and help her to understand the love that he had for her, that she may be desirous to follow him and become his wife.

21 So when the Pharisees continued asking him, he lifted up himself, and said unto them: He that is without sin among you, let him first cast a stone at her.

22 And again he stooped down and wrote upon the ground, waiting for a reaction among them. For each of them knew that he had been with Mary and had paid her. And each of them knew of one other among them who had been with her.

23 And they who heard it, being convicted by their own guilt, by their conscience, went out one by one, beginning at the eldest, even unto the last of them who had sinned with Mary; and Jesus was left alone with the woman standing in the midst.

24 When Jesus had lifted up himself, and saw none but the woman, he said unto her: Mary, where are those thine accusers? Hath no man condemned thee?

25 And Mary marveled that Jesus knew her name. And when she looked into his eyes, he smiled upon her. And Mary was instantly drawn to Jesus, for the Father had opened her mind that she knew him and believed in him. And she said: No man is left that hath condemned me, Lord.

26 And Jesus said unto her, Neither do I condemn thee for that which these men have done unto you, but them I condemn. Now go, and sin no more. And when Jesus had said these things unto her, Mary fell at his feet and wept upon them that he would forgive her for all that she had done.

27 And the Lord knelt down before Mary and lifted her to his breast and wiped away her tears and comforted her. And Mary looked again into the eyes of her Savior and felt his exceeding love for her. And Jesus smiled upon her and wept upon her neck, for he knew that she would be with him in the kingdom of his Father forever.

28 But these things he could not tell unto Mary at this time, because he was already married to Martha according to the laws of the Jews, and to Mary according to the law of the Father. And Mary had to make her own choice concerning him according to her own free will, and for this reason Jesus said nothing unto her.

29 But it came to pass that Mary followed him thereafter and was with no other man, for Jesus had commanded his apostles to watch out for Mary and give unto her of their bread and their money that she would not have to take it from another man.

30 And now, I, Moroni, would ask of you who now have the truth regarding that which occurred between Jesus and Mary Magdalene. Yea, do ye not see why those who brought forth the accounts of these things unto you in the Bible excluded these things? Do ye see why they would not want the people to know that the eternal wife of the Son of God, even our Savior Jesus Christ, was a woman who they would consider the lowliest and most vile of all the women among them?

31 And in this there was similitude given by the Father, so that all of you should know that love that He hath for all of His children, more especially for those of His children who have chosen to be women in mortality. For He cherisheth the woman, and knoweth that only in them, can a man be like unto Him.

32 And what say ye of the latter days of those women among you who are forced by no want of their own to do that which Mary was forced to do to survive? Now, what say ye of them? For they are more precious before God than ye who would profess to be of God.

33 And when the Lord cometh in all the glory of the Father unto you of the latter days, he shall have Mary at his side, and ye shall look upon her as his eternal wife. Then what shall ye say unto her, knowing that which she was forced to do during the days of her probation?

34 Will ye look upon her as ye look upon those among you who do in their probation what she was forced to do in hers because of the wickedness of the lusts of men? I say unto you, that in that day shall all those whom ye call whores and prostitutes, yea, even all those who have abused their bodies because of the lusts of men; in that day they shall rejoice and fall down and worship the Lord.

35 And he shall call them forth and embrace them and forgive them and exalt them above those of you who have abased them all the days of their lives. And they shall be received of him, while ye who have judged them shall be rejected by him.

36 Therefore, repent of the judgments that ye have rendered unto these, and embrace them and lift them up and give unto them that of which they are in need, that they need not do that which is abominable both to them and to their Father who loveth all of His children and judgeth none of them who are forced to sin because of the wickedness of others.

37 And now, I return once again to the account of John concerning that which Jesus taught unto the Jews in the temple:

38 Then spake Jesus again unto them, saying: I am the light of the world that the Father hath given unto the world that lieth in darkness. And he that followeth me shall not walk in darkness, but shall have the light of life.

39 The Pharisees therefore said unto him: Thou bearest record of thyself, and thou hast already said unto this people that whosoever bearest record of himself, that record is not true. Therefore, thy record is not true.

40 And Jesus answered and said unto them: Though I bear record of myself, yet my record is true; for I know from whence I came, and whither I go; but ye cannot tell from whence I come, and whither I go. For ye have said that my brothers and sisters according to the flesh are among you, but ye have not inquired of my mother from whence I came. And if ye would inquire of her, she will testify unto you that I was conceived not of the flesh, but of the Spirit of God.

41 But ye judge me after the flesh and bear record of yourselves because ye know that your fathers are of the flesh. But I judge no man after the flesh, but I judge according to the Spirit of my Father, which is in me.

42 And yet if I judge, my judgment is true, for my judgment is not from your fathers, which words ye have among you, but my judgment is from my Father, whose words ye cannot receive in the flesh, because they are given by the Spirit, which ye have not among you.

43 For I am not alone, but I am one with the Father who sent me. It is also written in the law of your fathers, that the testimony of two men is true. I am one that beareth witness of myself, and the Father who sent me beareth witness of me through the Spirit.

44 Then said they unto him, Where is thy Father? Jesus answered them, saying: Ye neither know me in the flesh, nor my Father, which is not of the flesh as your fathers are. And if ye had known me, ye should have known my Father also. But ye shall not know my Father except He maketh Himself known unto you by the Spirit.

45 And ye cannot have this Spirit that would bear witness unto you of the Father, unless ye first accept the Son, who is before you in the flesh.

46 These words spake Jesus in the treasury, as he taught in the temple, where he preached to the Jews that their offerings of money and sacrifice were not the commandments of God, but the commandments of men.

47 And many of the poor among the people rejoiced in the things which he taught, they not having sufficient money to buy that which was needed for the sacrifices and ordinances of salvation that was commanded of them by their leaders.

48 And because many people believed in him, no man laid hands on him; for his hour was not yet come.

49 Then said Jesus again unto them, I go my way, and ye shall seek me, and shall die in your sins; because I go unto the kingdom of my Father to prepare a place for those who hear my words and keep the commandments of the Father, which I give unto them, and that are necessary that ye also can dwell with the Father with me.

50 Nevertheless, whither I go, ye cannot come because ye refuse to listen to the commandments and will of the Father pertaining to His kingdom.

51 Then said the Jews, Will he kill himself, because he saith, Whither I go, ye cannot come?

52 And he said unto them: Ye are from beneath, for in this world ye bury your fathers. But, I am from above where my Father liveth forever in worlds without end. Yea, ye are of this world wherein your fathers were born. But I am not of this world, and my Father was not born into this world, but created this world that he might give it as an inheritance unto His children.

53 I said therefore unto you, that ye shall die in your sins and be buried with your fathers in the earth. For if ye believe not that I am he whom the Father hath sent to save you by my words, then ye shall die in your sins; and where I and my Father are, ye cannot go thither.

54 Then said they still unto him, because they did not believe in his words: Who art thou?

55 And Jesus saith unto them: Even the same that I said unto you from the beginning and ye still do not understand. And if what I have told you since the beginning, ye do not believe, then why should I say these things unto you a second time that ye believe them not again?

56 Behold, I have many things to say and to judge of you, which ye cannot understand unless this understanding is given unto you from Him who hath sent me. And He that sent me is true, for He is God, our Eternal Father. And I speak to the world those things which I have heard of Him.

57 And this he said unto them because they understood not that he spake to them of the Father.

58 Then said Jesus unto them, When ye have lifted up the Son of man, then shall ye know that I am he, and that I do nothing of myself, but only do and speak as my Father hath given unto me.

59 And He that sent me is with me; for the Father hath not left me alone at anytime, because I do always those things that please Him. And if ye would also do those things that please Him, even those things which I have taught unto you, then He would be with you always.

60 And as he spake these words, many believed on him. Then said Jesus to those Jews who believed on him: If ye continue in my word, then are ye my disciples indeed, and ye shall know the

truth, and the truth shall make you free.

61 And they answered him, saying: We be the seed of Abraham, and were never in bondage to any man. How sayest thou that, Ye shall be made free?

62 Jesus answered them, saying: Verily, verily, I say unto you, the traditions of your fathers which have been taught unto you by the leaders of your church, are those things that hold you in bondage.

63 For they cause you to commit sin before the Father. And whosoever committeth sin is the servant of sin and is therefore in bondage to sin. And the servant of sin abideth not in the house of my Father forever.

64 But the Son abideth there forever, because I know the will of the Father and do not sin. If the Son, therefore, shall make you free by teaching you that which is the will of the Father, so that ye do not sin, then ye shall be free indeed.

65 I know that ye are the seed of Abraham, and that ye believe more in the words that ye perceive to be the words of Abraham than ye do in the words of the true Father which I give unto you. But ye seek to kill me, because my word hath no place in you because I have testified unto you that I have fulfilled all the words and the law of Abraham.

66 I speak only that which I have seen when I was with my Father in heaven. But ye do that which ye have seen when ye are with your fathers, having been taught by them that which ye believe and accept as the truth.

67 Then they answered and said unto him: Abraham is our father and we will do what is of Abraham as our fathers have taught us.

68 And Jesus saith unto them: If ye were the children of Abraham, ye would do the works of Abraham. But now ye seek to kill me, a man that hath told you the truth, which I have heard of God—this did not Abraham. You do not the works of Abraham but ye do the deeds of your fathers.

69 Then said they to him justifying in themselves that they served the only true God: We be not born of fornication; we have one Father, even God.

70 And Jesus said unto them: If God were your Father, ye would love me, for I proceeded forth and came from God; neither came I of myself, but He sent me.

71 Why do ye not understand my manner of speech? Even because ye cannot bear my word, which is only accepted and borne by those who have the Spirit of God within them.

72 Ye are of your father the devil, and the lusts of your father ye will do. He was a murderer

from the beginning, and abode not in the truth, because there is no truth in him. When he speaketh a lie, he speaketh of his own, for he is a liar, and the father of all lies.

73 And because I tell you the truth, ye believe me not. Which of you convinceth me of sin? And if I have not sinned against God, then I have His Spirit within me and speak unto you the truth. And if I say the truth, why do ye not believe me?

74 He that is of God receiveth the words of God. Ye therefore receive them not, because ye are not of God.

75 Then answered the Jews, and said unto him: Say we not well that thou art a Samaritan, for thou wast among them and learned of them who are unclean according to our law, and thou hast a devil?

76 Jesus answered, saying: I have not a devil, but ye are of the devil, who is your father which ye honor by your works. But I honor my Father, and ye do dishonor me because ye know not my Father. And I seek not mine own glory, but the glory of Him who hath sent me.

77 And there is only one that seeketh out His children and judgeth them according to His words. And if they keep His commandments, then they shall have eternal life in His kingdoms.

78 Verily, verily, I say unto you, if a man keep my sayings, which are the commandments of the Father, he shall never see death.

79 Then said the Jews unto him: Now we know that thou hast a devil. For Abraham is dead, and the prophets are also dead, yet thou sayest: If a man keep my saying, he shall never taste of death. Art thou greater than our father Abraham, who is dead, and the prophets who are also dead? Whom makest thou thyself?

80 Jesus answered, saying; If I honor myself, my honor is nothing. I do not give honor and glory unto myself, but it is my Father that honoreth me, of whom ye say, that He is your God. Yet ye have not known Him. But I know Him. And if I should say, I know Him not, I shall be a liar like unto you, because I do know Him, and keep His commandments. But ye do not know Him because ye keep not His commandments.

81 Behold, your father Abraham and all the holy prophets of old rejoiced to see my day; and they truly saw it when they were dead, living according to the spirit, and were glad.

82 Then said the Jews unto him: Thou art not yet fifty years old, and hath thou seen Abraham?

83 Jesus said unto them: Verily, verily, I say unto you, Before Abraham was, I was in the spirit world with Abraham and all the holy prophets and was given all power and authority therein by the Father. I am he who gave the promises of God unto Abraham and commanded him in all things.

84 And these sayings enraged the anger of the Jews, for now he had testified unto them that he was the Son of God and also the Spirit of God. And then took they up stones to cast at him because of the testimony of himself that he gave unto them.

85 But Jesus hid himself, and went out of the temple, going through the midst of them, and so passed by without them noticing him, because in their intense anger they were blinded.

86 And as Jesus passed by, he saw a man who was blind from his birth. And his disciples asked him, saying: Master, who did sin, this man, or his parents, that he was born blind? And this they said because they believed that the infirmities of the flesh were cursings of God.

87 But Jesus answered them, saying: Neither hath this man sinned, nor his parents: but that the works of God should be made manifest in him that all might give glory unto the Father.

88 I must work the works of Him who sent me while I am with you; the time cometh when I shall have finished my work, then I go unto the Father; but while I am here, it is the light of the day.

89 For the night cometh wherein there shall be much darkness because of the wickedness of men, when no man can do the work of the Father, for the power of the Father shall no longer be with the children of men upon the earth.

90 As long as I am in the world, I am the light of the world and will do the work of the Father according to the commandments and the power which He hath given me. For men shall not always have the power of God with them to heal the infirmities of the flesh.

91 But this ye shall know, that if a man healeth by the power of God, it is because he doeth the will of the Father in all things. For the Father shall not give His power unto any man who will not keep His commandments and do His will in all things.

92 When Jesus had thus spoken, he spat on the ground, and made clay of the spittle, and he anointed the eyes of the blind man with the clay, and said unto him: Go, wash in the pool of Siloam—which had been thus named by the prophet Elias of old, having seen in a vision that which the Lord would one day do to the blind.

93 And the man went his way therefore, and washed, and came seeing. The neighbors therefore, and they which before had seen him that he was blind, said: Is not this he who sat and begged?

94 Some said, This is he, and others said, He is like him. But the man answered them all, saying: I am he. Therefore said they unto him, How were thine eyes opened? He answered and said: A man who is called Jesus made clay, and anointed mine eyes, and said unto me, Go to the pool of Siloam, and wash. And I went and washed, and I received sight.

95 Then said they unto him, Where is he? And the man said, I know not. Then they brought to the Pharisees him that aforetime was blind. And it was the sabbath day when Jesus made the clay, and opened his eyes, therefore the people had aught against Jesus to condemn him according to the commandments of the church.

96 Then again the Pharisees also asked him how he had received his sight, and the man said unto them: He put clay upon mine eyes, and I washed, and do see.

97 Therefore said some of the Pharisees: This man is not of God, because he keepeth not the sabbath day. But others of them said: How can a man who is a sinner do such miracles? And there was a division among them.

98 Then they say unto the blind man again: What sayest thou of him, that he hath opened thine eyes? And he answered them, saying: He is a prophet.

99 But the Jews did not believe concerning him, that he had been blind, and received his sight, until they called the parents of him who had received his sight. And they asked them, saying: Is this your son, who ye say was born blind? How then doth he now see? His parents answered them and said: We know that this is our son, and that he was born blind, but by what means he now seeth, we know not; or who hath opened his eyes, we know not; he is of age, ask him: he shall speak for himself.

100 And these words spake his parents, because they feared the Jews. For the Jews had agreed already, that if any man did confess that Jesus was Christ, he should be put out of the synagogue. Therefore said his parents: He is of age; ask him.

101 Then again called they the man who was blind, and said unto him: Give God the praise for the miracle that thou hast received, for we know that this man is a sinner.

102 But he answered them, and said: Whether he be a sinner or no, I know not; but one thing I know, that whereas I was blind, now I see.

103 Then said they to him again, What did he to thee? How opened he thine eyes? And the man answered them, saying: I have told you already, and ye did not hear. Therefore, if ye would hear it again, will ye also be his disciples?

104 Then they reviled him, and said: Thou art his disciple, but we are the disciples of Moses. We know that God spake unto Moses and hath given us His word through him. But as for this fellow, we know not from whence he is.

105 The man answered and said unto them: Why; herein is a marvelous thing, that ye know not from whence he is, and yet he hath opened mine eyes. And ye have said already that he hath sinned. Now, we know that God heareth not sinners because they do not His will. But if any man be a worshipper of God, and doeth His will, him He heareth.

106 Since the world began was it not heard that no man can open the eyes of one who was born blind, except he be of God and one who hath His power. And if this man were not of God, he could do nothing that would require the power of God. For I was born blind by the will of God, and only by this same will can I see.

107 And they answered and said unto him: Thou wast altogether born in sins, and dost thou teach us? And they cast him out from among them.

108 And Jesus heard that they had cast him out, and when he had found him, he said unto him: Dost thou believe on the Son of God? And the man answered and said: Who is he, Lord, that I might believe on him?

109 And Jesus said unto him: Thou hast both seen him and heard him, and it is he who talketh with thee.

110 And he answered Jesus, saying: Lord, I believe. And he worshipped him.

111 And Jesus said unto all those present: For that the judgment of God might come upon all men, I am come into this world, that they which see not, might see according to the power of God. And that they which think that they see might be made blind because they have not the power of God within them.

112 And some of the Pharisees which were with him heard these words, and said unto him: Are we blind also, for we see perfectly with our eyes?

113 Jesus said unto them: If ye were blind as this man is blind, then ye should have no sin. But ye are blind as to the things of God, which blindness causeth you to sin. But now ye say, We see and know the things of God. Therefore your sin remaineth with you because ye are blind to the will of the Father.

CHAPTER 55

Jesus begins to speak in parables to the people because they can't accept his words in simplicity and plainness. Parable of the good shepherd. He raises Lazarus from the dead. The words of Alma concerning the spirit world and the resurrection are given again by Moroni.

And now, it came to pass that because the Jews had not received the words of Jesus when he spoke unto them in plainness, he began to speak unto them in parables, so that hearing they would not hear, and seeing, they would not see, they being blind anyways; and thus Christ became a stumbling block unto them.

2 And he continued speaking unto them, saying: Verily, verily, I say unto you, He that entereth not by the door into the sheepfold, but climbeth up some other way, the same is a thief and a robber.

3 But he that entereth in by the door is the shepherd of the sheep. And to him the porter openeth; and the sheep hear his voice; and he calleth his own sheep by name, and leadeth them out. And when he putteth forth his own sheep, he goeth before them, and the sheep follow him; for they know his voice.

4 And a stranger will they not follow, but will flee from him; for they know not the voice of strangers.

5 Now this parable spake Jesus unto them, but they understood not what things they were which he spake unto them.

6 Then said Jesus unto them again: Verily, verily, I say unto you, I am the door of the sheep. All that ever came before me, who testified not of me, are thieves and robbers. But the sheep did not hear them and follow them to their destruction.

7 Behold, I am the door; by me if any man enter in, he shall be saved, and shall go in and out, and find pasture.

8 The thief cometh not to give, but to steal, and to kill, and to destroy. But I am come that they might have life, and that they might have it more abundantly.

9 I am the good shepherd, and the good shepherd giveth his life for the sheep. But he that is an hireling, and not the shepherd, whose own the sheep are not, seeth the wolf coming, and leaveth the sheep, and fleeth; and the wolf catcheth them, and scattereth the sheep. And the hireling fleeth, because he is an hireling, and careth not for the sheep.

10 I am the good shepherd, and know my sheep, and am known of mine own who hear my voice and followeth after me. As the Father knoweth me, even so know I the Father. And the Father hath commanded me that I be willing to lay down my life for the sheep.

11 And other sheep I have, which are not of this fold, which the Father hath given me and hath taken away from this fold that they might not be devoured by the wolves who are in the clothing of sheep among them.

12 For there hath not been a true shepherd among them for many years. And these other sheep that the Father hath given me, them also I must bring, and they shall hear my voice; and there shall be one fold, and one shepherd.

13 And all of them shall be led through the same door into pasture; and I will watch over them and chase out the wolves who are among them.

14 Therefore doth my Father love me, because I lay down my life for my sheep, who are those who follow me, that I might take it again as an example of that which the Father hath prepared for all those who hear His voice and do His will.

15 And no man taketh it from me, but I lay it down of myself. For I have power to lay it down, and I have power to take it again. And this commandment have I received of my Father, who hath given me unto you.

16 And there was a division therefore again among the Jews because of his sayings. And many of them said: He hath a devil, and is mad. Why then do ye hear him? But others said: These are not the words of him who hath a devil. Can a devil open the eyes of the blind?

17 And it was at Jerusalem the feast of the dedication, and it was winter. And Jesus walked in the temple in the porch of Solomon. Then came the Jews round about him, and said unto him: How long dost thou make us to doubt? If thou be the Christ, tell us plainly and speakest thou not unto us in parables.

18 And Jesus answered them, saying: I told you, and ye believed not. But ye believe on the works that I have done, which ye believe because ye see them with your own eyes. And I do all these things in the name of my Father.

19 And the works that I do in the name of my Father, they bear witness of me. But ye believe not, because ye are not of my sheep, as I have said unto you. For, my sheep hear my voice, and I know them, and they follow me because they recognize the voice by which they are called.

20 And I give unto them eternal life; and they shall never perish, neither shall any man pluck them out of my hand. For my Father gave me to them that I might teach them His commandments, which will assure them eternal life. He is greater than all; and no man is able to pluck them out of the hand of my Father, or out of my own hand, because I and my Father are one.

21 Then the Jews took up stones again to stone him. And Jesus said unto them: Many good works have I shewed you from my Father; therefore, for which of those works do ye stone me?

22 The Jews answered him, saying: For a good work we stone thee not; but for blasphemy against God we stone thee because that thou, being a man, makest thyself equal with God.

23 And Jesus answered them, saying: Is it not written in your law, I said, Ye are gods? If he called them gods, unto whom the word of God came, and the scripture cannot be broken according to your traditions; then how can ye say of him, whom the Father hath sanctified, and sent into the world, Thou blasphemest; because I said, I am the Son of God?

24 If I do not the works of my Father, then believe me not. But if I do, though ye believe not me, believe the works, that ye may know, and believe, that the Father is in me, and I in him.

25 And all those who do the works of God are the sons and daughters of God. And what son or daughter is there that doth not have the potential to be equal with their father and become like their father? And if ye are in the Father, by doing His works, then are ye all equal with him indeed.

26 Now, these sayings were too much for the Jews to hear, for they did not believe that any man could become as God; therefore, they sought again to take him, but he escaped out of their hand, and went away again beyond Jordan into the place where John at first baptized; and there he abode.

27 For there were many people in this place who had been converted by the words of John. And many resorted unto him because of the words which John testified of him, and said: John did no miracle, but we still believed on his words. And all things that John spake of this man were true. And many believed on him there.

28 Now a certain man whom Jesus loved, named Lazarus, of Bethany, the town of Mary and her sister, Martha, the wives of Jesus; and he was sick. And Mary, his sister, who anointed the Lord with ointment and wiped his feet with her hair, lived with her sister Martha, in whose house her brother Lazarus was sick.

29 And these lived in their own house because Jesus could not provide for them that which was required of a husband according to the laws of the Jews. Nevertheless, in this Martha and Mary were not disappointed because they knew who their husband was and what the Father had commanded of him.

30 And because Lazarus fell ill, therefore his sisters sent unto Jesus, saying: Lord, behold, he whom thou lovest is sick.

31 When Jesus heard that, he said: This sickness is not unto death, but for the glory of God, that the Son of God might be glorified thereby according to the will of the Father.

32 For the Lord had received a commandment of the Father upon the mount to perform this miracle that the people might know of the flesh, that He had given all power unto His Son, even the power to raise the dead.

33 Now, Jesus loved Martha and her sister, and Lazarus. And when he had heard, therefore, that he was sick, he abode two days still in the same place where he was waiting for Lazarus to give up the ghost.

34 Then after he had waited the two days, he saith to his disciples: Let us go into Judea again.

35 But his disciples were afraid of the Jews and said unto him: Master, the Jews of late sought to stone thee; and goest thou thither again?

36 And Jesus answered them, saying: Are there not twelve hours in the day? If any man walk in the day, he stumbleth not, because he seeth the light of this world. But if a man walk in the night, he stumbleth, because there is no light in him. But if he walketh with the light of God within him, he shall not stumble in the darkness.

37 These things said he concerning the Jews and the spiritual condition that he saw of those who wanted to kill him among the Jews, but could not do so until his hour had come. And his hour would come in the twelfth hour according to that which he spoke

38. And he said these things unto his disciples so that they might know to trust in him, he being the light of the world by which they would not stumble if they followed him. But after he should be gone from among them, he knew that there would be darkness; and he impressed upon their minds that if they continued in the Spirit of God, which he would send to them after his ascension into heaven, then they would never stumble in the darkness.

39 And after that he saith unto them: Our friend Lazarus sleepeth; but I go, that I may awake him out of sleep. Then said his disciples: Lord, if he sleepeth, he shall do well, then let him sleep, Lord, that the Jews might not have you.

40 But Jesus spake of his death, which in the eyes of God is only a brief sleep to those who love Him. But they thought that he had spoken of the taking of rest in sleep.

41 Then said Jesus unto them plainly: Lazarus is dead. And I am glad for your sakes that I was not there to save him from death, to the intent that ye may believe in my words when ye shall see that he hath already died according to my word. Nevertheless let us go unto him.

42 Then said Thomas, which is called Didymus, unto his fellow disciples: Let us also go, that we may die with him. For they feared lest the Jews should take Jesus and put him to death; for as yet, they did not understand the power of God that had been given to Jesus by the Father.

43 And when Jesus came to Bethany, to the house of Martha, Lazarus had already been in the grave four days. Now, Bethany was nigh unto Jerusalem, about fifteen furlongs off, so many of the Jews who were wont to persecute Jesus came to Martha and Mary, to comfort them concerning their brother.

44 For the Jews had not abandoned Martha and Mary for their relationship with Jesus, for they believed that Jesus had deceived them, and the Jews were trying to win their hearts once again to their own ways.

45 And as soon as Martha heard that Jesus was coming, she went out and met him and greeted him openly among the Jews, for the Jews knew that Martha was his legal wife. But Mary they did not know had also been betrothed to Jesus according to the Holy Spirit of promise by which Jesus did his work among the people. Therefore, Mary sat still in the house where she would not be seen by the Jews who had gathered.

46 Then said Martha unto Jesus: Lord, if thou hadst been here, my brother would have not died. But I know, that even now, whatsoever thou wilt ask of God, God will give it thee.

47 And Jesus saith unto her: Thy brother shall rise again. And Martha saith unto him, I

know that he shall rise again in the resurrection at the last day, but if thou wouldst have been here, he would have still lived among us here in the flesh.

48 And Jesus said unto her: I am the resurrection, and the life. He that believeth in me and keepeth the commandments which I have given unto him, though he were dead, yet shall he live in the spirit. And whosoever liveth and believeth in me shall never die. Believest thou this?

49 She saith unto him: Yea, Lord, I believe that thou art the Christ, the Son of God, which should come into the world to save all men from their sins and bring the resurrection and eternal life to all who believe on thee.

50 And when she had so said, she went her way, and called Mary her sister secretly, saying: Our husband is come, and calleth for thee, for he desireth to see thee. And as soon as she heard that, she arose quickly, and came unto him.

51 Now, Jesus was not yet come into the town, so as not to be discovered by the Jews who sought him, but was in that place where Martha met him. And the Jews then which were with her in the house, and comforted her, when they saw Mary, that she rose up hastily and went out, followed her, saying: She goeth unto the grave to weep there.

52 Then when Mary was come where Jesus was and saw him, she fell down at his feet, saying unto him: Lord, if thou hadst been here, my brother had not died. When Jesus therefore saw her weeping, and the Jews also weeping which came with her, he groaned in the spirit, and was troubled; for he loved Lazarus and also loved his wives, but he was troubled because they lacked faith.

53 For he had taught them that the spirit world was a wonderful place where the spirits of the righteous would rest from all of their labors in a state of happiness until the resurrection.

54 And now, I, Moroni, would that ye should once more have the words of Alma concerning the spirit world and also concerning the resurrection, for they are nearly exact to those words which the Lord had given unto the people during his ministry.

55 And his words are great concerning these things, and for this reason I include them again in this sealed part of this record.

56 And my father wrote the words of Alma, which saith: Behold, I say unto you, that there is no resurrection, or, I would say, in other words, that this mortal doth not put on immortality, this corruption doth not put on incorruption until after the coming of Christ.

57 Behold, he bringeth to pass the resurrection of the dead. But behold, the resurrection is not yet. Now, I unfold unto you a mystery; nevertheless, there are many mysteries which are kept, that no one knoweth them save God himself. But I show unto you one thing which I have inquired diligently of God that I might know—that is concerning the resurrection.

58 Behold, there is a time appointed that all shall come forth from the dead. Now, when this time cometh no one knoweth; but God knoweth the time which is appointed. Now, whether there shall be one time, or a second time, or a third time, that men shall come forth from the dead, it mattereth not; for God knoweth all these things; and it sufficeth me to know that this is the case—that there is a time appointed that all shall rise from the dead.

59 Now, there must needs be a space betwixt the time of death and the time of the resurrection. And now, I would inquire what becometh of the souls of men from this time of death to the time appointed for the resurrection?

60 Now, whether there is more than one time appointed for men to rise it mattereth not; for all do not die at once, and this mattereth not; all is as one day with God, and time only is measured unto men. Therefore, there is a time appointed unto men that they shall rise from the dead; and there is a space between the time of death and the resurrection.

61 And now, concerning this space of time, what becometh of the souls of men is the thing which I have inquired diligently of the Lord to know; and this is the thing of which I do know. And when the time cometh when all shall rise, then shall they know that God knoweth all the times which are appointed unto man.

62 Now, concerning the state of the soul between death and the resurrection—Behold, it hath been made known unto me by an angel,

that the spirits of all men, as soon as they are departed from this mortal body, yea, the spirits of all men, whether they be good or evil, are taken home to that God who gave them life.

63 And then shall it come to pass, that the spirits of those who are righteous are received into a state of happiness, which is called paradise, a state of rest, a state of peace, where they shall rest from all their troubles and from all care, and sorrow.

64 And then shall it come to pass, that the spirits of the wicked, yea, who are evil; for behold, they have no part nor portion of the Spirit of the Lord; for behold, they chose evil works rather than good; therefore the spirit of the devil did enter into them, and take possession of their house—and these shall be cast out into outer darkness; there shall be weeping, and wailing, and gnashing of teeth, and this because of their own iniquity, being led captive by the will of the devil.

65 Now, this is the state of the souls of the wicked, yea, in darkness, and a state of awful, fearful looking for the fiery indignation of the wrath of God upon them; thus they remain in this state, as well as the righteous in paradise, until the time of their resurrection.

66 Now, there are some who have understood that this state of happiness and this state of misery of the soul, before the resurrection, was a first resurrection. Yea, I admit it may be termed a resurrection, the raising of the spirit or the soul and their consignation to happiness or misery, according to the words which have been spoken.

67 And behold, again it hath been spoken, that there is a first resurrection, a resurrection of all those who have been, or who are, or who shall be, down to the resurrection of Christ from the dead. Now, we do not suppose that this first resurrection, which is spoken of in this manner, can be the resurrection of the souls and their consignation to happiness or misery. Ye cannot suppose that this is what it meaneth. Behold, I say unto you, Nay; but it meaneth the reuniting of the soul with the body, of those from the days of Adam down to the resurrection of Christ.

68 Now, whether the souls and the bodies of those of whom it hath been spoken shall all be reunited at once, the wicked as well as the righteous, I do not say; let it suffice that I say that they all come forth; or in other words, their resurrection cometh to pass before the resurrection of those who die after the resurrection of Christ.

69 Now, my son, I do not say that their resurrection cometh at the resurrection of Christ; but behold, I give it as my opinion, that the souls and the bodies of the righteous are reunited at the resurrection of Christ and his ascension into heaven.

70 But whether it be at his resurrection or after, I do not say; but this much I say, that there is a space between death and the resurrection of the body, and a state of the soul, in happiness or in misery, until the time which is appointed of God that the dead shall come forth and be reunited, both soul and body, and be brought to stand before God, and be judged according to their works.

71 Yea, this bringeth about the restoration of those things of which have been spoken by the mouths of the prophets. The soul shall be restored to the body, and the body to the soul; yea, and every limb and joint shall be restored to its body; yea, even a hair of the head shall not be lost; but all things shall be restored to their proper and perfect frame.

72 And now, my son, this is the restoration of which hath been spoken by the mouths of the prophets; And then shall the righteous shine forth in the kingdom of God. But behold, an awful death cometh upon the wicked; for they die as to things pertaining to things of righteousness; for they are unclean, and no unclean thing can inherit the kingdom of God; but they are cast out, and consigned to partake of the fruits of their labors or their works, which have been evil; and they drink the dregs of a bitter cup.

73 And now, these are the things that Jesus had taught unto the people concerning death and the resurrection, but they believed him not; and for this reason, he was troubled in the Spirit because of their unbelief; for they knew that Lazarus was a righteous man who would be received into the spirit world in a state of happiness.

74 And Jesus was greatly perplexed as to why

the people weeped for Lazarus when they should have been rejoicing for him because he was a righteous man.

75 And he said unto those who attended to the body of Lazarus: Where have ye laid him? And they said unto him: Lord, come and see. And as Jesus approached the tomb in which lay the body of Lazarus, Jesus wept.

76 Then said the Jews: Behold, how he loved him. And some of them said, Could not this man, who opened the eyes of the blind, have caused that even this man whom he loved so much should not have died?

77 And Jesus, therefore again was groaning in himself because of their lack of faith and understanding; for he did not cry tears of sorrow for Lazarus, but for them he did cry in sorrow, because they would not come unto the Father, except they see miracles and signs among them.

78 And Jesus cometh to the grave, and it was a cave, and a stone lay upon it. And Jesus said: Take ye away the stone.

79 But Martha, the sister of him who was dead, saith unto him: Lord, by this time he stinketh; for he hath been dead four days. And again Jesus was troubled, even that his own wife did not believe in him as she had said. And he saith unto Martha: Said I not unto thee, that, if thou wouldst believe, thou shouldst see the glory of God?

80 Then they took away the stone from the place where the dead was laid. And Jesus lifted up his eyes, and said: Father, I thank Thee that Thou hast heard me. And I knew that Thou hearest me always; but because of the people which stand by I said it, that they may believe that Thou hast sent me and that they might give all glory unto Thee and not to me.

81 And when he thus had spoken, he cried with a loud voice: Lazarus, come forth! And he who was dead came forth, bound hand and foot with grave clothes according to the traditions of the Jews. And his face was bound about with a napkin, and Jesus saith unto them: Loose him, and let him go.

82 And then many of the Jews which came to Mary, and had seen the things which Jesus did, believed on him. But some of them went their ways to the Pharisees, and told them what things Jesus had done.

CHAPTER 56

The leaders of the church conspire to kill Jesus. Jesus prophesies of his own death. He is the light of the world. The last supper where Jesus washes the disciples' feet is mentioned.

AND it came to pass that the chief priests and the Pharisees gathered in a council, and said: What do we now; for behold, this man doeth many miracles. If we let him thus alone, all men will believe on him, and will call him our king and our Christ.

2 And if we allow the people to do this thing it shall offend Caesar, and the Romans shall come and take away both our place in the church and our power in the nation, for the people shall believe that he is the Christ who should save us from the Romans. And the Romans believe that there is save one king only, and that king is Augustus Caesar.

3 And one of them, named Caiaphas, being the High Priest that same year, said unto them: Ye know nothing at all, nor do ye consider that it is expedient for us, that one man should die for the people, and that the whole nation perisheth not if we offer him up to the Romans as that man who should die because of his crimes among us.

4 And this spake he, not of himself, for as High Priest that year, he prophesied in the name of the Lord that Jesus should die for that nation; and not for that nation only, but also for all those who he should gather together in one, even all of the children of God that were scattered abroad.

5 And when the High Priest spoke prophecy unto the people in the name of the Lord, then the words were not of himself, but his words were considered the words that were given unto the people directly from God, therefore, they were the words of God.

6 And Caiaphas knew not that he had spoken the truth concerning that which would come to pass regarding Jesus; but these things he spoke of him, who the Romans would kill for them according to their customs and the law of the land.

7 But Nicodemus, who secretly believed in the Lord, stood forth and asked of the other high priests: What crime shall we say that this man

hath done to the Romans that he should be worthy of death? For they shall not crucify one who hath not broken their law.

8 And Caiaphas mocked Nicodemus and said unto him: Wouldst thou have him as thy king also? Behold, he hath spoken against Caesar, and we shall prove this to them that they might take him and punish him according to their laws.

9 And then, from that day forth, they took counsel together to put him to death.

10 And Nicodemus met with the disciples of Jesus secretly and told them all things that the priests were wont to do to him. For the high priests had gone to the authority of the Romans and sought out a warrant from them, even one that had to be executed in the name of Caesar, which the soldiers would seek out to serve upon whomever against whom the warrant was issued.

11 Jesus therefore walked no more openly among the Jews; but went thence unto a country near to the wilderness, into a city called Ephraim, and there hid himself in secret and continued with his disciples.

12 And the Passover of the Jews was nigh at hand, and many went out of the country up to Jerusalem before the Passover to purify themselves according to their traditions.

13 Then sought they for Jesus, and spake among themselves as they stood in the temple, some saying: What think ye, that he will not come to the feast? Now both the chief priests and the Pharisees had given a commandment, that, if any man knew where he was, he should shew it, that they might take him.

14 Then Jesus six days before the Passover came to Bethany, which was nigh unto Jerusalem, and where Lazarus was, who had been dead, whom he raised from the dead. And he came up that he might be with his wives whom he had not seen for many days.

15 And Mary Magdalene was with them and lived also in the house of Martha with those who had accepted her. There they made him a supper; and Martha served the twelve, but Lazarus was one of them that sat at the table with him. And Mary Magdelane sat close unto the Lord and would not leave his side to help Martha, for she truly loved the Lord and had remembered all the things which he had promised her.

16 Then took Mary, the sister of Martha, a pound of ointment of spikenard, very costly, and anointed the feet of Jesus, and wiped his feet with her hair: and the house was filled with the odor of the ointment.

17 Then saith one of his disciples, Judas Iscariot, the son of Simon, which should betray him: Why was not this ointment sold for three hundred pence, and given to the poor? This he said, not that he cared for the poor; but because he was a thief, and had the bag, and bore what was put therein.

18 But he said these things to please the ears of those who were in the house, for they knew that the Lord owned no precious things and had commanded those who had the precious material things of the world to sell them and give unto the poor who had not that which would sustain their lives.

19 Then said Jesus unto Judas: Let her alone. For she hath preserved this ointment until now, that she might anoint me in token of my burial as I have asked of her, even against the day of my burying hath she kept this. For the poor always ye have with you, and them shall ye continue to serve according to the commandments of the Father; but me ye have not always.

20 And it was noised abroad that Jesus was come unto the house of Martha, and many people of the Jews therefore knew that he was there; and they came not for the sake of Jesus, but that they might see Lazarus also, whom he had raised from the dead.

21 But the chief priests consulted that they might put Lazarus also to death. Because that by reason of him, many of the Jews went away from the church and did not follow their leadership, and believed on Jesus.

22 On the next day, many people came to the feast when they heard that Jesus was coming to Jerusalem. And they did not come up according to the traditions and ordinances of the church of the Jews, for they had forsaken the church because of the words of Jesus, which he spoke concerning the church and its leaders.

23 And these many people took branches of palm trees, and went forth to meet him, and cried: Hosanna! Blessed is the King of Israel that cometh in the name of the Lord.

24 And Jesus, when he had found a young ass, sat thereon; as it is written: Rejoice greatly, Oh, daughter of Zion; shout, Oh, daughter of Jerusalem; behold, thy King cometh unto thee; he is just, and having salvation; lowly, and riding upon an ass, and upon a colt the foal of an ass.

25 Now these things which Jesus did, understood not his disciples at the first, for they knew not why he sought out an ass and rode it into Jerusalem, allowing the people to praise him and worship him and give unto him glory as he had forbidden them to do, being taught that all glory should be given to the Father and not the Son.

26 Nevertheless, when Jesus was glorified, then remembered they that these things were written of him in the prophecies of the scriptures, and that they had done these things unto him.

27 The people, therefore, that were with him when he called Lazarus out of his grave and raised him from the dead, bare record unto the rest of the Jews. For this cause, many of the people also met him, for they heard that he had done this miracle.

28 And the Pharisees, therefore, said among themselves: Perceive we how we prevail nothing against this man? For behold, the world is gone after him.

29 And there were certain Greeks among them who came up to worship at the feast, that the words which Caiaphas prophesied in his ignorance should be fulfilled, when he said: And not for that nation only, but also for all those who he should gather together in one, even all of the children of God that were scattered abroad.

30 And these same Greeks came therefore to Philip, which was of Bethsaida of Galilee, and desired to speak unto him, saying: Sir, if it were possible, we would see Jesus.

31 And Philip cometh and telleth Andrew; and again Andrew and Philip telleth Jesus about all those who had come up to Jerusalem to glorify him.

32 And Jesus answered them, saying: The hour is come that the Son of man should be glorified. Verily, verily, I say unto you, Except a corn of wheat fall into the ground and die, it abideth alone in the stalk in which it was formed. But if it falleth from the stalk and die, it bringeth forth much fruit.

33 Even so must I die that others might have life through me. And I die because of the things which I have taught unto this people, which things they could not accept from my mouth, even though they were given unto me of the Father.

34 And I have hated my life because of the persecutions that I have endured, but in all these things, I have kept the commandments that were given of me by the Father in all things.

35 Verily, verily, I say unto you, He that loveth his life shall lose it; and he that hateth his life in this world shall keep it unto life eternal.

36 And if any man among you shall serve me, let him follow me and do those things which I have done, and teach the things that I have taught. And if ye do these things, which ye have seen me do, then the world will want to kill you also, like it doth me.

37 But ye can also be saviors of men, if it so be that ye do as I have done and go unto this people and teach unto them the things that I have taught unto you, even the things that the Father requireth of all those who would live in His kingdoms.

38 For the Father hath spoken and hath said: Where I am, there shall also my servant be. And if any man serve me, whom the Father hath sent, him will my Father honor and give unto him what He hath given unto me. For we are all equal in the eyes of God, even the Son like unto his Father.

39 And now is my soul troubled because I must give my life for the work of the Father. And what shall I say? Father, save me from this hour for I cannot bear it? But for this cause came I unto this hour. Therefore, I will praise the Father and say unto him: Father, glorify thy name in me.

40 And after Jesus had raised his arms towards heaven and said these things, then came there a voice from heaven, saying: I have both glorified it, and will glorify it again.

41 The people, therefore, that stood by, and heard it, said that it thundered; but others said that an angel spake to him.

42 Jesus answered and said unto them: This voice came not because of me, but for your sakes, for I know of the work of the Father and of the glory of which He hath spoken, which is His glory and not mine own.

43 But for your sake, and the sake of all those who cannot bear to see the Father and hear His voice, He hath given me His glory for a time.

44 Behold, the time shall come that the Father alone shall be glorified when the Son presenteth this kingdom back to the Father and saith unto Him, Father Thy work is done.

45 Now is the judgment of this world because of the things that shall be done unto me. And in the day of my glory shall the prince of this world be cast out. And because of the wickedness of the world, I shall be lifted upon the cross. And I, if I be lifted up from the earth, will draw all men unto me. This he said, signifying what death he should die.

46 And when the people heard him speak these words, they answered him, saying: We have heard out of the law that Christ abideth forever: and how sayest thou, The Son of man must be lifted up? Who is this Son of man of whom thou speakest?

47 And they remembered not the words that Jesus had spoken to them, saying: the Son of man I call myself because I am a servant to all men—for he knew that the Spirit which was within each man would testify of him according to that spirit that was in that man.

48 Then Jesus said unto them, Yet a little while is the light with you, therefore, walk while ye have the light, lest darkness come upon you; for he that walketh in darkness knoweth not whither he goeth. While ye have light, believe in the light, that ye may be the children of light.

49 These things spake Jesus, and he departed, and did hide himself from them.

50 And though he had done so many miracles before them, yet they believed not on the words that he gave unto them. And the words that he gave unto them were the words of salvation that would save them in the kingdom of God. But the people believed them not, that the saying of Isaiah the prophet might be fulfilled, which he spake, saying: Lord, who hath believed our report? And to whom hath the arm of the Lord been revealed?

51 Therefore, they could not believe because of that which Isaiah said again: He hath blinded their eyes, and hardened their heart; that they should not see with their eyes, nor understand with their heart, and be converted, and I should heal them. These things said Isaiah, when he saw his glory, and spake of him.

52 Nevertheless among the chief rulers also many believed on him; but because of the Pharisees, they did not confess him, lest they should be put out of the synagogue. For they loved the praise of men more than the praise of God.

53 And after the Lord had found himself among his disciples away from the people, even in that place where they were hiding from the warrant that had been issued against him, the Lord broke down and cried mightily on behalf of all the people whom he had taught.

54 For even though he loved them and taught them the things of the Father, which were words of love and peace, they did hate him and persecute him.

55 And Jesus cried and said to his disciples: I do not do this work of myself, neither do I want the glory thereof. And he that believeth on me, believeth not on me, but on Him who sent me. And he that seeth me seeth Him who sent me.

56 I am come a light into the world, that whosoever believeth on me should not abide in darkness. And if any man hear my words, and believe not, I judge him not according to that which he hath not heard.

57 For behold, I came not to judge the world, but to save the world from sin by teaching the world the things that would be required of them by the Father before they can receive eternal life in His kingdom.

58 For this reason am I the Savior of the world. But I can save none who rejecteth the words of the Father. Yea, he who rejecteth me and receiveth not my words hath one who judgeth him, even the Father shall judge him according to the words that I have spoken.

59 And the words that I have spoken, the same shall judge him in the last day. For I have not spoken of myself; but I have spoken the word of the Father who sent me; yea, He gave me a commandment, what I should say, and what I should speak.

60 And I know that His commandment is life everlasting unto all those who hear my words and obey the commandments that I have given them. And whatsoever I speak, therefore, even as the Father said unto me, so I speak.

61 And thus cried Jesus with many tears among his disciples, for it burdened him of that which the people had done with the words of the Father.

62 And his disciples gathered around him, all except Judas who was off seeking out the Chief Priest that he might betray his Lord.

63 But the rest embraced their Lord and comforted him, promising that when he was gone, that they would continue the work of the Father and teach the commandments of the Father to the people as Jesus had done.

64 Now, before the feast of the Passover, when Jesus knew that the hour was come that he should depart out of this world unto the Father, having loved his own which were in the world; and he loved them unto the end, and had called them together at a supper which would be his last among them.

65 And supper being ended, the devil having now put into the heart of Judas Iscariot, the son of Simon, to betray him; but Jesus, knowing that the Father had given all things into his hands, and that he was come from God, and went to God upon his death;

66 Therefore, knowing these things which should shortly come to pass, he riseth from supper, and laid aside his garments; and took a towel, and girded himself. And after that, he poureth water into a basin and beginneth to wash the feet of his disciples, and to wipe them with the towel wherewith he was girded.

67 Then cometh he to Simon Peter, and Peter saith unto him: Lord, dost thou wash my feet? Jesus answered and said unto him, What I do thou knowest not now because ye do not yet have the spirit of understanding which the Father shall send unto you when I am gone. But thou shalt know hereafter why I do these things, because it shall be revealed unto you by the Spirit which ye shall receive of the Father.

68 Peter saith unto him, Thou shalt never wash my feet. But Jesus answered him, saying: If I wash thee not, thou hast no part with me. For this thing I do in similitude of that which ye must do for one another when I am gone.

69 For behold, thy feet have carried thee forth whithersoever thou hast gone all the days of thy life. And I wash from thee the sins which thou hast done in the path that these feet have followed. Therefore, these things are in similitude of the new path, on which these feet, which are now clean by my works, shall carry you forth unto righteousness, which righteousness is the example that I have set for you.

70 Therefore, go forth, all of you, with the clean feet that ye now have and follow this path that will lead you to eternal life.

71 And Simon Peter saith unto him: Lord, not my feet only, but also my hands and my head, because my hands have done not the works of righteousness and my head hath not thought always of the example that thou hast shown unto me.

72 And Jesus saith unto him: He that is washed needeth not save to wash his feet, but is clean every whit. For the feet are those that have carried you forth from the works that ye have done in your past.

73 And your former sins have been forgiven you and shall come no more against you, if it so be that ye follow in cleanliness the path that I have set before you. And ye are clean, but not all. For he knew who should betray him; therefore said he, Ye are not all clean.

74 So after he had washed their feet, and had taken his garments, and was set down again, he said unto them: Know ye what I have done to you? Ye call me Master and Lord; and ye say well; for so I am.

75 If I then, your Lord and Master, have washed your feet; ye also ought to wash the feet of one another, even that ye should support one another in your tribulations as I have supported you. For I have given you an example, that ye should do as I have done to you.

76 Verily, verily, I say unto you, The servant is not greater than his lord; neither is he that is sent greater than He that sent him, for we are all, everyone of us, equal to the Father.

77 And If ye know these things, happy are ye if ye do them. I speak not of you all, for I know whom I have chosen, and there is one among you who hath the desire of Satan in his heart and shall betray me, so that the scripture may be fulfilled, which saith: He that eateth bread with me hath lifted up his heel against me.

78 Now, I tell you this thing before it happens, that, when it is come to pass, ye may believe that I am he of whom all of the holy prophets have written and of whom the scripture speaketh.

79 Verily, verily, I say unto you, He that receiveth whomsoever I have sent before me, receiveth me; and he that receiveth me, receiveth Him who sent me. And the words of those whom I have sent before have testified of me.

80 And if ye receive their words, then ye shall believe in me and receive all of my words. And if ye receive all of my words, then shall the Father send forth His Spirit unto you and ye shall be one with the Father as I am one.

81 And if ye are one with me, then shall I send ye forth to find those who shall receive my words through you. And he that receiveth you, whom I send forth, receiveth me. And he that receiveth me, receiveth the Father and shall also be one with us.

82 And when Jesus had thus said, he was troubled in spirit, and testified, and said: Verily, verily, I say unto you, that one of you shall betray me. Then the disciples looked one on another, doubting of whom he spake.

83 Now, there was leaning on his bosom one of his disciples, whom Jesus loved, even he who hath given this account of the Lord. And Simon Peter, knowing that the Lord loved John, therefore beckoned to him in secret with his hand, that he should ask who it should be of whom the Lord spake that would betray him.

84 John, then lying on his breast, whispered unto him, Lord, who is it? Jesus answered quietly, saying: He it is, to whom I shall give a sop when I have dipped it. And when he had dipped the sop, he gave it to Judas Iscariot, the son of Simon.

85 And after the sop was given to Judas, Satan entered into him. And Jesus knowing this said unto him: That which thou hast put in thy heart to do, do quickly, for my time is at hand.

86 Now, no man at the table knew for what intent he spake this unto him, except Peter who had given the sign, and John who had received the answer from the Lord.

87 For some of them thought, because Judas was appointed by the Lord to be the treasurer and had the bag, that Jesus had said unto him, Buy those things that we have need of against the feast; or, that he should give something to the poor.

88 For Jesus had taught his disciples that the money which they received should only be used for their simple needs and to help the poor and the needy in their want.

89 He then having received the sop went immediately out from among them at the word of the Lord; and it was night.

CHAPTER 57

Jesus teaches his twelve apostles what they should do when he is gone. He promises to send the Holy Ghost to teach them all things.

AND it came to pass that when Judas was gone out from among them, Jesus said unto those apostles who remained: Now is the Son of man glorified, and God is glorified in him. And if God be glorified in him, then God shall also glorify him Himself, and shall straightway glorify him, for the Son shall take no glory for himself, but hath given all glory unto God.

2 For this reason God glorifieth the Son, who shall receive no glory except it be given him of God, who is his Father.

3 Behold, I would that ye should be like unto little children, even yet this little while that I am with you. For little children, when they are with their father, glorifieth their father and cling to him. But when he is gone, they seek for him, not knowing where he hath gone.

4 And after I have gone, ye shall seek me as a child seeketh its father, whom it glorifieth. Thus have I said unto the Jews, Whither I go, ye cannot come unless ye keep the commandments that I have given unto you.

5 And I have given many commandments unto you, which are the commandments of the Father. And all these commandments are new and not like those of old, on which believeth the

Jews, but these things are encompassed in one commandment, which is from the Father.

6 So now I say to you: A new commandment I give unto you, that ye love one another as ye would have them love you. And as I have loved you in this way, ye should also love one another. And by this shall all men know that ye are my disciples, if ye have love one to another.

7 And the apostles, each one, came unto Jesus and wept upon him. And when Simon Peter came to him, he said unto him: Lord, whither goest thou? Jesus answered him, Whither I go, thou canst not follow me now; but thou shalt follow me afterwards.

8 And Peter said unto him: Lord, why cannot I follow thee now? I will lay down my life for thy sake.

9 Jesus answered him, saying: One day thou shalt lay down thy life for me, even as I lay down my life, so shall thee. But now thou canst not lay down thy life for me, because my life is not mine, but His who sent me.

10 And Peter was angered, in love, for his Lord, and said: Surely I will lay down my life for thee this very night.

11 And Jesus smiled upon him, and looked into his eyes, and said: Wilt thou lay down thy life for my sake? Verily, verily, I say unto thee, The cock shall not crow, till thou hast denied me thrice.

12 And then Jesus turned to all of his apostles who were surrounding him and said unto them: Let not your hearts be troubled because I have said unto you that I must now lay down my life. But if ye believe in God, believe also in me, whom God hath commanded to lay down his life that he may take it up again and go unto the Father for you.

13 And fear not for those by whose hands I shall die, neither fear for those who have not kept the commandments of the Father. For behold, in the house of my Father there are many mansions where these may dwell after they have repented and have received of the glory of the Father.

14 But ye, who have been given me by the Father, shall be with me in the house of my Father, if it were not so, I would have told you. I go to prepare a place for you. And if I go and prepare a place for you, I will come again, and receive you unto myself through the power of the resurrection; that where I am, there ye may be also.

15 And whither I go, ye know, and the way that ye shall get there, ye also know, because I have told you.

16 Then Thomas saith unto him: Lord, we know not whither thou goest; and how can we know the way?

17 And Jesus saith unto him: I am the way, the truth, and the life, and what ye have seen me do, do ye, even as I have commanded you. For I go unto the Father to dwell in His kingdom, and no man cometh unto the Father, but by me.

18 If ye had known me, ye should have known my Father also; and from henceforth ye know him, and have seen him.

19 And Philip saith unto him: Lord, shew us the Father, and it sufficeth us. And Jesus saith unto him: Have I been so long a time with you, and yet hast thou not known me, Philip?

20 Behold, he that hath seen me hath seen the Father. And he that witnessed my example, hath seen the example of the Father. And how sayest thou then, Shew us the Father? Believest thou not that I am in the Father, and the Father in me?

21 The words that I speak unto you, I speak not of myself, but I have given you the words that I have received of the Father. And the Spirit of the Father that dwelleth in me causeth me to do the works that ye have witnessed me do.

22 Believe me that I am in the Father, and the Father in me. And if ye cannot believe me at this time, then believe me because ye have seen the works that I have done. For the works that I have done are the works of the Father, in whom ye already believe.

23 And ye know that the works that I have done cannot be done except the Father hath given me the power to do these works. Verily, verily, I say unto you, He that believeth on me, the works that I do shall he do also, because the Father shall also be with him and give unto him His power.

24 And greater works than these shall he do, because the Father shall send forth the Holy Ghost, which shall testify to the spirits of His children of His words and of the works that those who believeth on me do, because I go unto my Father and can no longer do the works in the flesh that ye can do.

25 And by the power of the Holy Ghost ye shall be able to convince many of my words which I have given unto you; even many of those who have rejected me shall accept you because of the power of the Holy Ghost, which the Father hath established to teach all of His children His will.

26 And my name shall remain among you as an example of those works which I did in the flesh. And if ye do the works that ye have seen me do, then ye act in my name. And if ye act in my name, the Father shall give unto you all that ye ask of Him. And whatsoever ye shall ask in my name, that will I do, that the Father may be glorified in the Son.

27 Yea, if ye shall ask any thing in my name, I will do it, if ye love me. And if ye love me, ye will keep my commandments. And I will pray that the Father shall give you another Comforter that he may abide with you forever.

28 And this Comforter is the Holy Ghost of whom I have spoken, even the Spirit of truth, who shall bear witness unto you of all things, and whom the world cannot receive, because it seeth him not with the eyes of flesh, for he is of spirit matter.

29 Neither knoweth they him, because their works are evil. But ye know him, because ye do the works of the Father, which ye have seen me do. And because of the works which ye do, His Spirit dwelleth with you, and shall be in you.

30 And this is why I said unto you, I will not leave you comfortless, but shall ask the Father to send His Spirit to comfort you when I am gone.

31 But one day, I will come to you again. Yet a little while, and the world seeth me no more. But in that day ye shall see me, because I shall live again, being resurrected by the power of the Father; and by this same power ye shall also live.

32 At that day ye shall know that I am in my Father, and ye in me, and I in you, for we shall all be one. Therefore, he that hath my commandments, and keepeth them, he it is that loveth me. And he that loveth me shall be loved of my Father, and I will love him, and will manifest myself to him by the gift of the Holy Ghost, which the Father shall send to you because of me.

33 And Judas, the brother of James, who did not betray the Lord, saith unto him: Lord, how is it that thou wilt manifest thyself unto us and not unto the world?

34 And Jesus answered and said unto him: If a man love me, he will keep my words, which are the words of my Father. And if he keep the words of my Father, then my Father will love him, and we will come unto him, and make our abode with him by giving unto him the Holy Ghost.

35 And as the Son witnesseth of the Father by the flesh, even so doth the Holy Ghost witnesseth of the Father by the Spirit. For the Son giveth an example of the Father by the works that he doeth in the flesh, and the Holy Ghost giveth an example of the Father by that which he giveth through the spirit.

36 He that loveth me not keepeth not my sayings and doth not follow the example of the Father, therefore, he doeth that which the world doeth, and not that which I have given unto him by my word.

37 And the word which ye hear is not mine, but the word of the Father who hath sent me. These things have I spoken unto you, being yet present with you. But the Comforter, which is the Holy Ghost, whom the Father will send in my name, he shall teach you all things, and bring all things to your remembrance whatsoever I have said unto you.

38 And now, I have said unto you that the Holy Ghost shall bring all things to your remembrance. And how shall he bring something to you that ye might remember it, except that ye have heard it before? And I say unto you, that ye have all before heard the things that I have given unto you by the command of the Father.

39 For these things are the same things that ye heard of the Father before ye entered into mortality; yea, even those things which he spake unto you in His kingdom before this world was created.

40 And as His children, ye heard all these things from the Father. And the Holy Ghost shall

bring these things which ye have heard to your remembrance. And when they are brought to your remembrance, ye shall feel peace, which is caused by the confirmation of the Holy Ghost that the things that ye remember are true.

41 And this peace I leave with you, my peace I give unto you through the Spirit. Not as the world giveth peace, give I unto you. But the peace which ye shall receive from the Spirit shall be an everlasting peace that shall dwell with you forever.

42 Therefore, let not your heart be troubled, neither let it be afraid. Ye have heard how I said unto you, I go away, and come again unto you. And if ye loved me, ye would rejoice, because I said, I go unto the Father to prepare a place for you.

43 And I can do nothing further for you in the flesh, for the work that I have been given to do by my Father is done. And now, the work of the Father for you must be done, for my Father is greater than I.

44 And now, I have told you before it cometh to pass, that, when it is come to pass, ye might believe. Hereafter I will not talk much with you according to the flesh, but I shall send forth the Holy Ghost to be with you that ye be not overcome by the world.

45 For the prince of darkness, who is of this world, cometh, but hath no power over me, but he hath power over you. But that the world may know that I love the Father, and as the Father gave me commandment, even so I do; Arise, let us go hence that it may be done to me according to the will of the Father.

46 But I would that ye should continue in the flesh and bring forth fruits worthy of me. For I am the true vine, and my Father is the husbandman.

47 Every branch in me that beareth not fruit, He taketh away and burneth. And every branch that beareth fruit, He purgeth it, that it may bring forth more fruit.

48 Now ye are clean through repentance and faith on the word which I have spoken unto you. Therefore, abide in me, and I shall abide in you. As the branch cannot bear fruit of itself except it abide in the vine; no more can ye bring forth fruit worthy of me except ye abide in me. I am the vine, ye are the branches; He that abideth in me, and I in him, the same bringeth forth much fruit, but without me ye can do nothing.

49 If a man abide not in me, he is cast forth as a branch that is withered; and as men gather the branches of the vine that bear not fruit and cast them into the fire and they are burned, even so shall it be unto those who do not abide in me.

50 If ye abide in me and my words abide in you, ye shall ask what ye will, and it shall be done unto you. Herein is my Father glorified, that ye bear much fruit which is worthy of me. And if ye bring forth this fruit, so shall ye be my disciples.

51 And as the Father hath loved me, so have I loved you; therefore, continue ye in my love. If ye keep my commandments, ye shall abide in my love; even as I have kept the commandments of my Father, and abide in His love.

52 These things have I spoken unto you, that my joy might remain in you and that your joy might be full. And this is my commandment unto you, even the same commandment that I received from my Father: That ye love one another as I have loved you.

53 And greater love hath no man than this, that a man lay down his life for his friends. Ye are my friends if ye do whatsoever I command you.

54 Henceforth, I call you not to be my servants, for the servant knoweth not what his lord doeth. But I have called you friends; for all things that I have heard of my Father, I have made known unto you; therefore, ye knoweth that which I do.

55 Ye have not chosen me, but I have chosen you and ordained you, that ye should go and bring forth fruit and that your fruit should remain because of the Holy Ghost that shall purify and sanctify the fruit. And by being purified and sanctified, whatsoever ye shall ask of the Father in my name, He shall give it you.

56 Again, these things I command you, that ye love one another, and do unto others what ye would have them do unto you.

57 And when ye shall teach these things in the world, ye shall be hated for that which ye teach. For those of the world do not love one another, and do unto others what they will. For they love themselves and those who are their friends and their families, and their sons and their daughters, and their husbands and their wives. But the stranger they do not love, and their enemy, they hateth.

58 And when ye teach them that it is the will of the Father that they love their neighbor and their enemy, then shall they hate you.

59 But if the world hate you, ye know that it hated me before it hated you. If ye were of the world, the world would love its own; but because ye are not of the world, but I have chosen you out of the world, therefore the world hateth you as it hateth me.

60 And in this ye shall know if ye truly are my disciples. For the world hateth my disciples and persecuteth them.

61 Remember the word that I said unto you: The servant is not greater than his lord. If they have persecuted me, they will also persecute you.

62 But the righteous shall hear your voice and keep your sayings; for if they have kept my sayings, they will keep yours also.

63 But all these things will the wicked do unto you for the sake of my name, or in other words, the things which I have done among them. And they do these things because they know not Him who sent me.

64 For if they knew the Father, then they would know that the Father loveth all His children and hath no enemies, but loveth them all.

65 And if I had not come and spoken unto them, then they would have not had sin, because the Father is merciful unto those who have not heard His voice. But now they have no cloak for their sin because they have heard His voice through me.

66 And he that hateth me hateth my Father also. If I had not done among them the works which none other man did, then they would have had no sin, because of the mercy of the Father. But now have they both seen and hated both me and my Father, for we are one.

67 But this cometh to pass, that the word might be fulfilled that is written in their law, which said: They hated me without a cause.

68 But when the Comforter is come, whom I will send unto you from the Father, even the Spirit of truth, which proceedeth from the Father, he shall testify of me unto those who do the will of the Father, even those who loveth his enemies and doeth unto others what he would have others do to him; for this is the commandment of the Father.

69 And ye also shall bear witness, because ye have been with me from the beginning. And ye shall write the witness that ye have seen that it might be brought forth to judge those who have received these things.

70 For I shall not write these things and send them forth. For I shall take no glory unto myself, except it be given me of the Father. Therefore, ye shall write and shall be given glory for that which ye shall write.

71 And all these things have I spoken unto you that ye should not be offended when ye are persecuted for the sake of my name. For they shall put you out of the synagogues because ye do not teach for doctrine the commandments of men, but preach unto them the commandments of the Father.

72 Yea, the time cometh, that whosoever killeth you will think that he doeth God service. And these things will they do unto you, because they have not known the Father, nor me.

73 But these things have I told you, that when the time shall come, ye may remember that I told you of them. And these things I said not unto you at the beginning, because I was with you always and it was I that the world hated and not you.

74 But now I go my way to Him who sent me; and none of you asketh me, Whither goest thou? But because I have said these things unto you, sorrow hath filled your heart. Nevertheless I tell you the truth so that ye might understand whither I go and why I go unto the Father.

75 Behold, it is expedient for you that I go away from you in the flesh. For if I go not away, the Comforter will not come unto you, because I am with you in the flesh. And because I am with you in the flesh, ye have no need of the Holy Ghost, for we are one and will give unto you the same words and the same understanding.

76 But if I depart, I will send him unto you, so that ye might know through the Spirit what ye could not understand in the flesh. For the flesh straineth against the spirit, even that the flesh understandeth not the spirit. But the spirit understandeth the flesh and doth not strain against it.

77 For this reason, ye understand not the things that I have said unto you in the flesh from the beginning. But the Holy Ghost I shall send unto you to give to your spirit the understanding that ye could not get from the flesh.

78 And when he is come, he will reprove the world of sin, and of righteousness, and of judgment; of sin, he reproveth because they believe not on me and the things that I have taught unto them; of righteousness he reproveth, because I go to my Father, and ye see me no more, and yet ye shall still believe that of myself all righteousness doth come, taking glory from the Father; and of judgment he reproveth, because the prince of this world is judged according to his works.

79 For the world shall judge that which is good and of God to be evil, and that which is evil and of the prince of darkness to be good.

80 And I have yet many things to say unto you, but ye cannot bear them now. Howbeit when he, the Spirit of truth, is come, he will guide you into all truth in that which he shall speak unto you.

81 For he shall not speak of himself, but of the Father. But whatsoever he shall hear from the Father, that shall he speak. And if ye ask of the Father in my name by keeping my commandments and following my example, then he will shew you things to come.

82 He shall glorify the Father through me; for he shall receive of mine, which I have received from the Father, and shall shew it unto you, who are mine.

83 All things that the Father hath are mine, because He hath given them unto me for your sakes. Therefore said I, that he shall take of mine, and shall shew it unto you.

84 A little while, and ye shall not see me; and again, a little while, and ye shall see me, because I go to the Father.

85 Then said some of his disciples among themselves, What is this that he saith unto us, A little while, and ye shall not see me; and again, a little while, and ye shall see me, because I go to the Father? They said therefore amongst themselves: What is this that he saith, A little while? We cannot tell what he saith.

86 Now Jesus knew that they were desirous to ask him, and said unto them: Do ye inquire among yourselves of that I said, A little while, and ye shall not see me; and again, a little while, and ye shall see me? Verily, verily, I say unto you, That ye shall weep and lament, but the world shall rejoice because I am gone unto the Father.

87 And ye shall be sorrowful, but your sorrow shall be turned into joy. A woman when she is in travail hath sorrow, because her hour is come; but as soon as she is delivered of the child, she remembereth no more the anguish, because of the joy that a child is born into the world.

88 And ye now therefore have sorrow. But I will see you again, and your heart shall rejoice, and your joy no man taketh from you.

89 And in that day ye shall ask of me nothing, for my glory shall be swallowed up in the glory of the Father; but of the Father ye shall ask all things and it shall be done unto you.

90 Verily, verily, I say unto you, Whatsoever ye shall ask the Father in my name, He will give it you. Hitherto have ye asked nothing of the Father in my name, because I have been with you in the flesh. But when ye have received the Holy Ghost, then ask, and ye shall receive, that your joy may be full.

91 These things have I spoken unto you in proverbs because of the wickedness of men; but the time cometh, when I shall no more speak unto you in proverbs. But when I have sent unto you the Comforter, I shall shew you plainly of the Father.

92 At that day ye shall ask in my name, but I shall say not unto you, but I will pray unto the Father for you, because ye yet do not understand that ye are equal to me in the eyes of the Father.

93 For the Father Himself loveth you, because ye have loved me, and have believed that I came out from God. I came forth from the Father, and am come into the world to save all men by giving them the commandments of the Father.

94 Again, I leave the world, and go to the Father who hath sent me. And his disciples said unto him: Lo, now speakest thou plainly, and speakest no proverb. Now are we sure that thou

knowest all things, and needest not that any man should ask thee, but have commanded us to ask all things of God, taking no glory unto thyself. And by this humility we believe that thou camest forth from God.

95 Jesus answered them, saying: Do ye now believe? Behold, the hour cometh, yea, is now come, that ye shall be scattered, every man to his own, and shall leave me alone; and yet I am not alone, because the Father is with me.

96 Behold, the things that I have spoken unto you, I have said unto you that in me ye might have peace. For in the world ye shall have tribulation. But be of good cheer; for I have overcome the world and have shown you the way that ye might also overcome the world.

97 And the Holy Ghost shall teach you all these things that ye might overcome the world and have peace with you always.

CHAPTER 58

The intercessory prayer in the garden of Gethsemane. The true nature of Christ's suffering in the garden. Moroni speaks in plainness concerning the true purpose and mission of the life of Christ, and of the things that were changed and deleted in the record of the Bible. (Compare John 17)

AND it came to pass that Jesus separated himself from the disciples and took with him into a more secluded part of the garden Peter, James and John. And he commanded them to watch for those who were coming for him.

2 And Jesus left them and went off a ways and kneeled before the Father.

3 And Jesus wept exceedingly, and sorrowed greatly because of the great wickedness of the world, and that he had been rejected by so many whom he loved so dearly.

4 And his agony because of these things was so great that he did weep exceedingly and every fiber of his being trembled; and he began to sweat because of his anguish. And the stress of his exalted soul upon his body caused him to bleed from his nose and his ears, even his eyes did issue forth tears of blood because of the turmoil of his spirit.

5 And now, I would that ye should understand that the Lord was not suffering because he was paying the penalty for the sins of others as ye have supposed—and this doctrine is what hath become a great stumbling block for you—for all those who sin shall suffer for their own sins. But he suffered because of these sins, or because of the wickedness of men and their inability to love each other and search for the Father who had created them.

6 And this is not the doctrine of Christ desired by those who shall canonize the accounts of the eye witnesses of the life and ministry of Christ into scripture. For they shall believe that Christ suffered and died for the sins of all men, even that all men might be saved if they would only accept Jesus into their hearts and believe in him.

7 Now, this doctrine might not be far from the truth, but these men shall not believe that man is saved by his works, but by grace alone. And this they shall believe that they might justify their own wickedness, because they shall not love each other as they would have another love them.

8 And they shall set themselves up above the people, and they shall desire glory and praise from the people whom they lead, and in many other ways shall they disobey the words of the Father given through Christ. And for these reasons shall they change the truth regarding the mission and purpose of the life of Christ.

9 And now, if a man hath accepted Jesus as his Savior, then that man would obey the commandments that Jesus hath given unto him. And if this man doth not obey the commandments, yet professeth to have taken upon him the name of Jesus, then hath he sinned, in that this man hath taken the name of the Lord in vain, and he shall not be held guiltless who taketh the name of the Lord in vain.

10 And this man can profess the name of Jesus forever, but he shall not be saved in the kingdom of God unless he can abide by the laws that govern the kingdom of God; and these laws are the commandments that Jesus taught to the people, and are the commandments that the apostles taught to the people, and are the same commandments that were given by the Father in the beginning, which He also giveth unto all of His children through the ministrations of the Holy Ghost, if it so be that they listen to His Spirit.

11 Therefore, I would that ye should know, that Christ did not suffer for your sins, but he suffered because of them.

12 For what man is there among you who hath a son who doeth those things which are not good, even those things that bring unhappiness upon him that he is miserable; yea, do ye take upon yourself the penalty for that which your son hath done; or is it not that ye do suffer because of the pain that ye know your son must go through because of that which he hath done, which hath brought upon himself the just penalty for what he hath done to himself?

13 And if ye take away the penalty for that which he hath done, how then can this son learn that he should not do this thing that hath caused him this unhappiness?

14 And if ye truly love your son, then ye would suffer because of his sins, but ye would not suffer for them, nor pay the penalty for which he is responsible, because he acted on his own with the free agency that hath been granted unto him.

15 And those of you who believe that the Lord Jesus Christ took upon himself your sins, and that ye shall not be responsible for that which ye have done, are in grave error, and if ye do not repent of your own sins and begin to do those things which the Lord hath commanded you, ye shall suffer for all of your sins and be kept out of the kingdom of God until ye have paid the last senine for that which ye have done.

16 And because of the great love that Jesus had for all men, he did suffer exceedingly in the garden because of their wickedness.

17 And after he had suffered exceedingly, he lifted up his eyes to heaven and prayed, saying: Father, the hour is come that Thou shalt glorify Thy Son, and that Thy Son also may glorify Thee. And Thou art glorified through Thy Son because Thou hast given him power over all flesh, that he should give eternal life to as many as Thou hast given him.

18 And this is life eternal, that they might know Thee the only true God, and Jesus Christ, whom Thou hast sent. I have glorified Thee on the earth by teaching the things that Thou hast commanded me to teach unto Thy children; that they might repent of their sins and do that which Thou requirest of them to prepare them to live in the kingdoms of glory that Thou hast prepared for them.

19 Yea, I have finished the work which Thou gavest me to do. And now, Oh, Father, glorify Thou me with Thine own self, even with the glory which I had with Thee before the world was.

20 I have manifested Thy name unto the men who Thou gavest me out of the world; Thine they were, and Thou gavest them me; and they have kept Thy word as I have commanded them. Now they have known that all things whatsoever Thou hast given me are of Thee and are not for mine own glory, but for Thine.

21 For I have given unto them the words which Thou gavest me; and they have received them, and have known surely that I came out from Thee, and they have believed that Thou didst send me.

22 I pray for them, Oh, Father. I pray not for the world, but for them which Thou hast given me out of the world; for they are Thine. And all mine are Thine, and Thine are mine; and I am glorified in them because they do the works that they have seen me do.

23 And now, I am no more in the world, but these are in the world. And I come to Thee, Holy Father, and pray that Thou keepest through Thine own name those whom Thou hast given me, that they may be one, as we are one.

24 While I was with them in the world, I kept them in Thy name by teaching them the things which Thou hast given me for them. And those that Thou gavest me I have kept, and none of them is lost, but the son of perdition; that the scripture might be fulfilled.

25 And now come I to Thee and leave them in the world. And these things I speak in the world, that they might have my joy fulfilled in themselves.

26 I have given them Thy word and the world hath hated them because of Thy word, because

they are not of the world, even as I am not of the world. I pray not that Thou shouldst take them out of the world, but that Thou shouldst keep them from the evil of the world. They are not of the world, even as I am not of the world.

27 Sanctify them, Holy Father, through Thy truth, which is given unto them by Thy Spirit. For they have received Thy word, and Thy word is truth.

28 As Thou hast sent me into the world to save it from all sin, even so have I also sent them into the world to save all of Thy children from the sins of the world.

29 And for their sakes I sanctify myself by my example and by my word, that they also might be sanctified through the truth. Neither pray I for these alone, but for them also who shall believe on me through their word.

30 And if they believe on me through the word of those who Thou hast given me out of the world, then they shall believe in Thee and keep Thy commandments which they shall receive through these; that they all may be one; as Thou, Father, art in me, and I in Thee, that they also may be one in us; that the world may believe that Thou hast sent me to make all of Thy children one with their Father.

31 And the glory which Thou gavest me, I have given them; that they may be one, even as we are one; yea, I in them, and Thou in me, that they may be made perfect in one; and that the world may know that Thou hast sent me, and hath loved them, as Thou hast loved me.

32 And that the world might know that Thou hast sent them, as Thou hast sent me to bring salvation unto all men according to their words, which is Thy word. That all men, Holy Father, might be one with us.

33 Oh, Father, I will that they also, whom Thou hast given me, be with me where I am; that they may behold my glory, which Thou hast given me; for Thou lovedst me before the foundation of the world; and Thou lovedst them also in the beginning and have called them as Thou hast called me.

34 Oh, righteous Father, the world hath not known Thee; but I have known Thee, and these have known that Thou hast sent me. And I have declared unto them Thy name, and will declare it always unto them that they might give glory to Thee and not to me; that the love wherewith Thou hast loved me may be in them, and the love wherewith I have loved them may be in the world.

35 And now, I, Moroni, have been commanded by the Lord to speak with plainness in this record, so all that shall receive it might understand the true mission and purpose of the life and ministry of Jesus Christ.

36 For behold, I have given unto you the account of John as it was given in its plainness, even before it shall be edited and changed by those who shall include it in the Bible that ye have before you.

37 And the words of the Savior which John hath given unto us are great and powerful to those who have the Holy Ghost to bear witness to them of their truthfulness and their meaning. But to those of you who do not have the Holy Ghost with you—and ye do not have the Holy Ghost because of your wickedness—these things shall not be made known unto you by the Spirit, but shall be to you as a parable, or a proverb, of which even the apostles spoke when they could not understand the meaning of the words of Jesus Christ.

38 But now, I give unto the world, in plainness, the meaning of his words. And then after I have given unto you in plainness the meaning of these things, then ye should go and read and ponder once again the words of the account of John, that ye might better understand that which was written concerning Jesus Christ in the flesh.

39 And when ye read the words of John again; yea, when ye read the words of the other accounts also in the Bible, then shall ye begin to understand the many plain and precious things that were taken out of this record because of the wickedness of men.

40 For behold, unless a man hath the Spirit of God to direct him in those things which he should write unto the world; yea, unless a man hath the inspiration of the Holy Ghost, he shall not write the word of God, but he shall write the words of men according to his own beliefs and desires.

41 Therefore, what ye believe in the latter

days as being the word of God, was written by the hand of a man. And in many instances, the words which ye have are the word of God as was given to those who wrote the scriptures by the Spirit of God.

42 But when these things were translated into different languages and interpolated and edited by those who did not have the Spirit of God, then they became dark and obscure and not the pure word of God, but a corrupted form based upon the understanding and opinions of man.

43 And for this purpose hath the Lord commanded my father to make this record. And he hath also commanded me to write those things that I have translated by the power of the Urim and Thummim which was written by the brother of Jared, who was given the vision of the world from the beginning of time to the end of time.

44 And now, I would that ye should know that the words Urim and Thummim, being interpreted, mean Lights and Perfections.

45 And now, here is a mystery unto those who shall receive these things, even those of you who have understanding, which understanding is not the knowledge of man, but the knowledge of God:

46 For in the book called Revelation of the Bible which came forth from the mouth of a Jew, which was also written by John, he wrote, saying: He that hath an ear, let him hear what the Spirit saith unto the churches: To him that overcometh will I give to eat of the hidden manna, and will give him a white stone, and in the stone a new name written, which no man knoweth saving he that receiveth it.

47 And now, I would that ye should know that this white stone is like unto the Urim and Thummim. In other words, he that overcometh the world and keepth the commandments of God in all things shall be given a new name. And this name is symbolic of the works of this man. And because his works are righteous, only he shall know the new name, or in other words, only he shall be able to do the works that he hath done.

48 And the hidden manna is that same manna of which Christ spoke when he said unto the Jews: Your fathers did eat manna in the wilderness and are dead. This is the bread which cometh down from heaven, that a man may eat thereof, and not die. I am the living bread which came down from heaven; if any man eat of this bread he shall live forever; and the bread that I will give is my flesh, which I will give for the life of the world.

49 And the bread of Christ is the works of the Lord and his example to us in the flesh. And if we do the works of Christ and follow his example, then are we given the white stone, or in other words a Urim and Thummim, which is Lights and Perfections.

50 Yea, when a man hath perfected his life, then shall the light of the Father shine within him and he shall be one with the Father and know all things that the Father knoweth, thus becoming perfected in the Father.

51 For light is truth and knowledge and shall be given to all those who have perfected their lives through the words, or manna, of Christ.

52 And now, my beloved brothers and sisters, what is it that the Lord requireth of us that we might be perfected, even as the Father which is in heaven is perfect?

53 Behold, he requireth that we first learn the words of Christ, then repent of our former ways and change them so that they conform to the words of Christ and the example that he hath set for us.

54 And now this is the thing that I have been commanded to explain to you: Behold, in the beginning we were all equal in the eyes of the Father, having been created by Him of His own will, and given the power of free agency to act and exist independent of Him that we might one day experience the happiness that we desire for ourselves.

55 And in order to experience this happiness, the Father gave unto us commandments in the beginning by which we needed to live in order to have this happiness.

56 And he taught us of His kingdom and the different degrees of glory, or of happiness, that we would one day inherit according to our individual desires of happiness. And He taught us that in order for us to live in these kingdoms, we needed to abide by certain eternal laws, or commandments, that would assure us that we would experience the happiness that we desire.

57 And if we cannot live by these laws, or these commandments, then we cannot live in these eternal kingdoms, because we would not be happy abiding by any other laws, which laws are not the eternal laws of the Father, which laws are the same laws by which He liveth in His kingdom and which bring Him His happiness.

58 And the Father explained to us that it was necessary that we experience life without these laws, even in a world where these laws would not always exist because of the different desires of happiness that each of us possesseth.

59 And in this world where these laws did not exist, we would learn for ourselves, firsthand, that the laws that we are required to live by in the kingdoms of God are indeed the laws of happiness that will assure us eternal happiness forever.

60 And because of His own experience, He knew that many of us would reject the laws of happiness and live according to the dictates of our own consciences, which are selfish in nature and are centered in our own individual happiness.

61 And He taught us that though we would all experience eternal happiness in His kingdom, that there were certain penalties, or denials of happiness, based upon what we would do with our free agency in choosing for ourselves which happiness best suiteth our own interests.

62 And I, Moroni, have already explained many of these things beforehand in this record. Therefore, I will not repeat that which I have already given unto you concerning these things.

63 Ye have the words which the Lord hath commanded me to write unto you; therefore, study them and ponder them, and ask the Father to give you an understanding of them.

64 But now, I have been commanded to explain unto you in simplicity and plainness the life and ministry of Jesus Christ:

65 Behold, Jesus Christ was he who was chosen in the beginning to represent the Father in this part of His kingdom. And he was called Jehovah by the Father; and he is our brother and equal to all of us before the Father, but hath been given the calling by the Father to assure that all of us receive the opportunity to learn the laws of happiness that we need to know and live by in order to live forever in the kingdom of the Father.

66 And Jehovah came into this world and became Jesus Christ for one purpose and one purpose only; yea, to teach us the laws of happiness, which were taught unto us by our Father, by which we must live that we might be saved in the kingdom of God. And also to show unto us an example of how these laws should be lived; he being this example of the Father.

67 Yea, he gave us the words and the commandments of the Father.

68 Yea, he gave us the example of his works and his actions among men in the flesh, even a perfect example of how these laws must be lived.

69 Yea, he even gave unto us the example of his reactions to the commandments and precepts of men that are not based upon the eternal laws of happiness.

70 And finally, he came into the world to teach the exact same things that we heard of the Father when we all listened to the Father as spirits in His kingdom where we were created, even when the Father presented unto us the fullness of His eternal plan of happiness for us.

71 And now, HEAR YE MY WORDS, my brothers and sisters; for if ye will not hear my words, ye shall be held responsible for that which ye do because ye will not hear my words.

72 Behold, I give not unto you of my own words, but the words that the Lord hath commanded me to give unto you in plainness:

73 Behold, Jesus Christ did not die for your sins, nor did he do anything that would take away your sins, except teach unto you the true commandments of the Father, that ye might repent of your sins and keep these commandments. For those things which are not a commandment of the Father are sins.

74 Behold, Jesus died because the world judged the things which he taught to be evil and of the devil; therefore, they crucified him.

75 Behold, he could have at any time used the power that he had been given by the Father to save his own life and kill those who wanted to kill him. Nevertheless, he was an example of the Father to us in all things, and he obeyed the commandments of the Father in all things, even until the end of his life.

76 And now, what are these commandments of the Father which shall save us in His kingdom?

77 Yea, what is the message of the life and example of Jesus Christ?

78 Yea, what was it that he commanded of the people when he said unto them: Except ye keep my commandments, ye shall in no wise inherit the kingdom of God?

79 Yea, what are these commandments and laws of happiness that we must live by in order to experience this happiness forever?

80 Behold, they are as simple as my words; but ye are blinded so exceedingly by your desires to make a mystery of God, that ye do not understand the simplicity and plainness of these things. And for this reason ye do not know Him; and this is life eternal that ye know the very Eternal Father, and His Son, Jesus Christ.

81 Behold, the great and everlasting commandment and eternal law of happiness of the Father who created us all is this: That ye love one another as ye would have them love you.

82 And on this one commandment alone, doth all other commandments and laws stand; and there is none other commandment by which ye must live.

83 Yea, this is the great standard of the Lord. This is the embodiment of the words of Christ and the all-encompassing message that the Father hath given to His children from the beginning.

84 And on this standard, or on the words of Christ, shall all the children of God, yea, even every one, be judged according to their works.

85 Behold, every action, every thought, every reaction, even every time that ye use your free agency to act in the independent state in which ye have all been created, ye shall be judged according to this standard.

86 And if ye cannot love another as ye would have them love you, then ye shall not inherit the kingdom of God, and there shall be found no place in His kingdom for you, but ye shall take your place with those who rebelled against the plan of the Father in the beginning, even with Lucifer and those who followed him.

87 And now, I would admonish you to read and reread the words of Christ, even in all the scripture that he hath suffered to be written of him, and see for yourselves if his message doth not say these things unto you.

88 He is our Savior because he teacheth us these things that we might be saved. And all those who teach his words are the saviors of men and are one in mind and mission with the Father, who gave these words unto us all in the beginning.

89 And the Holy Ghost, who is one with the Father and the Son, shall teach these things unto all of us, even by giving us peace and happiness when we keep this great commandment of God.

90 And when the Spirit hath withdrawn itself from us, because we do not keep this commandment, then we are left unto ourselves and feel misery, strife, depression, loneliness, and pain.

91 Therefore, judge ye yourselves whether ye are at peace with yourselves and whether ye are happy. And if ye are honest with yourselves, then ye can judge righteously whether or not ye are prepared to enter into the kingdom of God and partake of His eternal happiness, which He hath offered us, forever.

92 And if ye are not at peace with yourself, ye shall be miserable and unsettled and continually searching for that peace and happiness that eludeth you.

93 Therefore, my beloved brothers and sisters, do unto others that which ye would have them do unto you, and ye shall be one with Christ, who is one with God, who is the Father who desireth that all of His children be one with Him.

94 This is the meaning and the message of the atonement of Christ. There is no other meaning, and there shall be no other meaning given forever. Amen.

CHAPTER 59

Moroni continues with the account of John. The death of the Lord is given according to the account of John. We are commanded to concentrate on the words of Jesus and not on his death.

AND now, I return again to the account of John, so therein, ye might read of the death of Christ and his resurrection; that ye might have joy in him and what he was commanded to do by the Father, who loveth us all, yea, even every one of us equally.

2 And it came to pass that after Jesus had spoken these words, which were his last words unto his disciples in the flesh, he went forth with his disciples over the brook Cedron, where there was a garden, into the which he entered with his disciples.

3 And this garden was the secret place of hiding for him because of the warrant for his arrest that had been obtained by the High Priest of the church at Jerusalem. And Judas also, which betrayed him, knew the place; for Jesus ofttimes resorted thither with his disciples, of which Judas was one.

4 And it came to pass that Judas went unto the High Priest and revealed unto him where Jesus and the other apostles were hiding. Judas then, having been paid the money, received a band of men and officers from the chief priests and Pharisees, went thither with lanterns and torches and weapons.

5 And they were led by Judas to the place of hiding. And when they came into the garden, Jesus therefore, knowing all things that should come upon him, went forth, and said unto them: Whom seek ye? They answered him: Jesus of Nazareth. Jesus saith unto them: I am he. And Judas also, which betrayed him, stood with them.

6 And as soon then as he had said unto them, I am he, the apostles went backward, and fell to the ground taking with them by force Jesus also to the ground that he might not be discovered among them.

7 But Jesus stood upon his feet and said again unto them: Whom seek ye? And they said, Jesus of Nazareth. Jesus answered, I have told you that I am he. If therefore ye seek me, let these go their way.

8 And this he said that the saying might be fulfilled, which he spake, saying: Of them which Thou gavest me have I lost none.

9 And Judas drew close to the Lord and kissed him on the cheek, which was the sign he had given to the priests and the soldiers, who were there to arrest him, of which among them was the Christ.

10 And as these came forth to take him, Simon Peter having a sword, drew it, and smote the servant of the High Priest, and cut off his right ear. And the name of the servant was Malchus, who was later converted unto the Lord by the apostles after he had received the Holy Ghost, and who was stoned by the Jews for apostacy.

11 Then said Jesus unto Peter: Put up thy sword into the sheath and do not sin in your anger by keeping me from doing the will of my Father. And remember, as it is written, that he who liveth by the sword, shall by it die. Behold, the cup which my Father hath given me, shall I not drink it?

12 Then the band and the captain and officers of the Jews took Jesus and bound him, and led him away to Annas first; for he was father-in-law to Caiaphas, who was the High Priest that same year.

13 For Annas wanted to behold the man who had caused so much contentiton and confusion among the Jews, and who had said that the church of God among them was corrupt, and that unless the people repent of their sins and follow not their leaders, but follow God, they would perish with their church.

14 And Annas was a great and powerful man among the Jews who dealt with the Romans in all things, and arbitrated that which the church needed from the Romans according to the needs and the wants of the church of the Jews.

15 Now Caiaphas was he who gave counsel to the Jews that it was expedient that one man should die for the people. And he was also that High Priest to whom went Joseph, the brother of Jesus, and who received the thirty pieces of silver that Joseph had given him

because of the miracle that Jesus had wrought, being in the employ of their father Joseph, and who then paid this money to Judas, who had betrayed Jesus.

16 And it came to pass that Simon Peter followed Jesus, and so did another disciple, even Nathanael, who was a learned man and revered and respected among the Jews because of his learning.

17 And Nathanael was known unto the High Priest, and went in with Jesus into the palace of the High Priest. But Peter stood at the door without. Then went out Nathanael, who was known unto the High Priest, and spake unto her that kept the door that she would allow Peter to also be brought in with them.

18 But Peter was afraid and dared not enter therein with Nathanael and Jesus. And when the damsel that kept the door said unto Peter, that he might be let in with them: Art not thou also one of the disciples of this man? He saith unto her: I am not.

19 And the servants and officers, who had brought Jesus into the palace, stood there and had made a fire of coals; for it was cold; and they warmed themselves; and Peter stood with them, and warmed himself.

20 And the High Priest then asked Jesus of his disciples, and of his doctrine, and why it was that Jesus was hiding and preaching in secret among the people.

21 Jesus answered him, saying: I spake openly to the world; I ever taught in the synagogue, and in the temple, whither the Jews always resort; and in secret have I said nothing. Why askest thou me of my doctrine? Ask them who heard me what I have said unto them. Behold, they know what I said.

22 And when he had thus spoken, one of the officers who stood by struck Jesus with the palm of his hand, saying: Answerest thou the High Priest so?

23 Jesus answered him, saying: If I have spoken evil, bear witness of the evil which I have spoken. But if I have spoken well, why smitest thou me?

24 Now, Annas had sent him bound unto Caiaphas, the High Priest, and he was knocked to the ground because his hands were tied and he could not catch himself.

25 And it came to pass that Nathanael stood forth boldly and defended Jesus to the High Priest according to his knowledge of the law of Moses and the law of the church. And he confounded the High Priest in all of his words.

26 But the High Priest had the hearts and the minds of the people, and when he became angry, because he could not stand up to the defense which was given by the mouth of Nathanael, he commanded that Nathanael be cast out from among them and cast off from the church forever.

27 And in this thing Nathanael did rejoice and said unto the High Priest as they led him out from among them: And what need thinkest thou that I have of this church and the wickedness that is taught herein. I need not the church or its leaders to assure me my salvation. For God hath sent His Son, and he is my friend; and in his words I have found my salvation.

28 And Simon Peter stood and warmed himself with the officers and the servants without. They said therefore unto him: Art not thou also one of his disciples? But Peter denied it, and said, I am not. But one of the servants of the High Priest, being his kinsman whose ear Peter cut off, saith: Did not I see thee in the garden with him?

29 Peter then denied again; and immediately the cock crew. And Peter remembered the words of the Lord concerning his own betrayal, even thrice before the crow of the cock. And Peter ran from among them and tore off his clothes and wept exceedingly because he had betrayed his friend and Lord.

30 Then led they Jesus from Caiaphas unto the hall of judgment of the Romans. And it was early during the time of the Passover; and they themselves went not into the judgment hall, lest they should be defiled; so that they might eat the Passover in righteousness according to their traditions.

31 Pilate then came out of the judgment hall unto them, and said: What accusation bring ye against this man? They answered and said unto him: If he were not a malefactor, we would not have delivered him up unto thee.

32 Then said Pilate unto them: Take ye him, and judge him according to your law. For Pilate

wanted nothing to do with Jesus, having been forewarned by his wife in a dream that he should have nothing to do with him because he was a righteous man.

33 But the Jews therefore said unto him: It is not lawful for us to put any man to death. For death is what the Jews sought for Jesus that the saying of Jesus might be fulfilled, which he spake, signifying what death he should die, saying: Behold, by the hands of my friends shall I be betrayed, and by the wicked delivered unto judgment; and by the hand of a stranger, shall I be slain.

34 Then Pilate entered into the judgment hall again, and called Jesus, and said unto him: Art thou the King of the Jews?

35 Jesus answered him, saying: Sayest thou this thing of thyself, or did others tell it thee of me?

36 Pilate answered, saying: Am I a Jew? Thine own nation and the chief priests have delivered thee unto me. What hast thou done?

37 Jesus answered him, saying: My kingdom is not of this world, but is the kingdom of my Father. Behold, if my kingdom were of
this world, then would my servants fight with the sword, that I should not be delivered to the Jews; for this is how the kings of the earth defend their kingdoms. But now is my kingdom not from hence, but from heaven, which is where my Father dwelleth.

38 Pilate therefore said unto him, Art thou a king then? Jesus answered, saying: Thou sayest that I am a king because thou hast heard these things from the Jews. And thou sayest that thou art not a Jew, therefore, how can I be a king unto thee? But thou art my brother because of my Father, and it is He that hath made me a king.

39 But to this end was I born, and for this cause came I into the world, that I should bear witness unto the truth, which I have received from my Father. Every one that is of the Father heareth my voice and findeth truth.

40 Pilate saith unto him: What is truth? And when he had said this, he went out again unto the Jews, and saith unto them: I find in him no fault at all. But ye have a custom, that I should release unto you one at the Passover.

41 And this was the custom that the Romans allowed for the Jews, even that in remembrance of the Passover, which was that day in which all the firstborn among the children of Israel were saved by an angel of God, that they would release one unto them who had been convicted of a crime.

42 And this the Romans did to pacify the Jews and keep them under subjection to them. And the Jews were fulfilling the portend that was given at the Passover, even that the firstborn of the Father should be killed among them, and they knew it not.

43 And therefore, Pilate said unto them: Will ye therefore that I release unto you the King of the Jews? And this he said to mock Jesus and their customs and also to gain popularity among them.

44 Then cried they all again, saying, Not this man, but Barabbas. Now, Barabbas was a robber.

45 Then Pilate therefore took Jesus, and scourged him according to their customs. And the soldiers mocked Jesus for saying that he was the King of the Jews, and platted a crown of thorns, and put it on his head, and they put on him a purple robe, and said, Hail, King of the Jews! And they smote him exceedingly with their hands.

46 Pilate therefore went forth again, and saith unto them: Behold, I bring him forth to you, that ye may know that I find no fault in him. Then came Jesus forth, wearing the crown of thorns, and the purple robe.

47 And Pilate saith unto them: Behold the man who is your king. And when the chief priests and officers saw him, they cried out, saying: Crucify him, crucify him.

48 And Pilate was astounded at their anger and vengeance towards Jesus, and saith unto them: Take ye him, and crucify him according to your law, for I find no fault in him that he should die by the hand of a Roman.

49 The Jews answered him, saying: We have a law, and by our law he ought to die, because he made himself the Son of God. When Pilate therefore heard that saying, he was the more afraid because of the warning that he had received from his wife.

50 And he went again into the judgment hall,

and saith unto Jesus: Whence art thou? But Jesus gave him no answer, for Pilate had scourged him and mocked him in the answers that he had given him before.

51 Then saith Pilate unto him: Speakest thou not unto me? Knowest thou not that I have power to crucify thee, and have power to release thee?

52 Jesus answered him, saying: Thou couldst have no power at all against me, except it were given thee from above by my Father. Therefore, fear not for that which thou hast done and that which thou must do; for they that delivered me unto thee hath the greater sin.

53 For they have heard my words and have rejected them, but thou hast not heard my words, therefore, the law hath not been given unto thee. And if thou hast not heard the law, then the punishment that is affixed to the law cannot be required at thy hand.

54 But woe unto them that have heard the law and have rejected it. But thou art also my brother, therefore, I give the law of the Father unto thee, even that thou art commanded by the Father to love thy neighbor as thyself and do unto them what thou wouldst have them do to you. This is the law of the Father, and the law which these have rejected.

55 And Pilate answered Jesus, saying: If this is the law that thou teacheth, and it is the law of thy father, and it is thy father who hath made thee King over this people to give them this law, then surely it is they who have sinned.

56 And from thenceforth Pilate sought to release him because he believed in the word of Jesus. But the Jews cried out, saying: If thou let this man go, thou art not a friend of Caesar and thou art not loyal to the law of Caesar, for thou believest in another king and another law. And whosoever maketh himself a king speaketh against Caesar.

57 When Pilate therefore heard that saying, he brought Jesus forth, and sat down in the judgment seat in a place that is called the Pavement, but in the Hebrew, Gabbatha. And it was the preparation of the Passover, and about the sixth hour: and he saith unto the Jews: Behold your King.

58 Behold, this man doth not teach the law of Caesar, but he teacheth a law by which ye should abide and ye shall have peace among you. But they cried out, Away with him, away with him, crucify him.

59 And Pilate saith unto them: Shall I crucify your King who giveth a righteous law to you according to your customs and traditons? And the chief priests answered, saying: We have no king but Caesar.

60 And in this the Jews spoke the truth; for behold, their king was the same king who ruled over and directed Caesar, even Satan.

61 Then delivered Pilate him therefore unto them to be crucified. And they took Jesus, and led him away. And he, bearing his cross, went forth into a place called the place of a burial, which is called in the Hebrew, Golgotha, where they crucified him, and two others with him, on either side one, and Jesus in the midst.

62 And Pilate wrote a title, and put it on the cross. And the writing was JESUS OF NAZARETH THE KING OF THE JEWS. This title then read many of the Jews; for the place where Jesus was crucified was nigh to the city; and it was written in Hebrew, and Greek, and Latin according to the command of Pilate that all might understand his words, for Pilate truly believed on the Christ, even though he did not understand all things concerning him.

63 Then said the chief priests of the Jews to Pilate: Write not, The King of the Jews; but that he said, I am King of the Jews. Pilate answered them, saying: What I have written, I have written.

64 Then the soldiers, when they had crucified Jesus, took his garments, and made four parts, to every soldier a part; and also his coat they did want as a souvenir. Now, the coat was without seam, woven from the top throughout and could not be torn. They said therefore among themselves: Let us not rend it, but cast lots for it, whose it shall be.

65 And this came to pass that the scripture might be fulfilled, which saith: They parted my raiment among them, and for my vesture they did cast lots. These things, therefore, the soldiers did, not knowing of those things which were written concerning him.

66 Now, there stood by the cross of Jesus his mother, and the sister of his mother, Mary, who was the wife of Cleophath, and Mary Magdalene, one of his wives.

67 And when Jesus therefore saw his mother, and the disciple standing by, whom he loved, even John from whose account this record is taken, he saith unto his mother: Woman, behold thy son.

68 Then saith he to the disciple: Behold thy mother. Honor her as I would have honored her, that her days may be long before God. And from that hour John took her into his own home and cared for Mary, because she had left her husband Joseph and her other sons because of their wickedness.

69 After this, Jesus knowing that all things were now accomplished, that the scripture might be fulfilled, saith: I thirst. Now there was set a vessel full of vinegar: and they filled a sponge with vinegar, and put it upon a hyssop branch, and put it to his mouth.

70 When Jesus therefore had received the vinegar, he said: Now, it is finished, even that which I have been given to do by the Father. And I have given unto the world of the cup that the Father hath given unto them through me, even a cup of pure water that shall quench their thirst forever.

71 But I have received from them a cup of vile water from which I receive no relief from my thirst.

72 And when the centurion heard these words, he took his spear and pierced the side of Jesus that he might no more speak such things.

73 And in his agony, the Lord cried out in pain: My Father, why hast Thou forsaken me in the greatest hour of my need. And after he had bowed his head for a short time in prayer, he raised his head for the last time in the flesh and smiled upon his beloved wife, Mary, and said: It is done. Now go I unto the Father. And with these words came his last breath, and he bowed his head, and gave up the ghost.

74 And now, I, Moroni, have read the account of the brother of Jared concerning the death of the Lord and many of the other things that occurred concerning those things that led up to his death and those things that transpired at the time he gave up the flesh and entered again into the spirit world.

75 But of his death the Lord hath commanded me to write little. For he knoweth that those of the latter days worship him because of his death and not because of those things that he taught to the people.

76 And the Lord would that ye should understand that his death meaneth nothing, except that the world had rejected him and killed him for that which he taught.

77 But his words are that which the Lord would have his people remember of him. For in the death of Christ there is no life, but only death. But in his words, there is life eternal.

CHAPTER 60

Moroni continues with John's account of the resurrection of Christ and concludes the account of his life.

AND it came to pass that the Jews, therefore, because it was the days of preparation, wanted not that the bodies of Jesus and those who had been crucified with him; and there were two others who were not yet dead; and that their bodies should not remain upon the cross on the sabbath day, (for that sabbath day was an high day,) which was esteemed greatly among them because of their traditions concerning the Passover.

2 Therefore, they besought Pilate that their legs might be broken, and that they might be taken away before the sabbath.

3 Then came the soldiers, and brake the legs of the first, and of the other who was crucified with him. But when they came to Jesus, and saw that he was dead already, they brake not his legs, so that the scripture and prophecy concerning him might be fulfilled. For these things were done, that the scripture should be fulfilled, which said: A bone of him shall not be broken.

4 And again that a another scripture should be fulfilled, which saith: They shall look on him whom they pierced and marvel at the sight;

therefore, one of the soldiers with a spear pierced his side again in the same wound that had been given unto Jesus before, and forthwith came there out blood and water, even the last mortal blood and water of the Lord.

5 And John saw all these things and beareth record of all that is written herein; and his record is true according to that which he saw. And he testifieth that it is true that ye might believe in that which hath been written concerning the Christ.

6 And after these things, Joseph of Arimathaea, being a disciple of Jesus, but secretly for fear of the Jews, he being one who had been converted by the words of Nicodemus who spoke secretly of him, besought Pilate that he might take away the body of Jesus.

7 And he said unto Pilate: Your Most Noble Honor, I have herewith much money that I might purchase of thee the body of the man that was called Jesus.

8 And Pilate being distraught because of everything that the Jews had desired of him, answered him, saying: I know that this man was a righteous man, and my hands I have washed clean from the works of your people who desired his death. And now, thou comest to me and tempt me with blood money? I want no further cause with this thing. Go, do that which thou desirest with his body, but bring this thing no more to my attention. And with those words, Pilate gave him leave.

9 He came therefore, and took the body of Jesus to a place that he had purchased for his own tomb, he being a very rich man among the Jews.

10 And there came also Nicodemus, which at the first came to Jesus by night, and brought a mixture of myrrh and aloes, about an hundred pound weight. Then took they the body of Jesus, and wound it in linen clothes with the spices, as the manner of the Jews is to bury.

11 Now in the place where he was crucified there was a garden; and in the garden a new sepulchre, wherein was never man yet laid, and it was this sepulchre that Joseph had purchased for himself. There laid they straightaway Jesus therefore, because of the preparation day of the Jews; for the sepulchre was nigh at hand.

12 And they rolled a stone of much weight before the tomb that no one could come there and disturb the body of Jesus. And after the body of Jesus lay in the tomb for three days, on the first day of the week cometh Mary Magdalene early to be close to him whom she loved with all of her soul.

13 And she came when it was yet dark, unto the sepulchre, that the Jews and others might not know of the place where they had laid the body. And she seeth the stone taken away from the sepulchre.

14 Then she runneth, and cometh to Simon Peter, and to John, whom Jesus loved, and saith unto them: They have taken away the Lord out of the sepulchre, and we know not where they have laid him.

15 Peter therefore went forth, and John, and came to the sepulchre. So they ran both together; and John did outrun Peter, and came first to the sepulchre. And he stooping down, and looking in, saw the linen clothes lying; yet went he not in, for he wept exceedingly for that which he believed had been the desecration of the grave of his Lord and his best friend.

16 Then cometh Simon Peter following him, and went into the sepulchre, and seeth the linen clothes lie, and the napkin, that was about his head, not lying with the linen clothes, but wrapped together in a place by itself.

17 Then went in also John, who came first to the sepulchre, and he saw, and believed that the body had not been desecrated, but carried off by one who loved Jesus, for the linens were folded neatly within the tomb.

18 And now, I would that ye should understand a thing concerning John, the beloved of the Christ. For ye shall notice in the account that hath been given unto you in the Bible that John doth not give mention of his name many times. And this he hath done that he might not take glory unto his own name, as do many who have been called by the Lord, not wanting to take away the glory that is deserved of the Father and the Son.

19 But in this record, I have given you his name, with a counsel that ye give no glory unto John; for he would not that any glory be given unto him.

20 And of the resurrection of Christ, he wrote very little. And I write very little according to the commandment of the Lord, in which he hath commanded me to not write for the same reason that I write little of the account of his death.

21 Yea, that ye might turn your attention and your minds and your hearts more towards the words of Christ, which he hath given unto you, giving glory to the Father for all things.

22 And again, this is the way ye are commanded to pray unto the Father in the name of Christ for all things, even that ye shall give glory to the Father by doing the things that Jesus did in the flesh, and having the same desires that Jesus had, and having the same responsibilities one to another of which Jesus spoke—this is praying in the name of Jesus.

23 And it came to pass that Peter and John had not yet received the Holy Ghost that would testify unto them concerning that which had taken place; for as yet, they knew not the scripture was fulfilled, which said that he must rise again from the dead.

24 Then the disciples went away again unto their own homes. But Mary stood without the sepulchre weeping. And as she wept, she stooped down and looked once again into the sepulchre where they had buried her Lord. And when she looked in this time, she seeth two angels in white sitting, the one at the head, and the other at the feet, where the body of Jesus had lain.

25 And they say unto her, Woman, why weepest thou? And she saith unto them, not knowing that they were angels, but believing that they were men who had come with Peter and John: Because they have taken away my Lord, and I know not where they have laid him.

26 And when she had thus said, she turned herself back out of the tomb. And when she turned around she saw Jesus standing there, and knew not that it was him because of her exceeding mourning and tears.

27 And Jesus saith unto her: Woman, why weepest thou? Whom seekest thou?

28 She, supposing him to be the gardener, saith unto him: Sir, if thou have borne him hence, tell me where thou hast laid him, and I will take him away.

29 And Jesus saith unto her: Mary, My Beloved Wife, look now upon me. And she turned herself and recognized him from his words, and saith unto him, Baal; which is to say, Husband.

30 And she was wont in her joy to throw herself upon him, but Jesus saith unto her: Touch me not; for I am not yet ascended to my Father and cannot touch thee as my wife with the body that I now possess.

31 But go to my brethren, and say unto them, I ascend unto my Father, and your Father; and to my God, and your God. And He hath given me my eternal body, which is Celestial like unto His. And I am the first fruits of the resurrection of the Father.

32 Fear not, My Beloved, for as I have promised you, so shall we be together forever in the kingdom of our Father.

33 And Mary Magdalene came and told the disciples that she had seen the Lord, and that he had spoken these things unto her.

34 Then the same day at evening, being the first day of the week, when the doors were shut where the disciples were assembled for fear of the Jews, came Jesus and stood in the midst, and saith unto them: Peace be unto you.

35 And when he had so said, he shewed unto them his hands and his side and the marks of his death. And he commanded them that they should come forth and feel his flesh that they might know that it was he.

36 And when the disciples had all come forth and touched him, except for Mary, who did not touch him according to that which he had commanded her in the garden, then were the disciples glad, when they saw the Lord.

37 Then said Jesus to them again: Peace be unto you. As my Father hath sent me to the world to save it from its sins, even so send I you to be saviors of men.

38 And when he had said this, he looked at them and placed his hands on each and ordained them, saying: Receive ye the Holy Ghost by doing the works which these hands which are placed upon you have done. For ye have seen my works and know of the commandments that I have been given by the Father to give to all of His children throughout the whole earth.

39 And ye shall go forth into the world and do the things that ye have witnessed that I have done among you in the flesh. And ye shall teach the things that I have taught and show the way of salvation unto those who shall hear your words, which by your mouth, or by my own, it is the same.

40 And those who hear your words and repent and begin to do the will of the Father, shall have their sins remitted unto them; and those who will not hear your words and reject the words of the Father shall have their sins retained.

41 But remember always the words which I spake unto you in the flesh, even the final words that I did give unto you. Behold, ye shall be known as my disciples if ye love one another.

42 And this ye shall teach to all men, that they should love one another, and this is the only thing that ye shall teach unto them, having everything point to this great commandment of the Father.

43 And now, I leave you and go unto the Father. And the disciples of Christ begged of him that he would stay among them. And there were some women among them who were also ordained by the Lord, and bidden to keep these things to themselves because of the Jews, but that they, too, should do what he had commanded them.

44 But because of the Jews and their traditions, even the beliefs of the world, which esteem men above women, the Lord commanded their ordinations to be held in secret.

45 But he commanded all of his disciples that they should show unto the world of the example that he had set for them by their works.

46 But to the twelve he gave specific instructions concerning the Jews. And after he had given these instructions, a pillar of light shown above him and he left them and went unto the Father.

47 But Thomas, one of the twelve, called Didymus, was not with them when Jesus came. And when the other disciples therefore said unto him, We have seen the Lord, he did not believe them. But he said unto them: Except I shall see in his hands the print of the nails, and put my finger into the print of the nails, and thrust my hand into his side, I will not believe that which ye tell me. For ye are all distraught, as I am, and your minds have played upon you this trick.

48 And after eight days again his disciples were within, and Thomas with them speaking of all things which had occurred, even for the whole week spoke they of these things.

49 Then came Jesus again, the doors being shut, and stood in the midst, and said: Peace be unto you.

50 Then saith he to Thomas, smiling upon him: Reach hither thy finger, and behold my hands; and reach hither thy hand, and thrust it into my side; and be not faithless, but believing.

51 And Thomas answered and said unto him, My Lord and my God, and fell to his knees and wept for his lack of faith.

52 And Jesus saith unto him: Thomas, because thou hast seen me, thou hast believed. But more blessed are they who have not seen, and yet have believed. Because they believe because the Father hath testified unto them by the power of the Holy Ghost.

53 And many other signs truly did Jesus in the presence of his disciples, which are not written in this book. And the Lord commanded his disciples to write only those things that would turn the hearts of the people to his words, and not to the greatness of the miracles that were wrought before them.

54 But these are written, that ye might believe that Jesus is the Christ, the Son of God; and that by believing ye might have life through his name.

55 And it hath already been explained unto you in this record what the name of Christ representeth; yea, it representeth his works. And except ye do the works of Christ, ye shall not have eternal life.

56 And after these things, Jesus shewed himself again a third time to the disciples at the sea of Tiberias; and on this wise shewed he himself. And at that place there were together Simon Peter, and Thomas called Didymus, and Nathanael of Cana in Galilee, and the sons of Zebedee, and two other of his disciples.

57 And Simon Peter saith unto them, I go a fishing. They say unto him, We also go with thee. They went forth, and entered into a ship immediately; and that night they caught nothing.

58 But when the morning was now come, Jesus stood on the shore: but the disciples knew not that it was Jesus, because he was disguised among them that he might observe their actions without them knowing he was there among them.

59 Then Jesus saith unto them: Children, have ye any meat? They answered him, Nay. And he saith unto them: Cast the net on the right side of the ship, and ye shall find. They cast therefore, and now they were not able to draw it for the multitude of fishes.

60 Therefore that disciple whom Jesus loved, who is John, saith unto Peter: It is the Lord.

61 Now when Simon Peter heard that it was the Lord, he girt his coat unto him, for he was naked, and did cast himself into the sea.

62 And the Lord laughed and smiled at that which Peter had done because he was naked. And the apostles saw the Lord, and laughed with him because of this thing.

63 And the other disciples came in a little ship; for they were not far from land, but as it were, two hundred cubits, dragging the net with fishes. As soon then as they were come to land, they saw a fire of coals there, and fish laid thereon, and bread, which Jesus had prepared for them.

64 And Jesus saith unto them: Bring of the fish which ye have now caught. And Simon Peter went up, and drew the net to land full of great fishes, an hundred and fifty and three; and for all there were so many, yet was not the net broken.

65 And Jesus saith unto them: Come and dine with me. And none of the disciples durst ask him, Who art thou? knowing that it was the Lord.

66 Jesus then cometh, and taketh bread, and giveth them, and fish likewise. Now, this was the third time that Jesus shewed himself to his disciples, after he had risen from the dead. And he showed himself thrice that all things of which the truth shall be established, shall be established by three witnesses.

67 So when they had dined and laughed with the Lord because of Peter, Jesus saith to Simon Peter: Simon, son of Jonas, lovest thou me more than these other of my disciples?

68 And Jesus said this thing because Peter had continually said amongst them that he loved the Lord more than any of them. And Peter saith unto him: Yea, Lord; thou knowest that I love thee.

69 And Jesus saith unto him: Feed my lambs. But Peter understood not that which the Lord had told him. And the Lord saith to him again the second time: Simon, son of Jonas, lovest thou me? And Peter answered again and saith unto him: Yea, Lord; thou knowest that I love thee.

70 And again Jesus saith unto him: Feed my sheep. And again the third time he saith unto Peter: Simon, son of Jonas, lovest thou me? And this the Lord did because thrice he was denied by Peter; but the purpose of the Lord was not known unto Peter; but the Lord smiled upon him because he knew for what purpose he asked thrice of Peter these things.

71 And Peter was grieved because he said unto him the third time, Lovest thou me? And he said unto him: Lord, thou knowest all things, therefore, thou knowest that I love thee. And then for the last time Jesus saith unto him: If thou lovest me, then feed my sheep.

72 For behold, many will say that they love me, and many will betray me as thou betrayed me thrice before my death. And they shall betray me because of the world; for they fear the world, that they might not receive from the world that which they need to make them happy.

73 But thou knowest the things that bring true happiness and which shall also bring eternal life. It is this food that my sheep desire. Therefore, have I said unto thee that if thou lovest me, then feed my sheep.

74 For my words are meat indeed unto all those who shall receive them. And if they eat of my flesh, which I have given them, then shall they never hunger again.

75 Fear not, therefore, the world, for the world cannot give unto you of this meat. For ye fished all day and could not find a fish to eat. But I have given unto you more fish than ye are able to eat; and even of them which ye caught with your one net by my command, I have not given unto you to eat, but had already prepared for you that which ye should eat with me.

76 And this I did that it might be in similitude

of that which ye shall now do for me, if thou truly lovest me. And I know that thou lovest me, but the other apostles also love me, and therefore, I would that ye all go into the world and give unto my sheep the food that they need that they might have eternal life.

77 And Peter, Verily, Verily, I say unto thee, When thou wast young, thou girdest thyself, and walkedst whither thou wouldst according to the desires of thine uncircumcised heart. But when thou shalt be old, thou shalt stretch forth thy hands, and another shall gird thee, and carry thee whither thou wouldst not.

78 For behold, when ye have received the testimony of the Spirit, it shall lead thee to do that which I now command of thee, and I shall gird thee and carry thee where thou wouldst not go except it be commanded of thee by the Spirit.

79 And the Spirit shall lead thee to do all things which thou hast observed that I have done, yea even unto death. And this spake he, signifying by what death Peter should glorify God.

80 And when he had spoken this, he saith unto him: Follow me as thou hast said of thy love.

81 Then Peter, turning about, seeth the disciple whom Jesus loved following; which also leaned on his breast at supper, and who had said, Lord, which is he that betrayeth thee?

82 Peter seeing him, and knowing that the Lord loved him greatly, saith unto Jesus: Lord, and what shall this man do? Shall he be commanded of thee to follow me and do that which thou hast commanded of me? And this Peter said having been made the chief apostle among them by the Lord.

83 And Jesus answered him, saying unto him: If I will that he tarry till I come, what is that to thee? Follow thou me as I have commanded thee, and he shall also follow me as I have commanded of him.

84 Then went this saying abroad among the brethren, that that disciple should not die; yet Jesus said not unto him that he shall not die; but, If I will that he tarry till I come, what is that to thee?

85 Behold, this is the disciple who testifieth of these things; and who wrote these things; and we know that his testimony is true, because he was alive to see that which hath been written by other men and attributed to him.

86 And that which I have written herein, hath been approved by him. And by him hath it been received.

87 And there are also many other things which Jesus did, the which, if they should be written every one, I suppose that even the world itself could not contain the books that should be written. Amen.

CHAPTER 61

Moroni recounts in brevity the desire of the apostles to form a church of God. A reiteration is made that a church is not needed to learn the things of God. The world rejects the prophets of God because of the works of men.

AND now, it is expedient, according to the commandment of the Lord concerning this record, that I give unto you a brief accounting of the works of the apostles who were sent forth by Christ to deliver his message to the world.

2 After these had received the Holy Ghost, who testified to them of the true mission of the Christ, they organized themselves into a group of disciples whose only purpose was to teach the people the things which the Lord had taught unto them.

3 And Peter was he who the Lord had chosen to administer in the line of authority that had been established, so that the apostles could work in order, one with another according to their traditions.

4 And previously in this record I have explained unto you the true purpose and meaning of the priesthood of God. And because it is the manner of men that this priesthood is frequently misused to benefit the agendas of those who claim this Priesthood; and these are the priestcrafts that are set up upon the earth among the children of men, so that the priests and leaders can get gain and power over the people; and because the Lord understood these things, he commanded his disciples that they should not use the authority that he gave to them, except to preach his gospel to the people.

5 And his gospel is nothing more or less than the words that he taught the people and the example that he set for them by his works. And by example he instructed Peter, James and John, who were the presidency of this first priesthood, to give unto others the authority to preach the gospel in the same manner that they had received their authority from him.

6 And this authority was given by the laying on of hands. Now, this priesthood ordinance of the laying on of hands was performed in similitude of the purpose for which this authority was given to another. For with our hands we do the works that we do.

7 And when a man putteth his hands upon the head of another in the manner that the Lord hath subscribed to authorize his disciples to preach his gospel, then the man who is administering the ordinance is symbolically passing on, through his hands, the works that he expecteth the person who is receiving the authority to do; in other words; to do the works that he hath done.

8 Now for this purpose, Christ put his hands upon the heads of his disciples, and not just upon the twelve did he place his hands and give unto them the priesthood, or in other words, the authority to do his works, but he placed his hands upon all of those who were desirous to do his will and preach his gospel, and show an example of him to others.

9 Yea, there were many women who also received this authority from the Lord. Yet, the women were commanded to keep their ordination from the Jews, so that they would not receive any more persecution than that which they would already receive, having accepted Jesus as the Christ who would save them.

10 And the ordination of women was an abomination to the Jews, who strictly observed the law of Moses as they had been taught by their customs and their traditions.

11 But the Lord taught his disciples that there was no difference to the Father between the authority of a man to act in the name of God, and the authority of a woman to act in the name of God; both genders being equal before Him.

12 Yea, the Lord taught his disciples that all of those who were willing to take upon them the name of Christ, and covenant to obey the words of Christ, and do what he hath done, then all these would belong to an Order of individuals who followed him in all things.

13 Yea, he taught them that this would be a Holy Priesthood called after the Order of the Son of God, which included all the men and women who were ordained unto this Holy Order because of their desire to serve God and keep His commandments, which were given through His Son, Jesus Christ.

14 Therefore, anyone, whether a man or a woman, could belong to this Holy Order by following Christ. And if this man or this woman followed Christ in all things, then he or she belongeth to this Holy Order and hath this Holy Priesthood conferred upon him or her.

15 And this thing was taught to the disciples of Jesus while he was yet with them in his ministry. And during his ministry, his disciples began to have some contention amongst them because of this doctrine which the Lord taught unto them, which was hard for them to accept because of the traditions concerning the priesthood of God to which they were accustomed.

16 And they were also accustomed that there should be one appointed among them who is always greater than the others, who was the leader of all.

17 And I have already explained unto you the desires of the Lord concerning these things; but again I will show unto you the teachings of the Lord, according to the record of the Bible that ye have before you, so that ye might not be contentious concerning these things.

18 And it came to pass that there was a time when the disciples were arguing amongst themselves as to who should be the greatest among them.

19 And when the Lord had entered into the house where they were arguing amongst themselves, the disciples became quiet and durst not say anything of their disputations to the Lord. But the Lord perceived their thoughts and knew straightaway the reason for their silence and their disputations.

20 And it is written in that record, saying: And he came to Capernaum; and being in the

house he asked of them: What was it that ye have been disputing among yourselves?

21 But they held their peace; for they were embarrassed that they had disputed amongst themselves, who should be the greatest of them.

22 And he sat down, and called the twelve unto to him, and said unto them: If any man desire to be the first, the same shall be the last of all, and the servant of all.

23 And he took a child, and set him in the midst of them and smiled upon the child and played with him for a time.

24 And when he had taken the child in his arms, he said unto them: Whosoever shall humble himself like one of these children, and receiveth me, ye shall also receive in my name. And whosoever shall receive me, receiveth not me only, but Him who sent me, even the Father.

25 And then the disciples knew of what the Lord spoke. For they knew that they had been called and ordained by the Lord to teach his gospel to all those who would receive them.

26 But because of the ordination that they had received of the Lord, even that he had called them, and placed his hands upon them, and ordained them to the office of an apostle, they were prideful and thought themselves above the other disciples who followed Jesus.

27 And it came to pass that on one occasion the apostles observed a woman healing others and casting out devils in the name of Jesus. And she was not ordained by the Lord to do such things as the apostles had supposed, not understanding these things.

28 And John said unto the Lord: Master, we saw one casting out devils in thy name, and she followeth not us, for thou hast not given this authority unto a woman. And we went to her and forbade her from doing that which she did, because she did not have the authority to do these things.

29 But Jesus, being perplexed by the lack of understanding of his apostles, answered John, saying: Forbid her not. For there is no man or woman who shall do a miracle in my name, that can lightly speak evil of me; because this power is given unto any of the children of God according to their faith in Him and their obedience to His commandments.

30 And now, I, Moroni, would that ye should observe this thing that those who canonized the New Testament of the Bible have changed and edited, even so that it might not be known that the Lord condoned and authorized women to be ordained in the Priesthood and have the power of God like unto any man.

31 And the Lord continued his instructions, saying: For he that is not against us is on our part and doing the will of the Father. For whosoever shall give unto another a cup of water to drink in my name, because he belongeth to Christ; and he giveth this cup of water, because of me, unto him who is thirsty, verily I say unto you, he shall not lose his reward in that which he hath done.

32 And whosoever shall offend one of these little ones that believeth in me, it is better for him that a millstone were hanged about his neck, and he were cast into the sea.

33 And ye have been called by my hand as my apostles to serve others by teaching them the things that I have taught unto you. And if there be any among you, either a man or a woman, who so desires to preach me unto the world, then ye shall not forbid them in this thing.

34 And it mattereth not to the Father whether it be a man or a woman who giveth unto others the gospel of His Son, only that they do so worthily and not in vain; in other words, that they live by His commandments, as an example of what they teach, and not as the hypocrites.

35 And if there are those among you who live by my gospel, then these same shall belong to my Holy Order and serve me as I serve the Father.

36 And there are those among you who offend the Spirit and do not those things which the Father hath commanded of them; these shall not abide in this Holy Order and shall be cast out that they might not corrupt the order of the kingdom of God.

37 Verily I say unto you, therefore, if thy hand offend thee, cut it off; or if thy brother offend thee and confess not and forsake not that in which he hath offended the Spirit of God, he shall be cut off. For it is better for thee to enter into life maimed, than having two hands, to go into hell.

38 For it is better for thee to enter into life without thy brother, than for thee and thy brother to be cast into hell; into the fire that never shall be quenched, where their worm dieth not, and the fire is not quenched.

39 For the works of thy hands shall be according to the Spirit of God, if it so be that ye belong to my Order. And it is better that I have only one to do my work, than for another that offendeth the Spirit to work in my name and corrupt the whole work.

40 And again, if thy foot offend thee, cut it off; for he that is thy standard, by whom thou walkest, if he become a transgressor, he shall be cut off. For it is better for thee, to enter halt into life, than having two feet to be cast into hell; into the fire that never shall be quenched.

41 Therefore, let every man stand or fall, by himself, and not for another; or not trusting another.

42 Seek unto my Father, and it shall be done in that very moment what ye shall ask, if ye ask in faith, believing that ye shall receive.

43 For ye have seen of the Jews that those who are their leaders, who lead them and are their standard, do mislead them and cause them to sin before the Father and disobey His commandments. And it is better that a man have no leader, than be led into the same hell with his leader whom he hath made his standard.

44 And if thine eye which seeth for thee, even him that is appointed to watch over thee to show thee light, becometh a transgressor and offend thee, pluck him out. For it is better for thee to enter into the kingdom of God, with one eye, than having two eyes to be cast into hell fire.

45 For it is better that thyself should be saved, than to be cast into hell with thy brother, where their worm dieth not, and where the fire is not quenched.

46 Now, these words the Lord spoke to his disciples concerning all those who had the desire to preach his gospel to the world. And there were many among them who were desirous that they might set up a church among them as a standard to which the people could see and follow.

47 And the Lord hath suffered that his servants set up churches among them for their sakes. And if it were that the children of men could always have the Spirit of God with them, then they would not need a church, or leaders, or prophets to give unto them the word of God.

48 For the Spirit of God giveth unto the children of God all of His words. But I have already explained these things in this record, and it sufficeth me to say that the Lord alloweth churches to be established among men that they might facilitate the hearing of his gospel.

49 Nevertheless, this is something that he suffereth, and is not his will, nor is it the will of the Father, but it is the desire of the children of men, who in and of themselves, do not recognize the voice of the Father as it is given unto them through the Spirit.

50 And even so, the twelve apostles organized a church among them and instituted certain ordinances for all those who were desirous to join the church, so that the people might be able to receive the words of the Father, which are given unto the world by His Son, Jesus Christ, in some form that they would more readily receive according to their traditions.

51 But ye shall see that because of these established religions, many of the plain and precious words of Christ have been changed and kept back from the children of men because of the wickedness of the leaders of the churches which the people have chosen for themselves as their standards.

52 And if the children of men would keep the commandments of God, then they would have the Spirit of God within them to guide them in all things.

53 And if the Spirit of God is within them to guide them in all things, then they would not be susceptible to the corrupt teachings and the doctrines of men that lead them away from the Father.

54 And in all generations of the children of men, the Lord hath suffered that churches be established among the people according to their desires. And in all these generations, yea, even in every one, the church of God hath become corrupted and beginneth to teach the people the doctrine and commandments of men, laying aside the true gospel of Christ which could save them.

55 For it is the nature of men that they seek for glory and honor among themselves. Therefore, when there is one who hath been set up as a leader of the people, or as the standard of truth to whom the people look for guidance, this man or woman, beginneth to exercise unrighteous dominion and teacheth the people that they should look to him or her for the word of God, and not to the Father who would freely give His word unto any of His children who would ask of Him.

56 And it came to pass that the apostles established churches throughout the land. And many people came to them and heard the words of Christ, which words were soothing to the souls of those who were poor, both as to the Spirit and as to the things of the world.

57 And those of the lower classes rejoiced in the words that they heard of Christ. For they were taught that they were equal in the eyes of God, and that God loved them and had prepared a place in His kingdom for all of them, regardless of their class, their knowledge, or the color of their skin.

58 And there began to be great success in the church among the people of the poorer classes. But among the rich, there was very little success.

59 For the apostles preached consistently against riches and the fine things of the world as they had heard from Jesus. And they commanded that any who would join the church should give of all that they had, so that it might benefit all.

60 But the rich would not give up their riches, for they were great. And the poor gave all that they had, for they had very little to give. And there were some who were poor who joined the church of God only to receive that which they did not have.

61 But these were soon discovered by the others in the church, who had joined the church because of what they could give, and not because of what they might receive. And if these wicked poor did not repent of that which they desired, then they were cast out of the church because they did not truly have the testimony of Christ.

62 But those who were the happiest and most righteous members of the church of God, were those who cared not for the things of the world, and who feasted upon the words of Christ and followed his example and did unto others what they would have done unto themselves.

63 And because of these righteous few, the church began to prosper, and many people came to the church and were baptized and received the gift of the Holy Ghost by the laying on of hands, it being given in similitude of doing the works of those who represented the Lord, and who administered the confirmation of the Holy Ghost unto them.

64 And now, it is expedient that ye understand that no man or woman, even those who have been given the authority of the Holy Order of the Son of God, or the Priesthood of God, hath the ability or the right to give unto another the gift of the Holy Ghost.

65 And this is not the purpose for which the Lord suffered that this ordinance be given to the church. For every ordinance that is given to the people by the church, is given in similitude of some part of the gospel of Christ, or the plan of salvation of the Father.

66 Yea, when a man presenteth himself to the leaders of the church of God that he might be baptized by immersion, thus following the example given to him by Christ, then this man hath already accepted the words of Christ, and hath repented of his sins, and hath come to make a covenant before God, in the presence of others, that he is willing to take upon him the name of Christ and do all things that are commanded of him by the words of Christ.

67 And when this man cometh forth from the waters of baptism, then he hath fulfilled the part of the plan of the Father that is necessary for him to fulfill in order for him to be worthy to receive the guidance and inspiration from the Holy Ghost.

68 And for this reason it is confirmed upon him, that he might have this privilege, or this gift, as long as this man obeyeth the words of Christ and his commandments in all things.

69 And if the man offendeth the Spirit, even by his actions, in not obeying the commandments of Christ in all things, then the Spirit withdraweth from him, and he is left to himself, where Satan can have much more power over him.

70 And though the Holy Ghost is confirmed upon this man, it is not sealed unto him, and therefore, is not promised to him, only upon his ability to abide by the laws that allow this gift of the Father.

71 And I have already explained in an earlier part of this record the difference between that which is confirmed and that which is sealed upon us.

72 Behold, that which is confirmed unto us, is guaranteed by the Father conditionally; yea, its realization being based upon our ability to obey the laws that determine our worthiness to receive it.

73 For this reason, in the Holy Endowment that is given unto the children of men to turn them towards the plan of the Father; yea, in this endowment our anointing to become Kings and Queens, Priests and Priestesses to the Most High God, is confirmed unto us and is not sealed.

74 For if it were sealed unto us, then it would be a promise that the Father hath made to us unconditionally, and to which He is bound forever.

75 And the confirmation of this anointing dependeth upon our worthiness to perform those things that are necessary in order to secure the anointing and have it sealed unto us.

76 And this is also the reason why we are symbolically washed and have the holy garments placed upon our bodies; which is sealed unto us. For these things represent our spiritual creation, which we have all received freely and unconditionally from the Father, and which can never be taken from us, forever; it being a promise that was sealed unto us by the Father from the beginning.

77 And it is necessary that I explain these things unto you who shall receive these things in the latter days. For in those days there shall be many churches set up among you with many leaders claiming to have the authority of God to teach the word of God.

78 And these shall have their priesthoods and their doctrines and their ordinances; and many shall claim that they have the Priesthood of God; and they shall lay their hands upon each other, giving authority to another to do the work of God, in the priesthood of God, according to the lines of authority of their churches.

79 And they shall claim that they have the power to give unto a man the gift of the Holy Ghost by the power of their words.

80 But they shall not give unto any the gift of the Holy Ghost as it hath been explained unto you, but they shall be passing to those upon whom they lay their hands, the authority to do the works that they do, which is the reason why the Lord placed his hands upon the apostles in the first place; but those in the latter days shall be giving authority to others to perform the works that they do, which are the works of Satan, and not the works of God.

81 And by the power of Satan, many shall be deceived, thinking that they are receiving the power of the Priesthood after the Holy Order of the Son of God, but in reality they are receiving the power of Satan, because they are doing the works of Satan and not the works of God.

82 And now, let me once again speak in plainness, so that none of you who receive these things shall have any more excuse why ye should not understand these things:

83 Behold, any man or woman who doeth the works of Christ, belongeth to the Holy Order of the Son of God. And if a man or a woman belongeth to this Holy Order, then he or she hath the power of His Priesthood, and can do anything that any prophet can do; yea, he or she can do anything that the Lord himself can do by the power of the Father.

84 And ye need not believe that it is necessary that another man lay his hands upon your head to give unto you this power. For this power is not given by men, but is given by the Father through the ministrations of the spirit world where the Holy Ghost resideth in the authority of the Father.

85 And those of you who cannot receive this power of the Father, even those of you who do not belong to the Holy Order of His son, can go to whatever man or woman; yea, to any church or religion of your choosing and receive from them their laying on of hands and their gifts of the Holy Ghost.

86 And ye shall indeed receive the power and authority and blessing that these have, which is their own power, and their own authority, and their own blessing, given unto them by Satan,

who would have all of us believe that we can have the power of the Father without going to the Father and getting it directly from Him.

87 And now, my brothers and sisters, I would that ye should know that the Lord hath already shown unto us the way that we might judge those who profess to have his authority and who profess to belong to his Holy Order; for ye shall judge them by their works alone.

88 Do not be deceived by their words, for their words are intended for your itching ears, and they will tell you all things which ye want to hear from them, so that ye will listen to them and support them and give them money that they might maintain power and their authority over you.

89 Judge them by their works. Behold, do they live like Christ? Yea, do they follow his example in all things? Do they teach unto you anything that is not the words of Christ? I say unto you, by this ye shall know them.

90 Behold, a true prophet and apostle of Christ will follow the example of Christ in all things and live his life as Christ lived. He will point you towards the words of Christ and will not take any money from you to point you to this standard that the Father hath given unto all of us freely, without charge.

91 And he shall not put himself above you, but will humbly serve you and abase himself that ye may be exalted. Behold, he shall not enjoy the uppermost rooms at the feasts and the chief seats in your churches and your synagogues.

92 Neither will he enjoy the greetings of Rabbi, Rabbi, or Prophet, Prophet, or Apostle, Apostle, or Elder, Elder, or any other name that would distinguish him above another.

93 And in the day of the Lord, he shall say unto all of these, even that which he said unto them in his own day, saying unto them: But woe unto you, scribes and Pharisees, hypocrites; for ye shut up the kingdom of heaven against men because of the things that ye have taught unto them, which are your commandments and not the commandments of God.

94 And because of the things which ye do teach, ye neither go into the kingdom of heaven yourselves, neither suffer ye them that come to you that they might enter therein, to go in, but ye have shut the doors against any who listen to you and believe in your precepts.

95 Woe unto you, scribes and Pharisees, hypocrites; for ye devour the houses of widows by requiring a tithe from them who do not have that which to pay you. But ye have convinced the widows and the poor, even all those who have not the money even to pay for their own houses, that they must pay a tithe unto you in order to be saved in the kingdom of God.

96 And ye require this sacrifice of them that they might receive the pretended ordinances of salvation that ye present to them as the saving ordinances of God.

97 And for a pretense ye make long prayer, causing them that follow you to believe that the Spirit of God is within you. But the Spirit of God is not within you, nor is it in the words that ye give unto them.

98 And if they follow your words and your examples, they shall be damned. But ye have led them into this damnation, therefore ye shall receive the greater damnation.

99 Woe unto you, scribes and Pharisees, hypocrites; for ye send out missionaries who compass sea and land to make one proselyte, and when he is made, ye make him twofold more the child of hell than yourselves because of those things which ye preach unto him, which are your teachings and not the true teachings of the Father.

100 Woe unto you, ye blind guides, who say, Whosoever shall swear by the temple, it is nothing; but whosoever shall swear by the gold of the temple, he is a debtor. For ye have made them that follow you believe that unless they can pay a tithe to you, they cannot enter into the temple and be saved. But if they pay a tithe to you, then ye take no thought of the wickedness of their disobedience of the laws which are taught to them within the walls of the temple.

101 Ye fools who are the blind leading the blind; for which is greater, the gold, or the temple that sanctifieth the gold? And ye teach, saying: Whosoever shall swear by the altar, it is nothing; but whosoever sweareth by the gift that is upon it, he is guilty.

102 Ye fools who lead the blind; for which is greater, the gift, or the altar that sanctifieth the

gift? Whoso therefore shall swear by the altar, sweareth by it, and by all things thereon. And whoso shall swear by the temple, sweareth by it, and by him that dwelleth therein. And he that shall swear by heaven, sweareth by the throne of God, and by him that sitteth thereon.

103 Woe unto you, scribes and Pharisees, hypocrites; for ye require a payment of tithe of mint and anise and cummin, and have omitted the weightier matters of the law, which are judgment, mercy, and faith, even those things of God which the temple supposeth to teach; these ought ye to have done, and not to leave the other undone.

104 Ye blind guides, which strain at a gnat, and swallow a camel. For ye preach the words of the Father unto the people and command them that they should obey these words. Yet they do not understand the words of the Father because they look to you as their example.

105 And do ye keep the words of the Father? I say unto you that ye do not keep the words of the Father, but ye strain to give unto the people those things that have nothing to do with righteousness, but cause them to sin against the whole law.

106 Woe unto you, scribes and Pharisees, hypocrites; for ye make clean the outside of the cup and of the platter, but within they are full of extortion and excess. And ye are the cup and the platter that ye present unto the people that they might drink and eat thereof.

107 And when they eat of that which ye offer unto them, they are cast out of the kingdom of the Father, because they do not know that which the Father doth require of them.

108 And your positions of authority cause you to put yourselves above those whom ye lead, even that you extort from them of their offerings to God that ye yourselves might live in excess, while those whom ye lead live in poverty. Thou blind Pharisee, cleanse first that which is within the cup and platter, that the outside of them may be clean also, that the people might eat thereon and live.

109 Woe unto you, scribes and Pharisees, hypocrites; for ye are like unto white painted sepulchres, which indeed appear beautiful outward, but are within full of the bones of dead men, and of all uncleanness. Even so, ye also outwardly appear righteous unto men, but within ye are full of hypocrisy and iniquity.

110 Woe unto you, scribes and Pharisees, hypocrites; because ye build the tombs of the prophets, and garnish the sepulchres of the righteous, and teach the people to hate the true word of God as it is given by these, even that the people begin to hate them and want to kill them and cast them from among them according to your words.

111 And then ye say, If we had been in the days of our fathers, we would not have been partakers with them in the blood of the prophets. Therefore by this saying, ye be witnesses unto yourselves, that ye are the children of them who killed the prophets. Fill ye up then, the measure of your fathers, for they also thought as they killed the prophets that they were not killing a righteous man of God.

112 Ye serpents, ye generation of vipers, how can ye expect to escape the damnation of hell? Yea, to help this people escape the damnation of hell, behold, I send unto you prophets, and wise men, and scribes, who are true revelators, who write the true word of God as they receive it from the Spirit of the Father.

113 And some of them ye shall kill and crucify; and some of them shall ye scourge in your synagogues, and persecute them from city to city until ye have cast them out from among you, or killed them. That upon you may come all the righteous blood shed upon the earth, from the blood of righteous Abel unto the blood of Zacharias son of Barachias, whom ye slew between the temple and the altar.

114 Verily I say unto you, All these things shall come upon this generation and upon all generations who cast out the prophets of God from among them.

115 Oh, Jerusalem, Jerusalem, thou that killest the prophets, and stonest them which are sent unto thee, how often would I have gathered thy children together, even as a hen gathereth her chickens under her wings, and ye would not.

116 Behold, your house is left unto you desolate. For I say unto you, Ye shall not see me henceforth, till ye shall say, Blessed is he that cometh in the name of the Lord.

117 And now, I, Moroni, testify that these

same things can be said of the religious leaders of the people of the latter days. And ye have been commanded to liken these things to the present day in which ye live. Therefore, liken them unto you, and ye shall come to know the gravity of the situation in which ye find yourselves, even those of you unto whom these things shall be revealed in the latter days.

118 And except ye repent, ye shall also be destroyed as were the Jews at Jerusalem. Perhaps ye shall also say, as did they of old, We shall not kill the prophets of God or cast them out from among us.

119 Yet I have already seen your day, and have witnessed that which ye have done to the first of these prophets who shall bring these things forth unto you. And ye rejected his message and cast him from among you and have killed him.

120 Yea, even the strength of your government, which was set up that ye might receive these things in freedom, did not save him from being murdered by you.

121 And this last, who shall give unto you these things which are sealed, ye shall say in your hearts, We have no desire to kill this prophet. But your leaders shall desire to kill him, and with their secret combinations they shall make an attempt to cast him from among them and kill him.

122 But the things which he would say unto you are those things which have been revealed unto you in this record. Therefore, if ye take his life, ye have sealed his work with his blood, as hath been done upon the earth since the beginning by all those who follow Satan.

123 But the Lord shall be with him, and he shall do all that which the Lord hath commanded him to do that he might give unto you this final testimony of the words of Christ, that ye might prepare yourselves for the coming of the Lord in the glory of the Father.

124 And those of you who receive these things shall seek to protect him from those who would kill him, even from the Pharisees and scribes of your day who are the hypocrites.

125 And this last prophet shall give unto you these things which shall be a means whereby ye might receive the words of the Father, by the Spirit of the Father, and not by the arm of the flesh, in which ye are accustomed to hearing that which ye believe is the word of God.

CHAPTER 62

The state of the spirit before birth and after death is further explained as well as the resurrection of the dead.

AND I have given unto you many things pertaining to the words of Christ, which were given unto him by the Father to prepare us to live in His kingdoms. And I have spoken in plainness unto you.

2 And the Lord hath commanded me to give unto you a further explanation of that which occureth immediately after our death, or the separation of our spirit from our body of flesh and bone.

3 But in order that ye might understand these things in their fullness, it is necessary that I speak somewhat of the state of the spirit after it hath been placed in this world by the Father.

4 For behold, all of our spirits were created on the world in which our Father and our Eternal Mothers reside. And when we have reached an age of maturity that is becoming of a spirit who is ready to enter into the second estate, or the state of our probation as it hath been explained unto you; yea, when we are ready for this second estate, the Father placed our spirits in this world in the part of His kingdom that He hath assigned to us.

5 And when He placed our spirits in this world, he caused that none of us could leave the boundaries that He hath set for the laws of nature that govern this world.

6 And even though our spirits are not subjected to the same laws of nature to which our mortal bodies are subjected, they are still subjected to the eternal laws of heaven to which all of these natural laws are subject.

7 Therefore, the elements that make up our spirits are confined to this earth and the atmosphere and gravity that keepeth all things upon this earth.

8 And in the latter days, many of these laws shall be made known unto you. And these laws have been known by all of the prophets of God since the world was created; nevertheless, they were commanded not to reveal these laws in their entirety to the people until the own due time of the Lord came in which he would allow these laws to be known among them.

9 And ye of the latter days shall witness that which occureth when the children of men begin to understand these laws. For they shall take these laws and begin to destroy the earth from which our bodies of flesh and bone are created.

10 But our bodies of spirit are made of elements that are not subjected to the same laws as our bodies of flesh and bone, as I have previously explained it unto you; and therefore, these bodies cannot be affected or destroyed like unto the elements of the earth, which are subjected to the lower laws of nature.

11 Yet, in a spiritual state, we are all consciously aware of all things that transpire in the mortal state. But those of a mortal state, are not aware of that which transpireth in a spiritual state. Therefore, in a spiritual state, or in the spirit world, we can observe and learn all things that all mortals can observe and learn during the days of their probation.

12 And we have the power to take upon ourselves flesh according to that which we need in order to teach us the things that we must learn in order to prepare ourselves for the kingdom of the Father.

13 And for this reason we are given the agency to chose for ourselves which gender we desire to be during the days of our probation.

14 Behold, we are also aware in the spirit of that which passes during the days of mortality, and therefore, we are in a better position to choose for ourselves in what mortal situation we are desirous to be born.

15 And if we are weak as a spirit, and know not in which situation that we should place ourselves, that we might better prepare ourselves to live in the eternal kingdoms of the Father, then there are those spirits in the spirit world who counsel with us and help us determine what is the best for us.

16 Now, all these things are according to the independent state in which the Father hath created all of us. For He created our spirits and gave us our free agency to act according to our own desires.

17 And He doth not force us to come into mortality and be rich or poor, bond or free, male or female, black or white, but hath given us the freedom to choose for ourselves the thing that we desire for each of us according to our individual desires of happiness.

18 Behold, the only concern of the Father is that we learn to love each other, and accept each other, and live with each other in peace and harmony, so that we will not disrupt His kingdom when we are finally put there forever by Him.

19 And now, this judgment of whether or not we are ready to enter into the kingdom of God is not given unto us to know, and is not something that we can determine for ourselves. Behold, this judgment can only be made by the Father and those whom He hath chosen to make this judgment for us.

20 For no man can say of himself, I am ready to live forever in the kingdom of God with an exalted body that will never die. For if we could determine this thing for ourselves, then many of us would deceive ourselves and take upon us a resurrected body that we could use to disrupt the kingdom and order of God.

21 And even though the Father doth not command us on how we must work out our own salvation, He doth, however, reserve the right and the power to determine whether or not we are ready to live in His kingdoms forever.

22 And this is what is meant by being judged by God and brought to stand before the judgment bar of Christ to be judged according to our works.

23 And we all know those things which are required of us by the Father in order that we might be resurrected into an eternal body that will never die, even a body that is perfected in every way; yea, a body that we are comfortable with according to our desires of happiness.

24 Nevertheless, only those spirits who are Celestial spirits shall have a body of a male or a female; yea, all those of the other kingdoms will have no choice of their gender, for there will be no gender among them.

25 Yea, we shall know when we are ready to present ourselves before the Father and say unto Him: Father, I have done all that which Thou requirest of me to enter into Thy presence, and am ready to accept that degree of glory that

Thou hast created for me, that I might find happiness therein forever.

26 But until the time that we can say these things in honesty, we shall be tried and tested and proven to see if we are truly ready to present ourselves to the Father and say these things.

27 And the days of our probation, or mortality, are the days in which we must prove to ourselves, and to our Father, that we are ready for His kingdom.

28 And we have the free agency to take upon us the type of body, male or female, which we feel will help us to prepare ourselves for the judgment bar of Christ.

29 And there are many spirits who have been upon the earth many times in order that they might prepare themselves more fully.

30 For those who are wicked cannot go to the Father and say unto Him: Father, I know that I was wicked during the days of my probation, and did not those things which Thou hast commanded of me; but as a spirit, I have come to know the error of my ways, and I am now ready to enter into Thy presence.

31 Now, the Father already knoweth if ye are ready or not, but this thing ye must know of a surety.

32 Therefore, if ye have not proven yourselves worthy during the days of your probation, then ye shall be given the opportunity to enter again into mortality and make another attempt to live by the commandments of the Father. And ye shall have as many attempts as ye need in order to prove yourself worthy of the kingdom of God.

33 Behold, there are those spirits in the spirit world who continually live in mortality because they have yet to learn the lessons that they need to know in order to prepare themselves for the kingdom of God. And there are also those spirits who followed Lucifer in the beginning, and who are denied the opportunity to take upon them the flesh, having rejected the plan of the Father from the beginning. These shall dwell in the spirit world until the Father casteth them out of His kingdom into their own place.

34 And there are many spirits who do not give heed to those in authority in the spirit world, and who take upon themselves a situation in mortality that doth not benefit them. Therefore, these return once again to the spirit world unprepared to be resurrected.

35 But once a spirit is prepared to receive its eternal body of flesh and bone, which shall be the house of its spirit forever, then this spirit can receive the gift of the Father in being resurrected.

36 And once these beings have been resurrected, then they are placed in a different place than the spirit world, for they can no longer abide in the spirit world, having received a body of flesh and bone, which can be seen and touched and sensed by the flesh of mortality.

37 And whether these resurrected beings are taken home to the planet of the Father and reside there until their kingdom of glory is prepared for them, or whether they are placed on one of the planets in our own solar system according to the power of God, I cannot say, for the Spirit forbiddeth me that I reveal this unto you.

38 But this I do say, that the resurrection is a continual process that goeth on eternally according to the worthiness of those beings who are ready to receive their eternal bodies.

39 And the Lord, even Jesus Christ, was the first to be resurrected on this planet, he being the first fruits of the resurrection and the example of the Father that all of us have been commanded to follow.

40 And after he gave up the ghost upon the cross, Jehovah immediately entered the spirit world. And in this world he was received with much gratefulness and adoration for that which he had done during the days of his probation.

41 For Jehovah gave his life as a sacrifice, or in other words, an example unto all those in the spirit world that it is possible that a child of the Father can live in mortality without sin. Therefore, he set the standard by which all of us will be judged; yea, this standard is the judgment bar of Christ.

42 And Jehovah only entered into mortality one time; and in this time, he proved himself worthy of the resurrected body that he received from the Father.

43 But before he was resurrected, even during the three days that his mortal flesh lay in its earthly tomb, he was in the spirit world giving

all of the authority that he had received from the Father to Michael, who is the Holy Ghost.

44 For with a resurrected body of flesh and bone, the Lord could no longer abide upon this earth. But he hath visited this earth at times, giving unto those whom he hath chosen to do his work instructions and strength in their times of need.

45 And he traveleth in such a way that the mortal eye cannot perceive him unless he desireth to manifest himself unto those in mortality. And further concerning these things, I am also forbidden that I should write more at this time.

46 And when he had given all authority of the Father unto Michael, the Lord called upon the power of the Father, which he possessed in a fullness, and created from the elements a perfected body that he would have forever.

47 And he formed this body according to the specifications that he desired for himself, having received these specifications directly from the Father, saving those wounds of his death, which he was commanded by the Father to keep as a remembrance to all of us of what he accomplished during the days of his probation.

48 And when his spirit had entered into the body that he had created by the power of the Father, he was able to observe all things both in mortality and in the spirit world with the perfected eyes that his eternal body possesseth.

49 And while still aware of those in the spirit world, he called forth all of those who had lived upon the earth from the days of Adam to his day; even all those who were ready to receive their eternal bodies; and he commanded, by the power of the Father, that their bodies be created and given unto them, as had been outlined in the plan of the Father from the beginning.

50 And there were bodies Telestial, which he created for those spirits who had proven themselves worthy and ready for their eternal state of existence from which they would never leave.

51 But the majority of those bodies which he created were Terrestrial bodies. And there were many spirits that day who were resurrected with Christ and who now live in the proper temporary place that was prepared for them by the Father until He hath finished His work and prepared the other worlds which these shall inhabit forever.

52 But those bodies that were Celestial were not created by the Lord. For all of those who were worthy of this glory knew all of the mysteries of the Father, and therefore could command the elements like unto the Son.

53 And each of these created the body that would suit its desires of happiness, whether it was male or female that each spirit desired for itself.

54 And thus it is with all those who have proven themselves worthy of a Celestial glory. Yea, all these shall have the power within them to resurrect at the time that they have chosen for themselves.

55 But those who are Celestial shall only be given this power from the Father, and they cannot receive this power and knowledge from the Lord, or any other, except it be from the Father.

56 For the Father overseeth the allocation of the powers of the Celestial glory, which are all the powers of the heavens, and are only relegated to those who have overcome all things and have proven themselves worthy of these things. And those who are Celestial beings are few.

57 And thus it is with the state of birth and death and the resurrection. For we are born according to our own desires to enter into mortality and prove ourselves worthy of the glory that we have chosen for ourselves in the kingdom of God.

58 And when we die, we are received back into the spirit realm with a realization that we did that which our Father had commanded us, or that which He did not command us.

59 And if we have disobeyed the commandments of the Father in mortality, then in misery we reside in this spiritual state until we are ready once again to take upon ourselves the trials and tribulations of the flesh, so that we might be proven therein.

60 Now, this is what the Lord meant when he said: For it is better for thee to enter into life without thy brother, than for thee and thy brother to be cast into hell; into the fire that

never shall be quenched, where their worm dieth not, and the fire is not quenched.

61 For, in the spirit world, ye cannot change that which ye have done in the flesh. And the torment of those things which ye have done in the flesh, which are contrary to the will of the Father, shall eat at you like unto a worm that dieth not. And the turmoil of your embarrassment for that which ye have done shall burn within you, and this fire cannot be quenched in the spirit world, even through repentance.

62 And the only way that this fire can be quenched, is that ye enter once again into mortality, and this time, obey the commandments of the Father in all things, proving that ye are worthy of the kingdom of God.

63 But if ye die and enter into the spirit world, and are received therein in a state of misery, there ye will have an opportunity to learn many things and change the nature of your spirit, but only in those things that ye need to change that pertaineth to the kingdom of glory that ye have already chosen for yourselves.

64 And when ye think that now ye are ready to prove to yourselves, and to your Father, that ye are ready for His kingdom, then ye will enter once again into the flesh and be proven to see if ye are correct in your assertion that ye are ready.

65 And if ye go through the days of your probation and learn the words of the Father, and live by them, then when ye die, the worm dieth and ye feel no more the fire that is unquenchable. And if ye choose, ye can then be resurrected into your eternal bodies.

66 And now, I have said unto you that there are those in the spirit world who are in authority and who can teach us and counsel us in that which we must do in order to prepare us to live in the eternal kingdoms of our Father.

67 And do ye not suppose that there are not also those who are sent unto us in mortality to help us prepare ourselves for this?

68 Yea, there are those among us who have been called of God to help us prepare ourselves for His kingdom. And these are the prophets and righteous men who have been sent to give unto us the words of the Father.

69 And His words are simple; yea, the very words that we are given by the Father, whether we receive them in the spirit world, or in the world of mortality, they are the same.

70 And they are, that we do unto others that which we would have them do unto us.

71 These are the words and the plan of salvation of the Father, and cannot be more simple to our understanding. And thus hath it been commanded me by the Lord to give unto you in this record.

CHAPTER 63

Moroni expounds upon Nephi's prophetic vision of the coming forth of the Book of Mormon and the Sealed Portion, and explains more about the plain and precious things taken out of the Bible. He explains the difference between an angel of God and the Spirit of God. The love of God is explained. The significance of the number of the twelve apostles is revealed.

AND it came to pass that the gospel of Jesus Christ spread throughout the land of Judea and unto all the earth by way of those who were chosen to preach this gospel to the people.

2 But there were others who were not known by the Jews, nor were they those who were descendants of Lehi, even those of whom the Lord said were his other sheep which must hear his voice, that there may be one shepherd. And of some of these I shall give a brief account hereafter.

3 But it is expedient that ye know the truth behind the beginnings of the scriptures which ye have before you, even that which is written in the Bible, which ye accept as the word of God. Yea, it is expedient that ye know from whence these things have come forth unto you, and that I expound more fully upon why the plain and precious things were taken out of this record according to the words of the angel unto Nephi.

4 And I will take much of my explanation from the words which ye have already received in the unsealed portion of this record. Nevertheless, the Lord hath commanded me to expound on the things that have already been given in the record of Nephi, which is upon the small plates of Nephi, which my father included with the remainder of his abridgment of the record of the children of Lehi.

5 Therefore, I shall give unto you the words of Nephi and expound upon them, that ye might know the truth regarding them and better understand that which hath been written unto you.

6 And Nephi wrote concerning the vision that he received of the latter days, even the days in which ye live; yea, the days in which these things shall be revealed unto you.

7 And he wrote, saying: For it came to pass after I had desired to know the things that my father had seen, and believing that the Lord was able to make them known unto me, as I sat pondering in mine heart, I was caught away in the Spirit of the Lord, yea, into an exceedingly high mountain, which I never had before seen, and upon which I never had before set my foot.

8 And the Spirit said unto me: Behold, what desirest thou? And I said: I desire to behold the things which my father saw. And the Spirit said unto me: Believest thou that thy father saw the tree of which he hath spoken? And I said: Yea, thou knowest that I believe all the words of my father.

9 And now, the angel of the Lord knew that Nephi believed in the words of his father. Nevertheless, it was necessary that Nephi proclaim his testimony by the words of his own mouth, which testifieth by the manner of the flesh, those things which are known of the spirit.

10 And Nephi continueth, saying: And when I had spoken these words, the Spirit cried with a loud voice, saying: Hosanna to the Lord, the most high God; for he is God over all the earth, yea, even above all. And blessed art thou, Nephi, because thou believest in the Son of the Most High God; therefore, thou shalt behold the things which thou hast desired.

11 And behold this thing shall be given unto thee for a sign, that after thou hast beheld the tree which bore the fruit which thy father tasted, thou shalt also behold a man descending out of heaven, and him shall thou witness; and after thou hast witnessed him, thou shalt bear record that it is the Son of God.

12 And it came to pass that the Spirit said unto me: Look. And I looked and beheld a tree; and it was like unto the tree which my father had seen; and the beauty thereof was far beyond, yea, exceeding of all beauty; and the whiteness thereof did exceed the whiteness of the driven snow.

13 And it came to pass after I had seen the tree, I said unto the Spirit: I behold thou hast shown unto me the tree which is precious above all. And he said unto me: What desirest thou? And I said unto him: To know the interpretation thereof; for I spake unto him as a man speaketh; for I beheld that he was in the form of a man; yet nevertheless, I knew that it was the Spirit of the Lord; and he spake unto me as a man speaketh with another.

14 And it came to pass that he said unto me: Look. And I looked as if to look upon him, and I saw him not; for he had gone from before my presence.

15 And now, this is the manner in which all visions are given unto those in the flesh. Behold, those in the flesh are able to see the visions that the Lord would give unto them by the power of the Spirit.

16 And Nephi hath herein given his testimony that the Spirit doth indeed appear like unto a man in appearance, and speaketh unto men according to their ability to understand him.

17 And this Spirit who spoke with Nephi, was Jehovah, who was the same Spirit who gave unto the brother of Jared the things which he saw. Nevertheless, Nephi was commanded at this time not to reveal the true identity of this Spirit, because of that which he beheld in the vision, which Jehovah had shown unto him.

18 And there is a difference between those who are spirits and those who are angels who are sent forth from the Father. For an angel is an exalted being who hath been given a body of flesh and bone, which is eternal, and who hath been given specific commandments by the Father for the purpose which the Father desireth of His angels.

19 And these angels, which are sent forth by the Father, do not dwell upon this earth, neither in the spirit world, nor in mortality, but they can travel to this world and react with the

elements thereof according to the command of the Father, they being like unto Him, having a body like unto His.

20 And Nephi seeth the vision which he is recounting by the power of the Spirit, which is introduced to him by Jehovah. But soon thereafter in the vision, an angel of the Father appeareth unto him and teacheth to him of Christ and his mission.

21 And Nephi continueth, saying: And it came to pass that I looked and beheld the great city of Jerusalem, and also other cities. And I beheld the city of Nazareth; and in the city of Nazareth I beheld a virgin, and she was exceedingly fair and white.

22 And it came to pass that I saw the heavens open; and an angel came down and stood before me; and he said unto me: Nephi, what beholdest thou? And I said unto him: A virgin, most beautiful and fair above all other virgins.

23 And he said unto me: Knowest thou the condescension of God? And I said unto him: I know that he loveth his children; nevertheless, I do not know the meaning of all things.

24 And he said unto me: Behold, the virgin whom thou seest is the mother of the Son of God, after the manner of the flesh. And it came to pass that I beheld that she was carried away in the Spirit; and after she had been carried away in the Spirit for the space of a time the angel spake unto me, saying: Look.

25 And I looked and beheld the virgin again, bearing a child in her arms. And the angel said unto me: Behold the Lamb of God, yea, even the Son of the Eternal Father.

26 Knowest thou the meaning of the tree which thy father saw? And I answered him, saying: Yea, it is the love of God, which sheddeth itself abroad in the hearts of the children of men; therefore, it is the most desirable above all things. And he spake unto me, saying: Yea, and the most joyous to the soul.

27 Now this love of which Nephi and the angel spake was the love of the Father that He hath for all of His children; yea, even every one of us who dwelleth on this planet in mortality and in the spirit world.

28 And this love of the Father bringeth joy and peace to our souls, and it is the fruit which is most desirable above all other fruit.

29 And this love is the same love that He commandeth all of us to have one for another, and is the love that we are required to attain before we can enter into His kingdom.

30 And this love is felt by each of us, in our hearts, as we care one for another. And as we care for one another, this love of the Father giveth us joy and peace, which indeed is the most joyous to our souls.

31 And it is this love that Jesus taught during his ministry, and which is his only message to us.

32 And Nephi continueth, saying: And after he had said these words, he said unto me: Look. And I looked, and I beheld the Son of God going forth among the children of men; and I saw many fall down at his feet and worship him.

33 And it came to pass that I beheld that the rod of iron, which my father had seen, was the word of God, which led to the fountain of living waters, or to the tree of life; which waters are a representation of the love of God; and I also beheld that the tree of life was a representation of the love of God.

34 And the angel said unto me again: Look and behold the condescension of God. And I looked and beheld the Redeemer of the world, of whom my father had spoken; and I also beheld the prophet who should prepare the way before him.

35 And the Lamb of God went forth and was baptized of him; and after he was baptized, I beheld the heavens open, and the Holy Ghost come down out of heaven and abide upon him in the form of a dove.

36 And I beheld that he went forth ministering unto the people, in power and great glory; and the multitudes were gathered together to hear him; and I beheld that they cast him out from among them.

37 And I also beheld twelve others following him. And it came to pass that they were carried away in the Spirit from before my face, and I saw them not.

38 And it came to pass that the angel spake unto me again, saying: Look. And I looked, and I beheld the heavens open again, and I saw angels descending upon the children of men; and they did minister unto them.

39 And now, these things which Nephi saw were in the very similitude of the way in which the Father prefereth that his children learn from him. For Nephi beheld the twelve apostles, who represent all of those who are called to teach the gospel of Jesus, which is this rod of iron that he beheld.

40 And then immediately these apostles were taken away from his view that he beheld them not. For their only mission is to teach the children of men to love one another, which is the only true gospel of Jesus Christ, and the rod of iron that leadeth to the tree of life, which representeth eternal life in the kingdoms of glory of the Father, which is also the love of God.

41 And when the children of men begin to love one another, then the Father sendeth forth His angels and His Spirit to minister unto them and giveth to them this joy of which the angel hath spoken.

42 But from the words of the apostles, even those who are servants of God who are sent unto His children to share His love with all of us, this joy shall not come; and this is the reason why they were taken away so suddenly from the sight of Nephi in the vision.

43 For the apostles can only preach repentance unto the people, and teach them the commandments of love which they have received from Christ.

44 And then, if the children of men repent and begin to love each other as the Father hath commanded, then they are ministered unto by the Father through the ministrations of His Holy Spirit.

45 And at no time shall the children of God receive this joy from any other, except from the Father who hath created them. And thus was the significance of this part of the vision of Nephi that I have been commanded to explain unto you.

46 And Nephi continued, saying: And he spake unto me again, saying: Look. And I looked, and I beheld the Lamb of God going forth among the children of men. And I beheld multitudes of people who were sick, and who were afflicted with all manner of diseases, and with devils and unclean spirits; and the angel spake and showed all these things unto me. And they were healed by the power of the Lamb of God; and the devils and the unclean spirits were cast out.

47 And it came to pass that the angel spake unto me again, saying: Look. And I looked and beheld the Lamb of God, that he was taken by the people; yea, the Son of the everlasting God was judged of the world; and I saw and bear record.

48 And I, Nephi, saw that he was lifted up upon the cross and slain for the sins of the world.

49 And now, I have already explained unto you that the Lord did not die for the sins of the world, but because of them; yea, because they judged him to be evil.

50 And this thing is easy to understand when ye take into consideration that which Nephi wrote, saying: And I looked and beheld the Lamb of God, that he was taken by the people; yea, the Son of the everlasting God was judged of the world.

51 And this judgment of the world was because of the things that Jesus taught; and it was because of these things, that he was killed by them who could not accept that which he taught.

52 And Nephi continueth, saying: And after he was slain I saw the multitudes of the earth, that they were gathered together to fight against the apostles of the Lamb; for thus were the twelve called by the angel of the Lord.

53 And the multitude of the earth was gathered together; and I beheld that they were in a large and spacious building, like unto the building which my father saw.

54 And the angel of the Lord spake unto me again, saying: Behold the world and the wisdom thereof; yea, behold the house of Israel hath gathered together to fight against the twelve apostles of the Lamb.

55 And it came to pass that I saw and bear record, that the great and spacious building was the pride of the world; and it fell, and the fall thereof was exceedingly great. And the angel of the Lord spake unto me again, saying: Thus shall be the destruction of all nations, kindreds, tongues, and people, that shall fight against the twelve apostles of the Lamb.

56 And now, ye already know that the

twelve apostles who were with the Lord during his ministry were all slain and cast out from among the people. Therefore, that which the angel spake concerning those that fight against the twelve apostles of the Lamb, was spoken in similitude of all those who fight against the gospel of Christ as it is given unto the world by those whom the Lord hath called to administer his word.

57 And these are the prophets and righteous men in all nations and among all the cultures of the world, let them be named that which they are named according to the traditions, customs and the language of the people to whom they are sent by the Lord.

58 And this pride of which the angel spoke and gave a similitude of in the great and spacious building, is the pride of the world that keepeth the children of men from accepting the message of those who are sent forth by the Lord.

59 And one day, the pride of the earth will fall, and great shall be the fall thereof when they come to a true understanding of the Lord and that which he hath been commanded of the Father to do for them in this part of His kingdom.

60 And Nephi continueth, saying: And it came to pass that the angel said unto me: Look, and behold thy seed, and also the seed of thy brethren. And I looked and beheld the land of promise; and I beheld multitudes of people, yea, even as it were in number as many as the sand of the sea.

61 And it came to pass that I beheld multitudes gathered together to battle, one against the other; and I beheld wars, and rumors of wars, and great slaughters with the sword among my people. And it came to pass that I beheld many generations pass away, after the manner of wars and contentions in the land; and I beheld many cities, yea, even that I did not number them.

62 And it came to pass that I saw a mist of darkness on the face of the land of promise; and I saw lightnings, and I heard thunderings, and earthquakes, and all manner of tumultuous noises; and I saw the earth and the rocks, that they rent; and I saw mountains tumbling into pieces; and I saw the plains of the earth, that they were broken up; and I saw many cities that they were sunk; and I saw many that they were burned with fire; and I saw many that did tumble to the earth, because of the quaking thereof.

63 And it came to pass after I saw these things, I saw the vapor of darkness, that it passed from off the face of the earth; and behold, I saw multitudes who had not fallen because of the great and terrible judgments of the Lord.

64 And I saw the heavens open, and the Lamb of God descending out of heaven; and he came down and showed himself unto them. And I also saw and bear record that the Holy Ghost fell upon twelve others; and they were ordained of God, and chosen.

65 And the angel spake unto me, saying: Behold the twelve disciples of the Lamb, who are chosen to minister unto thy seed. And he said unto me: Thou rememberest the twelve apostles of the Lamb? Behold they are they who shall judge the twelve tribes of Israel; therefore, the twelve ministers of thy seed shall be judged of them; for ye are of the house of Israel.

66 And these twelve ministers whom thou beholdest shall judge thy seed. And, behold, they are righteous forever; for because of their faith in the Lamb of God their garments are made white in his blood.

67 And now, it is expedient that ye understand the significance of the number twelve, and the similitude in which the Lord useth this number to call those who preach his words unto the children of men.

68 Behold, I have already explained unto you in this record, that in the kingdom of the Father there are three degrees of glory, and in each degree, there are three degrees; therefore, there are nine degrees of glory, or planets, wherein the children of the Father shall dwell in eternity.

69 Now, to each of these planets the Father will assign two, who shall be in authority over these kingdoms of glories and assure that the laws are abided by which are set for each kingdom.

70 And for this same reason both Jehovah, the Christ, and Michael, the Holy Ghost, were given authority in the beginning and became part of a Holy Trinity, the Father being the First, and these other two being in authority according to the eternal laws of heaven, under the Father.

71 Nevertheless, in the Celestial glories, there is no authority given to two, because those who are Celestial need not that any have authority over them, for they are like unto the Father in all things.

72 But in the other two kingdoms, it is necessary that two in authority be assigned by the Father to oversee those glories. Therefore, without the Celestial glories, there remaineth six glories, which need the authority of two who have been given that commission by the Father.

73 And this is where the similitude of the number twelve cometh from when the Lord calleth forth those who would lead his people.

74 And now, Nephi seeth in this part of his vision the land of promise on which the children of Lehi are led and dwell according to the promises that the Lord made unto Nephi. And these ye now know are some of the other sheep that the Lord was commanded by the Father to visit and give His gospel.

75 But these were not the only sheep that he visited after his death and resurrection in the land of Jerusalem. For after the Lord visited my fathers, he went to all parts of the world, wherever there were gathered together a group of righteous people who were obeying the commandments of the Father, even those who were loving each other and abiding by the words that they had been taught by the prophets that the Lord had sent unto them.

76 And as I have said unto you before, I will give an accounting of some of these other peoples in a later part of this record. But it is expedient that ye understand that the gospel of Christ was taught throughout the whole earth by the Son of God, who was commanded by the Father to give unto all of His children the same opportunity to hear His voice; for the Father respecteth none of His children above another, and giveth liberally unto all who call upon Him; behold, in whatever name or language that they call Him; He loveth them and answereth them according to the Spirit.

77 And in person, Jesus did visit all the peoples of the earth, and called forth many apostles so that they could teach the people that which he hath given unto all people. And in this way there shall be one fold and one shepherd, according to his own words.

78 And Nephi continueth, saying: And the angel said unto me: Look. And I looked, and beheld three generations pass away in righteousness; and their garments were white even like unto the Lamb of God. And the angel said unto me: These are made white in the blood of the Lamb, because of their faith in him. And I, Nephi, also saw many of the fourth generation who passed away in righteousness.

79 And it came to pass that I saw the multitudes of the earth gathered together. And the angel said unto me: Behold thy seed, and also the seed of thy brethren. And it came to pass that I looked and beheld the people of my seed gathered together in multitudes against the seed of my brethren; and they were gathered together to battle.

80 And the angel spake unto me, saying: Behold the fountain of filthy water which thy father saw; yea, even the river of which he spake; and the depths thereof are the depths of hell. And the mists of darkness are the temptations of the devil, which blindeth the eyes, and hardeneth the hearts of the children of men, and leadeth them away into broad roads, that they perish and are lost.

81 And the large and spacious building, which thy father saw, is the vain imaginations and the pride of the children of men. And a great and a terrible gulf divideth them; yea, even the word of the justice of the Eternal God, and the Messiah who is the Lamb of God, of whom the Holy Ghost beareth record, from the beginning of the world until this time, and from this time henceforth and forever.

82 And now, this terrible gulf which divideth the children of men is that which I must explain unto you in plainness. For this gulf is the justice of the Lord who cometh between those that keep his commandments and those who do not.

83 For those who are prideful and vain and centered upon themselves, evensomuch that they do not care about their neighbor, neither do they love others as they would have others love them; yea, these have no part of the Holy Ghost, which rendereth unto all the children of men the peace and joy of the Father.

84 And even though the vision that Nephi received hath spoken specifically concerning his own people, who are the descedants of Lehi, these things were given in similitude of the whole earth, even all the nations of the earth.

85 For thus shall come to pass in all nations of the world according to the words of the angel. And this great gulf is what separateth the wicked from the righteous.

86 For the wicked are forever miserable, and are angry, and unsettled, and judgeth their neighbors and hateth them because of their words, which do not agree with their own.

87 Yea, these are those who are saddened in their countenances, and depressed in their spirits, and have not the light of Christ within them.

88 But those who are righteous are happy and content with their lives; and these do not judge their neighbor, but loveth their neighbor as themselves, and are not angry, and loveth their enemies as they do their friends.

89 These receive the gift of the Holy Ghost that the Father hath provided so that the souls of all of His children can experience joy and peace forever.

90 And Nephi, continueth, saying: And while the angel spake these words, I beheld and saw that the seed of my brethren did contend against my seed, according to the word of the angel; and because of the pride of my seed, and the temptations of the devil, I beheld that the seed of my brethren did overpower the people of my seed.

91 And it came to pass that I beheld, and saw the people of the seed of my brethren that they had overcome my seed; and they went forth in multitudes upon the face of the land. And I saw them gathered together in multitudes; and I saw wars and rumors of wars among them; and in wars and rumors of wars I saw many generations pass away.

92 And the angel said unto me: Behold these shall dwindle in unbelief. And it came to pass that I beheld, after they had dwindled in unbelief, they became a dark and loathsome and a filthy people, full of idleness and all manner of abominations.

CHAPTER 64

Moroni continues expounding upon Nephi's vision. The great and abominable church is explained and compared to the LDS Church. The rewards of Satan are compared to the rewards of the Spirit.

AND it came to pass that the angel spake unto me, saying: Look. And I looked and beheld many nations and kingdoms. And the angel said unto me: What beholdest thou? And I said: I behold many nations and kingdoms. And he said unto me: These are the nations and kingdoms of the Gentiles.

2 And it came to pass that I saw among the nations of the Gentiles the formation of a great church. And the angel said unto me: Behold the formation of a church which is most abominable above all other churches, which slayeth the saints of God, yea, and tortureth them and bindeth them down, and yoketh them with a yoke of iron, and bringeth them down into captivity.

3 And it came to pass that I beheld this great and abominable church; and I saw the devil that he was the founder of it. And I also saw gold, and silver, and silks, and scarlets, and fine-twined linen, and all manner of precious clothing; and I saw many harlots.

4 And the angel spake unto me, saying: Behold the gold, and the silver, and the silks, and the scarlets, and the fine-twined linen, and the precious clothing, and the harlots, are the desires of this great and abominable church. And also for the praise of the world do they destroy the saints of God, and bring them down into captivity.

5 And now, I, Moroni, have been commanded to explain unto you the true meaning of this great and abominable church which came forth from the Gentiles.

6 Behold, there are many of you of the latter days that shall believe that this church is a church that hath been established and set up among you and to which many go believing that they are receiving the word of God, but are not receiving the truth, but are being misled by the leaders of this church.

7 Behold, I say unto you that this great and

abominable church is not a religion, nor is it one particular church; but it is the same beast of which John speaketh in his great revelation; and also it is the mist of darkness and the fountain of filthy water of which Nephi spoke, which I have already explained unto you.

8 For behold, there is no one particular religion, or church, that hath been set up among you which slayeth the saints of God, yea, and tortureth them and bindeth them down, and yoketh them with a yoke of iron, and bringeth them down into captivity; but there are many doctrines and commandments taught in many of the churches of the latter days that doeth these things unto the saints of God.

9 Behold, if I could choose for an example a church among you that more appropriately representeth the great and abominable church which Nephi describeth in his vision, then I would give unto you that church which was set up by the coming forth of this record unto them, even this church which shall be called the church of Jesus Christ of the latter day saints.

10 For behold, there are truly no saints among them that are not being held in captivity because of the things which are taught unto them by this church and its leaders.

11 Yea, the gold, and the silver, and the silks, and the scarlets, and the fine-twined linen, and the precious clothing, and the harlots, are the desires of this latter day church. And also for the praise of the world do they destroy the saints of God, and bring them down into captivity.

12 And this captivity is that which I have spoken of before, even by the words of Alma which he spoke unto the people, saying: And they that will harden their hearts, to them is given the lesser portion of the word until they know nothing concerning his mysteries; and then they are taken captive by the devil, and led by his will down to destruction.

13 Now this is what is meant by the chains of hell and captivity. For the leaders and the members of this church have hardened their hearts against the true words of Christ, and seek after the vain things of the world, and glorify themselves in the praise of the world, and the honors that men give unto them.

14 And they are dressed exceedingly fine, evensomuch that they look down upon any that would enter into their synagogues to listen to the vain words of their leaders, that they might not have those come into their synagogues who are not dressed exceedingly fine like unto them.

15 And I say unto any church that would do these things: Yea, is not your manner of fine dress that which is acceptable and praiseworthy of the world?

16 Behold, look around you. Do ye not notice that those in power in the world, even in the kingdom of Satan, do they not dress like unto you when ye enter into your churches to worship God?

17 And ye are like unto the scribes and the Pharisees and the hypocrites, who dress themselves in white that they might give a demonstration of their purity to others. Yet, ye go beyond that which they do, even that ye wear your shirts that are white and then place a suit of darkness over this whiteness, unknowingly showing forth the nature of your works.

18 And then, if this was not enough that ye should do, ye wrap around your neck, even upon the whiteness of the shirts that ye wear, a sash of darkness that chokes off your whiteness from your head, which representeth the kingdom of God, which hath been given unto you.

19 And even by having my words already among you, which ye testify of to the world; yea, these same words that say unto you: For behold, ye do love money, and your substance, and your fine apparel, and the adorning of your churches, more than ye love the poor and the needy, the sick and the afflicted.

20 Oh, ye pollutions, ye hypocrites, ye teachers, who sell yourselves for that which will canker, why have ye polluted the holy church of God? Why are ye ashamed to take upon you the name of Christ? Why do ye not think that greater is the value of an endless happiness than that misery which never dies, because of the praise of the world?

21 Do ye not know what it meaneth to rob the poor because of your fine clothing?

22 Yea, let me speak once again unto you in plainness that perhaps ye may understand: If ye buy a suit of clothes that is valued at the same price as two sets of a less finer cloth, but

covereth the body in the exact same manner, then ye have robbed the poor by purchasing the more expensive cloth because of the praise of the world, when ye could have purchased two suits of clothes of a lesser cloth and given one unto him who hath none.

23 Oh, the misery of my soul when I contemplate the great wickedness of this church, yea, even of all the churches of the latter days. For they all belong to the church of the devil, which is this great and abominable church described in the vision of Nephi.

24 And none of them understandeth the commandments and will of the Father. And their hearts and desires are continually upon the things of the world, which things give them a moment of joy, even in the moment that they experience them, but then these things causeth them to suffer and become miserable because of them.

25 For the devil will not stand behind the promises that he maketh unto his children, but he giveth the things of the world as a reward unto them for not following the plan of salvation that was given unto us by the Father.

26 And his rewards, or the desires of this great and abominable church, are temporal rewards, or rewards of the flesh, which moth and rust doth corrupt and thieves break through and steal.

27 And I say unto you, that when ye receive these rewards from Satan, do ye not rejoice in that which ye receive from him? But when a moth doth enter into your closet and beginneth to consume the reward that ye have received, even the clothes that ye have purchased, keeping back the money that ye could have used to love one another; do ye not suffer in misery because of this thing?

28 Do ye not curse the moth for that which it hath done unto you by destroying the reward that ye have received from Satan?

29 And when those rewards of Satan, which can rust, begin to rust and deteriorate, do ye not become distraught and unsettled, even that ye become greatly concerned that ye must replace that which the rust hath corrupted?

30 And do ye not stress and concern yourselves in misery that thieves should take the rewards that Satan hath given unto you? Do ye not become afraid of your neighbor, instead of loving him, because he might take from you that with which Satan hath rewarded you?

31 And now my brothers and sisters, I again ask of you, why do ye not think that greater is the value of an endless happiness than that misery which never dieth? Yea, ye have received the desires of your church, which is this great and abominable church, even the church of the devil.

32 And its desires have become your desires, and ye shall be rewarded with the same reward that she shall receive, even the whore of the whole earth.

33 And Nephi continueth the relation of his vision, saying: And it came to pass that I looked and beheld many waters; and they divided the Gentiles from the seed of my brethren.

34 And it came to pass that the angel said unto me: Behold the wrath of God is upon the seed of thy brethren. And I looked and beheld a man among the Gentiles, who was separated from the seed of my brethren by the many waters; and I beheld the Spirit of God, that it came down and wrought upon the man; and he went forth upon the many waters, even unto the seed of my brethren, who were in the promised land.

35 And it came to pass that I beheld the Spirit of God, that it wrought upon other Gentiles; and they went forth out of captivity, upon the many waters. And it came to pass that I beheld many multitudes of the Gentiles upon the land of promise; and I beheld the wrath of God, that it was upon the seed of my brethren; and they were scattered before the Gentiles and were smitten.

36 And I beheld the Spirit of the Lord, that it was upon the Gentiles, and they did prosper and obtain the land for their inheritance; and I beheld that they were white, and exceedingly fair and beautiful, like unto my people before they were slain.

37 And it came to pass that I, Nephi, beheld that the Gentiles who had gone forth out of captivity did humble themselves before the Lord; and the power of the Lord was with them. And I beheld that their mother Gentiles were gathered together upon the waters, and upon the land also, to battle against them. And I beheld that the power of God was with them, and also that the wrath of God was upon all those who were gathered together against them to battle.

38 And I, Nephi, beheld that the Gentiles who had gone out of captivity were delivered by the power of God out of the hands of all other nations. And it came to pass that I, Nephi, beheld that they did prosper in the land; and I beheld a book, and it was carried forth among them.

39 And the angel said unto me: Knowest thou the meaning of the book? And I said unto him: I know not. And he said: Behold it proceedeth out of the mouth of a Jew. And I, Nephi, beheld it; and he said unto me: The book that thou beholdest is a record of the Jews, which containeth the covenants of the Lord, which he hath made unto the house of Israel; and it also containeth many of the prophecies of the holy prophets; and it is a record like unto the engravings which are upon the plates of brass, save there are not so many; nevertheless, they contain the covenants of the Lord, which he hath made unto the house of Israel; therefore, they are of great worth unto the Gentiles.

40 And the angel of the Lord said unto me: Thou hast beheld that the book proceeded forth from the mouth of a Jew; and when it proceeded forth from the mouth of a Jew it contained the fullness of the gospel of the Lord, of whom the twelve apostles bear record; and they bear record according to the truth which is in the Lamb of God.

41 Therefore, these things go forth from the Jews in purity unto the Gentiles, according to the truth which is in God.

42 And after they go forth by the hand of the twelve apostles of the Lamb, from the Jews unto the Gentiles, thou seest the formation of a great and abominable church, which is most abominable above all other churches; for behold, they have taken away from the gospel of the Lamb many parts which are plain and most precious; and also many covenants of the Lord have they taken away. And all this have they done that they might pervert the right ways of the Lord, that they might blind the eyes and harden the hearts of the children of men.

43 Therefore, thou seest that after the book hath gone forth through the hands of the great and abominable church, that there are many plain and precious things taken away from the book, which is the book of the Lamb of God.

44 And after these plain and precious things were taken away it goeth forth unto all the nations of the Gentiles; and after it goeth forth unto all the nations of the Gentiles, yea, even across the many waters which thou hast seen with the Gentiles who have gone forth out of captivity; thou seest, because of the many plain and precious things which have been taken out of the book, which were plain unto the understanding of the children of men, according to the plainness which is in the Lamb of God; because of these things which are taken away out of the gospel of the Lamb, an exceedingly great many do stumble, yea, insomuch that Satan hath great power over them.

45 Nevertheless, thou beholdest that the Gentiles who have gone forth out of captivity, and have been lifted up by the power of God above all other nations upon the face of the land, which is choice above all other lands, which is the land that the Lord God hath covenanted with thy father that his seed should have for the land of their inheritance; therefore, thou seest that the Lord God will not suffer that the Gentiles will utterly destroy the mixture of thy seed, which are among thy brethren. Neither will he suffer that the Gentiles shall destroy the seed of thy brethren.

46 Neither will the Lord God suffer that the Gentiles shall forever remain in that awful state of blindness, which thou beholdest they are in, because of the plain and most precious parts of the gospel of the Lamb which have been kept back by that abominable church, whose formation thou hast seen.

47 Therefore saith the Lamb of God: I will be merciful unto the Gentiles, unto the visiting of the remnant of the house of Israel in great judgment.

48 And it came to pass that the angel of the Lord spake unto me, saying: Behold, saith the Lamb of God, after I have visited the remnant of the house of Israel—and this remnant of whom I speak is the seed of thy father—therefore, after I have visited them in judgment, and smitten them by the hand of the Gentiles, and after the Gentiles do stumble exceedingly, because of the most plain and precious parts of the gospel of the Lamb which have been kept back by that abominable church, which is the mother of harlots, saith the Lamb; I will be merciful unto the Gentiles in that day, insomuch that I will bring forth unto them, in mine own power, much of my gospel, which shall be plain and precious, saith the Lamb.

49 For, behold, saith the Lamb: I will manifest myself unto thy seed, that they shall write many things which I shall minister unto them, which shall be plain and precious; and after thy seed shall be destroyed, and dwindle in unbelief, and also the seed of thy brethren, behold, these things shall be hid up, to come forth unto the Gentiles, by the gift and power of the Lamb.

50 And in them shall be written my gospel, saith the Lamb, and my rock and my salvation. And blessed are they who shall seek to bring forth my Zion at that day, for they shall have the gift and the power of the Holy Ghost; and if they endure unto the end, they shall be lifted up at the last day and shall be saved in the everlasting kingdom of the Lamb; and whoso shall publish peace, yea, tidings of great joy, how beautiful upon the mountains shall they be.

51 And it came to pass that I beheld the remnant of the seed of my brethren, and also the book of the Lamb of God, which had proceeded forth from the mouth of the Jew, that it came forth from the Gentiles unto the remnant of the seed of my brethren.

52 And after it had come forth unto them I beheld other books, which came forth by the power of the Lamb, from the Gentiles unto them, unto the convincing of the Gentiles and the remnant of the seed of my brethren, and also the Jews who were scattered upon all the face of the earth, that the records of the prophets and of the twelve apostles of the Lamb are true.

53 And the angel spake unto me, saying: These last records, which thou hast seen among the Gentiles, shall establish the truth of the first, which are of the twelve apostles of the Lamb, and shall make known the plain and precious things which have been taken away from them; and shall make known to all kindreds, tongues, and people, that the Lamb of God is the Son of the Eternal Father, and the Savior of the world; and that all men must come unto him, or they cannot be saved.

54 And they must come according to the words which shall be established by the mouth of the Lamb; and the words of the Lamb shall be made known in the records of thy seed, as well as in the records of the twelve apostles of the Lamb; therefore they both shall be established in one; for there is one God and one Shepherd over all the earth.

55 And the time cometh that he shall manifest himself unto all nations, both unto the Jews and also unto the Gentiles; and after he hath manifested himself unto the Jews and also unto the Gentiles, then he shall manifest himself unto the Gentiles and also unto the Jews, and the last shall be first, and the first shall be last.

56 And it shall come to pass, that if the Gentiles shall hearken unto the Lamb of God in that day that he shall manifest himself unto them in word, and also in power, in very deed, unto the taking away of their stumbling blocks; and harden not their hearts against the Lamb of God, they shall be numbered among the seed of thy father; yea, they shall be numbered among the house of Israel; and they shall be a blessed people upon the promised land forever; they shall be no more brought down into captivity; and the house of Israel shall no more be confounded.

57 And that great pit, which hath been digged for them by that great and abominable church, which was founded by the devil and his children, that he might lead away the souls of men down to hell; yea, that great pit which hath been digged for the destruction of men shall be filled by those who digged it, unto their utter destruction, saith the Lamb of God; not the destruction of the soul, save it be the casting of it into that hell which hath no end.

58 For behold, this is according to the captivity of the devil, and also according to the justice of God, upon all those who will work wickedness and abomination before him.

59 And it came to pass that the angel spake unto me, Nephi, saying: Thou hast beheld that if the Gentiles repent it shall be well with them; and thou also knowest concerning the covenants of the Lord unto the house of Israel; and thou also hast heard that whoso repenteth not must perish.

60 Therefore, wo be unto the Gentiles if it so be that they harden their hearts against the Lamb of God. For the time cometh, saith the Lamb of God, that I will work a great and a marvelous work among the children of men; a work which shall be everlasting, either on the one hand or on the other; either to the convincing of them unto peace and life eternal, or unto the deliverance of them to the hardness of their hearts and the blindness of their minds unto their being brought down into captivity, and also into destruction, both temporally and spiritually, according to the captivity of the devil, of which I have spoken.

61 And it came to pass that when the angel had spoken these words, he said unto me: Rememberest thou the covenants of the Father unto the house of Israel? I said unto him, Yea. And it came to pass that he said unto me: Look, and behold that great and abominable church, which is the mother of abominations, whose founder is the devil.

62 And he said unto me: Behold there are save two churches only; the one is the church of the Lamb of God, and the other is the church of the devil; therefore, whoso belongeth not to the church of the Lamb of God belongeth to that great church, which is the mother of abominations; and she is the whore of all the earth.

63 And it came to pass that I looked and beheld the whore of all the earth, and she sat upon many waters; and she had dominion over all the earth, among all nations, kindreds, tongues, and people. And it came to pass that I beheld the church of the Lamb of God, and its numbers were few, because of the wickedness and abominations of the whore who sat upon many waters; nevertheless, I beheld that the church of the Lamb, who were the saints of God, were also upon all the face of the earth; and their dominions upon the face of the earth were small, because of the wickedness of the great whore whom I saw.

64 And it came to pass that I beheld that the great mother of abominations did gather together multitudes upon the face of all the earth, among all the nations of the Gentiles, to fight against the Lamb of God.

65 And it came to pass that I, Nephi, beheld the power of the Lamb of God, that it descended upon the saints of the church of the Lamb, and upon the covenant people of the Lord, who were scattered upon all the face of the earth; and they were armed with righteousness and with the power of God in great glory.

66 And it came to pass that I beheld that the wrath of God was poured out upon that great and abominable church, insomuch that there were wars and rumors of wars among all the nations and kindreds of the earth.

67 And as there began to be wars and rumors of wars among all the nations which belonged to the mother of abominations, the angel spake unto me, saying: Behold, the wrath of God is upon the mother of harlots; and behold, thou seest all these things; and when the day cometh that the wrath of God is poured out upon the mother of harlots, which is the great and abominable church of all the earth, whose founder is the devil, then, at that day, the work of the Father shall commence, in preparing the way for the fulfilling of his covenants, which he hath made to his people who are of the house of Israel.

68 And it came to pass that the angel spake unto me, saying: Look. And I looked and beheld a man, and he was dressed in a white robe. And the angel said unto me: Behold one of the twelve apostles of the Lamb. Behold, he shall see and write the remainder of these things; yea, and also many things which have been. And he shall also write concerning the end of the world.

69 Therefore, the things which he shall write are just and true; and behold they are written in the book which thou beheld proceeding out of the mouth of the Jew; and at the time they proceeded out of the mouth of the Jew, or, at the time the book proceeded out of the mouth of the Jew, the things which were written were plain and pure, and most precious and easy to the understanding of all men.

70 And behold, the things which this apostle of the Lamb shall write are many things which thou hast seen; and behold, the remainder shalt thou see. But the things which thou shalt see hereafter thou shalt not write; for the Lord God hath ordained the apostle of the Lamb of God that he should write them.

71 And also others who have been, to them hath he shown all things, and they have written them; and they are sealed up to come forth in their purity, according to the truth which is in the Lamb, in the own due time of the Lord, unto the house of Israel.

72 And I, Nephi, heard and bear record, that the name of the apostle of the Lamb was John, according to the word of the angel.

73 And behold, I, Nephi, am forbidden that I should write the remainder of the things which I saw and heard; therefore the things which I have written sufficeth me; and I have written but a small part of the things which I saw.

74 And I bear record that I saw the things which my father saw, and the angel of the Lord did make them known unto me. And now I make an end of speaking concerning the things which I saw while I was carried away in the spirit; and if all the things which I saw are not written, the things which I have written are true. And thus it is. Amen.

75 And now, I have given unto you many of the words of Nephi so that ye of the latter days who have now received these things, which have been sealed up to come forth in their purity according to the truth which is in the Lamb, in the own due time of the Lord unto the house of Israel; yea, so that ye who receive these things can know of a surety that the Father hath commenced His work in gathering the elect out of this great and abominable church of which Nephi hath spoken.

76 And there are those of you in the latter days who shall receive these things and believe that the Father hath already begun His work, and that ye belong to the church that carrieth forth His work, even this church that is called the church of Jesus Christ of the latter day saints.

77 O, how ye have misunderstood the words of Nephi and interpreted them to consume them on the pride of your hearts, which pride causeth you to believe that ye belong to the church of the Lamb, and that everyone else belongeth to the church of the devil.

78 Behold, ye do not understand the words of Nephi, even though they are given in plainness unto those who have the Spirit of the Lord to receive the true meaning of them.

79 Behold, if ye read the words of Nephi, ye shall see that the unsealed portion of the record of my father, which ye already have among you, is that which was to come forth to testify of the gospel which is contained in the book that proceedeth forth from the mouth of the Jews.

80 For in the portion of this record which was unsealed, my father hath given unto you the account of the visit of the Christ to the children of Lehi and the establishment of his gospel among them, which are the words of Christ which he spoke both to them as well as to the Jews.

81 But the words that Nephi hath given unto you do not say that that which shall testify of the first

record, which is the record that proceedeth forth from the mouth of a Jew, or the Bible, as ye call it according to your language, shall give unto you those things which were taken out of this record, even those plain and precious things that were lost because of the great and abominable church that existeth in the world to bring into captivity, or take the saints of God away from the truth, which is given in the church of the Lamb of God.

82 But the words of Nephi saith unto you: And also others who have been, to them hath he shown all things, and they have written them; and they are sealed up to come forth in their purity, according to the truth which is in the Lamb.

83 And I, Moroni, am he who these things refer to, and also the brother of Jared is one of them to whom the Lord hath shown all things in their purity, that have been sealed up to come forth to give back those plain and precious things which have been taken out of the record of the Jews.

84 Behold, the unsealed portion of this record doth not give unto you in purity the things that were taken out of the record of the Jews, or out of the revelation that was given unto John, as the words of Nephi explain.

85 But the unsealed part, which containeth the record of my father, testifieth of those things which ye have already before you, even the Bible, and giveth not unto you all things in their purity, but it testifieth of the words of Christ which were given unto the people.

86 But these things which ye are receiving in this part which hath been sealed are the things which shall give unto you the gospel of Jesus Christ in its purity, even those things that shall take away your stumbling blocks as it hath been explained to you; yea, even in plainness all these things shall be given unto you.

87 And the sealed portion of this record shall not come unto you at the time of the unsealed portion, so that the words of Nephi can be fulfilled, which he wrote, saying: And it came to pass that I beheld that the wrath of God was poured out upon that great and abominable church, insomuch that there were wars and rumors of wars among all the nations and kindreds of the earth. And as there began to be wars and rumors of wars among all the nations which belonged to the mother of abominations, the angel spake unto me, saying: Behold, the wrath of God is upon the mother of harlots; and behold, thou seest all these things; and when the day cometh that the wrath of God is poured out upon the mother of harlots, which is the great and abominable church of all the earth, whose founder is the devil, then, at that day, the work of the Father shall commence, in preparing the way for the fulfilling of his covenants, which he hath made to his people who are of the house of Israel.

88 And now, do ye of the latter days see that the wrath of God is beginning to be poured out upon this great and abominable church of which Nephi hath spoken? Do ye not see that there are wars and rumors of wars throughout the entire earth, even amongst all the nations of the earth that belongeth to the church of the devil?

89 Do ye not see that the Lord hath blessed this land of promise that it might be a way whereby these things shall come unto you?

90 But after ye, who are the Gentiles, shall receive the part of this record which was unsealed, and which shall testify of the record of the Jews, or the Bible; do ye not see that at this time the wrath of God was not poured out upon this great and abominable church?

91 For behold, your nation, even the nation that was established in the beginning upon righteous principles, shall become the seat of Satan, or the catalyst for the church of the devil throughout the whole world.

92 And these are the things that Nephi was forbidden to write unto you. But these things are explained in the revelations and writings of John, and an explanation of which I have somewhat given unto you already in this record.

93 And when your nation begins to fail; yea, when the economy of the beast, or the economy of this great and abominable church which is among you shall begin to fail those of you who have received the mark of the beast in your right hand, and also the mark of the beast in your foreheads; yea, when Satan turneth his back on you and ye begin to feel the wrath of God poured out upon you because of your riches and your pride and your envyings and covetness of gold and silver and the precious things of the earth, which are the desires of this great and abominable church;

94 Yea, when your hearts are full of depression and anger towards your neighbor, even that ye live in fear that your neighbor taketh from you that which he desires of the beast; yea, will ye then believe that the work of the Father hath commenced, and that He hath given unto you this record that ye might depart from this great and abominable church, which is the church of the devil, and join the church of the Lamb of God?

95 Behold, if ye shall depart from this great and abominable church, and give up the blessings of this church, which are its desires, or the rewards of Satan; yea, if ye come unto the church of Christ, then ye shall receive the joy that the Father hath promised unto you.

96 Then shall ye be at peace in your heart. Then shall ye be a witness of those things which Nephi wrote when he said: And it came to pass that I, Nephi, beheld the power of the Lamb of God, that it descended upon the saints of the church of the Lamb, and upon the covenant people of the Lord, who were scattered upon all the face of the earth; and they were armed with righteousness and with the power of God in great glory.

97 And if ye are armed with righteousness and with the power of God, then ye shall not suffer with those who belong to the great and abominable church of the devil when the wrath of God is poured out upon it.

98 But those who belong to the church of the devil shall suffer and fill up that great pit, which hath been digged for them by that great and abominable church, which was founded by the devil and his children, that he might lead away the souls of men down to hell; yea, even that great pit which hath been digged for the destruction of men shall be filled by those who digged it, unto their utter destruction, saith the Lamb of God; not the destruction of the soul, save it be the casting of it into that hell which hath no end.

99 For behold, this is according to the captivity of the devil, and also according to the justice of God, upon all those who will work wickedness and abomination before him.

100 And now, my brothers and sisters, ye have now received those things which have been sealed up to come forth by the power of God for your salvation. Therefore, read them and pray that ye might understand them and be saved.

CHAPTER 65

The great apostasy is touched upon. The first principles of the gospel are set forth pertaining to the church of God. The worldwide Catholic Church is introduced. How the plain and precious things of the Bible were taken out.

AND now, I would that ye should understand that after the apostles of the Lord had been killed, and the Gentiles had set up many different churches among them; and many of them claiming to be the true church of Christ; yea, even after these things had been done, those that were the true saints of God were cast out of the churches of the rich, even by those men who were rich and powerful and who had set themselves up as leaders of the people who had the authority of God, which they believed that their leaders had received by the laying on of hands from the direct line of Priesthood which was given unto Peter, James, and John by the Lord.

2 And the true saints of God, who were His elect, were persecuted and slain by the hands of the Romans and by the consent of those leaders of the Christian faith who had made alliances with the Romans and the other governments of the earth.

3 And after only a few generations, the word of God became corrupt; yea, even after the same amount of time, which Nephi saw in his vision concerning his own people; in which he wrote, saying: And the angel said unto me: Look. And I looked, and beheld three generations pass away in righteousness; and their garments were white even like unto the Lamb of God. And the angel said unto me: These are made white in the blood of the Lamb, because of their faith in him. And I, Nephi, also saw many of the fourth generation who passed away in righteousness.

4 And these things were also true of the Jews who were in Jerusalem, and the Gentiles who received the gospel by the preaching and works of the apostles of the Lord in that part of the earth, even those at the same time period in which the children of Lehi were blessed with righteousness according to their desires to keep the commandments of God.

5 But the churches began to become corrupt and follow not the gospel of Christ, but follow the counsels of men, who had set themselves up above the people as the mouthpieces of God, even those who were the bishops and evangelists, and the elders of the churches.

6 For these men thought that they were given special authority over the children of men to counsel with them and give unto them the revelations of God as they received them from Him.

7 And the people began to believe these things and look to the leaders of their churches as those who had been called of God to guide them in all things.

8 But this was not the intent of the gospel of Jesus Christ, nor was it the intent of the Priesthood that was suffered to be established among them so that the fullness of the gospel could be given unto the people.

9 For the first principle of the gospel was that the people should have faith in the Lord Jesus Christ, even that they should listen to the words that he taught unto them and follow the example that he hath set for them.

10 Then after they have accepted these things of Christ, that they might repent and forsake the things that they were doing that were not in conformity with the words of Christ.

11 And then after repenting and forsaking these things, that they should make a covenant before God and before all men that they are willing to take upon them the name of the Son, and keep his commandments which he hath given unto them, that they may have the Spirit to be with them always, which Spirit giveth unto them this peace and joy, which is the love of the Father.

12 And this covenant was made by and through the ordinance of baptism. And after they are baptized and have made this covenant with the Father, then they receive the gift of the Holy Ghost that He hath promised to all of His children who worship Him and keep His commandments, which commandments He hath given unto them through His Son.

13 And now, there are no other principles or doctrine of the gospel that should have been given unto the people in regards to what should be offered unto them by the leadership of a true church of Christ.

14 Nevertheless, the people began to listen more to the words of their leaders, who had been ordained to the Priesthood of God, but who had been denied the power thereof because of their wickedness.

15 And their wickedness was in their examples; for they taught the words of Christ, yet they sought for the things of the world and the honor and praise of men, thus offending the Spirit of God, who would give the power to act in the name of God unto them, if they were like unto Christ in all things.

16 And these leaders begin to excommunicate those from the church who came to them with a broken heart and a contrite spirit seeking for forgiveness from the Lord for that in which they had sinned against him.

17 And these leaders thought of themselves as righteous and full of the power of God to deny salvation to any of those who they chose to excommunicate from the church of God.

18 And now, do ye suppose that the Father condoneth this of those who act in His name? Do ye suppose that if His child cometh unto Him and seeketh forgiveness for that which this child hath done against the Father, that He will cast this child away from Him, or disfellowship this child from His Spirit?

19 I say unto you that He would not do such a thing, and hath commanded those who He suffereth to lead in the church of God to forgive all those who come unto them seeking forgiveness from Him.

20 And the Lord did give commandments unto the apostles concerning those things which were sins that were punishable by an excommunication from the church, which he suffered to be established among them. But in all these commandments, he commanded his disciples to forgive all of those who came unto them for all things, except it be for murder, which shall not be forgiven in this world.

21 But if a man or a woman hath not committed murder, then anything that he or she hath committed, for which they seek forgiveness from the church, they shall be forgiven and not be cast out of the church or disfellowshipped from its blessings.

22 But as the church corrupted itself, these leaders began to cast out all those who questioned their authority, or who committed a sin according to their own commandments, which were the commandments and precepts of men.

23 And it came to pass that because the church began to embrace the world and teach for commandments the doctrines of men, Satan began to reward the church and its leaders and give unto them the prosperity and power that he giveth unto all those who follow him.

24 And in not too many years, the church became rich and powerful. And when Satan saw that he now had complete control over the church, he left the governments of men that he had set up to control the hearts and desires of the children of men, and gave his power and attention to the church, which became great and powerful, even a world-wide church, which being interpreted is Catholic.

25 And after this church had overthrown the governments of men by the power of Satan, it began to persecute all those who did not belong to the church. And it sent its armies and its navies, which were under the control of the leaders of the church, into all the world to subdue the world and bring all under the subjection of the church of the devil, which this great world-wide church promulgated.

26 And it was some of the leaders of this church that ordered that all the scriptures that were read concerning the life and ministry of Christ should be brought before them, that they might determine that which they would canonize and give unto the world as the official doctrine of Christ.

27 And when they had chosen these things, they excluded many things that did not agree with their own doctrines and principles, believing that the records had been corrupted by those who first wrote them.

28 But these records were not corrupted, but were given in their purity by many of the apostles, who were eyewitnesses to the life and ministry of Christ and the words which he spoke.

29 But because these pure words of the apostles did not agree with the corrupted doctrine of this great church, these leaders deleted those things which did not agree with them, thus were the plain and precious parts of the gospel lost among men.

30 And they would have been lost forever had not the Lord foreseen these things and prepared this record that it might come forth to give once more unto the children of men the things that were taken out of that which he had suffered to be written concerning his gospel.

31 For the original documents that were written by the hands of the apostles were destroyed. And various translations of their words survived, and it was from these documents that survived that the leaders of the church took their official version of the New Testament of the Bible, which ye have before you.

32 And there was none who could stand against Satan and the power that he gave unto the church. For the leaders of all nations were chosen by Satan and became his followers. And great and powerful kings and queens, who were ordained and confirmed by the church and its leaders, ruled and reigned over the people perpetuating the works and will of Satan throughout the whole earth.

33 And these kings and queens would do nothing except first it be sanctioned by the leaders of the church, who the people accepted as the mouthpieces of God in all things.

34 And during this time, the Spirit of the Lord had withdrawn itself from the whole earth. Thus began the days of darkness and obscurity upon the earth.

35 And though the gospel of Christ had spread throughout the world, there were few who were the humble followers of Christ. Yea, this was the period of time between the times and the half of time of which the prophet Daniel and John have spoken. He who hath understanding let him understand these things.

36 But before the Lord withdrew the Spirit from the earth, he made an attempt among the children of Israel in that part of the world to once again establish his gospel among them.

37 And now, I would that ye should understand what it meaneth when the Lord withdraweth His Spirit from off the face of the earth.

38 And ye should remember that I have spoken unto you concerning Lucifer and his plan of salvation that he presented before the Father in the beginning.

39 Now, the Father did not condemn Lucifer for using his free agency to speak that which he desired. And because of the words of Lucifer, many of the spirit children of God followed him and were desirous to accept the plan of salvation that he had offered unto them.

40 And the Father doth not force His children in anything, and according to the eternal laws, can never force them, but giveth unto them the ability to pursue that which they desire, that they might come to a better understanding of why the eternal plan that He hath given unto them is that plan that will give them the greatest source of eternal happiness and joy.

41 But if by their free agency they choose to live by another plan, He doth not interfere, but alloweth them the opportunity to learn for themselves.

42 And when it is said that the Spirit is withdrawn from the world, then these are the times that the Father commandeth that His Spirit is not given to any upon the earth, or in other

words, that the ministrations of the spirit world cease, even the communication between those in the spirit world who instill in the hearts of the children of men the plan of the Father, and those who are the children of men in mortality.

43 In other words, the Holy Ghost no longer maketh an effort to give the plan of the Father unto the children of men, so that they might experience an existence according to the laws by which Lucifer would have them live.

44 And this is the only reason why the Father would command that His Spirit not be given unto His children, whom He loveth.

45 And so it is that there have been times upon this earth when the Spirit of the Father hath not been given to the children of men, so that they might learn from their own experiences.

46 And when they are left to themselves, then they are subjected unto that spirit that would want us all to believe that his plan is a righteous plan that will give unto us more joy than the plan of the Father.

47 And since the time of Abraham, the Spirit hath been given and hath been available to the children of men, first for a time, and then it was taken from them, and then for times, that was twice as long as the first; and then it was taken from them; and finally for a time that shall be one half the time of the first.

48 And at the end of this half of time, shall the Lord come in the glory of the Father to give the plan of the Father once again to His children, so that they might experience it in its fullness.

49 And at this time, the Father shall never again withdraw His Spirit from among His children. For at this time, they will have learned through experience that His plan is the best plan for them, even the only plan that can assure them eternal peace and happiness forever.

50 And before the Spirit of the Lord shall be withdrawn from the world the second time; yea, even at the end of the times of which I have spoken, the Lord once again shall stretch forth his arm of mercy unto the world and call a prophet, who shall be the final prophet of that dispensation of time, through whom he shall give his gospel once again unto the children of men.

CHAPTER 66

The prophet Mohammed is introduced and his life and purpose is expounded on according to what Moroni received from the vision of the brother of Jared.

AND now, I, Moroni, I return once again to the words of the brother of Jared which he wrote concerning the last of the holy prophets that was called by the Lord as the last prophet of the times, which I have mentioned.

2 And it came to pass that the Lord had chosen a man and woman who were desirous to be husband and wife, who were one a Jew, and the other a Christian who followed the sect of the Gnostics, who were those who had separated themselves from the orthodox Christian church that was in the infancy of its power among the nations of the world.

3 And the families of this man and this woman were contentious one with the other over the religions to which they had dedicated their lives. But this man, whose name was Ismabil, cared not for that which his family thought concerning his love for this woman, whose name was Shamira.

4 But the family of Shamira, who were of the Christian faith, were sore against the marriage of their daughter to a Jew, and they set about to kill Ismabil before he could marry Shamira.

5 And a day for their marriage had been set. But during the night before the day that had been set, a brother of Shamira went in darkness unto the bed of Ismabil and slew him in his sleep.

6 And in the morning, when Shamira found him dead, she took up a dagger that she might thrust it deep into her own heart and join the man whom she loved.

7 But the Lord sent an angel unto her and stopped her in that which she was about to do. And the angel spoke unto her, saying: Behold, thou hast been chosen by God to bring forth a son of Ismabil, that he might be a great prophet among this people and bring many to salvation because of his words.

8 And he shall be set as a standard among the people that shall be given unto the world that they might have the word of God given unto them in darkness, that they might have a light by which they can see.

9 And Shamira spoke to the angel, saying: I have known Ismabil only one time, wherewith then shall I conceive by him?

10 And the angel answered her saying: Believest thou that Ismabil was a righteous man? And Shamira answered him, saying: Yea, I know he was a righteous man, who loved God with all of his heart, and also the Christ who should come and save his people. And he tried to live his life after the laws of this God, and in this he was righteous.

11 And the angel answered her, saying: And dost thou believe in this Christ of whom Ismabil hath spoken? And she saith: I do not know his Christ, but I believe in the Son of God according to that which I have learned of my father. But I know that Ismabil believed in a Christ, and it is him that I loved.

12 And the angel, saith unto her: Behold, his Christ truly is the Son of God that did come into the world to teach the will of God to all men. And he hath called others to help him teach this will. And in thy womb he hath given unto thee a son by Ismabil, even that thou shouldst teach unto thy son the things which his father believed, which is the righteousness of the Son of God.

13 And she saith: I know that thou hast been sent from God unto me, for I behold that thou art an angel. And if thou hast been sent from God, then those things which thou hast spoken unto me are the words of God, therefore, I believe that they are true.

14 And it came to pass that Shamira kept these things in her heart and revealed them unto no one in her family. But when her family found that she was with child from Ismabil, who was dead, they mourned exceedingly for her and prayed that the child might not be born among them.

15 And it came to pass that Shamira left her family and wandered in the wilderness until the time of the birth of her son had arrived. And when the time had arrived for the birth, she traveled to the city of Mecca and there had the child in the stall of an animal, she being an outcast because she did not have a husband, but was with child.

16 And so it was that a great prophet was born like unto the Christ at Jerusalem. And it was this same prophet, who as a spirit, guided his mortal mother in all things that she should do.

17 And after she had given birth to her son, the angel of God that had previously appeared unto her came down and blessed the child and gave unto him his name, which was Mohammed.

18 And his mother could not care for Mohammed, and took him unto one of her sisters who had compassion on her. But this sister could not show compassion openly unto Shamira, having been commanded by her family to have nothing to do with her.

19 And the sister of Shamira hid the boy from the knowledge of her family, her own husband being sympathetic towards all men, he being an unbeliever. Nevertheless, in time, it was revealed to the father of Shamira that she had taken Mohammed into her house.

20 And it came to pass that her father befriended Mohammed and loved him and raised him up according to the customs of his people.

21 And immediately after Shamira had given her son to her sister, she went back into the wilderness and took no food or water with her, and was desirous to leave this world and be with Ismabil again.

22 And Ismabil was allowed by the administration in the spirit world to come to his wife in her weakened state and speak comfort to her as she left the flesh and entered into the spirit world to be with Ismabil.

23 And together they were present in the spirit world as Mohammed grew in the days of his youth. And they observed all things which were done through the administrations of the spirit world to prepare Mohammed for the mission that he would perform in the flesh. And in this, Ismabil and Shamira remained in a state of happiness in the spirit world observing all things that their son of the flesh did in mortality.

24 And Mohammed grew up in a similar fashion like unto Jesus among those who did not understand the greatness for which the Father had prepared him and foreordained him.

25 And during the years of his youth, Mohammed learned many things by watching the examples of those with whom he lived. And it came to pass that when he had reached the age of maturity, he began to reason within himself of those things which he observed among the people.

26 For he saw the hate that the Jew had for the Christian, and also the hate which the Christian had for the Jew, both sects claiming that they were in possession of the truth. And having seen this hate and the cause that it had upon the people, Mohammed thought within himself that the truth could not be had among a people who thought themselves above another.

27 And he was a righteous man all the days of his life, and looked out for the well being of others and did all things according to the Spirit of God which was within him.

28 Nevertheless, the Lord had not manifested himself unto Mohammed in any manner except through the ministrations of the spirit world, which are given unto the children of men by faith, even that which they do not see but in which they have a hope.

29. And it came to pass that Mohammed became saddened by that which he beheld among the people. And he was exceedingly prosperous among the people because of his honesty and good works among them.

30 And he worked with a woman who had much business among the people in trade, and who was esteemed above many in that part of the land. And it came to pass that Mohammed married this woman and raised children according to the customs of the people of that area, which customs were influenced by the traditions of the Christians and also of the Jews.

31 Nevertheless, Mohammed was not influenced by the pride and prestige of the rich, neither did he put his family above his neighbor and thought of all people as equal before God.

32 And he did not know God, but knew that the love in his heart would be the love of God, if He truly existed.

33 And the wife of Mohammed, whose name was Khadija, was particular to the Christian faith and would encourage Mohammed to visit the Christian church and learn of their ways. Nevertheless, he did not know of a surety in himself which of the many religious beliefs was the true belief of God.

34 And because of the confusion of the different sects that were among the people, Mohammed became depressed in the Spirit, this having been the plan of the Lord at the time that Mohammed was ready to be called to his foreordained calling as a prophet of the Lord.

35 And it came to pass that Mohammed would for many days retreat unto the cave called Hira, and therein contemplate the truths that the Spirit was giving unto him, he not knowing consciously that he was receiving this light and knowledge from the ministrations of the Spirit.

36 And this same mountain in which the cave of Hira was found was called the Mountain of Light by those who would follow the teachings of Mohammed in later times.

37 And Mohammed wandered in the Spirit for many years, searching within himself for the truths which were made evident unto him by the Holy Ghost.

38 And when he was near unto forty years, Mohammed retired once again into the cave, being depressed in the spirit because of the many disputations that he had witnessed among his people. And he, for the first time since those days of his childhood when he was taught to pray to a God in whom he did not believe; neither did he understand this God to whom he was taught to pray;

39 Notwithstanding, Mohammed knelt before God and prayed unto him, saying: Great God, all power and glory be to Thy Holy Name. I know Thee not; but this I do know, even that Thou wouldst not have that there exist among Thy children the contention that causeth hate and persecution of brothers and sisters, all who believe in Thee and seek for Thy truths.

40 And when he had spoken these words, a pillar of light appeared directly above him, which light was brighter than the sun at noon day and which did light the cave that it shown in brilliant white; yea, even the rocks did glow exceedingly because of this light.

41 And within the light Mohammed beheld two personages, whose light and brilliance exceeded even the light of the pillar in which they were suspended.

42 And the first spoke unto him and said: Behold, This is my Beloved Son, in whom I am well pleased because of the things which he hath done in my kingdom. Hear him.

43 And now, I would that ye should know that this was the very Eternal Father who had accompanied the Son, even Jesus Christ, who was appointed by the Father to administer His plan to His children in this part of His kingdom.

44 And Jesus spoke unto Mohammed, calling him by name and teaching many things unto him which he had taught to his disciples during the days of his earthly ministry.

45 And now, I, Moroni, do not recount all of the words which Jesus spake unto Mohammed, for many of them, if not all, were the same words which he hath given unto all of the holy prophets whom he hath called to teach his will unto the children of men; and all of these words have I given in this record.

46 But in one thing the Lord did command Mohammed that he had not commanded to his apostles at Jerusalem. And that which the Lord commanded him was that which I have already given unto you in this record concerning the name of Jesus and the insignificance of this name, or any name by which God is called by the different cultures and people of the world.

47 And I have written already unto you, saying: And according to these cultures and traditions, we have been taught the gospel of Jesus Christ. Nevertheless, this gospel is not called the gospel of Jesus Christ according to the traditions and customs of the many different peoples of the world.

48 And it doth not matter to the Lord in what name he is called, for it is his desire to give unto all the laws of his gospel, let these laws be called by whatever name they might be called. And also, let him be called by whatever name he may be called according to the different cultures and traditions of the children of men

49 And the Lord spoke unto my fathers when he visited them after his resurrection and ascension, and he said unto them: And verily, verily, I say unto you that I have other sheep, which are not of this land, neither of the land of Jerusalem, neither in any parts of that land round about whither I have been to minister.

50 For they of whom I speak are they who have not as yet heard my voice; neither have I at any time manifested myself unto them.

51 But I have received a commandment of the Father that I shall go unto them, and that they shall hear my voice, and shall be numbered among my sheep, that there may be one fold and one shepherd, therefore I go to show myself unto them.

52 Now I, Moroni, ask of you, Do ye know the name by which the Lord is called by these other sheep who had not yet heard his voice at the time he presented himself to my fathers? Do ye not know that his name is not important to him, if it so be that they believe in him and keep his commandments?

53 And what say ye, even of those who are reading this record that the Lord hath commanded me to make, and hath instructed me to write the things that the Spirit whispereth unto me; again, what say ye, if ye heard me pronounce the name of the Lord Jesus Christ according to my own language, which was taught to me by the traditions and culture of my fathers? Would ye understand of whom I speak?

54 Behold, I say unto you, that ye would not understand the words that I would speak, and likewise, I would not understand the words that ye would speak. And if I pronounce the name of the Lord in a different manner, or if I call him by a different name than you, what think ye then about the name of Jesus Christ?

55 And if my Lord and my God is called Cummenkinin, and it is this being whom I worship and obey, what say ye of my righteousness then? And if it so be that Cummenkinin hath established a church among my people, which is established according to our traditions and our culture, which of a surety is different than your own, is it then a sin to worship our God in this manner, who is not called Jesus Christ by us, but who is the same God whom ye worship according to your traditions?

56 And if our prophets, whom we call Serihlibiem, teach us the law of Cummenkinin, and teach us that we should love our enemies and do good to them that hate us and persecute us, and if we live our lives in harmony with the spirit of Cummenkinin, as we are taught by our Serihlibiem, are we to be condemned for not taking upon us the name of Jesus Christ only because we do not understand this name, and it cannot be understood by us according to our language and our culture?

57 Behold, I say unto you, that when the Lord visiteth these people, who are some of the other sheep that have not heard his voice, he shall allow them to call him Cummenkinin, or by whatever name they have been taught to worship by their Serihlibiem.

58 And this doth not take away the efficacy of the holy name of Christ, by which all men shall be saved. For I have written upon this record the meaning of the symbolism of which a name is given. And again I say unto you, that all names are symbolic of the works that are associated with that name.

59 And is it not by the works of Christ, or Cummenkinin, or by whatever name he might be called, that we are saved? I say unto you, that it is by the works, which the name of Christ symbolizeth, by which we are saved. Behold, we are not saved by his name, but by that which he hath accomplished for us.

60 Therefore, it mattereth not unto the Father by what name we call Him or those whom He hath commissioned to serve us and bring us back to His kingdom.

61 And if there are churches and religions that are named according to the customs and traditions of the different peoples of the world; and if these have their own written word, which is their holy scripture, then what difference would they have in the eyes of the Lord, if it so be that they teach his gospel?

62 I say unto you, that there is no difference. And if these teach the words of the gospel of Christ, then they are accepted by him.

63 And now, the Lord did not want Mohammed to use the name of Jesus Christ among the people to whom he would be sent to teach his gospel. And the reason for which he commanded this of Mohammed, was because those who professed to be followers of Jesus Christ, even the Christians who were already many upon the earth, had corrupted the true gospel of the Father by the name of Jesus Christ.

64 And many of their leaders had taught the people erroneous doctrine regarding the name of Jesus; and therefore, to avoid any conflict with the Christians, that they might think of themselves above the Jews, Mohammed was prohibited from using the name of Jesus, or the Christ, as he went about to teach the gospel to the people.

65 Nevertheless, Mohammed was commanded to instruct the people to maintain great respect for any of the true parts of the gospel that still remained among the Christians who professed to follow Jesus Christ, and also those truths that remained among the Jews.

66 And he was commanded to make no mention of the visitation of the Father, or of the appearance of Jehovah, who was known as Jesus Christ in the flesh, so that no more conflict concerning these things would come to pass among the people.

67 But since both the Jews and the Christians believed in the appearance of angels, and since one of the most accepted names of an angel among both of these sects was the angel Gabriel, Mohammed was therefore commanded that he should recount the visitation of the Father and the Son to the people as a vision and visitation from Archangel Gabriel, who he would testify told him that he was to be a prophet of the Almighty God.

68 And the Lord instructed Mohammed in many things, and sent other angels down unto him to give unto him the authority and commission to preach the gospel to the people.

69 And it came to pass that after three days of visitation from these heavenly messengers, Mohammed returned to the house of Khadija, his wife, and related that which he was commanded to give unto the people. And his wife from that moment believed on the words of Mohammed and became his disciple.

70 And it came to pass that Mohammed went forth among the people and taught them the gospel of Jesus Christ, or the gospel of Allah, as he had been instructed by the Lord to give unto the people.

71 And the people mocked Mohammed for those things which he taught unto them. But among the poor and outcasts he did gain much success in those things which he taught unto them.

72 And again, I say unto you, that I shall not give herein a detailed explanation of those things which he taught to the people; for he taught the exact same gospel that Jesus had taught during his ministry, changing nothing, except for the names by which he called the Father and the Son, from whom he had received these things.

73 And it came to pass that over the course of a few years, Mohammed received many revelations from the Holy Ghost and caused that they should be written by scribes, who would hear his words and write them as he spoke them unto the scribes.

74 And he became like unto Moses, in that he was not strong in writing, nor could he read a language, but he spoke with power, being filled with the gift and power of God.

75 And from the revelations that Mohammed received from the Spirit, he brought forth a record of the teachings that he would have those that followed him learn and understand. And this record became known as the Quran.

76 And Mohammed proclaimed that the Quran was the last revelation that God would give unto the people of that time. And he also taught unto the people that he himself was the last holy prophet, who was called of God to save the people, in that dispensation of time.

77 And I have already explained unto you that he truly was the last prophet of the time period revealed in the revelations of Daniel and John as the times, which time period would precede a time of great darkness upon the earth when the Holy Ghost was commanded by the Father to withdraw His Spirit from the children of men.

78 And then in the latter days, even at the beginning of the half of time, which I have explained unto you, the gospel of the Lord shall once again be revealed in its fullness to the first of these two final prophets who shall be sent forth among the people to restore the truth of all things unto them.

79 And like it was with the message of Moses among the Jews, and the message of Jesus among the Christians, even the message of all the holy prophets of God; yea, in the days following the death of Mohammed the people shall also corrupt his message and do those things which are most abominable in the sight of God, and change the meaning of the Holy Quran, which shall be given unto the people who would become known of themselves as Muslims, being called this because of their belief in the religion of Islam, which shall be that which is like unto the religion of the Jews, and the religion of the Christians, and the religions that came to be because of the followers of the prophets of God, who have been called to teach the gospel of the Father unto the people of their own cultures.

80 And as soon as these great prophets left the people—most of them being killed by those who would not accept their teachings of the word of God—their followers corrupted the word of God and set themselves up above their neighbors and proclaimed that their prophet was he who was greater than the last, or greater than the prophet of their neighbor.

81 And thus in the effort of the Lord to make all people of the earth his sheep, and teach his sheep one doctrine, which was the doctrine of the Father, even that His children should love one another; yea, in spite of his efforts, the people reject the shepherd and become prideful and put themselves firmly in the grasp of Satan.

82 And Satan useth these religions of men to make war and reign with blood and horror upon the earth as he had promised to do in the beginning.

CHAPTER 67

Moroni expounds upon the other sheep to which the gospel hath been taught. The prophets Kung-fu-tse, Lao-tse, Buddha and Rishabha are introduced. Moroni expounds further on time, times, and half of time as the timetable of the history of humankind. He explains what is good and evil to the Father.

AND now, there are other sheep that the Lord visited to whom he taught the will of the Father in all things. For the Father had commanded His Son to give His gospel unto all of His children.

2 And ye know of those who are the descendants of Jacob, and their record ye have in the account of the Jews. And those who followed the teachings of Zarathustra, and many of the other holy prophets sent unto the house of Israel, are also those of the descendants of Jacob. And all of the children of men scattered throughout the whole earth are the descendants of Adam and Eve.

3 Nevertheless, so that ye in the latter days can know of the great love and mercy that the Father hath for all of His children, I have been commanded to give unto you a brief accounting of that which the brother of Jared saw concerning those who had separated themselves from the other sons of Adam, or those who were separated from the children of men that came forth from the loins of Abraham, whose record hath been given unto you from the mouth of a Jew.

4 And these who were separated from the descendants of Abraham were some of those whose bodies had been affected by interbreeding with the order of the lower creatures from which Beneli was born in the beginning, even many of those who were the descendants of the Cainites and the Benelites, who lived in and around the land of Eden in the beginning.

5 However, all of their spirits, regardless of their flesh, were children of the Father, and were like unto the Father in all the things according to the likeness of the spirit.

6 And it came to pass that some of the Cainites, who had escaped destruction, went into the land northward and found a land from which they could see across the great waters of the oceans. And they beheld, across the great waters, this land, which was even greater than the land on which they stood.

7 And there were those who constructed rudimentary ships that they might cross this narrow gap of water and go into the great land which they beheld.

8 And when they had reached this land, they begin to travel southward, staying close unto the borders of the great ocean. And this they did so that they would not be lost in their way, thinking in themselves that they would explore this strange new land, and if it was not inhabitable, then they could easily follow the shoreline of the great ocean and find their way back to the land from whence they came.

9 And these that traveled in the borders of the seashore into the land southward continued their journey for a great distance. And many of them found the land to be very verdant and comfortable for their existence. And after many generations, there began to be many of the descendants of the Cainites that inhabited many parts of the great land that they had discovered.

10 And it came to pass that very few of the descendants of the Cainites, and only a few of the Benelites, who had escaped destruction, stayed in the land of Eden. But there were those who did stay in the land northward. And it was this people who eventually came down near the land of Lehi-Nephi, and who joined with the families of Laman and Lemuel and the sons of Ishmael who had rebelled against Nephi, thus perpetuating the dark skin that came from the effects of the sun and the interbreeding with those who were descendants of Beneli.

11 And after the majority had left the land of Eden and traveled to this new land, it came to pass that they began to separate themselves and form nations and cities amongst them, some of which became great and powerful civilizations.

12 And it came to pass that the Lord sent forth his prophets also unto these peoples and taught the gospel unto them. And for a time, many of the descendants of Cain repented and turned to the Father and received of His spirit, even so much that they had exceeding peace among them and did prosper in the land.

13 And two of the greatest prophets among them were named Kung-fu-tse, and another named Lao-tse, they being the principle ones from whose teachings most of the cultures of these peoples began to be influenced by the word of God. For behold, the teachings of Kung-fu-tse and Lao-tse truly were the teachings of the gospel, which both of these were taught as they grew in their childhood in the like manner which I have shown unto you in the accounting of many of the other prophets who were called by God to give His commandments unto His children.

14 And these two prophets were called at the beginning of the times, in which the Father had commanded that His Spirit once more be had in its fullness upon the earth for the sake of all of His children.

15 And now, it is important that I once again touch upon that which is written concerning the time, and times, and half a time, so that ye might have a better understanding of the marvelous works of the Father concerning His children.

16 And I have already explained unto you that these are the periods of time that the gospel was preached throughout the earth through the ministrations of the Holy Ghost, and through the Holy Order of the Son of God, by which were called forth prophets, seers and revelators who were given the fullness of the gospel so that they might give it in its fullness unto the children of men.

17 And now, I have been commanded to expound further upon these things so that ye might know the mysteries of God pertaining to the manner in which He alloweth all of His children to experience the flesh, so that they might know that which is best for them, even that which will bring them the most happiness.

18 For behold, the Father taught all of His children His plan, which is this gospel. But because of our free agency, He could force none of us to accept His plan.

19 And for this reason, Lucifer had a right to present unto us his plan, that we might consider it and weigh it against the plan of the Father, determining for ourselves which plan would bring the most happiness to us.

20 Now, the Father knew that His plan was the only plan that was acceptable according to the eternal laws of heaven. Nevertheless, so that we might learn this without doubting for ourselves, He hath allowed Satan to incorporate his alternate plan into our lives in mortality, so that we might know from our own experience that the plan of the Father is the only way to eternal happiness and salvation.

21 And now, the prophets have spoken much; yea, they have written much concerning righteousness and wickedness, and keeping the commandments of God and sinning; even there have been many things written and spoken of concerning that which is good and that which is evil.

22 And I have explained many of these things in this record, that ye might come to a better understanding of that which is good and that which is evil. Nevertheless, I have also shown you herein that what is evil to some, might be good to others; and likewise, what is good to some, might be evil to others.

23 Now, these things that are good to some and evil to others, cannot be that which is righteousness and that which is wickedness in the plan of the Father. For in the plan of the Father, that which is righteous is always righteous and shall be righteous forever, even for all of His children.

24 And that which is wickedness is always wickedness and shall be wickedness forever. But the things which cause ye such contention, even that which some of you believe to be righteous, which others of you believe to be wickedness, and also that which some of you believe to be wickedness, and which others of you believe to be righteous; yea, this contention is not part of the plan of the Father, and never will be.

25 And for this reason, He hath commanded us to not judge one another, but that we should love each other and mete out for a measurement of judgment against another that which we would have them measure unto us.

26 And now, I will explain unto you in plainness and simplicity so that there shall be no more contention among you, and also that ye might have a better understanding of that which is truly good and that which is truly evil to God, our Father.

27 And then if ye know the good and evil which concerneth our Father, that ye might stop your judgments of your neighbor and love him as yourself, this being the great commandment of the Father.

28 Behold, since the plan of the Father is to give unto us eternal happiness, then anything that goeth contrary to this eternal happiness is that which is evil to the Father.

29 And likewise, anything that bringeth us joy and causeth us a happiness that is eternal, this is what is good to the Father.

30 And that which is good for us and causeth us to experience joy, and remain in a state of happiness forever, is that which we should do unto others, and that which we should expect that others should do unto us; for these things are good and righteous before the Father.

31 However, my brothers and sisters, the plan of Lucifer also provideth us with joy and happiness. But the joy and happiness that we receive from his plan are temporary and last only for a few moments, and cannot give unto us any joy outside of the flesh.

32 And now, all of us know those things which cause us enduring happiness, and also those things which cause us a moment of happiness, which things are temporary, and afterwards reward us with misery, which is the absence of happiness.

33 And these things which give unto us this temporary happiness and then give back unto us misery thereafter, are sins against God. These are those things which are wickedness and unrighteousness, and against that which the holy prophets and the scriptures speak.

34 But that which bringeth us continual joy and placeth us in a state of happiness that is never ending; yea, these things are the righteous things of God, and have been given unto us by the Father for our happiness.

35 Behold, the Father desireth us to be happy forever. He doth not want us to experience misery, and then at times fleeting joy that doth not remain with us. For this purpose were we created by Him, even that we might have joy and remain in a state of happiness forever.

36 And now, there are many who say that there doth not exist upon the earth those things that bring continual happiness unto us. Yea, they say that the world is full of misery and strife, and all manner of vicissitudes and evil; and that the joys that we experience are all temporary, and last only for a short time before misery once again claimeth its permanent place in our hearts.

37 And that which they say is true, and is not said in hypocrisy, but wisdom. But of this wisdom, there are few who understandeth that which they speak.

38 For behold, the works of the children of men are wicked and bring forth the rewards that are associated with these wicked works, even this fleeting joy of which they speak, which is replaced with continual misery thereafter.

39 And do ye think that this would be the case if ye obeyed the commandments of God and did that which is good and righteous in His sight? Of a surety the children of men suffer all manner of vicissitudes and sadness and misery among them; but these things they suffer because they are wicked, and not because the word of God is not sure in that which He hath promised those who keep His commandments.

40 And is it so hard to understand that if ye are happy, then ye are doing those things which are good before the Father; that is, I say, if the happiness that ye are experiencing is a continual happiness that lasteth forever.

41 And if ye are sad and miserable, then ye are doing those things which are evil and contrary to the plan of the Father.

42 And now, I have been commanded by the Spirit to give unto you an example of that which ye can do to have this eternal happiness with you always.

43 Yea, ye already know that the commandments of the Father are all related to the great commandment which He hath given unto us, which is that ye love one another as ye would have them love you.

44 Therefore, a sin is anything that ye do to another that ye would not have him do unto you. And a righteous work is anything that ye would do to another that ye would have him to do unto you.

45 And if ye do unto another what ye would want him to do to you, and he doth likewise unto you, then wherein can there exist a semblance of misery of any kind?

46 Would not, then, this happiness last forever in that which ye have done unto each other?

47 And are not the vicissitudes and miseries that we experience in mortality only those things that others do unto us?

48 For the sun continueth to shine in its fullness everyday, giving light unto the world according to the laws of nature in which it hath been established. Therefore, it is giving unto us, and taketh nothing from us, therefore, is it capable of sinning against us?

49 And do any of those things which God hath provided for us on this earth, even the fruits and plants that provide us with nourishment, do any of these sin against us and cause us misery?

50 Yet, if our neighbor taketh more of the fruits and the plants than are necessary for his own nourishment, even that there is none left for another, doth this not create misery and strife among us?

51 And if he who hath nothing to eat cometh to him who hath taken more than that which he needeth for his own nourishment, and asketh of him something to eat; and if he who hath an abundance saith unto him who hath none, I have nothing to give to you, doth this not cause misery and unhappiness?

52 Doth this not cause him who hath none to rise up against his neighbor, who hath an abundance, and take by force that which he requireth to satisfy his hunger? Is this not a cause of misery?

53 Yea, it is true that when the man took more of the fruits and the plants than that which he needed to sustain himself, he began to feel a temporary joy and a satisfaction that he had an abundance and a security of his future needs. But this temporary joy perpetuateth an even greater misery when he turneth away his neighbor and keepeth this abundance for himself.

54 And if the man gave unto his neighbor of his abundance so that they both were filled, then how great would be the gratitude of one and the satisfaction of the other, knowing that he saved the life of his neighbor—and this joy would never be forgotten, nor would it end.

55 Therefore, I would that ye should know, that a sin is anything that is contrary to the plan of happiness that the Father taught unto us in the beginning.

56 And in order for the Father to teach us that His plan was the only way that we could possibly find this eternal happiness, He commanded that there be times upon the earth when His children are left to themselves, and that Satan might have an opportunity to give his plan unto the children of men without the interference of prophets of God and the ministrations of the Holy Spirit, which turn the hearts of the children of men from evil to good.

57 And these are the times inbetween the time at the beginning, and the times in the meridian of the time of the history of the children of men, and the half of time that shall be in the last days of the history of the children of men in this world.

58 Yea, these are the times of great wickedness, or sin and misery, as I have explained it unto you. Or in other words, these are the times that the children of men live contrary to the plan of the Father; and by living contrary to the plan of the Father, they experience great misery and unhappiness among them.

59 And I have already related to you in this record a brief history of many of these peoples that lived upon the earth during the time, and times, and also those who lived upon the earth in between these two different time periods.

60 And now, I have also explained unto you that the time of my making of this record is near unto the end of the times of which I have spoken. And the time is not yet, but is soon to come that the end of the times shall come, and the beginning of the period of time between the times and the half of time shall commence upon the earth.

61 And I have abridged the words of the brother of Jared concerning this Mohammed, who shall be the last prophet in the dispensation of the times.

62 And now, I would that ye should know more concerning the beginning of this period known as the times, and other of the holy prophets that the Lord called at the beginning of this time to teach the plan of the Father to all those upon the earth.

63 For it was at the beginning of this time, which is the times, that Zenos and Zenock were prepared and sent to the Jews at Jerusalem, and of whom Lehi testifieth according to the record of Nephi.

64 And I also have mentioned to you of Kung-fu-tse and Lao-tse, who were sent unto the people who are the descendants of Beneli and Cain; and these were sent at the beginning of the period known as the times.

65 And it is also important that those of you who shall receive these things in the latter days know of two other great prophets who were called by the Lord to administer his word unto the people of the cultures in which they lived.

66 And they were called Gautama, who was later called Buddha, and Rishabha.

67 And these were both holy prophets who taught the people the plan of the Father, having received their instruction and their callings from the Lord in their own times.

68 And it is expedient that ye should have mention of these because of their influence of the cultures among the children of men, and because of the way in which they are perceived in the latter days.

69 And in the latter days there shall be many religions and divers churches which preach many forms of these religions. But the main religions of the latter days shall be those which are based upon the corrupted teachings of these holy prophets that I have mentioned in this record.

70 Behold, these religions shall be known as the Muslim, and the Hindu, and the Buddhist and the Jew, and the Christian. And from these shall come forth many sects, each teaching many different forms of these religions.

71 And now, these things have been made known unto you that ye might know the mind and the will of the Father concerning all of His children.

72 Yea, did not the Lord call these holy prophets and give unto them his commandments and teach unto them his gospel, which is the plan of the Father? And are we not all children of one God, even the Creator of our spirits, and the Creator who set in motion this system and order of nature that revolveth around the sun that He created to give life unto this planet on which we live?

73 And did not the Lord say unto his disciples that he had other sheep which were not of this fold, and that he must bring them also unto the Father by teaching them his gospel?

74 Do ye not see what the Father hath done for His children in mercy and in patience? Do ye not see that He hath given us His gospel during the time, and times, and half of time; and that during these times, were there not at least some of His children who found continual happiness when they followed His plan of happiness for them?

75 And during the times that He withdrew His Spirit and left the children of men unto themselves, were not these time periods increased in misery and in turmoil and in wickedness among the children of men? Yea, could there be found any righteous and happy people upon the face of the earth during these times?

76 Hath not our own history testified unto us that the plan of the Father is the only plan that we can follow if we want to experience joy and happiness forever?

77 Is this not why our Father hath provided the opportunity for us to experience mortality, even that we might prove to ourselves that all of His words are true?

78 And it came to pass that when these great prophets of whom I have made mention died, their followers began to corrupt their teachings, and in many ways changing the pure gospel that was given unto them by these prophets.

79 And after they had corrupted their teachings, they began to teach for doctrine the precepts and commandments of men mingled with the enlightened words of wisdom given by these prophets.

80 And in this way Satan was able to subvert the plan of God and put in place his own plan, which plan hath caused exceedingly misery and pain among the children of men.

81 And now, I will give unto you my final words concerning the time, and times and half of time. For the Lord hath forbidden me from giving unto you anything further than that which I have given you, and that which I am about to give you concerning these things.

82 For if ye truly had the Spirit to be with you, then ye would know these things. And if ye would listen to the prophets who have been sent unto you, then ye would know these things, if it so be that ye are too weak in the Spirit to understand them for yourselves.

83 Behold, after the period of the times hath ended, there shall be a great period of time when the Spirit shall not be upon the earth, even a time when no prophets of God shall be called to give the fullness of the gospel to the people of the earth.

84 But at the beginning of the half of time shall this first prophet of the latter days, even he who shall be called Joseph after the name of his father; yea, he shall be called and shall give unto the world the fullness of the gospel once again.

85 And in the meridian of the half of times shall this final prophet be called forth to establish the truth of the first and take away all the stumbling blocks that have been put in place by the Lord because of the wickedness of men. And he shall be called Christopher, being a bearer of Christ, and shall be he who shall bring forth this record unto you.

86 And this record shall be the final written revelation given by the Father to prepare the world for the coming of Christ in the glory of the Father.

87 And Christ shall come at the end of the half of time. And at this time there shall be no more need of prophets or scriptures, or holy men to teach the fullness of the gospel to the world. For Christ shall reign supreme; and he shall throw down all the governments and the religions of the world which have been set up according to the precepts and commandments of men, which are wicked.

88 And the Lord shall cause to be set up the final government of God, which shall be established according to the plan of the Father.

89 And now, it is expedient that ye should know the times of Satan and his power, that ye might realize that the Father hath given Lucifer, who is Satan according to the spirit, a fair opportunity to show forth his plan upon the earth.

90 And since the beginning of time Satan hath been trying to win over the hearts of the children of men to his plan and turn their hearts from the plan of the Father.

91 And he hath done this through the ministrations of the spirit world, where he resideth with those who follow him, as I have already explained it unto you.

92 But in all the time periods of the earth, the Lord hath forbidden Satan from using all of his knowledge of the power of God, which is the ability to understand the laws of nature and to control them to bring happiness to the children of God.

93 And part of the argument of Lucifer is that all of the children of God should have the privilege to become like their Father and have His power, so that they can give themselves this happiness. But the plan of the Father doth not allow those who are Terrestrial or Telestial spirits to have this power. And this He forbideth, because of that which these spirits would do with this power.

94 But Lucifer disagreeth with the Father, and maintaineth that all the children of God should have the same opportunity to enjoy all the benefits of being an exalted being like unto the Father in all things.

95 And in the beginning, even as a spirit, Lucifer argued this point successfully, because none of the children of God had yet experienced the effects of the flesh on their spirits.

96 And the Father knew that those who had chosen for themselves those glories in His kingdoms where they did not serve others, but were served themselves forever, could not have His powers and knowledge bestowed upon them because they would misuse these powers and destroy themselves and create imbalance and chaos in His kingdoms.

97 Nevertheless, because none of His children had experienced mortality, or the effects of the flesh as I have mentioned, there was no way that He could convince Lucifer or those who followed him, nor could any of us know for a surety until we experienced the effects of the flesh firsthand, as was provided in the plan of the Father from the beginning.

98 But during the times of the earth when Satan went to and fro upon the earth deceiving the children of men and turning them from God to his plan, he was forbidden by the Father to give much knowledge of the powers of God unto them.

99 And this the Father forbade because He knew that with this knowledge, the children of men would destroy themselves.

100 Nevertheless, so that none of His children would question the exactness of His plan and the wisdom of it, the Father shall allow Satan to have complete control over the hearts of the children of men during the half of time during the latter days, while at the same time allowing the Spirit and the Holy Order of the Son to dwell with those who choose to do the will of God.

101 And at that time, he shall be allowed to give unto the children of men some of the knowledge of God and the understanding of the laws of nature, so that they may use these laws according to the dictates of their own wills and pleasures. And of these things I shall make an account later in this record.

102 And now I end my words which I have been commanded to give unto you concerning the time and times and half of time, which have been spoken of and written of by the holy prophets.

CHAPTER 68

Moroni continues his explanation of the timetable of the Lord. The times of many of the events of the history of the world are explained, and the exact year of the Second Coming can be ascertained by this revelation and the Spirit.

BEHOLD, before I end my words concerning these time periods, the Lord hath commanded me to give unto you a better insight into some things which are unclear to many of you in the latter days.

2 For it came to pass, that after the Lord had taken his Spirit from the earth and left the children of men to themselves; and after Satan began to have exceedingly great power over the hearts and minds of the children of men; yea, at this time the whole earth became wicked, denying the plan of the Father in all things.

3 And the brother of Jared wrote concerning many of the things that the children of men began to do contrary to the plan of the Father.

4 And I have already explained unto you that the plan of Lucifer is not an evil plan to those who have made it their plan and follow it. Yea, when those who follow the plan of Lucifer incorporate the whole plan into their lives, they begin to think that they are a righteous and a blessed people.

5 And when they have used their free agency to choose the plan that they are desirous to follow, then the promulgator of this plan becometh their God.

6 And in this way Satan became the God of the whole earth. And he began to put his plan into the hearts and minds of the children of men, and seal in their foreheads his name; and in their hand, according to their works, they have received his mark, which is the mark of the beast of which John hath spoken.

7 And John also wrote of the fall of the Roman Empire and the beginning of the time that Satan would have power over all the earth, even concerning the time period between the times and the half of time as I have explained it unto you.

8 And John wrote saying: And I saw one of his heads as it were wounded to death. Now, this was the Roman Empire of which John wrote. And his vision continued, saying: and his deadly wound was healed; and all the world wondered after the beast.

9 And they worshipped the dragon which gave power unto the beast and to them that were their leaders. And they worshipped the beast, saying, Who is like unto the beast? Who is able to make war with him?

10 And there was given unto him a mouth speaking great things and blasphemies; and power was given unto him this time to continue forty and two months.

11 And he opened his mouth in blasphemy against God, to blaspheme his name, and his tabernacle, and them who dwell in heaven. And it was given unto him to make war with the saints, and to overcome them by the words of the leaders of the nations to whom he had given his power.

12 And power was given him over all kindreds, and tongues, and nations. And all that dwell upon the earth shall worship him, whose names are not written in the book of life of the Lamb slain from the foundation of the world.

13 If any man have an ear, let him hear. He that leadeth into captivity shall go into captivity; he that killeth by the sword must be killed with the sword. Here is the patience and the faith of the saints.

14 And now, I, Moroni, have been instructed to give unto you a clearer meaning of the words of John, and also to put back those plain and precious things which the great and abominable church hath taken away from the words of John.

15 And I have been commanded to do these things, so that those of you who receive these things in the latter days might have no more excuses for your wickedness; and that ye might see the error of your ways and repent and turn again to the plan of the Father.

16 For behold, after the fall of the Romans, the formation of this great and abominable church began of which Nephi hath written.

17 But this is only according to the time of John, for this abominable church hath existed since the beginning when it was first established by Beneli during the days of Adam.

18 But John writeth of that which is pertinent to his time, which is the time given in the revelation that he received. And Nephi also wrote those things that were pertinent to his own vision.

19 And the Spirit hath commanded me to explain this unto you, so that ye might not misunderstand the purpose of the words of Nephi, or the words of John.

20 For that great and abominable church is the plan of Lucifer, and its doctrines and precepts create the abomination of desolation of which the ancient prophets have written.

21 And its foundation was formed at the time that Lucifer rebelled against the plan of the Father and presented his own plan before all the children of God who were spirits.

22 Therefore, be careful that ye do not suppose that the formation of this church of the devil began at the time in which Nephi hath prophesied according to the vision that he received from God.

23 For this great and abominable church, as I have explained it unto you, is also the beast that receiveth its power from the dragon, who is Lucifer.

24 And now, of these things I have been instructed to tell you more concerning the times of which I have written.

25 Behold, the ending of the times began—according to the reckoning of time of the latter days—at the birth of the holy prophet Mohammed, he being the last prophet sent forth into the world in that dispensation of time.

26 And from the ending of the times to the beginning of the half of time shall be the equivalent—according to the words of John and your own reckoning of time—to forty and two months, or in other words, one thousand two hundred and sixty days.

27 And these days that are mentioned of John, are years according to the reckoning of time that ye shall have in the latter days.

28 And in the same month in which Mohammed was born; even after exactly one thousand twelve hundred and sixty years have passed—yea, the forty and two months mentioned by John—then shall the commencement of the half of time begin.

29 And the half of time shall be ushered in with the fullness of the gospel being once again given to all the inhabitants of the earth by the work of the first of these latter day prophets who shall live among you, even he who shall bring forth the unsealed portion of this record, which shall testify to the world of the words of Christ, which are the fullness of the plan of the Father.

30 And now, if ye read the words of John, it shall be revealed unto you therein more concerning this time.

31 For John also wrote concerning the forty and two months, saying: And there appeared a great sign in heaven, in the likeness of things on the earth; a woman clothed with the sun, and the moon under her feet, and upon her head a crown of twelve stars.

32 And the woman being with child, cried, travailing in birth, and pained to be delivered. And she brought forth a man child, who was to rule all nations with a rod of iron; and her child was caught up unto God and His throne.

33 And there appeared another sign in heaven; and behold, a great red dragon, having seven heads and ten horns, and seven crowns upon his heads. And his tail drew the third part of the stars of heaven, and did cast them to the earth.

34 And the dragon stood before the woman which was ready to be delivered, for to devour her child after it was born. And the woman fled into the wilderness, where she had a place prepared of God, that they should feed her there a thousand two hundred and threescore years.

35 And there was war in heaven; Michael and his angels fought against the dragon; and the dragon and his angels fought against Michael; And the dragon prevailed not against Michael, neither the child, nor the woman which was the church of God, who had been delivered of her pains, and brought forth the kingdom of our God and His Christ.

36 Neither was there place found in heaven for the great dragon, who was cast out; that old serpent called the devil, and also called Satan, which deceiveth the whole world; he was cast out into the earth; and his angels were cast out with him.

37 And I heard a loud voice saying in heaven, Now is come salvation, and strength, and the kingdom of our God, and the power of Christ; for the accuser of our brethren is cast down, which accused them before our God day and night.

38 For they have overcome him by the blood of the Lamb, and by the word of their testimony; for they loved not their own lives, but kept the testimony even unto death. Therefore, rejoice, Oh heavens, and ye that dwell in them.

39 And after these things I heard another voice saying, Woe to the inhabiters of the earth, yea, and they who dwell upon the islands of the sea; for the devil is come down unto you, having great wrath, because he knoweth that he hath but a short time.

40 For when the dragon saw that he was cast unto the earth, he persecuted the woman which brought forth the man child. Therefore, to the woman were given two wings of a great eagle, that she might flee into the wilderness, into her place, where she is nourished for a time, and times, and half a time, from the face of the serpent.

41 And the serpent casteth out of his mouth water as a flood after the woman, that he might cause her to be carried away of the flood. And the earth helpeth the woman, and the earth openeth her mouth, and swalloweth up the flood which the dragon casteth out of his mouth.

42 Therefore, the dragon was wroth with the woman, and went to make war with the remnant of her seed, which keep the commandments of God, and have the testimony of Jesus Christ.

43 And he also wrote, saying: And there was given me a reed like unto a rod that is used to judge the world. And the angel stood, saying, Rise, and measure the temple of God, and the altar, and them that worship therein. But the court which is without the temple leave out, and measure it not; for it is given unto the Gentiles in their own time. And at this time the holy city shall they tread under foot forty and two months.

44 And I will give power unto my two witnesses, and they shall prophesy a thousand two hundred and threescore days, clothed in sackcloth.

45 Now, I, Moroni, have already given somewhat of an explanation of these things already in this record. Nevertheless, I have been commanded to give unto you more information concerning these times of the Lord, so that ye of the latter days might see the words of John being fulfilled as they have been given.

46 Now the rod of iron of which John hath written is the fullness of the gospel of Jesus Christ which came forth from the child, who is the Christ. And as soon as the fullness of the gospel was given to the world, or according to the words of John, as soon as the child was to be delivered, Satan was there to deceive all those who hear the gospel; and he causeth them to not believe in that which they hear.

47 And the record of the Jews containeth the fullness of this gospel. And the record of my father, which is this record, also containeth the fullness of this gospel as I have explained it unto you previously in this record.

48 But during the forty and two months, or the one thousand two hundred and threescore days, or the three days and an half, which also representeth three years and an half, which is also one thousand two hundred and sixty days;

yea, during this time the records that contain the fullness of the gospel shall prophesy covered in sackcloth, or in other words, be covered from the eyes of all the world, so that if they read their words, they might not understand that which they read, because they do not have the Spirit to bear witness unto them of the truthfulness of these things.

49 And the record of my father shall be covered in that it shall be hid up and not come unto the world until the time appointed by the Lord, which is the time after the forty and two months that the Gentiles shall tread under foot the holy city.

50 And this is the time of the great apostasy of which the holy prophets have prophesied concerning the latter days.

51 And because the words of John, which ye have in the latter days, have passed through the hands of the great and abominable church, many of his words were taken out of the context in which they were given; because those who lacked the Spirit made an attempt to put them in the order that they thought supported those things that they believed according to their corrupted understanding of the truth.

52 And for this reason, the Lord hath commanded me to explain these things unto you in plainness.

53 Behold, ye of the latter days can call upon those who ye believe are learned among you, and inquire of them that they research the dates of all of these things according to the accounting of time that ye have among you.

54 And if ye research these things in truth, ye shall find indeed that exactly one thousand two hundred and sixty years have passed from the time of the birth of the last prophet of the dispensation of the times, even the prophet Mohammed, and the coming forth of this record by the hand of the first of the latter day prophets.

55 And the reckoning of your time is somewhat correct, according to the true time of the Lord, after the birth of this last prophet. But a few generations before this time, there was a discrepancy of circa ten years in the reckoning of your time, which discrepancy was adjusted and accounted for by those who were in power in the world and who brought forth the canonized record of scripture that ye have among you, and which ye call the Bible.

56 Therefore, taking this into consideration, ye shall begin to see the fulfillment of all the prophecies that have been given by the holy prophets.

57 Behold, I have already given unto you the exact date that this sealed portion of this record shall be published to the world. Yea, exactly two thousand years from the birth of Christ—and this time is within the ten years that ye have not reckoned by the mistakes that were made in the days of old—shall these things come forth unto you by the second of the two prophets of the latter days.

58 And the Lord shall call forth the last of the two prophets among you at the meridian of the half of time, and shall begin to prepare him to bring forth unto you this record, which shall be the marvelous work and wonder that the Father hath prepared for you.

59 And if ye are wise and follow the Spirit and pray for an understanding of these things, then ye shall know the time that the Lord hath given for all things, even ye can know of the year in which the Lord shall come in the glory that the Father hath given unto him.

60 Of the hour and the day, no man knoweth, not even the Son, but the Father knoweth this day and this hour. But the year and its month have now been revealed unto you. He who hath an ear let him hear and understand.

61 And now, this period after the times shall be the same length of time, according to your reckoning, as the period of the times, or in other words, one thousand two hundred and sixty years.

62 And therefore, the period of the time is six hundred and thirty years, and the period of the half of time is three hundred and fifteen years.

63 Now, it is expedient that ye understand the event that marketh the beginning of this manner of reckoning. For the Lord hath marked all of the dispensations of time with an event that is only known unto him and those to whom he revealeth his will.

64 Behold, this time of reckoning began at the time Abraham received the covenant and promise of the Lord, that through his lineage, the Christ would come forth in the flesh.

65 And the day that the Lord made this covenant and promise to Abraham marked the beginning of the time.

66 Therefore, from the time of the covenant of Abraham, six hundred and thirty years passed in which the Father gave of His Spirit freely unto all of the inhabitants of the earth, both by the power and ministrations of the Spirit world, and also by the voice of the holy prophets whom the Lord had chosen to preach unto the people.

67 And after the period of the time had ended, then the Spirit of the Father was taken from the earth for the same amount of time, or for another six hundred and thirty years.

68 And this He did so that Lucifer might have the same amount of time to incorporate his plan into the hearts of the children of men, giving fairly unto him his opportunity to prove the worthiness of his plan.

69 And then when the period of the times began, even the dispensation of time in which He again sent forth prophets and His Spirit into the world, it lasted for one thousand two hundred and sixty years; this period being twice the time of the first period of time.

70 And for the same amount of time, or one thousand two hundred and sixty years, shall the length of time be of the great apostasy, or the greatest amount of time that the Father hath withdrawn His Spirit and direction from off of the earth, allowing Lucifer to freely administer his plan without competition from the word of God.

71 And after one thousand two hundred and sixty years of not having the fullness of the plan of the Father given unto the children of men, neither by the Spirit nor by the mouth of a prophet, then shall the half of time begin, in which the fullness of the gospel shall once more be given unto the earth, never to be taken off again until the Lord hath finished his work.

72 And now, during these three hundred and fifteen years of the half of time, the Spirit shall strive to influence the hearts of the children of men to choose the plan of the Father over the plan of Lucifer.

73 And all of the scriptures shall be available during the half of time, which are the words of the prophets that have been given unto the children of men throughout all the dispensations of time. And these scriptures shall teach the fullness of the plan and will of the Father.

74 And because an equal amount of time was given unto Lucifer to prove his plan before the dispensation of the half of time, he and those who follow him might protest that they do not have a fair chance during this last period of time

75 Nevertheless, the Father shall release Satan, who hath been bound in that which he can reveal of the knowledge of the powers of God unto the children of men. And he shall be released by the Father, so that he might have power over his own dominions.

76 And now, I would that ye should understand that even though the Father hath stopped His work during these time periods that are in between the time and times and half of time, this doth not mean that a righteous man cannot live in the world.

77 For behold, the Father would never deny any of His children a right to the blessings of His Spirit, if it so be that they comply with the laws that afford these blessings.

78 Nevertheless, during these times, the Father doth nothing to entice His children to accept His plan. For this reason, the two prophets of whom John hath spoken, prophesy covered in sackcloth for forty and two months.

79 And Satan shall be released by the Father at the beginning of this half of time. And with this freedom and the power that he hath been allowed to use upon the earth, he shall begin to deceive the children of men according to the words of John, which he wrote, saying: And he deceiveth them that dwell on the earth by the means of those miracles which he had power to do in the sight of the beast; saying to them that dwell on the earth, that they should make an image to the beast, which had the wound by a sword, and did live.

80 And now, it is expedient that ye understand somewhat more concerning the reckoning of time which I have given unto you in this record.

81 For behold, in the latter days there shall be some contention and disputation among you as to the exact reckoning of times which the Lord hath given to his holy prophets concerning that which occureth upon the earth.

82 And the manner of reckoning of the Lord is one way, and is the only way that the true measure of time can be given in order to understand those things which have been prophesied by the mouth of the prophets.

83 And there shall be many in the latter days who think that they are learned, and that they know a reckoning of time that doth not agree with the time that the Lord hath set in the holy scriptures. And they shall believe these things because of the records that they shall have concerning the histories of the nations and peoples upon the earth that came before them.

84 But these accounts shall not agree one with another, and shall be the means of much contention among you. And this contention shall confuse many, and cause some strife among those who concern themselves of the times mentioned in the holy scriptures.

85 But I say unto you, the reckoning of time that I have given unto you herein is the true time of the Lord, which he hath revealed unto all the holy prophets since the beginning of time.

86 And if the reckoning of time that ye accept doth not agree with the time that I have given you herein, then ye shall know that these times are not the true time of the Lord which he intended for his prophets of old.

87 And many of the prophets were not learned men according to the reckoning time of men, but being inspired by the Holy Ghost, they were given the dispensations of time which they have given in their prophecies.

88 And ye shall see that the times that they have given are correct and correspond precisely to the event that each time describeth.

89 And if ye know the mysteries of God, then ye also know that ye have not received an explanation of these mysteries by the words and by the learning of men. But ye can only receive an explanation of these things through the same Spirit by which these things were received, even the Holy Spirit, who revealed them unto the prophets.

90 And a great revelation was given unto the prophet Daniel in the record of the Jews. And it is written: Go thy way, Daniel, and touch not that which thou shalt see hereafter; for the words are closed up and sealed till the time of the end.

91 And at that time many shall be purified, and made white, and tried according to their faith; but the wicked shall do wickedly and shall not have the Spirit with them. And none of the wicked shall understand; but the wise shall understand.

92 And from the time that the daily sacrifice was taken away, and the abomination that maketh desolate set up, there shall be a thousand two hundred and ninety days.

93 And blessed is he that waiteth, and cometh to the thousand three hundred and five and thirty days. But go thou thy way till the end be; for thou shalt rest, and stand in thy lot at the end of the days.

94 And now, I, Moroni ask of you: Do ye understand these words? I say unto you that I know that ye do not understand that of which Daniel hath spoken, unless ye have the Spirit to give unto you the meaning of these things.

95 For thus it is written, and none of the wicked shall understand; but the wise shall understand.

96 And if ye are reading my words that are given in this record, then ye are wise and have been guided in the Holy Spirit. And these things which have been sealed are the things which Daniel was not allowed to write and are the words that are closed up and sealed till the time of the end.

97 And now, so that ye might know that the things which I have written unto you concerning the time, and times, and half of time are true; even that they are the true reckoning of time of the Lord; I shall give unto you this sign, even an explanation of these final things that Daniel was allowed to give unto you concerning his vision.

98 Behold, these things concern the daily sacrifice that was offered up according to the law of Moses, which was kept in the temple of God, or in the ark of the covenant in the time of Moses.

99 And the time periods that are described by Daniel are the years between the time that the ark of the covenant was first destroyed— even a few years before the ending of the dispensation called the time—and the year in which the great king of Jerusalem began his reign, so that the temple at Jerusalem could once again be rebuilt, so that the daily sacrifice could once more be performed by the Jews. And this great king was Herod, in whose heart the Lord put the desire to do all these things for the house of Israel according to the prophecies of the holy prophets.

100 And it was the destruction of the ark of the covenant that took away the ability of the Jews to perform the daily sacrifice according to their traditions, and this event marked the beginning of the end of the time.

101 And if ye research your histories, ye shall find circa the time in which the ark of the covenant was first destroyed and the daily sacrifice taken away.

102 And then if ye add a thousand two hundred and ninety years to this time, ye shall find the year in which King Herod began his reign so that the temple could be rebuilt, thus enabling the Jews to perform the daily sacrifice once again according to the law that Moses had given unto them.

103 And then if ye add another forty and five years to this time, which would then be a thousand three hundred and five and thirty years from the time the ark was first destroyed, ye shall then arrive at the year of the birth of the Lord Jesus Christ.

104 And surely, blessed is he that waiteth, and cometh to the year in which the Son of the Father was born into the flesh.

105 He who hath understanding, let him understand that which I have written and revealed unto you concerning the true time of the Lord.

106 And now I make an end of my sayings concerning these things, but exhort you who receive these things to ponder upon all of the words of the holy prophets, and more especially those things which are written in this sealed part that shall come forth unto you in the last days.

107 And when ye have pondered upon these things, I would exhort you to ask the Father in the name of Christ, that He might send His Spirit unto you, and that ye might understand all of His words which He hath suffered to be given to the prophets of God for the benefit of all of His children that pertain to this part of His eternal kingdom.

CHAPTER 69

The works of humankind are predictable to God because of an eternity of experience in dealing with His children in mortality. All things have existed forever—there was no beginning to the nature of things. Our memories record our works. The book of life is explained. The Lord calls prophets because his arm of mercy is extended to us. Only the names of the righteous are written in the book of life. Moroni reiterates the words of Alma. (Compare to Alma chapter 5.)

AND now, the Spirit hath commanded me to give unto those of you who have received these things in the latter days an explanation of more of the prophecy of John which ye have before you.

2 And I know that because ye are reading these things, it is because ye have been wrought upon by the Holy Ghost and have been inspired to seek out the truth of all things pertaining to the kingdom of God.

3 And this record which hath been sealed to come forth unto you hath been prepared by the Father for the latter days, so that His children might have access to His love and His mercy, and a clearer understanding of all of His works; so that they might come unto Him and accept the plan that He hath outlined for their happiness.

4 For behold, the Father hath had endless experience in giving life to His children in their first estate, which is the creation of their spirits in His kingdom, and also the kingdom of their Eternal Mothers.

5 And this endless experience He hath also gained by giving unto His children their second estate, which is the state of the flesh which they have been given in mortality.

6 And I say unto you, that the experience of the Father is endless, or in other words, that He hath experienced it endlessly in the eternity where He dwelleth.

7 But I did not say that it was eternal, which meaneth that it hath no beginning and it hath no end. This I did not say, but I said that His experience in these things is endless.

8 For behold, as we are in the spirit, and also in mortality, our Father once was in the same manner—His spirit being created by His own Father, who is like unto to our Father in all things.

9 Nevertheless, we consider our Father to be our Eternal Father, because His works are eternal, in other words they have no beginning and they have no end.

10 For there hath always been a Father, or a God, who hath existed and hath given life unto others for the sake of His own glory, which giveth Him His happiness.

11 And not at anytime hath there been a space of time when there hath not been a God. Thus the state of a God, or the position and authority of an Eternal Father, is without a beginning and is without an end.

12 Likewise are the elements eternal. For there hath never been a time when there were no elements from which all things are created; even the spirits which we have are created from these same elements because of the Father.

13 Therefore, as I have said that our Father is eternal and His experience is endless, the Spirit giveth me understanding that the title and role of our Father, who is our God and our Creator is eternal. But our Father in heaven is not eternal, or in other words, He was also created by His Father. Nevertheless, He is eternal to us, because He hath always been before us since the beginning of our own existence.

14 And when His Eternal Father created His spirit, then began the experience of our Father.

15 And because we are His children and have the potential to become like Him, therefore as He is, we may become.

16 And our experience also started when our Father and our Mothers created our spirits, this creation being our beginning.

17 But like the Father, we are now endless and cannot be destroyed. And if we could be destroyed, then we are not endless. And if we are not endless, then our Father is not endless; for we are His children, created in His own image.

18 And if the Father is not endless, then one day He must end, or cease to exist. And if He ceaseth to exist, then He shall become nothing, therefore, all things would follow the pattern of their Creator and become nothing, and all would cease to exist.

19 But all will not cease to exist; for if all ceased to exist, then nothing would exist presently, because we cannot be if we do not exist. But we are, and we know that we are. And if we know that we are, then we do exist. And if we do exist, then it must needs be that we were created. And if we were created, then someone must have created us. And He who created us is our Eternal Father, who is as endless as we now are.

20 And now, concerning the experience of our Father. His experience is endless and not eternal, because it began when He was created by His Father and will continue forever without end.

21 Therefore, His experience will always be greater than our own experience, for we were created after Him, by Him, so that we could become like Him. And as our experience groweth, so doth the experience of our Father.

22 And if we have a little experience and add to it, this experience becometh greater. But it can never become as great as the experience of our Father, who already had much experience when our own experience began.

23 And so it is that our Father knoweth all that shall occur in our existence because of the experience that He hath in these things. For our world is not the only world of the Father, neither is it His first world. And even if it were His first world, He would still know everything that would come to pass in our world, because He hath learned all that His Father knoweth, which is eternal knowledge and experience that hath been passed down from Father to Son and given to those who have the power of a God and belongeth to the Celestial kingdom.

24 And because the Father knoweth all things whatsoever that shall come to pass in our world, or in our own experiences, He giveth us warnings from time to time to prepare us for that which is to come.

25 And He doeth this so that we might find joy and happiness in the hardships and vicissitudes of life, which He knoweth shall beset us all and add to our own experience.

26 And if He gave no warning or portend as

to that which is to come to pass among us, then when it cometh to pass, we will not understand why this thing hath come to pass, and this will cause us misery and unhappiness.

27 Behold, I have already explained to you that we have not been created to experience misery and unhappiness; but we have been created to have joy. Therefore, to help us have this joy and remain in a state of happiness through all the experiences through which we must pass during the days of our probation, which is our second estate, the Father hath revealed to us that which shall come to pass among us.

28 And those to whom He revealeth these things are the prophets which the Lord hath chosen to give to the children of men an understanding of all the things that we must go through to give us the experience that we need that will eventually guarantee us this eternal happiness promised to us by our Father.

29 And if we listen, and read, and understand the words of the prophets which are the revelations and prophecies of those things that shall come to pass during our lives, then we shall know the way in which the Father instructeth us by them.

30 For they are like unto a book, which can appropriately be called the book of life. Yea, everything that the Father knoweth that shall come to pass in our lives is in this book of life. And if ye read the words of the prophets, ye shall have somewhat of an idea of the book of life of which they speak.

31 And I know that ye have read that when the end cometh, then shall a judgment cometh, and the books shall be open and all shall be judged out of these books. These are the books of our lives, even the very works and thoughts that we have experienced during the days of our probation.

32 Now, it is expedient that ye understand that these books are figurative in the expressions used in the words of the prophets. For there are no books wherein a scribe shall make an exact accounting of that which we do during the days of our mortality.

33 Nevertheless, there is an accounting and a recording made of all of our thoughts and actions. And this recording is made within us according to the structure and engineering of our spirit, which recordeth all things that we experience.

34 Now, this thing should not be hard for you to understand; yea, even I do not understand all the ways and means of the Lord in all things. But this I do understand; that even as ye remember that which ye did and thought yesterday, so shall ye remember all things concerning you when ye no longer have the flesh, which weakness of the flesh inhibiteth our ability to remember all things; and this is the veil that hath been placed over our mortal minds according to the plan and design of the Father as I have explained it unto you previously.

35 And now, ye know that ye can remember many things because they have been recorded in the cerebrum of the flesh. But this cerebrum that is of the flesh is patterned like unto the cerebrum of the spirit, except that it is not as refined or as advanced in its nature as that of the spirit.

36 And whatever is recorded by the flesh, is also recorded by the spirit. Nevertheless, that which hath been recorded by the spirit, even all of our experiences that we acquired before entering into the flesh, cannot be accounted for by the flesh because of its weakness, but remaineth recorded in the spirit, where it can be recalled effortlessly and completely, outside of the flesh.

37 For this reason, if we have done evil during the days of our probation, and have not repented of that which we have done, or have not reconciled with the spirit for that which we have done in the flesh; then when we leave the flesh, all these things will come immediately to our minds and we will be tormented for that which we have done which is contrary to those things that our spirit remembereth that the Father hath commanded of us.

38 Now, this is the state of misery and unhappiness, or better, the state of hell in which ye shall find yourselves, if ye do not reconcile the flesh with the spirit.

39 And now, I have written these things that ye might understand how your works are recorded in the record of the Father.

40 For behold, the Father hath an exalted body of flesh and bone which hath been given all the powers and knowledge of a God. And with this power and knowledge, our Father can read the books of our lives, or in other words, He can know and understand our memories and get a full accounting of our lives directly from our spirits where this accounting is recorded.

41 For this reason, nothing can be hidden from the Father, for He knoweth all things pertaining to His children. And because He knoweth all things, He doeth that which is necessary to help us learn the things that we must learn in order to find the happiness for which we were created.

42 Therefore, as I have told you, He hath revealed many things unto His holy prophets who have seen the works of the children of men from the beginning of time to the end of time. And there have been many prophets who have seen these things and have gone forth unto the people and prophesied the things which they learned from the Father.

43 But in most instances, the people refuse to listen to the voice of the prophets, because they prophesy against that from which the people receive their temporary happiness.

44 And the people receive their happiness from the temporal rewards that Satan giveth unto them because they follow him.

45 And if a prophet cometh and preacheth that which is contrary to the way in which the people have already experienced happiness, then their words are rejected by the people, who see with their eyes, and hear with their ears, but do not understand with their hearts, which is the Spirit of God that they have rejected, or have not remembered, which is within them.

46 And if the people would listen to the spirit of God which is within them, then they would find this never ending happiness, or endless happiness of which I have written previously in this record.

47 And if they would listen to the Spirit within them, then the Lord would bless them and take them under his wing and protect them and give them all things which they need for their own happiness.

48 And for this reason the Lord cried over the great city Jerusalem, saying: Oh, Jerusalem, Jerusalem, thou that killest the prophets, and stonest them which are sent unto thee, how often would I have gathered thy children together, even as a hen gathereth her chickens under her wings, and ye would not.

49 Behold, the Lord loveth all of the children of God and desireth them all to be happy; and for this reason he hath called forth prophets and sent them unto the people to bring them this good news, or rather, his gospel.

50 Yea, he would speak unto them by his own voice, which is the voice of the spirit; but because of their experience, even the only experience that they can remember, they trust in the arm of the flesh, or in those things that bring them the temporary joy that they can remember from day to day.

51 Yea, they are encircled about by the chains of hell and led into captivity by Satan away from the Father. Nevertheless, the Lord trieth with all of his power to turn the people to the Father.

52 And now, I will repeat the words of Alma, for they are some of my favorite words which the prophets of old have spoken unto the people; for he spoke of the book of life in which are written all the names of the righteous who shall be saved in the kingdom of God.

53 And he prophesied, saying: And now behold, I say unto you, my brethren, have you sufficiently retained in remembrance the captivity of your fathers? Yea, and have you sufficiently retained in remembrance his mercy and long-suffering towards them?

54 And moreover, have ye sufficiently retained in remembrance that he hath delivered their souls from hell? Behold, he changed their hearts; yea, he awakened them out of a deep sleep, and they awoke unto God.

55 Behold, they were in the midst of darkness; nevertheless, their souls were illuminated by the light of the everlasting word; yea, they were encircled about by the bands of death, and the chains of hell, and an everlasting destruction did await them.

56 And now I ask of you, my brethren, were they destroyed? Behold, I say unto you, Nay, they were not. And again I ask, were the bands of death broken, and the chains of hell which encircled them about, were they loosed?

57 I say unto you, Yea, they were loosed, and their souls did expand, and they did sing redeeming love. And I say unto you that they are saved.

58 And now I ask of you on what conditions are they saved? Yea, what grounds had they to hope for salvation? What is the cause of their being loosed from the bands of death, yea, and also the chains of hell?

59 Behold, I can tell you: did not my father Alma believe in the words which were delivered by the mouth of Abinadi? And was he not a holy prophet? Did he not speak the words of God, and my father Alma believe them?

60 And according to his faith there was a mighty change wrought in his heart. Behold I say unto you that this is all true. And behold, he preached the word unto your fathers, and a mighty change was also wrought in their hearts, and they humbled themselves and put their trust in the true and living God.

61 And behold, they were faithful until the end; therefore they were saved. And now behold, I ask of you, have ye spiritually been born of God? Have ye received His image in your countenances? Have ye experienced this mighty change in your hearts? Do ye exercise faith in the redemption of Him who created you?

62 Do you look forward with an eye of faith, and view this mortal body raised in immortality, and this corruption raised in incorruption, to stand before God to be judged according to the deeds which have been done in the mortal body?

63 I say unto you, can ye imagine to yourselves that ye hear the voice of the Lord, saying unto you in that day: Come unto me ye blessed, for behold, your works have been the works of righteousness upon the face of the earth?

64 Or do ye imagine to yourselves that ye can lie unto the Lord in that day, and say, Lord, our works have been righteous works upon the face of the earth; and that he will save you?

65 Or otherwise, can ye imagine yourselves brought before the tribunal of God with your souls filled with guilt and remorse, having a remembrance of all your guilt, yea, a perfect remembrance of all your wickedness, yea, a remembrance that ye have set at defiance the commandments of God?

66 I say unto you, can ye look up to God at that day with a pure heart and clean hands? I say unto you, can you look up, having the image of God engraven upon your countenances?

67 I say unto you, can ye think of being saved when ye have yielded yourselves to become subjected to the devil? I say unto you, ye will know at that day that ye cannot be saved; for there can no man be saved except his garments are washed white; yea, his garments must be purified until they are cleansed from all stain, through the blood of him of whom it hath been spoken by our fathers, who should come to redeem his people from their sins.

68 And now I ask of you, my brethren, how will any of you feel, if ye shall stand before the bar of God, having your garments stained with blood and all manner of filthiness? Behold, what will these things testify against you?

69 Behold will they not testify that ye are murderers, yea, and also that ye are guilty of all manner of wickedness? Behold, my brethren, do ye suppose that such an one can have a place to sit down in the kingdom of God, with Abraham, with Isaac, and with Jacob, and also all the holy prophets, whose garments are cleansed and are spotless, pure and white?

70 I say unto you, Nay; except ye make our Creator a liar from the beginning, or suppose that He is a liar from the beginning, ye cannot suppose that such can have place in the kingdom of heaven; but they shall be cast out for they are the children of the kingdom of the devil.

71 And now behold, I say unto you, my brethren, if ye have experienced a change of heart, and if ye have felt to sing the song of redeeming love, I would ask, can ye feel so now? Have ye walked, keeping yourselves blameless before God? Could ye say, if ye were called to die at this time, within yourselves, that ye have been sufficiently humble? That your garments have been cleansed and made white through the blood of Christ, who will come to redeem his people from their sins?

72 Behold, are ye stripped of pride? I say unto you, if ye are not, ye are not prepared to meet

God. Behold ye must prepare quickly; for the kingdom of heaven is soon at hand, and such an one hath not eternal life.

73 Behold, I say, is there one among you who is not stripped of envy? I say unto you that such an one is not prepared; and I would that he should prepare quickly, for the hour is close at hand, and he knoweth not when the time shall come; for such an one is not found guiltless.

74 And again I say unto you, is there one among you who doth make a mock of his brother, or who heapeth upon him persecutions? Woe unto such an one, for he is not prepared, and the time is at hand that he must repent or he cannot be saved.

75 Yea, even woe unto all ye workers of iniquity; repent, repent, for the Lord God hath spoken it. Behold, he sendeth an invitation unto all men, for the arms of mercy are extended towards them, and he saith: Repent, and I will receive you.

76 Yea, he saith: Come unto me and ye shall partake of the fruit of the tree of life; yea, ye shall eat and drink of the bread and the waters of life freely; Yea, come unto me and bring forth works of righteousness, and ye shall not be hewn down and cast into the fire.

77 For behold, the time is at hand that whosoever bringeth forth not good fruit, or whosoever doeth not the works of righteousness, the same have cause to wail and mourn.

78 Oh, ye workers of iniquity; ye who are puffed up in the vain things of the world, ye who have professed to have known the ways of righteousness nevertheless have gone astray, as sheep having no shepherd, notwithstanding a shepherd hath called after you and is still calling after you, but ye will not hearken unto his voice.

79 Behold, I say unto you, that the good shepherd doth call you; yea, and in his own name he doth call you, which is the name of Christ; and if ye will not hearken unto the voice of the good shepherd, to the name by which ye are called, behold, ye are not the sheep of the good shepherd.

80 And now if ye are not the sheep of the good shepherd, of what fold are ye? Behold, I say unto you, that the devil is your shepherd, and ye are of his fold; and now, who can deny this?

81 Behold, I say unto you, whosoever denieth this is a liar and a child of the devil. For I say unto you that whatsoever is good cometh from God, and whatsoever is evil cometh from the devil.

82 Therefore, if a man bringeth forth good works, he hearkeneth unto the voice of the good shepherd, and he doth follow him; but whosoever bringeth forth evil works, the same becometh a child of the devil, for he hearkeneth unto his voice, and doth follow him.

83 And whosoever doeth this must receive his wages of him; therefore, for his wages he receiveth death, as to things pertaining unto righteousness, being dead unto all good works.

84 And now, my brethren, I would that ye should hear me, for I speak in the energy of my soul; for behold, I have spoken unto you plainly that ye cannot err, or have spoken according to the commandments of God.

85 For I am called to speak after this manner, according to the holy order of God, which is in Christ Jesus; yea, I am commanded to stand and testify unto this people the things which have been spoken by our fathers concerning the things which are to come.

86 And this is not all. Do ye not suppose that I know of these things myself? Behold, I testify unto you that I do know that these things whereof I have spoken are true.

87 And how do ye suppose that I know of their surety? Behold, I say unto you, they are made known unto me by the Holy Spirit of God.

88 Behold, I have fasted and prayed many days that I might know these things of myself. And now I do know of myself that they are true; for the Lord God hath made them manifest unto me by his Holy Spirit; and this is the spirit of revelation which is in me.

89 And moreover, I say unto you that it hath thus been revealed unto me, that the words which have been spoken by our fathers are true, even so according to the spirit of prophecy which is in me, which is also by the manifestation of the Spirit of God.

90 I say unto you, that I know of myself that whatsoever I shall say unto you concerning that

which is to come, is true; and I say unto you, that I know that Jesus Christ shall come, yea, the Son, the Only Begotten of the Father, full of grace and mercy and truth.

91 And behold, it is he that cometh to take away the sins of the world, yea, the sins of every man who steadfastly believeth on his name.

92 And now I say unto you that this is the order after which I am called, yea, to preach unto my beloved brethren, yea, and every one who dwelleth in the land; yea, to preach unto all, both old and young, both bond and free; yea, I say unto you, the aged, and also the middle aged, and the rising generation; yea, to cry unto them that they must repent and be born again.

93 Yea, thus saith the Spirit: Repent, all ye ends of the earth, for the kingdom of heaven is soon at hand; yea, the Son of God cometh in his glory, in his might, majesty, power and dominion.

94 Yea, my beloved brethren, I say unto you, that the Spirit saith: Behold the glory of the King of all the earth; and also the King of heaven shall very soon shine forth among all the children of men.

95 And also the Spirit saith unto me, yea, crieth unto me with a mighty voice, saying: Go forth and say unto this people, Repent, for except ye repent ye can in nowise inherit the kingdom of heaven.

96 And again I say unto you, the Spirit saith: Behold, the ax is laid at the root of the tree; therefore every tree that bringeth not forth good fruit shall be hewn down and cast into the fire, yea, a fire which cannot be consumed, even an unquenchable fire. Behold, and remember, the Holy One hath spoken it.

97 And now my beloved brethren, I say unto you, can ye withstand these sayings; yea, can ye lay aside these things, and trample the Holy One under your feet; yea, can ye be puffed up in the pride of your hearts; yea, will ye still persist in the wearing of costly apparel and setting your hearts upon the vain things of the world, upon your riches?

98 Yea, will ye persist in supposing that ye are better one than another; yea, will ye persist in the persecution of your brethren, who humble themselves and do walk after the holy order of God, wherewith they have been brought into the church of the Lamb, having been sanctified by the Holy Spirit, and they do bring forth works which are meet for repentance?

99 Yea, and will ye persist in turning your backs upon the poor and the needy, and in withholding your substance from them?

100 And finally, all ye that will persist in your wickedness, I say unto you that these are they who shall be hewn down and cast into the fire except they speedily repent.

101 And now I say unto you, all you that are desirous to follow the voice of the good shepherd, come ye out from the wicked, and be ye separate, and touch not their unclean things; and behold, their names shall be blotted out, that the names of the wicked shall not be numbered among the names of the righteous, that the word of God may be fulfilled, which saith: The names of the wicked shall not be mingled with the names of my people; for the names of the righteous shall be written in the book of life, and unto them will I grant an inheritance at my right hand.

102 And now, my brethren, what have ye to say against this? I say unto you, if ye speak against it, it matters not, for the word of God must be fulfilled.

103 For what shepherd is there among you having many sheep doth not watch over them, that the wolves enter not and devour his flock? And behold, if a wolf enter his flock doth he not drive him out? Yea, and at the last, if he can, he will destroy him.

104 And now I say unto you that the good shepherd doth call after you; and if you will hearken unto his voice, he will bring you into his fold, and ye are his sheep; and he commandeth you that ye suffer no ravenous wolf to enter among you, that ye may not be destroyed.

105 And now I, Alma, do command you in the language of him who hath commanded me, that ye observe to do the words which I have spoken unto you. I speak by way of command unto you that belong to the church of the Lamb; and unto those who do not belong to this church, I speak by way of invitation, saying: Come and be baptized unto repentance, that ye also may be partakers of the fruit of the tree of life.

CHAPTER 70

Moroni expounds upon the book mentioned in Revelation that is sealed with seven seals. He gives an introduction of each of the seven thousand years of the history of the human race since Adam and Eve were expelled from the garden of Eden. Moroni saves the revelation of the last part of the history of humankind until the end of The Sealed Portion.

AND now, I, Moroni, continue with an explanation of the prophecy of John. Behold, in this great revelation of the prophet, the Lord revealeth many things that concern that which hath occurred, and that which is now occurring, and that which shall occur in the latter days.

2 And the revelation of these things are given figuratively in the prophecy of John, saying: And I saw in the right hand of him who sat on the throne, a book written within and on the backside, sealed with seven seals.

3 Now, John speaketh of the Father as He who holdeth the book in His right hand. And I have already explained unto you that our works are symbolic of that which we do with our right hand.

4 Therefore, the Father holdeth the book in His right hand, which containeth all of His works concerning us.

5 And John mentioneth that he seeth writing on the backside, because the book is full, written within and on the back, because no page remaineth whereon can anymore be written.

6 And this book containeth the knowledge of the Father, which He knoweth shall come to pass in mortality as soon as he placeth His children in their second estate.

7 Behold, everything that is written within the book and on its backside was revealed to all of us as spirits in the kingdom of the Father. For behold, the Father did not hold anything back from us in the beginning and taught us all the things that He knew would come to pass concerning us as we go through the days of our probation in mortality. And this He knoweth from His own experience.

8 And now, John giveth a relation of four beasts which are likened unto animals, which are figurative expressions used by John in describing all the creatures that live by their own instinct, not having the free agency that God hath given unto his children.

9 Thus are these beasts bound together in the vision of Ezekiel, which was written, saying: Thus were their faces; and their wings were stretched upwards—signifying their obedience and honor of the God who created them—two wings of every one were joined one to another, and two covered their bodies—signifying the dependence of one order of nature upon one of the other orders of nature to be able to fulfill the measure of their creation and find joy therein.

10 And they went every one straight forward; whither the spirit was to go, they went; and they turned not when they went—thus signifying their instincts which are programmed into them and commanded by the God who created them.

11 And these hath God created to come down into mortality and do what he commandeth them to do for our sakes.

12 And these four beasts represent certain natural orders of the creatures that God hath placed upon this earth, of which our flesh is also a part.

13 And there is one that representeth those beasts—even the calf or the ox— that eateth the plants that were first placed upon the earth to provide the necessary elements which would be needed so that other life might live upon the earth. These receive their power and life from the sun, which is the great light that giveth its life-giving power to all of the earth.

14 And another beast representeth those beasts—the lion—that were placed on the earth to eat the flesh of another for their sustenance, thus maintaining a proper balance within the order of nature to which all things are subjected.

15 And the eagle representeth the nature of the fowls of the air, which exist in the order of their nature, being seemingly unrestricted in certain laws of nature that make their conveyance through the air unlike the means of conveyance of all other creatures. And they are from both the earth and also the air, being dependent on both for their state of happiness.

16 And the final beast hath the face of man, which representeth those creatures who were

like unto men after Lucifer had caused them to be influenced and refined over many years by his own hand, they being first upon the earth before Adam and Eve, and becoming like unto the children of men in all things according to the flesh.

17 And from these creatures came forth the corruptible nature of our bodies as I have explained it unto you in the beginning of this record.

18 Thus there are four orders of creatures which have been established by the Father to do His will and provide for the plan of salvation that He hath established for His children.

19 And each of these creatures, in their own order, existeth for their own enjoyment, according to their desires of happiness, which have been given them by God; yea, the order of those creatures who eat that which groweth of itself—thus the eating of these plants which fulfilleth their desires of happiness;

20 And the order of those creatures that eat the flesh of other creatures, thus maintaining an order in nature—they also fulfill their desires of happiness within their own order; and likewise is the order of nature for the fowls of the air;

21 And finally, the order of the creatures which provided the bodies for the children of men in which the spirits of the children of God are placed during the days of their probation—they finding happiness in their carnality.

22 And all of these orders work as one according to the commandments that each have received of the Father. And without one, none of the others can exist and fulfill the measure of their creations.

23 Thus were these symbolic beasts before the throne of God in the vision of John; for they are all the creations of God for His own will and pleasure.

24 And now, that which is written next by John concerneth that of which I have already explained in this record concerning the calling of Jehovah in the beginning to be the leader over all the children of God in this part of His kingdom.

25 For behold, he was found worthy of the Father to accomplish His will concerning us in all things—as it is written: And he came and took the book out of the right hand of Him who sat upon the throne.

26 And at that time, we all rejoiced in the election of Jehovah as our representative of the Father, he becoming our God in this part of the kingdom of the Father. And in the book, which he received from the Father, was written all those things that would come to pass upon the earth according to the knowledge and experience which the Father had written in the book concerning our second estate—these things being figurative.

27 And there is an exact timetable of the Father that must be followed according to the eternal laws of heaven.

28 And the timetable of any planet which is used for the purpose of the probationary state of the children of God is seven thousand years.

29 And the beginning of these seven thousand years beginneth when the first of us, who are spirits, enter into mortality, or rather, when our incorruption, or eternal spirits that exist in the state of their creation forever, put on corruption, or the corruptible flesh that is subject to the laws of nature, which include the death of this corruptible flesh.

30 And this time period, even the beginning of the first of the seven thousand years, began when Adam and Eve were cast out of the garden of Eden and given a body of corruption.

31 And for a period of seven thousand years shall this earth remain in the state at which it had arrived at the first of the seven thousand years, even at the time of the expulsion of Adam and Eve from the garden of Eden.

32 And after seven thousand years, this earth shall be made into one of the Celestial kingdoms of the Father, it being the third planet from the sun, and having fulfilled the measure of its creation, thus becoming the third kingdom of glory in the Celestial realm.

33 And while the earth is going through these seven thousand years, we shall be upon it passing through the days of our probations.

34 And Christ is he who is responsible to the Father that His will be done on this earth. Therefore, according to the vision of John, only he hath the power and authority to open each seal of the book, or in other words, direct the will of the Father as it is given in each dispensation of time.

35 And now, when Christ openeth the first seal of the book, a beast speaketh to John and commandeth him to come and see. And also when the second seal is opened; and the third; and also when the fourth seal is opened a beast speaketh and commandeth that John come and see.

36 But when the fifth, and the sixth, and the seventh seals are opened, behold, there is no beast that speaketh unto John.

37 Now, the reason for this symbolism is that during the opening of the first four seals, or in other words, during the first four thousand years of the existence of the children of men, all of the warnings and prophecies concerning them are because of those things which have been caused among the children of men by their own hand, being enticed by the instincts of the flesh; even those things that the children of men cause because of their own works by using the free agency that they have been given by the Father.

38 Behold, the beasts represent the works of the children of men by their own hands.

39 But those things which shall come to pass in the opening of the fifth, and the sixth, and the seventh seals, are those things that shall come to pass by nature, or by the hand of the Lord; men having no power to cause or prohibit these things from occurring unto them.

40 And this power shall the Lord demonstrate, showing unto the children of men that he hath all power to shut up the heavens, or open them up like unto a scroll at his will; to seal up unto life, or to cast down to the regions of darkness, according to his own will and not according to the works of men.

41 And those things which the children of men have caused among themselves during the first four thousand years could have been avoided had they abided by the word of God which was given unto them during the time, and the times.

42 And that which I have revealed unto you concerning the time, and times, and half of time, are those things that concern the spirits of the children of men, even the salvation of the soul.

43 But those things which are revealed unto you in the opening of the seals, are those things which affect the physical flesh; yea, those things that can harm the flesh, even unto death.

44 And during the first thousand years, the white horse and its rider are sent forth, which is the color of righteousness, which was set forth by father Adam and his righteous sons, who taught all of their children the ways of God, which were given unto him from the beginning.

45 And the white horse and its rider meaneth that all were pure and righteous in the beginning, the majority following after the things that they had been taught by the patriarch Adam.

46 And they went forth into the world according to the commandment of the Lord to have dominion over all the earth—thus signifying the crown that was given unto the children of men to go forth conquering and to conquer.

47 And then the people of the earth began to divide themselves into families and nations and kindreds and peoples. And each nation went forth to overrun another and bring the weakest among them under the subjection to the will of the strongest.

48 And then peace was taken from off of the earth because the children of men began to kill one another during their many wars and contentions. And so it was, by the hand of the children of men, war began to destroy them and take away their peace and happiness.

49 Thus, during the second thousand years were the horse and its rider brought forth, and they were of the color red, symbolizing the blood that was spilled of the people of the earth.

50 And when the third seal was opened, then begin the children of men to do all manner of wickedness among them concerning that which they would take from the earth and place a value upon according to their own judgments of these things—symbolized by the pair of balances in his hand—selling and buying with money those things among them that are a necessity for life.

51 And during this time shall the great trading nations of the earth be established, and they shall begin to accumulate riches and strength and they shall begin to take advantage of the poor so that they might be rich.

52 And the commerce and economy of the beast, seen by the holy prophets, were introduced; and the abomination that maketh desolate came forth; even the desires for riches which make the house of one man full and the house of another empty.

53 And it was during this time that the abomination of desolation spoken of by the mouth of the prophet Daniel was set up for the first time among the children of men.

54 And the reason why this great abomination maketh desolation, is because the economy of men beginneth to make them completely desolate of the Spirit of God. For their hearts become so set upon the things of the world and the honors of men, that their spirits are left desolate as to things pertaining to righteousness.

55 And by their wickedness, a few men are rich, but by the course of their riches, the majority of men are left desolate of the Spirit.

56 And this inequality is a great abomination before God and hath been, and is, and shall be the abomination that brings the most misery and unhappiness among the children of men.

57 For this reason the horse and its rider are black and are brought forth during the time of the third seal, signifying the great wickedness of the children of men because of their commerce set up among them.

58 For they sell that which would feed a man—wheat and barely—for money, and keep that which is valuable safe—the oil and the wine—for themselves.

59 And when the fourth seal is opened, a pale horse and its rider are brought forth signifying the death of the flesh. And John herein speaks definitively of the great Roman Empire, which is also the first beast of which he maketh mention later in his vision.

60 For the Roman Empire had power over the fourth part of the earth, and caused many to die by the sword, and from hunger, and with the beasts of the earth.

61 And this great Empire came to power during the fourth thousand years of the time of the earth and gave Satan his greatest power and control over the hearts and minds of the children of men that had ever been experienced among them up until this time.

62 And now, all these things that occurred during the first four thousand years, came to pass because of the wickedness of the children of men. For they had rejected the plan of the Father and followed the plan of Lucifer instead, bringing upon themselves their own destruction and captivity.

63 But there are no horses or riders, nor do any beasts speak when the fifth, and the sixth, and the seventh seals are opened.

64 For during these next two thousand years shall be the coming forth of many natural disasters that shall perplex the kingdoms of the earth and cause the kings of the earth, and the great men, and the rich men, and the chief captains, and the mighty men, and every bondman, and every free man, yea, even every person upon the earth to ponder upon the destructions that shall come to pass, which occur by the force of nature.

65 For they shall know that these things do not come by their own hand, therefore, they must come by the hand of God, who is the God of nature.

66 And these natural disasters shall come to pass during this time, so that the children of men might consider that which they do not consider, even that which pertaineth to the heavens and those things that have nothing to do with the lusts and envyings of the flesh.

67 Therefore, these things are set to come to pass in hope that the children of men might once again turn to the God who created them, and who created all things upon the earth; for it is by these things that their destruction shall come during these last days.

68 But the Lord shall not destroy the earth until the righteous have been given a chance to repent of their sins and turn their thoughts towards God. In other words, the Lord shall command that: Hurt not the earth, neither the sea, nor the trees, till we have sealed the servants of God in their foreheads.

69 And at this time the fullness of the gospel shall once more be given to the world, starting with the last of the holy prophets of the times, and then with the first and the last of these two prophets who shall come forth in the latter days during the half of time as I have already explained it unto you.

70 And there shall be many who shall receive the mark of the Father in their foreheads and begin to bring forth righteous works upon the earth.

71 Nevertheless, their numbers shall be few in comparison with the rest of those who reside in the world. For at that time, the world shall be filled with many people, even upon all the continents of the earth shall there be many nations, and kindreds, and peoples, and tongues.

72 And there shall be many from among all these nations, and kindred, and peoples, and tongues who shall wash themselves clean, and who have forsaken the great beast which shall arise up among them.

73 And they shall be those who, although they are forced to receive the mark of the beast in their right hand, nevertheless, they are marked with the seal of God in their foreheads.

74 And once all of the righteous have been marked in the forehead, then shall the time of the seventh seal come to pass. And after the seventh seal is opened; yea, even at the beginning of the seventh thousand years pertaining to the history of the children of God upon this earth; then shall there come upon the earth that which hath never before been experienced by the children of men.

75 For Satan shall rise up with his minions and control the hearts of those who have received his mark in their right hand and in their forehead. And with the power that Satan hath given unto them by the means of those miracles which he performeth before them, even the great scientific knowledge and technology as it shall be given in the latter days; he shall call forth his armies and his navies and all the means of force that he controlleth, and shall make one last stand against all righteousness before the great and dreadful day of the Lord cometh.

76 Yea, he shall come forth and begin to destroy all the inhabitants of the earth, even all those who do not have the mark of the Lamb written in their foreheads.

77 And after the seventh seal is opened, he shall wage war unlike any war that hath ever been experienced among the children of men since the beginning. And for five months he shall wage this battle and destroy much of the earth, even a third of all the earth, with the great power that he hath given unto men.

78 And then cometh the Lord in his glory, and with him the angels of God. And they shall destroy all of those who destroy and kill the children of men by the power of Satan.

79 And his power shall be the power of the Father, which shall be far greater than any power that hath been given unto the children of men by Satan.

80 And these are the things that John was forbidden to write, which were the trumpets that sounded long and loud, even all things that shall be accomplished by the Lord until the end of the seventh thousand years, or the end of time.

81 And now, I, Moroni, have seen these things and have read concerning these things in the words of the brother of Jared. And I have received a commandment of the Spirit that I not give unto you these things at this time, so that ye might see the unfolding of the great mysteries of God that have been revealed unto his prophets since the world began.

82 But after I have given unto you more of the abridgment of the words of the brother of Jared, and also an accounting of the things that the Lord hath commanded me by his own voice to give unto you, then I shall reveal unto you that which shall come to pass during the seventh seal of which John hath written.

CHAPTER 71

The fall of the Roman government, which is the beast in John's day, is touched upon and the meaning of the beast in John's revelation is explained. The United States is the great beast of the latter days. The God that the people worship in the latter days is actually Satan, and the devil that the people are taught to believe in by Satan is the true Christ.

BUT now, it must needs be that I return once again to the time period of the Romans of which John hath written, and whose history I have seen in the words of the brother of Jared. And it is this thing that is expedient that I explain unto you regarding the beast, who had the wound by the sword and did live.

2 For the beast to which John refereth is the Roman government and the principles upon which this government is established. For the Romans are an exceedingly proud and prosperous people according to the things of the world, which are the blessings of Satan, the God of the world.

3 And when the Roman government fell, all the nations of the world were astounded at its fall and wondered after it, even reasoning amongst themselves what was the cause of its fall from the power and glory that it had received from the dragon.

4 But the world was under the power of Satan, therefore, the nations of the world did not believe that it was Lucifer who had given these things unto the Romans, but that they had received these things from God.

5 And in this they were correct. Nevertheless, the God who gave them these things was Lucifer, the dragon of whom John speaketh, whose tail drew the third part of the stars of heaven—or in other words, the Spirit children of the Father who followed Lucifer—and cast them to the earth; yea, these are the devil and his angels.

6 And the principles of the government of Rome were those things which were coveted by other nations. For other nations began to study the formation of the Roman Empire and take from it the basis for the foundations of their own governments.

7 And the great European Empire of the latter days shall be established and formed according to many of the things that it shall learn from the form of government of the Romans, whose great empire shall be wounded by the sword, but then healed by the great and abominable church that was formed by the devil.

8 And from this seventh empire, according to the words of John, the eighth beast shall come forth and establish itself as the seat in which Satan shall wield his power in the last days.

9 And in that day, even in the day when these things shall come forth unto you, Satan shall have great power over the whole earth. And the people of the latter days shall believe that they are worshipping the Father, when in reality, they are worshipping Lucifer and following the course that he hath set for them by his power and according to his plan.

10 And in that day, Satan shall be the God in whom they trust. And Satan shall convince the world that he is not the devil, but that he is the God of the world; and he shall also convince them that the Lord is not the Christ, but that he is the devil.

11 For they shall change the words of Christ and misinterpret them, and begin to live their lives according to the commandments which they shall receive from their god, who is Lucifer. And by the words of Christ they shall not abide; and any who do abide by the words of Christ shall be mocked and persecuted and judged that these works of Christ, which they do, are the works of the devil—the true Christ being the devil unto the world according to the convincing power that Satan hath over them.

12 And I have already explained unto you the meaning of the mark of the beast and the number of his name. And these things pertain to gold and silver, which is the money and the possessions of those who dwell upon the earth.

13 And it shall come to pass that all the nations of the earth shall be in pursuit of money and lands and the fine things of the world. And in their desires for these things, they shall separate themselves into these great nations that shall make war one with another and cause that many of the inhabitants of the earth shall perish in the wickedness of their hearts.

14 And the reasons for many of these wars, if not all of them, is because of money and pride, and the loss of love that one should have for another. For the children of men, being divided into these great nations, shall begin to think of themselves above those of the other nations of the earth.

15 And the accumulation of wealth shall be the desires of all the inhabitants of the earth. And those that have not shall envy that which they do not have. And those who have, shall not be satisfied with their abundance, but shall continually strive for more riches, that they might be set alone in the earth and receive the honors that other men shall bestow upon them because of these riches.

16 And now, John explaineth all of these things in the revelation that he hath given concerning the latter days and the end of the world. Yea, all of the holy prophets, who have seen the last days, have testified of the great wickedness that shall exist upon the whole earth in the latter days.

17 And there hath not been any prophet who hath prophesied that righteousness shall increase in the latter days, and that those of the latter days are the most blessed of all the children of God. But they have prophesied of the great wickedness that shall abound before the coming of the Lord, in the glory that the Father hath given unto him.

18 And the prophets were forbidden that they should reveal these things in their visions, except it be through symbolism, so that only the righteous might receive their words and understand.

19 Yea, these prophets also saw the miracles of science and technology that Satan shall introduce in the last days, being allowed by the Father to give these things unto the world that he might have this final chance to prove his plan.

20 And these prophets understood this power of God and could have revealed this great power and knowledge at any time unto the children of men, if it would have helped them to become more righteous.

21 But these things that are given to the world in the latter days by Satan have not made the people more righteous, but have caused them even more wickedness than at any other time in the history of the children of men.

22 And I shall write unto you much more concerning these things later in this record. But now it is expedient that we return once again to the abridgment that I have been commanded to make of the words of the brother of Jared, and follow the course of the history of the world, so that it might be revealed unto you how Satan managed to turn the hearts of the children of men from the Father.

23 And upon the earth there was no nation like unto the Roman Empire that filled a fourth part of the earth with its power and its glory. And at the time of its glory, it became the throne of Satan.

24 And John maketh mention of the beginnings of the principles of the government and the monetary economy of the great Roman Empire. For the Greeks were those who first introduced many of these principles to the world.

25 And John wrote of Pergamos, calling it the seat of Satan, because of its works. And now, my brothers and sisters, do ye not know that all nations of the world looked to the Romans as the standard of peace and prosperity and righteousness that should be followed by the whole world?

26 Do ye not know that the Romans were the envy of all other nations upon the earth, and also the envy of the people of the earth, because of that which the people believed were the highest standards and quality of living upon the earth?

27 Yet, even so, their manner of government and the principles of the republic for which they stood were an abomination before God.

28 And the Lord condemned the seat of Satan, according to the words of John, specifically denouncing the works of they who hold the doctrine of Balaam, which was that doctrine that was passed down by Beneli through Cain.

29 And it was written of them saying: Woe unto them; for they have gone in the way of Cain, and ran greedily after the error of Balaam. For these are murmurers and the complainers, walking after their own lusts; and their mouth speaketh great swelling words, holding the persons of men in admiration because of the advantage that they have over another.

30 And the Lord also condemneth the works of the Nicolatians, who were an order of men after the order of Cain that represented the hierarchy of a ruling class over the rest of the people, developing an unrighteous order of fleshly leadership dedicated to the secret combinations of old, which were mentioned throughout the record of my father.

31 And these are the same orders of men set up among the Romans, having their Caesars, and their senators, and their councilmen, and the definers of the law, who deceive and manipulate the people for their own gain.

32 And they had their censors, and consuls and their proconsuls, and their praetor and propraetor. And thus were the leaders of the people called who were elected by the voice of the people to serve them.

33 And these were of the rich, who were called patricians by the Roman people. And these were the few who owned all the land and sought gain from the laws which they enacted among the people.

34 But these did not serve the true needs of the people, but were elected by them because of their flattering words and their rhetoric, which enticed the people and deceived them into thinking that their ways were righteous and just.

35 And unto those of you of the latter days, who are the citizens of that great nation which shall rise out of the earth with a horn like a lamb, deceiving the people that it is a lamb, but being the seat of Satan of the latter days:

36 Behold, the leaders of this great nation shall also follow the ways of the Nicolatians and follow the course of Balaam, which was passed down to them from one generation of the earth to the other from Beneli and Cain, who first established this order of government among the children of men.

37 And I have seen your works, and know that your works are even more deceitful and wicked than the works of the secret combinations of old, which deceive the people for great personal gain and power.

38 And ye have your republicans and your democrats, your presidents and vice presidents and senators and congressmen, and all those who support the principles of Satan, which are principles of the rich ruling over the poor and taking advantage of another because of the blessings of wisdom and power that they have received from your god, who is Satan.

39 And this great nation of the latter days shall be like unto the Roman Empire in the day of its grandeur. And for a time, the world shall behold this great latter day nation with great wonder, and the world shall hold it above all other nations of the earth as the standard that it hath set above all others.

40 And the people of this nation shall be like unto the Romans, who thought of their nation as the greatest nation upon the face of the earth, and their Caesar as the most powerful leader upon the earth.

41 And like unto the Romans, it shall have the power of its armies and its navies to destroy any nation that cometh up to battle against it. And it shall go to battle with all the nations of the earth, even against those that raise up a standard which is contrary to the standard that they have set for the world.

42 And the standard that they shall set shall be a standard of material pleasures and easiness of living, and a promise to the whole earth that all can be rich and powerful, like unto it, if the people will fall down and worship the beast, whom it worshipeth.

43 And the people of this nation, like unto the Romans, shall believe that their nation is a nation united, under God, and that it cannot be divided or conquered because of its great armies and navies.

44 And it shall deceive the people into believing that it offereth liberty and justice for all. Now, even these words which I have written shall be the pledge of allegiance to this nation that those who worship this nation shall say with their own mouths.

45 And with this pledge they deceive themselves and know not that they are pledging their allegiance to Satan. And this they do because they have his mark in their right hands and in their foreheads, and have denied the true words of Christ and follow after a god and a Christ that have been given unto them by Satan; for he is the great deceiver, and the beast, and the false prophet who shall issue forth the

flattery of his words unto the people, even those words that the people will accept.

46 And I have seen the flag which this great nation shall raise in its land to show unto the earth the works which it hath done. And the people shall worship this flag as a representation of the standard that they have accepted for themselves.

47 And the flag shall be white, symbolizing the righteousness that is claimed of this nation. And this righteousness shall be stained with the blood of the righteous, whom it persecuteth; and also of its own sons, who have ignorantly fought that this standard might prevail over all other standards of the earth.

48 And this blood shall be symbolized on their flag as red stripes that lay over the background of righteousness that it proclaimeth.

49 And in the corner thereof, there shall be stars, which represent the people, even according to the words of John which he wrote, saying, And his tail drew the third part of the stars of heaven, and did cast them to the earth.

50 And these stars shall be of the white background, or of the righteousness that they have proclaimed in and of themselves. But they shall be found in a field of darkness, which symbolizeth the great deception and ignorance of the people who honor and pledge allegiance to this flag; all the people being in darkness and in captivity by the chains of Satan.

51 And these things are in the exact likeness of those things which existed during the greatness of the Roman Empire.

52 And now, my beloved brothers and sisters, can ye now see how much power and control over the minds and hearts of the children of men that Satan hath? Do ye not see how ye have been deceived by him?

53 And there will be those who wonder how these great nations which I have mentioned can be so prosperous, yet be so wicked.

54 And now, I have already explained to you that the blessings of Satan are prosperity for those who follow his plan and do his will. But peace they shall not have.

55 And ye shall see that any nation that followeth the plan of Lucifer shall not have peace. Yea, a nation might think that it hath peace because it is powerful and no other nation can stand against it in war.

56 But this is not the peace that the Father hath promised to those who follow His plan. And if ye look at the people of these nations which seem to be peaceful and prosperous, ye shall find that the people within them are not peaceful, but are unhappy and disconcerted with their lives.

58 Behold, Satan can most assuredly bless a nation with wealth and security from other nations, and give unto the people of a nation a great sense of patriotism and respect for their nation, and this he accomplisheth through the emotions of their hearts.

59 But the people of this nation of Satan shall not love one another according to the words of Christ. And because they cannot love one another, they shall never find the peace and happiness that they desire.

60 And because they cannot find this happiness according to things which are spiritual, they shall seek this happiness from the things of the world, which are the many blessings that Satan shall give unto them.

61 But I have already explained to you that these blessings are temporary reprieves from the causes of misery that a nation under Satan shall experience.

62 But if a nation followeth after the plan of God and keepeth the commandments that He hath given to His children that will lead them to everlasting peace and happiness, then it would not matter if their enemies rose up against them and killed them, for they would die in the Lord.

63 Now, this is the thing that was mentioned in the record of my father concerning the Lamanites who laid down their arms and would not defend themselves against those who were wont to destroy them. And was it not said of them, that they were the most righteous souls that ever lived upon the earth?

64 Yea, they truly lived in happiness and died in happiness, and shall be raised in happiness according to all their desires of happiness, which have been promised them by the Father.

65 But those who follow Satan, do the will of Satan, not the will of the Father, therefore they shall experience the happiness of him whom they serve.

66 And Satan shall set up this great nation of the latter days and deceive all the children of men therein. And there shall be some who have the mark of the lamb in their foreheads, but they shall be few. And those who do not belong to the great and abominable church of the devil shall have the peace of the Spirit that the Father hath promised to all of His children who keep His commandments.

67 And John wrote further concerning this great nation under Satan in the last days. And he wrote, saying: And the beast that was, and is not, and yet is, hath given his full power unto an eighth, and this eighth is of the seventh, and this eighth shall worship the beast. And this beast is he that goeth into perdition.

68 And the ten horns which thou sawest are ten kings, which have received no kingdom as yet; but receive power as kings one hour with the beast. These have one mind, and shall give their power and strength unto the beast.

69 And these things have I already given an explanation of previously in this record. But there are words of John that I have not yet explained unto you. And he wrote saying: These shall make war with the Lamb, and the Lamb shall overcome them at the last day; for he is Lord of lords, and King of kings; and they that are with him are called, and chosen, and faithful.

70 And he saith unto me, The waters which thou sawest, where the whore sitteth, are peoples, and multitudes, and nations, and tongues. And the ten horns which thou sawest upon the beast, these shall hate the whore, and shall make her desolate and naked, and shall eat her flesh, and burn her with fire.

71 For God hath put in their hearts to fulfill His will, and to agree, and give their kingdom unto the beast, until the words of God shall be fulfilled.

72 And the woman which thou sawest is that great city, which reigneth over the kings of the earth.

CHAPTER 72

The United States is the great whore of the latter days. All other nations shall hate the United States because of its pride. All nations and kingdoms will be in turmoil before the coming of the Lord; and all will fall before him.

AND now, my beloved brothers and sisters, I say unto those of you who have received this record and are reading the words which I have been commanded to write unto you by the Lord, behold, the woman and the great city, which reigneth over the kings of the earth is this great nation which shall rise forth in the latter days, even the nation which is called the United States by you.

2 And this nation shall be like unto the Roman nation in all things. And like the great Roman Empire, it shall fall, and great shall be the fall thereof.

3 And during the last days there shall be other nations upon the earth which shall also belong to the church of the devil, or the great and abominable church of which Nephi hath given an account.

4 And these shall also be under the influence of the beast and shall be consumed by their desires and interest in money, and in gain, and in the fine things of the world.

5 And there shall be ten great nations that shall be upon the earth at the same time that the United States shall wield its power and influence over the world. And these are the ten horns of which John hath written that shall hate the whore.

6 For behold, these nations shall agree and give their kingdom unto the beast, or in other words, be under the influence of Satan like unto the United States.

7 But these other nations shall hate the United States and abhor that for which it standeth; for these shall see the influence of the great whore upon the whole earth and the cause of her wickedness, because of the greatness of her strength, which is the strength of her armies and her navies, which shall subdue all those who rise up against her.

8 And she shall be prideful and arrogant in

that which she claimeth of herself, even that she saith in her heart: I sit a queen, and am no widow, and shall see no sorrow, and this according to the prophecy of John.

9 For the United States shall raise its head above all other nations and proclaim its dominance over all the nations of the earth.

10 And the leaders and the people of this great nation shall think of themselves as the most powerful nation upon the earth, against which no other nation shall rise and prosper.

11 And the other nations of the earth shall commit fornication with this nation, or this great whore of which John speaketh; and this meaneth that they shall take part of the economy of this nation and wax rich through the abundance of her delicacies.

12 Behold, the people of this nation shall consume more of the earth and its resources than all the other nations of the earth. And their appetite for the things of the world shall go contrary to the laws of nature that have been established for its survival since the beginning. And the health of the earth itself shall be affected because of the wants of this nation.

13 And its people shall believe that they are special, yea, a chosen people above all others, and this because of their prosperity and their riches and the fine things of the earth which they lust after and desire.

14 And the youth of this nation shall be unlike any other since the world began. For they shall be consumers of their lusts, having been taught these things by their parents.

15 And there shall be great markets set up in which are displayed all the fine things of the world. And the youth of this nation shall gather themselves to these markets and envy that which they do not possess and buy all that they can purchase with the money that their hearts are set upon.

16 And virtue and righteousness, and honesty and integrity, and hard work and sacrifice, yea, even all those things that are the fruits of righteousness shall be a thing of the past.

17 And the youth of this nation shall oppress their elders and cause great turmoil for their parents. For these youth shall desire all the fine things of the earth and center their hearts and thoughts upon these things and care not for the poor and the needy, the sick and the afflicted that are among them.

18 And the women of this nation shall rise up in power against the men and began to control their husbands, and look down upon them, and set their hearts upon all the fine things of the world that they can get from their husbands, each lusting after these things in her heart.

19 And the young woman shall lust after that which an older man can give unto her to make her comfortable and give her security in the lusts of the flesh.

20 And these women shall rule over their husbands and live in misery with them, lusting only after those things that they receive because of the money of their husbands.

21 And the men of this nation shall think of nothing but those things which they must do in order to acquire more material goods and get more gain that they might, in their pride, have more than their neighbor, and be looked upon as one who hath gained the success of the world because of his hard work and his industry.

22 And these men shall engage in all manner of business to get gain. And their desires shall be set in lasciviousness and in envy of the honors and glories of men.

23 And their money, and their possessions, and the security of the blessings that they receive from Satan shall be the desires of their hearts.

24 And then shall the words of the prophet Isaiah come to pass in the latter days, even as he said: The shew of their countenance doth witness against them; and they declare their sin as Sodom, they hide it not. Woe unto their soul; for they have rewarded evil unto themselves.

25 Say ye to the righteous, that it shall be well with him; for they shall eat the fruit of their doings. Woe unto the wicked; for it shall be ill with him; for the reward of his hands shall be given him.

26 As for my people, children are their oppressors, and women rule over them. Oh, my people, they which lead thee cause thee to err and destroy the way of thy paths.

27 And now my brothers and sisters, I have seen your day and know of your wickedness, even that every soul upon the face of the earth is wicked in some manner, having made Satan their God, and money, which is the number of the beast, their desire.

28 And because of these things, and the pride of this great whore, the other nations of the world shall hate her.

29 And according to the words of John: These have one mind, and shall give their power and strength unto the beast. For God hath put in their hearts to fulfill his will, and to agree, and give their kingdom unto the beast, until the words of God shall be fulfilled.

30 And now, John continueth his prophecy describing many of the things that I have explained unto you concerning the beast, and the great city, or the whore, as I have explained it unto you.

31 And it is that great city of Babylon, or the city that is the whore of all the earth, even these United States of which John wrote, when he said: And after these things I saw another angel come down from heaven, having great power; and the earth was lightened with his glory.

32 And he cried mightily with a strong voice, saying, Babylon the great is fallen, is fallen, and is become the habitation of devils, and the hold of every foul spirit, and a cage of every unclean and hateful bird.

33 For all nations have drunk of the wine of the wrath of her fornication, and the kings of the earth have committed fornication with her, and the merchants of the earth are waxed rich through the abundance of her delicacies.

34 And I heard another voice from heaven, saying, Come out of her, my people, that ye be not partakers of her sins, and that ye receive not of her plagues. For her sins have reached unto heaven, and God hath remembered her iniquities.

35 Reward her even as she rewarded you, and double unto her double according to her works, in which she hath filled the cup of the indignation of the wrath of God; yea, in the cup which she hath filled, fill to her double.

36 How much she hath glorified herself, and lived deliciously, so much torment and sorrow give her because of the pride of her heart; for she saith in her heart, I sit a queen, and am no widow, and shall see no sorrow.

37 Therefore shall her plagues come in one day: death, and mourning, and famine; and she shall be utterly burned with fire: for strong is the Lord God who judgeth her.

38 And the kings of the earth, who have committed fornication and lived deliciously with her, shall bewail her, and lament for her, when they shall see the smoke of her burning; standing afar off for the fear of her torment, saying: Alas, alas that great city Babylon, that mighty city; for in one hour is thy judgment come.

39 And the merchants of the earth shall weep and mourn over her; for no man buyeth their merchandise any more; yea, the merchandise of gold, and silver, and precious stones, and of pearls, and fine linen, and purple, and silk, and scarlet, and all fine wood, and all manner of vessels of ivory, and all manner of vessels of most precious wood, and of brass, and iron, and marble, And cinnamon, and odours, and ointments, and frankincense, and wine, and oil, and fine flour, and wheat, and beasts, and sheep, and horses, and chariots, and slaves, and souls of men.

40 And the fruits that thy soul lusted after are departed from thee, and all things which were dainty and goodly are departed from thee, and thou shalt find them no more at all.

41 The merchants of these things, which were made rich by her, shall stand afar off for the fear of her torment, weeping and wailing, and saying: Alas, alas that great city, that was clothed in fine linen, and purple, and scarlet, and decked with gold, and precious stones, and pearls; for in one hour so great riches is come to naught.

42 And every shipmaster, and all the company in ships, and sailors, and as many as trade by sea, stood afar off, and cried when they saw the smoke of her burning, saying: What city is like unto this great city? And they cast dust on their heads, and cried, weeping and wailing, saying: Alas, alas that great city, wherein were made rich all that had ships in the sea by reason of her costliness; for in one hour is she made desolate.

43 Rejoice over her, thou heaven, and ye holy apostles and prophets; for God hath avenged you on her.

44 And a mighty angel took up a stone like a great millstone, and cast it into the sea, saying, Thus with violence shall that great city Babylon be thrown down, and shall be found no more at all. And the voice of harpers, and musicians, and of pipers, and trumpeters, shall be heard no more at all in thee; and no craftsman, of whatsoever craft he be, shall be found any more in thee; and the sound of a millstone shall be heard no more at all in thee;

45 And the light of a candle shall shine no more at all in thee; and the voice of the bridegroom and of the bride shall be heard no more at all in thee; for thy merchants were the great men of the earth; for by thy sorceries were all nations deceived.

46 And in her was found the blood of prophets, and of saints, and of all that were slain upon the earth.

47 And now, I, Moroni, mourn exceedingly for that which I have seen with my own eyes concerning you, and also that which I have read of the words of the brother of Jared, which he wrote concerning you.

48 Behold, ye have had the words of John among you all the days of your lives. Yea, ye have also the testimonies of the other prophets of God, and also the testimonies of the prophets that testified unto you in the record of my father.

49 And now, how can ye not understand the words of John concerning you? Behold, Nephi gave a testimony of the importance of the prophecy of John, when he wrote, saying: And it came to pass that the angel spake unto me, saying: Look! And I looked and beheld a man dressed in a white robe. And the angel said unto me: Behold one of the twelve apostles of the Lamb.

50 Behold, he shall see and write the remainder of these things which have been. And he shall also write concerning the end of the world.

51 And now, are not the words of John correct in that which he hath prophesied concerning ye of the latter days? Doth not his words ring true to your souls, even that upon reading them your bosoms burn within you; thus the Holy Ghost testifieth unto you concerning the truthfulness of his words?

52 Behold, the words of John are a prophecy in two-fold, or in other words, they are prophetic regarding the great Roman Empire that rose up during the days of John, and the great nation of the United States that ye have in the latter days.

53 For their histories are the same, and their powers and influence are the same throughout the earth. And John was commanded to speak unto you symbolically of one that ye might apply the meaning of his words unto the other.

54 And I testify unto you that the words of John shall all be fulfilled which he hath written concerning these great nations, which each is the seat of the beast in its own time.

55 And when these shall be upon the earth, their power shall be given unto them during the time that the Father hath commanded that His gospel be given to the world both by His own mouth, which is the mouth of His Holy Spirit, and also by the mouth of His holy prophets, who are called after the order of His Son.

56 And the Roman Empire shall rise up and shall be completely destroyed during the dispensation of time known in the prophecies of the holy prophets as the times.

57 And the United States shall rise out of obscurity and have its power and dominion, and shall eventually be destroyed during the dispensation of time known as the half of time.

58 And so shall all the nations of the earth be destroyed before the great and dreadful day of the Lord.

59 And the prophet Daniel gave a similitude of these things when he interpreted the dream of the king of Babylon. And he interpreted the dream, saying: This is the dream; and we will tell the interpretation thereof before the king.

60 Thou, Oh, King, art a king of kings among the nations of the earth; for the God of heaven hath suffered that thou art given a kingdom, power, and strength, and glory. And wheresoever the children of men dwell, the beasts of the field and the fowls of the heaven hath he suffered to be given into thine hand, and hath made thee ruler over them all. Thou art this head of gold.

61 And after thee shall arise another kingdom inferior to thee, and another third kingdom of brass, which shall bear rule over all the earth.

62 And the fourth kingdom shall be strong as iron, forasmuch as iron breaketh in pieces and subdueth all things; and as iron that breaketh all these, shall it break in pieces and bruise.

63 And whereas thou sawest the feet and toes, part of the clay of a potter, and part of iron, the kingdom shall be divided; but there shall be in it of the strength of the iron; forasmuch as thou sawest the iron mixed with miry clay.

64 And as the toes of the feet were part of iron, and part of clay, so the kingdom shall be partly strong, and partly broken. And whereas thou sawest iron mixed with miry clay, they shall mingle themselves with the seed of men, but they shall not cleave one to another, even as iron is not mixed with clay.

65 And in the days of these kings shall the God of heaven set up a kingdom, which shall never be destroyed: and the kingdom shall not be left to other people, but it shall break in pieces and consume all these kingdoms, and it shall stand for ever.

66 Forasmuch as thou sawest that the stone was cut out of the mountain without hands, and that it brake in pieces the iron, the brass, the clay, the silver, and the gold; the great God hath made known to the king what shall come to pass hereafter: and the dream is certain, and the interpretation thereof sure.

67 And John also gave the description of the fall of these kingdoms of men in this way, when he wrote, saying: And I saw heaven opened, and behold a white horse; and he that sat upon him was called Faithful and True, and in righteousness he doth judge and make war.

68 His eyes were as a flame of fire, and on his head were many crowns; and he had a name written, that no man knew, but he himself. And he was clothed with a vesture dipped in blood: and his name is called The Word of God.

69 And the armies which were in heaven followed him upon white horses, clothed in fine linen, white and clean.

70 And out of his mouth goeth a sharp sword, that with it he should smite the nations and divide the wicked from the righteous. And he shall rule them with a rod of iron, which is the word of God that proceedeth out his mouth. And he treadeth the winepress of the fierceness and wrath of Almighty God.

71 And he hath on his vesture and on his thigh a name written, King of Kings, and Lord of Lords.

72 And I saw an angel standing in the sun; and he cried with a loud voice, saying to all the fowls that fly in the midst of heaven: Come and gather yourselves together unto the supper of the great God; that ye may eat the flesh of kings, and the flesh of captains, and the flesh of mighty men, and the flesh of horses, and of them who sit on them, and the flesh of all men, both free and bond, both small and great.

73 And I saw the beast, and the kings of the earth, and their armies, gathered together to make war against him who sat on the horse, and against his army.

74 And the beast was taken, and with him the false prophet who wrought miracles before him, with which he deceived them that had received the mark of the beast, and them who worshipped his image. These both were cast alive into a lake of fire burning with brimstone.

75 And the remnant were slain with the sword of him who sat upon the horse, which sword proceeded out of his mouth: and all the fowls were filled with their flesh.

CHAPTER 73

Little children are given as an example of how our attitude towards life should be. When the Lord comes, doctors, businessmen, religious leaders and politicians will suffer great sorrow and embarrassment because of the things that they hear coming from the Lord's mouth. Television is used by Satan to project his image to the world.

AND now, all ye of the latter days unto whom these things shall be revealed in this sealed portion of this record; yea, do ye not see the great destruction that shall come upon the nations of the earth at the coming of the Lord in his glory? How many more words must I use to give unto you in plainness that which shall come to pass because of your wickedness and abominations before God?

2 Behold, all the nations upon the face of the earth shall be in a constant state of turmoil and unrest until the coming of the Son of God in his righteousness.

3 Yea, Satan shall have great power over the hearts of the leaders of these nations; and the few, who are the rich and powerful, shall rule and reign over the majority of the people, who are those of you who support your leaders in their wickedness and give unto them their power.

4 For behold, these leaders would not have any power except it be given unto them by the people whom they lead.

5 And ye are this people who have given them their power. And ye listen to their words of flattery, and ye see their lives, which are lives of wealth and leisure, and ye worship them and envy that which they possess.

6 And they make vain promises unto you that ye also can have all that they have, which ye begin to believe, dedicating your lives and your desires to becoming like your leaders.

7 And ye shall think that they are righteous and good and honorable men of the earth because of their success and their power that ye have given unto them. But ye shall not know of their secret combinations which they have established among them to maintain control over your hearts and your minds.

8 And like sheep who have lost their way, ye shall follow these wolves, who are dressed in the skins of sheep so that they might not be discovered among the flock; and ye shall follow them to your own destruction.

9 And now, my beloved brothers and sisters, think in and of the Spirit for a moment. Yea, take no thought of the world for a moment, but listen to the words that I am commanded to give unto you by the power of the Holy Spirit which is with me.

10 Ye know that your hearts and desires are set upon the things of the world. Ye know that ye do aspire for the honors and glories of men, which ye believe shall give you the fine things of the world and make your life happier and more at peace.

11 But I ask of you, are ye at peace having these things? Yea, doth not your souls become burdened because of your desires for the things of the world? Do ye not see how the soul is corrupted when it desireth these things?

12 And if ye have these things; yea, if all the riches and glory and honors of men were given unto you, then do ye think that ye would be happy? I say unto you that ye would not be happy.

13 And ye need not take my opinion of this, but look at those who have the power and the riches and all the fine things of the world. Are they happy? Ye know that they are not happy, even though they have all the things that ye desire and on which ye have set your hearts.

14 Behold, can ye find one of them among you who is happy and righteous? I say unto you that ye cannot find one of them among you. And if there is one among you that claimeth that he is happy because of the things which he hath accumulated for himself, or the power that hath been given him, then ye can know of a surety that he lieth to you and covereth up a multitude of his sins, that they might not be known unto you.

15 And now, I ask of you, who among you is truly happy in all things? Yea, who is there among you that loveth his life and cherisheth the hours of each day that they are alive and smileth upon the thought that they exist, and not upon the thought of how they should exist by consuming the things of the world upon their flesh?

16 Behold, who among you can be given a rock of no value and find joy with that rock, and cherisheth it and throweth it to the pleasure of his soul?

17 Yea, who among you is not concerned about money, or prestige, or the honors and glories of men?

18 Yea, these whom ye find among you who are this way are those who are truly happy. And these are your little ones, your children, the flesh of your flesh, even those who have been given to you by the Father to be an example unto you in all things. Yea, these are the happiest among you.

19 These are they who live without hatred one towards another. These are they of whom the Lord spoke when he said, except ye become as a little child, ye shall in no wise inherit the kingdom of God.

20 And now my brothers and sisters, how many among you are like unto your little children? I say unto you that ye are not like unto little children, but ye teach your children to become like unto yourselves; ye being miserable and dissatisfied with the life that the Father hath given unto you.

21 And ye show an example unto your children of how they should be, which example is given unto your children by your works, which are the works of Satan that can only bring temporary joy to you in that moment that ye receive the reward for your works.

22 And ye teach your children to do the works that ye do, or the works of Satan, that they, too, might have this temporary joy that cometh from the blessings of Satan for doing his works and keeping his commandments.

23 And the blessings of Satan are your fine clothing that ye wear, the fine houses that ye live in, the money that ye have, which can purchase any of the fine things of the world.

24 And your children see your examples in these things and your desires to have these things. And they see that ye spend all the days of your lives in search of these temporal blessings of Satan, which he giveth to you as ye deserve them.

25 And your children witness when ye receive these things from Satan; and they see the temporary joy that these things seem to bring unto you when ye receive them. But ye do not show unto your children the misery that cometh from these things.

26 Yea, your children do not know of the wickedness that ye harbor in your hearts in your pursuit of these things. Neither do they know of their fathers who lust after other women who are not the mothers of their children, and the mothers who lust after the things of the world for themselves.

27 Yea, your children do not see that which is in your foreheads, or the thoughts of your minds, even the mark of the beast that is in your foreheads and in your right hands. And the misery that cometh from your pursuit of these things, they see not.

28 Behold, they cannot see these things, for ye hide them from your children. And because they only see the temporary happiness that cometh from acquiring the things of the world, they do not understand the eternal peace and happiness that they are promised by their God, who is their Father in heaven.

29 And ye take them to your churches and teach them to listen to the leaders of your churches, whom ye present unto them as the mouthpieces of God on earth.

30 And these leaders also are the successful and affluent men of the earth, as ye have taught your children that they should become; and they begin to do the things which ye teach them to do by your own example and also by the example of those who ye claim are the examples of God upon the earth.

31 Behold, how many of you teach your children to pattern their lives after Christ and his teachings? Yea, how many of you teach these innocent ones, who were happy in the beginning, that Christ hath given already unto them an example that they should follow in all things?

32 Yea, there are many of you who say these things to your children, yet by your examples and the examples of the leaders of your churches, your children become confused and know not where to find the true example of the way in which they should live their lives.

33 But ye have the scriptures before you, and many of you proclaim to your children that the scriptures are the word of God, and that they should live by the scriptures, and do that which is commanded of them therein. Yet, do ye live by these same words?

34 I say unto you that ye do not, for ye are hypocrites, and do not read and understand the scriptures for yourselves. And because of your wickedness as parents, ye have offended the little ones of whom Christ spoke when he said: Verily I say unto you, except ye be converted, and become as little children, ye shall not enter into the kingdom of heaven.

35 Whosoever therefore shall humble himself as this little child, the same is greatest in the kingdom of heaven. And whoso shall receive one such little child in my name receiveth me. But whoso shall offend one of these little ones which believe in me, it were better for him that

a millstone were hanged about his neck, and that he were drowned in the depth of the sea.

36 Woe unto the world because of offenses; for it must needs be that offenses come; but woe to that man by whom the offense cometh. Take heed that ye despise not one of these little ones; for I say unto you, That in heaven their angels do always behold the face of my Father which is in heaven.

37 Behold, all of you who have received my words in this record that hath been sealed to come forth at the time of the greatest wickedness that hath ever existed upon the face of the earth; know ye not that ye are offending the children, even all those who have the countenance of the Father written upon them?

38 Know ye not that when these children grow up and become like unto you that they shall suffer as ye have suffered?

39 And if ye have not suffered in the flesh, because ye believe that ye have prospered and have lived peacefully all the days of your lives, truly ye shall suffer when ye are dead and have given up the flesh; and as a spirit, ye see the fruits of the works of your flesh and the way that ye have offended your little ones.

40 For your children and the children of your children shall be those who suffer at the great and dreadful day of the Lord. They are the ones who shall live upon the earth at a time of exceedingly great turmoil and unhappiness because of the works of their parents before them.

41 And ye who shall be dead, shall see the fruits of your works and the turmoil and pain of the suffering of your children, and shall not be able to take back the example that ye have given unto them in the flesh, neither shall ye be given the power to teach them according to the things of the spirit.

42 For during the days of your flesh with your children, ye taught them to set their hearts upon the things of the world and the desires and honors of men. And since their hearts are continually concentrating on these things, do ye think that they shall listen to the Spirit and receive guidance from God?

43 And if they do not listen to the Holy Ghost and those who have been commissioned to minister from the spirit world to your children in the flesh, do ye think that they shall listen to you?

44 Yea, those of you who have spent the days of your probation constantly denying the Holy Spirit because of your pursuit of the fine things of the world; yea, ye shall be in a state of unquenchable hell and torment as ye witness that which shall come to pass to your children in the flesh.

45 For your children shall see the great and terrible day of the Lord. Yea, they shall be in the flesh when the Lord cometh and with his mouth, which is the sword of his power, he shall subdue the nations of the earth and cause that your children shall drink of the cup of his indignation and feel of his wrath.

46 Now, do ye think that his wrath shall be a wrath of anger? Do ye think that the sword which proceedeth forth from his mouth shall be wielded in anger? I say unto you that it is impossible for the Lord to become angry as ye are accustomed to become angry one with another, but his anger is a righteous indignation, which is wielded in love for all men.

47 And John hath given you the revelation and hath told you that his name is called The Word of God. And it is the word of God that shall cause your children to weep and wail and gnash their teeth in pain and misery and be tormented by that which cometh out of the mouth of the Lord at that time.

48 For your children shall hear the words of the Lord and shall begin to see the enormous error of the things that ye have taught unto them and the deceptions that they were led into because of your examples.

49 For they shall hear that their honors and their glories, which they receive from men, and also the precious and fine things of the world that they were taught by you to desire, are the things which the Lord hateth and which he despiseth according to his words.

50 And they shall see that the Lord shall call forth the poor and the meek, and those who did not receive the mark of the beast in their forehead, and were those whom your children mocked and ridiculed and imprisoned for the way in which they desired to live their lives, even according to the Spirit of God that was in them.

51 And your children who have spent the days of their probation pursuing the honors and the degrees of a lawyer or a doctor, or a businessman adroit in the economy of the beast, and who have all lived deliciously with the whore of the earth and have acquired many things because of the whore; yea, these shall the Lord despise.

52 For they have spent their lives in pursuit of those things which brought riches unto them, when they could have used their talents and their time and the intellect of their spirit to bring peace upon the earth.

53 And your children shall witness all the great leaders among men, and all those who have received praise and adoration from men, even those who are set up because of their popularity in athletics, and in the image of the beast which shall be broadcast upon the housetops of all the people of the earth.

54 Behold, this image shall be broadcast by way of what ye shall call that which shall give unto you a vision, or an image of the beast, by way of the undulations of natural impulses that are cast in the air and underground and received into each household of the earth, even upon the housetops, deceiving those who have given their hearts and minds to the beast who hath caused this miracle and given his image unto them.

55 And by this means shall the whole earth be deceived by Satan; and the people of the earth shall learn of him those things which he would teach unto them.

56 And there shall be many who are made popular and rich from the transmissions of the image of the beast upon the world; and these shall be despised by the Lord when he cometh to judge the world.

57 And your children who honor and give adoration unto them shall suffer with them; for they shall see the error of their ways and will not be able to look upon the Lord in their wickedness, having desired the things of Satan all the days of their lives.

58 And those among you who are doctors of the flesh and have spent all the days of your youth in pursuit of the knowledge of medicine so that ye might become rich and be set up above others; yea, what shall ye think when the Lord shall come forth and heal with only his touch?

59 Of what use then is the waste of your lives in pursuit of these things, which ye believe are noble and great? Yea, there are many of you who believe that which ye pursue is noble and great and is necessary so that the children of men might be healthy and happy.

60 But I say unto you that they are not healthy and happy, because they follow the course that Satan hath set before them, which is a course of indulgence and laziness, which causeth the people of the earth to need the doctors that are taught the ways of Satan, so that they can heal the rewards of these ways.

61 And when the Lord cometh in the glory of the Father, what then shall ye doctors say unto him? Shall ye say unto him that ye have created more happiness upon the earth because of your knowledge and the way that ye have deceived those who look up to you as the saviors of the flesh?

62 Shall ye say these things when ye realize that the spirit world is a place of a much greater peace and happiness than mortality, and had ye not healed many of the people of those ailments that would have caused them to go home to the spirit world from whence they came, then they would have been much happier as spirits there than the life that ye have given unto them because of your medicines and your ways, which keep them alive that they might pay you for your services and enrich you with the fine things of the world, which ye desire?

63 Woe unto the doctors of the flesh when the Lord cometh in his glory.

64 Yea, woe unto the doctors of the soul, or those of you who have set yourselves up as counselors and the spiritual advisers of another. And the leaders of every church that hath been set up among men shall also be despised by the Lord and cut asunder by the sword that cometh forth from his mouth.

65 For he shall witness in that day against them because of their works. And your children shall see the Lord ignore those who thought of themselves as his prophets and apostles, his ministers, and his evangelists, his priests and his popes, his bishops and his pastors.

66 And all those who have enriched themselves because of the word of God shall be cast down and tormented by that which the Lord shall tell them in that day.

67 And they shall come forth and kneel before him, crying: Lord, Lord, have we not prophesied in thy name; and in thy name have cast out devils; and in thy name done many wonderful works?

68 And then shall the Lord command them to arise and depart from before him, for he shall not recognize their works, which are not his works, but the works of Satan.

69 For those who profess to be his prophets and apostles, his ministers, and his evangelists, his priests and his popes, his bishops and his pastors, who do not live their lives as he lived his, are not his servants.

70 And therefore, he hath said, By their works ye shall know them. And now, look at those who profess to you in the latter days that they are the servants of the Lord and the prophets and the seers and the revelators of the will of God. Yea, how do these men dress? Yea, in what manner of houses do they live? Yea, how much money and honor and status do they receive in the world? Yea, in fine, how much do they actually live as our Lord and Savior Jesus Christ lived?

71 I say unto you that they do not live like Jesus lived, nor do they teach the things that Jesus taught by their examples, but they give unto the people of the earth an example of the works and glory of Satan.

72 For it is Satan who desireth the prestige and honor and glory of men. It is Satan who desireth gold and silver and the fine and precious things of the earth. And all of these things he hath given unto those who serve him and keep his commandments.

73 And there shall not be any religion upon the face of all the earth that shall be the religion that shall be accepted by the Lord when he cometh, but all of them shall be rejected by him, because their works are evil and are not based upon the word of God, as it was given by Christ.

74 And in the day of the Lord shall the leaders of the governments of men come unto the Lord for his blessing and his acceptance of him. But in their desire they shall be sorely disappointed, for the sword of his mouth shall tell them that they have been the leaders of the nations of Satan, and have done those things that Satan hath commanded them and inspired them to do.

75 For these are the men who have received greatness and honor from those whom they lead, having deceived those whom they lead by their riches and their flatterings and their promises of peace and prosperity.

76 And when these leaders die, they receive great honor and praise from the world. Yea, they have long funeral processions which those who loved them and followed after them give unto them in a memory of their works.

77 And now, I would ask of those of you in the latter days, who honor and praise your leaders and give them great glory; yea, what do ye think of the manner in which Christ was honored and praised by the world?

78 Yea, how doth the funeral procession of the greatest soul who ever lived in the flesh compare to that of your leaders, who are the perpetuators and promulgators of the plan of Lucifer?

79 I say unto you, that every one of your leaders who receiveth the glories and honors of men, receiveth these things from Satan, who is the God that they followed while they led you.

80 For the world loveth them and giveth them the honor which they sought. And ye can assure yourselves, that the greater the glory and honor that they received of the world, the more wicked they were in the leadership that they gave unto the people.

81 And ye should judge all men according to the life of Christ and his works, and not according to the works and lives of those whom ye have accepted as the great men among you. For these same great men shall not be able to stand in the presence of the Lord when he cometh in the glory of the Father.

82 And those of you who are the businessmen and the merchants of the earth, who have gained your wealth by the economy of the beast and the blessings that Satan affordeth to all those who seek to perpetuate his plan; yea, do ye think that ye shall escape the wrath of God at that day? Do ye think that ye shall find any justification of your riches?

83 Behold, as the history of the peoples of the earth is revealed unto you in this record, ye shall see that the merchants and rich men of the earth are those who caused most of the misery and unhappiness that is experienced in mortality.

84 And there shall not be one of you who is considered rich by the standard of the world, yea, no not one, that shall be justified in your riches in the day of the Lord. And ye shall not be able to stand before the Lord because of your riches.

85 And ye are those of whom the Lord made reference when he spoke to the Jews, saying: When the Son of man shall come in his glory, and all the holy angels with him, then shall he sit upon the throne of his glory, which the Father hath given unto him.

86 And before him shall be gathered all the nations of the earth; and he shall separate them one from another, as a shepherd divideth his sheep from the goats when they come unto him to feed. And he shall set the sheep on his right hand, but the goats on the left.

87 Then shall the King say unto them on his right hand, Come, ye blessed of my Father, inherit the kingdom prepared for you from the foundation of the world, even the glories of the kingdom of my Father.

88 For I was an hungred, and ye gave me meat. I was thirsty, and ye gave me drink. I was a stranger, and ye took me in; naked, and ye clothed me. I was sick, and ye visited me and in prison, and ye came unto me.

89 Then shall the righteous answer him, saying, Lord, when saw we thee an hungred, and fed thee? or thirsty, and gave thee drink? When saw we thee a stranger, and took thee in? or naked, and clothed thee? Or when saw we thee sick, or in prison, and came unto thee?

90 And the King shall answer and say unto them, Verily I say unto you, Inasmuch as ye have done it unto one of the least of these my brethren, ye have done it unto me.

91 Then shall he say also unto them on the left hand, Depart from me, ye cursed, into everlasting fire prepared for the devil and his angels, which is the kingdom that ye have chosen for yourselves.

92 For I was an hungred, and ye gave me no meat. I was thirsty, and ye gave me no drink. I was a stranger, and ye took me not in; naked, and ye clothed me not; sick, and in prison, and ye visited me not.

93 Then shall they also answer him, saying, Lord, when saw we thee an hungred, or athirst, or a stranger, or naked, or sick, or in prison, and did not minister unto thee?

94 Then shall he answer them, saying, Verily I say unto you, Inasmuch as ye did it not to one of the least of these, ye did it not to me. And these shall go away into everlasting punishment: but the righteous into life eternal.

95 And thus shall it be unto all of you who have great riches of the latter days. Yea, even those of you who have two coats and imparteth not to him that hath none; ye shall suffer the same; even all of you who have made money from your businesses and your merchandise; ye shall suffer for that which is of an abundance that ye keep for yourselves when there are others who are in need.

96 A word of wisdom I give unto those of you who are rich as to the things of the world, remember the widow and her mite, for in this is the foundation of righteousness.

97 He who hath an ear to hear, let him hear and understand.

CHAPTER 74

Judges and lawyers will suffer the most when the Lord comes because of the misuse of their power over the lives of others. The righteous should not go to court, but should love all men and let their light shine by their examples.

AND those who make the laws of Satan and administer these laws unto the children of men shall come forth at the day of the Lord in hopes that they, too, might receive a justification and a reward for that which they have done during the days of their probation.

2 Then shall the sword of his mouth condemn them above all others who have set themselves up in the glories and honors of men.

3 And these are those who cover their righteousness by the blackness of the robes that they symbolically wear when they administer the laws and justice of Satan unto the children of men.

4 For they do not see that they put on a robe of darkness when they administer justice, as they suppose, to their other brothers and sisters, and take away from them their liberty and their possessions, and their lives according to the laws of Satan, whose works they represent in their darkened robes of black.

5 And they shall not see those whom they judge as their brothers and sisters, but they shall condemn them and think of them as the dross of the earth, because of the wickedness that is in the souls of them who judge, they having been deceived by Satan, because of the power that they have been given by him.

6 For behold, all of the servants of God have worn light colors, or pure white, when available to them according to their tradition and customs, that they might be a witness unto the people of that which the Lord requireth of them.

7 But the judges of the latter days shall put on a cloak of darkness and sit in judgment upon the lives of those who are weak and poor among them.

8 And with their robes of darkness, they shall think of themselves above all others upon the face of the earth, they alone wielding the power of Satan in his kingdom.

9 And because of their judgments and their ways, even the power given unto them by Satan to take away the free agency of man, which hath been given unto all by the Father, these above all others shall be condemned exceedingly by the Lord.

10 And those who are the lawyers shall also suffer exceedingly; even those who stand before the judges and who are of the judges, who make their penitence on behalf of those who pay them their wages of sin before the law of the land, which they have convinced the people is a law of righteousness and justice.

11 And these shall claim in that day that the law was necessary that there might be order and peace established and maintained among the people of the earth.

12 And of this principle of order they speak the truth, but in hypocrisy.

13 Yea, the Father abideth by the eternal laws of heaven that have been established for the purpose of creating order and maintaining the peace that existeth in His kingdom among His children.

14 And for this purpose is all law given, that it might protect the rights of one from that which another might do unto him that taketh away from his free agency.

15 And righteous law is established to protect the rights of all and to maintain peace and order among the people.

16 But I have said that these lawyers and these judges receive their wages of sin, for that is what they receive by disregarding the law of Christ, which he hath given unto us that we might have true peace among us.

17 For the law of the latter days shall be set up for those who administer the law and act under its name to get gain and power over others.

18 And the lawyers shall incite the people to sue one another and make another an offender for a word so that the case might be brought before a judge and argued by a lawyer, who is paid well for his words, which are honored in a court of law to which both the lawyer and the judge belongeth.

19 And these shall be a secret combination in and of themselves, in that they shall not give honor and respect to a man who representeth himself before a judge and cometh to defend his cause before the law of the land without paying the wages of sin according to the requirement of the court.

20 For if all people were allowed to give their case in truth and honesty before a righteous judge, who judgeth not by that which he seeth, nor by the manner of the case that is brought before him, but judgeth a righteous judgment, rendering the same justice to all;

21 Yea, if a man could come before a judge in this manner, then there would be no need for a lawyer, who useth his cunningness and his expertise in the law that was created for him to get gain.

22 And now, if all law was based upon the commandments of God, even the greatest of all commandments, yea, that a man should love his neighbor as himself; and if each judge would render judgment based solely on this great commandment, then the law would be just.

23 But the words of Christ condemneth the laws of men, because he hath given the commandment of the Father, saying: And if any man sue thee at the law and take away thy coat, let him have thy cloak also.

24 Now, this is the law of the Father. And it is this law by which the judges and lawyers of the nations shall be judged.

25 For the Lord forbiddeth those who follow him from suing another in a court of law. And if a true follower of Christ is brought before a judge by another to take away any of his earthly possessions, then this humble follower of Christ would not fight the case, but give unto him who hath sued him all that is requested of him.

26 And if the children of men obeyed the law of Christ, then they would surely have peace among them, for there would be no need of lawyers.

27 And if there were honest and righteous judges, then all men would be judged by the words of Christ, which are the laws that the Father hath given unto him to teach unto us.

28 And if we were judged by the laws of the Father, then we would receive a just punishment, if it so be that we disobeyed His laws.

29 But the laws of Satan are not the laws of God. And his laws are set up so that one man might gain power and control over another, and that another might gain money by suing his neighbor for whatever cause, taking that which he envieth of his neighbor.

30 And there shall be no love in the hearts of the children of men in the latter days. For if a man offendeth another, then the man who is offended shall seek out a counselor of the law of the land that he might sue him who offended, that he might take his money.

31 And in this way there is no peace among the children of men of the latter days because of the law and the lawyers and the judges who are among you; and this is why I have said unto you that lawyers and judges are hypocrites in that which they believe to be their righteous works.

32 And these all shall be condemned exceedingly by the Lord and suffer the wrath of his indignation, which shall issue forth by the words of his mouth.

33 And all of you who have found cause against you neighbor, who have paid money to a lawyer to represent you against your neighbor in a court of law, do ye think that ye are justified in this thing and shall remain spotless before the Lord when ye know that ye have disobeyed his commandments concerning these things?

34 Behold, ye shall also suffer exceedingly, both those of you in the spirit world who shall witness the coming of the Lord from there, and also those of you who are the children of those who taught you by their example that ye must sue your neighbor and bring a cause of action against him in a court of Satan.

35 And if ye are a true follower of Christ, then ye would not enter into a court supporting the laws of Satan for any reason. Nevertheless, there shall be some of you who are forced into these courts by others; and if ye are forced into these courts by others, do not fight them therein, but give unto them that which they desire of you.

36 And if ye are living by the words of Christ, then ye shall not have that which another would desire to take from you in court.

37 And there shall be some who are forced into court by the laws of Satan, which ye are not abiding by, thinking that ye should not abide by them because they are contrary to the law of God, by which ye supposedly live.

38 But I say unto you, that if ye live by the law of God, there should be no reason why the courts of men should have reason to carry you forth. For the law of God is righteous and doeth those things which create peace and harmony and love and happiness upon the earth.

39 And if ye live your life in bitterness towards your enemies, which ye might perceive are Satan and his followers, then ye are not living by the command of God, but by your own commandment; for the Lord hath commanded you to love your enemies and do good to those who persecute you and hate you and despitefully use you.

40 And this the Father hath commanded you because ye are all His children, and there is no place for hate and pride and disrespect in His kingdom.

41 And this I say unto you of the latter days who think in and of yourselves that ye are above

the laws of men, whether they be the laws of Satan or not, it mattereth not, for ye are subjected to these laws until the Lord cometh to set up his laws of righteousness.

42 And he hath commanded you, like he commanded the Jews, to obey these laws and give unto Caesar that which is of Caesar and unto God that which is of God.

43 And if ye are keeping the commandments of God in all things, then ye shall have the Spirit of God with you. And the Spirit of God shall teach you to love one another and to do good to one another and pray for those who misuse you and abuse you.

44 Do not think that the Lord hath called you out of Babylon, or the world, that ye should isolate yourselves and disregard the rights of others to obey the laws of Satan, if that is what they choose for themselves.

45 For this is not the will of God, but the subtle deceptions of Satan that he hath used to bind your hearts also and bring you down into captivity.

46 For if ye are true followers of Christ, then ye would let your light shine unto your brothers and sisters and love them and be an example unto them.

47 For even Satan is a son of God, and he is also your brother. Behold, his plan is not such a one that the Father would never allow to be followed. For his plan is good to those who follow after him, and cannot cause any harm to the souls of those who follow the plan of the Father, except it be that if ye follow the plan of Lucifer, ye cannot inherit a kingdom of the Father.

48 For this reason the Father alloweth the plan of Lucifer to be incorporated into the days of our probation, so that we might see for ourselves which plan bringeth forth happiness and which plan bringeth forth misery.

49 Therefore, love your neighbor and do good to those who are following the plan of Lucifer and creating unhappiness for themselves. Do not condemn them, but love them. For they shall bring upon themselves their own condemnation according to that which I have told you, even at the time that they shall see the Lord in his glory and hear the law of the Father from his own mouth.

50 Therefore, if they shall suffer at this time, why should ye, who are their brothers and sisters, heap upon them your own judgment and condemnation?

51 I say this unto those of you who think that ye are following the commandments of God, yet ye judgeth and condemneth your neighbors because they followeth after Satan in desiring the things of the world.

52 Behold the words of the Lord shall not directly condemn anyone, but those who hear his words shall condemn themselves.

53 And I have already revealed unto you in this record those things which the Lord shall say in the day of judgment, which shall come at the beginning of the seventh thousand years, which shall mark the end of the half of time and the beginning of a time of great peace and love among all the children of God upon the earth;

54 For those things are the same words that he hath spoken to all of the children of men since the world began. They are the words of the Father, and the only words that we need to listen to in order to be saved in the kingdom of God.

55 And when the Lord speaketh these words again, all those who have not abided in these words shall condemn themselves, even like unto that which was prophesied by John when he said of those who are the kings of the earth, and the great men, and the rich men, and the chief captains, and the mighty men, and every bondman, and every free man, even those who shall hide themselves in the dens and the rocks of mountains away from the presence of the Lord.

56 And they shall say to the mountains and rocks, Fall upon us, and hide us from the face of him who sitteth on the throne, and from the wrath of the Lamb.

57 And these are those of whom I have spoken. And in that day their condemnation shall be their own.

58 But woe unto those who shall condemn them, for ye have sinned also and shall not be ready to stand blameless before the Lord.

59 And now, for this reason the Lord hath commanded these things to come forth unto you of the latter days, even that ye might know of those things which are to come to pass, and that ye might know of the plan of Lucifer which the majority of you follow in the latter days.

60 Now, the Father doth not condemn you if ye follow the plan of Lucifer, if that is what bringeth happiness to you, but He hath commanded the Lord to give His own plan unto you, so that ye might compare the two and know of a surety which one truly bringeth the most happiness to you.

61 And this record was prepared as a voice of warning to all of you who shall receive these things, that ye might know of that which shall shortly come to pass among you.

62 For ye of the latter days who shall receive these things are already in the final half of the half of time of which I have written.

63 And the time is short when the great and dreadful day of the Lord shall come upon all the inhabitants of the earth.

64 And this record is sent forth not to condemn the world for its wickedness, for what good would the condemnation of their wickedness be, if they do not desire to change that which they are experiencing, believing that they are righteous and happy?

65 Behold, for this reason it hath been written that these things shall come unto the elect, who are already written in the book of the Lamb, and who have overcome the world because of the words of Christ which they understand and follow in all things.

66 And because the power of Satan is great upon the earth, most of the elect, at the time this record shall be revealed to the world, shall be ready for these things and shall accept them with an open mind and a glad heart. For they shall read of all the works of the children of men that have led up to the end of the world and the coming of the Son of God to the earth to prepare this earth for its place in the kingdom of the Father.

67 And those of you who shall receive these things with gladness, are commanded to teach these things unto your children in gladness, and they shall rejoice with you.

68 And when ye are dead, ye shall not suffer for that which ye shall observe that your children of the flesh doeth during the days of their probations. For ye shall know of all things that shall come to pass, and ye shall prepare your children for these things.

69 And now, I say unto you who receive these things with gladness: Behold, if ye have received these things with gladness, then in this gladness share these things with the rest of your brothers and sisters who have not received these things.

70 Do not condemn them for their ignorance and their captivity in the chains of Satan, but let the word of God condemn them.

71 But ye are commanded to rejoice in that which hath been revealed unto you. And if ye rejoice in that which hath been revealed unto you, then it might be the cause of your neighbor wondering the reason of your rejoicing.

72 And if your neighbor wondereth of the cause of your great joy, then he might, for the first time during the days of his probation, open up his mind to the things that he hath never heard, nor hath he ever considered.

73 For there are those who profess to be the followers of Christ who condemn others and ridicule them for the path that they have chosen for themselves to follow.

74 And if a man feeleth that he is condemned by another, he will have no cause to want to know the judgment by which he is condemned, and will shun him who condemneth this man.

75 But if this same man seeth that another rejoiceth in that which he hath received from God, then this man shall not feel condemned, but he shall want to experience that which he seeth in which another rejoiceth.

76 And if ye of the latter days, who are the elect, have the Spirit of God, ye shall be happy and full of joy all the days of your lives; for there shall be no reason that ye should be miserable.

77 For misery cometh of the plan of Lucifer, but hath no part of the plan of the Father. Therefore, I say unto you, rejoice in these things and share your rejoicing with the world, that they, by your example, might glorify your Father in heaven because of that which He hath given unto you that causeth your rejoicing.

CHAPTER 75

Moroni returns to the history of the world. The kings and queens of medieval times are established. The people are taught by their religions to reverence the royal families of the earth. The arts and thought of the Renaissance are caused by the influence of Satan.

AND now, I will return once again to the abridgment of the vision of the brother of Jared concerning the latter days and those things that shall transpire in those days that shall cause so much misery and unhappiness among the children of men.

2 And it came to pass that after the great Roman Empire had fallen; and its fall was not of a sudden, but it continued to be diminished in its strength and its glory over many years.

3 And it shall come to pass that it shall be dissolved into many nations, each taking a part of it and forming their own government based upon that which they believe shall best suit them. And many great kings and queens and many kingdoms shall rise up throughout the earth, each sufficiently strong within its own borders to protect itself and maintain order among the people who accept the leadership of the kings that rule over them.

4 And these kings and queens shall begin to think of themselves as those who are special and blessed and chosen by God. And they shall deceive the people and compel them to believe that they are of a royal bloodline; and this belief will ensure them their positions and authority among the people forever.

5 Nevertheless, these royal families cannot be established and maintained if they are not accepted and supported by the people.

6 And the hearts of the people shall turn to their religions and to their beliefs in God. And most of their beliefs and faith are products of the hopes and prayers of the poor, who are the majority of the people who work the land and provide the kings and queens with riches and the fine things of the world.

7 And these poor shall become the property of the kingdom and be subjected to the will of the ruling class, which are the kings and the queens, and the nobles, and those who have been appointed by and received their glory from the royal families.

8 But the poor, who are the majority of the people, are those who shall give unto the royal families their prestige and their power. For without subjects to rule, there could be no kingdom and no royalty to rule it.

9 And for this reason the churches during this time period shall become prosperous and important to the royal families. For the people shall believe in the leaders of their churches, and shall be taught to believe that their leaders are the mouthpieces of God for them.

10 Therefore, anything or anyone that is sanctioned by the leaders of the church, is accepted by the people as that which God hath sanctioned.

11 And the kings and the queens and the royal families depend upon the blessings of the church to maintain their power over the people.

12 Thus shall the kings and queens be ordained and prospered by the churches of the land in sight of the people, that they might know that these kings and queens are called of God to rule and reign over them.

13 And I have already explained unto you that during this time of darkness, which shall be known in the latter days as the medieval times, the Father shall give Lucifer his equal time to present his plan to the children of men.

14 And for this reason, the people shall be left to themselves and the light of Christ that is within them, if they are righteous; and these shall not be helped by the Holy Ghost, nor shall they be inspired and guided by the ministrations of those spirits in the spirit world who were under his direction.

15 And the children of men shall be left unto themselves at this time so that they might learn from their experience that which is good, and that which is evil.

16 Nevertheless, it is expedient that ye understand that each person still possesseth the conscience, or the light of Christ as it hath been explained unto you, that the Father hath given to each of His children in mortality.

17 And I have explained unto you that this is the enmity that the Father hath placed between the sons and daughters of Adam and Lucifer.

18 But Lucifer began to fulfill the promise that he made to the Father when he said: And with the enmity that thou hast placed between me and the children of men, I will take the treasures of the earth, and with gold and silver I will buy up armies and the means of force, and priests and religions, and I will reign with blood and horror on this earth.

19 And these things Satan began to do without the Spirit upon the earth to aid the children of men to be able discern between that which is of God and is good, and that which is of Satan.

20 And the leaders of the church shall become the emissaries of Satan in all things. And they shall be paid well by him, having received many of the fine things of the earth from the kings and the queens whom they support.

21 And the people shall be taught by their religious leaders that the kings and queens, who the people are deceived into believing have been called of God, deserve the best parts of the land and the best part of all the fine things of the earth, which the people can produce and provide for them.

22 And thus are the principles of priestcraft that Satan hath established among the children of men.

23 For behold, if a people believe that their possessions and their property, and the things that they produce by the sweat of their own brow, do not belong to them, but to God, then it is easy for them to give up these things to those whom they believe have been called of God to lead them and protect them.

24 And the people of the various kingdoms know that they are threatened at the border of their lands by those who are marauders and who are desirous to take their lands and their possessions by force.

25 And in this way the people become dependent upon their king and his armies for their protection. And when their king goeth up to battle against their enemies and is victorious, then the people believe that their king is blessed by God and hath been given the power of God to protect them.

26 And the kings shall begin to amass strong armies to protect the people. And there shall be some times that there is no threat at the border of their lands. Nevertheless, the kings shall seek to incite the people to believe that they are in danger of an imaginary enemy, so that the kings can keep the people believing in them and in need of their protection.

27 And in this way the royal families are able to justify the great tax burden that is placed upon the people.

28 But in many instances the individual kingdoms are threatened by a stronger kingdom, or a larger one that hath more powerful armies that could conquer the weaker kingdom.

29 And when the kings are weakened in their state of popularity among the people, they call upon the leaders of the religions to speak to the people and assure them that God is with them.

30 And thus shall the church which shall be established during the end times of the Roman Empire begin to exercise its authority and its power in all aspects of the lives of the people of the earth.

31 And among all the nations of the earth, the sword shall wield the power and bring the people under the submission of the kings and the queens who command the means of force that Satan hath caused to be set up among all the kingdoms of the earth.

32 And now, I, Moroni, have read of all these things which shall come to pass among the nations of the earth in the words of the brother of Jared, which he wrote of the vision that he received from the Lord.

33 And I do not take credit of myself for that which I write, except it be for those things which I speak unto you by the power of the Holy Ghost, which is in me, or for those things that the Lord, himself, commanded me that I should write.

34 And my abridgment of these things is taken from the vision of the brother of Jared. And there are times that I have used his own words, but much of the time I have written an abridgment of that which he hath already written concerning these things, so that I might emphasize those things that the Spirit commandeth me to emphasize for the sake of those of you of the last days, to whom these things shall be revealed; even those things

which are pertinent to your salvation and the times of the latter days.

35 Behold, if ye liken unto yourselves all of the things that I have written in my abridgment of the words of the brother of Jared, then ye shall see the great importance of these things to you.

36 And there are many of you of the latter days who shall not believe that ye are like unto the people before you, who were subjected to kings and queens and the royalty of monarchs who received their gain by the power and control that they had over the people.

37 And if ye believe this, then ye are deceived by Satan who hath established his kingdom in the same manner throughout the history of the earth. For are ye not also burdened with great taxes because ye have been convinced by your leaders that if ye do not maintain a powerful army your nation and your families shall be destroyed?

38 And have not your leaders in many instances created the wars among you against enemies that did not exist, so that they could control you and show forth the greatness of their leadership and their powers? For they care not for the lives of the people of other nations, but care only for their own power which they hold over the hearts and the minds of the people of their own nation.

39 And ye of these nations ignorantly follow the course that Satan hath set before you. For when Satan reigneth over his dominions, and hath power over all the nations of the earth, then they are in his hands and he doeth with them what he will.

40 And if there be a nation under his power that is at peace, and he thinketh that this nation is in need to be reminded of his strength and his power over them, then he will raise up another nation and direct that nation to throw itself upon a peaceful nation to subdue it and destroy it.

41 And when another strong nation under the power of Satan witnesseth that a weaker nation, that is under the same power of Satan, is being overcome, then this stronger nation riseth up and destroyeth the nation that is attempting to overcome a weaker nation.

42 And when this great nation succeedeth in the battles that Satan hath caused it to fight, then the people gain trust in their leaders and in their nation, and then their hearts are more fully dedicated to their nation and to their leaders, which are the servants of Satan.

43 Thus doth Satan cause one nation to rise up and destroy another that he might keep all nations in his power, as he desireth, in order to keep all people under his power. And during the time of his power, he doeth this thing that he might maintain control over the hearts and minds of the children of men.

44 Behold, first he causeth them to separate themselves into families, and cities, and nations; then he causeth them to seek for riches to care for their families and make their own nation better than that nation of their brothers; then he causeth the leaders of this nation to instill fear and patriotic duty in the hearts of its citizens, so that they will do his will in all things.

45 For the nations and kingdoms of the earth care not for the doings and the welfare of another nation, for Satan hath put it in their hearts to hate all other nations and think that only their nation is a blessed nation under God.

46 And if the people of a nation or a kingdom began to question the position of their own nation and kingdom, then Satan seeth that he is losing power over the hearts of this people, therefore he causeth war with another nation, so that the people feel fear for their safety and the safety of their families, thus winning over the hearts of the people again to hate and fight each other and live in fear of each other.

47 And when their nation hath risen up and destroyed another nation, then they thank God and praise the greatness of their nation for that which they have done unto another.

48 And now my brothers and sisters, do ye think that the Father of this earth condoneth war in any manner? Do ye believe that He would command one of His children to rise up and kill another? Do ye think that He hateth one nation because of their works, more than another, even if their works be the works of Satan?

49 I say unto you that the true God doth not condone war, neither doth He condone that one nation shall think of itself above another.

50 Even in the defense of your life, when another nation cometh upon you to destroy you, doth God condemn the use of force and anger in your defense.

51 Yea, He suffereth that ye defend yourselves from another, but He doth not condone this thing. And that is what the Lord meant when he said, He who saveth his life shall lose it. And he who loseth his life for my sake, shall find it.

52 Therefore, when a people support their leaders in war, and in the pride of their hearts they look down upon another nation, and think of themselves as a better nation, ye can know of a surety that these people belong to a nation under Satan. For a nation under God would do no such thing.

53 Now, during the times of peace when Satan is not causing war and strife among you to keep you in his power, he beginneth to reveal unto the children of men the things that bring moments of peace and happiness, or this temporary peace and happiness that I have explained is the reward, or one of his blessings.

54 Therefore, during this dark period of time in which the Spirit of God is not upon the earth in all its power and purpose, Lucifer beginneth to introduce into the world many wonderful things, pertaining to the flesh, even in the arts, and in theater, and in music, and in dance, and in sculpture, and in the architecture of the buildings that he causeth to be constructed by the poor for the needs and wants of the rich.

55 And from the time that Adam and Eve were banished from the land of Eden, the children of men began to be influenced by Satan to bring forth the fruits of his own blessings unto them.

56 And remember that which I have said unto you concerning the temporality of the blessings of Satan, even that the effect of the happiness that ye receive from one of his blessings lasteth for but a moment, and then returneth you to the misery that ye feel because of him.

57 And now, since the plan of Lucifer is to circumvent the plan of the Father, which offereth eternal happiness to those who follow after it; yea, Lucifer hath introduced many things into the world to change the focus of the minds of the children of men from the things of God to the things that he helpeth them create with their own hands, even that which bringeth to them a temporary joy.

58 And when the people are burdened exceedingly because of the causes of the plan of Lucifer, he giveth unto them a reprieve from their pain and their sorrow and the unhappiness that they feel from him.

59 And for this reason he also introduced wine and the means of other stimulants that relieve the souls of men from the daily drudgeries of their mortal lives, which would not be miserable if they followed the plan of the Father.

60 And he also inspireth the minds of men in their inventions of painting and sculpture and of other arts that are the creations of their own hands.

61 For behold, what man among you can create the beauty and splendor of nature? Yea, look at the animals and the plants that the Father hath created in all their beautiful forms and placed upon this earth for our enjoyment.

62 And how can ye say that ye receive the same enjoyment from a painting or a sculpture as that which ye receive from observing the beauty and perfect order of nature in all of its glory?

63 And when ye walk in a forest among the trees and the plants that the Father hath placed there; and ye behold the peace and serenity of nature in all of its glory, do ye not come away from this experience with a joy and a happiness which lasteth forever? Doth it not last much longer than that which ye experience in a gallery of the paintings that ye suppose are great works of art, given unto you by the hands of man?

64 Behold, it is the desire of Lucifer to mimic the things that the Father hath given unto us to bring us joy and happiness. But the things that Lucifer causeth to come forth to mimic these things, are things made by the arm of flesh.

65 And because they are made by the arm of flesh, he who hath made these things receiveth the honor and glory that cometh from that which he hath created with his own hands, and thus is the plan of Lucifer fulfilled.

CHAPTER 76

The works of humans are temporary and bring temporary satisfaction and glory to them, but the works of God are eternal. The rich rule the government of the people with their secret combinations.

AND now, it is necessary that I explain unto you more concerning the periods of time when the Spirit of God doth not interact with the spirits of the children of men and guide them in that which they should do.

2 Behold, I have explained these time periods unto you, but it is expedient that ye understand that all the children of God have been blessed with this conscience that enableth them to know the good from the bad, or in other words, that which bringeth happiness and that which bringeth misery.

3 And if a man doth not have the companionship of the Holy Ghost, this doth not mean that he doth not understand that which is good and that which is evil. Behold, all of us understand these things from our own experience, and also because of the blessing of a conscience that the Father hath given unto us.

4 And when a man doth not have the Spirit of God, he can still do that which is good and bringeth happiness to his soul. But that which he doeth, he doeth of himself, and therefore, bringeth joy and glory to himself.

5 Now, this is part of the plan of Lucifer, even that a man should bring glory to himself and the works of his own hands, instead of giving the glory and honor to the Father, who created him.

6 And without the Father, this man could not exist to experience happiness of any kind, therefore the honor and glory of all things should be given unto God.

7 And the works of man will always receive the honors and glories of man, but the works of God will always demonstrate the glory and honor that is in Him.

8 And the plan of Lucifer indeed provideth joy and happiness to those that follow it, but as I have said before, his plan doth not account for those things which are not temporal, even those things which are eternal.

9 For the works by the hands of a man shall end when that man dieth and leaveth this temporal existence and entereth into an eternal realm that hath nothing that bringeth a temporary joy, but bringeth an eternal joy in all things.

10 And the works of God cannot be destroyed, for they are eternal; but the works of man, which are temporal, are always destroyed through the effects of the actions of other men, or through the effects of the actions of those things which are eternal, or by nature.

11 So it is that Lucifer hath provided for the happiness of his children, so that they might have their consciences satisfied enough to continue in the course of his plan.

12 And during this medieval time, Satan shall cause to be developed many great cities in all the nations of the earth that shall flourish and prosper in the temporal blessings that he hath promised those who follow his plan.

13 And the people of the earth shall begin to fall further away from their dependence on the natural order of things which God hath ordained for them, and they shall depend upon the things that Satan hath offered them in his plan.

14 And because the things of the earth have a value placed upon them, the people shall begin to horde these things and take more than what is necessary to sustain their lives.

15 And the rich shall begin to depend upon their money, which is their gold and their silver, and their precious gems. And this money shall begin to be the most prized possession of all the people of the earth.

16 For with gold and silver and precious gems, the people shall trade for that which their hearts desire.

17 And the poor shall become many, because of the wants and the needs of the few, who are rich, and who control the wealth and the money and the prices which are paid for the things of the earth.

18 Yea, there shall be many poor because of their inability to have money and purchase that which they create with their own hands for the rich.

19 Behold, the poor shall work all the days of their lives providing the rich with the things that they need to live in easiness and leisure.

20 And when the poor, through their hard labor, produce a thing, then the rich shall place a price on it which is already predetermined by them so that they might receive some sort of gain from it.

21 And during the medieval times, there were those who did not want to produce through their labors that which would support the rich in their luxury. And these would make an attempt to live in all things according to the laws of nature, taking from the earth only that which they needed to sustain their lives and the lives of their children.

22 And these wanted nothing to do with the system of economy of the beast, which system was based on the money that the rich invented and controlled.

23 Nevertheless, the rich are powerful and have their secret combinations, and develop a way whereby all the people would be forced to produce that which they need for their own comfort.

24 Behold, first, there were few land owners who were not rich. And the rich would make contracts with the poor, giving unto the poor a portion of their land as a grant, with the stipulation that in payment for the land, a part of that which the poor produced would be given unto the rich, who own the land, as a rent.

25 And then the king would demand of the poor a portion of that which they produced as a tax, which was to be used, according to the pretenses of the king, to defend the land of the poor against their enemies as I have explained it unto you.

26 And if the poor did not produce that which was wanted by the rich, or by the king, in order that they might pay their taxes, then they would be forced to exchange that which they produced for the money of the rich, which could then be traded for anything upon which the rich had already placed a predetermined value.

27 And since the rich set the value for all things; and since they also demand of the poor those things which they want to satisfy their lusts and their easiness of living without working by the sweat of their own brow, the poor are forced into submission to the will of the rich, even for their very existence.

28 And if a man refuseth to pay his taxes, or refuseth to provide for the rich those things that are demanded of him, then the rich would pay money to others who would come and take the man and cast him into prison, or kill him.

29 And in this manner the rich fix the laws of the land, which laws are established and enforced by the means of the secret combinations among them.

30 Now, I have already given unto you in this record an explanation of these secret combinations which were established in the beginning to protect one group of people and bring them gain without the need to work by the sweat of their own brow thereby suffering the anguish of physical labor to bring them their riches.

31 And it sufficeth me to say that any government, any religion, any group, any organization that doeth anything in secret, or when it withholdeth the true nature of its works from the rest of the people, so that they are not discovered, then it is a secret combination.

32 And in the latter days these secret combinations shall abound in wickedness. For they shall exist in many forms upon the earth. And many, if not all, of the governments, and religions, and practices of business that are among you in the latter days, belong to these secret combinations, which are set up so that it is not known among the people about the general operations of these combinations, or the means that each of them useth to obtain the end of its desires, which end is profit and gain and power and control over the people.

33 And in the nation that is the seat of the beast in the latter days, these secret combinations shall be rampant. For your government shall act in secret meetings that are not held before the public, that they might hide the way in which they control and manipulate the hearts and minds of the people.

34 And the religions of the world shall not disclose the riches that they possess, which are generated from the tithing of the people that is given unto their churches by the people who believe that they are donating their money to God for His purposes.

35 And the leaders of the religions shall also

separate and exclude themselves from the people and hold their meetings in secret that the people may not discover their works.

36 And the businesses that are set up among you to get gain; are they not also secret combinations? Doth he who selleth you a thing disclose unto you how much profit he is making from that which he selleth unto you? Doth he not sell unto you a thing for the price that ye are willing to pay unto him?

37 And in that day ye shall see that your money shall be valued according to the desires and whims of the rich, who are your leaders.

38 For I have seen your time, and see that it is by these secret combinations that it is determined what value is placed upon the money of the nations among you.

39 And in considering all these things in secret, the rich do not take into account those who produce the things that are sold and purchased by this money, nor do they consider how the decisions of their secret combinations might affect the lives of the poor.

40 But when a determination is made on the value of the money of a nation, it is made on how the value of this money shall effect the rich and the powerful.

41 And ye have witnessed these secret combinations among you. And your laws, which are established by the rich, are established to protect these secret combinations and assure their prosperity.

42 Behold, how can it be that a man who hath a certain amount of money with which he can buy a certain quantity of bread one day, shall wake up in the next morning and find that the money which he hath from yesterday cannot buy on this new day that which it could buy yesterday?

43 And how can ye allow the rich, who do not work by the sweat of their brows, to change the value of the money that the poor receiveth for their labors?

44 And it shall be that a poor man shall work one day for a wage that he thinketh shall provide that which he requireth for the needs of his family; and in going to his bed, he is satisfied by the labors of his own hands, knowing that his family shall eat on the morrow.

45 And then in the morning, when the man ariseth to labor again, he findeth that that for which he labored yesterday doth not provide for the needs of his family as he had supposed.

46 Yet when the man reporteth to his employer, he is not given an increase in the wage of the day for that which he lost in value of yesterday, which would be a just compensation because of the decision of the rich to value the money that he useth to provide for the needs of his family.

47 And this causeth the man to be angry and curse the secret combinations that he upholdeth with his gratitude and patriotism, which is given to the nation that he hath been convinced protecteth his life and the lives of his children.

48 And when the people begin to rebel against these secret combinations, their governments begin to seek for that which will turn the hearts of the people again unto them. And this they do in many instances by war and through national pride, which is instilled in the people by the flattering words of the rich.

49 And so, my beloved brothers and sisters, if ye know of a government, or a religion, or a practice of business that doth not disclose unto you all things; yea, if they do not let you be in attendance at all of their meetings that ye might know their agendas and the purpose of their meetings, then ye shall know of a surety that these are the secret combinations that Satan hath set up in his kingdom to give glory to those who follow him and bring under his power those who think that they are not following him.

50 Thus shall Satan rule over the earth during the time that the Father hath allotted him to prove his plan unto us.

51 And during this time, the cities of the earth shall grow as the children of men begin to increase in a great number. And because of their cities and their increase in number, great famines and pestilence shall come upon them and destroy many of them.

52 But the rich shall not be destroyed so easily by these things, for they shall keep themselves isolated away from the majority of the people in the splendor of the fine things which they have taken from the people by the greatness of the riches and money that they possess.

53 Now, all these things that I saw in the record of the brother of Jared, and of which I am now giving my abridgment, shall be in fulfillment of the words of John, which he wrote, saying: And he had power to give life unto the image of the beast, that the image of the beast should both speak, and cause that as many as would not worship the image of the beast should be killed.

54 And he causeth all, both small and great, rich and poor, free and bond, to receive a mark in their right hand, or in their foreheads. And that no man might buy or sell, save he that had the mark, or the name of the beast, or the number of his name. Here is wisdom. Let him that hath understanding count the number of the beast: for it is the number of a man; and his number is Six hundred threescore and six.

55 And now, do ye see how the number of the beast is money? Do ye not see how all are forced to have money and be engaged in the economy that hath been set up by Satan, or be killed?

56 And most importantly, do ye see how ye all have the mark of the beast in your right hands? And those who are not elect, do ye see that they also have this mark in their foreheads?

57 Yea, even the whole earth is under the power of Satan, and shall continue to be until the time the Lord cometh in the glory of the Father.

CHAPTER 77

Satan perpetuates peace and replaces war with secular learning of the sciences and technology. The Father gives Lucifer a chance to repent and forsake his plan for His children.

AND now, Satan shall begin to see that the cause of all the wars among the children of men shall be the means of their destruction.

2 And when we are witnessing the plan of Lucifer unfold before us, both in the spirit world by those who are dead, and by those of us who are experiencing the effects of the plan of Lucifer still in mortality, we shall begin to see that his plan doeth nothing more than cause great turmoil and wars and rumors of war throughout the whole earth.

3 And Lucifer shall begin to realize that his plan is failing to bring forth the fruits that he had promised those who followed him away from the plan of the Father.

4 And now, I will include herein some of the words of the brother of Jared concerning that which he saw in the vision concerning the time that Lucifer shall begin to realize that his plan is not succeeding as he had intended for it to succeed in the beginning:

5 And I saw in the Spirit of the Lord, Lucifer stand up before those who followed him in the realm of the spirits where they are kept locked in prison of their own accord and unable to take upon them the second estate that would be necessary for their progression in the eternal worlds of the Father.

6 And there were many of these spirits who complained to Lucifer that that which was promised by him was not giving to them the happiness that they desired, even the happiness and joy that he had promised them.

7 And Lucifer cursed the earth and sent forth a command to all of those who followed him that they should stop their wars for a time and bring to pass the things that would bring temporary happiness to the people.

8 And among all the great nations and kingdoms that were set up, the wars did stop for a time, and Satan went to and fro upon the earth giving inspiration and
revelation to the children of men concerning their plights as mortals.

9 And there were schools of thought set up among them, and great institutions of learning and practice that enabled them to bring more of the promise of Satan to fruition, that they might begin to enjoy their lives in mortality.

10 And the people began to seek out the knowledge that would ease their lives of the burdens that had been placed upon them by the works of their leaders.

11 And the leaders of the nations began to send forth explorers and scientists to solve the mysteries that nature presented to them. And a period of time known as the great Renaissance came forth upon the earth, giving to the children of men a great sense of themselves and their own natures.

12 And once Satan had influenced the people to think in the manner that he would have them think, he led them down any path that they would follow in search for the meaning of life and for the happiness for which their souls craved.

13 And it came to pass that there arose out of this time many wise and talented men, as far as the arm of the flesh is concerned, or as far as the knowledge of man is given unto them.

14 And Satan continued to have great power over the hearts and minds of men, even as he was giving them peace for a time.

15 But Lucifer was dissatisfied with the way in which his plan was unfolding upon the earth, because he was still prohibited from revealing unto men the great powers of nature that were a prerequisite to understanding the great powers that the Father possesseth.

16 And Lucifer complained to the Father that in order for his plan to take its full effect, he needed to be able to give to the earth a portion of the power of a God, so that he could show the other spirit children of the Father the full effect of the happiness that they would receive from following him as their God.

17 And he spoke in the spirit unto the Father, saying: Oh, Father, until this time have I been forbidden by Thee to show forth a portion of Thy power unto those of us who would have all Thy children possess the power of the Gods.

18 And Thou knowest that the end is near, as Thou hast set the order of all things for us. How then, Oh, Father, can I prove the worthiness of my plan, unless Thou releasest me and allowest me to give unto the earth the beginnings of Thy power, that they might know the righteousness of that which I have proposed before them?

19 And I know that Thou art a fair God, but I also know that when the last time cometh that Thou shall send forth Thy spirit unto the earth to influence the children of men, it shall be the end of time, and there shall be no more time given unto me to exercise the ability to show forth the righteousness of my plan, without the interference of Thy Spirit.

20 Therefore, Oh, Father, in all fairness before the laws of heaven, I ask of Thee that I be released from these bonds and be allowed to introduce Thy power upon the earth so that I might prove my words therein.

21 And I saw the Father call forth Lucifer from the spirit world into His own kingdom to answer his prayer.

22 And Lucifer stood before the Father. And the Father took Lucifer by himself and said unto him: My Son, that which thou hast done in the world which I have caused to be created for my children hath proven that thy plan cannot work to the benefit of the happiness of all of my children.

23 And is not the fruits of thy works proof enough unto thee that the eternal plan which I have given unto all of my children is the only plan that can provide them eternal happiness?

24 Please, my Son, go to those that follow after thee and have them return unto me and follow the plan that I have set forth before you, and ye shall all be saved in my kingdom. For behold, I will give unto you this chance to repent of your misdoings and once again accept the eternal laws of heaven.

25 Nevertheless, my Son, because of the eternal laws of heaven that govern me, thou art forbidden forever from having a Celestial body and partaking of its power and glory, because of the things which thou hast desired for thine own glory and happiness.

26 And when Lucifer heard these things, he turned away from the Father and demanded of the Father that he be allowed to do what had been done in other worlds, and that he be allowed to prove his plan to those that followed him.

27 And the Father wept for Lucifer, but commanded his angels to give unto him that which he desired to help him for the last time to make an attempt to prove the worthiness of his plan.

28 And the Father did this so that none of his children could ever proclaim that Lucifer was not given every opportunity available to use his free agency to create the happiness that he desired according to his own plan.

29 And now, I, Moroni, have given you the time period of the time and times and half of time; and it was at the beginning of the half of time that the Father released Lucifer to allow him

to introduce to the world many of the mysteries of nature that would be necessary for the children of men to understand so that they could begin to use the power of God among them.

30 And it was just before this time, even at the very end of the times, that the full effect and greatness of science and technology was first introduced to the children of men.

31 And I have seen your day and have the words of the brother of Jared before me. And I have been instructed at this time in this record to reveal unto you in plainness many of the mysteries of nature that Satan was forbidden to give unto you in past generations of the children of men.

32 And the greatest mystery among you, even that mystery which shall be the cause of much turmoil and misery among you, is the mystery of the power of electricity, as it is known among you, even a great power of nature that shall be used in the latter days to deceive the people of the earth and turn all of the children of men away from the plan of the Father.

33 And before Lucifer was released to give this knowledge unto the world, he began, during this time that the brother of Jared hath written as the time of the Renaissance, to influence the minds of some men in that which he could reveal unto them of science and of the knowledge that would lead them to the revelations that they would eventually receive when he was released from the restrictions that were placed upon him by the Father.

34 And there were many men who made great strides in the introduction of these things of Satan.

35 And now, these same men have become renown and great in the eyes of all other men in the latter days who have benefited from their works.

36 And I have seen some of their names in the words of the brother of Jared, nevertheless, I will not include their names in this record, because they are servants of Satan, and deserve no more honor for that which they have done, except that which hath already been given unto them by Satan and those who follow him.

37 And now, ye of the latter days should know why these men are considered servants of Satan when they are instrumental in bringing forth the truths of the power of God.

38 Behold, all of the holy prophets knew of the great power of electricity and the power that was held in nature to create many miracles among the children of men. Yea, these holy men saw all of the great advancements of the plan of Lucifer in the latter days.

39 Yea, they saw the extraordinary and seemingly miraculous means of transportation that ye have among you, even by ground and by air and by sea; even up into the heavens beyond the boundaries of this earth.

40 Yea, they saw the miraculous means by which ye communicate and speak one to another, and the ease of your lives in so many ways.

41 Yea, they saw your attempts to colonize the planets and make them into the kingdoms of men, without the aid of the Father.

42 In fine, they saw all the miracles of science and technology that the Father hath allowed Satan to give unto you in the latter days.

43 And these are the things that they were forbidden to speak of and of which they could not write. For behold, they knew how these things would affect the minds and hearts of the children of men; and that they would create great wickedness and misery among them.

44 But even more, they knew that as soon as these things are introduced unto the children of men, there should only be a short time until they take the power of these things and use them to destroy themselves and turn their hearts completely away from the purpose of the plan of the Father.

45 And for this same reason have all the holy prophets testified of the great wickedness that would be upon the earth in the latter days before the great and dreadful day of the Lord.

46 And now, ye of the latter days have seen that the words of the prophets are true concerning these things. For ye know that the cause of your misery and the degradation of the natural health of the earth is caused by the misuse of this power that hath been given unto you.

47 And ye have harnessed even greater power than that which electricity hath given

unto you; for ye have developed nuclear power, which is a power much greater than the power of electricity.

48 And ye shall also discover that there is still an even greater power that ye have among you. But the knowledge of this greater power that shall be given unto you shall be restricted in its use by the Lord.

49 For if ye understood the fullness in the way in which this power is used by the Gods, then ye would use it to destroy the earth in one day.

50 For by this power was the great sun created that giveth light unto the world. But the Father hath limited the ability of Satan to give unto you this greater power, so that ye might not destroy yourselves before the Lord is able to once again establish peace upon the earth and reign among you for a thousand years, showing forth the plan of the Father for the last time without the influence of Satan against you.

51 And during this thousand years of peace, this great power shall be used to heal the earth and bring things to the earth that have never been known by the children of men.

CHAPTER 78

The histories of the world are often incorrect and one sided. We are admonished to seek truth in righteousness according to the words of Christ.

AND now, I have given you an accounting of the history of the world up until the beginning of the half of time.

2 And because there was no work of the Lord accomplished since the works of the prophet Mohammed, there hath been nothing of the work of the Lord to account for in this record. But these final things I say unto you concerning these days of darkness:

3 Behold, during this time, Satan hath prepared the earth and the hearts of the children of men to bring them into the last days, in which he shall have power over his own dominions as I have explained it unto you.

4 And most of what ye know of these medieval times in the latter days hath been given unto you by those who were not present when the course of the history of the earth was being fulfilled.

5 And the things that ye have are only those things which the rulers and the rich would have you know concerning their works during these times. But of the poor and the masses of the majority, few things are written.

6 And if it could be written, even a full accounting of all the works of the rich and powerful during this time, even according to the experiences of the poor, ye would know of the exceeding wickedness of the kings and queens, the popes and priests, even of all those who have been given honor by those who have written the accounts of the histories which ye have among you.

7 Therefore, believe not in the things which are given unto you, for they are a biased accounting given by those from whom ye receive them.

8 Remember the words of Christ in which he hath commanded you to not judge; but if ye do judge, then make a righteous judgment. And since ye do not have before you a full accounting of the ways in which the rich and powerful, yea, those honored by your histories, have plundered and abused and taken advantage of the poor, do not give unto them the honor and glory that they do not deserve.

9 Behold, ye are commanded to seek out truth through study and also through the Spirit. And if ye study the opinions of men, remember that they are only their opinions, and often not the truth as it was, or as it is, or as it shall be.

10 Behold, the truth is things as they were, as they are, and as they are to come; and anything other than this truth, is conceived of Satan and used to deceive you.

11 Remember these things, my brothers and sisters, and seek for truth in all things, believing not in the word of man or trusting in the arm of flesh.

CHAPTER 79

The Americas are discovered and conquered in wickedness. The American Revolution was fought under the influence of Satan to reward the rich. The Gentiles shall receive the beginnings of the fullness of the gospel through Joseph Smith. The Gentiles shall be smitten because of their rejection of the gospel and the Book of Mormon. The work of the gathering shall commence with the work of Christopher Nemelka and the coming forth of the Sealed Portion.

AND it shall come to pass among the nations of this great European Empire, which shall be formed from other nations and kingdoms of the earth, that a group of people who shall travel across the great oceans and establish themselves in the land of my fathers; yea, these shall begin to prosper exceedingly in all things.

2 And there shall also be the rich among them who shall become rich from the land and the things that they shall take from the land of my fathers.

3 For behold, the Lamanites shall be upon the land when it is discovered by these great European nations of the latter days. And at this time, they shall be a humble people, having their own tribes and nations upon the land.

4 And though the Spirit of the Lord shall not be with them directly, they shall remember many of the teachings of their fathers and begin to establish peace amongst themselves according to their traditions and the customs which shall be passed down to them from generation to generation.

5 And it shall come to pass that Lucifer shall influence the discovery of the land of promise, which is filled with all manner of precious things which are the desires of this great and abominable church of which I have spoken.

6 And when the promised land is discovered by the people of the great European Empire, they shall begin to search for gold and silver and for anything that is of value to them.

7 And it shall come to pass that they shall begin to destroy the Lamanites and take from them their lands and force them into places which are desolate and void of the precious things that these European nations desire.

8 And the Lamanites shall begin to dwindle in numbers and lose their nations and their lands to the effects of the lusts of the great and abominable church.

9 And the men who shall destroy the Lamanites shall think that they are doing God a service, because they believe that the Lamanites and all those who are of a dark skin are those who have been cursed of God and not worthy of the full blessings of the Father.

10 And this wickedness shall be taught unto them by their leaders and their priests, who are all servants of Satan and shall follow his will in all things.

11 And thus the eighth beast of which John wrote shall begin to rise up out of obscurity and gain power for itself.

12 And those who shall colonize the land of promise shall begin to have much disputation and contention with the government that controlleth them from across the oceans, which government shall be set up amongst the nations in the great European Empire.

13 And the rich men of the colonies who shall rebel against their king, shall rise up and conspire against the laws of their government, because they desire to keep more of that which they gain from the service of the poor who shall be among them.

14 And many of these rich men shall unite together and form an alliance, even according to the covenants and bonds of the secret combinations of old.

15 And these rich men shall be desirous to rebel against the laws that shall be established among them so that they can establish their own laws that will serve them in their desires for more gain.

16 And these men shall be men of great intelligence who have much power in speaking and in writing.

17 And they shall begin to influence the poor among them, who shall be the majority, to join their cause and fight for them against the government to which they belong.

18 But the rich shall not fight, but shall establish a law amongst themselves, that for the

payment of money—even three hundred dollars, as the number of the beast shall be called by this great and final beast—they shall be exempt from conscription.

19 And these same men shall be inspired by Lucifer to set up their nation and their laws in such a way that they can maintain control over the minds and hearts of the poor and the majority.

20 And now, ye of the latter days shall also give praise and honor to those whom ye refer to as the fathers of your nation. Yea, truly they are the fathers of your nation, but wherein is their righteousness according to the words of Christ?

21 Behold, as I have told you to not judge unless it is done according to the Spirit in righteousness, ye must know that these men shall be servants of Satan who shall set up the government of your nation to get gain for themselves.

22 And like those leaders in the kingdoms of Satan before them, they have done all things that they might get gain and protect themselves and their families.

23 Know ye not that many of these founding fathers that ye hold in such high esteem held men of dark skin in servitude?

24 Behold, there is no man that is influenced by the Spirit of Christ who can hold another man in servitude, so that he might get gain.

25 And I have shown unto you that the beginning of the half of time had not yet begun when these men brought forth the nation which would become the eighth beast of which John speaketh.

26 And because the Father had not yet released the Holy Ghost to send his ministrations unto the children of men, then how do ye suppose that it was possible that the fathers of your nation could have been inspired by the Spirit of the Father?

27 Behold, they were indeed inspired; and the God from whom they received their inspiration was Lucifer. For it is a nation of Satan that shall be created. Nevertheless, all these things shall be done by the power and according to the great wisdom of the Father; for it is his desire that Lucifer be allowed to do these things so that this great nation could be a free nation in the beginning, offering unto all the ability to act according to the free agency that the Father hath given unto all of His children, that they might be more fully tried and tested during the final days of their probation.

28 And if ye of the latter days are not deceived by the accounts of the actions of these fathers, which are contained in the histories that ye have accepted among you, then ye will know of their wickedness and the misery that they have caused many people because of their works.

29 And this I can tell you, that the only interest of any of these men was for their own gain and the protection of their own families and their own property and their own possessions. For they did not care for the poor or the needy among them, neither did they care about the great suffering of the humble Lamanites who were forced out of their land by them.

30 And now this is the thing for which I must repent, even for the anger that swelleth up in my soul because of that which shall come to pass to the Lamanites, who are my brothers and of my own flesh, even the flesh of our father Lehi.

31 For behold, their plight shall be miserable in the last days, and this because of the exceeding wickedness of this great beast of the latter days.

32 And my soul doth cry for them. For even in my own day they are a proud and a noble people. And it is because of the sins of their fathers and the traditions that have been taught unto them that have caused them to come up to battle against us and destroy us.

33 And if the Nephites would have given heed unto the words of Christ, then they would not have been destroyed.

34 But even so, the Lamanites shall be a peaceful people amongst themselves at the day that they are discovered by the European nation of which John hath written.

35 And the vengeance for that which shall be done to my brothers is not mine to give, but shall be given unto the Gentiles, who have destroyed the Lamanites, by the hand of the Lord, if it so be that they do not repent and return unto the Lord.

36 For it shall come to pass that just before the beginning of the half of times, the Lord shall call forth the first of these latter day prophets to bring the fullness of the gospel to the people of the earth. And this is he who shall be called Joseph after the name of his father.

37 And he shall bring forth the unsealed portion of this record and establish upon the earth another testimony of the gospel of Jesus Christ.

38 And in the record that he shall be commanded to bring forth, shall be the words of Christ, which he spoke unto the Nephites when he appeared unto them in the land of Bountiful.

39 And the Lord spoke of the great blessings that shall come forth to the Gentiles in the last days, even the coming forth of this entire record in its fullness, if it so be that they repent and receive these things. And I have already repeated these things once in this portion of the record that I shall seal up according to the commandment of the Lord. But because of their great importance to those of you of the latter days, I give these words unto you again, that I might expound further upon them.

40 And the Lord spoke, saying: And verily I say unto you, I give unto you a sign, that ye may know the time when these things shall be about to take place, even that I shall gather in, from their long dispersion, my people, Oh, house of Israel, and shall establish again among them my Zion;

41 And behold, this is the thing which I will give unto you for a sign; for verily I say unto you that when these things which I declare unto you, and which I shall declare unto you hereafter of myself, and by the power of the Holy Ghost which shall be given unto you of the Father, shall be made known unto the Gentiles that they may know concerning this people who are a remnant of the house of Jacob, and concerning this my people who shall be scattered by them;

42 Verily, verily, I say unto you, when these things shall be made known unto them of the Father, and shall come forth of the Father, from them unto you; for it is wisdom in the Father that they should be established in this land, and be set up as a free people by the power of the Father, that these things might come forth from them unto a remnant of your seed, that the covenant of the Father may be fulfilled which he hath covenanted with his people, Oh, house of Israel;

43 Therefore, when these works and the works which shall be wrought among you hereafter shall come forth from the Gentiles, unto your seed which shall dwindle in unbelief because of iniquity; for thus it behooveth the Father that it should come forth from the Gentiles, that he may show forth his power unto the Gentiles, for this cause that the Gentiles, if they will not harden their hearts, that they may repent and come unto me and be baptized in my name and know of the true points of my doctrine, that they may be numbered among my people, Oh, house of Israel;

44 And when these things come to pass that thy seed shall begin to know these things, it shall be a sign unto them, that they may know that the work of the Father hath already commenced unto the fulfilling of the covenant which he hath made unto the people who are of the house of Israel.

45 And when that day shall come, it shall come to pass that kings shall shut their mouths; for that which had not been told them shall they see; and that which they had not heard shall they consider.

46 For in that day, for my sake shall the Father work a work, which shall be a great and a marvelous work among them; and there shall be among them those who will not believe it, although a man shall declare it unto them.

47 But behold, the life of my servant shall be in my hand; therefore they shall not hurt him, although he shall be marred because of them. Yet I will heal him, for I will show unto them that my wisdom is greater than the cunning of the devil.

48 Therefore it shall come to pass that whosoever will not believe in my words, who am Jesus Christ, which the Father shall cause him to bring forth unto the Gentiles; and shall give unto him power that he shall bring them forth unto the Gentiles, and it shall be done even as Moses said, they shall be cut off from among my people who are of the covenant.

49 And my people who are a remnant of Jacob shall be among the Gentiles, yea, in the midst of them as a lion among the beasts of the forest, as a young lion among the flocks of sheep, who, if he go through, both treadeth down and teareth in pieces, and none can deliver. Their hand shall be lifted up upon their adversaries, and all their enemies shall be cut off.

50 Yea, woe be unto the Gentiles except they repent; for it shall come to pass in that day, saith the Father, that I will cut off thy horses out of the midst of thee, and I will destroy thy chariots; and I will cut off the cities of thy land, and throw down all thy strongholds; and I will cut off witchcrafts out of thy land, and thou shalt have no more soothsayers;

51 And thy graven images I will also cut off, and thy standing images out of the midst of thee, and thou shalt no more worship the works of thy hands; and I will pluck up thy groves out of the midst of thee; so will I destroy thy cities.

52 And it shall come to pass that all lyings, and deceivings, and envyings, and strifes, and priestcrafts, and whoredoms, shall be done away.

53 For it shall come to pass, saith the Father, that at that day whosoever will not repent and come unto my Beloved Son, them will I cut off from among my people, Oh, house of Israel;

54 And I will execute vengeance and fury upon them, even as upon the heathen, such as they have not heard.

55 But if they will repent and hearken unto my words, and harden not their hearts, I will establish my church among them, and they shall come in unto the covenant and be numbered among this the remnant of Jacob, unto whom I have given this land for their inheritance;

56 And they shall assist my people, the remnant of Jacob, and also as many of the house of Israel as shall come, that they may build a city, which shall be called the New Jerusalem.

57 And then shall they assist my people that they may be gathered in, who are scattered upon all the face of the land, in unto the New Jerusalem. And then shall the power of heaven come down among them; and I also will be in the midst.

58 And then shall the work of the Father commence at that day, even when this gospel shall be preached among the remnant of this people. Verily I say unto you, at that day shall the work of the Father commence among all the dispersed of my people, yea, even the tribes which have been lost, which the Father hath led away out of Jerusalem.

59 Yea, the work shall commence among all the dispersed of my people, and the Father shall prepare the way whereby they may come unto me, that they may call on the Father in my name.

60 Yea, and then shall the work commence with the Father among all nations in preparing the way whereby his people may be gathered home to the land of their inheritance. And they shall go out from all nations; and they shall not go out in haste, nor go by flight, for I will go before them, saith the Father, and I will be their rearward.

61 And now, I know that there are those among you of the latter days that shall believe that the work of the Father shall commence when the first of these latter day prophets shall come forth among you.

62 And it shall be a beginning in that he shall prepare the world for the coming forth of the sealed portion of this record that shall be that which is the most instrumental in fulfilling the words of the Lord which he hath spoken.

63 For behold, ye who receiveth these things knoweth that this first prophet shall come forth in the latter days shall be killed by the Gentiles, and that the church that he shall make an attempt to establish shall be destroyed from off the face of the earth.

64 And the Lord hath said that the life of his servant shall be in his hand; therefore they shall not hurt him, although he shall be marred because of them. Yet I will heal him, for I will show unto them that my wisdom is greater than the cunning of the devil.

65 Now, this the Lord hath said concerning the second of these latter day prophets who shall come forth among you. For the first of these shall be murdered by you after he hath accomplished that which he came upon the earth to do.

66 Yea, he was called in the spirit of Elias, if ye can receive this, to prepare the way for the second prophet who shall be among you.

67 And this second latter day prophet shall be called in the spirit of Elias to prepare the people for the coming of the Lord in his glory.

68 And at the great day of the Lord shall he establish his church among the people and gather the elect from the four corners of the earth.

69 And the life of this second latter day prophet shall be in the hands of the Lord. And he shall be marred by the world, but not killed like unto the first, but shall be the means of bringing many people to the true Christ.

70 And he shall bring forth this sealed portion of this record which shall teach unto the whole earth the truth in all things pertaining to the gospel of Jesus Christ.

71 Therefore, those of you who belongeth to this great church that is called after the name of Jesus Christ of the latter days, do not be deceived into believing that your church is the true church of God as was attempted to be established by this first prophet among you.

72 For your church is nothing like unto the church that Joseph attempted to establish among you. And there shall be no true church of Christ in the latter days until he cometh in his glory to set it up for himself.

73 Nevertheless, this first prophet shall make an attempt to establish a church of God among you, but it shall fail because of the wickedness of the Gentiles.

74 And because of the wickedness of the Gentiles of the latter days, all of the words of the Lord shall be fulfilled concerning them.

75 And the blood of the righteous Lamanites shall be avenged upon their heads by a remnant of the house of Jacob that shall be among the Gentiles, yea, in the midst of them as a lion among the beasts of the forest, as a young lion among the flocks of sheep, who, if he go through, both treadeth down and teareth in pieces, and none can deliver. Their hand shall be lifted up upon their adversaries, and all their enemies shall be cut off.

76 And now, ye of the latter days know that these things did not come to pass in the days of this first latter day prophet. But these things shall come to pass during the days of this second prophet of God, even the bearer of Christ, who shall be known among you as Christopher.

CHAPTER 80

The United States is set up so that free agency is protected, somewhat, by the government. Experience is the most proficient teacher. Lucifer's plan is in its full effect upon the earth during the last days. Lucifer's plan vs. God's plan.

AND now, it is expedient that I give unto you an accounting of the life and ministry of this first prophet among you, even he who is called Joseph after his father.

2 And it shall come to pass that after this great nation shall begin to establish itself upon the land of my fathers, even among all the other great nations of the earth, the principles of freedom and liberty shall be more fully instated in the principles of its government.

3 And because they shall be somewhat protected by the constitution and articles of this great nation during this half of time, all the children of God shall begin to see the reasons why there are different degrees of glory in the kingdom of the Father, according to the eternal laws of heaven; and also that they might know for themselves that the kingdom which they have chosen for themselves is the kingdom that shall bring them the greatest amount of joy and eternal happiness.

4 Behold, up until this time, the Father shall restrict the free agency of His children in some things. And that in which He hath restricted them is in the knowledge and understanding of the natural laws of heaven that control the elements and control the principles of the temporal nature that we are experiencing in mortality.

5 For behold, the Father knoweth that Lucifer, who is also one of his children, who hath been granted the right to his free agency, should be given the ability to introduce many of these eternal laws to men upon the earth, according to the conditions of his own plan, so that he might have the opportunity to see his plan tested in its full effect.

6 And now, it is exceedingly important that ye understand more concerning the power that Satan hath over those of you who shall receive

these things in the latter days; and also that ye might know more fully the purpose and principles of the plan of Lucifer that he useth to show an alternate course to joy and happiness than that which the Father presented to us in the beginning.

7 Behold, it is not the desire of Lucifer that we argue and fight and become contentious, because he knoweth that these things cause us tremendous unhappiness. And the end of the plan that Lucifer desireth for us is that we all have the eternal joy and felicity of the Celestial kingdom, and also that we might have all the power and all the glory that our Father hath without the responsibility of proving ourselves worthy of such power.

8 Therefore, it is the desire of Lucifer to show unto us his alternate plan, which he hath been trying to incorporate into the mortal existence of the children of men since the beginning.

9 And during the time, and times, and also during this last half of time, as well as the time before the accounting of the times given in the revelations that the prophets revealed unto us for our own instruction and learning, or before the covenant was given unto Abraham; yea, even while the Father commanded His gospel to be given to the children of men through the ministrations of the spirit world and by the mouth of his holy prophets, Satan hath been allowed to use his influence over the hearts of the children of men to incorporate his plan into their lives.

10 Therefore, the Father hath given him much opportunity to prove his plan unto us. Now, here is a mystery that ye of the latter days have not known, and which is necessary to know that ye might more fully understand all things according to the truth of God, and not the opinions and imaginations of men, which cause all truth to become mysterious unto them.

11 Behold, Satan desireth all people to be happy living according to the precepts and conditions of his plan. He doth not want us to hate each other and cause each other to experience misery and pain. Yea, he doth not want us to suffer from the vicissitudes of life to such an extent that we are miserable enough to know that the course of our lives is not producing the happiness that we all desire.

12 For if we experience life and realize that there is no peace and happiness in the life that we have chosen to live for ourselves, then we must ask ourselves why we are not experiencing happiness, and which plan are we following that bringeth this misery unto us.

13 Yea, are we following the plan of the Father, which giveth this peace and happiness without price, without strain and toil, and is a peace and happiness that lasteth forever?

14 Or are we following the plan of Lucifer, which ensureth us the temporary joy and happiness that we experience while benefiting from the blessings that he hath given unto us; but afterwards, we find no peace or happiness that remaineth in our souls; but we find an emptiness and a sorrow, which is as if a man who dreameth, and in his dream he eateth all that his heart desireth. But when he awaketh from the dream, he seeth himself and remaineth empty and unsatisfied.

15 And Christ spoke of this hunger many times as he taught the Jews. And he spoke of the blessings that the plan of Lucifer offereth to the children of men; and many times he made a contrast between these blessings and the blessings that were given of the Father.

16 And he taught the people, saying: Woe unto you that are rich, for ye have received your consolation. Woe unto you that are full, for ye shall hunger. Woe unto you that laugh now, for ye shall mourn and weep. Woe unto you, when all men shall speak well of you, for so did their fathers to the false prophets.

17 And now, I have already explained unto you that the fruits that ye shall receive by following the plan of Lucifer are riches, honors and the glories of men, and a temporary joy that ye feel when ye find happiness in those things which are temporary, yet your happiness remaineth not thereafter.

18 And now, it is the desire of the Lord that ye know this of Satan and his plan, even that it is a good and a righteous plan to those whom he hath convinced to follow him.

19 And it is not Satan that causeth the wars among men, nor doth he cause their unhappiness and their misery. Behold, why do ye think that he would cause such things, when

he hath made a promise unto those that follow him that they shall not suffer these things, but shall be happy following his plan?

20 And do ye think that Satan can command your spirits and that they will obey his commands and do what he desireth of them?

21 I say unto you that he cannot give a command unto your spirit and cause you to do that which ye do not want to do.

22 Behold, he can inspire you to follow him and give unto you feelings and thoughts that would entice you to follow him, but he cannot go against the eternal law of free agency that hath been given to all the children of God in their independent state of existence.

23 And because he cannot force us in any way, therefore, he is not responsible for our sins and the evil which we do during the days of our probation.

24 And again, his desire is to give happiness unto us and cause us to rejoice in the plan that he hath presented to us, that we might reject the plan of the Father and follow his plan.

25 And the wars and rumors of wars, and all contention, and the misery that we suffer during the days of our probation are because we are trying to follow the plan of Lucifer, which seemeth the right plan to the flesh.

26 And now, Satan hath convinced our flesh that his plan can give us the happiness that we desire. Yet, when we follow the enticements of the flesh, which are the enticements of the plan of Lucifer and his blessings, we cause the wars, and the contention, and the misery among us.

27 Thus we are learning from experience during the days of our probation that it is impossible for us to gain the eternal joy and happiness that hath been promised us by the Father by following the plan of Lucifer.

28 And we have been given ample examples of the way in which our spirits learn. For what child that belongeth unto you, according to the flesh, listeneth to all of your counsel and believeth that which ye already know from your own experience?

29 Do they not fight you in that which ye attempt to teach unto them, and claim that ye are unwise and that ye do not understand them? Yea, do they not want to follow their own course in life, according to their understanding, and listen to their own hearts before considering that which ye have taught unto them?

30 Ye know that the children of men do not learn through reason and trust, but must be taught through experience that which they shall accept as the truth.

31 And thus it is with our spirits, who are the literal children of the Father. Yea, He hath taught us what will bring us happiness and hath shown us the path that we should follow to find this happiness. But He doth not condemn us for not understanding His ways and accepting His experience and wisdom in all things, but he loveth us and giveth us every opportunity that we need to learn for ourselves what bringeth happiness and what bringeth misery unto us.

32 And He alloweth us to use our free agency to pursue whatever course we might think is better than the course that He hath set before us, which is the only way to eternal life and happiness.

33 For this reason it was symbolically taught unto us, and passed down from Adam, concerning the first commandments that the Father gave unto Adam and Eve.

34 At first He commanded them that they should not eat of the tree of knowledge of good and evil, or in other words, that they should not give into the enticements of the flesh, but maintain control over it according to His commandments.

35 But then He commanded them to multiply and replenish the earth, which would have required them to partake of the fruit of the tree of knowledge of good and evil.

36 Now, they could not obey both of the commandments of the Father. But Eve chose the more righteous commandment for herself and the joy that she wanted to experience; for she wanted to be a mother and learn by experience that which she should know and understand in order to become an Eternal Mother in the Celestial kingdom, where she would rejoice in her children forever.

37 Therefore, she chose to disobey the Father and partake of that which was not commanded by the Father, thus enabling her to become a mother. And in this choice, she was blessed above Adam.

38 And Satan encourageth the children of

men to seek other ways to obtain the happiness that they can experience from the flesh without obeying the commandments of the Father. And the Father hath allowed his children to do this that we might all learn by our own experience the difference between His plan and the plan of Lucifer, or in other words, the difference between good and evil.

39 And now, for this reason Lucifer demanded of the Father that he be allowed in the last days to introduce some of the knowledge of the power of God into the world, so that he might show forth his plan more fully to the children of men.

40 And with the ability that this power would allow him, Satan would be able to give unto them more of the fine things of the earth, and make their lives easier to live without the toil and struggle of the work that they were commanded to do by the sweat of their own brow for the sake of their own experience, which commandment was given by the Father in the beginning.

41 And ye shall see the great effects of this power that Satan shall introduce into the world in the last days. Yea, ye shall see the imminent destruction that hangeth over the heads of the children of men in the last days because of this knowledge and this power that Satan hath been allowed to give unto them.

42 And in those days ye shall see the rich and the proud rise up above their brothers and their sisters; and ye shall also see the poor, that they shall envy that which the rich are experiencing, which they believe shall give them happiness and the easiness of life.

43 Yea, ye shall see that the plan of Lucifer shall again fail miserably because of the things that he shall be allowed to give unto those who follow his path, which hath a gate that is broad and is easy into which to enter; that upon entering this wide gate, they might follow the broad way to their own destruction.

44 But before this day, it shall be expedient that the Father once again establisheth His plan also into the hearts of those who have the desire to follow Him and enjoy the fruits of the spirit which are promised to all those who follow His plan.

45 And it shall be expedient that His gospel be restored in its fullness to the earth to begin the last time period known as the half of times.

CHAPTER 81

The life and mission of Joseph Smith. The rise and fall of the Church of Jesus Christ of Latter Day Saints. The Church splits into two factions, according to Satan's desires. The three Nephites are introduced and will aid Joseph and Christopher in their missions. Christopher will have the power to confound those who mock the word of God.

AND it shall come to pass that the Lord shall instruct those in the spirit world to prepare the first of these final two prophets who shall bring forth the words of this record unto the world.

2 And from the time of his birth, Joseph shall be watched over by those in the spirit world who will assure that the experiences of his youth shall sufficiently prepare him to have the necessary characteristics and attributes that he will need to fulfill the mission that shall be required of him.

3 And it was determined by the Lord that Joseph should be born into a poor family who shall live among the people of the states that shall be established among this great nation of the United States of which I have written.

4 And it shall be in his youth that Joseph shall begin to be prepared to be the first of these final prophets of the latter days.

5 And before Joseph is born, an elder brother according to the flesh shall be born unto his father and prepared also by the Lord to learn those things of his family; and that he might learn of their ways and their customs, so that he might assist in the education and inspiration of his mortal brother.

6 And the Lord shall prepare his brother in this thing and command that Joseph shall not come into mortality until his brother reacheth an age of responsibility and understanding, so that he might know and remember all things concerning the mission and life of his younger brother Joseph.

7 And in the eighth year of the life of his elder brother, Joseph shall be born into the world.

8 And now, it shall be a tradition among the children of men at this time, that the Father give unto his oldest son, who is his first born, his own name, thus passing on this name through the lineage of his posterity.

9 But the father of Joseph shall not give his name to his oldest son, who shall be called Alvin, who is the one who hath been chosen to assist in the care of Joseph. And to his next son he shall not give his name. But the Lord hath given commandments to those in the spirit world to assure that his next son, who would be the prophet Joseph, should receive his name.

10 And it shall also be customary at this time that the children of men be given a last name, which will distinguish them from others who have also been given the same first name at birth.

11 And there shall be many names among the people at this time, but the last name of this first of the two final prophets shall be a very common name among the people that he might not stand out, even as the name Jesus was given unto the Christ, that it might be known unto the world that he was born among common men, so that the words of the prophets might be fulfilled when they wrote, saying:

12 For ye see your calling, brethren, how that not many wise men after the flesh, and not many mighty, and not many noble, are called of God to preach his words. But God hath chosen the foolish things of the world to confound the wise; and He hath chosen the weak things of the world to confound the things which are mighty, and the base things which are despised, hath God chosen, yea, and things which are not glorified by the flesh, to bring to naught things that are glorified by God; that no flesh should glory in His presence.

13 But of Him are ye in Christ Jesus, who of God is made unto us wisdom, and righteousness, and sanctification, and redemption, so that according as it is written, he that glorieth, let him glory in the Lord.

14 And now, Joseph shall grow in the spirit of the Lord in his youth. And Alvin shall be there at his side all the days of his youth to encourage him and give unto him strength in that which he hath been called to do.

15 And the spirit of Alvin shall be commanded to return to the spirit world where he might better inspire his brother, but he shall remain upon the earth in mortality with Joseph until the time that Joseph shall be ready and accepted as a mature adult among the rest of the people of this nation in which he shall be born.

16 And after Joseph hath reached nigh unto the age of eighteen, then shall Alvin be called back into the spirit world to aid in his instruction and care there.

17 And it shall come to pass that the people of the United States shall begin to exercise the freedom that they have been granted, to set up many religions and faiths according to the dictates of their own consciences, not being afraid to express that which their spirit speaketh unto them.

18 And this was the thing that Satan wanted of the Father, so that he could have more opportunity to bring the children of men to his plan. And Satan began to create a great excitement of religious thought among the people.

19 And with this excitement, the people of the United States shall begin to establish these religions in such a way that the people shall be divided greatly in that which they believe.

20 And this division causeth the love of all men to wax cold. And there shall be great contentions among them and much confusion as one church attempteth to gain converts from another by the preaching and flattering words of its ministers and its priests.

21 And none of these shall follow the words of Christ, in that they should love one another as they would have another love them, but every priest shall contend against another in hopes that he might convince the people to join his church and listen to his words and interpretations of the word of God, which the people shall accept in the Bible, which are the words that proceedeth out of the mouth of the Jew as spoken by the words of Nephi.

22 And the Spirit shall bear down greatly upon Joseph in the days of his youth and cause him to seek for the truth in all things.

23 But he shall not find this truth in the religions of men that are set up before him, nor shall he be taught this truth by his father, Joseph, or by his mother, both of them differing in their own opinions, even as the parents of Mohammed, who shall be the last prophet of God, who shall be called forth by and through the Holy Order of the Son of God before Joseph.

24 And the course of his inquiry of truth shall be the same as that which Mohammed shall follow to find the truth for himself. And in the same manner in which Mohammed shall be given instruction and revelation from God, so shall Joseph be given this knowledge of God through the same means.

25 Behold, the Father and the Son shall also reveal themselves unto Joseph and manifest the actuality of their beings unto him that he might no longer live by faith in this thing; and also, that he might not be deceived by the words and precepts of those men who think they are learned, and who think that they know the will and mind of God concerning that which the Father would have His children know of Him during the days of their probations upon the earth.

26 And the Lord shall command Joseph to hide the true nature of the visitation that he shall receive from the Father and the Son until he hath established a means whereby the fullness of his gospel might come forth unto the children of men.

27 And the Lord shall suffer once again that a church be established among the Gentiles that they might have an opportunity to know the true gospel of Jesus Christ, and have the truth of all things taught to them by the Spirit of God, once they have perfected their lives to such a degree that the Spirit is able to bear Its witness unto them.

28 And if the children of men were righteous, then they would have the Spirit to teach unto them all things that would lead them safely down the straight and narrow path which leadeth to eternal life and happiness.

29 But the children of men have never been of such a righteous state that they could have the great blessing of the Spirit.

30 And for this purpose the Lord shall suffer that Joseph establish a church in the latter days, that these things might more easily be accepted by those who are accustomed to receiving their instructions from God from a church, or from a man, or a prophet, who shall be like unto Moses.

31 Now, I have already explained unto you that this is not the way the Lord would teach us his ways, but he suffereth it because of your wickedness in denying the power of the Holy Spirit and in not keeping the commandments which are given in the words and gospel of Christ.

32 And the Father shall allow the rising up of this latter day church so that He can show by an example the great weakness and frailities of the children of men in complying with His plan while they choose to follow the course which Satan hath set for them.

33 For ye cannot serve God and Mammon. He who hath ears that hear, let him understand.

34 And it shall come to pass that this church, which shall be established by Joseph, shall be established in righteousness in the beginning.

35 And after it hath been established in righteousness, the people of the church shall begin to rebel against Joseph. And when they shall begin to rebel against this prophet of God, the church that was suffered by the Lord to be built up for the sanctification and instruction of the saints of God, and its authority, shall be taken from the earth.

36 And in its stead there shall rise up two more churches, which shall both claim the power and authority that the Lord gave unto Joseph in the beginning to establish a church of God among the people.

37 But the Lord shall take the power and authority of the priesthood, which is after his Holy Order, from off the earth when the first church shall be destroyed; and this power and authority to establish a righteous church shall not be given again unto the children of men upon the earth.

38 And Satan shall take the remnants of the church of God and they shall be under his power. And he shall see which church shall give unto him his authority, or in other words, which church shall seek after the things of the world and the pride and honor of the men of the earth.

39 And there shall be one of these two that shall rise up above all other churches of the latter days. Nevertheless, it shall not rise up in righteousness, but in wickedness, for those who shall belong to this church shall also belong to the church of the devil and desire the blessings of this great and abominable church.

40 And ye shall witness hereafter in this record the rise of this great church which shall be called the Church of Jesus Christ of Latter-day Saints. And ye shall see the way in which Satan in subtleness overcometh this church and taketh control of its leaders, so that it becometh a powerful church that shall wield the power that it shall receive from Satan, who shall be its God and its Christ.

41 But in the beginning it was not so. And I have shown unto you that the record of my fathers shall come forth unto Joseph, and he shall translate the part which is unsealed and publish it to the world, so that all might know of the work of the Father, which was wrought upon the land of Eden, which is this promised land, which shall be called in the latter days, the United States of America.

42 And the unsealed portion of this record shall come forth by the power of God, which the Lord hath promised unto me, that I might be the protector and overseer of these plates, that they might not fall into the hands of the wicked and be destroyed.

43 And it shall come to pass that I shall die; and then, according to the promise that the Lord gave unto me when he was in my presence, immediately I shall resurrect and go to the kingdom of the Father and receive the glory that I have desired for myself.

44 And then the Lord shall command me that I should watch over the work that shall come forth from my own hand unto Joseph.

45 And there shall be others, who are not exalted, even those three apostles who were among those whom the Lord called forth when he visited my people in the land of Bountiful;

46 And these three shall be upon the earth until the end of time. And they shall not be known among men, having hidden themselves from the sight of men all the days of their lives.

47 Now, I say hidden because they disguise themselves and act in a way that others shall not discover who they are, so that they might oversee the work of the Lord in all things in the latter days.

48 And my father was forbidden to write their names in the record that was unsealed, but in this record their names are given. And these are the brother of Nephi, who was named Timothy, whose body was transformed at the time he was raised from the dead by the word of Nephi; and also Mathoni and his brother Mathonihah; yea, these are those apostles who remain upon the earth in a state of mortality, but cannot grow old, having received this blessing according to their desires of the Lord.

49 And they shall give much strength to these last two latter-day prophets who shall bring forth this record unto the people of the earth.

50 For behold, I shall not be able to abide upon the earth once I have brought forth this record unto Joseph, who is the first among them, because I shall have an exalted body of flesh and bone like unto the Father in that day; and because of the body that I shall possess at that time, I cannot sojourn among them and give them assistance at that time.

51 But I shall come down at the set time of the Lord when the prophet Joseph shall be ready to receive the record that my father and I have prepared according to the commandments of the Lord.

52 And I shall instruct Joseph in many things and teach him many things concerning this record and the way in which it should be translated and come forth unto the world.

53 And I shall command him to not break the bands which I shall make to seal this portion of the record concerning the vision of the brother of Jared. And this portion of the record shall contain the mysteries of God that He would have His children know in the last days of the half of time, which is the end of time before He shall send His Son in all of His glory to reign upon the earth.

54 And Joseph shall prepare the world to receive these things which are sealed. And he shall take part in the coming forth of this sealed portion, even by bringing the plates which have been made by my own hands and the hands of my father, and delivering them unto the last of these final prophets, whose name beareth the name of Christ.

55 And it shall come to pass that in the very same year that Joseph shall establish the church of God in the last days, yea, in this same year shall begin the half of times of which I have spoken.

56 And in the same month as the birth of

Mohammed, which was the mark of the end of the times, shall this church be presented to the world as the only true church of God upon the earth.

57 And now, these times and events are given unto you who lack faith and do not believe in these things. For there shall be many of you who shall mock these last prophets and shall say that of themselves these things have come forth from their own hand that the children of men might be deceived.

58 And I say unto you, Woe unto you who shall say these things and shall lead others to believe in your words. For do ye not also have the Bible with you? And would ye convince others that these last two prophets wrote the Bible also?

59 Yet, in this record shall all the signs of the great revelations be revealed unto you, which are given by the prophets of God in the Bible.

60 And when ye have an explanation of the symbolism and the allegories that were given in the words of the ancient prophets of God, will ye then say that these two prophets have invented these things to deceive you?

61 And as ye read the words of this record; behold, what do these words say unto you? Do they not make an attempt to push you towards Christ and to love your neighbor as yourself, and to forsake the world and become one with the Father in all things?

62 Yea, ye know that they preach these things, for this is the only message of God that should be taught among you. And those of you who have received these things and who doubt within yourself of whence they came; yea, have ye read all of these words?

63 Yea, have ye spoken to the last of these two latter-day prophets about these things? Can ye confound him in his words? I say unto you, that ye cannot confound him in his words, because he speaks according to the Spirit of God, which is within him; and he who speaketh according to the Spirit of God, cannot be confounded in that which he speaketh.

64 But ye who condemn them and who believe that these things were invented by them that they might deceive you, why do ye not speak with the prophet of God that is now among you upon the earth?

65 Behold, I shall prophesy unto you and tell you why ye do not speak to him: Yea, Satan hath great power over your hearts and ye are filled with anger and hate towards him, even with the same anger and the hate that the Jews had against Jesus when he spoke unto them.

66 And Satan shall inspire you to not seek out this last prophet and speak to him of these things, for Satan knoweth that he shall confound you in your words. And if ye are confounded in your words, then what shall ye say of your understanding and your knowledge and the spirit which ye harbor inside of you?

67 Behold, ye shall go away knowing that ye do not know truth, and ye shall be empty and afraid to speak unto this latter-day prophet, even as ye shall be afraid to be in the presence of the Lord and listen to his words when he cometh in his glory.

68 And ye shall seek to kill this prophet and rid the world of him, because he condemneth you in your wickedness and casteth down your pride and your arrogance in those things which ye think ye understand of God.

69 And when the Lord cometh in his glory and calleth forth the plates of ore that my father and I have made with our own hands; yea, and ye have the Urim and Thummim explained and shown unto you, then what shall ye say?

70 Will ye look upon the Lord and say unto him, We do not believe these things, for they came forth from the writings of a man?

71 Behold, in that day when all the books shall be opened unto you, those of you who have doubted these things shall be ashamed and disgraced in the glory that ye have received from Satan in the church of the devil to which ye belong.

CHAPTER 82

The rise and fall of the original LDS Church. Joseph tries to establish a church by Celestial laws, but it fails. Brigham Young becomes an emissary and leader under the power of Satan. Salt Lake City is established similar to Jerusalem and is one of the many seats of Satan in the latter days. The LDS Church will send the Book of Mormon into all of the earth because of the pride of its members.

AND it shall come to pass that Joseph shall establish the church of God among the people and shall once again introduce into the world, the fullness of the gospel of Jesus Christ to them.

2 And Joseph shall desire of the Lord that the church be set up according to the principles of the eternal laws of heaven, which are Celestial.

3 And the Lord shall say unto him at that day: Behold, my servant Joseph, thy calling is not that this people shall have the things of the Celestial kingdom of the Father, for many are not of this kingdom and cannot abide therein and find their happiness.

4 But thou shalt establish this church for the sake of all of the children of God, so that all might partake of His goodness and mercy and prepare themselves for the kingdom of glory that they have chosen for themselves.

5 Behold, there shall be many called by thee to help thee bring forth this church that thou desirest to establish among the people of the earth according to the principles of heaven, and these shall be of a Terrestrial and a Telestial nature, because of the desires of their hearts.

6 Nevertheless, it is better that the people be led by those to whom they can relate and understand according to the glory to which they pertain, instead of feeling miserable and tormented because of the glory of the Father, which shall torment them as they hear thy words, which are the words of a true prophet of God, who knoweth the laws that pertaineth to the Celestial kingdom of the Father.

7 Therefore, seek not to establish the laws of the Celestial kingdom among them, for they shall not abide by them, and it shall lead to their destruction.

8 And it shall come to pass that Joseph shall be like unto Moses and Samuel, and other prophets who, in their desire to bring the people to repentance, disregarded the counsel of the Lord and did that which they thought was best for the people, according to the desires of the people.

9 And it shall come to pass that Joseph shall begin to set up the church of God according to the principles that he shall learn from the Spirit, and also from the mouths of the holy angels, which are the principles of the Celestial kingdom.

10 And the Father knew that Joseph would do this thing, for this reason he was chosen. For it was expedient of the Father that the children of men be given the opportunity to live by these principles so that they might know that these Celestial principles are not those things which all desire to make them happy.

11 And it shall come to pass that Joseph shall introduce the law of consecration among the people.

12 Now this was the same law that the twelve apostles of Christ set up in the church that they established among the people of the Jews.

13 And this law is based upon the principles that they have been given by the Lord, which are principles of the kingdom of God. And these same principles were instituted into the first church of God which was established by Adam and his sons in the land of Eden.

14 And these principles take from those who have an abundance and give to those who have less. And the commandment is given that, if a person would live by this law, then he would give willingly of his abilities to all according to their needs.

15 And this is the law of communal living, which if lived in righteousness and in its fullness, shall bless a people with exceeding peace and happiness as long as they live this law in righteousness.

16 And those who are rich are those who feel that they sacrifice the most by living this law, for they give of all that they have, and receive only what they need, like unto the poor, who do not have what they need and take much from that which is given by the rich.

17 And now, the rich, who think that they are righteous, have always complained of this inequality pertaining to this great law of heaven, which is not only a Celestial law, but is lived in many of the kingdoms of the Father.

18 And now, how can ye that are rich think that this is an inequality? Do ye not realize that ye would not be rich except for the poor who have given unto you your riches and have supported you in all that ye have?

19 And now, where do ye suppose that the fine things of the earth that ye enjoy come from? Yea, how are they manufactured and produced? Do ye think that a drop of your own sweat fell in acquiring the materials for all of the fine things that make you rich?

20 I say unto you that ye do not sweat at all, but the sweat cometh from the brows of the poor, with whom ye should be glad to share the abundance which ye have.

21 And now, those of you who are rich, and who have a hard time giving up that which ye have in order to live by the principles of the kingdom of God; behold, do ye not see that ye are not ready for the kingdom of God, and will not be ready until the riches which ye have mean nothing to you.

22 And if they meant nothing to you, then ye would not have acquired them, and therefore, ye would not be rich. Alas, well did the Lord speak of you when he said: It is harder for a rich man to enter the kingdom of heaven than for a camel to go through the gate of the eye of the needle.

23 Behold, all ye that are rich shall never be of the kingdom of God and follow His plan, but are of the kingdom of Satan, whose plan hath made you rich.

24 And the record of the Bible readeth concerning the first church that was suffered to be set up by the twelve apostles of the Lord among the Jews, saying: And the multitude of them that believed were of one heart and of one soul; neither said any of them that ought of the things which he possessed was his own; but they had all things in common.

25 And with great power gave the apostles witness of the resurrection of the Lord Jesus; and great grace was upon them all.

26 Neither was there any among them that lacked: for as many as were possessors of lands or houses sold them, and brought the prices of the things that were sold, and laid them down at the feet of the apostles; and distribution was made unto every man according as he had need.

27 And it shall come to pass that Joseph shall attempt to institute this same law among those who shall join the church of God in the latter days. And it shall come to pass that this shall fail because of the wickedness of the members of the church, especially among those who are rich as to the things of the world.

28 And the church shall begin to come forth in that day, but it shall not come forth in righteousness as ye would suppose the church of God would come forth.

29 And now, this is the thing that ye should know who shall receive these things in the latter days: Behold, Joseph shall not be called forth upon the earth to establish a church, yea, this is not his main mission; but the Lord shall suffer that a church be established to prove all of his words which he hath spoken concerning the great wickedness of the Gentiles in the latter days.

30 For there shall be much rebellion and strife among the leadership of the church that Joseph shall establish, and many shall fall away because of their pride and their desires to have the glories of men, which they should not desire according to the commandments of the Lord.

31 And even Joseph himself shall become overcome for a time by the pride of his own heart, which pride ariseth in the hearts of all men when they gain power and control over the hearts of those who believe in them.

32 Nevertheless, the Lord shall chastise him and cause him to repent and teach the people only the words of Christ.

33 And it shall come to pass that the people of the church of God shall prosper when they are at peace, even when their leaders are humble and are following the Lord in all his ways.

34 But when they are wicked and contentious and seek more for the things of the world than they do for the things of God, then shall the Lord withdraw his help so that they cannot prosper in peace and be happy.

35 And there shall be those of the church of God who shall be humble followers of Christ, who shall learn the true gospel and find happiness in that which they shall learn.

36 But many of the leaders of this church shall not listen to the words of the prophet Joseph and shall be desirous to establish the church and the Holy Order of the Son of God in their own way. And when Joseph standeth against them in their wicked desires, they shall rebel against him, proclaiming that he is a false prophet who would mislead the people.

37 Now, there are many of you who shall receive these things in the latter days who shall believe that ye are of the church that was established by Joseph in the beginning. But I say unto you, that the true church of God shall not exist upon the earth in the latter days because of the great wickedness of the children of men in following the plan of Lucifer instead of the plan of God.

38 And the people of the church, which shall be recognized among you as the Church of Jesus Christ of Latter-day Saints, shall be misled and deceived by their leaders.

39 For their leaders shall not give unto the people of their church the true history of the beginnings of this church, nor will they allow them to question the corrupted and manipulated history that they shall teach to the people in their churches.

40 Behold, my beloved brothers and sisters, your leaders do not want you to know the truth behind the history of your church, because they know that ye shall begin to question their authority and wonder why they have corrupted the history and have hidden it from you.

41 And they have done these things so that they might maintain control over your hearts and minds and keep you within the church, so that ye might continue to give unto them praise and glory; and also that ye might continue to give unto them your tithing that they might create a kingdom for themselves upon the earth.

42 And I would admonish those of you who shall receive these things to seek out the truth and know of those things that transpired among the people of the church of God that was established by Joseph in the beginning.

43 And I have been commanded to reveal many of these things to you, so that ye might no longer be deceived by your leaders, and that ye might leave the church of the devil and become members of the church of the Lamb of God, which shall give you the opportunity to have the Spirit of God, which shall bring you the peace and happiness that ye desire.

44 And it shall come to pass that the government of the beast that shall be established in the latter days shall rise up against the people of this church and against Joseph and shall persecute them and desire to cast them out from among the rest of its people.

45 And in this way, Satan shall influence his leaders so that the church of God shall not have a chance to come forth in righteousness.

46 And Joseph shall do all that is in his power to teach the people the things that he hath learned from the Spirit. And he shall make many attempts to live at peace with the government of the United States, calling upon its protection of the rights of all of its citizens to be protected in their right to worship God according to the dictates of their own conscience.

47 And now, Satan gladly desireth that all people worship him according to the dictates of their own conscience. But if there ariseth a religion, or a thought, that is contrary to his plan, or that supporteth the plan of the Father, then he inspireth those over whom he hath power and causeth them to persecute and destroy those who do not want to follow his plan.

48 Therefore, it shall come to pass that the United States shall not protect the church of God from the persecutions of others, but shall hinder the church in its formation and its right to establish itself, because it is not a church that followeth the plan of Lucifer.

49 And it shall come to pass that all of the other religions that shall be set up in the United States shall be protected by the principles of this nation. But the church of God, which shall be established by Joseph, shall not be protected, but shall be persecuted and destroyed.

50 And thus it shall come to pass to any church, or a people, who make an attempt to usurp the power of Satan and cause commotion in his kingdom.

51 And Joseph shall be under a strict command of the Lord that he shall not reveal unto the world all of the knowledge that he shall receive from the Spirit and also from the voice of the angels, and from the servants of God that dwell among men, for much of this knowledge shall be contained in these things which are sealed.

52 But he shall be allowed to give unto men that which they are ready to receive and that which is expedient that they receive according to the commandments of the Lord.

53 For the Lord knoweth all that which is to come to pass among the children of men. And this he doth not know, except it be by the experience that the Father hath shared with him of those things which have occurred many times before on other worlds like unto this one.

54 And the Lord gave revelations unto Joseph so that the things that were supposed to occur in his time would come to pass. But of himself, Joseph thought that he could establish Zion and bring peace and happiness to the world by the principles of this peace and happiness which he had been given by God.

55 Nevertheless, the Gentiles shall be wicked and shall be so entrenched in the kingdom of Satan, that they shall not be worthy of a righteous church of God among them.

56 And it shall come to pass that Joseph shall be murdered for the sake of his word, and also because of the great wickedness of the members who belongeth to the church which he shall cause to be set up among them. And he shall seal his testimony of the truthfulness of his mission with his blood.

57 Nevertheless, the world shall hold his name in contempt, and the church which he shall cause to be established shall be overcome by Satan and led by him.

58 For it shall come to pass that after his death, the church shall be divided in itself as I have explained it unto you. And those who are in possession of more of the riches and property of this church, and who have more knowledge and familiarity with the beginnings of the church, yea, even the family of Joseph, shall attempt to continue his teachings and reestablish the church once again upon the earth.

59 And these shall know more of the truths of the history of Joseph and his teachings and the beginnings of the church, than those who refuse to follow them, who are the unlearned and meek among them.

60 And they shall separate themselves from the poor and the meek of the church, who shall be the majority of those who have joined this church in the latter days.

61 And the church that they shall establish among them shall rise up and be lost in obscurity, having not the strength and power to combat Satan and his will concerning them.

62 And in that day Satan shall have great power over the hearts of the rest of the people who shall be left in this church; and he shall make one of them his own leader and raise him up; and Satan shall pretend to be the God of the people of the Saints, which is the name by which they shall call themselves after the name of the church that Joseph shall establish among them.

63 And this leader who he shall raise up shall speak with authority and much power and flattery unto the people. And his name shall be Brigham.

64 And he shall deceive the poor and the meek and shall lead them into the wilderness, pretending to be an emissary of the Lord.

65 And he shall be like unto King Noah, whose only desire was to set up a kingdom for himself and bring glory to himself by captivating the hearts and the minds of the people with his flattering words.

66 And it shall come to pass that Brigham shall lead the people to a land of wilderness near unto the remnants of a great lake which once covered that part of the land when the earth was in its infancy.

67 And the remnant of this lake shall be of no worth, and shall be of salt, and the people shall cause to come forth a city that they shall call, the city of Salt Lake.

68 Now, this shall come to pass according to the mind and the will of Satan in all things. For he knoweth that the poor and the meek of the church of God cannot read, nor can they write, but that they are strong in their backs. Therefore they would need a leader to lead them and teach unto them the things of God.

69 And Satan knew that if he could raise up a leader among them, then he could give unto the people the blessings that he hath given to all of those who worship him and follow the course of his plan.

70 And the area in which this great city shall be established shall be like unto the area that surroundeth Jerusalem. Behold, both being established near the borders of a sea of salt, which provideth no life to the children of men.

71 And these things shall also be according to the knowledge and purpose of the Lord. For as the waters of the earth giveth life unto the world, so also shall the word of God. But the Jews and those who shall inhabit the city of Salt Lake shall not have the pure waters that flow forth from the mouth of God, but the stench that cometh forth from the sea of salt, which are the precepts and commandments of men.

72 And the people of Salt Lake shall be like unto the people of Jerusalem and shall be reminded by the stench of that great salt lake which is near unto their city, even that they should keep in remembrance that they do not have this pure and refreshing water that can give life unto them.

73 And Brigham shall use his power over the people to build a temple like unto the temple at Jerusalem. And in all things shall this people be like unto the Jews.

74 Now, this is the will of the Lord, so that he can one day show forth his power unto them as he did unto the Jews. For the great temple which shall be established among them shall one day be destroyed, like unto the temple at Jerusalem, and all these things shall come to pass because these people of the city of Salt Lake shall be like unto the Jews in every way.

75 And Brigham shall become great and glorious as the servant of Satan, and shall do whatsoever thing that he is commanded by Satan.

76 And the city of Salt Lake shall become a great city of commerce and business, even so much that the government of the United States shall take notice of its greatness.

77 And now, the sole purpose of Brigham shall be to get gain and set himself up above the people so that he might be worshipped by them and receive of their glory. And by the works of Brigham, Satan shall establish himself powerfully amongst those who think of themselves as the righteous saints of God.

78 And from his works, shall rise forth one of the most powerful religions that the world hath ever known. Yea, it shall be more powerful, even than the great Catholic Church that shall cover the earth during the days in between the times and the half of time.

79 And though its numbers shall be few in comparison with other religions that Satan shall cause to rise up in the latter days, with his subtle ways, shall Satan begin to use this church as one of the means that he hath set up to perpetuate his plan and bring all men under his power and his control.

80 For behold, in the last days this church shall show forth the glory of the blessings that it hath received from Satan by its great temples and its churches and the great amount of money and property which pertaineth unto it.

81 And its members shall pursue the things of the world and aspire to the honors of men; and many shall receive these honors from Satan, who they believe is their God. Nevertheless, they do not recognize their God as Satan, for he hath deceived them with the riches and the power that they shall possess.

82 And in his pride Satan shall laugh at the Father and he shall also laugh at all the holy prophets who have been upon the earth who have testified against the great wickedness that shall be established in the last days among the children of men. For behold, this church shall demonstrate to all the children of God that a people can seem prosperous and righteous and have peace if they follow his plan.

83 And now, it shall be revealed further unto you in this record more of this great and abominable church which shall be known among you as the Church of Jesus Christ of Latter-day Saints.

84 Yea, it shall be revealed further unto you of their hypocrisy and their wickedness, and their secret combinations, and also of their downfall as the great day of the Lord approacheth.

85 And I have explained many things regarding this church unto you in this record; for this church shall have the record of my father

among them, but they shall be like unto the Jews of old, who had the records of all the holy prophets, yet they did not read them, nor did they understand them.

86 And the Father shall use this church and its greatness and its glory and its money and the deception of its people to allow this record to be given unto all the earth.

87 For these people shall believe that they are the only righteous children of God upon the earth, and that a man cannot be saved unless he joineth their church and receiveth the ordinances that its leaders have prescribed for the salvation of the people.

88 And because of this pride, many people shall carry the record of my people to others upon the earth, who are the elect of God and are searching for the truth of God in all things.

89 And these shall join this church, but shall come to know that its works are evil, and then they shall depart from it. Nevertheless, they shall take with them the record of my fathers, which Joseph was commanded to bring forth unto them.

90 And after they have received a testimony of the things that are written in the part of the record which is not sealed, then shall their hearts and minds be ready to receive these things, which are sealed, and have been preserved for them, who are elect, even those who shall have the name of the Lord written in their hearts and in their foreheads.

91 And they shall know that the things revealed unto them are true, because they testifieth of the wickedness of the world and the great corruption of the children of men as they live by the plan of Lucifer.

92 But these things which have been sealed up shall come forth and give unto them a better understanding of the plan of the Father that they did not consider.

93 And if they are elect, and do not belong to the church of the devil, then they shall be received by the Father into the church of the Lamb, and therein they shall find the peace and the happiness, and the righteousness that they have desired all the days of their lives.

CHAPTER 83

Satan uses truth to deceive. The members of the LDS Church live the word of wisdom in hypocrisy. The lost 116 page manuscript is discussed—Christopher brings it again to the world in the latter days to prove the veracity of The Sealed Portion. Moroni testifies of the mission of Joseph Smith and Christopher Marc Nemelka. The desire of wealth and not taking care of the poor and needy are sure signs that a person is following the plan of Lucifer. The mentally handicapped are given as examples by the Father.

AND now, it hath always been the plan of Lucifer to take the eternal truths and laws that he learned as a spirit child in the kingdom of the Father and make them a part of his eternal plan. Nevertheless, only those truths and laws that satisfieth his needs and desires doth he introduce into his plan for happiness.

2 And because of this, it is a hard thing for a man to distinguish between the plan of Lucifer and the plan of the Father. For a mortal man hath forgotten the plan of the Father, and therefore knoweth not the eternal laws and truths that the Father gave unto His children as spirits in His kingdom.

3 But Satan hath not forgotten any of the promises made by the Father, nor hath he forgotten the eternal plan of the Father which he rebelled against in the beginning.

4 And there are many parts of the plan of the Father which are taught by Lucifer and used to bring the joy and happiness that all of our souls desire. And because of the many truths of the Father that he useth in his plan, many times a man can be deceived into thinking that the plan and course of life that the devil hath laid out for us is a righteous plan of God.

5 And because the plan of Lucifer provideth much of the temporary happiness in the flesh for the children of men, they begin to believe that it is a righteous plan, because of the goodness that they perceive in their hearts, which they believe cometh from the course of life that they live according to the plan of Lucifer, which they are deceived into believing is righteousness before God.

6 Now, I have already explained unto you that the plan of Lucifer provideth blessings of happiness to those who follow his plan. Nevertheless, there are great differences between the plan of Lucifer and the plan of the Father.

7 And I have explained unto you one of these differences, even that the joy and happiness that ye receive from following the plan of Lucifer is a temporary joy that doth not last forever, but endeth as soon as the experience of the blessing is complete.

8 And as an example of this thing, the Lord made an attempt to teach this unto the people when he said unto them: Lay not up for yourselves treasures upon earth, where moth and rust doth corrupt, and where thieves break through and steal; but lay up for yourselves treasures in heaven, where neither moth nor rust doth corrupt, and where thieves do not break through nor steal; for where your treasure is, there will your heart be also.

9 And now, when ye receive the treasures of the earth, which are those things with which Satan doth bless you for following his plan, do they not bring immediate joy to your heart when ye receive them?

10 But after ye have received them for awhile, doth the same joy exist in your heart that existed in the beginning when ye received these things?

11 And when they begin to rust, or when moths eat them, or when thieves steal them, do ye not feel miserable and have a great cause to mourn and be unhappy because of the effect that your loss hath upon your soul?

12 Now, this is what is meant by the temporary joy and happiness that ye receive from these things; for it is a feeling of joy that doth not last; and this same joy hath the power to cause you misery after the initial joy hath ended.

13 And it shall come to pass in the latter days that all the people of the whole earth shall begin to search after its treasures; and the desires of all the children of men shall be set upon their money and the things that they can purchase with their money.

14 And the elect shall see that this is the case; and they shall see the great cause of misery and unhappiness that cometh from the treasures of the earth and the pursuit of them.

15 And they shall witness the rich and the powerful among them, who would pretend to present themselves as happy, because they possess great riches and power.

16 Yet, ye shall see that they are not happy. For they shall give their lives to eating and drinking and making themselves merry in any way possible to assuage the misery that cometh from their riches.

17 And there shall be many poor upon the earth who also follow the plan of Lucifer. And these shall covet and envy that which the rich hath received from Satan, believing that if they are rich, then they shall be happy like unto the rich and powerful, who they believe are happy because of their riches, which appear before men in public to bring happiness unto them.

18 But when they are alone in their great houses surrounded by the many fine and precious things that their money hath provided for them, they shall be in misery alone; for they are away from the eye of the public, which would see them in the miserable state that they have caused for themselves because of their riches.

19 And because of the knowledge of the laws of heaven that Satan shall be allowed to introduce among the children of men in the last days, many of the children of men shall be inspired to invent the medicines that these rich can purchase, which shall give unto them the continued happiness that they do not receive from their riches, or a reprieve from their misery that they shall long for because of them.

20 And the brother of Jared hath written of these things and hath called them according as they shall relieve the symptoms that are caused because of the unhappiness of those of the latter days.

21 And not only the rich shall be miserable and in need of the stimulants that Satan shall provide for them, but also the poor who envy and covet the rich; yea, these shall also be miserable in that which they desire; and these also shall need the drugs and the anti-depressants, and the other stimulants that Satan shall inspire the children of men to create to give

them a temporary joy, or a temporary reprieve from the misery that they shall feel.

22 And now, my brothers and sisters, how can ye say that the plan which ye follow in the latter days is the plan of God, when the things which ye believe are the blessings of God, cause you such heartache and misery?

23 How can ye say that ye are a righteous people who live in a righteous nation under God, when there existeth no lasting happiness among you? Yea, do ye not see the abuse among you of these stimulants that shall be prevalent in the latter days?

24 And it shall come to pass that this church of which I have spoken, that which shall carry forth the unsealed portion of this record into the world, shall command its people to not partake of the alcohol, and the wine, and other of the stimulants that shall be produced from the natural course of nature; yet, they shall condone the use of the stimulants that their doctors shall prescribe for them, which are made from the knowledge of science and medicine that Satan hath given unto them in the latter days.

25 And they shall judge and condemn those that take natural drugs, and that drink wine, and that take into their bodies those things which they have been taught by their leaders are not permitted by their church.

26 But it shall come to pass that they shall consume more of the medicines made by the hand of men than any other people upon the earth.

27 Now, what say ye of this church which thinketh that it is the only church of God upon the earth? What say ye of the course which ye of this church shall follow to obtain your happiness? Do ye not now know that ye are indeed following the plan of Lucifer, even more so than the rest of the people of the earth?

28 And how do ye think that ye can justify the stimulants and the drugs that your doctors prescribe for you, yet ye judge and ridicule those who take substances of the earth, that do the same thing to the body that do those things which have been prescribed by your doctors, in whom ye trust, as a remedy for their misery?

29 Oh, ye hypocrites! My soul is burdened greatly because of you; for ye have the record of my father and have been given much more knowledge and testimony of the plan of the Father than the rest of your brothers and sisters who are upon the earth in the latter days, yet ye are worse than they.

30 Woe, woe unto you who are not pure in heart but are hypocrites, even those of you who consider yourselves righteous before God, but are filthy still. Behold, if ye do not see the error of your ways and refrain from the judgment of others, then it shall be measured unto you that which ye measure to another.

31 And in the latter days ye shall be stricken in your health. And ye shall become fat with excess, and ye shall groan within yourselves because of your depression, and your loneliness, and your lack of righteousness. And your leaders shall grow old and age in the progression of their wickedness, for they are the examples of wickedness that ye have chosen for yourselves.

32 And ye have been given a promise by the Lord through the prophet Joseph, that if ye obey his laws of health, then ye shall receive health in your navels and marrow to your bones; and ye shall find wisdom and great treasures of knowledge, even hidden treasures; and ye shall run and not be weary, and shall walk and not faint.

33 And now, look at the leaders who have set the example for you? Do they run and not weary, do they walk and not faint? Do they give unto you any treasures of knowledge that ye do not already have among you, which have not come from them, but from the corrupted doctrines and principles of Joseph that they have changed and doctored and presented unto you as the truth?

34 And are not many of them old men who speak only as they need to speak according to the desires and guidelines of the church? Behold, do they not lose their capacity to think and function without the aid of the doctors in whom they have put their trust?

35 And when they are old, are they not kept alive by the miracles that Satan hath introduced into the world to save your lives, so that ye might continue to live according to his plan in the flesh, when ye could have had faith in the Lord and died and entered into the rest and peace that the Lord hath promised unto those who live by the words of Christ and keep the commandments of the Father?

36 But I say unto you, that it is better for you that ye are kept alive by the means of Satan, because it might give unto you more of a chance to see the error of your ways and repent of the hypocrisy and wickedness that shall condemn you before the Lord.

37 For behold, if ye were to die, ye would die in your wickedness and your deception, and ye shall be received back into the spirit world in a state of misery and hell, which ye shall not be able to assuage by the means of your doctors and your prescribed medicines, which only affect the flesh and do nothing to relieve the pain and misery of your souls.

38 Behold, ye seek more for the things of the world and the honors of men than any other people upon the earth. Yea, your hearts and desires are set upon these things in the like manner as were the leaders of the Jews who were at Jerusalem when the Lord sent his prophets unto them in the days of my father Lehi.

39 And ye have this record in your church, which giveth unto you more of a responsibility to live by the word of God and keep the commandments of Christ which he hath given unto you by the two testimonies which ye shall carry forth to the world in your pride.

40 And it shall come to pass that the Lord shall allow the translation of the first part of the record of my father to fall into the hands of wicked men, who shall have it in their hearts to destroy the work of the Lord, if he would allow them to do so.

41 And it shall come to pass that Joseph shall give the manuscript on which he hath translated the first part of the abridgment which my father hath written upon these plates to his scribe, who shall be deceived by wicked men who shall steal the manuscript so that they might prove to the world that Joseph cannot translate the first part of this record again.

42 And this they shall believe, because Joseph was laid under a strict commandment that he should not show unto any man the plates upon which these things are written.

43 Now, neither my father nor I knew of the will of the Lord concerning these things when my father Mormon, included the small plates of Nephi with the remainder of the abridgment that he made of the records of the Nephites.

44 But I have the words of the brother of Jared, which give an accounting of all things that have happened and all those things which shall happen unto the ends of the earth.

45 And I read his words concerning the things that shall transpire concerning this record in the latter days. And I know that it was the will of the Lord that the wicked desires of these men in stealing this first manuscript from Joseph come to pass, that the Lord might hide from you of the latter days many of the words of my father which he wrote pertaining to the state of wickedness in which the Jews found themselves at Jerusalem.

46 For the church of God at Jerusalem at the time of Lehi shall be in the same state of wickedness as the church of God, as the Gentiles suppose, which shall be established in the great city of Salt Lake in the latter days.

47 And if ye of this church of the latter days would have had the first part of the translation of the record of my father, then ye would have known that which ye should not become, having a witness of these things before you.

48 But this great leader that shall be led by a flaxen cord by Satan, who shall be known among you as Brigham, he shall not know these things, and shall establish the foundations of the church that Satan desireth to establish among you in the latter days.

49 Behold, it shall come to pass that when the final of the two of these latter day prophets shall receive the plates upon which is written this record, even that he may fulfill the will of the Lord concerning these things which are sealed; yea, when he shall receive these plates, he shall be commanded to give unto you once again a translation of the first part of these plates, which translation shall be lost by Joseph to the hands of wicked men.

50 And it shall come to pass that these wicked men shall preserve that which they shall steal from Joseph and guard it up, and pass it from one generation to another, so that they might have a means whereby they might destroy the testimony of those who shall receive these things in the latter days.

51 For these men shall not believe that there are plates of gold which have these things written upon them. And they shall believe that Joseph made up the translation of these plates, and the proof that they shall present to the world is in the manuscript that was translated which they have guarded and kept among them; for they shall believe that if Joseph were to retranslate the first part of these plates, that the translation would not be the same, and therefore, they could prove to the world that he is a false prophet who hath set out to deceive the world.

52 And now, the Lord could command Joseph to retranslate the first part of these plates through the Urim and Thummim, and his translation would be the same, except it be for errors that are caused because of the weakness of men in the writing of their own language.

53 And if these wicked men would change or doctor the words of the original translation in any form, it would be made known unto any who observe the manuscript, because of the difference in the writing and the words of the scribe who wrote the original words that he received from Joseph as he translated them with the Urim and Thummim.

54 Nevertheless, the Lord shall command that these things shall not be given at that time for the reason that I have explained unto you.

55 Behold, this thing shall also be a witness against those wicked men and their children who shall receive these things from their fathers, who have the original manuscript which was written by the scribe of Joseph at the time he began the translation of these things.

56 Behold, ye have the manuscript before you; And now, I say unto you, bring it forth unto the world, so that it might be examined and verified by the means of science that ye shall have in those days.

57 For by the means of your science, ye shall know that it was indeed written by the hand of the scribe of Joseph in his day.

58 And it shall come to pass that ye shall have the translation of these same things given unto you by Christopher, having been commanded by the Lord to bring these things forth again unto the world along with the translation that he shall make of the portion of this record which shall be sealed.

59 Yea, ye shall know these things, and ye shall see that which Christopher shall bring forth, which is the lost part of the manuscript of Joseph. And ye shall compare the two translations, and ye shall see that they are nearly word for word in their construction and in their meaning, except for the weakness of writing that each of these latter day prophets shall have during the process of their own translation through the Urim and Thummim.

60 And now, what say ye of these things? Ye shall see that they are the same words, therefore, ye know that Christopher shall take his translation from the same plates from which Joseph shall take his translation.

61 But ye are wicked men who have been misled and deceived by Satan, therefore, ye shall not bring forth the manuscript at that day, but shall cause it to be destroyed, because of the verification that it can make of the truthfulness and correctness of the translation of these plates given by Christopher.

62 Woe unto you, ye wicked men. Behold, ye shall have proof of the truthfulness of these things before you, yet ye shall continue to deny these things and take it upon yourselves to continue to corrupt the work of God and mislead the people.

63 And there shall be others in the latter days who shall make an attempt to invent the contents of this portion of my record that is sealed. And Satan shall come unto them and deceive them as an angel of light, and give unto them a Urim and Thummim that they shall believe shall have the power to know the contents of these things

64 But how can ye who have been deceived think that ye can translate something that ye do not have? For ye do not have the plates of gold that my father and I have prepared for these things. And without the plates that we have prepared, what is it that ye think ye are translating with your Urim and Thummim?

65 And ye who have done these things shall also be condemned by the Lord for your deception and your weakness in allowing Satan to deceive you and give you his revelations, so

that he might mislead you also and bind you with his chains that shall lead to the destruction of your souls.

66 And I say unto all of you of the latter days, there shall not be but two latter-day prophets who shall be given the power and the authority to bring forth these things unto the world. The first shall be called Joseph after his father, and he shall only give unto you that which is required of him by the Lord.

67 And the second shall be Christopher, a bearer of Christ, who shall give unto you the translation of the sealed portion of this record, and he shall also give unto you only those things which the Lord shall command him.

68 And there shall be no other from whom shall come forth anything that pertaineth to this record, except these prophets of whom I make mention upon these plates.

69 And in the latter days Christopher shall be born into this great church of which I have spoken. And he shall be raised up and given the experiences that are necessary for him to accomplish those things which the Lord shall require of him.

70 And he shall be persecuted and reviled by those of his own household, and rejected by those of his church. And Satan shall make every effort to tempt him and steer him in a course of life that shall take him away from the great mission that he shall perform for the people of the earth in the latter days.

71 For he shall have all the attributes of the great men of the earth, even in his intelligence that shall be far greater than many upon the earth. And Satan shall give unto him many opportunities, and shall tempt him to follow his plan of happiness and become his servant, and receive the blessings that come from following his plan.

72 And he shall experience much tribulation and sorrow because of the wickedness of the people of the earth, and also by the misuse of his own free agency, which he shall use to shrink from the calling that he shall receive from the Lord.

73 Nevertheless, in the end, even at the time that the Lord hath appointed that these things shall come forth to the world, Christopher shall be taken from the refining fire from which he hath been cast and prepared, and he shall be ready and not afraid, and he shall do all things that he is commanded pertaining to this work.

74 And the Lord shall bless him with righteousness and wisdom and much knowledge of those things that are necessary for the children of men to know for their happiness and their salvation in the latter days.

75 Nevertheless, he shall be as harmless as a dove, and shall love all men, and seek for the good of his neighbor, never harming another as they would harm him, even as he shall be harmed by them.

76 And he shall hide among the Gentiles that he might not be discovered and made known to the world until the own due time of the Lord. And when he shall make himself known, there shall be many who are wicked who shall hate him and persecute him and lay a snare for him that they might show unto the world that he cannot be a prophet of God.

77 But his testimony shall stand in that which he shall translate from these plates, even the words that I am writing unto you at this time.

78 And there shall be no man who can deny the power of the things which he shall bring forth unto the world that have been sealed up by the command of the Father.

79 And he shall testify unto all those who seek him out and are desirous of his testimony. And he shall turn many to the words of Christ and to the happiness that cometh from following the plan of the Father.

80 And that great church which calleth itself the only true and living church of God upon the earth, shall be discovered by the people in the day that these things shall come forth. And the leaders of this church shall be old and uneasy men, who are kept alive by the blessings of Satan, and who have not the power of God within them.

81 And when the people of the latter days shall receive these things, then shall they discover their great wickedness and the many things that Satan hath caused to come forth among them.

82 Nevertheless, only the elect shall hear the voice of the Father, which shall be given unto them by the whisperings of the Holy Spirit, which shall testify unto them of the truthfulness of these things, and also of the wickedness of the world, which is under the power of Satan.

83 And many shall reject these things because these words shall testify that their riches and the desires of their hearts are evil, and that the great nation to which they have given their lives and their devotion is the seat of Satan, which perpetuateth his plan and bringeth all the earth under his power.

84 And now, I have explained unto you that a desire for the fine things of the world and the pleasure of these things are a way in which ye might tell if ye are following the plan of Lucifer or not.

85 And ye shall know that your nation and its people are following the plan of Lucifer because of their desires of these things.

86 But behold, there is another sure way in which ye might know for a surety that a nation and its people are following the plan of Lucifer. For ye shall behold that the nation of the United States shall raise up a standard to the whole world, which shall invite all the world to be like unto them, if the world is willing to do the things that they do.

87 And it shall proclaim that all people shall have the opportunity to become rich and have the fine things of the world by following its plan, which consisteth of its government and its laws.

88 And now, this is the other way that ye might know that this nation is following the plan of Lucifer, because it shall promise unto the people that which it cannot give unto them.

89 And if any nation among you hath those who are poor and who have not the means to feed themselves properly, and clothe themselves properly, and who do not have a place where they might rest, that they might call a home; yea, if any nation among you denieth its citizens the necessities of life, then ye may know of a surety that it followeth the plan of Lucifer; for the plan of the Father would not allow such things.

90 For behold, this is the greatest sin of all, even that ye do not love one another as ye would have others love you.

91 And if ye did not have food to eat, or clothes to wear, or a place to lay your head at night, would ye not want to be given the opportunity according to your abilities to have these things?

92 And now, this is where Lucifer made his greatest error of judgment when he considered the plan that he would offer unto us as an alternative plan than the plan of the Father.

93 For he did not take into account that we are all different in our own desires of happiness, and that to some of us, working according to the way in which we are required to work to obtain the fine things of the world, or even to support our own lives, is not that which bringeth happiness unto us.

94 But Lucifer sought to require these things from all of us. Yea, it was his desire to force us to live according to the principles and the commandments of the Celestial kingdom, so that we could all have that glory and partake of the exceeding power and glory of a God.

95 And if we did not want to follow his plan and become a God, as he wanted for us all, then he thought that we should not be, or that we should not be allowed to inherit any kingdom of glory, where we would be blessed for something that we did not deserve, or that we did not earn.

96 And he established his plan to compensate a man for his knowledge and his willingness to abide by the principles of his plan, which were given that each man might get power and glory and have all the riches of the world.

97 And this plan is contrary to the plan of the Father, which alloweth the full effect of our free agency and rewardeth us according to our desires of happiness, we, having been created by Him for this end.

98 And I have already explained unto you in this record the way that the Father expecteth us to be. Behold, He doth not care if we are desirous all the days of our lives to be beggars and sit at the gate of the rich begging for the crumbs that might fall from their tables.

99 Yea, he doth not care if our happiness is gained by having all things provided for us without our putting forth a concerted effort to obtain these things.

100 Behold, the Father hath caused that some of our brothers and sisters come down upon this earth and give unto us an example of these types

of His children, which He loveth, and who have already proven themselves worthy of His kingdom and the glory that they have chosen for themselves to bring them happiness.

101 And many of these spirits shall come into mortality in the flesh and shall not have the capability to seek after the things of the world, nor care for themselves.

102 And in the beginning, they shall be like unto the rest of the children of men, but their bodies shall grow into their spirits, instead of their spirits growing into their bodies.

103 And they shall all have an appearance that is similar in the physical nature of their bodies of flesh, indicating that they have been blessed by the Father as an example to show unto us the purpose of His plan for our eternal happiness.

104 And these shall not be able to exist upon the earth without their wants and their needs being provided for by others. And they shall be those upon whom Satan shall have no effect, for he cannot tempt them.

105 And now, these are they which are the true children of God and are following His plan in all things.

106 And now, I ask of you in the latter days, do these suffer unhappiness, except it be the unhappiness that ye cause them because of your mistreatment of them? Yet, even when ye mistreat them, do they judge you or mistreat you and cause misery to come upon you?

107 Behold, these do not suffer unhappiness, but are blessed by the Father and given unto us as an example of the purity of the souls of those who would enter into His kingdom.

108 And ye who follow the plan of Lucifer shall look upon these as incompetents and retarded in their progression, they not having the capacity or the ability to desire the things of the earth as ye do, for they shall be satisfied with the food that ye give unto them.

109 And they shall not concern themselves with the clothes that they wear, but only if ye teach them these things shall it matter unto them. And they shall not understand the significance of money, for it shall make no sense unto them, they being pure souls unable to be tempted in this way by Satan.

110 And now, this is the way that ye might know that ye are following the plan of Lucifer. For if ye find your happiness in seeking for the things of the world, and when ye find these things, the joy that accompanieth these things is only temporary, after which ye are forced to search for more of these things which provideth for you this temporary joy; and if ye need to use other means to relieve you of your misery, which is caused because of the temporary joy that hath ended, then ye shall know of a surety that ye follow the plan of Lucifer.

111 And if ye have any among you that ye do not feed, and clothe, and house, and ye judgeth them because they do not desire the things of the world as ye do, then ye shall also know that ye are the children of Satan and follow his plan.

CHAPTER 84

The discovery and formation of the United States as the seat of Satan. War is further condemned as the wickedness of political leaders. The American Indians are gentle and peaceful at first because of the teachings of the three Nephites, who are named. Christopher Columbus was not the man mentioned by Nephi in the Book of Mormon.

AND now, I shall return once again to the beginning of the nation which shall be known as the United States of America, and show unto those of you who shall receive these things, which have been sealed, the easy way that Satan shall have convincing power over the hearts and minds of all the people of the earth, convincing them that his plan is more righteous than the eternal plan of the Father.

2 And now, the United States shall not be the only nation upon the earth that shall follow after the plan of Lucifer, for all nations shall be under his power. But this nation shall become the most powerful nation among all the nations of the earth, and its influence shall be felt in all parts of the earth because of the beast and the foundation of the number of its name that shall be set up in the latter days in this great nation.

3 And all the economies that shall be set by all

the nations of the world shall be affected by this beast; and nothing that shall be done in the world regarding the monetary affairs among the children of men shall be done without the consideration and control of this beast, who shall be the fiduciary of the number of the beast throughout the whole world.

4 And now, it is easier for Satan to concentrate upon one nation and bring it under his control than it is for him to control all the nations of the earth in all things.

5 For behold, those in the spirit world who follow Satan and his plan are a finite number of souls whose works, according to the inspiration that they can give unto the children of men in mortality, can be better used on a small nation of people who are desirous to follow Satan, than they can be used on a nation of many people.

6 Nevertheless, it doth not take a large nation to control the rest of the world, but it taketh a powerful nation. And this power is in the strength of a nation, or in its ability to kill others, or defend itself by force from another.

7 Behold, in all the kingdoms of Satan, the means of force, which is concentrated in its armies and its navies and in any organization that it createth to wage the sin of war, shall always be a measure of its power.

8 But a nation under God attributeth its power to the righteousness and the peace and the happiness that is found among its people. Yea, nowhere in a nation under God can there be found weapons of warfare, for they shall not exist.

9 And for this reason it hath been written that when the Lord cometh in the glory of the Father to establish His kingdom upon the earth, it is written, saying: And many people shall go and say, Come ye, and let us go up to the mountain of the Lord, to the house of the God of Jacob; and he will teach us of his ways, and we will walk in his paths; for out of Zion shall go forth the law, and the word of the Lord from Jerusalem.

10 And he shall judge among the nations, and shall rebuke many people; and they shall beat their swords into plowshares, and their spears into pruninghooks; and nation shall not lift up sword against nation, neither shall they learn war any more.

11 And now, this is the plan of the Father; yea, this is what the Lord shall teach, even the sharp sword with two edges that proceedeth forth out of his mouth, which are his ways and his paths that he would have the children of men follow according to the eternal plan of the Father that shall give unto them happiness.

12 And many of the wicked in the latter days shall believe that it is necessary that they build up a great means of force and strength that they might protect their nation from other nations that might come upon them.

13 Now, this thing is that which Satan would have them believe so that he might have the means of force to conquer any who come against him, and that he might put down any usurpations of his power and authority throughout the earth.

14 And in the latter days, the United States of America shall be the most powerful nation upon the earth. And it shall also be the most wicked because it followeth in every way the plan of Lucifer and persecuteth those who would follow the plan of the Father, even those who would sue for peace and righteousness throughout the earth.

15 For it shall come to pass, that all those who rise up against this great nation shall be subdued by its great armies and navies and means of force.

16 Even those who are its citizens who sue for peace, and who petition the government against war, shall be overcome by the passions of the wicked who think that the killing of their brothers and sisters of other nations is justifiable to save their own lives.

17 And this great patriotism shall blind the minds and harden the hearts of the citizens of this nation. And it shall come to pass that they shall put their trust in their leaders and cast out from among them all those who speak against its power and its glory.

18 And there shall be exceedingly powerful advancements in the weaponry of war of this nation, and its power shall be glorified by these great weapons, which have been built to murder through war any that speak against the beast.

19 And the leaders of this nation shall take pride in their weapons of war, and their names

shall adorn them, and the people shall worship their leaders whose names shall adorn these great machineries of death that they shall cause to be built up among them.

20 And woe unto the leaders who have been sanctioned by the beast to stand among the people and gain their trust, and who use this trust to wage war against the children of God; yea, ye shall be in a state of exceeding torment and misery as ye watch from the spirit world, and witness the great destruction of your brothers and sisters, as the weapons which bear your names destroy them, and maim them, and blind them, and cause all manner of destruction to them.

21 And in your names shall these great weapons go forth and cause great turmoil throughout the earth. And they shall be the cause of many widows and orphans, and homelessness, and poverty and all manner of affliction among the children of men throughout the world; for in your ignorance, ye worship the beast, and ye destroy in the name of Satan.

22 And ye shall fulfill the prophecy of John in which he hath described you as a great beast who hath two horns like a lamb, and speaketh as a dragon.

23 For ye shall pretend that the wars that ye wage are wars for the sake of peace and righteousness, like unto a lamb, who is gentle in nature, but possesses its horns only to dissuade its enemies from harming it, thinking that these horns, which are on the head of the lamb, can inflict pain if it were attacked.

24 But ye are the beast, and speaketh by the mouth of Satan, which is the dragon; and all the wars that ye shall wage in the latter days shall be wars to protect your riches and those things which ye have received from Satan, because ye worship him and follow his broad way.

25 And all of your leaders and your politicians shall be from those who are rich, whose interests are served by the wars that they shall wage to destroy the other nations of the earth.

26 And woe unto all those of you who support your leaders in the spread of war and misery throughout the earth, because ye think in your hearts that ye are more righteous than the rest of the world.

27 Behold, the Father loveth all of His children throughout the whole earth; and hath he not commanded you to love one another and do unto them what ye would have them do unto you?

28 And what say ye if one of your neighbors, who is much stronger than you, cometh into your house and commandeth of you that ye worship as he worshippeth, and that ye follow in his ways, because he believeth that his ways are more righteous, and that your ways are wicked; and that if ye are left to pursue your ways without his intervention, then ye will destroy his righteousness and cause his children to suffer?

29 Yea, what say ye if he cometh into your house with his great weapons and subdueth you because ye cannot stand against his strength and power? Would ye think that this neighbor is righteous? Would ye do this to your neighbor?

30 And what of the great commandment of the Father that ye should love your enemies and do good to them that hate you and persecute you and despitefully use you, that ye may all be the same children of the one and only true God of heaven and earth, who is your Eternal Father? Do ye not understand this commandment and realize that He hath given this commandment unto you for your happiness?

31 Behold, it shall come to pass that your pride and your arrogance and your hate for your enemies shall be the means of your own destruction in the latter days.

32 And when ye should have been constructing houses, and gardens, and naming these things after your leaders, which would do good unto the people of the world and would not destroy them; yea, instead of doing these things, ye shall be destroying the fathers and mothers, and the sisters and the brothers, the uncles and the aunts of your enemies.

33 And when ye have destroyed them, then their sons and daughters, and their sisters and brothers, and their nieces and nephews shall rise up against you and hate you.

34 And because ye are more powerful than they shall be, they shall not come up against you in open, but shall come in among you in those parts of your society that are weak and vulnerable to their attacks.

35 And in spite of your technology and your

great weapons of destruction, in their vengeance they shall begin to kill your children, and your brothers and your sisters, and your loved ones.

36 And now, do ye not know that I have seen the same thing pass among my own people, the Nephites? Do ye not know that I not only speak these things as a prophecy concerning you, but that I speak these things from my own experience?

37 Behold, the Nephite people were a great nation, and they had pride in their nation and in their leaders who led them into war against the Lamanites, who they looked upon as their enemies.

38 And now, if a leader would go to war with another nation, then this leader should send forth his own children to fight for the peace which he supposeth justifieth this war.

39 For behold, my father hath sent me forth to fight the Lamanites, and he hath given up his own life fighting, not for the sake of righteousness, but so that he could live another day. For at the present time, the Nephites are not righteous, and we have no hope in the war which we have waged against the Lamanites.

40 And if a leader is not willing to send forth his own sons and daughters and sacrifice them to fight a war that he hath decided to pursue, then why should the poor and those who give unto him his power be required to fight in this war for him?

41 And ye can know for a surety the righteous desires of any leader to wage war on another people, if that same leader is willing to sacrifice his own sons and daughters, even his own life to fight the war that he hath caused.

42 And ye of the latter days should require this thing of any leader who goeth forth to war and bringeth under conscription your sons and daughters that they might die for his cause.

43 And your wars shall not be righteous wars, but wars that are set up to protect the blessings that ye shall receive from Satan, who is the god in whom ye shall trust to fight your wars for you.

44 And after my own people, the Nephites, began to set their hearts upon the fine things of the world and the glories and honors of men, they began to follow the plan of Lucifer, which requireth them that they raise up a means of force to protect their riches and their families from their enemies.

45 And ye have the history of my people in the record that the Lord hath already caused to come forth among you. And if ye have read the record of my father, then ye would know of the many wars and the misery that my people have brought upon themselves because of their wickedness.

46 And now, this is the exact reason why my father was commanded by the Lord to include so much concerning these wars among the Nephites and the Lamanites, so that ye might learn from the mistakes that they have made.

47 And it shall come to pass that after all the Nephites are destroyed, the Lamanites shall have many wars among them for a time. But after many years, they shall learn peace again, and turn to the traditions of their fathers in the things that brought unto their fathers the peace and happiness of the Lord.

48 And they shall not have the Spirit to guide them in these things, but they shall be guided by the light of Christ which is given to all the children of men throughout the whole earth.

49 And with the light of Christ, the Lamanites shall become once again a very peaceful and good-natured people who shall find much joy and harmony in following the light of Christ which helpeth them to know those things that bring them happiness, and also those things which bring them misery.

50 And it shall come to pass that after many years of wars among them, they shall divide themselves upon the land according to their families and their tribes; and their economy shall not be based upon gold and silver, for these things shall come to mean nothing to them, as they were in the beginning in the time of Adam.

51 And they shall learn to take from the earth only that which they need to sustain their lives. And they shall see that living in harmony with nature shall eliminate much of the misery that their fathers experienced because they would not live in this way.

52 And they shall come to an understanding that the family unit doth not bring peace and happiness, but that all should love each other and treat all as brothers and sisters.

53 Now I have explained unto you previously that the Father commanded that His Spirit be withheld from the earth during the periods in between the time, and times, and half of time, and that no prophets would be called to go forth among the people at these times.

54 But He did not command that there should not be righteousness among men, if there were those among them who understood the plan of the Father and lived by His commandments.

55 And after the Lamanites shall began to once again live in peace one with another; and when they shall put down their weapons of war and make covenants among themselves that they will not go to war again and take the life of another for any reason; yea, at this time, Timothy and Mathoni, and Mathonihah shall go forth upon the land among them and begin to preach the gospel of Jesus Christ once again unto the people.

56 Now, if they did not preach unto this people how would ye suppose that they should be taught the things of God? Neither did they do anything contrary to the will of the Father, during the time in between the times and half of time.

57 Behold, they shall teach the people according to their own languages and the customs that they shall establish among them, which customs are not according to the Holy Order of the Son of God.

58 And it shall be these three Nephite apostles that shall be the means whereby the Lamanites shall become once again a peaceful and loving people, who shall live upon the earth according to the commandments of God. And truly, there shall not be a more righteous and peaceful people among all the nations of the earth.

59 And it shall come to pass that Timothy shall leave the land of our fathers and cross the many seas to be among the other nations, so that he might do what he can to inspire others to use the light of Christ, which hath been in them since their birth into mortality, to find the truth, and follow the plan of the Father. And this he shall not do according to the Holy Order of the Son of God, which shall be taken from the earth at this time.

60 But Mathoni, and Mathonihah shall stay for many years among the people of the land of our fathers, which is the same land that ye call in the latter days, the Americas.

61 And it shall come to pass that as the people begin to prosper in peace and happiness, there shall arise some chief men among them who shall be influenced once again by the ways of Satan to build up great cities and highways, and these shall establish commerce that they might get gain.

62 And these Lamanites shall stay generally in the land southward, while the more peaceful of the Lamanites shall live in the land northward, and also upon the isles of the oceans that are near unto the land of the Americas, as ye shall call it.

63 And it shall come to pass that the nations of the Gentiles shall not know of the Americas until the time just before the Lord alloweth Satan to exercise his authority and power. And Satan shall be allowed to cause the nations that belong to the great and abominable church to discover the land that the Lord hath hid from them.

64 And this is one thing that Lucifer complained of to the Father, even that he did not have the finest parts of the earth in which to bring forth his plan and bring happiness to those who would follow him.

65 And for this reason, the Lord shall allow Satan to inspire the explorers of the great nations of the Gentiles to discover the land of the Americas, which is the land of my fathers.

66 And now, I have read in the words of the brother of Jared that which ye perceive is the meaning of the words of Nephi, which he wrote concerning the vision that he had of the latter days, in which he wrote, saying: And it came to pass that I looked and beheld many waters; and they divided the Gentiles from the seed of my brethren.

67 And it came to pass that the angel said unto me: Behold the wrath of God is upon the seed of thy brethren. And I looked and beheld a man among the Gentiles, who was separated from the seed of my brethren by the many waters; and I beheld the Spirit of God, that it came down and wrought upon the man; and he went forth upon the many waters, even unto the seed of my brethren, who were in the promised land.

68 And it came to pass that I beheld the Spirit of God, that it wrought upon other Gentiles; and they went forth out of captivity, upon the many waters.

69 And it came to pass that I beheld many multitudes of the Gentiles upon the land of promise; and I beheld the wrath of God, that it was upon the seed of my brethren; and they were scattered before the Gentiles and were smitten. And I beheld the Spirit of the Lord, that it was upon the Gentiles, and they did prosper and obtain the land for their inheritance; and I beheld that they were white, and exceedingly fair and beautiful, like unto my people before they were slain.

70 And it came to pass that I, Nephi, beheld that the Gentiles, who had gone forth out of captivity, did humble themselves before the Lord; and the power of the Lord was with them.

71 And I beheld that their mother Gentiles were gathered together upon the waters, and upon the land also, to battle against them. And I beheld that the power of God was with them, and also that the wrath of God was upon all those who were gathered together against them to battle.

72 And I, Nephi, beheld that the Gentiles who had gone out of captivity were delivered by the power of God out of the hands of all other nations.

73 And now, ye would believe that this man of whom Nephi hath written is the explorer that shall be known among you as a bearer of Christ, like unto the final prophet of the latter days. But this is not the man of whom the words of Nephi referreth, and this Christopher is not like unto the final of the two prophets who shall bring this record to you in the latter days.

74 For behold, this explorer shall be sent forth to discover the land of my fathers for the sole purpose to get gain for himself and those who shall send him, even one of the great nations of the Gentiles that belongeth to the great and abominable church, whose desires are the gold, and the silver, and the silks, and the scarlets, and the fine-twined linen, and the precious clothing, and the harlots.

75 And this was the only purpose of this explorer, even that he might get these things for himself and for those who shall send him.

76 And he shall come upon the land of my fathers at the time when the Lamanites shall be a peaceful and a good-natured people, who shall give freely of all that they possess; yea, they shall give of their gold and their silver and all those things which are found upon the land of promise, which shall have no value placed upon them.

77 And this explorer shall kill them in their innocence and take them in captivity back to those who sent him to get gain. And the Lamanites shall suffer exceedingly because of these things.

78 And it shall come to pass that many of the Lamanites shall throw themselves into the depths of the sea, so that they might not have to suffer death by the hand of the Gentiles who shall overcome them.

79 And in great wickedness shall the nations of the Gentiles overrun the land of the Lamanites and destroy their peace and their homes, and their righteousness.

80 And now, I ask of ye of the latter days who think that the man of whom Nephi hath written is this explorer Christopher of whom I have mentioned; yea, how can this be the man who was inspired by the Spirit of God to come across the waters and destroy the Lamanites for the want of gold and silver and the precious things of the earth, which are the desire of the great and abominable church?

81 And how is it that ye can believe this when Nephi hath written that these Gentiles who shall be wrought upon by the Holy Spirit shall come forth out of captivity?

82 Behold, this explorer Christopher did not come forth out of captivity, nor did those who followed him. Behold, they crossed the many waters because of greed and the want and desire for money and the desires of the great and abominable church. Now this is not the man of whom Nephi hath written.

83 And the captivity which Nephi hath mentioned is the captivity of the souls of the children of men by the great and abominable church which shall rise up among the Gentiles.

84 And I have already explained unto you that the Father shall not allow the Spirit to inspire the children of men until the beginning of the half of time as I have explained it unto you.

85 And this half of time shall not come to pass until a later day during the latter days than that day that the land of my fathers shall be discovered by the other nations of the Gentiles.

86 And if ye read all the words of Nephi, ye shall see that he hath written: And it came to pass that I beheld many multitudes of the Gentiles upon the land of promise.

87 Now, in the day that the people of the other nations of the Gentiles shall discover this land, there shall not be many Gentiles upon the land. And when they come upon the land they shall not be coming forth out of captivity.

88 But the things which Nephi beheld were an overview of the whole history of the nation of the United States and that which shall come to pass upon it.

89 And those who shall come forth out of captivity are those who shall come forth after this great nation shall be established as a power among all other nations of the earth.

90 And the United States shall be established as a separate nation from their mother Gentiles, or the other nations from which shall come forth many people out of the captivity that they feel holdeth them bound in their freedom to worship God according to the dictates of their own conscience.

91 For among the nations of the Gentiles, the power shall be held in the hands of the leaders of the religions established among them, who shall keep the hearts of all the children of men in the bondage of their power and their desires. And this is what Nephi meant when he said that they shall come forth out of captivity.

92 And when the United States shall begin to prosper, there shall be many upon the land who are humble and who want no part of the great and abominable church, but only want peace and happiness, which they shall expect that they shall receive under the protection of these United States.

93 And as they come forth upon the land, they shall scatter the Lamanites who remain, and who once again turned against the counsel that was given unto them, even that they shall take up arms against the Gentiles to slay them and drive them out of the land of their fathers.

94 And Nephi saw that the wrath of God was upon them because they did not do those things which were taught unto them by their fathers, who had received their instruction from the three Nephites who dwelt among them for many years.

95 And when they rebelled against the message of peace, which was testified of by the light of Christ within them, they shall be destroyed by the sword, as shall be all nations that live by the sword.

96 And this man of whom Nephi made mention was a great reformer of religion who prayed mightily unto God that he might leave the nations of the Gentiles and find a land where he could worship God according to the dictates of his own conscience, which was the light of Christ that was within him.

97 And he crossed the many waters and came unto the land of promise and began to preach that which he felt was the gospel of Christ unto the Lamanites. And this man was prepared by the Lord through the ministrations of Timothy, who had left Mathoni and Mathonihah and crossed the great oceans until he came to the land from which Lehi came in the beginning.

98 And I was about to write his name in this record, but the Spirit of the Lord hath forbidden me in this thing because of the contention that would arise because of his name and the things which he shall accomplish among the Gentiles in the land of promise in the latter days.

99 And it sufficeth me to say that this man shall not be an explorer as many of you suppose, but shall be a great reformer of religion that shall do that which shall establish a foundation of much good in the latter days.

100 And ye shall see that the rest of the words of Nephi shall be fulfilled in that which he prophesied concerning any other nation that might rise up against this great nation, that any nation that riseth up against it shall be destroyed; and this shall come to pass according to the power of God, or the knowledge that God hath allowed Satan to use to bring forth his plan in its fullness.

CHAPTER 85

The humble come from Europe to America to seek religious freedom. American government is set up to cater to the rich. Slavery is introduced as the greatest sin next to murder. The US Constitution was created by, for, and because of the rich. Latter day family values are from Satan.

FOR it shall come to pass that many of the poor and the needy and those who are persecuted in the other nations of the earth, shall flee the captivity of their souls and come forth to the land of promise.

2 And there shall be many who shall begin to humble themselves before the Father and desire the eternal happiness that is the blessing that He giveth by the fruits of the Spirit which is given unto them who follow his plan.

3 But because the plan of Lucifer alloweth those who follow it to aggrandize themselves and get gain according to each of their abilities to get gain, and also power and glory over others, the great nation that shall be established as a land of the free shall be corrupted from its beginnings.

4 And I have already mentioned in this record how the rich shall rise up and make law and policy over the poor that they might acquire more gain and more power over the people of the land.

5 And now, the rich are not the only people who shall bring forth much misery among the children of men in the latter days. Yea, before the establishment of this nation, even soon after the arrival of some Gentiles, who shall come upon the land immediately after it is discovered by their explorers, there shall be many who are pious and the hypocrites, who think of themselves as the purest of the children of God, and that their faith and their religion is the only one of God upon the earth.

6 And when a people beginneth to believe this of themselves, they become exceedingly wicked in their judgments of others. And it shall come to pass that there shall be upon this land those who profess to follow the words of Christ, but shall not do those things which he hath commanded of them, because his spirit shall not be with them.

7 For they shall persecute and cause to be killed anyone who doth not bow down to their religious leaders and abide by the precepts that these leaders shall introduce among the people.

8 And they shall cause many of the Lamanites to be killed, whose only crime unto them is their desire to be left alone and live in peace in the lands that they had inherited from their fathers. But these hypocrites shall persecute them and hate them and cause them to be destroyed by their weapons of war, which weapons shall be unlike any other weapons that the world hath ever known up until this time.

9 And these weapons shall be called flintlocks, and rifles, and all manner of guns, which by very little effort, can take the life of another by him who raiseth one of these weapons against another.

10 And with these weapons shall the Gentiles begin to destroy the Lamanites, and also all those who do not abide by the commandments and precepts taught unto them by the leaders of their churches.

11 And with these weapons, Satan shall cause to be introduced into this land the means of the greatest wickedness that one human can commit against another, except it be for murder.

12 For the Gentiles shall go into other nations of the earth and by force enslave the inhabitants of these nations that are poor as to the things of the world. And without the weapons to stand against those of the Gentiles, many souls of the children of God shall be subjected to slavery and torn away from their wives and their children and their own country and placed on great ships to be traded and bartered upon by the rich, that they might have slaves to work and to get them gain.

13 Now, this thing is most abominable before God. And the brother of Jared wrote, saying: Never in all the history of the world have I seen such brutality by the children of God against others. And the victims of this servitude crieth to the God who had created them that they should die and not be led into slavery to work in a strange land away from the nation of their births, having no hope of freedom.

14 And this great sin upon the earth caused my soul to be burdened in that I could no longer bear to witness the great wickedness of the rich in purchasing as merchandise the souls of men who they thought were beneath them.

15 And I cried unto the Lord: Oh, Lord, how canst thou suffer that these things come to pass among the children of God upon the earth? Cannot the Father show forth His omnipotence and stop this treatment of one child to another?

16 And the Lord said unto me: Behold, it is not the will of the Father that these things shall come to pass, but He hath granted all of His children their free agency to do that which they want for their own happiness.

17 And these things which thou hast beheld are those things which are most abominable before Him. Nevertheless, He shall have mercy on His children, even those who shall be held in slavery by their brothers and sisters, even that they shall be strong in spirit and shall rise up in power one day according as they have been cast down to be trodden upon by the foot of man.

18 Fear not for their souls, for they are children of the Father and He hath prepared a place for them. And He alloweth these things that His children might understand that which is capable of coming to pass when they follow the plan that Lucifer hath outlined for them.

19 For behold, none of the blessings of happiness that Lucifer hath promised unto those who follow him shall come without another being taken advantage of in some way.

20 And all these miseries shall be upon the heads of the rich and the powerful, as thou art about to observe in vision concerning those things of the latter days.

21 And now, I, Moroni, also have great cause to sorrow because of those things which I have read concerning these things which shall come to pass among the Lamanites, and also among the people of a dark skin who shall be brought into this promised land in chains that they might serve the lusts and the greed of the rich.

22 And these are not the only ones who shall suffer at the hands of the rich, but there shall be many poor who shall suffer in their poverty in the other nations of the European Empire, and these shall be desirous to come into this land and partake of the freedom that shall be promised to them.

23 But they shall sign over their lives to the rich, and subject themselves to indenturement, which shall endure for many of the good years of their lives. And these who are thus indentured shall also be bought and sold as the property of the rich, who shall justify their abuse and wickedness by declaring that they are the more righteous lot of the creations of God because of their knowledge and their seemingly endless blessings from God—and thus it shall be because Satan is their God.

24 And when any of these shall rise up in defiance of their mistreatment by the hands of their masters, they shall be killed by the guns that the rich shall have among them in abundance, whether of their own person, or by the command of the government that hath sworn to protect them.

25 And there shall be no man that shall stand against the fire of a gun in the latter days, for these weapons shall cut the flesh and destroy anything within its path.

26 And it shall come to pass that as the rich grow in their abundance, the poor also shall grow and become more numerous than the rich. And if these poor rise up against the rich, then they shall be deterred in their desires for their lives by the weaponry of the armies that are hired and controlled by the rich, which are mandated by the judicial system of their government.

27 And when they cannot justify their murders of the poor and their servants, they shall cause prisons to be built up that they might enclose the passions for freedom of the poor within, and that they might subdue the desires of the poor to go against the laws of the land which shall be established for the rich, by the rich, and because of the rich.

28 And it shall come to pass that because of the rebellions of the poor who shall be among them, many of the rich shall band together and desire to form a nation, which shall be a symbol of their power wherein they can establish laws so that they can control the uprisings and the profits and the political power of the poor, who are the majority.

29 Yea, these rich men, who ye of the latter days honor and call the founding fathers of your nation, shall create among you a national system of ways in which they might maintain their riches and also maintain their power over the poor.

30 And with this power that they shall have over the hearts of the poor, whom they have deceived with their pretended illusions of freedom and prosperity that they shall create for the poor, the rich shall engage in war against any who oppose them.

31 And in this way the captains of their armies shall gain the glory that they desire by the blood of their soldiers, which are from the families of those who are poor.

32 And the great merchants of the earth shall rise up and increase their wealth as the souls of men are enslaved further under their power. In fine, the fruits of the plan of Lucifer shall begin to show forth even at the beginning of your nation.

33 And it shall come to pass that the rich shall call upon those of their class who are great orators and who are skilled at using great words which shall deceive the people and hypnotize them and bring them under the power of their desires.

34 And this shall be the great purpose for the patriotism of a nation as I have explained it unto you previously in this record.

35 And the poor shall be led to believe, that if they support the policies and the laws of the rich, then they, too, might become rich by these same policies and laws.

36 And because of their envy and their own greed, the poor shall allow themselves to be persuaded by the cunningness of the politicians who shall be selected from among them, who are already rich, very much like unto the Romans at the beginning of their government.

37 And it shall come to pass that those who shall be the leaders among the rich at the beginning of this great nation shall convince the poor, who are the majority among them, that all of their problems are because of the mother nation, which is that great European Empire that requireth taxes from the people without representing their interests across the great oceans.

38 And this plan they shall devise to deceive the poor into taking up arms against their own government, so that the rich might control the revenue of taxes themselves, thus bringing their own laws and policies more in line with their own personal wealth and gain.

39 And thus it shall be, as these men, whom ye of the latter days have honored with great glory, set up the seat of Satan of the latter days.

40 And it shall come to pass that with their cunningness and their expertise in deceiving those who cannot read, and are generally the poor among them, the rich shall produce a declaration of independence from the mother nation that requireth a tax of their riches.

41 And this declaration shall further deceive the poor into thinking that the rich care for them and look out for their best interests, and that the rich are only doing what is good for all in equality.

42 And it shall come to pass that by the blood of the poor, the rich merchants of the United States shall establish themselves as a great nation.

43 And with the continued flattery and admonitions of their politicians, the rich shall continue to rule and wield great power over the poor.

44 And the poor shall be convinced that this new form of government is wise and inspired by God, so that liberty and justice for all might come to pass.

45 And there shall be liberty and justice; yea, but not for all. For the enslaved, and the poor, and all the women of this nation shall have no voice in the government of the people.

46 And they shall establish a constitution which shall offer the people the opportunity to observe the actions of these politics in service to all. And a democracy shall come forth in which all might have a voice in the way in which they are governed, except it be for the poor, and the enslaved, and the women.

47 And after many years a voice shall be given unto all the citizens of this great nation, that they might feel in their hearts that they are a part of the government that shall create the laws that shall govern them and control their lives.

48 And ye of the latter days shall be continually deceived by those who are your leaders, and ye shall not notice the ways in which Satan shall take control over you and bind you with the chains of iniquity.

49 And ye shall begin to wonder of what cause is your wickedness before the Lord. And have I not been plain in my words? Have I not given unto you in plainness the reasons for your great wickedness? Yea, doth not this record cry forth unto you in plainness, that ye should not be deceived and wonder any longer?

50 Yea, your family units are the beginning of your wickedness before the Lord. And I have already shown unto you the great wickedness that can arise by separating yourselves into these family units and forgetting to love your neighbors and doing unto them what ye would do unto the members of your own family.

51 And because of your love of your families, ye shall seek for the riches of the earth to give unto them that their lives might be easy and blessed with happiness, as ye suppose.

52 And as ye seek for that which will sustain your families, ye suffer the poor and the needy and those whom ye have caused to be imprisoned because of your families and your desires for riches, to pass by you that ye notice them not because ye are concentrating on your own family.

53 And ye want your own family to be protected; therefore, ye shall support your governments in their wars that are waged against the families of other nations, who also are children of the same God as ye all are.

54 And ye shall justify the righteousness of your wars against them, because ye are led to believe that they are a threat to your own family.

55 And if ye followed the plan of God, then ye would realize that these other nations are of your family, and therefore, ye would not take up arms against them to destroy them. And your wickedness before the Lord doth not end with your families, but it beginneth with your families.

56 And because ye have isolated your children away from the rest of their brothers and sisters, which are all the children of God, they shall begin to believe that they are a special people and that they deserve to be treated better than those who are not of their own family.

57 And they shall seek for the things of this world, which ye have taught them shall give unto them the happiness that they desire. And they shall not care for another if he should die; yea, if the death of a brother or sister in God doth not affect their lives and their happiness, then they shall not take notice of this death.

58 But if a member of their own family should die, then they shall suffer in misery and sorrow for the loss that they suppose hath affected their own happiness.

59 And now, it is in acquiring the things of the world that the children of men shall cause the most sin among them. For it shall come to pass that the people of the United States shall have an abundance of all that which they desire.

60 And they, being a small number of people in comparison with the rest of the other nations of the world, shall consume upon their lusts and greed more than all other nations.

61 And when they shall sit down at their tables and partake of the food that they eat, they shall take no thought of him who made possible the food that they eat, even that which they need to live.

62 For the poor among you shall work in the fields under the heat of the torrid sun and harvest that which ye need for your nourishment.

63 And then these poor shall return to their houses after working all the hours of the day trying to provide for their own sustenance by the wages that ye shall pay them to harvest the food for your own bellies.

64 And their houses shall not be like unto your own, but shall be of a poor construction, because of their inability to earn that which they would need to have a house like unto yours, because ye have kept back from their wages that which would give unto them of these things.

65 And ye shall think of them as those that do not deserve that which ye are blessed with because of their words, or the lack of the knowledge that they would need to be one who deserveth to sit at a table made of the fine things of the earth, even as a rich man who laboreth not for that which he eateth.

66 Behold, how many of you of the latter days

are willing to labor in all the hours of a day in the heat of the sun to obtain the food that ye need to sustain your lives?

67 I say unto you that none of you who are rich shall have a desire to do this thing, but thinketh that this type of work is below the dignity that ye have supposed for yourselves.

68 But I say unto you, when the Lord cometh in the glory of the Father, he shall employ himself as a laborer in the fields amongst those who are his friends and whom he loveth because of their humility and love for him.

69 And these are those of whom he hath spoken when he said that the poor, and the meek, and the lowly of heart shall inherit the earth and sit in the houses that are left desolate by the rich, even those of you who would not labor by the sweat of your own brow to provide your own table with those things that ye would eat.

70 And now, there shall be many of you who shall read these things and shall think in your hearts that ye do another type of work that is important to the world, instead of working in the fields to produce the food that ye do eat.

71 But I say unto you, of what importance is the work that ye do? Do ye do anything that produceth that which ye need to sustain your lives, even that which can feed you, or clothe you, or provide you with a shelter from the natural elements of the world?

72 I say unto you that ye do not employ yourselves in any of these things that would sustain your lives. And if ye were to do one of these things, then ye would not be rich, for ye would not have the glory and honor of men, which is that which ye would need to be given of those things that have made you rich.

73 For it shall come to pass that this great beast of the latter days shall place a value upon all aspects of the lives of the children of men.

74 And there shall be a value placed upon all the things of the earth, even a value that shall be determined by the merchants and the leaders who shall fornicate lavishly with the whore of the latter days.

75 And this great beast of which John hath given you an example in his words, which ye have among you in the Bible, and also of which I have given you an explanation, shall set a value upon the whole world because of the wickedness that shall issue forth from its mouth.

76 And this great beast of the latter days, of which John hath written, shall begin to prosper and spread its borders throughout the entire land of my fathers, and Satan shall begin to introduce many powers of the eternal laws of nature into the minds of those men who shall take these powers and control them for their own gain.

CHAPTER 86

Great inventions and technological advancements are established by Satan to control the world and institute his plan in its fullness. Most of the advancements come from the desires of the United States. The world lies under great sin because of these advancements.

AND now, there shall be much confusion in the latter days because of these blessings which Satan shall give unto those who follow his plan; or rather, there shall be much confusion because of the power of nature that Satan shall use to institute the giving of his blessings to those who follow him.

2 Behold, it is the design of the plan of Lucifer to make the days of our probation easy and labor free, so that we might partake of his blessings without toil or labor, enjoying the fruits that he provideth for us by following his plan.

3 Now, in this thing Satan hath used some principles of the plan of the Father in his own plan. For the Father hath also promised that in His kingdoms, there shall be no more toil or labor, and that all shall enjoy the eternal blessings of peace and happiness forever.

4 Nevertheless, it shall be shown unto you that the plan of Lucifer shall fail miserably in his promises of providing eternal peace and happiness as we have been promised by the Father

5 And in the latter days Satan shall be given power over his own dominions at the beginning of the half of times. Nevertheless, the Lord shall keep him bound for a short time at the beginning so that he can allow Joseph, the first of these last latter day prophets, to set up a church according to the desires of Joseph, and this the Lord shall suffer so that his words shall be fulfilled regarding the Gentiles.

6 For the Gentiles shall have the same opportunity to live by the gospel of Jesus Christ as did the Jews and those other Gentiles who were taught the gospel by the twelve apostles who were with Christ during the days of his ministry.

7 And the Gentiles of the last days shall reject the fullness of his gospel just as the Jews did, who were the first, thus fulfilling the word of the Lord when he said that the first shall be last, and the last shall be first, both receiving an equal opportunity in all things.

8 And it shall come to pass that after this church shall be established by Joseph in the latter days; and after the Gentiles have rejected the fullness of this gospel, then shall Satan have complete power over his own dominions according to the words given by the Lord to Joseph in which he said:

9 And again, verily I say unto you, Oh, inhabitants of the earth: I the Lord am willing to make these things known unto all flesh; for I am no respecter of persons, and will that all men shall know that the day speedily cometh; the hour is not yet, but is nigh at hand, when peace shall be taken from the earth, and the devil shall have power over his own dominion.

10 And also the Lord shall have power over his saints, and shall reign in their midst, and shall come down in judgment upon Idumea, or the world.

11 And now, my brothers and sisters of the latter days, I would that ye should find the date when this revelation and these words of the Lord are given unto Joseph. Yea, ye shall see that they shall be given unto him after he hath established the church of God for the last time upon the earth.

12 And ye shall see that Satan hath not yet, at that time, been released to have complete power over his own dominions according to the words of the Lord.

13 And if ye know this time, ye shall also realize that up until this time throughout the history of the children of men, very little progress was made in the advancements of science and technology, even in the understanding of the powers of nature and how to control these powers in mortality.

14 Nevertheless, after Satan shall be released from the restrictions that the Father hath placed upon him concerning these things; yea, even shortly after the fullness of the gospel shall be once again taken from off the face of the earth after the death of Joseph, then shall great advancements in science and technology be made throughout the whole earth, but more especially among the people who live in the United States, which Satan hath chosen for himself to set up his final kingdom and in which he shall establish his seat.

15 And then when he hath established his seat, and after the restrictions that were placed upon him by the Father have been lifted, then shall he begin to introduce these exceedingly miraculous advancements in science and technology that shall revolutionize the manner of living throughout the whole earth; yea, but in the beginning, only among those of the earth who are rich.

16 For the purpose of introducing these miracles among the children of men, is so that their lives might be more easily lived, and that they might pursue the selfish desires of their own happiness, without laboring so tediously by the sweat of their own brows as they were commanded by the Lord in the beginning.

17 And ye shall know from this record that this hath been the plan of Lucifer from the beginning, even the power and the blessings that he hath given unto the rich and powerful who have followed his plan and have been given their rewards for following him.

18 And one of these blessings is the easiness and leisure of life which the rich enjoy in all things. Nevertheless, the manner of life of the rich, since the beginning until the time that Satan shall have the restrictions of the Father lifted from him, is not as easy and as leisurely as the life that they shall lead in the latter days when Satan shall show forth his power by using the miracles of science and technology to reward those who follow him.

19 And since the beginning, there have been

many men who have known of the laws of nature and who have introduced some of their knowledge of these laws among the children of men. And Satan hath also inspired many men since the beginning with the same knowledge that the prophets of God receive through the ministrations of the Holy Spirit.

20 Nevertheless, the prophets of God do not reveal any of these things to the world, for they are forbidden to by the Lord, as I have explained it unto you previously in this record.

21 But those who follow Satan know nothing of the things of God and do not understand that which can take place upon the earth when these eternal laws of nature are misused in unrighteousness.

22 For this reason, even though there were many who understood the nature of these laws, none were given the ability to use this knowledge to control the power of these laws. And it is the power to use these eternal laws from which the Father had restricted Satan until the latter days.

23 For the Father knew that once a knowledge of this power was given to the world, then it would be used in unrighteousness by those who follow the plan of Lucifer, which plan offereth all of the powers of God to any who follow him.

24 And I have already explained unto you that when the wicked use these powers for their own purposes, which are the purposes that Satan would allow them according to his plan, then great misery and destruction shall come upon the earth.

25 And if these powers are left unchecked by righteousness, they would soon destroy the earth, which the Father hath created to bring happiness to His children, not the misery that they shall suffer by the misuse of these laws.

26 And it shall come to pass in the latter days, when the Father shall no longer hold him bound, that Satan shall have no further restrictions upon him, and he shall begin to use this power to reward them that follow him.

27 And in that day that he shall begin to rage in the hearts of the children of men and have power over them, there shall be many who shall introduce into the world their inventions, and their ideas, and their contraptions which shall use the laws of nature to do the bidding of Satan in all things.

28 For these things, which shall be introduced by the power of Satan, shall be used by those who have invented them and introduced them into the world to get gain and to become rich. And much of the inspiration that they shall receive in inventing these things shall come from their desire to not work by the sweat of their own brow and perform manual labor all the days of their lives.

29 And now, the Father gave the commandment to Adam and Eve that they should work and eat by the sweat of their brow all the days of their lives for a righteous purpose. And this purpose was so that we might learn through experience how glorious and wonderful His kingdoms of glory shall be unto us when we inherit them and do not have to work therein to sustain our lives.

30 And we saw these eternal worlds as spirit children of the Father; but as spirit children who did not have the knowledge of good and evil, or the knowledge that the Father possesseth, we could not understand how glorious these kingdoms are.

31 For this reason we are placed upon this earth to pass through the days of mortality and experience labor and toil, and sweat and languor, so that we might appreciate and be happy with all that the Father hath provided for us in His kingdoms.

32 And now, this is where Lucifer disagreed with the Father in the beginning and then presented his own plan, in which we would not have to suffer these things during mortality. And because of the plan that he presented to us, many of our brothers and sisters accepted it as a righteous plan, believing that it would ultimately bring eternal happiness to those who follow him according to the promises that Lucifer made unto them.

33 And it is this plan that many have followed upon this earth during the days of their probation. And these are the rich and the powerful who have set themselves up above all others, and who have enslaved others to labor by the sweat of their brows, so that these do not have to labor and become languorous.

34 Now, herein is the greatest problem with the plan of Lucifer compared in point with the plan of the Father. Behold, in the plan of Lucifer, only a few can have the riches and the glory and the power, and they shall be given glory and power over others because of what they perceive as being their righteous desires, which are the righteous desires of Lucifer and not the desires of the Father.

35 Behold, according to the plan of the Father, all are created equal and none is set up above another. And those who have the knowledge and power of the Gods, shall be servants to those who do not have this power.

36 And those who have this great eternal power, have been given this power only that they might serve others and provide them with the happiness that the Father hath promised to all of His children who choose Him as their God and follow the plan that He hath outlined for them.

37 But according to the plan of Lucifer, this power is given to all without regard to their righteous natures, or the desires of their hearts, whether these desires only serve their own selfish interests or not.

38 And according to his plan: in order for us to have this great power, it becometh a necessity that there are others who are our servants, or who do not have this power and authority, but shall remain servants to the gods of Lucifer forever.

39 Now, this is the great difference between the plan of the Father and the plan of Lucifer. For the plan of the Father maketh servants of those who have the power, of an Eternal God, and the plan of Lucifer maketh servants for those who have this same power.

40 And it is also a part of the plan of Lucifer that there shall never be suffering, nor shall there be a commandment of labor like unto the commandment that was given to Adam and Eve in the beginning.

41 And it is because of the inexperience of Lucifer that caused him to rebel against the Father and cause others to follow him in his rebellion of the plan of God.

42 And the Father knew that the only way that He could prove that His plan was the most righteous plan, yea, even the only plan that can be followed to find eternal happiness, is if He allowed Satan to be upon the earth and incorporate all aspects of his plan among the children of men.

43 And it shall come to pass that ye of the latter days shall see the fruits of the plan of Lucifer. Yea, ye shall see the nations of the earth lust after the blessings of Satan that come from following his plan.

44 And ye shall think that ye are happy following this plan, but in this ye are deceived, for ye know that ye are not happy. Yea, ye receive the temporary happiness of your fruits, but ye do not receive the eternal happiness that lasteth forever, which is the happiness that the Father hath promised unto you.

45 And it shall come to pass that the people of the United States shall raise up their standard of living above all other standards throughout the world. And they shall have an abundance of all the fine things of the world. And Satan shall begin to introduce his ideas into this great society and he shall be their god.

46 And to mock the plan of the Father, yea, even to show forth his power among the people of the United States in the latter days, Satan shall cause that they shall inscribe upon their money the words: In God We Trust.

47 And I have already explained this unto you that they shall trust in their money above anything else upon the earth.

48 And because of the miracles of their technology and their sciences, many of the people of the United States shall not know what it is to sweat by their own brow to sustain their lives, but they shall spend all the days of their lives in pursuit of money and the fine things of the world and the honors and glories that they shall set upon themselves.

49 And they shall cause many wars and rumors of wars because of this standard of living that they shall establish for themselves. And their children shall abuse and dishonor their parents; and they shall desire only to have the money of their parents as their own that they might have more of the fine things of the earth without laboring with their own hands to obtain these things.

50 And in that day a man shall rise from his bed in the morning and think of that which he must do so that he can obtain more money and increase the abundance of the things that he shall already have. And he shall do whatever he can in order to get this money and increase his abundance and give unto those of his family, whom he loveth, all the things that he believeth are the blessings from God.

51 And it shall come to pass that the parents shall give all these fine things unto their children while they are young, thus teaching their children that they do not need to work by the sweat of their own brows to obtain these things, but that these things are given to them freely.

52 And because they follow the plan of Lucifer and give these things freely unto their children without requiring a sacrifice on the part of their children in obtaining these things, their children shall become dissatisfied with that which they have and shall not appreciate that which they have received of their father and their mother, believing that these things are freely given unto them without their own toil, and that these things should be expected all the days of their lives.

53 But if they would have required a sacrifice of their children, and had they not given these things freely unto them, then their children would appreciate that which they have worked for with their own hands.

54 And after they have experienced what is necessary to obtain these things, then when these things are given unto them by their parents, then shall they honor their parents and know from their own experience the sacrifice that their parents have made for them in giving these things unto them freely.

55 Now, this is the exact reason why our Father requireth us to come down into mortality and work by the sweat of our own brows and experience life without the glorious blessings that He hath prepared for us in His kingdoms.

56 Now, all these things that shall come to pass in the latter days shall come to pass in fulfillment of the words of John, which he wrote, saying: And he doeth great wonders, so that he maketh fire come down from heaven on the earth in the sight of men. And deceiveth them who dwell upon the earth by the means of those miracles which he had power to do in the sight of the beast; saying to them that dwell on the earth, that they should make an image to the beast, which had the wound by a sword, and did live.

57 And he had power to give life unto the image of the beast, that the image of the beast should both speak, and cause that as many as would not worship the image of the beast should be killed.

58 And now, this image of which John hath spoken is the standard of living that ye shall think in the latter days is the standard that should be set for all the people of the earth. And those who do not want to live by the standard that ye shall set, ye shall go forth in battle against them and slay them and cause them to bow down to your nation, which causeth that this standard be given unto all.

59 And the beast shall promise this standard unto all those who worship it. And it shall say unto all: Peace, and liberty, and justice for all. Yea, seek ye for the fine things of the world and establish yourselves by my standards and ye shall be happy as all those who follow me are happy.

60 And it shall come to pass that all the words of John shall be fulfilled in those days. Yea, even those words which condemneth the beast and the great nation of the United States upon which the beast sitteth in all of His glory.

61 For it shall come to pass that all the people of the world shall be under the great bondage of sin. And there shall be many nations upon the earth who are under the power and authority of the beast. And there shall arise many leaders who shall set themselves up above the people whom they shall lead and to whom these leaders shall cause exceeding sorrow and misery because they have set themselves up according to the will and the ways of Satan.

62 For these leaders shall seek for power and for riches; and by the flattery of their mouths shall they obtain all these things by deceiving the poor into giving these things unto them without the sweat caused by the labors of their own hands.

63 And there shall be some nations which shall rise up which shall come up to battle against the seat of Satan, or the United States, because of the power of Satan that shall be upon this seat. But these nations shall be subdued and driven back before his seat, and Satan shall overcome the whole world for many years.

64 And when the United States shall subdue all other nations upon the earth; yea, when this nation becometh the greatest and most powerful nation upon the earth, then shall the power of Satan begin to be seen among all the nations of the earth.

65 For there shall be great wickedness and deception among the people of this nation. And they shall begin to spend all the hours of the day consumed by the desire for the fine things of the earth. And they shall not be able to sleep because of them.

66 And the laws of nature shall be in great turmoil because of their inventions and the miracles of their technology which Satan shall cause to come forth among them.

67 And the love of all men shall wax cold and there shall not exist upon the earth a love for another, except it be for those who are members of their own families, or those who do those things which are acceptable in the sight of the beast.

68 And it shall come to pass that happiness shall be defined as the amount of success that one man hath over another in those things which he possesseth. And there shall be no lasting happiness upon the earth.

69 Nevertheless, Satan shall find ways to assuage the unhappiness of those who follow him. And he shall do this by misdirecting the cause of their misery. And because of his expertise in misdirecting the people according to his will, the people of the earth shall not know of themselves, neither shall they understand that they are equal, and that they are all the children of an Eternal Father in heaven who loveth them and desireth that they find the happiness which they desire.

70 For every man shall have his hero in the flesh, and every woman her heroine in the flesh, that each looketh to as an example of what each desireth to become.

71 And there shall be few among them who looketh to Christ as their example, nor shall any of them give heed to the words of Christ which would lead them to the eternal happiness that they all desire.

72 For in that day there shall be the rich and the famous, and those who are well known because of the means of the technology that shall broadcast the image of the beast upon every housetop throughout the land. And these shall present an image of their persona that others shall see and after which others shall pattern their lives.

73 And the whole earth shall begin to worship the image of the beast in such a way that they shall forget about the Father, and know not from whence they came, and by whose hand they came into being.

74 For there shall be many in the latter days who shall believe that they are learned as to the things of the world. And they shall be known as great scientists and researchers, doctors and philosophers, and athletes and actors; and all these, yea, even every one shall be under the power and control of Satan and shall do his bidding in all things.

75 And these shall turn the hearts of the children of men away from the plan of the Father and create their own plans for the people of the earth according to the plan of Lucifer which they shall follow and by which they shall be rewarded with great success.

76 And the children of men shall begin to desire to become like unto these rich and successful and shall pattern their lives after them, that they might have the happiness that they believe these enjoy.

77 And the people shall begin to fear one another; and they shall fear death also, for they shall not believe that there existeth life after the life that they shall live in mortality.

78 Yea, there shall be many who shall claim that they believe in God, and that they believe that there is life after death, but they say these things because of what they have heard in the world, and not from the testimony of the Spirit, who would teach them the truth of God in all things, if it so be that they would listen to his promptings.

79 Behold, in the last days there shall be all manner of ways in which death shall be postponed and fought against by the miracles that Satan shall introduce among you.

80 And now, if ye believe that ye have a loving Heavenly Father, do ye not also believe that He knoweth the time in which ye have been appointed to die? And if the time which hath been appointed by Him arriveth, and a man is called home by the Father, then why do ye think that it is a good thing that ye save the life of this man and fight against the will of God?

81 And I have touched upon this thing in this record, yet in the latter days, your lack of faith in the Father concerning death shall be the means of much misery and unhappiness among you.

82 Behold, ye have the words of Christ in the Bible, therefore, have ye read the words of Christ pertaining unto those who are dead? Is it not written, saying: And another of his disciples said unto him, Lord, suffer me first to go and bury my father. But Jesus said unto him, Follow me; and let the dead bury their dead.

83 Behold, ye of the latter days shall trust more in your doctors and the medicines that ye shall create by the means of the miracles that Satan shall give unto you, than ye do in the Lord, who is the giver of life and the one appointed over death.

84 Yea, ye do not have faith in the Lord, for if ye had faith in him, then ye would not suffer when one of your loved ones dieth and entereth again into the spirit world and is received therein in the love of the Father.

85 But ye do suffer because of death, and the cause of your suffering is your lack of faith. For ye do not want to know the Father and His plan of salvation for you.

86 For if ye knew of His plan, then ye would know of your great wickedness, and it would give you a cause to change the course of your lives, which course ye have chosen for yourselves as the only means of your happiness.

87 And those whose lives you save, having fought the will of the Father, shall remain among you and shall be a burden unto you. And ye shall also suffer many of them to suffer exceedingly because of the choices that ye have made for them by fighting against the will of God by keeping them in mortality when they could be enjoying peace and happiness in the spirit world.

88 Behold, I give it as my opinion that it is good that ye save your lives with your doctors and your medicines and the miracles that Satan hath provided for you. And because your lives are saved, ye have more time to repent of your wickedness and prepare yourselves better for a state of death and hell which shall accompany the wicked after death in the spirit world.

89 For ye shall give thanks to the doctors and the medicines which have saved you. Yea, there are many of you who might say that it was God who saved your life by the means of the doctors and medicines that ye have among you.

90 But I say unto you, truly it was your god who hath saved you, but it was not the Eternal Father who hath promised you eternal life and happiness, but it was the god of the world, who giveth unto you his own blessings according to your desires to serve him and keep his commandments.

91 And as ye save your lives, ye shall lose them to him who desireth to hold you captive in his chains and bind you tighter still until you are defenseless before him as he leadeth you down to destruction.

CHAPTER 87

An easy life turns a person's heart away from God's plan. Temporal immortality will be achieved in the latter days. The human race will temporarily experience the effects of living forever in sin. Moroni is burdened by the wickedness of the latter days and explains who is righteous and who is wicked.

AND now, I, Moroni, am nearing the end of this abridgment which I have been commanded by the Lord to make of the record of the brother of Jared. And as I have read the words of the brother of Jared concerning those of you in the latter days, unto whom these things shall come, my soul sorroweth exceedingly because of you.

2 Yea, my heart is exceedingly heavy because of that which hath been written concerning you by the brother of Jared. For in the vision that the Lord gave unto him, he truly saw the great wickedness of your day.

3 And he wrote many words of sorrow concerning your wickedness and the deceptions of your hearts that cover and hide the wickedness of your souls from your own consciousness.

4 And there shall be many of you who shall reject these things which I have written concerning this earth and its history from the time that the Father placed Adam and Eve upon the earth to the time that the Lord shall finish the work of the Father as it pertaineth to this earth, even when he shall present to the Father this earth and all of its habitants that have been, and all that are, and all that shall live upon the earth, to be judged by Him.

5 And now, it is expedient that ye understand that most of the people of the latter days are those who have lived before and who have died in their sins, being unable to live by the gospel and the laws of the Father that they might prepare themselves and be ready for their resurrection into the body of glory that they have chosen for themselves.

6 And there shall come a point in the history of the earth when all the spirits that need to return to the earth, so that they might be tried and tested again, shall be upon the earth, and few shall remain in the spirit world, except it be for the righteous souls who remain there under the guidance and power of the Holy Ghost, and also those who are Lucifer and his followers, who are not allowed by their own choosing to take upon them their own flesh in mortality.

7 And this shall come to pass because of the technology and the understanding of the power and laws of God that Satan shall give unto the world in the latter days.

8 For it shall come to pass that through the advancements of technology that shall be given to the children of men in those days, that their scientists shall discover the secret to the laws of heaven pertaining unto death. In other words, they shall discover the means whereby the body of man shall no longer grow old and age, thus dying from the effects of the aging flesh caused by mortality.

9 For they shall discover the knowledge of what ye shall call among you as biogenetics which is the study of the process in which life beginneth and formeth the flesh into which is placed the spirits of the children of God. And this process of life is passed down from one generation to the next reflecting the pattern of life and death that a parent passeth on to its child.

10 And now, this great power and knowledge is like unto the power of eternal resurrection which the Father shall use to give each of us the eternal body that we desire to fulfill the desires of happiness that we desire for ourselves.

11 And the Father knoweth all the eternal laws; and he shall allow Satan to introduce some of these laws into the world, so that we might see the effects of these laws upon us in unrighteousness; or in other words, so that we might see the effects when there exist wicked people who follow the plan of Lucifer and who can live forever.

12 And the technology that ye shall have shall stop the aging process of your flesh. But this aging process is not the only way that death shall come upon you in the latter days. For ye shall still die from sickness and from pestilence, and from murder, which is perpetuated by the hand of another and also by your wars, or by accidents, which shall be caused because of the technology that Satan hath introduced to you.

13 And so it shall be that ye shall develop the

ability to live forever young in the flesh. And if ye learn to obey the laws of nature that perpetuate the continual regeneration of the flesh, then ye shall also live forever without sickness and pestilence among you.

14 Nevertheless, these laws of nature ye shall know, but ye shall not live by them, choosing instead to enjoy the temporary joy that the blessings of Satan shall bring to you.

15 And because ye shall live in this state of eternal youth, as ye shall call it, ye shall not have children, and shall use the power of creation and the blessings that come with this power for your own selfish pleasures, which shall be accentuated by the temporary joy and happiness that Satan shall bless you with because ye follow his plan.

16 And in the day that ye shall be given the knowledge and power of these things by Satan, there shall be a great division among you, even a great gulf between those of you that are rich, and those of you that are poor.

17 And the rich shall begin to think highly of themselves and shall make it a law among them that the poor shall not have the power to live upon the earth with eternal youth, except it be those who are the servants of the rich and bring them the riches that they desire.

18 And it shall come to pass that the rich shall reserve the right and the power of the regeneration of the flesh for themselves, and this they shall do because they shall place an exceedingly great monetary value upon this power, which the poor in their want shall not be able to afford.

19 And the poor shall rise up against the rich and complain unto them that they should also have this power. And they shall seek redress for that which shall be held back from them through the courts of law that shall be set up among them.

20 Oh, ye fools! Do ye believe that ye shall be given redress in a court of law that is filled by and controlled by those from whom ye seek your redress? Do ye think that ye shall obtain justice from the laws that are set up to grind your faces into the dust from which ye were made poor?

21 Behold, waste not your time in anger against those who have withheld from you the power that Satan hath given unto them. But live righteously, and learn to love your neighbor and prepare yourselves for death, that ye might die and go into the spirit world prepared and ready to meet God, that ye might be received therein in a state of never ending happiness.

22 Yea, why do ye think that ye shall be happy living forever in the miseries that shall be the fruits of the plan of Lucifer, who hath given his blessings to those who follow him, and whose blessings ye go to his court to obtain through the administration of his laws?

23 Seek ye first the kingdom of God and His righteousness and ye shall not suffer in the end as those shall suffer from whom ye seek the blessings of Satan.

24 And it shall come to pass that the poor that shall not give heed unto my words, but shall continue to rise up against the rich, because they shall continue to covet the blessings of Satan that they suppose would bring happiness to them; yea, these shall suffer with the rich.

25 And in those days, the poor shall not raise up arms against the rich as hath been the case in much of the history of the earth, because of the great strength and power of the armies and the navies and the means of force which shall be under the control of the rich.

26 And the value of the life of a man shall be determined by the rich and powerful. And these shall allow the poor to reproduce and bear children that they might enslave them to work in their fields and in their mines, and in the cramped quarters of their markets, so that they might continually get gain without sweating by their own brows.

27 But the poor shall grow old and die for many years, while the rich shall enjoy the benefits, as they suppose, of this eternal youth.

28 And after a time, there shall be no more need for the poor, for the flesh of the slave shall be replaced with the technological and scientific advancements of the latter days, even with metals made from the elements of the earth, that can think for themselves and walk and move by themselves without the hand of man to guide them. And these machines shall do the work of the poor and provide the service of labor for the rich.

29 And when the poor are no longer needed by the rich to perform the menial tasks of their labors, then shall the poor be killed by the rich, or rather, they shall be allowed to die because of that which the rich shall withhold from them in that day.

30 But there shall be many poor who shall not suffer that they are destroyed. And these shall organize themselves in secret against the rich and shall be among them in disguise and in hiding.

31 And they shall begin to murder the rich from their hiding places, and take from them their medicines and their food, and all their fine things.

32 But the rich shall seek them out, and there shall be a continual war between the rich and the poor, for both shall be following the plan of Lucifer and doing his will in all things. And there shall be no peace upon the whole face of the earth.

33 Yea, there shall be a temporary peace for a time among the rich, for they shall control all things by the means of the power that Satan shall give unto them. But this shall be a temporary peace, because they shall fear the poor and those who seek to kill them, whom they shall not find in their hiding places.

34 And those days shall be like unto the days of the power of the Gadianton robbers, who were among the Nephites because of their wickedness. And my father wrote concerning them, saying: And these Gadianton robbers, who were among the Lamanites, did infest the land, insomuch that the inhabitants thereof began to hide up their treasures in the earth; and they became slippery, because the Lord had cursed the land, that they could not hold them, nor retain them again.

35 And it came to pass that there were sorceries, and witchcrafts, and magics; and the power of the evil one was wrought upon all the face of the land, even unto the fulfilling of all the words of Abinadi, and also Samuel the Lamanite.

36 And it shall come to pass in the latter days that the people of the earth shall begin to believe that they have been blessed by God with riches, and with power, and with the knowledge that they shall have to remain in their youth seemingly forever.

37 Behold, these things shall surely come to pass among you of the latter days. And when these things shall come to pass among you, yea, when ye can live forever in a youthful state, shall ye then experience eternal happiness?

38 I say unto you that ye shall not be a happy people, but ye shall be a miserable people because ye are following the plan of Lucifer in all these things. And ye shall become dependent on the things which Satan shall provide for you for the happiness that ye shall experience.

39 And the drugs, and the alcohols, and the wines, and the foods that ye shall eat to give unto you the temporary reprieve of the misery that ye shall cause to come upon yourselves; yea, is this that which ye would call eternal peace and happiness?

40 In that day there shall be great lasciviousness upon the earth, and ye shall have no closeness with another of the opposite sex, or even of the same sex, because of the multiple partners that ye shall have because of the perpetuity of your youth.

41 And ye shall find the temporary joy that ye desire by having these multiple partners with whom ye partake of the blessings of procreation, which blessing shall be taken from you when ye enter the Terrestrial and the Telestial kingdoms of the Father; and there, finally dwell forever, knowing that ye shall never experience the blessings of procreation again.

42 Yea, ye know that ye do not find joy and happiness in these things. And why is it that ye would want to live forever according to the plan of Lucifer, when ye could repent and live according to the plan of the Father and find exceedingly great peace and happiness therein?

43 How is it that ye think that ye can live in joy and happiness when all around you are those who do not love you, nor do they care of your plight?

44 And in that day that ye shall live in your youth without growing old, ye shall still hate your neighbor, and ye shall still desire more than that which your neighbor shall have; and when ye do not have that which is obtained through

the blessings of Satan by your neighbor, ye shall still envy and covet that which ye do not have, and ye shall be miserable still in your efforts to obtain those things.

45 Yea, in that day ye shall long to hold a child in your arms and listen to the laughter of innocence once again among you, knowing that only from the innocence of a child did you at one time feel the hope of the peace and happiness that ye desire for yourselves.

46 But there shall not be many children at that day, and those that shall be upon the earth shall be protected and brought up so that they shall have no innocence from their birth until they reach the age of maturity at which time they shall remain like yourselves, suffering the same miseries that ye suffer.

47 Behold, I have already explained unto you the great blessing that the Father hath given to us by allowing us to experience the gentleness and innocence of a child. Behold, I have told you that only in the face of a child shall ye learn to know your Eternal Father who hath created you.

48 And in those days when there shall not be many children upon the earth, then shall the people of the earth be alienated that much further from the Father and His plan.

49 And now, this was the design of Satan in the beginning. Yea, it was his desire to take us away from the Father that we should not know Him and understand Him and accept the plan that He presented to us in the beginning.

50 And in the latter days the people of the whole earth shall worship Satan as their God. But they shall not see him for who he really is; for in that day Satan shall deceive the children of men and cause them to believe that the devil hath horns and a tail and is a monster of a gruesome appearance; and that hell is a place of fire and brimstone where the wicked are cast and are continually burned forever.

51 Now, this he shall cause to be taught unto you because he doth not want you to know the true nature of his being. And one day ye shall all see him for who he truly is and then ye shall wonder after him because ye shall see that he is like unto you, and that he is your brother and a son of the same God who created all of the spirits that exist in this world.

52 And ye shall exclaim: How could this, our brother, deceive us and bring us under his power that we could not understand his deceptions and his ways?

53 Behold, ye do understand his deceptions and his ways, for they are the ways that ye have chosen for yourselves to live upon the earth that the Father hath created for you.

54 And now, I, Moroni, will not dwell further upon the exceedingly great wickedness of the latter days, so that I might finish these plates which I have made with my own hands with an abridgment of the wonderful words of hope that the brother of Jared hath written concerning that part of his vision in which he saw the coming of the Lord, Jesus Christ to the earth to establish the plan of the Father in its fullness, and to reign upon the earth among the children of men for a thousand years of peace and continual happiness. For these things cause my soul to rejoice exceedingly.

55 Behold, it burdeneth my soul to continually relate to you in this record the great wickedness that shall exist in the latter days. Nevertheless, before I end my abridgment of the great wickedness of the latter days, let me give unto you who shall receive these things a few more words of advice and warning.

56 Behold, this great church that shall be among you and known as the Church of Jesus Christ of the latter days shall subtly gain much power and control among the rich and the powerful of the United States.

57 And this shall come to pass in the exact same manner as the rise of power of the great Catholic church. For behold, both of these churches were established in their foundations upon the fullness of the gospel of Christ, their founders having been called by God after the Holy Order of His Son, to preach the gospel throughout the world.

58 Yea, the Lord suffered that the foundations of these churches be established that it might be proven through our experience that the church of the Lamb cannot exist in righteousness upon an earth that hath been corrupted and is controlled by the power of Satan.

59 Behold, the foundations of Christianity shall be the basis and the beginnings of the great

Catholic church which shall rule the people in open for many years, and all shall see its greatness and glory.

60 But in the latter days, the Church of Jesus Christ of Latter-day Saints shall rise up in obscurity, and its foundation shall be upon the record that it shall receive of my father, which shall be another testimony of Christianity. And because of this record, its people shall be called Mormons, which shall disgrace the name of my father.

61 For the foundation of what ye shall call Mormonism shall be the basis and the beginnings of this great latter day church. Nevertheless, it shall remain in somewhat obscurity among you, and shall not be popular among you.

62 And this is the desire of Satan so that he might continue to perform his labors within this church without its secret acts being discovered, and its deceptions revealed to the people.

63 And its leaders shall deceive many by claiming that they are not wicked, but that they belong to the only true church of God upon the earth. And these shall be some of the most wicked upon the earth, according to the plan of Lucifer, because of their desire for wealth and power.

64 And in their hearts they shall be like unto the Zoramites whose history ye have in the record of my father. For they shall see themselves as the most blessed people upon the earth, and shall be deceived in this pride and led down to the destruction of their souls by the god whom they worship.

65 Therefore, I give unto those of you who shall receive these things which are sealed, and which should have been given through this church, if it had been righteous; yea, I give unto you these words of wisdom: Leave this church and do not support it in its wickedness, for it shall never give unto you the happiness that ye desire.

66 Seek out its secret combinations and compare the lives of its leaders to the life of Christ, and then ye shall know of the great hypocrisy of this latter day church.

67 For its power shall reach into all aspects of the government of the United States because of its exceedingly great wealth. And the beast shall use this church to spread its image throughout the whole earth.

68 And this is the thing that burdeneth my soul more than any other; for this church hath the unsealed portion of this record; and because it hath these things, ye would expect it to be righteous. Nevertheless, because it hath these things doth not mean that it is a righteous church, for it is not.

69 Search the scriptures in all things, and ye shall learn the truth of which I have written. Behold, ye have the scriptures before you; yea, even in all parts of the world the Father hath caused that His gospel be given to the children of men through the mouths and the words of the holy prophets that he hath caused to be sent among you.

70 And in all things that ye shall read, liken them unto yourselves. And if ye liken them unto yourselves, then ye shall understand the will of the Father concerning you that ye might obey the commandments that are given therein.

71 And any commandment that is given therein, if it was given by a true prophet of God, then it shall point you towards the example that Christ hath set for us. And the example that he hath set for us is that we should love one another and do unto each other what we would have others do unto us.

72 And if ye pattern your lives after this commandment, ye shall find the peace and happiness that ye shall desire.

73 And those of you who are wicked, yea, even those of you who think more of your own families than ye do of your neighbors; yea, those of you who have set your hearts and desires upon the things of the world and the honors and glories of men;

74 Behold, if ye do not come to know the Father, so that ye might have His Spirit to be with you, then ye shall not only suffer the consequences of following the plan of Lucifer during the days of your probation, but when ye die, ye shall suffer exceedingly in a state of hell for that which ye should have done in mortality.

75 And those of you who live in the time when ye cannot die, if ye do not abide by the counsel and words that the Lord hath commanded me to write unto you in this record, and learn from them, then ye shall suffer in the flesh; and if ye live until the coming of the Lord in the glory of the Father, then ye shall feel the exceeding torment of those who suffer in a state of hell in the spirit world.

76 For ye shall not be able to stand and face the Lord at that day because ye shall realize that ye have spent all the days of your probation in wickedness. And your degrees of education, and your riches, and all the miracles and advancements of your sciences and technologies shall not hide your great wickedness from before the face of the Lord. And ye shall be tormented with an anguish that is like unto fire and brimstone, which ye shall feel in the presence of the holy angels, and in the presence of the Lamb of God.

77 And there is a sure way that ye shall know if ye are righteous or if ye are wicked. Behold, if ye are righteous, then ye shall take no part of the things of the earth, except it be to sustain your lives.

78 And ye shall not take upon you the honors and glories of men, but ye shall be rejected by the world and cast out from among the wicked, which shall be the rich and powerful among you. And if ye are rejected by the world, then ye shall know that ye do not follow the plan of Lucifer.

79 But remember the commandment of the Lord in which he hath commanded you that ye should love your enemies and do good to those who hate you and persecute you. Behold, if ye are righteous, ye would give up your life before ye would hate or harm another.

80 And those of you who are wicked shall know that ye are wicked if ye belong to any of the organized religions upon the earth in the latter days, for they are all abominations before God, teaching for doctrine the commandments and precepts of men, who are followers of the plan of Lucifer.

81 Yea, ye shall know that ye are wicked if ye hate one another and judgeth another because of his own beliefs which differ from your own.

82 Yea, ye shall know that ye are wicked if ye become angry with your neighbor and envious of the things which he hath acquired of the things of the world which ye do not have.

83 And if ye sue in a court of law, then ye are wicked.

84 And if ye trust in your money and in the knowledge of man for the management of your future, then ye are wicked.

85 Behold, and if ye shall reject these things which are contained in this sealed portion of this record, which shall be revealed unto you in the latter days, then ye shall know of a surety that ye are wicked.

86 And those of you who live upon the earth at the time of the last of these two latter day prophets, even at the time that Christopher shall be upon the earth; yea, seek him out and know him, and he shall tell you if ye are wicked or if ye are righteous by the words which he shall speak unto you.

87 And ye shall know him by his works, for they shall testify of him and show unto you that they are the works of Christ and not the works of men. For he shall possess none of the things of this world, nor shall any of these things be important to him.

88 And he shall not seek for money or power or the honors and glories of men, but shall give all the glory to the Father, whom he serveth by the works that he shall do before you.

89 And if ye are wicked ye shall be angry at him and seek to destroy him because ye do not understand him, for thus have the wicked done unto all the prophets of God since the beginning.

90 But if ye are righteous, ye shall know him and love him and learn of him according to the Spirit that shall reside in him.

91 And finally, I say unto those of you who shall receive these things: If ye think that ye are not deceived by Satan, then ye may know of a surety that ye are.

92 And if ye know that ye have been deceived by him, then I say unto you, repent ye, all the ends of the earth, and come unto Christ so that ye might know the Father who hath created us all. And when ye shall know the Father, then ye shall find the happiness that ye desire.

CHAPTER 88

Humankind causes God's judgments that will precede the second coming of Christ to the earth according to the book of Revelation. Those who want to know can find the exact year of the coming of the Lord by studying the scriptures.

AND now, the Lord shall come in the year after the end of the half of times as I have explained it unto you. And before he cometh into the world, all the prophecies that are written in the book of Revelation, that came forth unto you from the mouth of a holy prophet of God, must needs be fulfilled.

2 And most of these prophecies I have explained unto you. And I have also explained unto you that there shall be many great and miraculous advancements upon the earth in science and technology. But these great advancements shall not save the world from the judgments of God that shall precede the second coming of the Lord to the earth.

3 For these great advancements, as ye suppose, shall be the cause of many of the destructions that shall come upon you in the latter days in fulfillment of the prophecy of John.

4 Behold, in the beginning the Father created the earth according to the principles and laws of nature, which are eternal. Now, these laws are powerful, and effectually maintain an order in nature that shall work forever.

5 But in your desires to follow the plan of Lucifer, and bring about the great and miraculous advancements in science and technology that ye of the latter days suppose bring unto you your happiness, ye shall disrupt the course of the laws of nature and cause that its eternal order becometh imbalanced.

6 And now, because of this imbalance in the natural laws that the Father hath set for this planet, ye shall begin to see the effects of the plan of Lucifer in using these laws for the purposes of his plan, which is a plan of selfishness.

7 And the causes of these unnatural imbalances in the perfect order of nature that the Father hath established in the beginning, shall be the means and the cause of the fulfillment of the words of John in the book of Revelation that ye have among you in the Bible.

8 Behold, these prophecies are written in symbolism according to the stumbling blocks that the Lord placed before you because of your inability to live according to the Spirit of God, which would make all things clear unto you; therefore, do not suppose that the Father would cause any of these things to come upon you; for He doth not punish His children in this manner, but alloweth them to punish themselves by the choices that they make for themselves according to their ability to act for themselves.

9 Now, this is what is always meant by the wrath of God. Behold, do ye think that the Father becometh angry with His children and is wont to hurt them in any manner? I say unto you that He doth not become angry with them, but in great sadness He witnesseth the destruction and misery that they bring upon themselves.

10 But when the prophets write concerning the destruction of things to come, they relate the inaction of the Father in interceding to prevent these destructions and miseries, as the wrath of God.

11 And it is written, saying: And I heard a great voice out of the temple saying to the seven angels: Go your ways, and pour out the vials of the wrath of God upon the earth.

12 And the first went, and poured out his vial upon the earth; and there fell a noisome and grievous sore upon the men which had the mark of the beast, and upon them who worshipped his image.

13 And now, this noisome and grievous sore is the many diseases that ye have amongst you in the latter days. And these are the cause of the effects of the poor and unnatural foods that ye shall consume in that day.

14 And I have already related to you in this record the effects of cooked food, which cooking with heat kills the natural process by which these foods are assimilated by the order of the flesh. And because ye eat food and flesh that is cooked, ye have caused an imbalance in your flesh, which is the cause of many of your diseases in the latter days.

15 And I would that ye should look into nature and to the other animals with which ye share the planet that the Father hath created for

us, where he hath given unto us this delicate balance of nature. Yea, do any of these causeth that their food pass through fire to destroy the purpose for which their food hath been created for them?

16 Ye know that they do not do these things, for they do not have the agency to perform these tasks, having been instinctually programmed by the Father in the beginning to obey, in all things, the laws of nature.

17 And do these other animals in nature have the noisome and grievous sore upon them as ye have; or in other words, do they have the diseases of the flesh that cause these unnatural and unhealthy sores that cause your suffering and your deaths? Behold, they do not.

18 Behold, even the food that ye eat that hath not passed through the heat of a fire and been destroyed, even these things have been contaminated by the unnatural attempts of men to get gain by providing these things unto you in abundance.

19 For in those days men shall obtain the knowledge of chemistry, as it shall be known among you, which shall aid them in their ability to use the natural elements which exist upon the earth to create concoctions and potions that shall kill the insects and the other animals that the Father hath placed in their own order to maintain a perfect balance of nature in all things.

20 And instead of working by the sweat of your brow to pull out the weeds that rise up in the crops that ye grow for yourselves, ye shall use these unnatural products of your chemistry to kill the weeds that grow among the plants that ye do eat as your food.

21 And do ye not realize that when these things are done unto nature, then its perfect balance is disrupted and the consequences of this disruption is the cause of the sores that shall come upon you?

22 And ye shall die of all manner of effects from your poor diets, having been provided these diets by the beast that ye worship.

23 And the prophecy of John continueth, saying: And the second angel poured out his vial upon the sea; and it became as the blood of a dead man, which is black in color and heavy in its consistency; and every living soul died in the sea.

24 And now, in the latter days ye shall began to use the resources of the earth to fulfill the plan of Lucifer. And he shall inspire you to seek out these resources of the earth that lie beneath its surface. And this shall be known among you as oil, but it shall not be the pure natural oils that are produced from the plants that the Father hath provided for our consumption. But this oil shall be black and heavy as the blood of a dead man, as John hath related to us.

25 And this oil which ye shall bring forth from its natural place, shall be the cause of much pollution and destruction of the oceans and great waters of the earth.

26 And now, what purpose do ye have of this oil except it be to consume it upon the lusts in the blessings which Satan hath given unto you? Why would ye cause that a natural process become something that ye desire to serve your selfishness, and in doing so, it becometh a cause of the destruction of the natural order of things that God hath established in its purity for you?

27 Yea, surely your turning of things upside down, relating to the natural order of things, shall not be unnoticed by you in the causes of the destruction that ye shall bring upon yourselves.

28 And those of you who shall bring these things forth into the world that ye might get gain, do ye not fulfill the words of the prophet Isaiah when he wrote, saying: Woe unto them who seek deep to hide their counsel from the Lord, and their works are in the dark, and they say, Who seeth us? and who knoweth us? Surely your turning of things upside down shall be esteemed as the clay of the potter; for shall the work say of him that made it, He made me not, or shall the thing framed say of him that framed it, He had no understanding?

29 Behold, in the day of the Lord, ye shall be judged for that which ye have done to the natural order that the Father hath set up for our progression in experiencing happiness.

30 And if ye do not repent of these things, and ye continue to pursue unnatural means whereby ye might get gain, then shall the rest of the words of John be fulfilled when he prophesied, saying: And the third angel poured out his vial upon the rivers and fountains of waters; and they became blood.

31 And I heard the angel of the waters say, Thou art righteous, Oh, Lord, which art, and wast, and shalt be, because thou hast judged thus. For they have shed the blood of saints and prophets, and thou hast given them blood to drink; for they are worthy. And I heard another out of the altar say, Even so, Lord God Almighty, true and righteous are thy judgments.

32 Now, the judgments that the Father hath made is that he shall stay His hand and not intervene in the destruction of nature in the latter days, allowing His children to experience for themselves that which occureth when the laws of nature are circumvented and used by wicked men for their own selfish purposes.

33 And John continueth, saying: And the fourth angel poured out his vial upon the sun; and power was given unto him to scorch men with fire. And men were scorched with great heat, and blasphemed the name of God, which hath power over these plagues according to His will but shall not stop them for the sake of man. And He stayed His hand because they repented not to give him glory.

34 Now, in the latter days the causes of the advancements that ye shall make in technology and science shall provide the means whereby the natural atmosphere of the earth shall begin to deteriorate in such a way that the heat of the sun shall be caused to do that which it was not intended according to the natural order for which the sun was created to give life unto the earth.

35 And because of the effect of the sun, the earth shall begin to warm exceedingly and cause misery and destruction upon the earth.

36 But even after these things shall come to pass, ye shall not repent, because of your desires for wealth and an easiness of life, which ye desire because ye worship the beast and desire the image that it hath created for you by the power of Satan.

37 And John continueth, saying: And the fifth angel poured out his vial upon the seat of the beast; and his kingdom was full of darkness; and they gnawed their tongues for pain, and blasphemed the God of heaven because of their pains and their sores, and repented not of their deeds.

38 And now, this is the destruction of the United States of America, which is the seat of the beast of the latter days. And this destruction shall come to pass in the same manner as the destruction of the great Roman Empire, which came to pass because of the wickedness of its citizens.

39 And ye have an account of the history of this Roman Empire among you; therefore, I would admonish you to study its downfall, so that ye might know the cause of the downfall of the seat of the beast in the latter days.

40 Behold, I have already shown unto you that Satan useth any nation that is under his power to do his will among the children of men throughout the whole earth. And when the Roman Empire fell, which was his seat in those days, he found another nation to raise up and implement his plan for the children of men.

41 And in the latter days when the United States shall fall, and great shall be the fall thereof, he shall gather all of his forces together upon the earth to prepare against the great day when the Lord shall come in the glory of the Father to cast Satan out and reclaim the earth for the purposes for which the Father caused it to be created.

42 And John wrote of this in his prophecy, saying: And the sixth angel poured out his vial upon the great river Euphrates; and the water thereof was dried up, that the way of the kings of the east might be prepared. And I saw three unclean spirits like frogs come out of the mouth of the dragon, and out of the mouth of the beast, and out of the mouth of the false prophet. For they are the spirits of devils, working miracles, which go forth unto the kings of the earth and of the whole world, to gather them to the battle of that great day of God Almighty.

43 And now, these three unclean spirits that shall come forth out of the mouth of all those who are unrighteous before God; yea, these are the spirit of selfishness; and the spirit of lust; and the spirit of hate; and these shall dwell in the hearts of the children of men and cause them to deny the Holy Spirit and worship the beast which issueth forth unto them the power of the dragon by way of the mouth of the false prophet.

44 And the beast is the governments that have been set up among you, that ostensibly

provide you with protection and the means whereby ye might have the blessings of freedom and liberty, and the power to pursue the fine things of the world, which the beast offereth unto you as a blessing for complying with its laws and its order.

45 And the false prophet is all of the organized religions upon the earth that have been organized by the hand of man, that they might subject the souls of the children of God to their pretended precepts and commandments, which do not create peace and happiness, but strife and misery among all nations of the earth.

46 And the great river Euphrates gave its life giving waters to the city of Babylon in times of old. And John hath used this city of Babylon as an example of the great wickedness and worldly desires of men. Therefore, when this angel poureth out his vial upon the great river Euphrates, this meaneth that the source of all of the worldliness and greatness of the world shall dry up and cease from giving unto the people of the earth the fine and precious things of the earth which their hearts desire and their souls are set upon.

47 And this shall affect greatly the economy of the beast throughout the world. And once the economy of the earth hath failed miserably, or once the waters of the great river Euphrates have dried up, so that they no longer give life to the great city of Babylon, then shall the world be prepared for the second coming of the Lord, and the people of the world shall also be prepared to receive the word of God which shall proceed forth from his mouth.

48 And John continueth his prophecy, saying: Behold, I come as a thief. Blessed is he that watcheth, and keepeth his garments clean, lest he walk naked, and they see his shame. And these are the elect of God which have received His mark in their foreheads. And He gathered them together into a place called in the Hebrew tongue: Armageddon.

49 And the seventh angel poured out his vial into the air; and there came a great voice out of the temple of heaven, from the throne, saying, It is done. And there were voices, and thunders, and lightnings; and there was a great earthquake, such as was not since men were upon the earth, so mighty an earthquake, and so great.

50 And the great city was divided into three parts, and the cities of the nations fell before it; and great Babylon came in remembrance before God, to give unto her the cup of the wine of the fierceness of his wrath.

51 And every island fled away, and the mountains were not found. And there fell upon men a great hail out of heaven, every stone about the weight of a talent; and men blasphemed God because of the plague of the hail; for the plague thereof was exceeding great.

52 And I know that ye have experienced the power of God in the earthquakes, and in the lightnings, and in the volcanoes, and in the whirlwinds which have destroyed many of your cities and many people throughout the history of the earth.

53 And the power of nature is held in the hand of God and is more powerful than any power that Satan shall be allowed to introduce among you in the latter days. And it is by this great power of nature that the Lord shall bring forth his judgments and prepare the earth for his coming.

54 Therefore, do not think that Satan shall be able to prepare you against the day that these judgments shall come forth against the world. Yea, he shall try his hand at this and give unto the rich and powerful many things that they shall believe shall save them from the power of nature; but in the end, the power of God given through the destructive force of nature, shall destroy them from off the face of the earth according to the prophecies given by John and the other holy prophets that the Lord hath sent to the earth to warn them.

55 And now, these things that shall come to pass shall be in fulfillment of the rest of the prophecy of John. For he prophesied concerning that which would come to pass as the final seals were opened, which represent the last days.

56 And he prophesied of the great natural destruction that shall come upon the earth, saying: And after these things I saw four angels standing on the four corners of the earth, holding the four winds of the earth, that the wind should not blow on the earth, nor on the sea, nor on any tree. And I saw another angel ascending from the east, having the seal of the living God in his right hand seeking throughout the whole earth for the elect of God.

57 And he cried with a loud voice to the four angels, to whom it was given to hurt the earth and the sea, saying: Hurt not the earth, neither the sea, nor the trees, till we have sealed the servants of our God in their foreheads. And I heard the number of them which were sealed; and there were sealed an hundred and forty and four thousand of all the tribes of the children of Israel.

58 And now, it shall come to pass in the latter days that the elect shall be upon the earth in every nation, among every people, and of every tongue; and every one of these shall be known and accounted for by the Lord.

59 And now, before these great natural disasters shall be allowed to occur by the command of the Lord to prepare the earth for his coming, the gospel of Christ shall be given to the elect of the earth, and their stumbling blocks shall be taken away so that they might see more clearly the true gospel of Christ.

60 And when the elect have received the fullness of the gospel, which is the seal of God in their foreheads, then they shall begin to prepare themselves for the coming of the Lord.

61 And there shall be some of the elect who shall gather together and unite in their desires to obey the commandments of the Father in following the example of Christ. Nevertheless, there shall not be a universal gathering of the elect into one place before the coming of the Lord, for there shall be many who shall be one, of a city, and a few of a nation, therefore, it shall not be wise for them to be gathered together at that time; for if they are all gathered together, then shall the beast destroy them.

62 And it shall come to pass that the elect of God shall begin to prepare themselves for the coming of the Lord in the glory of the Father. And they shall have the Holy Ghost with them to teach them whatsoever is required of them, so that they may be prepared for those events that shall lead up to the great and dreadful day of the Lord.

63 And to the elect, this day shall not be dreadful, but in that day they shall rejoice and praise God for the gift of His Son.

64 And so that ye might have no more confusion among you concerning the number of one hundred and forty and four thousand who shall be sealed in their foreheads, I would that ye should know that John used these numbers symbolically as a representation of all the nations of the earth who shall have the gospel among them.

65 And this reference of symbolism is given that it might be shown that the elect are scattered throughout the nations of the earth, as are the twelve tribes of Israel, but from each tribe, or from each nation, there shall be those who are elect who give heed to the word of God and receive His Spirit, that they might not suffer from the coming of His Son into the world.

66 Now the number of these is not significant, but is used as an example; for there shall be many elect upon the earth, even many more than one hundred forty and four thousand, but their numbers shall be small in comparison to the numbers of those who are not elect and do not have the seal of God written in their foreheads. Nevertheless, the elect are numbered and known by the Lord and his holy angels.

67 And now, the sealed portion of this record shall go throughout the world, as well as the unsealed record of my father, and all the elect shall know of the great blessings that are contained herein, even the truth of all things since the beginning of time until the end of time.

68 And because they shall know these things, both by the words of this record and also by the voice of the Spirit which shall be with them, they shall be prepared in all things, and they shall not suffer the wrath of God as it is poured out upon the kingdom of Satan.

69 And then shall the words of Christ unto his disciples be fulfilled which he spoke concerning the days prior to his coming, when he said: For I say unto you, that ye shall not see me henceforth and know that I am he of whom it is written by the prophets, until ye shall say: Blessed is he who cometh in the name of the Lord, in the clouds of heaven, and all the holy angels with him.

70 Then understood his disciples that he should come again on the earth, after that he was glorified and crowned on the right hand of God. And Jesus went out, and departed from the temple; and his disciples came to him, for to hear him, saying: Master, show us concerning the buildings of the temple, as thou hast said, They shall be thrown down, and left unto you desolate.

71 And Jesus said unto them: See ye not all these things, and do ye not understand them? Verily I say unto you, there shall not be left here, upon this temple, one stone upon another that shall not be thrown down.

72 And Jesus left them, and went upon the Mount of Olives. And as he sat upon the Mount of Olives, the disciples came unto him privately, saying: Tell us when shall these things be which thou hast said concerning the destruction of the temple, and the Jews; and what is the sign of thy coming, and of the end of the world, or the destruction of the wicked, which is the end of the world?

73 And Jesus answered, and said unto them: Take heed that no man deceive you; for many shall come in my name, saying, I am Christ, and shall deceive many. And then shall they deliver you up to be afflicted, and shall kill you, and ye shall be hated of all nations, for the sake of my name.

74 And then shall many be offended, and shall betray one another, and shall hate one another; and many false prophets shall arise, and shall deceive many.

75 And because iniquity shall abound, the love of many shall wax cold; but he that remaineth steadfast and is not overcome, the same shall be saved.

76 When ye, therefore, shall see again the abomination of desolation, spoken of by Daniel the prophet, concerning the destruction of Jerusalem, then ye shall stand in the holy place; whoso readeth let him understand.

77 Then let them who are in Judea flee into the mountains; and let him who is on the housetop flee, and not return to take anything out of his house; neither let him who is in the field return back to take his clothes. And woe unto them who are with child, and unto them who give suck in those days.

78 Therefore, pray ye to the Lord that your flight be not in the winter, neither on the sabbath day; for then, in those days, shall be great tribulation on the Jews, and upon the inhabitants of Jerusalem, such as was not before sent upon Israel, of God, since the beginning of their kingdom until this time; no, nor ever shall be sent again upon Israel.

79 All things which have befallen them are only the beginning of the sorrows which shall come upon them. And except those days should be shortened, there should none of their flesh be saved; but for the sake of the elect, according to the covenant, those days shall be shortened.

80 Behold, these things I have spoken unto you concerning the Jews; and again, after the tribulation of those days which shall come upon Jerusalem, if any man shall say unto you, Lo, here is Christ, or there, believe him not. For in those days there shall also arise false Christs, and false prophets, and shall show great signs and wonders, insomuch, that, if possible, they shall deceive the very elect, who are the elect according to the covenant.

81 Behold, I speak these things unto you for the sake of the elect; and you also shall hear of wars, and rumors of wars; see that ye be not troubled, for all I have told you must come to pass; but the end is not yet.

82 Behold, I have told you before; wherefore, if they shall say unto you, Behold, he is in the desert; go not forth, or if they shall say, Behold, he is in the secret chambers; believe it not. For as the light of the morning cometh out of the east, and shineth even unto the west, and covereth the whole earth, so shall also the coming of the Son of Man be.

83 And now I show unto you a parable. Behold, wheresoever the carcass is, there will the eagles be gathered together; so likewise shall mine elect be gathered from the four quarters of the earth.

84 And they shall hear of wars, and rumors of wars. Behold I speak for the sake of mine elect; for nation shall rise against nation, and kingdom against kingdom; there shall be famines, and pestilences, and earthquakes, in divers places.

85 And again, because iniquity shall abound, the love of men shall wax cold; but he that shall not be overcome, the same shall be saved.

86 And again, this Gospel of the kingdom shall be preached in all the world, for a witness unto all nations, and then shall the end come, or the destruction of the wicked; and again shall the abomination of desolation, spoken of by Daniel the prophet, be fulfilled.

87 And immediately after the tribulation of those days, the sun shall be darkened, and the moon shall not give her light, and the stars shall fall from heaven, and the powers of heaven shall be shaken.

88 Verily, I say unto you, this generation, in which these things shall be shown forth, shall not pass away until all I have told you shall be fulfilled. Although, the days will come, that heaven and earth shall pass away; yet my words shall not pass away, but all shall be fulfilled.

89 And, as I said before, after the tribulation of those days, and the powers of the heavens shall be shaken, then shall appear the sign of the Son of Man in heaven, and then shall all the tribes of the earth mourn; and they shall see the Son of Man coming in the clouds of heaven, with power and great glory.

90 And whoso treasureth up my word, shall not be deceived, for the Son of Man shall come, and he shall send his angels before him with the great sound of a trumpet, and they shall gather together the remainder of his elect from the four winds, from one end of heaven to the other.

91 Now learn a parable of the fig tree: When its branches are yet tender, and it beginneth to put forth leaves, ye know that summer is nigh at hand; so likewise, mine elect, when they shall see all these things, they shall know that he is near, even at the doors; but of that day, and hour, no one knoweth; no, not the angels of God in heaven, but my Father only.

92 But as it was in the days of Noah, so it shall be also at the coming of the Son of Man; for it shall be with them, as it was in the days which were before the flood; for until the day that Noah entered into the ark they were eating and drinking, marrying and giving in marriage; and knew not until the flood came and took them all away; so shall also the coming of the Son of Man be.

93 Then shall be fulfilled that which is written, that in the last days, two shall be in the field, the one shall be taken, and the other left; two shall be grinding at the mill, the one shall be taken, and the other left.

94 And what I say unto one, I say unto all men; watch, therefore, for ye know not at what hour your Lord doth come. But know this, if the good man of the house had known in what watch the thief would come, he would have watched, and would not have suffered his house to have been broken up, but would have been ready.

95 Therefore be ye also ready, for in such an hour as ye think not, the Son of Man cometh. Who, then, is a faithful and wise servant, whom his lord hath made ruler over his household, to give them meat in due season?

96 Blessed is that servant whom his lord, when he cometh, shall find so doing; and verily I say unto you, he shall make him ruler over all his goods.

97 But if that evil servant shall say in his heart: My lord delayeth his coming, and shall begin to smite his fellow-servants, and to eat and drink with the drunken, then the lord of that servant shall come in a day when he looketh not for him, and in an hour that he is not aware of, and shall cut him asunder, and shall appoint him his portion with the hypocrites; and there shall be weeping and gnashing of teeth.

98 And thus cometh the end of the wicked, according to the prophecy of Moses, saying: They shall be cut off from among the people; but the end of the earth is not yet, but by and by.

99 And now, the Lord spoke these things unto his disciples that they might have a better understanding of the will of the Father concerning the destruction of Jerusalem in those days, and also of the last days. And for the sake of the elect he hath said these things.

100 And also for the sake of the elect have these things which have been sealed come forth unto them. For there shall be none but the elect of God who shall receive these things and believe in them, that they might prepare themselves more fully for the coming of the Lord.

101 And in this record shall the elect have the time given, within the year, of the coming of the Lord, if it so be that ye shall ponder upon the things which the Lord hath commanded me to write unto you.

102 And there shall be those of the latter days who shall claim that the Lord hath said that no man shall know of the time of his coming. Yea, the Lord did not say that no man shall know of the time of his coming, only that no man shall know the day and the hour of his coming.

103 And when the year hath arrived that hath been revealed unto you in this record, then shall it come to pass as in the days of Nephi, when the prophecy was given by the prophet Samuel, the Lamanite, in which he prophesied, saying: Behold, I give unto you a sign; for five years more cometh, and behold, then cometh the Son of God to redeem all those who shall believe on his name.

104 And now, my brothers and sisters, yea, even all ye of the latter days who shall receive these things, did not Samuel give unto the people the exact year in which the Lord was to come into the world?

105 And even though the people were given this sign, they did not repent at that day. For when that year came, the people began to doubt and say amongst themselves: Behold the time is past, and the words of Samuel are not fulfilled; therefore, your joy and your faith concerning this thing hath been vain.

106 And now, this they said because they did not know the day and the hour of his coming, nevertheless, they did know the exact year, as had been prophesied by Samuel the Lamanite.

107 And now, my brothers and sisters, I would that ye should search these things which the Lord hath commanded me to give unto you in this record. Behold, they are faithful and true, and every word shall be fulfilled which is written upon these plates.

108 And if ye search these things, ye shall come to know many of the mysteries of God, and also the will of the Father concerning all of His children upon this earth.

CHAPTER 89

Moroni tells the world that there is a chance to repent and keep the prophecies of destruction from being fulfilled. All prophecy given is conditional.

AND now, it is expedient that ye understand one thing that I have not yet explained unto you in this record: Behold, all prophecy that proceedeth forth from the mouths of all the holy prophets are given unto the children of men as portends and cautions, and words of warning to prepare them for the things which shall come.

2 But most importantly, the words of the prophets are given to prepare your souls to meet the Father and live in one of His many kingdoms of glory.

3 And this is the thing that ye should understand: Yea, even though a prophet shall prophesy in the name of the Lord of the great destruction and tribulation that shall come to pass, this doth not mean that it shall have to come to pass according to his words; or in other words, it doth not mean that ye do not have your free agency to change the course of the events of the future so that these things do not come to pass.

4 For the words of the prophets are given unto you to warn you of the dangers ahead of you for living in wickedness and sin. And the prophets do not know the exactness of the destructions and tribulations that shall come upon you, but they give a generalization of those things which shall come to pass according to the words of prophecy that they receive from the Holy Ghost.

5 And the Holy Ghost receiveth all of his knowledge directly from the Son, who receiveth this knowledge from the Father. And it is the great knowledge and the vast experience of the Father that maketh it possible that things are known of the future.

6 And the Father loveth all of His children, and it is not His desire that we suffer in misery and tribulation upon this earth. And the only times that we suffer in misery is when we do not follow His plan. But He cannot force us to follow His plan, but hath given unto each of us our individual free agency to act according to our own desires and live the course of life that we choose for ourselves.

7 Therefore, all things which are done upon the earth, which maketh us miserable, are from our own doing, and are not the punishments or doings of the Father. Behold, the Father punisheth no one, because He knoweth that we will punish ourselves, if we do not listen to His Spirit and do those things which He knoweth will bring us joy and happiness.

8 But when we choose to go against His plan, then He also knoweth that which will come to pass because of our choice to go against Him. And this is the reason why He suffereth prophets to come among us and preach repentance unto us and try to persuade us to listen to the Holy Spirit, which giveth the peace and happiness that we desire.

9 Therefore, if ye of the latter days repent of your wickedness and turn again to the Father and follow His plan, then the words of the prophets shall not be fulfilled concerning you, and ye shall not suffer the misery and tribulation that ye shall suffer if ye reject His gospel.

10 And so that ye of the latter days might know more fully of His gospel, and also of the things which shall be taught by Christ when he cometh to the earth to set up the kingdom of the Father for the last time, the Lord hath commanded me to finish this record by explaining the gospel of Christ as it is intended for the daily lives of the children of men, which is also the will of the Father concerning those of you who live upon the earth in the last days, as it hath been since the beginning concerning all of His children.

11 And I have been commanded to give unto you what hath been written by the hand of the brother of Jared concerning the time when the Lord shall be upon the earth to teach the people his laws and to set up a righteous government that shall rule the people in peace and righteousness for the last thousand years of the existence of mortality upon this earth.

12 And as I abridge the words of the brother of Jared, I shall give unto you an explanation of these things according to the Spirit, which hath been strong within me during the course of this entire abridgment, which I have added to the record of my father Mormon, but shall cause to be sealed up according to the commandment of the Lord.

13 Therefore, the things that I am about to write unto you are those things that ye can do to bring much peace and happiness upon the earth in the latter days, and cause that the tribulations and destruction that have been prophesied against you shall not come to pass.

14 But if ye reject the things that I am about to write unto you according to the command of the Lord and the promptings of the Holy Ghost; yea, if ye refuse to incorporate them into your lives, then ye shall suffer all things which the prophets have prophesied against you.

15 Therefore, read these words; yea, take them into you hearts so that ye might understand their meaning. Implement the great counsel that shall be given unto you into your daily lives. Yea, require these things of your leaders and those whom ye have given power over you, that ye might have the peace and happiness that the Father hath promised to all of us.

16 Behold, Satan shall fight the implementation of these things into your daily lives, because they are not the principles and purposes of his plan.

17 But it should not matter what Satan desireth of you, for ye have your free agency to act and choose for yourselves that which ye will do during the days of your probation.

18 And a promise I give unto all the people of the world in the latter days: Yea, if ye do these things, then ye shall be a happy people and ye shall not want or suffer for anything all the days of your lives.

19 And if ye do these things, then shall the words of the prophets be fulfilled when they gave unto you the will of the Lord, saying: I will cut my work short in righteousness, for the days come that I will send forth judgment unto victory.

20 And now, this hath been the desire of all the holy prophets of God; even that they should establish righteousness upon the earth among the children of men. And this shall also be the desire of these last two prophets who shall be among you in the latter days.

21 And the first shall do all in his power to implement the fullness of the gospel of Jesus Christ into the daily lives of those who shall give heed unto his words.

22 And this prophet shall pray unto the Lord, saying: We ask thee to appoint unto Zion other stakes besides this one which thou hast appointed, that the gathering of they people may roll on in great power and majesty, that thy work may be cut short in righteousness.

23 And the Lord shall promise Joseph, this first prophet among you, that if Zion is established and the people repent and work righteousness in all things whatsoever that they shall be commanded by the mouth of Joseph, then he would cut his work short in righteousness; even saying unto his servant Joseph: For I, the Almighty, have laid my hands upon the nations, to scourge them for their wickedness. And plagues shall go forth, and they shall not be taken from the earth until I have completed my work, which shall be cut short in righteousness.

24 And now, these are promises of the Lord, if the people are righteous before him. Behold, Enoch preached the gospel unto the people in his day and they became an exceedingly righteous people; and all the days of their lives they remained righteous. And when the world rose up against them, the Lord caused that they should be taken from off of the earth because of the promises which he made unto them.

25 But the people of the church that Joseph shall establish upon the earth shall not remain in righteousness, and thus the promises of the Lord shall not be fulfilled concerning them.

26 And these promises also pertain unto you who have received this record. Behold, if ye repent and begin to work righteousness upon the earth, then shall the promises of the Lord be fulfilled in you.

27 And now, my brothers and sisters, yea, even all of you upon the face of the whole earth, read these things that I am about to give unto you. Know that the Lord will come one day and open up all the books which have been written by his power, and ye shall be judged by the words that are written in these books.

28 And this book, which shall be sealed to come forth at this time, is the greatest of all the books that have ever been written, because of the plainness of the words and the clarity of the things which the Father would have His children know concerning Him.

29 Therefore, I say unto you, give strict heed to the things that are written herein, for they shall either bless your lives exceedingly on one hand, or on the other, they shall condemn you to everlasting condemnation.

CHAPTER 90

Having no money or a value placed upon the necessities of life will create much peace and happiness in society. The businesses and corporations are tools used by the rich to grind the faces of the poor. The Lord shall destroy all business that do not do something to provide for the necessities of life, or the happiness of humankind.

AND now, the first thing that shall be done when the Lord cometh upon the earth, is that he shall rebuke all those who have placed a value upon, not only the things of the earth—its gold and its silver, and its fine and precious things—but also the values that have been placed upon the souls of the children of men.

2 Behold, in that day there shall be no money, which is the number of the beast, and which createth and sustaineth the value that hath been placed upon all things upon the earth, and also upon the souls of men, which lead to the wickedness of slavery.

3 And if there is no money, and no value is placed upon the things of the earth, or upon the souls of men, then there shall be no rich and poor, but all shall have all things in common.

4 And the brother of Jared wrote concerning this, saying: And the Lord took away the power and control of the rich by taking away the value that had been placed upon the money system that is established among the children of men.

5 For in that day, all the world shall be under one monetary system, which shall be controlled by the rich. And when the Lord devalues the worth of all things, then there shall be no gold, or silver, or paper money of any kind in that day.

6 For the value of the riches that a man possesseth is counted unto him by machines that hold the accounting of his wealth within them, which is the number of his name, or his works. And the number of his name is distributed to all those who have access to these machines, so that all might know the number by which he is named.

7 And each man, woman, and child upon the earth is given an account that is held within this machine. And when a man is employed at a business, a value is placed upon that in which he hath been employed. And when he works for a time, then the number of his worth, or this value, is credited to his account that is held within these machines.

8 And when he maketh a purchase of whatever his heart desireth, then is the value that is placed upon this thing taken away from the account that giveth unto him his worth and the number of his name.

9 And it is required of all upon the earth, who are of age, to work in some manner that they might have a number in their accounts that provideth for them all the things that they need to live.

10 And when a man or a woman desireth that which they cannot afford because of the insufficiency of the number in their account, then they borrow against their account and are forced to pay usury for that amount that is above the number in their account.

11 And there are many who have little in their accounts because of the value that hath been placed upon the things that they need to eat, and to wear, and upon a home in which to live.

12 And the value of these things are determined by the rich among them, that they might get continual gain from those who seeketh only that they can survive by the necessities of life.

13 And the poor rebel against the value that hath been placed upon the things that sustain their lives so that the rich might get gain from them. But when they rebel against these things, then they are taken by the rich and placed in prisons away from the rest of the people as a punishment for disobeying the laws of the rich.

14 And while in these prisons, the poor become hardened in their hearts against the rich, and imagine up in their hearts all manner of evil that they would do to the rich who have placed the value upon the necessities of life and also upon their souls.

15 And I beheld that there were many prisons set up among them, and many in the process of being built to punish the poor who would rebel against the will of the rich.

16 And there existed no love among the people of the earth, for there was no trust one for another, because of the desires of all to obtain the fine things of the world by the number of their accounts that are maintained in the machines that I beheld.

17 And when the Lord came among them, he commanded his holy angels to destroy all the machines that held the accounts of all the inhabitants of the earth and the number of their names.

18 And when he had destroyed these machines, all the people of the earth became equal, having no value placed upon them by the number of their names.

19 And the rich lamented of that which the Lord had done, and cursed his name and hid themselves from the face of the Lord in their mansions, and in their grand estates, and in their lavish houses and domiciles.

20 But the poor rejoiced exceedingly in that which the Lord had done. And the poor were those who were responsible for the maintenance and the upkeep of the lifestyles that the rich had created for themselves.

21 And the rich had maintained control over the poor because of the accounts and the number of their names, which gave unto each man, woman, and child the ability to purchase that which they needed to survive.

22 For the rich had placed a value upon the food, and the raiment, and the houses of the poor, and paid them in wages for their employ only that which the poor could afford to sustain their lives.

23 And the poor were forced to work for the rich to obtain a number that would be placed in their account, which number was controlled by the rich.

24 And the rich had placed a value upon the worth of a soul of a man and a woman who would perform work for them.

25 But the Lord commanded that there shall be no more an account given of the worth of a man, and a woman, or a child, but that all

should be provided for equally in all that they needed to sustain their lives, all being equal in the eyes of the Lord.

26 And then did the rich lament exceedingly because they could no longer make a profit from the desire of another to sustain his life.

27 And the Lord commanded that all of the prisoners inside of the prisons be released and given their freedom in all things, and also be made equal like unto all others upon the earth.

28 And the prisoners that were being held by the rich came forth and knelt before the Lord and praised his name and made a covenant to obey him and keep his commandments in all things.

29 And he commanded the people to continue in the business that they were accustomed to do, so that the same economy would survive by which the people were accustomed to living. But he commanded his angels to go throughout the earth and change the course of all employment that did not provide an opportunity for the happiness, or for the necessities of life, of the people of the earth.

30 And the majority of all the merchants and the business that were set up among them, were those that had nothing to do with the production of food, raiment, or shelter, but were set up to manage and account for and maintain the accounts and the numbers held within their machines.

31 And the rich had set up an ingenious system of stocks and bonds, whereby they might gain more numbers in their accounts without working for them. And if a man invested his number into a company, he was promised by the company that he would be returned a greater number than that which he invested.

32 And the company would take the money that was invested into it and seek for means and ways whereby it might make more profit and increase its own number so that it might give back to the investor that which it had promised unto him.

33 Nevertheless, the companies were like unto the accounts and the numbers of the rich, in that they were not actual people, but entities of incorporation which had been developed by the laws of the rich to get gain.

34 And when a man would invest his number with a company, and the company could not increase the number of its name sufficiently to pay back a dividend to the investor, then there was no course of redress given that the man might receive back the money that he had given, because the company was not responsible as one man might be to another, because it was not a man, but a number.

35 And when a company desired to make a profit so that it might pay dividends to those who invest in it, then it grindeth upon the face of the poor and taketh more from the poor and useth its power over them to make the profit that it desireth.

36 And the Lord shall never again allow a man to make a profit by the labor of another man, but all shall give equally of their time to have the things that they all can share to bring happiness to them equally.

37 And if a man hath increased in his abilities and can provide them as a benefit to others, then he shall do so whether he hath much to give, or little to give, according to the abilities that he hath received from the blessing of existence that the Father hath given to all of us.

38 And in the last days the rich shall enforce their laws and their ways upon the poor by the means of force that Lucifer hath used to reign over them.

39 But in the day of the Lord, the armies and navies and all the means of force of all the governments throughout the world shall be disbanded and become obsolete against the power of the Lord and his holy angels; for with the command of his word, the Lord can cause a mountain to rise up and cover an entire battalion of soldiers and all of their weapons of war.

40 And the Lord shall cause to be set up places of employ for all the people of the earth. And no value shall be placed upon that which one would do in his employ, but all shall be equal before the Lord.

41 And all food, and raiment, and houses shall become free to all.

42 And now, I, Moroni, say unto those of you who shall receive these things before the prophecy concerning that day of the Lord described by the brother of Jared shall come to pass:

43 Behold, the first thing that ye must do amongst yourselves is to establish a principle and law that guaranteeth to all the necessities of life.

44 And now, I ask this thing of you: Is it fair that any among you be forbidden these things? Behold, the choice of their existence was not made by them, but was made by the parents who created them.

45 Therefore, none of them should be responsible to suffer for a want of any of these things to sustain their lives in the existence in which they were created. Now, I have already explained this unto you in this record, even that none of us made a conscious choice to come into existence, but we were created by the will and pleasure of the Father.

46 And for this reason, the plan of the Father provideth for us all those things which we need to remain in the existence in which we were created.

47 And in the kingdom of the Father there is no monetary value placed upon the things which He hath given unto us, neither is that which any of us do, according to our individual desires of happiness, valued more than that which another doeth.

48 For behold, when our basic needs are guaranteed unto us, then we have a hope that our existence is fair and just, and we begin to believe by this hope that those who created us love us and care about us.

49 But when we are forced to provide these things for ourselves, then we think that it is not fair that we came into existence because of the desires of another, and then are forced against our free will to labor for that in which we had no choice, but for that which we need to labor in order to continue in the existence in which we were created.

50 Therefore, my brothers and sisters, call upon the rich and the governments that have power over you and demand of them, in righteousness, that they provide for you the necessities that ye require to sustain your lives.

51 Yea, demand that there exist laws prohibiting the creation of a child, if it is not the intent of those who have created it to provide for its needs all the days of its life.

52 For this reason none can create life in the kingdom of the Father except it be those who have already proven that they are worthy parents, and that they will provide for the happiness of their creation in all things. Yea, is not this fair and just?

53 And the plan of Lucifer would not have it this way, for he believeth that we should create others to serve us. And for this reason, he putteth in the hearts of the children of men to exalt themselves one above another, so that one is forced to serve the other.

54 And when one is forced to serve another, this shall always create misery and despair unto those who are forced to serve by no choice of their own.

55 And ye of the latter days, are not ye servants of those who give you the money so that ye might live? Are not ye their indentured slaves that they might get gain from your employ? Are ye not required to work all the days of your lives under their subjection, because of the power that they have over you in the money that ye receive from them?

56 Now, if ye had a righteous government that provided you with food and clothing and shelter, then ye would not be the servant to any man, for he could not command you in anything, knowing that ye could leave his employ and still be able to survive and be happy.

57 Do ye not see the guise of the rich in enslaving you that they might get gain from you and not work for themselves? Is not this the image of happiness that the beast hath deceived you into believing is the only way to peace and happiness?

58 And those of you who are rich and employ the souls of the children of men that they might get gain for you, what say ye of yourselves? How can ye justify that which ye do to maintain the image of the beast?

59 Yea, I have read that which ye say in the words of the brother of Jared; and ye speak, saying: I am rich because I deserve the blessings of God, because I provide for those who are in my employ with the things that they need to live.

60 And if I did not provide them with employment, then they would not have the necessities of life and would die. Therefore, I deserve to be exalted above them, because of that which I do for them.

61 Woe unto the rich who think in this manner, for ye shall be condemned greatly for that which ye do. Yea, how many of those whom ye employ would work for you if they were always guaranteed that which they needed to survive? Do ye think that they would remain in your employ when ye treat them with disrespect and put yourselves above them?

62 Do ye think that they are happy in your employ? I say unto you that they are not happy in your employ, but of a necessity they are forced to be your slaves.

63 Now, it is not a hard thing for a government of a nation to set up a system whereby all of the people can have those things which they need to sustain their lives.

64 And now, I have seen the latter days and the nation of the United States, which is the most wicked nation upon the earth in regards to those who seeketh to enslave the souls of the children of men so that they might get gain and not be required to work by the sweat of their own brow.

65 Yea, ye complain in this nation of the poor and the needy, whom ye believe are lazy and undeserving of the fine things of the world. And ye have many of them in your prisons because of the imagined threat that ye suppose they have caused you because of that which they do to their own bodies.

66 Behold, I have seen the great abuse that many of the poor do to their bodies with drugs, which ye have made illegal by the laws that ye have established among you.

67 Now, why is it that ye imprison these who take these illegal drugs, when the reason why they take them is because they are in search of a temporary happiness and an escape from the drudgery of the employ that is forced upon them by your desires to get gain?

68 Behold, ye have many drugs which ye take that are prescribed to you by your doctors which are more harmful than these drugs which are distributed and consumed by the majority of those whom ye imprison.

69 And many of those whom ye have imprisoned have been convicted of crimes that ye have caused them to commit because of the unrighteous laws that ye have established for yourselves. Do ye think that by placing them in these prisons that ye shall solve the unhappiness and problems of your society? I say unto you that it shall not solve any of your problems, but shall make them worse for you.

70 And what shall ye say when the Lord cometh in the glory of the Father and commandeth that all the prisons be destroyed and all the prisoners therein be released? What then shall ye think of your laws?

71 Behold, if ye want to help your brothers and sister who are imprisoned because of you, then ye should seek out the reasons for the which they have broken the laws that ye have established against them.

72 Behold, why do ye not think that it would be more beneficial to you if ye found the source of their desires to commit these crimes, or the reason why they have broken your laws, instead of treating the symptom that ye know a prison will not cure?

73 And now, I shall give unto you the will of the Lord concerning these things, that if ye desire, that ye might make the necessary changes in your laws and your government that shall solve these problems which ye have before you.

74 In the day of the Lord, he shall place a great emphasis on the food that is produced for consumption in those days. And he shall make it a priority that the farms and gardens of the earth begin to produce all manner of fruits and foods which are pleasing to the eye and refreshing to the taste.

75 And He shall command that this food be that which all should have according to their needs and their wants.

76 And these fruits and foods shall be natural foods which are created according to the laws of nature as they were in the beginning when the sons and daughters of Adam lived for many years in health and happiness.

77 And no man or woman or child shall go without enough food to eat; nevertheless, the food that they shall eat shall be only that food that shall be beneficial to their bodies, even that food that shall cure all manner of ills within them.

78 And now, because there shall be no value placed upon the food that shall be available for all to eat, there shall be no reason why one would steal for this food.

79 And if a man stealeth any of this food, then what shall he say to another: Buy this food from me for a price? And another will say unto him: What price thinkest thou that I would give unto thee for something that I can obtain without price?

80 And furthermore, there shall be no money to exchange for the food, therefore, there is no incentive given to steal this food.

81 And when a man knoweth that he hath sufficient food that he might live, then this man beginneth to believe that he is happy and that those who have provided this food for him value him as a man who is equal to them.

82 And when a man feeleth that he is valued and is equal to all others, then he is happy and hath no desire to hurt others, or steal from them, or cause pain upon them for any reason.

83 And when ye all feel of equal importance one to another, then shall hope rise among you and ye shall be happy and at peace.

CHAPTER 91

Hope plus faith equals good works and is the formula set forth for righteousness and happiness. The reasons why people commit crimes against humanity are explained. The form of government that will be upon the earth during the millennium is introduced. The exalted shall be abased and the abased shall be exalted. Latter-day humans are encouraged to set their governments up according to the government of heaven.

AND now my brothers and sisters, if there existeth hope among you in abundance, then there shall also be an exceedingly strong faith in that which hath created this hope.

2 Therefore, if it is a government that perpetuateth and giveth unto a man this hope, then this man will have faith in this government and support it, and if necessary, give his life for it.

3 And now, the governments of men are led by leaders who speak flattering words of hope unto the people; and because of their words of flattery and promises of hope, they deceive the people and manipulate them into believing that the hope that they promise the people with their flattery will come to fruition.

4 But when the hope in which the people have placed their trust is not realized, then the people do not have faith in their government and do not support it. And when the people do not support it, the government shall fail.

5 Therefore, the most important thing to a man is his hope, which bringeth to him the faith that causeth his works.

6 And now, a government that expecteth the people to support it and trust in it, should be able to guarantee the people that for which they hope. Nevertheless, there hath been no government upon the face of the earth since the beginning of the accounted history of man that hath given all the people that for which they hope.

7 Yea, it is true that the governments of men have provided an opportunity for the few, who are rich and who hold power over the poor, to realize the hope that bringeth joy to them, but no government based upon the principles and precepts of men, which are given unto them according to the plan of Lucifer, can provide a hope for all of the people.

8 And because these governments have not provided this hope for all of the people, many of them do not have faith in these governments, but are forced by the power of these governments, which is held in the hands of those whose hope is fulfilled, to support the government that the rich and the powerful have established for themselves.

9 And if the majority, who are poor, do not support the government, then by the power of its force, these are imprisoned, or killed, thus fulfilling the words of John, which he wrote, saying: And he had power to give life unto the image of the beast, that the image of the beast should both speak, and cause that as many as would not worship the image of the beast should be killed.

10 And when the people have lost hope in their government, then they no longer have faith in it, and their works become contrary to the principles and laws that these governments have set up.

11 Now, these are the reasons for the crimes that are committed by the poor against the rich in the governments of men. Behold, the poor have lost faith in the rich because they do not care for them, nor do they represent their causes and their needs in their governments.

12 And when they have lost the hope that their faith can be realized, according to their desires of happiness, then their works seem to be evil in the eyes of the government that hath set itself up as an entity from which they should receive the desires of their faith.

13 And when their works are evil according to the government, then these that have lost hope are imprisoned for that which they do contrary to the laws of the land established by these corrupt governments.

14 And it shall come to pass that when the Lord cometh upon the earth, he shall throw down all the governments of men which have made empty promises by the flattering words of their leaders.

15 And he shall establish his government, which shall guarantee unto all the fulfillment of the hope of all their desires. And this hope is that we might be happy in the state of existence in which we have been placed by God, our Heavenly Father.

16 Therefore, in the day that he shall cast down all the governments of men, he shall release all the prisoners being held in all of the prisons that shall be established throughout the earth.

17 And it shall not matter to the Lord for what crime these have been charged, or for what purpose they have been caused by their governments to be incarcerated in prisons; for all the people of the earth shall know that the new government of the Lord is a righteous government, which giveth to all equally those things which will sustain their lives and bring them happiness.

18 And when those that were once prisoners realize that they are now being led by a righteous leader, and that the government of the earth is a government set up for the sake of all of the people, and not for the sake and purpose of the rich only, then shall these begin to have an exceedingly great faith in the government, and then they shall not be desirous to commit any crime against it.

19 And it shall come to pass that the whole earth shall be under one government; and it shall fill the entire earth with its laws and its principles.

20 And those who were chosen as leaders of the governments of men shall have their nakedness revealed unto them in that day. In other words, the whole world shall see the wickedness of the manner in which they led the people and held power in their governments.

21 And none of these shall receive the honor and respect that they once received among men. And all the leaders of the governments throughout the history of the earth shall lose the respect and adoration of the people of the earth; and their names and their works shall not be known again throughout the earth.

22 And then shall the words of the Lord be fulfilled, when he said: He who is exalted shall be abased, and he who is abased shall be exalted.

23 Behold, in the day of the reign of the Lord, the works of men shall be discovered for what they are; yea, the whole world shall know that every government set up among the children of men since the days of Adam, were governments which followed the plan of Lucifer and exalted the rich and powerful and abased the poor, and the meek, and the humble among men.

24 And now, it is for this reason, which I knew before I started this abridgment of the record of the brother of Jared, that I have not included in this record the names of any of the leaders of the governments of men which have lived upon the earth, except it be those who have been wrought upon by the Lord, or used by him, to do his will for the people, even those elect who honored the Lord and obeyed his commandments.

25 Therefore, all ye leaders of the governments of men who shall receive these things; yea, even all ye who have given great accolades to the leaders of your governments and your nations, which ye thought were

righteous and noble men among you; behold, I say unto all of you that ye are wicked men and did nothing to perpetuate the plan of the Father upon the earth.

26 Yea, ye have led the rich and those whose hope was satisfied by you. But the poor, and the needy, the widow, and the orphan, and those who are imprisoned, ye did nothing for, except it be that ye fed them from the scraps that fell from your tables.

27 And the honor and glory that ye received from men shall be as the sand that bloweth off the palm tree in the desert. Yea, the sand covereth the palm, so that the glory of its life is hidden from view. And the wind bloweth off the sand revealing the glory and beauty of the tree.

28 But the sand that covered up the tree is cast amongst the rest of the grains of sand, which is plentiful, and of which there is no distinction, all grains being equal one to another.

29 For in the day of the Lord, no man who hath received glory and honor of men shall maintain that same glory in that day.

30 And the Lord shall call forth those whom he hath chosen to be the leaders of his government, which is the government that supporteth the plan of the Father. And when the people of the world shall behold those whom he calleth forth from among them to be the leaders of his government, they shall be astonished at those whom he shall ordain to this power and authority.

31 And then shall the words of the prophets be fulfilled when they prophesied, saying: The weak things of the world shall come forth and break down the mighty and strong ones, that man should not counsel his fellow man, neither trust in the arm of flesh; but that every man might speak in the name of God the Lord, even the Savior of the world.

32 For there shall be some called from among the poor, who are cast out by the rich and their governments; and there shall be some called who have been imprisoned by the governments of men.

33 Behold, then he shall call forth those who shall be the principle leaders over the people of the whole earth. And these are many of the prophets who have been cast out and slain by the governments and the religions of men which existed upon the earth since the beginning.

34 And then shall the leaders of the governments and religions of men look upon the leaders whom the Lord hath chosen from among them, and they shall say of them like was said of the apostles of the Lord, which is written, saying: Now when they saw the boldness of Peter and John, and perceived that they were unlearned and ignorant men, they marveled.

35 And there shall be great torment among the prideful, and the rich, and the learned, and those who once held a position of power over the children of men. For these shall know that they are nothing in the sight of God, but that the Lord hath exalted those who were once abased by them.

36 And he shall exalt these that were once perceived as unlearned and ignorant and weak among men, and he shall give them power over the rich, and the prideful, and those who held honor and glory among the kingdoms and nations of the earth.

37 And at that day, the Lord shall cause that there shall be no body hair upon the face, or the bodies of those who have not been ordained by him to have power over the people. And by this shall the people know that a man hath been chosen by God to lead the people.

38 Behold, only those men who can grow a beard and who have body hair shall be those who have been chosen by the Lord to lead the people. And in this way there shall be no more deception among the people of the earth as to who is a leader and doeth the will of the Father, and who is not.

39 Behold, at that day, the Lord shall establish his government and his laws and call forth those who shall be in different parts of the world to govern under his authority. And because they shall have a beard, then shall the people know that they have been chosen by God to serve them and lead them in the plan of the Father.

40 And the Lord shall not allow a wicked man to wear a beard, nor shall a wicked man be capable of growing one by nature.

41 And these leaders who are called by the Lord shall set up the kingdom of God according to the things which they shall be taught by the Lord.

42 And it shall come to pass that the entire world shall be ruled under one government, even a new world order of government which shall be led by the Lord. And there shall be no bureaucracy in the government of the Lord, for there shall be no need for one man to tell another that which he should do, for all shall be taught the law of the Father, which shall be a universal law that all shall obey.

43 And the reasons why all shall obey this law, is because it is a righteous law which was given unto the people by the Lord, who shall come to the earth in all the glory and power of the Father.

44 And the people shall know that his law is a righteous law because it guaranteeth unto them the fulfillment of their hopes of peace and happiness.

45 And because the people know that it fulfilleth their hopes, then they have exceeding faith in this law; and their faith shall bring forth works which are meet for this law.

46 And if it is a righteous law, then it shall bring forth righteous works; and from the righteous works of all the people of the earth, shall peace and happiness reign upon it.

47 And now, I would that ye should understand something more concerning the day of the Lord. For I know that there shall be many of you who think that when the Lord cometh in the glory of the Father that all the wicked shall be destroyed. And this ye believe because ye are taught the precepts of men, and do not understand the plan of the Father concerning His children.

48 Behold, it was given unto you in an allegory concerning these things that shall come to pass in the day of the Lord by the prophet Zenos, when he spoke, saying: And it came to pass that the Lord of the vineyard said unto the servant: Let us go to and hew down the trees of the vineyard and cast them into the fire, that they shall not cumber the ground of my vineyard, for I have done all. What could I have done more for my vineyard?

49 And now, my beloved brothers and sisters, I, Moroni, have received a commandment of the Lord that I should give unto you an explanation of this parable that Zenos used to teach the people the things that were to come to pass pertaining to the kingdom of God upon the earth.

50 Therefore, I shall give unto you the meaning of all of these things according to the Holy Spirit which is in me. For behold, after the gospel shall be given unto the Gentiles in the latter days, even through Joseph, the first of these last two prophets of God, the church that he shall set up upon the seat of the beast of the latter days shall become exceedingly prideful and shall fulfill the words of Zenos when he said:

51 And it came to pass that the servant said unto his master: And now, behold, notwithstanding all the care which we have taken of my vineyard, the trees thereof have become corrupted, that they bring forth no good fruit; and these I had hoped to preserve, to have laid up fruit thereof against the season, unto mine own self.

52 But, behold, they have become like unto the wild olive-tree, and they are of no worth but to be hewn down and cast into the fire; and it grieveth me that I should lose them. But what could I have done more in my vineyard? Have I slackened mine hand, that I have not nourished it, Nay, I have nourished it, and I have digged about it, and I have pruned it, and I have dunged it; and I have stretched forth mine hand almost all the day long, and the end draweth nigh.

53 And it grieveth me that I should hew down all the trees of my vineyard, and cast them into the fire that they should be burned. Who is it that hath corrupted my vineyard?

54 And it came to pass that the servant said unto his master: Is it not the loftiness of thy vineyard; have not the branches thereof overcome the roots which are good? And because the branches have overcome the roots thereof, behold they grew faster than the strength of the roots, taking strength unto themselves. Behold, I say, is not this the cause that the trees of thy vineyard have become corrupted?

55 And now, this Zenos said concerning the church that shall rise up in the latter days and take upon itself the name of the Church of Jesus Christ of Latter-day Saints. Behold, these are they who have preserved the root of the tree, which is the true gospel of Jesus Christ.

56 And this they have preserved in the pride of their hearts; for they have the record of my father in which is given the fullness of the gospel and all the words of Christ; and they also have the words of the Bible, which proceedeth forth from the mouth of the Jew.

57 And this former testifieth of the latter, giving testimony to the whole world of the truthfulness of the gospel of Jesus Christ, which are the words which he gave unto the Jews, first, and then unto my fathers, who were the Nephites in the land of Bountiful.

58 And this great church of the latter days hath preserved the roots of the gospel, but the branches of the tree, which are the leaders and the members of this church, have taken strength unto themselves, in the pride and arrogance that they show forth because of the true gospel which they have among them.

59 And because they have taken strength unto themselves, the fruit which these branches bear is a corrupted and an evil fruit, which the Lord hateth.

60 For behold, it is the position and authority of Jehovah to prepare the world for the Father and teach the people the will of the Father in all things. In other words, it is his commission from the Father to prepare the vineyard that it might bring forth righteous fruit.

61 And after the Gentiles shall corrupt the work of the Lord; yea, even after much patience and mercy hath been shown unto them by the Lord, then shall the Lord be dismayed in his efforts to fulfill the will of the Father in all things which he was commanded by the Father in the beginning concerning the children of God that pertain unto this earth.

62 And when the Lord showed forth his dismay at the great wickedness of the children of men, he called forth all of his holy prophets, even all those who had been upon the earth, and counseled with them.

63 And at the time that he shall call together all those who have been called to the office of a prophet, there shall only be one of them, who hath been called of God to perform the labors of a prophet of God, left upon the earth.

64 And this shall be Christopher, the last of the two latter-day prophets that shall be among you. And the Lord shall call forth his prophets, all of whom shall be resurrected at this time and residing in the kingdom of the Father, except it be for the last of them, who shall be still upon the earth among you.

65 And the Lord shall counsel with them about that which they should do in order to complete the will of the Father concerning this world.

66 And the Lord knew that the time of the end was near and that it was expedient that the will of the Father be completed according to the timetable that the Father had set down in the beginning.

67 Therefore, the Lord was saddened that it should be necessary to hew down all the trees of his vineyard, and cast them into the fire that they should be burned.

68 And the words of Zenos continue, saying: But, behold, the servant said unto the Lord of the vineyard: Spare it a little longer. And the Lord said: Yea, I will spare it a little longer, for it grieveth me that I should lose the trees of my vineyard. Therefore, let us take of the branches of these which I have planted in the nethermost parts of my vineyard, and let us graft them into the tree from whence they came; and let us pluck from the tree those branches whose fruit is most bitter, and graft in the natural branches of the tree in the stead thereof.

69 And this will I do that the tree may not perish, that, perhaps, I may preserve unto myself the roots thereof for mine own purpose. And, behold, the roots of the natural branches of the tree which I planted whithersoever I would are yet alive; therefore, that I may preserve them also for mine own purpose, I will take of the branches of this tree, and I will graft them in unto them.

70 Yea, I will graft in unto them the branches of their mother tree, that I may preserve the roots also unto mine own self, that when they shall be sufficiently strong perhaps they may bring forth good fruit unto me, and I may yet have glory in the fruit of my vineyard.

71 And it came to pass that they took from the natural tree which had become wild, and grafted in unto the natural trees, which also had become wild. And they also took of the natural trees

which had become wild, and grafted into their mother tree.

72 And the Lord of the vineyard said unto the servant: Pluck not the wild branches from the trees, save it be those which are most bitter; and in them ye shall graft according to that which I have said. And we will nourish again the trees of the vineyard, and we will trim up the branches thereof; and we will pluck from the trees those branches which are ripened, that must perish, and cast them into the fire.

73 And this I do that, perhaps, the roots thereof may take strength because of their goodness; and because of the change of the branches, that the good may overcome the evil.

74 And because that I have preserved the natural branches and the roots thereof, and that I have grafted in the natural branches again into their mother tree, and have preserved the roots of their mother tree, that, perhaps, the trees of my vineyard may bring forth again good fruit; and that I may have joy again in the fruit of my vineyard, and, perhaps, that I may rejoice exceedingly that I have preserved the roots and the branches of the first fruit.

75 Therefore, go to, and call servants, that we may labor diligently with our might in the vineyard, that we may prepare the way, that I may bring forth again the natural fruit, which natural fruit is good and the most precious above all other fruit.

76 Therefore, let us go to and labor with our might this last time, for behold the end draweth nigh, and this is for the last time that I shall prune my vineyard. Graft in the branches; begin at the last that they may be first, and that the first may be last, and dig about the trees, both old and young, the first and the last; and the last and the first, that all may be nourished once again for the last time.

77 Therefore, dig about them, and prune them, and dung them once more, for the last time, for the end draweth nigh. And if it be so that these last grafts shall grow, and bring forth the natural fruit, then shall ye prepare the way for them, that they may grow.

78 And as they begin to grow ye shall clear away the branches which bring forth bitter fruit, according to the strength of the good and the size thereof; and ye shall not clear away the bad thereof all at once, lest the roots thereof should be too strong for the graft, and the graft thereof shall perish, and I lose the trees of my vineyard.

79 For it grieveth me that I should lose the trees of my vineyard; therefore ye shall clear away the bad according as the good shall grow, that the root and the top may be equal in strength, until the good shall overcome the bad, and the bad be hewn down and cast into the fire, that they cumber not the ground of my vineyard; and thus will I sweep away the bad out of my vineyard

80 And the branches of the natural tree will I graft in again into the natural tree; And the branches of the natural tree will I graft into the natural branches of the tree; and thus will I bring them together again, that they shall bring forth the natural fruit, and they shall be one.

81 And the bad shall be cast away, yea, even out of all the land of my vineyard; for behold, only this once will I prune my vineyard.

82 And it came to pass that the Lord of the vineyard sent his servant; and the servant went and did as the Lord had commanded him, and brought other servants; and they were few.

83 And the Lord of the vineyard said unto them: Go to, and labor in the vineyard, with your might. For behold, this is the last time that I shall nourish my vineyard; for the end is nigh at hand, and the season speedily cometh; and if ye labor with your might with me ye shall have joy in the fruit which I shall lay up unto myself against the time which will soon come.

84 And it came to pass that the servants did go and labor with their mights; and the Lord of the vineyard labored also with them; and they did obey the commandments of the Lord of the vineyard in all things.

85 And now, my brothers and sisters, these words of Zenos shall not come to pass until the Lord cometh in the glory of the Father to labor with the servants whom he shall call forth to help him teach the gospel throughout the world. And these are those whom I have mentioned who shall have facial hair and be known as the servants of the Lord and the leaders of the nations of the world.

86 And all of the wicked shall not be destroyed at his coming, for they are the bad fruit which shall be allowed to stay upon the earth and shall be removed as the good shall grow.

87 For behold, the wicked of the earth shall be taught the gospel of Christ according to their ability to understand it and abide by its precepts. But as righteousness beginneth to sweep the earth, the wicked will no longer remain thereon, having been taught the gospel and been overcome by its power.

88 And the rest of the words of Zenos shall come to pass, which he spoke, saying: And there began to be the natural fruit again in the vineyard; and the natural branches began to grow and thrive exceedingly; and the wild branches began to be plucked off and to be cast away; and they did keep the root and the top thereof equal, according to the strength thereof.

89 And thus they labored, with all diligence, according to the commandments of the Lord of the vineyard, even until the bad had been cast away out of the vineyard, and the Lord had preserved unto himself that the trees had become again the natural fruit; and they became like unto one body; and the fruits were equal; and the Lord of the vineyard had preserved unto himself the natural fruit, which was most precious unto him from the beginning.

90 And it came to pass that when the Lord of the vineyard saw that his fruit was good, and that his vineyard was no more corrupt, he called up his servants, and said unto them: Behold, for this last time have we nourished my vineyard; and thou beholdest that I have done according to my will; and I have preserved the natural fruit, that it is good, even like as it was in the beginning.

91 And blessed art thou; for because ye have been diligent in laboring with me in my vineyard, and have kept my commandments, and have brought unto me again the natural fruit, that my vineyard is no more corrupted, and the bad is cast away, behold ye shall have joy with me because of the fruit of my vineyard.

92 For behold, for a long time will I lay up of the fruit of my vineyard unto mine own self against the season, which speedily cometh; and for the last time have I nourished my vineyard, and pruned it, and dug about it, and dunged it; therefore I will lay up unto mine own self of the fruit, for a long time, according to that which I have spoken.

93 And when the time cometh that evil fruit shall again come into my vineyard, then will I cause the good and the bad to be gathered; and the good will I preserve unto myself, and the bad will I cast away into its own place. And then cometh the season and the end; and my vineyard will I cause to be burned with fire.

94 And now, my beloved brothers and sisters, there are few parables as powerful as the words which Zenos spake unto the leaders of the Jews at Jerusalem. And all of his words shall come to pass.

95 And the Lord shall set up his government when he cometh to rule and reign upon the earth. And he shall labor side by side with the prophets who have died and have been resurrected to come forth in that day and labor with him in his vineyard.

96 And now, I have something more to say unto you regarding the government of the Lord which shall be established at the beginning of the last thousand years, or after the end of the half of times, as it hath been explained unto you.

97 Behold, this government shall be established according to the principles and laws of a righteous government which I have already given unto you and explained in this record. Nevertheless, so that it might be possible that the Lord shall cut his work short in righteousness and come down among you and begin his reign here again upon the earth before the appointed time of the Father, it is expedient in the hope that I have for the governments of the latter days, that I give unto you again these eternal principles that ye of the latter days might use to demand these things from the leaders whom ye shall choose to serve you.

98 Behold, I wrote unto you already, saying: And there existeth only one pure form of government that hath always existed, and shall continue to exist in worlds without end, and it is this form of government that ye should demand of your politicians and the leaders of all the nations of the earth.

99 For this is the form of government that the Lord shall establish upon the earth when he

cometh in the glory of the Father, for it is the government of the Father which is in heaven.

100 And this government hath one purpose and priority, in which are incorporated all the eternal laws that manage this government and cause it to function for the purpose for which it existeth. And that purpose for which it should exist upon the earth in mortality is for the temporal happiness of those whom it serveth.

101 And the first principle and law of this government, is that this government shall never be self-serving, or in other words, it shall never act in and of itself and of its own accord for the sake of its own existence.

102 And this government should be restricted in its power according to the restrictions that are necessary to ensure that it abideth by this first principle and law.

103 And this government should serve those who benefit from its existence; and those who benefit from its existence are those who give it the power that it hath received. And the power that it hath received hath been given to this government to serve those who have given it its power.

104 And this government should assure each of us the happiness that each of us desireth according to each of our individual desires of happiness.

105 And the second principle and law of this eternal government, is that it will guarantee the freedom, or the free agency, of all those whom it serveth.

106 And this free agency that it guaranteeth, restricteth those that it serveth from infringing upon the free agency of another, or from having another infringe on the free agency that each of those it serveth possesseth.

107 And this government will do nothing that infringeth upon the free agency of those whom it serveth, except in defending the free agency of another from being infringed upon.

108 And the third principle and law of this eternal government, is that it shall provide the means whereby those whom it serveth may have an equal opportunity to experience the happiness that they desire.

109 And because it was not the choice of those whom it serveth to exist, this government must provide those things that are necessary to fulfill the measure and purpose of their creation, which purpose is their individual happiness.

110 And this government should not compel any to use those things which it hath provided for its people so that they might find the happiness that they desire. For if this government were to compel the people in any of these things, then it would break the second law that governeth it, by taking away their free agency.

111 And these are the three main principles and laws of a righteous and just government. And these principles and laws of government should exist to serve those who have established this government. And they should exist to assure the freedom of those whom this government serveth. And they should exist to provide equality for all those whom this government serveth.

112 And I have explained unto you previously that under these three main principles and laws, are sub-laws, and sub-principles, which should be set forth to assure the adherence to these three main laws.

113 And I wrote unto you more concerning these things, saying: And this same government which is in heaven hath been explained and given unto the children of men through the prophets of God who have lived among them, and also from the ministrations of the Holy Ghost.

114 And the prophets have instructed the children of men to pattern their governments after the government which is in heaven, even the eternal government that assureth peace and order in all the eternal worlds that exist, which worlds are without end.

115 And according to the words of the brother of Jared, yea, even according to the words of my ancestors, and also according to my own experience, when the children of men attempt to pattern their governments after the pattern that hath been revealed unto them, then peace existeth upon the earth.

116 But if they stray from the pattern that hath been shown unto them, then there are wars, and chaos, and famine, and all types of destruction among them.

117 And the reason why they stray from the pattern shown unto them, is because they reject the words of the holy prophets, or they offend the Spirit, in that it withdraweth Itself from them. And when the Spirit withdraweth from them, then they shall have no ministrations to teach them the proper way that a government should work.

118 And when this pure form of government hath been established among them by those in authority, even those who have listened to the voice of the prophets, or who have the Holy Ghost as their constant guide, then peace and prosperity reign among them, evensomuch that there existeth no poor or needy among them.

119 And now, this shall be the state of the government during the time that the Lord shall reign upon the earth. And because of this form of government, there shall be no rich and poor, bond and free, but all shall be made free, and partakers of the heavenly gift.

120 Behold, my brothers and sisters of the latter days, I say unto you, always retain within you this hope of a government that patterneth itself after these principles.

121 And if ye have this hope, then ye can strive to establish this form of government among you.

122 And if ye cannot establish this form of government among you, because of the power and the wickedness of your leaders who depend on their own wisdom and the flesh of their own arm, and cast out the holy prophets, giving no attention to their words, and who seek after gold and silver and all the vain things of the earth; yea, then ye must wait upon the Lord; and in the power and glory of the Father shall the purpose of your hope be fulfilled, and the patience and faith of the saints shall be revealed.

CHAPTER 92

During Adam's days there was righteousness and happiness without technology. Healthy living and exercise are essential for good health. During the millennium there will be no more death or the eating of flesh. At that time, all will follow the laws of health provided in God's plan for his children.

BEHOLD, this form of government was upon the earth in the days of Adam and was established by him for the benefit of all of his children. And in the beginning, Adam and all of his children followed the plan of the Father and were an exceedingly happy and righteous people. Yea, there were no poor among them, and each of them was valued equally to every other soul upon the earth.

2 And at that time there had been no value placed upon the things of the world so that one thing might be sold for a profit, or that a man might gain power and control over another because of the riches that he possessed.

3 And in these early years of the life of Adam and Eve, the people were like unto the people of the city of Enoch, which was taken from off the earth because of its righteousness in living according to all the commandments and laws of the Father.

4 And now, ye of the latter days should understand this thing, even that in the early years of the life of Adam and Eve, the whole earth and its inhabitants were righteous and happy.

5 Now, did they have the technology and the advancements of science which ye of the latter days have? Yea, did they have the art, and the music, and the theater, and the sports, and the games, and all of those things which ye of the latter days believe bring you happiness?

6 And those things which ye believe bring you the comforts of life, did Adam provide these things for his children? Behold, Adam was a prophet of God and was like unto many of the prophets of old who saw the future of his children, even unto the latter days. Yea, he saw the great technology and the scientific advancements that would one day be upon the earth and instituted among all of his descendants according to the plan of Lucifer.

7 And when he saw these things, he also witnessed the great wickedness and abominations that were brought out into the world because of these things. And in the things which he saw, he was saddened greatly because of the choices that would be made by his descendants when they used this power of God to serve their own selfish needs.

8 And he saw the great destruction of the earth and its environs because of these things. And it was for this reason that Adam revealed none of these things unto his children.

9 Now, Adam had his free agency and could have taught his children concerning this power of God that would bring about these scientific advancements and this technology, if he had not been commanded by the Lord to keep the knowledge of these things away from his children.

10 And even if Adam had not received this commandment of the Lord, he would not have revealed these things unto his children, knowing that they would misuse the power of God, as his descendants would in the latter days, and bring upon themselves misery, and sickness, and inequality, and all the vicissitudes of the body and soul from which those of the latter days shall suffer.

11 Now, in the days of Adam the people lived for many years in health and strength, even for hundreds of years did they live at this time. But in the latter days, the days of a man shall be shortened exceedingly because of the laws of health which all of the people of the earth disobey and do not understand. And those days shall also be shortened for the sake of the elect who shall be forced to suffer exceedingly because of the wickedness of those days.

12 Nevertheless, as I have explained unto you, that the technology and the knowledge of these things shall be given unto you in the last days by Satan, so that it shall be possible that ye do not grow old in the state of the flesh in which ye shall find yourselves. But if ye receive by this technology the ability to live forever in a state of youth, this doth not necessarily mean that ye shall exist in a state of health and happiness.

13 Behold, I have explained unto you that the laws of health of the Father forbideth the cooking of food which destroyeth the natural order that hath been established for those things that were created to bring nourishment to our bodies.

14 And in the latter days most of the food that shall be consumed shall be those things which are processed by those who seek to get gain. And there shall be laws set up among you that shall require that any food that is sold unto you must be heated to kill those things which ye believe can cause sickness to the flesh.

15 Now, if the fire that ye apply to your food killeth those things which might be harmful unto you, according to your understanding, then do ye not suppose that those things which are most beneficial to you shall also be killed when this heat is applied? I say unto you that any food that passeth through the process of heat shall be no good for your bodies and shall be the means and cause of all of your infirmities in the latter days.

16 And even those of you who shall choose to live in your youth without experiencing the effects of the natural aging process, yea, ye shall also die because of the disease and pestilence that shall come from cooking your food.

17 And in the latter days there shall be many people who shall be unhealthy and sick because of the food which they eat. And there shall be many others who shall be sick and afflicted because of the technology that ye have developed among you that causeth you to become inactive and overweight because of the easiness of your lives, which Satan hath given unto you according to his plan.

18 Now, if ye are young and are excessively overweight, what cause of joy do ye have to live? Do ye enjoy the bodies that ye have, which shall not grow old, yet are obese and susceptible to all manner of disease that can end your life anyway? Yea, is the quality of your life sufficient unto you to bring you the happiness that ye desire?

19 I say unto you that ye are not happy, but are miserable; and if it were not for the things that Satan hath provided for you to assuage your unhappiness, then ye would have no desire to live.

20 And now I shall give unto you a description of the lifestyle and manner of living of those during the time that the Lord shall be upon the earth in the power of the Father. And in this description ye shall see the great benefits of health and strength that shall come to all of those who follow the plan of the Father.

21 And if ye were to follow the plan of the Father in all things, then ye would know true happiness, which is a joy that lasteth forever under the eternal plan that our Father hath given us to provide this never ending happiness.

22 Behold, in that day there shall also be no death; and the reason why there shall be no death is because none who are upon the earth shall grow old. And all shall grow to the age of their maturity and remain in that state forever.

23 And the Lord shall begin to cleanse the earth from the manner in which technology and science is used to bring happiness to those of you in the latter days. For behold, any use of this technology or science that destroyeth the natural order of the earth, shall no longer be permitted to remain upon the earth.

24 Yea, the oil which ye of the latter days take from the earth, shall be used no more; even all of the waste byproducts of your efforts to provide energy for the function of those things which ye have developed because of your advancements in science and technology, even all these things shall be taken from off the earth.

25 For in the day of the Lord, the power of the natural sun shall be used to give to the earth all things which are necessary for the happiness and enjoyment of its inhabitants.

26 Behold, it is this power that giveth life unto the plants which provide the foods that we should eat to maintain our strength and our health. And the process by which these plants captivate and use the power of the sun shall be introduced and used by the Lord and his servants to provide the people of the earth with all the energy that they need to be happy.

27 And Satan shall strive to give this knowledge of the power of the sun to the children of men in the latter days before the coming of the Lord. But the knowledge that he shall give unto those who worship him and receive his mark shall be a knowledge that affecteth the natural state in which the earth was created. And this knowledge that they shall receive from Satan shall begin to destroy the earth and kill the people of the earth.

28 And now, it is important to understand that the powers of the Father should do nothing but give happiness to His children. Behold, none of these powers should be used to hurt any of the creations of God; and the earth and all of its inhabitants are the creations of God.

29 And in the day of the Lord, the great power of the process that is used by the vegetation of the earth to maintain a healthy living environment shall be used by the Lord to heal the earth and provide fresh water, and clean air, and delicious and plentiful food for all the inhabitants of the earth.

30 And there shall be no need for fires or heat to cook food, for the natural state of all things shall be maintained for the health and enjoyment of all.

31 Behold, in the beginning the Father commanded that the seeds of the plants from his own planet be brought upon this planet and planted to bring forth the eternal perpetuation of themselves that existeth in these seeds. For behold, all plants are eternal in and of themselves. For the seed shall grow into a mature plant and cast it seeds again to perpetuate itself continually forever.

32 Now, this great power which is contained in all the seeds that giveth life unto the world shall be harnessed according to the knowledge and command of the Lord. And he shall command the balance of nature to once again become like it was in the garden of Eden, in which were placed Adam and Eve.

33 For all noxious weeds and plants which were put upon the earth to inhibit the happiness of the children of men for their own sake and experience, shall be taken off the earth. Nevertheless, if a plant supporteth the balance and order of nature in its production of food for the consumption of the people of the earth, then it shall remain, whether it is an edible plant or not.

34 And there are many plants which survive in the environment in which they are created to purify the air that we breathe and maintain a constant order in the atmosphere that alloweth

for life to perpetuate itself. And these plants shall remain, not only for their purifying abilities in the order of their nature, but also for their beauty, which is beheld by the children of God, and in which they receive much joy.

35 But every plant that doth not benefit the happiness of the children of God, shall no longer be upon the earth in the day of the Lord, for he shall command them to be destroyed that they shall no longer inhibit the joy and happiness experienced by the people of the earth.

36 And the trees and plants that produce food shall be placed once again in their natural state, which state shall be overseen by those who have been chosen by the Lord to produce food in its abundance. And this process of food production shall be according to the laws of nature, and not the laws of men.

37 For the laws of men cause chaos in the laws of nature and bring forth fruits and the produce of plants that are deficient in the natural nutrients that provide for the health and strength of those for whom these plants are intended.

38 And if these foods are produced in their natural states, then the natural nutrients are maintained therein, and then these foods shall provide for the bodies of the people of the earth so that they might live in their youth without sickness and pestilence and the diseases that would kill them.

39 Now, this perpetual youth is not the resurrection of the body to its eternal state, but is a state of mortality only. For in an eternal state, the spirits of the children of God shall not be able to leave the flesh that they shall receive in the resurrection according to the kingdom which they shall inherit according to their individual desires for happiness.

40 And during the time of the Lord, all spirits shall be brought forth into the earth to live in mortality according to the days of their probation, which days are necessary for them to show unto them that the degree of glory in the kingdoms of the Father that they have chosen for themselves, is the kingdom that fulfilleth all of their desires for happiness.

41 Behold, during the final reign of the Lord upon the earth, all bodies of flesh and bone that have not been resurrected, shall be in a state that is similar to the state of those bodies which shall reside in the Telestial kingdom of glory.

42 Nevertheless, there shall be some among them upon the earth that shall have perfected bodies that have received the resurrection that pertaineth to the glory that they have chosen for themselves.

43 Yea, these are those who were resurrected with Christ, and also all those who have proven themselves worthy of the resurrection after the first resurrection occurred.

44 Now, I have already touched upon these things in this record—concerning the resurrection—but it sufficeth me to say that the majority of all the mortal bodies that the spirits of the children of God shall inhabit in mortality during the great millennium of the Lord, shall be liken unto those bodies of a Terrestrial and of a Telestial nature. And all these bodies shall be healthy bodies which shall reach the age of maturity and never grow old again.

45 And they shall eat of the fruit and the foods that shall be produced for them by the industry of production that the Lord shall set up throughout the whole earth. And these foods shall be available to all people without price and whenever their hearts so desire them.

46 And there shall be no more eating of flesh upon the earth. Yea, ye have in the words of the prophets that which they wrote, saying: But with righteousness shall he judge the poor, and reprove with equity for the meek of the earth; and he shall smite the earth with the rod of his mouth, and with the breath of his lips shall he slay the wicked.

47 And righteousness shall be the girdle of his loins, and faithfulness the girdle of his reins. The wolf shall dwell with the lamb, and the leopard shall lie down with the kid; and the calf and the young lion and the fatling shall play together, and a little child shall lead them. And the cow and the bear shall feed upon the plants of the earth from which all things receiveth their life; and their young ones shall lie down together; and the lion shall eat straw like the ox.

48 And the sucking child shall play on the hole of the asp, and the weaned child shall put his hand on the den of a cockatrice. They shall not hurt nor destroy in all my holy mountain; for the earth shall be full of the knowledge of the Lord, as the waters cover the sea.

49 Behold, how blessed shall be the day of the Lord and the establishment of the plan of the Father upon the earth. How glorious shall be that time when there existeth no more death, nor the murder of an animal for food, neither by the hand of man, nor by the order of nature which causeth one animal to eat another to maintain the balance therein.

50 Yea, during these days the animals upon the earth shall not fear man, neither shall man fear any animal. And all animals shall be changed by the command and knowledge of the Lord, which shall fill the earth and instruct his holy angels and servants to change the nature of the bodies of the animals of the earth by his command.

51 And when the change hath come upon them, then shall all animals eat from the fruits and plants that taketh their power from the sun and provideth nutrients for all life. And the fish of the sea shall not consume one another anymore, but they shall be like unto the great leviathan who eateth the order of plants that the Lord hath provided in the sea in an abundance, and from which these great beasts of the sea receive their nutrients. And all fish in the sea shall receive their nutrients in this manner, not hurting or destroying in any form throughout the entire earth.

52 And when all the animals of nature begin to eat those things which are of a different order, even the plant life which hath been provided for them by the Lord to exist in the environs in which they were placed to fulfill the measure of their creation, then shall the fear diminish and disappear among all the creatures of the earth.

53 Now, all creatures are created for the benefit of the children of God. Behold, they are not created to act independently of themselves, so that they might be like unto the souls of men, who act consciously in their individual desires of joy and happiness. But these shall exist to provide this joy to those of a higher order, who are the children of God who have been made in His own image.

54 Therefore, all those animals that do not bring forth joy and happiness to the children of God in their interactions with them, according to the happiness that a man or a woman might receive from an animal; yea, all those that serve no purpose to generate a state of happiness for the children of God, shall be taken from off the earth.

55 For behold, these were placed here in the beginning to be an example unto the children of the Father of the difference between the plan of Lucifer, which would allow one creature to be more powerful than another and consume the weaker creature at the pleasure of the stronger one, and the plan of the Father, which provideth all things in equality for the enjoyment and happiness of all of His creations.

56 And now, I say unto you of the latter days who shall live upon the earth before the great day of the Lord, yea, why do ye not see the great benefits of eating healthy according to the laws of nature, which would give you the health and strength that ye desire?

57 Yea, why do ye allow those things which are processed by the hand of man and given unto you after they have passed through the destroying heat of fire, which taketh from them their beneficial nutrients, to be taken into your bodies?

58 Why do ye cause yourselves to depend upon the doctors and physicians that have set themselves up above you to maintain power over you and get gain from you?

59 Behold, if ye would eat those things which are natural, then ye would not be sick and ye would not have a need for a doctor. And if ye are sick, and would die, except it be that ye are saved by the hand of a doctor, why is it that ye have no faith in God, in that, if ye die, ye die unto Him?

60 Know ye not that your Father loveth you, and that He would take you unto Himself in love and mercy in the death of the mortal body which is causing you pain and sorrow? Why do ye trust in the arm of flesh and use these doctors to save the flesh that it might be a continual burden unto you, when ye could enjoy the peace of the Father that he hath promised the righteous through the peace of death?

61 Behold, I know why ye trust in these doctors and physicians among you; yea, ye trust in them because ye do not have faith in God; and because ye do not have faith in God,

ye fear death; and it is this fear of death that causeth you to seek out your doctors and your physicians that they might heal the infirmities that ye have brought upon yourselves because of the food that ye eat and the lack of exercise that causeth your bodies to rot away in a state of lethargic misery.

62 Do ye think for a moment that there shall be doctors and physicians during the time that the Lord reigneth upon the earth, even when he shall introduce the commandments of the Father pertaining to health and strength?

63 I say unto you, that there shall not be a doctor or a physician anywhere upon the earth. And those who exist upon the earth at the great and dreadful day of the Lord, shall be those who shall suffer the indignation of the wrath of God that shall be given unto them by the rod of his mouth; and with the breath of his lips shall he slay all the doctors and physicians upon the earth.

64 Behold, I have seen the great wickedness in the latter days pertaining to the state of health that shall be among you. And never hath there been a more discontented people upon the earth because of the unhealthy state of the bodies that ye maintain during the days of your probation in mortality in the latter days.

65 Yea, ye have the scriptures before you, yet ye do not understand them, and ye read those things only which speaketh gentle words to your souls and causeth you to justify the wickedness of your hearts.

66 Behold, the prophet Daniel gave unto you an example of the law of the Lord pertaining to the foods which ye should eat among you. And it is written, saying: And the king spake unto Ashpenaz the master of his eunuchs, that he should bring certain of the children of Israel, and of the seed of the king, who were the princes; yea, children in whom was no blemish, but well favored, and skillful in all wisdom, and cunning in knowledge, and understanding science, and such as had ability in them to stand in the palace of the king, and whom they might teach the learning and the tongue of the Chaldeans.

67 And the king appointed them a daily provision of the meat of the king, and of the wine which he drank that they might be nourished for three years; and that at the end thereof they might stand before the king.

68 Now among these were of the children of Judah, Daniel, Hananiah, Mishael, and Azariah; unto whom the prince of the eunuchs gave different names than those that had been given them by their fathers; for he gave unto Daniel the name of Belteshazzar; and to Hananiah, of Shadrach; and to Mishael, of Meshach; and to Azariah, of Abednego.

69 But Daniel, knowing the law of the Lord in all things, purposed in his heart that he would not defile himself with the portion of the meat of the king, nor with the wine which he drank; therefore he requested of the prince of the eunuchs that he might not defile himself with these things.

70 Now, God had brought Daniel into favor and tender love with the prince of the eunuchs. And the prince of the eunuchs said unto Daniel: I fear my lord, the king, who hath appointed your meat and your drink that ye might be nourished before him; for why should he see your faces worse looking than the children which are his princes and not of your sort? If he seeth this in you, then shall ye make me endanger my head to the king.

71 Then said Daniel to Melzar, whom the prince of the eunuchs had set over Daniel, Hananiah, Mishael, and Azariah: Prove thy servants, I beseech thee, ten days; and let them give us pulse to eat, and water to drink. Then let our countenances be looked upon before thee, and compare them to the countenance of the children that eat of the portion of the meat of the king; and as thou seest, deal with thy servants.

72 So he consented to them in this matter, and proved them ten days. And at the end of ten days their countenances appeared fairer and fatter in flesh than all the children which did eat the portion of the meat of the king and who drank his wine.

73 Thus Melzar took away the portion of their meat, and the wine that they should drink; and gave them pulse. As for these four children, God gave them knowledge and skill in all learning and wisdom; and above them all Daniel had understanding in all visions and dreams because he was called as a prophet of God.

74 Now at the end of the days that the king had commanded his servant to bring them in, then the prince of the eunuchs brought them in before Nebuchadnezzar. And the king communed with them; and among them all, was found none like Daniel, Hananiah, Mishael, and Azariah; therefore stood they before the king.

75 And in all matters of wisdom and understanding, that the king inquired of them, he found them ten times better than all the magicians and astrologers that were in all his realm.

76 Now, Daniel could not have been a prophet if he did not understand the mysteries and the laws of God pertaining to all things. And he did understand these things, and for this reason he introduced the laws of health to the king and his house that they might know the power of God which was in him.

77 And now, the Lord is not so much concerned with that which ye consume to live, but he is more concerned with that which ye do with the life and the energy that ye receive from the food that ye eat.

78 Nevertheless, during the millennium, there shall be no more taking the life of an animal for its flesh, nor shall any be allowed to cook their food for nourishment of the bodies that shall be provided in those days for the children of men.

CHAPTER 93

The error of cosmetic surgery because of vanity is touched upon. The relationships between all human beings during the millennium are described. The nations of the Telestial, Terrestrial, and Celestial kingdoms will be established, with the city of Zion and Jerusalem being the main cities of the Lord's government. The gospel will spread throughout the earth and the people will choose for themselves in which nation they will live. Only the Celestial people will be allowed to have children.

AND now, the consumption of food is not the only thing in which ye sin grossly in the latter days as pertaining to the laws of health and happiness; but there are other ways that shall be introduced among you by the plan of Lucifer that shall cause you to destroy the order of nature by which ye were created.

2 Behold, in the latter days there shall be great pride and vanity throughout the earth because of the image that the beast shall present unto you and cause you to worship. Yea, the image of the beast shall cause that there shall be a standard set for the appearance of a man and a woman.

3 And the people of the earth shall begin to worship this image and do all in their power to follow this image and reach this standard of beauty that hath been set for them.

4 And there shall be many who again deny the power of God, and also their faith in God, in that which they have been given according to the natural order of all things. For the standard of beauty that shall be set by the image of the beast shall be that which all desire.

5 And if by the course of nature this beauty is not had by many of those of the latter days, then shall they go to the doctors and the physicians who shall receive a knowledge and an expertise from Satan to change the form of their faces, and their bodies, and their natures to conform to the standard that the beast hath set for them.

6 And I say unto you, that ye that doeth these things denieth the power of the Father and shall be condemned for that which ye have done to yourselves, which is contrary to the order of nature that maintaineth a balance in all things. And these changes which ye shall make for yourselves shall cause you more misery than the temporary joy that they shall give unto you when ye look into a mirror and behold the image of that which ye have been convinced is the standard of beauty that should be maintained.

7 Behold, God loveth all of his children and will give unto each of them according to their needs to learn during the days of their probation. And many of these shall not reach the standard of beauty that hath been set for them by the beast; and they shall not have the means whereby they might make the change to their appearance to conform to this standard; yet, do ye think that the Father loveth them less than those who have been given this standard of beauty by nature?

8 I say unto you that He doth not love them less, but shall bless them exceedingly if they

will but have faith in Him and His will. Behold, it shall come to pass in the day of the Lord that all of those who have changed their bodies to conform to the standard set for them by the image of the beast; yea, these shall be the ugliest among all the children of men upon the earth.

9 For in that day, all of the unnatural parts of their bodies shall fail them, and they shall no longer function as they should function. And those who have deformities, or who have been burdened with what they perceive as levels of beauty that are below the standard of beauty that giveth them their happiness, these shall the Lord bless and cause by his power that they receive the body and the beauty that they desire for their happiness.

10 And these desires of happiness cometh from the natural sexual desires that all shall experience according to the laws of nature. Nevertheless, in that day, there shall only be a few who shall have the bodies necessary to create children and be parents. Yea, these are those who have proven to themselves that the sacrifice of their own selfishness bringeth more happiness to them, than the fulfillment of their own selfish desires.

11 Yea, in that day only those women shall have breasts and the beauty of a natural woman that can produce a child. And only those men who are worthy shall have the parts of the male body that are necessary so that they might create children.

12 But the majority of the people of the earth at this time shall be like unto a eunuch, or shall have those bodies that shall exist in the Terrestrial and Telestial kingdoms of glory. At that day there shall be no distinction between a man and a woman except it be among those who are worthy of this distinction.

13 Behold, the spirits of the children of God shall inhabit the body that they have chosen for themselves as their desires of happiness. And if their desires of happiness are not Celestial in nature, then they shall not have a body of a male or a female, which body dependeth on the choice of the spirit who would be a male or female according to that which bringeth to them the most happiness.

14 And in those days that shall continue in the course of mortality, there shall only be a few who shall be given the power and the authority to provide the mortal bodies for the spirits who shall still be in the spirit world awaiting another chance in mortality to experience the days of their probation.

15 For behold, during the millennium of the Lord, all the spirits of the children of God shall be upon the earth in mortality. And there shall be none left in the spirit world except Lucifer and those who chose to follow him in his plan. And these shall remain in the spirit world and shall observe all things that shall transpire upon the earth as the children of God live according to His plan.

16 And at this time Lucifer shall be bound and shall not be permitted to inspire the hearts of the children of men to follow his plan. For six thousand years the plan of Lucifer was tried and tested upon the earth. And for all of these years there was turmoil, and strife, and all manner of wickedness upon the earth.

17 And during the millennium of the Lord, Lucifer and those that follow him shall see the effects of the plan of the Father that shall be implemented by the Son according to the will of the Father in all things.

18 And at that day shall the desire for sexual relations be taken from off the earth except it be among those who have the power in their own bodies to produce the mortal bodies for the spirits who must enter again into mortality from the spirit world.

19 And now, these sexual desires have been the means of much wickedness during the first six thousand years of the existence of the children of men upon the earth; yea, these natural enticings, being that which overcame Eve because of her desire to bear children and keep the commandment of the Father in this thing; even these things are the enticings of the flesh of those who have the body parts that are designed to produce children.

20 And as the children of men go through the days of their probation upon the earth, they are tested and proven to see if they are worthy to have this great power. And the means of their tests are the enticements of the flesh in the want of sex and the enjoyment that these enticements provide to all of the children of men.

21 And there have been none, save a few only, who have proven themselves worthy of this great power. And with this power, the enticement and gratification of sex is continued for the benefit and the blessing of those who have proven themselves worthy of this power.

22 But the majority of the children of God who shall be upon the earth during the millennial reign of the Lord, shall not have this power, neither shall they have these enticements which caused them so much wickedness during the early days of their probation, or during these first six thousand years. And without the parts of the body that are required to produce children, the desire to do so shall no longer be with them.

23 And in that day there shall be no more family units, nor shall there be any nations or kingdoms, or borders of any kind, except it be those that shall be established by the Lord according to the laws of the Father. And all the people of the earth shall speak the same tongue and all will understand their neighbor as they are understood.

24 And there shall be no partnerships, or companionships, or husbands and wives, or sisters and brothers who belong to a separated family that hath set itself apart from the earth; for all the inhabitants of the earth shall be brothers and sisters, yea, children of the Father, their God and Creator.

25 And the children that shall come forth in that day shall be cared for by all the inhabitants of the righteous nation in which they shall be created, but more especially by the mothers who created them.

26 And now, there shall be friendships that rise up among all the people of the earth, but there shall be no isolation in these friendships; in other words, all shall be friends with their neighbors. And those neighbors who are not known intimately by one, shall become known, for the love that shall abide in the hearts of all the people shall be equal one towards another

27 Yea, at this time there shall be upon the earth all of the children of God who have chosen for themselves that kingdom in which they have chosen to reside in the eternal kingdoms of the Father.

28 And these groups shall be the only division made among the inhabitants of the earth. And there shall be seven parts of the world that shall have a border, of sorts, between them. And these shall be the only borders that shall exist upon the earth, but they shall not be borders established by one people to keep another people from coming into their nation, but they shall be for the distinction of the place upon the earth that the Lord shall establish for the people of the different kingdoms of glory that they have chosen for themselves.

29 And there shall exist three separate kingdoms of those who are Telestial people. And there shall be three separate kingdoms for those who are Terrestrial people. And these people shall divide themselves into these kingdoms according to their desires of happiness.

30 And the laws that shall be established in these separate kingdoms shall be the laws that are like unto those eternal laws that shall govern the planet on which they shall be placed to live forever after the resurrection, having eternal life and enjoying the state that they have chosen for themselves.

31 And these kingdoms shall be called nations. And these six nations shall be called Telestialand, and Telestialnom, and Telestialsan, according to those borders in which reside those of a Telestial state.

32 And the nations of those who desire the laws of happiness of a Terrestrial state shall be called Terrestrialand, and Terrestrialnom, and Terrestrialsan.

33 And the Lord shall command that the governments of these kingdoms be set up according to the laws of happiness that shall exist in these kingdoms of glory in the eternal kingdom of the Father.

34 And the seventh nation shall be the governing nation in which shall dwell all those who pertain to the Celestial kingdom of glory. Behold, these are the righteous who have lived upon the earth. These are those who are some male and others are female according to their desires for happiness.

35 And by these shall the rest of the people of the earth be served. For they shall be the servants of those who belong to the other six nations of the earth.

36 And the Lord shall appoint twelve from among them to be the governors of these nations. And these twelve shall rule and reign in these kingdoms under the direction of the Lord, who shall establish his government in both hemispheres of the world, one of these capitals being called the City of Zion, which shall be upon this land; and the other being called Jerusalem after the city in which the Lord came down during the days of his own probation.

37 And then shall the words of the prophets be fulfilled, which were written, saying: And it shall come to pass in the last days, that the mountain of the house of the Lord shall be established in the top of the mountains, and shall be exalted above the hills; and all nations shall flow unto it.

38 And many people shall go and say, Come ye, and let us go up to the mountain of the Lord, to the house of the God of Jacob; and he will teach us of his ways, and we will walk in his paths; for out of Zion shall go forth the law, and the word of the Lord from Jerusalem.

39 And he shall judge among the nations, and shall rebuke many people; and they shall beat their swords into plowshares, and their spears into pruninghooks; nation shall not lift up sword against nation, neither shall they learn war any more.

40 And it shall come to pass in that day that the people of the earth shall look to Zion and to Jerusalem for the law of the Lord. And the people shall know the twelve who have been chosen by the Lord to rule over the other nations of the earth.

41 And all people shall be given the freedom to travel in all parts of the earth, visiting all the different kingdoms and living among the people according to their desires.

42 And now, this is the will of the Father concerning this thing, for this is the final opportunity for His children to know for themselves which kingdom of glory best suiteth their desires for happiness.

43 For those who are Telestial shall travel into the lands of those who live by the laws of the Terrestrial kingdom; and when they come into the land, they shall not feel as comfortable or at ease with these laws and this manner of living as they do with the laws and the manner of living of their own kingdom.

44 And those who are both Telestial spirits and Terrestrial spirits shall travel to Jerusalem and to Zion and shall see the Celestial people in their manner of living; and they shall know for themselves that the kingdom which they have chosen for themselves is truly that which will bring them the most happiness.

45 For the people of the Celestial cities shall be servants who shall have the power and the authority of the Lord to spend all the days of their lives in the service of others, for this is what bringeth them their own happiness.

46 And those of the Telestial kingdoms and the Terrestrial kingdoms, yea, these shall not have the desire to serve others all the days of their lives, but they shall have the desire to be served and receive from another those things that make them happy.

47 And it shall come to pass that there shall exist an attitude of extraordinary love and respect for one another, and all shall respect the rights of another to live their lives the way that they have chosen for themselves.

48 And now, it is expedient that ye understand why it is that the Father hath commanded the Lord to establish the kingdoms of His glories upon the earth in these final days. Behold, when we lived as spirits in the kingdom of our Father, we were raised by our Eternal Mothers and taught all those things which were necessary to allow us to grow as a spirit and to understand the plan of the Father in all things.

49 And the choices of the different kingdoms of glory were explained unto us, and we understood them, having been taught these things by our Mothers. Nevertheless, because we were spirits, we did not understand all things pertaining to these different kingdoms of glory; or in other words, we did not know from our own experience what it would be like to exist in these kingdoms with a body of flesh and bone that would provide our spirits with the eternal joy and happiness that our Eternal Father and Mothers enjoy in their kingdom.

50 Yet, we made our choice according to our understanding. But also, our Eternal Parents helped us in our determination of which kingdom of glory would be the one that would bring our particular spirit and its own individual characteristics and personality the greatest amount of happiness.

51 For They knew us better than we knew ourselves as Their spirit children, because They have the experience that we did not yet have because of the state of existence in which we resided in the preexistent state in the kingdom of our Father. And They had already passed through this state and were exalted beings who knew in and of Themselves all things that pertain to all of the glories of the kingdom of God.

52 And it was our Eternal Mothers who knew which of us would be Celestial, and which of us would be Terrestrial, and which of us would be Telestial, because They were with us from the beginning of our existence and watched us grow and use our free agency to act and think for ourselves and make our own choices based upon this free agency.

53 Therefore, because we knew by the word of our Eternal Parents, and also by our own choice, which kingdom of glory would best suit us forever, we were ready to enter into our second estate, which is the state in which we would receive our bodies of flesh and bone and prove to ourselves further, that the kingdom of glory that we had chosen to reside in forever, was that kingdom that would bring us the most happiness of all the kingdoms of God.

54 And I have already explained unto you how Lucifer rebelled against the plan of the Father and introduced his own plan for our eternal salvation. And if it was that easy for Lucifer to convince one third of all the children of the Father that his plan might provide more happiness for us, then we can see, that in the beginning, many of us were not convinced of our final choice of our eternal kingdom of glory.

55 And there were many who did not follow Lucifer, but followed Jehovah in his desire to follow the plan that the Father presented unto us; and these were still unsure of themselves, but they loved the Father, and knew their Mothers, who pleaded with them to follow the Father.

56 And there shall be many still, even after the days of their probation, who shall doubt within themselves whether or not the kingdom of glory that they have chosen for themselves is the right one for them.

57 And for this reason, the Father hath commanded the Son to establish these kingdoms upon the earth in similitude of what they shall be like when the planets are transformed into these kingdoms in the own due time of the Father.

58 Now, during the millennium of the Lord, all of the children of God shall have the opportunity to live for many, many years; yea, even for the better part of one thousand years upon the earth in peace and happiness; and during this millennium be allowed to experience, in the flesh, the kingdom that they have chosen for themselves.

59 However, even during these days, they shall not know for a surety which kingdom shall bring them the most happiness. But after they have lived according to the laws of the Father, and after they have been able to see for themselves the institution of these laws in their lives upon the earth with a body of flesh and bone, which shall be similar to the body that they have chosen for themselves; yea, after so many years of this experience, then shall they know for a surety that the plan of the Father is just, and that kingdom which they have chosen for themselves is the eternal kingdom that shall provide for them the greatest source of happiness according to their individual desires of happiness.

60 And it shall come to pass at this time, that Lucifer and those spirits who followed him in the beginning; yea, these shall also have the opportunity to witness from the spirit world the plan of the Father in full effect upon the earth. And these will be able to choose for themselves whether they will follow the plan of the Father, or continue to follow the plan of Lucifer.

61 And if these repent, then they, too, shall be given the chance to come into mortality and take upon them the flesh and bone prepared by the Father, and experience the kingdoms of God upon the earth, so that they can know for a surety that the plan of the Father is just and true.

62 And now, this is the mystery that the Lord hath commanded me to give unto you; yea, I

have read concerning all of these things in the words of the vision of the brother of Jared concerning the end of time; and I know that in the end, most of the children of the Father shall choose His plan over the plan of Lucifer and shall receive their inheritance in His kingdom.

63 And there shall be some who shall continue to support Lucifer in his desires and shall be held in the captivity of the spirit world until the Lord hath finished his work upon the earth.

64 And at the end of the last millennium, these shall once again be released and given the chance to convince any that will give heed unto them to reject the plan of the Father and follow the plan of Lucifer.

65 And there shall be few who shall be deceived this time by the flattering words of Lucifer, having seen the effects of his plan during the first six thousand years of their existence upon the earth in mortality and in the spirit world.

66 But those who choose to follow him, shall be gathered together and cast out of the kingdom of the Father.

67 And now, at this time, I have been commanded to explain unto you what it meaneth to be cast out of the kingdom of God, and what shall be the end of Lucifer and those that follow him.

68 Yea, after so many years of experience that they shall have upon this earth in mortality; yea, even after all the patience and the mercy that the Father shall show unto them, giving unto them chance after chance to accept His eternal plan and live by the eternal laws that govern the whole universe and all of the planets, and all of the stars, and all of the kingdoms that exist therein; yea, even after all of this pure knowledge which they shall have, they shall reject the Father and not accept the exceeding love that He hath offered them.

69 And they shall become as the wood of a beloved tree, which a man planted as a seedling and watched grow for many years. And the man watered it and dunged it, and pruned it, and kept it warm in times of cold, and cool in times of heat.

70 And when the tree grew tall, even that its branches spread forth exceedingly, the man knew that it was time to make use of the tree that it might serve him and provide for his comfort all the days of his life.

71 And with gentle care the man cut down the tree and sawed its many branches and formed it into a chair that it might support him in his old age and provide for him the comfort that he desired.

72 And with great care he built a chair in which he could sit. And it was a beautiful chair, but when he sat thereon, it would not support his weight, and fell apart underneath him.

73 And when the man realized that the wood from the tree could not be made into a chair to support him, he did not have the desire to burn or throw out the wood, because it was the wood from his beloved tree.

74 Therefore the man with care again took the wood that was once a chair and shaped it into something that would serve him and comfort him in his old age.

75 And now, my beloved brothers and sisters, here is the end of those who choose for themselves not to serve the God who created them and gave them life and an independent existence wherein they might find happiness; behold, these who were created from the eternal elements of which all things are created, yea, from which all of our spirits were created, shall be broken apart, or destroyed in the form of the existence in which the Father had created them to bring them happiness.

76 And they shall be no more. And the matter from which they were created cannot be destroyed; and even it could be destroyed, the Father would not destroy it because of His love for that which hath brought him so much joy.

77 But Lucifer and those that follow him shall cease to exist, and the elements from which their spirits were formed shall be used to form other spirits that shall start their existence in the womb of an Eternal Mother, who shall wean them, and coddle them, and enjoy their birth again into existence by the power and will of the Father.

78 And these shall grow into mature spirits and be given the opportunity to follow the plan of the Father and receive the happiness for which He hath created them.

79 Now, this is according to the great mercy and justice of the Father; for He knoweth that there cannot exist those beings in the eternities that would disrupt the order of all things.

80 And this order hath existed forever, having no beginning, and no end. And it is the duty of any God to maintain this order, and in justice establish the laws of this order and assure that these laws are followed in righteousness.

81 But the Father knoweth that in order for us to follow any law in righteousness, we must first understand this law. And to understand this law in its fullness, we must be given the chance to disobey this law and reap the consequence of our disobedience, that we might know of our own experience that the eternal laws of heaven are indeed righteous—And this, my brothers and sisters, is the purpose of life and the reason that we exist in a mortal state and go through the days of our probation.

82 And this is also the reason why the Lord shall establish his kingdom upon the earth so that we can garner from it the experiences that we need in order to understand all of these eternal laws.

83 And in that day all of the different nations of the earth shall be under one law. And this law which the whole earth shall be under is the law of the Father that pertaineth to all of the kingdoms of glory in the kingdom of God.

84 And this is the law of the gospel that I have explained unto you throughout this record. And it is the law that was given by Christ in the flesh among the Jews, and also which he gave to my fathers in the land of Bountiful.

85 And it is by obedience to this law that peace and righteousness shall be established throughout the land.

86 And now, I have given you this law in this record, therefore, I will not repeat again this law unto you, but would admonish you to read the words which I have written concerning the law that Adam gave unto his children in the land of Adamondiahman.

87 For the words of Adam are great and were recorded by the brother of Jared who witnessed the great meeting in which he gave this law unto his children.

88 Study these words, my beloved brothers and sisters, for it is by this law that ye shall live upon the earth in the days of the Lord; and it is by this law that ye shall be judged; and it is also by this law that ye shall live in the latter days, if it be your desire that the Lord cut short his work in righteousness and come unto you before the appointed time of the Father.

89 And it is this law that was lived in its fullness by Enoch and those of the city of Enoch who were taken to the kingdom of the Father.

90 Behold, after the Lord hath established his law throughout the whole earth, yea, after Zion is established upon this land, then shall Enoch and all the people of his city which were raised up by the Father, be brought back to this earth; and they shall establish themselves in the nations in which each of them findeth the joy which each desireth.

91 And those of the city of Enoch who have chosen the Celestial kingdom for themselves, shall enter into the city of Zion, which shall be known as the New Jerusalem, then shall they meet the other elect of God who have been gathered out of all the earth, and they shall receive them into their bosoms and shall fall upon their necks and shall kiss them, and thus shall it be according to the words of the prophets.

92 And the law of the Lord shall be taught throughout the world. And the wicked who shall remain upon the earth shall be forced to live this law or they shall be cast out of the land and be put into prisons where they shall be taught this law.

93 And if they do not abide by this law still, they shall die in the prisons that they might not corrupt the earth. And upon their death they shall enter again into the spirit world and join Lucifer and his angels, who awaiteth the last judgment of God that shall be wrought upon them.

94 But it shall come to pass that the majority of the wicked shall see the error of their ways and shall repent of their sins and turn away from their wickedness and begin to trust in the law of the gospel that the Lord shall give unto them in that day.

CHAPTER 94

Moroni uses many of Jacob's words to teach what the Spirit hath commanded him to write concerning the gospel of Jesus Christ.

AND now, my beloved brothers and sisters, I would that ye should know more concerning the law of the Lord that he shall teach unto the whole world during the blessed millennium in which he shall dwell upon the earth with us in the flesh to teach us the will of Father in all things that we might have peace and happiness among us.

2 Yea, I would that ye should understand the very way in which he shall make us one with the Father, thus fulfilling the covenant that he hath made with us, that by his atonement, we shall come once again into the kingdom of God and live forever in eternal happiness.

3 And in this way Jesus Christ becometh our God and our Creator, or in other words, he maketh us one with him as he is one with the Father.

4 And now, Jacob, the brother of Nephi, gave many words of instruction to the people in his day. And when I read the words of Jacob, my heart rejoiceth in that which he speaketh unto the people in plainness and purity, except it be those things that he was commanded to withhold from the knowledge of the people because of the stumbling blocks that the Lord had placed before them.

5 Behold, my soul doth not rejoice in the stumbling blocks that are placed before the wicked, which are not placed there by the Lord, nevertheless, they are not taken away by him because of the wickedness of the people.

6 But my soul rejoiceth in the pure word and truth of God. Behold, the words of Jacob which he gave unto the people were the words of wisdom that would save them from their sins, if it so be that they would have given heed unto them.

7 And because my soul delighteth in his words, I give unto you again in this sealed portion of the record of my father the words which cause my soul to rejoice because of the great wisdom that is given therein.

8 For behold, Jacob also saw the beginning of time to the end of time. And he saw the great day of the Lord when he would reign upon the earth in the glory of the Father; nevertheless, he likened all things unto the people whom he taught in his day.

9 And Jacob taught the people, saying: Behold, my beloved brethren, I speak unto you these things that ye may rejoice, and lift up your heads forever, because of the blessings which the Lord God shall bestow upon your children.

10 For I know that ye have searched much, many of you, to know of things to come; therefore I know that ye know that our flesh must waste away and die; nevertheless, in our bodies we shall see God.

11 Yea, I know that ye know that in the body he shall show himself unto those at Jerusalem, from whence we came; for it is expedient that it should be among them; for it behooveth the great Creator that he suffereth himself to become subject unto man in the flesh, and die for all men, that all men might become subject unto him.

12 For as death hath passed upon all men, to fulfill the merciful plan of the great Creator, there must needs be a power of resurrection, and the resurrection must needs come unto man by reason of the fall; and the fall came by reason of transgression; and because man became fallen they were cut off from the presence of the Lord.

13 Therefore, it must needs be an infinite atonement; and save it should be an infinite atonement this corruption could not put on incorruption. Therefore, the first judgment which came upon man must needs have remained to an endless duration.

14 And if so, this flesh must have laid down to rot and to crumble to its mother earth, to rise no more. Oh, the wisdom of God, his mercy and grace. For behold, if the flesh should rise no more our spirits must become subject to that angel who fell from before the presence of the Eternal God, and became the devil, to rise no more.

15 And our spirits must have become like unto him, and we become devils, angels to a devil, to be shut out from the presence of our God, and to remain with the father of lies, in

misery, like unto himself; yea, to that being who beguiled our first parents, who transformeth himself nigh unto an angel of light, and stirreth up the children of men unto secret combinations of murder and all manner of secret works of darkness.

16 Oh, how great the goodness of our God, who prepareth a way for our escape from the grasp of this awful monster; yea, that monster, death and hell, which I call the death of the body, and also the death of the spirit.

17 And because of the way of deliverance of our God, the Holy One of Israel, this death, of which I have spoken, which is the temporal, shall deliver up its dead; which death is the grave.

18 And this death of which I have spoken, which is the spiritual death, shall deliver up its dead; which spiritual death is hell; therefore, death and hell must deliver up their dead, and hell must deliver up its captive spirits, and the grave must deliver up its captive bodies, and the bodies and the spirits of men will be restored one to the other; and it is by the power of the resurrection of the Holy One of Israel.

19 Oh, how great the plan of our God. For on the other hand, the paradise of God must deliver up the spirits of the righteous, and the grave deliver up the body of the righteous; and the spirit and the body is restored to itself again, and all men become incorruptible, and immortal, and they are living souls, having a perfect knowledge like unto us in the flesh, save it be that our knowledge shall be perfect.

20 Therefore, we shall have a perfect knowledge of all our guilt, and our uncleanness, and our nakedness; and the righteous shall have a perfect knowledge of their enjoyment, and their righteousness, being clothed with purity, yea, even with the robe of righteousness.

21 And it shall come to pass that when all men shall have passed from this first death unto life, insomuch as they have become immortal, they must appear before the judgment seat of the Holy One of Israel; and then cometh the judgment, and then must they be judged according to the holy judgment of God.

22 And assuredly, as the Lord liveth, for the Lord God hath spoken it, and it is his eternal word, which cannot pass away, that they who are righteous shall be righteous still, and they who are filthy shall be filthy still; therefore, they who are filthy are the devil and his angels; and they shall go away into everlasting fire; prepared for them; and their torment is as a lake of fire and brimstone, whose flame ascendeth up forever and ever and hath no end.

23 Oh, the greatness and the justice of our God. For he executeth all his words, and they have gone forth out of his mouth, and his law must be fulfilled.

24 But, behold, the righteous, the saints of the Holy One of Israel, they who have believed in the Holy One of Israel, they who have endured the crosses of the world, and despised the shame of it, they shall inherit the kingdom of God, which was prepared for them from the foundation of the world, and their joy shall be full forever.

25 Oh, the greatness of the mercy of our God, the Holy One of Israel. For he delivereth his saints from that awful monster the devil, and death, and hell, and that lake of fire and brimstone, which is endless torment.

26 Oh, how great the holiness of our God. For he knoweth all things, and there is not anything save he knoweth it. And he cometh into the world that he may save all men if they will hearken unto his voice; for behold, he suffereth the pains of all men, yea, the pains of every living creature, both men, women, and children, who belong to the family of Adam.

27 And he suffereth this that the resurrection might pass upon all men, that all might stand before him at the great and judgment day.

28 And he commandeth all men that they must repent, and be baptized in his name, having perfect faith in the Holy One of Israel, or they cannot be saved in the kingdom of God. And if they will not repent and believe in his name, and be baptized in his name, and endure to the end, they must be damned; for the Lord God, the Holy One of Israel, hath spoken it.

29 Therefore, he hath given a law; and where there is no law given there is no punishment; and where there is no punishment there is no condemnation; and where there is no condemnation the mercies

of the Holy One of Israel have claim upon them, because of the atonement; for they are delivered by the power of him.

30 For the atonement satisfieth the demands of his justice upon all those who have not the law given to them, that they are delivered from that awful monster, death and hell, and the devil, and the lake of fire and brimstone, which is endless torment; and they are restored to that God who gave them breath, which is the Holy One of Israel.

31 But woe unto him who hath the law given, yea, who hath all the commandments of God, like unto us, and who transgresseth them, and who wasteth the days of his probation, for awful is his state.

32 Oh, that cunning plan of the evil one. Oh, the vainness, and the frailties, and the foolishness of men. When they are learned they think they are wise, and they hearken not unto the counsel of God, for they set it aside, supposing they know of themselves, therefore, their wisdom is foolishness and it profiteth them not; and they shall perish.

33 But to be learned is good if they hearken unto the counsels of God.

34 But woe unto the rich, who are rich as to the things of the world. For because they are rich they despise the poor, and they persecute the meek, and their hearts are upon their treasures; therefore, their treasure is their God. And behold, their treasure shall perish with them also.

35 And woe unto the deaf who will not hear; for they shall perish. Woe unto the blind who will not see; for they shall perish also. Woe unto the uncircumcised of heart, for a knowledge of their iniquities shall smite them at the last day. Woe unto the liar, for he shall be thrust down to hell. Woe unto the murderer who deliberately killeth, for he shall die. Woe unto they who commit whoredoms, for they shall be thrust down to hell. Yea, woe unto those who worship idols, for the devil of all devils delighteth in them.

36 And, in fine, woe unto all those who die in their sins; for they shall return to God, and behold His face, and remain in their sins.

37 Oh, my beloved brethren, remember the awfulness in transgressing against that Holy God, and also the awfulness of yielding to the enticings of that cunning one. Remember, to be carnally-minded is death, and to be spiritually-minded is life eternal.

38 Oh, my beloved brethren, give ear to my words. Remember the greatness of the Holy One of Israel.

39 Do not say that I have spoken hard things against you; for if ye do, ye will revile against the truth; for I have spoken the words of your Maker. I know that the words of truth are hard against all uncleanness; but the righteous fear them not, for they love the truth and are not shaken.

40 Oh, then, my beloved brethren, come unto the Lord, the Holy One. Remember that his paths are righteous. Behold, the way for man is narrow, but it lieth in a straight course before him, and the keeper of the gate is the Holy One of Israel; and he employeth no servant there; and there is none other way save it be by the gate; for he cannot be deceived, for the Lord God is his name.

41 And whoso knocketh, to him will he open; and the wise, and the learned, and they that are rich, who are puffed up because of their learning, and their wisdom, and their riches; yea, they are they whom he despiseth; and save they shall cast these things away, and consider themselves fools before God, and come down in the depths of humility, he will not open unto them.

42 But the things of the wise and the prudent shall be hid from them forever; yea, that happiness which is prepared for the saints.

43 Oh, my beloved brethren, remember my words. Behold, I take off my garments, and I shake them before you; I pray the God of my salvation that he view me with his all-searching eye; therefore, ye shall know at the last day, when all men shall be judged of their works, that the God of Israel did witness that I shook your iniquities from my soul, and that I stand with brightness before him, and am rid of your blood.

44 Oh, my beloved brethren, turn away from your sins; shake off the chains of him that would bind you fast; come unto that God who is the rock of your salvation.

45 Prepare your souls for that glorious day when justice shall be administered unto the righteous, even the day of judgment, that ye

may not shrink with awful fear; that ye may not remember your awful guilt in perfectness, and be constrained to exclaim: Holy, holy are thy judgments, Oh, Lord God Almighty, but I know my guilt; I transgressed thy law, and my transgressions are mine; and the devil hath obtained me, that I am a prey to his awful misery.

46 But behold, my brethren, is it expedient that I should awake you to an awful reality of these things? Would I harrow up your souls if your minds were pure? Would I be plain unto you according to the plainness of the truth if ye were freed from sin?

47 Behold, if ye were holy I would speak unto you of holiness; but as ye are not holy, and ye look upon me as a teacher, it must needs be expedient that I teach you the consequences of sin.

48 Behold, my soul abhorreth sin, and my heart delighteth in righteousness; and I will praise the holy name of my God.

49 Come, my brethren, every one who thirsteth, come ye to the waters; and he that hath no money, come buy and eat; yea, come buy wine and milk without money and without price. Therefore, do not spend money for that which is of no worth, nor your labor for that which cannot satisfy.

50 Hearken diligently unto me, and remember the words which I have spoken; and come unto the Holy One of Israel, and feast upon that which perisheth not, neither can be corrupted, and let your soul delight in fatness.

51 Behold, my beloved brethren, remember the words of your God; pray unto him continually by day, and give thanks unto his holy name by night. Let your hearts rejoice.

52 And now, my beloved brothers and sisters of the latter days, even all of you who shall receive these glorious words of the prophet Jacob. Do ye understand his words? Do they not ring in perfect understanding to your ears? Doth he not point your souls towards the words of Christ and plead with you to obey these words?

53 Behold, the words of Christ are these things which he hath commanded you to feast upon, even that which perisheth not, neither can be corrupted.

54 And this is the gospel of Christ that containeth in and of itself all of the saving principles and ordinances that any child of God shall need in order to enter once again into the kingdom of the Father.

CHAPTER 95

The evils of modern day secular educational pursuits. The Lord will destroy all of the institutions of learning that have been established by the human race. We are admonished to seek for the kingdom of God above all else.

AND now behold, in the latter days Satan shall begin to use the power that he hath gained over the hearts and minds of the children of men to turn them away from the law of the Lord.

2 For behold, in those days there shall be many institutions of learning established in all the corners of the earth. And the people shall be deceived into believing that the most important thing that they can acquire for themselves is an education from one of these institutions.

3 And these institutions shall be set up to get gain by those who organize them and seek a profit from them. For they shall not give knowledge without price. But behold, the knowledge that they shall teach shall be worthless in the kingdom of God.

4 Behold, the knowledge that shall be taught unto the students of these institutions shall be the knowledge that Satan hath given unto the world that all might know of his plan, and that all might learn the things that they must do in order to make his plan successful.

5 And Satan shall promise all those who attend these institutions of learning, even these colleges, and universities, and schools, as they shall be known among you; yea, Satan shall promise them glories and honors of men, if it so be that they abide by the requirements of these institutions and pay the money that is required of them.

6 And in that day the wicked shall rejoice in their knowledge that they have gained from these institutions, and they shall praise each other in their accomplishments which they have obtained by attending these institutions of learning.

7 And the knowledge that shall be taught therein shall support the functions of the blessings that Satan hath given to those who follow him and keep his commandments.

8 And the children of the world shall be taught by their parents to trust in the knowledge that they shall receive therein. Behold, the children shall be given praise from their parents for the marks that they shall receive and the degrees upon which they shall set their hearts.

9 And when their hearts are set upon obtaining the glories and honors of men, then shall their righteous acts towards the poor, and the sick, and the inflicted, and those who are in prison because of their lack of knowledge; yea, then shall their concern for their neighbor cease.

10 And thus Satan shall again show forth his power over the children of men in fulfilling the words of John, when he spoke of the beast and its image and the acceptance and worshipping of this image, which is established and influenced through these institutions of learning.

11 Now, in the days of Adam there were no schools where one might go to learn the things and knowledge of the world. But all the children of Adam were taught the plan of the Father, which is that they should love one another and do unto each other what they would have done unto them.

12 And in the city of Enoch, which was the most righteous city that hath ever been upon the earth; yea, in this city there were no institutions of secular learning established among the people.

13 And these people were the most beloved and respected of all the children that God hath placed upon this earth. And they truly experienced eternal peace and happiness among them.

14 And now, I ask of ye of the latter days: Yea, what good is the knowledge that is taught to you in your schools of learning? Doth the knowledge that ye learn point you towards loving your neighbor and doing good unto them, or doth it not teach you to exalt yourself above your neighbor?

15 Yea, doth it not teach you that which ye must do in order to get more gain than that which the poor and the meek receive because they do not attend these schools?

16 And what of the poor? Are not they the ones that work in your fields, and sew your clothes, and do all manner of manual labor that provideth you with a house in which to live?

17 And what have these, who are the most important people in the sustaining of your daily lives; yea, what have they learned in your institutions? Behold, not attending your institutions causeth them to be humble before God and work by the sweat of their own brow, which was commanded of them by the Lord.

18 Yea, these are the poor, and the meek, and the humble whom ye have abased because ye have lifted yourselves above them and pay them a low wage for which ye would not work.

19 And many of the poor shall desire to attend these schools that they might also participate in the economy of the beast and take its image upon them. But because they are poor, they shall not have the means whereby they can pay for the education that the rich have placed a value upon to get gain.

20 Behold, these institutions shall be set up to enrich those who invest in them and pay the salaries of the professors and administrators, who are emissaries of Satan and share in the glory and blessings that he hath promised them.

21 Behold, these have been convinced by Satan that without an education that can only be received in an institution of learning that is set up to get gain, the image of the beast cannot be realized, neither shall the great standard of excellence that they have been deceived into thinking should be the desire of every heart, come to pass.

22 Yea, these are the learned of whom the prophets have testified shall persecute the poor and the needy because of their words; or in other words, because of their lack of the education offered in these institutions.

23 And now, the Lord offereth his truth and his understanding of knowledge unto all without price. Yea, this is what was meant by Jacob when he said: Come, my brethren, every one who thirsteth, come ye to the waters; and he that hath no money, come buy and eat; yea, come buy wine and milk without money and without price. Therefore, do not spend money for that which is of no worth, nor your labor for that which cannot satisfy.

24 And now, how can your degrees, and your honors, and the glories of men which ye shall receive in these institutions satisfy your desires of happiness? Yea, the only desire that they shall satisfy is your lust for power and gain according to the plan of Lucifer and the blessings that he as promised you by following his plan.

25 Yea, even after ye have obtained all the glories of men, are ye then happy and satisfied with your lives? I say unto you, that ye are not satisfied with your lives.

26 For behold, I have seen your day and have read much concerning your great wickedness in the words that have been written by the brother of Jared; and we know that ye are not happy. For even after ye have received all these things, ye still seek for those things which Satan hath provided for you to ease the pain and misery of your souls.

27 And your children; behold, do they not use the freedom that they have away from the auspices of their parents to drink wine, and use those things which ease the pain and misery of the pressure and burden that these institutions of learning place upon them? Behold, what happiness do ye find in these things?

28 And now, of what use are many of the courses of learning that ye are required to take in order that ye might obtain a degree and an honor that ye might perform your duties in a profession that will never utilize any of the knowledge that ye receive from these required courses?

29 Behold, this is the desire of the rich who have set up these institutions to get gain and power over you. For behold, the more knowledge that is required of you, the more ye are forced to pay to those who shall reward you with the glories and honors of men.

30 Behold, why do ye allow another to indoctrinate you and control your thinking, when that in which they have indoctrinated you shall do nothing to give unto you the peace and happiness that ye desire?

31 Behold, why do ye trust in the professors, and the teachers, and the educators of these accepted learning institutions among you, yet deny the power of the Holy Ghost, which could teach you all the things that ye need to find happiness and be saved in the kingdom of God?

32 Do ye not know that the prophets of old knew and understood many of the things which are much greater than the things that ye are taught in the schools of men?

33 And when the Lord Jesus Christ was upon the earth, did he attend these institutions of learning? Yea, did he desire any of the honors and glories of men?

34 And Joseph and Christopher, who are the last prophets who shall be among you upon the earth before the coming of the Lord, what do ye think they learned in these institutions?

35 Behold, the former shall not have more than the education that is required of a young child, yet he shall bring forth truths unto you that the world hath never known.

36 And the latter shall attend this institution of secular learning during the time of his refinement, having been influenced by Satan to follow the course of his plan. But he shall overcome the temptations of Satan, and shall mock the ways of this institution, and shall prove therein that the wisdom of man is nothing compared to the wisdom of God.

37 And it shall come to pass that when the Lord cometh upon the earth to reign during the millennium, he shall cause to be destroyed all of the institutions of learning and all of the books contained therein that teacheth unto the children of men the lies that Satan desired them to know concerning his plan.

38 Behold, he shall teach all the inhabitants of the earth the gospel which he taught before, which taught a man that he should love his neighbor and his enemies as much as he loveth himself.

39 Yea, and upon this foundation shall the inhabitants of the earth learn all of the truths which are necessary for their salvation and eternal happiness in the kingdoms of the Father.

40 And he shall teach them the truths concerning the order and laws of nature, which shall be presented and taught in such a manner that even a young child shall understand and be able to use the knowledge that shall be given unto him by the Lord, for the sake of its own happiness.

41 And now, I have already explained unto you that only those who are Celestial in their desires shall be given the knowledge and power over the elements that will allow them to create worlds and the environs that are required by these worlds in order to allow life to begin thereon.

42 Therefore, if only those who are Celestial shall have this knowledge; and this knowledge shall be taught unto them by the Lord in its pure form; of what use shall it be for others to study the functions and laws of nature, when they shall be forbidden from using this knowledge in any kingdom that is not Celestial, which kingdom of glory they have chosen for themselves because of their free agency?

43 Behold, during the last days, Satan shall have the ability and the power to give unto the children of men many of the powers of God and give them a limited understanding of these powers, as I have already explained it unto you. And ye of the latter days shall see the great destruction that shall come upon the inhabitants of the earth because of this knowledge and these powers that Satan shall be allowed by the Father to give unto them.

44 Therefore, ye shall see how wicked and selfish men use these powers for their own gain. And the knowledge that they shall receive from Satan shall be taken from them during the last millennium of the earth, and shall only be given to those who are righteous and who would use these powers for the benefit and happiness of all the children of God.

45 And thus we can see the great wisdom of God in allowing Satan to have access to these powers to incorporate into his plan in the latter days. For it shall be proven that the desire of Lucifer in the beginning to give unto all of the children of God the powers that the Father possesseth can only lead to chaos and misery because of the selfish way in which these powers are used by those who are not Celestial beings.

46 Therefore, my beloved brothers and sisters, seek not for the knowledge of the world, for it shall not lead you down the path of righteousness, which path shall bring you the happiness that ye desire.

47 But before ye seek for knowledge, seek ye first for the kingdom of God, and all these things shall be given unto you.

48 And when ye understand the Father and know Him, then ye are at one with Him, and the purpose of the great atonement hath been fulfilled in saving your souls from the misery that ye would have experienced by following the plan of Lucifer.

49 Behold, do not seek for an education that ye might become rich and receive the honors and glories of men; for in this thing ye shall become prideful and shall offend the Spirit of God.

50 Behold, here are more of the words of Jacob which have been given in the unsealed portion of this record and which bring great joy to my soul.

51 For behold, the Nephites were like unto ye of the latter days, in that they had acquired many of the fine things of the world. But the Lord caused that Jacob should speak unto the people regarding these things. Therefore, I would that ye of the latter days liken his words unto you, for they were written and preserved and sealed up to come forth unto you for your instruction.

52 And it is written, saying: I must tell you the truth according to the plainness of the word of God. For behold, as I inquired of the Lord, thus came the word unto me, saying: Jacob, get thou up into the temple on the morrow, and declare the word which I shall give thee unto this people.

53 And now behold, my brethren, this is the word which I declare unto you, that many of you have begun to search for gold, and for silver, and for all manner of precious ores, in the which this land, which is a land of promise unto you and to your seed, doth abound most plentifully.

54 And the hand of providence hath smiled upon you most pleasingly, that you have obtained many riches; and because some of you have obtained more abundantly than that of your brethren, ye are lifted up in the pride of your hearts, and wear stiff necks and high heads because of the costliness of your apparel, and persecute your brethren because ye suppose that ye are better than them.

55 And now, my brethren, do ye suppose that God justifieth you in this thing? Behold, I say unto you, Nay. But he condemneth you, and if ye persist in these things his judgments must speedily come unto you.

56 Oh, that he would show you that he can pierce you, and with one glance of his eye he can smite you to the dust. Oh, that he would rid you from this iniquity and abomination.

57 And, Oh, that ye would listen unto the word of his commands, and let not this pride of your hearts destroy your souls.

58 Think of your brethren like unto yourselves, and be familiar with all and free with your substance, that they may be rich like unto you.

59 But before ye seek for riches, seek ye for the kingdom of God. And after ye have obtained a hope in Christ ye shall obtain riches, if ye seek them; and ye will seek them for the intent to do good; to clothe the naked, and to feed the hungry, and to liberate the captive, and administer relief to the sick and the afflicted.

60 And now, my brethren, I have spoken unto you concerning pride; and those of you who have afflicted your neighbor, and persecuted him because ye were proud in your hearts of the things which God hath given you, what say ye of it?

61 Do ye not suppose that such things are abominable unto him who created all flesh? And the one being is as precious in his sight as the other. And all flesh is of the dust; and for the selfsame end hath he created them, that they should keep his commandments and glorify him forever.

62 And now behold, my brothers and sisters, do ye not yet understand the great words of Jacob which the Lord commanded him to give unto the people? Are they not plain enough so that ye might understand them?

63 Do ye not see that it is a hope in Christ which ye should desire above all other things upon the earth? Behold, if ye have a hope in Christ, then ye shall know Christ; and if ye know him, then ye shall know the Father by the power of the Holy Ghost which shall give unto you all the knowledge that ye desire to make you happy.

64 Again, I say unto you, seek ye first the kingdom of God and all these things shall be given unto you.

CHAPTER 96

The care of nature and all of its environs shall be a priority during the millennium. The earth will be restored to a state similar to the garden of Eden.

AND it shall come to pass that the Lord shall begin to once again restore the earth to its natural state in which it existed at the time Adam and Eve were placed in the garden of Eden, even at the time when death did not exist among all the creations of the earth.

2 For behold, the reproductive process of all the orders of animals of the earth shall be changed to conform to the plan of the Father. For behold, if the animals were allowed to reproduce and create offspring, and there were no more of those animals that eat their flesh to curtail the increase in their population, then this order of creatures would overrun the earth, and there would be no place left for the children of men.

3 Therefore, at that day the creatures of the earth will become eternal in their nature, or in other words, by the same means that our bodies shall grow to maturity and never age, so shall it be among all the creatures of the earth.

4 And all the creatures shall live in the environment that shall provide for them the joy that they have been programmed by their instincts to desire.

5 For behold, all creatures shall exist for the joy and happiness of the children of God, as this is the purpose for which they were created.

6 And many of the animals that shall be upon the earth shall serve the children of God; and these animals shall provide instinctual devotion and love for all the children of God, even like unto that which a man receiveth from the animals that he hath established as his pets.

7 And it shall come to pass that throughout all of the earth the orders of all animals shall be protected by the power and the word of the Lord.

8 And the insects shall continue to do that which they have been designed to do for the benefit of the plants which they aid in the process of their existence. And those insects that do not benefit a plant, shall be changed in their nature and reprogrammed in their instinct that they might serve the happiness of man and not cause affliction upon him; or they shall be taken off of the earth because they are no longer needed thereupon.

9 For behold, it is in the wisdom of the Father that nature is maintained in a balance and an order that alloweth it to fulfill the measure of its creation in all things.

10 And now, I have somewhat to say unto you concerning the manner in which the animals and creatures of the earth are created.

11 Behold, for the pleasure, and at times, for the humor of the Father were these things created and placed upon the earth to perform their individual functions within the order of nature and according to the instincts which God gave unto them to maintain a perfect balance.

12 And when the Father createth one of these, He patterneth it after the desires of His heart, which oft times are influenced by His happiness that includeth a humorous side that He hath demonstrated by example in the spirits that He hath given to all of His children.

13 And nature is set up for His enjoyment, after it hath served the purpose of fulfilling the needs of happiness of His children.

14 Now, if ye were to watch carefully the animals that go about their daily lives upon the earth, ye would see the way that they have been programmed in their instincts according to the good will and humor of the Father.

15 And in your observations of many of these animals, ye could come to know your Father better.

16 And the plants, and the flowers, and the vines, and the mosses, yea, even all of the beautiful verdant areas of the world have been organized and contrasted according to the power and the will of the Father.

17 And in all these things, He obeyeth the eternal laws of nature, which govern these things.

18 Behold, I have said that it is by the power and the will of the Father, but in most cases it is not His will that is being done in these things. For behold, our Eternal Mothers are those whose concepts and understanding of the beauty of nature surpass the interest of the Father in these things.

19 And it is these blessed Eternal Mothers who many times give their opinions and advice to the Father on the way in which the earth and its order of nature should be organized to bring to pass a state of beauty and wonder that shall bring happiness to Their children.

20 For the power to accomplish these things resideth in the Father, but the way in which these things are accomplished is greatly influenced and overseen by our Eternal Mothers.

21 And it shall come to pass during the millennial days of the Lord, that he shall counsel with many of the women of the world, and also those who have no gender, but who have the desires to beautify and decorate the world with plants, and flowers, and with the creatures that share the environs of the earth; yea, he shall counsel with these concerning the way in which they would have him restore the earth in all of its natural beauty and glory.

22 And the words of the brother of Jared describe the greatness and beauty of the world after the Lord hath once again restored it to its original state. And he wrote, saying: The waters upon the earth once again run pure and undefiled, from the mountain tops where they are spawned, to the great oceans of the earth, where they provide life and refreshment to all the creatures of the earth.

23 And these great oceans shall once again be filled with undefiled and pure water that shall give life unto all creatures upon the earth.

24 And there are wide areas of verdant lands that are lush with all manner of vegetation and flowers, which give beauty and provide food for the creatures of the earth.

25 And there shall be few deserts and places of desolation upon the earth, except it be in a few areas that are within the borders of the land called Telestialsan, because of the desires of happiness of the citizens of this nation.

26 And the birds of the air fly aimlessly throughout the heavens in search of the desires of their happiness. And these are beautiful birds, made especially for the eye to behold, and for the hand to touch and caress and admire in the order of their creation.

27 And I saw the fish of the great waters that were changed by the Lord to swim openly upon all the waters of the earth. And the inhabitants of the earth in all of the kingdoms swim with the fishes of the waters, and they also fly in the air with the birds after the manner of the technology that the Lord giveth unto those with this desire, so that they might experience this thing and have joy therein.

28 And the grasses that grow in the vast lands of the earth are soft and supple and are created to bring joy to the animals that seek nourishment from them; and these are also enjoyed by those who run thereon with no covering upon their feet, enjoying the softness and gentleness of their touch upon the flesh.

29 And the sight which I beheld was of such an astounding sight, that I wept in joy for the greatness of the blessings of the Father in providing this order of nature in all of its glory for the benefit of His children.

30 And I marveled at the sight which I beheld. And the Lord smiled upon me and looked upon me in the countenance of his smile, and spoke unto me, saying: Behold, my beloved brother, this is the glory of the Father in its fullness.

31 And in this glory hath He provided these wonderful blessings for all of His children. Behold, blessed be the Father in this thing, for what He hath done for all of those who believe in Him and keep His commandments.

32 Behold, by Him is the nature and order of all things established for our sake and our happiness. And by Him shall all things be given unto us forever in the worlds which He hath created for us.

33 And the glory and honor and thanksgiving be given to Him forever.

34 And it came to pass that the brother of Jared smiled with the Lord as he observed the wonderful blessings of nature that would come to pass during the last millennium of the Lord.

35 And now, I, Moroni, cannot write all of the words of the brother of Jared which he saw concerning these things. But his description caused me to fall to my knees and rejoice in my soul with exceeding joy because of those things which I read concerning the millennial reign of the Lord.

36 For behold, never hath there been upon the earth, nor shall there ever be upon the earth until that time, the wonderful and fascinating blessings of nature which God hath provided for us.

CHAPTER 97

Planetary exploration and archeology in the latter days are condemned as worthless to the happiness of humankind. The Lord's knowledge and power shall be used during the millennium to prepare the planets as the degrees of glory in the kingdom of God. Moroni uses Joseph Smith's revelation to describe the inhabitants of the different degrees of glory. Humankind should use their knowledge of science to do good to others.

AND it shall come to pass that this great and wondrous order of nature shall be established in all of the eternal kingdoms of glory in the kingdom of the Father.

2 And I have already explained unto you that the planets that are fixed in their rotation around the sun shall become these kingdoms of God, each planet assigned to a different degree of glory in the Celestial, Terrestrial, and Telestial orders.

3 And it shall come to pass in the latter days, that Satan shall begin to use the power that he is allowed to introduce into the minds of the children of men to inspire them to set their hearts upon understanding the planets, and the stars, and the sun which giveth life to the earth; yea, there shall be many among the children of men who shall spend all the days of their lives in pursuit of an understanding of the mysteries of the universe.

4 And this thing Satan shall inspire them to do that they might come to an understanding of the mysteries of God without being worthy of receiving them by the Spirit of God, which is the way that the Father revealeth these things unto the elect.

5 And with the understanding that they shall receive from Satan, they shall begin to explore

the universe in search of answers and ways that would justify and give credence to the plan of Lucifer.

6 Behold, Lucifer knoweth that it is by the power and knowledge of the Father that the worlds were created; and he also knoweth that without this power and knowledge, these things cannot be created and organized in the manner that they have been placed in the universe, so that their order and balance can be maintained.

7 And it is the desire of Lucifer that perhaps he might circumvent the power and authority of God by inspiring men to use the knowledge that they shall receive from him to understand the laws of nature pertaining to the creation of the planets, so that through those men whom he hath inspired, he might organize and establish a kingdom apart from the kingdom of the Father where he and those that dwell with him might live under the laws that he hath introduced in his plan.

8 And in the latter days the children of men shall use many of the resources of the world, and they shall spend a great amount of time and a great amount of money on the research and exploration of space, believing that by doing so, they might receive the honor and glory of those who look to them for knowledge and understanding of these things.

9 And they shall compete with one another in this thing that they might receive this glory, if it so be that they make a discovery that no other man before them hath made.

10 And instead of using their time, and their talents, and their resources to care for the poor and the needy, and the sick and the afflicted, and also caring for those who are imprisoned because of them; yea, instead of using their knowledge of the laws of nature to improve the situation of the planet on which they live, these shall waste away their time ever learning and never coming to a knowledge of the truth.

11 And then shall the words of the prophets be fulfilled concerning them, which are written, saying: This know also, that in the last days perilous times shall come. For men shall be lovers of their own selves, covetous, boasters, proud, blasphemers, disobedient to parents, unthankful, unholy, without natural affection, trucebreakers, false accusers, incontinent, fierce, despisers of those that are good, traitors, heady, high-minded, lovers of pleasures more than lovers of God; having a form of godliness; but denying the power thereof.

12 From these the elect are commanded to turn away. For of this sort are they which creep into houses, and lead captive silly women laden with sins, led away with divers lust, ever learning and never able to come to the knowledge of the truth.

13 Now, as Jannes and Jambres withstood Moses, so do these also resist the truth; they being men of corrupt minds, reprobate concerning the faith. But they shall proceed no further in their knowledge and understanding of the mysteries of God; for their folly shall be manifest unto all men, as theirs also was.

14 Now, Jannes and Jambres were Egyptian sorcerers who were learned men in the arts of science and magic, and who were trusted in the court of the Pharaoh because of their secular learning and their education among the people.

15 Yea, these mocked Moses and the power and knowledge of God that Moses received from the Spirit by the order of his calling as a prophet of God. For they did not believe that Moses could know the principles and laws of science that they believed could only be learned by experience and experimentation and by the means of science to which these men had devoted their lives.

16 And these men had convinced the Pharaoh that their knowledge was great and important to the people, and that without their knowledge, the people could not be guided properly by the Pharaoh.

17 For they had convinced the Pharaoh and the people that their gods would not reveal themselves unto the people and bless them, except it be through the power and knowledge that these priests possessed.

18 And these stood forth in the court of Pharaoh and boasted of their great knowledge of the stars and the planets that existed in the universe.

19 And by their cunning words and pretended theories of knowledge, the Pharaoh was deceived and gave unto these men great riches and glory among the people.

20 And this was their craft, even that which they had refined and in which they had become exceedingly adroit so as to be able to fool the Pharaoh and the people with their pretended learning.

21 And now, it is not hard to deceive the people with theories and presentations of hypothesis regarding those things which the majority of them know nothing about. Yea, it is easy to persuade the people to give their money to the pursuit of these theories and hypothesises of truth by cunning words and great promises of invention and discovery that will provide more happiness to the people.

22 And the people in awe look to these sorcerers, and these scientists, and these learned men for an understanding of the seemingly endless magic that existeth in the universe. And it is mystical and magic to the people because they do not understand it.

23 And if the people were to understand these things, then they would not be mystical or magic, and they would see through the guise of those who mislead them and take their money that they might gain a profit and have power over the lives of the people.

24 And Moses stood forth boldly in the court of Pharaoh and rebuked Jannes and Jambres, saying: These men in whom ye have put your trust; know ye not that they understand nothing of the laws of God and the order of nature in which He hath placed us?

25 Know ye not that they are deceiving you because of their desire for riches and glory, which ye give unto them because of their pretended learning?

26 Yea, of what use is their counsel unto thee, Oh, great Pharaoh, when your people suffer because of famine, and pestilence, and from the wickedness of their own souls?

27 Yea, of what use is their knowledge of the universe and the course of nature which holdeth it in its boundaries when thy people suffer so exceedingly?

28 Behold, I say unto you, that the God of nature knoweth and understandeth the laws by which He hath created all things. And this understanding He doth not give to wicked men who desire it so that they might get gain and glory and power from the people.

29 And thou, Oh, great Pharaoh, dost thou not know, that by the power of my word, which is the power of God that hath been given unto me, thy kingdom shall be cursed by the nature which is held in the power of the only true God?

30 And this shall be done unto you because of the suffering of the children of God who are under your power, and to whom thou givest nothing in comparison to that which thou givest to these pretended men of great learning.

31 Behold, it mattereth not to God if ye understand the laws of His nature, for they are His laws, and He giveth a full understanding of them to those who He hath chosen to serve His people.

32 But it mattereth to God that His people are suffering exceedingly by your hand and by the hands of those whom thou hast given power and placed over them.

33 Behold, those things which thy counselors, and thy scientists, and they magicians give unto thee as the truth, are not the full truth. Yea, they have a form of godliness, but they deny the power therein; and this power shall only be given unto those who shall use this power to serve the children of God in righteousness, which is the only purpose for which this power and knowledge were given unto Him, yea, that He might serve us.

34 And it came to pass that the advisers and counselors of the court of Pharaoh were sorely offended at what Moses said concerning them; and they sought from that time forth to lay a snare for him and catch him in a lie that they might rebuke him before the Pharaoh.

35 But Moses withstood all of the machinations of these wicked men; and by the power of his word, did the plagues and curses of nature come upon Pharaoh and all of his house.

36 And now, I, Moroni, have included these things which are contained in the record of the brother of Jared; yea, I have included them in this record that ye of the latter days might not be deceived by those who are among you who take of your money and your substance to invent pretended hypothesis and theories of truth regarding the universe in which ye live.

37 For behold, though these shall have the portion of the truth that Satan shall be allowed to

give unto them in the latter days, they shall never come to an understanding of the full truth. Therefore, they shall be ever learning and never able to come to a knowledge of the truth.

38 Behold, I would that ye of the latter days should be more concerned with the plight of your daily lives and that which transpireth day by day upon the earth which ye live.

39 Behold, look around you and see the great poverty and the necessity of so many of your brothers and sisters. Yea, ye know that there existeth no love or peace among any of you upon the earth in the latter days; and ye are those of whom the prophets make mention.

40 Behold, why do ye allow yourselves to be deceived by those who seek for a knowledge of something that God hath created for you so that ye might be happy?

41 Yea, if ye would take the money and the time that ye spend on the pursuit of those things which ye shall never be given, yea, even the knowledge and power of God over the universe, and use them to find ways to feed the hungry and administer to the relief of those in need, then ye shall be making an effort in fulfilling the laws of God concerning the love that ye should have one towards another.

42 And only by obeying the law of God, can ye find the happiness and the knowledge that ye desire.

43 And there shall be many of you in the latter days who shall be called archeologists, and paleontologists, and geologists, who think in your learning that ye are providing a valuable service to your fellowmen by that which ye spend your efforts and your money.

44 But I say unto you, let the dead bury their own and leave these things of the past so that they do not become a burden to you in the future.

45 For behold, there is nothing of the past that ye can change, but of the future ye are responsible and shall be held accountable for by those things which ye accomplish in the present.

46 For behold, the past hath shaped the present, and the present shall shape the future, and the future shall judge the works which ye have done in the past, and which ye do in the present.

47 Think not of yourselves that by digging up the past and reflecting on it that ye can change the future in any way, for ye shall not. Only that which ye do today shall effect the morrow.

48 Behold, it is better that ye put your efforts of time and money and the learning that ye have received into the problems that ye have created for yourselves by your works of the past.

49 Behold, in the day of the Lord none of those things which ye have done in the past shall effect the future paradise which shall be created for you by the Father.

50 And it shall come to pass that during the last thousand years of the days of your probation, or the days of your mortality in which the Father hath placed you, the Lord shall begin to use the power and knowledge that he hath received from the Father to begin to change the planets that belong to the system of stars that are held in their course by the power of the sun. Behold, each planet shall be transformed into the kingdom of glory to which it pertaineth.

51 And now, I, Moroni, have been commanded to speak plainly unto you according to the words of the brother of Jared which he wrote concerning you, and also according to my own understanding which I have received by and through the Spirit of prophecy that hath been given unto me.

52 Behold, nearest unto the sun is the planet Mercury, as it shall be known among you in the latter days. And this planet shall be transformed into a state that shall be the eternal world of those who belongeth to the highest degree of glory of the Celestial kingdom.

53 And it shall be called, Shinehahsan, like unto the kingdom of glory in which the Father dwelleth. And upon this planet shall an atmosphere be created by the power of God that shall shield it from the heat of Kolob, which is the name by which the sun in its final glory shall be known in the eternal kingdoms of the Father.

54 And the rotation of this planet shall be set according to the time of reckoning that shall be established upon it. And its time of reckoning shall be a thousand years of the time which ye consider a day, or as a completed rotation on its axis.

55 And the reckoning of time on this planet shall be set according to the desires of happiness of those who dwell upon this planet, who are the exalted Gods and Goddesses, who are united as one flesh and who have chosen to serve in the kingdom of God forever.

56 And this planet shall have an order of nature placed upon it that shall fulfill the desires of happiness of those who shall inherit this kingdom of glory.

57 And the next planet in its order from the sun, which is known among you as Venus; yea, this planet shall be known in the eternities as Shinehahsein, and it shall be the middle kingdom of the Celestial glory.

58 And it shall also be changed in its nature and be prepared for those who shall inhabit it according to their desires of happiness.

59 And these shall be Goddesses who have chosen to be female, and who have a desire to raise the spirits of the children of God, and who find the source of Their joy therein. Yea, these are They who do not desire an eternal partnership with one man, but have chosen to follow the course of the eternal laws of heaven in the use of Their bodies to bring forth spirits that will inhabit the worlds that shall be created for them by the Father whom each of these Goddesses hath chosen to be the Father, or the God, of Her children.

60 And this world shall be organized in such a manner that the ability to raise children upon it shall bring exceedingly great joy to those Goddesses who have chosen this world for Themselves.

61 And the earth on which our spirits have been confined for seven thousand years is the third planet from the sun, and shall be known in the eternities as Shinehahsum.

62 And this earth shall also be changed and receive its paradisiacal glory as the third kingdom in the Celestial glory.

63 And now, even though one of these planets is closer than the other to the sun in its order, yea, this doth not mean that one of these planets of the Celestial glory shall be greater than the other; for this shall not be the case; but all the planets that pertain to the Celestial kingdom shall be equal in power and in authority.

64 Nevertheless, upon each shall be found those beings who have chosen for themselves different ways in which they shall serve in the eternities, each according to their individual desires of happiness.

65 For behold, upon Shinehahsum shall be the angels of God, who have not the desire to be Eternal Fathers and Eternal Mothers of children, but shall have the desire to do the bidding of the Gods, having the same power and glory as the Gods, that will be used to benefit and bring happiness unto the children of God.

66 Now, these are those who, unseen, come into this world and keep the balance of things in order according to the plan of the Father. Yea, these are those who cause the power of the Father to be exercised upon the earth by their command, having received their command, or commission, from the Father to serve the needs of His children.

67 And in this way, these angels of God receive their happiness and live upon this planet, which shall become their eternal world.

68 And the fourth planet from the sun, which is known among you as Mars, shall be the first kingdom of the Terrestrial glory, and shall be known as Oleasan throughout eternity.

69 And this planet shall also be changed and organized according to the laws of the Terrestrial glory, which shall provide the inhabitants thereof with all that which they need to fulfill their desires of happiness.

70 And the fifth and sixth planets from the sun, which are known as Jupiter and Saturn among you, shall be transformed into the rest of the kingdoms of the Terrestrial glory.

71 And these shall be known as Oleasein, and Oleasum respectively, in the order of the manner of their reckoning of time according to the desires of happiness of those who shall live upon these two great planets.

72 Behold, these two are the largest of all the planets that God hath created; and they are large enough that they might provide for the spirits of the children of God who have chosen these degrees of glory for themselves.

73 For behold, the majority of the children of God shall desire one of these two Terrestrial glories; and the things that shall be provided

thereupon shall fulfill their desires of happiness forever.

74 And the next planet, which ye call Uranus, shall be the first kingdom of the Telestial glory; and it shall be called Kokobsan.

75 And the last two planets which ye call Neptune and Pluto are those that have been placed in the orbit of this system under the power of the sun, according to the will of the Father, to house those souls who have chosen these degrees of glory for themselves.

76 And Neptune shall be called Kokobsein; and Pluto shall be called Kokobsum, each being named according to the names which the Father hath given unto each of them in the order in which He hath created them.

77 And now, my beloved brothers and sisters, ye have the words of the prophets before you which they have spoken concerning the kingdoms of the Father. And none of the revelations that ye have had among you is greater than that which the prophet Joseph gave unto you concerning the inhabitants of the kingdoms of glory of the Father.

78 And he wrote, saying: Hear, Oh, ye heavens, and give ear, Oh earth, and rejoice ye inhabitants thereof, for the Lord is God, and beside him there is no Savior. Great is his wisdom, marvelous are his ways, and the extent of his doings none can find out.

79 His purposes fail not, neither are there any who can stay his hand. From eternity to eternity he is the same, and his years never fail.

80 For thus saith the Lord: I, the Lord, am merciful and gracious unto those who fear me, and delight to honor those who serve me in righteousness and in truth unto the end. Great shall be their reward and eternal shall be their glory. And to them will I reveal all mysteries, yea, all the hidden mysteries of my kingdom from days of old, and for ages to come, will I make known unto them the good pleasure of my will concerning all things pertaining to my kingdom.

81 Yea, even the wonders of eternity shall they know, and things to come will I show them, even the things of many generations. And their wisdom shall be great, and their understanding reach to heaven; and before them the wisdom of the wise shall perish, and the understanding of the prudent shall come to naught.

82 For by my Spirit will I enlighten them, and by my power will I make known unto them the secrets of my will; yea, even those things which eye hath not seen, nor ear heard, nor yet entered into the heart of man.

83 And these things were given unto Joseph and his servant by the Spirit of God which was with the church that he had established in the beginning.

84 And he continued this revelation, saying: By the power of the Spirit our eyes were opened and our understandings were enlightened, so as to see and understand the things of God, even those things which were from the beginning before the world was, which were ordained of the Father, through his Only Begotten Son, who was in the bosom of the Father, even from the beginning; of whom we bear record; and the record which we bear is the fullness of the gospel of Jesus Christ, who is the Son, whom we saw and with whom we conversed in the heavenly vision.

85 For while we were doing the work of translation, which the Lord had appointed unto us, we came to the twenty-ninth verse of the fifth chapter of John, which was given unto us as followeth—speaking of the resurrection of the dead, concerning those who shall hear the voice of the Son of Man: And shall come forth; they who have done good in the resurrection of the just; and they who have done evil, in the resurrection of the unjust.

86 Now this caused us to marvel, for it was given unto us of the Spirit. And while we meditated upon these things, the Lord touched the eyes of our understandings and they were opened, and the glory of the Lord shone round about.

87 And we beheld the glory of the Son, on the right hand of the Father, and received of his fullness; and saw the holy angels, and them who are sanctified before His throne, worshiping God, and the Lamb, who worship Him forever and ever.

88 And now, after the many testimonies which have been given of him, this is the testimony, last of all, which we give of him:

That he lives. For we saw him, even on the right hand of God; and we heard the voice bearing record that he is the Only Begotten of the Father.

89 That by him, and through him, and of him, the worlds are and were created, and the inhabitants thereof are begotten sons and daughters unto God.

90 And this we saw also, and bear record, that an angel of God who was in authority in the presence of God, who rebelled against the Only Begotten Son whom the Father loved and who was in the bosom of the Father, was thrust down from the presence of God and the Son; and was called Perdition, for the heavens wept over him; for he was Lucifer, a son of the morning.

91 And we beheld, and lo, he is fallen; yea, he is fallen, even a son of the morning. And while we were yet in the Spirit, the Lord commanded us that we should write the vision; for we beheld Satan, that old serpent, even the devil, who rebelled against God, and sought to take the kingdom of our God and his Christ.

92 Therefore, he maketh war with the saints of God, and encompasseth them round about.

93 And we saw a vision of the sufferings of those with whom he made war and overcame, for thus came the voice of the Lord unto us, saying: Thus saith the Lord concerning all those who know my power, and have been made partakers thereof, and suffered themselves through the power of the devil to be overcome, and to deny the truth and defy my power.

94 They are they who are the sons of perdition, of whom I say that it had been better for them never to have been born; for they are vessels of wrath, doomed to suffer the wrath of God, with the devil and his angels in eternity; concerning whom I have said there is no forgiveness in this world nor in the world to come; having denied the Holy Spirit after having received it, and having denied the Only Begotten Son of the Father, having crucified him unto themselves and put him to an open shame.

95 These are they who shall go away into the lake of fire and brimstone, with the devil and his angels; and the only ones on whom the second death shall have any power; yea, verily, the only ones who shall not be redeemed in the due time of the Lord, after the sufferings of his wrath.

96 For all the rest shall be brought forth by the resurrection of the dead, through the triumph and the glory of the Lamb, who was slain, who was in the bosom of the Father before the worlds were made.

97 And this is the gospel, the glad tidings, which the voice out of the heavens bore record unto us; even that he came into the world, even Jesus, to be crucified for the world, and to bear the sins of the world, and to sanctify the world, and to cleanse it from all unrighteousness; that through him all might be saved whom the Father had put into his power and made by him.

98 And who glorifies the Father, and saves all the works of His hands, except those sons of perdition who deny the Son after the Father hath revealed him. Therefore, he saveth all except them; and they shall go away into everlasting punishment, which is endless punishment, which is eternal punishment, to reign with the devil and his angels in eternity, where their worm dieth not, and the fire is not quenched, which is their torment.

99 And the end thereof, neither the place thereof, nor their torment, no man knoweth; neither was it revealed, neither is, neither will be revealed unto man, except to them who are made partakers thereof; nevertheless, I, the Lord, show it by vision unto many, but straightway shut it up again. Therefore, the end, the width, the height, the depth, and the misery thereof, they understand not, neither any man except those who are ordained unto this condemnation.

100 And we heard the voice, saying: Write the vision, for lo, this is the end of the vision of the sufferings of the ungodly.

101 And again we bear record; for we saw and heard, and this is the testimony of the gospel of Christ concerning them who shall come forth in the resurrection of the just:

102 They are they who received the testimony of Jesus, and believed on his name and were baptized after the manner of his burial, being buried in the water in his name, and this according to the commandment which he hath given; that by keeping the commandments they might be washed and cleansed from all their sins, and receive the Holy Spirit by the laying on of the hands of him who is ordained and sealed unto this power; and who overcome by faith, and are sealed by the Holy Spirit of promise, which the Father sheds forth upon all those who are just and true.

103 They are they who are the church of the Firstborn. They are they into whose hands the Father hath given all things.

104 They are they who are priests and kings, who have received of his fullness, and of his glory, and are priests of the Most High, after the order of Melchizedek, which was after the order of Enoch, which was after the order of the Only Begotten Son.

105 Therefore, as it is written, they are gods, even the sons of God. Therefore, all things are theirs, whether life or death, or things present, or things to come, all are theirs and they are of Christ, and Christ is of God. And they shall overcome all things.

106 Therefore, let no man glory in man, but rather let him glory in God, who shall subdue all enemies under his feet.

107 These shall dwell in the presence of God and his Christ forever and ever. These are they whom he shall bring with him, when he shall come in the clouds of heaven to reign on the earth over his people. These are they who shall have part in the first resurrection. These are they who shall come forth in the resurrection of the just.

108 These are they who are come unto Mount Zion, and unto the city of the living God, the heavenly place, the holiest of all. These are they who have come to an innumerable company of angels, to the general assembly and church of Enoch, and of the Firstborn.

109 These are they whose names are written in heaven, where God and Christ are the judge of all. These are they who are just men made perfect through Jesus the mediator of the new covenant, who wrought out this perfect atonement through the shedding of his own blood.

110 These are they whose bodies are Celestial, whose glory is that of the sun, even the glory of God, the highest of all, whose glory the sun of the firmament is written of as being typical.

111 And again, we saw the Terrestrial world, and behold and lo, these are they who are of the Terrestrial, whose glory differs from that of the church of the Firstborn who have received the fullness of the Father, even as that of the moon differs from the sun in the firmament.

112 Behold, these are they who died without law; and also they who are the spirits of men kept in prison, whom the Son visited, and preached the gospel unto them, that they might be judged according to men in the flesh; who received not the testimony of Jesus in the flesh, but afterwards received it.

113 These are they who are honorable men of the earth, who were blinded by the craftiness of men. These are they who receive of his glory, but not of his fullness. These are they who receive of the presence of the Son, but not of the fullness of the Father.

114 Therefore, they are bodies terrestrial, and not bodies Celestial, and differ in glory as the moon differs from the sun.

115 These are they who are not valiant in the testimony of Jesus; therefore, they obtain not the crown over the kingdom of our God.

116 And now this is the end of the vision which we saw of the Terrestrial, that the Lord commanded us to write while we were yet in the Spirit.

117 And again, we saw the glory of the Telestial, which glory is that of the lesser, even as the glory of the stars differs from that of the glory of the moon in the firmament.

118 These are they who received not the gospel of Christ, neither the testimony of Jesus. These are they who deny not the Holy Spirit. These are they who are thrust down to hell. These are they who shall not be redeemed from the devil until the last resurrection, until the Lord, even Christ the Lamb, shall have finished his work.

119 These are they who receive not of his fullness in the eternal world, but of the Holy Spirit through the ministration of the Terrestrial; and the Terrestrial through the ministration of the Celestial.

120 And also the Telestial receive it of the administering of angels who are appointed to minister for them, or who are appointed to be ministering spirits for them; for they shall be heirs of salvation.

121 And thus we saw, in the heavenly vision, the glory of the Telestial, which surpasses all understanding; and no man knoweth it except him to whom God hath revealed it.

122 And thus we saw the glory of the Terrestrial which excels in all things the glory of the Telestial, even in glory, and in power, and in might, and in dominion.

123 And thus we saw the glory of the Celestial, which excels in all things; where God, even the Father, reigns upon His throne forever and ever; before whose throne all things bow in humble reverence, and give Him glory forever and ever.

124 They who dwell in His presence are the church of the Firstborn; and they see as they are seen, and know as they are known, having received of His fullness and of His grace; and He maketh them equal in power, and in might, and in dominion.

125 And the glory of the Celestial is one, even as the glory of the sun is one. And the glory of the Terrestrial is one, even as the glory of the moon is one. And the glory of the Telestial is one, even as the glory of the stars is one; for as one star differs from another star in glory, even so differs one from another in glory in the Telestial world;

126 For these are they who are of Paul, and of Apollos, and of Cephath. These are they who say they are some of one and some of another; yea, some of Christ and some of John, and some of Moses, and some of Elias, and some of Esaias, and some of Isaiah, and some of Enoch; but received not the gospel, neither the testimony of Jesus, neither the prophets, neither the everlasting covenant.

127 Last of all, these are they who will not be gathered with the saints, to be caught up unto the church of the Firstborn, and received into the cloud.

128 These are they who are liars, and sorcerers, and adulterers, and whoremongers, and whosoever loveth and maketh a lie. These are they who suffer the wrath of God on earth. These are they who suffer the vengeance of eternal fire. These are they who are cast down to hell and suffer the wrath of Almighty God, until the fullness of times, when Christ shall have subdued all enemies under his feet, and shall have perfected his work;

129 When he shall deliver up the kingdom, and present it unto the Father, spotless, saying: I have overcome and have trodden the wine-press alone, even the wine-press of the fierceness of the wrath of Almighty God.

130 Then shall he be crowned with the crown of his glory, to sit on the throne of his power to reign forever and ever.

131 But behold, and lo, we saw the glory and the inhabitants of the Terrestrial and Telestial and worlds, that they were as innumerable as the stars in the firmament of heaven, or as the sand upon the seashore.

132 And we heard the voice of the Lord saying: These all shall bow the knee, and every tongue shall confess to him who sits upon the throne forever and ever; for they shall be judged according to their works, and every man shall receive according to his own works, his own dominion, in the mansions which are prepared; and they shall be served by the Most High; but where God and Christ dwell they cannot come, worlds without end.

133 Behold, this is the end of the vision which we saw, which we were commanded to write while we were yet in the Spirit.

134 But great and marvelous are the works of the Lord, and the mysteries of his kingdom which he showed unto us, which surpass all understanding in glory, and in might, and in dominion; which he commanded us we should not write while we were yet in the Spirit, and are not lawful for man to utter; neither is man capable to make them known, for they are only to be seen and understood by the power of the Holy Spirit, which God bestoweth on those who love Him, and purify themselves before Him; to whom He granteth this privilege of seeing and knowing for themselves; that through the power and manifestation of the Spirit, while in the flesh, they may be able to bear His presence in the world of glory.

135 And to God and the Lamb be glory, and honor, and dominion forever and ever. Amen.

136 And now, if it so be that the Lord shall not reveal the mysteries of the eternal laws unto a man except he be a man who hath purified himself before the Lord by keeping his commandments, then how can ye of the latter days suppose that your theories and understanding of the laws of nature are true?

137 Behold, I know that Satan hath deceived you in that which ye think ye know concerning your science and your technology. Yea, Satan hath given unto you a portion of the knowledge and understanding of these laws, but shall not be allowed by the Father to give unto you the whole law; neither shall any man upon the earth in the latter days understand the power that the Father possesseth, by which power He hath created and hath organized the planets which shall house the souls of all of His children when His work is completed in this part of the universe.

138 For behold, no man in his wickedness shall have this power of creation.

139 But ye of the latter days shall come to understand many things; and ye shall learn many things which ye shall use to follow the plan of Lucifer. But when the Lord cometh upon the earth in the glory of the Father, all of your supposed learning shall be for naught; and those of you who thought that ye understood the truths of nature, shall be stricken with great anguish and turmoil when the Lord beginneth his work with the power that he possesseth.

140 For what man among you can command the elements with the sound of his voice? Yea, what man among you can cause the world to change its pattern of rotation so that it appeareth unto the inhabitants of the world that there is no night? Yea, what man among you can cause a mountain to remove itself from off the earth and cast itself into the depths of the sea? Yea, what man among you can heal all manner of sickness and affliction with his touch?

141 I say unto you, that though ye suppose that ye know much concerning the world and the laws that govern it, ye know nothing in comparison to the great knowledge that shall be given unto the righteous who will only use this knowledge to serve others.

142 Behold, perhaps ye shall understand some things, which understanding far surpasseth the understanding of your ancestors who lived upon the earth before the days of your mortality.

143 And why do ye suppose that your ancestors did not understand these things for thousands of years before you, but then in seemingly no time, ye find this knowledge and use this knowledge to benefit you, as ye suppose?

144 Do ye now realize that Satan was forbidden until the latter days to give unto you this knowledge? Do ye now see whom ye serve?

145 And ye who think that ye understand the laws of science and nature, whom do ye serve in righteousness, except it be your own selfish interests of glory and honor and gain? Behold, in the day of the Lord ye shall suffer with the hypocrites.

146 And now, I would admonish those of you who have received this knowledge and understanding from Satan in the latter days; yea, ye know that this knowledge hath been used to cause much misery and commotion upon the earth.

147 Yea, ye have seen the many souls that have been sent home prematurely to the God who gave them life because of the causes of this knowledge that ye have among you.

148 And Satan cannot take back the knowledge that he hath revealed unto you, therefore, repent and use your knowledge for good, and for the purposes which the Lord would have you use this knowledge.

149 Behold, if ye begin to use this knowledge to feed the hungry, clothe the naked, and provide shelter for him who hath no house; yea, if ye use this knowledge to do good to your fellowman; even if ye use this knowledge to obey the words of Christ in all things, which are the commandments of the Father; I say unto you, if ye begin to use this knowledge in righteousness, then shall the Lord bless you and give unto you more knowledge that he might cut his work short in righteousness.

150 Remember my words, my brothers and sisters; Yea, prepare yourselves to meet God and give unto Him an accounting of all that ye did with the knowledge and blessings that ye have received.

151 And if ye can stand in front of Him and declare unto Him that ye have not hurt another because of your works; yea, if ye can say that all of your brothers and sisters had food, and clothing, and shelter in the same abundance that ye had, then shall ye be justified before the Lord for that which ye do with your time, and your money, and the knowledge that ye have.

152 Remember my words, and perish not.

CHAPTER 98

The religions of the world are all corrupt, yet have good roots, which is the primary gospel that they teach. The practice of religion during the millennium is discussed. Prayer will no longer be needed in the Celestial kingdom, but the beings in the other kingdoms will still pray in righteousness and give thanks to the Father for all that they have received from Him. Humans will worship God by their works.

AND it shall come to pass in the latter days that the people shall not receive their knowledge and understanding from these institutions of learning only, even those that have been set up among them, which shall teach them those things which pertain to worldly things, or secular studies, which deal with matters unassociated with faith.

2 For faith is the substance of things hoped for; things unseen that work to benefit the souls of the children of men.

3 And these things of faith shall be taught throughout the world in the many religions that shall be set up in the latter days.

4 And these religions shall also have a form of godliness, because they shall have the roots of the gospel, which are true, because they were given unto the people by the prophets of God who were assigned to their specific cultures and period of time. Nevertheless, in the latter days they all shall deny the power of God, because of the great wickedness and deceptions of their leaders.

5 And in those days shall all the religions of the world be corrupt, because the people of these diverse religions are taught the precepts and concepts of faith by men who are uninspired, and who do not have the true Spirit of God to guide them in their own understanding of His will.

6 For behold, no man can have the Spirit of God unless he liveth his life one with God. Yea, unless a man abideth by the laws of Christ, he cannot have the Spirit of God with him.

7 And because the power of Satan shall abound in the latter days, all the people of the earth shall be deceived in the matters of faith, in the same manner that they shall be deceived by their supposed knowledge of science and technology which they shall receive from Satan.

8 Behold, the inhabitants of the earth shall worship Satan as their God; and they shall call him their Father, and their Christ.

9 And because of the great power that Satan shall have over their minds, they shall not know that it is Satan whom they worship, because they shall be led to believe that they are worshiping the true God.

10 Behold, instead of the religions of the world uniting the souls of all men and women upon the earth, they shall divide them; and they shall be at war one with another for dominance and preeminence among all the earth.

11 And the Christian shall rise up in his pride and condemn any who do not believe in Christ.

12 And the Muslim shall rise up and condemn all those who do not believe in Allah, and his prophet Mohammed.

13 And the people of the great church of the beast, even the church known among you by the name of my father, shall believe that they alone have the truth, and that unless a man joineth this church, he shall not be saved.

14 And thus shall the god of the earth rule and reign over the people of the latter days. Behold, Satan shall begin to divide the nations unto themselves, and cause great pride and boasting of one nation above another because of the blessings which he hath given to the nations of the earth.

15 And the seat of Satan shall be glorified in the latter days above all other nations of the world; and from this throne, shall Satan rule the world and cause all to bow down before him and worship him.

16 Yea, Satan shall inspire the children of men to separate their lives from God, having God in their thoughts and in their lives only when they are not dealing in secular matters of government, education, and the course of activities that bringeth the temporary joy that is received from the blessings of Satan.

17 And the leaders of all the religions of the earth shall establish themselves with the beast; and they shall dress like the beast; and they shall perform all their works with the beast, so that

they might be accepted by and given honor from the image of the beast that they represent in their examples to the members of their churches.

18 Behold, ye shall know these leaders by their works. Yea, judge them by the words that ye have received in this record, even the words of Christ which he hath spoken unto you, and of which ye have two testimonies in the book of the Jews, and also in the record of my father which was unsealed and given unto you by the prophet Joseph.

19 I say unto you, set this as your standard of judgment. And if the leaders of your religions do not meet this standard set by Christ, then ye may know of a surety that they are servants of Satan, and that which they promote shall not give you the eternal peace and happiness that ye desire.

20 Behold, ye shall believe that ye feel of the Spirit of God in your churches when ye listen to the flattery and the deceitful words of your religious leaders; yea, Satan shall mimic the Spirit of God and cause you to weep and feel a burning in your bosom that the church to which ye belong, or the religion which ye follow, is the true church of God.

21 Nevertheless, there is only one way that ye can be assured that the church to which ye belong is a true church of God: Yea, doth your church teach the words of Christ? Do your leaders follow the example of Christ in how they live their lives? Yea, do they have the power that Christ had, which is the same power that the twelve apostles had when they went throughout the land healing the sick and preaching the gospel without price to all those who would hear them?

22 Yea, is it required of you that ye give of your money to hear the word of God? I know that ye believe that it is not required of you to give, but that ye are asked to give by your leaders, so that God might fill your souls with His unspeakable mercy, which mercy your leaders do not speak of in truth, because they do not understand it.

23 And when they have received your money, what manner of lifestyle do your leaders pursue? Do they live like Christ? Do ye know of their houses and their fine things of the world, which they receive from the money that ye give unto them?

24 And there shall be some religious leaders upon the earth who shall deceive you in following them by their pretended works of Christ. Yea, they shall live poorly and dress humbly that they might prove to you of the dedication of their hearts to God.

25 But these shall not teach you to love one another and bless your enemies and do good to them that hate you and persecute you; yea, they shall teach you to defend the holy name of your God, and give your life by taking the lives of others in the defense of your God.

26 Now, these are not the works of Christ, nor are they the words that he hath given unto you. Behold, ye have the words of Christ, and now ye have my own testimony of these words, and also the testimony of the brother of Jared, who was accompanied by Jehovah in the vision which he received from the Father pertaining unto all things that shall come upon this earth since the days of its creation until the time that it shall become a glory in the Celestial kingdom.

27 Yea, ye have all of these testimonies. And ye also have the testimony of the Spirit that whispereth to you that these things are true; and ye know that these things which have been revealed unto you in the portion of this record which I shall seal up unto you are true.

28 Yea, when ye read these things your heart burneth within you and ye marvel at the simplicity and truthfulness of these things.

29 Yet, even though ye shall know that these things are true by the manifestations of the Spirit which shall testify of these things, many of you shall deny them and reject them because of the many stumbling blocks that have been placed before you because of your wickedness.

30 But this thing I shall prophesy unto those of you who receive these things, and who read them: Yea, after ye have read these things, ye shall no longer be able to find peace in any of the religions of the earth. Yea, ye shall begin to see the leaders of your religions and their works, and ye shall know that they fulfill all of the prophecies of the Lord concerning their wickedness, which are contained in the holy scriptures.

31 And ye shall begin to see things that ye have never beheld; and understand things that ye have never considered before.

32 And now, my beloved brothers and sisters, when my words are fulfilled within you, or when ye have felt these things, will ye still continue to deny the truthfulness of these things which the Lord hath prepared for you that ye might not suffer at his coming?

33 Behold, if ye deny these things and go back to the evil of your ways, then ye shall never have peace again in your heart, and Satan shall try harder still to deceive you and keep you in his fold.

34 Behold, if ye want the peace that the Father hath promised to all of His children, then ye must look to Christ and the things which he taught.

35 Do not look to the words of men for this comfort, for it shall not come from the words of any man.

36 Come out of the corrupt religions that are organized upon the earth and prepare yourself for the day of the Lord, or for the day that ye shall die and know of a surety that these things are true.

37 And now, during the millennium there shall be no religions upon the earth. Yea, there shall be no governments upon the earth, except it be that government which the Lord shall establish himself when he cometh.

38 And there shall be institutions of learning set up throughout the earth, and these shall be the churches, and the colleges, and the universities that shall teach the students and members thereof the truth in all things whatsoever the Lord shall command to be taught according to the nation, or the kingdom in which each person shall choose to live.

39 And in the Celestial nation, they shall be taught the power and knowledge of God, so that they might use this power to help in the transformation of the planets into the kingdoms of the Father.

40 And these shall be taught how to command the elements; yea, how to heal with a touch, even they shall be taught all things pertaining to the righteous works of the Lord.

41 And those who shall be set apart by the Lord to be the leaders over these seven nations that shall exist upon the earth, shall teach and administer the words of Christ in all things. And these are the only things that they shall teach the people, except it be the particular laws that pertain to the kingdom in which they live according to their desires of happiness.

42 And the power of the Lord shall spread throughout the whole earth, and the manner that the children of men have been taught to worship the Father shall cease among them. For they shall no longer worship the Father upon their knees, but they shall worship Him by their works.

43 For behold, the Father rejoiceth when He seeth that His children love one another and care for one another in all things. And in this way shall all the inhabitants of the earth worship the Father. And they shall be doers of the word, and not only hearers.

44 And then shall the words of the prophets be fulfilled when they wrote, saying: Pure religion that is undefiled before God, the Father is this: To visit the fatherless and widows in their affliction, and to keep oneself unspotted from the world.

45 Behold, my brothers and sisters, this is not only the pure religion, but it is the only religion that hath been, and is, and shall ever be accepted by the Father, even that ye should love one another as ye would have them love you.

46 Behold, do not think that ye shall fall down before the Lord in the day of his power to worship him with your tears and your humility; for if ye do this before him, he shall command you to arise and depart from before him.

47 And he shall command you to go and do good to your neighbor and love your enemy and praise the Father for the wonderful blessings of life that He hath given to you.

48 For the Lord will not suffer his merciful smile to grace the eyes of a hypocrite, who in an effort to ease the pain and anguish of his misery, desireth a smile from the Lord.

49 But the righteous shall be constantly engaged in the work of the Lord, in doing good to others; and they will not think that it shall be necessary to fall down before him and weep upon him; but they shall see his smile as

he passeth by them and witnesseth them engaged in his work, which is a work of love one for another.

50 And all the inhabitants of the earth shall know his name and understand his words, for they shall be spoken unto all in plainness, so that there might be no error in the interpretation of them.

51 And they shall be written upon their hearts, and in their minds, and every knee shall bow, and every tongue confess that he is the Son of the living God, who hath saved us from our sins, and hath come to prepare us to meet the Father, so that we might be ready to dwell in the kingdom of glory that we have chosen for ourselves.

CHAPTER 99

The children of God must have certain needs met in order for them to realize that they are children of God and find eternal happiness, and also so that they can ascertain properly which kingdom of glory best suits their desires of happiness. The Lord will provide all of these needs during the millennium. The earth will be prepared to receive the Father and all of our Eternal Mothers in a grand family reunion.

AND now, my beloved brothers and sisters, it is expedient in that which the Lord hath commanded me concerning the organization of this abridgment of the vision and words of the brother of Jared; and also those things which I have included herein of my own words, according as I have received them from the Holy Spirit, and also from the mouth of the Lord himself; yea, it is expedient at the conclusion of this record that it is explained unto you that which must surely come to pass in the kingdom of God in order for His plan to take its full effect upon all of His children.

2 For behold, it hath been explained unto you that before any spirit is ready to enter into immortality and receive eternal life, through the resurrection of the body of flesh and bone with the spirit matter from which we have been created; yea, it is necessary that we understand fully the plan of the Father in all things and prove ourselves worthy of living in His kingdom with a body that shall be the home of our spirit forever, never again being separated from it.

3 Behold, the days of probation which we pass through during our sojourn in mortality; and also our observations and experience in the spiritual dimension that holdeth our spirits upon this planet while others journey through mortality; give us an indication of our worthiness and readiness to partake of the blessings of the resurrection.

4 In other words, the seven thousand years of our confinement to this planet in mortality with flesh and bone, and in the spirit dimension as eternal matter, give us the opportunity to prove to ourselves that the kingdom of glory that we would exist in forever is just and proper for us, according to our desires of happiness.

5 And now, I have written much concerning our individual desires of happiness; and these desires pertain to each of us individually, according to our free agency to act in the state of independence in which we were created by the Father.

6 And ye know from the experience that ye have, that each of us perceiveth happiness in our own way, depending on the gender that we have chosen for ourselves. Behold, even the gender that we choose for ourselves shall be according to each of our individual desires of happiness.

7 And ye shall have those among you upon this earth who shall enter into mortality with a gender that they have chosen for themselves as a spirit. But when they begin to experience the effects and nature of the gender that they have chosen for themselves, they shall realize that this gender is not that which bringeth them joy. And these shall live trapped in mortality in a body of flesh and bone that doth not give unto them a complete fulfillment of the joy that they should feel.

8 And in the latter days many of these shall take it upon themselves to change the manner of their dress, or with the technology that Satan shall introduce in those days, change the structure of their bodies from one gender to another.

9 And there shall be those among you who lack the understanding and spirit of God; and ye shall mock these brothers and sisters of yours for desiring this change.

10 But I say unto you, have they sinned against their Father for desiring that which would make them happy? Behold, they have not sinned, but ye who mock them and judge them unrighteously are those who sin against God.

11 For ye are commanded to love them and do good to them, whether ye agree with their desires of happiness or not.

12 And this hath been the cause of most of the hatred and misery among you in mortality, even your inability to understand the plan of the Father, in that it giveth unto all their free agency to act as they choose in their search for happiness.

13 For behold, the purpose for our placement upon this earth is to find ourselves and understand who we are, and more importantly, find that which bringeth happiness unto us.

14 And now, in order for any of us to come to a realization of ourselves and our individual desires of happiness, we must have certain rights to pursue this understanding, and we must also be provided with the proper means and environment in which this search might be performed in fairness and equity for all.

15 And this is the reason for the gospel of Jesus Christ. Behold, his message was one that, if followed, would provide us fairly and equally with the environment that we would need to find ourselves.

16 And for this same reason, he shall come down upon the earth and establish his gospel throughout the world, thus creating this environment for all of the children of God.

17 For behold, during the first six thousand years of our mortality, as Lucifer made his attempts to show us that his plan would create for us this environment, very few of us were able to come to the certain realization of who we are and what our happiness is.

18 And the reason why most of the children of men shall fail to come to this self-realization during these first six thousand years, is because they do not have the environment in which they can know these things.

19 Behold, all the spirits of the children of men are motivated in their works, or in the choices that they make according to their free agency, by certain needs of the flesh. And before the needs of the spirit can be satisfied, these fleshly needs must be satisfied.

20 Behold, all animals which have been placed upon this earth, both for our instruction, and also for our happiness, have the same needs of the flesh as the children of men. Nevertheless, these creatures of a lower order do not have the same spiritual needs, because they are not children of God, and do not have the desire to know themselves and pursue their own individual desires of happiness.

21 Yea, these act in the order of nature in which they have been placed by God to be led instinctually in the works which they accomplish in mortality by the commands which God hath placed in their bodies of flesh.

22 And the basis of their works, or the reason for their instincts, which are these commands that God hath placed in them, is to fulfill these lower needs of the flesh.

23 Behold, if there existeth an environment around a spirit that is confined to the order of mortal flesh, then the needs of the flesh begin to take precedence over the needs of the spirit, because the desires of the flesh are strong and enticing.

24 And for this reason, the children of men seek for the things of the flesh before they seek for the kingdom of God.

25 And now, the plan of Lucifer doth not provide a fair environment in which all might equally receive the fulfillment of the needs of the flesh, so that all might concentrate more fully upon the desires of the spirit.

26 For this reason, we as supposed rational beings, act contrary to the nature of our spirits, which spirits were created in the image of God, who is righteous. And by acting contrary to our holy natures we bring upon us our own unhappiness and misery.

27 For while we are seeking to satisfy the lower needs of the flesh, we do nothing to satisfy the higher needs of the spirit. And when our environment doth not allow us to find the means to satisfy the lower needs of the flesh, then we are constantly engaged in seeking satisfaction of these needs, which satisfaction is only temporary, causing the needs of the flesh to continue with us, unsatiated and seeking always to be fulfilled.

28 And now, since it was the desire of the Father from the beginning to give us the opportunity to satisfy the needs of the spirit, which was the order of creation in which we were created by Him in the beginning; therefore, He hath commanded that we be given the opportunity in the flesh to know those things that we must do to satisfy the higher needs of the spirit.

29 For this reason holy prophets have been sent throughout the world in all periods of time upon the earth to teach us the proper ways in which we can fulfill the needs of our spirits.

30 And during the millennium, or the last thousand years upon the earth, all of our lower needs shall be met by the government and laws that the Lord shall establish throughout the world.

31 And when all or our lower needs are met, then we will exist in an environment where we can concentrate completely upon the needs of our spirit, so that we can come to know ourselves; and also that we might more fully understand and realize the needs of our individual happiness.

32 And after we have come to this self-realization, then we shall know without a doubt that the kingdom of glory that the Father hath prepared for us is the only kingdom of glory in which we could live forever and experience eternal peace and happiness.

33 And now, the Spirit constraineth me that I should write upon this last plate of ore, which is the last one that I have been able to make with my own hands—ore being scarce—and also because I have lost the mold and the pattern that I received of my father to make more plates; yea, even for many days have I hidden from the Lamanites that I might not be destroyed before I complete the work which the Lord hath given me to do.

34 And Timothy, and Mathoni, and Mathonihah have taken the plates of Nephi, and also the record of the brother of Jared. And I have still with my person these plates which my father and I have made with our own hands, and also the interpreters which I have used to read the great words of the brother of Jared, and which shall be used to translate this record; but except for these things, I have none of the records with me.

35 Behold, if the Lamanites were to find me and these records, then they would destroy them. And for this reason, Timothy, and Mathoni, and Mathonihah have taken the records of my people and will do with them what the Lord shall command them.

36 And I know that they shall hide them up so that they shall not be discovered until the Lord shall call for them in his own due time, to prove to the children of men that all of his words are true, which have been written by my father and me.

37 Behold, when the Lord cometh in his glory, he shall uncover all things and show unto the children of men that which he hath done for their salvation.

38 And when the Lord shall present unto the world the records of my people, then shall ye know that the record of my father is true; and ye shall also know that this record which I shall seal up is true.

39 And because of the things which are written herein, many of you, who have mocked these things, shall weep and wail and gnash your teeth because of that which ye would not accept when it was given unto you in plainness.

40 And now, the room on this last plate is scarce; therefore, let me return once again to the explanation that the Lord hath commanded me to write hereupon concerning the realization of the spirit.

41 And now, these lower needs, which are the basic needs of the flesh, are the desire to satisfy our hunger and our thirst, which hunger and thirst are caused because of the flesh; and our desire to rest the flesh, and sleep to maintain our strength, which is debilitated by the lusts of the flesh; and our desire to satisfy the cravings of sex, which are set within us that we might fulfill the measure of our creation and multiply and replenish the earth with the mortal bodies necessary to house the spirit children of God.

42 And it is also a need to preserve our lives and feel safe in the environment in which we exist. For this reason the birds have nests, the foxes have holes, and the children of men search for a place upon the earth that they can make their home and feel safe within its walls.

43 Now, these lower needs are also instinctual, or programmed into our flesh as they are in all of the animals that God hath put upon this earth.

44 Behold, when these are not satisfied, we may feel sickness, irritation, pain, and discomfort, which are the effects of the wants of the flesh commanding us to satisfy these basic needs.

45 Behold, these feelings motivate us to alleviate them so that we might establish a homeostasis, which is the balance and order of the nature in which we were created.

46 Yea, once we have reached a homeostasis of the flesh, then we will begin to concentrate more fully on the things of the spirit, which things separate us from the other animals that have been placed in the same order of nature in which our mortal bodies have been placed.

47 Behold, I have already explained unto you that the countenance of the Father can be seen in a child, and that upon entering into mortality as a newborn infant, we are born in the semblance of the Father in all things which are spiritual.

48 And when ye look upon the countenance of a child, ye shall see the potential of your spirits; for behold, we were spawned from Eternal Parents, who are righteous.

49 And these infants are innocent from the beginning and depend upon others to provide them with the fulfillment of these lower needs of the flesh that they might grow and gain experience.

50 And in the beginning of our mortal lives our natures were trustworthy, and given to love and forgiveness, and tenderness and mercy. Yea, nothing compareth in spiritual satisfaction than the smile and attitude of a child.

51 Behold, a child is prone to growth and to love, which it instinctively pursueth, enticed by the spirit within the flesh. And while the needs of our flesh were being met, we remained in this state.

52 Nevertheless, when these needs are thwarted and are not fulfilled, then we seek by whatever means we might find available to satisfy these needs.

53 And thus doth the innocence of human nature turn selfish, and self-serving, and the fruits of the flesh begin to manifest themselves in our search for the fulfillment of these lower needs.

54 And in the pursuit of these needs, we lose the innocence that we once had as a child; and the cycle of our misery and destruction followeth in the constant need to satisfy these lower needs of the flesh.

55 Yea, war, and murder, and deceit, and lies, and lasciviousness, and all manner of sin beginneth to overcome the spirit because of the desires of the flesh to be satiated.

56 And these things are contrary to the happiness of our spirits, which spirit desireth peace, and happiness, and love.

57 Yea, a man doth not sin to be happy, but he sinneth only to satisfy the needs of the flesh. And when the needs of the flesh are satisfied, then he feeleth a moment of joy in the satisfaction of his fleshly need; but afterwards he is left empty and again desireth the satisfaction of the flesh, because this temporary happiness is all that he knoweth and understandeth.

58 Nevertheless, his spirit constantly yearneth for fulfillment. Yea, it desireth to be loved by others and accepted, and appreciated for what it offereth to those who love and accept this man.

59 Now, these are the higher needs of the spirit, even that a man be loved and accepted by others.

60 And if this man, in a desire to satisfy the needs of his flesh, is involved with others who have the same desire, then there is a bond created, or a love generated between them that fulfilleth the need of the spirit.

61 Therefore, there existeth a bond between a parent and a child in the satisfying of these needs. But as the child groweth, the needs of the spirit remain, and the child searcheth for the fulfillment of these needs.

62 And for this reason, the children of men divide themselves into families, and

communities, and cities, and nations, wherein the need for love and belonging is satisfied.

63 But when they have divided themselves in this manner, then they begin to place the needs of their own family, and their own community, and their own city, and their own nation above the same needs of other families, and other communities, and other cities, and other nations; and in this way do the wars and contentions begin among the children of men.

64 And when the children of men have satisfied the desire of their heart to belong to a group, or a club, or a gang, which have desires like unto their own; yea, when they are comfortable therein, then they begin to seek to satisfy the need to be recognized above another, or acknowledged in some special way that alloweth them to stand out in their group, thus assuring themselves of their own worth.

65 And now, this is the reason that the children of men seek for the honor, and the glory, and the power of the world. For behold, they have been convinced by the very nature of their desires for self-realization, that in order for them to be accepted and recognized as an individual, they must be exalted above another, showing forth their value and thereby justifying their existence.

66 Behold, for this reason the children of men seek after the fine things of the world, and money, and those things which would define them as rich and prosperous. And when they are rich, then they can look down upon the poor, and further exalt themselves above another so that they might feel good about themselves.

67 And after this spiritual need of acceptance and belonging is met, even when a man feeleth that he is accepted and honored within the group to which he belongeth, then it becometh his desire to be loved.

68 Yea, the spirit hath the need to be convinced that that which it doeth is righteous and good, and is accepted as righteous and good by those from whom it seeketh this love.

69 And now, after all these lower needs are met, or when a man hath gained for himself a security in the things of the flesh, and also a security that he is loved and accepted by others, then he shall be left unto himself to find out his true nature, or the desires of happiness that determine who he truly is.

70 And it is in this state, when a man beginneth to search for the promptings of the spirit within him; or in other words, it is in this state of security that he seeketh for the reason of his creation, or why he existeth.

71 Now, these promptings of self-realization are fruits of the spirit; for behold, our spirits were created in the image of our Father.

72 And when we were created, we began to experience the effects of our creation, or we began to grow in knowledge and experience.

73 And since we were born of God, then it must needs be that we become like Him. And it is this thing that our spirit whispereth to us all the days of our lives.

74 Behold, again I say unto you, this is life eternal, that ye know the only wise and true God, and Jesus Christ, whom He hath sent. He who hath wisdom, let him understand.

75 And now, my beloved brothers and sisters, the essence of the gospel of Jesus Christ is that ye know the Father.

76 And in all the works of Christ he hath pointed us to the Father, giving glory to the Father in all things. And the commandments of Christ, which were given unto us by commandment of our Father, is that we should all have the opportunity to know Him.

77 But in order to know Him, we must first satisfy the needs of the flesh, as well as the needs of the spirit, as I have explained them unto you.

78 And for this reason, when the Lord cometh in the glory of the Father and dwelleth among the children of men upon the earth during the last thousand years, he shall provide for all the needs of the flesh, and also the needs of the spirit, that all might have an equal and fair opportunity to realize who they are and that which are their true desires of happiness.

79 And the Lord shall give food, and clothing, and shelter freely to all the inhabitants of the earth, according to the laws that he shall establish throughout the land.

80 And the need for sex shall be taken away from all those who are not worthy of this blessing, which blessing is reserved for those who seek to use it to selflessly serve others by providing the materials necessary for the bodies of the children of God.

81 And when these fleshly needs have been guaranteed unto us, then shall the Lord exalt those who have been abased, and abase those who have exalted themselves above others.

82 And there shall exist no inequality among the inhabitants of the earth, for all shall see the Lord, who hath all the power of the Father, and they shall witness his example among them.

83 And they shall see that he is approachable, and loving, and humorous, and kind unto all. Yea, they shall see that he shall labor with those who were once poor, because of the labor which they performed in the fields, and in the factories, and in the businesses of the rich. But all these merchants who have made themselves rich by the labor of the poor, and who have exalted themselves above others, shall be removed from off of the earth.

84 Yea, in that day we shall see the Lord abase himself before us, so that all of us might be exalted above him.

85 And now, when ye shall behold the self abasement of the Lord, even the Son of God that reigneth upon the earth in the glory of the Father, what then shall ye say of your glories and your honors which ye received before he came into the world?

86 Yea, when ye see the Son of God exalt the beggar, who begged all the days of his life for that for which he had no desire to work, what shall ye that are rich say then?

87 And when he releaseth the prisoners of your prisons, who have defied your laws, which laws were based upon your desire to follow the plan of Lucifer instead of the plan of God; yea, when he bringeth these forth and exalteth them, and maketh them equal to all, then what shall ye say of your laws?

88 Behold, in the day of the Lord shall all the inhabitants of the earth, who were once abased by those who exalted themselves above them; yea, these shall sing praises of joy unto the Lord, who hath given them the means by which they can find the happiness that is the purpose for their creation.

89 And during the course of the millennium shall all the children of God come to know their Father through the Son; for he shall shine unto them as a perfect example of the Father.

90 And the Father loveth all of His children, and is no respecter of any one above another.

91 And thus shall the spiritual needs of all the inhabitants of the earth be fulfilled, so that they can know for themselves that they are all children of one God, even our Eternal Father.

92 And now my brothers and sisters, even ye of the latter days that shall receive these things, ye now know that which is required of a man that he might find joy and happiness in mortality; therefore, why do ye prolong the days of mortality and continue to live in pain, and misery, and unhappiness, because your needs are not being properly met?

93 Behold, ye have these things which I have been commanded to write unto you, and if ye understand these things, then seek to establish these things among you.

94 Yea, seek to give to all the inhabitants of the earth the fulfillment of their needs. Make the poor, rich, make the bond, free; make the outcasts and imprisoned among you feel like they are important, and that they are your brothers and your sisters.

95 For behold, if their needs are fulfilled, then no man or woman would have cause to do evil unto you and follow the plan of Lucifer, but shall rejoice in the plan of their Father, which can provide for them a constant state of happiness in all things.

96 And now, throughout this record I have shown unto you the effects of the children of men in their attempts to satisfy these needs of which I have spoken according to the plan of Lucifer.

97 And ye have seen that when they seek to fulfill these needs selfishly, then there existeth great unhappiness upon the earth among you.

98 Therefore, become the children of God and follow the plan that He hath established for you from the beginning, and ye shall be blessed by him.

99 Behold, when the Father looketh upon a man, He doth not behold the evil works that this man hath done, but He beholdeth the infant child that He held in His arms upon its creation.

100 Yea, the Father doth not see a murderer in the face of a man who hath slain another, nor doth he see the face of a sinner who hath wasted away the days of his mortality in exceeding sin.

101 Behold, the Father seeth his child, whom He loveth and cherisheth with all of His soul.

102 And when your own children have grown and become old like unto you, do ye not remember the times when they were young? Yea, do ye not remember the times when ye held them in your arms and witnessed their tender smiles as they clung to you and depended on you for their happiness?

103 Do ye not remember the young child who held your hand, and sat upon your lap, and put its head upon your shoulder, showing unto you the unconditional love that only a child can give?

104 Yea, these things ye can remember. And which of your children, when they are old, shall ye not love because of the knowledge that remaineth in your heart of their youth?

105 I say unto you, that the Father loveth all of His children in this manner; good or bad, rich or poor; He loveth them as He did when they were created.

106 And for this reason He shall send His Only Begotten Son once again to the world to save His children and show unto them the exceeding greatness of this love which He hath for them.

107 And the Lord shall turn the hearts of the children of men to their Heavenly Father, and they shall yearn to know Him and become a part of Him.

108 And it shall come to pass, that after the last millennium hath passed away, even after the Lord hath cleansed the whole earth of its sin, and prepared it to receive the Father; yea, even after all these wonderful things shall come to pass among the children of men, then shall the greatest blessing of all come to pass.

109 Then shall the day come that all the holy prophets have looked forward to since the beginning of time, in faith, having an eye single to the glory of the Father.

110 Behold, at that time shall the very Eternal Father and all of the Eternal Mothers who have created the spirits of all men, come down upon the earth and receive Their children upon Their breasts, and talk with them, and coddle them, and laugh with them, and play with them.

111 And we shall see our Eternal Parents as They truly are. And They smile upon us and receive us into Their arms, where we shall weep, because we have missed Them for these many years of our preparation to come home to Them once again.

112 Yea, great and glorious shall be the day, when at last, we are all once again reunited to the only family that we have ever been a part of—the Eternal Family of God.

CHAPTER 100

Moroni's epilogue: Love one another as ye would have them love you.

BEHOLD, my soul is overcome at this time by the Spirit of God. For behold, I know that I am done fulfilling the commandment that I have received of the Lord, and that for which the Spirit hath prepared me all the days of my life.

2 And I know that I shall shortly die and return once again to the spirit world; for behold, the Lamanites are all around me, and they have promised to avenge their fathers by my death.

3 And when I have sealed these things up and hid them in the earth, I shall not run any longer, but I shall let them capture me and do to me what they will.

4 And I will follow the example of my Lord and Savior, Jesus Christ, and submit unto their hate, even unto death.

5 But as they end my life, I will love them and forgive them for that which they do to my flesh, knowing that they shall have no more power over me, forever.

6 And my eyes and face are wet with tears, for I am saddened that I must end this record and end my words unto you, my beloved brothers and sisters of the latter days.

7 Behold, I love you all. I have come to know you through the greatness of the words of the brother of Jared, and also through the visions and the revelations that I have received from the Holy Spirit concerning you.

8 And I know that I have been hard at times, because of the plainness of those things which the Lord hath commanded me to reveal unto you according to the office and calling that I have received as a prophet of God.

9 But in all these things, I have never ceased to love you, for I am also your brother. And it is this exceeding love that engulfeth my soul at this time.

10 Behold, I have seen the beginning of our existence as the spirit children of the Father, even at the beginning in His kingdom until the end of time when we shall inherit the kingdom that shall bring us eternal joy and happiness forever.

11 And my soul rejoiceth because of the things which I have seen; for I know that most of you; yea, even the majority of the children of God shall be saved in one of His kingdoms.

12 And though at times the days of your probation might seem overwhelming in body and soul, I pray, my beloved brothers and sisters, that ye do not give up a hope in that which ye do not see and understand by the nature of the flesh that ye have.

13 Behold, the future is wondrous and glorious. And it shall come to pass that good shall overcome evil in all things; and peace, and happiness, and order shall be the state of the universe as it hath always been, and shall always be, worlds without end.

14 And now, with my parting words unto you I leave you my blessing and my love.

15 Yea, love one another. Do good to all.

16 Look at your neighbors and imagine them as a child of God. Know that each of you is a child of God, and that He loveth each of you, and hath done all these things for your good.

17 Remember the words of Christ which have been given unto you. Remember them, my beloved brothers and sisters; for in them ye shall know peace and happiness.

18 And one day we shall meet in the kingdoms of the Father, where we shall receive eternal life. Amen.

APPENDIX 1

The Coming Forth of The Sealed Portion

Throughout the history of humankind, prophets, seers, and revelators have emerged in all epochs, eras, cultures, and diverse geographical areas of our small planet. There have been many that were and are presently self-proclaimed—desirous to claim a title that rightfully belongs to those who have truly received such a calling from a higher source with the authority to bestow it properly.

It is easy to discern a man or woman who has bestowed the title upon themselves, yet lacks the actual authority to act upon it. He or she becomes selfish and self-centered in their efforts to gain followers. They usually isolate themselves and their followers from mainstream society in an effort to guard their presupposed doctrines and beliefs; thus avoiding the scrutiny of others who have not fallen for their invented revelations, dreams, and prophecies.

By doing this, false prophets have caused considerable damage to the emotional well-being of many human beings and have been the cause of much, if not all, of the world's misery, poverty, and general hopelessness. Their designs, however, were not intended to be evil or to cause misery. In fact, most truly believe they are inspired to act and preach the things that they do and that they have been called of God to do so.

In order to understand the necessity of true prophets, seers, and revelators, one has to take a hard look at exactly why the human species exists. Because we know that we do exist, one must consider the possibility that there is a viable reason as to why we exist. We know we exist because we know—reiterating what the philosopher, Rene Descartes proclaimed: "I think, therefore I am."

Contrary to the belief of those who love and protect the wonderful animals with which we share this small planet, we are the only species that truly knows that we exist. All other species are driven by natural instincts directing them throughout their existence. In essence, they have been programmed to function in certain ways and for certain purposes. They have very little conscious choice as to how they act or what they should do with their lives. Some species of animals have greater instincts than others and still others can be trained and adapted to have extraordinary skills. However, none have the reasoning capacity of human beings. All animals are programmed to do whatever is necessary in order to stay alive—all animals, except humans.

Unlike all other creatures on earth, we have the capacity and ability to take our own lives any time we choose. We can stop eating at any time just by willing and choosing to do so. Unfortunately for our species, we often choose to overeat and abuse our natural state of health. Distinct of every other living creature in nature, some of us make the conscious choice of committing suicide, and ending our lives prematurely. We have a power that no other creature has—the power of free agency.

Because animals have natural instincts to guide and direct them through life—telling them exactly what they must do in order to survive—they have no need for anyone or anything outside of their natural programmed instincts to command them. It seems nature has provided the perfect instructions for all animals—that is, again, except humans. Though we have a few innate, natural instincts (i.e., sex, sleep, and food), we still also have the unique power to control each of these at our discretion.

Therefore, it would seem reasonable to assume that if nature has provided animals with the instructions and guidance needed to exist, then the same provisions are available to us. Nevertheless, instincts do not come with instruction manuals, but rather are programmed into the creature. Based on thousands of years of experience, humans, left on their own accord to come up with the instructions for their survival, inevitably seem to be the cause of their own extinction. Whereas animals would survive perpetually by following their instincts, humans would last but a few thousand years.

Though there are countless theories and ideas about nature and how it works, few reasonable explanations clarify why nature is and where it came from. All we know for sure is that there are natural laws to which all living things are subject, and these laws have certain conditions and restrictions that cannot be overlooked or disobeyed. Like all animals, we are subject to the eternal laws of nature. Nevertheless, unlike other animals (that survive solely on their ability to abide by the promptings of their instincts given to them by these laws), we have the desire and capacity to understand the laws of nature and to manipulate them for our benefit. Other animals can learn rudimentary manipulations of these laws in order to fulfill the desires of their natural instincts, but no other animal looks up at the dark night sky and wonders what a star is; and they most certainly do not have the desire to visit one.

Of all the evolutionary theories that humankind has invented to explain who we are and why we are, none can describe how we evolved to a state of yearning—a state of desire that entices us not only to understand how we exist, but why we exist. These differences between humans and other animals can only make one wonder if we are indeed aliens to the planet earth that we call home. Natives of this planet (other animals) seem to get along quite fine here and have done so for millions of years. However, as soon as we showed up on the scene, all the problems started. Because we aren't subject to the restrictions of natural instincts, we use the earth and its resources in any manner that will bring us more happiness and pleasure. Other animals kill only to eat and protect. We kill because we want to. Other animals have sex to produce offspring. We have sex for enjoyment only. (Imagine a buffalo saying to its partner: "I'd better use contraceptives because the herd's getting pretty large." Or, "I don't like the looks of those buffalo with droopy eyes. Let's make them stay over on their side of the prairie and kill them if they try to come over and eat on ours.")

Not being completely subject to the laws of nature, yet having the ability to control such for our enjoyment, reasonably, we should have other laws that are not instinctual, but necessarily establish order among ourselves in order to assure our species will perpetuate itself forever.

If we truly are aliens to this planet (and our actions seem to confirm so), then wherever we are from must have certain laws established that would guide and tell us what we need to do so that we can fulfill the reason for our existence, i.e., happiness. Furthermore, whoever put us on this planet must know these laws and have some way to communicate them to us. We already realize that these laws are not going to be given to us like the rest of the animals (through instinct), so it seems reasonable that these laws should be given to us in some other way.

The way in which we receive these laws must compliment the type of beings that we actually are. Since we are free beings able to act according to our own will and pleasure, these laws cannot be forced upon us, but must be given in a way that fairly ensures us the choice to obey them or not. Upon obeying them, we will find peace, prosperity, and happiness. Disobeying them will cause misery and strife, and will eventually be the demise of our species.

We are aliens to this planet and have been placed here to experience things that other animals will never experience. Those responsible for our placement here have no other object in mind than to grant us the ability to have what they already enjoy—eternal peace and happiness. They know we need the laws they live by so that we, too, can enjoy this peace and happiness. They understand that we must be given these laws freely and without manipulation on their part, so that we can eventually learn that they are the right laws to live by and will give us the greatest amount of happiness possible. Because we have free will, we do not have to live by these laws. On our native planet, we grew up around the laws these creators (or euphemistically stated, these Gods) live by. Yet, having free will, we did not have to abide by them.

To help us understand that these laws are good and necessary in order to assure our eternal happiness, the Gods knew it was necessary to place us in a world where these laws do not exist. In this world we would experience other living beings that do not live by these laws, but live by instinct only. We would also be given the opportunity to live with each other without these laws. Nevertheless, in order to truly understand the eternal laws of happiness, we needed these laws given to us in such a way that it would seem completely arbitrary (thus assuring us our free agency) whether we obeyed them or not. We could not receive these laws directly from beings who had supernatural powers over the laws of nature and were continually experiencing eternal happiness. Were this the case, we would obviously be convinced by their mere presence to obey the laws that they gave us, or else; thus taking away some of the free will that makes us who we are.

We are given these laws from sources that cannot possibly make us think that we had better obey or else. Instead, we are given individuals whom we have properly named prophets and revelators—men and women like ourselves who are weak and mortal, and subject to all the same vicissitudes and problems of human nature as we are. Revelators are people who don't seem to fit in with the majority, but usually stand alone in their demeanor and desires. They are humans who easily learn and understand the eternal laws of the Gods and are able, without reservation, to incorporate these laws into their lives and teach others to do the same without regard to their own personal safety, material possessions, or worldly honors. In other words, the meekest, kindest, most compassionate, yet most courageous human beings the world has to offer. One who would dress oneself in the basest of human coverings, eat locust and honey if necessary, preach with the tenacity and courage of the fiercest lion, yet have said about him, "Among them that are born of women there hath not risen a greater…notwithstanding he that is least in the kingdom of heaven is greater than he." Yes, the least of the Gods is greater than the best we humans have to offer.

I did not choose to be a revelator. In fact, I've spent a great deal of my life running from the calling. I spent countless years rebelling against all the eternal laws that I'd been taught, in hope that the Gods would choose someone else. (For simplicity of understanding, I will use the terms "God" and "the Lord" to describe the Gods that I have mentioned.) I wish to this day that, "if it be possible, let this cup pass from me." Unlike the Christ, if I could get out of doing the "Father's will," I would run as fast as I could the other way. But I have tasted a fruit that very few people have tasted. I've seen things that most people will never be allowed to see. I have been taught and received things that most have a hard time learning. I've experienced things that few will ever experience (and I doubt many would want to). In fine, I've learned that if I want to enjoy happiness, my only option is to fulfill my calling or be racked with endless torment and misery.

I've spent many years deceiving and manipulating others into thinking that I am evil and undeserving of any special calling from God. Nevertheless, in all my machinations to rebel against the reality of my destiny, I have never intentionally hurt anyone. I have protected my calling and kept it hidden deep inside of me, hoping that one day another might be found more worthy and courageous than me; one who could stand up against a world that desires to be rid of anyone that questions its orthodoxy. It was hard for me to stand up and be counted among the insane and be seen as a blasphemous apostate—an atheist who had no hope of ever seeing heaven. But as the very mouth of hell would gape open to devour my soul, the Lord would pull me away and reassure me there was no other that could do what needed to be done.

Among humans I find very few friends. I have lost family, wives, children, brothers, and sisters because of what I have been called to do. But of the truly righteous, I find a friend, a special sister, and some special children who love me unconditionally; and no matter what the world might do to me, they will remain loyal.

As my experiences come to life in my biography, the reader will soon realize why each and every experience I went through taught me an important lesson and prepared me for the day when I would reveal to the world what the Lord has assigned me to do. Each experience taught me something different and gave me better insight into why the eternal laws the Gods live by are so vital to our happiness. My understanding of human nature far surpasses that of average human beings and is accentuated by the understanding that I receive through revelation. Nevertheless, none of this understanding has anything to do with my calling—the devil understands everything a lot better than I do. Yet, what makes him the devil? His works—in other words, what he does with his knowledge. One can know everything that the Gods know, yet still be locked out of eternal happiness because he or she refuses to abide by the laws that pertain to this happiness.

My calling is to bring to the world one of the greatest revelations that humankind has ever known. An ancient revelator tried desperately to teach the world the truths he was taught and received. He recorded this revelation, but found very little success among the majority of the people he preached to in his day. He was able to convince one of his brothers and a few others that what he understood was the only way any of them was going to find peace and happiness in a world that was in disarray. He was given this revelation at a time in history when the human race was ripe for destruction by wars, pestilence, and self-induced famine.

His revelation is one of the greatest revelations ever given to human beings. It reveals the truth from the beginning to the end of time, reviewing the nature of humankind and the great destruction brought upon itself by not abiding by the eternal laws of heaven. It also recounts the times when humans obeyed these eternal laws and had peace and happiness among them. His revelation reveals the secret acts of men of power, who disregard the eternal laws and enact laws of men and women upon humankind, in order to deceive and subject others under them for their own gain. It reveals more about the history and future of the human race than any other theory, prophecy, revelation, or speculation that any human has ever had.

Luckily for us all, this revelation was written and passed down from generation to generation unadulterated by human hand. It was written in a language that has long since been lost from among us, and purposefully so; so that in the end, the words of this book would come forth in their purity and show us the fallacies and corruption of the human race. Upon reading of our ignorance and lack of respect for the laws of nature and the eternal laws of peace and happiness, humankind will be brought under judgment and weep, wail, and gnash their teeth in embarrassment for what they have done to each other.

There were means provided by the Lord to translate this great revelation when the time was right. Two stones known as the Urim and Thummim are made of elements that are not tarnished or changed by time or the effects of nature. The Urim and Thummim are clear and ordinary to the human eye, appearing to be nothing more than rocks found by the thousands upon many of earth's mountains. However, these seemingly ordinary rocks have one special quality that none other of their kind have—they've been touched by the hand of God. In other words, inside their molecular structure, the Gods have implanted special devices that can be best related to our modern-day computer chips, yet far beyond any technology that we could possibly imagine. These miniscule devices use reflected light to actuate them and cause the meaning of any written language to come to light. They work very similar to a projection screen where the meanings of the words are miraculously transposed into pictures that only a chosen revelator can see.

Not every human that holds the Urim and Thummim can get it to work. Inside each of us are fractions of light that are distinct to each individual. (These fractions of light can be more easily described as "spirit" matter—and we've scientifically named these "electrical impulses." Some call this light an aura.) All fractions of light undulate, or move in a wavelike manner, according to their makeup and purpose. Like our fingerprints, our own light undulations are unique to each of us and give us our individuality and distinctiveness. There have only been a handful of men and women whose DNA has been programmed, so that the waves of their unique light meet the actuating specifications and parameters programmed into the Urim and Thummim.

When I first held the Urim and Thummim, it worked perfectly and actually scared me senseless. As soon as my hands touched it, it began to glow exceedingly and was set in motion to be used for the purpose of translating a source of revelation written upon very thin plates of gold that time has had no ill effect upon. I had previously been given the gold plates and soon thereafter was led to the Urim and Thummim. It was necessary I get the Urim and Thummim away from those who had it in their possession, but could not make it work. (Since those who were in possession of it couldn't make it work, they were skeptical of what it actually was. Many of them touched it and admired the clarity of its form, yet none had the spiritual design to actuate the molecules that were programmed into the stones in order to see what it presents.)

I have continually hid the gold plates and the Urim and Thummim from the sight and knowledge of all those who have shared my life and become close to me. I was instructed to test each person who came into my life and receive reassurance that they would not betray me and cause me to leave the calling I was appointed to do. There were not a few women that enticed my heart to follow the ways of the world and its human relationships instead of fulfilling the calling I had before me. I told no one the truth regarding the actuality of my possession of the gold plates and the Urim and Thummim. The reasons for my deception were obvious from the beginning: these people needed to prove to themselves that they would gladly obey the eternal laws because these laws are righteous and good and not because they were convinced by the seemingly miraculous things that I could have shown to them. To the date of this writing, I have found none yet ready to see what I have seen and touch what I have touched.

In almost every case that the test was given, my partners, friends, and intimates rebelled against me and caused me exceeding pain and misery. They failed to prove to me or to themselves that kindness, compassion, mercy, and forgiveness are far better than vengeance, vindictiveness, strife, and persecution. When I failed (many times on purpose) to give these companions of the filial and friendly persuasion that each of them wanted, he or she turned from me and became my enemy. My only desire was to find someone, anyone, who would not become self-serving because his or her needs were not being met. The only need I had (which ironically seemed to be instinctual, or programmed within me) was to fulfill my calling.

I am a man. I have the same passions and needs of any mortal man. I want to be loved and to love. I am no different from any of my fellow human beings. If I could give them what I have, I would do so freely without any expectation of receiving anything in return. I would embrace them as my brothers, sisters, relatives, and friends, and I know we would have the peace and happiness that we all desire.

I now know the importance of my calling and am ready and willing to reveal to the world what has been made known to me. My biography will be available to any and all who want to know what the Lord has done to prepare a revelator in these modern times for the incredibly important job he must accomplish.

The message must go out to the world. The eternal laws of happiness must be taught. The good news must be spread throughout the world. And this great revelation from God must be given to humankind the only way it has ever been given since the human species was placed upon this earth—through a mortal revelator.

One of those revelators is me, Christopher—a bearer of Christ.

How I Received The Gold Plates Of Mormon

It is not illegal, nor is it unethical, to present to the world my view of the gospel of Jesus Christ. The religions of the world have evolved to a point of precise targeting of many diverse groups of people, who in their search to understand themselves better, have turned to religion for their answers. Each group has its own answers; therefore, many religions, churches, and other organizations have been formed based on the inalienable right that we have to find out for ourselves the answers to life's mysteries.

In the early 1800's, in our newly-found nation that boasted itself as the first free country in the civilized world (the U.S.), a young man named Joseph Smith presented his view of religion to a world desperately seeking for the right answers. From that young man's inquiries burst forth a religious view that has affected the lives of millions of people worldwide. His ideas and perceptions were based on a book that eventually became the cornerstone of The Church of Jesus Christ of Latter-day Saints and The Reorganized Church of Jesus Christ of Latter Day Saints, currently known as the Community of Christ. This book is called the *Book of Mormon*.

The *Book of Mormon* has been a source of guidance and inspiration to millions of people who believe with all of their hearts that they have found the truth. Their willingness to share this truth with others has brought on undeserved persecutions and turmoil, the likes of which have seldom been experienced in other religious venues of the American nation.

When Joseph Smith received the calling to translate the ancient plates, he found that only 1/3 of the plates were unsealed and ready for translation. With the Urim and Thummim, a device prepared and blessed by the power of God, he proceeded to translate the plates that were unsealed and subsequently presented to the world what has become known as the *Book of Mormon, Another Testament of Jesus Christ*—the cornerstone of the LDS and RLDS faiths.

The Lord promised that one day the plates would be given back to mortal man so that the remaining sealed portion could be translated through the same means that were used to translate what was not sealed. In the sealed portion of these plates the answers to all of humankind's questions, from the beginning of time to the end thereof, would be given, and the revelations of God brought forth to prepare the world for the Second Coming of Jesus Christ. No other set of scriptures would match the extraordinary content of *The Sealed Portion*.

As Joseph Smith was given the authority and ability to bring about the *Book of Mormon* by way of translating the unsealed portion of Mormon's ancient plates, I have also been given the authority and calling to do the same thing, in the same way, with the sealed portion of these gold plates, thus bringing to the world *The Sealed Portion of the Book of Mormon, The Final Testament of Jesus Christ*.

There have been attempts made by others to invent the contents of the sealed portion and lift themselves up as ones who have authority from God to do so. Nevertheless, the mere reading of these feeble attempts leaves one dismayed at the idea that anyone would attempt such a thing.

The mainstream LDS Church would have the world believe that the introduction and translation of the plates would only come through a leader who has been called and set apart by those having the proper Priesthood authority within the LDS Church. Thus also believed the Jews when Jesus began his ministry and proclaimed his message without the sanction of the mainstream church. Likewise, Samuel, a Lamanite prophet of the *Book of Mormon*, was called to preach repentance to the Church and its leaders. Samuel was not the ordained and chosen President of the Church in his time; Nephi was. Yet Samuel's mission was one of the most important events of his day.

As Samuel, Abinadi, Jonah, and even Jesus Christ himself wanted desperately to be relieved of the missions they had been given, so too have I made many attempts to convince myself and others that I am not worthy or ready for such a calling. Like these great men, I could not escape the fulfillment of my mission.

The dark side uses its forces to hunt me down and make it seem virtually impossible to do what I have been assigned to do. I have been in jail for long periods of time due to the lies and disparagement that others have forced upon me because of their lack of understanding and support for what I am destined to do. Mormon judges and lawyers prosecute me any way they can, and would do anything within their power to stop the translation, publication, and eventual distribution of *The Sealed Portion* throughout the world. Mean and unsavory men and women pursue me and ridicule my name in an attempt to cause me enough harm so as to inhibit my ability to bring forth that, which in the end, will confound them before God.

Yet in all my experiences, I have never hurt another human soul. The depth of my compassion for my fellow human beings is hard to imagine when one considers the effect that others' lies and behavior have had upon me. There are many who consider me their enemies, but I love them all and wish no ill upon them. I have lost wives, children, and all of my personal effects, and have been persecuted by those who once loved me. But in spite of all of these negative experiences in my life, I have yet to turn against another and harbor ill feelings toward him or her. In other words, my conscience is clean and pure before my God and my fellow human beings.

There is no doubt that the future holds further persecutions and mistreatment by those who do not understand my mission and want to destroy me because of *The Sealed Portion, The Final Testament of Jesus Christ*.

Oh, how many times I have wished that someone would have taken my life and lifted the burden that this calling has brought upon me. Oh, if God would only have left me to myself so that I might pursue a normal existence like the rest of my brothers and sisters on earth. So many times I have tried to get out of my calling. So many times I attempted to sin in the eyes of God and present myself as a sinner to my fellow beings, in hopes that someone more worthy than I would be called to take my place. Yet in my heart, I knew that only I could accomplish what I had been raised and foreordained to do.

There are two sides to me that I perpetuated in the past in hopes that I might relieve myself of the burden of translating the plates, or at least, protect myself in doing so. As Peter cursed and denied the Christ when confronted by those who would have mocked and hurt him for believing in the Savior, I too have made myself seem a miserable sinner to others in hopes that they would not see the divine light that shines in my soul. Lucifer himself has tempted me many times to follow him and acquire all the riches, beauty, and glory of the world. In temptation I tried his hand and found that his promises were true. I could have had anything that I wanted in this world, but no matter how hard I tried to run from my calling, I was sucked into the depths of a whale's hell, and spit out only when I reconfirmed within my own soul what I was called to do.

Here I am, presenting to the world one of the greatest revelations that humankind has ever been given. Whether the world believes it or not does not matter to me. What matters to me is fulfilling my mission.

If Joseph Smith was a fraud, as some suppose, then so am I. The *Book of Mormon* stands as a testament to the authenticity of Joseph Smith's mission. Likewise, *The Sealed Portion* will stand as a testament of my mission. If Joseph received the plates of Mormon and translated them into the

Book of Mormon by the calling and power of God, then what the world is about to receive through me will be the most beneficial work the world has ever known.

Only the reader who asks God in faith can hope to find the truth for him or herself. No matter what one might conclude from his or her own inquiry, I stand unwavering and give my solemn testimony of the following:

In the early summer of 1987 I was employed as a Security Officer for The Church of Jesus Christ of Latter-day Saints. I was assigned to the Genealogical Library and the Church Museum located in downtown Salt Lake City, Utah. It was customary in the Security Department to cross-train in all areas of Church Security. One night I was assigned to the Salt Lake Temple. My orders were to make rounds in all areas of the temple and assure its safety.

Prior to this time, I had become disillusioned with the Church because of the great hypocrisy that I experienced being involved with and working for its leaders. This disillusionment caused me to do some tremendous soul searching and eventually led me to start investigating the Church to which I had dedicated my life. My investigations led me to many parts of the headquarters of the Church where no lay member had access. I was a friend with the other Security Officers, and was able to go anywhere I wanted with the help of my fellow officers who were sympathetic to my cause. The officers in the security control room would disengage the alarms in the areas that I wanted to go in search of information. (To protect these individuals, many who continue to work for the Church, I will give no specific dates or times when the following incidents took place.)

During the course of many hours of investigation, I found some very interesting information that convinced me that I knew very little about the Church that I had been taught to love and honor. However, none of the information I uncovered suggested that the leaders of the Church were maliciously misleading the members. On the contrary, I found that these Brethren were doing the best they could in spite of the members that they represented. It soon became apparent to me that the Church was not being guided by the Lord nor any portion of His Spirit. I was able to obtain the personal notes and thoughts of some very prominent leaders that indicated that the Church had fallen into tremendous wickedness of which the Lord was very displeased.

At this point, I began to mention my concerns to my superiors in the Security Department. I was told to either keep quiet or I would be terminated. I was greatly saddened by the apathy of the leaders and the members of the Church. On Tuesday, June 16th, 1987, while doing my security rounds in the Salt Lake Temple (the graveyard shift), the following took place:

There is a room on one of the upper floors of the Temple where only the Twelve Apostles meet. When I entered this opulent room, I found twelve chairs of considerable quality, and I noticed that each individual Apostle had a 3' X 4' hand-painted portrait of himself hanging upon the walls.

I could not hold back my turmoil and anguish any longer. I wept; and I wept bitterly. I fell to my knees and asked God with all of my soul if the Brethren whose pictures decorated the walls of this room were His chosen leaders, and what I should do in my disillusionment.

In this great moment of despair, I heard a soft but firm voice that penetrated to the very depths of my being, say to me, "Who else would you have me lead this people?"

I then looked around the room and it came to my mind the occupation of each of these men.

"Of course!" I exclaimed, "A doctor, a lawyer, an insurance man, a businessman!" As I thought of their worldly occupations, I realized the great success of each of these in his chosen field of worldly praise and glory. I then realized why the Lord had suffered these men to be chosen—because they were and are the kind of leaders that the members want to lead them.

I then proceeded to ask what it was that I could do to improve my doubts of the veracity of the Church. I had no sooner arranged these thoughts in my head, than I found it impossible to speak any of the words that I attempted. At that moment, a tremendously bright light began to fill the room. I became very frightened, not knowing if I was to be reprimanded or killed for what I had thought.

Before I could think another thought, a personage appeared before me who I immediately recognized as the Prophet Joseph Smith. (I recognized him not only by how he looked, as I was familiar with the descriptions given of him by the Church, but something inside of me assured me that it was truly him.)

I didn't have the slightest idea how to react. I simply knelt there astonished. He smiled the kindest smile I had ever seen and said the following to me:

"Christopher, do not be afraid; for it is I, Joseph, whom you have been taught to honor as a prophet of God."

I guess he could perceive my doubts of his presence, because he reached out his hand, lifted me up, and placed me in one of the chairs that was in the room. He told me that the Lord was well aware of me and that I demonstrated the faith and strength of few men. He told me that I would perform a tremendous work for my fellow men if I remained faithful to the commandments that he was about to give to me. At that moment, my grandfather also appeared from within the light that still filled the whole room with its brilliance.

I wanted to embrace my grandfather, but was told I could not; because he had not yet received a body that mortals could feel. He also smiled and assured me that he was sent from the Spirit World to comfort me and to help teach me the things I needed to know in order to perform the work that the Lord would require of me.

I began to cry profusely, knowing that I was a frequent sinner, who at many times had broken the commandments of God. I expressed my fear that I would not be able to do the things that would be required of me. My grandfather told me that I would be taught many things in the future that would prepare me for the work that I was commanded to do. He said that I would be guided as necessary to bring about this work.

Joseph Smith then told me that I was chosen to bring about the sealed portion of the plates of Mormon that he had not translated while he was on earth. He explained many things to me about the wickedness of the Saints in his time; and that the Lord saw fit to take him from among them because they would not hearken to his commands and abide by his teachings.

I asked why I had been chosen for this work and what would be required of me. Joseph responded that I was one of the very few who was not affected by the material things and honors of this world. He told me that I would be tested many times in the future to see if I would be willing to sacrifice all, even my own life if necessary, for the sake of the kingdom of God.

At this point, I began to express my doubts and my unworthiness to fulfill such a calling. My grandfather assured me that I would not have been chosen unless I could accomplish the work given to me.

A flash of brilliant light appeared directly between Joseph Smith and me, and to my surprise, there were the gold plates of Mormon. I didn't dare touch them until I was instructed to do so by the Prophet. I slowly turned each leaf and was astonished at the preciseness of the writing. As I turned the pages, I thought about how much these plates would be worth. No sooner had I thought these things, than Joseph warned me that this temptation would always be with me, as it was with him, and that I should cast it out of my mind if it ever came again. As I sat in front of these two glorious beings, I was embarrassed greatly for what I had thought.

Both of these men were dressed in white robes that covered their whole bodies except for their ankles, wrists, and necklines. Their robes were each tied by a white sash, similar to the sash used in the modern LDS temple ceremony. They were both very pleasant to look upon, and my fear of them at this point was completely gone.

I then received many instructions and was told that I would lose all my friends, family, and close associations before I would be ready to present the translation of the plates to the world. I asked these beings what further would be required of me and whether I should tell my family and friends.

I was instructed to leave the employment of the LDS Church and to give no indication as to why, or tell anyone what had taken place. I was not even to tell my wife, for she was to be tested to prove her worthiness and ability to support me in this work. I was told that I would travel extensively in preparation of doing this work and that I would become known as an apostate of the Church, but that I should allow the Church to do with me as they wished, for its own sake. I was told that I would be given many opportunities to meet those who were being prepared at this time to aid me in this work, but I was cautioned to test each one, so as not to be deceived or betrayed by them. I was also instructed in many other things that I cannot reveal at this time.

I wondered greatly about the condition of the Church and the righteousness of its leaders, seeing as this was the cause for my prayers that led to the heavenly vision. Joseph Smith proceeded to quote me some scriptures, which he told me to remember and present to the world along with the translation of the plates when it was ready to come forth. I asked if I would translate the record myself, or if someone else would give the translation to me. I was told that I could not translate the record at this time, for it was the position and authority of Joseph Smith to determine when the time was right. He told me that when the time came for the record to come forth, that he would visit me and give me further instructions.

I expressed my doubts in withstanding the inevitable mocking that would come because of my claims, and that not being able to show the plates to the world would greatly hinder my ability to do the work. Joseph laughed a most sincere laugh and my grandfather smiled profusely.

Joseph replied, "Do you think that your persecutions will be any greater than mine were?"

At this, I smiled and began to understand.

Many years passed by, and I went through some important growing and refining experiences that would further prepare me for my mission. For many years I ran from this calling, not being able to handle the persecution that was heaped upon me. Indeed, I have been alienated from all of my loved ones. I have become totally unattached to all worldly possessions and filial relationships. I was given tremendous wisdom and knowledge, and was instructed to do many things that would help me accomplish the work that I had been given to do. I was put in jail twice, changed my name for a time to protect myself, and have been rejected by the Church as an apostate.

Finally, the time arrived when Joseph Smith again visited me, and I began to write down the translation of the sealed portion of the plates of Mormon.

After this visit, and the commencement of the translation of the plates, I was overcome with tremendous pride and arrogance at the greatness of the things that I had written and with the calling I had received. I then became overwhelmed and distraught because of the persecution and the sacrifices that were being required of me. In this state of depression, I made some bad mistakes in my arrogance and almost lost my soul in the process. However, the Lord has tremendous patience and mercy, and before long I was again visited by Joseph Smith and other servants of the Lord who are assigned to aid me in this work; and finally the sealed portion of the plates of Mormon will come to the world to all those who are ready and willing to receive it.

The following are a few of the scriptures that Joseph Smith quoted to me during our first meeting, which I was told to ponder and remember:

> *Forasmuch as this people draw near unto me with their mouth, and with their lips do honor me, but have removed their hearts far from me, and their fear towards me is taught by the precepts of men—Therefore, I will proceed to do a marvelous work among this people, yea, a marvelous work and a wonder, for the wisdom of their wise and learned shall perish, and the understanding of their prudent shall be hid. And wo unto them that seek deep to hide their counsel from the Lord! And their works are in the dark; and they say: Who seeth us, and who knoweth us? And they also say: Surely, your turning of things upside down shall be esteemed as the*

potter's clay. But behold, I will show unto them, saith the Lord of Hosts, that I know all their works. For shall the work say of him that made it, he made me not? Or shall the thing framed say of him that framed it, he had no understanding? But behold, saith the Lord of Hosts: I will show unto the children of men that it is yet a very little while and Lebanon shall be turned into a fruitful field; and the fruitful field shall be esteemed as a forest. And in that day shall the deaf hear the words of the book, and the eyes of the blind shall see out of obscurity and out of darkness. And the meek also shall increase, and their joy shall be in the Lord, and the poor among men shall rejoice in the Holy One of Israel. For assuredly as the Lord liveth they shall see that the terrible one is brought to naught, and the scorner is consumed, and all that watch for iniquity are cut off; And they that make a man an offender for a word, and lay a snare for him that reproveth in the gate, and turn aside the just for a thing of naught. Therefore, thus saith the Lord, who redeemed Abraham, concerning the house of Jacob: Jacob shall not now be ashamed, neither shall his face now wax pale. But when he seeth his children, the work of my hands, in the midst of him, they shall sanctify my name, and sanctify the Holy One of Jacob, and shall fear the God of Israel. They also that erred in spirit shall come to understanding, and they that murmured shall learn doctrine. (2 Nephi 27:25-35)

For they have strayed from mine ordinances, and have broken mine everlasting covenant; They seek not the Lord to establish his righteousness, but every man walketh in his own way, and after the image of his own god, whose image is in the likeness of the world, and whose substance is that of an idol, which waxeth old and shall perish in Babylon, even Babylon, the great, which shall fall. (D&C 1:15-16)

They wear stiff necks and high heads; yea, and because of pride, and wickedness, and abominations, and whoredoms, they have all gone astray save it be a few, who are the humble followers of Christ; nevertheless, they are led, that in many instances they do err because they are taught by the precepts of men. (2 Nephi 28:14)

And I know that ye do walk in the pride of your hearts; and there are none save a few only who do not lift themselves up in the pride of their hearts, unto the wearing of very fine apparel, unto envying, and strifes, and malice, and persecutions, and all manner of iniquities; and your churches, yea, even every one, have become polluted because of the pride of your hearts. For behold, ye do love money, and your substance, and your fine apparel, and the adorning of your churches, more than ye love the poor and the needy, the sick and the afflicted. O ye wicked and perverse and stiffnecked people, why have ye built up churches unto yourselves to get gain? Why have ye transfigured the holy word of God, that ye might bring damnation upon your souls? Oh, ye pollutions, ye hypocrites, ye teachers, who sell yourselves for that which will canker, why have ye polluted the holy church of God? Why are ye ashamed to take upon you the holy name of Christ? Why do ye not think that greater is the value of an endless happiness than that misery which never dies—because of the praise of the world. Why do ye adorn yourselves with that which hath no life, and yet suffer the hungry, and the needy, and the naked, and the sick and the afflicted to pass by you, and notice them not? Yea, why do ye build up your secret abominations to get gain, and cause that the widows should mourn before the Lord, and also the orphans to mourn before the Lord. (Compare Mormon 8:33-40)

The years passed, and I did many things that I am not proud of in hopes of finding those who would help me in my calling. I wanted desperately to find a partner to help in the translation, and a woman to be my companion. I had many opportunities and tried and tested many individuals, in hopes that I would find just one to help. In my desperation and lack of companionship of the Spirit, I was left lonely and afraid.

After I finally realized that the Lord would not provide a companion or partner to help me in the translation, I humbled myself enough to allow a servant of the Lord to aid me in hiding the plates from the world and give me much needed encouragement from time to time. With the increased frequency of his visits, the translation of the gold plates began to come forth.

I was commanded to start the translation at the beginning of the plates and to first translate the part that was lost through the transgression of Martin Harris, whom Joseph had entrusted with 116 pages of handwritten manuscript when he began to translate in his day. I was told that the retranslation of the beginning of the gold plates would give the world a better insight of the mission and life of Lehi and the beginnings of the record of Mormon. It seems that Mormon abridged the record of Lehi and Lehi's mission up to a certain point before he found the Small Plates of Nephi among the many records that he had in his possession, which plates Mormon also included in his abridgment.

What was even more interesting to me was what the lost 116 pages of manuscript had contained. After finishing the first few pages that were given to me, I was astounded at how much prophetic prose was in the lost manuscript. It generally depicted the condition of the church in Jerusalem during Lehi's day as a close replica of the church in Salt Lake City during the present day. It quickly became apparent that the Lord had allowed the manuscript to be lost so that the modern church would have no reference to what it shouldn't be like, so that it could be tried and tested by faith. With Joseph's concurrence, I realized the great wisdom of the Lord in keeping this scripture from the Church until this time. There are few other passages of scripture that shed a greater light on the misdoings and hypocrisy of the modern LDS Church. I was instructed to first introduce the retranslation of the beginning of the gold plates, which was once translated by Joseph Smith and written in manuscript form by Martin Harris, who subsequently lost it.

Then, for the benefit of the whole world, I will present the most phenomenal scripture and revelation ever given to the children of God. After I have presented these things to the world, then whatever the Lord would have me do, that I will do. If any man or woman wants to mock me, that I will accept of myself. But if any of you mock these things, which are now revealed to you, then you will mock God; for these things are not mine, but they are His. If you mock God, then He will judge you according to your works. But the work that I have been given by Him to do pertaining to these things…is done.

Christopher Marc Nemelka

APPENDIX 2

The Book of Lehi
The Lost 116-Page Manuscript

The following is the official introduction to the *Book of Mormon* as given by the modern LDS Church. Its contents are suitable enough for the purposes of introducing the reader to the significance of the lost 116-page manuscript:

> *The Book of Mormon is a volume of holy scripture comparable to the Bible. It is a record of God's dealings with the ancient inhabitants of the Americas and contains, as does the Bible, the fullness of the everlasting gospel.*
>
> *The book was written by many ancient prophets by the spirit of prophecy and revelation. Their words, written on gold plates, were quoted and abridged by a prophet-historian named Mormon. The record gives an account of two great civilizations. One came from Jerusalem in 600 B.C., and afterward separated into two nations, known as the Nephites and the Lamanites. The other came much earlier when the Lord confounded the tongues at the Tower of Babel. This group is known as the Jaredites. After thousands of years, all were destroyed except the Lamanites, and they are the principal ancestors of the American Indians.*
>
> *The crowning event recorded in the Book of Mormon is the personal ministry of the Lord Jesus Christ among the Nephites soon after his resurrection. It puts forth the doctrines of the gospel, outlines the plan of salvation, and tells men what they must do to gain peace in this life and eternal salvation in the life to come.*
>
> *After Mormon completed his writings, he delivered the account to his son Moroni, who added a few words of his own and hid up the plates in the hill Cumorah. On September 21, 1823, the same Moroni, then a glorified, resurrected being, appeared to the Prophet Joseph Smith and instructed him relative to the ancient record and its destined translation into the English language.*
>
> *In due course the plates were delivered to Joseph Smith, who translated them by the gift and power of God. The record is now published in many languages as a new and additional witness that Jesus Christ is the Son of the living God and that all who will come unto him and obey the laws and ordinances of his gospel may be saved.*
>
> *Concerning this record the Prophet Joseph Smith said: "I told the brethren that the Book of Mormon was the most correct of any book on earth, and the keystone of our religion, and a man would get nearer to God by abiding by its precepts, than by any other book.*

As Joseph Smith began the translation of the gold plates, he received help from a few scribes who would write down the words that he translated. These words were written on British foolscap, which was a popular writing paper used during that time period and was approximately 13" X 16" in size. These papers were folded to make a page that was 13" X 8". There were generally about 225 words per page that were translated by the prophet and written down by each scribe, depending upon the particular writing style of each.

The first 116 pages of the original manuscript of Joseph Smith's translation of the *Book of Mormon* from the plates of Mormon are commonly known as "the lost 116 pages" or the "lost manuscript." They were hand-written in Harmony, Pennsylvania by Martin Harris, being the principal, but not the only scribe to write for the prophet on these manuscripts.

Martin Harris met Joseph Smith sometime after 1816, when the Smith family moved to Palmyra, New York. He first met Joseph Smith's father, Joseph Smith, Sr., who told him about the angel Moroni's appearances and the golden plates. The Smiths moved to Manchester in 1820, where Joseph obtained the plates in 1827. Because of persecution, he was forced to go to Harmony, Pennsylvania, to begin the translation of the plates. Sometime in the fall of 1827, Martin consented to help with the translation, both financially as well as serving as a scribe.

From about April 12 to June 14, 1828, Martin Harris served as Joseph Smith's primary scribe, subsequently producing 116 manuscript pages. Because he was using a lot of his own money to help in the translation, Harris' family soon became suspicious of exactly what was going on between him and Joseph. In order to gain his family's support, Martin Harris persuaded Joseph to let him take the 116 pages that they had completed to Palmyra to show his family. Purportedly, during a three-week period when Harris visited his relatives, attended to business, and served jury duty, the 116 pages were stolen. Martin's wife, Lucy Harris, allegedly stated that she had burned them, claiming that they would lead to her family's financial ruin.

When Harris failed to return to Harmony as promised, Joseph became extremely agitated and filled with great anxiety, and was forced to make an arduous journey to Manchester to see what was going on. Harris reluctantly reported that someone had stolen the manuscript from his home after he had broken his promise and indiscriminately showed the manuscript to others outside of his family. Devastated (I understand exactly how he was feeling), Joseph Smith approached the Lord in prayer and accepted his responsibility in the loss of the manuscript.

In consequence of his disobedience and the loss of the manuscript, Joseph temporarily lost custody of the plates and the Urim and Thummim. But following many days of incredible misery and humbling pain, Joseph Smith again received the plates as well as the Urim and Thummim and all of his gifts were restored.

However, Joseph Smith was forbidden by the Lord to retranslate the part of the record he had previously translated. This was because, as he was told, those who had stolen the manuscript had made secret plans to publish it in an altered form in order to discredit his ability to translate accurately. Having foreseen this tragic event, knowing full well that his prophets and revelators are fallible men at times, the Lord instructed Mormon to insert certain plates in with the plates that he had made to abridge the history of his people. These plates are known as the Small Plates of Nephi and they cover approximately the same time period as the lost manuscript did.

As Joseph Smith explained in the preface to the first (1830 A.D.) edition of the *Book of Mormon*, the 116 pages contained materials *"from the Book of Lehi, which was an account abridged from the plates of Lehi, by the hand of Mormon."* Lehi's record is mentioned in 1 Nephi 1:17, and is referred to at times by Nephi throughout his writings. Mormon explained his decision to include the Small Plates of Nephi:

> *And I do this for a wise purpose; for thus it whispereth me, according to the workings of the Spirit of the Lord which is in me. And now, I do not know all things; but the*

Lord knoweth all things which are to come; wherefore, he worketh in me to do according to his will. (Words of Mormon 1:7)

The Lord's true purpose for the loss of the manuscript was to chastise the LDS Church for its extreme wickedness in modern times, and to prepare a way so that I could prove to the world that I, in fact, was in possession of the gold plates and the Urim and Thummim.

If I truly had the gold plates of Mormon, the same ones that Joseph had in his possession, then it would be logical that I was looking at the exact same plates. If I began at the very first plate in my translation, then it would translate the exact same way that it did for Joseph when he began his translation, owing to the fact that we both used the same Urim and Thummim. Therefore, I would have the ability to retranslate the part that was lost with the 116-page original manuscript.

The enemies of truth and righteousness know this. They also know that if anyone would ever make the claim to be in possession of the gold plates, then this claimant could ostensibly translate the first part of the plates and come up with the exact same words that these evil, conspiring cohorts have in their possession as the original hand-written manuscripts, that just so happen to be written in the verifiable handwriting of Martin Harris.

The original 116-page manuscript still exists today. It has been passed down from generation to generation by these misled humans who have no other interest in mind than to stop the work of God. It is hidden away from the world to be brought out in hopes of destroying the credibility of the one chosen to translate the sealed portion of the plates.

I have met these men under the guise that I was an atheist and that I did not believe that Joseph Smith actually had any gold plates, but that he made the whole thing up. I have seen the first few manuscript pages and have verified that they are indeed mostly written in the handwriting of Martin Harris. I know that through technology, science could easily prove them to be original and undoctored and unchanged since their creation. This group of vengeful human beings is waiting for their trap to be sprung upon the prophet and revelator that has been called to bring forth *The Sealed Portion*. They now know who that revelator is.

They will compare what I have translated with what they possess, and they will find that the words are nearly exact, allowing for minor differences in the editing personalities between me and Joseph Smith (because our spirits are unique and different); the Urim and Thummim giving the translation in the same manner each time, with the meaning never different.

This highly recognized group of human beings, which will go unnamed for my own protection, will suppose that I had remembered the words of the manuscript that they had shown to me years before, and would be wont to make an attempt to discredit me and claim that I did nothing more than write down what I had remembered. However, they will recall vividly that I did not even handle the manuscript with my own hands, and that I saw maybe a few of the very first pages that were laid before my eyes on a table. The manuscript was preserved in a special container that was sealed in such a way as to preserve it as much as possible from contamination and the effects of time. They will quickly realize that it would be impossible for me to remember any of the words that I saw, let alone know what the thousands of words were that were written on the pages that I was unable to see underneath the few that were visible in the container.

They will read the retranslation that I am now revealing to the world for the very first time, and they will gasp in horror that the words match the manuscript precisely. Suddenly, their trap will fall apart. The very existence of the manuscript will be a vital proof that I indeed had the ancient plates, and that the *Book of Mormon* that has been given to the world is indeed a direct translation from the plates of gold received by Joseph Smith and subsequently given to me. They will not know what to do. How can they allow the manuscript to come to light in a scientific world? Surely technology would prove its reality and origins. And if the manuscript is proven to be true, then my retranslation is also true, and they will begin to see the extremity of their sins. They know that they have continually fought the Mormon faith from its beginnings and have entered into secret alliances with each other, and have made promises to their ancestors and to their diabolical friends that they will eventually bring about the demise of Mormonism and show it for what it really is—lies and deception. They had no idea that I had infiltrated their group (very similar to the way that Joseph infiltrated the secret Mason Society), and discovered their secret works, and that I would one day bring about their secret society's demise.

I give to this secret group a stern warning: You will not stop the work of God. He is much smarter than you. I challenge you to bring the manuscript out into the light so that it can be seen and verified by the world that it is true. This is the work of God, and if you are not engaged in the work of God, then you must be working for the devil, who has hardened your hearts and blinded your minds to such an extent that your souls are in jeopardy of eternal damnation. Do not fight the work of the Lord. Repent of your sins and bring the manuscript forth, for it can become a testimony to the world of this work, and you will be given the glory that you deserve. But also, you will be on the side of the Lord, and will not suffer as you will, if you continue to fight against him.

Sadly, I write the above words in vain. There will be few of these people who will come forth and admit what they have done. I am sure they will destroy the manuscript so that it doesn't come to light to be a witness to the world of the truthfulness of my calling and the calling that Joseph Smith received from the Lord. Many of them will come forth and claim allegiance to their group, and make futile attempts to discredit me by claiming that they have read the 116-page manuscript and that it is very different from what I have retranslated. This they will do to discredit my calling and continue working for the demise of the truths that are revealed to the world through Mormonism. Nevertheless, the world will see them for who they really are, and they will become a thing of naught—having their darkness illuminated by the light of the true gospel of Jesus Christ.

This group of humans, however, I do not fear nearly as much as I do the modern Church of Jesus Christ of Latter-day Saints. This church as a whole is much more powerful than this isolated group of individuals, which, in reality, has been an enemy of the Church ever since Brigham Young moved the Saints out West and founded the state of Utah. Ironically, it is possible that these two groups of humans will now become allies in attempting to stop the world from receiving the sealed portion of the gold plates of Mormon.

I say that it is possible that the Church becomes my enemy, but not necessary, because there is a chance that will be given to the Church of Jesus Christ of Latter-day Saints to repent and begin to work righteousness before the Lord. The Church will have the chance to have *The Sealed Portion* controlled and presented to the world the way that the leaders of the Church determine is in the best interests of the Church, so that the Saints may be edified and glorified, instead of being damned by its revelations.

The First Presidency and General Authorities of the Church will be given the opportunity to accept the translation of the plates as I give it to them according to the time frame and commandments of the Lord. They will be counseled on the best way to introduce it to the world, and the best way to begin the transformation of the Church—from one of an extreme worldly and materialistic nature and standing in the world, to the true church of Christ as it should be—thus preparing the world for the coming of the Lord, Jesus Christ, in His glory.

If the LDS leaders shall accept this work, the general membership of the Church and the world at large will not know my name or recognize me. I will continue my guise as a lowly member of the Church and will not set myself above any other. I will not be a prophet to the church or receive any leadership position therein. I will remain secluded behind the scenes of the Church and be had in a position of counselor only. Nevertheless, only I will have the power and ability to use the Urim and Thummim for the sake of inquiry of the Lord—and I will use it wisely and only at the times the Lord will permit. I will counsel regularly with the leadership of the Church and will not overstep the bounds of their offices in the Church. In order and calmness *The Sealed Portion* will be revealed to the world under the direction of the First Presidency of the Church, and none other. The President will present it to the world as if he had received it from the Lord, which in truth, he did. He received it from the Lord through me—the one who has been called to bring it forth. However, my name will never come up, giving all the glory to the Father and His righteousness.

Eventually, the gold plates will be given to the leadership of the Church so that they might stand as a testimony of what they will already know in their hearts to be true. However, the gold plates shall not be shown to the world until the Lord comes in His glory. He will then call for the gold plates of Mormon to be brought forth and set before the whole world as a testimony in and of themselves. And then shall the scripture be fulfilled that says, "*for out of the books which shall be written I will judge the world, every man according to their works, according to that which is written.*" (2 Nephi 29:11)

It could be possible that very few humans will ever read these words. If the Church accepts what they will be offered, this book will not be given to the world or be published or known in any form outside the higher leadership circles of the LDS Church. But if the leadership of the LDS Church refuses the offer that they shall receive through me from the Lord, then they will see the beginning of the end of their pride and their glory. They will see this work come forth to the world and it will mark the beginning of the demise of the current Church of Jesus Christ of Latter-day Saints, and the wickedness and hypocrisy of its leaders and members.

Thus will begin the separation of the sheep from among the goats. The sheep will hear the good shepherd calling their names and beckoning them to come out of the stalls that have held them captive in guilt and misery for so many years. They will be able to purchase the fruits of Christ, which include salvation without a price (tithing). They will no longer be under the spell of a self-righteous and worldly church that has corrupted the word of God and teaches for doctrine the commandments of men. They will know the truth and the truth will set them free.

I am not a man that wants to be a martyr for any cause. It is my hope and prayer that the burden of my calling can be relieved by the intercession of the powerful LDS Church, which has the means and the ability to get the message of *The Sealed Portion* out to the world in a much more organized and timely manner than I would be able to organize. This hope comes in light of the fact that I have not received a calling to organize a church or an organization (except for The Worldwide United Foundation) to teach the contents of *The Sealed Portion*. I was commanded to translate it and get it published to the world expounding on the mysteries of godliness as I am commanded. I have asked the Lord's servants many times what I need to do when the record is translated and complete; and how I should go about presenting it to the world, and what my role should be thereafter. I have been told to remain at peace and be patient for the will of the Lord to work itself out without the trust that I have in my own flesh or in the arm of another.

I don't think I am supposed to know. Because if I knew for a surety that they would not accept it, then why in the world would I set myself up for considerable persecution and possibly a martyr's noose at the hands of the Church? And if I knew that they would accept it, then owing to my rebellious and nonconformist nature, I would probably mess up the design of the Lord because of my human weaknesses of impatience and zealousness, thereby disregarding the timetable of the Lord and forcing the work upon the LDS Church.

By way of commandment I wrote the following letter to the First Presidency of the Church of Jesus Christ of Latter-day Saints and had it delivered in late March 2004 along with a copy of *The Book of Lehi*, certified and registered by way of the United States Postal Service:

The First Presidency of the
Church of Jesus Christ of Latter-day Saints
47 East South Temple
Salt Lake City, UT 84150

To Those Brethren That It May Concern:

Enclosed with this letter you will find a concise and truthful biography of my life and the calling that have I received to bring to the world the sealed portion of the gold plates of Mormon.

With an honest effort on your part, you may investigate the facts and the claims made therein. The last names of all the individuals have been excluded, but I am sure with a little effort, your investigators can determine who these individuals are. And with a continued honest effort, you will also determine that every fact presented in this biography is true and verifiable. I trust that you will use the utmost caution and abide by the laws of our country as you send forth those who will verify the facts and report their findings to your office.

It would benefit us both if you took the time to read the book before you make a judgment of how you are going to proceed from this point. After reading its contents and discussing the matter amongst yourselves, I expect that an opinion and a decision will be rendered appropriately by you. Until that decision is rendered, I will not act in any way on the publication of the things revealed herein, nor will I reveal to any other individual or group the contents of this letter or the biography of my life until I hear, or do not hear, directly from your office. Your silence on the matter will indicate your decision to disregard this letter and the important contents of the book included.

You may respond to this letter by electronic E-mail at the following address: sealedportion@yahoo.com.

If I receive a notice of your indication to discuss this matter further, I will respond to your E-mail and give you further instructions on how to contact me.

As you read the enclose material, you will soon ascertain that I am not seeking money, prestige, honor, glory, or any other kind of acknowledgement of my person. In fact, it will become vividly apparent to you that I wish I had nothing to do with this. But as it is, I do.

Please read the book carefully, paying special attention to appendixes I & II. You will begin to see the ramifications of what is about to occur. I can only hope that there exists among you, noble and righteous leaders who can see what is about to take place. And if it is in the best interests for all, I would hope that we can become friends instead of enemies. I would want nothing more than to have the Church on my side rather than fighting against me. Nevertheless, I am not afraid of the Church and its power. I am ready and willing to see the fruition of the calling that I have received with or without your help.

I know that the General Conference of the Church is close, and that your time is limited. (And please, please, Brethren, DO NOT put the gospel of Jesus Christ into the fray of prejudice, hate, and bigotry that homosexual marriage is creating. Any comments that the leadership of this church makes to the members during Conference will add to their erring *hearts, which are already brimming with hate, prejudice and intolerance against anyone that is not a member of the Church. The Lord's gospel is a message of love and acceptance. You would be wise to reach out with love to those who you believe live in sin and error. No where in His teachings to the Jews or to the Nephites did our Savior teach against homosexuality, but he adamantly commanded us to love our neighbor and our enemies, and refrain from judging one another. Remember this counsel, my brethren, it could save the souls of millions and perpetuate peace in a world that lacks it.)*

Owing to the pending conference and the demand that it has on your time, and also the time that it will take for you to investigate these things, I will not expect an answer, or the lack of an answer, from your office for at least 60 days. If by the 1st day of June, I have received no communication from you, I will assume that you have determined that it is not in the best interest of the Church, owing to its present state, to have further communication with me. If this be the case, then I will counsel with the Lord's servants who guide and protect me to determine the best way to bring to the world one of the greatest sources of scripture it has ever known, and unfortunately for us both, you will come to consider me an enemy. However, unlike the examples that I have personally witnessed in the Church, I will remain steadfast and immovable in keeping the commandments of the Lord, and I will love you and do good to you and pray for you, knowing that in the end, we will all see each other as brothers and sisters, children of the One Almighty God.

I am your humble servant,

Christopher

It should be obvious to the reader that if he or she is reading these words, then the Church declined the offer to take control of *The Sealed Portion* under my empirically invisible direction and counsel. The reader should note that I would have given anything to become a friend to the Church and help its leaders straighten out the corrupt spiritual state in which the members of the Church unknowingly find themselves.

I expect the leaders of the LDS Church to not let go of their pride, their arrogance, and their blatant hypocrisy regarding the true gospel and teachings of Jesus Christ. Yet, at the time of this writing, the Spirit leans me in neither direction. I can only hope and pray for the millions of LDS members, and remain ready and willing to do what I am commanded to do.

Martin Harris eventually apostatized from following Joseph Smith and became a critic who disagreed with the manner in which Joseph was allowing the LDS faith to grow and prosper. What was it that Martin knew that no other person knew? Martin knew what the 116-page manuscript contained. He knew that the LDS Church was in every way a latter-day copy of the ancient Jewish Church that had corrupted the true gospel of Christ and turned the people against the *true* prophets of God. Martin knew of the prophecies contained in the *Lost Manuscript* that expressly denounced organized religion, and specifically, the latter-day Church of Jesus Christ of Latter-day Saints, which would one day receive the record of Mormon. When Harris voiced his opinion to Joseph, he was quietly commanded to keep what he knew of the 116-page manuscript to himself.

Now the whole world will have the chance to read what Martin Harris read. The reader will understand the dilemma Martin faced, and the true reason he left Joseph and the LDS Church. There will be little doubt about what the ancient prophets knew of the latter days in which the people of the earth would be leading each other astray. They prophesied that the latter-day leaders would offer for truth the commandments and precepts of men and corrupt the gospel of Jesus Christ. Martin Harris wanted Joseph Smith to stop the corruption and not allow it to continue. He wanted Joseph to tell the people what both of them knew was contained in the manuscript he had lost. Joseph knew better. Joseph Smith let the people have the desires of their hearts.

Because of this *marvelous work and a wonder*, which is the *only* latter-day work directed by the Lord, all of those who become familiar with it who are currently members of the Church of Jesus Christ of Latter-day Saints, and anyone else who might obtain it in this world, will never be the same again.

Now, without further adieu, here is the first part of the record known as the *Book of Mormon*, translated by the Urim and Thummim from the first plate made by the hand of Mormon *after* the words given and known as the Title Page of the *Book of Mormon* already published by the Mormon faith:

The Book of Lehi

An Abridgment Taken From the Plates of Nephi

The life and ministry of Lehi, the son of Jeshron, who lived and preached in Jerusalem. An account of his miraculous conversion and his many persecutions and sufferings at the hands of the Jews because of the things that he both saw and heard of the Lord. An account also of his wanderings in the wilderness with his wife, Sariah, and his children, who consisted of his sons, Laman, Lemuel, Sam, Nephi, Jacob, and Joseph, and also his daughters, Lenrah and Sira. An account also of many of the visions of Lehi and his blessings and admonishings to his children. Also an account of his journey in the wilderness and his arrival at the great waters, which he crosses with his family and discovers the land of promise. Also an account of the rebellion of Laman and Lemuel and their separation from Nephi, thus forming two peoples called the Nephites and the Lamanites.

CHAPTER 1

Mormon prepares the plates of gold by commandment of God and begins his abridgment of the Large Plates of Nephi. The genealogy of Lehi and his standing in the Jewish priesthood is explained. The prophets Zenos and Zenock are introduced. The preaching of Zenock is given.

I, MORMON, according to the commandment of the Lord, have made these plates of ore according to the knowledge and understanding that the Lord hath given unto me. And I write the things that I have been instructed to write, having received this instruction from the Holy Spirit.

2 For behold, the plates of Nephi are numerous and contain the entire history of Lehi and his life and mission. They also contain the writings of Nephi and other prophets of God who were given a strict commandment by the Lord that they should record their history and the history of their children. And this he hath commanded them to do so that the Lord might show unto future generations the many great and marvelous things that he hath done for the children of Lehi according to their faith and obedience towards him.

3 And because the plates of Nephi are many, I, Mormon, have been instructed of the Lord to include only those things which will be beneficial unto future generations; yea, even unto those who shall receive these plates. And whosoever shall receive these plates shall be given the commandments of God pertaining unto them.

4 For behold, it is wisdom in the Lord that the world should not have these plates, so that the faith of all men can be tried and tested to see if they are willing to do all things in faith whatsoever the Lord shall command them. And if they keep the commandments of God as they shall be given unto them, even according to the commandments written upon these plates, then shall the greater things concerning the kingdom of God be made known unto them, until they know the mysteries of God in full.

5 And the Lord hath shown unto me many of these mysteries of God and hath laid me under strict command to show them to no man. And because of this commandment I do not write all the things that I have been shown and which have been revealed unto me by the power of the Holy Spirit. But the things that the Spirit whispereth unto me, these things I shall write.

6 And these are the generations of Lehi. And I take these things from the record that Nephi hath written upon plates of ore, and which are found among the records that I received from Ammoron.

7 And Lehi was the son of Jeshron, a High Priest among the Jews, who lived in Jerusalem. And Lehi was also a High Priest like his father before him. And they were High Priests after the order of Aaron, who received instructions of the Lord from the mouth of Moses at the time the Israelites wandered in the wilderness.

8 And Jeshron was the son of Emrish. And Emrish was the son of Nathaniel. And Nathaniel was the son of Chemish. And Chemish was the son of Alabash. And Alabash was the son of Minorech, a High Priest who was much beloved of the people in the land of the Israelites.

9 And Minorech was the son of Libnah. And Libnah was the son of Joshua. And Joshua was the son of Gilead. And Gilead was the son of Shechem, who was also a great High Priest and was known throughout the lands of Israel as a righteous man of God.

10 And Shechem was the son of Shiloh. And Shiloh was the son of Abinadi. And Abinadi was the son of Benjamin. And Benjamin was the son of Ebal. And Ebal was the son of Joshua. And Joshua was the son of Kolesh. And Kolesh was the son of Tershis. And Tershis was the son of Gerizim. And Gerizim was the son of Malachi. And Malachi was the son of Saresh.

11 And Saresh was the son of Judah, who was the son of Ephraim, who was the son of Joseph.

12 And it was this same Joseph who was sold into Egypt by his brothers, the sons of Israel. And the genealogy of Joseph to Adam, a son of God, is found upon the plates of brass which shall be preserved among the Jews. Therefore, I, Mormon, do not include the rest of the lineage of Lehi upon these plates.

13 And Lehi lived in Jerusalem all of his days. And he was the son of Jeshron, a High Priest. And Lehi followed in the footsteps of his father and was called and anointed according to the priesthood of Aaron that was taught and accepted among the Jews who belonged to the church of God at Jerusalem.

14 And it came to pass that during the time that Lehi was a High Priest, the Lord sent many prophets to the people of Jerusalem to persuade them to repent of their sins and to obey the commandments of God.

15 And many of these prophets were bound by the Jews and carried forth unto the High Priests to see what should be done with them. For the people of Jerusalem mocked the prophets and ridiculed their authority to preach the word of God. For behold, the Jews were not familiar with these prophets, as they had not been acknowledged by the proper authority of the priesthood of Aaron, which the people believed resided only in the High Priests who were called to serve in the church at Jerusalem by lineage of the priesthood, and also by the laying on of hands by those who were in authority.

16 For the people had been taught that there were none, save he who had been chosen and set apart by a sacred anointing, who could administer the word of God unto the people. And the prophets who were sent by the Lord to Jerusalem were not members of this priesthood that was accepted by the people of the church at Jerusalem, nor were they recognized as one having authority to preach the word of God to the people.

17 And it came to pass that it fell upon Lehi and others of the High Priests to try and test those who professed to be prophets of God. And this they did that they might catch those who professed to be prophets in a lie and prove to the people that they were not men sent by God, but that they were servants of Satan, who had sent them to deceive the people of God and pervert the right ways of the priesthood and authority of Aaron.

18 And there were many prophets sent forth by the Lord to bring the people of Jerusalem unto repentance. And when these prophets were bound and set before the chief priests of the people they were chastised and commanded to recant their prophecies and their testimonies and their preachings against the people.

19 For behold, the prophets did truly testify of the iniquities of the church at Jerusalem. For the people of the church were corrupted by the examples of their leaders who had the priesthood of God but lacked the power thereof, which power can only be exercised through the Holy Spirit; and this Spirit can only be controlled upon the principles of righteousness of him who was anointed to this priesthood. For the leaders were rich and popular men among the people, and had set themselves up above the people, even unto the envying of their positions by the people. And the leaders chose other leaders who were also rich and popular men among them. And in this way, the leaders of the Jewish people assured that all men who were chosen to the Priesthood would be like unto themselves.

20 And the people justified their own wicked state because of the examples of their leaders. Nevertheless, the leaders did not think of themselves as wicked, but as men whom God had blessed with riches and wisdom. And since the people believed that their leaders were indeed men of God, they were deceived into believing that riches and power and worldly glory were blessings of God. And in this way did Satan deceive the leaders; and the leaders did deceive the people.

21 And because the leaders did not believe that they were wicked, they taught the people that God would not speak to the people unless He did so through the channels of the priesthood of Aaron, which was established for this purpose. And the leaders taught the people that no High Priest belonging to the order of Aaron would be allowed by God to deceive the people. And in this way the High Priests assured themselves that the people would not be swayed by a doctrine outside of the church at Jerusalem, nor by other preaching that was not approved by them.

22 And the leaders of the people taught them the sacraments and the offerings and the ordinances of the church, which was established among the people according to the laws of Moses and according to the traditions of the Jews.

23 And it came to pass that there were two prophets that were bound and carried up before the High Priests to be judged for their crimes. And their names were Zenos and Zenock.

24 And they stood forth boldly in their chains before the counsel of High Priests that had assembled to judge them. And Lehi was among these priests who were assigned by the church to judge anyone professing to be a prophet of God.

25 And it came to pass that Zenock stood before the priests and began to speak unto them, being filled with the Spirit of God. And he spake boldly unto them saying:

26 Oh ye wicked and perverse generation. Why have ye polluted and corrupted the holy church of God? Why have ye led this people in such a way that the wrath of God will soon visit them even unto their own destruction? Behold, I say unto you, that their blood will be required at your hands because of your example and the things that ye have taught them. Nevertheless, their sins will be their own and they will also suffer because of them. But ye shall also suffer with them because ye have set yourselves up as the mouthpiece of God and have lied unto them by telling them that the Lord will not allow you to mislead them.

27 Behold, ye know not the words of God, but speak vanity and foolishness unto this people. Ye have taught this people that they should worship the church and the ordinances and the traditions thereof, and yet they deny the Spirit of God that will only dwell with the children of men in righteousness.

28 Do ye not remember the words of the prophet, Isaiah? Ye have them before you, yet ye understand them not. Ye hear them, but ye do not hear their true meaning. Ye read them, but ye do not understand that which ye have read, but ye have changed the doctrine of God to conform to your own selfish interests and desires.

29 Behold, did not Isaiah say unto this church: Thus saith the Lord, To what purpose is the multitude of your sacrifices unto me? Saith the Lord: I am full of the burnt offerings of rams, and the fat of fed beasts; and I delight not in the blood of bullocks, or of lambs, or of he-goats.

30 When ye come to appear before me, who hath required this at your hand, to tread my courts?

31 Bring no more vain oblations; incense is an abomination unto me; the new moons and sabbaths, the calling of assemblies, I cannot abide them; away with them; it is iniquity, even the solemn meeting.

32 Your new moons and your appointed feasts my soul hateth; they are a trouble unto me; I am weary to bear them.

33 And when ye spread forth your hands, I will hide mine eyes from you: yea, when ye make many prayers, I will not hear: your hands are full of blood.

34 Wash you, make you clean; put away the evil of your doings from before mine eyes; cease to do evil;

35 Learn to do well; seek judgment, relieve the oppressed, judge the fatherless, plead for the widow.

36 Come now, and let us reason together, saith the Lord: though your sins be as scarlet, they shall be as white as snow; though they be red like crimson, they shall be as wool.

37 If ye be willing and obedient, ye shall eat the good of the land;

38 But if ye refuse and rebel, ye shall be devoured with the sword; for the mouth of the Lord hath spoken it.

39 And it came to pass that as Lehi heard the words of Zenock, he was filled with great anguish, for he knew that Zenock spoke the truth unto them. For Lehi had known previously that the things that he was doing as a leader of the people were not the things of God. Nevertheless, he did the things that were expected of him by the people, and also those things that the church had instructed him to do.

40 And Lehi was a rich man who had acquired many riches by business among the Jews at Jerusalem. And he saved many of his riches and imparted them not unto those who were poor and needy. Neither did he impart of all his substance unto the widows and the orphans and those that were oppressed. For he had been taught that his riches were a blessing from God because of his own righteousness.

41 And it had been a tradition among the Jews, or rather, a commandment of the church, that each member pay a tithe to the church of all their increase. And this tithing was great, and was only used for the purposes of the church. And also, it was required of the members of the church to give regularly to the benefit of the poor and the needy. Yet, this offering, which the people made to the poor, was only a small part of their increase; the majority of their increase the people kept for themselves and their families, thus being taught by the words and the examples of their leaders.

42 And it did not matter if one man had an increase of a much greater worth than another, for the same offerings were required of them all. Thus the rich were allowed to keep their riches and set themselves up above those who had less than they.

43 And the poor and needy were also required to give a tithe and an offering to others who were poorer than they. This they had been taught was the commandment of God pertaining to the people of His church.

44 And in this manner the church of God justified the division of the rich and the poor—the inequality between those that had much and those that had little.

45 And Lehi knew of himself how the members of the church had submitted unto the teachings of the church and its doctrines and ordinances and denied the true doctrine of God of which Zenock spoke.

46 For Zenock said unto the priests: Know ye not that the ordinances and sacraments, and offerings, and institutions, and traditions of this church are not the gospel of the Lord, but were intended to point a man towards this gospel? And that this gospel was given to us in its pure form by the mouth of the prophet, Moses? Yet, the children of Israel could not abide by this pure gospel, but required signs and symbols, and ordinances, and endowments, to teach them and keep them in remembrance.

47 And the Lord in his frustration with the children of Israel gave the children of Israel the things which they desired, and commanded Moses to set up the ordinances and endowments of the church, so that the children of Israel would remember him and keep his commandments.

48 Nevertheless, these ordinances and traditions of this church are not the things that the Lord requireth of his people. But he requireth of them righteousness and humility before him.

49 Behold, it mattereth not unto the Lord whether or not a man belongest to this church, or hath the priesthood of Aaron as ye claim that ye have; for the Lord judgeth a man by his works—the desires of his heart. And if his works are good, then the Lord will accept this man. But if his works are evil, then he shall have no part of the Spirit of God.

50 And your works are evil before the Lord. For behold, ye do teach this people to respect and worship the church, and the requirements of the church, and teach them not the pure gospel and commandments of God; and the church was established to teach these things symbolically through its ordinances and services. Thus ye deceive this people and have opened the door to their destruction.

51 Behold, I am not a member of your church, nor do I have the priesthood that ye claim giveth you the power and authority to act in the name of

God, so that a man can teach this people His words. Nevertheless, God hath called me through the administrations of His holy angels, and also by the Spirit of God that dwells within me. And by these things ye shall know me, and by my works ye shall judge.

52 Behold, because of the mercy and goodness of the Lord, I was snatched from the bitterness that awaited me if I would have continued to follow the course of life that I was following before I was called to come unto you and testify of your wickedness.

53 For behold, I was rich and popular, like unto yourselves, among those that resided in the city in which I lived. And I was a man who many looked up to and praised for the great things that I had accomplished among them. But all this praise and glory was the praise and glory of men. And the things for which I was praised were the things of this world.

54 And God sent his servant, Zenos, unto me and he met me in my house and spoke unto me about the things of God. And while he spoke to me, I was filled with the Spirit of the Lord, even so much, that I wept bitterly because of my many iniquities and my sins.

55 And after experiencing a bitterness of soul that I had never before felt, I called upon God for a remission of my sins, even upon the Son of God who is to come into the world to save the righteous from the corruptness thereof.

56 And as I called upon the Lord in my agony, I was visited with a gentle and quiet spirit that took away my pain and my anguish and filled my soul with an unspeakable joy that I cannot describe with my own words. And it is this joy that turned my sins from crimson into wool as the prophet Isaiah hath written.

57 And it is because of the Son of God that this mercy was given unto me. For I beheld a vision while in the Spirit that showed unto me the condescension of God, or in other words, the coming of His Son into this world.

58 And I have seen the coming of the Son of God in vision and have witnessed the mission of the Lord. And he shall come unto this people and show unto them the things that they must do in order to be saved in the kingdom of God. And he shall live among them and preach the word of God unto the Jews who are here at Jerusalem.

59 And he shall further witness against this church and its leaders. And the leaders of the church shall rise up against him and turn the people from him, contriving all types of lies and falsehoods in order to keep the people from accepting the gospel that he shall teach unto them.

60 For the church at Jerusalem will deny that even the Son of God doth not have the authority to preach the word of God, because he doth not have the permission of the church or its authority to do so. Nor will he be given this authority by the laying on of hands by the High Priest of this church. And for this reason shall he be rejected by the Jews.

61 And the Lord shall go forth among the people and establish his own truth. And his church shall be established according to the Spirit of God and not according to the commandments and traditions of men.

62 And he shall call others to a ministry, or to preach the gospel that he shall give unto them, both by his own mouth and by the mouth of his spirit which he shall leave with them.

63 And the gospel that they shall teach shall be the words that they shall hear the Son speak while he dwelleth among them. And they shall add nothing to, nor shall they take anything away from this gospel. For it is an everlasting gospel, yea, a gospel that was preached before this world was created.

64 And because of the things that they shall teach, they shall be persecuted and rejected by the Jews at Jerusalem. And they shall be cast out and slain. Behold, even the Son of God shall be taken up by the leaders of this people and crucified before them.

65 And the leaders of this church shall mock the Lord and spit upon him in the presence of the people. And the people shall also deny their Lord because of the example of their leaders.

66 And it came to pass that Zenock stood forth boldly before the High Priests of the church. And Lehi was astonished at what Zenock had testified concerning the Son of God and also concerning the wickedness of the church.

CHAPTER 2

The preaching of Zenos—Laban rejects the preaching of Zenos and Zenock and demands their death—Lehi stands forth and pleads with Laban, the chief High Priest, and testifies against the church of God.

AND it came to pass that after Zenock had ended his exhortation and preaching unto the leaders of the Jews, Zenos stood forth and began to expound further upon the things which Zenock had said concerning the coming of the Son of God to the world and the destruction of the Jews.

2 And I, Mormon, cannot write all the words that the prophets Zenock and Zenos preached unto the Jews at Jerusalem, for they did truly speak many things unto the Jews; and many things did they also speak unto the leaders of the Jews. And Nephi hath recorded upon his record all of the words that Zenos and Zenock spake according to the memory of his father Lehi, who was present when they stood before the High Priests at Jerusalem.

3 And the words of these two prophets are great and wonderful and have been preserved for the generations of the sons and daughters of Lehi and their descendants, and also for all those who shall receive this record in the last days. But a portion of their words I have been commanded by the Lord to include in my abridgment of the plates of Nephi, which plates I have before me.

4 And of all the words and prophecies that are recorded upon these plates of Nephi, none are as great as those that were spoken by Zenock and Zenos.

5 And it came to pass that Zenos also stood forth boldly and spake unto the High Priests, which were assembled before him. And Zenos expounded unto them a parable of an olive tree and likened the house of Israel unto this olive tree.

6 And this he did that he might show unto the Jews that which was to befall them if they continued in their wicked ways and continued to deny the gospel of the Son of God.

7 And it came to pass that Zenos likened the children of Israel unto a tame olive tree that the Lord nourished in his vineyard, or in other words, in the land of promise. And this he meant so that it might be understood that the Lord had blessed the house of Israel and had given them the land in which they dwelt, and had driven out their enemies and sent his Spirit to dwell among them.

8 And the tree became corrupt and began to decay. And the Lord commanded his servants, who were the prophets of God, to go into the vineyard and attempt to nourish the olive tree and bring back the good fruit thereof.

9 And he commanded his servants to prune it, and dig about it, and nourish it for a time to see if it would once again bring forth its natural fruit.

10 And Zenos prophesied in the parable about the destruction of the Jews; and that the Lord shall withdraw the righteous from among them and send them to other parts of the world where they would not be destroyed. This he would do to preserve unto himself the roots of the tree, or in other words, the true gospel of the Son of God.

11 And these things had reference to the children of Lehi and other people whom the Lord would lead out of the land of Israel before its destruction by its enemies.

12 And the parable spoke of the restoration of the gospel among the Jews at the time of the coming of the Lord into the world. Nevertheless, because the trees of the vineyard are so corrupt, the Lord commands his servants to graft in the wild olive branches in hopes that he might preserve the good fruit of the tree unto himself. And the wild olive branches are the Gentiles who shall have the gospel preached unto them by the servants of God.

13 And it came to pass that after the gospel is preached unto the Gentiles, there shall be peace for a time among them. And after a space of a time the trees of the vineyard shall once again bring forth corrupted fruit.

14 And Zenos spoke of this land, which is a promised land unto the Nephites and also unto the Lamanites and unto others whom the Lord shall bring into this land. And the gospel shall be given to the people on this continent as well as it was given unto the Jews at Jerusalem.

15 And there shall be all manner of trees throughout the vineyard of the Lord, in other words, there shall be many people upon all the continents of the world that shall hear the gospel of the Son of God and repent of their

sins. And there shall be many churches that shall claim to be the pure olive tree that the Lord grew in his vineyard.

16 And in the latter days before God once again sendeth His Son among the people, yea, even in all his glory like unto the glory that he showed unto the Nephites and the Lamanites in the land of Bountiful, God shall once again bring the knowledge of His gospel unto the Gentiles and then unto the Jews, that the last may be first, and the first may be last.

17 And it shall come to pass that the gospel shall be established in all the parts of the world; in other words, the Lord shall graft in the wild branches into the natural olive trees and the natural branches into the wild trees, that he might once again obtain fruit that is pleasing unto him.

18 And after this gospel shall be preached in all the parts of the world, yea, even after the voice of Jesus Christ shall be heard among all men; then still shall the Lord of the vineyard weep and say unto his servants: What could I have done more for my vineyard?

19 For behold, all the trees of the vineyard shall be corrupt. And the Lord shall ask of his servants what was the cause of the corruptness of his vineyard.

20 Then shall the servant of the Lord say unto his master: Is it not the loftiness of thy vineyard— have not the branches thereof overcome the roots which are good? And because the branches have overcome the roots thereof, behold they grew faster than the strength of the roots, taking strength unto themselves.

21 And it came to pass that Zenos expounded the meaning of the parable unto the High Priests, saying: Behold, in the latter days the church of God shall be like unto this church at Jerusalem. For the Lord will give unto them the pureness of his everlasting gospel and provide for them a way whereby they might be saved in the kingdom of God at the last day.

22 Nevertheless, because of the branches, or in other words, because of the church of God and its supposed greatness, the roots of the tree, which is the pure gospel of God, shall be overcome. The leaders and members of the church of God shall become lofty and prideful, and their desires shall be towards the church and not set upon the gospel, which is the root of the tree, thus the branches overcoming the roots that are good.

23 And they shall be like unto you, and also like unto those who will be at Jerusalem when God sendeth His Son among them. For behold, they shall not understand the gospel that the Son of God, shall preach unto them. And because of the examples of the leaders of the church of God the people shall harden their hearts towards the gospel and turn their hearts towards the church for their salvation, thus denying the power of the Holy Spirit and its righteousness.

24 And their hearts and their minds shall be set upon the things of this world and the honors and glories of men. Then shall the words of Isaiah again be fulfilled among them when he spoke unto the house of Israel, saying:

25 Woe unto the wicked for it shall be ill with him: for the reward of his hands shall be given him.

26 As for my people, children are their oppressors, and women rule over them. Oh, my people, they which lead thee cause thee to err, and destroy the way of thy paths.

27 The Lord standeth up to plead, and standeth to judge the people.

28 The Lord will enter into judgment with the ancients of his people, and the princes thereof: for ye have eaten up the vineyard; the spoil of the poor is in your houses.

29 What mean ye that ye beat my people to pieces, and grind the faces of the poor? saith the Lord God of hosts.

30 Moreover the Lord saith, Because the daughters of Zion are haughty, and walk with stretched forth necks and wanton eyes, walking and mincing as they go, and making a tinkling with their feet;

31 Therefore the Lord will smite with a scab the crown of the head of the daughters of Zion, and the Lord will discover their private parts.

32 In that day the Lord will take away the bravery of their tinkling ornaments about their feet, and their cauls, and their round tires like the moon,

33 The chains, and the bracelets, and the mufflers.

34 The bonnets, and the ornaments of the legs, and the headbands, and the tablets, and the earrings,

35 The rings, and nose jewels,

36 The changeable suits of apparel, and the mantles, and the wimples, and the crisping pins,

37 The glasses, and the fine linen, and the hoods, and the veils.

38 And it shall come to pass, that instead of sweet smell there shall be stink; and instead of a girdle, a rent; and instead of well set hair, baldness; and instead of a stomacher, a girding of sackcloth; and burning instead of beauty.

39 Thy men shall fall by the sword, and thy mighty in the war.

40 And her gates shall lament and mourn; and she being desolate shall sit upon the ground.

41 And it came to pass that Zenos continued his prophecies in front of the High Priests. And he prophesied concerning the second coming of the Son of God, even when he shall appear in his power and his glory to prune his vineyard for the last time.

42 And the Lord shall once again set his hand for the last time to prune his vineyard and attempt to bring forth good fruit from the trees thereof.

43 And he shall call his servants to work at his side. And he will allow the good and the bad to continue to grow together. Nevertheless, he shall clear away the bad as the good groweth, making sure that the branches will never again overrun the strength of the roots.

44 And it shall come to pass that the trees of his vineyard shall once again bring forth good fruit for the space of many seasons. And when evil fruit shall once again come into the vineyard, then will the Lord cause to be gathered all of the fruit of his trees. And the good he shall preserve unto himself, and the bad he will cast away in its own place. And then the end of the world shall come; and the Lord will cause his vineyard to be burned with fire—and all these things according to the parable and prophecy of Zenos.

45 And it came to pass that after Zenos had testified of the end of the world and the destruction of the wicked, Laban, the chief high priest, stood forth and commanded that Zenos be struck down for his blasphemy against the church of God. For behold, Laban denied that the church of God was corrupt and that the leaders thereof were misleading the people. And Laban stood forth and testified of the righteousness of the church and its leaders.

45 And upon his command one of the guards who had carried Zenock and Zenos into the chamber of the High Priests put forth his sword to silence Zenos.

47 And Lehi sprang forth from his seat, which was set high above the assembly of the people and was among those of the other High Priests. And Lehi stood between the sword of the guard and Zenos.

48 And Lehi pleaded with the other High Priests that no harm should come to these two prophets of God. And he pleaded unto them, saying: What cause have we against these two men? Do they not speak the truth concerning us? Do they not speak unto us of our iniquities and corruption? Know we not that they have been sent by God to preach repentance unto us that we might not experience the pain and anguish of the wrath of God because of our sins?

49 Behold, my soul hath been burdened much because of the ways of this church and those things which we teach unto the people. And have we not set ourselves up above the people, even so much that when we walk by them on the street or in the synagogue that they do worship us and bow down before us? How can we not see that these things are an abomination before God and that we are misleading this people to trust more in the church and its leaders than in the gospel that we are supposed to be teaching unto them?

50 And have we not taken the money that hath been given to the church, because of the commandment of the Lord regarding the tithing of his people, and have we not used this money to build great synagogues and great temples, yet we suffer that there remain the poor and needy among us? Doth this not bear testimony that we do love our money and our substance, and our fine apparel, and the adorning of our churches, more than we love the poor and the needy, the sick and the afflicted?

51 And in our solemn assemblies do we not justify our actions and doings because of the praise of the world? Do we not make concessions to the word of God because we believe that we will be mocked and ridiculed by the pride and ignorance of the world? In fine, do we not change the precepts and doctrines of God, and even the pure ordinances that were given unto us

by the prophet, Moses; do we not change them to suit our whims and satisfy the desires of the world that we may be accepted by it?

52 Behold, my soul is racked with anguish because I know that these things are true, and I also know that these two men are prophets of God who have been sent unto this church to bring us unto repentance so that we might not be destroyed.

53 And it came to pass that Lehi did have success with some of the other High Priests who were present in the chambers, and also with many of the people who attended the inquisition of Zenos and Zenock.

54 Nevertheless, Laban, who was the Chief High Priest, did stand forth to confound Lehi; and he commanded that Lehi should be bound also and judged for his testimony against the church of God and its leaders.

55 But Lehi was beloved by the people and there were none who wanted to see him cast out from among them.

56 And there was another High Priest who knew that the things that Lehi had spoken were true. And his name was Ishmael; and he had for a long time known Lehi and his family. And they were friends who had shared many times together united with their families. But Ishmael dared not to say anything in the defense of Lehi; for Ishmael feared Laban.

57 And it was Laban who also had the loyalty and the trust of the captain of the guard and the soldiers who were assigned to administer the law in that part of the land of Israel.

58 And it came to pass that Lehi could see the hardness of the heart of Laban, and he also could see that the people began to be swayed by the words of Laban.

59 And Lehi left the chamber and went out into the street and knelt down and prayed unto the Lord in behalf of his people. And he prayed with all the energy of his soul, yea, even with all of his heart; for great was his anguish for the sins of the people.

CHAPTER 3

The conversion and calling of Lehi—he preaches to and is rejected by the Jews. Lehi is commanded to leave Jerusalem with his family and flee into the wilderness.

AND it came to pass that as Lehi prayed unto the Lord, he was visited by the Spirit of God and was shown a marvelous vision in which appeared before him a pillar of fire. And the pillar of fire was seen by those who were around the place where Lehi had fallen to the ground.

2 And it came to pass that a voice spoke unto Lehi from within the pillar of fire. Nevertheless, those who were around Lehi, even those that beheld the pillar of fire, could hear no voice from within.

3 And I, Mormon, have been commanded by the Lord not to write the things which Lehi heard from the voice within the pillar of fire. For the things which he heard are many things that the Lord hath commanded to be sealed up and kept from the eyes of the world until the time that these things shall come forth unto the children of men at the appointed time of the Lord.

4 But because of the things that Lehi did see and hear, he did fear exceedingly for his people and for all the world.

5 And it came to pass that Lehi, being overcome by the Spirit because of the things that he had both seen and heard in the vision, returned to his home and laid himself upon his bed.

6 And Lehi cried unto the Lord that he might be forgiven for his many sins and that he might understand further what the Lord would require of him.

7 And it came to pass that he was once again carried away in a vision in which he saw many of the things of which Zenock and Zenos had testified.

8 For he truly beheld the coming of the Son of God to the earth. And he saw the Lord go out among the people at Jerusalem and begin to preach his gospel unto them. And he saw others who the Lord had called to help him teach the people his gospel.

9 And one of the servants of the Lord came and stood before Lehi and gave unto him a book and

commanded him that he should read the book. And as Lehi read the book he was filled with the Spirit of the Lord and rejoiced exceedingly.

10 And Lehi was called of God to go unto the people of Jerusalem and teach unto them the things which he had read in the book.

11 And it came to pass that Lehi went forth again unto the people of Jerusalem and began to expound on the things which had been testified of by Zenos and Zenock, and also on the things which he had read in the book that was given unto him in his vision.

12 And Lehi preached many things unto the people of Jerusalem, and to his friends, and to his relatives, and to his family, which consisted of his wife, Sariah, and his sons and his daughters.

13 And it came to pass that the people of Jerusalem rejected the words of Lehi and cast him out from among them and mocked him. For behold, the people at Jerusalem were hardened by their pride, and also by the pride that they had in the church of God to which they belonged.

14 And they mocked Lehi, saying: How can thee, being one man alone, claim that the church of God is corrupt? Dost thou not believe that the Lord hath prospered this church and sanctified it because of its righteousness? Do we not attend regularly to the ordinances and traditions that Moses handed down to us? And we know that Moses was a prophet of God and that he showed us all things that we must do in order to be saved in the kingdom of God at the last day. And do we not do all the things that he hath commanded us?

15 And Lehi rebuked them, saying: Know ye not that the Lord suffered Moses to give unto you a lower law because of your wickedness? And this lower law is the law that this church teacheth unto the people.

16 For behold, the sacraments and the ordinances and all the rituals thereof are symbols and representations of the pure gospel of the Lord. And the commandments that ye have been given have been given unto you because of your inability to live the higher law, which law is this gospel of which the prophets of old have spoken.

17 And if there was no law given unto the children of Israel at the time they rebelled against the Lord in the wilderness, then they would have been left unto themselves and they would have never had the opportunity to inherit the promised land.

18 And it was this law that brought peace among them and suffered them to live one with another without violence and without all manner of wickedness that would surely have led to their destruction.

19 But behold, this law that was given unto the children of Israel was a law of ordinances and sacrifice that they might not forget the Lord their God who had led them forth to the land of promise.

20 And these laws and ordinances were types and portents of those things that would come to pass in eternity. And it is this eternal law that ye cannot understand. Yea, I say unto you, that this eternal law is the gospel of the Lord Jesus Christ, even he who shall come into the world, and the only way whereby man might be saved in the eternal kingdom of God. And ye do not understand this gospel because ye have hardened your hearts against the Spirit of the Lord, which teacheth this pure gospel.

21 And this church and all churches that the Lord suffereth to be built up on this earth to turn the hearts of the children of men towards him, are not this gospel, nor do they represent this gospel. But they are set up among men to point them towards this eternal gospel, which is the only gospel of eternal salvation.

22 And it shall come to pass that the Lord himself shall come down amongst his people in the flesh and teach this eternal gospel unto them. And they shall reject him and kill him because they do not understand his gospel, and this they do because they do not have the Holy Spirit with them.

23 And the Lord hath sent many prophets unto us to preach repentance and prepare us to meet the Lord and hear his gospel, whether in this flesh, or as a spirit when we die.

24 And we have cast out these holy men of God because we could not understand the things that they have preached unto us. And the blood of these men shall be upon our hands. And we shall suffer the wrath of God because of them.

25 And it came to pass that the people were angry with Lehi and sought from that time forth to take him and bind him and carry him up unto the chamber of the High Priests, so that he, too, might be tried for heresy and blasphemy before the church.

26 And they sought to take away his life as they did the lives of Zenos and Zenock. For behold, Laban had delivered up Zenos and Zenock to be killed by the hands of the people. And the people took Zenos and Zenock, and after they had stoned them, they hung them by the neck until they were dead.

27 And there were many of the people who loved Lehi and his family and did not desire that he be destroyed or cast out from among them. But the greater part of the people wanted Lehi cast out from among them or bound and taken before the other High Priests where he would surely be sentenced to death.

28 And it came to pass that Lehi fled from before the people and went unto his family and told them all the things that had befallen him.

29 And it came to pass that Lehi gathered up his family and some provisions and fled with them into the wilderness before the more wicked part of the people could alert the High Priests of his plans to flee Jerusalem.

30 For behold, the Lord had warned Lehi in a dream that he should take his family and flee into the wilderness. And Lehi was promised that if he would keep the commandments of God in all things, he would be blessed; and also his wife and his children would be saved.

31 And it came to pass that Lehi left his gold and his silver and all of his material possessions and fled with his family into the wilderness.

32 And he traveled many days in the wilderness until he came down unto the borders of the Red Sea.

33 And it came to pass that Laman and Lemuel, the elder sons of Lehi, began to mock their father and murmur against him. For they did not want to leave the land of their inheritance and their gold and their silver and all their precious things. And they murmured and complained that their father was a visionary man who had dreams and visions that they did not understand.

34 And Laman and Lemuel spoke to their father, saying: Why hast thou judged the people of the church at Jerusalem? Thou also were a great leader among them and also a priest after the order of Aaron. And did not the Lord promise his people that he would never allow them to be led astray by those who lead his church? And we know that the leaders of the people are righteous men because they have been called of God by the laying on of hands, and also by the Spirit of God.

35 And thou hast judged them and pronounced evil upon their heads because of the foolish dreams and visions which thou hast had, which we believe are the imaginations of thy heart.

36 For behold, how could it be possible that they be wicked men when the Lord hath shown his acceptance of them by granting them with prosperity and happiness? And they teach the people the words that are written, which are the words of the Lord which were written by the hand of Moses for the salvation of all Israel.

37 And thus Laman and Lemuel did murmur against Lehi and desired to return again to the Land of Jerusalem. For behold, the family of Lehi did indeed suffer many things in the wilderness; and because of these sufferings, Laman and Lemuel did rise up and murmur against their father.

38 And it came to pass that Lehi stood forth before his sons and rebuked them, being filled with the power and Spirit of God. And he confounded them, evensomuch that they did shake and tremble before their father, even that they dared not speak nor murmur anymore against him.

39 And it came to pass that the two younger sons of Lehi, yea, even Sam and Nephi, did give heed unto the counsel of their father and believed the things that he said unto them.

40 For behold, the Lord had chosen Nephi, the youngest, to lead his elder brothers. And for this purpose the Lord sent his Spirit unto Nephi and blessed him with wisdom and understanding that far exceeded that of his older brethren.

41 And the Lord promised Nephi that he and his posterity would be a great blessing unto his father Lehi and unto all of the children of Lehi, even unto the generations of Laman and Lemuel, if it so be that he keepeth the commandments of the Lord.

42 And it came to pass that Lehi commanded his sons to return to Jerusalem and seek the plates of brass which contained the genealogy of his forefathers and also a record of the Jews. And he commanded his sons to go unto Laban and ask him for the plates of brass.

43 And it came to pass that Laman and Lemuel once again murmured against their father and called him a fool for sending them to the house of Laban to obtain the record of the Jews. For the plates of brass were most precious unto the Jews, and they did not believe that Laban would give the plates unto them.

44 Nevertheless, they remembered the things that their father had said unto them. And they also remembered the power of the Spirit that they felt that had caused their frames to shake before him. And Laman and Lemuel kept their murmurings to themselves and gathered up provisions and their younger brothers, Sam and Nephi, and went back into the wilderness towards Jerusalem.

45 And it came to pass that the lot fell to Laman, the eldest, to go into the house of Laban and ask of him the plates of brass, which contained the record of the Jews and the genealogy of Lehi.

46 And it came to pass that Laban mocked Laman and sought to take away his life. For Laban had hardened his heart against Lehi because he had taken his family and fled into the wilderness. Nevertheless, Laban feared the part of the people that loved Lehi and those that listened to what Lehi had said about the wickedness of the church and its leaders.

47 And Laban called to his servants that they might take Laman away and imprison him according to the laws of the land. For Laban had lied to his servants, convincing them that Laman had tried to steal the plates from him. And Laban convinced his servants that Laman would steal the plates of brass that were of great worth unto the people of Jerusalem, telling his servants that Laman asked for the records without payment.

48 And Laman fled from before Laban and went unto his brethren who were hiding outside the city of Jerusalem in the wilderness and told unto them all that had happened in the house of Laban.

49 And it came to pass that the sons of Lehi returned again to the land of their inheritance and gathered together all their gold and their silver, and everything that they had owned before they had fled into the wilderness. And there was much substance because of the riches that Lehi had acquired while he served as a Priest in the church at Jerusalem.

50 And they returned to the house of Laban and desired of him that they might buy the plates of brass for the amount of all their possessions.

51 And it came to pass that Laban saw the riches that the sons of Lehi presented before him. And he desired to have the riches, but had no desire to give unto them the plates of brass as they had requested.

52 And Laban sent his servants to slay the sons of Lehi. But behold, the sons of Lehi fled again into the wilderness leaving behind in the possession of Laban all their gold and all their silver and all their precious things.

53 And it came to pass that the sons of Lehi became exceedingly sorrowful and desired to return to the tent of their father.

54 And it came to pass that Nephi, the youngest of the sons of Lehi, stood forth and pleaded with his brothers that they should not return to the tent of their father without the plates of brass which the Lord had commanded them to obtain from Laban.

55 And Laman and Lemuel became exceedingly angry with Nephi and began to beat him with a rod and cause him great pain. And Sam stood forth against his elder brothers and pleaded with them to cease from smiting their younger brother.

56 And it came to pass that Laman and Lemuel would not heed the words of Sam and continued to smite their brother, and also they did smite Sam with a rod.

57 And it came to pass that the Lord sent an angel unto the sons of Lehi and rebuked Laman and Lemuel. Behold, the angel did speak many things unto them about their younger brother Nephi who one day would rule over them. And the angel of the Lord did also tell them that the Lord would deliver Laban and the plates of brass into their hands. And after all these things, the angel of the Lord departed.

CHAPTER 4

Nephi returns to Jerusalem and slays Laban to obtain the plates of brass. The Lord prepares Zoram to be a scapegoat for the sons of Lehi—they are, therefore, able to return to Jerusalem and bring Ishmael and his family with them into the wilderness.

AND it came to pass that when the sons of Lehi returned again outside the walls that surrounded Jerusalem, they were sore afraid. And Laman and Lemuel once again doubted the promise of the angel of the Lord when it was promised that Laban and the plates of brass would be delivered unto them.

2 But Nephi did not doubt the words of the angel and rebuked his brothers, saying: How can ye deny the power of the Lord when it hath been demonstrated to you time and time again? Yea, ye have seen an angel, and the angel hath rebuked you and caused your frames to shake before him? How can ye continually deny the power of God when it hath been made known unto you in such great and marvelous ways? Why should ye suffer that I, your younger brother, rule over you because of your lack of faith and your iniquities?

3 Know ye not that the Lord can command his angels and they will come to our aid, if it so be that we demonstrate our faith and our worthiness in keeping his commandments? Ye know that this is true; and ye also know that an angel hath spoken it unto you; therefore, how can ye doubt?

4 And Nephi spake many words of encouragement unto his older brothers. Nevertheless, they were still afraid and would not go into Jerusalem again.

5 And Nephi became angry with his brothers; yea, even a righteous indignation came over him and he stood forth and rebuked his brothers being wrought upon by the Holy Spirit.

6 And it came to pass that Nephi went forth to Jerusalem at night; and his brother, Sam, also wanted to go with Nephi unto Jerusalem. For behold, Sam did truly love his brother and wanted to protect him from any harm that might befall him.

7 But Nephi did not desire that Sam should accompany him into the city at night. And Nephi told Sam that he should stay with his elder brothers, Laman and Lemuel, and ensure that they did not go into the city and alert the Jews that he was going again unto the house of Laban. This Nephi did because his older brothers had threatened to confess to the Jews that their father was foolish, and also because of their desire to once again be part of the people at Jerusalem.

8 And Sam heeded the words of Nephi and stayed outside the walls of Jerusalem with his older brothers, Laman and Lemuel.

9 And it came to pass that Nephi went forth unto the house of Laban, and he found Laban drunk with wine outside his house.

10 And the Spirit commanded Nephi to kill Laban and dress in his clothes that he might gain entrance into the house of Laban, in disguise, without the guards of Laban knowing that it was not their master.

11 And Nephi fought the promptings of the Spirit, for he had never so much as harmed another person, or another living creature, without just cause at any time in his life. And Nephi doubted the promptings that the Spirit of the Lord gave unto him.

12 But after continual promptings from the Spirit, and after his own reflections on the treatment that he and his brothers had received at the hand of Laban, and also remembering the threats of Laban towards his father, Nephi realized that the Lord had delivered Laban into his hands, and that it would be better that Laban perish than for the commandment of the Lord to go unfulfilled.

13 And Nephi also knew that the Jews would wake up the morning of the next day and find Laban slain. And the Jews would know that the sons of Lehi had killed Laban, for they had visited Laban the previous day and had requested the plates of brass from him.

14 And the Jews would know that it was the sons of Lehi who had done this unto Laban, because the plates of brass would be gone and Laban would be found dead. And because of this, Nephi did again doubt the Spirit, and he began to shrink from the commandment that he had been given.

15 And it came to pass that the Spirit of the Lord once again came unto Nephi and told him to

slay Laban and keep the commandments of God, or his family would not prosper and that they would be destroyed in the wilderness. And the Spirit told Nephi that the Lord had prepared a way whereby the sons of Lehi would not be blamed by the Jews for the death of Laban, or for stealing the plates of brass.

16 And Nephi believed the words of the Spirit, he having had many such manifestations in his youth and many presently, therefore he could feel the sanctification of the Spirit of that which he was about to do.

17 And Nephi took the sword of Laban and smote off his head with his own sword.

18 And it came to pass that Nephi put on the clothes of Laban and went into the house of Laban. And the guards of Laban were also drunken with wine and knew not that Nephi was not their master returning home, because Nephi was dressed in the clothes and in the robes of Laban.

19 And it came to pass that Nephi entered the inner chambers of the house of Laban and commanded the servant of Laban to take up the plates and carry them forth outside the walls of the city to his brethren.

20 And Nephi spoke in the voice of Laban. And the servant of Laban thought that Nephi was speaking of the brethren of the church, among whom Laban had been with that night.

21 And it came to pass that the servant of Laban followed Nephi out of the city of Jerusalem, and Nephi led the servant to where his older brothers were hiding.

22 And when Laman and Lemuel and Sam saw Nephi, who was clothed in the robes of Laban, coming with the servant of Laban, they were afraid and fled from before them.

23 But Nephi took off the headdress of Laban and called to his brethren.

24 And when the servant of Laban saw that Nephi was not his master, he also attempted to flee. But Nephi grabbed hold of the servant of Laban and held him tight and would not allow him to flee from before him. And the servant of Laban began to call out loud for help that others inside the city walls might hear his cries.

25 And Nephi drew the sword of Laban and told the servant of Laban that he would slay him if he did not give unto them the plates and return with them to the tent of their father in the wilderness.

26 And Nephi pleaded with the servant of Laban that they would not harm him, and that he would no longer be a servant to any man as long as he abided with them in the wilderness.

27 And the Spirit of the Lord came over the servant of Laban. And his name was Zoram. And Zoram fell at the feet of Nephi and covenanted with him that he would be his servant from that time forth, if he would spare his life.

28 And Nephi lifted Zoram up and embraced him and said unto him: My brother, knowest thou not that thou art my brother and that we are all children of the same God? Knowest thou not that the same creator who gave me power to slay your master and obtain these plates hath spared thy life and hath from this day forth set thee free? Thou shalt be my brother and my friend.

29 And Zoram believed Nephi and was wrought upon by the Spirit of God so exceedingly that he wept on the shoulder of Nephi and promised to obey all the commandments of God from that time forth.

30 And it was in this way that the Lord prepared a means whereby the sons of Lehi would not be blamed for the murder of Laban, or for stealing the plates of brass, as the people of Jerusalem would believe.

31 For behold, the next morning the Jews did find the body of Laban; and they did also discover that the plates of brass were missing and had been taken from his house. Nevertheless, they knew also that Zoram was missing from among them. And it came to pass that the Jews believed that Zoram had stolen the plates of brass from Laban after he had killed his master. And the Jews attributed no blame to Lehi or to his sons.

32 And it came to pass that the sons of Lehi did return to the tent of their father in the wilderness.

33 And after they had returned to their father in the wilderness, their mother Sariah did rejoice exceedingly. And this she did because of the anguish that she was caused by the commandment of the Lord in sending her sons back to the city of Jerusalem to obtain the plates of brass from Laban.

34 For Sariah had complained considerably to

her husband Lehi, saying: I know that thou art a man of God, and that thou hast served the Lord all the days of thy life. And I know that thou believest that we have been led out of the land of our inheritance because of thy dreams and thy visions. Yea, I know that the things which thou speaketh about the church at Jerusalem are true, for I have felt these things many times during my own life.

35 And I also know that the people of Jerusalem did seek thy life, and that thy life would have been in their hands if we had not fled into the wilderness.

36 Nevertheless, how canst thou say that the Lord hath commanded thee to send our sons to their deaths? And my daughters do suffer day and night because of the loss of their brothers, and also because of their hunger and their thirst which we have suffered these many days in the wilderness.

37 Knowest thou not that I am even at this time ripe with child and that I will deliver this child in the wilderness? And my daughters; what shall they do when they are grown and have no man to choose from to be a husband? Shall they be single and barren all the days of their lives and perish in the wilderness?

38 And Sira, one of the daughters of Lehi, rebuked her mother and embraced her father Lehi, who also was depressed in spirit because of the things that were required of his sons by the Lord.

39 And Sira spoke consoling words unto her father and rebuked her mother for the things that she had said. For behold, Sira was greatly blessed by the Spirit of the Lord and understood many things which she kept secret and unto herself because of her respect for her father and his authority in the priesthood. For Sira truly understood many of the mysteries and things of God.

40 And Sira brought great joy and refreshment unto her father, and he embraced her and rebuked his wife Sariah for her lack of faith and doubts.

41 And it came to pass that when the sons of Lehi returned to the tent of their father, their mother and sisters did rejoice exceedingly. And Sariah did humble herself before the Lord, and also before her husband; and she begged forgiveness for her doubts and offered thanks and sacrifice unto the Lord for the safe return of her sons.

42 And now I, Mormon, having been wrought upon by the Spirit, include in my abridgment an explanation of the importance of the plates of brass that Nephi and his brethren obtained from Laban.

43 Behold, it is not the intent or purpose of the Lord to destroy any man to accomplish his purposes. And after Nephi had taken the life of Laban, he was promised by the Spirit of the Lord that the blood of Laban would not be required at his hand. Also, that no man shall shed the blood of another from that time forth, except it shall be in the defense of his life, or the life of his family.

44 Behold, the Spirit hath shown unto me the destruction of Jerusalem and the carrying away of the people into foreign lands. And had the plates of brass been allowed to remain in the possession of Laban, they would have been destroyed.

45 And also, the plates of brass are a record of the Jews, and also a record of the laws of Moses that were established among the Jews for the sake of righteousness, and for the guidance of the church that was established among the children of Israel. And they also contain many of the prophecies and the words of the great prophets who preached unto the Jews. And these things were necessary that Lehi might teach his children the things that were taught to the children of Israel so that they could be more correctly taught in the ways of the Lord.

46 And Jerusalem was destroyed, thus fulfilling the word of the Lord as was prophesied by the mouth of his holy prophets.

47 And when Jerusalem was destroyed, many of the pure records and the scriptures of the Jews were also destroyed. Nevertheless, because the plates of brass were preserved by the hand of the Lord by way of the sons of Lehi, a more perfect record of the words of the prophets and also of the commandments of God were preserved for future generations.

48 And thus doth the Lord preserve the words that he giveth unto the children of men in all dispensations of time. And one day shall all the books which have been written by the commandment of the Lord be opened, and all the children of men shall see that the Lord hath been just and merciful unto his children by giving unto them, in every generation, his words and his

commandments by way of scripture, and also by the mouths of his holy prophets.

49 And in this way he shall judge all men according to the same laws and the same commandments that they received from Him in their own dispensation of time. And if these commandments were not preserved from one generation to the next, then the children of the future generations would have cause for contention when they stand before the Lord to be judged of their works in the flesh. For the children could claim innocence from the strict commandments of God that were given unto their fathers but not given unto them. And in this way doth the Lord turn the heart of the fathers to the children and the hearts of the children to their fathers, that they may all be judged by the same laws and by the same commandments.

50 For behold, the Lord judges all of his children according to the same laws, which are the eternal laws decreed from before the foundation of the world as the only laws of salvation whereby the children of men shall be saved in the kingdom of God.

51 And this is the importance and significance of the plates of brass that Nephi obtained from Laban.

52 And it was the wisdom of the Lord in the placement of Zoram as the servant of Laban, and also the way in which Zoram was used to procure the plates of brass without the blame being put upon the sons of Lehi by the Jews at Jerusalem.

53 For behold, the Lord commanded Lehi to once again send his sons to Jerusalem to convince Ishmael and his family to join them in the wilderness. And had the sons of Lehi returned unto the land of Jerusalem they would have been bound and brought before the judge of the land to be tried for the murder of Laban. But the Jews were convinced of the guilt of Zoram, because he had the keys to the vaults of Laban and was the only one who could obtain the plates. And in this way the Lord prepared a way that the sons of Lehi could once again return to Jerusalem.

54 And it came to pass that the sons of Lehi returned again unto Jerusalem to the house of Ishmael. But Zoram did not return with them again to Jerusalem and remained hidden in the tent of Lehi in the wilderness.

55 And it came to pass that the sons of Lehi persuaded Ishmael to leave the land of Jerusalem and join them in the wilderness. And Ishmael had also been affected by the words that were spoken by Zenos and Zenock. And he also knew of the wickedness and hypocrisy of the leaders of the church. And because of these things Ishmael had left the priesthood and was cast out of the church, and also his family was cast out with him.

56 And it came to pass that Ishmael and his family journeyed with the sons of Lehi down into the wilderness. And the family of Ishmael consisted of Ishmael, his wife, his two sons, and his five daughters. And this was again the wisdom and providence of the Lord in preparing a way whereby the family of Lehi would have spouses and families in the Promised Land. For behold, the sons of Lehi were four, and with Zoram, there were five men who had no spouse. And the daughters of Lehi were two, and there were two sons of Ishmael who did not have spouses. And in this way the Lord assured the posterity of Lehi and Ishmael in the land of promise.

57 And it came to pass that the sons and some of the daughters of Ishmael began to complain against their father for his foolishness in leaving Jerusalem and the comfort of their home and their riches. For behold, Ishmael was also a very rich man, yea his riches were even greater than those of Lehi.

58 And these children of Ishmael begin to stir up the elder brothers of Nephi, even Laman and Lemuel, to harden their hearts and desire once again to return to the land of their inheritance. And the two daughters of Ishmael, who had been chosen by Laman and Lemuel to be their wives, stirred up the brothers of Nephi, even so much that they rebelled again against the commandments of God and would not return to the wilderness unto the tent of their father.

59 And Nephi was exceedingly sorrowful for the continued rebellion of his brethren and stood forth and rebuked them for their rebellion. And the sons of Ishmael who were not present when an angel of the Lord rebuked Laman and Lemuel, stood before Nephi and derided him for desiring to be their leader. And these sons of Ishmael did inspire Laman and Lemuel to stand against their brother saying:

60 How is it that God would choose your

younger brother to rule over us? How can ye be convinced that your younger brother is blessed and called by God to be your head, and also our head? Ye are the elder brothers and have the right of leadership according to the customs and traditions of our fathers, which we know to be just and true.

61 And in this way were the sons of Ishmael and also two of his daughters swayed to harden the hearts of Laman and Lemuel to the point that they took Nephi and bound him with cords and were wont to leave him to be devoured by the beasts of the wilderness.

62 And it came to pass that the power of the Spirit of the Lord was with Nephi and he broke the bands that held him prisoner before his brethren. And Nephi stood forth and began to rebuke his brethren again for their doubts and their rebellion.

63 And Laman and Lemuel became even more hardened against Nephi and were desirous to murder him in the wilderness. And as they put forth their hands to take Nephi and put him to death, Rachael, one of the daughters of Ishmael, and also her mother, Habasha, pleaded with Laman and Lemuel that they would spare the life of Nephi. But Laman and Lemuel were past feeling and put forth their hands against Nephi.

64 And it came to pass that one of the sons of Ishmael, being of great strength, even of a strength greater than that of many men, began to have compassion on Nephi, and also compassion on his mother who he loved with all of his heart. And also Ishmael, being bent over with great age, did plead with his son to help Nephi. And this son of Ishmael, and his name was Barhanas, did take a hold on the brothers of Nephi, and with his exceedingly great strength, restrained Laman and Lemuel from murdering their brother.

65 And Barhanas became grieved because of his own wickedness and the hurt that he brought upon his mother and also upon his father. And the Spirit of the Lord was with Barhanas and he began to rebuke Laman and Lemuel, and also his other brother. And he knelt before Nephi and begged for his forgiveness and also for the forgiveness of the Lord. And seeing this enormous man kneeling before their brother, Laman and Lemuel knelt down before Nephi and also begged for his forgiveness. And thus we can see the influence that other men have over Laman and Lemuel, who of themselves possess no strength in righteousness.

66 And it came to pass that the sons of Lehi did continue their journey with the family of Ishmael down into the wilderness until they came to the tent of their father.

CHAPTER 5

Lehi and Ishmael continue their journey in the wilderness. Lehi continues to have visions and revelations. The Lord prepares a compass to guide them in the wilderness. Their sufferings and trials in the wilderness. Laman and Lemuel continue to rebel.

AND it came to pass that Lehi and Ishmael went into a tent together to pray to the Lord and receive inspiration from the Spirit as to where they should go and how they should govern their families while they were traveling in the wilderness towards the land that the Lord had promised unto them.

2 And the Spirit of the Lord spoke unto Ishmael that Lehi should lead their families down into the wilderness in the borders of the sea, which land was prepared with the many provisions that they would need. And Lehi was appointed as the leader of both his family and the family of Ishmael as they traveled in the wilderness.

3 And Ishmael gathered his family together and commanded them to follow Lehi and keep the commandments that he would receive from the Lord concerning them. And he also spake of the righteousness of Nephi, and that Nephi was also chosen by the Lord to lead this people after the death of Lehi. And Ishmael assured his family that if they kept the commandments of the Lord in all things, they would inherit a land of promise that was set aside for their posterity.

4 And Ishmael did these things because he knew that he would soon die and return to the God who gave him life. And he blessed each of his children and admonished them to be faithful to Lehi and also to Nephi. And it came to pass

that the children of Ishmael covenanted with their father that they would keep the commandments of the Lord and follow Lehi and Nephi wherever they would lead them.

5 And Lehi received many dreams and visions. And many of them were great and marvelous. Nevertheless, I, Mormon, do not write in this record all of the dreams and visions of Lehi, for they are many. But of one dream I do write in this abridgment. And I write this dream because of its exquisite beauty and symbolic representation of the goodness and the greatness of the love of God. And also because of its prophetic meaning concerning all of the children of men from the beginning of time to the end thereof.

6 For behold, Lehi saw in vision a large and spacious field that representeth the world and the vastness thereof. And Lehi wandered in a dark and dreary place for what seemed to him as the space of many hours—this representing the beginning of the life of Lehi and his transgression and ignorance as a High Priest appointed by the church at Jerusalem.

7 And Lehi prayed for forgiveness in his vision, even that the Lord would forgive him for his many sins and transgressions. And it came to pass that Lehi was introduced into the large and spacious field.

8 And in the midst of this field Lehi beheld a tree whose beauty and wonder surpassed any that he had ever seen before. And the fruit of the tree was delicious and desirous to make one happy—this signifying the gospel of Jesus Christ and the great joy it giveth to him who partaketh of it. And Lehi describeth the fruit as being sweet and most desirable above any that he had before tasted. And the whiteness, or purity thereof, exceeded anything that he had seen before.

9 And as he partook of the fruit of the tree, it brought him great joy, evensomuch that he called to his family that they might also partake of the delicious and desirable fruit. And his family stood at the head of a great river of water—which representeth the temptations and wickedness of the world. And Lehi was forced to cry aloud to his family that they might hear him above the sound of the mighty river running near unto the tree of which he spoke.

10 And it came to pass that his family came forth and partook of the fruit of the tree and rejoiced with him in the taste thereof. But Laman and Lemuel would not heed his voice, nor could they hear him above the roar of the turbulent water.

11 And it came to pass that Lehi beheld a rod of iron that extended the entire length of the river and led to the tree. And along the rod of iron was a straight and narrow path that also led to the tree of which he spake—this signifying the word of God and the straight and narrow path that one must follow in keeping His commandments.

12 And Lehi saw many other people pressing forward towards the path and the rod of iron that led to the tree whose fruit was desirable to make one happy. And many people grabbed hold of the rod of iron and pressed forth towards the tree. But as they pressed forward, mists of darkness arose and caused many to become afraid and lose their way.

13 But others he saw pressing forward steadfastly until they came to the tree and partook of the fruit thereof. Nevertheless, after they had partaken of the fruit of the tree, they cast their eyes across the river and lowered their heads in shame.

14 And Lehi beheld the cause of their shame. For behold, Lehi beheld across the river a large and spacious building that was filled with all manner of people, both young and old, male and female. And these people were dressed in fine clothes and accessories, and were pointing their fingers and mocking any who partook of the fruit of the tree.

15 And those who had partaken of the fruit and lowered their heads in shame did cast the fruit that they were eating away from them and fell into forbidden paths and were lost from sight.

16 And Lehi beheld many people pressing forth to gain entrance into the large and spacious building—which is a representation of the pride, and honor, and glory, and prestige of the world. And many others came forth and started out on the straight and narrow path, but were soon lost from sight because of the darkness caused by the mist that arose from the great river. And many were lost in the depths of the river, and also in a great fountain, that was filled by the river.

17 And there were others who came forth and

held fast to the rod of iron and paid no attention to the mocking and ridicule of the many people in the large and spacious building. And they came through the dark mists that rose up from the river and also from the fountain. And they came forth and partook of the fruit of the tree and were happy, nevertheless, their numbers were very few.

18 And now I, Mormon, write the things which I have learned from the vision of Lehi, and also from the Spirit who giveth understanding unto all those who obey the commandments of God and honor Him. And the Lord hath commanded me to write somewhat concerning the end of the world and the condition of the world as it hath been presented to Lehi in this glorious vision.

19 For behold, I have seen the beginning and the end of the world, having been shown these things and having understood these things by the gift and power of the Holy Spirit. And there are many things that I am forbidden to write, because the Lord shall try the faith of men and give understanding only to those who keep his commandments and have faith in him.

20 Behold, it is sad to report the situation of the children of men and their continued rebellion against the commandments of God and the gospel of His Son, which commandments are given for the happiness of His children. But because the pride and riches of the world entice many of the children of men to discount the commandments of God and deny the Holy Spirit, the whole world lieth in sin and groaneth under the burden of wickedness and unhappiness.

21 Behold, I have seen the great wickedness of the last days in which the Lord will set again a rod of iron and establish the path of righteousness that will lead his children to happiness. I have seen the majority of the children of men pursue the wealth and pride of the world more than they seek the Lord and his righteousness.

22 And because of the deceptions of Satan and his angels, the children of men know not that they are disobeying the commandments of God and wandering in forbidden paths. The mists of darkness are great and cause most of the children of men to lose their way. And those that come unto the tree of life and partake of the fruit thereof are misled by the precepts and pride of men, even until they discard the fruit that will assure them of their happiness.

23 Behold, the Savior of the world came to the Jews, and also to my fathers, the Nephites, and gave unto them the rod of iron and this straight and narrow path that they should follow, which is His gospel. And this gospel will cause all those who eat thereof to rejoice exceedingly. Nevertheless, the church of God in the last days hath become corrupt; yea, the leaders thereof and the condition thereof are like unto the church at Jerusalem at the time that our father Lehi was commanded to leave that great city and go into the wilderness.

24 And like the Jews of old, the members of the church of God put their trust in men and deny the literal gospel of Jesus Christ that he gave unto them in a like manner as he gave it unto the Jews and also unto the Nephites. In fine, the members think they are righteous because they are following the counsel of their leaders and performing the ordinances and commandments of the church.

25 Oh, my beloved brothers and sisters, do ye not understand that it is because of your wickedness that ye have ordinances and commandments given unto you by the church? Do ye not see the turmoil and strife in your lives because ye follow not the gospel of Jesus Christ? Why do ye dress yourselves in costly apparel and mock and ridicule those who are really the humble followers of Christ? Why do ye think money and the pursuit thereof is more important than the gentle commands that the Savior hath given unto you by way of his gospel?

26 My soul is burdened at this time because I know your fate. I have seen the frustration and turmoil in your hearts as ye try to live according to the commandments of God that are given unto you, which commandments are not of God, but of your church, or in other words, of the leaders of your church.

27 Behold, ye have the record of the Jews, and ye will also have this record, which the Lord hath commanded to be written as a second testament of his gospel. And now that ye have these two testimonies of the words of Christ, why are ye so blind that ye will not see? Yea, what were the words that the Lord spake to my fathers, the Nephites? Were they not the same words that he spake unto the Jews at Jerusalem?

28 Oh my beloved brothers and sisters, read his words. Ponder his gospel and pray for understanding. Your church meetings, your ordinances, your genealogies, your tithes, your offerings, your temples, your churches, your rituals, and your prayers are not sanctioned by the Lord or His Spirit, because all of these things cause you to reject and deny the true gospel of Jesus Christ. Read the words of Isaiah that the prophet Zenock spoke unto the Jews at Jerusalem and liken them unto yourselves, for your plight is much worse than theirs.

29 And now, I, Mormon, do prophesy unto you in the name of the Lord, even Jesus Christ, that these things that I write to you at this time shall be withheld from you until there be found some who are righteous enough to read and understand them.

30 For behold, the Lord hath shown me that these things shall be withheld from the children of men because of wickedness. Nevertheless, much of my abridgment of the plates of Nephi will be translated and given unto the world. But these words of prophecy will be taken because of wickedness, and will not be given unto the children of men until the church of God hath become like unto the large and spacious building of which Lehi hath spoken in his vision.

31 And at that time, these things shall come forth as a testament against the church of God and its wickedness. And when these things that have been withheld come forth, the righteous of the church shall have these things and understand them and leave that great and spacious building and grasp to the rod of iron that will lead them to the fruit of the tree of happiness.

32 Behold, it hath been shown unto me that there are many in the church of God that shall deny these things and claim that they are not the words of God, but the words of the devil to deceive the people of the church. And this they will say because these things shall not come by way of the church of the last days, but shall come by another way that the Lord shall prepare.

33 And when ye receive these things, I would ask you to ponder them carefully and pray for the Spirit to bear witness of their truthfulness. Compare these words to the words of Jesus Christ, even those that He gave unto the Jews at Jerusalem and also unto the Nephites, who are my ancestors, and who also have denied them and cast them aside causing their own destruction.

34 Yea, compare the gospel of Jesus Christ to the gospel of your church. Where are the desires of your hearts placed, my beloved brothers and sisters? Doth not your church cause many to suffer because of your pride and your arrogance? Have ye truly tasted of the fruit of happiness of which Lehi speaketh by following the commandments of the church? I say unto you that ye cannot be happy.

35 Yea, there are many of you who have riches and power and the glory of the world, and there are many more of you who pursue after these things. But are these things providing you the sweetness of the fruit of the gospel of Jesus Christ? And again, I say unto you, that these things are not blessings from God. Behold, the Lord doth not bless one of his children so that this child will be able to set him or herself above another, whether it is in riches, or in power, or in glory. But all are the same in the gospel of Jesus Christ.

36 The church of Jesus Christ should teach his gospel and only those things that he taught when he was ministering unto the people. Anything other than these things is not of his gospel, but is of the precepts and commandments of men.

37 And now I, Mormon, will proceed with the account of Lehi and his family in the wilderness. Behold, it is my desire to continue to preach repentance to all of those who receive this record and read my writings. Nevertheless, I know the Lord hath prepared other means whereby he will prepare the righteous for His coming, yea, even for his arrival in all the power and glory of the Father. And I have been commanded to abridge the record of the Nephites, and so I continue:

38 And it came to pass that when Lehi awoke in the morning he found a ball of curious workmanship outside the door of his tent. And Lehi took the ball in his hands and wondered on its creation and also on its exquisite beauty and craftsmanship, of such he had never before seen.

39 And the ball had two pointers that pointed in a determined direction according to the design of the compass. Also, there were words that appeared on the ball that gave specific directions to the person who held the ball. And when my father Lehi held the ball in his hands, the pointers began to move until they became stationary. And the Spirit of the Lord came to Lehi and commanded him to follow the course in the wilderness directed by the pointers in the ball.

40 And Laman took interest in the curious ball and took it in his hands to examine its beauty and curious workmanship. And immediately the pointers began to spin and would not come to rest at any given direction. And when Laman gave the ball again to Lehi, the pointers once again pointed steadfastly in the direction that they should go.

41 And it came to pass that Lehi led his company into the wilderness according to the directions of the ball. And they carried seeds of every kind so that they could plant the seeds when they came to the land where the Lord would lead them. Nevertheless, they were not able to stay in one place long enough for them to plant the seeds and partake of their harvest.

42 And the Lord commanded Lehi not to make any fire in the wilderness; for he was warned by the Lord that there was an army of men sent from Jerusalem in search of Zoram and the brass plates, and any fire might lead the army to them. And Lehi and his family and Ishmael and his family ate their meat raw in the wilderness. And the Lord blessed their meat and made it sweet to the taste.

43 And it came to pass that Sariah gave birth to a son. And they called his name Jacob. And Sariah gave birth to another son in the wilderness, and they called his name Joseph. And Sariah bore these two sons to Lehi in the wilderness without the comforts that she was accustomed to at her home in Jerusalem. And the Lord blessed Sariah and her daughters, and also the wife of Ishmael and her daughters with much strength and stamina, even so much that they were strong like unto the men with whom they journeyed, and this because of the raw meat that they did eat.

44 And Nephi and his brothers took the daughters of Ishmael to wife. And Zoram was also married to a daughter of Ishmael. Thus were the families of Lehi and Ishmael divided. Yet, they had everything in common according to the commandments of the Lord. And they also followed the commandments and directions that Lehi received from the Spirit, and also from the ball which directed them into the most fertile parts of the wilderness where they could find an abundance of food.

45 And it came to pass that they traveled many days in the wilderness before they pitched their tents and rested for the space of a few days. Nevertheless, the Lord commanded Lehi to continue to travel until they came to a land bordering the seashore, which they called Bountiful.

46 And there were many times when food was scarce. And during these times Laman and Lemuel and some of the children of Ishmael began to murmur because of the hardness of their travels and their afflictions in the wilderness.

47 And Ishmael grew old and died in the wilderness. And the children of Ishmael began to complain against Lehi because of the loss of their father.

48 And Lehi began to murmur against the Lord also. And when Lehi doubted the Lord, the pointers on the ball stopped working and no steady direction could be found. And the families wandered aimlessly for many days in the wilderness.

49 And it came to pass that they had eaten all of the provisions that they had with them, and also the men were unsuccessful in their attempts to hunt wild game.

50 And their murmurings became exceeding. And the murmurings of Lehi became more frequent before the Lord. But Nephi stayed faithful and full of trust in the Lord. And he stood forth and rebuked his father with the gentleness and respect that he was commanded to give unto his father. And Nephi asked his father to repent of his murmurings and take the ball again in his hand and ask the Lord to point the directors where he must go to hunt for food.

51 And it came to pass that Lehi humbled himself before the Lord and repented of his murmurings. And Lehi took the ball into his hands and the pointers began to work and to point in a steady direction where Nephi was to go in search of food.

52 And it came to pass that Nephi was successful in acquiring enough food for everyone. And this brought more faith and joy to the families of Lehi and Ishmael.

53 And the Lord chastised Lehi for his murmurings and commanded him to look to the ball for directions always. And the Lord commanded Lehi to remain faithful always and keep his commandments in all things, and if he would do these things, his family would never again want for anything.

54 And there appeared on the ball writing from time to time. And this writing gave instruction to Lehi in the ways of the Lord. Nevertheless, the pointers or the written directors would not work without faith and adherence to the commandments of the Lord.

55 And it came to pass that Laman and Lemuel and their wives and one of the sons of Ishmael did rebel and murmur exceedingly against Lehi and Nephi because of their afflictions in the wilderness. And they were desirous to return to the land of Jerusalem. But Nephi attempted to reason with them to no avail. And Laman and Lemuel began to stir up the hearts of the others to anger against Nephi and their father, evensomuch that they sought once again to take the life of Nephi and also the life of their father Lehi.

56 And the Lord knew of the hardness of the hearts of Laman and Lemuel. And the Lord also knew that without his divine help, Laman and Lemuel would accomplish their design and kill their father and their brother.

57 And the Lord spoke forth from the heaven and caused the earth to shake around where Laman and Lemuel stood. And they fell to the ground, and also many of the others who stood next to them.

58 And the Lord spoke unto them, saying: Laman and Lemuel why have ye cursed your brother and your father and sought to take away their lives? Know ye not that I chose these? And I have chosen them to lead this people to a land of promise which I have kept from the knowledge of the rest of my children that it might be a land of promise unto those who serve me and keep my commandments.

59 Behold, I have sent an angel unto both of you and ye have heard the angel speak unto you. Behold, ye have felt the power of my Spirit that your younger brother doth possess. Yet, ye still doubt my commandments and ye seek to take away his life. Yea, I have chosen him to rule over thee, and this because of his righteousness.

60 And now I say unto you, if ye put forth your hand to slay my servants, I will smite you even to the earth from whence ye were made, and ye shall be no more.

61 And now ye have heard my voice, and a commandment I give unto you that ye shall follow the counsel of your father, and also of your younger brother, and ye shall be saved. But if ye continue to deny me and my power, which both of them have in abundance from me, ye shall be destroyed; and if your posterity shall deny me they shall be cursed throughout all generations of time and throughout all eternity. And thus have I commanded it.

62 And it came to pass that when Laman and Lemuel received strength again that they might stand, they repented of the things that they had done and also of the things that were in their hearts. But they continued to deny the Spirit of the Lord and believe that Nephi had an evil power that they could not understand. Yet they feared Nephi and also their father. And their fear was for their own lives and not for the salvation of their souls.

63 And now I, Mormon, being commanded by the Spirit, give an explanation of the compass that was given unto Lehi and his family to guide them in the wilderness.

64 For behold, all of the mysteries of godliness are given unto those who worship him and obey his commandments. But to others are given signs and symbols and representations that are not easy to understand; and this the Lord hath done because of the hardness of their hearts and their lack of faith in understanding the promptings of the Holy Spirit, which are given to all of his children equally.

65 And because of these signs and symbols and representations, many of his children stumble and fall, and many are led away by the enticings and the promptings of the devil, whose only desire is to confuse and deceive all that shall give heed unto him.

66 For behold, the compass that was given unto Lehi is like unto the Spirit of God who giveth instruction to those who are faithful and heed his commandments and warnings. And those that do not heed the commandments of God, whether they are written commandments that can be read, or commandments given unto them by the power of His Spirit, shall not receive directions from the Spirit during the course of their lives.

67 Therefore, the compass is like unto the Holy Spirit that leadeth the faithful throughout their course in life. And this Spirit is always with them as long as they heed the commandments and warnings that it giveth unto them.

68 And those who do not heed the promptings of the Holy Spirit will be left unto themselves. And these shall wander throughout their lives as Lehi and his family wandered—aimlessly and helplessly—when they had not the compass of the Lord to guide them.

69 And now, I, Mormon, give unto all those who shall read these things some counsel and warning pertaining to those things that are received through the gift of the Holy Spirit, like unto those things which were written upon the compass that the Lord prepared for Lehi and his family.

70 Behold, the Lord hath caused his gospel to be written so that there can be no confusion among men as to its meaning. Nevertheless, there shall be many, who, being deceived by the devil, shall prophesy and command those things that are not revelations from God, as if they were.

71 For this reason the Lord hath commanded me and others, who were eyewitnesses to his life and ministry, to only record those things which are most pertinent to his gospel.

72 And this gospel shall be written the same in this record as well as it is written in the record that shall come forth from the Jews.

73 And with these two records shall all heresy and false doctrine be confounded. Behold, no revelation that cometh forth from the mouth of God by the power of His Spirit shall contradict or add to the words that Jesus spoke both to the Jews at Jerusalem, and also to the Nephites and Lamanites that were spared in the land of Bountiful.

75 And again I say unto you, search these words and live by them. For behold, only in them shall be found the true commandments and counsel of God.

CHAPTER 6

Nephi is commanded to build a ship to cross the waters to the land of promise. Rebellion at sea. Their arrival in the promised land.

AND it came to pass that Lehi and his family reached the great waters that separate the great lands that the Lord hath prepared for the inhabitants of the world, on which the sons and daughters of man reside.

2 And now it is expedient for me to explain that there were many things written by the hand of Nephi upon plates of ore pertaining to the struggles and sufferings of his father Lehi and his family in the wilderness. Nevertheless, the plates that I have made to abridge the record of Nephi are few, and therefore, I cannot write even a small part of their experiences in the wilderness.

3 And it came to pass that Nephi was commanded to build a ship to take Lehi and his children, and also the children of Ishmael, across the many waters into the land of promise.

4 And it came to pass, that once again, Laman and Lemuel, and one of the sons of Ishmael, and some of the daughters of Ishmael, began to mock Nephi, and they were desirous to return to the land of their inheritance.

5 And they were again desirous to take the life of Nephi and their father Lehi, and take their wives and their children and return to the land of Jerusalem.

6 And it came to pass that Zoram stood forth and took up a staff against the enemies of Nephi. For behold, Zoram was a great and loyal friend to Nephi, and the Spirit of the Lord was with him as it was with Nephi.

7 And Zoram fought with great strength and dexterity against Laman and Lemuel and one of the sons of Ishmael, Barhanas not being present at the time.

8 And it came to pass that these enemies of Nephi were astounded and amazed at the strength of Zoram, who with the end of his staff defended every blow that they put forth against Nephi.

9 And it came to pass that Zoram struck down the son of Ishmael and was about to strike down Laman and Lemuel, but Nephi stood forth and embraced his friend and begged for the safety of his brothers.

10 Behold, never hath one man been more dedicated as a friend than Zoram was to Nephi. And Nephi loved Zoram as his own brother. And he did also love Sam, who had also stood against his enemies for his protection.

11 And it came to pass that Nephi began to construct the ship according to the promptings of the Spirit.

12 And it came to pass that as the ship began to take form, even a most curious form that had never before been seen among men, Laman and Lemuel were exceedingly amazed and gave up their plans to harm their brother, even so much that they did offer their hands to labor on its construction.

13 And when the ship was completed, they were struck with awe by the craftsmanship and preciseness of its construction, and they praised their younger brother for what he had accomplished.

14 And Lehi was pleased that his older sons were once again unified with Nephi, and he had great hope that the Lord would spare them from future wickedness.

15 But in this Lehi was sorely disappointed. For behold, his sons did once again rebel against their brother and sought to take away his life after they had embarked on the great waters and journeyed towards the promised land.

16 For it came to pass that they set out on the great waters not knowing which way that they should go, having faith in the Lord that he would lead them safely to the land of promise.

17 And Nephi had constructed a platform that was affixed to the bow of the ship. And Nephi was commanded by the Spirit to place the compass thereon and secure it that it might not be removed until they reached dry land again.

18 And Nephi did that which the Spirit had instructed him to do.

19 And it came to pass that once again Laman and Lemuel and one of the sons and some of the daughters of Ishmael rebelled against Lehi and Nephi and were desirous to kill him and take control of the ship.

20 And they did confine Sam and Barhanas and Zoram below the deck of the ship so that they could not come to the aid of Nephi. And they bound Nephi and held him captive for many days.

21 And because of their wickedness, the compass stopped working. And it came to pass that the Lord caused an exceedingly great storm to rise up and threaten the destruction of the ship and all of those on board.

22 And Laman and Lemuel were desirous to throw Nephi into the great waters, believing him to be the cause of all of their problems.

23 And it came to pass that as Laman and Lemuel were about to throw Nephi into the depths of the water, Lehi stood forth on the deck of the ship and held strong to the coat of his son Nephi.

24 And in a loud voice he cried through the fierce wind that he would not be a witness to the death of his beloved son, and that if Laman and Lemuel would throw Nephi into the depths of the great waters, then he also would go with him.

25 And it came to pass that Laman and Lemuel would not hearken unto their father, but took hold upon him that they might throw him also into the waters.

26 And Sira, the daughter of Lehi, and the younger sister of Laman and Lemuel, forced her way onto the deck of the ship from the place where she was being held and guarded by a son of Ishmael. And she took hold of the bosom of her father and would not let him go. And she threatened to throw herself into the water if Laman and Lemuel did not let go of her father and her brother.

27 And Sira was the wife of Barhanas, one of the sons of Ishmael. And she was exceedingly beautiful, insomuch that her husband loved her with all of his soul, and he was also a friend to Nephi.

28 And it came to pass that upon hearing the desperate pleas of his wife, Barhanas broke forth from the place where he was being held and took hold of Laman and Lemuel and was about to throw them into the depths of the ocean.

29 And the hearts of Laman and Lemuel were filled with fear and they pleaded for their lives. But Nephi was bound and could not stop Barhanas from doing to them what they had wanted to do unto him. Nevertheless, Sira pleaded with her husband for the lives of her brothers. And Barhanas did listen to the pleas of his wife and released Laman and Lemuel.

30 And Sira lifted her father off the deck of the ship and tended to his bruises, which were great due to the harsh treatment that he had received from Laman and Lemuel, and also because of his old age.

31 And Barhanas broke the bonds that held Nephi. And as soon as Nephi was released from his bonds, the compass once again began to work. And it came to pass that Nephi prayed that the Lord would forgive the actions of his brothers, and that they might reach the land of promise safely.

32 And it came to pass that the Lord had mercy upon the brothers of Nephi, but not because of their own righteousness, but because of his love of Nephi. And also that his words might be fulfilled which were promised to Lehi, that all of his children would inherit a land of promise.

33 And it came to pass that after many days and much suffering at sea because of the wickedness of Laman and Lemuel, they reached the promised land.

34 And now I, Mormon, cannot write the words to describe the exceeding joy that Lehi and his family felt when they reached the promised land. For it was a beautiful land, full of many plants, and there were many animals in the forest that were of great use to Lehi and those that were with him.

35 And it came to pass that they found gold and silver and all manner of precious stones and ores that were beneficial to them.

36 And there could not be found any other land upon the earth that could compare to the wondrous beauty and exceedingly abundant food and raiment that was found in the land that the Lord had set aside for those who heeded him and obeyed his commandments.

CHAPTER 7

The death of Lehi. Laman and Lemuel continue their rebellion against Nephi. The formation of two groups of people: the Nephites and the Lamanites. Wars and contention begin among them. Nephi is commanded to hand down the record of his people to his brother, Jacob. The succession of the plates is set forth.

AND it came to pass that Nephi and his brethren began to plant the seeds that they had brought with them from the land of Jerusalem. And they began to till the earth and harvest the fruit thereof, insomuch that there began to be an abundance of all things throughout the land.

2 And Lehi began to weaken; and before his death, he called all of his children together, and even those children of Ishmael did gather to hear the words of Lehi, their father Ishmael having died during their journeys in the wilderness.

3 Behold, Ishmael was a loyal friend to Lehi until his last day. And Lehi had many visions concerning Ishmael that warned him of the consequences if he or his children failed to follow the counsel and guidance of Lehi and his son, Nephi.

4 And Sariah had taken Habasha, the wife of Ishmael, and given her unto Lehi that he might care for her for the remainder of her days.

5 Therefore, Lehi was considered as a father to the sons and daughters of Ishmael, especially by those who had not rebelled against Nephi during their journeys through the wilderness.

6 And Nephi took Rachael, the daughter of Habasha and Ishmael, as his wife; and she bore four daughters unto him. And they were all beautiful like unto their mother and wise like unto their father. And the daughters of Nephi were greatly desired by many of the sons of Laman, Lemuel, and also by the grandsons of Ishmael. Nevertheless, they were very wise in their youth and wanted no man until they were old enough to choose for themselves by their own wisdom.

7 And it came to pass that the daughters of Nephi chose the sons of Zoram, and also one of the sons of Barhanas. And this they did because of their great love and respect for their father—Zoram and Barhanas having been lifelong friends and protectors of their father, Nephi.

Lehi 7:8–7:24

8 And it came to pass that the sons of Laman and Lemuel were angry with the daughters of Nephi, for they were exceedingly desirous to have them as their wives. And Laman and Lemuel complained against Nephi, that he had put himself above them, insomuch that his daughters thought themselves above their sons.

9 And this was a source of much contention during the last days of Lehi, he being very weak and near unto death.

10 And it came to pass that Lehi called all of his children to come before him; and when they had come before him, he spoke to each one and prophesied many things concerning them.

11 And it came to pass that Lehi left his blessing on Nephi, that he should be the leader of the people, and that Laman and Lemuel and the sons of Ishmael should honor him and obey him in all things whatsoever the Lord should command him.

12 And it came to pass that after the death of Lehi, Laman and Lemuel rebelled against their brother for the last time. For behold, the Lord will suffer the wicked to dwell among the righteous that the righteous might be an example and an influence unto them. Nevertheless, he will not suffer the righteous to be destroyed completely because of the actions of the wicked.

13 And it came to pass that Laman and Lemuel began to separate themselves from the people of Nephi; and they called themselves Lamanites. And the people of Nephi were called Nephites.

14 And the Nephites were an industrious people who engaged in all manner of commerce and industry for the benefit of all the people.

15 And the Lamanites became lazy and adulterous and would not wear clothes to cover their naked bodies, thus allowing the sun to change their skin to a darkness that was passed on to their children. And after each generation, the skin of the Lamanites and their children became darker, evensomuch that there began to be a great distinction between the Nephites and the Lamanites.

16 For behold, the Nephites wore clothing that protected their bodies from the light of the sun, therefore, they were a white and delightsome people.

17 But because of their wickedness, the Lamanites developed a tolerance to the light of the sun and in this way darkened their own bodies. And thus were they fulfilling the words of Lehi that he prophesied against them saying: Oh, my pain is great because of the visions I have had concerning Laman and Lemuel. For the Lord hath shown me the curse that shall come upon them, even that they shall become a dark and loathsome people, except they repent and obey the commandments of the Lord.

18 And it came to pass that the Nephites began to hire guards to watch the Lamanites and keep them from stealing the fruits of their industry and labor.

19 And Nephi pleaded with his brethren to repent and turn again to the Lord that he might have mercy on them and save them from their own destruction.

20 But Laman and Lemuel refused to listen to their younger brother and wanted nothing more to do with him. And the Lamanites rose up against Nephi and his people and began to slay the guards that were set to keep the Lamanites from stealing from the Nephites.

21 And Nephi knew in his heart that his brethren were past feeling, and that the Spirit of the Lord no longer dwelt among them. And in his anguish, Nephi cried unto the Lord:

22 Oh, my Eternal Father, how can I make the choice to take the lives of my brethren that I might preserve my own life and the lives of my own children? How can the devil have so much power over the hearts of men that they cannot seek to live in peace and harmony one with the other? Why is it my burden to take the lives of the wicked that the lives of the righteous might be preserved? How many times must Thy great mercy be bestowed upon my brethren before they will repent and work righteousness before Thee? Please, my Father, give me the strength to do what I know must be done.

23 And it came to pass that Nephi commanded his best foundry men and his strongest guards to take the sword of Laban and construct other swords like unto it that they might protect themselves from the Lamanites.

24 And the Nephites did arm themselves and began to kill any Lamanite that attempted to rob and steal from them.

25 And the Lamanites were sore afraid of the weapons of the Nephites, and they fled into the wilderness.

26 Now, I, Mormon, do not know what happened among the Lamanites from the time that they fled from before the Nephites and went into the wilderness, to the time that Ammon traveled among them in the land of Lehi-Nephi. For behold, they did not keep records according to the commandment that Nephi had received from the Lord.

27 Nevertheless, I know they became a wild and ferocious people who despised the Nephites and tried many times to war against them only to be driven back and slain. And they were taught by their fathers that Nephi had stolen their authority and had driven them out of the land of their inheritance, which was the most choice land in all the land roundabout, and was promised to their fathers, the elder brothers of Nephi. And thus did they harbor an exceeding hatred for the Nephites.

28 And instead of becoming an industrious, hardworking people, the Lamanites hunted wild beasts in the wilderness and depended on plunder to support them in their needs.

29 And it came to pass that the Nephites began to prosper exceedingly throughout the land. And they began to build machines and all manner of devices to help them produce their food, and manufacture their clothes, and provide them with many precious things. And their armies grew and became strong in their weaponry, insomuch that there was no threat from the Lamanites again.

30 And Nephi instructed his people to build a house of God like unto the temples of old. And this he did that he might keep the people in remembrance of the law of Moses, which they had covenanted to honor and obey.

31 And Nephi was the High Priest having been ordained by his father, Lehi, who had received his authority from the church at Jerusalem at the time when he was a member of the High Priesthood. And according to the law of Moses, this priesthood was passed down from generation to generation by way of a sacred anointing, which is the ordination that Lehi received from his father Jeshron.

32 And according to this law of Moses, only the Lord can give or take away the authority of this priesthood; the authority of which can be bestowed upon men whether they are righteous or wicked. Nevertheless, this power can only be controlled and granted to the bearer upon the principles of righteousness. Behold, though there have been many wicked men who have had the authority of the priesthood bestowed upon them, none of these had the power associated with this authority, which power can only come from God.

33 And only by the authority of tradition, or in other words, the lineage of the priesthood, can the ordinances of the law of Moses be performed and sanctioned by the church of God.

34 Nevertheless, in many instances the Lord will call prophets and ordain them by his own hand. And these prophets have all the authority to act with the power of God, having not been sanctioned by the church and the law of Moses, but being sanctified by the Holy Spirit, which sanctification is binding on all those who call themselves children of God.

35 For behold, the church of God will not always be righteous. Yea, it will not always follow the commandments of God and will suffer itself to become corrupt through the craftiness and wickedness of men.

36 For this reason the Lord calleth prophets who are not members of the church of God, who are sent to preach repentance unto the church. Nevertheless, these prophets have no authority from God to lead the church, which hath been set up according to the lower law of Moses, which Jesus Christ fulfilled during his earthly ministry among the Jews.

37 Yea, the lower law is necessary for the perfection of the children of God, to teach them the things that they need to know in order to prepare themselves to receive the higher laws, which are the laws of heaven.

38 And Moses taught the children of Israel the higher law of God, but they could not abide therein; and therefore, they were given a lower law that they could abide by until they were ready to receive the higher laws of salvation.

39 And in the condescension of God was the lower law fulfilled and the higher law given unto the children of men.

40 Nevertheless, this higher law was rejected by the people; and the lower laws were once again established for the edification and purification of the children of God until they are worthy enough to accept and live the higher laws of heaven.

41 And now, I, Mormon, am desirous that ye know the whole law and the other mysteries that relate to it. But behold, the Spirit hath constrained me from writing more than what I have just written. And if the children of men have the desire to know the mysteries pertaining to the priesthood and the higher laws of heaven, then I would beseech you to ask God, in faith, living by every word and commandment that he hath given you through his Son, Jesus Christ.

42 And it came to pass that Nephi was not allowed to teach the people the higher laws of heaven. Yea, he was commanded to construct temples and churches among them so that the people could go and partake of the sacrifices and ordinances that pertain to the lower law of Moses.

43 And it came to pass that the people wanted Nephi to be their king and their lawgiver, and this because of the tremendous love that they had for Nephi. And it became customary among them to make the High Priest their king also. And thus was Nephi their king and their High Priest.

44 And Nephi taught many things unto his people and established righteous laws that brought equality to every man and woman throughout his kingdom.

45 And Nephi had many visions and dreams like unto his father, Lehi, and he prophesied much concerning the Jews and the Nephites and also concerning the Lamanites.

46 And again, I, Mormon, am constrained by the Spirit to write all the prophecies of Nephi, wanting to save these plates for the more secular part of the history of the children of Lehi, in an attempt to demonstrate how easily the children of God are led to destruction because they will not heed the counsel and commandments of God.

47 For it came to pass that Nephi grew old and was about to die, and not having any sons to confer the kingdom upon, he was desirous to confer the kingdom upon his brother Jacob.

48 But Jacob refused to become a king among the Nephites; for behold, Jacob began to see great wickedness swell up in the hearts of the Nephites because of their exceedingly great riches and prosperity, and therefore, he wanted to dedicate his time to the preservation of the bounteous spiritual blessings that were bestowed upon the Nephite people. And Jacob knew that the only way the people were going to have continual peace and prosperity was for them to keep the commandments of God in all things.

49 And it was the desire of Jacob to spend the rest of his life working in the church as a High Priest, continually bringing the people to a remembrance of their sins and iniquities that they might repent and be saved.

50 And it came to pass that both Jacob and Joseph were anointed and consecrated by the hand of Nephi as High Priests and teachers of the people.

51 And the people elected another leader to be their king. And this king was also called Nephi in honor of their beloved first king, who was Nephi, the son of Lehi. And from that time forth were the kings of the Nephites called by the title of Nephi.

CHAPTER 8

The Nephite kings keep the record of the people. The Nephites become corrupt, and wars with the Lamanites increase. Many prophets are sent to preach repentance to the people—they are rejected by the Nephites. The Lamanites begin to take the possessions and lands of the Nephites.

AND it came to pass that the records of the people of Nephi and their history were entrusted into the hands of the kings of the Nephites who handed them down to the next king that was called to reign by the voice of the people. And there were many records which were written upon plates of ore. And I, Mormon, have been entrusted with these records, which have been given unto me by Ammaron.

2 And I have read them all and have taken my abridgment from them. Nevertheless, my abridgment is a very small part of all the records of the Nephites. And under the direction of the Spirit and through Its inspiration I know what things I should write upon these plates, which I have made with my own hands. And these plates are made of gold mixed with another ore that we are familiar with, and therefore these plates are of great worth. Nevertheless, I did not choose these ores because of their worth, but because of their lightness and the easiness of writing upon them, and also that they might last forever.

3 Behold, I am an old man and cannot transport all of the plates of Nephi wherever I should go to hide myself from the Lamanites who are continually pursuing me.

4 And I have hidden the plates in a large crevasse of a rock, and it is in this crevasse that I am writing this abridgment. And I have spent many days searching through all the plates of Nephi and other plates that have fallen into my hands that I might know what I should abridge and what I should not.

5 And I do not leave this rock except when I am hungry or thirsty and am in need of sustenance. Nevertheless, Moroni, my son, knoweth where I am hiding and he visiteth me from time to time bringing me food and news about the war with the Lamanites.

6 And now I will continue with the abridgment of the history of the people of Nephi: For behold, many years passed in peace and happiness among the Nephites. And all of their enemies were swept away from among them.

7 And it came to pass that the people began to spend their days in pursuit of gold and silver, and other precious ores that gave no sustenance to their lives, except to their pride and to their arrogance.

8 For behold, the people began to believe that their gold and their silver, and their precious things were gifts from God because of their righteousness. And the church of God was becoming like unto the church that was at Jerusalem when Lehi was commanded to leave.

9 And it came to pass that the people began to separate themselves into groups according to the amount of gold and silver and precious things that they had accumulated.

10 Now this would not have been such a gross sin in the eyes of the Lord had it been an accumulation that was made through their own industry and hard work. But their accumulation of wealth was from the sweat and work of others who were the less fortunate and had not the ability to accumulate wealth due to the scarcity of the gold, and the silver, and the precious ores; and also because they were the more ignorant part of the people. Nevertheless, these more ignorant ones were more righteous in keeping the commandments of God—their ignorance coming in worldly affairs only.

11 And it came to pass that a small group of Nephites had accumulated most of the wealth among them, and the other Nephites were forced to labor continuously for this minority who owned the machinery and the tools and the businesses and the crafts on which they were all dependent for their survival.

12 And thus did the Nephites divide themselves into a rich class and a poor class, thus denying the commandments of God in which they were commanded to be equal in all things.

13 And the rich class refused to do manual labor, but hired out all manner of work that required sweat to those who were poor and in need of that which the rich provided for them.

14 And the rich controlled the guards that kept watch at the borders of the city. And the leaders of the people began to become rich, leading the people to believe that because they were leaders, they deserved more sustenance than others.

15 And it came to pass that the guards began to exercise authority over the Nephites under the direction of the rich. And any Nephite who complained against the rich was arrested by the guards and brought forth to be judged according to the Nephite system of justice, which was set up and controlled by the rich.

16 Nevertheless, the guards had no authority over the church, nor did they have any authority over the High Priests, who had also set themselves up as leaders of the people and convinced the people that they deserved more sustenance than the average Nephite, like unto the rich class. And in this way did the leaders of the church of God begin to separate themselves from the people.

17 And in this way did pride and envying enter into the hearts of the Nephites. And this pride began to threaten and destroy the very foundation of truth and righteousness, which foundation was set up in the beginning by Nephi and his brothers Jacob and Joseph, and which was based upon the commandments of God.

18 For behold, because the church was not accountable to the laws of justice established by the Nephites and enforced by the guards, the leaders of the church began to become the most wicked of all the leaders of the people. Yea, because these leaders were not accountable to the people, they were left to do whatever their hearts desired. And the church became more wicked than the church at Jerusalem at the time of Lehi and his ministry unto the Jews.

19 And it came to pass that the Lord sent prophets to the Nephite people to preach repentance unto them and turn the hearts of the people back to righteousness.

20 And the prophets were rejected and cast out from among the people. And those prophets that would not leave their preaching were arrested and brought before the judges of the land. And the judges found no just cause to hold the prophets, nevertheless, these judges held the prophets bound and commanded their guards to carry them forth to the High Priests of the church to see what the church would do with them.

21 And it came to pass that the prophets were mocked by the leaders of the church and were commanded by these leaders to repent of their sins—the High Priests believing that the prophets were sinning by preaching against the church, and that they were pretending to be prophets of God to stir up the people to anger. And the High Priests ridiculed the prophets for condemning the people for living in sin when the people were enjoying many years of peace and happiness.

22 And it came to pass that the people rejected the prophets and would not listen to their words. And the Nephites hardened their hearts against the prophets because their leaders told them to pay no attention to anyone who was not ordained and sustained by the church.

23 And in this way did the devil gain control over the hearts and blind the minds of the Nephites to the truth; in other words, the people were led by the precepts of men, which denied the power of the priesthood of the Son of God that can only be controlled upon the principles of righteousness.

24 And they were all deceived, save a few only, who humbly followed the law of Moses and kept the commandments of God. Nevertheless, many of these humble ones were led that they did err because they did listen to the precepts of men and follow the dictates of the leaders of the church who had convinced them that they were righteous, instead of listening to the peaceful words that were given unto these humble ones by the Spirit of God.

25 And it came to pass that there was a man living among the Nephites and his name was Mosiah. And Mosiah was a direct descendent of Zoram, the servant of Laban who delivered the brass plates unto Nephi and his brethren.

26 And Mosiah listened to the voice of the prophets and recognized the wickedness of the pride and envying of his people because of their exceeding possessions, and their gold, and their silver and the classes in to which they had divided themselves.

27 And it came to pass that the Lord sent an angel unto the house of Mosiah to speak with him in a dream. And Mosiah became heavy of heart and his countenance fell because of the things that he both saw and heard in his dream.

28 For behold, Mosiah beheld the downfall of the Nephite nation and its captivity by the Lamanites who were living just outside the borders of the Nephite land and were readying their armies to come up with their numerous hosts to destroy the Nephites.

29 And the Nephites were unaware that the Lamanites were amassing forces just outside the borders of their land. For behold, their time was spent in continual pursuit of riches. Yea, even every day did the Nephites count their riches and spend the majority of their time devising ways and means that they might gain more riches. And thus were they engaged while their enemies were planning their destruction.

30 And it came to pass that Mosiah went forth among those of his own family in faith that he could convince them of their wickedness before the Lord. And his family rejected the words of Mosiah and mocked and chastised him saying:

31 Behold, thou art envious of our riches and the success that we have had because thy own riches have not come to thee as ours have. For behold, thy struggles and efforts are barely sufficient to bring food to thy family and to thy wife, who even at this time is desirous to find another husband who can support her with the fine things with which the Lord hath blessed us.

32 And is it not a blessing from the Lord that we have acquired these things? Is it not that we have paid our offerings and tithing to the church, that the Lord hath promised us these riches? And thou art poor of thy own will and choosing; for behold, thou spendeth thy time in what thou perceiveth are the problems of others, when thy own problems are not attended to. Is this not the reason that thy wife desireth to leave thee? Doth she not pay her tithes and offerings to the church in faith, believing that the Lord will bless her with the things that we have been blessed with?

33 And it came to pass that Mosiah did not give heed unto the words of the people, for he knew that they were deceived by their own pride and also by their associations with the church and its leaders.

34 And it came to pass that Mosiah departed into the wilderness taking with him all those who were humble and contrite, yea, even all those who believed the words of the prophets and were convinced of the sins of the church and also of their own sins.

35 And it came to pass that Mosiah and his followers traveled deep into the wilderness not knowing where they should go, being led by the Spirit of God, which was a constant companion of Mosiah, he being a righteous man of God.

36 And another record of the people of Nephi was recorded upon plates of ore, and this record I have in my possession. And this particular record was made by the hand of Nephi and handed down from father to son according to the commandment that Nephi had received from the Lord. Nevertheless, the majority of the history of the Nephite people was written on other plates of ore and handed down through the lineage of Nephite kings that had received this commandment from Nephi.

37 And Abinadom, who was named after his father, and who was a direct descendant of Lehi, took his family and fled into the wilderness with Mosiah. And Abinadom had many of the records of the Nephites in his possession.

38 Behold, Abinadom was one of the captains of the guards and had great authority among the Nephites. Nevertheless, he was a humble man who gave much to the poor and needy of his people and he found no place among the rich class to which those in similar positions of authority belonged.

39 And it came to pass that the Nephite king had placed Abinadom in charge of the records of the Nephites that he might protect them. And Abinadom took these records also with him into the wilderness.

40 And it came to pass that Abinadom organized a small army of guards from among those who had fled with Mosiah to protect them in their journeys in the wilderness.

41 And it came to pass that the people of Mosiah, for that is what they called themselves in order to separate themselves from the Nephites who stayed in the land of Nephi, traveled many days in the wilderness.

CHAPTER 9

Mosiah discovers the people of Zarahemla. He teaches them and discovers that they are descendants of Zedekiah, the last king of Judah. Mosiah is made king over the people and confers the kingdom upon his son Benjamin.

AND it came to pass that after many days of wandering in the wilderness, the people of Mosiah came into a land that was inhabited by other people who were strangers to them.

2 For behold, the Lamanites who had separated themselves from the Nephites were becoming a dark skinned people because of the effects of the sun on their nakedness. But these strange inhabitants of the land northward were white and delightsome like unto the Nephites.

3 And it came to pass that Mosiah sent Abinadom with a group of armed guards in among the people to attempt to talk to their leader and see if they were at peace, and also if they were friendly towards them.

4 And it came to pass that Abinadom returned to Mosiah and reported that he and his guards could not understand the language of this people, and that they had a leader among them who was called Zarahemla, and that they were a very friendly people.

5 And it came to pass that the people of Zarahemla rejoiced exceedingly at the arrival of the people of Mosiah, even though they could not communicate with each other. And their rejoicing was caused by the physical similarities that they shared—both groups being a white and delightsome people.

6 And it came to pass that Mosiah taught Zarahemla and his people in the language of the Nephites, and they began to understand each other from that time forth.

7 And Mosiah learned that Zarahemla was a descendant of Mulek, one of the sons of Zedekiah, king of Judah, who was carried away by his nephew, the king of Babylon, shortly after Lehi had left the city of Jerusalem.

8 Behold, Zedekiah rebelled against the king of Babylon and began to believe in a creator and the things that the prophets were preaching unto the Jews at Jerusalem. And Zedekiah took compassion upon the Jews and was wont to protect them from the king of Babylon.

9 And because of his righteousness, the Lord came to him in a dream and showed unto him the destruction of Jerusalem and also that his sons would all be slain if he stayed in the land of Jerusalem.

10 And it came to pass that Mulek, the son of Zedekiah, heeded the words of his father and took many of his riches and gathered up all those who would listen to him and fled into the wilderness before the king of Babylon could destroy him.

11 And it came to pass that the spirit of God led Mulek to the same waters that Lehi and his family had crossed. And Mulek built ships that carried his people across the many waters until they came to the promised land.

12 And Mulek had a son and called his name Mattaniah after the name of his father. And Mattaniah begot Timrah.

13 And Timrah begot Sandesh, and Sandesh begot Helekiah. And Helekiah had a son whom he called Joshua, who was the father of Jerosham. And Jerosham was the father of Zarahemla.

14 And behold, it was the wisdom of the Lord that he should send Mulek out of Jerusalem. For behold, the people of Mosiah learned from the descendants of Mulek that all of the prophecies that were prophesied concerning the destruction of Jerusalem had come to pass.

15 And Zarahemla did rejoice exceedingly for he had no record of his ancestors with him. And because they had no written record, the people of Zarahemla could not read or write. And in this manner did their language become corrupt.

16 And it came to pass that the people of Zarahemla did unite with the people of Mosiah and they did make Mosiah their king and ruler over them.

17 And it came to pass that the people of Zarahemla brought forth some old records that had been written upon stone and gave them unto Mosiah that he might know the meaning thereof.

18 And it came to pass that Mosiah was given the gift of translation by the power of the Holy Spirit that was in him.

19 And the record contained a history of some other inhabitants of the promised land who had come over across the many waters many years before the people of Mulek, or before the people of Lehi had reached the promised land.

20 And the record was given unto the people of Zarahemla by Coriantumr, who was the last known descendant of the people who had been destroyed by wars and pestilence, and whose bones lay in the land northward.

21 And this Coriantumr died among the people of Zarahemla during the time that Mattaniah, the son of Mulek, was the leader of the people.

22 And Mattaniah could not understand the words of Coriantumr, but he did receive the record of the people of Coriantumr, which was engraven upon stone. And it was this same stone that Zarahemla gave unto Mosiah.

23 And it came to pass that there were other records that were also discovered among the ruins in the land northward that were later given unto king Mosiah, who was the grandson of Mosiah, the first king of Zarahemla, so that he might translate them. And an account of these other records will I save for another part of this abridgment.

24 For behold, I, Mormon, do not know beforehand what I am about to write in the abridgment that I am engraving upon these plates of ore. Nevertheless, this I do know: that the Spirit of God is within me and I write those things which God wants to preserve for those who will find these plates and bring forth the words which I have written.

25 Behold, for this reason the interpreters have been passed down from generation to generation until they have fallen into my hands. And I will seal up this record along with these interpreters when I have finished what the Lord would have me write in this abridgment. And these are the same interpreters that king Mosiah had in his possession during his reign and ministry, which were given to him by the people of Limhi who had found them with the records of the people who had perished in the land northward, an account of which I will give in another part of my abridgment.

26 And it came to pass that the people of Zarahemla were taught the law of Moses and the gospel of the coming of the Son of God into the world to save his people.

27 And the people of Zarahemla began to understand the words of Mosiah, their king. And they did repent of their sins and began to live in righteousness.

28 And it came to pass that king Mosiah was loved by his people, and he spent all the days of his life teaching them to live at peace and with love one towards another.

29 And he did teach the people of the coming of Christ to the world. And he did expound upon the scriptures that they had among them, explaining them to the people so that they could understand the meaning thereof.

30 And it came to pass that the people in the land of Zarahemla began to increase exceedingly. Nevertheless, they were constantly taught the gospel of Christ and by the law of Moses, which pointed them towards the acceptance of the Son of God and his gospel message for them.

31 And there arose some contention among the people as to why they could not return to the land of Nephi and reclaim the land of their inheritance. And many men in their pride went back into the wilderness against the counsel of king Mosiah, who had warned them that the time was not right for them to do so.

32 And it came to pass that king Mosiah called the people together to speak with them one last time before his death.

33 And when the people had gathered to hear their leader, Mosiah set his son Benjamin before them and consecrated and anointed him to reign in his stead.

35 And king Mosiah stood forth and spoke unto his people, saying: My beloved brothers and sisters; Behold, ye are all truly my brothers and sisters, for in God our Father, we have our affiliation.

36 Ye have made me your king and granted me the opportunity to serve you all the days of my life. And for this service I have taken nothing from you except it be to sustain my own life and the lives of my wife and my children.

37 Many years ago I heeded the promptings of the Holy Spirit, which hath been my constant companion all the days of my life. Behold, it was this same spirit that led me out of the land of our fathers and into the wilderness.

38 And it is the same spirit that led many of your fathers to follow me and leave the land of Nephi so that we would not be subjected to the same punishments as our brethren who stayed in the land of Nephi.

39 Behold, we would not have had to leave the land of our inheritance if we had not fallen into sin and corruption. Yea, even the very church of God that was established by our father Nephi became corrupt in the eyes of the Lord.

40 And do ye know the reason for the corruption of our people? Can you begin to see what causeth such great calamity to any society of the children of God that refuseth to live by His commandments? Even if I speak plainly unto you by the power of the spirit of God that engulfeth my soul at this time and giveth me great strength even, in my old age, will ye understand?

41 Oh, my beloved brothers and sisters, know ye not that the devil is a deceiver and hath the cunningness to make us think that sin is righteousness and that righteousness is sin? Know ye not that he can present himself as a God and a savior of the world, and then present the true God and His Son as the devil? Know ye not that when ye least expect it the devil will take power over you and turn your minds and your hearts against the truth?

42 I know this to be true, for behold, it hath happened in Jerusalem; it hath happened in the land of Nephi; and it will happen unto you if ye do not watch yourselves carefully and live by the precepts of truth and righteousness.

43 Behold, how will ye know that the precepts that ye are taught by your leaders are precepts of truth and righteousness? Yea, how will ye know if the God that ye are following is the true God and not the devil in disguise? How will ye know that ye are being misled by your leaders in whom ye trust to teach you these precepts of truth and righteousness?

44 Alas, how shall ye keep this destruction and unhappiness from coming upon you like it hath come upon our brothers and sisters who stayed in Jerusalem and are in the land of Nephi at this time?

45 The answer is simple. Oh, that ye would open your hearts to the simplicity of the answer. Oh, that ye would not look beyond the mark, which mark hath been set since the beginning of time to teach the children of God all things that they need to know in order to have peace and happiness forever.

46 Behold, it is the standard of God and the only way that happiness and peace can be obtained. Yea, it was taught to you by all the holy prophets that have preached unto you. Behold, it shall be taught to the Jews at Jerusalem when the Son of God cometh unto them in the flesh and teacheth them this thing.

47 Yea, it shall be taught to our descendants who shall witness the resurrected Savior of the world who shall come down among them after his resurrection.

48 And my soul crieth in exceeding joy to know that it shall be taught when the Lord cometh in all his power and glory to set up his kingdom for the last time upon this earth. And this kingdom shall last forever.

49 Behold, my soul is overpowered by the spirit at this time, evensomuch that I am wont to shout aloud the glorious message of this standard of God unto you, that ye might remember it and live by it always; that ye might always have peace and happiness among you, and that the Spirit of the Lord might abide with you forever.

50 And these are the commandments of God, yea, even the only way unto salvation:

51 Love your neighbor as yourself. And do unto others as you would have them do unto you—this is the mark, my brothers and sisters; this is the standard by which ye shall be judged and by which ye shall live in the eternities.

52 This is the foundation of the law and commandments of God. There is no other. All commandments, and laws, and ordinances, and sacrifices, and sacraments, and endowments, and duties should lead the children of God to this eternal standard.

53 And if ye shall not live by this standard, ye shall be destroyed. Ye shall end up in bondage and suffer without peace and with no happiness.

54 Do not let the pride and riches of the world keep you from reaching this simple mark. Do not let the devil deceive you into thinking that it is righteous to own more than another, or that ye deserve more than your neighbor. Do not think that ye are justified to set yourselves up above another class of people.

55 For behold, when the Lord shall come in his glory and set this standard as the only standard that shall be followed, the poor in spirit shall rejoice, and they that mourn shall be comforted, and the meek shall be exalted, and the merciful shall obtain mercy, and there shall be no rich or poor among any of the people of the Lord.

56 Listen to the words of my son, for he is a righteous man who hath the Spirit of the Lord within him.

57 Live peacefully one with another and seek not to destroy your enemies, but to teach them the commandments of God and show them by your example the standard by which they can also find peace and happiness.

58 May God be with you all, my beloved brothers and sisters.

59 And it came to pass that the people of Zarahemla were overcome by the words of king Mosiah and they wept exceedingly for their king. And king Mosiah died and was buried close to the burial place of his friend Zarahemla.

60 And it came to pass that though the people of the land of Zarahemla loved their king, they loved their riches and their pride and their houses and their precious things more than they loved their fellowmen.

61 And it came to pass that the Lamanites came into the land of Zarahemla and began to kill the Nephites and take their possessions. And the Nephites fought back with exceeding strength and drove the Lamanites out of their lands.

62 And there arose much contention throughout the land of Zarahemla. Yea, everyone blamed another for the wars with the Lamanites. Yea, every man accused his neighbor of sinning against God and bringing the wrath of God upon them, thus denying his own wickedness.

63 And it came to pass that king Benjamin pleaded with the people to repent of their sins and remember the things that his father had spoken unto them.

APPENDIX 3

The First Vision
Introduction

The most defining event in Mormon religious history is the appearance of God, the Father, and Jesus Christ to the young boy, Joseph Smith. From this vision, the Mormon faith was born.

The Mormon faith consists of many churches that claim to have the authority of God to proclaim His truths to the world. The largest and most influential of these sects is known as The Church of Jesus Christ of Latter-day Saints, and was established, not by the will of the Lord, but "suffered" to come forth by the insistence of Joseph Smith and those who had gained a testimony of the *Book of Mormon*. The translation of the "unsealed" portion of Mormon's plates was Joseph's ONLY *divine* calling.

When Joseph Smith received what has become known in early Mormon History as *The First Vision*, he was NOT commanded to establish a church, or any other organization for that matter. He gives his relation of this event in his own words, saying:

> *My object in going to inquire of the Lord was to know which of all the sects was right, that I might know which to join. No sooner, therefore, did I get possession of myself, so as to be able to speak, than I asked the Personages who stood above me in the light, which of all the sects was right (for at this time it had never entered into my heart that all were wrong)—and which I should join. I was answered that I must join none of them, for they were all wrong; and the Personage who addressed me said that all their creeds were an abomination in his sight; that those professors were all corrupt; that: 'they draw near to me with their lips, but their hearts are far from me, they teach for doctrines the commandments of men, having a form of godliness, but they deny the power thereof.' He again forbade me to join with any of them; and many other things did he say unto me, which I cannot write at this time.* (*Pearl of Great Price*, Joseph Smith History 1:18-20)

What was it that Joseph was forbidden to write at the time he gave this accounting of *The First Vision*?

Keep in mind that this *official* version of *The First Vision* was NOT given until 1838. The enemies of Mormon doctrine point to varying accounts of this important vision given by Joseph Smith prior to the *official* declaration given in 1838. The existence of these accounts is indeed true, and upon studying the different accounts, which are easily available upon honest research, one will come to the conclusion that no mention of the Father and the Son together was made by Joseph Smith until 1838, eight years after the LDS Church was first organized.

Why did Joseph Smith lie? What was the purpose in keeping the true nature of *The First Vision* from the members of the Church and the world? What were these "*other things*" that he could not reveal to the members of the Church when he gave the true nature of *The First Vision* in 1838? The answer rests in the "many other things did he say unto me, which I cannot write at this time."

Keep in mind that Joseph Smith knew what was written on the 116-page manuscript (*The Book of Lehi*) that Martin Harris had lost. He also knew that the things revealed in that manuscript were supposed to be withheld for a "wise purpose in the Lord." (Doesn't it seem reasonable that there would be a "*wise purpose*" in not bringing forth the contents of the 116-page lost manuscript, as the Lord knows his work and would never allow the foolishness of a man to keep it from coming forth?) Unless one reads *The Book of Lehi*, and *The Sealed Portion, The Final Testament of Jesus Christ*, he or she cannot properly understand the things which Joseph Smith was forbidden to give to the Church in 1838. It would behoove the honest researcher to read these works for a clearer understanding of these things.

Here are the complete words of the Lord given to Joseph Smith in **The First Vision**:

The First Vision

The words of Jesus Christ, the Beloved Son of God, given to Joseph Smith Jr. near Manchester Township, Ontario County, New York, in the early morning hours of April 6, 1820. Commanded not to be revealed to the world until all things in their fullness are given to the inhabitants of the world according to the own due time of the Lord. Now given to the world by way of commandment; quoted by Joseph Smith to Christopher Nemelka on December 23, 2004.

BEHOLD, Joseph, with diligence and proper faith thou hast inquired of our Father concerning these churches and creeds, which are an abomination in His sight, having a form of godliness, as they pretend, but denying the power of the Holy Ghost, which the Father hath given to this world as a witness of His will concerning its inhabitants.

2 Behold, these teach for commandments the doctrine and precepts of men, who deny the Holy Ghost and seek not the Lord to establish his righteousness, but each man therein walketh after the manner of the flesh which he hath received in this world.

3 Behold, they draw near to me with their lips but their hearts are far from me, knowing not me, nor the Father, which denieth unto them eternal life in His kingdoms.

4 Behold, thou hast been chosen to bring salvation to many of the children of God in this world, even those who seek the Father diligently as thou hast sought after him, and who keep His commandments, which He hath given unto them through me, their Savior.

5 Verily I say unto thee, the formation of a church is not that which the Father requireth of His children; nevertheless, this He suffereth that His word might go forth among His children in the manner that they have accepted for their own learning.

6 And I came down in the flesh as the Son of God and fulfilled all things which were given me of the Father to do for the world, insomuch that it might be saved from the sins of its generations.

7 And I was persecuted and rejected and lifted up upon the cross for the things which I taught unto the Jews, which things were the words that the Father sent me to give to the world. But the world knoweth not the Father, but hath invented many gods and beliefs that take away the plainness of the plan that our Father hath established for this part of His kingdom, over which He hath placed me as your Lord and God.

8 And He hath commanded all the ends of the earth to come unto me and receive the words which He hath given me to give to the children of men that they might be saved in His eternal kingdoms.

9 And He hath suffered prophets to be called among men that they might hear His words; they, because of their wickedness, unable to learn these things from the Holy Ghost, which was given unto them by the Father to teach them all things whatsoever are expedient for their salvation.

10 But they have cast out the holy prophets and changed the doctrine and ordinances given of them to point the children of men towards me and the commandments that I have given unto them.

11 Behold, great darkness covereth the whole earth, and there are none, save a few only, who do not defile themselves by the flesh; and the works thereof doth condemn them, taking away from them the power of the Holy Ghost to be with them and give them the fruits of the Spirit.

12 For except they obey the commandments of the Father, they shall not have the power to receive of the Holy Ghost, who giveth only unto those who are one with Us; they then being one with Us.

13 Behold, Joseph, my Son, thou shalt be prepared in thy youth to bring forth more of the

word of God that shall be revealed to you in due time, that it might testify of the words, which I have already suffered to be given unto the world and which the children of men carry forth among them, and which they preach in their churches, and which they ponder in their hearts, ever learning but never coming to a knowledge of the Father, and the Son.

14 Behold, this is eternal life, that ye might know the only wise and true God, and Jesus Christ, whom He hath sent. I am he. Receive ye, therefore, my law.

15 For straight is the gate, and narrow the way that leadeth unto eternal life in the kingdom of our Father, and few there be that find it, because they receive me not in the world, neither do they know me or Him who hath sent me.

16 But if the children of men receive me in the world, then they shall know me, and shall receive eternal life in the eternal worlds of the Father.

17 Behold, because the religious sects of this world do not know me, they cannot receive eternal life, for they are led by men who deny the power of the Holy Ghost because they do not the works that I have done, neither do they teach the things that I have taught unto them, and which they have in the testimony of the word that hath already been given unto them.

18 And it is the will of the Father that all the children of men come unto the Father through me that they might have this eternal life of which I have spoken. Behold, there is no other way except by me that this salvation shall come unto them.

19 And I came unto the Jews that I might teach them that they did not need to follow the leaders of their churches to destruction, but that if they seek the Holy Ghost and keep my commandments, then they would find peace and rest in me, having the fullness of my gospel revealed unto them.

20 But the Jews rejected me because of the things that I taught unto them, desiring rather to follow the course of their churches and their leaders, which they looked to for the words of salvation.

21 Behold, the religions and churches of men have always been an abomination before God, for He despiseth them, because they put one man above his neighbor in the things which they believe.

22 And these churches lead the children of God away from the Father because of the leaders who put themselves above the members of these churches, teaching for commandments the doctrines and precepts of men.

23 And the people are led to believe that their church is greater than that of another, thus causing a division among them, who should have all things in common before the Father.

24 Behold, in time it shall be given unto thee—the mysteries of God and the path that He desireth that His children should follow to eternal life; and not only eternal life, but for the establishment of peace and happiness upon the earth.

25 And thou shalt desire to establish a church among men according to the commandments and the words that thou shalt receive concerning these things as they shall be given unto thee. But this thing is not that which shall bring happiness unto you; for this reason, I forbid this thing. But unto you it shall be given according to the desires of the Gentiles.

26 And thou shalt desire to do this to prove the Gentiles herewith. and show unto them that they are not above the Jews, and that the Jew is not above the Gentile, that all might know that God is no respecter of persons, and would that all of His children seek not the arm of flesh, but Him and His righteousness.

27 And thou shalt be called as a prophet among them, being the first who shall prepare the way for the last, that the children of men might have the opportunity to know the Father and receive eternal life as I have explained it unto thee. And the Gentiles shall reject that which shall be given them through you; and they shall cast you out from among them and listen not to your precepts and counsel.

28 And thou shalt lead those that listen to thy words like my servant Moses led those of the house of Israel, and give unto them my words as thou receivest through me, like unto Moses and

Aaron. But the Gentiles shall reject thee, as did the Israelites the law that Moses brought down unto them, that they might have known me and the Father who sent me unto them.

29 And thou shalt be commanded to give unto them a lower law of ordinances and sacrifice like unto those which Moses gave unto the rebellious house of Israel, who would not hear my words from my own mouth, but wanted that they be given unto them through Moses.

30 And when they rejected me and trusted more in the arm of the flesh than they did in me, I took the plainness of my gospel from among them and allowed them to be led according to their own desires, which were unrighteous before God. And they did stumble exceedingly because of their wickedness.

31 And the fullness of my gospel was among them, but they did not understand it, trusting more in their fleshly ordinances and the sacrifices that pointed them towards this gospel.

32 And when I came down among them, they could not give up the traditions and doctrines of men that had crept in among them and deceived their souls, causing them to trust in their church and its leaders for their salvation.

33 And behold, as I was led, so shalt thou be led like a lamb to the slaughter, being innocent of the sins of this generation, having given unto them the opportunity to receive the fullness my gospel and establish the kingdom of God upon the earth for the last time.

34 And the Gentiles shall be led like unto the Jews of old, and they shall do all things in the likeness of the Jews, that the first may be last and the last may be first, showing that the weaknesses of men are the same yesterday as they are today.

35 And then shall the Father put forth His hand for the last time upon the earth and begin to gather the wheat from among the tares, and cause the tares that they shall be bundled together, and the wheat shall be gathered into the barn where it shall be safe from the fire which shall soon come to consume this world, destroying the churches and doctrines of them who teach falsehoods and lead the children of men away from the Father.

36 And when the work of the Father commenceth upon this earth, then shall the light of my gospel once again shine forth its light, that those who shall see it might follow it into the barn of the Lord, where they shall be safe.

37 And there shall be one like unto you, who shall be the last, who shall be called forth to give unto the Gentiles the fullness of my gospel as I gave it unto the Jews.

38 And he shall not be like unto Moses, but he shall be like unto me, having my countenance upon him for the sake of the work of the Father.

39 And he shall do that which I have done, and preach against the religions of men and their doctrines, calling upon all men to repent and come unto me and be saved.

40 And there shall be many that shall receive the words that he shall give unto them, which have been prepared to come forth in their fullness. And these words shall come forth from thy own works, which shall be given unto thee in mine own time, as thou shalt be prepared.

41 And his work shall testify of thy work, and thy words shall testify of his words, giving unto the children of men the testimony of two, that the fullness of my gospel might come forth to prepare the world for my coming.

42 Behold, Joseph, thou art in thy youth; therefore, concern not thyself with the particulars of these things, for all shall be given you according to my command and that which I have been given of the Father.

43 Thou shalt receive the keys of authority to do these things when thou hast been prepared to receive these things.

44 And when thou shalt be rejected by the Gentiles, then shall the keys that shall be given unto thee be taken from off the earth until the last, who shall be given these same keys to bring forth the mysteries of God in their plainness, that the children of men might have no more excuses in not understanding the plan of the Father.

45 And now, my son, keep all these things in thy heart and reveal them to no man. And a commandment I give unto thee, that thou shalt not reveal unto the world the true nature of our beings—my Father and I being exalted beings

The First Vision 1:46–1:57

made of flesh and bone like unto other men, except for the exalted nature of our flesh.

46 For behold, this is a mystery that the world shall not have until thou hast caused the fullness of my gospel to come forth unto the world to prepare them for these things.

47 For in the day that thou shalt be commanded to reveal these things unto the world, thou shalt be persecuted and hated, and thy work shall be cut short because of these things and the other mysteries that shall be given unto thee.

48 And thou shalt not reveal all of these things unto those who shall follow thee, until it be commanded by me under the direction of the Father. For in that day He shall commence His final work among the children of men.

49 For if the Gentiles shall have these things, then they shall not proceed with faith; and that which they would do cannot come to pass because of their knowledge of these things.

50 And when they shall receive these things, then shall they know that the work of the Father hath commenced upon the earth for the last time.

51 Behold, if the Gentiles shall reject the fullness of my gospel given unto them through you, then shall they set up their churches and their sects, like unto those that exist in this day, but they shall be more numerous, and their doctrines more corrupt before God.

52 But that church which shall come forth because of thee shall become like unto the church that came forth from the Jews because of Moses. And in all these things there shall be a symbol and a type—the first being last and the last being first.

53 Behold, thou art Joseph, and hast been called of God to go forth in the calling of Elijah and turn the hearts of the children to their fathers as foretold by my holy prophets.

54 Seek not for the wisdom of men; for all things whatsoever thou shalt be in need of pertaining to this calling shall be given unto thee.

55 Remember my words and my commandments this day, my Son, and thou shalt be commanded to bring these things forth in mine own due time.

56 Remember me and the Father who smileth upon thee at this time. Know us, Joseph, and where we are, thou shalt one day come.

57 Peace be unto thee; therefore, we leave with thee the Comforter, who shall now begin to teach thee all things for thy salvation. We love thee, Joseph.

APPENDIX 4

The Fullness of the Gospel of Jesus Christ

When Joseph Smith was visited by Moroni, he was told specifically what his work would be and what purpose the record known as the gold plates of Mormon had:

*He called me by name, and said unto me that he was a messenger sent from the presence of God to me, and that his name was Moroni; that God had a work for me to do; and that my name should be had for good and evil among all nations, kindreds, and tongues, or that it should be both good and evil spoken of among all people. He said there was a book deposited, written upon gold plates, giving an account of the former inhabitants of this continent, and the source from whence they sprang. He also said that **the fulness of the everlasting Gospel was contained in it, as delivered by the Savior** to the ancient inhabitants;* (Pearl of Great Price, Joseph Smith—History [JSH] 1:33-34)

Moroni also quoted the eleventh chapter of Isaiah (see JSH 1:40), but gave the correct translation as follows:

*1 And there shall come forth **a rod** out of the stem of Jesse who shall strengthen the house of Israel by **his word**. And **his word** shall establish the roots of the kingdom of heaven; and a Branch shall grow out of his roots, which shall shine forth among all kingdoms and all nations.*
2 And the spirit of the Lord shall rest upon him, even the spirit of wisdom and understanding, the spirit of counsel and might, and the spirit of knowledge which is given to all those who do not fear the Lord and keep His commandments.
3 And this spirit shall make him of quick understanding; and he shall reprove all nations of the earth which live in fear of the Lord. And he shall not judge after the sight of his eyes, neither reprove after the hearing of his ears; for thus doeth those who feareth the Lord and keep not His commandments.
*4 But with righteousness shall he judge the poor, and reprove with equity for the meek of the earth, rebuking those who have judged them with an unrighteous judgment; and he shall smite the earth with the **rod of his mouth**, and with the **breath of his lips** shall he slay the wicked.*
5 And righteousness shall be the girdle of his loins, and faithfulness the girdle of his reins; for all that which the Lord shall send him to do shall be done.
6 And in that day when he shall establish his righteousness, the wolf who devoured his sheep shall dwell with the lamb; if not, the wolf shall be destroyed. And truth in equity shall abase those who possess power over another and who have exalted themselves above others; and they shall be as a leopard that lieth down with the kid; and as the calf and the young lion and the fatling lie together in peace and equality of strength. And behold, those who are as a little child shall lead them all.

7 And the cow who feedeth from the pasture given to the sheep, and also the bear who eateth the cow and the sheep, shall feed together from the same pasture; and their young ones shall lie down together in equity and peace; and all shall eat from the same pasture, even the lion shall eat straw like the ox in that day.

8 And the sucking child who is without knowledge shall play on the hole of the asp, who are the serpents that afflict wounds in the heels of all the children of God. Yea, those who have been filled with the milk of the Lord shall no longer be in need of nourishment; and the weaned child shall put his hand on the cockatrice's den because it shall be filled with the spirit and knowledge of the Lord.

9 Behold, thus saith the Lord, They shall not hurt nor destroy the little ones in all my holy mountain; for the earth shall be full of the knowledge of the Lord, as the waters cover the sea.

10 And in that day **the root which shall be established by the stem of Jesse shall stand for an ensign unto all the people**; *from it shall the Gentiles seek shelter from the tribulations of the world; and they shall find rest in the branches established by the roots of the tree of life, which is the stem of Jesse; and his rest shall be glorious.*

11 And it shall come to pass in that day when the Lord shall establish **His ensign** *unto the people, this stem of Jesse shall set his hand again the second time to recover the remnant of his people, who shall be left, from Assyria, and from Egypt, and from Pathros, and from Cush, and from Elam, and from Shinar, and from Hamath, and from the islands of the sea, yea, even from the four corners of the earth.*

12   And he shall set up **the ensign of the Lord God** *for all the nations, and shall assemble those who have been cast out of Israel, and gather together the dispersed of Judah from the four corners of the earth.*

13 The envy also of Ephraim shall depart, and the adversaries of Judah shall be cut off because of the ensign of peace and equity which shall be given. Ephraim shall not envy Judah, and Judah shall not vex Ephraim any longer, but they shall lie down together in the shade of the tree. And eagles shall come down and lodge in the branches of the tree protecting those who seek shade from the heat of the day.

14 And the eagles shall fly upon the shoulders of the Philistines toward the west; and they shall lay spoil to them and to them of the east together. And they shall lay their hand upon Edom and Moab, who have exalted themselves above those of the land of Ammon; and the children of Ammon shall lead those who once abased them, and they who were exalted shall obey them.

15   And the LORD shall utterly destroy the power and the word of all nations of the earth, even as he did the tongue of the mighty Egyptian nation which exalted itself in the earth and whose river ran over all nations of the earth and into the sea; and the **breath of his lips** *shall be as a mighty wind, and he shall shake his hand over the river of filthy water, and shall smite it into seven streams, which shall carry the pure water* **from his mouth** *unto the whole earth. And he shall make highways and roads, which shall lead all men dryshod across the filthy waters.*

16 And there shall be an highway built for the remnant of his people, which shall be left, from Assyria; like as it was to the house of Israel in the day that they came up out of the land of Egypt led by the chosen servant of the Lord, who said to the people, **A prophet shall the Lord your God raise up unto you of your brethren, like unto me; him shall ye hear in all things whatsoever he shall say unto you**. *And it shall come to pass, that every soul, which will not hear that prophet, shall be destroyed from among the people.*

In his book of Revelation, John also referred to the "**rod** out of the stem of Jesse" mentioned by Isaiah, saying:

"*And she brought forth a man child, who was to rule all nations with a rod of iron:*" (Revelation 12:5)

Moroni explained to Joseph that "the prophet" mentioned by Isaiah in verse 16 of chapter 11 was "*Christ; but the day had not yet come when 'they who would not hear his voice should be cut off from among the people,' but soon would come.*" (See JSH 1:40)

It should be of no surprise then, that when, as a young boy, Joseph sincerely inquired as to which religion was true, he was told that none were, and that all were an abomination. These religions included every major Christian faith then and all those that are still upon the earth today. These are an abomination because they do not teach "**the root which shall be established by the stem of Jesse [which] shall stand for an ensign unto all the people.**" They do not teach the "**rod of his mouth**," or that which came from "**the breath of his lips**," as pointed out in Isaiah above. These Christian faiths fail to point out a significant fact to the millions of people who go to their churches and listen to their vain and foolish interpretations of the scriptures. The "breath" of the pastors', ministers', and leaders' lips have convinced the people that the actual "blood of Christ" saves them; failing to point out that Jesus Christ *fulfilled* his mission long before he was killed upon the cross. These uninspired leaders cannot teach their followers of *life eternal* because they themselves do not know the only true God, and Jesus Christ, whom God has sent. Well did John record the words of Christ **before** Christ's death:

> *And this is life eternal, that they might know thee the only true God, and Jesus Christ, whom thou hast sent. I have glorified thee on the earth:* ***I have finished the work which thou gavest me to do***. (John 17:3-4)

Before Christ was killed by those who rejected his message, he accomplished his mission and left his testimony of what the Father intended him to do. The majority of the people choose a different god than the one of whom Christ spoke. Despite this, Jesus left his example and gave the commandments of God he was instructed to give to the world. His gospel ("the rod of iron") was revealed to the world and transcribed as Matthew chapters 5, 6, and 7 in the New Testament; although these and his other teachings were rejected by the majority of the people during his lifetime. After his resurrection, in fairness to all the people in every other part of the world, Christ taught the ***exact same*** teachings to the people of other parts of the world, fulfilling the words he had thus spoken:

> *And other sheep I have, which are not of this fold: them also I must bring, and they* **shall hear my voice**; *and there shall be one fold, and one shepherd.* (John 10:16)

These teachings were what Moroni was referring to when he gave instruction to Joseph Smith "*that the fulness of the everlasting Gospel was contained in it, as delivered by the Savior to the ancient inhabitants.*" This fullness is found in the *Book of Mormon*, 3 Nephi, chapters 12, 13, and 14. When Joseph translated the record of the people of the Western Hemisphere, he found that the words that the Savior delivered in Jerusalem had been misquoted, mistranslated, and incorrectly presented in the New Testament record. However, he was instructed to use the King James Version of Matthew, as this was the translation that most people accepted as being a true reflection of Christ's words. Joseph was also instructed to interpolate the words of Isaiah from the accepted King James Version of the Bible, as quoted throughout the *Book of Mormon*.

When I translated the sealed portion of the record, I too was instructed to interpolate the accepted King James Version of the Bible when quoting similar passages of scripture. I was also told to include Moroni's quotes (that are in the sealed portion) word for word from the unsealed portion, as they are currently given in the published *Book of Mormon*. Both Joseph and I saw the exact same translation of the words of Christ published as 3 Nephi 12, 13, and 14, and Matthew 5, 6, and 7. We were both perplexed at the *plain and precious* parts that were excluded by modern translations and unscrupulous editors, but even so, we each did as we were commanded.

Being raised a member of the Church of Jesus Christ of Latter-day Saints, I (like Joseph in his day) was confused by the hypocrisy and blatant disregard the Church had for *"the fulness of the everlasting Gospel...delivered by the Savior to the ancient inhabitants."* I, too, sincerely inquired if the LDS Church was indeed true. The visitation of the resurrected Joseph Smith answered my question and brought forth the publication of *The Sealed Portion—The Final Testament of Jesus Christ*.

The translation of both of these records came by use of the Urim and Thummim. The Urim and Thummim consists of two stones, which act as a computer-like translating device and also an advanced cell phone that can communicate with beings on another planet. If Jesus is resurrected, then he must be somewhere, upon some other planet in the Universe, awaiting his Second Coming. If that is the case (and it is), then it would seem plausible that he could communicate with a person upon this earth. Just like a person in the Western Hemisphere can instantaneously connect to and communicate with a person in the Eastern Hemisphere today, in the same way there exists advanced technology that allows a person of one planet to communicate with a person of another. This is exactly what the Urim and Thummim is: an advanced cell phone technology hidden in the form of two stones.

With the ability to use the Urim and Thummim, I simply asked to know the true and complete words that Jesus spoke to the people the day he gave what is known as the Sermon on the Mount. I was instructed to place the Urim and Thummim over the words given in Matthew. Upon doing so, the correct translation of the Gospel of Jesus Christ was given from the "breath of the lips" of the resurrected Christ, though through the technology of an advanced cell phone known as the Urim and Thummim.

Now presented for the first time are the true and complete words Christ gave to the people when he fulfilled his mission and delivered the fullness of his gospel to the people of the earth:

(The parts changed from the King James Version are given in **bold text**.)

CHAPTER 5

1 AND seeing the multitudes, he went up into a mountain **to teach unto them the things which the Father had commanded of him;** and when he was set **in the place where he would teach the people, he called forth** his disciples **and they** came unto him **that they might hear more clearly the things that he would command the people, so that they could teach these same things unto the people as they had been given authority to do.**

2 And **after he had presented his disciples before the people,** he opened his mouth, and taught them, saying, **Blessed are ye if ye shall give heed unto the words of these twelve whom I have chosen from among you to minister unto you, and to be your servants; and unto them I have given power that they may baptize you with water, if ye repent and believe on the things which I shall give unto you from my Father; and after that ye are baptized with water, which is the covenant ye shall make before God that ye shall do the things which I shall command you this day; behold, I will baptize you with fire and with the Holy Ghost, which shall cause you to know that the things that I shall give unto you are true. And this fire shall burn within you, giving you a remission of your sins by the peace that ye shall find in your souls. For ye are poor in spirit and seek for the kingdom of heaven. And it is this kingdom that I shall give unto you this day.**

3 Blessed are the poor in spirit **who come unto me and learn that which the Father hath given me for them; for their spirits shall be filled and they shall enter into** the kingdom of heaven.

4 And **again,** blessed are they that mourn **because they seek for more righteousness, but cannot find it in the doctrines and precepts of men which they have been given;** for they shall be comforted **by the words which I give unto them this day.**

5 Blessed are the meek **who seek to do the will of the Father in all things;** for they shall inherit the earth **that hath been prepared for them.**

6 **And** blessed are they **who** do hunger and thirst after righteousness **in meekness and lowliness of heart;** for they shall be filled **with the Holy Ghost who shall teach them all things.**

7 **And** blessed are the merciful **who love others and extend to them no judgment for what they do, which is evil;** for they shall obtain mercy **for that which they do, which is evil.**

8 **And** blessed are **all** the pure in heart **who in righteousness seek to know God and His ways, that they might understand truth, and not to consume it upon their lusts as do they who are impure; behold,** they shall **know** God.

9 **And** blessed are the peacemakers **who contend with no man over doctrine. Yea, these shall come to know the true doctrine, and then** they shall be called the children of God.

10 **And** blessed are they which are persecuted **and mocked by others because of their righteous works; for they shall find their peace and happiness in** the kingdom of heaven.

11 **And** blessed are ye, when men shall revile you, and persecute you, and shall say all manner of evil against you falsely, **because of that which ye do** for my sake.

12 Rejoice, and be exceeding glad **in your persecutions and afflictions;** for so persecuted they the prophets **who** were before you, **who I sent unto the people to teach them these things;** for your reward **shall be given you from** heaven **by receiving peace and comfort from the Spirit of God.**

13 Ye are the salt of the earth, **even as ye are given as examples unto all men of the peace that ye receive from the Father;** but if the salt **hath** lost **its** savor, wherewith shall **the earth** be salted? It is thenceforth good for nothing, but to be cast out **again into the earth from whence it came,** and to be trodden under foot **by** men. **For the Father will not have those whom He hath chosen give a false example of Him.**

14 **I am the light of the world that the Father hath given unto the world that lieth in darkness. And he that followeth me shall not walk in darkness, but shall have the light of life. And ye have been given me of the Father, therefore,** ye **also** are the light of the world; **and with the light that the Father hath given unto us, we shall be as a city of lights set on a hill that giveth light unto all the world.** A city that is set on an hill cannot be hid **because it is in the view**

of all the world. Therefore, men who have received light cannot hide it from the world.

15 Neither do men light a candle, and **make a measure of that light unto others by putting** it under a bushel, **for the light cannot be measured to any man in a portion**; but **he putteth it** on a candlestick **so that all may partake equally thereof**; and it **shall give** light unto all that are in the house.

16 Let your light so shine before **all** men **by the** good works **that ye do because of the light that the Father hath given unto you; that** they **might** see your good works, and glorify your Father which is in heaven.

17 Think not that I am come to destroy the law **that hath already been given you of Moses**, or **of** the prophets **who have come before me**. I am not come to destroy **the law or the prophesies**, but to fulfil **them every wit. For behold, the law of Moses and the prophets pointed all men to me, giving in darkness what ye now see in the light**.

18 For verily I say unto you, Till heaven and earth pass, **if it were possible, not** one jot or one tittle shall in no wise pass from the law **which hath been given** till all be fulfilled. **For this is the law and the prophets, even all the commandments that have been given by the Father: that ye should worship God with all your heart, might, mind, and soul by keeping His commandments; and this is His commandments, that ye do unto others what ye would have them do unto you. And there shall be no more law given except those commandments that I give unto you this day.**

19 Whosoever therefore shall break **any** of these commandments **that I give unto you**, and shall teach men **to do** so **by his example**, he shall **in no wise be saved** in the kingdom of heaven, **for these commandments is the law that ye shall also keep there**; but whosoever shall do **these commandments of the law until it be fulfilled** and teach them, the same shall be called great **and be saved** in the kingdom of heaven.

20 For I say unto you, That except your righteousness shall exceed the righteousness of the scribes and Pharisees, ye shall in no case enter into the kingdom of heaven. **For the scribes and Pharisees sit in the seat of Moses and teach the** commandments, but they do not abide by them, and by their example teach many to break these commandments; therefore, I have said unto you, that whosoever shall do these commandments and teach them shall be saved in the kingdom of heaven. And behold, I shall give unto you the law and the commandments of my Father, that ye shall believe in me, and that ye shall repent of your sins, and come unto me with a broken heart and a contrite spirit. Behold, ye have the commandments already before you, and ye must now know that in me is the law fulfilled. Therefore come unto me and be ye saved; for verily I say unto you, that except ye shall keep my commandments, which I have been commanded to give unto you at this time, ye shall in no wise enter into the kingdom of heaven.

21 **Behold**, ye have heard that it was said **of** them of old time, Thou shalt not kill; and whosoever shall kill shall be in danger of the judgment; **and this is the law that the scribes and Pharisees teach unto you, and which they do not understand; for they have said, An eye for an eye and a tooth for a tooth, and that ye shall stone and kill those who violate the law. But wherein shall the commandment be fulfilled if ye kill him who hath killed? Are not ye both then of the same sin?**

22 But I say unto you, **he that killeth in any manner and for whatever reason lieth in sin; and** whosoever is angry with his brother **for any reason** shall be in danger of the **same** judgment, **because the anger in his heart might lead to the death of his brother**; and whosoever shall **hold his brother in contempt or ridicule** shall be in danger of **the law that hath been given by** the council **which rendereth the law**; but whosoever shall say **to his brother for any reason**, Thou fool, shall be in danger of **a** hell **like unto** fire, **which shall burn in his soul because of that which he thinkest of his brother**.

23 Therefore if thou **presentest thyself at** the altar **as a righteous offering to God**, and there rememberest that thy brother hath ought against thee **because of that which thou hast done unto him**;

24 Leave there thy gift before the altar, and go thy way **until thou canst offer up a gift in**

righteousness; and before thou offerest thyself as a gift to God, first be reconciled to thy brother, and then come and offer thy gift.

25 Yea, be kind to thy brother and respect the opinion of he who disagreeth with thee and considereth thee his adversary, whiles thou art still in his good graces, that thou mightest remain in the way with him; lest at any time he who considereth thee an adversary causeth thee to sin; for in whatsoever sin thou shalt be found, thou shalt be delivered to the judge, and the judge deliver thee to the officer, and thou be cast into prison.

26 For I am thy righteous judge, and by my words shalt thou be judged; and if it so be that thou hast offended thy brother in anger, thou shalt not be delivered from the anguish of thy soul until thou hast suffered for that which thou hast done. This is the state in which thou shalt find thyself in the kingdom of my Father; and this state is like unto a prison. Verily I say unto thee, Thou shalt by no means come out thence, till thou hast paid the uttermost farthing.

27 Behold, ye have heard that it was said by your leaders that they of old time commanded, Thou shalt not commit adultery; but the scribes and Pharisees have given you their unrighteous example in this thing, because they look upon women and lust after them, having many concubines and wives, justifying their wickedness by them of old time;

28 But I say unto you, That whosoever looketh on a woman to lust after her hath committed adultery with her already in his heart; therefore, your leaders have caused you to err because of their examples. Ye look at them as your guides who have eyes that see for you, and hands that do for you that which ye believe God hath commanded of them.

29 For ye have seen of the Jews that those who are their leaders, who lead them and are their standard, do mislead them and cause them to sin before the Father and disobey His commandments. And it is better that a man have no leader, than be led into the same hell with his leader whom he hath made his standard. And if thine eye which seeth for thee, even him that is appointed to watch over thee to show thee light, becometh a transgressor and offend thee, pluck him out. For it is better for thee to enter into the kingdom of God, with one eye, than having two eyes to be cast into hell fire. For it is better that thyself should be saved, than to be cast into hell with thy leaders where their worm dieth not, and where the fire is not quenched.

30 And if thy right hand offend thee, cut it also off, and cast it from thee; for the works that thy leaders do by their unrighteous example causeth thee to stumble in darkness; for it is more profitable for thee that one of thy members should perish, in that thou leavest those who do the works of God for thee, and not that thy whole body should be cast into hell.

31 It hath been said, Whosoever shall put away his wife, let him give her a writing of divorcement, and this they have said to justify the lust that they have for another woman who is not their wife, thinking that with a divorcement, they shall be free of sin;

32 But I say unto you, That whosoever shall put away his wife, so that he might be justified in the lust of his heart and his fornication, hath committed adultery and is not free from sin because of the covenant that he made with his wife; and whosoever shall marry her that is not divorced committeth adultery. And this I say because your leaders justify themselves in their lust for women who are not their wives, but condemn those caught in fornication, who are not married by their laws.

33 Again, ye have heard that it hath been said by them that they of old time commanded, Thou shalt not forswear thyself, but shalt perform unto the Lord thine oaths; and this they have said unto you that they might keep you in bondage to them who have set themselves upon the throne of God.

34 But I say unto you, make no oaths to any man and forswear not at all; neither by heaven; for it is God's throne upon which only He can perform His oaths, and your leaders cannot perform His oaths in unrighteousness upon this earth;

35 Nor should ye forswear yourselves by the earth; for it is his footstool where His oaths shall be fulfilled even as I am here to fulfill them; neither should ye forswear yourselves by

Jerusalem; for it is the city of the great King, **who is not of heaven, but is here now upon the earth to fulfill all things sworn by the Father**.

36 Neither shalt thou by thy head **commit thyself to any matter**, because thou canst not make one hair **of thy head** white or black.

37 But let your communication **among each other** be, Yea, yea, **this I can do**; or, Nay, nay, **this I cannot do**; for whatsoever is more than these **can cause** evil.

38 **And again,** ye have heard that it hath been said, An eye for an eye, and a tooth for a tooth, **doing unto another what he hath done unto you**.

39 But I say unto you, That ye **shall** not resist this evil **that another doeth unto you, because I have commanded you to do unto another what ye would want him to do unto you; and ye would not want to lose an eye, if yours was taken; or a tooth, if one was lost by the hand of another;** but whosoever shall smite thee on thy right cheek, turn to him the other also **that he might see thy love for him and stop that which he doeth unto thee**.

40 And if any man will sue thee at the law, and take away thy coat, **do not fight for that which he desireth of thee, but** let him have thy cloak also.

41 And whosoever shall compel thee to go a mile, go with him twain, **showing that your love is greater than the vengeance of him who compeleth thee to do a thing againt thy will**.

42 **If thou hast that which thou canst give, then** give to him that asketh **of** thee, and from him that would borrow of thee turn not thou away **lest he esteem thee as his enemy**.

43 Ye have heard that it hath been said **of your leaders that ye shall** love **your** neighbour **who is like unto you and believeth as ye believe**, and **that ye should** hate **your** enemy **and cast him out from among you, even he that doth not believe as ye believe, that ye be not misled by the hand of an enemy**.

44 But I say unto you, Love your enemies, bless them that curse you, do good to them that hate you, and pray for them **who** despitefully use you, and persecute you;

45 That ye may **become** the children of your Father **who** is in heaven, **who is no respecter of persons**; for he maketh his sun to rise on the evil and on the good, and sendeth rain on the just and on the unjust—**all being His beloved children**.

46 For if ye love **only** them **who** love you, what reward have ye **of your Father in heaven**? Do not even the publicans **do** the same? **And ye know that they are wicked; yet your Father loveth them still**.

47 And if ye salute your brethren only, what do ye more than **the** others **who ye condemn as sinners**? Do not even the publicans so **salute only those who are their friends**?

48 **Behold, those things which were of old time, which were under the law that ye have been taught by your leaders, in me are all fulfilled. And for this reason hath the Father sent me to you, that ye might repent and do the works that I have commanded you to do, and follow the example that I have given unto you, that** ye **might**, therefore, be **commanded to be** perfect **in the love that ye have one for another,** even as your Father which is in heaven **hath a** perfect **love for you**.

CHAPTER 6

AND it came to pass that as Jesus taught his disciples, he said unto them, teach this people, saying, Take heed that ye do not your alms before men, to be seen of them **and receive the honor and praise of the world**; otherwise ye have no **need for a** reward of your Father which is in heaven, **which He shall give unto you, not as the honors of men are given, but by the peace of His Spirit**.

2 Therefore when thou doest thine alms, do not sound a trumpet before thee, as the hypocrites do in the synagogues and in the streets, that they may have glory of men. Verily I say unto you, They have their reward, **for it is given them of men from whom they desire it**.

3 But when thou doest alms, let not thy left hand know what thy right hand doeth; **for if thou givest of unrighteousness, by that which thou doest with thy left hand, to receive the glory of men, then thy righteous act, which thou doest of thy right, shall not be acceptable as a**

righteous offering to thy Father; for thou dost not do this thing for the benefit of another as thou would want another to do so to thee, but thou doest this to be seen and rewarded openly by men.

4 Therefore, so that thine alms may be in secret **and for the benefit of he who receiveth of thy alms, let not thy left arm of unrighteousness influence the secret work of thy right arm**; and thy Father **who** seeth in secret, Himself shall reward thee openly.

5 And when thou prayest, be thou not as the hypocrites are **when they pray out loud to be heard of another;** for they love to pray standing in the synagogues and in the corners of the streets, that they may be seen of men. Verily I say unto you, They have **the** reward **that they seek.**

6 But thou, when thou prayest, enter into **the** closet **of** thy **heart, where others cannot hear thee,** and when thou hast shut **thine own** door **to be alone in the Spirit**, pray to thy Father **who seeth** in secret; and thy Father **who** seeth in secret shall reward thee openly **through the ministrations of the Spirit.**

7 But when ye pray, use not vain repetitions, as the heathen do **in sackcloth and ashes upon the ground;** for they think that they shall be heard for their much speaking; **and they ask according to their wants and their needs, demanding of the Father that which they should not.**

8 Be not ye therefore like unto them **who ask according to their needs and wants;** for your Father knoweth what things ye have need of, before ye ask Him. **And if ye ask for that which is not the will of the Father, then ye ask amiss and shall not receive as the Father would give unto you according to His own will; ye therefore, fight the will of God and grieve the Spirit.**

9 After this manner therefore pray ye **always that ye be not led into temptation**: Our Father who art in heaven, Hallowed be thy name.

10 **Bless us that we may know and do Thy works, that** thy kingdom **may** come **among us, and that** Thy will be done **on** earth, as it is **done** in heaven.

11 **We ask Thee only to** give us this day our daily bread **that we may have the strength to do Thy works.**

12 And forgive us our **trespasses against Thy will, only** as we forgive **those who have trespassed against us.**

13 And **suffer** us not **to be led** into temptation, but deliver us from **the evil of this world and the works that we do therein; And help us always to do Thy will and keep Thy commandments;** for thine is the kingdom, and the power, and the glory, for ever. Amen.

14 For if ye forgive men their trespasses, your heavenly Father will also forgive you **by giving you the fruits that ye deserve of the Spirit.**

15 But if ye forgive not men their trespasses, neither **can** your Father forgive your trespasses.

16 Moreover when ye fast, be not, as the hypocrites, **who pretend to be** of a sad countenance; for they disfigure their faces **so that it may appear that they sacrifice much of the flesh**, that they may appear unto men to fast. Verily I say unto you, They have their reward.

17 But thou, when thou fastest, anoint thine head **in remembrance of the commandments of the Father, and keep them, that thou might keep thyself unspotted from the world;** and wash thy face **and be of a happy countenance**, that thou appear not unto men to fast.

18 But unto thy Father, **who seeth** in secret, **thou shalt present thyself unspotted and clean from the sins of this world;** and thy Father, **who** seeth in secret, shall reward thee openly **for the works which thou hast done.**

19 Lay not up for yourselves treasures upon **this** earth, where moth and rust doth corrupt, and where thieves break through and steal **the treasures of your hearts, which are the desires that ye have.**

20 But lay up for yourselves **these** treasures in heaven, where neither moth nor rust doth corrupt, and where thieves do not break through nor steal;

21 For where your treasure is, there will your heart be also.

22 **But that which bringeth forth** light **into** the body is the eye; if therefore thine eye be single **to the glory of God,** thy whole body shall be full of light, **for that light which ye shall see is given of the Father, and how great is that light.**

23 But if thine eye be evil, **then it shall be shut up against the light, and** thy whole body shall be full of darkness. If therefore **thou hast shut**

thine eyes to the light, **then** that **which** is in thee is darkness, **and** how great is that darkness!

24 And it came to pass that Jesus spoke to his disciples of that which would be required of them when they went forth to teach the people his gospel. And he spoke, saying, Behold, it is impossible for a man to serve two masters **and be equally loyal to each**; for either he will hate the one **more than** the other; or else he will hold **fast** to the one, and despise the other. Ye cannot serve God and mammon.

25 And, again, I say unto you, go ye into the world, and care not for the world; for the world will hate you, and will persecute you as it does me, and will turn you out of their synagogues. Nevertheless, ye shall go forth from house to house, teaching the people; and I will go before you. And your heavenly Father will provide for you, whatsoever things ye need for food, what ye shall eat; and for raiment, what ye shall wear or put on. Therefore I say unto you, Take no thought for your life, what ye shall eat, or what ye shall drink; nor yet for your body, what ye shall put on. Is not the life that **I have offered unto you of the Spirit** more than **the** meat **that ye eat to sustain your life**; and the body, **is it more** than raiment **for your spirit**? **If the Father hath given you your spirit and feedeth it, shall He not also provide for its raiment?**

26 Behold the fowls of the air, **which were also created by your Father**; for they sow not, neither do they reap, nor gather into barns; yet your heavenly Father feedeth them. Are ye **who are in His service** not much better than they?

27 Which of you by taking thought **of himself** can add one cubit unto his **own** stature? **Yet, your Father can add that which He desireth to your body, which houses the spirit He loveth and hath created in His own image.**

28 And I have said that this body is only **raiment for this spirit; Therefore,** why take ye thought for raiment? Consider the lilies of the field, how they grow; they toil not, neither do they spin **to provide raiment for their body;**

29 And yet I say unto you, That even Solomon in all his glory was not arrayed **by the Father** like one of these. **But Solomon was arrayed in raiment of his own hand, choosing to cover his body as the grass covereth the field and chokes the lilies arrayed in the glory of God.**

30 Wherefore, if God so clothe **the lilies, and suffereth that** the grass of the field **covereth them; and that same grass** which to day is, to morrow **shall be** cast into the oven; **how much more will he not provide for you, if ye are not of little faith and keep your eye single to the glory of God**?

31 Therefore take no thought, saying, What shall we eat? or, What shall we drink? or, Wherewithal shall we be clothed?

32 (For after all these things do the Gentiles seek **that they might live without God**;) for your heavenly Father knoweth that ye have need of all these things.

33 Therefore, seek not the things of this **world,** but seek ye first **to build up** the kingdom of God, and **to establish** his righteousness; and all these things shall be added unto you.

34 Take therefore no thought for the morrow **and that which shall come to pass**; for the morrow shall take thought for the things of itself. Sufficient unto the day is the evil thereof. **Therefore, teach this people that they should fast and pray always as I have commanded you that ye be not led into the temptations and evil of the day.**

CHAPTER 7

1 BEHOLD, **the temptations of the flesh cause this people to judge one another, and anger and strife enter into their hearts, therefore they sin and keep not the great commandment that I have given unto you. Therefore, teach this people, saying,** Judge not, that ye be not judged.

2 For with what judgment ye judge **another**, ye shall be judged **of the same. Behold, ye should discern that which is good and that which is evil, but make this judgment in righteousness according to the commandments I have given you of the Father. For which one of you, being evil, can set a measure of righteousness for another? With the measure of righteousness that I have given you, ye shall judge the**

actions of another, and with this measure that ye mete, it shall be measured to you again when the Son of Man cometh in his glory.

3 And many times thy brother might not see clearly because of his blindness that hath been caused by his traditions and beliefs. And again, ye shall say unto them, Why is it that thou beholdest the mote that is in thy brother's eye, but considerest not the beam that is in thine own eye?

4 Or how wilt thou say to thy brother, Let me pull out the mote out of thine eye so that thou might see more clearly the measure of the Lord; and canst not behold, a beam is in thine own eye because neither do ye see clearly, nor do ye understand the true measure of the Father?

5 And Jesus said unto his disciples, Beholdest thou the Scribes, and the Pharisees, and the Priests, and the Levites? They teach in their synagogues, but do not observe the law and the commandments; and all have gone out of the way, and are under sin. Go thou and say unto them, Why teach ye men the law and the commandments, when ye yourselves are the children of corruption? Say unto them, Ye hypocrites, first cast out the beam out of thine own eye by learning of me and keeping the commandments that I have given unto thee; and then shalt thou see clearly to cast out the mote out of thy brother's eye and twain ye shall enter into my rest.

6 Go ye into the world, saying unto all, Repent, for the kingdom of heaven hath come nigh unto you. And the mysteries of the kingdom ye shall keep within yourselves; for it is not meet to give that which holy unto the dogs; neither cast ye your pearls unto swine, lest they trample them under their feet. When ye have learned these things and keep them, then ye shall receive the Holy Ghost who shall teach you the mysteries of God and all things necessary for your salvation. For the world cannot receive that which ye, yourselves, are not able to bear; therefore ye shall not give your pearls unto them, lest they turn again and rend you.

7 And when they shall approach you and seek out your pearls, ye shall not give them unto them, but shall say unto them, Ask of God, and it shall be given you according to the heed that ye give to His commandments; seek to do the will of God and not your own will, and ye shall find; knock, and it shall be opened unto you according to the desire that ye have in approaching God to receive of Him. And if ye knock in vain to consume it upon your lusts, then He shall not open unto you, and the door to an understanding of His mysteries shall be closed before you.

8 For every one that asketh in righteousness receiveth in righteousness; and he that seeketh in righteousness, findeth in righteousness; and to him that knocketh in righteousness with a broken heart and a contrite spirit, the mysteries of the kingdom shall be opened up unto him.

9 And then said his disciples unto him: They will say unto us, We are righteous, and need not that any man should teach us. God, we know; we have heard Moses and accept his laws for salvation; and the prophets have been given us from whom we hear the word of God; but to us, God will not hear or speak. And they will say, We have the law for our salvation, and that is sufficient for us.

10 Then Jesus answered and said unto his disciples, Thus shall ye say unto them, What man among you, having a son, and he shall be standing out, and shall say, Father, open thy house that I may come in and sup with thee, will not say, Come in, my son; for mine is thine, and thine is mine?

11 Or what man is there of you, whom if his son ask bread, will he give him a stone? Or if he ask a fish, will he give him a serpent? If ye then, being evil, know how to give good gifts unto your children, how much more shall your Father which is in heaven give good things to them that ask him in rigtheousness? But if ye ask not in righteousness, then He cannot give to you of righteousness. And I have given unto you the standard by which ye shall measure your righteousness. And this is the standard and law taught by all the holy prophets.

12 Therefore, all things whatsoever ye would that men should do to you, do ye even so to them as I have commanded you; for this is the law and the prophets and the gate by which ye shall enter the kingdom of God.

13 Yea, enter ye in at the strait gate **that leadeth to salvation**: for wide is the gate, and broad is the way, that leadeth to destruction, and many there be which go in thereat; **for they do not unto others what they would have others do unto them; and they shall not enter through the gate into the kingdom of God.**

14 Because strait is the gate, and narrow is the way, which leadeth unto life, and few there be that find it. **Behold, they do not find it because they are led by the precepts and doctrines of men that teach them to trust in the arm of flesh; yea, they are led down the broad way, through the wide gate that is easy to enter, because there are those who claim that they know the way, but do not, who show them the gate.**

15 Beware of **these** false prophets, which come to you in sheep's clothing, but inwardly they are ravening wolves, **who sneak in among the flock to devour the souls of men by placing them under their authority that they might get praise and gain.**

16 **Be not, therefore, deceived by men. For any that come among you and add to or take away from that which I have given you this day, and who seek for gain or glory by teaching these things unto you, are those whose fruit is corrupt. Behold,** ye shall know them by their fruits. Do men gather grapes of thorns, or figs of thistles?

17 Even so every good tree bringeth forth good fruit **in abundance**; but a corrupt tree bringeth forth evil fruit.

18 A good tree cannot bring forth evil fruit, neither can a corrupt tree bring forth good fruit. **And the fruit of a good tree bringeth forth the fruits of the spirit, which cause a man to love one another and do unto another that which he would have done unto him. And an evil tree causeth a man to set himself above another, and hate another, and causeth strife and contention, and all things contrary to the Spirit of God.**

19 And when the Son of man cometh in his glory to prune the vineyard of the Father, every tree that bringeth not forth good fruit **shall be** hewn down, and cast into the fire.

20 Wherefore by their fruits ye shall know them; **yea, even by the way that they keep these commandments that the Father hath given unto me to give to you, that ye might go forth among them and prepare them to enter the kingdom of heaven.**

21 And not every one that saith unto me, Lord, Lord, shall enter into the kingdom of heaven; but he that doeth the will of my Father **who** is in heaven. **For this reason came I into the world, that all men might come unto me and be saved by the commandments that I give unto them. And these commandments are that which will prepare them to live in the kingdom of the Father.**

22 **And the Son of man shall come to judge each man according to the way that he hath treated his fellowman. And at** that day many will say to me, Lord, Lord, have we not prophesied in thy name **and taught the people the things that they should do to be saved in thy name**? And in thy name have **we not** cast out devils? And in thy name have **we not** done many wonderful works **that glorify thee**?

23 And then will I profess unto them, I never knew you; **for I did not require any of these things at your hands; and the glory that ye gave unto me, was that glory that ye sought for yourselves; for there is but one God, and Him only did I command that ye should glorify, by keeping His commandments. And this ye should have done and not left the other undone; even that which I commanded you to do, ye did not do; for behold, I commanded that ye should love one another, and that ye should do unto one that which ye would have him do unto you; and of these things ye did none; therefore,** depart from me, ye that work iniquity.

24 Therefore whosoever heareth these sayings of mine, and doeth them, I will liken him unto a wise man, **who buildeth** his house upon a rock; **behold, I am this rock, and upon this rock will I gather all those who come unto me and hear the things that I have taught unto them this day, and who keep these sayings of mine. Behold, this is my doctrine, and whoso buildeth upon this buildeth upon my rock, and the gates of hell shall not prevail against them.**

25 And whoso shall declare more or less

than this, and establish it for my doctrine, the same cometh of evil, and is not built upon my rock. Therefore, build a house upon my rock; and the rain **shall** descend, and the floods **shall come**, and the winds **shall blow**, and beat upon that house; and it **shall not fall**; for it **is** founded upon **this** rock.

26 And every one that heareth these sayings of mine, and doeth them not, shall be likened unto a foolish man, **who** built his house upon the sand, **who said to himself, the rock is too hard to build upon, but this sand is soft and shall provide me with more comfort;**

27 And the rain descended, and the floods came, and the winds blew, and beat upon that house; and it fell **because its foundation was soft and not founded upon a rock. And the foundation was washed away by the torrents of storms that cometh forth out of the earth; and because the foundation was washed away, the house fell**, and great was the fall of it.

28 And it came to pass, when Jesus had ended these sayings, the people were astonished at his doctrine **and the simplicity of the things that he taught unto them; for the scribes and Pharisees taught the people to believe in their doctrine and perform those things which were required of them by the law of Moses by the church which gave them their authority**.

29 **But Jesus** taught them as one having **no** authority **of the church, but as one who received his authority from God,** and not as the scribes **and Pharisees of the church.**

a practical plan to end poverty...

wwunited.org
888.499.9666

www.ingramcontent.com/pod-product-compliance
Lightning Source LLC
Chambersburg PA
CBHW080857230426

43663CB00013B/2560